Release 14

AutoCAD
and its applications
Basics

by

Terence M. Shumaker
Manager
Autodesk Premier Training Center
Clackamas Community College, Oregon City, OR

David A. Madsen
Chairperson
Drafting Technology
Autodesk Premier Training Center
Clackamas Community College, Oregon City, OR
Former Board of Director
American Design Drafting Association

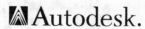

Registered Author/Publisher

Publisher
The Goodheart-Willcox Company, Inc.
Tinley Park, Illinois

Library of Congress Catalog Number 97-20232
International Standard Book Number 1-56637-409-X (Softcover)
International Standard Book Number 1-56637-421-9 (Loose-leaf drilled)

6 7 8 9 10 98 02 01 00 99

Cover image: The Stock Market, Will Ryan © 95

Library of Congress Cataloging-in-Publication Data
Shumaker, Terence M.
  AutoCAD and its applications—basics: release 14 /
by Terence M. Shumaker, David A. Madsen.

    p. cm.
  Includes index.
  ISBN 1-56637-409-X

  1. Computer graphics. 2. AutoCAD (Computer file) I. Madsen, David A. II. Title.
T385.S46162 1998
604.2'0285'5369—dc21   97-20232
                                                        CIP

Introduction

AutoCAD and its Applications—Basics, Release 14 is a write-in text that provides complete instruction in mastering AutoCAD® Release 14 commands and drawing techniques. Typical applications of AutoCAD are presented with basic drafting and design concepts. The topics are covered in an easy-to-understand sequence, and progress in a way that allows you to become comfortable with the commands as your knowledge builds from one chapter to the next. In addition, *AutoCAD and its Applications—Basics, Release 14* offers the following features:

- Step-by-step use of AutoCAD commands.
- In-depth explanations of how and why commands function as they do.
- Extensive use of font changes to specify certain meanings.
- Examples and discussions of industrial practices and standards.
- Actual screen captures of AutoCAD and Windows features and functions.
- Professional tips explaining how to use AutoCAD effectively and efficiently.
- Over 200 exercises to reinforce the chapter topics. These exercises also build on previously learned material.
- Chapter tests for review of commands and key AutoCAD concepts.
- A large selection of drafting problems supplement each chapter. Problems are presented as 3D illustrations, actual plotted industrial drawings, and engineering sketches.

With *AutoCAD and its Applications—Basics, Release 14*, you not only learn Auto-CAD commands, but you also become acquainted with information in other areas:

- Office practices for firms using AutoCAD systems.
- Preliminary planning, sketches, and drawing plan sheets.
- Linetypes and their uses.
- Drawing geometric shapes and constructions.
- Special editing operations that increase productivity.
- Making multiview drawings.
- Dimensioning techniques and practices, based on accepted standards.
- Drawing section views and designing graphic patterns.
- Creating shapes and symbols for different uses.
- Creating and managing symbol libraries.
- Sketching with AutoCAD.
- Basic 3D drawing and display.
- Plotting and printing drawings.
- Using Windows NT Explorer for organizing and managing files and directories.

Fonts used in this text

Different typefaces are used throughout this text to define terms and identify AutoCAD commands. Important terms always appear in ***bold-italic face, serif*** type. AutoCAD menus, commands, variables, dialog box names, and tool buttons are printed in **bold-face, sans serif** type. File names, directory folder names, paths, and keyboard-entry items appear in the body of the text in Roman, sans serif type. Keyboard keys are shown inside of square brackets [ ] and appear in Roman, sans serif type. For example, [Enter] means to press the Enter key.

Prompt sequences are set apart from the body text with space above and below, and appear in Roman, sans serif type. Keyboard entry items in prompts appear in **BOLD-FACE, SANS-SERIF** type, capital letters. In prompts, the [Enter] key is represented by the ⏎ symbol.

In addition, commands, menus, and dialog boxes related to Microsoft Windows appear in Roman, sans serif type.

Checking the AutoCAD reference manuals

No other reference should be needed when using this text. However, the authors have referenced relevant topic areas to the *AutoCAD User's Guide* and the *AutoCAD Customization Guide*. An icon in the margin identifies the specific chapter within the reference where additional information can be found. For example, the icon next to this paragraph tells you that you can find more information in chapter 5 of the *AutoCAD User's Guide*.

The *AutoCAD User's Guide* and *AutoCAD Customization Guide* are part of the help file installed with AutoCAD. To reference these materials, select **AutoCAD Help Topics** from the **Help** pull-down menu.

The AutoCAD help also includes the *AutoCAD Command Reference*. Commands and variables are presented in alphabetical order in this manual. Refer to it for additional information on specific commands and system variables.

Other text references

For additional information, standards from organizations such as ANSI (American National Standards Institute) and ASME (American Society of Mechanical Engineers) are referenced throughout the text. These standards are used to help you create drawings that follow industrial, national, and international practices.

Also for your convenience, other Goodheart-Willcox textbooks are referenced. Textbooks that are referenced include *AutoCAD and its Applications—Advanced, Release 14*; *AutoCAD and its Applications* (Releases 10, 11, 12, and 13); *AutoLISP Programming—Principles and Techniques*; and *Geometric Dimensioning and Tolerancing*. All of these textbooks can be ordered directly from Goodheart-Willcox.

Introducing the AutoCAD commands

There are several ways to select AutoCAD drawing and editing commands. Selecting commands from the toolbars, pull-down menus, or the digitizer tablet template menu is slightly different than entering them from the keyboard. All AutoCAD commands and related options in this text are introduced by providing all of the commonly active command entry methods.

Unless otherwise specified, command entries are shown as if they were typed at the keyboard. This allows the text to present the keyboard shortcuts and full command name and the prompts that appear on screen. Commands, options, and values you must enter are given in bold text, as shown in the following example. The available keyboard shortcuts are given first to reinforce the quickest way for you to enter commands at the keyboard. Pressing the [Enter] (return) key is indicated with the ⏎ symbol.

```
Command: L or LINE↵
From point: 2,2↵
To point: 4,2↵
To point: ↵
```

General input, such as picking a point or selecting an object, is presented in *italic, serif font*, as shown below.

```
Command: L or LINE↵
From point: (pick a point)
To point: (pick another point)
To point: ↵
```

The command line, pull-down menu, and toolbar button menu entry methods are presented throughout the text. When a command is introduced, these methods are illustrated in the margin next to the text reference. The toolbar in which the button is located is also identified. The example in the margin next to this paragraph illustrates the various methods of initiating the **LINE** command.

The AutoCAD digitizer tablet template is presented in Chapter 29 and Appendix J. This gives you the opportunity to become familiar with other input formats before using the template menu. Experiment with all command entry methods to find the most convenient way for *you* to enter commands.

Features new for Release 14

Autodesk has introduced many new features in Release 14 of AutoCAD. When a new or updated feature is presented in this text, the AutoCAD R14 icon appears in the margin next to the material. This serves as an aid to users upgrading to Release 14 from earlier releases. Refer to Appendix A for a complete list of new features.

Flexibility in design

Flexibility is the key word when using *AutoCAD and its Applications—Basics, Release 14*. This text is an excellent training aid for individual instruction, as well as classroom instruction. *AutoCAD and its Applications—Basics, Release 14* teaches you AutoCAD in the Windows environment and how to apply AutoCAD to common drafting tasks. It is also an invaluable resource for any professional using AutoCAD.

When working through the text, you will see a variety of notices. These notices include Professional Tips, Notes, and Cautions that help you develop your AutoCAD skills.

PROFESSIONAL TIP These ideas and suggestions are aimed at increasing your productivity and enhancing your use of AutoCAD commands and techniques.

NOTE A note alerts you to important aspects of a command, menu, or activity. These aspects should be kept in mind while you are working through the text.

CAUTION A caution alerts you to potential problems if instructions or commands are used incorrectly, or if an action can corrupt or alter files, folders, or disks. If you are in doubt after reading a caution, always consult your instructor or supervisor.

AutoCAD and its Applications—Basics, Release 14 provides several ways for you to evaluate your performance. Included are:

- **Exercises.** Each chapter contains in-text Exercises. These Exercises instruct you to perform tasks that reinforce the material just presented. You can work through the Exercises at your own pace.
- **Chapter Tests.** Each chapter includes a written test at the end of the chapter. Questions require you to give the proper definition, command, option, or response.
- **Drawing Problems.** There are a variety of drafting and design problems at the end of each chapter. These are presented as real-world CAD drawings, 3D illustrations, and engineering sketches. The problems are designed to make you think, solve problems, use design techniques, research and use proper drawing standards, and correct errors in the drawings or engineering sketches. Each drawing problem deals with one of seven technical disciplines. Although doing all of the problems will enhance your AutoCAD skills, you may be focusing on a particular discipline. The discipline related to a problem is indicated by a graphic in the margin next to the problem. Each graphic and its description is as follows:

 These problems address *mechanical* drafting and design applications, such as manufactured part designs.

 These problems address *architectural* and *structural* drafting and design applications, such as floor plans and presentation drawings.

 These problems address *electronics* drafting and design applications, such as electronic schematics, logic diagrams, and electrical part design.

 These problems address *civil* drafting and design applications, such as plot plans, plats, and landscape drawings.

 These problems address *graphic design* applications, such as text creation, title blocks, and page layout.

 These problems address *piping* drafting and design applications, such as piping flow diagrams, pump design, and pipe layout.

 These problems address a variety of *general* drafting and design applications.

NOTE

Some problems presented in this text are given as engineering sketches. These sketches are intended to represent the type of materials a drafter is expected to work from in a real-world situation. As such, engineering sketches often contain errors or slight inaccuracies, and are not drawn according to proper drafting conventions and applicable standards. Errors in these problems are *intentional* to encourage the user to apply appropriate techniques and standards in order to solve the problem. As in real-world applications, sketches should be considered to be preliminary layouts. Always question inaccuracies in sketches and designs, and consult the applicable standards or other resources.

Disk Supplements

To help you develop your AutoCAD skills, Goodheart-Willcox offers a disk supplement package to use with *AutoCAD and its Applications—Basics, Release 14*. The AutoCAD Release 14 software is required for Goodheart-Willcox software to operate properly.

The *Student Work Disks* contain additional AutoCAD pull-down menus with a variety of activities. These activities are intended to be used as a supplement to the exercises and activities found in the text. These activities allow you to progress at your own pace. The student work disks can be purchased from Goodheart-Willcox.

About the Authors

Terence M. Shumaker is Manager of the Autodesk Premier Training Center and a Drafting Technology Instructor at Clackamas Community College. Terence has been teaching at the community college level since 1977. He has professional experience in surveying, civil drafting, industrial piping, and technical illustration. He is the author of Goodheart-Willcox's *Process Pipe Drafting*, and is coauthor of the *AutoCAD and its Applications Release 13* series, *AutoCAD and its Applications* (Release 10, 11, and 12 editions), and *AutoCAD Essentials*.

David A. Madsen is the Chairperson of Drafting Technology and the Autodesk Premier Training Center at Clackamas Community College. David has been an instructor/department chair at Clackamas Community College since 1972. In addition to community college experience, David was a Drafting Technology instructor at Centennial High School in Gresham, Oregon. David also has extensive experience in mechanical drafting, architectural design and drafting, and construction practices. He is the author of several Goodheart-Willcox drafting and design textbooks, including *Geometric Dimensioning and Tolerancing*, and is coauthor of the *AutoCAD and its Applications Release 13* series, *AutoCAD and its Applications* (Release 10, 11, and 12 editions), and *AutoCAD Essentials*.

Notice to the User

AutoCAD and its Applications—Basics, Release 14, covers basic AutoCAD applications. For a text that covers the advanced AutoCAD applications, please refer to *AutoCAD and its Applications—Advanced, Release 14*. Copies of any of these texts can be ordered directly from Goodheart-Willcox.

Acknowledgments

The authors and publisher would like to thank the following individuals and companies for their assistance and contributions.

Special recognition

The authors are indebted to Rod Rawls for his professional expertise in providing in-depth research and testing, technical assistance, reviews, and development of new materials for use throughout the text. Rod is an AutoCAD consultant and principal instructor at the AutoCAD Premier Training Center, Clackamas Community College. He is also the coauthor of *AutoLISP Programming: Principles and Techniques* published by Goodheart-Willcox.

Technical assistance and contribution of materials

Margo Bilson of Willamette Industries, Inc.
Fitzgerald, Hagan, & Hackathorn
Dr. Stuart Soman of Briarcliffe College
Gil Hoellerich of Springdale, AR

Contribution of materials

Cynthia B. Clark of the American Society of Mechanical Engineers
Marty McConnell of Houston Instrument, A Summagraphics Company
Grace Avila and Wayne Hodgins of Autodesk, Inc.
Dave Hall of the Harris Group, Inc.

Contribution of photographs or other technical information

Amdek Corporation
Applications Development, Inc.
Arthur Baker
Autodesk, Inc.
CADalyst magazine
CADENCE magazine
CalComp
Chris Lindner
Computer-Aided Design, Inc.
Digital Equipment Corp.
EPCM Services Ltd.
Far Mountain Corporation
FLIR Systems Inc.
Gateway 2000
GTCO Corporation
Harris Group, Inc.
Hewlett-Packard
Houston Instrument, A Summagraphics Company
International Source for Ergonomics

IOLINE Corporation
JDL, Inc.
Jerome Hart
Jim Webster
Kunz Associates
Matt Slay
Mark Stennfeld
Mitsubishi Electronics America, Inc.
Microsoft Corporation
Mouse Systems Corporation
Myonetics Inc.
NEC Technologies, Inc.
Norwest Engineering
Schuchart & Associates, Inc.
Summagraphics Corporation
The American Society of Mechanical Engineers
The Xerox Engineering Systems Weiser, Inc.
Willamette Industries, Inc.

Technical assistance and reviews

Rod Rawls, Autodesk Premier Training Center, Clackamas Community College
Bryan Kelley, KETIV Technologies
Keith McDonald, FLIR Systems, Inc.
J.C. Malitzke, Autodesk Premier Training Center, Moraine Valley Community College
Tim Brooks and Tim Gabriel for technical drawings

Trademarks

Autodesk, AutoCAD, and AutoLISP are registered in the U.S. Patent Trademark Office by Autodesk, Inc.

Autodesk Animator Pro, Autodesk 3D Studio, and DXF are trademarks of Autodesk, Inc.

dBase is a registered trademark of Ashton Tate

IBM is a registered trademark of International Business Machines

Windows, Windows 95, and Windows NT are trademarks of Microsoft Corporation

Pizazz Plus is a registered trademark of Applications Software Corporation

RenderMan is a registered trademark of Pixar used by Autodesk, Inc. by license

Microsoft Word is a trademark of Microsoft Corporation

MS-DOS is a registered trademark of Microsoft Corporation

Contents

EDITING THE DRAWING

AUTOCAD APPLICATIONS

DIMENSIONING AND TOLERANCING

ADVANCED DRAWING CONSTRUCTION

BASIC THREE-DIMENSIONAL DRAWING

ADVANCED APPLICATIONS

APPENDICES

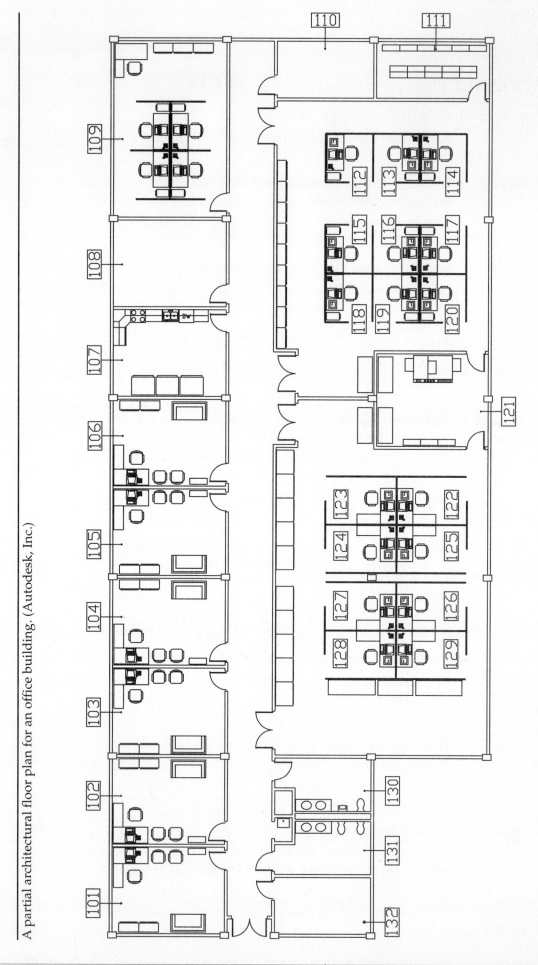

A partial architectural floor plan for an office building. (Autodesk, Inc.)

Introduction to AutoCAD Features

Learning Objectives

After completing this chapter, you will be able to:
- ○ Describe the methods and procedures used in computer-aided drafting.
- ○ Explain the value of planning your work and system management.
- ○ Describe the appropriate locations for saving drawing files.
- ○ Identify the meaning of DOS disk drive prompts.
- ○ Load AutoCAD from the Windows Desktop.
- ○ Describe the AutoCAD screen layout and user interface.
- ○ Describe the function of dialog boxes.
- ○ Use the keyboard and an input device to select commands, enter text, and pick locations on the screen.
- ○ Use the **HELP** command for on-line assistance.
- ○ Define the use of function, control, and shortcut keys.

The Tools of CAD

The computer and software are the principal components of the present-day design and drafting workstation. These tools make up a *system* referred to as CAD—Computer-Aided Design, or Computer-Aided Drafting. CAD is used by drafters, designers, and engineers to develop designs and drawings, and to plot them on paper or film. Additionally, drawings and designs can be displayed as 3D models and animations, or used in analysis and testing.

CAD has surpassed the use of manual drafting techniques because of its speed, power, accuracy, and flexibility, but is not totally without its attendant problems and trade-offs. Although the uses of CAD designs are limited only by the imagination, it should be remembered that the computer hardware is sensitive to the slightest electrical impulses, and the human body is sensitive to the repetitive motions required when using the tools.

The AutoCAD Toolbox

Drawings and models are constructed in AutoCAD using XYZ coordinates. The *Cartesian (rectangular)* coordinate system is used most often, and is discussed in Chapter 4. Angular layouts are created by measuring angles in a counterclockwise direction. Drawings can be annotated with text and described with a variety of dimensioning techniques. In addition, objects can be given colors, patterns, and textures. The tool you will use the most often is the ability to view the entire drawing or model, or its smallest feature from any direction. AutoCAD also provides you with the tools to create basic pictorial drawings called *isometrics*, and powerful 3D surface models and solids.

The Applications of AutoCAD

Using AutoCAD software and this text, you will learn how to construct, lay out, dimension, and annotate two-dimensional drawings. Should you wish to continue your study into 3D rendering and customization, *AutoCAD and its Applications—Advanced, Release 14* provides you with detailed instruction. Your studies will enable you to create a wide variety of drawings, designs, and 3D models in any of the drafting, design, and engineering disciplines.

The drawings can have hundreds of colors, and *layers* that contain different kinds of information. Objects can also be shown as exploded assemblies or displayed in 3D. See Figure 1-1.

In addition, objects in the drawing can be given "intelligence" in the form of *attributes*. These attributes are various kinds of data that turn a drawing into a graphical database. You can then ask questions of your drawing and receive a variety of information.

Using AutoCAD, you have the ability to construct 3D models that appear as wireframes or have surface colors and textures. The creation of solid models that have mass properties and can be analyzed is also possible with AutoCAD. The display in Figure 1-2 is an example of a solid model created in AutoCAD. 3D drawings and models can be viewed in several ways. These models can also be colored and shaded, or *rendered*, to appear in a realistic format.

Figure 1-1.
A nozzle shown as a 2D drawing and as a 3D model. (Autodesk, Inc.)

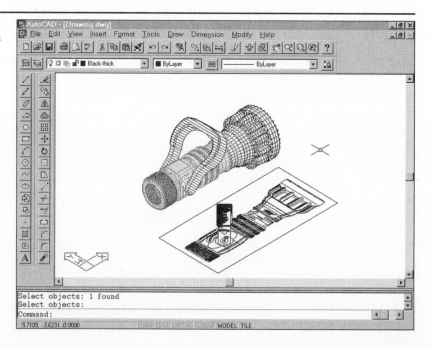

Figure 1-2.
A 3D model of a control rod. A—Model shown as a wireframe, with edges marked by lines.
B—Color and shading are added when the model is rendered. (Autodesk, Inc.)

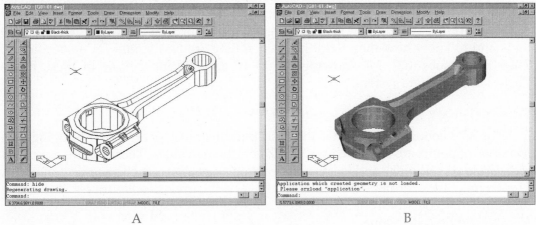

A   B

A powerful application of CAD software and 3D models is animation. The simplest form of animation is to dynamically rotate the model in order to view it from any direction. See Figure 1-3. Drawings and models can also be animated so that the model appears to move, rotate, and even explode into its individual components. An extremely useful form of animation is called a *walkthrough*. Using specialized software, you can plot a path through or around a model and replay it just like a movie. The logical next step in viewing the model is to actually be inside it and have the ability to manipulate and change the objects in it. This is called *virtual reality*, and is achieved through the use of 3D models and highly specialized software and hardware.

Figure 1-3.
This 3D piping model can be rotated and viewed from any location in 3D space. (Autodesk, Inc.)

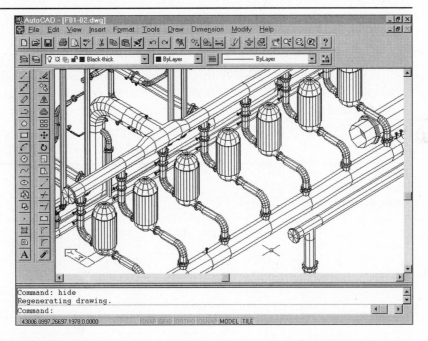

Graphics cards called *accelerator boards* may allow 1600 × 1200 resolution and up to 16.7 million colors. Older computers may have VGA (Video Graphics Array) resolution that supports only 16 colors. However, the most common resolution is Super VGA, which supports up to 16.7 million colors. Also, many industrial applications now need high-end graphics accelerator boards because of the complexity of the models, renderings, and animations.

Establishing an AutoCAD Drawing Method

All aspects of the project must be considered when developing a drawing plan. This requires careful use of the CAD system and detailed standards for the planning and drawing process. Therefore, it is important for you to be familiar with the AutoCAD tools and to know how they work and when they are best suited for a specific job. There is no substitute for knowing the tools, and the most basic of these is the Cartesian coordinate system.

Learn the XYZ coordinate system

The XYZ coordinate system is the basic building block of any CAD drawing. The locations of points are described with XYZ coordinate values. These values are called *rectangular coordinates* and locate any point on a flat plane, such as a sheet of paper. The *origin* of the coordinate system is the lower-left corner. See Figure 1-4. A distance measured horizontally from the origin is an X value. A distance measured vertically from the origin is a Y value.

Figure 1-4.
The 2D rectangular coordinate system.

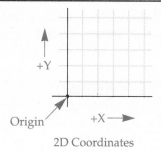

2D Coordinates

Rectangular coordinates can also be measured in three-dimensional space. In this case, the third dimension rises up from the surface of the paper and is given the Z value. See Figure 1-5. When describing coordinate locations, it is proper to give the X value first, Y second, and Z third. Each number is separated by a comma. For example, the value of 3,1,6 represents three units from the X origin, one unit from the Y origin, and six units from the Z origin. A detailed explanation of rectangular coordinates is provided in Chapter 4.

Figure 1-5.
The 3D rectangular coordinate system.

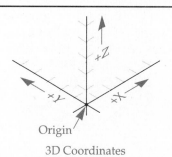

3D Coordinates

Planning your drawing

Drawing planning involves looking at the entire process or project that you are involved in. A plan determines how a project is going to be approached. It includes the drawings to be created, how they will be titled and numbered, the information to be presented, and the types of symbols needed to show the information.

More specifically, drawing planning applies to how you create and manage a drawing or set of drawings. This includes which view or feature you draw first and the coordinates and AutoCAD commands you use to draw it.

Drafters who begin constructing a drawing from the seat of their pants—creating symbols and naming objects, shapes, and views as they go—do not possess a good drawing plan. Those who plan, use consistent techniques, and adhere to school or company standards are developing good drawing habits.

Throughout this text you will find aids to help you develop good drawing habits. One of the first steps in developing your skills is to learn how to plan your work. The importance of planning cannot be emphasized enough. There is no substitute.

Using drawing standards

Standards are guidelines for operating procedures, drawing techniques, and record keeping. Most schools and companies have established standards. It is important that standards exist and are used by all CAD personnel. Drawing standards may include the following items:

- Methods of file storage: location and name.
- Dimensioning techniques.
- File naming conventions.
- Text styles.
- Drawing sheet sizes and title blocks to be used.
- Linetypes.
- Drawing symbols.
- Color schemes for plotting.
- File backup methods and times.

Your standards may vary in content, but the most important aspect of standards is that they are used. When standards are used, your drawings are consistent, you become more productive, and the classroom or office functions more efficiently.

Planning your work

Study the planning pyramids in Figure 1-6. The horizontal axes of the pyramids represent the amount of time spent on the project. The vertical axes represent the life of the project. The top level is the planning stage and the bottom level is the final execution of the project.

The pyramid on the right is pointed at the top and indicates a small amount of planning. As the project progresses, more and more time is devoted to planning and less time is available for other tasks. This is *not* an ideal situation. The inverted pyramid on the left shows a lot of time devoted to initial planning. As the project advances, less planning time is needed, thus freeing more time for tasks related to the completion of the project.

Figure 1-6.
Planning pyramids illustrate time required for well-planned and poorly-planned projects.

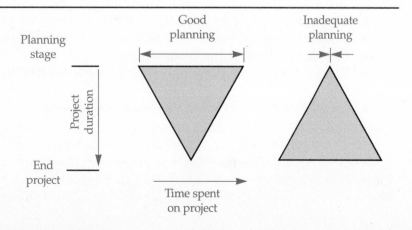

As you begin your CAD training, plan your drawing sessions thoroughly to organize your thoughts. Sketch the problem or design, noting size and locations of features. List the drawing commands needed in the order they are to be used. Schedule a regular time to use the computer and adhere to that time. Follow the standards set by your school or firm. These might include specific drawing names, project planning sheets, project logs, drawing layout procedures, special title blocks, and a location for drawing storage. Standards and procedures must be followed by everyone using the computers in your school or company. Confusion may result if your drawings do not have the proper name, are stored in the wrong place, or have the wrong title block.

Develop the habit of saving your work regularly—at least every 10 to 15 minutes. The **SAVETIME** system variable can be set to automatically save your drawings at predetermined intervals. **SAVETIME** is covered in detail in Chapter 3. Drawings may be lost due to a software error, hardware malfunction, power failure, or your own mistakes. This is not common, but you should still be prepared for such an event.

You should develop methods of managing your work. This is critical to computer drafting and is discussed throughout the text. Keep the following points in mind as you begin your AutoCAD training.

✓ Plan your work and organize your thoughts.
✓ Learn and use your classroom or office standards.
✓ Save your work often.

If you remember to follow these three points, your grasp of the tools and methods of CAD will be easier. In addition, your experiences with the computer will be more enjoyable.

Remember the planning pyramids as you begin your study of AutoCAD. When you feel the need to dive blindly into a drawing or project, restrain yourself. Take the time needed for development of the project goals. Then proceed with the confidence of knowing where you are heading.

During your early stages of AutoCAD training, write down all of the instructions needed to construct your drawing. Do this especially for your first few assignments. This means documenting every command and every coordinate point (dimension) needed. Develop a planning sheet for your drawings or use an example shown below. Your time spent at the computer with AutoCAD will be more productive and enjoyable.

Using drawing plan sheets

A good work plan can save drawing time. Planning should include sketches and drawing plan sheets. A rough preliminary sketch and completed drawing plan sheet help in the following ways:

* Determines the drawing layout.
* Sets the overall size of the drawing by laying out the views and required free space.
* Confirms the drawing units based on the dimensions provided.
* Predetermines the point entry system and locates the points.
* Establishes the **Grid** and **Snap** settings.
* Presets some of the drawing variables, such as **LINETYPE**, **FILL**, and polyline width.
* Establishes how and when various activities are to be performed.

- Determines the best use of AutoCAD.
- Results in an even work load.
- Provides maximum use of equipment.

Drawing plan sheets range in content, depending on the nature of the drafting project. One basic drawing plan sheet is shown in Figure 1-7.

Figure 1-7.
A drawing plan sheet and project log combination. They are generally printed on the front and back of one piece of paper. (Courtesy of Harlton Terrie Gaines; Palmer, Alaska)

```
╔═══════════════════════════════════════════════════════════════════════════╗
║          DRAWING PLANNING SHEET              Page 1 of 2                     ║
╠═══════════════════════════════════════════════════════════════════════════╣
║ The following information is to be furnished by the Assigned Project        ║
║ Engineer requesting design support:                                         ║
║                                                                             ║
║              PROJECT TITLE: _____         ║
║                 DISCIPLINE: _____                                     ║
║               PROJECT NO. : _____    A.F.E. NO. : _____        ║
║           PROJECT ENGINEER: _____    PHONE NO. : _____         ║
║                     CLIENT: _____               ║
║      DRAWING SCOPE OF WORK: _____               ║
║                             _____               ║
║                             _____               ║
╠═══════════════════════════════════════════════════════════════════════════╣
║ The following information will be furnished by the assigned Lead Designer:  ║
║                                                                             ║
║              LEAD DESIGNER: _____    PHONE NO. : _____         ║
║                  DISK NAME: _____                                     ║
║                  FILE NAME: _____    DRAWING NO.: _____        ║
║  DWG. GHOST (SIZE & FORMAT): _____                                    ║
║                                                                             ║
║                    DRAFTER: _____    PHONE NO. : _____         ║
║              DATE ASSIGNED: _____    DATE REQUIRED: _____       ║
║                 DATE I.F.A. : _____  DATE I.F.C. : _____        ║
║              ESTIMATED M.H. : _____  ACTUAL M.H. : _____        ║
║           DRAWING STANDARD: _____    MAT'L SPEC.: _____         ║
║           AFFECTED TAG NO'S:                REFERENCE SHEETS                 ║
║  _____  _____  _____     _____  _____  _____         ║
║  _____  _____  _____     _____  _____  _____         ║
╠═══════════════════════════════════════════════════════════════════════════╣
║ Freehand sketch by drafter:                                                 ║
║                                                                             ║
║                                                                             ║
║                                                                             ║
║                                                                             ║
║                                                                             ║
║                                                                             ║
║                                                                             ║
║     Approved by: _____     Date: _____                ║
╚═══════════════════════════════════════════════════════════════════════════╝
```

Figure 1-7.
(Continued)

| DRAWING PLANNING SHEET | Page 2 of 2 |

Drafters notes: _____
_____
_____
_____
_____
_____
_____
_____
_____
_____

Commands used by the drafter:

	Commands	Values		Commands	Values
1.			34.		
2.			35.		
3.			36.		
4.			37.		
5.			38.		
6.			39.		
7.			40.		
8.			41.		
9.			42.		
10.			43.		
11.			44.		
12.			45.		
13.			46.		
14.			47.		
15.			48.		
16.			49.		
17.			50.		
18.			51.		
19.			52.		
20.			53.		
21.			54.		
22.			55.		
23.			56.		
24.			57.		
25.			58.		
26.			59.		
27.			60.		
28.			61.		
29.			62.		
30.			63.		
31.			64.		
32.			65.		
33.			66.		

Planning checklist

In the early stages of your AutoCAD training, it is best to plan your drawing projects carefully. There is a tendency to want things to happen immediately—for things to be "automatic". But if you hurry and do little or no planning, you will become more frustrated. Therefore, as you begin each new project, step through the following planning checklist so that the execution of your project goes smoothly.

✓ Analyze the problem.
✓ Study all engineering sketches.
✓ Locate all available resources and list for future use.
✓ Determine the applicable standards for the project.
✓ Sketch the problem.
✓ Decide on the number and kind of views required.

✓ Determine the final plotted scale of the drawing, and of all views.

✓ Determine the drawing sequence (lines, features, dimensions, notes, etc.).

✓ List the AutoCAD commands to be used.

✓ Follow the standards and refer to resources as you work.

PROFESSIONAL TIP

AutoCAD is designed so that you can construct drawings and models using the actual dimensions of the object. Therefore, *always draw in full scale*. The proper text and dimension size is set using scale factors. This is covered in detail in later chapters. The final scale of the drawing should be planned early, and is shown on the plot. Always plot the drawing to a specific scale if plotting a model space layout. Always plot the drawing at a scale of 1:1 if plotting a paper space layout.

Working procedures checklist

As you begin learning AutoCAD, you will realize that several skills are required to become a proficient CAD user. The following list provides you with some hints to help you become comfortable with AutoCAD. They will also allow you to work quickly and efficiently. The following items are discussed in detail in later chapters.

✓ Plan all work with pencil and paper before using the computer.

✓ Check the **Object Properties** toolbar at the top of the display screen and the status bar at the bottom to see which layer(s) and drawing aid(s) are in effect.

✓ Read the command line at the bottom of the display screen. Constantly check for the correct command, instructions, or proper keyboard entry of data.

✓ Read the command line after keyboard entry of data before pressing the [Enter] or [Return] key. Backspacing to erase incorrect typing is quicker than redoing the command.

✓ If using a multibutton puck, develop a good hand position that allows easy movement. Your button-pressing finger should move without readjusting your grip of the puck.

✓ Learn the meanings of all the buttons on your puck or mouse and use them regularly.

✓ Watch the disk drive lights to see when the disks are being accessed. Some disk access may take a few seconds. Knowing what is happening will lessen frustration and impatience.

✓ Think ahead. Know your next move.

✓ Learn new commands every day. Don't rely on just a few that seem to work. Find commands that can speed your work and do it more efficiently.

✓ Save your work every 10 to 15 minutes in case a power failure or system crash deletes the drawing held in computer memory.

✓ If you're stumped, ask the computer for help. Use the on-line help to display valuable information about each command on the screen. Using AutoCAD's on-line help is discussed in detail later in this chapter.

Starting AutoCAD

AutoCAD Release 14 is designed to operate with Windows 95 or Windows NT. With the introduction of Windows NT version 4.0, the two interfaces are nearly identical. Therefore, if you see illustrations in this text that appear to be NT, do not be concerned, for the 95 version of the AutoCAD feature is the same.

When AutoCAD is first installed, Windows creates a ***program icon*** that is displayed on the desktop. An *icon* is a small picture that represents an application, accessory, file, or command. In addition to the icon, the program name is listed as an item in the Start menu under the Programs item.

NOTE   AutoCAD must first be installed properly on the computer before it can be used. Refer to *Appendix C* for detailed instructions on AutoCAD installation and configuration of peripheral devices such as plotters, printers, and digitizers.

AutoCAD can be started using three different techniques. The quickest way to start AutoCAD is to double-click on the AutoCAD R14 icon on the Windows desktop. See Figure 1-8.

Figure 1-8.
Double-click the AutoCAD R14 icon on the Windows desktop to start AutoCAD.

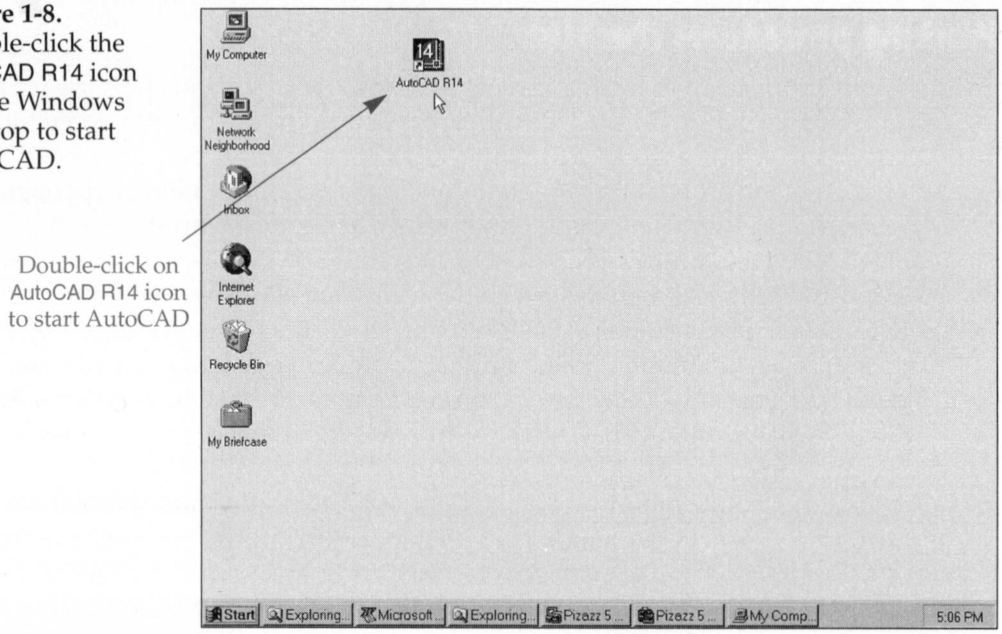

PROFESSIONAL TIP   When AutoCAD is installed using unaltered settings, the label for the AutoCAD icon is AutoCAD R14. The name can be quickly changed by picking the label, typing a new name, and pressing [Enter].

The second method for starting AutoCAD is to pick the Start button at the lower-left of the Windows screen. This displays the Start menu. Next, move the pointer to Programs and either hold it there or pick to display the Programs menu. Now move the pointer to the AutoCAD R14 item and click. This displays all of the items in the AutoCAD R14 program group. Pick on AutoCAD R14 to load the software. See Figure 1-9.

Figure 1-9.
Pick AutoCAD R14 in the Programs menu to load AutoCAD.

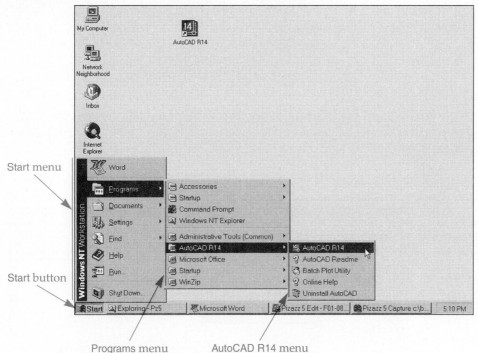

Five items are listed in the AutoCAD R14 menu.
- **AutoCAD R14.** Loads AutoCAD.
- **AutoCAD Readme.** Opens a text file that gives information on important items that may not be covered in the printed documentation or the on-line help files. Also provides links to other topics such as "What's New in AutoCAD Release 14".

NOTE
A Windows *link* is identified by green, underlined text. The pointer changes to a hand icon when it is moved over link text. A new page of information is displayed when you pick a link.

 ▶ To access Help topics

- **Batch Plot Utility.** This temporarily loads AutoCAD and enables you to plot a group of files at one time. You cannot edit drawings with this utility. It can run in the background while you do other work. This is discussed in Chapter 10.
- **On-line Help.** This provides access to all of the documentation for AutoCAD R14. It is discussed later in this chapter.
- **Uninstall AutoCAD.** Enables you to remove AutoCAD from your computer.

The third method for loading AutoCAD is the most cumbersome, and is the same process used to install software. Using this method you must locate and run the acad.exe file. To begin this process as follows:
1. Pick the Start button then pick Run... to display the Run dialog box. See Figure 1-10.
2. Enter the drive and directory location of the acad.exe file in the Open: text box.
3. Pick the OK button or press [Enter]. If you do not know the exact location of the acad.exe file, use the Browse... button. The acad.exe file is always located in the main AutoCAD directory folder. If the defaults were used during installation, this folder should be named AutoCAD R14.

Figure 1-10.
The Run dialog box allows you to load programs such as AutoCAD.

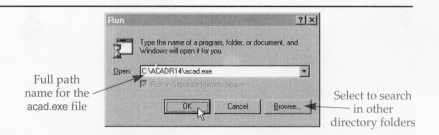

Full path name for the acad.exe file

Select to search in other directory folders

AutoCAD is loaded and the **Start Up** dialog box is displayed. See Figure 1-11. The functions of this dialog box are discussed thoroughly in Chapter 2. Pick the **OK** button to clear the dialog box.

Figure 1-11.
The **Start Up** dialog box is displayed when AutoCAD is loaded.

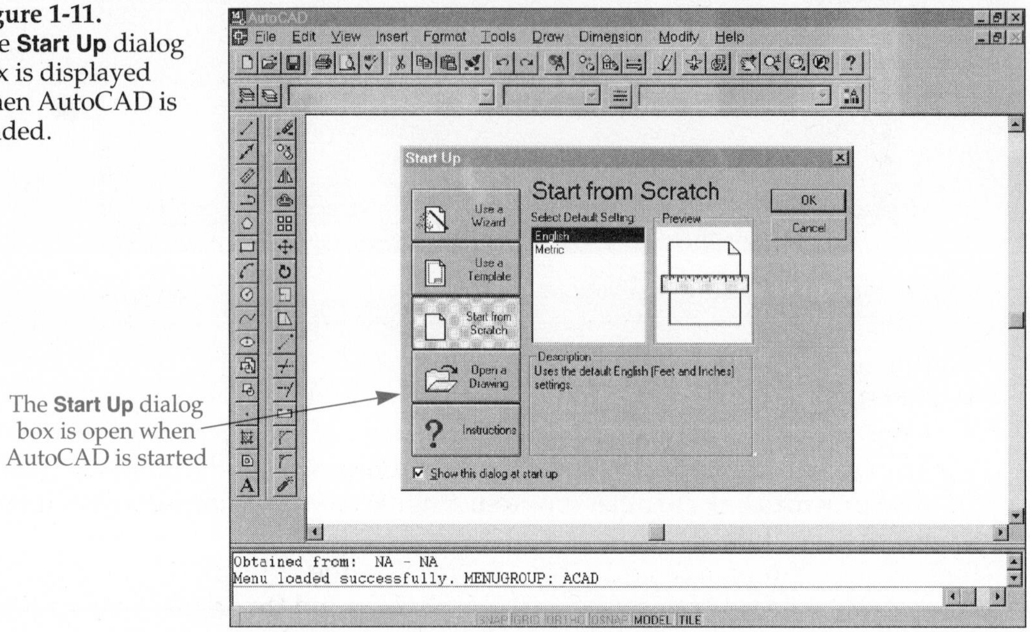

The **Start Up** dialog box is open when AutoCAD is started

The AutoCAD Graphics Window

The AutoCAD graphics window is similar to any other window within the Windows operating system. Picking the small control icon in the upper-left corner displays a standard window control menu, and the icons in the upper-right corner are used for minimizing, maximizing, and closing the window. See Figure 1-12.

Window sizing operations are done as with any other window. AutoCAD uses the familiar Windows style interface, with buttons, pull-down menus, and dialog boxes. Each of these items are discussed in detail in this chapter. Learning the layout, appearance, and proper use of these features allows you to master AutoCAD quickly.

Standard screen layout

The standard screen layout provides a large graphics, or drawing, area. The drawing area is bordered by the *toolbar* at the top and the *command line* at the bottom. Look at your screen now and study the illustration in Figure 1-12. Note that the proportional size of the AutoCAD graphics window features may vary depending on the display resolution of your computer system.

Figure 1-12.
The standard AutoCAD graphics window.

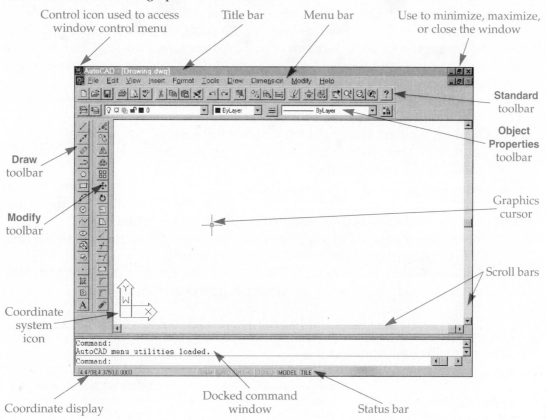

Many of the elements of the AutoCAD graphics window are referred to as *floating*. This means that the item can be freely moved about the screen into new positions. When an item is floating, it has a standard Windows border and title bar. Floating windows are moved and adjusted for size in the same manner as any other window. Items that are floating can also be *docked* around the edges of the graphics window. To dock an item, drag it to the edge of the graphics window (top, bottom, left, or right). When an item is docked, it loses its border and title bar and becomes a part of the graphics window. Moving a docked item away from the edge of the graphics window restores its title bar and border. Objects may be moved or docked at any time as needed.

Become familiar with these unique areas of the graphics window and the information provided by each. The following list describes the function of each area. Each of these features will be discussed in detail later in this text.

- **Floating command window.** In its default position, this window is docked at the bottom of the graphics window. It displays the Command: prompt and reflects any command entries you make. It also displays prompts that supply information to you or request input. This is where your primary communications with AutoCAD are displayed, so watch for any information shown on this line.

- **Menu bar.** The menu bar appears just below the title bar and displays a number of menu names. As with standard Windows menus, use the cursor to point at a menu name and press the pick button. This causes a *pull-down menu* to be displayed. Any time you pick an item followed by an *ellipsis* (…), a dialog box is displayed. A *dialog box* is a rectangular area that appears on the screen after you type or select certain commands. It contains a variety of options related to a specific command or function, and provides a convenient means of supplying information to AutoCAD.

- **Scroll bars.** The scroll bars allow you to adjust your view of the drawing area.
- **Graphics cursor.** This is your primary means of pointing to objects or locations within a drawing. The length of the graphics cursor crosshairs can be quickly changed. Pick **Preferences...** in the **Tools** pull-down menu, then pick the **Pointer** tab. Change the number in the **Cursor size** text box at the bottom of the tab to suit your needs. A 5% setting is default, and a 100% value extends the crosshairs to the limits of the graphics window.
- **Coordinate system icon.** This indicates the current coordinate system and helps to determine point locations.
- **Floating toolbar.** Floating toolbars contain various buttons that activate AutoCAD commands. These toolbars can be moved, resized, modified, hidden, or docked as needed.
- **Status bar.** This contains several display fields that reflect the current state of specific drawing control features. When a menu item is highlighted or you are pointing at a button, a brief explanation of the item is shown here.
- **Coordinate display.** This display field, found on the status bar, shows the XYZ cursor location according to the current settings.
- **Standard toolbar.** In the default AutoCAD screen configuration, the **Standard** toolbar appears just above the **Object Properties** toolbar. When you move

---

Figure 1-13.
The **Standard** toolbar and its components.

A—**New.** Begins a new drawing session.

B—**Open.** Allows existing drawings to be opened for editing and revision.

C—**Save.** Writes the drawing information currently in memory to a file.

D—**Print.** Sends drawing information to a hardcopy device, such as a printer or plotter.

E—**Print Preview.** Displays a preview of the drawing layout prior to printing.

F—**Spelling.** Performs a spell-check of the text in your drawing.

G—**Cut to Clipboard.** "Cuts" a specified portion of your drawing geometry, storing it on the Windows clipboard.

H—**Copy to Clipboard.** Copies a specified portion of your drawing geometry, storing it on the Windows Clipboard.

I—**Paste from Clipboard.** "Pastes" the contents of the Clipboard to a specified location in your drawing.

J—**Match Properties.** Copies the properties from one object to one or more objects.

K—**Undo.** Cancels the effect of the last command or operation.

L—**Redo.** Can be used after **Undo** to redo the previously canceled operation.

M—**Launch Browser.** Launches the Internet browser software that is defined in your Windows system registry.

N—**Object Snap Flyout.** Presents a series of buttons that activate the tracking and object snap tools for accessing specific geometric points within a drawing.

O—**UCS Flyout.** Presents a series of buttons that activate various coordinate system options.

P—**Inquiry Flyout.** Presents a series of buttons that activate various drawing inquiry commands.

Q—**Redraw All.** Redraws the display in all viewports.

R—**Aerial View.** Activates the **DSVIEWER** command, which displays the **Aerial View** dialog box.

S—**Named Views Flyout.** Various options for changing the current view of your drawings are presented by this flyout.

T—**Pan Realtime.** Displays the hand icon cursor and moves the display in the current viewport dynamically in real time.

U—**Zoom Realtime.** Displays the zoom icon and increases or decreases the displayed size of objects in the current viewport.

V—**Zoom Flyout.** Displays a series of buttons that activate **ZOOM** command options.

W—**Zoom Previous.** Returns the previous display to the graphics area.

X—**Help.** Activates AutoCAD's online help facility.

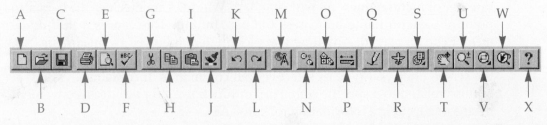

your pointing device to the toolbar, the crosshairs change to the familiar Windows arrow pointer. Holding the cursor over a button for a moment displays ToolTips, which show the function of the button. Some buttons show a small black triangle in the lower-right corner. These buttons are called *flyouts*. Press and hold the pick button while pointing at a flyout to display a set of related buttons. The **Standard** toolbar contains a series of buttons that provide access to several of AutoCAD's drawing setup and control commands. Each of these features is identified and briefly described in Figure 1-13. These features are discussed in detail later in this text.

- **Object Properties toolbar.** In the default AutoCAD screen configuration, the **Object Properties** toolbar appears just above the graphics area with the **Standard** toolbar. This toolbar contains buttons and display fields for commonly used AutoCAD commands. Each of these features is identified and briefly explained in Figure 1-14.

Figure 1-14.
The **Objects Properties** toolbar and its components.

A— **Make Object's Layer Current.** Allows selection of a drawing object to change the current layer to that of the selected object.

B— **Layers.** Accesses the **Layer & Linetypes Properties** dialog box, where you can create and manage drawing layers and linetypes.

C— **Layer Control.** Shows the current layer and its properties. Picking on the down arrow on the right side of the **Layer Control** field shows information on all drawing layers and provides a handy shortcut to common layer control options.

D— **Color Control.** Displays the current object creation color and when picked displays the four most recently used colors and the seven standard colors. Also allows access to the **Select Color** dialog box.

E— **Linetype.** Accesses the **Layer & Linetype** Properties dialog box for selecting and loading object linetypes.

F— **Linetype Control.** Displays the current object linetype. Clicking on the down arrow to the right allows you to select a new linetype from the currently loaded linetypes.

G— **Properties.** Allows modification to the properties of existing objects in a drawing.

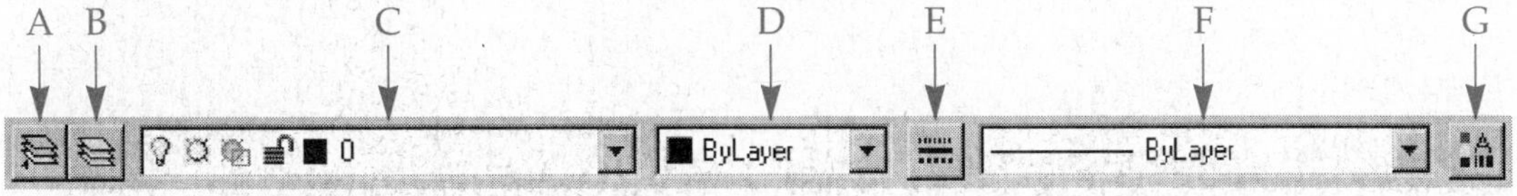

Pull-down menus

The AutoCAD pull-down menus are located on the menu bar at the top of the screen. As with a toolbar, when you move your pointing device to the menu bar, the crosshairs change to the arrow pointer. From Figure 1-15, you can see that the default menu bar has ten pull-down menu items: **File**, **Edit**, **View**, **Insert**, **Format**, **Tools**, **Draw**, **Dimension**, **Modify**, and **Help**.

Figure 1-15.
The AutoCAD menu bar. Pull-down menus are accessed by picking the words in this bar.

By default, AutoCAD divides the command set between menus and toolbars, with some commands occurring in both. To see how a pull-down menu works, move your cursor to the **View** menu and press the pick button. A pull-down menu appears below **View**, Figure 1-16A. Commands are easily selected by picking a menu item with your pointing device.

Notice that several of the commands in the **View** pull-down menu have a small arrow to the right. When one of these items is selected, a *cascading menu* appears. A cascading menu has additional options for the previous selection, Figure 1-16B.

Some of the menu selections are followed by an ellipsis (...). If you pick one of these items, a dialog box is displayed. If you pick the wrong pull-down menu, simply move the cursor to the one you want. The first menu is removed and the new menu is displayed. The pull-down menu disappears after you pick an item in the menu, pick a point in the drawing area, or type on the keyboard.

Figure 1-16.
Using the pull-down menus. A—When you pick **View**, this pull-down menu is displayed. B—A pull-down menu item followed by an arrow indicates a cascading menu. Selecting the item displays the cascading menu (shown here highlighted).

A

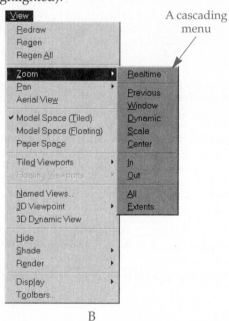
B

A cascading menu

PROFESSIONAL TIP You can also select a pull-down menu item by holding the pick button down while moving the pointer to the desired selection and releasing the pick button.

Accessing pull-down menus from the keyboard. As you move through the pull-down menus, note that one character of each pull-down menu title is underlined. This allows access to any pull-down menu selection using an [Alt]+[*key*] combination on the keyboard. For instance, the **File** menu can be accessed by pressing [Alt]+[F]. Pressing [Alt]+[D] accesses the **Draw** menu, and so on.

Once a pull-down menu is displayed, a menu item can be selected using a single character key. For example, suppose you want to zoom in closer to your work. Referring once again to Figure 1-16B, first press [Alt]+[V] to access the **View** menu. Then, press Z to select the **Zoom** command. Finally, press I to select the **In** option. These shortcut keystrokes for accessing pull-down menu items are called *menu accelerator keys*.

PROFESSIONAL TIP

Once a pull-down menu is displayed you can use the up, down, right, and left cursor arrow keys to move to different items in the menu and to display cascading menus. When an item followed by an arrow is highlighted, press the right arrow key to display the cascading menu. Remove the menu by pressing the left arrow. Press [Enter] to select a highlighted item.

NOTE

There are many individual character key and key combination shortcuts available for Windows and Windows-based applications. Refer to your Microsoft Windows documentation for a complete list of keyboard shortcuts.

Dialog boxes

One of the most important aspects of AutoCAD Release 14 is the Graphical User Interface (GUI) offered by the Microsoft Windows operating environment. A *graphical user interface* is how information, options, and choices are displayed for you by the software. The most common component of the GUI is the dialog box. A *dialog box* is a box that may contain a variety of information. You can set variables and select items in a dialog box using your cursor. This eliminates typing, saving time and increasing productivity.

A pull-down selection that is followed by an ellipsis (...) displays a dialog box when picked. An example of a simple dialog box is shown in Figure 1-17. This dialog box is displayed when you pick **Open...** from the **File** pull-down menu.

Figure 1-17.
A dialog box appears when you pick an item that is followed by an ellipsis. The dialog box shown here appears after you select **Open...** from the **File** pull-down menu.

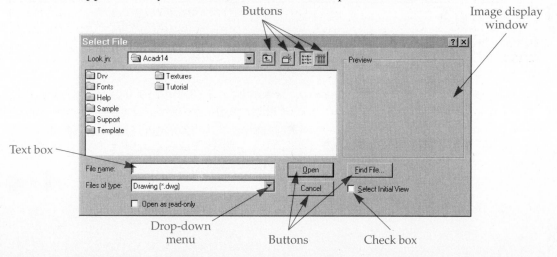

Buttons in a dialog box that are followed by an ellipsis (...) display another dialog box when they are picked. The second dialog box is displayed on top of the original dialog box, much like laying a sheet of paper on top of another. You must make a selection from the second dialog box before returning to the original dialog box.

There are standard parts to all dialog boxes. If you take a few minutes to review the brief descriptions here, you will find it much easier to work with the dialog boxes. Detailed discussions are provided in later chapters. You can become efficient in your use of dialog boxes by remembering two things—pick a button and enter text in a text box.

- **Command buttons.** When you pick a command button, something happens immediately. The most common buttons are **OK** and **Cancel**. Another common button is **Help**. See Figure 1-18. If a button has a dark border, it is the default. Pressing the [Enter] key accepts the default. If a button is "grayed-out" it cannot be selected. Buttons can also lead to other things. A button with an ellipsis (...) leads to another dialog box. A button with an arrow symbol (⟩) requires that you make a selection in the graphics window.
- **Radio buttons.** When you press a selector button on your car radio, the station changes. Only one station can play at a time. Likewise, only one item in a group of radio buttons can be highlighted or active at one time. See Figure 1-19.
- **Check box.** A check box, or toggle, displays a "✓" when it is on (active). If the box is empty, the option is off. See Figure 1-20.
- **List box.** A list box contains a list of items or options. You can scan through the list using the scroll bar (if present) or the keyboard arrow keys. Either highlight the desired item with the arrow keys and press [Enter], or simply select it using your pointing device. See Figure 1-21.
- **Drop-down list box.** The drop-down list box is similar to the standard list box, except only one item is initially shown. The remaining items are hidden until you pick the down arrow. When you pick the down arrow, the drop-down list is displayed below the initial item. You can then pick from the expanded list, or use the scroll bar to find the item you need. See Figure 1-22.

Figure 1-18.
When you select a button, something immediately happens. Three common buttons found in dialog boxes are the **OK**, **Cancel**, and **Help...** buttons. Note the dark border around the **OK** button. This means that this is the default button.

Figure 1-19.
Only one radio button in a group can be highlighted at a time.

Only one option can be active

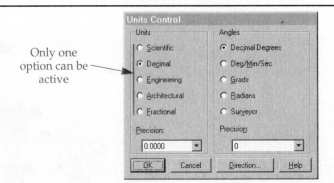

Figure 1-20.
A "✓" in a check box indicates that the item is active (on). Any number of check boxes can be active in a given group.

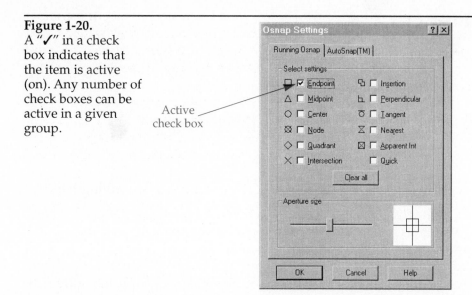

Active check box

Figure 1-21.
A list box contains a list of items related to the dialog box. Here, the list shows the views defined for the current drawing.

Hilighted item

List box

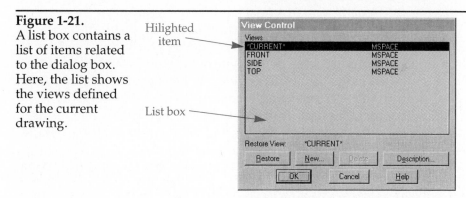

Figure 1-22.
A drop-down list box is displayed when you pick the drop-down arrow.

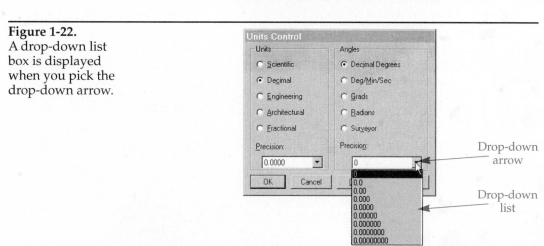

Drop-down arrow

Drop-down list

- **Text box.** You can enter a name or single line of information using the text box. See Figure 1-23. When a text box is empty, the cursor appears as a flashing vertical bar positioned at the far left side of the box. If there is existing text in the box, that text appears highlighted. Any characters you then type will replace the highlighted text. Pressing either the [Backspace] key, space bar, or the [Delete] key deletes all of the highlighted text. You can edit existing text using the cursor keys [Home], [End], right arrow, and left arrow. The [Home] key moves the cursor to the beginning of the line of text and the [End] key moves to the end of the line. The right arrow and left arrow keys move the cursor one

Figure 1-23.
You can enter a name, number, or single line of information in a text box. Several text boxes are shown here highlighted.

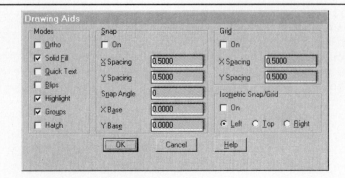

character to the right or to the left, respectively. By using the [Ctrl] key in conjunction with the right arrow or left arrow key, you can move the cursor to the next word or the previous word, respectively.

- **File dialog.** The file dialog provides a simple means of locating and specifying file names using the familiar Windows style dialog. The example in Figure 1-24 shows a file dialog for drawing file names. By *double-clicking* a folder name in the list, you can "open" it. Its contents are then displayed in the list box where items can be selected. The **Look in:** drop-down list displays the directory tree and allows you to browse for a storage device or a folder. The **Files of type:** drop-down list is used to specify the type of file being searched for. Once a file name is selected in the list box, it appears in the **File name:** text box, and its image appears in the **Preview** box. The four buttons above the upper-right corner of the list box allow you to back up one folder level, create a new folder, and display the files as a list of icons and names or with all file details. The **Find File...** button allows you to browse for a file. If the path and file name are already known, simply type it into the **File name:** text box and pick **Open** or press [Enter].

Figure 1-24.
The file dialog provides a simple means of locating files. The list box of this dialog box is highlighted.

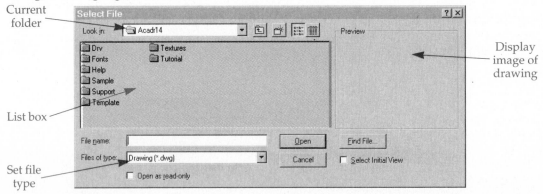

- **Scroll bars and buttons.** The scroll bar can be compared to an elevator sitting next to a list of items. The top arrow, or scroll button, points to the top floor, and the bottom arrow points to the basement. The box in the middle is the elevator. If you pick the elevator and hold down the pick button, you can move the box up or down. This displays additional items in the upper or lower floors of a list box. Pick the blank area above the elevator box to scroll up one page. Pick below the elevator box to scroll down one page. If you want to scroll up or down one file at a time, simply pick the up or down arrows. Horizontal scroll bars and buttons operate in the same manner. See Figure 1-25.

Figure 1-25.
Use scroll bars and
buttons to scroll
through a listing or
to view sections of a
drawing.

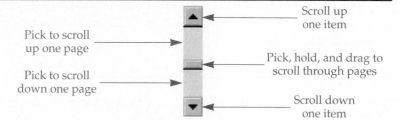

Pick to scroll
up one page

Pick to scroll
down one page

Scroll up
one item

Pick, hold, and drag to
scroll through pages

Scroll down
one item

- **Preview box or image tile.** A preview box is an area of a dialog box that displays a "picture" of the item you select, such as a hatching style, linetype, or text font. See Figure 1-26. For many image tiles, you can actually pick the image, or part of it, to adjust the selection.

Figure 1-26.
An image tile
displays the
selected setting.
Many image tiles,
such as the ones
shown here, can be
picked to change
the setting.

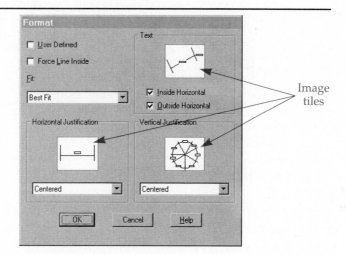

Image
tiles

- **Tab.** A dialog box tab is much like an index tab used to separate sections of a notebook, or like the label tabs on the top of a manila file folder. Many dialog boxes in AutoCAD contain two or more "pages" or "panels", each with a tab at the top. Each tab displays a new set of related options. While the dialog box is displayed, you can pick any number of tabs in order to select options. The dialog box will only be dismissed when the **OK** button is picked. See Figure 1-27.

Figure 1-27.
A dialog box tab is
much like an index
tab used to separate
sections of a
notebook. Each tab
displays a new set
of related options.

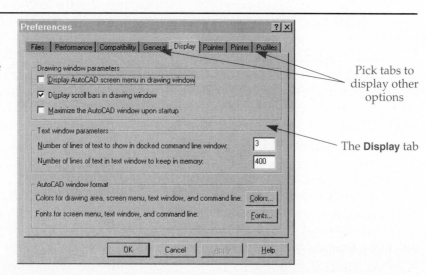

Pick tabs to
display other
options

The **Display** tab

- **Alerts.** Alerts can be displayed in two forms. A note may appear in the lower-left corner of the original dialog box or a separate alert dialog box may appear. See Figure 1-28.

Figure 1-28.
Alerts. A—An alert may appear as a note in the corner of a dialog box.
B—An alert may appear in a separate dialog box.

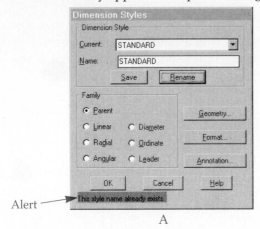

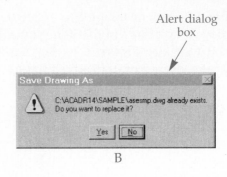

Alert dialog box

Alert

A

B

AutoCAD Release 14 makes extensive use of right-click menus. These are often referred to as *cursor menus* or *shortcut menus*. They are accessed by right-clicking. They are discussed throughout the text where they apply. Spend some time clicking the right mouse button while using a command or dialog box. You can increase your productivity by using these features.

AutoCAD tablet menu

The digitizer tablet can accept an overlay or menu that contains most of AutoCAD's commands. Other specialized programs that operate with AutoCAD may have similar menus.

This text presents commands as if they are typed at the keyboard or selected from menus, dialog boxes, or toolbars. If you wish to use your digitizer tablet to pick commands, the tablet must first be configured (arranged) before the menu can be used. See Chapter 29 for information on tablet configuration.

When you use a digitizer with AutoCAD, the cursor can only be moved within the active drawing area on-screen. Therefore, menu selections can only be made from the tablet menu overlay. Since all of the AutoCAD commands do not fit on the tablet, you will still need to select toolbar buttons, or to make selections from the pull-down menus on the menu bar. In addition, using the tablet requires that you take your eyes off the screen and look down at the overlay. After picking a tablet command, look at the command line to be sure you picked what you desired.

The AutoCAD tablet menu is shown in Figure 1-29. If you plan on using a digitizer with a tablet menu, take some time and study its arrangement. Become familiar with the command groups and try to remember where each command is located. The quicker you learn the layout of the menu, the more efficient your drawing sessions will be.

Figure 1-29.
The AutoCAD tablet menu. (Autodesk, Inc.)

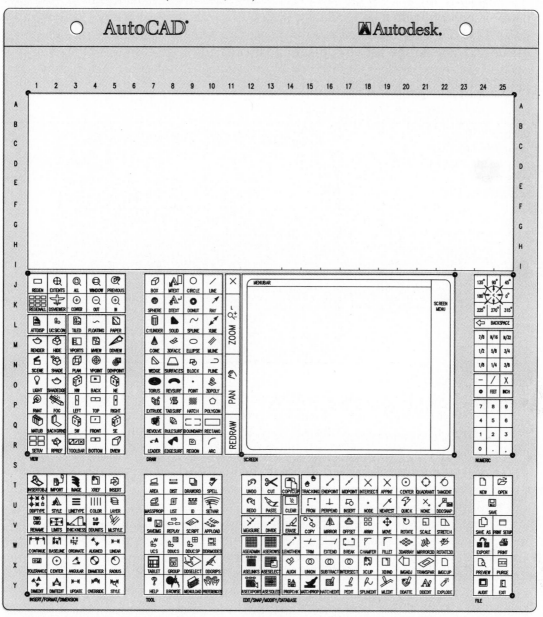

NOTE

Certain types of digitizer tablets can be configured to work both as a Windows system pointer (a mouse) and a digitizer. This type of configuration is called *absolute mode.* In order to operate in absolute mode, you must have a Wintab Compatible Digitizer. Windows NT requires both a Wintab System driver and an ADI Wintab driver to function. See the *AutoCAD Installation Guide* for more information.

Image tile menus

An image tile is the same as a preview box, and displays an image of the object, pattern, or option that is available. AutoCAD uses several menus composed of images. See Figure 1–30. To choose the object you want to use, simply pick the image tile or text label in the list box. Image tile menus allow for easy selection, since you can see the shape or item represented by the image. To select an image, move your pointing device to it and pick.

Figure 1-30.
Image tile menus graphically display options or selections.

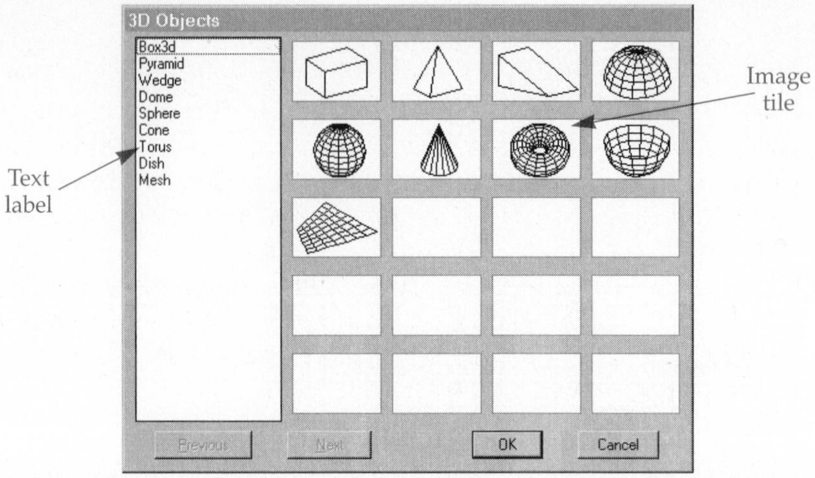

Text label

Image tile

Selecting AutoCAD Commands

AutoCAD commands may be selected in four different ways:
- Executed by picking a toolbar button or icon.
- Selected from one of the pull-down menus (or screen menus, if so configured).
- Selected from the digitizer tablet menu overlay.
- Typed at the keyboard.

The advantage of using toolbar buttons and on-screen menus is that you do not need to remove your eyes from the screen. Typing commands may not require that you turn your eyes from the screen. You can also learn commands quickly by typing them. However, when using a digitizer tablet, you must look down to pick tablet menu commands. On the other hand, a tablet menu overlay can show almost every command. Also, when configured as both a windows pointer and a digitizer (absolute mode), a tablet is a powerful and efficient input device.

> **NOTE** The examples shown in this text illustrate each of the AutoCAD commands as they appear when typed at the Command: prompt and when picked from toolbars and pull-down menus.

Command line editing

AutoCAD Release 14 provides you with the ability to select previously used commands simply by using the up and down arrow keys. For example, if you wanted to use the **CIRCLE** command that was used a few steps prior to your present position, simply press the up arrow key on the keyboard until the command you need is displayed on the Command: line, then press [Enter] to activate it.

This capability can be used to execute a typed command that is misspelled. For example, suppose you type LINE\ and press enter. The following message appears:

Unknown command "LINE\". Press F1 for help.

Just press the up arrow key, then press [Back space] to delete the backslash (\) and [Enter] to execute the **LINE** command. This is a time-saving feature if you like to type commands at the Command: prompt.

Getting Help

If you need help with a specific command, option, or program feature, AutoCAD provides a powerful and convenient on-line help system. There are several ways to access this feature. The fastest method is to simply press the [F1] function key. This displays the **Table of Contents** for the help system in the **AutoCAD Help** window, Figure 1-31. You can also display the **Table of Contents** by selecting the question mark icon at the right end of the **Standard** toolbar, by picking **AutoCAD Help Topics** from the **Help** pull-down menu, or by typing ? or HELP at the Command: prompt.

It is not necessary that AutoCAD be running in order to get help. The on-line help facility is available directly from the Windows desktop. Pick the Start button, pick Programs, pick AutoCAD R14, and finally select On-line Help. This displays the **AutoCAD Help** dialog box. See Figure 1-31.

Figure 1-31.
The help contents are displayed when you select **AutoCAD Help Topics...** from the **Help** pull-down menu or press the [F1] function key.

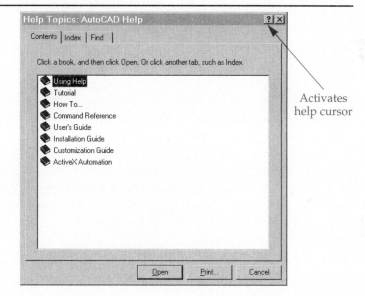

Activates help cursor

If you pick the question mark icon (What's this?) at the upper-right corner of the dialog box next to the close icon, it displays a cursor with a "?" attached to it. Pick on any item in the dialog box to get a brief explanation of what that feature is.

PROFESSIONAL TIP   If you are unfamiliar with how to use a Windows help system, it is suggested that you spend time now exploring all of the topics under **Using Help** in the **Contents** tab.

Exploring the contents of help

The **Contents** tab displays a list of eight book icons and topic names. The first book, **Using Help**, provides you with detailed information on using the Windows help system. To open a help topic simply double-click on the topic name or the book icon that precedes it. Figure 1-32A shows the list of items displayed when the **Using Help** book is opened. Double-click the **Using a Windows Help System** item and the two items shown in Figure 1-32B are displayed. Double-click the **Using Help** item and a list of help topics preceded by question mark icons are displayed. See Figure 1-32C.

Figure 1-32.
Using help. A—Double-click the book icon to open it and reveal the topics.
B—Double-clicking a topic can lead to other books. C—Double-clicking the **Using Help** item presents another list of help topics.

Picking one of the items preceded by the question mark displays a **Windows Help** dialog box. See Figure 1-33. Step-by-step instructions are provided in this window, as well as useful tips. Three buttons are located at the top of this window:

- **Help Topics.** Returns to the **Help Topics** dialog box.
- **Back.** Flips back to the previous **Windows Help** page. If no pages were previously displayed, this button is grayed-out.

AutoCAD and its Applications—Basics

Figure 1-33.
Opening a topic
displays a help
window.

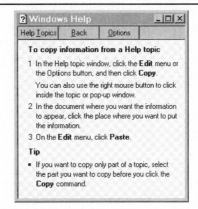

- **Options.** Picking **Options** displays the following selections:
  - **Annotate...**—Allows you to write a note that relates to the current help topic. See Figure 1-34. Picking **Save** in the **Annotate** dialog box attaches your note to the help topic with a paper clip icon. To read your annotation, simply click once on the paper clip. This note can also be copied to another document, or text from another document can be pasted into it. When the note is no longer needed it can be deleted.
  - **Copy**—Copies the entire content of the **Windows Help** dialog box to the Clipboard. If you wish to copy only specific text, select it first then use **Copy**.

Figure 1-34.
Using the **Annotate** option. A—You can write a note in the **Annotate** dialog box.
B—The paper clip icon appears when there is a note associated with a topic.

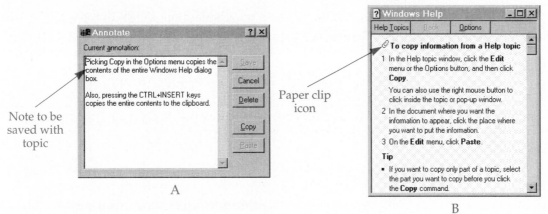

A

B

NOTE

Remember, the key combinations [Ctrl]+[C] and [Ctrl]+[V] can be used to quickly execute the **Copy** and **Paste** commands, respectively.

PROFESSIONAL TIP

All of the text inside the **Windows Help** box can be copied to the clipboard by pressing the [Ctrl]+[Insert] keys. Use the paste function to insert this text into a new document.

- **Print Topic...**—Displays the **Print** dialog box, and allows you to send the contents of the **Windows Help** dialog box to the system printer.
- **Font**—Allows you to select between small, normal, and large fonts for the display of **Windows Help** dialog box text.
- **Keep Help on Top**—Allows you to keep the **Help** window on top of all other windows. The **Default** setting allows the window to remain in its selected order of open windows on the desktop.
- **Use System Colors**—Returns the help windows to the default Windows system colors.

PROFESSIONAL TIP   While a help dialog box is displayed, pressing the right mouse button displays a cursor menu that contains all the items in the **Options** pull-down menu.

The topics **Concepts** and **How To...** are listed in the **Contents** tab shown in Figure 1-31. These are topics to assist you in understanding and using AutoCAD drawing concepts and techniques.

The last five topics in the **Contents** tab represent the printed *AutoCAD Release 14 Documentation Pack*, of which only the *Installation Guide* and the *User's Guide* are shipped with the software. The *Command Reference, Customization Guide*, and *OLE Automation Guide* must be ordered through your Authorized Autodesk Dealer or Reseller.

Using the Index tab

Although the **Contents** tab is useful for displaying all of the topics in an expanded table of contents manner, it is not that useful when searching for a specific item. In this case, most people refer to the index. This is the function of the **Index** tab. See Figure 1-35.

Figure 1-35.
The **Index** tab displays an index listing.

Enter topic in text box

Alphabetical list of topics

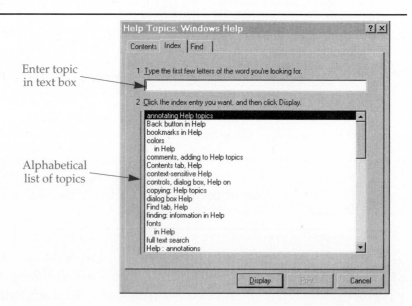

The index can be used in two ways. The first is to just scroll through the alphabetical list of items in the list box. This is tedious because the list is lengthy. The second way is to follow the instructions above the text box: Type the first few letters of the word you're looking for. As you type each new character, the lower list changes to match your entry as close as possible. Test this by slowly typing the letters lin and notice the entry that appears highlighted at the top of the list. See Figure 1-36. If you were searching for information on drawing lines you could now double-click on the specific item in the list.

Figure 1-36.
The **Index** tab with lin entered in the text box.

AutoCAD selects topic that most nearly matches text box entry

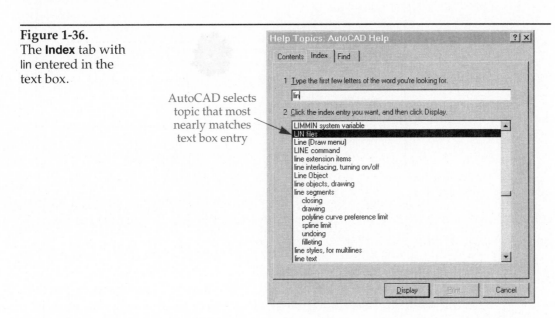

Some items refer to several topics. In this case, the **Topics Found** dialog box is displayed. See Figure 1-37. Click on the topic you wish to see and pick the **Display** button. When you display the topic, a help screen is presented that may include text, hypertext links, and graphics.

Figure 1-37.
The **Topics Found** dialog box.

Select one of the topics

Pick to display help window for selected topic

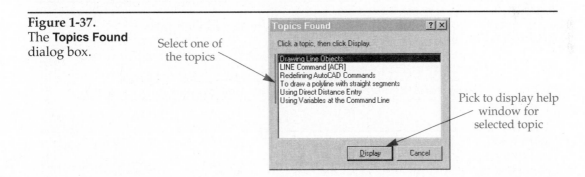

Hypertext is green underlined text. If a hypertext item is selected, it automatically displays the help screen it is linked to. When the cursor is on hypertext, it becomes a hand, Figure 1-38. Picking with the hand displays specific help related to the hypertext.

Figure 1-38.
AutoCAD Help
dialog box for the
LINE Command with
pointer on continue.

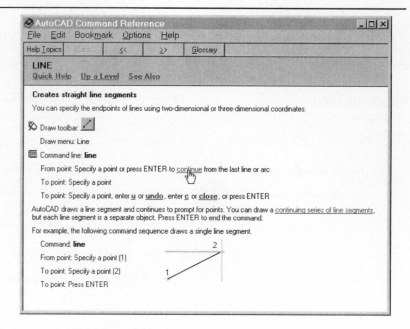

An item that is underlined with a solid line jumps to another topic. An item that is underlined with a dashed line displays a pop-up topic. When one of these items is picked, a pop-up topic box is displayed. See Figure 1-39.

AutoCAD help screens that display information about a command also display the following items just below the command name:

- **Quick Help.** Displays a pop-up topic box that provides definitions of the buttons in the **AutoCAD Help** dialog boxes. This display is shown in Figure 1-40.
- **Up a Level.** Displays an alphabetical listing of AutoCAD commands and system variables.
- **See Also.** Displays a pop-up topic box that provides links to commands and variables that are related to the one currently displayed. Refer again to Figure 1-39.

Figure 1-39.
A pop-up topic box is displayed when a green hypertext word with a dashed underline is selected.

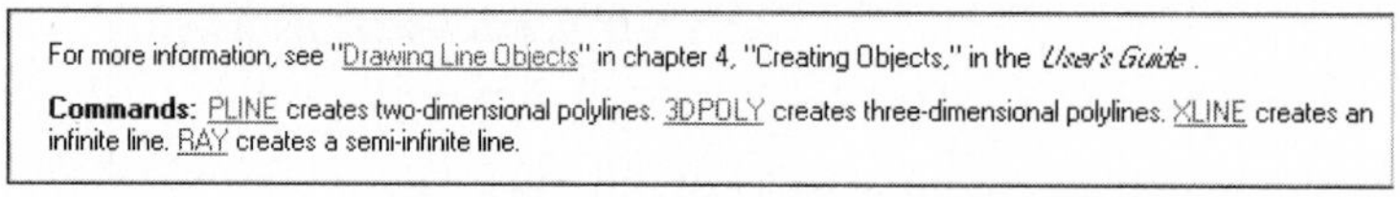

> For more information, see "Drawing Line Objects" in chapter 4, "Creating Objects," in the *User's Guide*.
>
> **Commands:** PLINE creates two-dimensional polylines. 3DPOLY creates three-dimensional polylines. XLINE creates an infinite line. RAY creates a semi-infinite line.

Figure 1-40.
The **Quick Help** pop-up window explains several buttons found in the help windows.

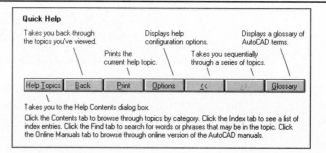

Using the Find tab

The **Find** tab enables you to conduct a detailed search based on one or more words. This should be your third choice for help after using the **Contents** and **Index** tabs. It is a more detailed search process because **Find** bases its search on words and word combinations. Therefore, it must first create its own word list, much like a super index.

The first time you select the **Find** tab you are presented with two displays of the **Find Setup Wizard**. See Figure 1-41. Pick the **Next** 〉 button to accept the defaults. This creates the minimum database size.

Figure 1-41.
The **Find Setup Wizard** creates a database to be used to find help.

When the word list is created, the display in the **Find** tab changes to that shown in Figure 1-42. This looks like a beefed-up **Index** tab, and in fact it is much more powerful. Use **Find** in the following manner:

1. Begin your search by typing the topic you are looking for. Unlike the **Index** help, you can type more than one word. For example, suppose you want to know how to erase lines. Just type erasing lines and watch the displays change. See Figure 1-43.

Figure 1-42.
The **Find** tab allows you to conduct a detailed search.

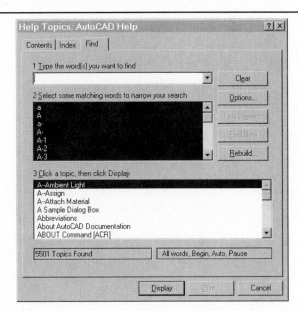

Figure 1-43.
Enter the topic you wish to search for in the first text box.

Enter topic in text box

Select or deselect related words

Search results

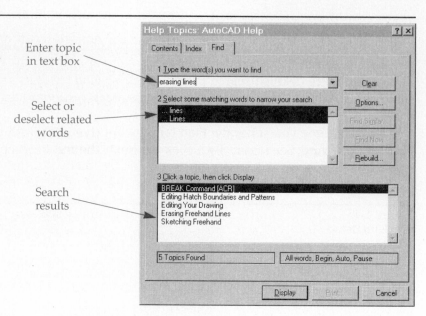

2. Select any of the additional modifying words in the list box in the center of the dialog box. All of the items in this box are highlighted and are deselected when you pick one. Remember to hold the [Shift] key down if you want to add words to the selected list.

3. Look in the bottom list box for the final list of contestants. Select the one that appeals to you, and pick the **Display** button or press [Enter] to read about the topic.

NOTE   Choosing to create the minimized version of the word list does not impair your ability to search for words in the AutoCAD documentation. It merely keeps the size of the word list file small until further additions are needed. If a **Find** search does not locate the specific topic you need, just pick on the **Rebuild** button in the **Find** tab and the word list will be rebuilt.

Find is set for optimal searching, and like **Index**, immediately displays characters and words as you type them. The words also do not have to be typed in a logical order. You could have entered lines erasing in the previous example and the topics displayed would have been the same.

The **Find** utility, by default, searches through all of the AutoCAD documentation. As a result, a wide variety of items may be displayed as a result of the search. You can limit the search to just the documents you need by picking the **Options...** button in the **Find** tab. This displays the **Find Options** dialog box. Pick the **Files...** button and the **File Options** dialog box lists all of the files that are searched. Deselect any of the references that do not need to be included in the search. Pick **OK** in both dialog boxes when done.

CAUTION

In many AutoCAD help windows a **Bookmark** menu item is displayed. Setting a bookmark in Windows was intended to be a convenient tool for quickly recalling specific help topics. But this feature does not work as intended in AutoCAD and other software that contains several documentation manuals. The AutoCAD help is composed of five manuals, hence there are five separate help files. When a bookmark is set in one of the manuals, it will not be listed when help from another manual is displayed. In other words, in the current release of AutoCAD, bookmarks are not added to a single list to reference all manuals quickly. This is a shortcoming of the Windows bookmark facility. Using **Index** and **Find** are the best methods of locating topics.

Using the glossary

The glossary is a list of AutoCAD terms. It can be accessed from any main help screen by picking the **Glossary** button. Glossary topics can be accessed by scrolling through the list, or by picking one of the alphabet buttons above the list. All of the items in the glossary are pop-up topics. These can be useful for obtaining a quick definition of a topic. See Figure 1-44.

Figure 1-44. The AutoCAD glossary. A—The Glossary window. B—Picking a topic displays a short explanation.

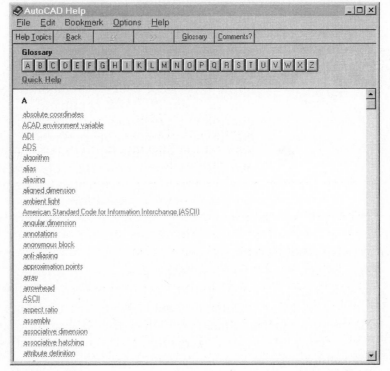

A

B

PROFESSIONAL TIP

You can get quick help when many of AutoCAD's file dialog boxes are open. Simply right-click on the item in the dialog box you wish information on and a **What's This?** button appears. Pick the button and a pop-up topic box is displayed that provides a brief explanation of the feature. Pick anywhere on the screen to clear the topic box.

New Features in Release 14

If you are curious about the changes that were made for the Release 14 version of AutoCAD, pick **What's New...** from the **Help** pull-down menu. This displays a main menu of eleven topics. Placing the pointer on each topic displays a pop-up topic box that provides a brief explanation of the topic. Picking a topic in the main menu starts a scripted presentation on the topic. It will advance automatically and return to the main menu when completed. Four buttons at the upper-right of the screen allow you to stop, step backward, pause, and step forward in the presentation. Pick the red square in the lower-left to exit the entire help presentation, or pick the main menu icon at the upper-left to return to the main menu.

Pick **Quick Tour** in the **Help** pull-down menu if you want to view a quick introduction to AutoCAD Release 14, or a glimpse of the new drawing capabilities. You can quickly jump between **What's New...** and **Quick Tour** by picking the **Show me** icon at the lower-right of the main menu of each feature.

PROFESSIONAL TIP

AutoCAD's **Help** function can also be used while you are in the process of using a command. For example, suppose you are using the **ARC** command and forget what type of information is required by AutoCAD for the specific prompts that are on-screen. Simply press the [F1] function key and the help information for the currently active command is displayed. This *context oriented help* saves valuable time, since you don't need to scan through the **Help** contents or perform any searches to find the information.

Learning assistance

AutoCAD Release 14 provides a powerful learning tool called **Learning Assistance** found in the **Help** pull-down menu. It is an interactive, multimedia facility composed of three parts: **Tutorials**, **Fast Answers**, and **Concepts**. Each section contains a wide variety of presentations complete with text, graphics, sound, and animations. They are highly informative, and will satisfy the needs of persons with different learning styles.

The first time **Learning Assistance** is selected, it is installed on your hard drive. You can use the default folder name or create one yourself. Once **Learning Assistance** is installed on the hard drive, pick **P**rograms in the Start menu, then pick AutoCAD Learning Assistance. It is suggested that you pick **Using Learning Assistance** from the **Help** pull-down menu and take a few minutes to familiarize yourself with how this learning tool functions.

After viewing and using these tools you can immediately apply them to your work. As you work through this text you can increase your AutoCAD skills by using **Learning Assistance**.

Bonus tools

This release of AutoCAD includes a set of Bonus Tools. These tools are not included in a typical installation but are included in a full installation.

If the Bonus Tools are installed, a **Bonus** pull-down menu is included in the menu bar. Four toolbars (**Internet Utilities**, **Bonus Standard**, **Bonus Text Tools**, and **Bonus Layer Tools**) appear on the right side of the graphics window.

Most of the Bonus Tools are AutoLISP routines or ARX applications designed to improve productivity. The tools allow you to use a single command in a situation where several commands are normally needed.

Individual tools are referenced in appropriate locations throughout this text. For a full discussion of all the Bonus Tools, refer to Appendix A.

Keys, Buttons, Functions, and Terminology

AutoCAD provides several ways of performing a given task. A variety of keys on the keyboard allow you to quickly perform many functions. In addition, multibutton pointing devices also use buttons for AutoCAD commands. Become familiar with the meaning of these keys and buttons.

The [Esc] key

Any time it is necessary to cancel a command and return to the Command: prompt, press the *escape key* on your keyboard. This key is found on the upper-left corner of most keyboards and is typically labeled [Esc]. Some command sequences may require that the [Esc] key be pressed twice to completely cancel the operation.

Control keys

Most computer programs use *control key* functions to perform common tasks. Control key functions are activated by pressing and holding the [Ctrl] key while pressing a second key. These are also called accelerator keys.

Keep the following list close at hand and try them occasionally. (If a command or key is noted as a "toggle," it is either on or off—nothing else.)

Key Combination	Result
[Ctrl]+[B]	**Snap** mode (toggle)
[Ctrl]+[C]	**Copyclip**
[Ctrl]+[D]	Coordinate display on status line (toggle)
[Ctrl]+[E]	Crosshairs in isoplane positions left/top/right (toggle)
[Ctrl]+[G]	**Grid** (toggle)
[Ctrl]+[H]	Same as backspace
[Ctrl]+[K]	**PICKADD** system variable toggle
[Ctrl]+[L]	**Ortho** mode (toggle)
[Ctrl]+[O]	**Open**
[Ctrl]+[P]	**Print** (Plot)
[Ctrl]+[R]	Toggle viewport
[Ctrl]+[S]	**Save**
[Ctrl]+[T]	**Tablet** mode (toggle)
[Ctrl]+[V]	**Paste clip**
[Ctrl]+[X]	**Cut clip**
[Ctrl]+[Y]	**Redo**
[Ctrl]+[Z]	**Undo**

PROFESSIONAL TIP

Computer users who are experienced in working with DOS or those who have used previous versions of AutoCAD may be familiar with using the [Ctrl]+[C] key combination as a **Cancel** command. However, in AutoCAD Release 14, the [Ctrl]+[C] key combination activates the **COPYCLIP** command. If you want to use the [Ctrl]+[C] key combination so that it activates the **Cancel** command, pick **Preferences...** in the **Tools** pull-down menu, then pick the **Compatibility** tab. Pick the **AutoCAD classic** button in the **Priority for accelerator keys** area then pick **OK**. You can now use [Ctrl]+[C] as a cancel. See *AutoCAD and its Applications—Advanced, Release 14* for information on customizing preferences.

Function keys

Function keys provide instant access to commands. They can also be programmed to perform a series of commands. The function keys are either to the left or along the top of the keyboard, Figure 1-45. Depending on the brand of keyboard, there will be either 10 or 12 function keys. These are numbered from [F1] to [F10] (or [F12]). AutoCAD uses only nine function keys. These are listed below. As you become proficient with AutoCAD, you might program the function keys to do specific tasks using other computer programs.

Figure 1-45.
Function keys are found along the top or side of a keyboard. In this photo,
the function keys are along the top and labeled [F1] through [F12].

Function keys [F1] through [F12]

Function Key	Result
[F1]	Help.
[F2]	Flip screen from graphics to text (toggle).
[F3]	**DDOSNAP**—displays the **Osnap Settings** dialog box.
[F4]	Tablet mode (toggle).
[F5]	Isoplane (toggle).
[F6]	Coordinate display (toggle).
[F7]	**Grid** (toggle).
[F8]	**Ortho** mode (toggle).
[F9]	**Snap** mode (toggle).

Button functions

If you are using a multibutton pointing device, you can select control key functions
by pressing a single button. The default settings of the pointing device buttons are:

Button	Result
0	Pick
1	Return
2	Object snap cursor menu displayed on-screen
3	**Cancel**
4	**Snap** mode (toggle)
5	**Ortho** mode (toggle)
6	**Grid** (toggle)
7	Coordinate display (toggle)
8	Crosshairs isoplane positions top/left/right (toggle)
9	Tablet mode (toggle)

Understanding terminology

The following terms are used throughout the text and will help you select
AutoCAD functions. Become familiar with them:

- **Default.** A value that is maintained by the computer until you change it.
- **Pick or Click.** Use the pointing device to select an item on the screen or tablet.
- **Button.** One of the screen toolbar or pointing device (puck) buttons.
- **Key.** A key on the keyboard.

- **Function key.** One of the keys labeled [F1]–[F10] (or [F1]–[F12]) along the top or side of the keyboard.
- **[Enter] (↵).** The [Enter] or [Return] key on the keyboard.
- **Command.** An instruction issued to the computer.
- **Option.** An aspect of a command that can be selected.

Avoiding "Disk Full" Problems

When you save a drawing, AutoCAD allows you to specify a name and a location for the drawing file. The drawing will be saved in the AutoCAD program folder AutoCAD R14 unless you specify a new one. You can also select the disk drive in which to save the drawing. The hard disk that contains the AutoCAD program folder is the default. New users to AutoCAD often want to save their drawings on a 3.5" disk instead of on the hard drive.

Saving a drawing to the 3.5" disk during a working session is not the most efficient way to operate AutoCAD. These drives are slow to store and access data. In addition, limited space on the 3.5" disk can eventually lead to a Not enough space on disk error. If you save your drawing directly to these disks, AutoCAD also places a backup drawing file with the same name in the same location as the original file. Each time you save the original drawing, the backup file is updated. Therefore, you actually have two drawing files instead of one. For additional information see Chapter 15, *Working with AutoCAD Files.*

Always save your work to the hard disk on a regular basis—every 10 to 15 minutes. If you must save a drawing to a 3.5" disk, make it the last thing you do before you exit AutoCAD. Additionally, you can use the Windows Explorer at any time to quickly see if drawings will fit on your disk, and then copy them to the disk. Refer to Chapter 30 for a discussion of using the Windows Explorer and the My Computer window. Chapters 2 and 3 discuss the techniques of starting and saving drawings properly.

PROFESSIONAL TIP

To ensure that your work is being saved on a regular basis, use the **SAVETIME** variable. Just enter **SAVETIME** at the Command: prompt, then enter the number of minutes between each automatic save. By default, your drawing file is saved with the name of auto.sv$. If for any reason the drawing file is damaged, the auto.sv$ can be renamed to a drawing file (.dwg) and loaded into AutoCAD.

NOTE

Most 3.5" disks are sold preformatted. But if you purchase unformatted disks, they must be formatted before they can be used by the computer. This process divides the disk into pie-shaped sectors, checks it for defects, and creates a file directory on the disk. This process is also useful for deleting all data from used disks. This is all accomplished in the My Computer window. See Chapter 30 for a complete discussion on this process.

Chapter Test

Write your answers in the spaces provided.

1. What system is used to construct drawings and models in AutoCAD? _____ *Cartesian (rectangular) coordinate system*

2. Basic pictorial drawings are called *isometrics*.

3. How would you write the proper notation of the following values using the system referred to in Question 1: Z=4, X=2, Y=5? *2,5,4*

4. Why is drawing planning important? *organize your thoughts, sketch problem, note size & locations of features. List dwg commands needed*

5. Why should you save your work every 10 to 15 minutes? *in case of system shutdown, software or hardware malfunct., power failure, own mistakes*

6. What is "drawing planning?" *sketch problem or design, note size & locations of features. List dwg commands needed in order used. Use computer @ reg. time, include specific dwg names, proj. plan, sheets, project logs, layout procedures*

7. What are standards? *guidelines for operating procedures, dwg techniques & record keeping*

8. What is the first thing you should do as part of your planning checklist? *plan dwg projects carefully (analyze problem)*

9. What scale should you use to draw in AutoCAD? *1:1*

10. Why should you read the command line at the bottom of the screen? *where primary communications w/ Autocad displayed, displays prompts which supply info. to you or request input*

11. How is AutoCAD represented on the Windows desktop? *program icon shown in windows selection*

12. What is the quickest method for starting AutoCAD? *double click on Autocad R14 icon*

13. What is a Windows link? *new page of info. that is attached or present info id by green underlined text & brought up by hand icon*

14. List four of the areas that compose the AutoCAD graphics window. *floating command window, menu bar, graphics cursor, floating tool bar, coordinate display*

15. Which area displays the communication between AutoCAD and the user? *floating command window*

16. What are the differences between a docked toolbar and a floating toolbar? *float - buttons activate commands, bars can be moved, resized, docked is default buttons*

17. What are menu accelerator keys? How are they used? Give an example. _____

_____

_____

_____

_____

p. 45

18. What is an option? *allows to write note that relates to current help topic*

19. List the ten AutoCAD pull-down menus. *File, edit, View, Insert Format, Tools, Draw, Dimension, modify, help*

20. What is a flyout menu? _____

21. What is the function of tabs in a dialog box? _____

22. What must you do to the tablet before it can be used? _____

23. What are the functions of the following control keys?
    A. [Ctrl]+[B] *Snap mode (toggle)*
    B. [Ctrl]+[C] *Copy clip*
    C. [Ctrl]+[D] *coordinate display on status Line (toggle)*
    D. [Ctrl]+[G] *Grid (toggle)*
    E. [Ctrl]+[O] *open*

24. Name the function keys that execute the same task as the following control keys.

    Control Key   Function Key
    A. [Ctrl]+[B] *F9*
    B. [Ctrl]+[D] *F6*
    C. [Ctrl]+[G] *F7*
    D. [Ctrl]+[L] *F8*
    E. [Ctrl]+[T] *F4*

25. What is the difference between a "button" and a "key"? _____

26. What do you call a value that is maintained by the computer until you change it? _____

27. What type of pull-down menu item has an arrow to the right? _____

28. What type of menu contains a group of symbols or patterns? _____

29. What is an image tile? _____

30. What is "content oriented help" and how is it accessed? _____

Problems

1. Interview your drafting instructors or supervisors and try to determine what type of drawing standards exist at your school or company. Write this down and keep it with you as you learn AutoCAD. Make notes as you progress through this text on how you use these standards. Also note how the standards could be changed to match the capabilities of AutoCAD.

2. Research your drafting department standards. If you do not have a copy of the standards, acquire one. If AutoCAD standards have been created, make notes as to how you can use these in your projects. If no standards exist in your department or company, make notes as to how you can help develop standards. Write a report on why your school or company should create CAD standards and how they would be used. Discuss who should be responsible for specific tasks. Recommend procedures, techniques, and forms, if necessary. Develop this report as you progress through your AutoCAD instruction, and as you read through this book.

3. Develop a drawing planning sheet for use in your school or company. List items that you think are important for planning a CAD drawing. Make changes to this sheet as you learn more about AutoCAD.

4. Load AutoCAD from the Windows desktop using one of the three methods discussed in the chapter. Perform the following tasks:
   A. Pick the **OK** button at the **Start Up** dialog box.
   B. Pick the minimize button at the upper-right of the AutoCAD graphics window.
   C. Pick the Start button on the Windows task bar, then pick Programs. Next, pick the AutoCAD R14 item, then pick Online Help.
   D. Pick the **Contents** tab if it is not displayed. Double-click the **User's Guide** item, then double-click **Chapter 1 — Getting Started**. Double-click **Accessing Information from the Help Menu**.
   E. Pick the green hypertext link **To access Help topics** and read the next help window.
   F. Dismiss the small help window by picking the "X" close button at the upper-right of the dialog box.
   G. Restore AutoCAD by picking the AutoCAD button on the task bar.
   H. Close AutoCAD by picking the control icon at the upper-left of the AutoCAD graphics window.

5. Load AutoCAD by selecting the proper items using the Start button on the Windows task bar.
   A. Pick the **OK** button at the **Start Up** dialog box.
   B. Move the pointer to a space between two buttons in the standard toolbar and read the note on the status bar at the bottom of the screen.
   C. Move the pointer to a space to the left of the **Color Control** drop-down list box and read the note on the status bar.
   D. Slowly move the pointer over each of the buttons on the **Standard** toolbar and **Object Properties** toolbar and read the ToolTips. Do the same on the **Draw** and **Modify** toolbars at the left of the screen.

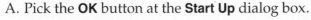

E. Pick the **File** pull-down menu to display it. Using the right arrow cursor key, move through all of the pull-down menus. Use the left arrow key to return to the **Draw** pull-down menu. Use the down arrow key to move to the **Circle** command, then use the right arrow key to display the **Circle** options.

F. Press the [Esc] key to dismiss the menu.

G. Close AutoCAD by picking **Exit** in the **File** pull-down menu.

6. Draw a freehand sketch of the screen display. Label each of the screen areas. To the side of the sketch, write a short description of each screen area's function.

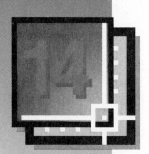

Chapter 2

Starting and Setting Up Drawings

Learning Objectives

After completing this chapter, you will be able to:
- ○ Plan an AutoCAD drawing.
- ○ Establish the drawing limits and set the units style.
- ○ Use the AutoCAD wizards.
- ○ Use the AutoCAD **Quick Setup** option.
- ○ Use the AutoCAD **Advanced Setup** option.
- ○ Use an AutoCAD template.
- ○ Start a drawing from scratch.
- ○ Use the **DDUNITS**, **UNITS**, and **LIMITS** commands to change a drawing setup.
- ○ Open an existing drawing.

Planning Your AutoCAD Drawing

Effective planning can greatly reduce the amount of time it takes to set up and complete a drawing. Drawing setup involves many factors that affect the quality and accuracy of your final drawing. AutoCAD helps make this planning process easy by providing a variety of automated setup options that help you begin a drawing. Even with these options, you still need to know the basic elements that make up your drawing. Some basic planning decisions include the following:
- The sheet size on which the drawing will be plotted.
- The units of measure being used.
- The precision required for the drawing.
- The name of the drawing.

This chapter discusses all of these AutoCAD setup options. It also provides an opportunity to experiment with them.

Starting a New Drawing

When AutoCAD is first started, the **Start Up** dialog box is automatically displayed. See Figure 2-1. In this dialog box several drawing setup options are available. These options define the drawing appearance by setting items such as dimensioning features, pattern scales, and text size to match the selected drawing units. In the **Start Up** dialog box the **Use a Wizard** button is the default. Two of the setup options are found in the **Select a Wizard:** list. A *wizard* consists of AutoCAD setup options that automatically control scale factors for dimension settings and text height based on the information you provide. The two wizard setup options are as follows:

- **Quick Setup.** This setup option allows a drawing to be quickly started by defining the drawing area, units, and scale. This is the default when AutoCAD is first started.
- **Advanced Setup.** This setup option provides the same options found in the **Quick Setup** but with additional control and flexibility. **Advanced Setup** also provides several border and title block options.

Figure 2-1.
The **Start Up** dialog box opens when you begin AutoCAD. This dialog box can be turned off and AutoCAD will start with the **Start from Scratch** drawing setup.

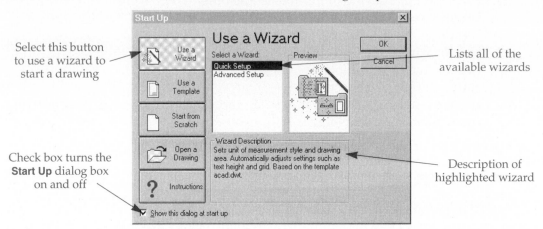

If more individual control over the setup of an AutoCAD drawing is desired, a template may be used or a drawing may be started from scratch. A *template* is a drawing file with standard settings. These two setup options are buttons located on the left side of the dialog box. These buttons are labeled as follows:

- **Use a Template.** This setup option offers a selection of standard sheet sizes with border and title block layouts.
- **Start from Scratch.** This setup option offers a selection of either English or metric units, and then you set up all other drawing specifications.

NOTE   In the lower-left corner of the **Start Up** dialog box is the **Show this dialog at start up** check box. It is checked by default, and the **Start Up** dialog box appears every time AutoCAD is started. Click on the check box to turn this dialog box off. To turn to dialog box back on, select **Preferences...** from the **Tools** pull-down menu. Then selet the **Compatibility** tab and pick the **Show the Start Up dialog box** check box.

New
[Ctrl]+[N]

File
→ New...

Standard
toolbar

New

If the **Start Up** dialog box is not on, a new drawing can still be started. The **Create New Drawing** dialog box is similar to the **Start Up** dialog box. See Figure 2-2. To access the **Create New Drawing** dialog box pick **New...** from the **File** pull-down menu, press the [Ctrl]+[N] key combination, or by typing NEW at the Command: prompt.

If the **Use a Wizard** button in the upper-left corner is selected, the **Select a Wizard:** list is shown. Highlight the desired setup option by picking either **Quick Setup** or **Advanced Setup**. The option used for the previous setup becomes the default for the next time AutoCAD is started. A description of the highlighted setup is given in the **Wizard Description** area. Look in this area for information provided by AutoCAD about any setup option chosen. Figure 2-1 shows the description for the **Quick Setup** and Figure 2-2 shows the description for the **Advanced Setup**.

Figure 2-2.
While in AutoCAD you can access the **Create New Drawing** dialog box by picking **New...** in the **File** pull-down menu. This dialog box is similar to the **Start Up** dialog box.

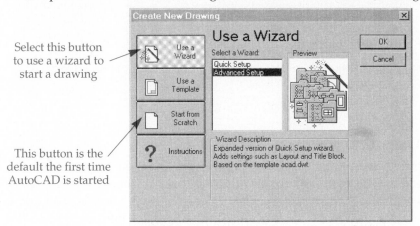

Select this button to use a wizard to start a drawing

This button is the default the first time AutoCAD is started

> **NOTE**
> The **Instructions** button in the lower-left corner of the **Start Up** and **Create New Drawing** dialog boxes is handy for giving you brief information about the different startup options.

Using the **Quick Setup** wizard

The following discussion explains how to start a new drawing using the **Quick Setup** option. To access this option in the **Start Up** dialog box, double-click on **Quick Setup** in the **Select a Wizard:** list, or highlight **Quick Setup** and pick **OK** or press [Enter].

> **NOTE**
> When using the **Create New Drawing** dialog box for the first time, **Start from Scratch** is the default. To access the wizard options, pick the **Use a Wizard** button. Then, select **Quick Setup** as just described.

The **Quick Setup** dialog box shown in Figure 2-3 should be on screen. The drawing units are set in the **Step 1: Units** tab, and area is set in the **Step 2: Area** tab. After the settings are made in the two tabs, AutoCAD sets up the drawing area.

Figure 2-3.
The **Quick Setup** dialog box contains the **Step 1: Units** and **Step 2: Area** tabs. The **Decimal** units is the **Step 1: Units** tab default.

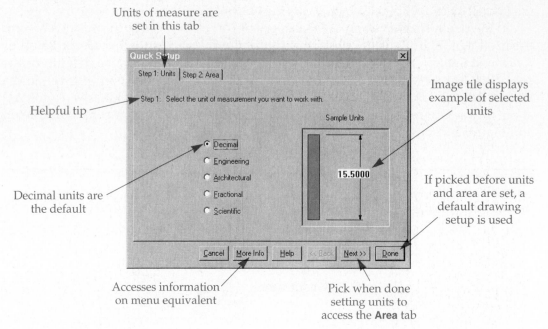

Setting units of measure

There are several options for setting drawing units in the **Step 1: Units** tab of the **Quick Setup** dialog box. The default setting is **Decimal** units. When using the **Quick Setup** dialog box, the default precision is given for all unit choices. There is an example of a typical decimal units and precision displayed in the **Sample Units** image tile. The units can be changed by picking the desired radio button. When a units radio button is picked, the selected option becomes active. An example of the new active option is then displayed in the **Sample Units** image tile. The units options are as follows:

- **Decimal.** These units are used to create drawings in decimal inches or millimeters. Decimal units are normally used on mechanical drawings for manufacturing. This option conforms to the *ASME Y14.5M* dimensioning and tolerancing standard. The default precision is four decimal places.
- **Engineering.** These units are often used in civil drafting projects such as maps, plot plans, dam and bridge construction, and topography. The default precision is four decimal places. The example from the **Sample Units** image tile is shown in Figure 2-4A.
- **Architectural.** Architectural, structural, and other drawings use these units when measurements are in feet, inches, and fractional inches. The default precision is to the half inch. The example from the **Sample Units** image tile is shown in Figure 2-4B.
- **Fractional.** This option is used for drawings that have fractional parts of any common unit of measure. The default precision is to one-half. The example from the **Sample Units** image tile is shown in Figure 2-4C.
- **Scientific.** These units are used when very large or small values are applied to the drawing. These applications take place in industries such as chemical engineering and astronomy. The default precision is four decimal places. The **Sample Units** image tile in Figure 2-4D shows 1.5500E+01. The E+01 means that the base number is multiplied by 10 to the first power.

Figure 2-4.
A—The **Engineering** units option shown in image tile. B—The **Architectural** units option shown in image tile. C—The **Fractional** units option shown in image tile. D—The **Scientific** units option shown in image tile.

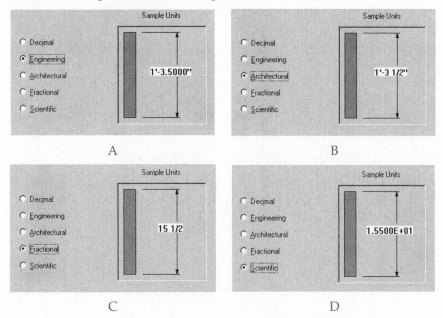

A   B

C   D

NOTE   Pick the **More Info** button at the bottom of the **Quick Setup** dialog box to get a dialog box with information about how to access the same AutoCAD feature using the pull-down menu equivalent. The information is provided for the specific tab where the button is active.

EXERCISE 2-1

❑ Open AutoCAD and look at the **Start Up** dialog box. If AutoCAD is already running, access the **Create New Drawing** dialog box.
❑ Pick the **Instructions** button and read the information about the different setup options.
❑ Pick the **Use a Wizard** button to return to the **Use a Wizard** options.
❑ Access the **Quick Setup** dialog box. **Decimal** units is the default units of measure in the this dialog box.
❑ Study the **Sample Units** image tile. Pick each of the unit options and notice how the **Sample Units** image tile changes.
❑ Pick the **Done** button.

Setting the drawing area

An AutoCAD drawing is created actual size using the selected units. *World size* indicates that the drawing is measured in the actual full-size units being used. If you are drawing an object that is measured in feet and inches, then you draw using feet and inches in AutoCAD. If you are creating a mechanical drawing for manufacturing, the drawing is full-size using decimal inches or millimeters. You draw the objects full-size regardless of the type of drawing, the units used, or the size of the final layout on paper.

Drafters often think of the drawing size as sheet size. The *sheet size* is the size of the paper that you use to plot the final drawing. The sheet size takes into account the size of the drawing and added space for dimensions, notes, and clear area between the drawing and border lines. The sheet size also includes the title block, revision block, zoning, and an area for general notes. AutoCAD refers to the sheet size as *area* or *limits*.

ASME/ANSI standard sheet sizes and format are specified in the documents ANSI Y14.1 *Drawing Sheet Size and Format* and ASME Y14.1M *Metric Drawing Sheet Size and Format*. The proper presentation of engineering changes are given in ASME Y14.35M *Revision of Engineering Drawings and Associated Documents*. ANSI Y14.1 lists sheet size specifications in inches as follows:

Size Designation	Size (in inches)
A	8 1/2 × 11 (horizontal format) 11 × 8 1/2 (vertical format)
B	11 × 17
C	17 × 22
D	22 × 34
E	34 × 44
F	28 × 40
Sizes G, H, J, and K are roll sizes.	

ASME Y14.1M provides sheet size specifications in metric units. Standard metric drawing sheet sizes are designated as follows:

Size Designation	Size (in millimeters)
A0	841 × 1189
A1	594 × 841
A2	420 × 594
A3	297 × 420
A4	210 × 297

Longer lengths are referred to as *elongated* and *extra-elongated* drawing sizes. These are available in multiples of the short side of the sheet size. Figure 2-5 shows standard ANSI/ASME sheet sizes.

Now you are ready to set the drawing limits. After setting the units of measure in the **Step 1: Units** tab, pick the **Step 2: Area** tab in the **Quick Setup** dialog box. See Figure 2-6. There is a **Width:** and **Length:** text box with default sheet size settings of 12″ × 9″. Change the width and length as desired by entering new values in the text boxes. The **Sample Area** image displays the sheet position and the limits dimensions. Pick the **Done** button when finished.

Figure 2-5.
A—Standard drawing sheet sizes (ANSI Y14.1) B—Standard metric drawing sheet sizes
(ASME Y14.1M).

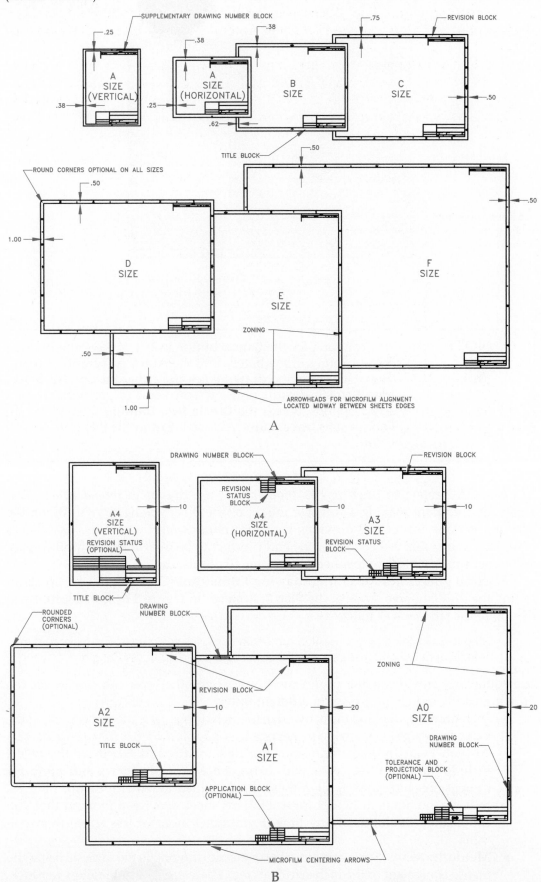

Figure 2-6.
The **Step 2: Area** tab. A 12 × 9 sheet size (limits) is the default.

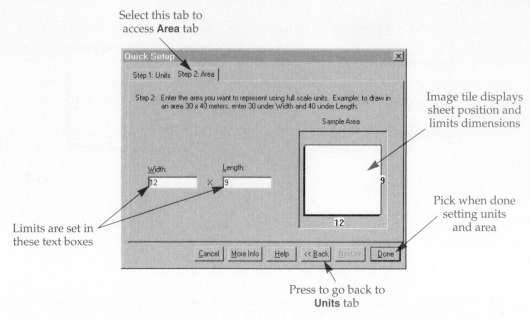

Select this tab to access **Area** tab

Image tile displays sheet position and limits dimensions

Limits are set in these text boxes

Pick when done setting units and area

Press to go back to **Units** tab

NOTE   You can pick the **Cancel** button in any of the setup dialog boxes to enter immediately into the AutoCAD graphics window. This starts the drawing session using the current **Start from Scratch** default units. If you want to get back to the setup options, access the **Create New Drawing** dialog box. If you want to leave AutoCAD, pick **Exit** in the **File** pull-down menu.

AutoCAD refers to drawings as *models* that are drawn in *model space*. This means that you are making a full-size model of the object being drawn. When the drawing is done, AutoCAD provides you with *paper space*, where the drawing is organized and scaled as needed for the end product to be put on paper. Model space and paper space are fully explained in Chapter 10 of this text.

Practical guidelines for setting drawing limits. AutoCAD provides a tip about setting the drawing area. Look at the **Step 2: Area** tab in Figure 2-6. The helpful tip at the top of the tab reads as follows:

Step 2: Enter the area you want to represent using full scale units. Example: to draw in an area 30 × 40 meters, enter 30 under Width and 40 under Length.

The following provides some professional guidelines that you can use to set the drawing width and length based on different units:

- **Inch drawings.** Setting the actual size for inch drawings is the same as using the exact sheet size measured in inches, such as 8.5 × 11, 11 × 8.5, 17 × 11, or 22 × 17. All you need to do is figure out the total width and length of the object included in all of the views with extra space between views and room for dimensions and notes. If all of these things added together measure 14″ × 9″, then set the limits to 17 × 11 for a standard sheet size. Keep in mind that you can change the limits at any time if you need more or less space than you think.
- **Metric drawings.** Setting an actual-size metric drawing is the same as using the metric equivalent of the inch-size drawing. There are 25.4 millimeters per inch.

So, if your units are in millimeters and you want the sheet size to be 17″ × 11″, multiply by 25.4 to get 431.8 × 279.4. Round this off to the next whole number to get metric limits of 432mm × 280mm. This works if you are using standard inch size drawing sheets. If you are using standard metric drawing sheets, calculate the size you need to fit the drawing and select one of the standard metric sheet sizes shown in Figure 2-5.

- **Architectural drawings.** The actual size of architectural drawings is based on feet and inch measurements. If you are drawing the floor plan that is 48′ × 24′, allow 10′ on each side for dimensions and notes to make a total drawing area 68′ × 44′. When you select architectural units, AutoCAD automatically sets up the drawing for you to draw in feet and inches.
- **Civil drawings.** The actual size of civil drawings that are used for mapping are often measured in units of feet. This allows you to set up the drawing limits similar to the architectural application just discussed. Civil drawings often represent very large areas, such as a plot plan that requires 200′ × 100′ to accommodate all of the property lines, dimensions, and notes.

EXERCISE 2-2

❏ Start AutoCAD if it is not already started. Access the **Quick Setup** dialog box. If you get an AutoCAD alert box that says: Save changes to unnamed?, pick the **No** button.
❏ Pick the **Step 2: Area** tab.
❏ Read the instructions at the top of the tab.
❏ The default limits are 12 × 9. Change the width to 17 and the length to 11 and notice the change in the **Sample Area** image.
❏ Change the width to 8.5 and notice the difference in the **Sample Area** image size and orientation.
❏ Pick the **Done** button.

Using the Advanced Setup wizard

The **Advanced** setup option is one of the wizards found in the **Start Up** and **Create New Drawing** dialog boxes. The **Advanced Setup** wizard provides more options and flexibility than the **Quick Setup** wizard. In the **Set Up** or **Create New Drawing** dialog box, double-click on **Advanced Setup,** or highlight **Advanced Setup** and pick the **OK** button or press [Enter]. The **Advanced Setup** dialog box is shown. See Figure 2-7. This dialog box has seven tabs. Use the tabs in progressive order or as needed to set up your drawing. The tabs are as follows:

- **Step 1: Units.** This tab is the same as the **Units** tab in the **Quick Setup** wizard. For the **Units** options, see Figures 2-3 and 2-4. Unlike the **Quick Setup**, the unit precision can be set using the **Precision**: drop-down list.
- **Step 2: Angle.** Pick this tab to select one of five angular unit options and the precision (display accuracy) of angles. Figure 2-8 shows the **Step 2: Angle** tab. The angle measurement options are accessed by picking the desired radio button. These options are as follows:
  - **Decimal Degrees**—This is the default setting. It is normally used in mechanical drafting where degrees and decimal parts of a degree are commonly used. The **Sample Angle** image in Figure 2-8 shows a representation of a decimal degree angle. Pick the **Precision**: drop-down arrow to open the drop-down list that contains angle precision ranging from the default of 0 to 0.00000000. Pick the desired angle precision and the **Sample Angle** image changes to represent the selected option.

Figure 2-7.
The **Advanced Setup** dialog box has seven tabs. This **Units** tab is the same as the **Units** tab in the **Quick Setup** dialog box with a **Precision:** drop-down list.

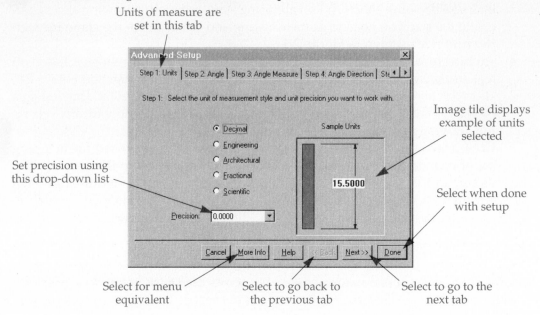

Units of measure are set in this tab

Image tile displays example of units selected

Set precision using this drop-down list

Select when done with setup

Select for menu equivalent

Select to go back to the previous tab

Select to go to the next tab

Figure 2-8.
The **Step 2: Angle** tab is used to set the type of angular units. Decimal degrees is the default.

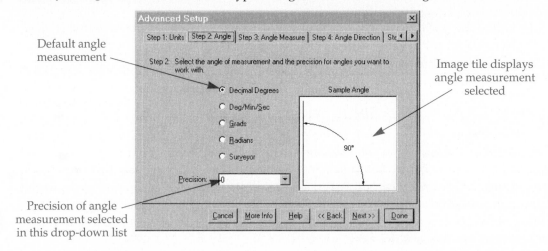

Default angle measurement

Image tile displays angle measurement selected

Precision of angle measurement selected in this drop-down list

- **Deg/Min/Sec**—This style is sometimes used in mechanical, architectural, structural, and civil drafting. The **Sample Angle** image tile in Figure 2-9A shows 90d, where the d is degrees. There are 60 minutes in one degree and 60 seconds in one minute. The **Precision:** drop-down list is used to select the display accuracy of minutes, seconds, and decimal seconds.
- **Grads**—*Grads* is the abbreviation for *gradient*. The angular value is followed by a g as shown in the **Sample Angle** image, Figure 2-9B. Gradients are units of angular measure based on one quarter of a circle having 100 grads. A full circle has 400 grads.
- **Radians**—A *radian* is an angular unit of measure where 2π radians = 360°, and π radians = 180°. For example, a 90° angle has $\pi/2$ radians and an arc length of $\pi/2$. The **Sample Angle** image tile in Figure 2-9C gives the default value of a 90° angle as 2r. Changing the display precision causes the radians to be rounded to the related decimal place.

Figure 2-9.
A—The **Deg/Min/Sec** angle option shown with the default precision. B—The **Grads** angle option shown with the default precision. C—The **Radians** angle option shown with the default precision. D—The **Surveyor** angle option shown with the default precision.

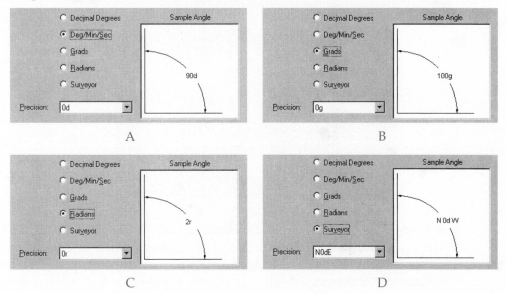

A   B

C   D

- **Surveyor**—Surveyor angles are measured using bearings. A *bearing* is the direction of a line with respect to one of the quadrants of a compass. Bearings are measured clockwise or counterclockwise (depending on the quadrant), beginning from either north or south. Bearings are measured in degrees, minutes, and seconds. An angle measured 55°45′22″ from north toward west is expressed as N55°45′22″W. An angle measured 25°30′10″ from south toward east is expressed as S25°30′10″E. Figure 2-9D shows the **Sample Angle** as N0dE. This represents the northeast quadrant of a compass. Use the **Precision:** drop-down list to set measurement to degrees, degrees/minutes, degree/minutes/seconds, or to set decimal display accuracy of the seconds part of the measurement.

NOTE   The values in the **Precision:** lists affect coordinate displays for units and angular measure but have no effect on the accuracy of your drawing. The high accuracy of AutoCAD is maintained regardless of the display precision.

- **Step 3: Angle Measure.** This tab lets you choose the compass orientation for measuring angles. The AutoCAD default is **East**. The angles are measured in a counterclockwise direction beginning at 0° to the east, or on the right side of the screen. Look at the **Angle Zero Direction** image in Figure 2-10 showing the 0° compass orientation. The orientation of the compass directions is the same as when you look at a map, with north at the top of the screen, east at the right, west at the left, and south at the bottom. Setting the angle measure establishes the direction for angle 0°. The **North, West**, and **South** radio buttons are used to place 0° at those orientations. The **Other** option requires that you type a desired starting angle.

Figure 2-10.
In the **Step 3: Angle Measure** tab, the default angle zero direction is **East**.

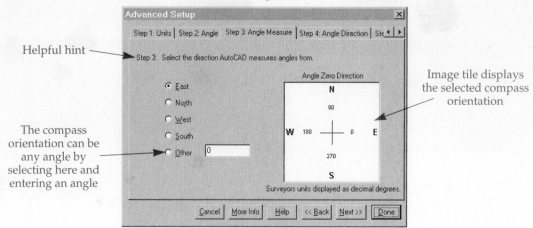

Helpful hint

The compass
orientation can be
any angle by
selecting here and
entering an angle

Image tile displays
the selected compass
orientation

- **Step 4: Angle Direction.** The **Angle Direction** tab allows you to select **Counter-Clockwise** or **Clockwise** angle direction. The angle direction originates from the compass position set in **Step 3: Angle Measure** tab. The default angle direction is **Counter-Clockwise**. Figure 2-11 shows the default and related **Angle Direction** image tile.

Figure 2-11.
In the **Step 4: Angle Direction** tab, the default is **Counter-Clockwise** angular measurement.

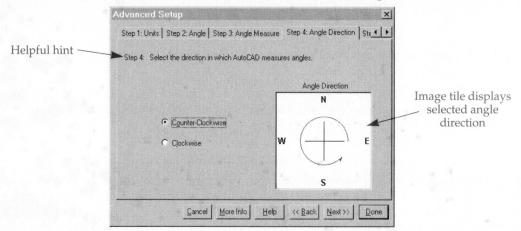

Helpful hint

Image tile displays
selected angle
direction

> **NOTE**
>
> If your operating system is set up with large fonts, some dialog boxes (including the **Advanced Setup** dialog box) may not be able to display all of the tabs at one time. When AutoCAD cannot display all of the tabs at once, a set of right and left navigational arrows appear at the right side of the tabs. Pick these to move through the tabs. The **Advanced Setup** dialog box also gives you the option of navigating between tabs with the ⟪**Back** and ⟫**Next** buttons.

- **Step 5: Area.** This **Area** tab works the same as in the **Step 2: Area** tab in the **Quick Setup** dialog box. See Figure 2-6. There is a **Width:** and **Length:** text box with default sheet size settings of 12″ × 9″. Change the width and length as desired by entering new values in the text boxes. The **Sample Area** image tile displays the sheet position and the limits dimensions.

- **Step 6: Title Block.** AutoCAD provides numerous standard title block and border formats in the **Step 6: Title Blocks** tab. The initial setting in the **Title Block Description:** and **Title Block File Name:** text boxes is No title block and None, respectively. Pick either down arrow to access the drop-down list with a variety of inch, metric, generic, and architectural title block and border options. The options are related to the inch and metric sheet sizes shown in Figure 2-5. Inch sheet sizes are referred to as ANSI A through ANSI V, Arch/Eng, and Generic. Metric sheet sizes DIN, ISO, and JIS A0 through JIS A4. When you pick a sheet format, the selection is identified in both text boxes and an example is displayed in the **Sample Title Block** image. See Figure 2-12.

Figure 2-12.
In the **Step 6: Title Block** tab, select a title block from the **Title Block File Name:** drop-down list and the **Sample Title Block** image tile displays the selection. Pick the **Add...** button to open the **Select Title Block File** dialog box.

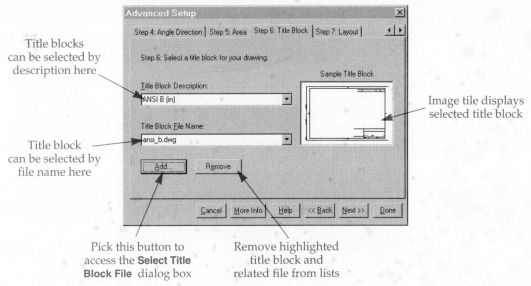

Title blocks can be selected by description here

Title block can be selected by file name here

Image tile displays selected title block

Pick this button to access the **Select Title Block File** dialog box

Remove highlighted title block and related file from lists

NOTE   *DIN* refers to the German standard *Deutsches Institut Fuer Normung*, which is established by the German Institute for Standardization. *ISO* is the International Organization for Standardization, and *JIS* is the Japanese Industry Standard.

The **Add...** and **Remove** buttons in the **Step 6: Title Block** tab are active when you select a title block from the list. The **Remove** button removes a highlighted title block from the list. The **Add...** button opens the **Select Title Block File** dialog box. In this dialog box, a title block format is picked from a directory folder. The search is done by using the **Look in:** drop-down list or by using the **Find File...** option button. See Figure 2-13. The **Find File...** option accesses the **Browse/Search** dialog box. This dialog box is discussed in Chapter 3 of this text.

Figure 2-13.
In the **Select Title Block File** dialog box, the desired title block is selected by highlighting a title block and then picking the **Open** button. The ansi_b title block is selected in this example.

Highlight file to be added
to title block lists

Select here to scroll through
the directory folder

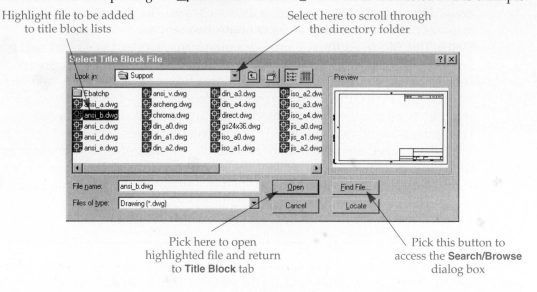

Pick here to open
highlighted file and return
to **Title Block** tab

Pick this button to
access the **Search/Browse**
dialog box

Once a title block format has been chosen, pick the **Open** button and the **Step 6: Title Block** tab returns. Add a description appears in the **Title Block Description:** text box. See Figure 2-14. A description, such as B size mechanical drawing, can be entered in the text box.

Figure 2-14.
After opening a title block in the **Select Title Block File** dialog box the **Step 6: Title Block** tab returns. The ansi_b title block selection is displayed in the **Title Block File Name:** text box. Add description is highlighted in the **Title Block Description:** text box.

Description of new
title block must
be entered

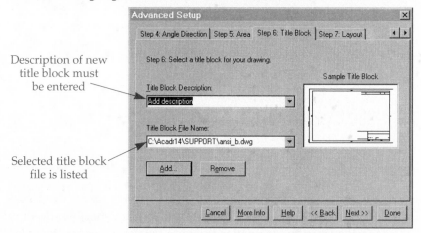

Selected title block
file is listed

CAUTION Use the **Remove** button with caution. Using it removes the title block description and the file from the description and file name drop-down lists.

- **Step 7: Layout.** This tab allows you to choose the manner in which you work on a drawing relative to the sheet layout. See Figure 2-15A. As previously mentioned, your drawing is referred to as a model, your drawing is done in model space, and paper space is where you create a layout of the drawing prior to

AutoCAD and its Applications—Basics

plotting. Paper space lets you create a layout of several different drawings and views with different scales. The **Layout** tab provides a definition of paper space, by picking the **What is paper space?** button. This accesses the **Information: Paper Space** dialog box, which shows examples of model space and paper space. See Figure 2-15B. Pick the **OK** button to return to the **Layout** tab.

Figure 2-15.
A—Picking the **What is paper space?** button in the **Step 7: Layout** tab opens the **Information: Paper Space** dialog box. B—The **Information: Paper Space** dialog box displays information about model space and paper space.

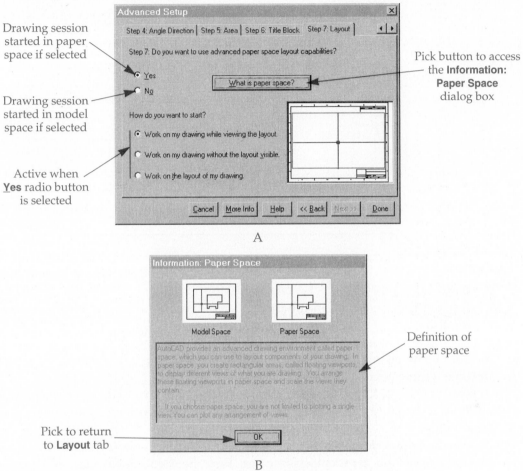

The **Yes** or **No** radio buttons determine the use of the advanced layout capabilities in paper space. If you pick **No**, you will begin the drawing session in model space. The three radio buttons listed under How do you want to start? are disabled. If you pick **Yes**, you will begin the drawing session in paper space and the three radio buttons are active:

- **Work on my drawing while viewing the layout.** Pick this option to work on a drawing with the border and title block displayed. The image in Figure 2-16 shows a single viewport inside the border and title block.
- **Work on my drawing without the layout visible.** Pick this option to work on a drawing without the border and title block displayed. The image displays the screen cursor without a border and title block.
- **Work on the layout of my drawing.** Pick this option to work on the layout without affecting the drawing in model space. You can add information such as general notes to the drawing.

Figure 2-16.
Picking **Work on my drawing while viewing the layout** option in the **Step 7: Layout** tab results in the title block and layout being visible in the graphics window.

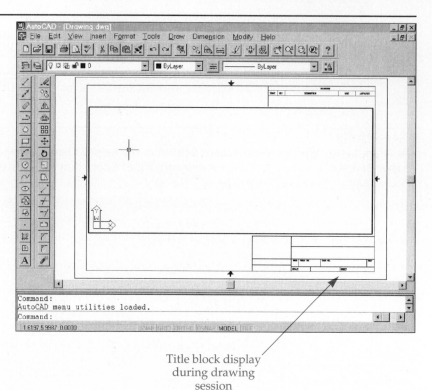

Title block display during drawing session

EXERCISE 2-3

❑ Start AutoCAD if it is not already started. Use the **Start Up** or **Create New Drawing** dialog box and select **Advanced Setup**.

❑ Review the features found in the **Step 1: Units** tab that were previously covered in Exercise 2-1.

❑ Access the **Step 2: Angle** tab. Change the precision to different settings. Look at the **Sample Angle** image tile as you pick each of the angle unit options. Now, pick **Decimal Degrees**.

❑ Access the **Step 3: Angle Measure** tab. Pick each of the four compass orientation options. Notice how the **Angle Zero Direction** image tile changes. Now, pick the **East** option.

❑ Access the **Step 4: Angle Direction** tab and notice the **Angle Direction** image tile for the default **Counter-Clockwise** option. Pick the **Clockwise** option and see the change in the image. Now, pick **Counter-Clockwise.**

❑ Review the features found in the **Area** tab.

❑ Access the **Step 6: Title Block** tab.

   ❑ Access the **Title Block Description** drop-down list and pick several different title block formats. Notice the change in the **Sample Title Block** image tile.

   ❑ Pick the **Add...** button to open the **Select Title Block File** dialog box. Pick one of the files, such as ansi_b.dwg and then pick **OK**. Enter a title block description, such as B size title block for mechanical drawings, in the text box.

❑ Access the **Step 7: Layout** tab. Pick the **What is paper space?** button and read the **Information: Paper Space** dialog box. Pick **OK**.

❑ Pick each of the How do you want to start? radio buttons. Notice how the image tile changes.

❑ Pick the **Work on my drawing while viewing the layout** option and pick the **Done** button. See the viewport displayed within the title block and border selected. Notice the differences between this setup and the results in Exercise 2-2, where the graphics window had no border and title block.

Using an AutoCAD template

In the **Advanced Setup** wizard, many standard border and title block formats are provided. AutoCAD refers to each of these standard formats as a *template*. A template is also referred to as a *prototype*. A template is a drawing file with pre-established settings.

These templates are accessed by picking the **Use a Template** button in the **Start Up** or **Create New Drawing** dialog box. The dialog box changes to show the **Use a Template** options, Figure 2-17. When a template is highlighted in the **Select a Template:** list, an image is displayed in the **Preview** image and a description is given in the **Template Description** area. To start a template, double-click on a template or highlight the template and pick the **OK** button or press [Enter].

Figure 2-17.
In the **Use a Template** start-up option, the template selected is displayed in the preview image and a description is provided.

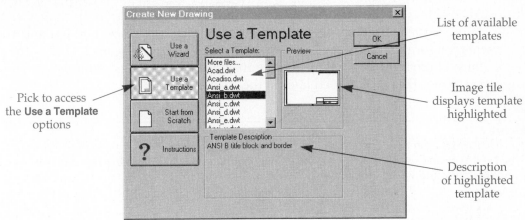

The ansi, din, iso, and jis options have a title block in the lower-right corner. The archeng.dwt option provides a title block on the right side of the sheet, which is common in the architectural industry. The **Select a Template:** list contains the acad.dwt option for starting a drawing using feet and inches, and the acadiso.dwt option for using metric units. These options do not have title blocks. The .dwt file extension stands for *drawing templates*.

When using a setup wizard, you enter values that define the drawing settings. When using a template, these values are automatically set. Templates usually have values for the following drawing elements:

✓ Standard limits with a border and title block.
✓ Grid and snap settings.
✓ Units and angle values.
✓ Text standards and general notes.
✓ Dimensioning settings.

The **Use a Template** option lets you move directly into a border and title block format. After entering the desired format, you can establish additional drawing settings that are considered common for the type of drawing being created. When going through this text, you will discover many ways to adjust AutoCAD to match individual needs and professional applications. Each of these applications can be used to build customized templates.

Using the **Start from Scratch** option

The **Start from Scratch** button in the **Start Up** and **Create New Drawing** dialog boxes is used if you want to set up a drawing on you own. When it is picked, AutoCAD displays the **Select Default Setting:** options where either English or metric units can be selected. The **Preview** image changes to match the units highlighted. The representation for the English and metric settings is shown in Figure 2-18. If a drawing is started from scratch, the limits and units must be established after the drawing has been started. This is discussed later in the chapter.

Figure 2-18.
A—In the **Start from Scratch** start-up option when **English** is selected, it is displayed in the **Preview** image and in the description. B—When **Metric** is selected, it is displayed in the preview image and in the description.

Select to start drawing from scratch

Description of highlighted setting

Image tile displays highlighted setting

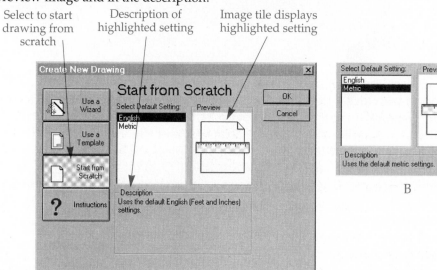
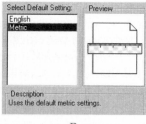

A

B

NOTE When you are in the **Start Up** or **Create New Drawing** dialog box, you can exit directly to the AutoCAD graphics window by picking the **Cancel** button.

What start-up option do I use?

Before starting an AutoCAD drawing, there should be some consideration of what startup option to use. Consider the following:

- **Wizards.** Wizards are often the best option when using AutoCAD as a design tool. In the design phase of a project, it may be too soon to be concerned about what the final drawing layout will look like. This option allows the size of the drawing area to be set up, including several of the drawing environment settings. It does not place a title block or border.

- **Templates.** Templates can be incredible productivity boosters. The provided template files may meet some personal needs, but creating new templates is where the greatest benefit is found. This allows you to use an existing drawing as a starting point for any new drawing. This option is extremely valuable for ensuring that everyone in a department, class, school, or company uses the same standards within their drawings.

- **Starting from scratch.** Use this option to "play it by ear" when just sketching or when the start or end of a drawing project is unknown. This is more frequently used by experienced AutoCAD users who are familiar with the settings that they like.

Changing Drawing Settings

AutoCAD User's Guide 2

After setting up AutoCAD, you are ready to begin drawing. The **Quick Setup** and **Advanced Setup** options provide a convenient way to initially set the drawing units and limits. However, these settings may need to be changed while working on the drawing or when the drawing is finished. The drawing units may be changed at any time with the **DDUNITS** or **UNITS** commands, and the limits can be changed with the **LIMITS** command.

Changing units

The **DDUNITS** command is the quickest way to set the units and angles. The **DDUNITS** command opens the **Units Control** dialog box for easy control of the settings. This command can be accessed by picking **Units...** in the **Format** pull-down menu or by typing UN or DDUNITS at the Command: prompt. The **Units Control** dialog box is shown in Figure 2-19A.

DDUNITS
UN

Units...
➥ Format

In the **Units Control** dialog box, pick one of the five radio buttons to select the desired units format and one of the five radio buttons to choose the desired format for angles. **Decimal** for units and **Decimal Degrees** for angles are the defaults, but the current values match the settings made while setting up. Access the **Precision:** drop-down lists in the **Units** and **Angles** areas to set the precision of the formats selected.

Pick the **Direction...** button to access the **Direction Control** dialog box. See Figure 2-19B. The standard **East**, **North**, **West**, and **South** options are offered as radio buttons. Pick one of these buttons to set the compass orientation. The **Other** radio button acti-

Figure 2-19.
A—The **DDUNITS** command accesses the **Units Control** dialog box. B—Picking the **Direction...** button accesses the **Direction Control** dialog box.

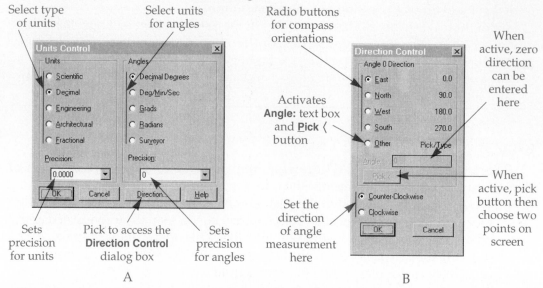

Select type of units

Select units for angles

Radio buttons for compass orientations

When active, zero direction can be entered here

Activates **Angle:** text box and **Pick ⟨** button

When active, pick button then choose two points on screen

Sets precision for units

Pick to access the **Direction Control** dialog box

Sets precision for angles

Set the direction of angle measurement here

A

B

vates the **Angle:** text box and the **Pick ⟨** button. The **Angle:** text box allows an angle for zero direction to be entered. The **Pick ⟨** button allows two points on the screen to be picked for establishing the angle zero direction. The direction of angle measurement can also be set in the **Direction Control** dialog box. Pick either the **Counter-Clockwise** or **Clockwise** radio button.

Unit-related values can also be set using the **UNITS** command. Entering UNITS at the Command: prompt opens the **AutoCAD Text Window**, Figure 2-20. Any of the listed formats can be selected.

These formats can be used with any basic unit of measurement, except for Engineering and Architectural formats, which are used specifically for measurements in the civil engineering and architectural fields. Decimal mode is used for metric units and decimal inch units. After selecting a format, precision can be set at the following prompt:

Enter choice, 1 to 5 ⟨2⟩: ↵
Number of digits to the right of decimal point (0 to 8) ⟨4⟩:

Figure 2-20.
The **UNITS** command accesses the **AutoCAD Text Window**. The unit-related values can be changed here.

Pick the close button when done

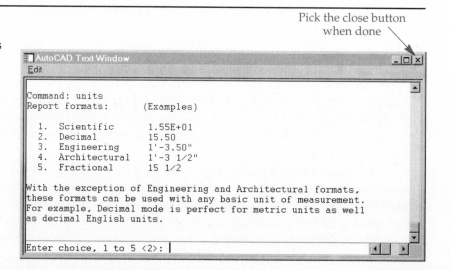

Press [Enter] to accept the default or type a new number of decimal places. The next prompts deal with angular measure. First set the units and then set the precision. The following shows an example:

```
Systems of angular measure:    (Example)
  1. Decimal degrees           45.0000
  2. Degrees/minutes/seconds   45d0'0"
  3. Grads                     50.0000g
  4. Radians                   0.7854r
  5. Surveyor's units          N 45d0'0" E

Enter choice, 1 to 5 ⟨1⟩: ↵
Number of fractional places for display of angles (0 to 8) ⟨0⟩: 2↵


Direction for angle 0.00:
  East                         3 o'clock = 0.00
  North                        12 o'clock = 90.00
  West                         9 o'clock = 180.00
  South                        6 o'clock = 270.00

Enter direction for angle 0.00 ⟨0.00⟩:↵
Do you want angles measured clockwise? ⟨N⟩:↵
Command:
```

If 4 for Architectural or 5 for Fractional units is entered, the next prompt is different from the previous example, because you are asked to decide the denominator of the smallest fraction. The default is 16. This makes the smallest fractional increments specified to 1/16th inch units. Select the default by pressing [Enter] or type one of the other options and press [Enter]. This sequence is as follows:

```
Enter choice, 1 to 5 ⟨2⟩: 4↵
Denominator of smallest fraction to display
(1, 2, 4, 8, 16, 32, 64, 128, or 256) ⟨16⟩:
```

When finished, press [F2] or pick the close button to close the **AutoCAD Text Window**. The close button is at the top of text window and has a large X on it.

Changing limits at the Command: prompt

Limits can be set after using **Quick Setup** and **Advanced Setup** by using the **LIMITS** command. The **LIMITS** command is accessed by entering LIMITS at the Command: prompt or by picking **Drawing Limits** in the **Format** pull-down menu.

LIMITS

Format
  ↪ Drawing Limits

The **LIMITS** command asks you to specify the coordinates for the lower-left corner and the upper-right corner of the drawing area. The lower-left corner is usually 0,0 but you can specify something else. Press [Enter] to accept the 0,0 value for the lower-left corner default, or type a new value. The upper-right corner usually identifies the upper-right corner of the sheet size. If you want a 17″ × 11″ sheet size, then the upper-right corner setting is 17,11. The first value is the horizontal measurement and the second value is the vertical measurement of the limits. Each value is separated by a comma. The command works like this:

```
Command: LIMITS↵
Reset Model space limits:
ON/OFF/⟨Lower left corner⟩ ⟨0.0000,0.0000⟩: ↵
Upper right corner ⟨12.0000,9.0000⟩: 17,11↵
Command:
```

The **LIMITS** command can also be used to turn the limits on or off by typing ON or OFF at the prompt.

Opening an Existing Drawing

Creating and saving drawings is discussed in detail in Chapter 3 of this text. Drawings that have been saved can be opened for additional work or for revisions. In the **Start Up** dialog box there is an **Open a Drawing** button. Pick this button to access the **Open a Drawing** options. See Figure 2-21. A **More files...** option and the last four files opened are listed in the **Select a File:** list. Any file listed can be opened by double-clicking on it.

Figure 2-21.
In the **Open a Drawing** options, the **Select a File:** list contains the **More files...** option and the last four drawings worked on.

Pick to open a recently opened file

Pick to access **Select File** dialog box

Select to open an existing drawing

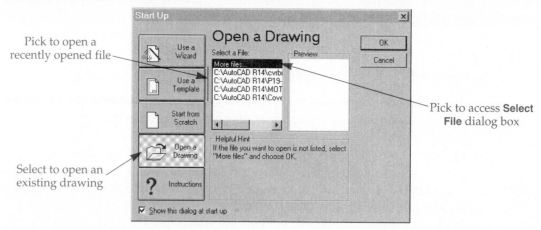

OPEN
[Ctrl]+[O]

File
➥ Open...

Standard
toolbar

Open

Double-clicking on **More files...** accesses the **Select File** dialog box, Figure 2-22. This dialog box can also be accessed by picking **Open...** in the **File** pull-down menu, using [Ctrl]+[O], entering OPEN at the Command: prompt, or by picking the **Open** button in the **Standard** toolbar.

The current folder shown in the **Look in:** text box is AutoCAD R14. Other folders and additional files can be accessed by double-clicking on a folder in the **Look in:** list. If you highlight a drawing file, a preview of the drawing is shown. To open a file, double-click on it, or highlight it and pick the **Open** button.

NOTE

If the file name and location is unknown, the **Find File...** button can be used to search for the file. Picking the **Find File...** button accesses the **Browse/Search** dialog box. In this dialog box, folders can be searched for specific files. This dialog box is discussed in Chapter 3 of this text.

Figure 2-22.
The **Select File** dialog box.

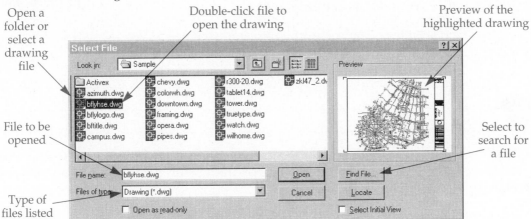

Open a folder or select a drawing file

Double-click file to open the drawing

Preview of the highlighted drawing

File to be opened

Select to search for a file

Type of files listed

To access additional drives, pick the down arrow next to the **Look in:** text box. The **Look in:** drop-down list appears as shown in Figure 2-23. Double-click on any of the drives to see the folders and files it contains. Access the desired folder or file, or close the dialog box.

When a drawing is open in the graphics window, you have the following options:
- Work on the drawing.
- Begin a new drawing by accessing the **NEW** command.
- Open another existing drawing.
- Exit AutoCAD by picking **Exit** in the **File** pull-down menu, or typing EXIT at the Command: prompt.

Figure 2-23.
Open the **Look in:** drop-down list to see the available drives and opened folder(s).

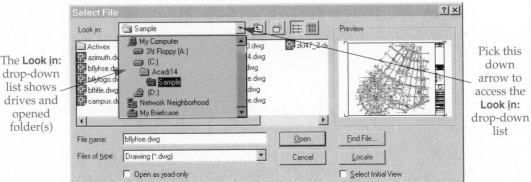

The **Look in:** drop-down list shows drives and opened folder(s)

Pick this down arrow to access the **Look in:** drop-down list

EXERCISE 2-7

❏ Open AutoCAD if it is not already open.
❏ Access the **Select File** dialog box.
❏ In the AutoCAD R14/Support folder, pick one of the files such as ansi_b. Display it in the **Preview** image tile. Open the file for display in the graphics window.
❏ Access the **Select File** dialog box again.
❏ If available, open the Sample folder. Pick each of the sample AutoCAD drawings. Look at the image of each in the **Preview** image tile.
❏ Open one of the sample drawings in the graphics window.
❏ Continue to use the **OPEN** command and look at different files.
❏ Exit AutoCAD when finished.

Chapter Test

Write your answers in the spaces provided.

1. Identify at least four basic planning decisions that need to be made before beginning a drawing._____

_____

_____

_____

2. How do you keep the **Start Up** dialog box from being displayed when you start AutoCAD?_____

_____

3. When in the **Start Up** dialog box, how can you immediately close the box and enter the AutoCAD graphics window? _____

_____

4. How do you return to the setup options if you are in the AutoCAD graphics window? _____

_____

5. What are AutoCAD wizards?_____

_____

6. This setup option allows you to quickly start a drawing by defining the drawing area, units, and scale. _____

7. This setup option provides units, angle control, area title blocks, and additional layout options. _____

_____

8. What is a template when used in AutoCAD? _____

_____

9. This setup option allows you to select from a list of standard sheet sizes with border and title block layouts. _____

_____

10. This setup option asks you to select either English or metric units before opening the AutoCAD graphics window. _____

_____

11. How do you open the **Start Up** dialog box? _____

_____

12. How do you open the **Create New Drawing** dialog box?_____

13. How do you open one of the wizards? _____
   _____

14. What is the purpose of the **Instructions** button in the **Start Up** dialog box? _____
   _____
   _____

15. List the options found in the **Step 1: Units** folder in the **Quick Setup** dialog box.
   _____
   _____

16. This is an example of which type of units: 15.500? _____

17. This is an example of which type of units: 1'-3 1/2"? _____

18. This is an example of which type of units: 15 1/2? _____

19. What are the purposes of the ⟨⟨**Back** and **Next**⟩⟩ buttons? _____
   _____
   _____

20. An AutoCAD drawing is created _____ size using the units you select.
   _____

21. Define world size. _____
   _____
   _____

22. What is sheet size? _____
   _____
   _____

23. AutoCAD refers to sheet size as area or _____.

24. What are the dimensions of an ANSI/ASME B size sheet? _____
   _____

25. Is the size of an ANSI/ASME A2 sheet specified in inches or millimeters?
   _____

26. AutoCAD refers to your drawing as a model that is drawn in _____.

27. What is the purpose of paper space? _____
   _____
   _____

28. 90.00° is an example of which angle units option? _____

29. 90°30'15" is an example of which angle units option? _____

30. N45°30'15"W is an example of which angle units option? _____

31. What is the AutoCAD default direction and compass orientation for measuring
   angles? _____

32. While in the **Advanced Setup** dialog box, what is the result of selecting ANSI B (in)
   in the <u>**Title Block Description:**</u> drop-down list of the **Step 6: Title Block** tab?
   _____
   _____
   _____

33. What is the purpose of the **Work on my drawing while viewing the layout** option in the **Step 7: Layout** tab? _____

_____

34. What is the purpose of the **Work on the layout of my drawing** option in the **Step 7: Layout** tab?_____

_____

35. What is another name for a template? _____

36. Which of the standard AutoCAD template files provides a border on the right side of the sheet for architectural applications?_____

_____

37. What does the .dwt file extension stand for? _____

38. List at least four types of values or drawing elements found in templates. _____

_____

_____

_____

_____

39. What are the items listed under **Select Default Setting:** when using the **Start from Scratch** options? _____

_____

40. What command opens the **Units Control** dialog box?_____

41. What happens when you enter UNITS at the Command: prompt?_____

_____

_____

42. The AutoCAD default for an angle is in a(n) _____direction.

43. What are the limits of an architectural drawing using a C-size (22 × 17) sheet and a scale of 4 feet per inch when plotted?

A. Lower-left corner _____

B. Upper-right corner _____

44. Name the pull-down menu that contains the **LIMITS** command. _____

45. Give the entries or commands needed to set the drawing units to three-digit decimal, two-place decimal degrees, East direction for angle 0, and to measure angles counterclockwise:

Command: _____

System of units: _____

Enter choice 1 to 5 ⟨*default*⟩: _____

Number of digits to right of decimal point (0 to 8) ⟨*default*⟩:_____

System of angular measure: _____

Enter choice, 1 to 5 ⟨*default*⟩:_____

Number of fractional places for display of angles (0 to 8) ⟨*default*⟩:_____

Enter direction for angle 0 ⟨*current*⟩: _____

Do you want angles measured clockwise? ⟨*current*⟩: _____

46. The display of a measurement will change when a different number of digits to the right of the decimal point is specified. If a 1.6250 dimension is to be displayed, and the number of digits to the right of the decimal point is as follows, what is actually displayed?

A. One digit_____

B. Two digits_____

C. Three digits _____

D. Four digits

47. Give the commands and coordinate entries to set the drawing limits to 22 × 17:

Command: _____

Reset Model space limits: _____

ON/OFF/⟨Lower left corner⟩⟨*current*⟩:_____

Upper right corner ⟨*current*⟩: _____

Drawing Problems

The following problems can be saved as templates for future use. You will be given instructions for saving, but saving drawings and templates is fully covered in Chapter 3 of this text.

For Problems 1–4, use the Quick Setup wizard.

1. Create a template with 11″ × 8.5″ area and decimal units. Name it QK A SIZE (H) INCHES.dwt and include QUICK A SIZE (H) SET UP for its description. You now have a template for doing inch drawings on 11 × 8.5 (horizontal) sheets.

2. Create a template with a 22″ × 17″ area and architectural units. Name it QK C SIZE ARCH.dwt and include QUICK C SIZE ARCHITECTURAL DRAWING SET UP for its description. You now have a template for doing architectural drawings on 22″ × 17″ sheets.

3. Create a template with an 8.5″ × 11″ area and decimal units. Name it QK A SIZE (V) INCHES.dwt and include QUICK A SIZE (V) INCHES SET UP for its description. You now have a template for doing inch drawings on 11″ × 8.5″ (vertical) sheets.

4. Create a template with a 594 × 420 area and decimal units. Name it QK A2 SIZE METRIC.dwt and include QUICK A2 SIZE METRIC SET UP for its description. You now have a template for doing metric (millimeters) drawings on 594 × 420 (A2) sheets.

For Problems 5–7, use the Advanced Setup wizard.

5. Create a template with a 17″ × 11″ area, decimal units with 0.000 precision; decimal degrees with 0.0 precision; default angle measure and orientation; and including the ANSI B (in.) title block. Set the template so the layout is not visible when you begin work on the drawing. Name it ADV B SIZE INCHES.dwt and include ADVANCED B SIZE INCHES SET UP for its description. You now have a template for doing inch drawings on 17 × 11 (B) sheets.

6. Create a template with a 420 × 297 (metric) area; decimal units with 0.0 precision; decimal degrees with 0.0 precision; default angle measure and orientation; and including the ISO A3 (mm) title block. Set the template so the layout is not visible when you begin work on the drawing. Name it ADV ISO A3 SIZE MM.dwt and include ADVANCED ISO A3 SIZE MILLIMETERS SET UP for its description. You now have a template for doing metric (millimeters) drawings on 420 × 297 (A3) sheets.

7. Create a template with a 22″ × 17″ area, architectural units with 1/16″ precision; degrees/minutes/seconds with 0d00′00″ precision; default angle measure and orientation; and including the Arch/Eng (in.) title block. Set the template so the layout is not visible when you begin work on the drawing. Name it ADV ARCH C SIZE INCHES.dwt and include ADVANCED ARCHITECTURAL C SIZE INCHES SET UP for its description. You now have a template for doing architectural drawings on 22 × 17 sheets with border and title block.

In Problems 8–10, create a new template using an existing template as a model.

8. Begin a new drawing and select the ansi_b.dwt template. Use the **DDUNITS** command to set decimal units with 0.000 precision and decimal angles with 0.0 precision. The direction control should be set to the default values. Set the limits to 0,0; 17,11. Name the drawing TEMP ANSI B.dwt and include ANSI B TEMPLATE SET UP for its description. You now have a template for doing inch drawings on 17 × 11 sheets with border and title block.

9. Begin a new drawing and select the iso_a3.dwt template. Use the **DDUNITS** command to set decimal units with 0.000 precision and decimal angles with 0.0 precision. The direction control should be set to the default values. Set the limits to 0,0; 420,297. Name the drawing TEMP ISO A3.dwt and include ISO A3 TEMPLATE SET UP for its description. You now have a template for doing metric (millimeters) drawings on 420 × 297mm sheets with border and title block.

10. Begin a new drawing and select the archeng.dwt template. Use the **DDUNITS** command to set architectural units with 1/16″ precision and degrees/minutes/seconds angles with 0d00′00″ precision. The direction control should be set to the default values. Set the limits to 0,0; 22,17. Name the drawing TEMP ARCH.dwt and include ARCHITECTURAL TEMPLATE SET UP for its description. You now have a template for doing architectural drawings on 22 × 17 sheets with border and title block.

In Problems 11 and 12, create templates from scratch.

11. Begin a new drawing and select the **Start from Scratch** button. Select 0.00 as decimal units, 0.00 as decimal degrees, and 90° (North) for direction of the 0° angle. Make angles measure counterclockwise. Set the limits to 0,0; 17,11. Save as a drawing template named SFS B SIZE INCHES and include START FROM SCRATCH B SIZE INCHES SET UP for its description. You now have a template for doing inch drawings on 17 × 11 sheets.

12. Begin a new drawing and select the **Start from Scratch** button. Select 0.00 as decimal units, 0.00 as decimal degrees, and 0° (East) for direction of the 0° angle. Make angles measure counterclockwise. Set the limits to 0,0; 420,297. Save as a drawing template named SFS A3 SIZE METRIC and include START FROM SCRATCH A3 METRIC SET UP for its description. You now have a template for doing metric (millimeters) drawings on 420 × 297mm sheets.

Introduction to Drawings, Saving Drawings

Learning Objectives

After completing this chapter, you will be able to:
- ○ Set up the drawing aids in a template drawing, including limits, units, grid, and snap.
- ○ Use the **LINE** command to draw several different geometric shapes.
- ○ Open a saved drawing.
- ○ Cancel a command.
- ○ Identify the function of the **FILEDIA** system variable.
- ○ Save a drawing under a different name.
- ○ Identify four ways to cancel a command.
- ○ Explain the difference between the **SAVE**, **SAVEAS**, and **QSAVE** commands.
- ○ Use the **SAVETIME** command to specify how often your work is automatically saved.
- ○ Determine the status of drawing parameters.

AutoCAD provides aids that help prepare the drawing layout, increase speed and efficiency, and ensure accuracy. These *drawing aids* include **GRID**, **SNAP**, and **ORTHO**. This chapter discusses each of these aids and how they are used to assist your drawing. AutoCAD automatically provides default drawing aids when you start a drawing, but you can change them to fit your own needs.

Establishing a Grid on the Screen

AutoCAD provides a grid or pattern of dots on the screen to help you lay out the drawing. The **GRID** command places this pattern of dots at any desired spacing, as shown in Figure 3-1. The grid pattern shows only within the drawing limits to help clearly define the working area. Entering the **GRID** command provides a prompt showing the default grid spacing and several other options. You can press [Enter] to accept the default spacing value shown in brackets, or enter a new value as follows:

    Command: **GRID**↵
    Grid spacing(X) or ON/OFF/Snap/Aspect 〈0.5000〉: **.25**↵

AutoCAD
User's
Guide 5

Figure 3-1.
The grid spacing is
represented by dots.

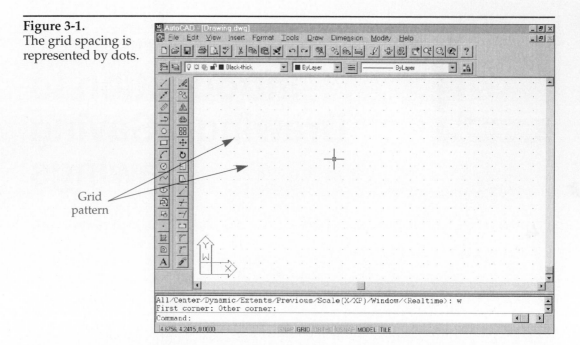

Grid
pattern

If the grid spacing you enter is too close to display on the screen, you get the "Grid too dense to display" message. In this case, a larger grid spacing is required.

The grid spacing can be changed at any time. Also, the grid can be turned on (displayed) or off (not displayed) using the **ON** and **OFF** options of the **GRID** command. Other methods for turning the grid on and off include double-clicking the **GRID** button on the status bar, the key combination [Ctrl]+[G], the [F7] function key, or pick button 6. The grid can also be turned on or off in the **Drawing Aids** dialog box, which is discussed later in the chapter.

Setting a different horizontal and vertical grid

Type A (for the **Aspect** option of the **GRID** command) to set different values for the horizontal and vertical grid spacing. For example, suppose you want a horizontal spacing of 1 and a vertical spacing of .5. Enter the following:

> Command: **GRID**↵
> Grid spacing(X) or ON/OFF/Snap/Aspect ⟨*current*⟩: **A**↵
> Horizontal spacing(X) ⟨0.5000⟩: **1**↵
> Vertical spacing(X) ⟨0.5000⟩: **.5**↵

This **Aspect** option provides the grid spacing shown in Figure 3-2.

AutoCAD and its Applications—Basics

Figure 3-2.
The X and Y grid spacing can be set to different values using the **Aspect** option. Notice that the horizontal spacing is greater than the vertical spacing.

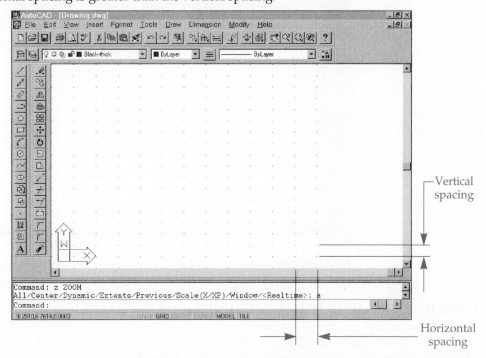

Introduction to Drawing Lines

This section gives a brief introduction to drawing lines so you can get started with AutoCAD drawing commands. You will see how the different drawing setup options affect the speed and accuracy of drawing lines. There are several ways to use the **LINE** command, but for now only one method is discussed. (The **LINE** command is explained in detail in Chapter 4 of this text.) Type L or LINE at the Command: prompt.

> Command: **L** *or* **LINE**↵
> From point: *(move the screen cursor to any position on the screen and pick that point)*
> To point: *(move the screen cursor to another location and pick a point)*

Notice that a line has been drawn between the two points. A "rubber band" line is attached to the last point selected and the cursor. The "rubber band" shows where the line will be drawn if you pick the current cursor location. The next prompt is:

> To point: *(pick the next point)*

You can continue to draw connected lines until you press the [Enter] key or space bar to exit the **LINE** command. The following command sequence is displayed in Figure 3-3.

> Command:**L** *or* **LINE**↵
> From point: *(pick point number 1)*
> To point: *(pick point number 2)*
> To point: *(pick point number 3)*
> To point: *(pick point number 4)*
> To point: ↵
> Command: *(meaning AutoCAD is ready for a new command)*

Figure 3-3.
Using the **LINE** command. Select the points in order from Point 1 to Point 4 to draw this three-segment line.

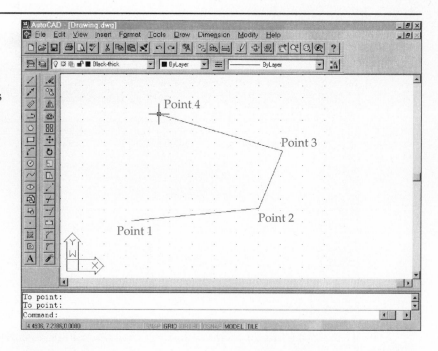

Canceling a Command

If you press the wrong key or misspell a word when entering a command or answering a prompt, use the backspace key to correct the error. This only works if you notice your mistake *before* the [Enter] key is pressed. If you do enter an incorrect option or command, AutoCAD usually responds with an error message. You are then given another chance to enter the correct data or returned to the Command: prompt. If you are not sure what has happened, reading the error message should tell you what you need to know.

Previous messages displayed in the floating command window are not always visible. Press the function key [F2] to display AutoCAD's text screen. This allows you to read the entire message. Also, you will be able to review the commands and options you entered. This may help you better understand what happened. You can press the [F2] key again to return to the graphics screen, or use your cursor to pick any visible portion of the graphics screen to make it current again.

It is often necessary to stop the currently active command and return to AutoCAD's Command: prompt to either reenter a command or use another command. This can occur if an incorrect entry is made and you need to restart the command using the correct method, or even if you simply decide to do something different. Some commands, such as the **LINE** command, can be discontinued by pressing the [Enter] key (or the spacebar). This exits the command and returns to the Command: prompt, where AutoCAD awaits a new command entry. However, there are many situations where this does not work. One example of this is using the **Window** option of the **ZOOM** command. Pressing [Enter] does not discontinue the command. In this case, you must cancel the command. (The **ZOOM** command is discussed in detail in Chapter 9.)

You can cancel any active command or abort any data entry and return to the Command: prompt by pressing the [Esc] key. This key is usually located in the upper-left corner of your keyboard. It may be necessary to press the [Esc] key twice to completely cancel certain commands. Many multibutton digitizer pucks use button number 3 to cancel a command. Additionally, most of the toolbar buttons and pull-down menu options automatically cancel any currently active command before entering the new command. So, in a case where you wish to abort the current command and start a new one, simply pick the appropriate menu option or toolbar button.

EXERCISE 3-1

❑ Start AutoCAD and use one of the start-up options discussed in Chapter 2.
❑ Set the grid spacing at .5.
❑ Use the **LINE** command to draw two sets of four connected line segments.
❑ Turn off the grid and draw two sets of three connected line segments. Notice how having the grid on provides some guidance for locating points.
❑ Enter the **LINE** command and then cancel the command before picking a point.
❑ Enter the **LINE** command, pick the first point, and then cancel the command.
❑ Enter the **LINE** command, pick the first and second points, and then cancel the command.
❑ Type SAVE at the Command: prompt. When the **Save Drawing As** dialog box appears, type EX3-1 in the **File name:** box to save this exercise on your hard disk. Press [Enter] or pick the **Save** button.
❑ Type QUIT at the Command: prompt and press [Enter] if you want to exit AutoCAD.

Setting Increments for Cursor Movement

When you move your pointing device, the cursor crosshairs move freely on the screen. Sometimes it is hard to place a point accurately. You can set up an invisible grid that allows the cursor to move only in exact increments. This is called the *snap grid* or *snap resolution*. The snap grid is different than using the **GRID** command. The snap grid controls the movement of the crosshairs. The grid discussed in the previous section is only a visual guide. However, the **SNAP** and **GRID** commands can be used together. The AutoCAD defaults provide the same settings for **GRID** and **SNAP.**

Properly setting the snap grid can greatly increase your drawing speed and accuracy. The **SNAP** command is used to set the invisible snap grid. Entering **SNAP** gives you the following prompt:

Command: **SNAP**⏎
Snap spacing or ON/OFF/Aspect/Rotate/Style ⟨*current*⟩:

Pressing [Enter] accepts the value shown in brackets. If a different snap spacing is required, such as .25, enter the new value as shown below:

Command: **SNAP**⏎
Snap spacing or ON/OFF/Aspect/Rotate/Style ⟨0.5000⟩: **.25**⏎

This sets up the invisible snap spacing at .25 increments both horizontally and vertically. The value that you set remains the same until changed.

The **OFF** selection turns snap off, but the same snap spacing is again in effect when you turn snap back on. The snap spacing can be turned on or off at any time by clicking the **SNAP** button on the status bar, pressing [Ctrl]+[B], pressing function key [F9], or pressing puck button 4. The snap grid can be turned on and off from the **Drawing Aids** dialog box, which is explained later in this chapter.

Different horizontal and vertical snap grid units

The **SNAP** command is usually set up with equal horizontal and vertical snap grid units. However, it is possible to set different horizontal and vertical snap grid units. This is done using the **Aspect** option of the **SNAP** command:

> Command: **SNAP**↵
> Snap spacing or ON/OFF/Aspect/Rotate/Style ⟨*current*⟩: **A**↵
> Horizontal spacing ⟨0.5000⟩: **.5**↵
> Vertical spacing ⟨0.5000⟩: **.25**↵

Rotating the snap grid

The normal snap grid pattern consists of horizontal rows and vertical columns. However, another option is to rotate the snap grid. This technique is helpful when drawing an auxiliary view that is at an angle to other views of the drawing. When the snap grid is rotated, you are given the option of setting a new base point. The base point is the pivot that the snap grid is rotated around. The base point of a normal snap grid is the lower-left corner. It may be more convenient to set the base point at the location where you will begin the view. You will also be asked to set the rotation angle. The command sequence is as follows:

> Command: **SNAP**↵
> Snap spacing or ON/OFF/Aspect/Rotate/Style ⟨*current*⟩: **R**↵
> Base point ⟨0.0000, 0.0000⟩: (*press* [Enter], *type a new coordinate value, or pick a new base point*)
> Rotation angle ⟨0⟩: **25**↵

The grid automatically rotates counterclockwise about the base point when a positive rotation angle is given, and clockwise when a negative rotation angle is given. Figure 3-4 shows the relationship between the regular and rotated snap grids. Remember, the snap grid is invisible.

Figure 3-4.
The snap grid is usually horizontal rows and vertical columns. However, it can be rotated to help you draw. Notice the angle of the crosshairs. (The snap grid is invisible, but represented here by dots.)

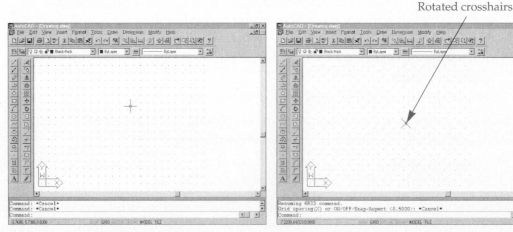

Default snap grid   Rotated snap grid

Setting the snap style

The **Style** option of the **SNAP** command allows you to set the snap grid to either a standard (default) or isometric pattern. The isometric pattern is useful when doing isometric drawings (discussed in Chapter 26). If the snap grid is set to **Isometric**, use the **Style** option to return it to the **Standard** mode, as shown below:

> Command: **SNAP**↵
> Snap spacing or ON/OFF/Aspect/Rotate/Style ⟨*current*⟩: **S**↵
> Standard/Isometric ⟨*current*⟩: **S**↵

Setting the grid spacing relative to the snap spacing

The visible grid can be set to coincide with the invisible snap grid by choosing the **Snap** option after entering the **GRID** command. You can also set the dot spacing as a multiple of the snap units by entering the number of snap units between grid points. For example, 2X places grid points at every other snap unit.

> Command: **GRID**↵
> Grid spacing(X) or ON/OFF/Snap/Aspect ⟨*current*⟩: **2X**↵

Therefore, if the snap units are .25 and you specify 2X at the Grid spacing: prompt, the grid spacing will be .5 units.

EXERCISE 3-2

❑ Start AutoCAD and use one of the start-up options discussed in Chapter 2.
❑ Set the units to decimal, with precision two digits to the right of the decimal point.
❑ Set the angular measure to decimal, one fractional place, 0 direction, and counterclockwise.
❑ Set the limits to an A-size (12 × 9) sheet. (Lower-left corner: 0,0; upper-right corner: 12,9.)
❑ Set the grid spacing to .5.
❑ Set the snap spacing to .25.
❑ Use the **LINE** command to draw two sets of four connected line segments.
❑ Turn **SNAP** off and draw two sets of three connected line segments. Notice how when **SNAP** is on, the cursor "jumps" exactly at .25 intervals.
❑ Type SAVE at the Command: prompt. Type EX3-2 in the **File name:** box. Pick the **Save** button or press the [Enter] key.
❑ Type QUIT at the Command: prompt and press [Enter] if you want to exit AutoCAD.

PROFESSIONAL TIP  The **SNAP** and **GRID** drawing aids may be set at different values to complement each other. For example, the grid may be set at .5 and the snap at .25. With this type of format, each plays a separate role in assisting drawing layout. This may also keep the grid from being too dense. You can quickly change these values at any time to have them best assist you.

Using the Drawing Aids Dialog Box

DDRMODES
RM

Tools
➡ Drawing Aids...

AutoCAD drawing aids can be set or changed using the **Tools** pull-down menu. Pick **Tools** in the menu bar, and then select **Drawing Aids...** from the pull-down menu. The **Drawing Aids** dialog box appears on the screen. Typing RM or DDRMODES at the Command: prompt also displays the same dialog box.

Use the dialog box to set or change the grid and snap spacing values. Place a check in the **Snap** or **Grid** toggle box as needed to turn the drawing aid on. Enter your desired grid and snap spacing in the **X/Y Spacing** boxes as needed. Look at Figure 3-5 and notice that **GRID** and **SNAP** are both on, as indicated by the check in the toggle boxes. The grid has equal horizontal (X) spacing and vertical (Y) spacing of 0.5000 units. The snap has equal X and Y spacing of 0.2500.

Figure 3-5.
The **Drawing Aids** dialog box. Notice the ✓s in the check boxes indicating options that are active. Also note the current **Snap** and **Grid** settings.

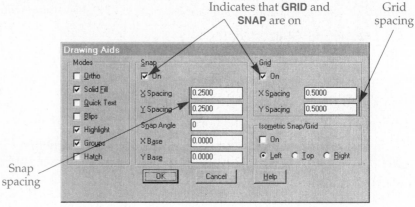

Indicates that **GRID** and **SNAP** are on

Grid spacing

Snap spacing

PROFESSIONAL TIP

The most effective use of **Snap** quite often comes from setting an equal X and Y spacing to the lowest, or near lowest, increment of the majority of the feature dimensions. For example, in a mechanical drawing this might be .0625 units, or 6″ in an architectural application. If many horizontal features conform to one increment and vertical features to another, then a corresponding snap grid can be set up using different X and Y values.

Factors to consider when setting drawing aids

The following factors will influence drawing aid settings:
- **The drawing units.** If the units are decimal inches, set the **Grid** and **Snap** values to standard decimal increments such as .0625, .125, .25, .5, and 1 or .05, .1, .2, .5, 1. For architectural units, use 1, 6, and 12 inches, or 1, 2, 4, 5, and 10-foot increments.
- **The drawing size.** A very large drawing might have a 1.00 grid spacing, while a small drawing may use a .5 spacing or less.
- **Value of the smallest dimension.** For example, if the smallest dimension is .125, then an appropriate snap value would be .125, with a grid spacing of .25.
- You can change the **Snap** and **Grid** values at any time without changing the location of points or lines already drawn. This should be done when larger or smaller values would assist you with a certain part of the drawing. For example, suppose a few of the dimensions are in .0625 multiples, but the rest of the dimensions are .250 multiples. Change the **Snap** spacing from .250 to .0625 when laying out the smaller dimensions.

- Always prepare a sketch before starting a drawing. Use the visible grid to help you place views and lay out the entire drawing.
- Use whatever method works best and fastest when setting or changing the drawing aids.

EXERCISE 3-3

☐ Start AutoCAD and use one of the start up options discussed in Chapter 2.
☐ Set decimal units precision three digits to the right of the decimal point.
☐ Set the angular measure to degrees/minutes/seconds, one fractional place, and default values for the rest of the options.
☐ Set the limits to 17,11. (Lower-left corner at 0,0 and upper-right corner at 17,11.)
☐ Zoom the screen using the **ZOOM All** option. To do this, type ZOOM at the Command: prompt, then enter A for the **ALL** option.
☐ Set the grid spacing at .5 units.
☐ Set the snap spacing at .25 units.
☐ Use the **LINE** command to draw two sets of eight connected line segments.
☐ Change the snap value to .125 and the grid spacing to .25. Draw several more lines and see what happens.
☐ Change the snap value to .5 and the grid spacing to 1. Draw several more lines and observe the results.
☐ Save the drawing as EX3-3.

Creating and Using Drawing Templates

Depending on the types of drawing projects you work with, there are many settings that are the same from one drawing to the next. This can include snap and grid settings, as well as many others. With most companies, standard borders and title blocks are used in all drawings. To save drawing setup time, templates are used.

The word *template* is defined as a model on which something is based. In AutoCAD, a *drawing template* is a model upon which other drawings are based. Templates were introduced in Chapter 2 with regard to starting an AutoCAD drawing. This discussion is a review of creating and using drawing templates. Depending on your specific needs, you can select from a number of predefined templates, or create your own.

Using an existing AutoCAD drawing template

To use a template to create a new drawing, select the **Use a Template** button in the **Start Up** or **Create New Drawing** dialog box. The **Create New Drawing** dialog box is shown in Figure 3-6A.

A number of predefined templates are available in the **Select a Template:** list box. When you highlight a template name, a brief description is provided in the **Template Description** area. These templates are based on different standards, including ANSI, ISO, DIN, and JIS. Two "normal" templates are provided: acad.dwt for English units and acadiso.dwt for metric units. A generic template and an architectural template are also listed. If you need to access an existing template that is not listed, pick More Files... to display the **Select Template** dialog box shown in Figure 3-6B. This dialog box allows you to look in other directory folders to find a template.

When you use a template, all of the settings saved in the template are applied to your drawing. The template file can supply any information that is normally saved in a drawing file, including settings and drawing objects. Many of the templates already have standard borders and title blocks, which are then created in your new drawing. The template drawing contains the setup options that you choose plus any snap and grid setting that you use.

Figure 3-6.
Templates make starting a new drawing more efficient. A—Pick the **Use a Template** button to list existing templates. B—Additional templates can be selected from the **Select Template** dialog box.

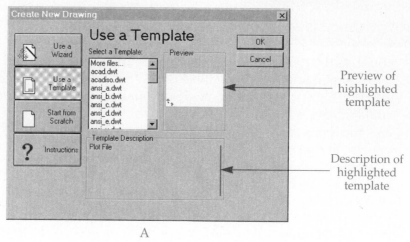

Preview of highlighted template

Description of highlighted template

A

Select location of template

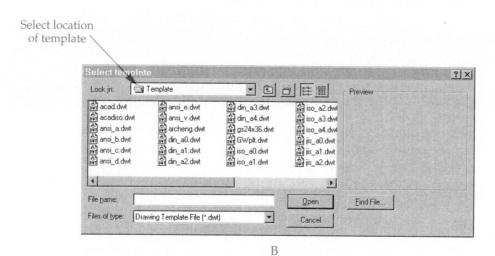

B

As you continue through this text, you can add items to your templates, such as layer settings; company information, logo and text styles; dimension styles; and bills of material. All of these settings are designed to your company or school specifications and based on your drawing applications.

When you have all of the desired items inserted and set, you can provide your template drawing with a name. The name should relate to the template, such as mechanical a size, for a mechanical drawing on an A-size sheet. The template might be named for the drawing application, such as architectural floor plans. The template name might be as simple as template 1. The name should be written in a reference manual along with documentation about what is included in the template. This provides future reference for you and other users. The template drawing you create is saved for you to open and use whenever it is needed.

Creating your own templates

If none of the predefined templates meet your needs, you can create and save your own custom templates. AutoCAD allows you to save *any* drawing as a template. A drawing template should be developed whenever a number of drawing applications require the same setup procedure. The template then allows the setup to be applied to any number of future drawings. Creating templates increases drafting productivity by decreasing setup requirements.

Some existing AutoCAD templates may be close to what you need and may simply need fine tuning. If the existing AutoCAD templates do not fit your needs, you may want to use a wizard to establish basic settings or even start from scratch. Some basic parameters that can be specified in a drawing template include units, limits, snap and grid. You can also draw your own border and title block. Review Chapter 2 for a complete discussion about setting up with a wizard or by scratch.

As you learn more about working with AutoCAD, you will find many other settings that can be included in your drawing templates. When you have everything in the template that is needed, it is ready to save. Use the **SAVEAS** command to save a drawing template. The **SAVEAS** command is accessed by picking **Save As...** from the **File** pull-down menu, or by typing SAVEAS at the Command: prompt. This command displays the **Save Drawing As** dialog box, as shown in Figure 3-7. To specify that the drawing is to be saved as a drawing template, pick **Drawing Template File(*.dwt)** from the **Save as Type:** drop-down list. The file list window then shows all of the drawing templates currently found in the Template folder. You can store custom templates in another location, but it is recommended that they be stored in the Template folder. This folder is displayed by default when the **Use a Template** option is selected in the **Create New Drawing** dialog box.

Figure 3-7.
Saving a template.

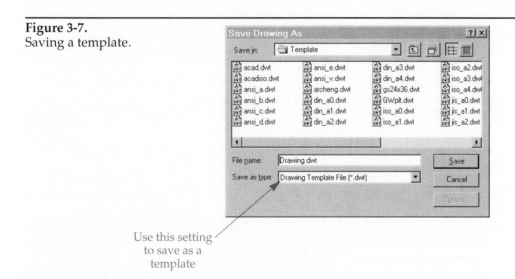

Use this setting
to save as a
template

After specifying the name and location for the new template file, pick the **Save** button in the **Save Drawing As** dialog box. The **Template Description** dialog box is now displayed, as shown in Figure 3-8. Use the **Description** area to enter a brief description of the template file you are saving. You can enter up to 200 characters, but a brief description usually works best. Under the **Measurement** drop-down list, specify whether the units used in the template are English or metric and then pick the **OK** button.

Now, you can exit AutoCAD and when you start up again, the template you created is ready for you to use for preparing a new drawing.

Figure 3-8.
Enter a description
of the new template
in the **Template
Description**
dialog box.

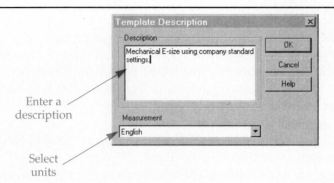

Enter a
description

Select
units

**PROFESSIONAL
TIP**

Generalized templates that set the units, limits, snap, and grid to specifications are useful, but keep in mind that you can create any number of drawing templates. Templates that contain more detailed settings can dramatically increase drafting productivity. As you refine your setup procedure, you can revise the template files. When using the **SAVE** command, you can save a new template over an existing one, or use the **SAVEAS** command to save a new template from an existing one.

EXERCISE 3-4

❏ Start AutoCAD to access the **Start Up** dialog box or pick **New...** from the **File** pull-down menu to open the **Create New Drawing** dialog box.
❏ Pick **Use a Template**.
❏ Create one of the following templates based on the type of drawing that you prefer:

    1. Name: MECHANICAL-IN-A
       Use: Mechanical drawings in inches on A-size sheet.
       Template: ansi_a.dwt
       Grid = .25
       Snap = .125
    2. Name: MECHANICAL-IN-B
       Use: Mechanical drawings in inches on B-size sheet.
       Template: ansi_b.dwt
       Grid = .5
       Snap = .25
    3. Name: MECHANICAL-MM-A3
       Use: Mechanical drawings in metric on A3-size sheet.
       Template: iso_a3.dwt
       Grid = 10
       Snap = 5
    4. Name: MECHANICAL-MM-A2
       Use: Mechanical drawings in metric on A2-size sheet.
       Template: iso_a2.dwt
       Grid = 20
       Snap = 10
    5. Name: ARCHITECTURAL-D
       Use: Architectural drawings on D-size sheet.
       Template: archeng.dwt
       Grid = 24
       Snap = 6

❑ Save the drawing template as explained in the previous discussion.
❑ Record the information about your template in a notebook.
❑ Create another new drawing template based on one of the previous options, but this time, design the template without a border and title block by using a setup wizard.
❑ Save the drawing template as explained in the previous discussion.
❑ Record the information about your template in a notebook.

Saving Drawings

Whether you start a new drawing from scratch or use a template, you need to assign a name for the new drawing and save it. The following discussion provides you with detailed information about saving and quitting a drawing.

When saving drawing files using either the **SAVE** or **SAVEAS** command, you can use a dialog box or type everything at the Command: prompt. Dialog boxes are controlled by the **FILEDIA** system variable. A *system variable* is a setting that lets you change the way AutoCAD works. These variables are remembered by AutoCAD and remain in effect until you change them again. There are two **FILEDIA** system variable options. The default is 1, which displays dialog boxes at the appropriate times. When **FILEDIA** is set to 0, dialog boxes do not appear. You must then type the desired information at the prompt line. You can quickly change the **FILEDIA** system variable as follows:

Command: **FILEDIA**↵
New value for FILEDIA ⟨1⟩: **0**↵

In the following discussion, the **FILEDIA** variable is set to 1, unless otherwise specified.

Naming drawings

Drawing names may be chosen to identify a product by name and number, for example, VICE-101, FLOORPLAN, or 6DT1005. Your school or company probably has a drawing numbering system that you can use. These drawing names should be recorded in a part numbering or drawing name log. This helps serve as a valuable reference long after you forget what the drawings contained.

It is important to set up a system that allows you to determine the content of a drawing by the drawing number. Although it is possible to give a drawing file an extended name, such as Details for Top Half of Compressor Housing for ACME, Inc., Part Number 4011A, Revision Level C, this is normally not a practical way of sorting drawing information. Drawing titles should be standardized and may be most effective when making a clear and concise reference to the project, part number, process, sheet number and revision level.

When a standardized naming system exists, a shorter name like ACME.4011A.C provides all of the necessary information. If additional information is desirable for the easier recognition, it can be added to the base name, for example: ACME.4011A.C.Compressor Housing.Top.Casting Details. Always record drawing names and provide information related to the drawings.

The following rules and restrictions apply to naming all files, including AutoCAD drawings:
- A maximum of 256 characters can be used.
- Alphabetical and numeric characters, spaces, along with most punctuation symbols can be used.
- The following characters cannot be used: quotation mark ("), asterisk (*), question mark (?), forward slash (/) and backslash (\).

Saving your work

The **SAVE** command allows you to protect your work by writing the existing status of your drawing to disk while remaining in the graphics window. While working in the graphics window, you should save your drawing every 10 to 15 minutes. This is very important! If there is a power failure, a severe editing error, or other problems, all of the work saved prior to the problem will be usable. If you save only once an hour, a power failure could result in an hour of lost work. Saving your drawing every 10 to 15 minutes results in less lost work if a problem occurs.

There are three commands that allow you to directly save your work: **QSAVE**, **SAVEAS**, and **SAVE**. Also, any command or option that ends the AutoCAD session provides a warning that asks if you want to save changes to the drawing. This gives you a final option to either save or not save changes to the drawing.

Using the QSAVE command

QSAVE
[Ctrl]+[S]

File
↳ Save

Standard
toolbar

Save

Of the three available saving commands, the most frequently used is the **QSAVE** command. **QSAVE** stands for *quick save*. The **QSAVE** command is accessed by picking the **Save** button from the **Standard** toolbar, picking the **Save** option from the **File** pull-down menu, typing QSAVE at the Command: prompt, or by pressing [Ctrl]+[S].

The **QSAVE** command response depends on whether the drawing already has a name. If the current drawing has a name, the **QSAVE** command updates the file based on the current state of the drawing. In this situation, **QSAVE** issues no prompts and displays no messages.

If the current drawing has not yet been named, the **QSAVE** command displays the **Save Drawing As** dialog box. This dialog box allows you to specify a file name and location for the current drawing. Refer to Figure 3-9 as you go through the following list detailing the use of the **Save Drawing As** dialog box:

- In this example, the current directory folder is AutoCAD R14. This is indicated by the listing in the **Save in:** drop-down list. The drawing file will be saved in this folder unless another location is specified. To specify a different disk drive, pick this drop-down list to see all of the available options.

Figure 3-9.
The **Save Drawing As** dialog box.

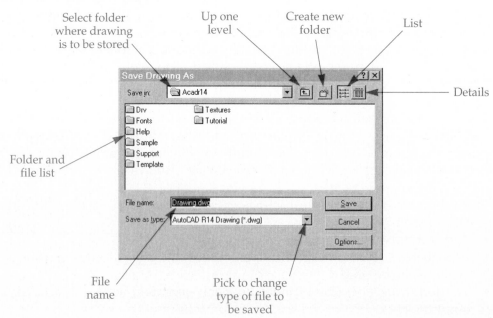

- To move upward from the current folder, pick the **Up One Level** button.
- To create a new folder in the current location, pick the **Create New Folder** button and type the name for the folder. To make the new folder the current location, double-click on the folder icon or pick it once and then pick the **Open** button. The **Save** button changes to an **Open** button when a folder is highlighted.
- The file listing area shows any folders or other drawing files found in the current folder. The default display style for the file dialog box is **List**. Pick the **Details** button to display additional file information, such as when it was last modified, file size, and file type. If some of the information is hidden, use the horizontal scroll bar to see more information. When the **Details** view is active, picking the **Name** label sorts the listing alphabetically in ascending order. Pick it again to change to a descending order. The **Size**, **Type**, **Modified**, and **Attributes** labels can also be used this way to sort the listing in the format identified by the title of the label.
- When the drawing has not yet been named, the name Drawing appears in the **File name:** text box. Change this to the desired drawing name.
- The **Save as type:** drop-down list offers options to save the drawing file in alternate formats. For most applications, this should be set to **AutoCAD R14 Drawing (*.dwg)** when saving drawings. When saving a template file, this is set as **Drawing Template File (*.dwt)**.
- Once you have specified the correct location and file name, pick the **Save** button to save the drawing file. Keep in mind that you can either pick the **Save** button or you can just press the [Enter] key to activate the **Save** button and save the drawing.

PROFESSIONAL TIP

While working in file dialog boxes, certain file management capabilities are available, similar to when you are using the Windows Explorer. To rename an existing file or folder, pick it once and pause for a moment, then pick the name again. This places the name in a text box for editing. Type the new name and press [Enter]. To delete a file or folder, highlight it and press the [Delete] key on your keyboard.

For a full listing of all of the available options, point to a desired file folder and then click and release the right mouse button. This displays a menu of available options for working with the file folder. Use one of the options or pick somewhere off the menu to close it.

CAUTION

Use extreme caution when deleting or renaming files and folders. Never delete or rename anything if you are not absolutely certain you should. If you are unsure, ask your instructor or system administrator for assistance.

If you accidentally delete a file or folder and you need to get it back, the Windows Recycle Bin can help you restore it. To use the Recycle Bin, open the Windows Explorer and pick Recycle Bin. The Recycle Bin files are displayed. Highlight the desired files and copy them back into the folder where they belong. Again, be sure to ask for assistance before doing anything if you are not absolutely certain.

Using the SAVEAS command

The **SAVEAS** command is used in the following situations:
- When the current drawing already has a name and you need to save it under a different name
- When you need to save the current drawing in an alternate format, such as a drawing file for AutoCAD Release 12 or 13, an AutoCAD LT drawing, or a drawing template file.
- When you open one of your drawing template files and create a drawing. This leaves the drawing template unchanged and ready to use for other drawings.

SAVEAS

File
 ↳ Save **A**s...

The **SAVEAS** command is accessed by picking **Save As...** from the **File** pull-down menu or by typing SAVEAS at the Command: prompt. This command always displays the **Save Drawing As** dialog box. If the current drawing has already been saved, the current name and location are displayed. Confirm that the **Save in:** box displays the current drive and directory folder that you want, and the **Save as type:** box displays **AutoCAD R14 Drawing (*.dwg)**. Type the new drawing name in the **File name:** box and pick the **Save** button.

Using the SAVE command

The third command provided for directly saving a drawing is the **SAVE** command. The **SAVE** command is not commonly used and is only available at the command line by typing SAVE. The **SAVE** command displays the **Save Drawing As** dialog box, regardless of whether or not the drawing has been previously saved. Because of this, the **QSAVE** command is better for saving a drawing in progress, and the **SAVEAS** command is better for saving a drawing with a new name.

If you try to save the current drawing using the same name and location as another drawing file, AutoCAD issues a warning message in an alert box and allows you to cancel the operation or replace the current drawing with the one you are working on. Figure 3-10 shows the alert box. If you actually need to replace the existing file, pick the **Yes** button to overwrite the file with the information in the current drawing. If you do not wish to overwrite the file or you are not sure, pick the **No** button to cancel the operation. Be very careful—if you pick the **Yes** button, the current drawing replaces the other drawing.

Figure 3-10.
This AutoCAD alert box appears when a drawing with the same name already exists in the specified directory.

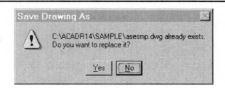

Saving your work automatically

AutoCAD provides you with an automatic work-saving tool called the **SAVETIME** system variable. All you need to do is decide how often you want your work saved, and enter the amount of time (in minutes) between saves. The following example tells AutoCAD to save the drawing every 15 minutes:

Command: **SAVETIME**↵
New value for SAVETIME ⟨*current*⟩: **15**↵

The **SAVETIME** timer starts as soon as a change is made to the drawing. The timer is reset when the **SAVE**, **QSAVE**, or **SAVEAS** command is used.

The drawing is saved when the first command is given after the **SAVETIME** value has been reached. For example, if you set **SAVETIME** to 15, work for 14 minutes, and then let the computer remain idle for 5 minutes, an automatic save is not executed until the 19 minute interval. Therefore, be sure to manually save your drawing if you plan to be away from your computer for an extended period of time.

The autosaved drawing is always saved with the name of auto1.sv$. If you need to use the autosaved file, it can be renamed with a .dwg file extension using the Windows Explorer. Refer to Chapters 15 and 30 for more information on the Windows Explorer. Renaming files from within the AutoCAD graphics window is covered in Chapter 15.

PROFESSIONAL TIP
While an automatic save is a safeguard, it is inconvenient to rename the auto1.sv$ file. Use the **QSAVE** command to continually save work in progress. A quick shortcut to the **QSAVE** command is the [Ctrl]+[S] key combination.

Where to save the drawing

When you save a drawing, it is stored in the current directory folder unless you specify a different location. To save a drawing to another disk drive, use the **SAVEAS** command to display the **Save Drawing As** dialog box. Pick the **Save in:** drop-down list to display all available disk drives and pick the desired drive icon. The **Save in:** list looks similar to the example shown in Figure 3-11, depending on what drives are available on your system or on your network. Using this option, you can save to any available hard disk, floppy disk, or network drive.

While your assignments should be saved in a file on the hard drive, you can save to a floppy disk for storage or transport to a remote system. The term *remote system* refers to a system that cannot be reached through a local network or an Internet connection. The example in Figure 3-11 shows the hard drive **(C:)** as the desired drive.

Figure 3-11.
Selecting the drive to save to.

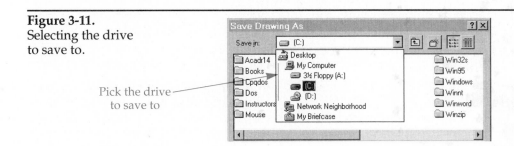

Pick the drive to save to

Unless otherwise specified by your instructor or CAD manager, it is best to do your assignment on the hard drive and then save to a floppy disk. In fact, save your work to two floppy disks so you have a backup in case something happens to one disk. After you save your work to a floppy disk and quit the drawing session, you will need to transfer the previous work from the floppy disk to the hard disk.

Saving Release 14 drawings for older releases

Your AutoCAD Release 14 drawings can be saved in a Release 12 or 13 format. This allows you to send Release 14 drawings to businesses where older releases of AutoCAD are being used, or if you use Release 14 at work or school and have Release 12 or 13 at home.

To save as an older release, use the **SAVEAS** command. The **Save Drawing As** dialog box appears. Using the **Save as type:** drop-down list, indicate whether you need to save as a Release 12, Release 13, or AutoCAD LT drawing by selecting one of the following options:

> AutoCAD R13/LT 95 Drawing (*.dwg)
> AutoCAD R12/LT 2 Drawing (*.dwg)

Next, specify the file name and location as previously discussed. When you save a version of a drawing in an earlier format, be sure to give it a different name than the Release 14 version uses. This prevents you from accidentally overwriting your working drawing with the older format. This is especially important when translating to Release 12. AutoCAD Release 13 and 14 can share all their information directly; however, some object types in Release 13 and 14 are not supported in Release 12 and are converted to older object types. These older object types may not be as easy to work with.

The information that is unique to Release 13 and 14 is lost in the Release 12 conversion. However, during the process a log lists changes and lost information for your reference. You can look at the log by pressing the [F2] key to get the text screen.

PROFESSIONAL TIP

Converting from Release 13 back to Release 12 adds handles to the drawing. *Handles* are an alphanumeric representation of the drawing in the AutoCAD database that can be accessed by other applications. Remove these handles using the **HANDLES** command in Release 12.

EXERCISE 3-5

❏ Start AutoCAD and use the template that you developed in Exercise 3-4.
❏ Use the **LINE** command to draw a simple object of your own design.
❏ Use the **SAVEAS** command to save the drawing with the name EX3-5.
❏ Draw another simple object of your own design.
❏ Use the **QSAVE** command.
❏ Draw another object and use the **QSAVE** command again.
❏ Put a floppy disk in the 3 ½" disk drive and use the **SAVEAS** command to save your drawing to the floppy disk.

AutoCAD User's Guide 1

OPEN
[Ctrl]+[O]

File
➥ Open...

Standard toolbar

Open

Opening an Existing Drawing

An existing drawing is one that has been previously saved. You can easily access any existing drawing with the **OPEN** command. To use the **OPEN** command, pick the **Open** button on the **Standard** toolbar, pick **Open...** from the **File** pull-down menu, press the [Ctrl]+[O] key combination, or type OPEN at the Command: prompt. If you are just starting AutoCAD, pick the **Open a Drawing** button in the **Start Up** dialog box and double-click on More files... in the **Select a File** list. The **Select File** dialog box appears, Figure 3-12.

The **Select File** dialog box contains folder and file lists, just as in the **Save Drawing As** dialog box. Double-click on a file folder to open it and then double-click on the

Figure 3-12.
The **Select File** dialog box is used to select a drawing to open. Notice the drawing asesmp has been selected from the files list box and appears in the **File Name:** text box.

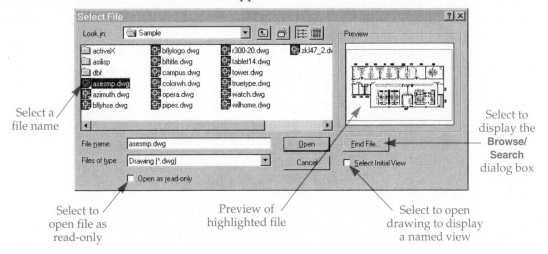

Select a file name

Select to open file as read-only

Preview of highlighted file

Select to display the **Browse/ Search** dialog box

Select to open drawing to display a named view

desired file to open it. The AutoCAD R14\Sample folder is open with the sample drawings displayed in Figure 3-12. You can also type the file name in the **File Name:** text box and pick the **Open** button (or press [Enter]) to open the file. If you specify a file name that does not exist, AutoCAD displays an alert box with the following messages:

File not found.
Please verify the correct file name was given.

If this happens, be sure you have correctly entered the file name and are in the appropriate directory folder. You cannot open a drawing file that does not exist, or is not in the folder you have specified.

When you pick an existing drawing that was created in AutoCAD Release 14 (or 13), a picture of the drawing is displayed in the **Preview** image tile. This is an easy way for you to get a quick look at the drawing without loading the files into the AutoCAD graphics editor. You can view each drawing until you find the one you want.

After picking a drawing file name to highlight it, you can quickly highlight another drawing in the list by using the keyboard arrow keys. Use the up and down arrow keys to move vertically between files and use the left and right arrow keys to move horizontally. This enables you to scan through the drawing previews very quickly.

An easy way to become familiar with the **Preview** image tile feature is to look at the sample drawings that come with AutoCAD. To do this exercise, the sample drawings must have been loaded during the AutoCAD installation process.

EXERCISE 3-6

❏ Start AutoCAD and use the setup option of your choice.
❏ Pick **Open...** from the **File** pull-down menu to access the **Select File** dialog box.
❏ Double-click on the directory that contains AutoCAD Release 14, such as AutoCAD R14, if it is not already open.
❏ Double-click on sample if it is displayed.
❏ The file list should display all of the sample AutoCAD drawing files.
❏ Pick any sample drawing and look at the **Preview** image tile. Pick as many as you like to preview. Use the cursor keys on your keyboard to scroll through the available files. Use the scroll bar to move the list from left to right as needed to display hidden files.
❏ Pick the **Cancel** button.
❏ Type QUIT at the Command: prompt and press [Enter] to exit AutoCAD.

Using select initial view and read only

When the **Select Initial View** check box in the **Select File** dialog box is activated you can select a named view to be displayed when you open the drawing. This feature is discussed in detail in Chapter 9, when you learn to establish different views of your drawing.

The **Open as read-only** check box will open the drawing as *read-only*. When this is active, any changes or modifications made to the drawing cannot be saved. In other words, the drawing can only be used for viewing purposes. This is one way to protect your drawing file from any changes made by an unauthorized user. You can also use this mode if you want to practice on your drawing without the fear of altering it. If you make changes that you want to save, you can still use the **SAVEAS** command to save under a different file name.

Searching for files

There may be instances when you need to edit an existing drawing file, but you cannot remember the drawing name or where the drawing resides on disk. A drawing file (or any other AutoCAD file type) may be located by its name, type, date created, or time created.

Pick the **Find File...** button in the **Select File** dialog box to display the **Browse/Search** dialog box. There are two sections to this dialog available by selecting the appropriate tab. When you are looking for a specific file, select the **Search** tab, as shown in Figure 3-13.

Figure 3-13.
The **Browse/Search** dialog box. To search for a file, select the **Search** tab. Search parameters can include drives, folders, and file types, and can be limited by the date or time the files were created.

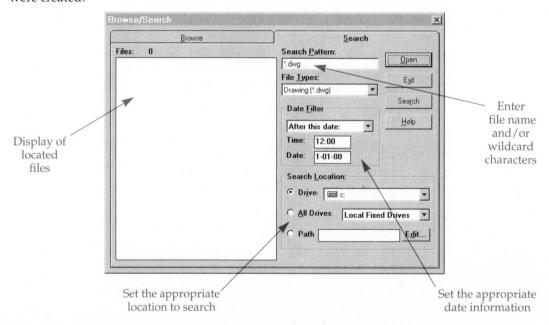

Display of located files

Set the appropriate location to search

Enter file name and/or wildcard characters

Set the appropriate date information

Set the **Search Pattern:** to look for the file you need. Either a complete file name can be specified or a partial name can be used with standard "wildcard" characters. For example, the default specification of *.dwg finds all files that have a .dwg file extension. The asterisk can be used alone, or after other characters. The file specification of floor*.dwg finds any drawing file that has the first five characters of floor. It would find floor_01.dwg, floor.dwg, and floorpln.dwg. Question marks can also be used to position wildcards in single character positions. For example, the specification fl??r.dwg would find floor.dwg and flyer.dwg, but not floor_01.dwg. Wildcard combinations can be used. For example, the specification fl??r*.dwg would find floor.dwg, flyer.dwg, floorpln.dwg, and floor_01.dwg.

The **File Types:** drop-down list displays the available options of file types for the current operation. Since you are opening a drawing, the only file type available is .dwg.

The **Date Filter** can be used to limit the search to files created within a specific date range. Selecting the drop-down list allows you to specify whether the search should include only files last edited before or after the date specified below. Note that the format for specifying time and date must be as follows:

    Date: mm-dd-yy
    Time: hh:mm or hh:mm:ss

The **Search Location:** allows you to limit your search to specific drives or directory paths. First, select the appropriate radio button, then set the required specifications. For example, to limit your search to the contents of one disk drive you must first select the **Drive:** radio button, then use the drop-down list to select the disk drive to search. Selecting the **All Drives:** drop-down list displays the options of searching only local fixed drives (hard disks) or searching all drives. Searching all drives will search all available hard and floppy disks, plus all available network drives.

If you wish to limit your search to specific directory paths, select the **Path:** radio button. For a single path, type your entry directly into the edit box. For multiple path entries, select the **Edit...** button. This displays the **Edit Path** dialog. Additional paths can be added or deleted from the search path list. See Figure 3-14.

Figure 3-14.
The **Edit Path** dialog box. The \acadr14\sample folder on the C: drive has been added to the search path. Additional paths can be entered in the **Path:** text box and added to the list by picking the **Add** button.

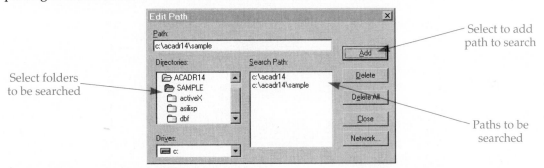

Select folders to be searched

Select to add path to search

Paths to be searched

Finally, pick the **Search** button to begin the search. A dynamic display above the **Files:** window counts the number of files found matching the current search criteria, while the path names of the folders being searched are displayed below. The **Search** button changes to a **Stop Search** button, and can be pressed at any time to halt the search.

Once the search is complete, the found files and their locations are displayed in the **Files:** window. Only Release 13 and 14 drawing files are displayed graphically; files from earlier releases are shown only as a rectangle with an "X" shape and the directory path location of the file. The scroll bars can be used to display the entire path or more file listings. To open a drawing in the **Files:** window, double-click on the desired file.

Browsing through drawing files

When the file name is not known and you would like to look through your drawing files to find a specific drawing, select the **Browse** tab. See Figure 3-15. This allows you to select folders and look through the drawing files found there. To browse through a folder of drawings, use the following procedure:

1. Use the **Directories:** window to navigate to the desired folder. Double-click on the folder you want to look through. If you need to change the current disk drive first, select the **Drives:** drop-down list and pick the appropriate disk drive. The **List Files of Type:** drop-down list shows only .dwg files since the active command is **Open**.
2. The **File Name:** edit box can be used to indicate specific files to display. Wildcard characters can be used here as well. For example, a*.dwg displays only drawing files that have a file name beginning with an "a".
3. Use the scroll bar to view more files. To open a file from the **Browse** tab, double-click on the drawing image, or pick the image and then pick the **Open** button. If you need to view another folder, simply double-click on the new folder, and the drawing files contained there are displayed. The browser displays only the contents of a single directory.
4. To change the size of the drawing image displayed, pick the **Size:** drop-down list. Selecting **Small** allows up to 30 drawings to be displayed at one time. However, there will be very little detail since they are so small. The **Medium** setting completely displays 9 to 12 files. The **Large** setting provides the best image, but only one drawing is completely displayed.

Figure 3-15.
When the file name is not known, select the **Browse** tab in the **Browse/Search** dialog box. Each individual drawing can be viewed.

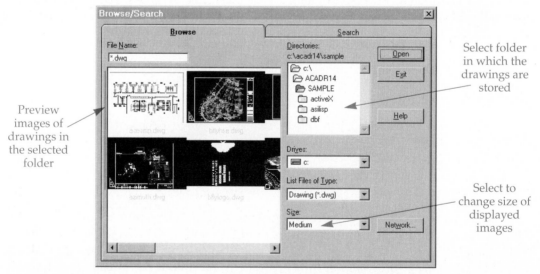

Opening Release 11, 12, and 13 drawings

You can open AutoCAD Release 11, 12, and 13 drawings in Release 14. When you open a drawing from a previous release and work on it, AutoCAD automatically updates the drawing to Release 14 standards when you save. After the previous release drawing is saved in Release 14, it can be viewed in the **Preview** image tile during future applications.

Opening a drawing from the <u>F</u>ile pull-down menu list

AutoCAD stores the names and locations of the last four drawing files opened in the graphics window. These file names are listed at the bottom of the **F**ile pull-down menu, as shown in Figure 3-16. Any one of these files can be quickly opened by picking the file name.

Figure 3-16.
The **F**ile pull-down menu contains a list of the last four edited drawings.

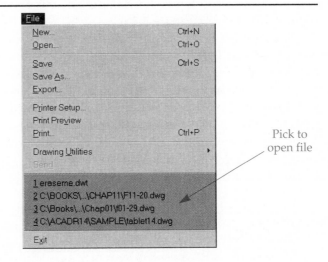

Pick to open file

Notice that the drive and directory for each drawing is included with the file name. If you try to open one of these drawing files after it has been deleted or moved to a different drive or directory, AutoCAD is unable to locate it. AutoCAD displays the message "Cannot find the specified drawing file" and opens the **Select File** dialog box.

When you are starting AutoCAD and pick the **Open a Drawing** button in the **Start Up** dialog box, the last four drawing files opened are listed in the **Select a File:** list. Pick the desired file to see its image in the **Preview** area. Press [Enter] or pick **OK** to open the drawing, or double-click on the file name.

Using the **Quit Command**

The **QUIT** command is the primary way to end a drawing session. You can close the program window by picking **E<u>x</u>it** from the **F**ile pull-down menu, or typing QUIT or EXIT at the Command: prompt.

If you enter the QUIT command before saving your work, AutoCAD gives you a chance to decide what you want to do with unsaved work. The AutoCAD alert box shown in Figure 3-17 appears. Press [Enter] to activate the highlighted **Yes** button. This saves the drawing. If the drawing is unnamed, the **Save Drawing As** dialog box appears. You can also pick the **No** button if you plan to discard any changes made to the drawing since the previous save. This is a good way to use AutoCAD for practice. Pick the **Cancel** button if you decide not to quit and want to return to the graphics window.

Figure 3-17.
This AutoCAD alert box is shown if you try to exit AutoCAD without saving the work. This is an opportunity to decide what will be done with unsaved work.

Determining the Drawing Status

While working on a drawing, you may want to refresh your memory about some of the drawing parameters, such as the limits, grid spacing, or snap values. All of the information about the drawing is displayed by typing STATUS at the Command: prompt. You can also select **Status** from the **Inquiry** menu item in the **Tools** pull-down menu. The graphics window automatically flips to the text window to display drawing information. See Figure 3-18.

The number of objects in a drawing refers to the total number of entities—both erased and existing. Drawing aid settings are shown, along with the current settings for layer, linetype, and color. These topics are discussed in later chapters of this text. Free disk space represents the space left on the drive containing your drawing file.

When you have completed reading the status information in the text window, press function key [F2] to flip back to the graphics window. This action automatically closes the text window and restores the inactive graphics window. You can also switch to the graphics window without closing the text window by clicking anywhere inside the graphics window.

Figure 3-18.
The **AutoCAD Text Window** displays drawing information listed by the **STATUS** command.

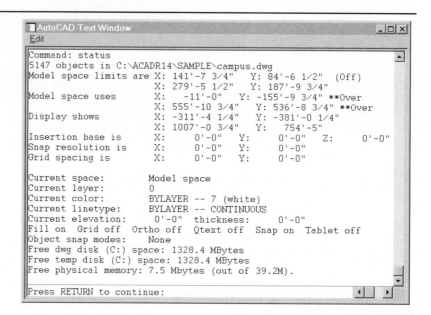

```
Command: status
5147 objects in C:\ACADR14\SAMPLE\campus.dwg
Model space limits are X: 141'-7 3/4"    Y: 84'-6 1/2"   (Off)
                        X: 279'-5 1/2"    Y: 187'-9 3/4"
Model space uses        X:    -11'-0"     Y: -155'-9 3/4" **Over
                        X: 555'-10 3/4"   Y: 536'-8 3/4"  **Over
Display shows           X: -311'-4 1/4"   Y: -381'-0 1/4"
                        X: 1007'-0 3/4"   Y:   754'-5"
Insertion base is       X:      0'-0"     Y:      0'-0"   Z:      0'-0"
Snap resolution is      X:      0'-0"     Y:      0'-0"
Grid spacing is         X:      0'-0"     Y:      0'-0"

Current space:          Model space
Current layer:          0
Current color:          BYLAYER -- 7 (white)
Current linetype:       BYLAYER -- CONTINUOUS
Current elevation:      0'-0"    thickness:      0'-0"
Fill on  Grid off  Ortho off  Qtext off  Snap on  Tablet off
Object snap modes:      None
Free dwg disk (C:) space: 1328.4 MBytes
Free temp disk (C:) space: 1328.4 MBytes
Free physical memory: 7.5 Mbytes (out of 39.2M).

Press RETURN to continue:
```

NOTE
Another way to move between the graphics window and the text window is provided with the AutoCAD commands **GRAPHSCR** and **TEXTSCR**. Typing TEXTSCR at the Command: prompt flips to the text window. Typing GRAPHSCR flips to the graphics window. You can also flip to the text window from the graphics window by selecting **Text Window** from the **Display** cascading menu in the **View** pull-down menu.

EXERCISE 3-7

❏ Start AutoCAD and open the drawing that you developed in Exercise 3-5.
❏ Use the **STATUS** command and read all of the items displayed in the **AutoCAD Text Window**.
❏ Press the [F2] function key to return to the graphics window.
❏ Open the **Select File** dialog box and pick the **Find File...** button.
❏ Open the **Search** tab in the **Browse/Search** dialog box. The **Search Pattern:** should be *.dwg, the **File Types:** should be Drawing (*.dwg), and the **Search Location:** should be C: or the drive where the AutoCAD sample drawings are located.
❏ Pick the **Search** button and see the results.
❏ Double-click on any desired AutoCAD sample file to open it, or pick the desired file followed by picking the **Open** button.
❏ Open the **Select File** dialog box and pick the **Find File...** button again.
❏ Find the directory with the AutoCAD sample drawings.
❏ Use the **Size:** list to pick the **Medium** and **Large** options to notice the difference. Pick the **Small** option again.
❏ Double-click on any desired AutoCAD sample file to open it.
❏ Use the **QUIT** command.
❏ Start AutoCAD again and pick the **Open a Drawing** button in the **Start Up** dialog box. Notice the last opened drawings displayed in the **Select a File:** list. Pick on one or more of the files and notice the **Preview** image displayed. Pick the **Cancel** button to close the **Start Up** dialog box.
❏ Select the **File** pull-down menu and notice the last opened drawings displayed near the bottom of the menu. Pick on one of the files to open the drawing.
❏ Exit AutoCAD.

Chapter Test

Write your answers in the spaces provided.

1. Give the command and value entered to set a grid spacing of .25:
   Command: _____
   Grid spacing(X) or ON/OFF/Snap/Aspect ⟨*current*⟩: _____

2. Give the command and value entered to set the snap spacing at .125:
   Command: _____
   Snap spacing or ON/OFF/Snap/Aspect/Rotate/Style ⟨*current*⟩: _____

3. Name the command used to place a pattern of dots on the screen. _____

4. Identify the pull-down menu used to select drawing aids. _____

5. How do you activate the snap grid so the screen cursor will automatically move in precise increments? _____

_____

_____

6. How do you set different horizontal and vertical snap units? _____

_____

_____

7. Name three ways to access the drawing aids. _____

_____

_____

8. Describe a template drawing. _____

_____

_____

_____

9. Identify the command that you use to leave the graphics window without saving.

_____

10. What command would you use to save an existing drawing with a different name? _____

_____

11. Identify at least four ways to cancel a command. _____

_____

_____

_____

_____

12. How do you change the name of a drawing while in the graphics window? ____

_____

_____

13. How often should work be saved? _____

14. Name the command that allows you to quickly save your work without displaying the dialog box. _____

15. The status of an AutoCAD drawing is currently displayed in the **AutoCAD Text Window**. List one method to get back to the graphics editor. _____

16. Name the system variable that allows you to control the dialog box display. ____

_____

17. List the settings for the system variable described in the previous question that is used to achieve the following results:

Dialog box displayed _____

Dialog box not displayed _____

18. Why is it important to record drawing names in a log? _____

_____

19. List at least three rules and restrictions for drawing names._____

_____

_____

_____

_____

20. Name the pull-down menu where the **SAVE**, **SAVEAS**, and **OPEN** commands are located._____

21. How do you exit AutoCAD without saving your work?_____

_____

_____

22. Name the command that allows AutoCAD to automatically save your work at designated intervals. _____

23. Explain how you can obtain a list of existing drawing templates to select one for opening. _____

_____

_____

24. What command do you use to save a drawing to a floppy disk?_____

_____

25. How do you access the **Preview** image tile and what is its purpose?_____

_____

_____

_____

_____

26. What does the **DDRMODES** command do?_____

27. Give the keyboard shortcut for the **DDRMODES** command. _____

28. What is the keyboard shortcut for the **LINE** command?_____

29. How do you turn **GRID** on and off at the status bar? _____

30. How do you turn **SNAP** on and off at the status bar?_____

31. What is the result of pressing the [Ctrl]+[B] keys or the [F9] function key?_____

32. Name the command that is accessed when you pick the **Save** button in the **Standard** toolbar._____

33. Which option in the **Save as type:** list in the **Save Drawing As** dialog box should be used when saving a drawing file? _____

_____

34. If a drawing has been previously saved, what is the difference between using the **QSAVE** or **SAVE** commands?_____

_____

_____

35. What safety precaution does AutoCAD provide if you try to save the current drawing using the same name and location as another drawing file?_____
_____
_____

36. How do you open a folder? _____
_____

37. When you save a version of a drawing in an earlier format, why is it a good idea to give it a different name than the Release 14 version uses? _____
_____
_____

38. Identify five ways to open the **Select File** dialog box. _____
_____
_____
_____

39. How do the arrow keys help you move between files in the **Select File** dialog box and how does this affect the previews? _____
_____
_____
_____

40. What happens if you pick the **Find File...** button in the **Select File** dialog box? ___
_____

41. What happens in the **Search** tab of the **Browse/Search** dialog box, if the **Search Pattern:** is *.dwg and the **File Types:** is Drawing (*.DWG), and you pick the **Search** button? _____
_____
_____
_____

42. How do you open a file in the **Files:** window of the **Search** tab in the **Browse/Search** dialog box? _____
_____

43. What is the purpose of the **Browse** tab in the **Browse/Search** dialog box? _____
_____
_____

44. What happens when you pick the different options in the **Size:** drop-down list in the **Browse** folder of the **Browse/Search** dialog box? _____
_____

45. If you want to exit AutoCAD, what are the two command names that can be typed at the Command: prompt?_____
_____

46. What command do you use if you want to refresh your memory about the drawing parameters? _____

Drawing Problems

1. Open one of your templates from Chapter 2 or Exercise 3-4. Draw the specified objects as accurately as possible with the **Grid** and **Snap** turned off. Use the **LINE** command to draw the following objects on the left side of the screen only:
   - Right triangle
   - Isosceles triangle
   - Rectangle
   - Square

   Save the drawing as P3-1.

2. Draw the same objects specified in Problem 1 on the right side of the screen. This time, make sure the **Snap** grid is turned on. Observe the difference between having snap on in this problem and off in the previous problem. Save the drawing as P3-2.

*The following problems can be done if the AutoCAD **Sample** file folder is loaded. In the following problems, use the **Browse/Search** dialog box to locate and open the specified drawing files, if needed, and complete the requested information:*

3. Locate and preview or open the campus drawing. Describe the drawing in your own words.

4. Locate and preview or open the watch drawing. Describe the drawing in your own words.

5. Locate and preview or open the azimuth drawing. Describe the drawing in your own words.

6. Locate and preview or open the tablet14 drawing. Describe the drawing in your own words.

7. Locate and preview or open the bflylogo drawing. Describe the drawing in your own words.

8. Locate and preview or open the opera drawing. Describe the drawing in your own words.

Elevations section. (Steve D. Bloedel)

Chapter 4

Drawing Lines, Erasing Objects, Using Layers, and Making Prints

Learning Objectives

After completing this chapter, you will be able to:
- ○ Use absolute, relative, and polar coordinate point entry systems.
- ○ Use the screen cursor for point entry.
- ○ Use the **Ortho** mode and coordinate display.
- ○ Select the **LINE** command to draw given objects.
- ○ Use direct distance entry.
- ○ Use a variety of linetypes to construct an object.
- ○ Make revisions to objects using the **ERASE** command and its options.
- ○ Make selection sets using the **Multiple**, **Window**, **Crossing**, **WPolygon**, **CPolygon**, and **Fence** options.
- ○ Use the **OOPS** command to bring back an erased object.
- ○ Draw objects in color.
- ○ Draw objects on separate layers using the **LAYER** command.
- ○ Create and manage drawing layers using a dialog box.
- ○ Remove and add objects to the selection set.
- ○ Use the **MULTIPLE** command modifier.
- ○ Clean up the screen with the **REDRAW** command.
- ○ Draw objects with different linetypes.
- ○ Make a print of your drawing.

Drafting is a graphic language that uses lines, symbols, and words to describe products to be manufactured or constructed. Line conventions are standards based on line thickness and type, which are designed to enhance the readability of drawings. This chapter introduces line standards and shows you how to use the AutoCAD drawing editor to perform basic drafting tasks.

Line Conventions

The American National Standards Institute (ANSI) recommends two line widths to establish contrasting lines on a drawing. Lines are described as thick and thin. Thick lines are 0.6mm wide and thin lines are 0.3mm wide. Figure 4-1 shows recommended line width and type as taken from ANSI Y14.2M, *Line Conventions and Lettering*.

Figure 4-1.
Line conventions. (ANSI Y14.2M)

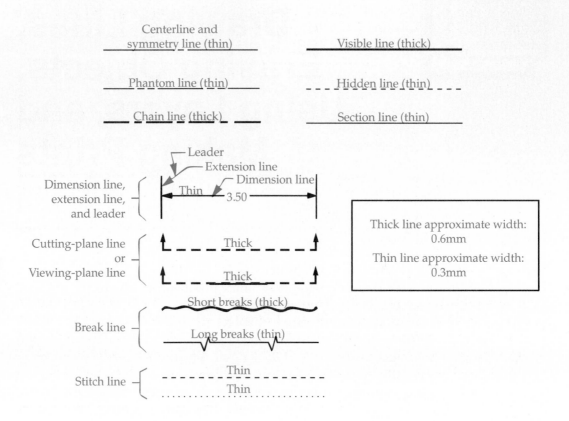

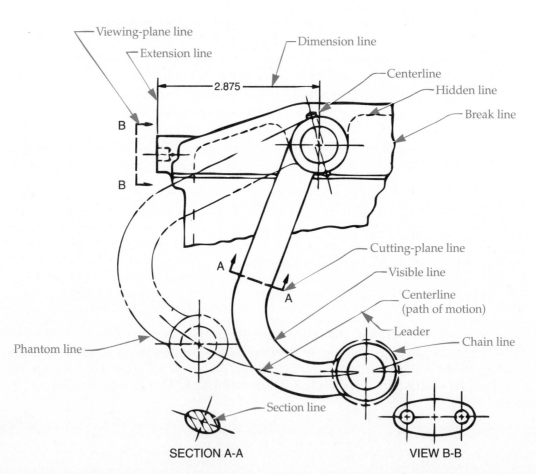

SECTION A-A

VIEW B-B

Object lines

Object lines, also called *visible lines*, are thick lines used to show the outline or contour of an object, Figure 4-2. Object lines are the most common type of lines used on drawings. These lines should be twice as thick as thin lines.

Figure 4-2.
Object line.

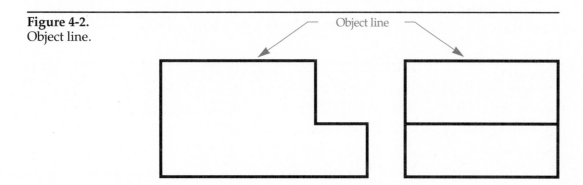

Hidden lines

Hidden lines, often called *dashed lines*, are used to represent invisible features of an object, as shown in Figure 4-3. Hidden lines are drawn thin so they clearly contrast with object lines. When properly drawn at full size, the dashes are .125″ (3mm) long and spaced .06″ (1.5mm) apart. Be careful if the drawing is to be greatly reduced or scaled down during the plotting process. Reduced dashes may appear too small.

Figure 4-3.
Hidden line.

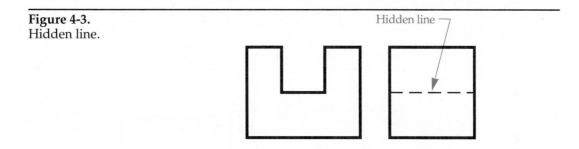

Centerlines

Centerlines locate the centers of circles and arcs and show the axis of a cylindrical or symmetrical shape, as shown in Figure 4-4. Centerlines are thin lines consisting of alternately spaced long and short dashes. The recommended dash lengths are .125″ (3mm) for the short dashes and .75″ to 1.5″ (19mm to 38mm) for the long dashes. These lengths can be altered depending on the size of the drawing. The dashes should be separated by spaces approximately .06″ (1.5mm) long. The small centerline dashes should cross only at the center of a circle.

Figure 4-4.
Centerline.

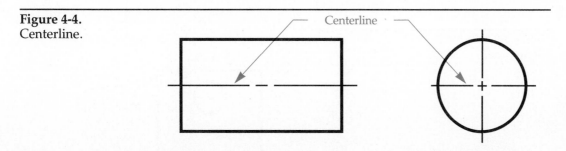

Extension lines

Extension lines are thin lines used to show the "extent" of a dimension, as shown in Figure 4-5. Extension lines begin a small distance from the object and extend .125" (3mm) beyond the last dimension line. Extension lines may cross object lines, hidden lines, and centerlines, but they may not cross dimension lines. Centerlines become extension lines when they are used to show the extent of a dimension. When this is done, there is no space where the centerline joins the extension line.

Figure 4-5.
Extension line.

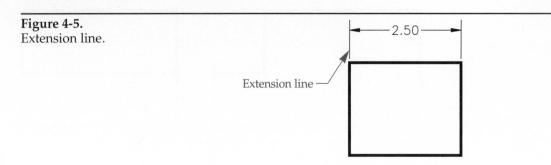

Dimension lines

Dimension lines are thin lines placed between extension lines to indicate a measurement. In mechanical drafting, the dimension line is normally broken near the center for placement of the dimension numeral, as shown in Figure 4-6. The dimension line normally remains unbroken in architectural and structural drawings. The dimension numeral is placed on top of an unbroken dimension line. Arrows terminate the ends of dimension lines, except in architectural drafting where slashes or dots are often used.

Figure 4-6.
Dimension line.

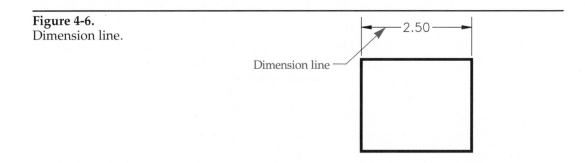

Leader lines

Leader lines are thin lines used to connect a specific note to a feature on a drawing. A leader line terminates with an arrowhead at the feature and has a small shoulder at the note, Figure 4-7. Dimension and leader line usage is discussed in detail in Chapters 18 and 19.

Figure 4-7.
Leader line.

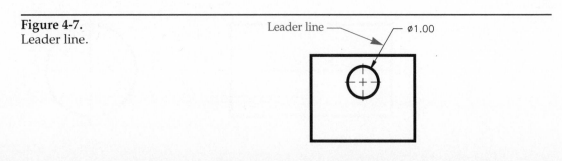

Cutting-plane and viewing-plane lines

Cutting-plane lines are thick lines that identify the location of a section. *Viewing-plane lines* are drawn in the same style as cutting-plane lines, but identify the location of a view. Cutting-plane and viewing-plane lines may be drawn one of two ways, as shown in Figure 4-1. The use of viewing-plane and cutting-plane lines is discussed in detail in Chapter 6 and Chapter 22.

Section lines

Section lines are thin lines drawn in a section view to show where material has been cut away, as shown in Figure 4-8. Types of section lines and applications are discussed in Chapter 22.

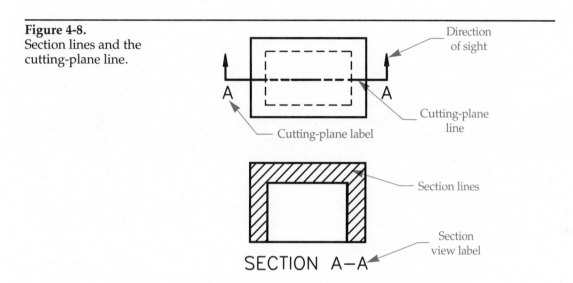

Figure 4-8.
Section lines and the cutting-plane line.

Break lines

Break lines show where a portion of an object has been removed for clarity or convenience. For example, the center portion of a very long part may be broken out so the two ends can be moved closer together for more convenient representation. There are several types of break lines shown in Figure 4-9.

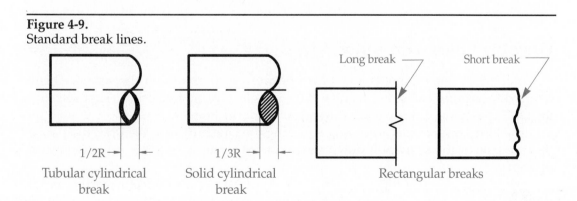

Figure 4-9.
Standard break lines.

Phantom lines

Phantom lines are thin lines with two short dashes alternately spaced with long dashes. The short dashes are .125″ (3mm) long and the long dashes range from .75″ to 1.5″ (19mm to 38mm) in length, depending on the size of the drawing. Spaces between dashes are .06″ (1.5mm). Phantom lines identify repetitive details, show alternate positions of moving parts, and locate adjacent positions of related parts, Figure 4-10.

Figure 4-10.
Phantom lines.

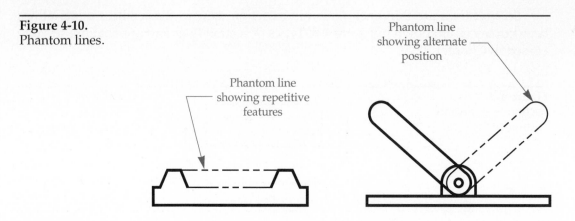

Phantom line
showing repetitive
features

Phantom line
showing alternate
position

Chain lines

Chain lines are thick lines of alternately spaced long and short dashes. They show that the portion of the surface next to the chain line has special features or receives unique treatment. See Figure 4-11.

Figure 4-11.
Chain lines.

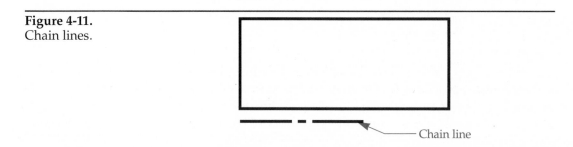

Chain line

Drawing Lines with AutoCAD

Individual line segments are drawn between two points on the screen. This is referred to as *point entry*. Point entry is the simplest form of drafting. After selecting the **LINE** command, simply enter the endpoints of the line.

The **LINE** command is accessed by picking the **Line** button in the **Draw** toolbar, by picking **Line** in the **Draw** pull-down menu, or by typing L or LINE at the Command: prompt.

When you use the **LINE** command, a prompt asks you to select a starting point. When the first point is selected (From point:), you are asked for the second point (To point:). When the next To point: prompt is given, continue selecting additional points if you want to connect a series of lines. When finished, press the [Enter] key or the space bar to get back to the Command: prompt.

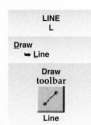

LINE
L

Draw
➥ Line

Draw
toolbar

Line

The following command sequence is used for the **LINE** command:

Command: **L** *or* **LINE**⏎
From point: *(select the first point)*
To point: *(select the second point)*
To point: *(select the third point, or press* [Enter] *or the space bar to get a new*
    Command: *prompt)*
Command: *(this appears if you pressed* [Enter] *or the space bar at the previous*
    prompt)

PROFESSIONAL TIP

AutoCAD provides a set of abbreviated commands called ***command aliases***. Command aliases are also called ***keyboard shortcuts***, because they reduce the amount of typing needed when entering a command at the keyboard. Using command aliases allows you to enter commands more quickly. For example, instead of typing LINE at the Command: prompt, it is faster to type L. Becoming familiar with the available command aliases can help you become more productive with AutoCAD.

Responding to AutoCAD prompts with numbers

Many of the AutoCAD commands require specific types of numeric data. Some of AutoCAD's prompts require you to enter a whole number. For example, later in this book you will learn how to draw a polygon using the **POLYGON** command. This command requires that you specify the number of sides as follows:

Command: **POLYGON**⏎
Number of sides ⟨*current*⟩: **6**⏎
Edge/⟨Center of polygon⟩: *(pick center of polygon)*
Inscribed in circle/Circumscribed about circle (I/C): *(respond with* I *or* C *and press*
    [Enter]*)*
Radius of circle: *(type the radius, such as* 2 *and press* [Enter]*, or pick a point on the*
    screen at the desired distance from the center)

The Number of sides: prompt illustrates the simplest form of numeric entry, in which any whole number may be used. Other entries require whole numbers that may be positive or negative. A number is understood to be positive without placing the plus (+) sign before the number. However, a negative number must be preceded by the minus (-) sign.

Much of your data entry may not be whole numbers. In these cases, any real number can be used, and can be expressed as decimals, fractions, or scientific notation. They may be positive or negative. Here are some examples of acceptable real numbers:

4.250
-6.375
1/2
1-3/4
2.5E+4 *(25,000)*
2.5E-4 *(0.00025)*

When entering fractions, the numerator and denominator must be whole numbers greater than zero. For example, 1/2, 3/4, and 2/3 are all acceptable fraction entries. Fractional numbers greater than one must have a dash between the whole number and the fraction. For example, 2-3/4 is entered for two and three quarters. The dash (-) separator is needed because a space acts just like pressing [Enter] and automatically ends the input. The numerator may be larger than the denominator, as in 3/2, *only* if a whole number is not used with the fraction.

When you enter coordinates or measurements, the value used depends on the units of measure.

- Values on inch drawings are understood to be in inches without placing the inch marks (") after the numeral. For example, 2.500 is automatically understood to be 2.500 inches.
- When your drawing is set up for metric values, any entry is automatically expressed as millimeters.
- If you are working in an engineering or architectural environment, any value greater than one foot is expressed in inches, feet, or feet and inches. The values can be whole numbers, decimals, or fractions.
  - For measurements in feet, the foot symbol (') must follow the number, as in 24'.
  - If the value is in feet and inches, there is no space between the feet and inch value. For example, 24'6 is the proper input for the value 24'-6".
  - If the inch part of the value contains a fraction, the inch and fractional part of an inch are separated by a dash, such as 24'6-1/2.

Never mix feet with inch values greater than one foot. For example, 24'18" is an invalid entry. In this case, you should enter 25'6.

PROFESSIONAL TIP   Placing the inch mark (") after an inch value at the prompt line is acceptable, but not necessary. It takes more time and reduces productivity.

Point entry methods

There are several point entry techniques for drawing lines. Being familiar and skillful with these methods is very important. A combination of point entry techniques should be used to help reduce drawing time.

Each of the point entry methods uses the Cartesian, or rectangular, coordinate system. The *Cartesian coordinate system* is based on selecting distances from three intersecting axes. A *location* is defined by its distance from the intersection point, called the *origin*, in respect to each of these axes. In standard two-dimensional (2D) drafting applications, objects are drawn in the X,Y plane and the Z axis is not referenced. Using the Z axis is discussed in Chapter 27 with three-dimensional (3D) drafting.

In 2D drafting, the origin divides the coordinate system into four quadrants within the X,Y plane. Points are located in relation to the origin, where X = 0 and Y = 0, or (0,0). Figure 4-12 shows the X,Y values of points located in the Cartesian coordinate system.

AutoCAD and its Applications—Basics

Figure 4-12.
The Cartesian
coordinate system.

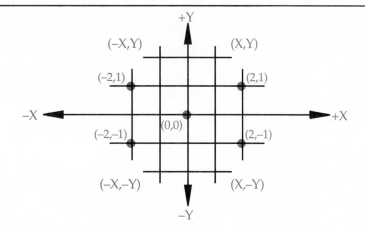

When using AutoCAD, the origin (0,0) is usually at the lower-left corner of the drawing. This point also coincides with the lower-left corner of the drawing limits. This setup places all points in the upper-right quadrant where both X and Y coordinate values are positive, Figure 4-13. Methods of establishing points in the Cartesian coordinate system include absolute coordinates, relative coordinates, and polar coordinates.

Figure 4-13.
The X,Y coordinate axes on the screen.

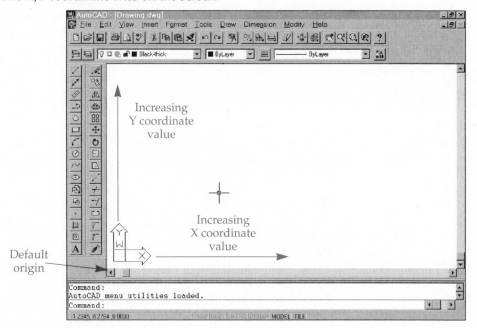

Using absolute coordinates

Points located using the absolute coordinate system are measured from the origin (0,0). For example, a point with X = 4 and Y = 2 (4,2) is located 4 units horizontally and 2 units vertically from the origin, as shown in Figure 4-14. Notice that the coordinate display window on the toolbar registers the location of the selected point in X, Y, and Z coordinates.

Figure 4-14.
Locating points with absolute coordinates.

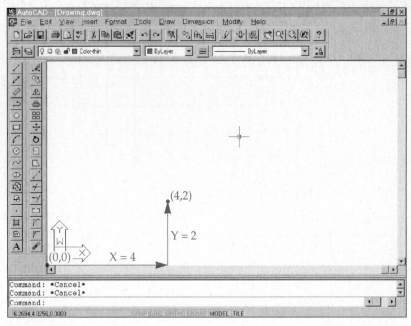

The discussion and examples in this chapter reference only the X,Y coordinates for 2D drafting. Also note that the coordinate display window reflects the current system of working units. Remember, when the absolute coordinate system is used, each point is located from 0,0. Follow through these commands and point placements at your computer as you refer to Figure 4-15.

Command: **L** *or* **LINE.**⏎
From point: **4,2.**⏎
To point: **7,2**⏎
To point: **7,6**⏎
To point: **4,6**⏎
To point: **4,2**⏎
To point: ⏎
Command:

Figure 4-15.
Drawing simple shapes using the **LINE** command and absolute coordinates.

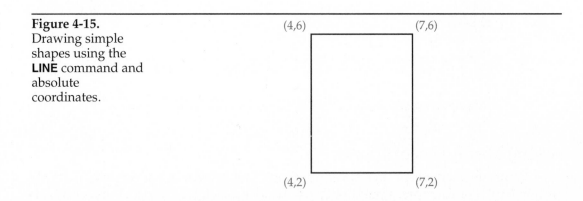

AutoCAD and its Applications—Basics

❏ Start a new drawing or use one of your templates.
❏ Given the absolute coordinates in the chart below, use the **LINE** command to draw the object.
❏ Save the drawing as EX4-1.

Point	Coordinates	Point	Coordinates
1	0,0	5	0,2
2	9,0	6	0,1.5
3	9.5,.5	7	.25,.5
4	9.5,2	8	0,0

Using relative coordinates

Relative coordinates are located from the previous position, rather than from the origin. The relationship of points in the Cartesian coordinate system shown in Figure 4-12 must be clearly understood before using this method. For relative coordinates, the @ symbol must precede your entry. This symbol is selected by holding the [Shift] key and pressing the [2] key at the top of the keyboard. Follow through these commands and relative coordinate point placements as you refer to Figure 4-16.

Command: **L** *or* **LINE**↵
From point: **2,2**↵
To point: **@6,0**↵
To point: **@2,2**↵
To point: **@0,3**↵
To point: **@–2,2**↵
To point: **@–6,0**↵
To point: **@0,–7**↵
To point: ↵
Command:

Figure 4-16.
Drawing a simple shape using the **LINE** command and relative coordinates. Notice that the coordinates are entered counter-clockwise from the first point (2,2)

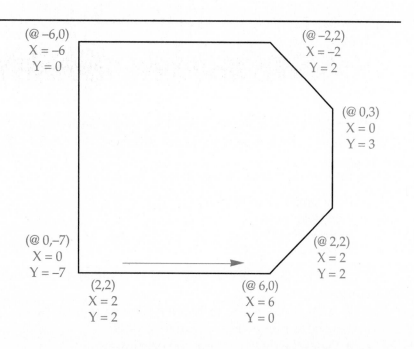

❏ Start a new drawing or use one of your templates.
❏ Use the **LINE** command to draw the object with the relative coordinates given in the chart below.
❏ Save the drawing as EX4-2.

Point	Coordinates	Point	Coordinates
1	1,1	5	@-9.5,0
2	@9,0	6	@0,-.5
3	@.5,.5	7	@.25,-1
4	@0,1.5	8	@-.25,-.5

Using polar coordinates

A point located using *polar coordinates* is based on the distance from a fixed point at a given angle. First the distance is entered, then the angle. The two values are separated by a ⟨ symbol.

The angular values used for the polar coordinate format are shown in Figure 4-17. Consistent with standard AutoCAD convention, 0° is to the right, or east. Angles are then measured counterclockwise.

Figure 4-17.
Angles used in the polar coordinate system.

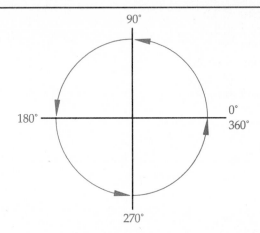

When preceded by the @ symbol, a polar coordinate point is measured from the *previous point*. If the @ symbol is not included, the coordinate is located relative to the origin. If you want to locate a point 4 units from point 1,1 at a 45° angle, the following information must be typed:

```
Command: L or LINE↵
From point: 1,1↵
To point: @4⟨45↵
To point: ↵
```

Figure 4-18 shows the result of this command. The entry @4⟨45 means the following:

- **@.** Tells AutoCAD to measure from the previous point. This symbol must precede nearly all polar coordinate inputs.
- **4.** Gives the distance from the previous point.
- **⟨.** Establishes a polar or angular increment to follow.
- **45.** Determines the angle, as 45° from 0°.

AutoCAD and its Applications—Basics

Figure 4-18.
Using polar
coordinates for the
LINE command.

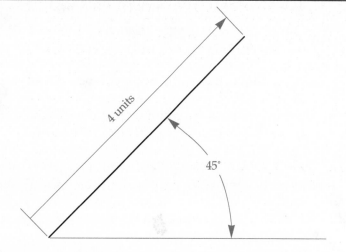

Now, follow through these commands and polar coordinate points on your computer as you refer to Figure 4-19.

Command: **L** *or* **LINE.**↵
From point: **2,6.**↵
To point: **@2.5⟨0.**↵
To point: **@3⟨135.**↵
To point: **2,6.**↵
To point: ↵
Command:↵
LINE From point: **6,6** ↵
To point: **@4⟨0.**↵
To point: **@2⟨90.**↵
To point: **@4⟨180.**↵
To point: **@2⟨270.**↵
Command:
To point: ↵

Figure 4-19.
Using polar
coordinates to draw.

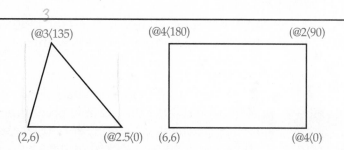

EXERCISE 4-3

❑ Start a new drawing or use one of your templates.
❑ Use the **LINE** command to draw an object using the polar coordinates given in the chart below.
❑ Save the drawing as EX4-3.

Point	Coordinates	Point	Coordinates
1	1,1	4	@1.5⟨90
2	@9⟨0	5	@9.5⟨180
3	@.7⟨45	6	@2⟨270

Picking points using the screen cursor

The pointing device can be used to move the crosshairs and pick points. The **GRID** and **SNAP** modes normally should be turned on for precise point location. This assists in drafting presentation and maintains accuracy when using a pointing device. With **SNAP** on, the crosshairs move in designated increments without any guesswork.

When using a pointing device, the command sequence is the same as using coordinates, except that points are picked when the crosshairs are at the desired location. After the first point is picked, the distance to the second point and the point's coordinates are displayed on the status line for reference. When picking points in this manner, there is a "rubberband" line connecting the "first point" and the crosshairs. The rubberband line moves as the crosshairs are moved, showing where the new line will be placed.

Drawing multiple lines

The **MULTIPLE** command modifier is a method used to automatically repeat commands issued at the keyboard. This technique can be used to draw repetitive lines, polylines, circles, arcs, ellipses, or polygons. For example, if you plan to draw several sets of line segments, type MU or MULTIPLE, press the space bar to add a space, and then type L or LINE at the Command: prompt. AutoCAD automatically repeats the **LINE** command until you have finished drawing all of the desired lines. You must cancel to get back to the Command: prompt. The **MULTIPLE** option is used as follows:

> Command: **MULTIPLE LINE**↵
> From point: *(pick the first point)*
> To point: *(pick the second point)*
> To point: *(pick the third point or press* [Enter]*)*
> To point: ↵
> LINE From point: *(pick the first point of the next line)*
> To point: *(pick the second point of the next line)*
> To point: *(pick the third point or press* [Enter]*)*
> To point: ↵
> LINE From point: *(press* [Esc] *to cancel)* *Cancel*
> Command:

As you can see, AutoCAD automatically reissues the **LINE** command so you can draw another line (or lines). Press [Esc] to cancel the repeating command.

The coordinate display

WHERE IS COORDS SYS. VARIABLE ON THE SCREEN ITSELF, MENU/STANDARD BAR?

The area to the left side of the status bar shows the coordinate display window. The number of places to the right of the decimal point is determined by the units setting. The coordinate display changes to represent the location of the cursor in relation to the origin. Each time a new point is picked or the pointing device moved, the coordinates are updated.

The coordinate display is turned on and off by double-clicking the coordinate display window, pressing the [Ctrl]+[D] key combination, function key [F6], or pick button 7. With coordinates on, the coordinates constantly change as the crosshairs move. With coordinates off, no coordinates are displayed.

There are three coordinate modes and they are controlled by the **COORDS** system variable. Set this variable to 0 for a static display. This displays coordinates only when points are selected. Set the **COORDS** variable to 1 for a dynamic absolute display. Set the variable to 2 for a dynamic length/angle (polar) display. A typical absolute coordinate display gives X, Y, and Z coordinates such as 6.2000,5.9000,0.0000. A polar coordinate display shows the distance and angle from the last point and the Z axis is distance, such as 3.4000⟨180, 0.0000.

❑ Start a new drawing, use one of your templates, or open a previous exercise.
❑ Draw rectangles 3" (76.2mm) wide by 2" (50.8mm) high using each point entry method from the following list. Experiment with the coordinate display options as you draw the rectangles.
  ❑ Absolute coordinates.
  ❑ Relative coordinates.
  ❑ Polar coordinates.
  ❑ Using the screen cursor.
❑ Use the **MULTIPLE LINE** command to draw several different lines and shapes. Notice the advantage of remaining in the **LINE** command when several different line segments or shapes must be drawn.
❑ Save the drawing as EX4-4.

Drawing in **ORTHO** mode

The term *ortho* comes from "orthogonal," which means "at right angles." The **ORTHO** mode constrains points selected while drawing and editing to be only horizontal or vertical. The directions are in alignment with the current **Snap** grid.

The **ORTHO** mode has a special advantage when drawing rectangular shapes because all corners are guaranteed to be square. See Figure 4-20. **ORTHO** can be turned on or off by typing O or ORTHO at the Command: prompt, by double-clicking **ORTHO** on the status bar, by using function key [F8], puck button 5, or [Ctrl]+[L] key combination.

> Command: **O** *or* **ORTHO**↵
> ON/OFF 〈*current*〉: (ON *or* OFF *as desired*)↵

Figure 4-20.
A—Angled lines cannot be drawn with a pointing device while **ORTHO** mode is turned on.
B—With **ORTHO** mode turned off, angled lines can be drawn.

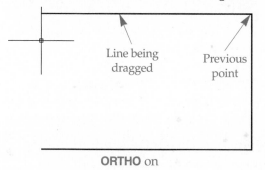

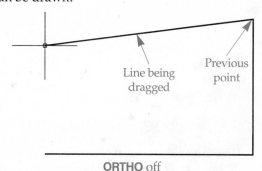

❑ Start a new drawing, use one of your templates, or open a previous exercise.
❑ Draw an equilateral triangle (three equal sides and angles). **ORTHO** must be off to do this.
❑ Draw a 3" (76mm) by 2" (50mm) rectangle using the screen cursor for point entry with **ORTHO** off. Draw a second rectangle with **ORTHO** on. Compare the difference.
❑ Save the drawing as EX4-5.

Using the Close Line option

A *polygon* is a closed plane figure with at least three sides. Triangles and rectangles are examples of polygons. Once you have drawn two or more line segments of a polygon, the endpoint of the last line segment can be connected automatically to the first line segment using the **Close** option. To use this option, type C or CLOSE at the prompt line. In Figure 4-21, the last line is drawn using the **Close** option as follows:

Command: **L** *or* **LINE**↵
From point: *(pick point 1)*
To point: *(pick point 2)*
To point: *(pick point 3)*
To point: *(pick point 4)*
To point: **C** *or* **CLOSE**↵
Command:

Figure 4-21.
Using the **Close** option to complete a box.

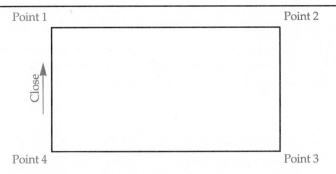

Point 1   Point 2

Close

Point 4   Point 3

Using direct distance entry

Direct distance entry is a method of entering points that allows you to use the cursor to specify the direction and keyboard entry to specify a distance. To draw a line using this point entry method, drag the cursor in any desired direction from the first point of the line. Then type a numerical value that indicates the distance from that point.

The direct distance entry method works best in combination with the **ORTHO** mode. Figure 4-22 illustrates how to draw a rectangle using direct distance entry. Note that the **ORTHO** mode is on for this example:

Command: **L** *or* **LINE**↵
From point: **2,2**↵
To point: *(drag the cursor horizontally, type* 6 *and press* [Enter]*)*
To point: *(drag the cursor vertically and type* 4 *and press* [Enter]*)*
To point: *(drag the cursor horizontally and type* 6 *and press* [Enter]*)*
To point: **C**↵
Command:

Figure 4-22.
Using direct distance entry to draw lines a designated distance from a current point. With **ORTHO** on, move the cursor in the desired direction and type the distance.

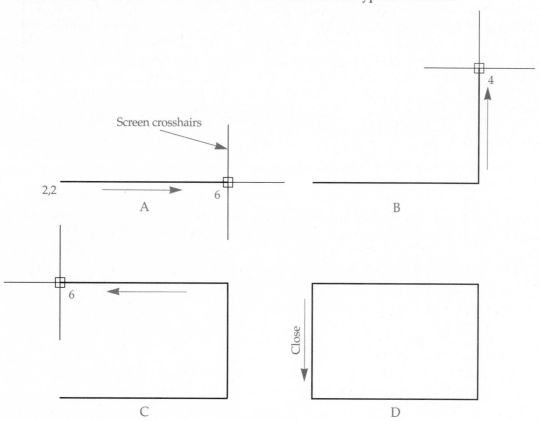

PROFESSIONAL TIP

Direct distance entry is a convenient way to find points quickly and easily with a minimum amount of effort. Use direct distance entry with **ORTHO** or **SNAP** on to draw objects with perpendicular lines. Direct distance entry can be used any time AutoCAD expects a point coordinate value, including both drawing and editing commands.

EXERCISE 4-6

❑ Start a new drawing, use one of your templates, or open a previous exercise.
❑ Use the **LINE** command and the **Close** option to draw a rectangle similar to Figure 4-21.
❑ Use direct distance entry to draw a rectangle similar to Figure 4-22.
❑ Use direct distance entry to start a new line a distance of your choice from the last point drawn, and then complete the line before returning to the Command: prompt.
❑ Save the drawing as EX4-6.

Using the Line Continuation option

Suppose you draw a line, then exit the **LINE** command, but decide to go back and connect a new line to the end of the previous one. Type L to begin the **LINE** command. Then, at the From point: prompt, simply press the [Enter] key or the space bar. This action automatically connects the first endpoint of the new line segment to the endpoint of the previous one, as shown in Figure 4-23. The **Continuation** option can also be used for drawing arcs, as discussed in Chapter 5. The following command sequence is used for continuing a line:

Command: **L** *or* **LINE**
From point: *(press* [Enter] *or the space bar and AutoCAD automatically picks the last endpoint of the previous line)*
To point: *(pick the next point)*
To point: *(press* [Enter] *or the space bar to exit the command)*
Command:

Figure 4-23.
Using the **Continue** option.

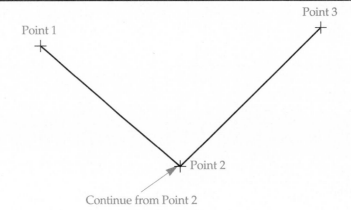

Point 1

Point 3

Point 2

Continue from Point 2

PROFESSIONAL TIP

Pressing the space bar or [Enter] repeats the previous command. If no other commands have been used since the line to be continued was drawn, pressing the space bar or [Enter] will repeat the **LINE** command.

Undoing the previously drawn line

When drawing a series of lines, you may find that you made an error. To delete the mistake while still in the **LINE** command, type U at the prompt line and press [Enter], or pick the **Undo** button in the **Standard** toolbar. Doing this removes the previously drawn line and allows you to continue from the previous endpoint. You can use **UNDO** repeatedly to continue deleting line segments until the entire line is gone. See Figure 4-24.

Command: **L** *or* **LINE**⏎
From point*: (pick point 1)*
To point: *(pick point 2)*
To point: *(pick point 3)*
To point: *(pick point 4)*
To point: **U**⏎
To point: **U**⏎
To point: *(pick revised point 3)*
To point: *(press* [Enter] *or the space bar to exit the command)*
Command:

Figure 4-24.
Using the **Undo** option while in the **LINE** command. Notice that the original points 3 and 4 remain as blips until the screen is redrawn.

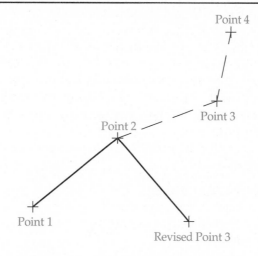

Point 4

Point 3

Point 2

Point 1

Revised Point 3

NOTE

When AutoCAD is configured to display screen menus in addition to the toolbar, the **Close**, **Continuation**, and **Undo** options appear in the **LINE** screen menu.

EXERCISE 4-7

❑ Start a new drawing, use one of your templates, or open a previous exercise.
❑ Experiment drawing lines using the following guidelines and options:
　❑ Draw one triangle and one rectangle using the **Close** option.
　❑ Draw two connected lines and end the **LINE** command. Then, repeat the **LINE** command and use the **Continuation** option to draw additional lines.
　❑ Draw eight connected lines. Then use the **Undo** option to remove the last four lines while remaining in the **LINE** command. Finally, draw four new connected lines.
❑ Save the drawing as EX4-7.

Introduction to Editing

Editing is the procedure used to correct mistakes or revise an existing drawing. There are many editing functions that help increase productivity. The basic editing operations **ERASE** and **OOPS** are introduced in the next sections.

To edit a drawing, you must select items to modify. The Select objects: prompt appears whenever you need to select items in the command sequence. Whether you select only one object or hundreds of objects, you create a *selection set*. You can create a selection set using a variety of selection options, including **Window**, **Crossing**, **WPolygon**, **CPolygon**, and **Fence**. When you become familiar with the selection set options, you will find that they increase your flexibility and productivity.

In the discussion and examples that follow, several of the selection set methods are introduced using the **ERASE** command. Keep in mind, however, that these techniques can be used with most of the editing commands in AutoCAD whenever the Select Objects: prompt appears. Any of the selection set methods can be enabled from the prompt line, or by picking the appropriate buttons in the **Select Objects** toolbar.

Using the ERASE Command

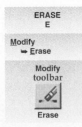

ERASE
E

Modify
➡ Erase

Modify
toolbar

Erase

The **ERASE** command is similar to using an eraser in manual drafting to remove unwanted information. However, with the **ERASE** command you have a second chance. If you erase the wrong item, it can be brought back with the **OOPS** command. Access the **ERASE** command by picking the **Erase** button in the **Modify** toolbar, picking **Erase** in the **Modify** pull-down menu, or by typing E or ERASE at the Command: prompt.

When you enter the **ERASE** command, you are prompted to select an object to be erased as follows:

> Command: **E** *or* **ERASE.**┘
> Select objects: *(select an object)*
> Select objects: ┘
> Command:

When the Select objects: prompt appears, a small box replaces the screen crosshairs. This box is referred to as the *pick box*. Move the pick box over the item to be erased and pick it. The object is highlighted. Then, press the [Enter] key or the right mouse button and the object is erased.

NOTE

The terms *entitiy* and *object* are interchangeable in AutoCAD. An entity or object is a predefined element that you place in a drawing by means of a single command. For example, a line, circle, arc, or single line of text is an entity or object.

After you pick the first object, the Select objects: prompt is redisplayed. You can then select another object to erase, as shown in Figure 4-25. If you are finished selecting objects, press the [Enter] key at the Select objects: prompt to "close" the selection set. The **ERASE** operation is completed and you are returned to the Command: prompt.

Figure 4-25.
Using the **ERASE** command to erase a single entity.

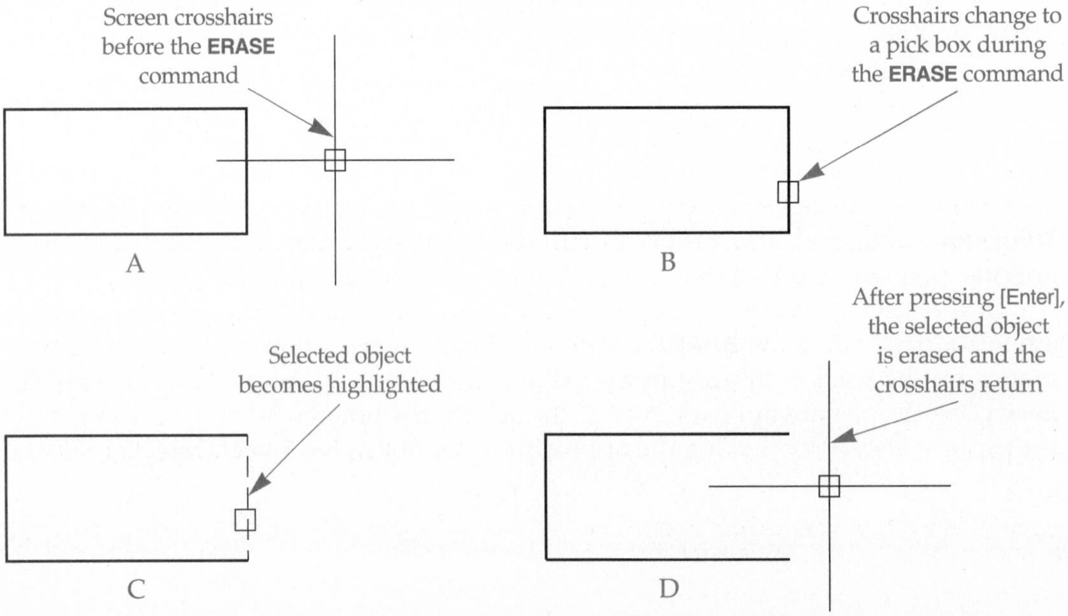

Screen crosshairs
before the **ERASE**
command

A

Crosshairs change to
a pick box during
the **ERASE** command

B

Selected object
becomes highlighted

C

After pressing [Enter],
the selected object
is erased and the
crosshairs return

D

Making a single selection automatically

Normally, AutoCAD lets you pick as many items as you want for a selection set, and selected items are highlighted to let you know what has been picked. You also have the option of selecting a single item and having it automatically edited without first being highlighted. To do this, enter SI (for single) at the Select Objects: prompt. To select several items with this method, use the **Window** or **Crossing** selection options (discussed later in this chapter). The command sequence is as follows:

Command: **E** *or* **ERASE.**↵
Select objects: **SI**↵
Select objects: *(pick an individual item, or use the **Window** or **Crossing** option to pick several items)*
Command:

Note that the Select objects: prompt did not return after the items were picked. The entire group is automatically edited (erased in this example) when you press [Enter] or pick the second corner of a window or crossing box.

PROFESSIONAL TIP  The **SI** (single) selection option is not commonly used as a command line option. This is because picking an object and pressing [Enter] requires less keystrokes than typing SI and pressing [Enter]. The **SI** option is most commonly used when developing menu macros that require single object selection.

Using the Last selection option

The **ERASE** command's **Last** option saves time if you need to erase the last entity drawn. For example, suppose you draw a line and then want to erase it. The **Last** option will automatically select the line. The **Last** option can be selected by typing L at the Select objects: prompt:

Command: **E** *or* **ERASE.**↵
Select objects: **L.**↵
1 found
Select objects: ↵
Command:

Keep in mind that using the **Last** option only highlights the last item drawn. You must press [Enter] for the object to be erased. If you need to erase more than just the last object, you can use the **ERASE** command and **Last** option repeatedly to erase items in reverse order. However, this is not as quick as using the **ERASE** command and selecting the objects.

EXERCISE 4-8

❏ Start a new drawing, use one of your templates, or open a previous exercise.
❏ Use the **LINE** command to draw a square similar to the ORIGINAL OBJECT in Figure 4-25.
❏ Type ERASE at the Command: prompt and erase two of the lines.
❏ Draw another square, similar to the previous one.
❏ Type ERASE at the Command: prompt and enter L at the Select objects: prompt.
❏ Press [Enter] again and enter L to erase one more line.
❏ Save the drawing as EX4-8.

Using the Window selection option

The **W** or **Window** option can be used with several commands. This option allows you to draw a box or "window" around an object or group of objects to select for editing. Everything entirely within the window can be selected at the same time. If portions of entities project outside the window, they are not selected. The command sequence looks like this:

Command: **E** *or* **ERASE.**⌟
Select objects: *(select a point to the left of the object or group of objects to be erased)*

When the Select objects: prompt is shown, select a point clearly outside and to the left of the object to be erased. After you select the first point, the screen crosshairs change to a box-shaped cursor. It expands in size as you move the pointing device to the right. The box is a solid line. The next prompt is:

Other corner: *(pick the other corner to the right of the object or group of objects)*
Select objects: ⌟
Command:

When the Other corner: prompt is shown, move the pointing device to the right so the box totally encloses the object(s) to be erased. Then pick to locate the second corner, as shown in Figure 4-26. All objects within the window become highlighted. When finished, press [Enter] or pick the right mouse button to complete the **ERASE** command.

Figure 4-26.
Using the **ERASE**
Window option.

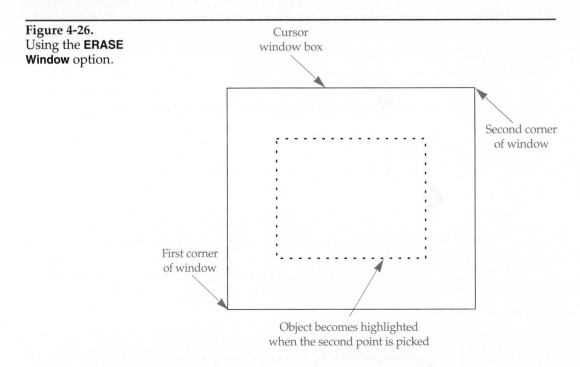

Cursor
window box

Second corner
of window

First corner
of window

Object becomes highlighted
when the second point is picked

You can also manually specify the **Window** option from the command line. You need to do this if the **PICKAUTO** variable (discussed later in this chapter) is set to 0. The command sequence is as follows:

Command: **E** *or* **ERASE.**⌟
Select objects: **W**⌟
First corner: *(select a point outside of the object)*

When you manually enter the **Window** option, you do not need to pick the first point to the left of the object(s) being erased. The "box" remains the **Window** box whether you move the cursor to the left or right.

Using the Crossing selection option

The **Crossing** selection option is similar to the **Window** option. However, entities within and those *crossing* the box are selected. The **Crossing** box outline is dotted to distinguish it from the solid outline of the **Window** box. The command sequence for the **Crossing** option is as follows:

> Command: **E** *or* **ERASE**⏎
> Select objects: *(pick a point to the right of the object or group of objects to be erased)*

When the Select objects: prompt is shown, select a point to the right of the object to be erased. After you select the first point, the screen crosshairs change to a box-shaped cursor. It expands in size as you move the pointing device to the left. The next prompt is:

> Other corner: *(move the cursor to the left so that the box encloses or crosses the object or group of objects to be erased and pick)*
> Select objects: ⏎
> Command:

Remember, the crossing box does not need to enclose the entire object to erase it as the window box does. The crossing box need only "cross" part of the object. Figure 4-27 shows how to erase three of four lines of a rectangle using the **Crossing** option.

Figure 4-27.
Using the **Crossing** box to erase objects.

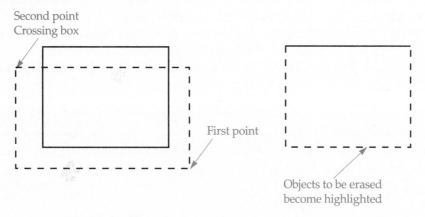

You can also manually specify the **Crossing** option from the command line. You need to do this if the **PICKAUTO** variable (discussed later in this chapter) is set to 0. The command sequence is as follows:

> Command: **E** *or* **ERASE**⏎
> Select objects: **C**⏎
> First corner: *(pick a point outside of the object)*

When you manually enter the **Crossing** option, you do not need to pick the first point to the right of the object(s) being erased. The "box" remains the **Crossing** box whether you move the cursor to the left or right.

Using the PICKAUTO variable

The **PICKAUTO** system variable controls automatic windowing when the Select Objects: prompt appears. By default, **PICKAUTO** is set to 1. At this setting, you can automatically use the **Window** or **Crossing** selection process. The **PICKAUTO** settings are: ON = 1 (default) and OFF = 0. Change the **PICKAUTO** value by typing PICKAUTO at the Command: prompt and then entering the new value.

You can use the automatic **Window** or **Crossing** option even if **PICKAUTO** is 0 (off). To do this, enter AU (for auto) at the Select objects: prompt, and then proceed as previously discussed.

PROFESSIONAL TIP With **PICKAUTO** set to 1, pick any left point outside the object and then move the cursor to the right for a **Window** selection. The **Window** box outline is a solid line. Pick any right point outside the object and move the cursor to the left for a **Crossing** selection. The **Crossing** box is a dashed line.

AutoCAD User's Guide **1**

Cleaning up the screen

After you draw and edit a number of objects, the screen is cluttered with small crosses or markers called *blips*. In addition, many of the grid dots may be missing. This can be distracting.

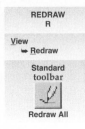

REDRAW
R

View
→ Redraw

Standard
toolbar

Redraw All

The **REDRAW** command cleans the screen in the current viewport. To access the **REDRAW** command, pick **Redraw** from the **View** pull-down menu, or type R or REDRAW at the Command: prompt. The **Redraw All** button on the **Standard** toolbar can be used to redraw the screen, but this uses the **REDRAWALL** command.

The screen will go blank for an instant, and the cleaned drawing and screen return. The **REDRAW** and **REDRAWALL** commands are discussed in Chapter 9.

EXERCISE 4-9

❑ Start a new drawing, use one of your templates, or open a previous exercise.
❑ Set the **PICKAUTO** system variable to 0 (off).
❑ Draw a square. Use the **LINE** command with relative coordinates and the **Close** option.
❑ Type ERASE at the Command: prompt and use the **Window** selection option. Place the window around the entire square to erase it. Enter OOPS at the next Command: prompt to have the square reappear.
❑ Now, erase three of the four lines using the **Crossing** selection. Type OOPS to bring the three lines back on the screen.
❑ Set the **PICKAUTO** system variable to 1 (on).
❑ Now, enter ERASE and automatically erase the square using a window. Type OOPS to get the square back again.
❑ Enter ERASE and erase three sides of the square using the automatic **Crossing** selection.
❑ Use the **REDRAW** command to clean up the screen.
❑ Save the drawing as EX4-9.

Using the WPolygon selection option

The **Window** selection option requires that you place a rectangle completely around the entities to be erased. Sometimes it is awkward to place a rectangle around the items to erase. When this situation occurs, you can place a polygon (closed figure with three or more sides) of your own design around the objects with the **WPolygon** option.

To use the **WPolygon** option, type WP at the Select Objects: prompt. Then, draw a polygon that encloses the objects. As you pick corners, the polygon drags into place. The command sequence for erasing the five middle squares in Figure 4-28 is as follows:

> Command: **E** *or* **ERASE**↵
> Select objects: **WP**↵
> First polygon point: *(pick point 1)*
> Undo/⟨Endpoint of line⟩: *(pick point 2)*
> Undo/⟨Endpoint of line⟩: *(pick point 3)*
> Undo/⟨Endpoint of line⟩: *(pick point 4)*
> Undo/⟨Endpoint of line⟩: ↵
> Select objects: ↵
> Command:

If you do not like the last polygon point you picked, use the **Undo** option by entering U at the Undo/⟨Endpoint of line⟩: prompt.

Figure 4-28.
Using the **WPolygon** selection option to erase objects.

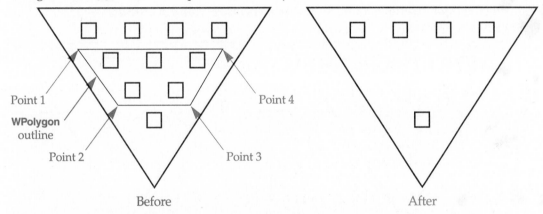

EXERCISE 4-10

❑ Start a new drawing, use one of your templates, or open a previous exercise.
❑ Draw an object similar to the one shown in Figure 4-28.
❑ Use the **WPolygon** selection option to erase the same items as shown in the figure.
❑ Use the **REDRAW** command to clean up the screen.
❑ Save the drawing as EX4-10.

Using the CPolygon selection option

The **Crossing** selection option lets you place a rectangle around or through the objects to be erased. Sometimes it is difficult to place a rectangle around or through the items to be erased without coming into contact with other entities. When you want to use the features of the **Crossing** selection option, but prefer to use a polygon instead of a rectangle, enter CP at the Select objects: prompt. Then, proceed to draw a polygon that encloses or crosses the objects to erase. As you pick the points, the polygon drags into place. The **CPolygon** line is a dashed rubberband cursor.

Suppose you want to erase everything inside the large triangle in Figure 4-29 except for the top and bottom horizontal lines. The command sequence to erase these lines is as follows:

```
Command: E or ERASE.↵
Select object: CP↵
First polygon point: (pick point 1)
Undo/⟨Endpoint of line⟩: (pick point 2)
Undo/⟨Endpoint of line⟩: (pick point 3)
Undo/⟨Endpoint of line⟩: (pick point 4)
Undo/⟨Endpoint of line⟩: ↵
Select objects: ↵
Command:
```

If you want to change the last **CPolygon** point you picked, enter U at the Undo/⟨Endpoint of line⟩: prompt.

Figure 4-29.
Using the **CPolygon** selection option. Everything enclosed within or crossing the polygon is selected.

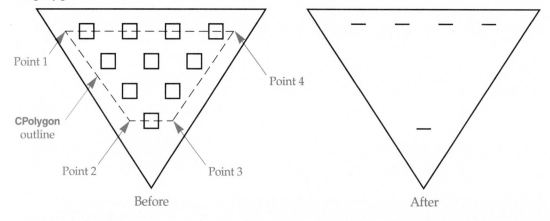

Before   After

PROFESSIONAL TIP

When using **WPolygon** or **CPolygon**, AutoCAD does not allow you to select a point that causes the lines of the selection polygon to intersect each other. Pick locations that do not result in an intersection. Use the **Undo** option if you need to go back and relocate a preceding pick point.

Using the Fence selection option

Fence is another selection option used to select several objects at the same time. When using the **Fence** option, you simply need to place a fence through the objects you want to select. Anything that the fence passes through is included in the selection set. The fence can be straight or staggered, as shown in Figure 4-30. Type F at the Select objects: prompt as follows:

    Command: **E** *or* **ERASE.**↵
    Select objects: **F**↵
    First fence point: (*pick the starting point of the first fence*)
    Undo/⟨Endpoint of line⟩: (*pick point 2*)
    Undo/⟨Endpoint of line⟩: (*pick point 3*)
    Undo/⟨Endpoint of line⟩: (*pick point 4*)
    Undo/⟨Endpoint of line⟩: (*pick point 5*)
    Undo/⟨Endpoint of line⟩: (*pick point 6*)
    Undo/⟨Endpoint of line⟩: ↵
    5 found
    Select objects: ↵
    Command:

Figure 4-30.
Using the **Fence** selection option to erase entities. The fence can be either straight or staggered.

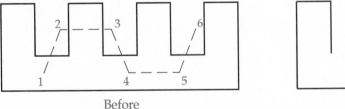
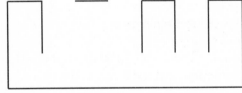

Before   After

Removing and adding objects to the selection set

When editing a drawing, a common mistake is to accidentally select an object that you do not want. The simplest way to remove one or more objects from the current selection set is by holding down the [Shift] key and reselecting the objects. This is possible only for individual picks and implied windows. For an implied window, the [Shift] key must be held down while picking the first corner, and can then be released for picking the second corner. If you accidentally remove the wrong object from the selection set, release the [Shift] key and pick it again.

To use other methods for removing objects from a selection set, or for specialized selection needs, you can switch to the **Remove objects** mode by typing R at the Select objects: prompt. This changes the Select objects: prompt to Remove objects: as follows:

Command: **E** *or* **ERASE**↵
Select objects: *(pick several objects using any selection technique)*
Select objects: **R**↵
Remove objects: *(pick the objects you want removed from the selection set)*

Switch back to the selection mode by typing A, for **Add**, at the Remove objects: prompt. This restores the Select objects: prompt and allows you to select additional objects. This is how the **Add** feature works:

Remove objects: **A**↵
Select objects: *(continue selecting objects as needed)*
Select objects: ↵
Command:

Using the OOPS command

The **OOPS** command brings back the last object you erased. It is issued by typing OOPS at the Command: prompt. If you erased several objects in the same command sequence, all are brought back to the screen. Only the objects erased in the most recent erase procedure can be returned using **OOPS**.

Using the previous selection

The object selection options given to this point in the chapter have used the example of the **ERASE** command. These selection options are also used to move objects, rotate objects, and perform other editing functions.

Often, more than one sequential editing operation needs to be carried out on a specific group of objects. In this case, the **Previous Selection** option allows you to select the same object(s) you just edited for further editing. You can select the **Previous Selection** set by typing P at the Select Objects: prompt. In the following example, a group of objects is erased and the **OOPS** command is used to recover them. Then, the **ERASE** command is issued again, this time using the **Previous Selection** option to access the previously selected objects:

Command: **E** *or* **ERASE**↵
Select objects: *(pick several items using any selection technique)*
n found.
Select objects: ↵
Command: **OOPS**↵
Command: **E** *or* **ERASE**↵
Select objects: **P**↵
n found.
Select objects: ↵
Command:

Selecting all entities on a drawing

Sometimes you may want to select every item on the drawing. To do this, type ALL at the Select objects: prompt as follows:

Command: **E** *or* **ERASE**↵
Select objects: **ALL**↵
Select objects: ↵
Command:

This procedure erases everything on the drawing. You can use the **Remove** option at the second Select objects: prompt to remove certain objects from the set. You can also enter ALL after typing R to remove all objects from the set.

EXERCISE 4-13

❑ Start a new drawing, use one of your templates, or open a previous exercise.
❑ Draw an object similar to the one shown in Figure 4-30.
❑ Use the **SI** selection option to erase one line.
❑ Use the **SI** selection option with a fence to erase any two lines.
❑ Experiment using the **Remove** and **Add** selection options by selecting six items to erase, removing two of the items from the selection set, and then adding three new entities.
❑ Use the **REDRAW** command to clean up the screen.
❑ Use the **ALL** selection option to erase everything from the drawing.
❑ Use the **UNDO** or **OOPS** command to get everything back that you erased.
❑ Save the drawing as EX4-13.

Using the **Box** selection option

Another way to begin the window or crossing selection option is to type BOX at the Select Objects: prompt. You are then prompted to pick the first corner, which is the left corner of a **Window** box or the right corner of a **Crossing** box. The command sequence is as follows:

Command: **E** *or* **ERASE**↵
Select objects: **BOX**↵
First corner: *(pick the left corner of a* **Window** *box or the right corner of a* **Crossing** *box)*
Select objects: ↵
Command:

Using the **Multiple** selection option

The **Multiple** option provides easy access to stacked objects. *Stacked objects* occur when one feature, such as a line, overlays another in a 2D drawing. These lines have the same Z values, so one is no higher or lower than the other. However, the last object drawn appears to be on top of all others.

When a point on an object is picked in select mode, the data base is scanned and the first object found is the object selected. Additional picks will only duplicate the original results. Unless **Window**, **Crossing**, **Fence**, or **Multiple** is used, the underlying objects are inaccessible.

Using the **Multiple** option allows multiple picks at the same point. The first pick finds the first object. A second pick in the same place ignores the already selected object and finds the next object. This process continues for each pick made. The **Multiple** option is used by typing M at the Select Objects: prompt. The command sequence used to erase two stacked lines with the **Multiple** option is as follows:

Command: **E** *or* **ERASE**↵
Select objects: **M**↵
Select objects: *(pick the stacked objects twice, then press the* [Enter] *key)*
2 selected, 2 found
Select objects: ↵
Command:

Notice that the *n* selected, *n* found prompt (in which *n* represents the number reported by AutoCAD) does not appear until you press the [Enter] key. This may make it difficult to select all overlapping objects if you do not know how many are there.

PROFESSIONAL TIP

When objects are selected using the **Multiple** option, the selected objects are not highlighted until the [Enter] key is pressed. This can speed up the selection process for text and other complex objects on workstations with slower display systems.

Often, you may want to modify an object underlying another without affecting the "top" object. To do this, enter the **Multiple** mode as previously discussed. For the previous example, pick a point on the object twice. Press [Enter] to end the multiple mode. AutoCAD tells you that both objects are selected. Now, use the **REMOVE** option and select the same point again. The "top" object is now removed from the selection set.

NOTE

When selecting objects to be erased, AutoCAD only accepts qualifying objects. *Qualifying object* refers to an object that is not on a locked layer and that passes through the pickbox area at the point selected. Layers are discussed later in this chapter.

Cycling through stacked objects

Another way to deal with stacked objects is to let AutoCAD cycle through the objects. *Cycling* is repeatedly selecting one item from a series of stacked objects until the desired object is highlighted. This works best when several objects cross at the same place or are very close together. To cycle through objects, hold down the [Ctrl] key as you pick the object.

For the objects in Figure 4-31, pick where the four circles intersect. If there are two or more objects found crossing through the pick box area, the top object is highlighted. Now, you can release the [Ctrl] key. When you pick again, the top object returns and the next one is highlighted. Every time you pick, another object becomes highlighted. In this way, you cycle through all of the objects. When you have the desired object highlighted, press [Enter] to end the cycling process and return to the Select Objects: prompt. Press [Enter] again to return to the Command: prompt.

The following command sequence is used to erase one of the circles in Figure 4-31, but you can use this for any editing function:

> Command: **ERASE**↵
> Select objects: *(hold down the* [Ctrl] *key and pick)* ⟨Cycle on⟩ *(pick until you highlight the desired object and press* [Enter]*)*
> ⟨Cycle off⟩1 found
> Select objects: *(select additional objects or press* [Enter]*)*
> Command:

Figure 4-31.
Cycling through a series of stacked circles until the desired object is highlighted.

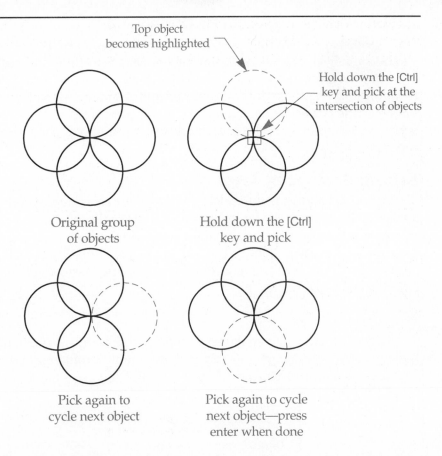

Top object becomes highlighted

Hold down the [Ctrl] key and pick at the intersection of objects

Original group of objects

Hold down the [Ctrl] key and pick

Pick again to cycle next object

Pick again to cycle next object—press enter when done

An Introduction to Layers

AutoCAD User's Guide **8**

In manual drafting, details of a design might be separated by placing them on different sheets of media. This is called *overlay* or *pin register* drafting. Each overlay is perfectly aligned with the others. All of the layers can be reproduced together to reflect the entire design. Individual layers might also be reproduced to show specific details. In AutoCAD, overlays are called *layers*. Using layers increases productivity in several ways:

✓ Specific information can be grouped on separate layers. For example, the floor plan can be drawn on one layer, the electrical plan on another, and the plumbing plan on a third layer.

✓ Drawings can be reproduced by individual layers or combined in any desired format. For example, the floor and electrical plans can be reproduced together and sent to an electrical contractor for a bid. The floor and plumbing plans can be reproduced together and sent to the plumbing contractor.

✓ Several drafters can work on a project at the same time to increase productivity.

✓ Each layer can be assigned a different color to help improve clarity.

✓ Each layer can be plotted in a different color or pen width.

✓ Selected layers can be turned off or frozen to decrease the clutter of information displayed on the screen and to speed up drawing regeneration.

✓ Changes can be made to a layer promptly, often while the client watches.

Layers used in different drafting fields

In mechanical drafting, views, hidden features, dimensions, sections, notes, and symbols might be placed on separate layers. In architectural drafting, there may be over one hundred layers. Layers can be created for floor plans, foundation plan, partition layout, plumbing, electrical, structural, roof drainage, reflected ceiling, and HVAC systems. Interior designers may use floor plan, interior partition, and furniture layers. In electronics drafting, each level of a multilevel circuit board is drawn on a separate layer.

Setting linetype by layer

AutoCAD allows you to select a linetype for each layer. Then, any item added to a layer is drawn with the linetype assigned to that layer.

As you have worked through the exercises in this book, you may have noticed that 0 appears in the **Layer Control** box on the **Object Properties** toolbar. Layer 0 is the AutoCAD default layer. It has a continuous linetype. Assigning linetype to layers is discussed later in this chapter.

Naming layers

Layers should be given names to reflect what is drawn on them. Layer names can have up to 31 characters and can include letters, numbers, and special characters. Typical mechanical, architectural, and civil drafting layer names are as follows:

Mechanical	Architectural	Civil
OBJECT	WALLS	PROPERTYLN
HIDDEN	WINDOWS	STRUCTURES
CENTER	DOORS	ROADS
DIMENSION	ELECT	WATER
CONSTR	PLUMB	CONTOURS
HATCH	FURNITURE	GAS
BORDER	LIGHTING	ELEVATIONS

For very simple drawings, layers can be named by linetype and color. For example, the layer name OBJECT-WHITE has a continuous linetype drawn in white. The linetype and color number, such as OBJECT-7, can also be used. Another option is to assign the linetype a numerical value. For example, object lines can be 0, hidden lines 1, and centerlines 2. If you use this method, keep a written record of the numbering system for reference.

Lastly, layers can be given more complex names. The name might include the drawing number, color code, and layer content. The name DWG100-2-DIMEN refers to drawing DWG100, color 2, and DIMENSIONS layer.

LAYER
LA

Format
→ Layer...

Object Properties
toolbar

Layers

Introduction to the LAYER Command

The **LAYER** command and all of its options can be used by accessing the **Layer & Linetype Properties** dialog box. To display this dialog box, pick the **Layers** button from the **Object Properties** toolbar, select **Layer...** from the **Format** pull-down menu, or type LA or LAYER at the Command: prompt.

There are two tabs shown in this dialog box, **Layer** and **Linetype**. When working with layers, the **Layer** tab should be displayed, as shown in Figure 4-32.

The only layer name present in a new drawing that has been started from scratch is the default layer 0. Notice layer 0 identified to the right of the **Current:** button and in the layer list. Newly created objects are placed on the current layer.

Figure 4-32.
The **Layer & Linetype Properties** dialog box with the **Layer** tab displayed.

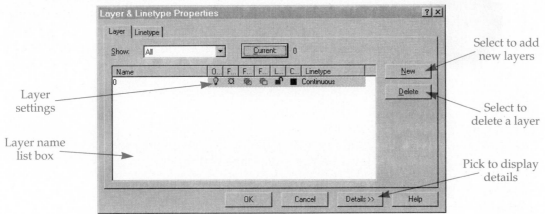

Select to add
new layers

Layer
settings

Layer name
list box

Select to
delete a layer

Pick to display
details

Layers should be added to a drawing to meet the needs of the current drawing project. To add a new layer, pick the **New** button. A new layer listing appears, using a default name of Layer1 as shown in Figure 4-33. The layer name is highlighted when the listing appears, allowing you to type in a new name.

Figure 4-33.
A new layer is
named Layer1 by
default.

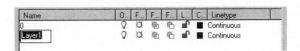

You can also enter several new layer names at the same time. This is done by typing a layer name followed by pressing the comma key. This drops the Layer1 listing below the previously entered name. Entering several layer names is much faster, because it keeps you from having to pick the **New** button each time. Pick the **OK** button when finished typing the new layer names. When you reopen the **Layer & Linetype Properties** dialog box, the new layer names are alphabetized. See Figure 4-34.

Figure 4-34.
Layer names are
automatically
placed in
alphabetical order.

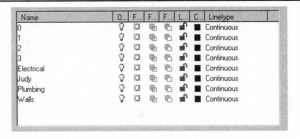

Deleting a layer that is no longer in use is a simple process. First, select the layer. Then, pick the **Delete** button. The layer is erased from the list box.

Setting a new current layer

You can set a new current layer by highlighting the layer name in the layer list and then picking the **Current:** button. To highlight the layer name, simply pick it. The newly selected layer name is now specified to the right of the **Current:** button.

❑ Start a new drawing or open one of your templates.
❑ Open the **Layer & Linetype Properties** dialog box.
❑ Start a list of layer names similar to Figure 4-34, or use other names of your own choosing. Enter a couple of the names by picking the **New** button after each entry.
❑ Continue the list of new layer names by pressing the comma key to enter several names.
❑ Pick the **OK** button when done.
❑ Open the **Layer & Linetype Properties** dialog box again and see how AutoCAD automatically lists the layer names in alphabetical order.
❑ Close the dialog box.
❑ Save as EX4-14.

Viewing the status of layers

The status of each layer is displayed with icons to the right of the layer name. See Figure 4-35. If you position the pointer over an icon for a moment, a ToolTip appears and tells what the icon refers to. Layer settings can be changed by picking the icon.

- **Changing the layer name.** The layer name list box contains all of the layers in the drawing. To change an existing name, pick the name once to highlight it, pause for a moment, then pick it again. When you pick the second time, the layer name is highlighted with a text box around it and a cursor for text entry to allow you to type in a new layer name. Layer 0 cannot be renamed.

Figure 4-35.
Layer settings can be changed by picking the icons in the list box of the **Layer & Linetype Properties** dialog box.

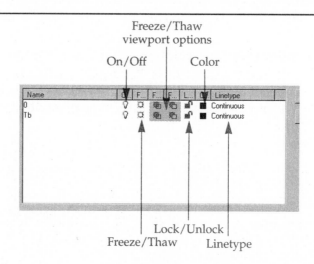

| NOTE | The On/Off, Freeze/Thaw, and Lock/Unlock settings in this dialog are toggles. This means that they have only two available settings, and adjusting the setting means switching it to the setting that is not currently set. For example, picking the yellow lightbulb turns the layer off, and the icon is updated to match. |

- **Turning layers on and off.** The lightbulb shows whether a layer is on or off. The yellow lightbulb means the layer is on; objects on that layer are displayed on-screen and can be plotted. If you pick on a yellow lightbulb, it turns gray, turning the layer off. If a layer is off, the objects on it are not displayed on-screen and are not plotted. Objects that are on a layer that has been turned off can still be edited when using advanced selection techniques, and are regenerated when a drawing regeneration occurs.   On   Off

- **Thawing and freezing layers.** Layers are further classified as thawed or frozen. Similar to the off setting, layers that are *frozen* are not displayed and do not plot. However, objects on a frozen layer cannot be edited and are not regenerated when the drawing regenerates. Therefore, freezing layers that contain objects that do not need to be referenced for current drawing tasks can greatly speed up your system performance. The snowflake icon is displayed when a layer is frozen. Layers are normally *thawed*, which simply means that objects on the layer are displayed on-screen. The sun icon is displayed for thawed layers. Picking the sun/snowflake icon will toggle it to the other icon.   Frozen   Thawed

- **Thawing and freezing layers in viewports.** These settings, for model space viewports viewed from paper space, are detailed in Chapter 24. If you select one of these options, a message is issued that the property is only valid when **Tilemode** is off.

- **Unlocked and locked layers.** The unlocked and locked padlock symbols are for locking and unlocking layers. Layers are unlocked by default, but you can pick on the unlocked padlock to lock it. A layer that is locked remains visible, but objects on that layer cannot be edited. New objects can be added to a locked layer. Locked Unlocked

- **Layer color.** The color swatch shows the current default color for objects created on each layer. When you need to change the color for an existing layer, pick the swatch to display the **Select Color** dialog box. Working with colors is discussed later in this chapter.

- **Layer linetype.** The current linetype setting for each layer is shown in the **Linetype** list. Picking the linetype name opens the **Select Linetype** dialog box, where you can specify a new linetype. Working with linetypes is discussed later in this chapter.

EXERCISE 4-15

❑ Open EX4-14.
❑ Open the **Layer & Linetype Properties** dialog box.
❑ Use one of the layers that you created in Exercise 4-14. Move your cursor to each of the icons as you read the ToolTip that appears.
❑ Pick each icon to see it change settings or give you an AutoCAD message. Change each back to the original setting.
❑ Pick on the color swatch to open the **Select Color** dialog box. Look at the dialog box and then pick **Cancel** when you have seen enough.
❑ Pick on a linetype name to open the **Select Linetype** dialog box. Pick the **Cancel** button when you have seen enough.
❑ Save your work and exit AutoCAD, or keep this drawing open for the next exercise.

Working with layers

Any setting that is changed affects all layer names that are currently highlighted. Highlighting layer names uses the same techniques used in file dialog boxes. You can highlight a single name by simply picking it. Picking another name de-highlights the previous name and highlights the new selection. You can use the [Shift] key to select two layers and all layer names between them on the listing. Using the [Ctrl] key allows even more flexibility. Holding the [Ctrl] key while picking layer names highlights or de-highlights each selected name without affecting any other selections.

A cursor menu is also available while your cursor is in the layer list area of this dialog box. Press the right mouse button to display the cursor menu shown in Figure 4-36. The options available on this menu are **Select All**, which selects all layer names, and **Clear All**, which clears all currently selected layer names.

Figure 4-36.
Right-clicking in the list box of the **Layer & Linetype Properties** dialog box produces this cursor menu.

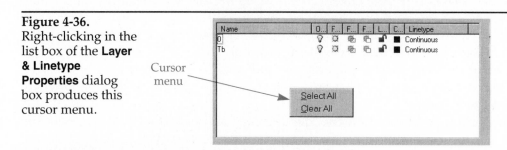

EXERCISE 4-16

❑ Open EX4-14 if it is not already open.
❑ Open the **Layer & Linetype Properties** dialog box.
❑ Pick layer names to highlight each individually.
❑ Use the [Shift] key to pick a group of consecutive layer names.
❑ Use the [Ctrl] key to pick a group of nonsequential layer names.
❑ Move the cursor inside the layer list area and pick the right mouse button. Pick **Select All** to highlight all layer names. Open the cursor menu again and pick **Clear All**.
❑ Save your work and exit AutoCAD, or keep this drawing open for the next exercise.

Setting the layer color

The number of layer colors available depends on your graphics card and monitor. A monochrome monitor displays only one color, usually white, amber, or green. Color systems usually support at least 256 colors. Many graphics cards support up to 16.7 million colors. Layer colors are coded by name and number. The first seven standard color numbers are given below

Number	Color
1	Red
2	Yellow
3	Green
4	Cyan
5	Blue
6	Magenta
7	White

Color settings affect the appearance of plotted drawings. Plotter pen widths are associated with drawing colors. Therefore, the colors you choose to use must correspond to the proper pen widths. This will be discussed in Chapter 10. Colors should also highlight the important features on the drawing and not cause eyestrain.

To change layer color, select the desired layer name or names and then pick the color swatch for one of the highlighted layer names. This displays the **Select Color** dialog box, as shown in Figure 4-37. The **Select Color** dialog box allows you to specify the default color for each layer.

Figure 4-37.
The **Select Color** dialog box.

Select color from any palette

Type color name or number

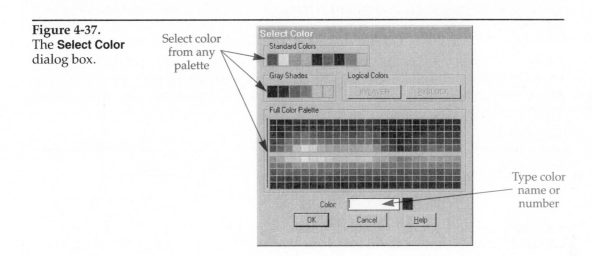

To select a color, you can either pick the color swatch that displays the desired color or type the color name or number in the **Color:** text box. The first seven basic colors were listed previously in the table. The color white (number 7) refers to white if the graphics screen background is black, and black if the background is white. All other colors can be accessed by their ACI (AutoCAD Color Index) number.

An easy way to investigate the ACI numbering system is to pick a color swatch and see what number appears in the **Color:** text box. Pick the **OK** button when ready after selecting a color. The color you picked in the **Select Color** dialog box is now displayed as the color swatch for the highlighted layer name in the **Layer & Linetype Properties** dialog box.

EXERCISE 4-17

❏ Open EX4-14 if it is not already open.
❏ Open the **Layer & Linetype Properties** dialog box.
❏ Highlight one or more layer names.
❏ Pick the color swatch of one of the highlighted layers to open the **Select Color** dialog box.
❏ Select a new color for the layer.
❏ Pick the **OK** button. Notice the layer color swatch is changed to match your color selection.
❏ Save your work and exit AutoCAD, or keep this drawing open for the next exercise.

Setting the layer linetype

Earlier in this chapter you were introduced to line standards. AutoCAD provides standard linetypes that can be used at any time. Standard AutoCAD linetypes are a single width. In order to achieve different line widths, it is necessary to use the **PLINE** or **TRACE** commands. These commands are introduced in Chapter 16 of this text.

Line width can also be varied using different plotter pen tip widths. To do this, draw different width lines on separate layers. Then, plot with the appropriate width of pen for each layer. This is discussed further in this chapter and in Chapter 10.

AutoCAD linetypes

AutoCAD maintains a standard library of linetypes in an external file called acad.lin. Before any of these linetypes can be used, they must be loaded into the drawing editor and then set current. You will note that a solid object line does not appear in the linetype library illustrated in Figure 4-38. The solid linetype is referred to as Continuous and is the default in AutoCAD. As the default linetype, it is always the current linetype when a new drawing is started and does not need to be loaded into the drawing editor.

Figure 4-38.
The AutoCAD linetype library contains ISO, standard, and complex linetypes.

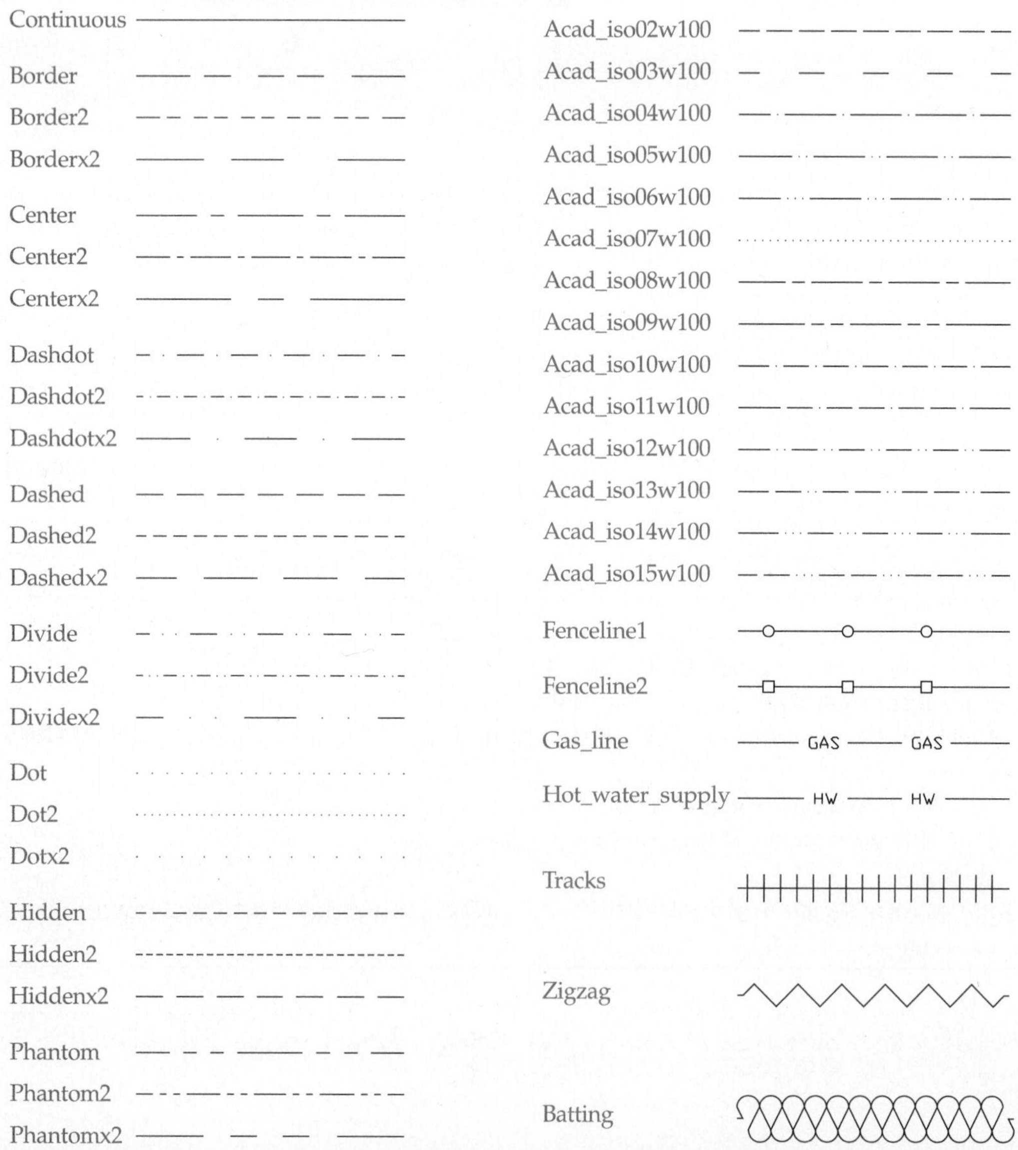

PROFESSIONAL TIP
Two linetype definition files are available, acad.lin and acadiso.lin. The ISO linetypes found in both files are identical, but the non-ISO linetype definitions are scaled up 25.4 times in the acadiso.lin file. The scale factor of 25.4 is used to convert from inches to millimeters. The ISO linetypes are for metric drawings.

Changing linetype assignments

To change linetype assignments, select the layer name you want to change and pick its linetype name. This displays the **Select Linetype** dialog box shown in Figure 4-39. The first time you use this dialog, you may find only the Continuous linetype listed in the **Loaded linetypes** list box. You need to load any other linetypes to be used in the drawing.

Figure 4-39.
The **Select Linetype** dialog box.

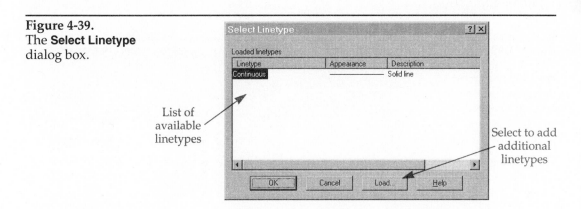

List of available linetypes

Select to add additional linetypes

If you need to add linetypes that aren't included in the list, pick the **Load...** button to display the **Load or Reload Linetypes** dialog box, shown in Figure 4-40. The ISO, standard, and complex linetypes are named and displayed in the **Available Linetypes** list. Standard linetypes use only dashes, dots, and gaps. Complex linetypes can also contain special shapes and text.

Figure 4-40.
The **Load or Reload Linetypes** dialog box.

Select file where linetype definitions are stored

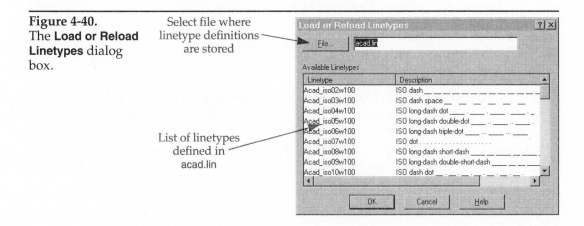

List of linetypes defined in acad.lin

Use the down arrow to look at all of the options. Select the linetypes you want to load. Pick the **OK** button to return to the **Select Linetype** dialog box, where the linetypes you selected will be listed. See Figure 4-41.

Figure 4-41.
Linetypes loaded
from the **Load or
Reload Linetypes**
dialog box are
added to the **Loaded
linetypes** list box.

Loaded
linetypes

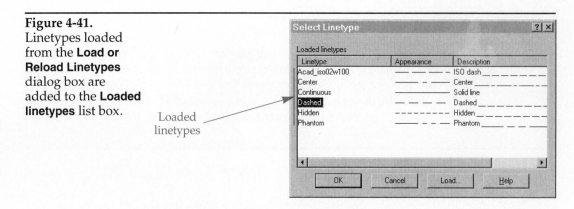

In the **Select Linetype** dialog box, pick the desired linetype and then pick **OK**, or
you can double-click on the desired name to automatically accept the selection and
return to the **Layer & Linetype Properties** dialog box. The Dashed linetype selected in
Figure 4-41 is now the linetype that is assigned to the Electrical layer, as shown in
Figure 4-42.

Figure 4-42.
Objects drawn on
the Electrical layer
will now have a
Hidden linetype.

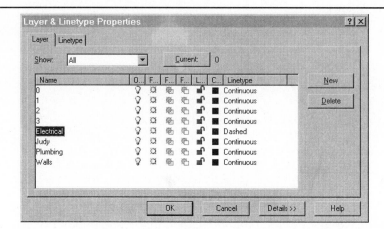

NOTE

The acad.lin file is used by default. You can switch to the
ISO library by picking the **File...** button. This displays the
Select Linetype File dialog box, where you can select the
acadiso.lin file.

Using the Linetype tab

LINETYPE
LT

Format
➥ Linetype...

Object Properties
toolbar

Linetype

The **Linetype** tab in the **Layer & Linetype Properties** dialog box is a convenient
place to load and access linetypes. This can be accessed by picking the **Linetype** tab in
the **Layer & Linetype Properties** dialog box, picking the **Linetype** button in the **Object
Properties** toolbar, selecting **Linetype...** from the **Format** pull-down menu, or typing
LINETYPE or LT at the Command: prompt. See Figure 4-43.

Picking the **Load...** button opens the **Load or Reload Linetypes** dialog box.
Picking the **Delete** button will delete any selected linetypes.

Figure 4-43.
The **Linetype** tab of the **Layer & Linetype Properties** dialog box.

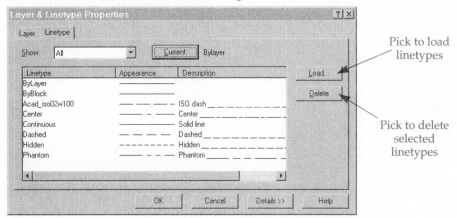

Pick to load linetypes

Pick to delete selected linetypes

EXERCISE 4-18

❏ Open EX4-14 if it is not already open.
❏ Open the **Select Linetype** dialog box and notice the default linetype.
❏ Pick the **Load...** button and load ISO02w100, Center, Dashed, Hidden, and Phantom.
❏ Pick the **OK** button.
❏ Apply the Dashed linetype to a layer of your choice.
❏ Save your work and exit AutoCAD, or keep this drawing open for the next exercise.

Customizing the layer listing

In some applications, large numbers of layer names may be used to assist in drawing information management. Having all layer names showing at the same time in the layer list can make it more difficult to work with your drawing layers. The **Show:** drop-down list box (Figure 4-44) provides options for filtering out unnecessary layer names from the list. *Layer filters* are used to screen, or filter, out any layers that have features that you do not want displayed in the **Layers & Linetype Properties** dialog box. The available options are explained in the following:

- **All**. This is the default option, and shows all defined layer names.
- **All in use**. The current layer and any layers that contain drawing objects are displayed.
- **All unused**. Displays all noncurrent layers that contain no objects.
- **All Xref dependent**. Xrefs are discussed in Chapter 24. This displays all layers brought in with externally referenced drawings.
- **All not Xref dependent**. Displays all layers native to the current drawing, and none that have been brought in with externally referenced drawings.

Figure 4-44.
The **Show:** drop-down list provides options for filtering layer names from the list.

Type of layers to be listed

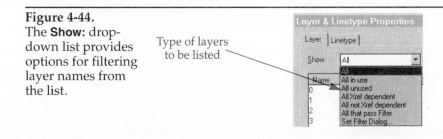

- **All that pass Filter**. Current filtering criteria is used to determine which layer names are displayed.
- **Set Filter dialog...**. Displays the **Set Layer Filters** dialog box.

Layer filters are set in the **Set Layer Filters** dialog box, Figure 4-45. Only the layers that possess the characteristics and settings defined by this dialog box are listed when the **All that pass Filter** option is selected in the **Show:** drop-down menu. The **Set Layer Filters** dialog box has the following components:

- **Layer Names: text box.** A single layer name can be entered in this text box if that is the only layer to be listed. Wildcard characters can be used to filter a specific group of layers. For example, the layer name W* would filter all layers beginning with *W*, such as Wall01, Wall02, and Wall03.
- **Layer settings drop-down menus.** These drop-down menus are used to specify certain types of layers to be listed. For example, selecting **On** from the **On/Off:** drop-down menu would cause only layers that are on to be listed. The default for all of the settings is **Both**.
- **Colors: and Linetypes: text boxes.** These text boxes are used to filter layers by their color or linetype. Only layers with colors and linetypes matching these selections will be listed. The default (*) represents all colors and all linetypes.
- **Reset button.** Picking this button returns all settings in this dialog box to the default values.
- **Apply this filter to the layer control on the Object Properties toolbar check box.** When this box is checked, only layers passing the filter are displayed in the **Layer Control** drop-down menu in the **Object Properties** toolbar.

Figure 4-45.
The **Set Layer Filters** dialog box.

Enter layer name(s) to be listed

Define settings for layers to pass filter

Select to filter layers in the **Layer Control** list in the **Object Properties** toolbar

Pick to change all settings to default values

Set color of layers to pass filter

Set linetype of layers to pass filter

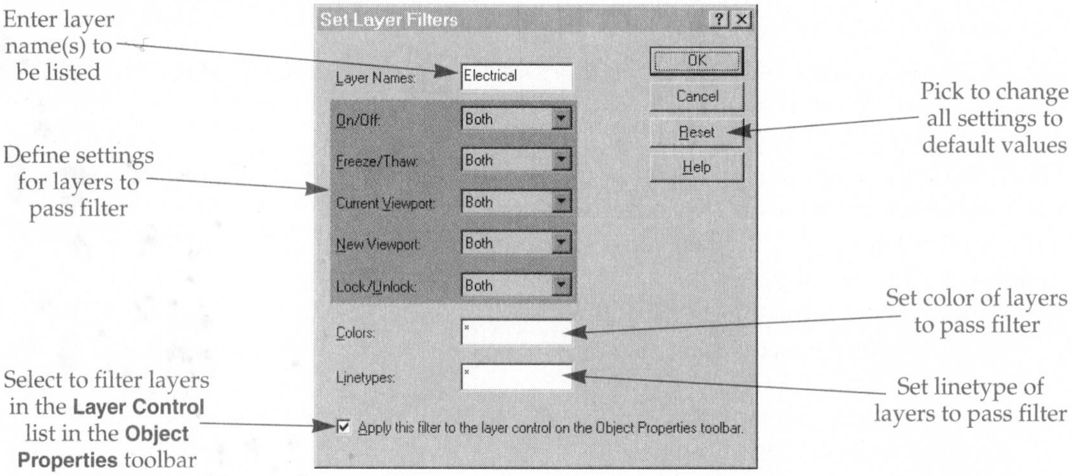

Using layer details

The **Layer & Linetype Properties** dialog box contains a **Details >>** button. The two greater than symbols show that selecting the button will expand the current dialog box. When selected, a new area is displayed at the bottom of the existing dialog box, Figure 4-46. The features of the **Details** area are inactive unless one of the layers is highlighted in the layer list. This area simply provides an alternate way of entering the same information that can be entered in the upper area, with the exception of the **Retain changes to xref-dependent layers** check box at the bottom. This toggle is off by default and is used to set the **VISRETAIN** system variable, which is discussed in detail in Chapter 24. Picking the **Details <<** button also hides the **Details** area.

Figure 4-46.
The **Details** area of the expanded **Layer & Linetype Properties** dialog box.

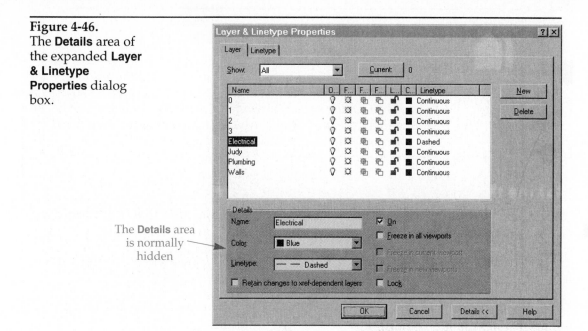

The **Details** area is normally hidden

Quickly setting a layer current

You can quickly change to another layer using the **Layer Control** drop-down list located in the **Object Properties** toolbar. The name of the current layer is displayed in the box. Pick the drop-down arrow and a layer list appears, as shown in Figure 4-47.

Figure 4-47.
The **Layer Control** drop-down list is located at the left side of the **Object Properties** toolbar. All layers are listed with icons representing their state and color. Double-click on a layer name to make it current.

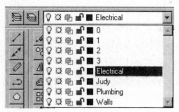

Pick a layer name from the list, and that layer is set current. When many layers are defined in the drawing, the vertical scroll bar can be used to move up and down through the list. Selecting a layer name to set as current automatically closes the list and returns you to the drawing editor. When a command is active, the drop-down button is grayed-out and the list is not available.

The **Layer Control** drop-down has the same status icons as the **Layers & Linetypes Properties** dialog box. By picking an icon, you can change the state of the layer.

You can also use the **CLAYER** system variable to make a layer current. Type **CLAYER** at the Command: prompt as follows:

    Command: **CLAYER.**⌐
    New value for CLAYER ⟨*current layer*⟩: (*enter the name of an existing layer and press* [Enter])

Object Properties toolbar

Make Object's Layer Current

Making the layer of an existing object current

You can select an object on the drawing and have the layer of that object become current. This is also a quick way to change the current layer. This works by picking the **Make Object's Layer Current** button in the **Object Properties** toolbar. When you pick this button, AutoCAD asks you to select the object:

> Command: (ai_molc)
> Select object whose layer will become current: *(pick an object to make its layer current)*
> PLUMBING is now the current layer.
> Command:

Changing Object Layers

You should always draw objects on their appropriate layer, but layer settings are not permanent. You can change an objects layer if needed. In addition, you can also change the object's color and linetype.

DDMODIFY MO

Modify
→ **Properties...**

Object Properties toolbar

Properties

To modify an object's properties, pick the **Properties** button in the **Object Properties** toolbar, select **Properties...** from the **Modify** pull-down menu, or type DDMODIFY or MO at the Command: prompt. When you do this, AutoCAD asks you to select the object(s) to be modified.

If you select one object, you get a dialog box that relates to that specific object. For example, if you pick a line, the **Modify Line** dialog box appears. If you pick a circle, the **Modify Circle** dialog box appears. These dialog boxes allow you to make several changes to the object, and among these changes are the layer, color, and linetype.

Figure 4-48 shows the **Modify Line** dialog box. The **Properties** area has a **Color...** button, which opens the **Select Color** dialog box for making a color selection. The **Layer...** button opens the **Select Layer** dialog box, where a new layer can be selected. The **Linetype...** button opens the **Select Linetype** dialog box, where you can select one of the previously loaded linetypes. The **Thickness:** text box is for 3D applications, and the **Linetype Scale:** box is used to change the linetype scale. Linetype scale is discussed later in this chapter.

The **Modify Line** dialog box and other similar **Modify** dialog boxes also allow you to edit features of the object. For example, the **Modify Line** dialog box allows you to change the From Point: and To Point: locations. This type of editing is explained in Chapter 12 of this text.

Figure 4-48.
The **Modify Line** dialog box is similar to all **Modify** dialog boxes.

Pick to
change color

Pick to
change layer

Pick to
change linetype

Edit features
of the object

Edit linetype
scale for the
object

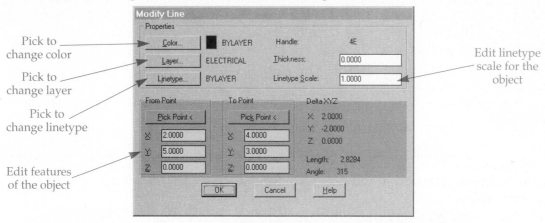

Figure 4-49.
The **Change Properties** dialog box.

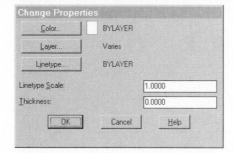

If you select more than one object, the **Change Properties** dialog box appears, Figure 4-49. This dialog box has the same **Color...**, **Layer...**, and **Linetype...** buttons, and the **Linetype Scale:** and **Thickness:** text boxes previously discussed.

EXERCISE 4-19

❏ Open EX4-14 if it is not already open.
❏ Use the **Layer Control** drop-down list in the **Object Properties** toolbar to experiment with making different layers current. Draw an object each time you change to a new current layer. Draw objects based on what you have already learned, such as line segments.
❏ Use the **Make Object's Layer Current** button to select an object in the drawing to make its layer current. Be sure the object you select is not on the current layer.
❏ Select an object and change its layer. Do this again, but this time select more than one object and change the layer in the **Change Properties** dialog box.
❏ Save your work and exit AutoCAD, or keep this drawing open for the next exercise.

Overriding Layer Settings

Color and linetype settings reference layer settings by default. This means that when you create a layer, you also establish a color and linetype to go with the layer. This is what it means when the color and linetype are specified as ByLayer. This is the most common method for managing these settings. Sometimes, however, you may need objects to reference a specific layer but have specific color and linetype properties that are different than the layer settings. In such a situation, the color and linetype can be set to an absolute value, and current layer settings will be ignored.

Setting the current object color

The current object color can be easily set by selecting the **Color Control** drop-down list from the **Object Properties** toolbar. See Figure 4-50. The default setting is ByLayer, which is also the recommended setting for most applications. To change this setting, pick another color from the list. If the color you want is not on the list, pick the item at the bottom of the list, labeled **Other...** to display the **Select Color** dialog box, or you can type COL at the Command: prompt. Once an absolute color is specified, all objects created are drawn in the specified color, regardless of the current layer settings.

Figure 4-50.
The current object color is easily set by opening the **Color Control** drop-down list in the **Object Properties** toolbar.

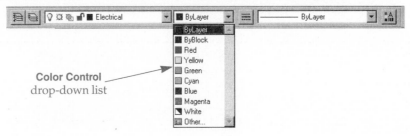

Another way to set the current object color is by using the **CECOLOR** system variable. **CECOLOR** stands for *current entity color*. This variable is set as follows:

Command: **CECOLOR.**↵
New value for CECOLOR 〈"BYLAYER"〉: *(enter new color value)*

To change this back to ByLayer, enter BYLAYER at the new value prompt.

Setting the current object linetype

Similar to the current object color, you can set the current object linetype to be separate from any layer settings. To set the current object linetype, pick the **Linetype Control** drop-down list from the **Object Properties** toolbar and select the desired linetype. See Figure 4-51. If the linetype that you want has not been loaded into the current drawing yet, it will not appear in the listing.

Figure 4-51.
The current object linetype is easily set by opening the **Linetype Control** drop-down list in the **Object Properties** toolbar.

You can also directly adjust the system variable that controls the current object linetype. This variable is called **CELTYPE**, for *current entity linetype*. Set the **CELTYPE** system variable in the same manner as the **CECOLOR** system variable.

Setting the linetype scale

The linetype scale sets the length of dashes and spaces in linetypes. When you start AutoCAD with a wizard or template, the linetype scale is automatically set to match the units you select. The default linetype scale factor is 1.0. However, just like layers, the linetype scale can be changed. One reason for changing the default line-type scale is to make your drawing more closely match standard drafting practices.

Earlier, you were introduced to the **Modify Line** dialog box and the **Change Properties** dialog box. Each of these dialog boxes has a **Linetype Scale:** text box. You can selectively change the linetype scale of objects by entering a new value. A value less than 1.0 makes the dashes and space smaller, while a value greater than 1.0 makes the dashes and spaces larger. Using this, you can experiment with different linetype scales until you achieve the desired results. Be careful when changing line-type scales to avoid making your drawing look odd, with a variety of line formats. Figure 4-52 shows a comparison of different linetype scale factors.

Figure 4-52.
Drawing the same linetype at different linetype scales.

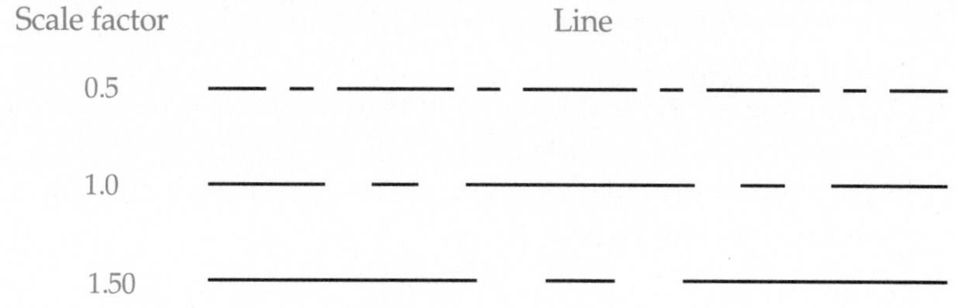

Scale factor	Line
0.5	
1.0	
1.50	

Changing the linetype scale at the Command: prompt

The **LTSCALE** variable can be used to make a global change to the linetype scale. *Global* means that the change affects everything in the current drawing. The default global linetype scale factor is 1.0. Any line with dashes initially assumes this factor.

To change the linetype scale for the entire drawing, type **LTSCALE** at the Command: prompt. The current value is listed. Enter the new value and press [Enter]. A Regenerating drawing message appears as the linetype scale is changed for all lines on the drawing.

Changing the linetype scale of individual objects

Sometimes you may want to change the linetype scale of an individual object or a select group of objects. One way to do this is by using the **CHPROP** command. This command allows you to change many properties, each of which is identified by name in a list of options. The **CHPROP** command is a handy tool that works like this:

```
Command: CHPROP↵
Select objects: (select the objects to change)
Select objects: ↵
Change what property (Color/LAyer/LType/ltScale/Thickness)? S↵
New linetype scale ⟨1.0000⟩: .5↵
Change what property (Color/LAyer/LType/ltScale/Thickness)? ↵
Command:
```

Using the CELTSCALE system variable

The **CELTSCALE** system variable controls the *current entity linetype scale*. The **LTSCALE** variable is a global setting that can be changed at any time and all objects in the drawing then use the new value. However, the **LTSCALE** variable is only a multiplier for the individual object linetype scale value. For example, if an object has an individual linetype scale of 0.5, and the **LTSCALE** is set at 0.5, then the apparent linetype scale displayed on screen is 0.25 for that object.

The **CELTSCALE** variable assigns a property directly to newly created objects, similar to the **COLOR** or **LINETYPE** commands. Subsequent changes to the variable do not affect already created objects, only objects that are created after the change is made. **CELTSCALE** may be set by typing CELTSCALE at the Command: prompt.

EXERCISE 4-20

❏ Start a new drawing, use one of your templates, or open a previous exercise.
❏ Draw the two objects shown below to approximate size.
❏ Change the linetype scale to .5, to 1.5, and then back to 1. Observe the effect each time it is changed.
❏ Change the linetype scale of only the hidden line to .5, to 1.5, and then back to 1.
❏ Change the linetype scale of only the center line to .5 to 1.5, and then back to 1.
❏ Experiment with other linetype scales if you wish and then change back to 1.
❏ Save the drawing as EX4-20.

Object 1   Object 2

Working with linetypes using the **Command:** prompt

The **-LINETYPE** command allows you to load different linetypes, change the current linetype, and create custom linetypes at the Command: prompt. This is a hyphen (-) typed before LINETYPE. The **-LINETYPE** command has several options:

- **?.** Lists the linetypes defined in a specified library file.
- **Create.** Allows creation of a new linetype and stores it in a specified library file.
- **Load.** Loads one or more linetypes from a specified library file.
- **Set.** Sets the current linetype used for newly drawn objects.

Listing linetypes. To get a listing of the available linetypes, type -LINETYPE at the Command: prompt. Then, use the ? option to open the **Select Linetype File** dialog box. The default linetype file name is acad.lin. Select a file and then press [Enter] to list the linetypes in that file.

Loading linetypes. To load linetypes, enter **-LINETYPE** at the Command: prompt and type L for the **Load** option. When loading multiple linetypes, separate each linetype name with a comma. In the following example, three linetypes are loaded:

```
Command: -LINETYPE↵
?/Create/Load/Set: L↵
Linetype(s) to load: CENTER,HIDDEN,PHANTOM↵
```

The **Select Linetype File** dialog box is displayed and the file containing the specified linetype must be selected.

Selecting a linetype. When drawing views of an object, you may need to draw hidden lines and centerlines. Select the linetype using the **Set** option of the **-LINETYPE** command. Type S at the prompt. You are then asked to name the linetype:

> Command: **-LINETYPE**↵
> ?/Create/Load/Set: **S**↵
> New object linetype (or ?) <BYLAYER>: **HIDDEN**↵
> ?/Create/Load/Set:

Press [Enter] to get the Command: prompt. Now, any lines you add are drawn with the new linetype. You must again use the **Set** option to draw continuous lines or set another linetype.

Loading custom linetypes. Many companies have custom linetypes. For example, cartographers may need special styles of lines to draw maps. These line-types are usually stored in library files other than the ACAD library. For example, if your company or school has installed a custom linetype library named maplines, then this file name is listed. Use the **Load** option and select the file containing the custom linetypes.

If you try to load a linetype that is already loaded, such as the standard AutoCAD Hidden linetype, you get this message Linetype HIDDEN is already loaded. Reload it? <Y>. Press [Enter] to reload the linetype, or type N and press [Enter] if you decide not to reload it.

EXERCISE 4-21

❏ Start a new drawing or use one of your templates.
❏ Set up seven new layers. Create some of the layers using the **Layer & Linetype Properties** dialog box and some at the Command: prompt. Use the following settings:

Layer name	Linetype	Color
Object	Continuous	White
Hidden	Hidden	Red
Center	Center	Yellow
Electric	Continuous	Green
Phantom	Phantom	Cyan
Dot	Dot	Blue
Dim	Continuous	Magenta

❏ Establish a new prototype with the specified layers by saving with a name of your choice. Record the prototype name and the settings in a notebook for future reference.
❏ Draw the objects shown below. Place objects on the layer that has their linetype. The dimension layer will not be used at this time.
❏ Save the drawing as EX4-21.

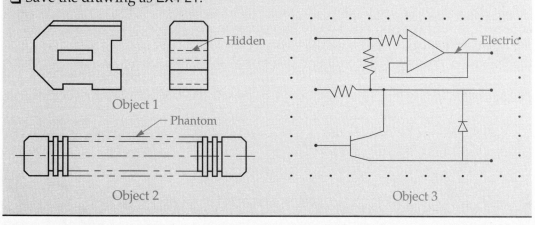

Object 1   Hidden   Electric

Phantom

Object 2   Object 3

Introduction to Printing and Plotting

A drawing created with CAD can exist in two distinct forms: hard copy and soft copy. The term *hard copy* refers to a physical drawing produced on paper by a printer or plotter. The term *soft copy* refers to the computer software version of the drawing, or the actual data file. The soft copy can only be displayed on the computer monitor, making it inconvenient to use for many manufacturing or construction purposes. If the power to the monitor is turned off, then the soft copy drawing is gone.

A hard copy drawing is extremely versatile. It can be rolled up or folded and taken down to the shop floor or out to a construction site. A hard copy drawing can be checked and red-lined without a computer or CAD software. Although CAD is the new standard throughout the world for generating drawings, the hard copy drawing is still a vital tool in industry.

AutoCAD supports two types of hard copy devices—printers and plotters. Printers and plotters take the soft copy images that you draw in AutoCAD and transfer them onto paper. There are several types of *printers*, including dot matrix, inkjet, laser, and thermal transfer. Dot matrix printers are normally used to make low-quality check prints, while the better quality inkjet, laser, and thermal printers may be used for quick check prints of formal drawings. Print size for most of these printers is 8.5" × 11" or 8.5" × 14".

Large format hard copy devices are commonly referred to as *plotters*. These include inkjet plotters, thermal plotters, electrostatic plotters, pen plotters, and pencil plotters. These plotters are capable of producing hard copy with varying line widths and color output. Pen plotters have been the industry standard for preparing large format hard copy. They are called pen plotters because they use liquid ink, fiber tip pens, or pens with pencil lead. Multipen plotters can provide different line thickness and colors. Even though pen plotters can plot very fast, it takes quite some time to plot a large, complex drawing. Since plotting with pen plotters can often be time-consuming, they are rapidly being replaced in industry by inkjet, thermal transfer, and laser plotters.

Laser printers and plotters draw lines on a revolving plate that is charged with high voltage. The laser light causes the plate to discharge while an ink toner adheres to the laser-drawn image. The ink is then bonded to the paper by pressure or heat. The quality of the laser printer or plotter depends on the number of dots per inch (dpi). Laser printers are commonly 300 and 600 dpi.

Thermal printers use tiny heat elements to burn dots into treated paper. The electrostatic process uses a line of closely spaced, electrically charged wire nibs to produce dots on coated paper. Inkjet plotters spray droplets of ink onto the paper to produce dot-matrix images.

This section introduces you to making prints and plots. Chapter 10 explores the detailed aspects of printing and plotting.

PLOT
[Ctrl]+[P]

File
↳ Print...

Standard toolbar

Print

Prints and plots are made using the **PLOT** command. The **PLOT** command is accessed by picking **Print...** in the **File** pull-down menu, by picking the **Print** button in the **Standard** toolbar, by pressing the [Ctrl]+[P] key combination, or by typing PLOT at the Command: prompt. This command displays the **Print/Plot Configuration** dialog box shown in Figure 4-53. Additional and advanced features of the **Print/Plot Configuration** dialog box are explained further in Chapter 10 of this text.

Figure 4-53.
The **Print/Plot Configuration** dialog box.

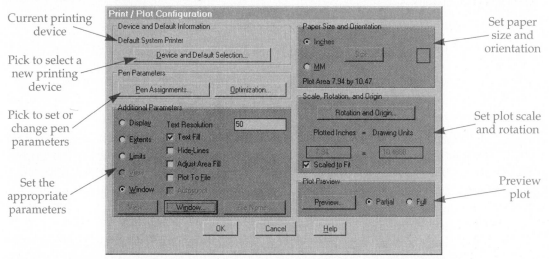

Current printing device

Pick to select a new printing device

Pick to set or change pen parameters

Set the appropriate parameters

Set paper size and orientation

Set plot scale and rotation

Preview plot

Device and default selection

As you look at the **Print/Plot Configuration** dialog box, notice the **Device and Default Information** area in the upper-left corner. This is where AutoCAD displays information about the currently configured printer or plotter. For now, it is assumed that your instructor or CAD systems manager has taken care of the device and default selections.

Pen parameters

The **Pen Parameters** area in the **Print/Plot Configuration** dialog box allows you to set pen parameters based on your drawing standards or the type of printer/plotter you are using. You should be able to make a print at this time without changing any pen parameters. If not, these settings should be set by your instructor or your CAD systems manager. You will learn to make your own settings in Chapter 10 of this text.

Additional parameters

Look at the **Additional Parameters** area of the **Print/Plot Configuration** dialog box. You can see the options for the part of a drawing to be plotted, and how it is to be plotted. The options are shown with radio buttons, and only one option can be selected at a time. The following describes the function of each option:

- **Display.** This option plots the current screen display.
- **Extents.** The **Extents** option plots only the area of the drawing where objects (entities) are drawn. Before using this option, zoom the extents to verify exactly what will be plotted. Be aware that border lines around your drawing (such as the title block) may be clipped off if they are at the extreme edges of the screen. This often happens because you are requesting the plotter to plot at the extreme edge of its active area.
- **Limits.** This option plots everything inside the defined drawing limits.
- **View.** Views saved with the **VIEW** command are plotted using this option. Until a view name has been provided, this option button is grayed-out.
- **Window.** This option button appears grayed-out until you pick the **Window...** button to display the **Window Selection** dialog box shown in Figure 4-54. This option requires you to define two diagonally opposite corners of a window around the portion of the drawing to be plotted. The corners can be chosen

Figure 4-54.
Specify a plot
window using the
Window Selection
dialog box.

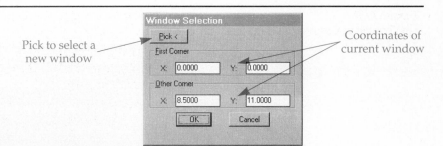

with your pointing device or entered as absolute coordinates. Enter the **First Corner** and **Other Corner** coordinates of the desired window in the appropriate **X:** and **Y:** text boxes. If you want to define the window with your pointing device, pick the **Pick** 〈 button. After you have picked the corners, the **Window Selection** dialog box is redisplayed. Pick **OK** to return to the **Print/Plot Configuration** dialog box.

- **Text Resolution.** This text box controls resolution of the plotted text. *Resolution* refers to the sharpness and clarity of the text characters, and how much detail you see. The default value is 50, which provides adequate resolution. Set a greater value for higher resolution.
- **Text Fill.** This check box is on by default. Some text characters are created with an outline and filled to provide a solid appearance. These text characters are printed solid when text fill is on. Only the outline is printed when text fill is off.
- **Hide-Lines.** Check this box if you want to plot a 3D drawing with hidden lines removed. This function works the same as the **HIDE** command. Do not check this box when plotting 2D drawings.
- **Adjust Area Fill.** Check this box if you want entities such as wide polylines, traces, doughnuts, and solids filled precisely.
- **Plot to File.** Check this box if you want to send the plot data to a file. This activates the **File Name...** button. Pick this button to get the **Create Plot File** dialog box.
- **Autospool**. This option is active only when plotting to an ADI (Autodesk Device Interface) device. When active, this allows you to automatically plot a specified file name or names.

Paper size and orientation

The upper-right area of the **Print/Plot Configuration** dialog box controls the paper size and orientation. Pick either the **Inches** or **MM** option button to make inches or millimeters the units for all plot specifications.

Pick the **Size...** button to access the **Paper Size** dialog box. You can only use the **Size...** button if your printer/plotter supports more than one size of media. This should already be set up by your instructor or CAD manager. You can make your own settings after studying Chapter 10. Also indicated is either landscape or portrait orientation. The orientation icon is a rectangle to the right of the **Size...** button. The term *landscape* comes from the idea that landscape artwork is normally displayed horizontally, while *portrait* artwork is usually prepared vertically.

Scale, rotation, and origin

Options to control the plot rotation and origin are located in the **Scale, Rotation, and Origin** area of the **Print/Plot Configuration** dialog box. Pick the **Rotation and Origin...** button to access the **Plot Rotation and Origin** dialog box shown in Figure 4-55.

Figure 4-55.
The **Plot Rotation and Origin** dialog box.

Select a rotation

Change the origin if necessary

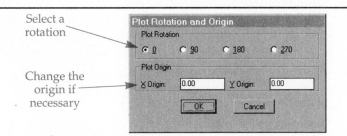

AutoCAD can rotate plots in 90° clockwise increments. The options are **0**, **90**, **180**, and **270** for rotation settings. These are located in the **Plot Rotation** area of the **Plot Rotation and Origin** dialog box. Figure 4-56 illustrates the result of the 90° increments of plot rotation.

Figure 4-56.
An example of a drawing plotted at various rotation angles.

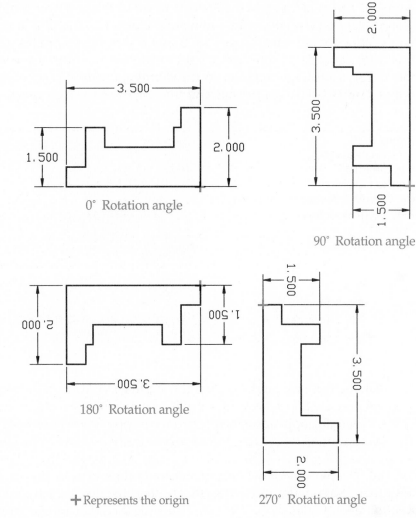

0° Rotation angle

90° Rotation angle

180° Rotation angle

+ Represents the origin

270° Rotation angle

The origin of a pen plotter is the lower-left of the plot media. To begin plotting a drawing at that point, leave the values shown in the **Plot Origin** text boxes at 0.00. If you want to move the drawing away from the default origin, set the required values in the text boxes accordingly. Remember that the units you enter should be consistent with the units specified with the option buttons in the **Paper Size and Orientation** area of the **Print/Plot Configuration** dialog box.

Scaling the plot

The **Plotted Inches = Drawing Units** text boxes (or **Plotted MM = Drawing Units** text boxes if using metric units) allow you to specify the plot scale as a ratio of plotted units to drawing units. Pick the **Scale to Fit** check box if you want AutoCAD to automatically adjust your drawing to fit on the paper. For now, pick this box. You will study the other options in Chapter 10 of this text.

Previewing the plot

The size and complexity of some drawings often makes the plotting time very long. By previewing a plot before it is sent to the output device, you can save material and valuable plot time. This feature is found in the **Plot Preview** area at the lower-right of the **Print/Plot Configuration** dialog box. Refer back to Figure 4-53. The **Partial** and **Full** preview options are each controlled with a radio button.

When the **Partial** option is activated and you pick the **Preview...** button, AutoCAD quickly displays the **Preview Effective Plotting Area** dialog box, Figure 4-57. The partial preview shows an outline of the paper size and an outline of the drawing on the paper. While this shows you how the drawing compares to the paper size, the final plot depends on how the printer or plotter is set up. If there is a problem with the setup, a message appears in the **Warnings:** box. These warnings give you an opportunity to make corrections and then preview the plot again.

Figure 4-57.
Selecting **Preview...**
when **Partial** is
checked displays
the **Preview Effective
Plotting Area** dialog
box.

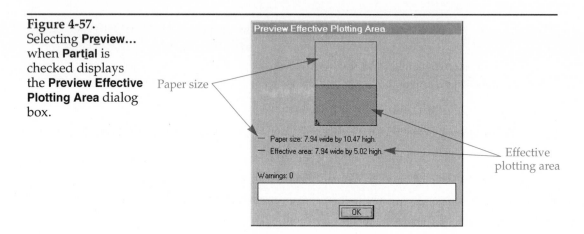

Paper size

Effective
plotting area

Pick the **Full** radio button, then the **Preview...** button, if you want a full preview. The **Full** preview takes more time, but it displays the drawing in the graphics window as it will actually appear on the plotted hard copy. See Figure 4-58. A full preview can also be performed by picking **Print Preview** from the **File** pull-down menu.

In the full preview, the cursor appears as a magnifying glass with a + and a – symbol. The plot preview image increases and reduces in size as you hold down the left mouse button and move the cursor. Press the [Esc] key to return to the **Print/Plot Configuration** dialog box. You can also pick the right mouse button to display the zoom cursor menu, which is discussed in Chapter 9. When the preview is initiated from the pull-down menu, the zoom cursor menu also includes a **Plot** option, which will plot the drawing.

If you are satisfied with the plot preview, return to the **Print/Plot Configuration** dialog box by pressing the [Esc] key. Pick the **OK** button in the **Print/Plot Configuration** dialog box to send the drawing to the printer or plotter.

Figure 4-58.
A full preview displays the paper sheet and drawing in the graphics window.

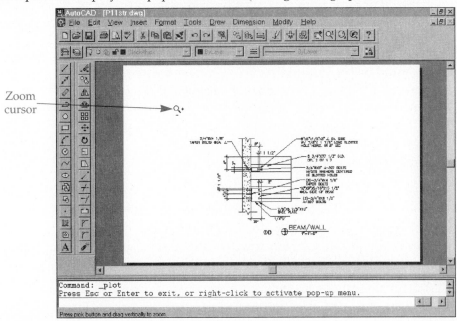

Completing the print process

Setting up the **Print/Plot Configuration** dialog box is easy. However, before you pick the **OK** button, there are several items you should check:

✓ Printer or plotter is plugged in.
✓ Cable from your computer to printer or plotter is secure.
✓ Printer has paper.
✓ Paper is properly loaded in the plotter and grips or clamps are in place.
✓ Plotter pens are inserted in the holder and the proper colors or thickness are in the correct places.
✓ Plotter area is clear for unblocked paper movement.

Pick the **OK** button when you are ready to send the print or plot to paper. You can also cancel or get help at any time by picking the **Cancel** or **Help** buttons. After you pick the **OK** button, you get one of the following messages:

Plot Complete, or
Position paper in plotter.
Press RETURN to continue or S to Stop for hardware setup.

If you get the second message, press the [Enter] key to send the drawing to the plotter.

PROFESSIONAL TIP
You can stop a plot in progress at any time by using the [Esc] key. Keep in mind that it may take awhile for some plotters or printers to terminate the plot, depending on the amount of the drawing file that has already been sent. Turning the plotter off purges all plot data from the plotter's internal buffer.

❑ Open any of your previous drawings.
❑ Access the **Print/Plot Configuration** dialog box.
❑ There should be a ✓ in the **Scale to Fit** check box, and the **Partial** and **Display** radio buttons should be highlighted.
❑ Pick the **Preview...** button and observe what happens. Press the [Esc] key.
❑ Pick the **Full** preview radio button and then pick the **Preview...** button to see the results. A full representation of your drawing should be displayed as it will appear when printed on the paper. Press the [Esc] key.
❑ Experiment by changing the rotation angle followed by doing a full preview each time.
❑ Pick the **Window...** button and then pick the **Pick ⟩** button in the **Window Selection** dialog box. Window a small portion of your drawing and then pick **OK**.
❑ Do another full preview to see the results. End the preview.
❑ Pick the **Display** radio button, preview the drawing to see if it is what you want, and make a print if a printer is available for your use.
❑ Exit AutoCAD.

Chapter Test

Write your answers in the spaces provided.

1. Give the commands and entries to draw a line from point A to point B, to point C, back to point A. Then, return to the Command: prompt:

   Command: _____

   From point: _____

   To point: _____

   To point: _____

   To point: _____

   To point: _____

   Command:

2. Give the command and actions needed to quickly connect a line to an existing line, and then undo it because it was wrong:

   Command: _____

   From point: _____

   To point: _____

   To point: _____

   To point: _____

3. Give the command sequence used to erase a group of objects at the same time and then bring them all back:

   Command: _____

   Select objects: _____

   First corner: _____

   Other corner: _____

   Select objects: _____

   Command:

4. Give the command necessary to clean the screen: _____

5. Identify the following linetypes:

A. _____

B. _____

C. _____

D. _____

E. _____

F. _____

G. _____

H. _____

I. _____

J. _____

K. _____

A ————————————

B – – – – – – – –

C ———————— – – ————————

D → F ← E

G ————————————

H ⌐– – – – – – –⌐

I —⌄——⌄——

J — – – — – – —

K ···························

6. List two ways to discontinue drawing a line. _____

_____

_____

_____

7. Name five point entry systems. _____

_____

_____

_____

8. Identify three ways to turn on the coordinate display._____

_____

_____

9. What does a coordinate display of 2.750⟨90 mean?_____

_____

_____

10. What does the coordinate display of 5.250,7.875 mean? _____

_____

_____

11. List four ways to turn on the **ORTHO** mode. _____

_____

_____

12. What do you enter at the Command: prompt if you want to have AutoCAD automatically repeat the **LINE** command? _____

_____

13. Identify three ways to continue drawing another line from a previously drawn line._____

_____

_____

14. Define stacked objects._____

    _____

15. How do you automatically use the **Window** selection method when you want to erase a group of objects? _____

    _____

    _____

16. How do you automatically use the **Crossing** selection option when you want to erase three out of four lines of a square? _____

    _____

    _____

    _____

17. How does the appearance of a window and crossing box differ? _____

    _____

    _____

18. Name the command that is used to bring back the last object erased before issuing another command. _____

19. List at least five ways to select an object to erase. _____

    _____

    _____

20. Define hard copy and soft copy._____

    _____

    _____

    _____

21. Identify four ways to access the **Print/Plot Configuration** dialog box. _____

    _____

    _____

    _____

    _____

22. Describe the difference between the **Display** and the **Window** options in the **Plot Parameter** section of the **Print/Plot Configuration** dialog box. _____

    _____

    _____

    _____

    _____

23. What is a major advantage of doing a plot preview?_____

    _____

    _____

    _____

24. What is the default linetype in AutoCAD? _____

25. Name at least ten of AutoCAD's standard linetypes.

_____

_____

_____

_____

_____

26. In the chart provided, list the seven standard color names and numbers.

Color Name	Color Number

27. How are the new layer names entered when creating several layers at the same time without using the **New** button in the **Layer & Linetype Properties** dialog box?

_____

28. Which pull-down menu contains the **Layer...** option? _____

29. Identify three ways to access the **Layer & Linetype Properties** dialog box. _____

_____

_____

30. What condition must exist before a linetype can be used in a layer?_____

_____

31. How do you make another layer current in the **Layer & Linetype Properties** dialog box? _____

_____

32. How do you change a layer's linetype in the **Layer & Linetype Properties** dialog box? _____

_____

33. How is the **Select Color** dialog box displayed from the **Layer & Linetype Properties** dialog box? _____

_____

34. How do you load several linetypes at the same time from the **Load or Reload Linetypes** dialog box? _____

_____

35. What is the state of a layer that is *not* displayed on the screen and *not* calculated by the computer when the drawing is regenerated? _____

36. Describe the purpose of locking a layer. _____

_____

_____

37. Are locked layers visible? _____

38. If you get the message Cannot freeze layer PROD002. It is the CURRENT layer, what should you do if you want to freeze the layer? _____

39. How do you easily select all of the layers in the **Layer & Linetype Properties** dialog box list at the same time? _____

_____

40. How do you know if a layer is either off, thawed, or unlocked in the **Layer & Linetype Properties** dialog box? _____

41. Describe the purpose of layer filters. _____

_____

42. Identify three ways to directly access property options for changing layer, line-type, or color of an existing object or objects: _____

_____

_____

43. Explain in general terms how direct distance entry works. _____

_____

_____

44. Why does direct distance entry work best with drawing aids such as **Ortho** and **Snap**? _____

_____

_____

45. What happens when the lines of the **WPolygon** or **CPolygon** cross, and how do you correct the problem? _____

_____

_____

46. The following command sequence is used for erasing lines, followed by removing objects from the selection set and then adding other objects back into the selection set. Provide the proper keyboard entry for removing and then adding objects:

Command: _____

Select objects: _____

Select objects: _____

Remove objects: _____

Remove objects: _____

Select objects: _____

Select objects: _____

Command:

AutoCAD and its Applications—Basics

47. Given the following layer status icons, write their meanings to the right of each symbol:

Symbol	Meaning
💡	
💡	
☼	
❄	
🔓	
🔒	

48. How do you make the layer of an existing object current? _____

49. How do you make another layer current by using the **Object Properties** toolbar?

50. How can you preview and create a plot while in the graphics window, without using the **Print/Plot Configuration** dialog box? _____

Drawing Problems

Before beginning these problems, set up template drawings with layer names, colors, and linetypes for the type of drawing you are creating. Review this chapter for information about setting up layering systems for different types of drawings. A basic layering format similar to the following can be used for some of the drawings:

Layer name	Color	Linetype
Object	White	Continuous
Hidden	Blue	Hidden
Center	Green	Center

Do not draw dimensions.

1. Draw an object by connecting the following point coordinates. Save your drawing as P4-1. Make a print of your drawing if a printer is available.

Point	Coordinates	Point	Coordinates
1	2,2	8	@-1.5,0
2	@1.5,0	9	@0,1.25
3	@.75⟨90	10	@-1.25,1.25
4	@1.5⟨0	11	@2⟨180
5	@0,-.75	12	@-1.25,-1.25
6	@3,0	13	@2.25⟨270
7	@1⟨90		

2. With the absolute, relative, and polar coordinate entry methods, draw the following shapes. Be sure to use a drawing plan sheet. Set the limits to 22,17, units to decimal, grid to .5, and snap to .0625. Draw rectangle A three times using a different point entry system each time. Draw object B once using at least two methods of coordinate entry. Do not draw dimensions. Save your drawing as P4-2. Make a print of your drawing if a printer is available.

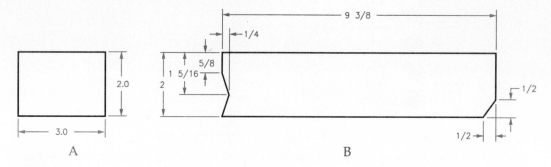

A   B

3. Draw the front elevation of this house. Create the dimensions proportional to the given drawings. Save the drawing as P4–3.

4. Draw the objects shown at A and B below using the following instructions:

A. Use a drawing plan sheet.

B. Draw each object using the **LINE** command.

C. Start each object at the point shown and then discontinue the **LINE** command where shown.

D. Complete each object using the **Continuation** option.

E. Do not draw dimensions.

F. Save the drawings as P4-4.

G. Make a print of your drawing if a printer is available.

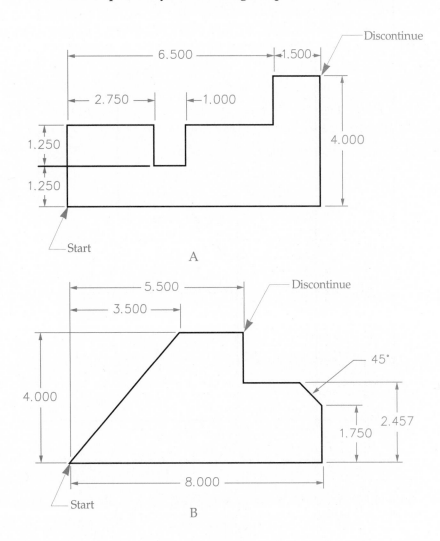

5. Draw the plot plan shown below. Use the linetypes shown, which include Continuous, Hidden, Phantom, Centerline, Fenceline2, and Gas_line. Make your drawing proportional to the example. Save the drawing as P4-5.

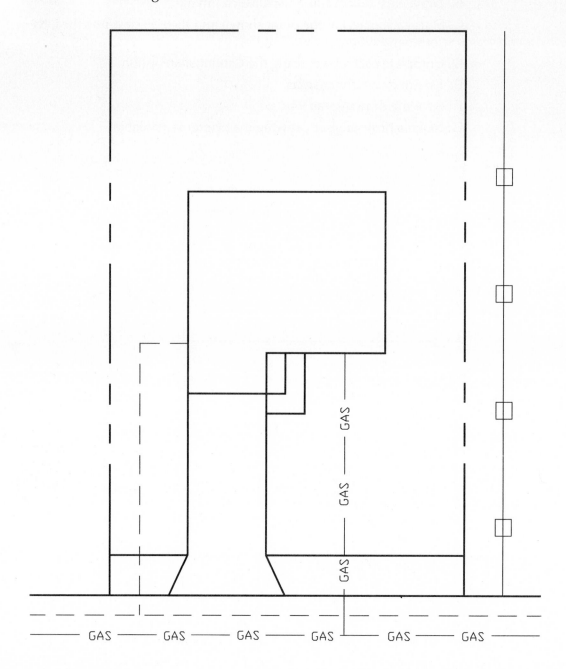

6. Draw the line chart shown below. Use the linetypes shown, which include Continuous, Hidden, Phantom, Centerline, Fenceline1, and Fenceline2. Make your drawing proportional to the given example. Save the drawing as P4-6.

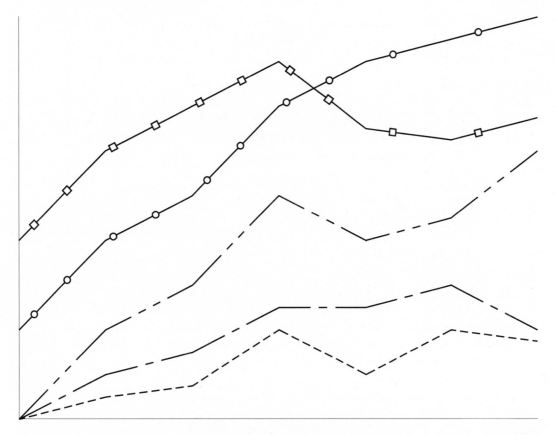

7. Draw the chart for the window schedule. Make the measurements for the rows and columns approximately the same as shown. Do not draw the hexagons or text. The hexagons are added in Chapter 5. The text will be added in Chapter 8. Save the drawings as P4-7.

WINDOW SCHEDULE

SYM.	SIZE	MODEL	ROUGH OPEN	QUAN.
(A)	12 X 60	JOB BUILT	VERIFY	2
(B)	96 X 60	W 4 N 5 CSM.	8'-0 3/4 X 5'-0 7/8"	1
(C)	48 X 6ᴏ	W 2 N 5 CSM.	4'-0 3/4"X 5'-0 7/8"	2
(D)	48 X 36	W 2 N 3 CSM.	4'-0 3/4"X 3'-6 1/2"	2
(E)	42 X 42	2 N 3 CSM.	3'-6 1/2"X 3'-6 1/2"	2
(F)	72 X 48	G 64 SLDG.	6'-0 1/2"X 4'-0 1/2"	1
(G)	60 X 42	G 536 SLDG.	5'-0 1/2"X 3'-6 1/2"	4
(H)	48 X 42	G 436 SLDG.	4'-0 1/2"X 3'-6 1/2"	1
(J)	48 X 24	A 41 AWN.	4'-0 1/2"X 2'-0 7/8"	3

8. Draw the chart for the door schedule. Make the measurements for the rows and columns approximately the same as in the given problem. Do not draw the text. The text will be added in Chapter 8. Save the drawing as P4-8.

DOOR SCHEDULE

SYM.	SIZE	TYPE	QUAN.
①	36 X 80	S.C. RP. METAL INSULATED	1
②	36 X 80	S.C. FLUSH METAL INSULATED	2
③	32 X 80	S.C. SELF CLOSING	2
④	32 X 80	HOLLOW CORE	5
⑤	30 X 80	HOLLOW CORE	5
⑥	30 X 80	POCKET SLDG.	2

9. Draw the chart for the interior finish schedule. Make the measurements for the rows and columns approximately the same as in the given problem. Do not draw the solid circles or the text. The solid circles will be added in Chapter 5. The text will be added in Chapter 8. Save the drawing as P4-9.

INTERIOR FINISH SCHEDULE

ROOM	FLOOR					WALLS				CEILING		
	VINYL	CARPET	TITLE	HARDWOOD	CONCRETE	PAINT	PAPER	TEXTURE	SPRAY	SMOOTH	BROCADE	PAINT
ENTRY					●							
FOYER		●				●			●			●
KITCHEN		●					●			●		●
DINING				●		●			●		●	●
FAMILY		●				●			●		●	●
LIVING		●				●		●			●	●
MSTR. BATH			●			●	●			●		●
BATH #2			●			●			●	●		●
MSTR. BED		●				●		●			●	●
BED #2		●				●				●	●	●
BED #3		●				●				●	●	●
UTILITY	●					●				●	●	●

AutoCAD and its Applications—Basics

10. Draw the kitchen range wall elevation using the given dimensions. Make all other features proportional to the given problem. Do not draw text or dimensions. Save the drawing as P4-10.

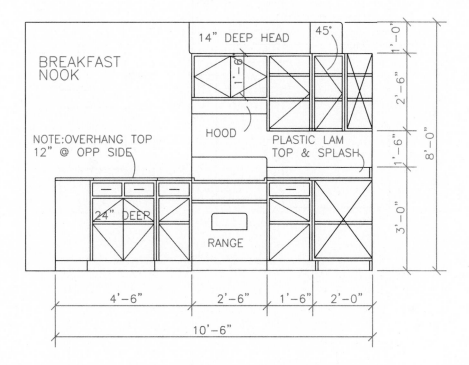

11. Draw the integrated circuit block diagram. Make your drawing proportional to the given problem. Do not draw the circle, line connections, or text. Save the drawing as P4-11.

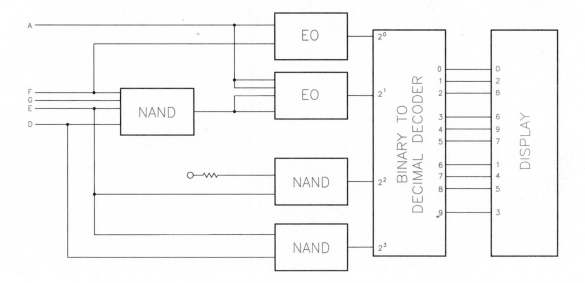

12. Draw the robotics system block diagram. Make your drawing proportional to the given problem. Do not draw the arrowheads or text. Save the drawing as P4-12.

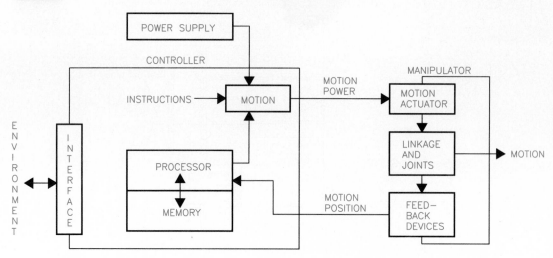

AutoCAD and its Applications—Basics

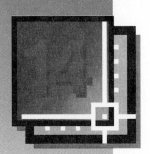

Chapter 5

Drawing Basic Shapes

Learning Objectives

After completing this chapter, you will be able to:
- O Use **DRAGMODE** to observe an object drag into place.
- O Draw circles using the **CIRCLE** command options.
- O Identify and use the @ symbol function.
- O Draw arcs using the **ARC** command options.
- O Draw an arc extending from a previously drawn arc.
- O Draw an arc extending from a previously drawn line.
- O Use the **ELLIPSE** command to draw ellipses and elliptical arcs.
- O Draw polygons.
- O Draw rectangles.
- O Draw rectangles with line width.
- O Draw rectangles with chamfered and rounded corners.
- O Explain and use the **MULTIPLE** command modifier.
- O Draw doughnuts.
- O Preset polygon and doughnut specifications.

The decisions you make when drawing circles and arcs with AutoCAD are similar to those when drawing the items manually. AutoCAD provides many ways to create circles and arcs using the **CIRCLE** and **ARC** commands. These include the center location and radius or diameter, or where the outline of the circle or arc should be located. AutoCAD also provides the **ELLIPSE**, **POLYGON**, **RECTANG**, and **DONUT** commands. These commands can be used to draw a wide variety of shapes.

Watching Objects Drag into Place

Chapter 4 showed how the **LINE** command displays an image that is "dragged" across the screen before the second endpoint is picked. This image is called a *rubberband*. The **CIRCLE**, **ARC**, **ELLIPSE**, **POLYGON**, and **RECTANG** commands also display a rubberband image to help you decide where to place the entity.

For example, when you draw a circle using the **Center Radius** option, a circle image appears on the screen after you pick the center point. This image gets larger or smaller as you move the pointer. When the desired circle size is picked, the dragged image is replaced by a solid-line circle. See Figure 5-1.

The **DRAGMODE** system variable affects the visibility of the rubberband. The **DRAGMODE** can be set to be on, off, or automatic by typing DRAGMODE at the Command: prompt and pressing [Enter] as follows:

Figure 5-1.
Dragging a circle to
its desired size.

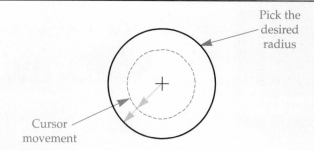

Pick the desired radius

Cursor movement

Command: **DRAGMODE**⏎
ON/OFF/Auto ⟨*current*⟩: *(type* ON, OFF, *or* A *and press* [Enter]*)*

The current (default) mode is shown in brackets. Pressing the [Enter] key keeps the existing status. When **DRAGMODE** is on, you must enter DRAG during a command sequence to see the objects drag into place. The following command sequence shows you how to activate the **DRAGMODE** while in the **CIRCLE** command.

Command: **CIRCLE**⏎
3P/2P/TTR/⟨Center point⟩: *(pick a center point)*
Diameter/⟨Radius⟩: **DRAG**⏎ *(the circle will drag into place as you pick the desired radius)*
Command:

Selecting **OFF** disables the **DRAGMODE**. This means that you will not see the objects drag into place. Even if you enter DRAG, AutoCAD ignores the request. When you set **DRAGMODE** to **Auto**, you see objects automatically dragged into place for all commands that support dragging. This is the default setting. Many users prefer to have the **DRAG-MODE** set to **Auto**. However, some computer configurations slow down the drag process. When this occurs, you may prefer to turn **DRAGMODE** on or off.

Drawing Circles

The **CIRCLE** command is used by picking the **Circle** button in the **Draw** toolbar, selecting **Circle** from the **Draw** pull-down menu, or by entering C or CIRCLE at the Command: prompt. The options available in **Circle** cascading menu are shown in Figure 5-2.

CIRCLE
C

Draw
↳ Circle

Draw
toolbar

Circle

Figure 5-2.
The **Circle** cascading
menu in the **Draw**
pull-down menu.

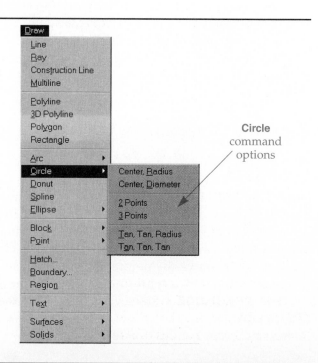

Circle command options

Drawing a circle by radius

A circle can be drawn by specifying the center point and the radius. The *radius* is the distance from the center to the circumference of a circle or arc. The *circumference* is the perimeter or distance around the circle.

Draw
➥ Circle
   ➥ Center, Radius

After accessing the **Center, Radius** option, you are asked to pick the center point followed by the radius. If the radius is picked on the screen, watch the coordinate display to help you locate the exact radius. The following command sequence is used to draw the circle in Figure 5-3:

    Command: **C** *or* **CIRCLE**↵
    3P/2P/TTR/⟨Center point⟩: *(select a center point)*
    Diameter/⟨Radius⟩: *(drag the circle to the desired radius and pick, or type the radius size and press* [Enter]*)*

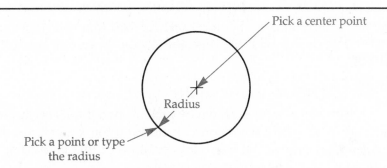

Figure 5-3.
Drawing a circle specifying the center point and radius.

The radius value you enter becomes the default setting for the next time you use the **CIRCLE** command. Use the **CIRCLERAD** system variable if you want to set a radius default. This provides you with the same circle radius default value each time you use the **CIRCLE** command. The **CIRCLERAD** system variable works like this:

    Command: **CIRCLERAD**↵
    New value for CIRCLERAD ⟨current⟩: *(set the desired default, .50 for example)*

The **CIRCLE** command sequence then looks like this:

    Command: **C** *or* **CIRCLE**↵
    3P/2P/TTR/⟨Center point⟩: *(pick the center point)*
    Diameter/⟨Radius⟩ ⟨.50⟩:↵
    Command:

When the **CIRCLERAD** system variable is set to a non-zero value, all you need to do is pick the center point of the circle and press [Enter] to accept the default value. You can always enter a different radius or pick a desired radius point if you want to ignore the default value. Set **CIRCLERAD** to 0 if you do not want a constant radius default.

Drawing a circle by diameter

A circle can be drawn by specifying the center point and the diameter. The command sequence for the **Center, Diameter** option is as follows:

Draw
➥ Circle
   ➥ Center,
     Diameter

    Command: **C** *or* **CIRCLE**↵
    3P/2P/TTR/⟨Center point⟩: *(select a center point)*
    Diameter/⟨Radius⟩: **D**↵
    Diameter: *(drag the circle to the desired diameter and pick, or type the diameter size and press* [Enter]*)*

Watch the screen carefully when using the **Center, Diameter** option. The pointer measures the diameter, but the circle passes midway between the center and the cursor. See Figure 5-4. The **Center, Diameter** option is convenient because most circle dimensions are given as diameters.

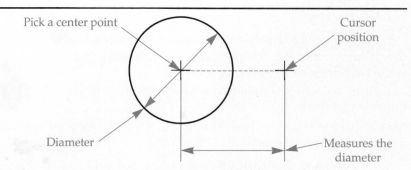

Figure 5-4.
Drawing a circle using the **Center, Diameter** option. Notice that AutoCAD calculates the circle's position as you move the cursor.

Pick a center point

Cursor position

Diameter

Measures the diameter

After you draw a circle, the selected radius becomes the default for the next circle (if **CIRCLERAD** is set to 0). If you use the **Diameter** option, the previous default setting is converted to a diameter. If you use the **Radius** option to draw a circle after using the **Diameter** option, AutoCAD changes the default to a radius measurement based on the previous diameter. If you set **CIRCLERAD** to a value such as .50, then the default for a circle drawn with the **Diameter** option is automatically 1.00 (twice the default radius).

Drawing a two-point circle

Draw
➥ Circle
➥ 2 Points

A two-point circle is drawn by picking two points on opposite sides of the circle. See Figure 5-5. The **2 Point** option is useful if the diameter of the circle is known, but the center is difficult to find. One example of this is locating a circle between two lines. The command sequence is as follows:

    Command: **C** *or* **CIRCLE.**⏎
    3P/2P/TTR/⟨Center point⟩: **2P**⏎
    First point on diameter: *(select a point)*
    Second point on diameter: *(select a point)*

AutoCAD automatically calculates the radius of the created circle. This is the default radius used the next time the **CIRCLE** command is used.

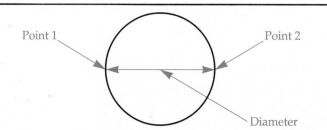

Figure 5-5.
Drawing a circle by selecting two points.

Point 1

Point 2

Diameter

Drawing a three-point circle

Draw
➥ Circle
➥ 3 Points

If three points on the circumference of a circle are known, the **3 Point** option is the best method to use. The three points can be selected in any order. See Figure 5-6. The command sequence is as follows:

    Command: **C** *or* **CIRCLE.**⏎
    3P/2P/TTR/⟨Center point⟩: **3P**⏎
    First point: *(select a point)*
    Second point: *(select a point)*
    Third point: *(select a point)*

AutoCAD automatically calculates the radius of the created circle. This is the default radius used the next time the **CIRCLE** command is used.

Figure 5-6.
Drawing a circle
given three points
on the circle.

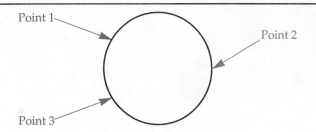

Drawing a circle tangent to two objects

The term *tangent* refers to a line, circle, or arc that comes into contact with an arc or circle at only one point. That point is called the *point of tangency*. A line drawn from the circle's center to the point of tangency is perpendicular to the tangent line. A line drawn between the centers of two tangent circles passes through the point of tangency. You can draw a circle tangent to given lines, circles, or arcs.

The **Tan, Tan, Radius** option is used to draw a circle tangent to two of these objects and to a specific radius. Once the **Tan, Tan, Radius** option is selected, select the lines, or line and arc, that the new circle will be tangent to. The radius of the circle is also required. To assist you in picking the three objects, AutoCAD uses the **Deferred Tangent** AutoSnap by default. (AutoSnap is covered in Chapter 6.) When you see the **Deferred Tangent** symbol, move it to the objects that you want to pick. The command sequence is as follows:

Draw
➥ Circle
➥ Tan, Tan,
Radius

> Command: **C** *or* **CIRCLE**↵
> 3P/2P/TTR/⟨Center point⟩: **TTR**↵
> Enter Tangent spec: *(pick the first line, circle, or arc)*
> Enter second Tangent spec: *(pick the second line, circle, or arc)*
> Radius ⟨*current*⟩: *(type a radius value and press* [Enter]*)*

If the radius entered is too small, AutoCAD gives you the message: Circle does not exist. AutoCAD automatically calculates the radius of the created circle. This is the default radius used the next time the **CIRCLE** command is used. Two examples of this option are shown in Figure 5-7.

Figure 5-7.
Two examples of
drawing circles
tangent to two
given objects using
the **Tangent,
Tangent, Radius**
option.

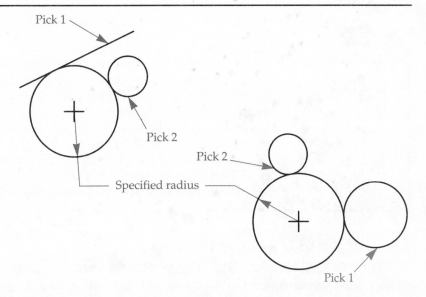

Drawing a circle tangent to three objects

The **Tan,Tan,Tan** option allows you to draw a circle tangent to three existing objects. This option creates a three-point circle using the three points of tangency. See Figure 5-8. Selecting the pull-down option is the same as using the **3 Point** option at the Command: prompt with the **TAN** object snap:

> Command: **C** *or* **CIRCLE**↵
> 3P/2P/TTR/⟨Center point⟩: **3P**↵
> First point: **TAN**↵
> to *(pick an object)*
> Second point: **TAN**↵
> to *(pick an object)*
> Third point: **TAN**↵
> to *(pick an object)*
> Command:

Figure 5-8.
Two examples of drawing circles tangent to three given objects.

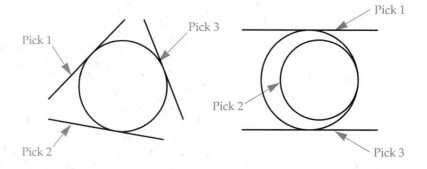

The Copy Rad option

The AutoCAD screen menu for the **CIRCLE** command also contains the **Copy Rad** option. This menu is not visible by default and must be activated before it can be used. The process for activating and customizing the screen menu is covered in detail in *AutoCAD and its Applications—Advanced, Release 14.*

To activate the screen menu, open the **Preferences** dialog box by picking **Preferences...** in the **Tools** pull-down menu. In the **Display** tab, place a check in the **Display AutoCAD screen menu in drawing window** check box. The screen menu now appears on the right side of the graphics window.

To access the **Copy Rad** option using the screen menu, pick **AutoCAD** at the top of the menu, followed by picking **DRAW 1**. Now pick **Circle**, followed by picking **Copy Rad.** Picking the **Copy Rad** option activates the AutoCAD geometry calculator, which is discussed in Chapter 7 of this text. The **Copy Rad** option allows you to draw a circle with exactly the same radius as an existing circle or arc, or a polyline arc segment.

Figure 5-9 shows how to use the **Copy Rad** option with an existing circle. First, pick **Copy Rad** from the **Circle:** screen menu. Then, use the following command sequence:

> New value for CIRCLERAD ⟨⟩: '_cal Expression: rad
> ⟩⟩Select circle, arc or polyline segment for RAD function *(pick the existing circle)*
> Command: **CIRCLE**↵
> 3P/2P/TTR/⟨Center point⟩: *(pick a center point for new circle)*
> Diameter/⟨Radius⟩ ⟨*current*⟩:↵
> Command:

Figure 5-9.
Drawing a circle with the same radius as an existing arc or circle using the **Copy Rad** option. Pressing [Enter] at the Radius: prompt draws the new circle. Note the screen menu (shown highlighted). This must first be turned on to use the **Copy Rad** option.

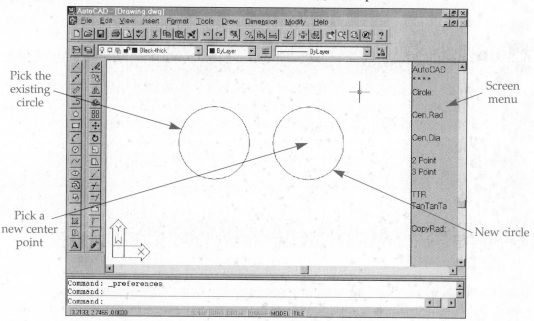

Using the @ symbol to specify the last coordinates

The @ symbol can be used to input the coordinates last entered. For example, suppose you want to draw a circle with a center at the end of the line just drawn. Enter the @ symbol when asked for a center point. The command sequence is as follows:

> Command: **L** *or* **LINE**↵
> From point: **4,4**↵
> To point: **8,4**↵
> To point:↵
> Command: **C** *or* **CIRCLE**↵
> 3P/2P/TTR/⟨Center point⟩: **@**↵

The @ symbol automatically issues the coordinate 8,4 (end of the last line) as the center of the circle. The 8,4 value is saved in the **LASTPOINT** system variable. The @ symbol retrieves the **LASTPOINT** value.

Another application of the @ symbol is drawing concentric circles (circles that have the same center). To do this, draw a circle using the **Center, Radius** or **Center, Diameter** options. Then, enter the **CIRCLE** command again and type @ when asked for the center point. This automatically places the center of the new circle at the center of the previous circle.

EXERCISE 5-1

❑ Begin a new drawing or use one of your templates.
❑ Set the **CIRCLERAD** system variable to 0.
❑ Use the **Center, Radius** option of the **CIRCLE** command to draw a circle similar to the one shown in Figure 5-3.
❑ Use the **Center, Diameter** option of the **CIRCLE** command to draw the circle shown in Figure 5-4.
❑ Draw two vertical parallel lines two units apart. Then use the two point option of the **CIRCLE** command to draw the circle tangent to the two lines.
❑ Use the three-point option of the **CIRCLE** command to draw the circle shown in Figure 5-6.
❑ Use the **Tangent, Tangent, Radius** option of the **CIRCLE** command to draw the circles shown in Figure 5-7.
❑ Use the **Tan,Tan,Tan** option to draw circles tangent to the existing objects as in Figure 5-8.
❑ Open the AutoCAD screen menu and then use the **Copy Rad** option to create a drawing similar to Figure 5-9. Close the screen menu.
❑ Draw a line. Use the **Center, Radius** option of the **CIRCLE** command and the @ symbol to place the circle's center at the endpoint of the line.
❑ Draw three concentric circles using @ and the **CIRCLE** command.
❑ Set **CIRCLERAD** to .5 and draw circles using each **CIRCLE** command option. Compare the prompts to those from the first circles drawn in this exercise.
❑ Save the drawing as EX5-1.

AutoCAD
User's
Guide 4

ARC
A

Draw
↦ Arc

Draw
toolbar

Arc

Drawing Arcs

An *arc* is defined as any part of a circle or curve. Arcs are commonly dimensioned with a radius, but can be drawn by a number of different methods. The **ARC** command can be accessed by selecting **Arc** from the **Draw** pull-down menu. There are eleven **ARC** construction options accessible in the **Arc** cascading menu, Figure 5-10. This is the easiest way to access the **ARC** command and an arc option. However, the **ARC** command and its options also can be accessed by picking the **Arc** button in the **Draw** toolbar, or by typing A or ARC at the Command: prompt. The three-point option is the default when using the toolbar button or the Command: prompt.

PROFESSIONAL TIP   It is easiest to select the desired **ARC** option using the **Arc** cascading menu in the **Draw** pull-down menu. When an **ARC** option is selected, AutoCAD automatically prompts you for the next required input.

Figure 5-10.
The **Arc** cascading menu in the **Draw** pull-down menu.

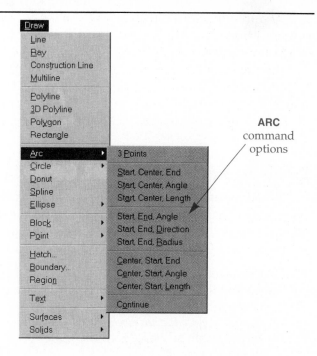

ARC command options

Drawing a three-point arc

The three-point option asks for the start point, second point along the arc, and then the endpoint. See Figure 5-11. The arc can be drawn clockwise or counterclockwise, and is dragged into position as the endpoint is located. The command sequence is as follows:

Draw
→ Arc
→ 3 Points

> Command: **A** *or* **ARC.⅃**
> Center/⟨Start point⟩: *(select the first point on the arc)*
> Center/End/⟨Second point⟩: *(select the second point on the arc)*
> End point: *(select the arc's endpoint)*
> Command:

Figure 5-11.
Drawing an arc by picking three points.

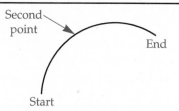

Second point
End
Start

Drawing arcs with the **Start, Center, End** option

Use **Start, Center, End** option when you know the start, center, and endpoints. Picking the start and center points establishes the arc's radius. The point selected for the endpoint determines the arc length. The selected endpoint does not have to be on the radius of the arc. See Figure 5-12. The command sequence is as follows:

Draw
→ Arc
→ Start, Center, End

> Command: **A** *or* **ARC.⅃**
> Center/⟨Start point⟩: *(select the first point on the arc)*
> Center/End/⟨Second point⟩: **C.⅃**
> Center: *(select the arc's center point)*
> Angle/Length of chord/⟨End point⟩: *(select the arc endpoint)*
> Command:

Figure 5-12.
Using the **Start, Center, End** option. Notice the endpoint does not have to be on the arc.

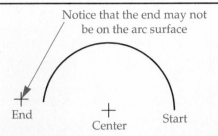

Drawing arcs with the Start, Center, Angle option

Draw
↳ Arc
  ↳ Start, Center, Angle

When the arc's included angle is known, the **Start, Center, Angle** option may be the best choice. The *included angle* is an angle formed between the center, start, and end-points of the arc. The arc is drawn counterclockwise, unless a negative angle is specified. See Figure 5-13. The following shows the command sequence with a 45° included angle:

Command: **A** *or* **ARC**↵
Center/⟨Start point⟩: *(select the first point on the arc)*
Center/End/⟨Second point⟩: **C**↵
Center: *(select the arc center point)*
Angle/Length of chord/⟨End point⟩: **A**↵
Included angle: **45**↵
Command:

Figure 5-13.
How positive and negative angles work with the **Start, Center, Angle** option.

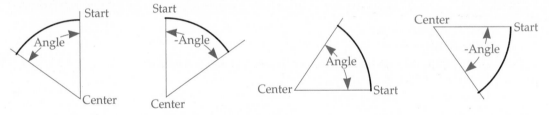

Drawing arcs with the Start, Center, Length option

Draw
↳ Arc
  ↳ Start, Center, Length

The chord length can be determined using a chord length table (see Appendix I). A one-unit radius arc with an included angle of 45° has a chord length of .765 units. Arcs are drawn counterclockwise. Therefore, a positive chord length gives the small-est possible arc with that length. A negative chord length results in the largest possi-ble arc. See Figure 5-14. The following shows the command sequence with a chord length of .765:

Command: **A** *or* **ARC**↵
Center/⟨Start point⟩: *(select the first point on the arc)*
Center/End/⟨Second point⟩: **C**↵
Center: *(select the arc center point)*
Angle/Length of chord/⟨End point⟩: **L**↵
Length of chord: *(type* **.765** *for the smallest arc, or* −.765 *for the largest arc, and press* [Enter]*)*
Command:

Figure 5-14.
How positive and
negative chord
lengths work with
the **Start, Center,
Length** option.

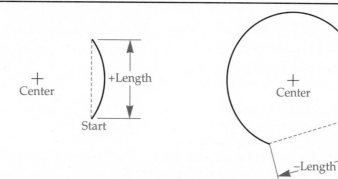

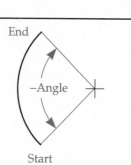

Drawing arcs using the Start, End, Angle option

An arc can also be drawn by picking the start point, endpoint, and entering the included angle. A positive included angle draws the arc counterclockwise, while a negative angle produces a clockwise arc. See Figure 5-15. The command sequence is as follows:

> Draw
> ➥ Arc
>   ↳ Start, En̲d,
>   Angle

```
Command: A or ARC↵
Center/⟨Start point⟩: (select the first point on the arc)
Center/End/⟨Second point⟩: E↵
End point: (select the arc endpoint)
Angle/Direction/Radius/⟨Center point⟩: A↵
Included angle: (type a positive or negative angle and press [Enter])
Command:
```

Figure 5-15.
How positive and
negative angles
work with the **Start,
End, Angle** option.

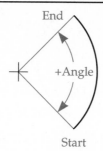

Drawing arcs using the Start, End, Radius option

Draw
➥ Arc
➥ Start, End,
Radius

A positive radius value for the **Start, End, Radius** option results in the smallest possible arc between the start point and endpoint. A negative radius gives the largest arc possible. See Figure 5-16. Arcs can only be drawn counterclockwise with this option. The command sequence is as follows:

> Command: **A** *or* **ARC**↵
> Center/⟨Start point⟩: *(select the first point on the arc)*
> Center/End/⟨Second point⟩: **E**↵
> End point: *(select the arc endpoint)*
> Angle/Direction/Radius/⟨Center point⟩: **R**↵
> Radius: *(pick, or type a positive radius or negative radius and press* [Enter]*)*

Figure 5-16.
Using the **Start, End, Radius** option with a positive and negative radius.

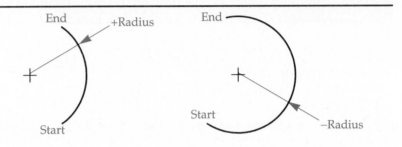

Drawing arcs using the Start, End, Direction option

Draw
➥ Arc
➥ Start, End,
Direction

An arc can be drawn by picking the start point, endpoint, and entering the direction of rotation in degrees. The distance between the points and the number of degrees determines the arc's location and size. The arc is started tangent to the direction specified, as shown in Figure 5-17. The command sequence is as follows:

> Command: **A** *or* **ARC**↵
> Center/⟨Start point⟩: *(select the first point on the arc)*
> Center/End/⟨Second point⟩: **E**↵
> End point: *(select the arc endpoint)*
> Angle/Direction/Radius/⟨Center point⟩: **D**↵
> Direction from start point: *(pick the direction from the start point, or type the direction in degrees and press* [Enter]*)*
> Command:

Figure 5-17.
Using the **Start, End, Direction** option.

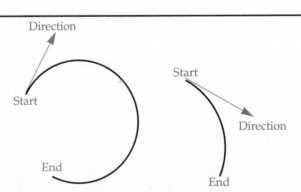

Drawing arcs using the Center, Start, End option

Draw
➥ Arc
➥ Center, Start, End

The **Center, Start, End** option is a variation of the **Start, Center, End** option. See Figure 5-18. Use the **Center, Start, End** option when it is easier to begin by locating the center. The command sequence is as follows:

Command: **A** *or* **ARC**↵
Center/⟨Start point⟩: **C**↵
Center: *(pick the center point)*
Start point: *(pick the start point)*
Angle/Length of chord/⟨End point⟩: *(pick the arc's endpoint)*
Command:

Figure 5-18.
Using the **Center, Start, End** option. Note that the endpoint does not have to be on the arc.

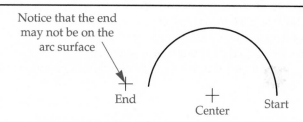

Notice that the end may not be on the arc surface

End   Center   Start

Drawing arcs using the **Center, Start, Angle** option

The **Center, Start, Angle** option is a variation of the **Start, Center, Angle** option. Use the **Center, Start, Angle** option when it is easier to begin by locating the center. Figure 5-19 shows how positive and negative angles work with this option. The command sequence is as follows:

Draw
➥ Arc
➥ Center, Start, Angle

Command: **A** *or* **ARC**↵
Center/⟨Start point⟩: **C**↵
Center: *(pick the center point)*
Start point: *(pick the start point)*
Angle/Length of chord/⟨End point⟩: **A**↵
Included angle: *(pick the included angle or type a positive angle or negative angle and press* [Enter]*)*
Command:

Figure 5-19.
How positive and negative angles work with the **Center, Start, Angle** option.

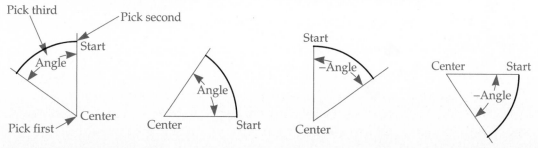

Drawing arcs with the Center, Start, Length of chord option

Draw
→ Arc
　→ Center, Start,
　　Length

The **Center, Start, Length** of chord option is a variation of the **Start, Center, Length** option. Use the **Center, Start, Length** option when it is easier to begin by locating the center. Figure 5-20 shows how positive and negative chord lengths work with this option. The command sequence is as follows:

```
Command: A or ARC↵
Center/⟨Start point⟩: C↵
Center: (pick the center point)
Start point: (pick the start point)
Angle/Length of chord/⟨End point⟩: L↵
Length of chord: (pick, or type the chord length and press [Enter])
Command:
```

Figure 5-20.
How positive and negative chord lengths work with the **Center, Start, Length** option.

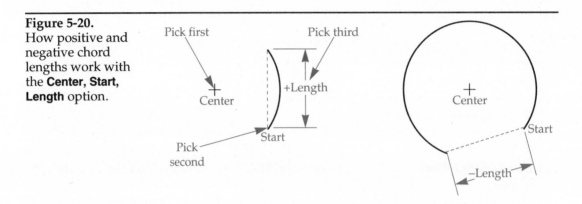

Continuing arcs from a previously drawn arc or line

An arc can be continued from the previous arc or line. To do so, pick **Continue** from the **Arc** cascading menu in the **Draw** pull-down menu, or press the [Enter] key, space bar, or right mouse button at the ⟨Start point⟩: prompt.

When a series of arcs are drawn in this manner, each consecutive arc is tangent. The start points and direction are taken from the endpoint and direction of the previous arc. See Figure 5-21.

Figure 5-21.
Using the **Continue** option to draw three arcs.

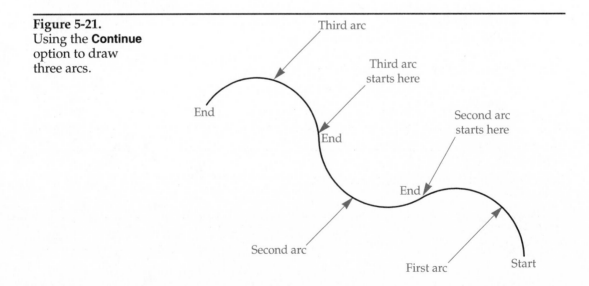

The **Continue** option can also be used to quickly draw an arc tangent to the end-point of a previously drawn line. See Figure 5-22. The command sequence is as follows:

Command: **L** *or* **LINE**↵
From point: *(select a point)*
To point: *(select the second point)*
To point:↵
Command: **A** *or* **ARC**↵
Center/⟨Start point⟩: *(press space bar or [Enter] to place start point of the arc at end of the previous line)*
End point: *(select the endpoint of the arc)*

Figure 5-22.
An arc continuing from the previous line. Point 2 is the start of the arc and Point 3 is the end of the arc.

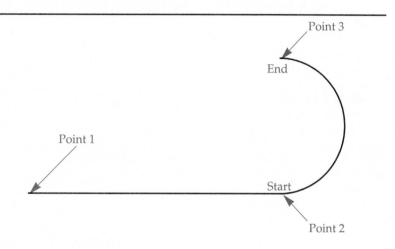

EXERCISE 5-4

- Begin a new drawing or use one of your templates.
- Use the **Center, Start, Angle** option of the **ARC** command to draw arcs similar to those shown in Figure 5-19.
- Use the **ARC** command and the **Continue** option to draw the arcs shown in Figure 5-21.
- Use the **ARC** command and the **Continue** option as described in the text to draw an arc connected to a previously drawn line as shown in Figure 5-22.
- Save the drawing as EX5-4.

Drawing Ellipses

ELLIPSE
EL

Draw
➥ **Ellipse**

Draw
toolbar

Ellipse

When a circle is viewed at an angle, an elliptical shape is seen. For example, a 30° ellipse is created if a circle is rotated 60° from the line of sight. The parts of an ellipse are shown in Figure 5-23. The **ELLIPSE** command can be accessed by selecting **Ellipse⟩** from the **Draw** pull-down menu, picking the **Ellipse** button in the **Draw** toolbar, or entering EL or ELLIPSE at the Command: prompt. An ellipse can be drawn using different options of the **ELLIPSE** command.

Figure 5-23.
Parts of an ellipse.

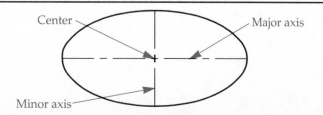

Drawing an ellipse using the Axis, Endpoint option

Draw
➥ Ellipse
   ➥ Axis, End

The **Axis, Endpoint** option establishes the first axis and one endpoint of the second axis. The first axis may be either the major or minor axis, depending on what is entered for the second axis. The longer of the two axes is always the major axis. After you pick the first axis, the ellipse is dragged by the cursor until the point is picked. The command sequence for the ellipses in Figure 5-24 is as follows:

Command: **EL** *or* **ELLIPSE**↵
Arc/Center/⟨Axis endpoint 1⟩: *(select an axis endpoint)*
Axis endpoint 2: *(select the other endpoint of the axis)*
⟨Other axis distance⟩/Rotation: *(select a distance from the midpoint of the first axis to the end of the second axis and press* [Enter]*)*

Figure 5-24.
Constructing the same ellipse by choosing different axis endpoints.

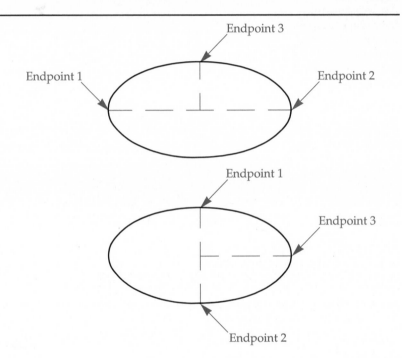

If you respond to the ⟨Other axis distance⟩/Rotation: prompt with R for rotation, AutoCAD assumes you have selected the major axis with the first two points. The next prompt requests the angle that the ellipse is rotated from the line of sight. The command sequence is as follows:

Arc/Center ⟨Axis endpoint 1⟩: *(select a major axis endpoint)*
Axis endpoint 2: *(select the other endpoint of the major axis)*
⟨Other axis distance⟩/Rotation: **R**↵
Rotation around major axis: *(type a rotation angle, such as* 30 *and press* [Enter]*)*

The 30 response draws an ellipse that is 30° from the line of sight. A 0 response draws an ellipse with the minor axis equal to the major axis. This is a circle. Any rotation angle between 89.42° and 90.57° or 269.42° and 270.57° is rejected by AutoCAD. Figure 5-25 shows the relationship between several ellipses having the same major axis length but different rotation angles.

Figure 5-25.
Ellipse rotation angles.

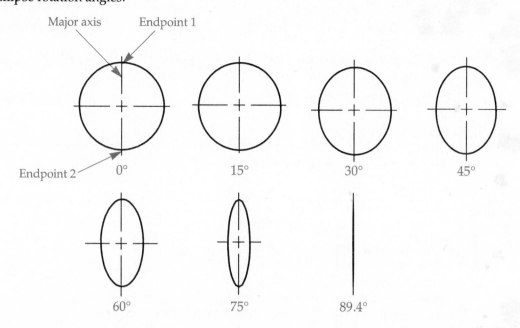

Major axis   Endpoint 1

Endpoint 2   0°   15°   30°   45°

60°   75°   89.4°

Drawing an ellipse using the Center option

An ellipse can also be constructed by specifying the center point and one endpoint for each of the two axes. See Figure 5-26. The command sequence for this option is as follows:

Draw
↳ Ellipse
↳ Center

> Command: **EL** *or* **ELLIPSE.**↵
> Arc/Center ⟨Axis endpoint 1⟩: **C.**↵
> Center of ellipse: *(select the ellipse center point)*
> Axis endpoint: *(select the endpoint of one axis)*
> ⟨Other axis distance⟩/Rotation: *(select the endpoint of the other axis)*

Figure 5-26.
Drawing an ellipse
by picking the
center and endpoint
of two axes.

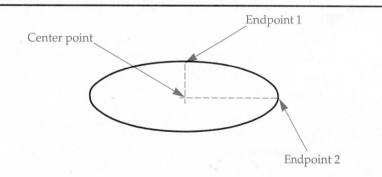

Center point   Endpoint 1

Endpoint 2

The rotation option can be used instead of selecting the second axis endpoint. The command sequence for a 30° rotation angle is as follows:

> Arc/Center ⟨Axis endpoint 1⟩: **C.**↵
> Center of ellipse: *(select the ellipse center point)*
> Axis endpoint: *(select the endpoint of one axis)*
> ⟨Other axis distance⟩/Rotation: **R.**↵
> Rotation around major axis: **30.**↵

Drawing elliptical arcs

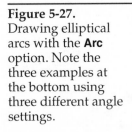

The **Arc** option of the **ELLIPSE** command is used to draw elliptical arcs. The command sequence for the **Arc** option is as follows:

```
Command: EL or ELLIPSE↵
Arc/Center/⟨Axis endpoint 1⟩: A↵
⟨Axis endpoint 1⟩/Center: (pick the first axis endpoint)
Axis endpoint 2: (pick the second axis endpoint)
⟨Other axis distance⟩/Rotation: (pick the distance for the second axis)
Parameter/⟨start angle⟩: 0↵
Parameter/Included/⟨end angle⟩: 90↵
Command:
```

Once the second endpoint of the first axis is picked, you can drag the shape of a full ellipse. This can be used to help you visualize the other axis. The distance for the second axis is from the ellipse center to the point picked. Then enter a start angle. The start and end angles are the angular relation between the ellipse center and where the arc begins. The angle of the elliptical arc is established from the angle of the first axis. A 0° start angle is the same as the first endpoint of the first axis. A 45° start angle is 45° counterclockwise from the first endpoint of the first axis. End angles are also established counterclockwise from the start point. Figure 5-27 shows the elliptical arc drawn with the previous command sequence, and displays samples of different start and end angle arcs.

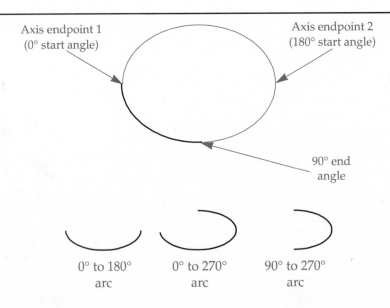

Figure 5-27. Drawing elliptical arcs with the **Arc** option. Note the three examples at the bottom using three different angle settings.

Using the Parameter option

The **Parameter** option requires the same input as the other arcs until the Parameter/⟨start angle⟩: prompt. The difference is that AutoCAD creates the elliptical arc using a different means of vector calculation. The results are similar, but the command sequence is as follows:

```
Parameter/⟨start angle⟩: P↵
Angle/⟨start parameter⟩: (pick the start point)
Angle/Included/⟨end parameter⟩: (pick the end point)
Command:
```

Using the Included option

The **Included** option establishes an included angle beginning at the start angle. An included angle is an angle that is formed by two sides, or in this case, an angle that is formed as a number of degrees from the start angle. This option requires the same input as the other arcs until the Parameter/Included/⟨end angle⟩: prompt. The command sequence is as follows:

```
Parameter/Included/⟨end angle⟩: I↵
Included angle ⟨current⟩: 180↵
Command:
```

Rotating an ellipse arc around its axis

The **Rotation** option for drawing an elliptical arc is similar to the **Rotation** option when drawing a full ellipse discussed earlier. This option allows you to rotate the elliptical arc about the first axis by specifying a rotation angle. Refer back to Figure 5-25 for examples of various rotation angles. This option requires the same input as the other arcs until the ⟨Other axis distance⟩/Rotation: prompt. The command sequence is as follows:

```
⟨Other axis distance⟩/Rotation: R↵
Rotation around major axis: 45↵
Parameter/⟨start angle⟩: 90↵
Parameter/Included/⟨end angle⟩: 180↵
Command:
```

Drawing an elliptical arc using the Center option

The **Center** option for drawing an elliptical arc lets you establish the center of the ellipse. See Figure 5-28. This option requires the same input as the other arcs until the ⟨Axis endpoint 1⟩/Center: prompt. The command sequence is as follows:

```
⟨Axis endpoint 1⟩/Center: C↵
Axis endpoint: (pick the first axis endpoint)
⟨Other axis distance⟩/Rotation: (pick the other axis distance)
Parameter/⟨start angle⟩: 0↵
Parameter/Included/⟨end angle⟩: 180↵
Command:
```

Figure 5-28.
Drawing elliptical arcs with the **Center** option.

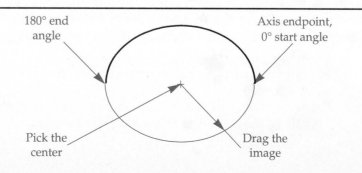

Setting the PELLIPSE system variable

PELLIPSE is an AutoCAD system variable having a value of either 0 or 1. When the value is 0, the object created using the **ELLIPSE** command is a true elliptical object. A true elliptical object can be grip edited while keeping the object elliptical. Grip editing is discussed in Chapter 12 of this text. If the **PELLIPSE** value is 1, the object created is a polyline ellipse. An elliptical polyline can be grip edited or edited with the **PEDIT** command, with each vertex able to move without maintaining the elliptical shape. The **Arc** option of the **ELLIPSE** command is not available when **PELLIPSE** is set to 1. The AutoCAD default is 0, but entering PELLIPSE and then entering 1 at the New value for PELLIPSE ⟨0⟩: prompt changes the value.

EXERCISE 5-6

❏ Begin a new drawing or use one of your templates.
❏ Use the **Arc** option of the **ELLIPSE** command to draw the following elliptical arcs:
  ❏ Use axis endpoints, axis distance, start angle = 0, and end angle = 90; similar to Figure 5-27.
  ❏ Use the same options as in the previous instructions to draw a 0° to 180° arc, 0° to 270° arc, and a 90° to 270° arc similar to the samples in Figure 5-27.
  ❏ Use the **Parameter** option to draw an elliptical arc of your own design.
  ❏ Use the **Rotation** option to rotate an elliptical arc 45° about its axis.
  ❏ Use the **Included** option to draw an elliptical arc with a 180° included angle and another with a 90° included angle.
  ❏ Use the **Center** option to draw an elliptical arc of your own design.
❏ Save the drawing as EX5-6 and quit.

POLYGON
POL

Draw
↳ Polygon

Draw
toolbar

Polygon

Drawing Regular Polygons

A *regular polygon* is any closed-plane geometric figure with three or more equal sides and equal angles. For example, a hexagon is a six-sided regular polygon. This command is used to draw any regular polygon with up to 1024 sides.

The **POLYGON** command can be accessed by selecting **Polygon** from the **Draw** pull-down menu, picking the **Polygon** button in the **Draw** toolbar, or entering POL or POLYGON at the Command: prompt. Regardless of the method used to select the command, you are first prompted for the number of sides. If you want an octagon (polygon with eight sides), enter 8 as follows:

> Command: **POL** *or* **POLYGON**↵
> Number of sides ⟨*current*⟩: **8**↵

The number of sides you enter becomes the default for the next time you use the **POLYGON** command. Next, AutoCAD prompts for the edge or center of the polygon. If you reply by picking a point on the screen, this point becomes the center of the polygon. You are then asked if you want to have the polygon inscribed within, or circumscribed outside of, an imaginary circle. See Figure 5-29. A polygon is *inscribed* when it is drawn inside a circle and its corners touch the circle. *Circumscribed* polygons are drawn outside of a circle where the sides of the polygon are tangent to the circle. You must then specify the radius of the circle. The command continues as follows:

> Edge/⟨Center of polygon⟩: *(pick center of polygon)*
> Inscribed in circle/Circumscribed about circle (I/C): *(respond with I or C and press [Enter])*
> Radius of circle: *(type the radius, such as 2 and press [Enter], or pick a point on the screen at the desired distance from the center)*

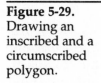

Figure 5-29.
Drawing an inscribed and a circumscribed polygon.

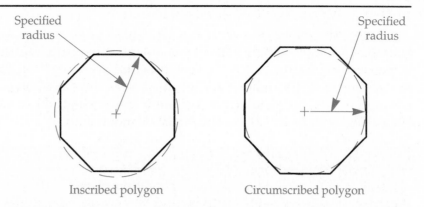

Specified radius   Specified radius

Inscribed polygon   Circumscribed polygon

The **I** or **C** option you select becomes the default for the next polygon. The Edge/⟨Center of polygon⟩: prompt allows you to pick the center or specify the edge. Notice that ⟨Center of polygon⟩ is the default. If you want to draw the polygon on an existing edge, specify the **Edge** option and pick edge endpoints as follows:

> Edge/⟨Center of polygon⟩: **E**↵
> First endpoint of edge: *(pick a point)*
> Second endpoint of edge: *(pick second point)*

After you pick the endpoints of one side, the rest of the polygon sides are drawn counterclockwise.

Polygons are polylines and can be easily edited using the **PEDIT** (polyline edit) command, which is discussed in Chapter 17 of this text. For example, a polygon can be given width using the **Width** option of the **PEDIT** command.

Hexagons (six-sided polygons) are commonly drawn as bolt heads and nuts on mechanical drawings. Keep in mind that these features are normally dimensioned across the flats. To draw a polygon to be dimensioned across the flats, circumscribe it. The radius you enter is equal to one-half the distance across the flats. The distance across the corners (inscribed polygon) is specified when the polygon must be confined within a circular area. One example is the boundary of a swimming pool in architectural drafting. Notice the distance across the flats and the distance across the corners in Figure 5-30.

Figure 5-30.
Specifying the distance across the flats and between corners of a polygon.

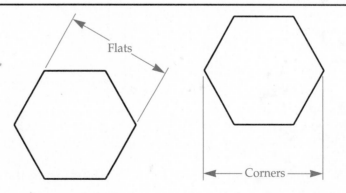

Flats

Corners

Setting the number of polygon sides

AutoCAD allows you to set the default number of polygon sides with the **POLYSIDES** system variable. This value can be set in your template for future use, but is automatically reset to 4 in a new drawing. Type POLYSIDES at the Command: prompt and enter the number of default sides for the **POLYGON** command. The value you specify for the default is used until you change the value again using the **POLYSIDES** system variable or the **POLYGON** command.

EXERCISE 5-7

❏ Begin a new drawing or use one of your templates.
❏ Draw a hexagon with a distance of three units across the flats. Then draw another hexagon measuring three units across the corners.
❏ Draw an octagon with a horizontal edge that is 1.75 units long.
❏ Draw a pentagon circumscribed about a circle having a 2.25 diameter.
❏ Save the drawing as EX5-7 and quit.

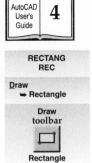

RECTANG
REC

Draw
➥ Rectangle

Draw
toolbar

Rectangle

Drawing Rectangles

AutoCAD's **RECTANG** command allows you to easily draw rectangles. When using this command, pick one corner and then the opposite corner. See Figure 5-31. The **RECTANG** command can be accessed by picking **Rectangle** in the **Draw** pull-down menu, by picking the **Rectangle** button in the **Draw** toolbar, or entering REC or RECTANG at the Command: prompt:

Command: **REC** or **RECTANG.**↵
Chamfer/Elevation/Fillet/Thickness/Width/⟨First corner⟩: *(select the first corner of the rectangle)*
Other corner: *(select the second corner)*
Command:

Figure 5-31.
Using the **RECTANG** command. Simply pick opposite corners of the rectangle.

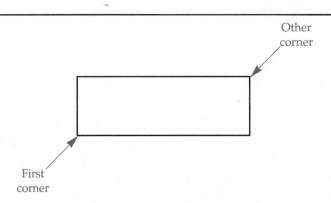

Rectangles are polylines and can be edited using the **PEDIT** command. Since a rectangle is a polyline, it is treated as one entity until exploded. After it is exploded, the individual sides can then be edited separately. The **EXPLODE** command is discussed in Chapter 17 of this text.

Drawing rectangles with line width

The **Width** option of the **RECTANG** command is used to adjust the width of the rectangle in the XY plane. Setting line width for rectangles is similar to setting width for polylines, which is discussed in Chapters 16 and 17.

The following sequence is used to create a rectangle with .03 wide lines:

Command: **REC** *or* **RECTANG**↵
Chamfer/Elevation/Fillet/Thickness/Width/⟨First corner⟩: **W**↵
Width for rectangles⟨*current*⟩: **.03**↵

You can press [Enter] at the Width for rectangles: prompt to have the rectangle polylines drawn with the default polyline width. If you enter a value at this prompt, the polylines are drawn with that additional width.

After setting the rectangle width, you can either select another option or draw the rectangle. Continue selecting options until you have set the characteristics correctly, then draw the rectangle.

Drawing chamfered rectangles

A *chamfer* is an angled corner on an object. Drawing chamfers is covered in detail in Chapter 11 of this text. This is a brief introduction to drawing chamfers on rectangles. To draw chamfers on rectangles, use the **Chamfer** option of the **RECTANG** command. The rectangle created will have chamfers drawn automatically.

After you select the **Chamfer** option, you must provide the chamfer distances, Figure 5-32. The command sequence is as follows:

Command: **REC** *or* **RECTANG**↵
Chamfer/Elevation/Fillet/Thickness/Width/⟨First corner⟩: **C**↵
First chamfer distance for rectangles ⟨*current*⟩: *(enter the first chamfer distance)*
Second chamfer distance for rectangles ⟨*current*⟩: *(enter the second chamfer distance)*

Figure 5-32.
A chamfer is an angled corner. An example of chamfer distance.

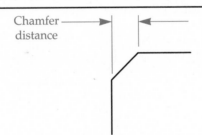

After setting the chamfer distances, you can either draw the rectangle or select another option. If you select the **Fillet** option, the chamfers will not be drawn.

The default chamfer distances are the chamfer distances or fillet radius used to draw the previous rectangle. If the default for the first chamfer distance is zero and you enter a different value, the new distance becomes the default for the second chamfer distance. However, if the default chamfer distances are nonzero values, a new value entered for the first distance does *not* become the default for the second distance.

Drawing filleted rectangles

A *fillet* is a slightly rounded corner on an object, Figure 5-33. Drawing fillets is covered in detail in Chapter 11 of this text. This is a brief introduction to drawing fillets on rectangles.

Figure 5-33.
A fillet is a rounded corner.

Fillet radius

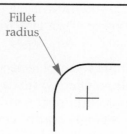

Fillets are automatically drawn on rectangles using the **Fillet** option of the **RECTANG** command. After selecting the option, you must enter the fillet radius:

Command: **REC** *or* **RECTANG.**↵
Chamfer/Elevation/Fillet/Thickness/Width/⟨First corner⟩: **F**↵
Fillet radius for rectangles ⟨*current*⟩: *(Enter a fillet radius or press* [Enter] *to accept the default)*

The default fillet radius is the radius of the previously drawn rectangle. Once a fillet radius is specified, the **RECTANG** command will automatically draw fillets on rectangles. In order to draw rectangles without fillets, the fillet radius must be set to 0. Figure 5-34 shows examples of rectangles drawn with chamfers and fillets.

Figure 5-34.
A—A rectangle drawn with chamfers.
B—A rectangle drawn with fillets.

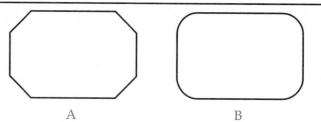

A   B

Additional **RECTANG** options

There are two other options available when using the **RECTANG** command. These options remain effective for multiple uses of the command:

- **Elevation.** This option sets the elevation of the rectangle along the Z axis. The default value is 0.
- **Thickness.** This option gives the rectangle depth along the Z axis (into the screen). The default value is 0.

A combination of these options can be used to draw a single rectangle. For example, a rectangle can have fillets and a 0.3 line width.

EXERCISE 5-8

❏ Begin a new drawing or use one of your templates.
❏ Use the **RECTANG** command to draw a rectangle.
❏ Use the **RECTANG** command to draw a rectangle with .03 line width.
❏ Use the **RECTANG** command to draw rectangles similar to Figure 5-34.
❏ Save the drawing as EX5-8.

AutoCAD and its Applications—Basics

Drawing Doughnuts and Solid Circles

Doughnuts drawn in AutoCAD are actually circular polylines. Drawing polylines is introduced in Chapter 16, and is covered in detail in Chapter 17. The **DONUT** command allows you to draw a thick circle. It can have any inside and outside diameter, or be completely filled. See Figure 5-35. The **DONUT** command can be accessed by selecting **Donut** from the **Draw** pull-down menu, or by entering DO, DONUT, or DOUGHNUT at the Command: prompt as follows:

Command: **DO**, **DONUT**, *or* **DOUGHNUT**↵
Inside diameter ⟨*current*⟩: *(specify a new inside diameter, or press* [Enter] *to accept the current value)*
Outside diameter ⟨*current*⟩: *(specify a new outside diameter, or press* [Enter] *to accept the current value)*
Center of doughnut: *(select the doughnut center point)*
Center of doughnut: *(select the center point for another doughnut, or press* [Enter] *to discontinue the command)*

Figure 5-35.
Examples of doughnuts.

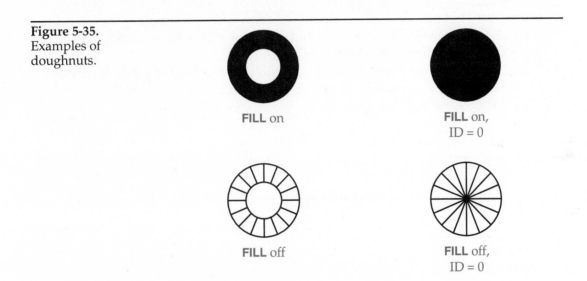

FILL on

FILL on,
ID = 0

FILL off

FILL off,
ID = 0

The current diameter settings are shown in brackets. New diameters can be entered, or press the [Enter] key to keep the current value. A 0 inside diameter produces a solid circle.

After selecting the center point, the doughnut appears on the screen. You may pick another center point to draw the same size doughnut in a new location. The **DONUT** command remains active until you press [Enter] or cancel by pressing [Esc].

When the **FILL** mode is turned off, doughnuts appear as segmented circles or concentric circles. **FILL** can be used transparently by entering 'FILL while inside the **DONUT** command. Then, enter ON or OFF as needed. The fill in previously drawn doughnuts remains on until the drawing is regenerated.

Presetting the DONUT options

AutoCAD allows you to preset the **DONUT** options so the inside and outside diameters have defaults. This saves time when you plan to draw only doughnuts with a given inside and outside diameter. To set **DONUT** to automatically issue a default inside and outside diameter, use the **DONUTID** and **DONUTOD** system variables. The **DONUTID** variable can be any value, including 0. The **DONUTOD** variable must be a nonzero value. If **DONUTID** is larger than **DONUTOD**, the two values are reversed by the next **DONUT** command. To set these variables, simply type the variable name at the Command: prompt, enter the desired setting, and press [Enter].

EXERCISE 5-9

❑ Begin a new drawing or use one of your templates.
❑ Draw a doughnut with a .5 inside diameter and a 1.5 outside diameter.
❑ Draw a doughnut with a 0 inside diameter and a 1.5 outside diameter.
❑ Turn the **FILL** mode off and enter REGEN to see what happens to the doughnuts.
❑ Set **DONUTID** to .25 and **DONUTOD** to .75.
❑ Enter DONUT at the Command: prompt and draw a doughnut using the defaults.
❑ Use a transparent **FILL** command (**'FILL**) to turn **FILL** on while in the **DONUT** command. Now, draw two more doughnuts.
❑ Select **Donut** from the **Draw** pull-down menu and draw three more doughnuts. Notice the inside and outside presets you set earlier are automatically used.
❑ Save the drawing as EX5-9 and quit.

Chapter Test

Write your answers in the spaces provided.

1. Give the command, entries, and actions required to draw a circle with a 2.5 unit diameter:

   Command: _____

   3P/2P/TTR/〈Center point〉: _____

   Diameter/〈Radius〉: _____

   Diameter: _____

2. Give the command, entries, and actions to draw a 1.75 unit radius circle tangent to an existing line and circle:

   Command: _____

   3P/2P/TTR/〈Center point〉: _____

   Enter Tangent spec: _____

   Enter second Tangent spec: _____

   Radius: _____

3. Give the command, entries, and actions needed to draw a three-point arc:

   Command: _____

   Center/〈Start point〉: _____

   Center/End/〈Second point〉: _____

   End point: _____

4. Give the command, entries, and actions needed to draw an arc, beginning with the center point and having a 60° included angle:

Command: _____

Center/⟨Start point⟩: _____

Center: _____

Start point: _____

Angle/Length of chord/⟨End point⟩: _____

Included angle: _____

5. Give the command, entries, and actions required to draw an arc tangent to the endpoint of a previously drawn line:

Command: _____

Center/⟨Start point⟩: _____

End point: _____

6. Give the command, entries, and actions needed to draw an ellipse with the **Axis, End** option:

Command: _____

Axis/Center/⟨Axis endpoint 1⟩: _____

Axis endpoint 2: _____

⟨Other axis distance⟩/Rotation: _____

7. Give the command, entries, and actions necessary to draw a hexagon measuring 4" (102mm) across the flats:

Command: _____

Number of sides: _____

Edge/⟨Center of polygon⟩: _____

Inscribed in circle/Circumscribed about circle (I/C): _____

Radius of circle: _____

8. Give the responses required to draw two doughnuts with a .25 inside diameter and a .75 outside diameter:

Command: _____

Inside diameter ⟨*current*⟩: _____

Outside diameter ⟨*current*⟩: _____

Center of doughnut: _____

Center of doughnut: _____

Center of doughnut: _____

9. Describe why the @ symbol can be used by itself for point selection. _____

_____

_____

_____

_____

_____

10. Define the term *included angle*. _____

    _____

11. List the three input options that can be used to draw an arc tangent to the end-point of a previously drawn arc. _____

    _____

    _____

12. Given the distance across the flats of a hexagon, would you use the **Inscribed** or **Circumscribed** option to draw the hexagon? _____

    _____

13. Describe how a solid circle can be drawn. _____

    _____

    _____

14. To use the **MULTIPLE** command modifier to draw a series of arcs, what command do you type? _____

    _____

15. Identify how to access the option that allows you to draw a circle tangent to three objects. _____

    _____

    _____

16. Describe the purpose of the **Copy Rad** option._____

    _____

    _____

    _____

17. Identify two ways to access the **Arc** option for drawing elliptical arcs._____

    _____

    _____

    _____

18. Name the AutoCAD system variable that lets you draw a true ellipse or a poly-line ellipse with the **ELLIPSE** command. _____

19. Name the pull-down menu where the **RECTANG** command is found. _____

    _____

20. What is the default option if the **ARC** command is typed at the Command: prompt?

    _____

21. Name the AutoCAD system variable that allows AutoCAD to automatically calculate the radius of the current circle and use this value as the default for the next circle.

    _____

22. Give the easiest keyboard shortcut for the following commands:

CIRCLE _____

ARC _____

ELLIPSE _____

POLYGON _____

RECTANG _____

DONUT _____

23. Name the command option that is designed specifically for drawing rectangles with line width. _____

24. Name the command option that is used to draw rectangles with rounded corners.

_____

25. Describe how you would draw a rectangle with different chamfer distances at each corner. _____

_____

26. What is the **ELLIPSE** rotation angle that causes you to draw a circle? _____

27. Explain how to turn the **FILL** mode off while inside the **DONUT** command. _____

_____

_____

28. Name the system variable used to set the default radius when drawing circles.

_____

29. Name the system variables used to preset the inside and outside donut diameters.

_____

Drawing Problems

Start AutoCAD and use one of the setup options or use a template. Do not draw dimensions or text. Use your own judgment and approximate dimensions if needed.

1. You have just been given the sketch of a new sports car design (shown below). You are asked to create a drawing from the sketch. Use the **LINE** command and selected shape commands to draw the car. Do not be concerned with size and scale. Consider the commands and techniques used to draw the car, and try to minimize the number of entities. Save your drawing as P5-1.

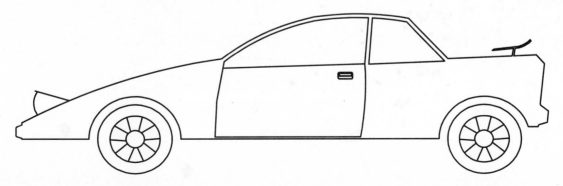

2. Use the **LINE** and **CIRCLE** command options to draw the objects below. Do not include dimensions. Save the drawing as P5-2.

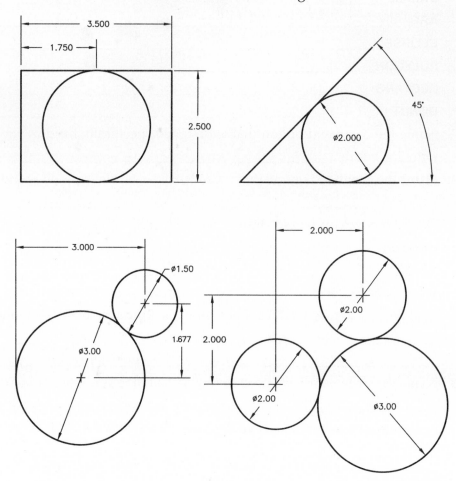

3. Use **CIRCLE** and **ARC** command options to draw the object below. Do not include dimensions. Save the drawing as P5-3.

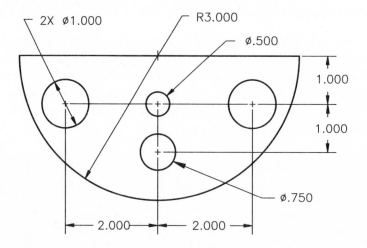

AutoCAD and its Applications—Basics

4. Draw the pressure cylinder shown below. Use the **Arc** option of the **ELLIPSE** command to draw the cylinder ends. Do not draw the dimensions. Save the drawing as P5-4.

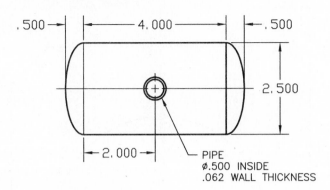

PIPE
∅.500 INSIDE
.062 WALL THICKNESS

5. Draw the hex head bolt pattern shown below. Do not draw dimensions. Save the drawing as P5-5.

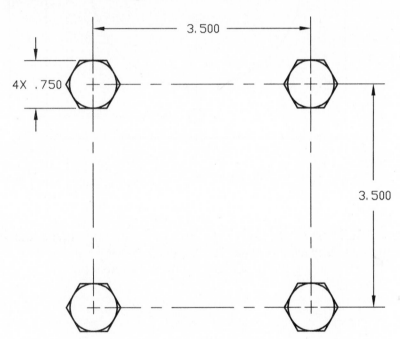

6. Draw the following object. Do not include dimensions.

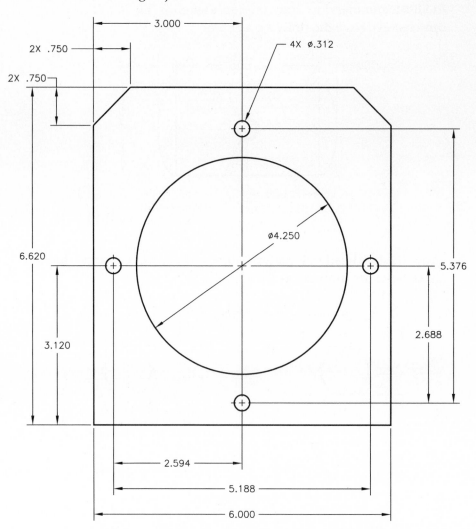

7. Draw the following object. Do not include dimensions.

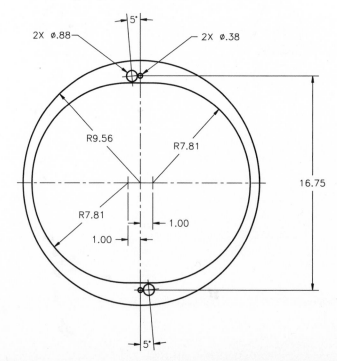

8. Draw the spacer below. Do not draw the dimensions.

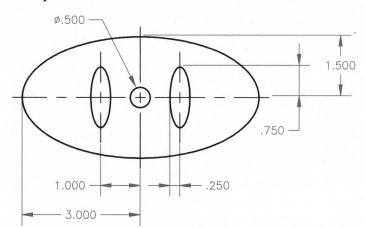

9. Create this controller integrated circuit diagram. Use a rule or scale to keep the proportion as close as possible. Do not include the text.

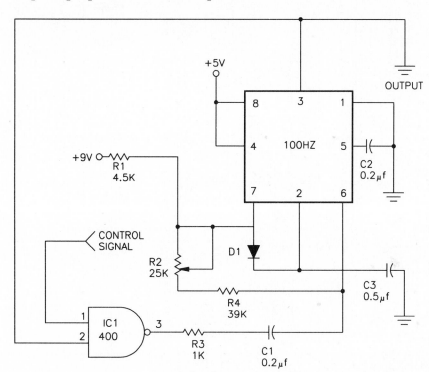

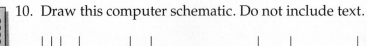

10. Draw this computer schematic. Do not include text.

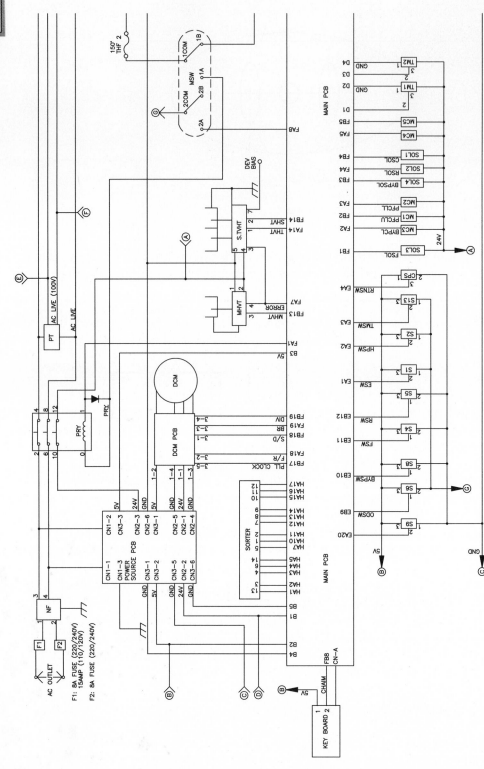

Object Snap, Geometric Constructions, and Multiview Drawings

Learning Objectives

After completing this chapter, you will be able to:
- ○ Use **OSNAP** command options to create precision drawings.
- ○ Use object snap overrides for single point selections.
- ○ Set running object snap modes for continuous use.
- ○ Describe the **Quick** object snap mode.
- ○ Adjust aperture size based on point selection needs.
- ○ Use the AutoSnap features to speed up point specifications.
- ○ Use the **OFFSET** command to draw parallel lines and curves.
- ○ Divide existing objects into equal distances using the **DIVIDE** command.
- ○ Use the **MEASURE** command to set designated increments on an existing object.
- ○ Use Tracking to locate points relative to other points in a drawing.
- ○ Use construction lines to assist in drawing multiviews and auxiliary views.

This chapter explains how the powerful **OSNAP** command features are used when creating and editing your drawing. **OSNAP** means *object snap*. Object snap allows you to instantly locate exact points relative to existing objects. A feature called *AutoSnap* can be used to visually preview and confirm snap point options prior to point selection. Other point selection methods, such as the Tracking tool and X and Y coordinate filters, allow you to locate points relative to existing points. This chapter continues with an explanation of how to create parallel offset copies, divide objects, and place point objects. Creating multiview drawings using orthographic projection and construction lines is also covered.

Snapping to Specific Features

Object snap is one of the most useful tools found in AutoCAD. It increases your drafting ability, performance, and productivity. The term *object snap* refers to the cursor's ability to "snap" exactly to a specific point or place on an object. The advantage of object snap is that you do not have to pick an exact point.

The AutoSnap feature is enabled by default. With AutoSnap active, visual cues are displayed while using object snap. This helps you in visualizing and confirming object snap candidate points.

These visual cues appear as markers displayed at the current selection point. Figure 6-1 shows two examples of visual cues provided by AutoSnap. The endpoint of a line object is being picked in Figure 6-1A. The visual cue for an endpoint object snap is shown as a square when the cursor is placed close to the line object. After a brief pause, a SnapTip is displayed. A *SnapTip* is a text listing at the cursor similar to the ToolTips displayed when pointing to toolbar buttons. In Figure 6-1B, a point that is tangent to an existing circle is being selected. The AutoSnap symbol for a tangency point is shown as a circle with a tangent horizontal line.

The default settings for AutoSnap are used for this discussion of the object snap features. Changing AutoSnap settings and features is discussed later in this chapter.

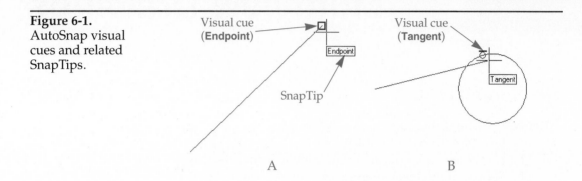

Figure 6-1.
AutoSnap visual cues and related SnapTips.

The Object Snap Modes

The object snap modes determine the point to which the cursor snaps. These modes can be activated using one of several different methods. An object snap override can be typed at the prompt line or selected from the *cursor menu*, shown in Figure 6-2. This menu is activated by first holding down the [Shift] key and then right-clicking your mouse or picking the [Enter] button on your puck. Object snap overrides are also available as buttons in the **Object Snap** toolbar, Figure 6-3. To activate the **Object Snap** toolbar, select **Toolbars...** from the **View** pull-down menu. Then, select **Object Snap** in the **Toolbars** dialog box.

Figure 6-2.
The cursor menu provides quick access to object snap overrides.

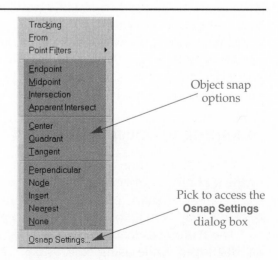

Figure 6-3.
The **Object Snap** toolbar.

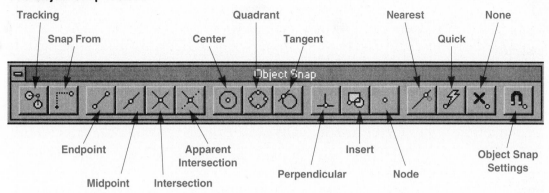

Object snap override refers to the entry of an object snap mode at a point specification prompt. A *point specification prompt* is any prompt that asks you to enter or pick a point coordinate. Object snap overrides are active for one point specification only, and they override any previously set object snap modes for that one entry.

A *running object snap* stays active for all point selections until it is changed. Running object snap modes are discussed later in this section.

NOTE   When AutoCAD is configured to display screen menus, the object snap modes screen menu can be accessed by picking "****" near the top of the current screen menu.

The table in Figure 6-4 summarizes the object snap modes. Included with each mode is the visual cue that appears on-screen and its button from the **Object Snap** toolbar. Each object snap mode selects a different portion of an object. When activated from the prompt line, only the first three letters are required.

Figure 6-4.
The object snap modes.

Object Snap Modes			
Mode	**Visual Cue**	**Button**	**Description**
Endpoint	☐		Finds the nearest endpoint of a line, arc, elliptical arc, spline, ellipse, ray, solid, or multiline.
Midpoint	△		Finds the middle point of any object having two endpoints, such as a line, arc, elliptical arc, spline, ellipse, ray, solid, xline, or multiline.
Center	○		Locates the center point of a radial object, including circles, arcs, ellipses, elliptical arcs, and radial solids.
Quadrant	◇		Picks the closest of the four quadrant points that can be found on circles, arcs, elliptical arcs, ellipses, and radial solids. (Not all of these objects may have all four quadrants.)
Intersection	✕		Picks the closest intersection of two objects.
Apparent Intersection	⊠		Selects a visual intersection between two objects that appear to intersect on screen in the current view, but may not actually intersect each other in 3D space.

(Continued)

Figure 6-4.
The object snap modes. *(Continued)*

Object Snap Modes			
Mode	**Visual Cue**	**Button**	**Description**
Insertion			Finds the insertion point of text objects and blocks.
Perpendicular			Finds a point that is perpendicular to an object from the previously picked point.
Tangent			Finds points of tangency between radial and linear objects.
Nearest			Locates the point on an object closest to the crosshairs.
Node			Picks a point object drawn with the **POINT** command.
None			Turns running object snap off.

PROFESSIONAL TIP
Remember that object snap overrides are not commands, but are used in conjunction with commands. If you type MID or PER at the Command: prompt, AutoCAD displays an "Unknown Command" error message.

Practice with the different object snap options to find which works best in various situations. Object snap can be used during many commands, such as **LINE**, **CIRCLE**, **ARC**, **MOVE**, **COPY**, and **INSERT**. The most common object snap uses are discussed in the following sections.

Endpoint object snap

In many cases, you need to connect a line, arc, or center point of a circle to the endpoint of an existing line or arc. Select the **Endpoint** object snap option and move the cursor past the midpoint of the line or arc toward the end to be picked. A small square marks the endpoint that will be picked.

In Figure 6-5, the following command sequence is used to connect a line to the endpoint of an existing line:

> Command: **L** *or* **LINE**↵
> From point: *(pick a point)*
> To point: *(pick the* **Endpoint** *button, type* END, *or pick* **Endpoint** *from the cursor menu)*
> of *(move the cursor near the end of line A and pick)*
> To point: ↵
> Command:

The **Endpoint** object snap can be used to quickly select the endpoints of all types of lines and arcs. It is often selected as a running object snap.

Figure 6-5.
Using **Endpoint**
object snap.

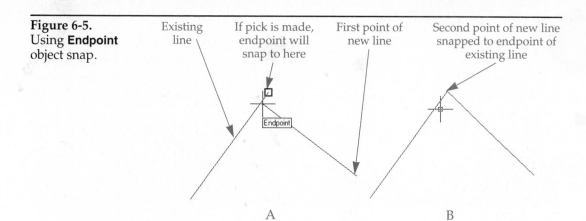

Midpoint object snap

The **Midpoint** mode finds and picks the midpoint of a line, polyline, or arc. Type MID at the prompt, pick the **Midpoint** button, or select **Midpoint** from the cursor menu to activate this object snap. Then position the cursor near the midpoint of the object, and a small triangle marks the midpoint where the line will snap. See Figure 6-6.

Figure 6-6.
Using **Midpoint**
object snap.

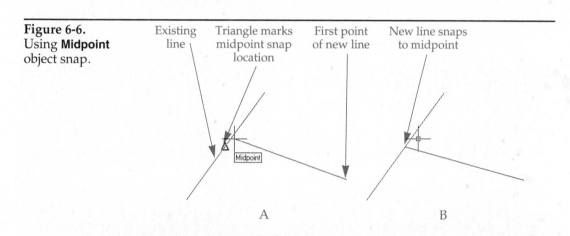

EXERCISE 6-1

❏ Start AutoCAD and use the setup option of your choice.
❏ Use the **Endpoint** and **Midpoint** object snap modes to draw the object shown below. Draw line 1, then line 2 connecting to the endpoint of line 1. Draw line 3 from the endpoint of line 2 to the midpoint of line 1. Draw arc A with one end connected to the endpoint of line 1.
❏ Save the drawing as EX6-1.

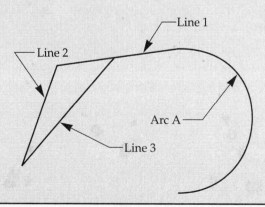

Center object snap

The **Center** option allows you to snap to the center point of a circle, doughnut, ellipse, elliptical arc, or arc. The mode is activated by typing CEN at the selection prompt, picking the **Center** button, or picking **Center** from the cursor menu. Then move the cursor onto the object whose center point is to be located. A small circle marks the center point.

Be sure to move the cursor near the object, not the center point of the object. For example, when locating the center of a large circle, the **Center** object snap mode will *not* locate the center if the cursor isn't near the circle. Even if the cursor is over the center of the circle, it may not be near enough to the circle to activate the snap point. In Figure 6-7, the **Center** object snap is used to draw a line to the center of a circle.

Figure 6-7.
Using **Center** object snap.

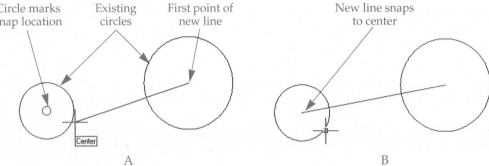

Circle marks snap location   Existing circles   First point of new line   New line snaps to center

Center

A   B

Quadrant object snap

A *quadrant* is a quarter section of a circle, doughnut, ellipse, elliptical arc, or arc. The **Quadrant** object snap mode finds the 0°, 90°, 180°, and 270° positions on a circle, doughnut, or arc, Figure 6-8.

Figure 6-8.
The quadrants of a circle.

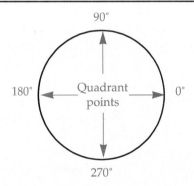

90°

180°   Quadrant points   0°

270°

When picking quadrants, locate the aperture on the circle, doughnut, or arc near the intended quadrant. For example, Figure 6-9 illustrates use of the **Quadrant** object snap mode to locate the center point of a new circle at the quadrant of an existing circle. The command sequence is as follows:

Command: **C** *or* **CIRCLE**↵
3P/2P/TTR/⟨Center point⟩: *(pick the **Quadrant** button, type QUA, or pick **Quadrant** from the cursor menu)*
of *(move the cursor to anywhere near the desired quadrant and pick)*
Diameter/⟨Radius⟩: *(pick a radius)*

Figure 6-9.
Using **Quadrant**
object snap.

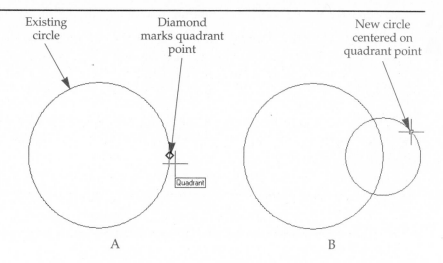

 NOTE   Quadrant positions are unaffected by the current angle zero direction, but always coincide with the current UCS (User Coordinate System). The UCS is discussed later in this chapter. The quadrant points of a circle, doughnut, or arc are at the top, bottom, left, and right, regardless of the rotation of the object. However, the quadrant points of ellipses and elliptical arcs rotate with the object.

EXERCISE 6-2

❏ Start AutoCAD and use the setup option of your choice.
❏ Use the **Center** and **Quadrant** object snap modes for the following:
   ❏ Draw two separate circles and refer to the one on the left as circle A and the other as circle B.
   ❏ Draw a line from the center of circle A to the 180° quadrant of circle B.
   ❏ Draw a line from the center of circle B to the 270° quadrant of circle B to the 270° of circle A, and finally to the center of circle A.
❏ Save the drawing as EX6-2.

Intersection object snap

The **Intersection** option is used to snap to the intersection of two or more objects. This mode is activated by typing INT at the selection prompt, picking the **Intersect** button, or picking **Intersection** from the cursor menu. Then move the cursor near the intersection. A small "X" marks the intersection. See Figure 6-10.

Figure 6-10.
Using **Intersection**
object snap.

Second point
will snap to this
intersection

First point of
new line

Existing line
and arc

Intersection

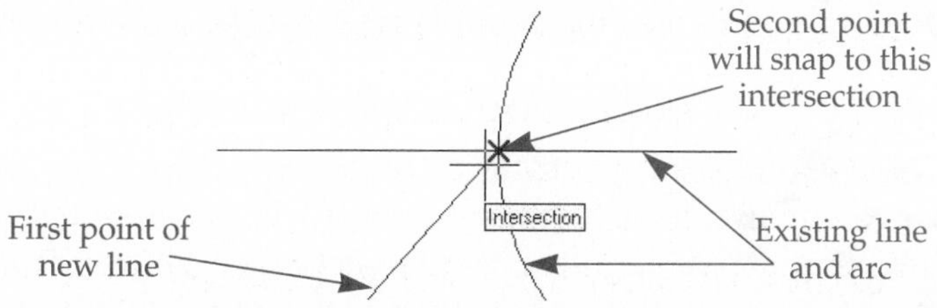

When picking a point for an **Intersection** object snap, the "X" appears only when the cursor is close to the intersection point of two objects. If the cursor is near an object, but not close to an actual intersection, the SnapTip reads Extended Intersection, and the AutoSnap symbol is followed by an ellipsis (...). When using **Extended Intersection**, you can select the objects one at a time and then the intersection point is found. This is especially useful when two objects do not actually intersect, and you need to access the point where these objects would intersect if they were extended. Figure 6-11 shows the use of **Extended Intersection** to find an intersection point between a line and an arc.

Figure 6-11.
Finding the extended intersection of two objects. A—Select the first object.
B—When the second object is selected, the extended intersection becomes the snap point.
C—The completed line.

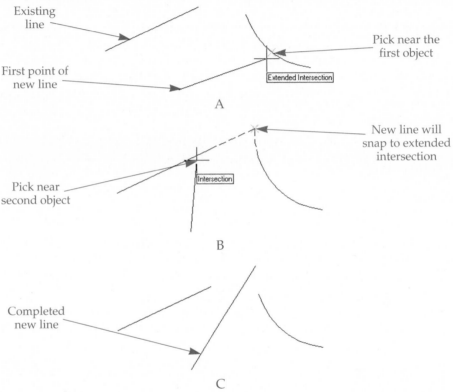

If the intersection point is not in the currently visible screen area, then the AutoSnap marker is not displayed when pointing to the second object. However, AutoSnap still allows you to confirm the point before picking. Keeping the cursor motionless for a moment still displays the SnapTip, and this supports the fact that the two objects do actually intersect somewhere beyond the currently visible area. When selecting two objects that could not intersect, no AutoSnap marker or SnapTip is displayed, and no intersection point is found if the pick is made.

Apparent intersection object snap

The *apparent intersection* is the point where two objects created in 3D space appear to intersect based on the currently displayed view. Three-dimensional objects that are far apart may appear to intersect when viewed from certain angles. Whether they intersect or not, this option returns the coordinate point where the objects appear to intersect. This is a valuable option when working with 3D drawings. Creating and editing 3D objects is discussed in Chapter 27.

Perpendicular object snap

A common geometric construction is to draw one object perpendicular to another. This is done using the **Perpendicular** object snap mode. This mode is activated by typing PER at the selection prompt, picking the **Perpendicular** button, or picking **Perpendicular** from the cursor menu. A small right-angle symbol appears at the snap point. This mode can be used with arcs, elliptical arcs, ellipses, splines, xlines, multi-lines, solids, traces, or circles.

Figure 6-12 shows an example of the **Perpendicular** object snap being used for the endpoint of a line. The endpoint is located so that the new line is perpendicular to the existing line. In Figure 6-13, the first point of the line is selected with the **Perpendicular** object snap. The SnapTip reads Deferred Perpendicular. The term *deferred perpendicular* means that the calculation of the perpendicular point is delayed until another point is picked. The second endpoint determines the location of the first endpoint.

Figure 6-12.
Drawing a line from a point perpendicular to an existing line.

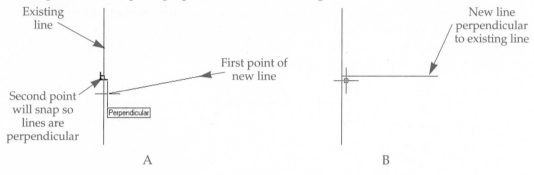

Figure 6-13.
Deferring the perpendicular location until the second point is selected.

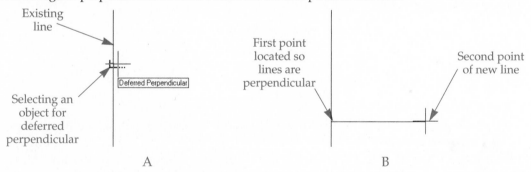

It is important to understand that perpendicularity is calculated from points picked, and not as a relationship between objects. Also, perpendicularity is measured at the point of intersection, so it is possible to draw a line that is perpendicular to a circle or an arc.

Tangent object snap

The **Tangent** object snap is similar to the **Perpendicular** object snap. However, instead of aligning the objects perpendicularly, it aligns objects tangentially. This mode is activated by typing TAN at the selection prompt, picking the **Tangent** button, or picking **Tangent** from the cursor menu. A small circle with a horizontal line appears at the snap point.

In Figure 6-14, the endpoint of a line is located using the **Tangent** mode. The first point is selected normally. Then the **Tangent** mode is activated and the cursor is placed near the tangent point on the circle. AutoCAD determines the tangent point and places the snap point (and the endpoint) there.

Figure 6-14.
Using **Tangent** object snap.

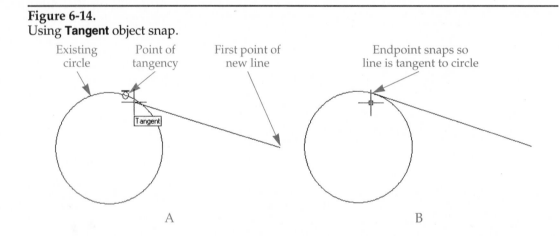

A   B

When creating an object that is tangent to another object, multiple points may be needed to fix the tangency point. For example, the point where a line is tangent to a circle cannot be found without knowing the locations of both ends of the line. Until both points have been specified, the object snap specification is for *deferred tangency*. Once both endpoints are known, the tangency is calculated and the object is drawn in the correct location. In Figure 6-15, a line is drawn tangent to two circles. The command sequence is as follows:

> Command: **L** *or* **LINE.**↵
> From point: *(pick the* **Tangent** *button, type* TAN, *or pick* **Tangent** *from the cursor menu.)*
> _tan to *(pick the first circle)*
> To point: *(pick the* **Tangent** *button, type* TAN, *or pick* **Tangent** *from the cursor menu.)*
> _tan to *(pick the second circle)*
> To point: ↵
> Command:

Figure 6-15.
Drawing a line
tangent to two
circles.

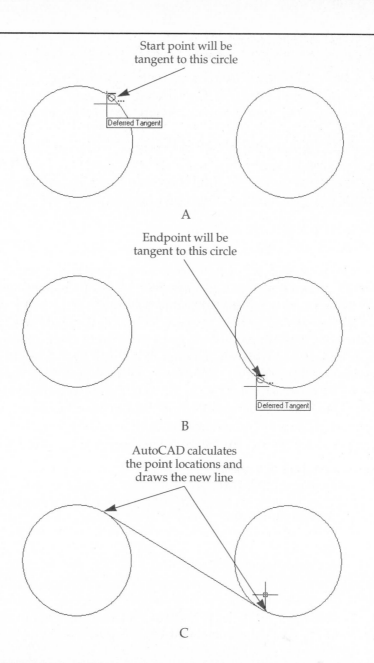

Start point will be
tangent to this circle

Deferred Tangent

A

Endpoint will be
tangent to this circle

Deferred Tangent

B

AutoCAD calculates
the point locations and
draws the new line

C

Node object snap

Point objects can be snapped to using the **Node** object snap mode. In order for object snap to find the point object, the point must be in a visible display mode. Controlling the point display mode is covered later in this chapter.

Nearest object snap

When you need to specify a point that is on an object but cannot be located with any of the other object snap modes, the **Nearest** mode can be used. This object snap locates the point on the object closest to the crosshair location. It should be used when you want an object to touch an existing object, but the location of the intersection is not critical.

Consider drawing a line object that is to end on another line. Trying to pick the point with the crosshairs is inaccurate because you are relying only on your screen and mouse resolution. The line you draw may fall short or extend past the line. Using **Nearest** ensures that the point is precisely on the object.

Using fast object snaps

When AutoCAD uses object snap modes, it searches the entire drawing database for the specified type of point nearest to the crosshairs. In a simple drawing, this process occurs very quickly. However, as your drawing becomes complex, it may take some time for the snap object to be found.

You can speed up the process by selecting the **Quick** object snap mode. To use this mode, select the **Quick** button from the **Object Snap** toolbar and then the desired object snap mode. You can also type QUI followed by a comma and the desired object snap option. The **Quick** mode directs AutoCAD to look only for the first point that satisfies the object snap mode. The only problem you may find is that the first AutoCAD selection may not be the best choice. However, in most cases the **Quick** mode works to your advantage and helps increase productivity. The following command sequence shows the **Quick** mode used on the example illustrated in Figure 6-15.

```
Command: L or LINE↵
From point: QUI,TAN↵
to (pick a point on the first circle near the intended point of tangency)
To point: QUI,TAN↵
to (pick a point on the second circle near the intended point of tangency)
To point: ↵
Command: ↵
```

NOTE   The **Quick** object snap mode is not effective for the **Intersection** object snap.

Using the From point selection option

The **From** point selection mode allows you to establish a relative, polar coordinate, or direct distance entry from a specified reference base point. Access the **From** option by selecting the **Snap From** button in the **Object Snap** toolbar, select **From** in the cursor menu, or type FRO at a point selection prompt. The example in Figure 6-16 shows the center point for a circle being established as a polar distance from the midpoint of an existing line. The command sequence is shown here:

```
Command: C or CIRCLE↵
3P/2P/TTR/⟨Center point⟩: FROM↵
Base point: MID↵
of (pick the line) ⟨offset⟩: @2⟨45↵
Diameter/⟨Radius⟩: .75↵
Command:
```

Figure 6-16.
Using the **From**
point selection
mode following the
command sequence
given in the text.

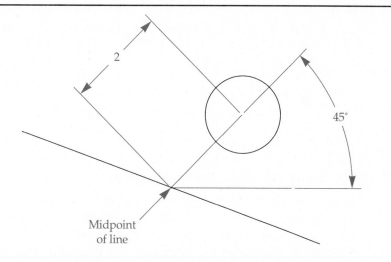

2

45°

Midpoint
of line

Setting Running Object Snaps

The previous discussion explained how to use object snaps by activating the individual mode at the selection prompt. However, if you plan to use object snaps continuously, you can set *running object snaps*. You preset the running object snap modes, and AutoCAD automatically activates them at all point selection prompts.

You can set a running object snap using the **Running Osnap** tab in the **Osnap Settings** dialog box. Pick **Object Snap Settings...** from the **Tools** pull-down menu, or pick the **Object Snap Settings** button from the **Object Snap** toolbar. You can also type OS, OSNAP, or DDOSNAP at the Command: prompt to access the dialog box.

The **Osnap Settings** dialog box is shown in Figure 6-17. Notice that the **Endpoint**, **Perpendicular**, and **Tangent** modes are active. You can use this dialog box at any time to discontinue a running object snap or to set additional modes.

DDOSNAP
OSNAP
OS

Tools
↳ Object Snap
Settings...

Object Snap
toolbar

Object Snap Settings

Figure 6-17.
Running object snap
modes can be set
using the **Osnap
Settings** dialog box.

Set running
object snap
modes

Deactivate
all modes

Change
aperature size

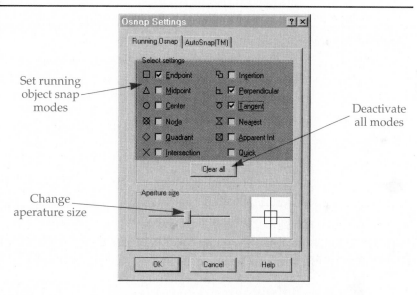

Toggling, disabling, and overriding running object snap

Running object snap is active at all point selection prompts, but is temporarily suspended when an object snap override is entered. The override is temporary, and is active for a single point selection only. Any currently running object snap mode is reactivated for the next pick.

To make a single point selection without the effects of any running object snap modes, enter the **None** object snap mode. When you need to make several point specifications without the aid of object snap, you can toggle it off by double-clicking the **OSNAP** button on the status bar at the bottom of the AutoCAD window. The advantages of this method are that you can make several picks, and you can restore the same running object snap modes by double-clicking **OSNAP** again.

You can remove the active checks in the **Osnap Settings** dialog box as needed to disable running object snaps. You can also pick the **Clear All** button to disable all running modes.

Using multiple object snap modes

As shown with the examples of running object snap, more than one object snap mode can be made active at once. When multiple modes are running at the same time, each of the modes is checked for possible points, and the closest point is selected.

For example, assume the **Endpoint** and **Midpoint** object snap modes are active. The AutoSnap marker locates either an endpoint or the midpoint of a line, depending on which is closest to the cursor location. This can cause conflicts between some object snap modes. For example, no matter where you pick a circle, the closest quadrant point is always closer than the center of the circle. This means that when quadrant and circle are both set active, a quadrant point is always selected.

The **Nearest** object snap mode causes conflicts with almost every other mode. The nearest mode does not move the selection point to a nearby feature of an object, but picks the point on the object closest to the current cursor location. This means that the **Nearest** mode always locates the closest point.

The **AutoSnap** tab in the **Osnap Settings** dialog box displays a tip, explaining that the [Tab] key can be used to cycle through available snap points. This works well when multiple object snap modes are active. For example, use this feature if you are trying to select the intersection between two objects where several other objects intersect nearby. To use this feature, when the AutoSnap marker appears, press the [Tab] key until the desired point is marked.

PROFESSIONAL TIP

By default, a keyboard entry of an absolute coordinate overrides any currently running object snap modes. This is controlled by the **OSNAPCOORD** system variable. The value of **OSNAPCOORD** can be set as follows:

- **0.** Running osnap settings override absolute coordinate entry.
- **1.** Keyboard entry overrides osnap settings.
- **2.** Keyboard entry overrides osnap settings except in scripts.

EXERCISE 6-5

❏ Start AutoCAD and use the setup option of your choice.
❏ Set the **Endpoint, Midpoint,** and **Perpendicular** running object snaps and practice using them in at least two situations. Drawings similar to Figure 6-5, Figure 6-6, and Figure 6-12 can be used.
❏ Change the running object snap to **Center** and **Tangent,** and use each twice in creating a simple drawing. Drawings similar to Figure 6-7 and Figure 6-15 can be used.
❏ Discontinue the running object snaps.
❏ Save the drawing as EX6-5.

Changing the aperture size

When selecting a point using object snap, the cursor must be within a specific range to a candidate point before it is located. The object snap detection system finds everything within a square area centered at the cursor location. This square area is called the *aperture* and is invisible by default.

To display the aperture, pick the **AutoSnap(TM)** tab (discussed on the following page) and activate the **Display aperture box** check box. Having the aperture visible may be helpful when you are first learning to work with object snap. To change the size of the aperture, go back to the **Running Osnap** tab and move the slider in the **Aperture size** area. Various aperture sizes are shown in Figure 6-18.

Figure 6-18.
Aperture box sizes are measured in pixels. The three examples here are not shown at actual size, but are provided to show the size relationship between different settings.

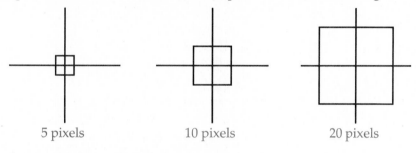

| 5 pixels | 10 pixels | 20 pixels |

The aperture size can also be set at the Command: prompt:

Command: **APERTURE.⏎**
Object snap target height (1-50 pixels) ⟨*current*⟩: **5.⏎**
Command:

The size of the aperture is measured in *pixels*. Pixels are the dots that make up a display screen.

Keep in mind that the *aperture* and the *pick box* are different. The aperture is displayed on the screen when object snap modes are active. The pick box appears on the screen for any command that activates the Select objects: prompt.

EXERCISE 6-6

❏ Open EX6-5.
❏ Display the aperture.
❏ Change the aperture size to 5 pixels. Draw lines to existing objects using the object snap modes of your choice.
❏ Change the aperture size to 20 pixels. Again, draw lines to the existing objects using the object snap modes of your choice.
❏ Observe the difference in aperture size. Determine your personal preference between the 5 and 20 pixel sizes as compared to the AutoCAD default of 10 pixels.
❏ Save the drawing as EX6-6.

AutoSnap Settings

The AutoSnap™ feature makes object snap much easier to use. However, if you do not wish to have the additional visual cues while using object snap, you can turn the AutoSnap feature off. AutoCAD also allows you to customize the appearance and functionality of the AutoSnap feature by using the **AutoSnap(TM)** tab in the **Osnap Settings** dialog box, shown in Figure 6-19. The settings are described as follows:

- **Marker.** Toggles the AutoSnap marker display.
- **Magnet.** Toggles the AutoSnap magnet. When active, the magnet snaps the cursor to the object snap point.
- **SnapTip.** Toggles the SnapTip display.
- **Display aperture box.** Toggles the display of the aperture.

The marker size and color can also be adjusted to suit your needs. For example, the default marker color is yellow, but this is difficult to see if you have the graphics screen background set to white. Pick the down arrow to access the **Marker color:** drop-down list, and select the desired color. At higher screen resolutions, a larger marker size improves visibility. Move the slider at the **Marker size:** area to change the size.

Figure 6-19.
Setting AutoSnap features.

AutoSnap options

Change marker size

Change marker color

EXERCISE 6-7

❏ Start AutoCAD and use the setup option of your choice.
❏ Open the **Osnap Settings** dialog box.
❏ Move the **Marker size:** slider and watch the image change to represent the marker size.
❏ Change the marker color to red.
❏ Use the newly revised marker size and color to draw objects of your choice with the object snaps.
❏ Save the drawing as EX6-7.

Using Tracking to Locate Points

Tracking is a system that allows you to visually locate points in a drawing relative to other points. Tracking creates a new point using the X coordinate of one tracking point and the Y coordinate of another. The tracking feature can be used at any point specification prompt, just like object snap. Tracking can also be used in combination with object snap.

To activate tracking, pick the **Tracking** button from the **Object Snap** toolbar, type TK or TRA at the point selection prompt, or pick **Tracking** from the cursor menu.

As an example, tracking can be used to place a circle at the center of a rectangle. See Figure 6-20. The center of the rectangle corresponds to the X coordinate of the midpoint of the horizontal lines. The Y coordinate corresponds to the Y coordinate of the vertical lines. Tracking can be used to combine these two points to find the center of the rectangle using this sequence:

Command: **C** *or* **CIRCLE**↵
3P/2P/TTR/<Center point>: **TRA**↵
First tracking point: **MID**↵
of *(pick one of the vertical lines and move the cursor horizontally)*
Next point (Press ENTER to end tracking): **MID**↵
of *(pick one of the horizontal lines)*
Next point (Press ENTER to end tracking): ↵
Diameter/<Radius> <0.2500>: ↵
Command:

Figure 6-20.
Using tracking to
locate the center of
a rectangle.

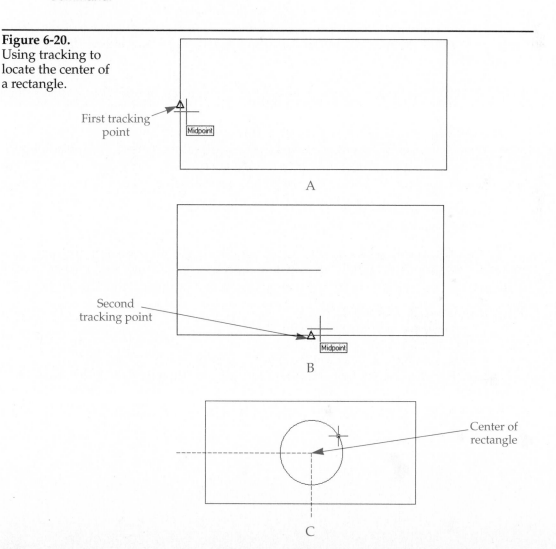

Once started, tracking remains active until you press [Enter] at a Next point: prompt. The direction of the orthogonal line determines whether the X or Y component is used. In the previous example, after picking the first tracking point, the cursor is moved horizontally. This means that the Y axis value of the previous point is being used and tracking is now ready for an X coordinate specification.

After moving the cursor horizontally, you may notice that movement is locked in a horizontal mode. If you need to move the cursor vertically, move the cursor back to the previously picked point and then drag vertically. Use this method any time you need to switch between horizontal and vertical movement.

EXERCISE 6-8

❏ Start AutoCAD and use the setup option of your choice.
❏ Draw a rectangle similar to the one in Figure 6-20.
❏ Use tracking to locate the center of the rectangle and draw a circle with its center at that location.
❏ Save the drawing as EX6-8.

Point filters

Tracking allows you to combine the X coordinate of one point and the Y coordinate of another point to locate a new point. You can also directly access the X or Y coordinates of a point by using point filters. *Filters* allow you to select any aspect of an object while filtering out other objects, items, or features.

There are many uses for filters. Filters used for layer control were introduced in Chapter 4. Point filters and object selection filters are completely discussed in Chapter 7.

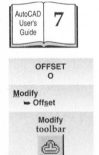

AutoCAD
User's   7
Guide

OFFSET
O

Modify
➥ Offset

Modify
toolbar

Offset

Drawing Parallel Lines and Curves

The **OFFSET** command can be used to draw concentric circles, arcs, curves, polylines, or parallel lines. This command is accessed by picking **Offset** in the **Modify** pull-down menu, picking the **Offset** button in the **Modify** toolbar, or typing O or OFFSET at the Command: prompt. When selected, the command produces the following prompt:

Command: **O** *or* **OFFSET**⏎
Offset distance or Through ⟨*current*⟩:

Type a distance or pick a point for the parallel object to be drawn through. The last offset distance used is shown in brackets. If you want to draw two parallel circles a distance of .1 unit apart, use the following command sequence. Refer to Figure 6-21.

Command: **O** *or* **OFFSET**⏎
Offset distance or Through ⟨*current*⟩: **.1**⏎
Select object to offset: *(pick the object)*
Side to offset? *(pick the side of the object for the offset to be drawn)*
Select object to offset: *(select another object or press* [Enter]*)*

Figure 6-21.
Drawing an offset
using a designated
distance.

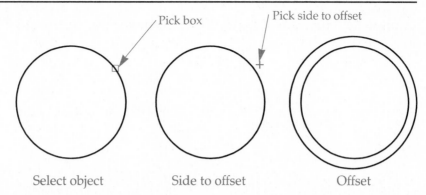

Figure 6-21.
Drawing an offset
using a designated
distance.

Pick box

Pick side to offset

Select object

Side to offset

Offset

When the Select object to offset: prompt first appears, the screen cursor turns into a pick box. After the object is picked, the screen cursor turns back into crosshairs. No other selection option (such as window or crossing) works with the **OFFSET** command.

The other option is to pick a point that the offset is drawn through. Type T as follows to produce the results shown in Figure 6-22:

Command: **O** *or* **OFFSET**↵
Offset distance or Through ⟨*current*⟩: **T**↵
Select object to offset: (*pick the object*)
Through point: (*pick the point that the offset will be drawn through*)
Select object to offset: ↵

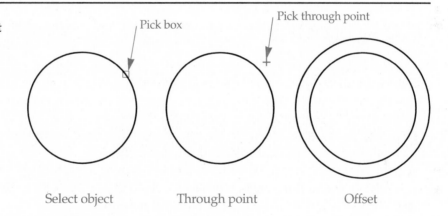

Figure 6-22.
Drawing an offset
through a given
point.

Pick box

Pick through point

Select object

Through point

Offset

Object snap modes can be used to assist in drawing an offset. For example, suppose you have a circle and a line and want to draw a concentric circle tangent to the line. Refer to Figure 6-23 and the following command sequence:

Command: **O** *or* **OFFSET**↵
Offset distance or Through ⟨current⟩: **QUA**↵
of (*pick the existing circle*)
Second point: **PER**↵
to (*pick the existing line*)
Select object to offset: (*pick the existing circle*)
Side to offset? (*pick between the circle and line*)
Select object to offset: ↵
Command:

Figure 6-23.
Using **OFFSET** to draw a concentric circle tangent to a line.

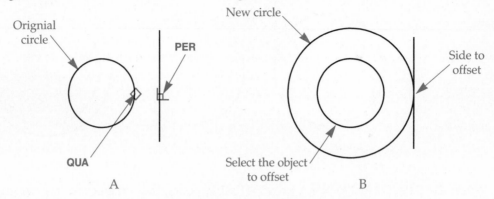

EXERCISE 6-9

❏ Start AutoCAD and use the setup option of your choice.
❏ Draw two circles and two objects made up of line and arc segments.
❏ Use the **OFFSET** command to draw parallels a distance of .2 units on the inside of one circle and one arc-line object.
❏ Use the **OFFSET** command again, this time specifying **Through** point on the outside of the other circle and arc-line object.
❏ Save the drawing as EX6-9.

AutoCAD
User's **5**
Guide

DIVIDE
DIV

Draw
→ Point
  → Divide

Dividing an Object

A line, circle, arc, or polyline can be divided into an equal number of segments using the **DIVIDE** command. To start the **DIVIDE** command, select **Divide** from the **Point** cascading menu of the **Draw** pull-down menu, or type DIV or DIVIDE.

The **DIVIDE** command does not physically break an object into multiple parts. It places point objects or blocks at the locations where the breaks would occur if the object were actually divided into multiple segments.

Suppose you have drawn a line and want to divide it into eight equal parts. Enter the **DIVIDE** command and select the object to divide. Then, enter the number of segments. Refer to Figure 6-24. The procedure is as follows:

> Command: **DIV** or **DIVIDE.↵**
> Select object to divide: *(pick the object)*
> ⟨Number of segments⟩/Block: *(enter the number of divisions and press [Enter])*

Figure 6-24.
Using the **DIVIDE** command. Note that the default marks (points) have been changed to X's.

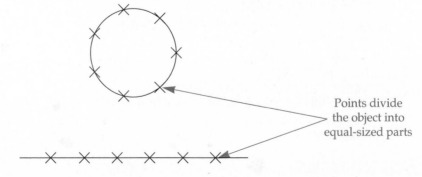

Points divide the object into equal-sized parts

The **Block** option of the **DIVIDE** command allows you to place a block at each division point. To initiate the **Block** option, type B at the prompt. You are then asked if the block is to be aligned with the object. A *block* is a previously drawn symbol or shape. Blocks are discussed in detail in Chapter 23 of this text.

After the number of segments is given, the object is divided with dots. However, the dots may not show very well. Notice in Figure 6-24 that the appearance of the marks has been changed. The marks placed by the **DIVIDE** command are controlled by the **PDMODE** (point display mode) system variable. Basic **PDMODE** values range from 0 to 4. Figure 6-25 shows points drawn using each **PDMODE** value. The **PDMODE** default value is 0. Use the following sequence to set the **PDMODE** value:

> Command: **PDMODE**↵
> New value for PDMODE ⟨0⟩: **3**↵

Type REGEN at the Command: prompt to change the **DIVIDE** points to reflect the new **PDMODE** setting.

Figure 6-25.
The five basic **PDMODE** values and the corresponding symbols.

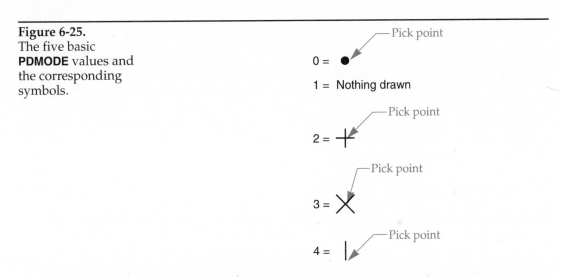

Dividing Objects at Specified Distances

Unlike the **DIVIDE** command, where an object is divided into a specified number of parts, the **MEASURE** command places marks a specified distance apart. The **MEASURE** command is accessed by picking **Measure** from the **Point** cascading submenu of the **Draw** pull-down menu, or by typing ME or MEASURE at the Command: prompt. The line shown in Figure 6-26 is measured with .75 unit segments as follows:

> Command: **ME** *or* **MEASURE**↵
> Select object to measure: *(pick an object)*
> ⟨Segment length⟩/Block: **.75**↵

Measuring begins at the end closest to where the object is picked. All increments are equal to the entered segment length except the last segment, which may be shorter. The **PDMODE** setting affects the marks placed on the object, just as it does with the **DIVIDE** command. Blocks can be inserted at the given distances using the **Block** option of the **MEASURE** command.

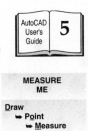

AutoCAD User's Guide **5**

MEASURE
ME

Draw
➡ Point
  ➡ Measure

Figure 6-26.
Using the **MEASURE** command. Notice that the last segment may be shorter than the others, depending on the total length of the object.

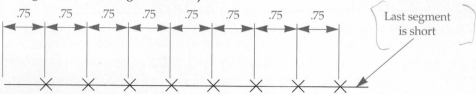

Last segment is short

EXERCISE 6-10

❑ Start AutoCAD and use the setup option of your choice.
❑ Set the **PDMODE** to 3 before marks are drawn in this exercise.
❑ Draw two circles of any diameter and two lines of any length.
❑ Use the **DIVIDE** command to divide one circle into 10 equal parts and one line into 5 equal parts.
❑ Use the **MEASURE** command to divide the other circle into .5 unit parts and the other line into .75 unit parts.
❑ Draw two parallel vertical lines. Make each line 3″ (76.2mm) long and space them 4″ (101.6mm) apart. Use the **DIVIDE** command to divide the line on the left into 10 equal increments. Draw horizontal parallel lines from each division on the left line over to the right line. Use the **Node** and **Perpendicular** object snap options to assist you.
❑ Save the drawing as EX6-10.

AutoCAD
User's
Guide **4**

POINT
PO

Draw
↪ P**o**int

Draw
toolbar

Point

Drawing Points

You can draw points anywhere on the screen using the **POINT** command. This command is accessed by picking the **Point** button from the **Draw** toolbar, typing PO or POINT at the Command: prompt, or selecting one of the options from the **Point** cascading menu in the **Draw** pull-down menu. The specific type of point drawn is controlled by **PDMODE**. The command sequence is as follows:

Command: **PO** or **POINT**⏎
Point: *(type point coordinates or pick with pointing device)*

When all you need to do is place a single point object, type PO or POINT at the Command: prompt or select the **Single Point** option from the **Point** cascading menu. After drawing a single point, you are returned to the Command: prompt. When you need to draw multiple points, use the **Point** button or pick **Multiple Point** from the **Point** cascading menu. Press [Esc] to exit the command.

NOTE   If **PDMODE** is set to 0 (dots) and blips are active, the blip covers the dot when the point is selected. Enter REDRAW at the Command: prompt to erase the blip.

Setting point style

The **PDMODE** system variable was mentioned briefly earlier in this chapter. The style and size of points can also be set using the **Point Style** dialog box, Figure 6-27. This dialog box is accessed by selecting **P**oint Style... from the **Format** pull-down menu or by entering DDPTYPE at the Command: prompt.

Figure 6-27.
The **Point Style** dialog box. This is a quick way to select the point style and to change the point size.

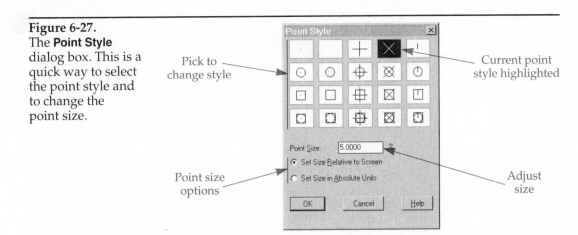

Pick to change style

Current point style highlighted

Point size options

Adjust size

The **Point Style** dialog box contains twenty different point styles. The current point style is highlighted. To change the style, simply pick the graphic image of the desired style.

These styles can also be set at the Command: prompt by entering PDMODE. Draw a circle by adding 32 to the original **PDMODE** value. Add 64 to draw a square. Add 96 to draw a circle and square. For example, a point display of an X inside a circle has a **PDMODE** value of 35. That is the sum of the X value of 3 and the circle value of 32. If you want to draw a point with an X inside of a circle and square, enter the **PDMODE** value 99. See Figure 6-28.

Figure 6-28.
By adding 32, 64, or 96 to the base **PDMODE** value, different symbols can be drawn.

PDMODE value		PDMODE value		PDMODE value	
32+0=32	⊙	64+0=64	▫	96+0=96	⊡
32+1=33	○	64+1=65	□	96+1=97	◎
32+2=34	⊕	64+2=66	⊞	96+2=98	⊕
32+3=35	⊗	64+3=67	⊠	96+3=99	⊠
32+4=36	◒	64+4=68	⊓	96+4=100	⊍

Set the point size by entering a value in the **Point Size:** text box of the **Point Style** dialog box. Pick the **Set Size Relative to Screen** option button if you want the point size to change in relation to different display options. Picking the **Set Size in Absolute Units** option button makes the points appear the same size no matter what display option is used.

The point size can also be modified using the **PDSIZE** (point display size) system variable. The default **PDSIZE** value is 0. Change the point size by typing PDSIZE at the Command: prompt and then entering the new value. The point retains the set **PDMODE** value, but the size changes.

Figure 6-29 shows the point sizes of different **PDSIZE** values. Positive **PDSIZE** values change size in relation to different display options. For example, if the view is enlarged with the **ZOOM** command, the point size also increases. (Zoom is discussed in Chapter 9.) A negative **PDSIZE** value makes the points appear the same size no matter how much you **ZOOM** the drawing.

Figure 6-29.
Point sizes of
different **PDSIZE**
values.

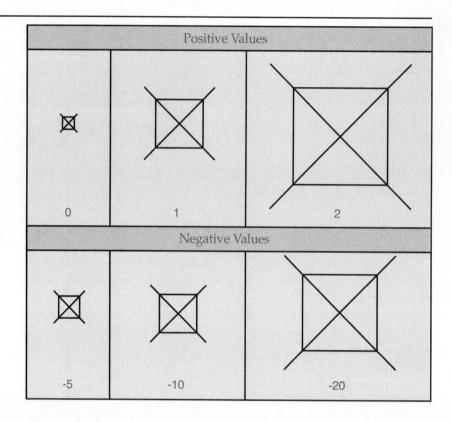

EXERCISE 6-11

❏ Start AutoCAD and use the setup option of your choice.
❏ Draw a point with **PDMODE** set to the following values: 0, 1, 2, 3, 4, 32, 33, 66, 67, 98, 99, and 100.
❏ Type REGEN and observe the results.
❏ Set **PDMODE** to a value of 35. Then draw a point using each of the following **PDSIZE** values: 0, 1, 2, –5, –10, and –20.
❏ Save the drawing as EX6-11.

Orthographic Multiview Drawings

Each field of drafting has its own method to present views of a product. Architectural drafting uses plan views, exterior elevations, and sections. In electronics drafting, symbols are placed in a schematic diagram to show the circuit layout. In civil drafting, contour lines are used to show the topography of the land. Mechanical drafting uses *multiview drawings*.

This section discusses multiview drawings. Multiview drawings are based on the standard ANSI Y14.3. Also explained is the use of construction lines for view alignment and use in geometric construction.

Multiviews are made using orthographic projection. *Orthographic projection* involves projecting object features onto an imaginary plane. This imaginary plane is called a *projection plane*. The imaginary projection plane is placed parallel to the object. Thus, the line of sight is perpendicular to the object. This results in views that appear two-dimensional, Figure 6-30.

AutoCAD and its Applications—Basics

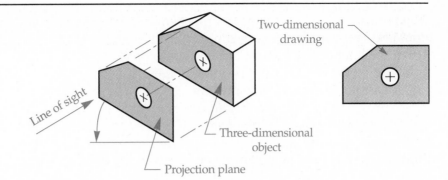

Figure 6-30.
Obtaining a front view with orthographic projection.

Two-dimensional drawing

Line of sight

Projection plane

Three-dimensional object

Six two-dimensional views show all sides of an object. The six views are the front, right side, left side, top, bottom, and rear. The views are placed in a standard arrangement so others can read the drawing. The front view is the central, or most important view. Other views are placed around the front view, Figure 6-31.

There are very few products that require all six views. The number of views needed depends on the complexity of the object. Use only enough views to completely describe the object. Drawing too many views is time-consuming and can clutter the drawing. In some cases, a single view may be enough to describe the object. The object shown in Figure 6-32 needs only two views. These two views completely describe the width, height, depth, and features of the object.

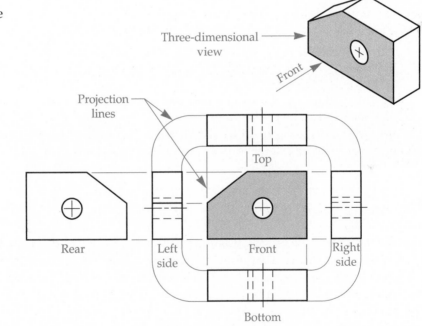

Figure 6-31.
Arrangement of the six orthographic views.

Three-dimensional view

Front

Projection lines

Top

Rear

Left side

Front

Right side

Bottom

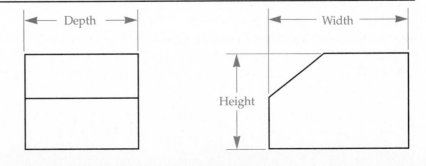

Figure 6-32.
The views you choose to describe the object should show all height, width, and depth dimensions.

Depth

Width

Height

Selecting the front view

The front view is usually the most important view. The following guidelines should be considered when selecting the front view:

✓ Look for the best shape or most contours.
✓ Show the most natural position of use.
✓ Display the most stable position.
✓ Provide the longest dimension.
✓ Contain the least hidden features.

Additional views are selected relative to the front view. Remember, choose only the number of views needed to completely describe the object's features.

Showing hidden features

Hidden features are parts of the object not visible in the view you are looking at. A visible edge appears as a solid line. A hidden edge is shown with a hidden line. Hidden lines were discussed in Chapter 4. Notice in Figure 6-33 how hidden features are shown as hidden lines. Hidden lines are thin to provide contrast to object lines.

Figure 6-33.
Hidden features are shown with hidden lines.

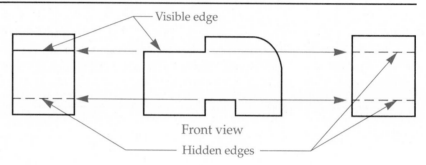

Visible edge

Front view

Hidden edges

One-view drawings

In some instances, an object can be fully described using one view. A thin part, such as a gasket, can be drawn with one view. See Figure 6-34. The thickness is given as a note in the drawing or in the title block. A cylindrical object can also be drawn with one view. The diameter dimension is given to identify the object as round.

Figure 6-34.
A one-view drawing of a gasket. The thickness is a given in a note.

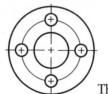

Thickness 1.5mm

Showing symmetry and circle centers

The centerlines of symmetrical objects and the centers of circles are shown using centerlines. For example, in one view of a cylinder, the axis is drawn as a centerline. In the other view, centerlines cross to show the center in the circular view. See Figure 6-35. The only place that the small centerline dashes should cross is at the center of a circle.

AutoCAD and its Applications—Basics

Figure 6-35.
Drawing
centerlines. A—For
a cylinder. B—For a
round hole.

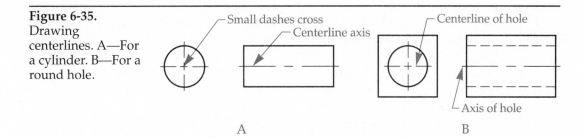

Drawing Auxiliary Views

In most cases, an object is completely described using a combination of one or more of the six standard views. However, sometimes the multiview layout is not enough to properly identify some object surfaces. It may then be necessary to draw auxiliary views.

Auxiliary views are typically needed when a surface on the object is at an angle to the line of sight. These slanted surfaces are *foreshortened*, meaning they are shorter than the true size and shape of the surface. To show this surface in true size, an auxiliary view is needed. Foreshortened dimensions are not recommended.

Auxiliary views are drawn by projecting lines perpendicular (90°) to a slanted surface. Usually, one projection line remains on the drawing. It connects the auxiliary view to the view where the slanted surface appears as a line. The resulting auxiliary view shows the surface in true size and shape. For most applications, the auxiliary view need only show the slanted surface, not the entire object. This is called a *partial auxiliary view* and is shown in Figure 6-36.

Figure 6-36.
Auxiliary views
show the true size
and shape of an
inclined surface.

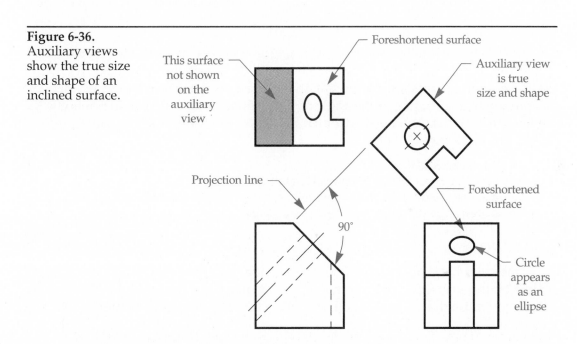

In many situations, there may not be enough room on the drawing to project directly from the slanted surface. The auxiliary view is then placed elsewhere, Figure 6-37. A viewing-plane line is drawn next to the view where the slanted surface appears as a line. The *viewing-plane line* is drawn with a thick dashed or phantom line in accordance with ANSI Y14.2M. It is terminated with bold arrowheads that point toward the slanted surface.

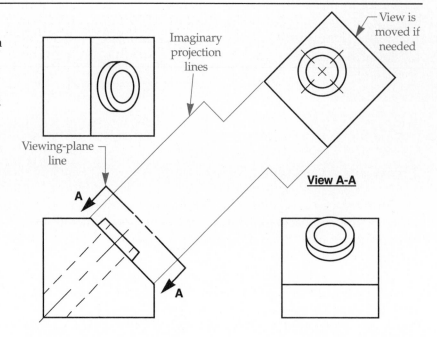

Figure 6-37.
Identifying an auxiliary view with a viewing-plane line. If there is not enough room, the view can be moved to a different location.

Each end of the viewing-plane line is labeled with a letter. The letters relate the viewing-plane line with the proper auxiliary view. A title such as VIEW A-A is placed under the auxiliary view. When more than one auxiliary view is drawn, labels continue with B-B through Z-Z (if necessary). The letters *I*, *O*, and *Q* are not used because they may be confused with numbers. An auxiliary view drawn away from the multiview retains the same angle as if it is projected directly.

Changing the snap grid rotation angle

Changing the rotation angle of the snap grid is especially useful for drawing auxiliary views. After the views have been drawn, access the **SNAP** command. Then, pick the base point for rotation on the line that represents the slanted surface. Enter the snap rotation angle equal to the angle of the slanted surface. If you do not know the angle, use object snap modes and pick points on the slanted surface to define the angle. The steps are as follows:

Command: **SNAP**↵
Snap spacing or ON/OFF/Aspect/Rotate/Style ⟨*current*⟩: **R**↵
Base point ⟨0,0⟩: (*pick an endpoint on the line that represents the slanted surface*)
Rotation angle ⟨0⟩: (*enter the angle of the slanted surface or pick two points on the surface*)
Command:

Once you have placed and rotated the snap grid, you may want to place grid points on the snap grid. Then, complete the auxiliary view as shown in Figure 6-38. When you finish drawing the auxiliary view, return the snap grid rotation value to 0°.

Figure 6-38.
Using the rotated
snap and grid
points to help draw
the auxiliary view.

Grid and snap
rotated for
auxiliary view

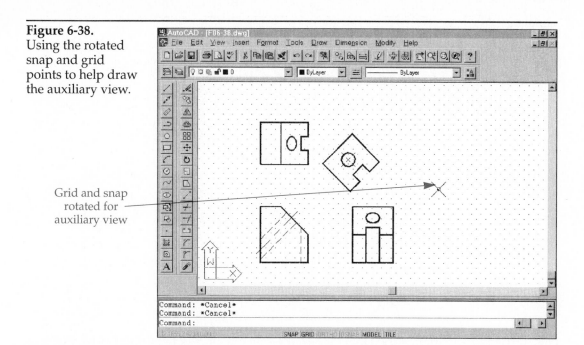

Using the User Coordinate System for auxiliary views

All of the features on your drawing originate from the *World Coordinate System (WCS)*. This is the X, Y, and Z coordinate values measured from the origin (0,0,0). The WCS is fixed. The *User Coordinate System (UCS)*, on the other hand, can be moved to any orientation. The UCS is discussed in detail in *AutoCAD and its Applications— Advanced, Release 14*.

In general, UCS allows you to set your own coordinate origin. The UCS 0,0,0 origin has been in the lower-left corner of the screen for the drawings you have done so far. In many cases this is fine, but when drawing an auxiliary view it is best to have the measurements originate from a corner of the view. This, in turn, makes all auxiliary view features and the coordinate display true as measured from the corner of the view. This method makes it easier to locate and later dimension the auxiliary view features.

First, draw the principal views, such as the front, top, and right side. Then, move the UCS origin to a location that coincides with a corner of the auxiliary view using this command sequence:

> Command: **UCS**↵
> Origin/ZAxis/3point/OBject/View/X/Y/Z/Prev/Restore/Save/Del/?/⟨World⟩: **O**↵
> Origin point ⟨0,0,0⟩: *(pick the origin point at the desired corner of the auxiliary view, as shown in Figure 6-39A)*

Next, realign the UCS grid with the angle of the auxiliary view by adjusting the Z axis to the same angle. For example, if the auxiliary view is projected at 45° from the slanted surface in the front view, then rotate the Z axis as follows:

> Command: **UCS**↵
> Origin/ZAxis/3point/OBject/View/X/Y/Z/Prev/Restore/Save/Del/?/⟨World⟩: **Z**↵
> Rotation angle about Z axis ⟨0⟩: **45**↵

The icon is rotated as shown in Figure 6-39A. If you want the UCS icon displayed at the current UCS origin, use the **UCSICON** command as follows:

> Command: **UCSICON**↵
> ON/OFF/ALL/Noorigin/ORigin/⟨ON⟩: **OR**↵

AutoCAD
User's
Guide **3**

Figure 6-39.
A—Relocating the origin and rotating the Z axis of the UCS system. Notice how the position of the UCS icon has been aligned with the auxiliary view angle. B—Moving the UCS icon display to the current UCS origin at the corner of the auxiliary view.

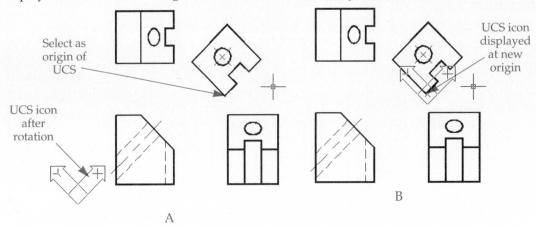

This automatically moves the UCS icon to the revised UCS origin at the corner of the auxiliary view, as shown in Figure 6-39B. Although this is not required, it is convenient to see the location of the UCS origin. Before you begin drawing the auxiliary view, use the **Save** option of the **UCS** command to name and save the new UCS:

> Command: **UCS**↵
> Origin/ZAxis/3point/OBject/View/X/Y/Z/Prev/Restore/Save/Del/?/⟨World⟩: **S**↵
> ?/Desired UCS name: **AUX**↵

Now, proceed by drawing the auxiliary view. When you have finished, use the **Previous** option of the **UCS** command to move the UCS icon to its previous position:

> Command: **UCS**↵
> Origin/ZAxis/3point/Object/View/X/Y/Z/Prev/Restore/Save/Del/?/⟨World⟩: **P**↵

You can also press [Enter] to accept the **World** default and send the UCS icon display back to the WCS origin:

> Command: **UCS**↵
> Origin/ZAxis/3point/Object/View/X/Y/Z/Prev/Restore/Save/Del/?/⟨World⟩: ↵

The **UCS** command options can also be used by selecting **UCS** from the **Tools** pull-down menu. You can also use the menu to turn the UCS icon off or move the icon to a new origin. Each of these options are covered thoroughly in *AutoCAD and its Applications—Advanced, Release 14*.

PROFESSIONAL TIP  Use the orthogonal mode (**ORTHO** command) to help align the projected auxiliary view with the slanted surface. Also, consider using object snap modes with X and Y filters to assist you in projecting the precise corners and features on the slanted surface to the auxiliary view.

Drawing Construction Lines

In drafting terminology, *construction lines* are lines used for layout purposes. They are not part of the drawing. In manual drafting, they are either drawn very lightly or removed so they do not reproduce.

AutoCAD has construction lines and rays that can be used for such purposes. For example, you can use construction lines and rays to project features between views for accurate placement, for geometric constructions, or to coordinate geometric locations for object snap selections. The AutoCAD command that lets you draw construction lines is **XLINE**, while rays are drawn with the **RAY** command. Both commands can be used for similar purposes, however, the **XLINE** command has more options and flexibility than the **RAY** command.

Using the XLINE command

The **XLINE** command creates xline objects. An *xline object* is an infinite length line designed for use as a construction line. Although these lines are infinite, they do not change the drawing extents. This means that they have no effect on zooming operations.

The xlines can be modified by moving, copying, trimming, and other editing operations. Editing commands such as **TRIM** or **FILLET** change the object type. For example, if one end of an xline is trimmed off, it becomes a ray object. A *ray* is considered semi-infinite because it is infinite in one direction only. If the infinite end of a ray is trimmed off, then it becomes a line object.

Construction lines and rays are drawn on the current layer and plot the same as other objects. This may cause conflict with the other lines on that layer. A good way to handle this problem is to set up a special layer just for construction lines.

The **XLINE** command can be accessed by picking the **Construction Line** button in the **Draw** toolbar, by picking **Construction Line** in the **Draw** pull-down menu, or by typing XL or XLINE at the Command: prompt. The **XLINE** command sequence appears as follows:

XLINE
XL

Draw
↳ Construction
Line

Draw
toolbar

Construction Line

```
Command: XL or XLINE↵
Hor/Ver/Ang/Bisect/Offset/〈From point〉:
```

The following **XLINE** options are available:

- **From point.** This **XLINE** default allows you to specify two points that the construction line passes through. The first point of an xline is called the *root point.* After you pick the first point, the Through point: prompt allows you to select as many points as you like. Xlines are created between every point and the root point. Use the object snap modes to accurately pick points:

```
Command: XL or XLINE↵
Hor/Ver/Ang/Bisect/Offset/〈From point〉: (pick a point)
Through point: (pick a second point)
Through point: (pick another second point)
Through point: (draw more construction lines or press [Enter])
Command:
```

Figure 6-40 shows how construction lines can be used to help project features between views.

- **Hor (H).** This option draws a horizontal construction line through a single specified point. It serves the same purpose as the default option, but the line is automatically drawn horizontally and you only have to pick one point.
- **Ver (V).** This option draws a vertical construction line through the specified point.

Figure 6-40.
Using the **XLINE** command default option. You can also use the **XLINE Hor** option.

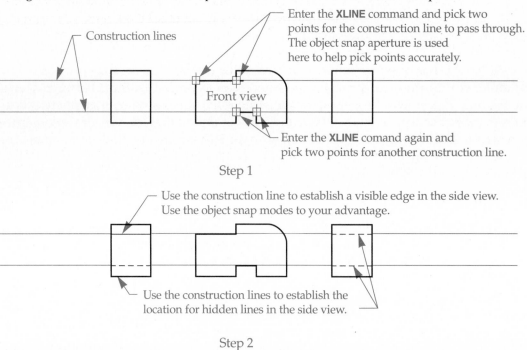

Construction lines

Enter the **XLINE** command and pick two points for the construction line to pass through. The object snap aperture is used here to help pick points accurately.

Front view

Enter the **XLINE** comand again and pick two points for another construction line.

Step 1

Use the construction line to establish a visible edge in the side view. Use the object snap modes to your advantage.

Use the construction lines to establish the location for hidden lines in the side view.

Step 2

EXERCISE 6-12

❑ Start AutoCAD and use the setup option of your choice. One of your templates may already have proper layers and line types.
❑ Set up layers and linetypes as needed. Review Chapter 4 if necessary.
❑ Draw the four views of the object shown below. Do not draw dimensions.
❑ The top and side views are currently incomplete. Use construction lines to help you complete all views by adding in the missing lines.
❑ Save the drawing as EX6-12.

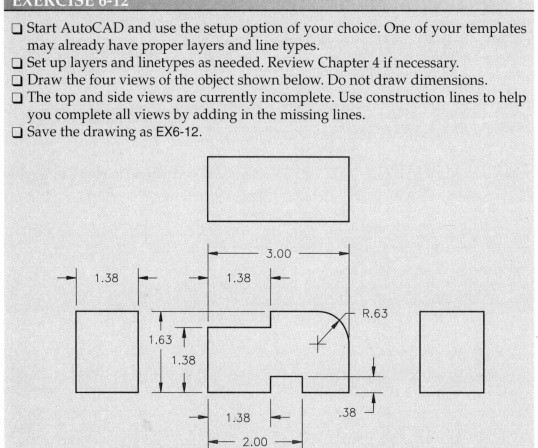

AutoCAD and its Applications—Basics

- **Ang.** This option draws a construction line at a specified angle through a specified point. The default lets you specify an angle and then pick a point for the construction line to be drawn through. This works well if you know the angle, or you can pick two points in the drawing to describe the angle:

> Command: **XL** *or* **XLINE**↵
> Hor/Ver/Ang/Bisect/Offset/⟨From point⟩: **A**↵
> Reference/⟨Enter angle (0.0000)⟩: *(enter an angle, such as 45)*
> Through point: *(pick a point)*
> Through point: *(draw more construction lines or press* [Enter]*)*
> Command:

A reference angle from the angle of an existing line object can be specified by using the **Reference** option. This can be used when you do not know the angle of the construction line, but you know the angle between an existing object and the construction line:

> Command: **XL** *or* **XLINE**↵
> Hor/Ver/Ang/Bisect/Offset/⟨From point⟩: **A**↵
> Reference/⟨Enter angle (45.0000)⟩: **R**↵
> Select a line object: *(pick a line)*
> Enter angle ⟨45.0000⟩: **90**↵
> Through point: *(pick a point)*
> Through point: *(draw more construction lines or press* [Enter]*)*
> Command:

Figure 16-41 shows the **Ang** option used to draw construction lines establishing the location of an auxiliary view.

Figure 6-41.
Using the **XLINE** command **Ang** option.

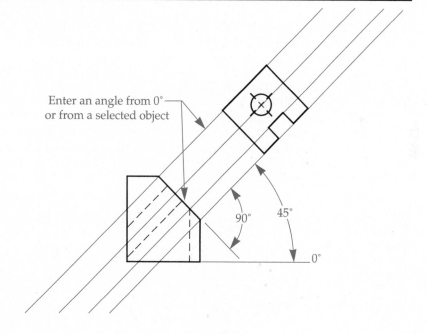

Enter an angle from 0° or from a selected object

90°   45°   0°

❏ Start AutoCAD and use the setup option of your choice.
❏ Draw the front and auxiliary views of the object shown below. Do not draw dimensions or the top view. The top view is given to help you visualize the object.
❏ The front view is currently incomplete. Use construction lines to help you complete the view by adding the missing lines.
❏ Save the drawing as EX6-13.

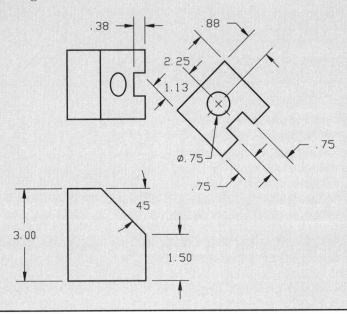

• **Bisect.** This option draws a construction line that bisects a specified angle. This is a convenient tool for use in some geometric constructions, as shown in Figure 6-42:

> Command: **XL** *or* **XLINE**↵
> Hor/Ver/Ang/Bisect/Offset/⟨From point⟩: **B**↵
> Angle vertex point: *(pick the vertex)*
> Angle start point: *(pick a point on a side of the angle)*
> Angle end point: *(pick a point on the other side of the angle)*
> Angle end point: *(draw more construction lines or press* [Enter]*)*
> Command:

Figure 6-42.
Using the **XLINE**
command **Bisect**
option.

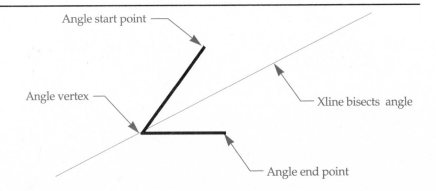

- **Offset.** This **XLINE** option draws a construction line a specified distance (offset) from a selected line object. It works just like the **OFFSET** command. You have the option of specifying an offset distance or using the **Through** suboption to pick a point for the construction line to be drawn through:

> Command: **XL** *or* **XLINE**↵
> Hor/Ver/Ang/Bisect/Offset/⟨From point⟩: **O**↵
> Offset distance or Through ⟨0.0000⟩: **0.75**↵
> Select a line object: *(pick a line)*
> Side to offset? *(pick any point on the side for the xline to be drawn)*
> Select a line object: *(draw more construction lines or press* [Enter]*)*
> Command:

EXERCISE 6-14

❑ Start AutoCAD and use the setup option of your choice.
❑ Draw the angle shown below using the given absolute coordinates.
❑ Use the **XLINE** command to bisect the angle and to draw a construction line parallel to the outer side of each leg of the angle offset at a distance of .525.
❑ Save the drawing as EX6-14.

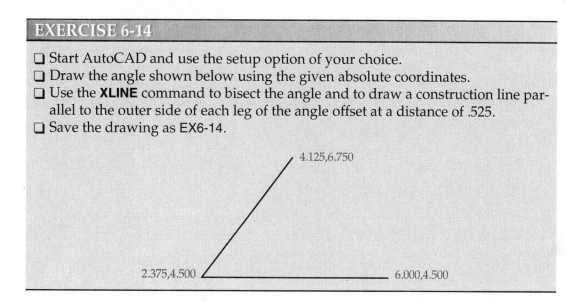

Using the RAY command

The **RAY** command is limited when compared to the **XLINE** command. The **RAY** command allows you to specify the point of origin and a point the ray passes through. In this manner, the **RAY** command works much like the default option of the **XLINE** command. However, the ray extends out beyond the second pick point only. The **XLINE** command results in a construction line that extends both ways from the pick points.

The **RAY** command can be accessed by picking **Ray** in the **Draw** pull-down menu, or by typing RAY at the Command: prompt. The **RAY** command sequence is as follows:

RAY

Draw
↦ Ray

> Command: **RAY**↵
> From point: *(pick a point)*
> Through point: *(pick a second point)*
> Through point: *(draw more construction lines or press* [Enter]*)*
> Command:

Both the **RAY** command and the **XLINE** command allow the creation of multiple objects. You must press [Enter] to end the command. They do *not* allow you to undo a construction line that you have already drawn.

Editing Construction Lines and Rays

The construction lines that you create using the **XLINE** and **RAY** commands can be edited and modified using standard editing commands. These commands are introduced in Chapter 11 and Chapter 12. The construction lines will change into a new object type when infinite ends are trimmed off. A trimmed xline becomes a ray. A ray that has its infinite end trimmed becomes a normal line object. Therefore, in many cases, your construction lines can be modified to become part of the actual drawing. This approach can save a significant amount of time in many drawings.

Chapter Test

Write your answers in the spaces provided.

1. Give the command and entries needed to draw a line to the midpoint of an existing line:

   Command: _____

   From point: _____

   To point: _____ of _____

2. Give the command and entries needed to draw a line tangent to an existing circle and perpendicular to an existing line:

   Command: _____

   From point: _____ to _____

   To point: _____ to _____

3. Give the command sequence required to draw a concentric circle inside an existing circle at a distance of .25:

   Command: _____

   Offset distance or Through ⟨*current*⟩: _____

   Select object to offset: _____

   Side of offset?: _____

   Select object to offset: _____

4. Give the command and entries needed to divide a line into 24 equal parts:

   Command: _____

   Select the object to divide: _____

   ⟨Number of segments⟩/Block: _____

5. Give the command and entries used to draw a point symbol that is made up of a circle over "X":

   Command: _____

   New value for _____ ⟨0⟩: _____

   Command: _____

   Point: _____

6. After drawing the point in Question 5, you find that it is too small. Give the command and prompts needed to draw the point larger:

   Command: _____

   New value for _____ ⟨0.000⟩: _____

7. Define object snap. _____

   _____

   _____

8. Define quadrant. _____

9. Describe the **Quick** mode. _____

   _____

   _____

10. Define running object snap. _____

    _____

    _____

11. How do you set running object snaps? _____

    _____

    _____

12. How do you access the **Osnap Settings** dialog box? _____

    _____

13. Describe the object snap override. _____

    _____

    _____

14. What command is used to change the aperture size? _____

15. In addition to the command identified in Question 14, what is another way to change the aperture size? _____

    _____

16. What value would you specify to make the aperture half the default value? ____

    _____

17. How is the running osnap discontinued? _____

    _____

18. List two ways to establish an offset distance using the **OFFSET** command. _____

    _____

19. The **DIVIDE** command is located in which pull-down menu? _____

20. What is the difference between the **DIVIDE** and **MEASURE** commands? _____

    _____

21. The **Quick** object snap mode is not effective on which object snap option? _____

    _____

22. If you use the **DIVIDE** command and nothing appears to happen, what should you do? _____

    _____

    _____

23. Name the system variable used to set a point style. _____

24. Name the system variable used to set a point size. _____

25. How do you access the **Point Style** dialog box? _____

    _____

26. How do you change the point size in the **Point Style** dialog box? _____

27. How do you activate the object snap cursor menu? _____

_____

_____

28. Define AutoSnap. _____

_____

_____

29. What is a SnapTip? _____

_____

_____

30. Name the following AutoSnap markers:

    A. ⬒ _____

    B. ◇ _____

    C. ○ _____

    D. ⊠ _____

    E. □ _____

    F. △ _____

31. What does it mean when the SnapTip reads Deferred Perpendicular? _____

_____

32. What is the situation when the SnapTip reads Extended Intersection? _____

_____

33. What conditions must exist for the SnapTip to read Tangent? _____

_____

34. What is a deferred tangency? _____

_____

35. If you are using running object snaps and you want to make a single point selection without the effects of the running object snaps, what do you do? _____

_____

36. If you are using running object snaps and you want to make several point specifications without the aid of object snap, but you want to continue the same running object snaps after making the desired point selections, what is the easiest way to temporarily turn the running object snaps off? _____

_____

_____

37. What do you do if there are multiple selection possibilities within range of the cursor and you want to select a specific one of the possibilities? _____

_____

_____

_____

AutoCAD and its Applications—Basics

38. Define tracking. _____

    _____

39. When can the tracking feature be used? _____

    _____

40. How do you turn AutoSnap off? _____

    _____

41. How do you change the color of the AutoSnap marker?_____

    _____

    _____

42. How do you draw a single point and how do you draw multiple points?_____

    _____

    _____

    _____

43. Provide at least four guidelines for selecting the front view of an orthographic
    multiview drawing. _____

    _____

    _____

    _____

44. When can a part be shown with only one view?_____

    _____

    _____

45. When is an auxiliary view needed?_____

    _____

46. What does an auxiliary view show? _____

    _____

47. What is the angle of projection from the slanted surface into the auxiliary view?

    _____

48. Name the **SNAP** command option used to change the snap grid rotation.

    _____

49. Name the AutoCAD command that allows you to draw construction lines.

    _____

50. What is the difference between the construction lines drawn with the command
    identified in Question 49 and rays drawn with the **RAY** command? _____

    _____

    _____

51. Why is it a good idea to put construction lines on their own layer? _____

    _____

52. Name the option that can be used to bisect an angle with a construction line.

    _____

Drawing Problems

Load AutoCAD for each of the following problems and use one of your templates or start a new drawing using your own variables.

1. Draw the object below using the object snap modes. Save the drawing as P6-1 (omit dimensions).

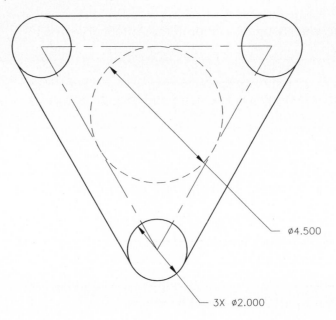

ø4.500

3X ø2.000

2. Draw the object below using the object snap modes indicated. Save the drawing as P6-2.

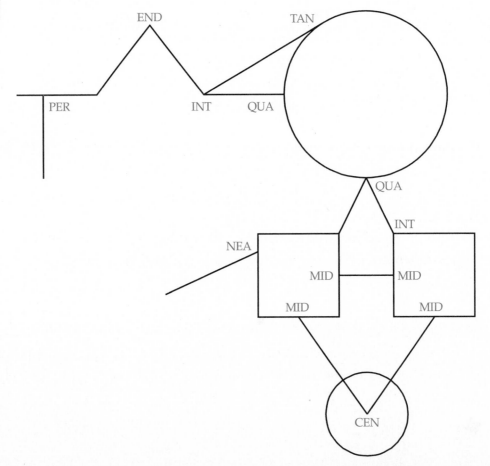

3. Draw the object below using **Endpoint**, **Tangent**, **Perpendicular**, and **Quadrant** object snap modes. Save the drawing as P6-3.

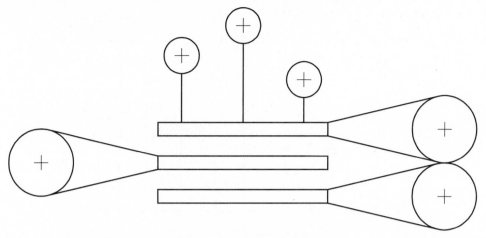

4. Use the **Midpoint, Endpoint,Tangent, Perpendicular** and **Quadrant** object snap modes to draw these electrical switch schematics. Do not draw text or arrowheads. Save the drawing as P6-4.

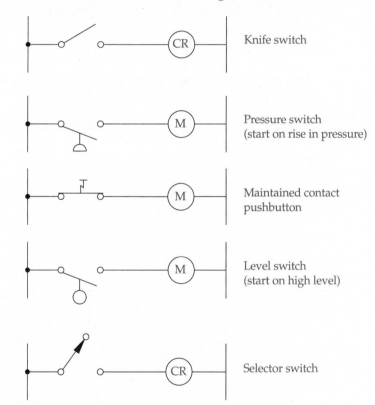

Knife switch

Pressure switch
(start on rise in pressure)

Maintained contact
pushbutton

Level switch
(start on high level)

Selector switch

5. Draw the front and side views of this offset support. Use construction lines. Do not draw the dimensions. Save your drawing as P6-5.

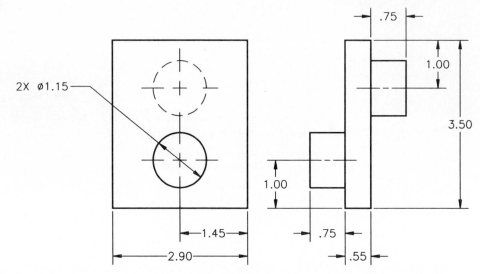

6. Draw the top and front views of this hitch bracket. Use construction lines. Do not draw the dimensions. Save your drawing as P6-6.

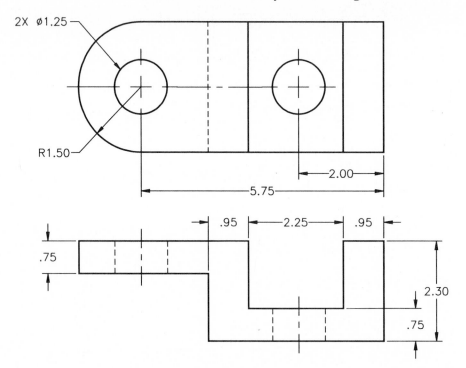

7. Draw this aluminum spacer. Use object snap modes and construction lines. Do not draw dimensions. Save the drawing as P6-7.

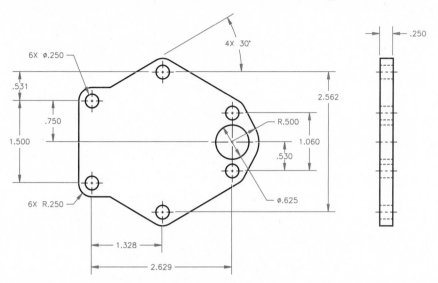

8. Draw this wiring diagram. Use object snap modes and construction lines. Do not draw text. Save the drawing as P6-8.

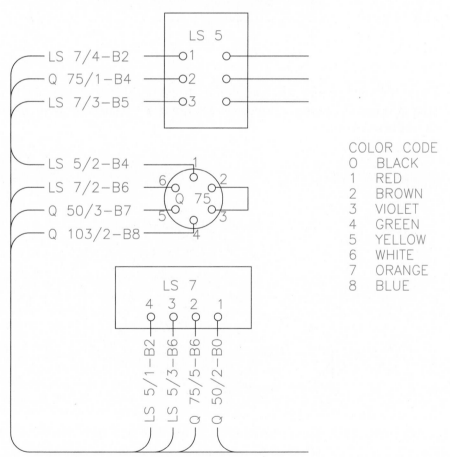

COLOR CODE
0   BLACK
1   RED
2   BROWN
3   VIOLET
4   GREEN
5   YELLOW
6   WHITE
7   ORANGE
8   BLUE

9. Draw the views needed to completely describe this brace. Use object snap modes and construction lines. Do not draw dimensions. Save the drawing as P6-9.

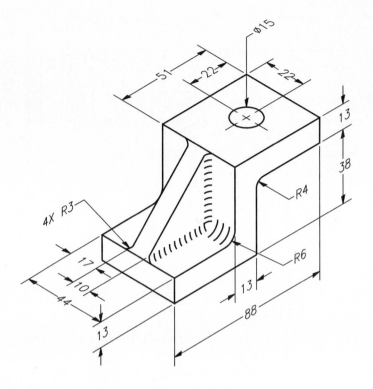

10. Draw the views needed to completely describe this brace. Use object snap modes and construction lines. Do not draw dimensions. Save the drawing as P6-10.

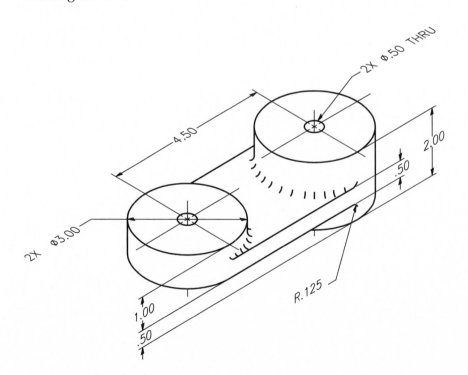

11. Use this engineer's sketch to create the views needed to describe this bracket. Do not draw the dimensions. Save the drawing as P6-11.

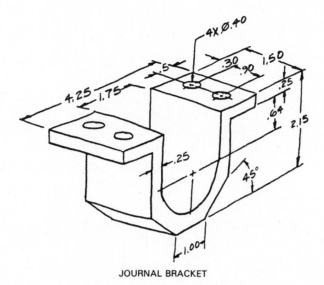

JOURNAL BRACKET

12. Use this engineer's sketch to create the views needed to describe this angle bracket. Do not draw the dimensions. Save the drawing as P6-12.

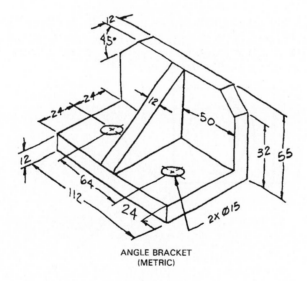

ANGLE BRACKET
(METRIC)

13. Use this isometric drawing to create the views needed to describe this hitch bracket. Do not draw the dimensions. Save the drawing as **P6-13**.

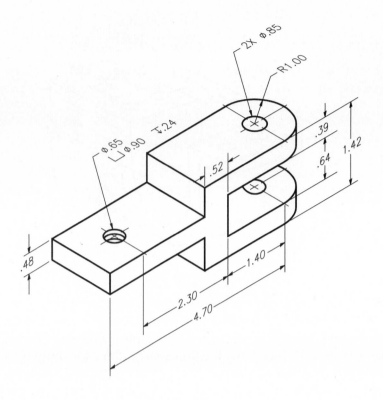

14. Draw the views of this pillow block, including the auxiliary view. Use construction lines. Do not draw the dimensions. Save your drawing as **P6-14**.

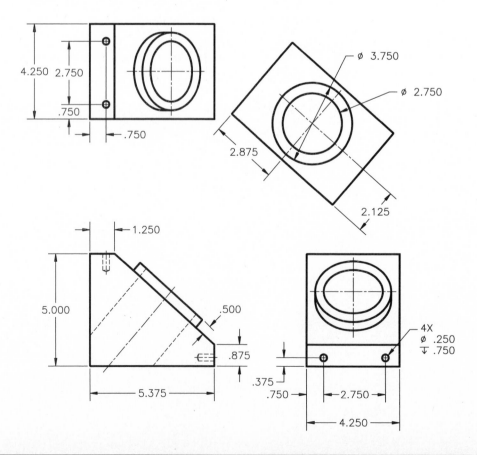

15. Use object snap modes to draw this elementary diagram. Do not draw the text. Save the drawing as P6-15.

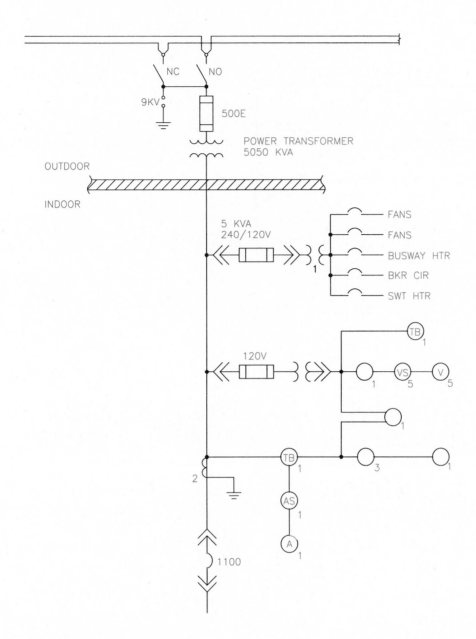

16. Draw the views of this V-block, including the auxiliary view. Use construction lines. Do not draw the dimensions. Save your drawing as P6-16.

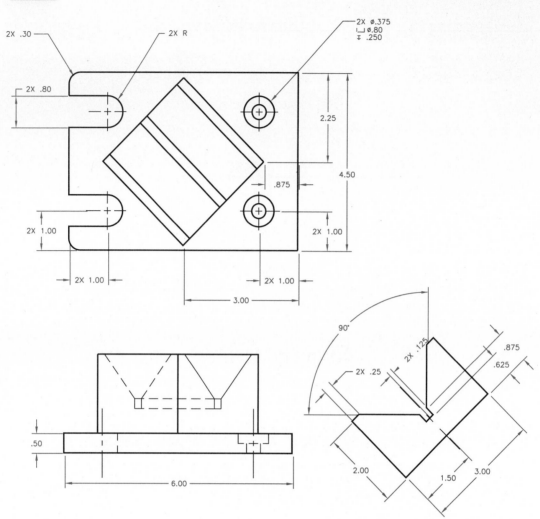

Chapter 7

Using the Geometry Calculator and Filters

Learning Objectives

After completing this chapter, you will be able to:
- ○ Use the geometry calculator to make mathematical calculations.
- ○ Make calculations and use information based on existing drawing geometry.
- ○ Add objects to drawings using the geometry calculator and object snaps.
- ○ Use selection set filters to create custom selection sets according to object types and object properties.

AutoCAD commands require precise input. Often, the input is variable and based on objects or locations within a drawing. AutoCAD provides a feature known as the *geometry calculator* to help find and use this type of information.

The geometry calculator and its use is explained in this chapter. Fundamental math calculations and drafting applications are presented. Complex mathematical calculations are also possible. Also covered in this chapter is the **FILTER** command, which allows you to customize a selection set by filtering objects based on object type and object properties.

Using the Geometry Calculator

AutoCAD's geometry calculator allows you to extract and use existing information in your drawing. The geometry calculator also allows you to perform basic mathematical calculations at the command line or supply an expression as input to a prompt.

The geometry calculator is accessed by typing CAL at the Command: prompt. You are then prompted for an expression. After you type the mathematical expression and press [Enter], AutoCAD automatically simplifies the expression, as shown in the following example:

> Command: **CAL**↵
> \>\> Expression: **2+2**
> 4
> Command:

Basics of the geometry calculator

The geometry calculator is more powerful than most hand-held calculators because it can directly access drawing information and can supply input to an AutoCAD prompt. The types of expressions that can be entered include numeric expressions and vector expressions. A *numeric expression* refers to mathematical process using numbers, such as the expressions solved using normal calculators. A *vector expression* is an expression involving a point coordinate location.

To use the geometry calculator, you must understand the ordering and format of an expression. The geometry calculator evaluates expressions according to the standard mathematical rules of precedence. This means that expressions within parenthesis are simplified first, starting with the innermost set and proceeding outward. Mathematical operators are evaluated in the standard order: exponents first, multiplication and division next, followed by addition and subtraction. Operators of equal precedence are evaluated from left to right.

Making numeric entries

The same methods of entering numbers used at AutoCAD prompts are also acceptable for calculator expressions. When entering feet and inches, either of the accepted formats can be used. This means that 5'-6" can also be entered as 5'6". The 5'-6" value can also be entered as inches (66). When a number expressed in feet and inches is entered, AutoCAD automatically converts to inches:

```
Command: CAL⏎
>> Expression: 24'6"⏎
294.0
```

 NOTE An entry at the Expression: prompt must be completed by pressing [Enter]. Pressing the space bar adds a space to your entry; it does not act as a return at this prompt.

Using basic math functions

The basic mathematical functions used in numeric expressions include addition, subtraction, multiplication, division, and exponential notation. Parenthesis are used to group symbols and values into sets. The symbols used for the basic mathematical operators are shown in the following table:

Symbol	Function	Example
+	Addition	3+26
-	Subtraction	270-15.3
*	Multiplication	4*156
/	Division	256/16
^	Exponent	22.6^3
( )	Grouped expressions	2*(16+2^3)

The following examples use the **CAL** command to solve each of the types of mathematical functions shown in the previous table:

```
Command: CAL⏎
>> Expression: 17.375+5.0625⏎
22.4375
```

```
Command: CAL↵
>> Expression: 17.375-5.0625↵
12.3125


Command: CAL↵
>> Expression: 12*18.25↵
219.0


Command: CAL↵
>> Expression: 27'8"/4↵
83.0


Command: CAL↵
>> Expression: 9^2↵
81.0


Command: CAL↵
>> Expression: (17.375+5.0625)+(4.25*3.75)-(18.5/2)↵
29.125
```

PROFESSIONAL TIP

The geometry calculator has limits when working with integer values. (An integer is a number with no decimal or fractional part.) Numeric values that are greater than 32,767 or less than -32,768 must be presented as real numbers. When working with values outside this range, type a decimal point and a zero (.0) after the value.

EXERCISE 7-1

❑ Open a drawing and use the **CAL** command to make the following calculations:
  ❑ 28.125+37.625 _____
  ❑ 16.875-7.375 _____
  ❑ 6.25+3.5 _____
  ❑ (25.75÷4)+(5.625×3) _____
  ❑ 3.625 squared. _____
  ❑ (12.125×3)+(24÷3+5.25)-(3.75÷1.5) _____

Making unit conversions

The calculator has a **CVUNIT** function that lets you convert one type of unit into another. For example, inches can be converted to millimeters, or liters can be converted to gallons. The order of elements in the **CVUNIT** function is:

    CVUNIT(value,from_units,to_units)

The following example converts 4.7 kilometers to the equivalent number of feet:

```
Command: CAL↵
>> Expression: CVUNIT(4.7,kilometers,feet)↵
15419.9
```

If the units of measure you specify are either incompatible or are not defined in the acad.unt file, the message >> Error: CVUNIT failed to convert units is displayed and the prompt is reissued.

The **CVUNIT** function can work with units of distance, angles, volume, mass, time, and frequency. The units available for conversion are specified in the file acad.unt found in the AutoCAD R14\Support directory folder. This file can be edited to include additional units of measure if needed.

EXERCISE 7-2

❏ Open a drawing and use the **CAL** command to make the following conversions:
  ❏ 8.625" to millimeters_____
  ❏ 34.5mm to inches _____
  ❏ 5.5 kilometers to miles _____
  ❏ 12 gallons to liters_____
  ❏ 47 hours to minutes

Point entry

While the numeric functions of the calculator provide many useful capabilities, the most powerful use of the geometry calculator is its ability to find and use geometric information. Information such as point coordinates can be entered as input to the geometry calculator.

A point coordinate is entered as two or three numbers enclosed in square brackets and separated by commas. The numbers represent the X, Y, and Z coordinates. For example [4,7,2], [2.1,3.79], or [2,7.4,0]. Any value that is zero can be omitted, as well as commas immediately in front of the right bracket. For example:

[2,2]	is the same as	[2,2,0]
[,,6]	is the same as	[0,0,6]
[5]	is the same as	[5,0,0]
[ ]	is the same as	[0,0,0]

Direction can be entered using any accepted AutoCAD format, including polar and relative coordinates as follows:

Coordinate system	Entry format
Polar Relative	[dist<angle] [@ x, y, z]

These options provide the ability to determine locations, distances, and directions within a drawing. For example, to determine a point coordinate value for a location that is 6 units from 2,2,0 at an angle within the X,Y plane of 45°, the following sequence is used:

Command: **CAL**↵
>> Expression: **[2,2,0]+[6<45]**↵
(6.24264 6.24264 0.0)

In an application of this type, the point answer is returned in parenthesis, with spaces to separate the numbers instead of commas.

Calculations can also be performed within the point coordinate specification, as shown in the next sequence:

>> Expression: **[2+3,2+3,0]+[1,2,0]**↵
(6.0 7.0 0.0)

AutoCAD and its Applications—Basics

A point location can be specified using the "@" symbol. Entering this symbol supplies the current value of the **LASTPOINT** system variable:

>   Command: **CAL**⏎
>   >> Expression: **@** ⏎
>   (*point coordinates*)

Besides entering coordinates at the prompt, you can also specify point coordinates by picking with the cursor. The **CUR** function is used to specify a point picked with the cursor, as shown in the following example:

>   >> Expression: **CUR**⏎
>   >> Enter a point: (*pick a point*)
>   (*point coordinates*)

This method can also be used as part of a calculation, as shown in the following sequence:

>   >> Expression: **CUR+[1,2]**⏎
>   >> Enter a point: (*pick a point*)
>   (7.09493 9.51857 0.0)

EXERCISE 7-3

❑ Open a drawing and use the **CAL** command to find the following point coordinates using the shortest entry format:
  ❑ [2,2,0]+[6<30]_____
  ❑ [4,3,0]+[2,2,0] _____
  ❑ Use your cursor to pick a point.
  ❑ Use your cursor to pick a point and add 3,2,0

Using the CAL command transparently

The **CAL** command can also be used transparently (within another command). To use the geometry calculator transparently, enter the command as 'CAL (an apostrophe followed by CAL). When the **CAL** command is used transparently, the result is supplied as input to the current prompt. This value is not displayed, however.

The following example uses direct distance entry combined with the geometry calculator to provide the correct length of a line. The line being drawn is 8.000 inches times 1.006:

>   Command: **L**⏎
>   From point: (*pick first point*)
>   To point: **'CAL**⏎ (*drag cursor in appropriate direction*)
>   >> Expression: **8*1.006**⏎
>   To point:

The calculator evaluates the expression and automatically supplies the result of 8.048 at the To point: prompt. When AutoCAD receives a single numeric value at a point prompt, it is automatically understood as a direct distance entry value. A calculation of this type might be a good way to include a shrinkage allowance for a casting or forging pattern.

EXERCISE 7-4

❑ Open an existing drawing or use one of your templates.
❑ Use the **CAL** command transparently to draw a line using direct distance entry from a point located at 2,4 to 6×1.0625.
❑ Save the drawing as EX7-4.

Using the object snap modes

Object snap points can also be specified as point coordinates to the geometry calculator. The object snaps provide the accuracy that is often needed when finding points on an object. The following example shows the **Endpoint** object snap mode being used to identify a specific point on an object:

```
Command: CAL↵
>> Expression: END↵
>> Select entity for END snap: (pick an object)
(point coordinates)
```

This example uses the **Endpoint** object snap to find the end of a line and add the point coordinate of 2 at 45°:

```
Command: CAL↵
>> Expression: END+[2<45]↵
>> Select entity for END snap: (pick an object)
(point coordinates)
```

You can use the geometry calculator to provide information based on selected points. For example, the following sequence can be used to find the point midway between two points selected with the cursor:

```
Command: CAL↵
>> Expression: (CUR+CUR)/2↵
>> Enter a point: (pick a point)
>> Enter a point: (pick a point)
(point coordinates)
```

This same technique can be used with any desired object snap mode. The following example is used to divide the distance between the center of a circle and the endpoint of a line by two:

```
Command: CAL↵
>> Expression: (CEN+END)/2↵
>> Select entity for CEN snap: (pick an object)
>> Select entity for END snap: (pick an object)
(point coordinates)
```

The next sequence starts a line halfway between the center of an existing circle and the endpoint of an existing line, as shown in Figure 7-1:

```
Command: L or LINE↵
LINE From point: 'CAL↵
>> Expression: (CEN+END)/2↵
>> Select entity for CEN snap: (pick the circle)
>> Select entity for END snap: (pick the line)
To point:
```

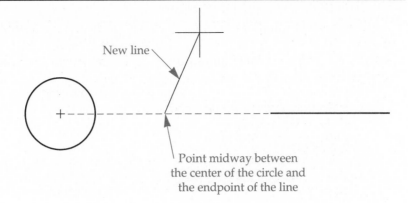

Figure 7-1.
Finding a point halfway between the center of a circle and the endpoint of a line.

New line

Point midway between the center of the circle and the endpoint of the line

The following sequence is used to create a circle with its center located two units along the X axis from the midpoint of an existing line, as shown in Figure 7-2:

```
Command: C or CIRCLE↵
CIRCLE 3P/2P/TTR/⟨Center point⟩: 'CAL↵
>> Expression: MID+[2,0]↵
>> Select entity for MID snap: (pick the line object)
Diameter/⟨Radius⟩ ⟨current⟩:
```

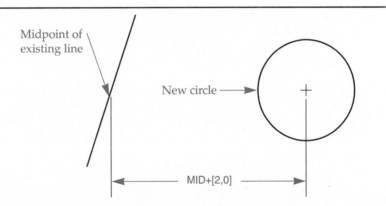

Figure 7-2.
Locating the center of a circle two units to the right of the midpoint of a line.

Midpoint of existing line

New circle

MID+[2,0]

The next sequence determines the centroid (center of mass) of a triangle, defined by picking three endpoints as shown in Figure 7-3:

```
Command: CAL↵
>> Expression: (END+END+END)/3↵
>> Select entity for END snap: (pick first corner of the triangle)
>> Select entity for END snap: (pick second corner of the triangle)
>> Select entity for END snap: (pick third corner of the triangle)
(12.4926 1.06199 0.0)
```

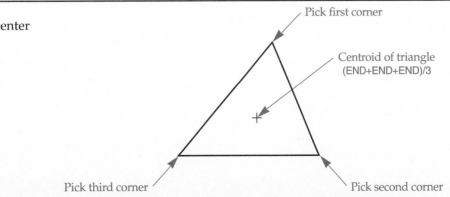

Figure 7-3.
Locating the center of mass of a triangle.

Pick first corner

Centroid of triangle (END+END+END)/3

Pick third corner

Pick second corner

❑ Open an existing drawing or use one of your templates.
❑ Use the **CAL** command and object snaps as needed to make the following drawings:
  ❑ Use (CEN+END)/2 to draw a line starting halfway between the center of a circle and the endpoint of a line, similar to Figure 7-1.
  ❑ Use MID+[2,0] to draw a circle 2 units on the X axis from the midpoint of a line, similar to Figure 7-2.
  ❑ Draw a triangle and find the center of mass, similar to Figure 7-3.
❑ Save the drawing as EX7-5.

Calculating distances

There are three basic calculator functions used to calculate distances in a drawing. These are the **DIST**, **DPL**, and **DPP** functions.

The **DIST** function is entered as DIST(P1,P2) where P1 = point 1 and P2 = point 2. The **DIST** function performs a simple distance calculation between the two specified points. Similar to all calculator functions, the points can be entered manually or picked. The **DIST** function is used in the following sequence to find a distance between two endpoints of a line:

> Command: **CAL**↵
> \>> Expression: **DIST(END,END)**↵
> \>> Select entity for END snap: *(pick an object)*
> \>> Select entity for END snap: *(pick an object)*
> *(distance)*

The **DPL** function is written as DPL(P,P1,P2) and calculates the perpendicular distance between a point P and a line passing through the points P1 and P2. See Figure 7-4. The following is an example using **DPL** with the endpoint object snap. The order of selection is P, P1, and then P2:

> Command: **CAL**↵
> \>> Expression: **DPL(END,END,END)**↵
> \>> Select entity for END snap: *(pick an object)*
> \>> Select entity for END snap: *(pick an object)*
> \>> Select entity for END snap: *(pick an object)*
> *(distance)*

Figure 7-4.
Finding the shortest distance between a point and a line.

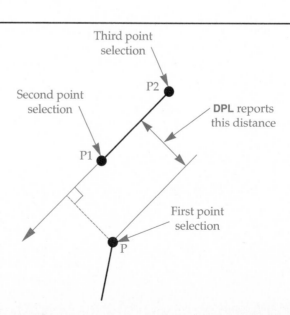

The **DPP** function is written as DPP(P,P1,P2,P3). **DPP** functions much like the **DPL** function except it finds the shortest distance between point P and a plane defined by P1, P2, and P3. See Figure 7-5. The points for **DPP** can be entered manually or picked. The following example shows a calculation of the distance between the point 2,2,6 and 3 points arbitrarily selected on the XY plane:

> Command: **CAL**↵
> >> Expression: **DPP([2,2,6],CUR,CUR,CUR)**↵
> >> Enter a point: *(pick a point)*
> >> Enter a point: *(pick a point)*
> >> Enter a point: *(pick a point)*
> 6.0

Figure 7-5.
Finding the shortest distance between a point and a plane.

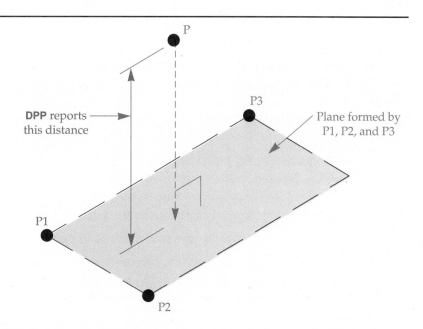

DPP reports this distance

Plane formed by P1, P2, and P3

EXERCISE 7-6

❏ Open an existing drawing or use one of your templates.
❏ Create the following drawings and make the required distance calculations:
   ❏ Draw a line. Find the distance between the ends.
   ❏ Find one-half the length of the line.
   ❏ Draw another line that is not parallel to the first line. Find the perpendicular distance between the endpoint of the second line and the first line.
❏ Save the drawing as EX7-6.

Finding intersection points

The **ILL** function locates an intersection point between two nonparallel lines. This function is written as ILL(P1,P2,P3,P4). The intersection of the line containing P1 and P2 with the line containing P3 and P4 is identified. An actual line between P1 and P2 (or P3 and P4) is not necessary. This function finds a hypothetical intersection, acting as though the lines are infinite in length. The following sequence shows the use of **ILL** to find the intersection of the lines shown in Figure 7-6:

> Command: **CAL**↵
> >> Expression: **ILL([2,5,0],[4,6,0],[4,5,0],[2,6,0])**↵
> (3.0 5.5 0.0)

Figure 7-6.
Finding the point of intersection between two nonparallel lines.

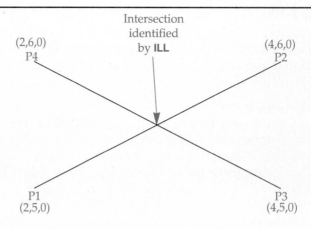

Finding a point on a line

The **PLD** function, written as PLD(P1,P2,Dist), finds a point along a line passing through P1 and P2, that is the specified distance from the start point. It is not necessary for an actual line to exist. The following sequence finds a point along a line passing through 0,0 and 3,1 that is 10 units from the start point, as shown in Figure 7-7:

> Command: **CAL.⏎**
> >> Expression: **PLD([ ],[3,1],10).⏎**
> (9.48683 3.16228 0.0)

Figure 7-7.
Finding a point along a line that is a specified distance from the start point.

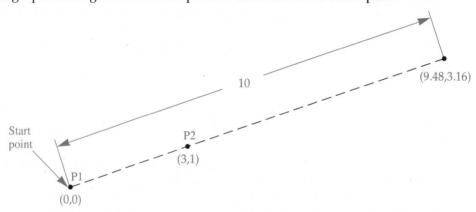

The **PLT** function provides another means of finding a point along a line. Written as PLT(P1,P2,T), this function finds a point along a line passing through P1 and P2. The point is located from the start point based on the T parameter. The T parameter is simply a scale factor relative to the distance between P1 and P2. If T=0, the point is P1, if T=1, the point is P2. A T value of .5 identifies the midpoint between P1 and P2, and a T value of 2.0 finds a point twice the length of the line. Figure 7-8 shows several examples. The following sequence locates a point that is three quarters of the way along the length of the specified line:

> Command: **CAL.⏎**
> >> Expression: **PLT([ ],[2,2],.75).⏎**
> (1.5 1.5 0.0)

Figure 7-8.
Finding a point
along a line based
on the scale of the
line length.

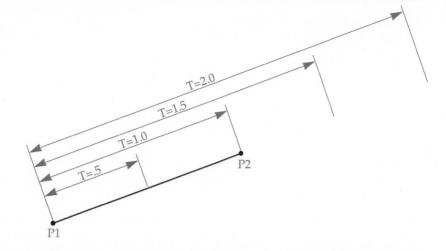

❑ Open EX7-3.
❑ Create the following drawings and make the required distance calculations:
  ❑ Draw a single line segment anywhere and then return to the Command: prompt. Use the @ symbol to find the distance between the last point and the point 4,4,0.
  ❑ Draw two lines that would intersect if they were extended. Use the **ILL** function to determine the point of intersection.
  ❑ Draw a line segment with two endpoints that are no more than 1″ apart. Use the **PDL** function to find the coordinates of a point that is 3.375″ from the start point.
  ❑ Draw a line and use the **PLT** function to find a point that is one-quarter of the distance from the start point.
❑ Save the drawing as EX7-7.

Finding an angle

The **ANG** function finds the angle between two lines. As with other calculator functions, the lines need not physically exist in the drawing. This function can be entered several different ways, depending on the nature of the angle you are trying to calculate.

To find the angle of a vector from the X axis in the X,Y plane, enter ANG(*coordinates*). The coordinate values are entered within parentheses. The coordinates can be manually entered or a point can be selected using object snap options. The following shows this method being used to enter the coordinates of a point along the line shown in Figure 7-9:

```
Command: CAL↵
>> Expression: ANG([1,1,0])↵
45.0
```

If the vector is not known, two points along a line can be used to determine the angle of the line in the X,Y plane from the X axis. The formula is ANG(P1, P2) as represented in Figure 7-10 and in the following sequence:

```
Command: CAL↵
>> Expression: ANG([2,2],[4,4])↵
45.0
```

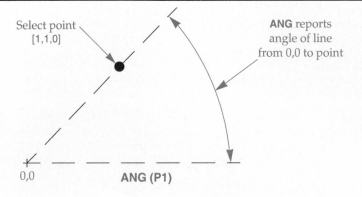

Figure 7-9.
Finding the angle of a line containing 0,0 and a point from the X axis.

Select point [1,1,0]

ANG reports angle of line from 0,0 to point

0,0   **ANG (P1)**

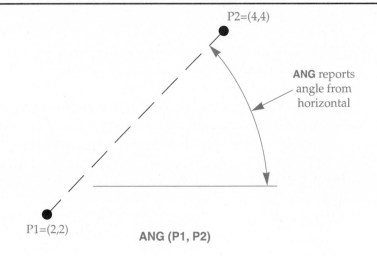

Figure 7-10.
Finding the angle of a line from the X axis given two points.

P2=(4,4)

ANG reports angle from horizontal

P1=(2,2)   **ANG (P1, P2)**

You can also calculate an included angle by specifying a vertex and a point on each side. A *vertex* is the intersection of two lines. An ***included angle*** is the angle formed between the vertex and the sides of the angle. The formula is entered as ANG(VERTEX,P1,P2), Figure 7-11. The following example determines the angle between two lines, selecting with the **Endpoint** object snap:

>   Command: **CAL**↵
>   >> Expression: **ANG(END,END,END).**↵
>   >> Select entity for END snap: *(pick apex)*
>   >> Select entity for END snap: *(pick end of first line)*
>   >> Select entity for END snap: *(pick end of second line)*
>   *(angle)*

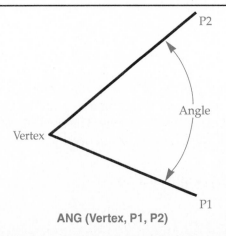

Figure 7-11.
Using the geometry calculator to determine the angle between lines in an XY plane.

P2

Angle

Vertex

P1

ANG (Vertex, P1, P2)

❑ Open an existing drawing or use one of your templates.
❑ Create the following drawings and make the required distance calculations:
  ❑ Draw a line using 0,0 as the start point. Do not draw a horizontal line. Use the **ANG** function to determine the angle of the line relative to horizontal.
  ❑ Draw a line at an angle to the XY plane. Use the **ANG** function to determine the angle.
  ❑ Draw an angle with a vertex and two sides similar to Figure 7-11. Use the **ANG** function to find the included angle.
❑ Save the drawing as EX7-8.

Finding a radius

You can use the **RAD** function to find the radius of an arc, circle, or 2D polyline arc. The command sequence works like this:

    Command: **CAL**↵
    >> Expression: **RAD**↵
    >> Select circle, arc or polyline segment for RAD function: *(select a circle)*
    (radius)

You can easily draw objects to match the radius of an existing object using the **RAD** function. The following example uses **RAD** to supply the radius value for a circle to match that of the existing circle, as shown in Figure 7-12:

    Command: **C** *or* **CIRCLE**↵
    3P/2P/TTR/⟨Center point⟩: *(pick center point)*
    Diameter/⟨Radius⟩ ⟨0.5000⟩: **'CAL**↵
    >> Expression: **RAD**↵
    >> Select circle, arc or polyline segment for RAD function: *(select a circle)*
    Command:

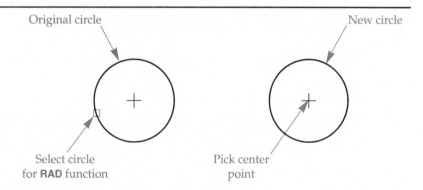

Figure 7-12.
Using the **RAD** function to create a circle equal in diameter to an existing circle.

Original circle   New circle

Select circle for **RAD** function   Pick center point

Calculator functions can be combined. For example, suppose you want to draw a new circle that is 25% the size of the original circle, placed in a new position that also needs to be calculated. Look at Figure 7-13 as you follow this command sequence:

    Command: **C** *or* **CIRCLE**↵
    3P/2P/TTR/⟨Center point⟩: **'CAL**↵
    >> Expression: **(MID+MID)/2**↵
    >> Select entity for MID snap: *(pick line 1)*
    >> Select entity for MID snap: *(pick line 2)*

Figure 7-13.
Combining
calculator functions
to revise a circle and
place it in a new
position.

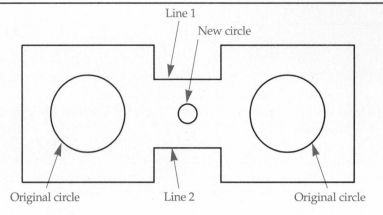

Now, instruct AutoCAD to calculate a new radius that is 25% of the size of the original circle like this:

> Diameter/⟨Radius⟩⟨*current*⟩: **'CAL**↵
> >> Expression: **.25*RAD**↵
> >> Select circle, arc, or polyline segment for RAD function: (*pick one of the original circles*)

The new circle is automatically drawn at the specified location, and at 25% of the size of the original circle.

Another application of the **CAL** command is shown in Figure 7-14, where a new circle is placed 3.00″ along a centerline from an existing circle. The new circle is 1.5 times larger than the original circle. The following command sequence can be used:

> Command: **C** *or* **CIRCLE**↵
> 3P/2P/TTR/⟨Center point⟩: **'CAL**↵
> >> Expression: **PLD(CEN,END,3.00)**↵
> >> Select entity for CEN snap: (*pick the original circle*)
> >> Select entity for END snap: (*pick near the right end of the centerline*)
> Diameter/⟨Radius⟩⟨*current*⟩: **'CAL**↵
> >> Expression: **1.5*RAD**↵
> >> Select circle, arc, or polyline segment for RAD function: (*pick the original circle*)

Figure 7-14.
Copying a circle
along a centerline
and resizing it.

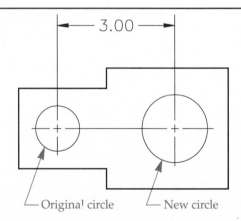

EXERCISE 7-9

☐ Open an existing drawing or use one of your templates.
☐ Draw a circle. Use the **RAD** function to draw another circle of equal diameter.
☐ Use the **CAL** command to assist you in making a drawing similar to Figure 7-13.
☐ Save the drawing as EX7-9.

Geometry calculator shortcut functions

To make using the geometry calculator as efficient as possible, some of the most commonly used calculator tasks have shortcuts to reduce your typing requirements. The basic abbreviations are shown in the following table:

Function	Replaces	Description
DEE	DIST(END,END)	Distance between two selected endpoints
ILLE	ILL(END,END,END,END)	Intersection of two lines defined by four selected endpoints
MEE	(END+END)/2	Point midway between two selected endpoints
NEE	NOR(END,END)	Direction vector in the XY plane and normal to two endpoints
VEE	VEC(END,END)	Vector between two selected endpoints
VEE1	VEC1(END,END)	Direction vector between two selected endpoints

These functions work exactly the same way as the longer format that you have already learned. Look at each of the shortcut options as you review earlier discussions covering the actual functions used by the shortcuts.

Use the following command sequence to determine the length of a line:

> Command: **CAL**↵
> \>> Expression: **DEE**↵
> \>> Select one endpoint for DEE: *(pick one end of the line)*
> \>> Select another endpoint for DEE: *(pick the other end)*
> *(distance)*

The following example shows how to use the **MEE** function to draw a circle at the center of a rectangle, as shown in Figure 7-15:

> Command: **C** *or* **CIRCLE**↵
> 3P/2P/TTR/⟨Center point⟩: **'CAL**↵
> \>> Expression: **MEE**↵

Figure 7-15.
Centering a circle within a rectangle using the **CAL** command.

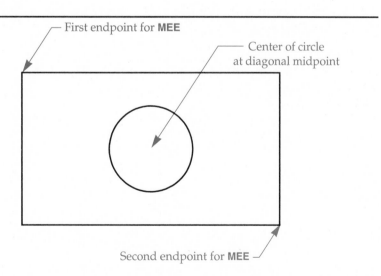
First endpoint for **MEE**
Center of circle at diagonal midpoint
Second endpoint for **MEE**

MEE is the midpoint between two endpoints. This expression allows you to pick the opposite corners of the rectangle to get the midpoint of the diagonal, which is the center of the rectangle.

> \>> Select one endpoint for MEE: *(pick one corner of the rectangle)*
> \>> Select another endpoint for MEE: *(pick the opposite corner of the rectangle)*
> Diameter/⟨Radius⟩⟨current⟩: *(type a radius and press* [Enter] *or pick a radius)*

❏ Open an existing drawing or use one of your templates.
❏ Draw a line and then use **DEE** to determine the length.
❏ Draw two intersecting lines and then use the **ILL** function to find the intersection point.
❏ Use the **MEE** function to help you create a drawing similar to Figure 7-15.
❏ Save the drawing as EX7-10.

Using advanced math functions

A number of advanced mathematical functions are also supported by the geometry calculator. These include logarithmic and exponential functions, as well as some data modification and conversion functions. The following table shows each of the advanced math operators supported by the geometry calculator:

Function	Description
ln(x)	Returns the natural log of a number.
log(x)	Returns the base-10 log of a number.
exp(x)	Returns the natural exponent (or antilog) of a number.
exp10(x)	Returns the base-10 exponent of a number.
sqr(x)	Returns a number squared.
sqrt(x)	Returns the square root of a number.
abs(x)	Returns the absolute value (magnitude) of a number.
round(x)	Rounds a number to the nearest integer value.
trunc(x)	Removes the decimal value of a number, returning the integer value.

An example of calculating the square root of 25 is as follows:

Command: **CAL**↵
>> Expression: **SQRT(25)**↵
5.0

Using trigonometric functions

When creating precision drawings, you often need to work with distances and angles. The geometry calculator supports several trigonometric functions for the calculations of distances and angles in a drawing. Figure 7-16 shows the basic trigonometric operators and formulae.

Figure 7-16.
The elements of a right triangle and related trigonometric functions.

$$\text{sine} = \frac{\text{length of opposite side}}{\text{length of hypotenuse}}$$

$$\text{cosine} = \frac{\text{length of adjacent side}}{\text{length of hypotenuse}}$$

$$\text{tangent} = \frac{\text{length of opposite side}}{\text{length of adjacent side}}$$

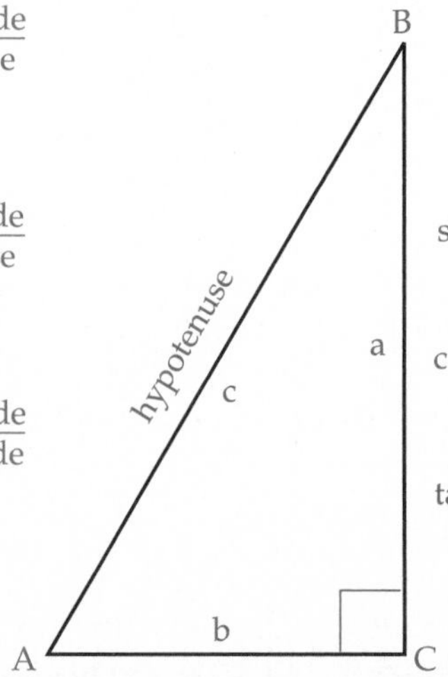

$$\sin A = \frac{a}{c}$$

$$\cos A = \frac{b}{c}$$

$$\tan A = \frac{a}{b}$$

The geometry calculator assumes that numeric input indicates degrees unless otherwise specified. This is regardless of the current angular units setting in AutoCAD. To enter angular data as degrees (d), minutes (') and seconds ("), use the format 30d45'15". If the minute or second value is zero, it can be omitted from the entry. For example, 42d0'30" can be written as 42d30". However, the degree value must be given, even if it is zero.

To enter a value in radians, use an *r* as a suffix for the number, such as 1.2r. A suffix of *g* indicates that the value is in grads, such as 50.00g. The geometry calculator output is always decimal degrees, regardless of the angular units style used for the input.

The available trigonometric operators are shown in the following table:

Function	Description
SIN(*angle***)**	Returns the sine of the angle.
COS(*angle***)**	Returns the cosine of the angle.
TANG(*angle***)**	Returns the tangent of the angle.
ASIN(*angle***)**	Returns the arcsine of the angle.
ACOS(*angle***)**	Returns the arccosine of the angle.
ATAN(*angle***)**	Returns the arctangent of the angle.
D2R(*angle***)**	Converts from degrees to radians.
R2D(*angle***)**	Converts from radians to degrees.
	Note: Do not use *r* suffix for this function.
PI	The constant pi (π, 3.14159...)

To provide an example of using trigonometric functions in the geometry calculator, the following sequence solves for angle A in Figure 7-16. The length of side a is 4.182 and side c is 5.136. Since the length of side a divided by the length of side c is equal to the sine of angle A, the arcsine of a/c is equal to angle A:

```
Command: CAL↵
>> Expression: asin(4.182/5.136)↵
54.5135
```

The returned value of 54.5135 indicates that angle A is 54.5135°. Using the information in Figure 7-16 and the geometry calculator, you can quickly solve for missing information needed to complete a drawing.

The constant *pi* (π) is presented in the trigonometry functions table. This constant is also used in circular formulae, such as πR^2 (circular area) or $2\pi R$ (circumference).

EXERCISE 7-11

❑ Open an existing drawing or use one of your templates.
❑ Solve the following math problems with the geometry calculator:
  ❑ Square root of 79.
  ❑ 23 squared.
  ❑ Sine of 30 degrees.
  ❑ Cosine of 30 degrees.
  ❑ Calculate the hypotenuse of a right triangle with side $a = 6$ and side $b = 2.5$.
  ❑ Calculate angle A of a right triangle with side $a = 6$ and side $b = 2.5$.
❑ Save the drawing as EX7-11.

Setting and using variables with the geometry calculator

In AutoCAD, many values are given a special name and stored for access whenever needed. These are called *system variables*, and their values depend on the current drawing or environment. The geometry calculator also has the ability to save values by assigning them to a variable.

A *variable* is a text item that represents a value stored for later use. Calculator variables can store only numeric, point, or vector data. The following example sets a variable named *X* to a value of 1.25:

```
Command: CAL↵
>> Expression: X=1.25↵
1.25
```

The variable can be recalled at a prompt by using the transparent **CAL** command:

```
Command: C or CIRCLE↵
3P/2P/TTR/⟨Center point⟩: (pick a center point)
Diameter/⟨Radius⟩: 'CAL↵
>> Expression: X
```

This extracts the value of the variable *X* (1.25) and uses this as the radius of the circle. The following example sets a variable named *P1* to a user-selected endpoint, then uses *P1* in the operation that follows:

```
Command: CAL↵
>> Expression: P1=END↵
>> Select entity for END snap: (pick an object)
(point coordinate)
Command: L or LINE↵
From point: 'CAL↵
>> Expression: P1↵
To point:
```

PROFESSIONAL TIP

The variables used by the geometry calculator are actually AutoLISP variables. *AutoLISP* is an easy-to-learn programming language for AutoCAD. An introduction to AutoLISP is given in *AutoCAD and its Applications—Advanced, Release 14*. For more detailed information on AutoLISP, see *AutoLISP Programming*, also from Goodheart-Willcox.

Using AutoCAD system variables in the geometry calculator

The geometry calculator has a specialized function named **GETVAR** that allows you to use values stored in AutoCAD system variables. To retrieve a system variable, type **GETVAR(***variable name***)** at the Expression: prompt. The following example shows the drawing area being increased by multiplying the upper-right limits by 4:

```
Command: LIMITS↵
Reset Model space limits:
ON/OFF/⟨Lower left corner⟩ ⟨0.0000,0.0000⟩: ↵
Upper right corner ⟨12.0000,9.0000⟩: 'CAL↵
>> Expression: 4*GETVAR(LIMMAX)↵
```

If you use the **LIMITS** command, you will see the upper-right value has increased to 48,36.

A complete listing of system variables is available by typing **SETVAR** at the Command: prompt, followed by typing ?. This gives you the Variables to list ⟨*⟩: prompt. The default lists all of the variables:

> Command: **SETVAR**↵
> Variable name or ?: **?**↵
> Variable(s) to list ⟨*⟩: ↵

This opens the **AutoCAD Text Window**, where all of the system variables and their settings are listed. Continue pressing [Enter] to see the complete list. Press the [F2] key to return to the graphics window.

Introduction to Filters

Filters allow you to select any aspect of an object on the screen while "filtering out" other objects, items, or features. A variety of applications for filters are covered in the rest of this chapter and throughout this text where specific applications are discussed. Filters used for layer control were introduced in Chapter 4.

Drawing with X and Y filters

This discussion involves using the **LINE** command with X and Y filters, which control X and Y coordinates. There is also a Z filter for the Z coordinate, but it is used in 3D applications. Enter 0 if prompted for a Z value when working in 2D.

Suppose you want to construct an isosceles triangle with a height of 2" on a baseline that already exists. Refer to Figure 7-17. First, use this command sequence to establish the base of the triangle:

> Command: **L** *or* **LINE**↵
> From point: **2,2**↵
> To point: **@3⟨90**↵

Figure 7-17.
Constructing an isosceles triangle using the Y filter.

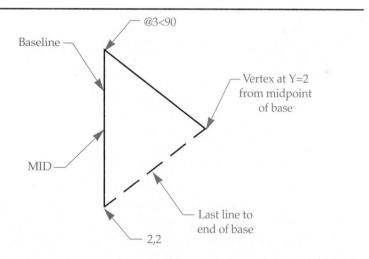

Now, place the vertex 2" from the midpoint of the baseline using this sequence:

> To point: **.Y**↵
> of **MID**↵
> of *(pick the baseline)*
> of (need XZ): **@2,0**↵

Finally, complete the triangle with the **Close** option:

> To point: **C**↵
> Command:

Earlier in this chapter you learned to construct a circle at the center of a rectangle using the geometry calculator **MEE** function. The same operation can be performed using X and Y filters. As an example, suppose you want to place the center of a circle at the center of a rectangle, as shown in Figure 7-18. The command sequence is as follows:

Command: **C** *or* **CIRCLE**↵
3P/3P/TTR/〈Center point〉: **.X**↵
of **MID**↵
of *(pick a horizontal line)*
of (need YZ): **MID**↵
of *(pick a vertical line)*
Diameter/〈Radius〉 〈*current*〉: *(type the desired radius or pick a point)*
Command:

In this example, the X value is filtered before the YZ value. However, the same operation can be performed by filtering the Y value first, and then the XZ value.

Figure 7-18.
Centering a circle inside a rectangle using X and Y filters.

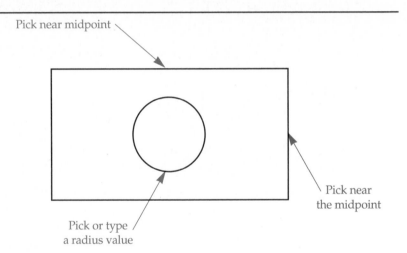

Pick near midpoint

Pick near the midpoint

Pick or type a radius value

Using X and Y filters to project views

If you draw the object shown in Figure 7-19 on a drafting board, you would probably draw the front view first. Then, using drafting instruments, you might project construction lines and points from the front view to complete the right side view.

Filters can be used to perform similar projection operations. The front view of a rectangular object can be drawn very efficiently using the **RECTANG** command. The circle can then be constructed using X and Y filters, as previously described. The command sequence to draw the side view is as follows:

Command: **REC** *or* **RECTANG**↵
First corner: **.Y**↵
of **END**↵
of *(pick near the endpoint of the bottom horizontal line)*
of (need XZ): *(pick a point to set distance between the views)*
Other corner: **@2.5,5**↵
Command:

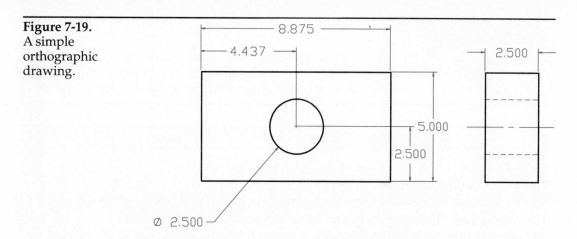

Figure 7-19.
A simple
orthographic
drawing.

8.875

4.437

2.500

5.000

2.500

Ø 2.500

The rectangle that represents the side view is now complete. Since the side view's lower-left corner is located by filtering the Y value of the front view's lower-right corner, it is aligned orthographically with that view. The @2.5,5 entry locates the upper-right corner of the side view rectangle relative to the filtered point.

It is also a simple matter to draw the hidden lines that represent the circle seen in the side view. This operation is performed using the object snap modes **Quadrant**, **Nearest**, and **Perpendicular**. First, change the current linetype to Hidden. Then, use the following command sequence. Refer to Figure 7-20.

> Command: **L** *or* **LINE.**↵
> From point: **.Y**↵
> of **QUA.**↵
> of *(pick near the 90° or 270° quadrant on the circle)*
> of (need XZ): **NEA.**↵
> of *(pick near one of the vertical lines of the side view)*
> To point: **PER.**↵
> of *(pick on the opposite vertical line in the side view)*
> To point: ↵
> Command:

Now that one of the hidden lines is drawn, you can repeat the procedure to draw the second hidden line. However, an easier way is to use the **OFFSET** command to offset the first hidden line at the required distance.

Figure 7-20.
"Projecting" lines
using X and Y
filters.

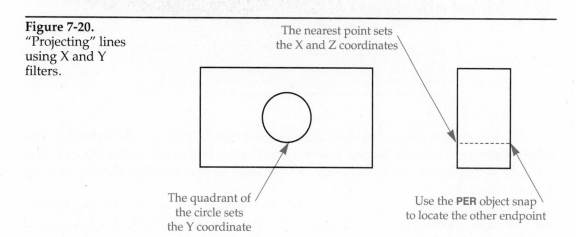

The nearest point sets
the X and Z coordinates

The quadrant of
the circle sets
the Y coordinate

Use the **PER** object snap
to locate the other endpoint

PROFESSIONAL TIP

You can greatly increase your productivity when you use object snap modes in conjunction with X and Y filters by setting running object snaps and using the AutoSnap feature.

EXERCISE 7-13

☐ Start AutoCAD and use the setup option of your choice.
☐ Turn off **Grid** and **Snap**.
☐ Draw the front view of the object shown in Figure 7-19 and locate the circle's center using the X and Y filter technique discussed in this chapter.
☐ Construct the right side of the object using the appropriate running object snap modes and X and Y filters.
☐ Save the drawing as EX7-13.

AutoCAD User's Guide 7

Using Filters to Create a Selection Set

The **FILTER** command is used to create a list of properties that are needed for a specific object to be selected. Filter lists can be created for use at any time. These filter lists are accessed at any Select object: prompt. The **FILTER** command can also be used transparently by typing '**FILTER** at the Select object: prompt.

The **FILTER** command is accessed by typing FI or FILTER. This opens the **Object Selection Filters** dialog box, Figure 7-21.

Figure 7-21.
The **Object Selection Filters** dialog box.

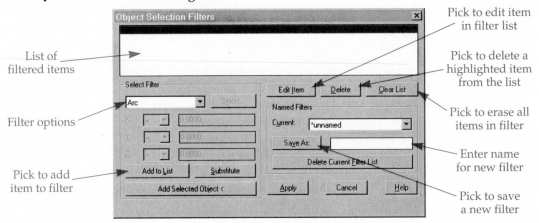

The three major areas of the **Object Selection Filters** dialog box are the list box, the **Select Filter** area, and the **Named Filters** area. The list box is where the current filter list data is displayed, the **Select Filter** area is used to specify filter criteria, and the **Named Filters** area is used to save filters for future use.

To introduce you to selection filters, the following example creates a simple filter list that selects only circle objects. To begin, the **SELECT** command is issued and '**FILTER** is entered transparently at the Select objects: prompt:

    Command: **SELECT**↵
    Select objects: '**FI** *or* '**FILTER**↵

This displays the **Object Selection Filters** dialog box. In the **Select Filter** area, pick the drop-down list to see the selection filter options. From this list, select **Circle**, Figure 7-22. To add this specification to the filter list, pick the **Add to List** button. The list box now displays this selection criteria as **Object = Circle**, to show that only circle objects are to be selected. To return to the **SELECT** command and use the selection filter, pick the **Apply** button, and the following prompt is issued:

    Applying filter to selection.
    Select objects:

Figure 7-22.
Items picked from
the drop-down list
appear in the
list box.

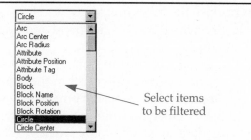

Select items
to be filtered

The prompt tells you that the filter is active. In Figure 7-23, a selection window is created around a group of lines, arcs, and circles. Because the filter is set to allow only circle objects, all other object types are filtered out of the selection. AutoCAD reports the number of objects found and the number selected:

    13 found 8 were filtered out.

Figure 7-23.
All objects are
filtered out except
for the circles.

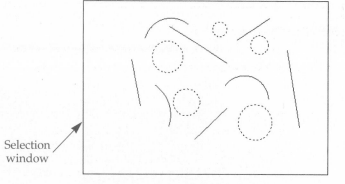

Selection
window

To exit the filtered selection and return to a normal selection mode, press [Enter] at the Select objects: prompt. You are then returned to a standard Select objects: prompt, and the filter is no longer applied. You can then make additional selections or complete the command.

NOTE   To remove an item from the filter list, highlight it and pick the **Delete** button. To clear the entire list and start over, pick the **Clear List** button.

❏ Start AutoCAD and use the setup option of your choice.
❏ Draw a group of lines, arcs, and circles similar to Figure 7-23.
❏ Use the **FILTER** command to create a filter that selects only circles.
❏ Use a selection window around all objects and observe which are selected.
❏ Save the drawing as EX7-14.

Filter lists can be expanded to select only objects with specific properties. The next example creates a filter list that selects only line objects that have a Center linetype. Use the following steps:

1. Start the **SELECT** command and enter the **'FILTER** command at the Select objects: prompt.
2. Clear the list box to start a new filter list by picking the **Clear List** button.
3. From the drop-down list in the **Select Filter** area, select **Line**. This adds the filter **Object = Line** to the list box.
4. Select **Linetype** from the drop-down list. When this is picked, notice two previously grayed-out items are now enabled: the **Select...** button and the text box to the right of the **X:** drop-down list.
5. Now you need to specify what linetype to add to the filter. Do this by typing the name of the linetype in the edit box, or by picking the **Select...** button to display the **Select Linetype(s)** dialog box.
6. Select the Center linetype and pick the **OK** button.
7. Finally, pick the **Add to List** button, and the **Object Selection Filters** dialog box should appear as shown in Figure 7-24.

Figure 7-24.
Line objects with Center linetype will be selected by this filter.

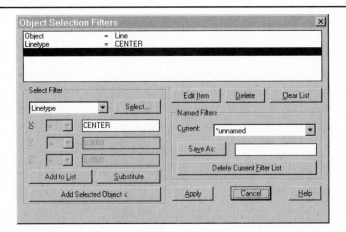

In Figure 7-25, the selection filter is applied to a window selection. Notice that only the lines with a Center linetype have been selected.

A filter list can be extremely specific when needed. Although this level of detail may seldom be needed, a very specific filter list is shown in Figure 7-26. This filter list will probably find only one object, because the filter specifies text content as well as the exact position of the text in the drawing.

Figure 7-25.
The selection filter
from Figure 7-24 is
applied to a
window selection.

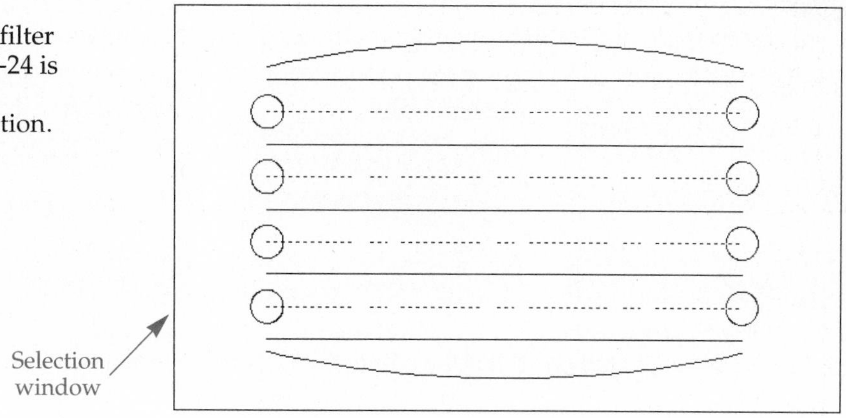

Selection
window

Figure 7-26.
This very specific
filter identifies only
one text object.

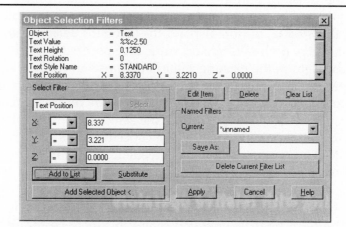

EXERCISE 7-15

❑ Start AutoCAD and use the setup option of your choice.
❑ Make a drawing similar to Figure 7-25. Do not draw the selection window.
❑ Use the **FILTER** command as previously discussed to create a filter that select only the centerlines.
❑ Save the drawing as EX7-15.

Entering filter data

The **Select Filter** area of the **Object Selection Filters** dialog box is where filter data is entered, as shown in previous examples. The drop-down list and edit boxes can be used to enter the values for the filters. Objects in a drawing can even be selected to develop a filter.

The three edit boxes correspond to X, Y, and Z point coordinates. They are enabled as needed for entering different types of filter information. When the filter drop-down list reads **Arc**, it refers to an object type. Since no further information is required about the object type, the edit boxes are all disabled.

Setting the filter to **Arc Center** enables all three edit boxes, which are used to define the center point. When **Arc Radius** is selected, only the top edit box is enabled because only a single value is required. An example of each of these situations is shown in Figure 7-27.

Figure 7-27.
This shows an example of filter items that access the **X:**, **Y:**, and **Z:** edit boxes.

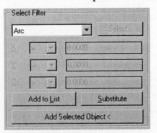  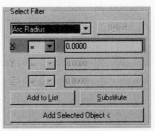

Object filter   Point filter   Distance/length filter
Edit boxes deactivated   All three edit boxes active   One edit box active

For many filter specifications, such as layers, linetypes, and other object properties, the **Select...** button is enabled. The **Select...** button displays the appropriate dialog box for showing the available options. For example, if **Color** is the specified filter, the **Select...** button displays the standard **Select Color** dialog box.

Once the desired filter and value are specified, pick the **Add to List** button to add the new item to the existing filter list. To use an existing object as a basis for a filter list, pick the button labeled **Add Selected Object** ⟨. This gives you a Select object: prompt, and once an object is selected, you are returned to the **Object Selection Filters** dialog box. The information from the selected object is placed in the filter list. Since you may not need all of the filter list specifications that result from picking an object, the filter list can now be edited as needed. Editing the filter list is covered later in this section.

Working with relative operators

The term *relative operator* refers to functions that determine the relationship between data items. These relationships include equality, inequality, greater-than, less-than, and combinations such as greater-than-or-equal-to and less-than-or-equal-to. Each of the three edit boxes in the **Select Filter** area are preceded by a relative operator drop-down list. An appropriate relative operator can be selected for each data field.

For example, a relative operator can be used to select all arcs that have a radius of 2.5 or greater. To do this, the filter specification is **Arc Radius** with 2.5 entered in the enabled edit box. Then, select the greater than or equal to symbol (**>=**) from the relative operator drop-down list. See Figure 7-28.

Figure 7-28.
The greater-than-or-equal-to filtering option.

Relative operator drop-down list

Enter setting value

Pick to select an object with properties to be filtered

Pick after editing an item from the filter list

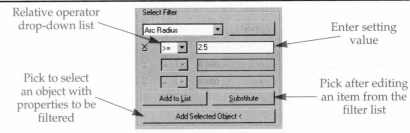 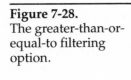 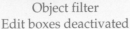

The following chart shows the relative operator functions:

Symbol	Meaning
=	Equal to
!=	Not equal to
<	Less than
<=	Less than or equal to
>	Greater than
>=	Greater than or equal to
×	Equal to any value

Editing the filter list

Editing capabilities are provided that allow you to modify and delete filter list items. If you accidentally enter an incorrect filter specification, you can easily correct it using these steps:

1. Pick the item in the filter list that you need to edit, then pick the **Edit Item** button. The values for the selected specification are then entered in the **Select Filter** area and can be freely edited.
2. Change the values as necessary.
3. Pick the **Substitute** button when finished. The edited filter specification is substituted for the highlighted item. Be sure to pick **Substitute**, and not **Add to List**; otherwise, you end up with two different values for the same filter specification in the filter list.

To remove an item from the filter list, highlight it and select the **Delete** button. Only one filter specification can be deleted at a time using this method. If you need to remove all of the current specifications and start over, pick the **Clear List** button.

Creating named filters

The most powerful feature of CAD is being able to benefit from work you have already done. By reusing previous work instead of repeating the work to produce duplicate results, you increase your efficiency and overall productivity levels.

Complex filter lists can be time consuming to develop. AutoCAD allows you to name and save filter lists. The **Named Filters** area of the **Object Selection Filters** dialog box is used to create and manage these lists.

When you have created a filter list that you plan to use again, it should be named and saved. When the filter list is completed and tested, follow these steps to name and save the list:

1. Pick the edit box to the right of the **Save As:** button to make it current.
2. Next, enter a short, descriptive name in the edit box. The name for a filter list can be up to 18 characters in length and cannot contain spaces. These named filters are stored in a file named filter.nfl and are available until deleted.
3. Pick the **Save As:** button to save the named filter.

To delete a filter list, make it current by picking the filter name from the **Current:** drop-down list, then pick the button labeled **Delete Current Filter List**.

EXERCISE 7-16

❑ Start AutoCAD and use the setup option of your choice.
❑ Establish the filter that was used in Exercise 7-14 and name it CIRCLE.
❑ Establish the filter that was used in Exercise 7-15 and name it CENTERLINE.
❑ Save the drawing as EX7-16.

Using filters on a drawing

Filters can increase productivity, but you must learn to recognize situations when they can be used. Imagine that you've just created the flow chart in Figure 7-29. You are then asked to change all of the Romans text inside the flow chart and in the note to a new layer and color for plotting considerations. You could use the **CHPROP** command and individually select each word on the chart, but you decide to use the **FILTER** command to make the job easier.

Figure 7-29.
Original flow chart requiring modification.

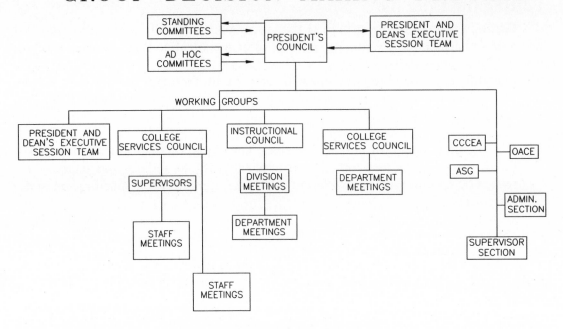

The **FILTER** command opens the **Object Selection Filters** dialog box, where you follow these steps:
1. Pick the **Add Selected Object** ⟨ button. The drawing returns with a Select object: prompt. Pick a text element within one of the boxes.
2. The dialog box returns and displays the characteristics of the text you picked. Highlight items such as **Text Position** and **Text Value**, and pick the **Delete** button for each. See Figure 7-30. These filters are not needed because they limit the filter list to specific aspects of the text.
3. Enter a filter name, such as TEXT, in the **Save As:** text box and then pick the **Save As:** button. TEXT becomes the current filter name.

Figure 7-30.
Deleting selection filters that are too specific.

Object Selection Filters				
Color	= 256 - By Layer			
Text Position	X = 3.8733069	Y = 7.383176	Z = 0.0000	
Text Style Name	= STANDARD			
Text Value	= PRESIDENTS			
Text Height	= 0.0750			
Text Rotation	= 0			

4. Pick the **Apply** button. The drawing returns and this prompt is given:

> Select object:
> Applying filter to selection.
> Select objects: *(window all of the drawing text to be included in the selection set)*
> Select objects: ⏎

The text within the flow chart is now highlighted, and you see this prompt:

> Select objects: Other corner: 144 found
> 106 were filtered out.
> Select objects: ⏎
> Command:

5. The highlighted text returns and the items that were previously highlighted become part of the selection set.

6. At the Command: prompt, enter the **CHPROP** command. Enter P when you get the Select objects: prompt. This retrieves the selection set that was previously established with the **FILTER** command:

> Command: **CHPROP**⏎
> Select objects: **P**⏎
> 106 found
> Select objects: ⏎
> Change what property (Color/LAyer/LType/ltScale/Thickness) ? **LA**⏎
> New layer ⟨0⟩: **COLOR**⏎
> Change what property (Color/LAyer/LType/ltScale/Thickness) ? ⏎
> Command:

The Color layer was previously created with a color of red. (You must create the layer before you can change to it.) Now all of the text within the flow chart is on the Color layer in red color. The revised flow chart is shown in Figure 7-31.

Figure 7-31.
Revised flow chart. All text in the flow chart is now red.

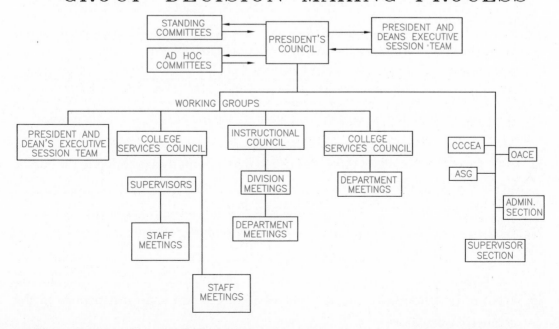

GROUP DECISION MAKING PROCESS

*NOTE: STANDING OR AD HOC COMMITTEES MAY BE FORMED AT ANY LEVEL.

Chapter Test

Write your answer in the space provided.

1. Identify the command that starts the geometry calculator. _____

2. Define expression. _____

   _____

3. What is the order of operations within an expression? _____

   _____

4. Give an example of an integer. _____

5. Give an example of a real number. _____

6. Show three examples of how the measurement *five feet six inches* can be entered when using the **CAL** command. _____

   _____

7. Give the proper symbol to use for the following math functions:

   A. Addition _____

   B. Subtraction _____

   C. Multiplication _____

   D. Division _____

   E. Exponent _____

   F. Grouped expressions _____

8. Give the expression used to calculate the conversion of 8″ to millimeters._____

   _____

9. Given the following geometry calculator point coordinate entries, provide the shorter format:

   A. [2,2,0]_____

   B. [0,0,6]_____

   C. [5,0,0]_____

   D. [0,0,0]_____

10. Show the entry format for the following coordinate systems:

    A. Polar _____

    B. Relative_____

11. What expression do you enter if you want to use the cursor to specify a point?__

    _____

12. Give the expression that you would use to find a point that is added to the cursor location at X=1 and Y=2. _____

13. How do you enter the geometry calculator transparently? _____

14. Why are object snaps often used when finding points for the geometry calculator?

    _____

    _____

15. What does AutoCAD recognize when entering object snap instructions in the geometry calculator? _____

    _____

16. Give the expression used to find the distance halfway between the endpoints of two lines. _____

    _____

17. Give the expression used to calculate the distance between the center of two circles.

    _____

    _____

18. Give the expression used to find the shortest distance from the end of a line to another line with two available endpoints. _____

    _____

19. Give the expression needed to find the distance between the last point used in AutoCAD and the point located at coordinates 4,4,0. _____

    _____

20. Identify the function that is used to find the intersection point between two non-parallel lines._____

21. Name the function that is used to find an angle._____

22. Give the expression used to identify the included angle when the vertex and sides are available. _____

23. Provide the function that is used to find the radius of a circle, arc, or 2D polyline.

    _____

24. Give the shortcut functions for the following applications:

    A. Distance between two selected endpoints _____

    B. Intersection of two lines defined by four selected endpoints _____

    C. Point midway between two selected endpoints _____

25. Give the function for the following math operations:

    A. Returns a number squared _____

    B. Returns the square root of a number _____

26. Give an example of the full format for entering degrees, minutes, and seconds in the geometry calculator. _____

27. Give the trigonometric functions for the following operations:

    A. Returns the sine of angle _____

    B. Returns the cosine of angle _____

    C. Returns the tangent of angle _____

28. Give the function for calculating the constant pi. _____

29. A _____ is a text item that represents another value that can be accessed later as needed._____

30. Define filters._____

    _____

    _____

31. How do you enter the **FILTER** command transparently?_____

32. What happens when you enter the **FILTER** command? _____

    _____

33. What is the purpose of the list box in the **Object Selection Filters** dialog box? ___
___

34. What is the purpose of the **Select Filter** area in the **Object Selection Filters** dialog box? ___
___

35. What is the purpose of the **Named Filters** area in the **Object Selection Filters** dialog box? ___
___

36. What do you do to exit the filtered selection and return to a normal selection mode? ___
___

37. How do you remove an item from the filter list? ___
___

38. How do you clear the entire filter list and start over again? ___
___

39. Name the command that is used to get a Select objects: prompt prior to using the **FILTER** command transparently. ___

40. Which relative operator is used to select all arcs that have a radius of 4.3 or less? ___
___

41. How many characters are allowed in a filter name? ___

42. If you want to use filters to make changes to the text on your drawing and you pick one of the text objects, the dialog box displays the characteristics of the text you picked. Why is it best to delete items such as **Text Position** and **Text Value**? ___
___
___

43. What is the purpose of X and Y filters? ___
___

44. If you add circles to the filter list, what happens when a selection window is placed around a group of lines, arcs, and circles? ___
___

45. Identify two ways to specify a linetype in a filter list. ___
___

46. Provide the following relative operator symbols:
    A. Not equal to ___
    B. Less than ___
    C. Less than or equal to ___
    D. Greater than ___
    E. Greater than or equal to ___
    F. Equal to any value ___

Drawing Problems

Use the **CAL** *command to calculate the following math problems:*

1. 27.375+15.875

2. 16.0625–7.1250

3. 5 × 17'-8"

4. 48'-0" divided by 16

5. (12.625+3.063)+(18.250–4.375)–(2.625–1.188)

6. 7.25 squared

7. Show the calculation and answer that would be used with the **LINE** command to make an 8" line 1.006 in./in. longer in a pattern to allow for shrinkage in the final casting. Show only the expression and answer.

8. Solve for the deflection of a structural member. The formula is written as $PL^3 / 48EI$, where P = pounds of force, L = length of beam, E = Modulus of Elasticity, and I = moment of inertia. The values to be used are P = 4000 lbs, L = 240", and E = 1,000,000 lbs/in². The value for I is the result of the beam (Width * Height³) / 12, where Width = 6.75" and Height = 13.5".

9. Convert 4.625" to millimeters.

10. Convert 26mm to inches.

11. Convert 65 miles to kilometers.

12. Convert 5 gallons to liters.

13. Calculate the coordinate located at 4,4,0 + 3<30.

14. Calculate the coordinate located at 3+5,1+1.25,0 + 2.375,1.625.

15. Find the square root of 360.

16. What is 3.25 squared?

Given the following right triangle, make the required trigonometry calculations:

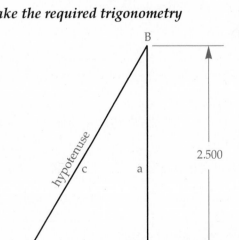

17. Length of side *c* (hypotenuse).

18. Sine of angle *A*.

19. Sine of angle *B*.

20. Cosine of angle *A*.

21. Tangent of angle *A*.

22. Tangent of angle *B*.

23. Create the following drawing using the **CAL** command and object snaps as needed to help you. Do not draw dimensions. Save the drawing as P7-23.

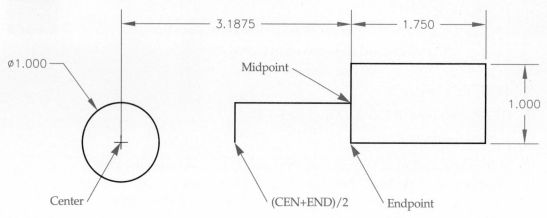

24. Open P7-23 and add the circle as shown below. Save the drawing as P7-24.

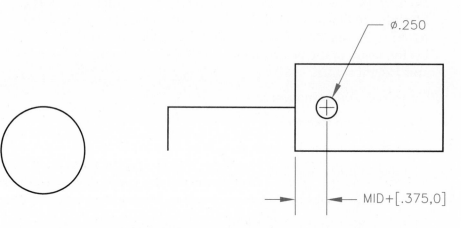

25. Create the following drawing using the **CAL** command and object snaps as needed to help you. Place the circle with its center at the center of mass of the triangle. Do not draw dimensions. Save the drawing as P7-25.

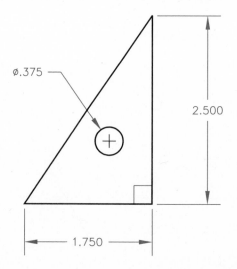

26. Draw the lines shown below using the dimensions given. Do not draw dimensions or labels. Calculate the following:

A. Length of line A.

B. Length of line B.

C. Shortest distance between point P and line B.

Write your answers and save the drawing as P7-26.

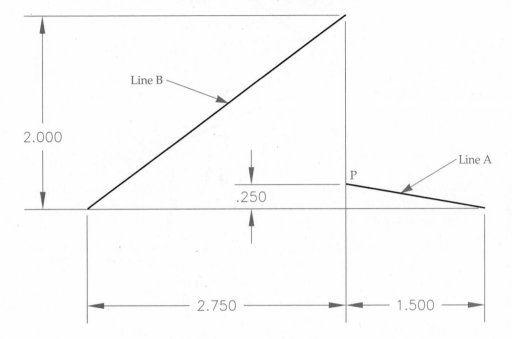

27. Line A has endpoints at 2.88,8.88 and 6.50,6.75. Line B has endpoints at 1.75,7.25 and 6.5,8.5. Determine the point where these lines intersect using the **CAL** command. Then draw the lines and check your solution graphically. Save the drawing as P7-27.

28. Draw the line shown below using the coordinates and dimensions given. Do not draw dimensions or labels. Calculate the coordinate at the other end of the line and the coordinate of a point along the line that is two and one-quarter times the length of the given line. Write your answer and save the drawing as P7-28.

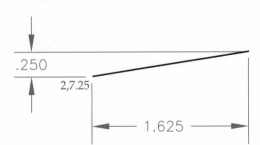

29. Draw the lines shown below. Use the **CAL** command to determine the angle between the lines. Save the drawing as P7-29.

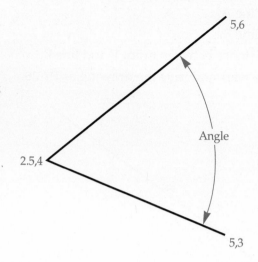

30. Draw a rectangle measuring 3.125 × 5.625. Use the **CAL** command to center a .75 diameter circle in the center of the rectangle. Save the drawing as P7-30.

31. Draw the following object. Then use the **CAL** command to add another circle with a diameter that is 30% of the size of the existing circle. Center the new circle between the midpoints of line 1 and line 2. Do not include dimensions. Save the drawing as P7-31.

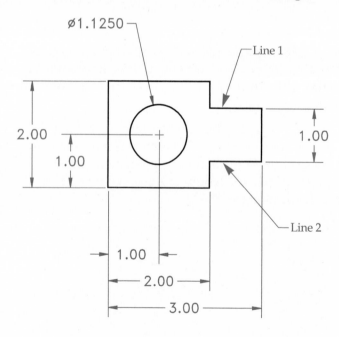

32. Draw the following object. Then use the **CAL** command to create another circle with the same diameter as the existing circle. Place the center of the new circle .5″ above a point that is midway between the center of the existing circle and the midpoint of the right line of the object. Do not include dimensions. Save the drawing as P7-32.

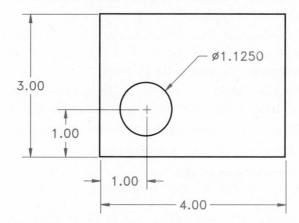

33. Use the X and Y filters to draw an isosceles triangle with a vertical baseline measuring 4.5″ long and 5.75″ high. Save the drawing as P7-33.

34. Draw the object shown below. Then use the **CAL** command to create another circle with a diameter which is 150 percent (1.5X) of the existing circle. Center the new circle 3″ horizontally to the right of the existing circle. Do not dimension the drawing. Save the drawing as P7-34.

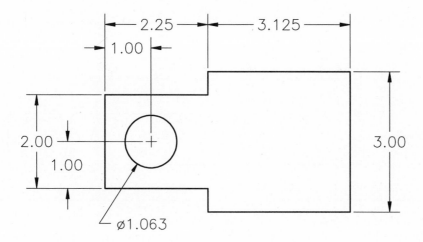

35. Use tracking, object snaps, and the geometric calculator to draw the following object based on these instructions:

A. Draw the overall object first, followed by the 10 φ.500 holes.

B. The B holes are located vertically halfway between the centers of the A holes. The B holes have a diameter one-quarter the size of the A holes.

C. The B holes that are located horizontally between the A holes are halfway between the centers of the A holes and also have a diameter one-quarter the size of the A holes.

D. The C holes are located vertically halfway between the A and B holes and have a diameter three-quarters of the B holes.

E. Draw the rectangles around the circles as shown.

F. Do not draw dimensions, notes, or labels.

G. Save the drawing as P7-35.

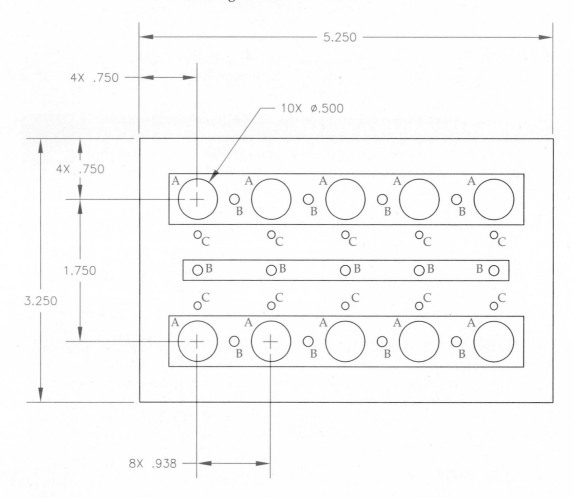

36. Open P7-35. Use a selection filter to erase all circles less than φ.500. Name and save the filter set. Save the drawing as P7-36.

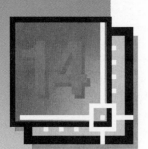

Placing Text on Drawings

Learning Objectives

After completing this chapter, you will be able to:
- ○ Use and discuss proper text standards.
- ○ Use the **DTEXT** command to display text on the screen while typing.
- ○ Make multiple lines of text with the **MTEXT** command.
- ○ Use the **TEXT** command to add words to a drawing.
- ○ Change text styles using the **STYLE** command.
- ○ Draw special symbols using control characters.
- ○ Underscore and overscore text.
- ○ Explain the purpose of the **Quick Text** mode and use the **QTEXT** command.
- ○ Design title blocks for your drawing template.
- ○ Draw objects with associated text.
- ○ Edit existing text.
- ○ Check your spelling.

Words and notes on drawings have traditionally been added by hand lettering. This is a slow, time-consuming task. Computer-aided drafting programs have reduced the tedious nature of adding notes to a drawing. In computer-aided drafting, lettering is referred to as *text*.

There are advantages of computer-generated text over hand-lettering techniques. When performed by computer, lettering is fast, easier to read, and more consistent. This chapter shows how text can be added to drawings. Also explained is the proper text presentation based on ASME Y14.2M-1992, *Line Conventions and Lettering*.

Text Standards

Company standards often dictate how text appears on a drawing. The minimum recommended text height on engineering drawings is .125″ (3mm). All dimension numbers, notes, and other text information should be the same height. Titles, subtitles, captions, revision information, and drawing numbers can be .188″ to .25″ (5 to 6.5mm) high. Many companies specify a .188″, or 5/32″ (5mm), lettering height for standard text. This text size is easy to read even after the drawing is reduced.

Vertical or inclined text may be used on a drawing, depending on company preference. See Figure 8-1. One or the other is recommended, but do not use both. The recommended slant for inclined text is 68° from horizontal. Computer-generated text offers a variety of styles for specific purposes, such as titles or captions. Text on a drawing is normally uppercase, but lowercase letters are used in some instances.

Numbers in dimensions and notes are the same height as standard text. When fractions are used in dimensions, the ANSI standard recommends that the fraction bar be placed horizontally between the numerator and denominator using full-size numbers. Notes placed on a drawing have fractions displayed with a diagonal (/) fraction bar, or the fractions can be stacked when using the **MTEXT** command. A dash or space is usually placed between the whole number and the fraction. See Figure 8-2.

Figure 8-1.
Vertical and inclined text.

ABC.. abc.. 123..
ABC.. abc.. 123..

Figure 8-2.
Examples of numbers for different units of measure.

Units	Example	
Decimal-inches	2.750	
Millimeters	3	0.5
Fractional inches	2 3/4	
	2—3/4	

Scale Factors for Text Height

Scale factors and text heights should be determined before beginning a drawing, and are best incorporated as values within your template drawing files. Scale factors are important because this value is used to make sure that the text is plotted at the proper height. The scale factor is multiplied by the desired plotted text height to get the AutoCAD text height. The AutoCAD setup wizards automatically control text height scale factors.

The scale factor is always a reciprocal of the drawing scale. For example, if you wish to plot a drawing at a scale of 1/2″ = 1″, calculate the scale factor as follows:

    1/2″ = 1″
    .5″ = 1″
    1/.5 = 2 The scale factor is 2.

An architectural drawing that is to be plotted at a scale of 1/4″ = 1′-0″ has a scale factor calculated as follows:

    1/4″ = 1′-0″
    .25 = 12″
    12/.25 = 48 The scale factor is 48.

The scale factor of a civil engineering drawing that has a scale of 1″ = 60′ is calculated as follows:

    1″ = 60′
    1″ = (60 × 12)
    720/1 = 720 The scale factor is 720.

If your drawing is in millimeters with a scale is 1:1, the drawing can be converted to inches with the formula 1″ = 25.4mm. Therefore, the scale factor is 25.4. When the metric drawing scale is 1:2, then the scale factor is 1″ = 25.4 × 2, or 1″ = 50.8. The scale factor is 50.8.

After the scale factor has been determined, you should then calculate the height of the AutoCAD text. If the text is to be plotted at 1/8″ (.125″) high, it should be drawn at that height. If the drawing scale is full (1″ = 1″), then the text height is 1/8″ (.125″). However, if you are working on a civil engineering drawing with a scale of 1″ = 60′, text drawn at 1/8″ high appears as a dot. Remember that the drawing you are working on is 720 times larger than it is when plotted at the proper scale. Therefore, you must multiply the text height by the 720 scale factor to get text that appears in correct proportion on the screen. If you want 1/8″ (.125″) high text to appear correctly on a drawing with a 1″ = 60′ scale, calculate the AutoCAD height as follows:

```
1″ = 60′
1″ = (60 × 12)
720/1 = 720 The scale factor is 720.
text height × scale factor = scaled text height
.125″ × 720 = 90″ The proper text height is 90″.
```

An architectural drawing with a scale of 1/4″ = 1′-0″ has a scale factor of 48. Text that is to be 1/8″ high should be drawn 6″ high.

```
1/4″ = 1′-0″
.25″ = 12″
12/.25 = 48 The scale factor is 48.
.125 × 48 = 6 The proper text height is 6″.
```

Text Composition

Composition refers to the spacing, layout, and appearance of the text. With manual lettering, it is necessary to space letters freehand. Spacing is performed automatically with computer-generated text.

Notes should be placed horizontally on the drawing. AutoCAD automatically sets lines of text apart a distance equal to one-half the text height. This helps maintain the identity of individual notes.

The term *justify* means to align the text to fit a given location. For example, left-justified text is aligned along an imaginary left border. Most lines of text are left-justified. Figure 8-3 shows the AutoCAD spacing between lines of left-justified text.

Figure 8-3.
Default spacing between lines of left-justified text.

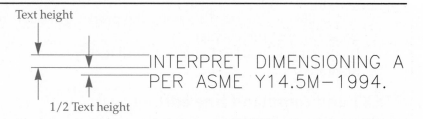

Using AutoCAD to Draw Text

AutoCAD provides you with two basic systems for creating text. There is line text for creating single-line text objects, and multiline text for preparing paragraph text. The **DTEXT** and **TEXT** commands are used to create single-line text where the text is entered at the prompt line. The **MTEXT** command is used to create paragraph text that is entered in the **Multiline Text Editor**. Each command is used differently, but the options are similar. Text styles allow you to make the text look the way you want.

Dynamic text

The **DTEXT** (dynamic text) command allows you to see the text on the screen as you type. The **DTEXT** command creates single-line text. This means that each line of text is a single text object. **DTEXT** is most useful for text items that require only one line of text. Whenever the text has more than one line or requires mixed fonts, sizes, or colors, multiline text should be used.

DTEXT
DT

Draw
↳ Text
  ↳ Single Line
    Text

The **DTEXT** command can be issued by picking **Single Line Text** from the **Text** cascading menu in the **Draw** pull-down menu, or entering DT or DTEXT at the Command: prompt as follows:

```
Command: DT or DTEXT↵
Justify/Style/⟨Start point⟩: (pick a starting point)
Height ⟨0.2000⟩: (enter a value, or press [Enter])
Rotation angle ⟨0⟩: (enter a value, or press [Enter])
Text: (type text)↵
Text: (type in next line of text or press [Enter] to complete)↵
Command:
```

When the Text: prompt appears, a text cursor equal in size to the text height appears on the screen at the text start point. **DTEXT** can be used to enter multiple lines of text simply by pressing [Enter] at the end of each line. The Text: prompt is repeated for the next line of text. Press [Enter] twice to exit the **DTEXT** command and keep what you have typed. You can cancel the **DTEXT** command at any time by pressing the [Esc] key. This action erases all of the text entered during the command.

A great advantage of **DTEXT** is that multiple lines of text can be entered. Simply press [Enter] at the end of each line. The text cursor automatically moves to the start point one line below the preceding line. Each line of text is a single object.

While in the **DTEXT** command, the screen crosshairs can be moved independently of the text cursor box. Selecting a new start point completes the line of text being entered and begins a new line at the selected point. Using **DTEXT**, multiple lines of text may be entered anywhere on the drawing without exiting the command. This saves a lot of drafting time. A few aspects of the **DTEXT** command to be aware of are:

✓ When you end the **DTEXT** command, the entered text is erased from the screen, then regenerated.

✓ Regardless of the type of justification selected, the cursor box appears as if the text is left-justified. However, when you end the **DTEXT** command, the text disappears and is then regenerated with the alignment you requested.

✓ When you use a control code sequence for a symbol, the control code, not the symbol, is displayed. When you complete the command, the text disappears and is then regenerated showing the proper symbol. Control codes are discussed later in this chapter.

✓ If you cancel the **DTEXT** command, all text entered while in the command is discarded.

DTEXT and command line editing

When using the **DTEXT** command, you can do command line editing. The following keys are used to edit the entered material:

• **[↑].** The up arrow key moves backward through previously entered commands, allowing them to become a text entry. You might think of it as moving *up* the list of previous commands.

• **[↓].** After moving backward through any number of previous lines, the down arrow key moves forward again. You might think of this as moving back *down* the list of previously entered commands.

- **[←].** The left arrow key moves the cursor left through the text currently on the command line. Doing this allows you to reposition the cursor to insert text or words that were skipped when entering the text.
- **[→].** After using the left arrow key, the right arrow key moves the typing cursor back to the right.
- **[Home].** Moves the cursor to the home position, which is in front of the first character typed at the command line.
- **[End].** Moves the cursor back to the far right, at the very end of the text typed at the command line.
- **[Insert].** Toggles the command line between **Insert** and **Overwrite** mode. When in **Insert** mode, any new text is inserted at the cursor position, and any text existing to the right of the cursor is moved to the right. When in **Overwrite** mode, new text entered replaces the character at the cursor position.
- **[Page Up].** Does not directly affect the actual command line, but moves the history lines (the lines that show the previous command lines) up whatever number of lines is currently displayed.
- **[Page Down].** Same as the page up key, except it moves back down the history list.
- **[Delete].** Deletes the character to the right of the text cursor.
- **[Backspace].** Deletes the character to the left of the text cursor.
- **[Space bar].** During **Insert** mode, inserts a space in text at the cursor position. During **Overwrite** mode, deletes the next character to the right of the cursor position.

The **Start point** option

After entering the **DTEXT** command, you are given the Justify/Style/⟨Start point⟩: prompt. The default option is **Start point**. This option allows you to select a point on the screen where you want the text to begin. This point becomes the lower-left corner of the text. If you do not like the start point that you pick, you can continue picking until you pick the desired point. After you pick the point, the prompt reads:

Height ⟨0.2000⟩:

This prompt allows you to select the text height. The default value is 0.2000. The previously selected letter height may be displayed as the current value. If you want letters that are .5 unit high, then enter .5. The next prompt is:

Rotation angle ⟨0⟩:

The default value for the rotation angle is 0, which places the text horizontally. The values rotate text in a counterclockwise direction. The text pivots about the starting point. See Figure 8-4.

NOTE If the default angle orientation or direction (**ANGBASE** and **ANGDIR** system variables) is changed, the text rotation is affected.

The last prompt is:

Text:

Type the desired text and press [Enter]. Text added with the **Start point** option is left-justified. See Figure 8-5.

Figure 8-4.
Different rotation angles for text. The starting point is indicated here with a plus sign.

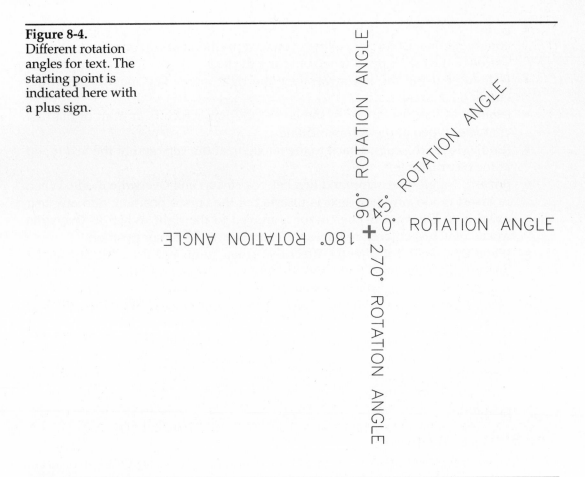

Figure 8-5.
Left-justified text using the **Start point** option.

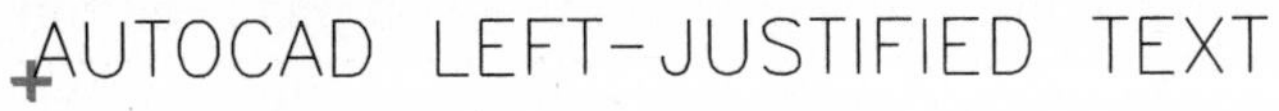

+AUTOCAD LEFT-JUSTIFIED TEXT

The Justify option

The **DTEXT** command offers a variety of justification options. Left-justification is the default. If you want another option, enter J at the Justify/Style/⟨Start point⟩: prompt. When you select the **Justify** option, you can use one of several text alignment options. These options can be seen in the command sequence below, and are explained in the next sections.

Command: **DT** *or* **DTEXT**↵
Justify/Style/⟨Start point⟩: **J**↵
Align/Fit/Center/Middle/Right/TL/TC/TR/ML/MC/MR/BL/BC/BR:

- **Align (A).** When this option is selected, you are prompted for two points between which the text string is confined:

  Align/Fit/Center/Middle/Right/TL/TC/TR/ML/MC/MR/BL/BC/BR: **A**↵
  First text line point: *(pick a point)*
  Second text line point: *(pick a point)*
  Text: *(type text)*

The beginning and endpoints can be placed horizontally or at an angle. AutoCAD automatically adjusts the text width to fit between the selected points. The text height is also changed with this option. The height varies according to the distance between the points and the number of characters. See Figure 8-6.

AutoCAD and its Applications—Basics

Figure 8-6.
Examples of aligned
text. Notice how
AutoCAD adjusts
the text height.

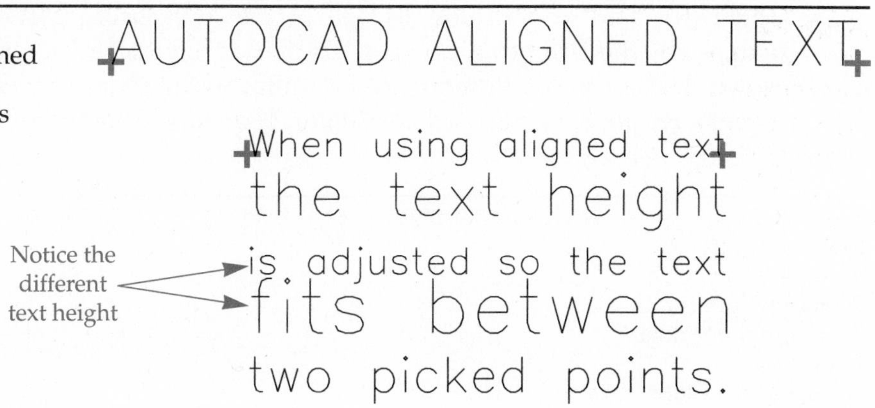

AUTOCAD ALIGNED TEXT

When using aligned text
the text height

Notice the
different ────→ is adjusted so the text
text height ────→ fits between
two picked points.

> **PROFESSIONAL TIP** **DTEXT** is not recommended for aligned text because the text height for each line is adjusted according to the width. One line may run into another.

- **Fit (F).** This option is similar to the **Align** option, except that you can select the text height. AutoCAD adjusts the letter width to fit between the two given points, while keeping text height constant. See Figure 8-7.

    Align/Fit/Center/Middle/Right/TL/TC/TR/ML/MC/MR/BL/BC/BR: **F.⏎**
    First text line point: *(pick a point)*
    Second text line point: *(pick a point)*
    Height ⟨*current*⟩: **.5.⏎**
    Text: *(type text)*

Figure 8-7.
Using the **Fit** text option. Notice how AutoCAD adjusts the letter width but keeps the letter height.

AUTOCAD FIT TEXT

AUTOCAD FIT TEXT

Notice
the different
letter width

- **Center (C).** This option allows you to select the center point for the baseline of the text. Enter the letter height and rotation angle after picking the center point. This example uses a .5 unit height and a 0° rotation angle. The prompts appear as follows:

    Align/Fit/Center/Middle/Right/TL/TC/TR/ML/MC/MR/BL/BC/BR: **C.⏎**
    Center point: *(pick a point)*
    Height ⟨*current*⟩: **.5.⏎**
    Rotation angle ⟨0⟩: .⏎
    Text: *(type text)*

- **Middle (M).** This option allows you to center text both horizontally and vertically at a given point. The letter height and rotation can also be changed. The command sequence is similar to the sequence for the **Center** option.

- **Right (R).** This option justifies text at the lower-right corner. The point is entered at the End point: prompt. The letter height and rotation can also be entered. The command sequence is similar to the sequence for the **Start point** option. Figure 8-8 compares the **Center**, **Middle**, and **Right** options.

Figure 8-8.
DTEXT options.
A—Using the **Center** text option.
B—Using the **Middle** text option.
C—Using the **Right** text option.

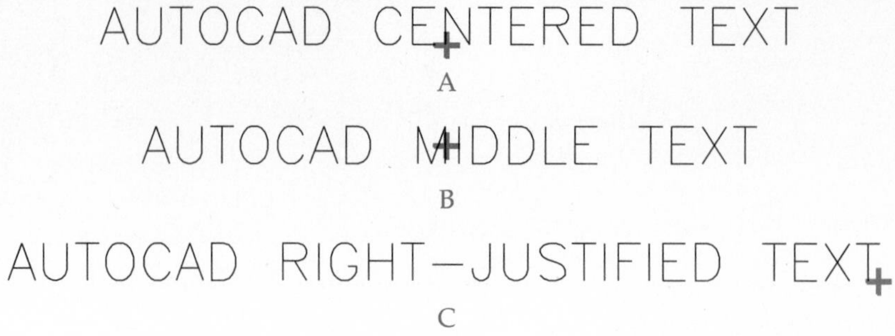

AUTOCAD CENTERED TEXT
A

AUTOCAD MIDDLE TEXT
B

AUTOCAD RIGHT—JUSTIFIED TEXT
C

PROFESSIONAL TIP   If you already know which text alignment option you want to use in your drawing, you can enter it at the Justify/Style/⟨Start point⟩: prompt without entering J. Just type the uppercase letter or letters of the desired option and press [Enter].

EXERCISE 8-1

❑ Start AutoCAD and use the setup option of your choice.
❑ Use the **DTEXT** command to type the following information. Each time, change the text option to obtain the format given. Use .5 (12mm) letter height and 0° rotation angle.

    AUTOCAD TEXT LEFT-JUSTIFIED USING THE START POINT OPTION.
    AUTOCAD TEXT RIGHT-JUSTIFIED USING THE RIGHT OPTION.
    AUTOCAD TEXT ALIGNED USING THE ALIGN OPTION.
    AUTOCAD TEXT CENTERED USING THE CENTER OPTION.
    AUTOCAD FIT TEXT USING THE FIT OPTION.
    AUTOCAD TEXT USING THE MIDDLE OPTION.

❑ Save the drawing as EX8-1.

Other text alignment options

There are a number of text alignment options that allow you to place text on a drawing in relation to the top, bottom, middle, left, or right side of the text. These alignment options are shown in Figure 8-9. These options are shown as abbreviations that correlate to the **TEXT** prompt line. To use one of these options, type the two letters for the desired option and press Enter:

    Command: **DT** or **DTEXT**↵
    Justify/Style/⟨Start point⟩: **J**↵
    Align/Fit/Center/Middle/Right/TL/TC/TR/ML/MC/MR/BL/BC/BR: (type the two letters for the desired option, such as TL, and press [Enter])

Figure 8-9.
Using the **TL**, **TC**, **TR**, **ML**, **MC**, **MR**, **BL**, **BC**, and **BR** text alignment options. Notice what the abbreviations stand for.

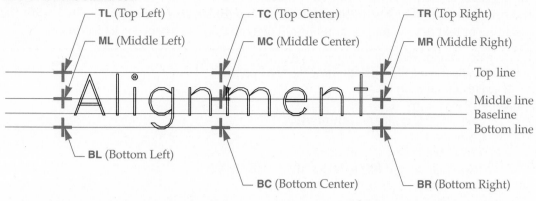

❑ Start AutoCAD and use the setup option of your choice.
❑ Use the **DTEXT** command to type the following information. Each time, change the text option to obtain the format given in each statement. Use .5 (12mm) letter height and 0° rotation angle.

    AUTOCAD TOP/LEFT OPTION.
    AUTOCAD TOP/CENTER OPTION.
    AUTOCAD TOP/RIGHT OPTION.
    AUTOCAD MIDDLE/LEFT OPTION.
    AUTOCAD MIDDLE/CENTER OPTION.
    AUTOCAD MIDDLE/RIGHT OPTION.
    AUTOCAD BOTTOM/LEFT OPTION.
    AUTOCAD BOTTOM/CENTER OPTION.
    AUTOCAD BOTTOM/RIGHT OPTION.

❑ Save the drawing as EX8-2.

Using the **TEXT** command

The **TEXT** command can also be used to draw single-line text. The **TEXT** command has the same options as the **DTEXT** command. However, the two commands have the following differences:

- After typing a line of text and pressing [Enter], the **TEXT** command returns you to the Command: prompt. The **DTEXT** command provides the Text: prompt again for another line of text.
- The **DTEXT** command displays text being typed at the prompt line and on the screen, while the **TEXT** command displays text only at the prompt line.

The following shows the use of the **TEXT** command for a single line of text:

Command: **TEXT**↵
Justify/Style/⟨Start point⟩: *(pick a start point or use a **Justify** option)*
Height ⟨0.2000⟩: ↵
Rotation angle ⟨0⟩: ↵
Text: *(type text and press [Enter])*
Command:

Additional lines of text can be made with the **TEXT** command. To do so, press [Enter] after the first line has been entered. This brings back the Command: prompt. A second [Enter] repeats the previous **TEXT** command. The Start point: prompt appears again and the previous line of text is highlighted. Press the [Enter] key to automatically justify the next line of text below the previous line. The command sequence is as follows:

    Command: **TEXT**⏎
    Justify/Style/⟨Start point⟩: *(pick the start point)*
    Height ⟨current⟩: **.5**⏎
    Rotation angle ⟨0⟩: ⏎
    Text: *(type text and press* [Enter]*)*
    Command: ⏎
    TEXT Justify/Style/⟨Start point⟩: ⏎
    Text: *(type second line of text and press* [Enter]*)*
    Command:

This method is far more cumbersome than using the **DTEXT** command.

Each line of text is an individual object when using the **TEXT** and **DTEXT** commands in AutoCAD. In order to move or erase a paragraph of text created by this method, you need to select each line of text. The **MTEXT** command discussed in the next section creates multiline text objects where one or more paragraphs can be created as a single AutoCAD object.

EXERCISE 8-3

❑ Start AutoCAD and use the setup option of your choice.
❑ Use the **TEXT** command to type the following multiple lines of text exactly as shown. Use .25 (6mm) letter height and 0° rotation angle.

> LETTERING HAS TYPICALLY BEEN A SLOW, TIME-CONSUMING TASK. COMPUTER-AIDED DRAFTING HAS REDUCED THE TEDIOUS NATURE OF PREPARING LETTERING ON A DRAWING. IN CAD, LETTERING IS REFERRED TO AS TEXT. COMPUTER-GENERATED TEXT IS FAST, CONSISTENT, AND EASIER TO READ.

❑ Save the drawing as EX8-3.

Making multiline text

The **MTEXT** command is used to create multiline text objects. Instead of each line being an individual object, all of the lines are part of the same object. The **MTEXT** command is accessed by picking the **Multiline Text** button in the **Draw** toolbar, picking **Multiline Text...** in the **Text** cascading menu of the **Draw** pull-down, or entering T, MT, or MTEXT at the Command: prompt.

After entering the **MTEXT** command, AutoCAD asks you to specify the first and second corners of the text boundary. The *text boundary* is a box within which your text will be placed. When you pick the first corner of the text boundary, the cursor changes to a box. Move the box until you have the desired size for your paragraph and pick the opposite corner. See Figure 8-10.

Figure 8-10.
The text boundary is a box within which your text will be placed. The arrow indicates the direction of text flow.

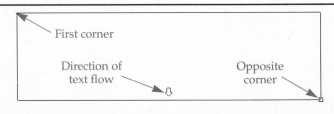

AutoCAD and its Applications—Basics

When drawing the boundary window for multiline text, an arrow in the window shows the direction of text flow. While the width of the rectangle drawn provides a limit to the width of the text paragraphs, it does not affect the possible height. The rectangle height is automatically resized to fit the actual text entered. When the text exceeds the height of the specified rectangle, the rectangle is automatically expanded to fit. The direction of the flow indicates where the rectangle is expanded if necessary. This is the command sequence:

Command: **T**, **MT**, *or* **MTEXT**↵
Current text style: STANDARD. Text height: 0.2000
Specify the first corner: *(pick the first corner)*
Specify opposite corner or [Height/Justify/Rotation/Style/Width]: *(pick the other corner)*

After picking the text boundary, the **Multiline Text Editor** appears. See Figure 8-11. The **Character** tab is used to enter text, change features (such as font, text height, color), and copy text. The **Properties** tab is used to change features such as the current text styles, justification, text boundary width, and rotation. The **Find/Replace** tab is used to replace selected words with new words.

Figure 8-11.
The **Multiline Text Editor**. Enter text in the text window (shown here highlighted).

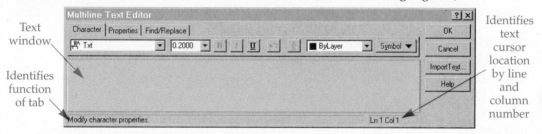

In the lower-right corner of the tab, there is a Ln 1 Col 1 message. This means that the text cursor is located at Line 1 Column 1. A *line* is created every time the text cursor moves down. A line can be full of text that you type or can be blank. You can move the text cursor down by pressing the [Enter] key, or by picking with your pointer. A new line is also created when you type to the right boundary and AutoCAD automatically moves the cursor to the next line.

The text window gets vertically bigger as new lines are added. When the text window fills the screen, previous lines begin to be hidden and a scroll bar is displayed at the right. Use the scroll bar to move up and down to access lines in the text window. A column is created every time the text cursor moves to the right. A column is one character wide, whether it is an actual text character or a space.

EXERCISE 8-4

❏ Start AutoCAD and use the setup option of your choice.
❏ Access the **MTEXT** command and create a text boundary that is 4″ (100mm) wide and 2″ (50mm) high.
❏ Pick each of the tabs: **Character**, **Properties**, and **Find/Replace** and just look at the features plus read the message in the lower-left corner of each.
❏ Type anything you want and press the [Enter] key to watch the line and column number change in the lower-right corner.
❏ Type enough text or press the [Enter] key enough times to see the text window increase in size until the scroll bar is displayed on the right.
❏ Pick the **OK** button when done to see the text displayed on the screen.
❏ Save the drawing as EX8-4.

Modifying character properties with the Multiline Text Editor

The **Multiline Text Editor** is displayed after you define the text boundary. The editing window is the primary feature of this dialog box. There are three tabs in this dialog box, by default the **Character** tab is open. This is where character standards are set and edited. Character standards refer to the content and appearance of the characters in the text object you are editing.

While in the **Multiline Text Editor** there are a number of keystroke combinations that are available. These combinations are as follows:

Keystroke	Function
[↑] [←] [↓] [→]	Arrow keys move the cursor through the text one position in the direction indicated by the arrow.
[Ctrl]+[→] [Ctrl]+[←]	Moves the cursor one word in the direction indicated.
[Home]	Moves the cursor to the start of the current line.
[End]	Moves the cursor to the end of the current line.
[Delete]	Deletes the character immediately to the right of the cursor.
[Backspace]	Deletes the character immediately to the left of the cursor.
[Ctrl]+[Backspace]	Deletes the word immediately to the left of the cursor.
[Ctrl]+[C]	Copy selection to Clipboard. The Clipboard is an internal storage area that temporarily stores information that you copy or cut from a document.
[Ctrl]+[V]	Paste Clipboard contents to the selection or current cursor location.
[Ctrl]+[X]	Cut selection to Clipboard.
[Ctrl]+[Z]	Undo.
[Ctrl]+[Spacebar]	Inserts a nonbreaking space.
[Enter]	Ends the current paragraph, starting a new one on the next line.
[Page Up] [Page Down]	These keys move the cursor up to 28 rows in the indicated direction.
[Ctrl]+[Page Up] [Ctrl]+[Page Down]	These keys move the cursor to the top or bottom of the currently visible page of text.
[Ctrl]+[Home]	Moves the cursor to line 1, column 1.
[Ctrl]+[End]	Moves the cursor to the last character position.
[Ctrl]+[A]	Selects all of the text in the current multiline text object.
[Shift]+[→] [Shift]+[←]	Selects or deselects text. Increases or decreases the selection by one character at a time, depending on the direction indicated.
[Shift]+[↑] [Shift]+[↓]	Selects or deselects text. Increases or decreases the selection by one line at a time, depending on the direction indicated.
[Ctrl]+[Shift]+[→] [Ctrl]+[Shift]+[←]	Selects or deselects text. Increases or decreases the selection by one word at a time, depending on the direction indicated.
[Esc]	Closes the **Multiline Text Editor** and loses any changes made.

PROFESSIONAL TIP

Text can be pasted from any text-based application into the **Multiline Text Editor**. For example, you can copy text from an application like Microsoft Word, and then paste it into the **Multiline Text Editor**. The pasted text retains its properties. Likewise, text copied or cut from the **Multiline Text Editor** can be pasted into another text based application.

As you move the cursor into the editing window, it changes shape. If you have used other windows text editors, this is a familiar text cursor shape. Pointing to a character position within the text and pressing the pick button causes the cursor to be placed at the selected location. You can then begin typing or editing as needed. If you begin typing where the text cursor is initially placed, your text begins in the upper-left corner of the text boundary.

Text is selected in the same way as with most standard Windows text editors. Place the cursor at one end of the desired selection, press and hold the pick button. Drag the cursor until the desired text is highlighted, then release the pick button. Now, any editing operations you perform affect the highlighted text. For example, a Copy or Cut operation places the highlighted text on the Clipboard. To entirely replace the highlighted text with new text, either paste the new text from the Clipboard or begin typing. The selection is erased and the new text appears in its place.

As you type in the **Multiline Text Editor**, the text cursor moves to the right. When the cursor gets to the end of the text window, the line of text moves to the left, allowing you to continue typing. Notice the scroll bar below the text window. Move the scroll bar to the left or right as needed to uncover hidden text.

Figure 8-12 illustrates the features found in the **Character** tab. Keep in mind that *selected text* refers to text that you have highlighted in the text window:

- **Font list.** A *font* is a family of text characters. Pick the down arrow to open the drop-down list of available text fonts, Figure 8-13. Picking one of the options allows the selected text to have its font changed. This overrides the font used in the current style. The AutoCAD default text style is named STANDARD. Txt is the default text font.

- **Font height.** This option allows selected text to have its height changed. This overrides the current setting of the **TEXTSIZE** variable and the text height set within the **STYLE** command for the selected text.

- **Bold.** Pick this button to have the selected text become bold. This only works with some TrueType fonts. The .shx fonts do not have this capability.

- **Italic.** Pick this button to have the selected text become italic. This only works with some TrueType fonts. The .shx style fonts do not have this capability.

- **Underline.** Picking this button allows selected text to become underlined.

Figure 8-12.
The **Character** tab.

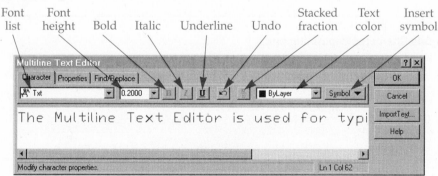

Figure 8-13.
The **Font** drop-down list.

NOTE If you select text that is already bold, picking the **Bold** button returns the text to its normal appearance. This is also true for italic and underline.

- **Undo.** Pick this button to undo the previous activity.
- **Stack/Unstack.** This button allows selected text to be stacked vertically. To use this feature for drawing a vertically stacked fraction, place a forward slash between the top and bottom items. Then select the text with your pointing device and pick the button. This button is also used for unstacking text that has been previously stacked. You can also use the caret (^) character between text if you want to stack the items without a dividing line.
- **Text color.** The text color is set ByLayer as default, but you can change the text color by picking one of the colors found in the **Text color** drop-down list.
- **Insert symbol.** The **Symbol** button opens the options for inserting symbols. See Figure 8-14. This option allows the insertion of symbols at the text cursor location. The **Non-breaking Space** option keeps two separate words together. The **Other...** option opens the **Unicode Character Map** dialog box, Figure 3-15. To use this dialog box, pick the desired TrueType symbols from the **Font:** drop-down list. The **Next** and **Previous** buttons cycle between the options in the **Subset:** list. The following are the steps for using a symbol or symbols:
    1. Pick the desired symbol and then pick the **Select** button. The selected symbol is displayed in the **Characters to Copy:** box.
    2. Pick the **Copy** button to have the selected symbol or symbols copied to the Clipboard.
    3. Pick the **Close** button to close the dialog box.

Figure 8-14.
The **Symbol** menu options.

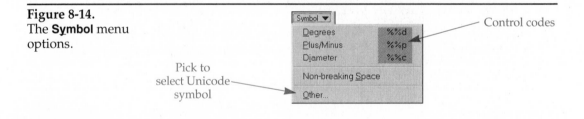

Figure 8-15.
The **Unicode Character Map** dialog box.

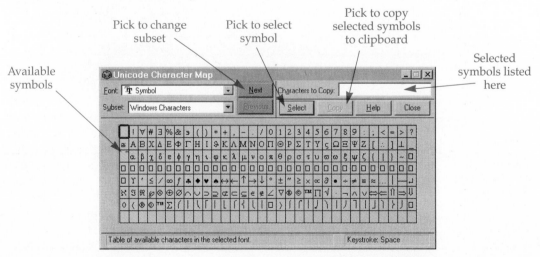

4. Back in the **Multiline Text Editor**, place the text cursor where you want the symbols displayed.
5. Point the screen cursor anywhere inside the text window and press the right mouse button to display the **Edit text** cursor menu shown in Figure 8-16.
6. Pick the **Paste** option to have the selected symbols pasted at the text cursor location.

Figure 8-16.
The **Edit text** cursor menu. When text is highlighted, the **Cut** and **Copy** options are active.

PROFESSIONAL TIP

When a symbol in the **Unicode Character Map** dialog box is highlighted, a keyboard shortcut appears on the right side of the status line. Many of these shortcuts involve the [Alt] key and a number, such as Alt+0175. These numbers match the decimal values for ASCII (American Standard Code for Information Interchange) character codes. To enter this symbol in the text window, hold the [Alt] key while typing 0175. Be sure the correct font is selected.

The listing may also specify a Unicode number. If so, the symbol can be entered by typing \U+ followed by the specified number, just as you would to enter a diameter or degree symbol.

- **Import Text... button.** This allows you to import text from an existing text file directly into the **Multiline Text Editor**. The text file can be either a standard ASCII text file or an .rtf (rich text format) file. The imported text becomes a part of the current multiline text object.

   When this option is selected, a standard file dialog box is displayed. Select the text file to be imported. You cannot import a file that is over 16K in size.

PROFESSIONAL TIP

To insert a text file that is over 16K in size, open it using the source application (the program where it was created), then select and copy the text to the Clipboard. Now it can be pasted into the **Multiline Text Editor**.

NOTE

The formatting of text within the **Multiline Text Editor** may not always appear exactly as it does in the drawing. This is most commonly true when a substitute font is used for display in the editor. A substitute font may be wider or narrower than the font used in the drawing. AutoCAD automatically reformats the text to fit within the boundary defined in the drawing.

Using the Edit text cursor menu

The **Edit text** cursor menu was briefly introduced in the previous discussion. The **Edit text** cursor menu is accessed by pressing the right mouse button when the **Multiline Text Editor** is open. Refer back to Figure 8-16. The following options are available:

- **Undo.** Select this option to undo the last operation. It may be a cut, a paste, or typing operation. Select **Undo** again to bring back the undone operation.
- **Cut.** Pick this option to have the selected text removed from the text window and placed in the Clipboard.
- **Copy.** Use this option to have the selected text copied to the Clipboard.
- **Paste.** This option places items from the Clipboard in the text window at the text cursor location. Anything that has been cut, copied, or imported to the Clipboard can be pasted into the text window.
- **Select All.** Pick this option to select and highlight the entire contents of the text window.

EXERCISE 8-5

- ❑ Start AutoCAD and use the setup option of your choice.
- ❑ Use the **MTEXT** command to create a text boundary that is 4″ (100mm) wide by 2″ (50mm) high.
- ❑ Type the following text paragraph:

   Entering a paragraph of text is quick and easy with the MTEXT command. The MTEXT command opens the Multiline Text Editor, where text is typed and edited as needed. The MTEXT command is accessed by picking Multiline Text in the Text cascading menu of the Draw pull-down menu, by picking the Multiline Text button in the Draw toolbar, or by entering MTEXT at the Command: prompt.

- ❑ Use the cursor menu to select all of the text in the paragraph and then change the height to .125 (3mm) and change the font from Txt to Romans.
- ❑ Select all of the text again and this time change the font to Arial. Now notice that the **Bold** and **Italic** buttons are active. This is because the Arial font is a TrueType font.
- ❑ Make the word MTEXT bold.
- ❑ Make the words Multiline Text Editor italic.
- ❑ Add the following statement to your paragraph:

   The Multiline Text Editor also makes it easy to enter the symbols for degrees (°), plus/minus (±), diameter (∅), greater than (≥), and Omega (Ω).

- ❑ Pick the **OK** button.
- ❑ Save the drawing as EX8-5.

Using the Properties tab

The **Properties** tab of the **Multiline Text Editor** dialog box is shown in Figure 8-17. The following drop-down lists are available:

- **Style.** This drop-down list displays the current text style. STANDARD is the default text style. Selecting a new style changes all the text in the window. All styles defined in the drawing are listed in the drop-down list. If text styles have not been created, then only the STANDARD style is listed.
- **Justification.** This drop-down list provides the list of multiline text justification options. See Figure 8-18. There is an icon to the left of each option name that identifies the option. The two letter abbreviation corresponds to the **DTEXT** and **TEXT** command justification options.

   The text is justified in relation to the boundary. Left-justified text is aligned along the left side, center-justified text is centered in the boundary, and right-justified text is aligned with the right side. See Figure 8-19.

Figure 8-17.
Parts of the **Properties** tab.

List of text styles   List of object alignments   Object widths   Rotation angle

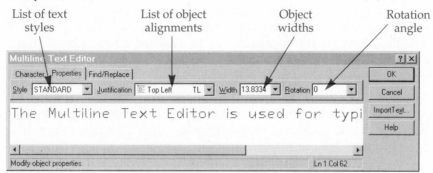

Figure 8-18.
The **Justification** drop-down list.

Figure 8-19.
The effects of the different **MTEXT** justification options.

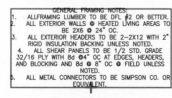
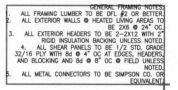

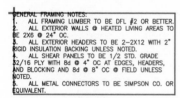
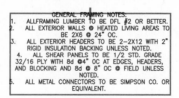

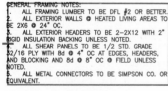

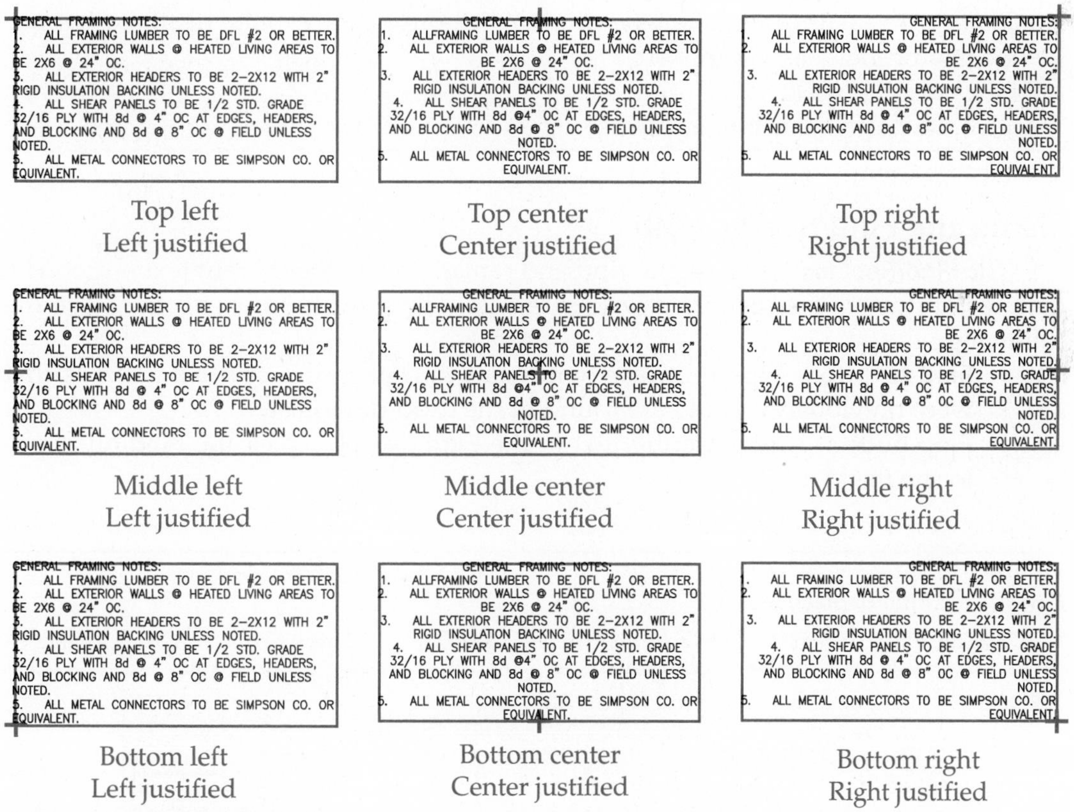

Top left
Left justified

Top center
Center justified

Top right
Right justified

Middle left
Left justified

Middle center
Center justified

Middle right
Right justified

Bottom left
Left justified

Bottom center
Center justified

Bottom right
Right justified

┼ This symbol represents the insertion point

When you are placing the text boundary window, the flow arrows also identify the justification. The flow arrow points downward for any top-justification option. When the text uses any bottom-justification option, the flow is upward so the arrow points upward. When middle-justification, the flow is in *both* directions, so both upward and downward arrows are displayed.

- **Width.** This option has a drop-down list and a text box. The value provided represents the current text boundary width. You can change this value to establish a new width. The **(no wrap)** option deactivates word wrap. When you are typing and reach the end of a line, *word wrap* automatically starts a new line. If you pick the **(no wrap)** option, each line of text continues beyond the right boundary until you press [Enter] to go to the next line.
- **Rotation.** Use this option to set the rotation of the paragraph.

EXERCISE 8-6

❏ Start AutoCAD and use the setup option of your choice.
❏ Use the **MTEXT** command to create a text boundary that is 4″ (100mm) wide by 2″ (50mm) high.
❏ Type the following text paragraph:

> Multiline text is created using the MTEXT command. This provides you with the opportunity to place several lines of text on a drawing and have all of the lines act as one text object. It also gives you the convenience of entering and editing the text in the Multiline Text Editor.

❏ Change the width to 2″ (50mm) and observe the effect.
❏ Change the width back to 4″ (100mm).
❏ Change the justification to a few different options just to see the results. Change the justification back to top left.
❏ Pick the **OK** button.
❏ Save the drawing as EX8-6.

Using the Find/Replace tab

The **Find/Replace** tab is used to find and replace text in the current text object. The features of this tab are identified in Figure 8-20. These features are explained in the following:

- **Find text box.** Type the word you want to find in this text box. Words that were previously entered are found in the drop-down list.
- **Find button.** After entering text in the **Find** text box, pick the **Find** button to locate the identified text.

Figure 8-20.
Parts of the **Find/Replace** tab.

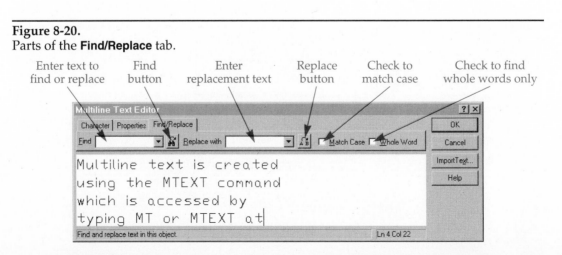

- **Replace with text box.** Type the text that you want to replace the text identified in the **Find** text box. In Figure 8-21A, Multiline is to be replaced with Paragraph.
- **Replace button.** Pick this button to have the selected text replaced with the new text. Figure 8-21B is the result of the replacement.
- **Match Case.** If this check box is activated, the search only finds text that matches the specification *exactly*, including specified uppercase and lowercase characters. If this box is unchecked, a search for HELLO finds Hello, hello, and heLLo.
- **Whole Word.** This check box is used to specify a search for a whole word, and not part of another word. For example, if **Whole Word** is not checked, a search for the would find those letters wherever they occur—including as part of another word, such as *other* or *weather*.

Figure 8-21.
A—Finding text. B—Replacing text.

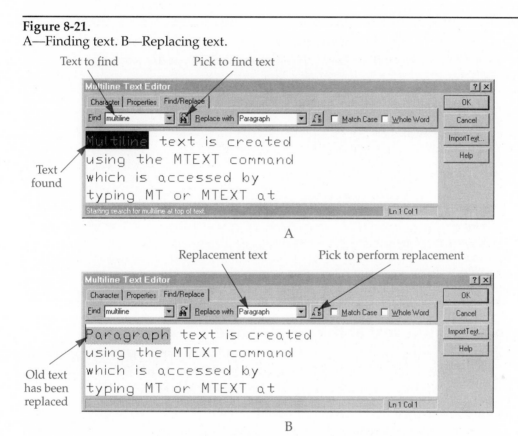

Setting multiline text options at the prompt line

You can set the **MTEXT** options at the Command: prompt. After picking the first boundary corner, select an option. The following command sequence shows an example:

```
Command: T, MT, or MTEXT↵
Current text style: STANDARD. Text height: 0.2000
Specify first corner: (pick the first boundary corner)
Specify opposite corner or [Height/Justify/Rotation/Style/Width]: H.↵
Specify height ⟨0.2000⟩: .125↵
Specify opposite corner or [Height/Justify/Rotation/Style/Width]: J.↵
Enter justification [TL/TC/TR/ML/MC/MR/BL/BC/BR] ⟨TL⟩: MC↵
Specify opposite corner or [Height/Justify/Rotation/Style/Width]: R.↵
Specify rotation angle ⟨0⟩: 30.↵
Specify opposite corner or [Height/Justify/Rotation/Style/Width]: S.↵
Enter style name (or '?') ⟨STANDARD⟩: ↵
Specify opposite corner or [Height/Justify/Rotation/Style/Width]: W ↵
Specify width: 4↵
```

A value specified in the **Width** option automatically sets the multiline text boundary width and opens the **Multiline Text Editor**.

PROFESSIONAL TIP

Multiple lines of text can be placed in a box format with the **Fit** option. This justifies the text on both the left and right. The letter height is the same for each line of text. However, the letter width is adjusted to fit the boundary. Refer to the example below.

EXERCISE 8-7

❑ Start AutoCAD and use the setup option of your choice.
❑ Use the **MTEXT** command and set the following options at the prompt line:

    Height = .125 (3mm)
    Justification = ML
    Rotation angle = 0
    Style = STANDARD
    Width = .5

❑ Type the following text:

    WORDS ON A DRAWING HAVE TRADITIONALLY BEEN REFERRED TO AS
    LETTERING. HAND LETTERING IS TYPICALLY A SLOW, TIME-CONSUMING
    PROCESS. COMPUTER-AIDED DRAFTING HAS REDUCED THE TEDIOUS
    NATURE OF PREPARING LETTERING ON A DRAWING.

❑ Pick the **OK** button.
❑ Save the drawing as EX8-7.

Entering multiline text at the prompt line

If you prefer to enter multiline text at the prompt line, use the **–MTEXT** command. That is a dash (–) entered before MTEXT. Instead of the **Multiline Text Editor** dialog box, an Mtext: prompt appears. The following is the command sequence:

    Command: **-MTEXT**↵
    Current text style: STANDARD. Text height: 0.2000
    Specify first corner: (pick the first text boundary corner)
    Specify opposite corner or [Height/Justify/Rotation/Style/Width]: (pick the other corner)
    MText: (type text)
    MText: (type text or press [Enter] to complete command)
    Command:

Setting a zero width causes lines of text to proceed in a continuous line until you press [Enter] (similar to the **DTEXT** command). When you do this, AutoCAD requests an insertion point. This is the command sequence:

    Command: **-MTEXT**↵
    Current text style: STANDARD. Text height: 0.2000
    Specify first corner: (pick the first text boundary corner)
    Specify opposite corner or [Height/Justify/Rotation/Style/Width]: **W**↵
    Specify width: **0**↵
    MText: (type text)
    MText: (type text or press [Enter] to end command)
    Mtext: ↵
    Command:

❑ Start AutoCAD and use the setup option of your choice.
❑ Type the following multiple lines of text at the prompt line:

> WHEN YOU TYPE THE MULTIPLE LINES OF TEXT DIRECTLY AT THE PROMPT LINE, AUTOCAD AUTOMATICALLY PLACES THE TEXT WITHIN THE BOUNDARY THAT YOU HAVE ESTABLISHED.

❑ Set a text boundary width of zero and then type the following multiple lines of text at the prompt line:

> ENTER THE DESIRED MULTIPLE LINES OF TEXT
> AT THE PROMPT LINE, BUT DO NOT FORGET TO
> PRESS ENTER TO HAVE THE TEXT GO TO THE
> NEXT LINE. PRESS ENTER AT THE MTEXT PROMPT
> TO GET BACK TO THE COMMAND: PROMPT.

❑ Save the drawing as EX8-8.

AutoCAD Text Fonts

A *font* is a particular letter face design. The standard AutoCAD text fonts are shown in Figure 8-22. These fonts have an .shx file extension.

The Txt font is the AutoCAD default. The Txt font is rather rough in appearance and may not be the best choice for your application, even though Txt requires less time to regenerate than other fonts. The Romans (roman simplex) font is smoother than Txt. It closely duplicates the single-stroke lettering that has long been the standard for most drafting. The complex and triplex fonts are multistroke fonts for drawing titles and subtitles. The gothic and italic fonts are ornamental styles. In addition, AutoCAD provides several standard symbol fonts. See Figure 8-23.

Figure 8-22.
Standard AutoCAD text fonts.

	Fast Fonts			Triplex Fonts
Txt	abcdABCD12345		Romant	abcdABCD12345
Monotxt	abcdABCD12345		Italict	abcdABCD12345
	Simplex Fonts			Gothic Fonts
Romans	abcdABCD12345		Gothice	abcdABCD12345
Scripts	abcdABCD12345		Gothicg	abcdABCD12345
Greeks	αβχδABXΔ12345		Gothicl	abcdABCD12345
Italic	abcdABCD12345			ISO Fonts
Simplex	abcdABCD12345		ISOCP	abcdABCD12345
	Duplex Font		ISOCP2	abcdABCD12345
Romand	abcdABCD12345		ISOCP3	abcdABCD12345
	Complex Fonts		ISOCT	a b c d A B C D 1 2 3 4 5
Romanc	abcdABCD12345		ISOCT2	a b c d A B C D 1 2 3 4 5
Italicc	abcdABCD12345		ISOCT3	a b c d A B C D 1 2 3 4 5
Scriptc	abcdABCD12345			
Greekc	αβχδABXΔ12345			
Complex	abcdABCD12345			

Figure 8-23.
Standard AutoCAD
symbol fonts.

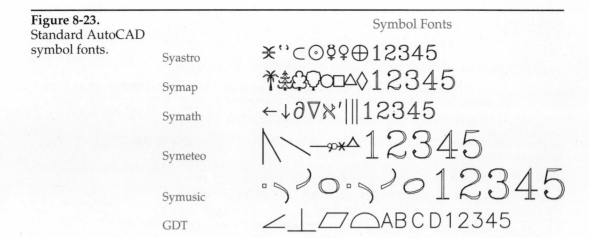

Symbol Fonts

Syastro	✳ '' ⊂ ⊙ ⚢ ⚢ ⊕ 12345
Symap	🌟 🌲 ♧ ▢ □ △ 12345
Symath	← ↓ ∇ ⋇ ' ‖ 12345
Symeteo	\ \ → ⊸⋇ △ 12345
Symusic	⸲ ⸲ ⸲ ⸲ ⊙ ⸲ ⸲ ⊙ 12345
GDT	∠ ⊥ ▱ � △ ABCD12345

Several additional AutoCAD fonts provide special alphabets or symbols that are accessed by typing specific keys. This is called ***character mapping***. Character mapping for non-Roman and symbol fonts is displayed in Figure 8-24.

TrueType fonts are scaleable and have an outline. *Scaleable* means that the font can be displayed on the screen or printed at any size and still maintain proportion. TrueType fonts have an outline, but they appear filled in the graphics window. When you plot or print, the fonts can be filled or shown as an outline. The **TEXTFILL** system variable controls this appearance. The **TEXTFILL** default is 1, which draws filled fonts. A setting of 0 draws the font outlines.

Samples of several TrueType fonts are shown in Figure 8-25. The architect's hand-lettered fonts Stylus BT is an excellent choice for the artistic appearance desired on architectural drawings. Try them and use the one you like the best.

PROFESSIONAL TIP

TrueType and other complex text styles can be very taxing on system resources. This can slow down display changes and increase drawing regeneration time significantly. Use these styles only when necessary. When you must use complex text styles, set your system variables to speed optimized settings.

The **TEXTQLTY** system variable controls how text affects drawing display speeds. Lower values for this variable reduce display quality and speed up display changes. Significant speed increases result from a setting of 0.

Figure 8-24.
Character mapping for non-Roman and symbol fonts.

	A	B	C	D	E	F	G	H	I	J	K	L	M	N	O	P	Q	R	S	T	U	V	W	X	Y	Z	[	\	]	^	_	'
Greekc	Α	Β	Χ	Δ	Ε	Φ	Γ	Η	Ι	ϑ	Κ	Λ	Μ	Ν	Ο	Π	Θ	Ρ	Σ	Τ	Υ	∇	Ω	Ξ	Ψ	Ζ	[	\	]	^	_	'
Greeks	Α	Β	Χ	Δ	Ε	Φ	Γ	Η	Ι	ϑ	Κ	Λ	Μ	Ν	Ο	Π	Θ	Ρ	Σ	Τ	Υ	∇	Ω	Ξ	Ψ	Ζ	[	\	]	^	_	'
Syastro	⊙	☿	♀	⊕	♂	♃	♄	♅	♆	♇	☾	⚹	✳	♈	♉	♊	♋	♌	♍	♎	♏	♐	♑	♒	♓	☋	[	\	]	^	_	'
Symap	○	□	△	◇	☆	+	×	*	●	■	▲	◀	▼	▶	★	⌐	⌐	↑	✶	♠	♣	♦	◆	♣	♠	△	[	\	]	^	_	'
Symath	ℵ	'	∣	‖	±	∓	×	÷	÷	=	≠	≡	<	>	≤	≥	∝	∼	√	⊂	∪	⊃	∩	∈	→	↑	[	\	]	^	_	'
Symeteo	·	·	·	·	▲	⸱	▲	^	⌒	∩	⌣	·	·	'	S	∼	∞	R	♭	—	/	∣	\	—	╱	/	[	\	]	^	_	'
Symusic	·	⸲	⸲	⸳	○	○	●	#	♮	♭	—	—	×	ꜱ	𝄞	𝄢	𝄫	·	·	—	⌐	^	⸤	▽			[	\	]	^	_	'

Figure 8-25.
Some of the many TrueType fonts available.

Swiss 721

Regular

swissl (light)	abcdABCD12345
swissli (light italic)	abcdABCD12345
swiss (regular)	abcdABCD12345
swissi (italic)	abcdABCD12345
swissb (bold)	abcdABCD1234
swissbi (bold italic)	abcdABCD12345
swissk (black bold)	abcdABCD12345
swisski (black bold italic)	abcdABCD12345

Condensed

swisscl (light)	abcdABCD12345
swisscli (light italic)	abcdABCD12345
swissc (condensed)	abcdABCD12345
swissci (italic)	abcdABCD12345
swisscb (bold)	abcdABCD12345
swisscbi (bold italic)	abcdABCD12345
swissck (black bold)	abcdABCD12345
swisscki (black bold italic)	abcdABCD12345

Expanded

swissel (light)	abcdABCD12345
swisse (expanded)	abcdABCD12345
swisseb (bold)	abcdABCD12345
swissek (black bold)	abcdABCD12345

Outline

swissbo (bold)	abcdABCD12345
swissko (black)	abcdABCD12345
swisscbo (bold condensed)	abcdABCD12345

Monospace 821

monos (monospaced)	abcdABCD12345
monosi (italic)	abcdABCD12345
monosb (bold)	abcdABCD12345
monosbi (bold italic)	abcdABCD12345

Dutch 801 (serif)

Regular

dutch (regular)	abcdABCD12345
dutchi (italic)	abcdABCD12345
dutchb (bold)	abcdABCD12345
dutchbi (bold italic)	abcdABCD12345

Expanded

| dutcheb (bold) | abcdABCD12345 |

Architect's Hand Lettered

| stylu (regular) | abcdABCD12345 |

Bank Gothic (all caps)

| bgothl (light) | ABCDABCD12345 |
| bgothm (medium) | ABCDABCD12345 |

Commercial Script

| comsc (regular) | abcdABCD12345 |

Vineta (shadow)

| vinet (regular) | abcdABCD12345 |

Commercial Pi

| compi (regular) | ©®©®±°′″●●-■ |

Universal Math

| umath (regular) | $\alpha\beta\psi\delta AB\Psi\Delta + - \times \div =$ |

Selecting AutoCAD Text Styles

Text styles are variations of fonts. A *text style* gives height, width, obliquing angle (slant), and other characteristics to a text font. You may have several text styles that use the same font, but with different characteristics. By default, the STANDARD text style uses the txt.shx font with 0.2000 height, 0 degrees rotation angle, width of 1, and 0 degrees obliquing angle.

If the **Style** option of the **TEXT** or **DTEXT** command is selected, you can select a previously created text style using the **Style** option:

> Command: **DT** *or* **DTEXT**↵
> Justify/Style/⟨Start point⟩: **S**↵
> Style name (or ?) ⟨*current*⟩:

Enter the name of an existing style, type ? to see a list of styles, or press [Enter] to keep the existing style. After entering ?, you can type the specific text style(s) to list, or press [Enter] to display all of the available text styles. The style name, font file, height, width factor, obliquing angle, and generation of each of the available text styles is then shown in the **AutoCAD Text Window**.

When you are using the **MTEXT** command, the available text styles are provided in the **Style** drop-down list of the **Properties** tab.

EXERCISE 8-9

❑ Start AutoCAD and use the setup option of your choice.
❑ Enter the **DTEXT** command and use the **Style** option to display the available text styles. Look through the list to see what is available. Press the [F2] key to return to the graphics window.
❑ Enter the **MTEXT** command and define a text boundary in order to open the **Multiline Text Editor**. Pick the **Properties** tab. Open the **Style** drop-down list and notice the list of available text styles.
❑ Exit AutoCAD or leave this drawing open for the next exercise.

STYLE
ST

Format
➥ Text Style...

Using and Creating Text Styles

The **STYLE** command is used to create new text styles and modify or list existing text styles. A *text style* is a set of text characteristics, such as font, height, width, and obliquing angle. The **STYLE** command allows you to customize one of the available fonts to create a new text style.

Access the **STYLE** command by picking **Text Style...** from the **Format** pull-down menu, or by entering ST or STYLE at the Command: prompt. The **STYLE** command opens the **Text Style** dialog box shown in Figure 8-26. The following describes the features found in this dialog box:

- **Style Name area.** Set a new current text style by making a selection from the drop-down list. Use the **New...** button to create a new text style and the **Rename...** button to rename a selected style. If you need to delete a style, use the **Delete** button.
- **Font area.** This area of the **Text Style** dialog box is where you select an available font, style of the selected font, and text height.
  - **Font Name:**—This drop-down list is used to access the available fonts. See Figure 8-27A. The default font is txt.shx. All .shx fonts are identified with an AutoCAD symbol, while the TrueType fonts have the TrueType symbol.

Figure 8-26.
The **Text Style** dialog box.

Set text style
Create new style
Rename a style
Delete a style

Set font name

Activate effects

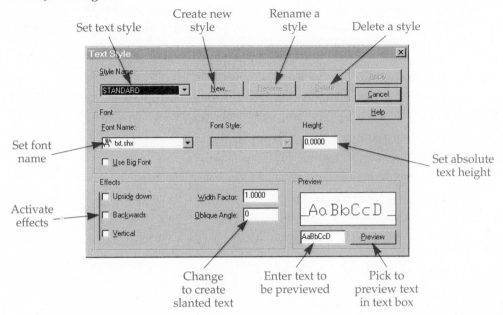

Change to create slanted text
Enter text to be previewed
Pick to preview text in text box
Set absolute text height

- **Font Style:**—This drop-down list is inactive unless the selected font has options available. None of the .shx fonts have additional options, but some of the TrueType fonts may. For example, the SansSerif font has Regular, Bold, BoldOblique, and Oblique options, as shown in Figure 8-27B. Each option provides the font with a different appearance.
- **Height:**—This text box is used to set the text height. The default is 0.0000. This allows you to set the text height in the **TEXT** and **DTEXT** commands. If you set a value such as .125, then the text height becomes fixed for this text style and you are not prompted for the text height. Setting a text height value other than zero saves time during the command process, but also eliminates your flexibility. ANSI recommended text heights were discussed earlier in this chapter.

Figure 8-27.
A—The **Font Name** drop-down list.
B—The **Font Style** drop-down list.

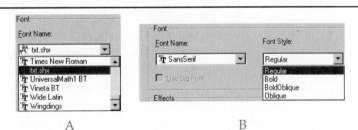

A

B

> **NOTE**
> The default text height is stored in the **TEXTSIZE** system variable. When a text style has a height other than 0, the style height will override any default value stored in this variable.

- **Use Big Font**—Asian and other large format fonts (called *Big Fonts*) are activated with this check box. The Big Font is used as a supplement to define many symbols not available in normal font files.

- **Effects area.** This area of the **Text Style** dialog box is used to set the text format.
  - **Upside down**—This check box is off by default. When it is checked, the text you draw is placed upside down, as shown in Figure 8-28A.
  - **Backwards**—When the box is checked, text that you draw is placed backwards, as shown in Figure 8-28B.
  - **Vertical**—This check box is inactive for all TrueType fonts. A check in this box makes .shx text vertical. See Figure 8-28C. Text on drawings is normally placed horizontally, but vertical text can be used for special effects and graphic designs. Vertical text works best when the rotation angle is 270°.

Figure 8-28.
A—Upside-down text.
B—Backward text.
C—Vertical text.

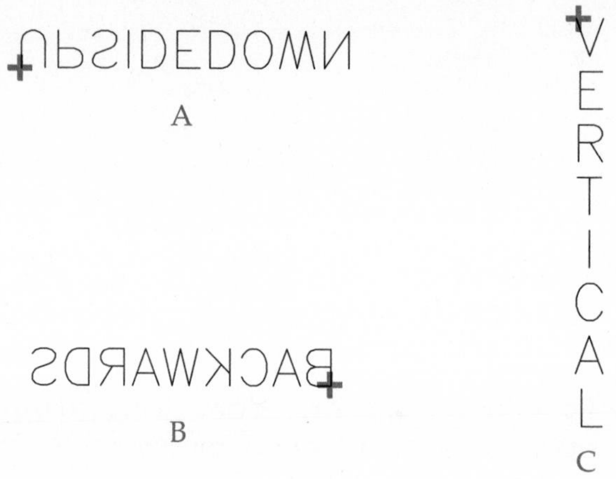

NOTE The **Multiline Text Editor** only displays the text horizontally, right-side up, and forward. Any special effects such as vertical, backwards, or upside down take effect when you pick **OK** to exit the editor.

- **Width Factor:**—This text box provides a value that defines the text character width relative to the height. A width factor of 1 is the default. A width factor greater than 1 expands the characters, and less than 1 compresses the characters. See Figure 8-29.
- **Obliquing Angle:**—This text box allows you to set an angle at which text is slanted. The zero default draws characters vertically. A value greater than 0 slants the characters to the right, while a negative value slants characters to the left. See Figure 8-30. Some fonts, such as italic.shx are already slanted.

Figure 8-29.
AutoCAD text width factors.

Width factor	Text
1	ABCDEFGHIJKLM
.5	ABCDEFGHIJKLMNOPQRSTUVWXY
1.5	ABCDEFGHI
2	ABCDEFG

Figure 8-30.
AutoCAD obliquing angles.

Obliquing angle	Text
0	ABCDEFGHIJKLM
15	*ABCDEFGHIJKLM*
–15	ABCDEFGHIJKLM

PROFESSIONAL TIP   Some companies, especially in structural drafting, like to slant text 15° to the right. Also, water features named on maps often use text that is slanted to the right.

- **Preview area.** The image allows you to see how the selected font name or style looks. This is a very convenient way to see what the font looks like before using it in a new style. Figure 8-31 shows previews of various fonts. Specific characters can also be previewed. Simply type the characters in the text box and then pick the **Preview** button. See Figure 8-31C.

Figure 8-31.
The **Preview** image shows a sample of the font. A—The Scripts font. B—The Gothice font. C—The Italic font.

      A   B   C

EXERCISE 8-10

- ❑ Start AutoCAD with the setup option of your choice.
- ❑ Open the **Text Style** dialog box.
- ❑ Access the **Style Name** drop-down list just to look through the available options. Select a few of the options that you want to see displayed in the preview image.
- ❑ Go to the **Font Name:** drop-down list and select a few different fonts to see their image in the preview tile. Pick the SansSerif font and then open the **Font Style:** drop-down list. Pick each of the options as you watch the preview image change to represent your selection.
- ❑ Turn the **Upside down** and **Backwards** check boxes on and then off while you watch the preview image.
- ❑ Change the width factor to 2, .5, and back to 1 while you watch the **Preview** image.
- ❑ Change the obliquing angle to 15, 30, –15, –30, and then back to 0 while you watch the **Preview** image.
- ❑ Type your own desired characters in the box to the left of the **Preview** button and then pick the button.
- ❑ Pick the **Close** button.
- ❑ Exit AutoCAD or leave this drawing open for the next exercise.

Creating a new text style

If you start a new drawing with the AutoCAD default template, the only text style that is available is the STANDARD style. The STANDARD text style is based on the txt font, which is not very attractive. This may not suit your needs.

What if you want to create a text style for mechanical drawings that uses the Romans font and the characters are .125 high? You want to have this available as the most commonly used text on your drawings. You decide to name the style ROMANS-125. This is a name that you can remember, because it uses Romans font characters that are .125" high. It is still a good idea to record the name and details about the text styles you create and keep this information in a log for future reference.

Text style names can have up to 31 characters, including letters, numbers, dashes (–), underlines (_), and dollar signs ($). You can enter uppercase or lowercase letters, but AutoCAD automatically changes to uppercase. The following explains the steps to use to create this text style:

1. Use the **STYLE** command to open the **Text Style** dialog box. STANDARD is the current style with txt.shx as the font, and a zero text height.
2. Pick the **New...** button. This opens the **New Text Style** dialog box shown in Figure 8-32A. Notice style1 is in the **Style Name:** text box. You can keep a text style name like style1 or style2, but this is not descriptive. Type ROMANS-125 in the box and then pick the **OK** button. See Figure 8-32B. ROMANS-125 is now displayed in the **Style Name** text box of the **Text Style** dialog box.
3. Go to the **Font Name:** drop-down list, find romans.shx, and pick it. The font is now romans.shx.
4. Change the value in the **Height:** text box to .125. Figure 8-33 shows the work done in Steps 2, 3, and 4.
5. Pick the **Apply** button followed by picking the **Close** button. The new ROMANS-125 font is now part of your drawing template.

Figure 8-32.
A—The **New Text Style** dialog box with the default entry. B—A new text style entered.

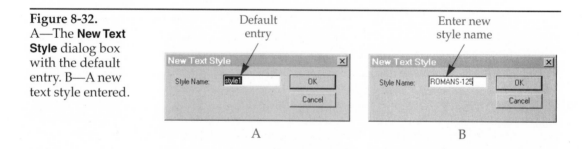

Figure 8-33.
The **Text Style** dialog box showing the changes in the style, font, and height.

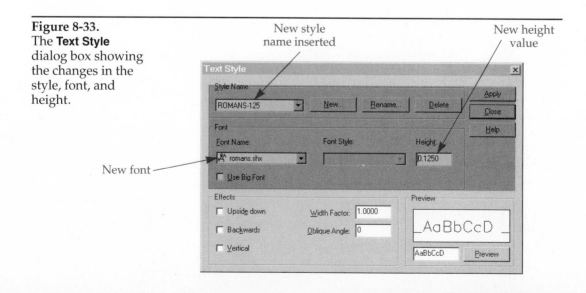

Now, ROMANS-125 is the default style when you use the **TEXT**, **DTEXT**, or **MTEXT** commands. If you want to create a similar text style for your architectural drawings, you might consider a style name called ARCHITECTURAL-125. For this style, set the font name to Stylus BT and the height to .125.

PROFESSIONAL TIP

You can make the text style name the same as the font name if you wish. In some cases, this is a clear and concise way of naming the style.

EXERCISE 8-11

❑ Start AutoCAD with the setup option of your choice.
❑ Open the **Text Style** dialog box with the **STYLE** command.
❑ Create a text style named ROMANS-125 if you commonly do mechanical drawings, or ARCHITECTURAL-125 if you commonly do architectural drawings.
❑ For ROMANS-125 set the font name to romans.shx and the height to .125.
❑ For ARCHITECTURAL-125 set the font name to Stylus BT and the height to .125.
❑ Pick the **Apply** button and then close the **Text Style** dialog box.
❑ Try out your new text style with the **TEXT**, **DTEXT**, and **MTEXT** commands.
❑ Create a text style named ROMANS if you commonly do mechanical drawings, or ARCHITECTURAL if you commonly do architectural drawings. For ROMANS set the font name to romans.shx and the height to 0. For ARCHITECTURAL set the font name to Stylus BT and the height to 0.
❑ Pick the **Apply** button and then close the **Text Style** dialog box.
❑ Try out your new text style with the **TEXT**, **DTEXT**, and **MTEXT** commands.
❑ Save the drawing as EX8-11.

NOTE

Unlike previous AutoCAD releases, Release 14 does not store the path to the font. This makes sharing drawings much easier. Previously, if the **STYLE** command was used on one computer, it may store the font as something like c:\fonts\romans.shx. When the drawing file is opened on another computer, it gives a message that it cannot find the desired font file, unless you give the complete path. This problem has been eliminated in Release 14, unless you are using the **-STYLE** command.

Renaming, changing, and deleting text styles

You can change text style without affecting existing text objects. The changes are applied only to added text using that style.

Existing text styles are easily renamed in the **Text Style** dialog box. Select the desired style name in the **Style Name** text box and pick the **Rename...** button. This opens the **Rename Text Style** dialog box, Figure 8-34. Change the text style name in the **Style Name:** text box and pick the **OK** button.

Figure 8-34.
The **Rename Text Style** dialog box.

Enter new style name

You can also delete an existing text style in the **Text Style** dialog box by picking the desired style name in the <u>**Style Name:**</u> drop-down list followed by picking the <u>**Delete**</u> button. If you try to delete a text style that has been used to create text objects in the drawing, AutoCAD gives you the following message:

> Style is in use, can't be deleted.

This means that there are text objects in the drawing that reference this style. If you want to delete the style, change the text objects in the drawing to a different style. You cannot delete or rename the STANDARD style.

If you enter the **Text Style** dialog box and make changes to the current text style, you can pick the <u>**Apply**</u> button followed by the <u>**Close**</u> button to have the changes take affect. If you make changes to the current style and pick the <u>**Close**</u> button, you get the following message:

> The current style has been modified. Do you want to save your changes?

Pick the <u>**Yes**</u> button to save the changes or pick the <u>**No**</u> button to decline.

Creating a text style at the prompt line

A new text style can be created at the prompt line by using the **-STYLE** command. That is a dash (-) entered before STYLE. Everything is done at the prompt line. You may recognize the following prompts from what you have already learned:

```
Command: -STYLE↵
Text style name (or ?) ⟨STANDARD⟩: ROMANS-125↵
Specify full font name or font filename ⟨txt⟩: ROMANS↵
Height ⟨0.0000⟩: .125↵
Width factor ⟨1.0000⟩: ↵
Obliquing angle ⟨0⟩: ↵
Backwards? ⟨N⟩: ↵
Upside-down? ⟨N⟩: ↵
Vertical? ⟨N⟩: ↵
ROMANS-125 is now the current text style.
Command:
```

Keep reference notes stating the name and features of text styles that you design. However, if you forget, enter ? at the Text style name ⟨ ⟩: prompt. A listing of created styles appears in the **AutoCAD Text Window**.

Special Characters

Many drafting applications require special symbols for text and dimensions. There are different methods for entering special characters, depending on if you are creating single-line text objects using the **TEXT** or **DTEXT** commands. Drawing symbols when using the **MTEXT** command was explained earlier in this chapter.

In order to draw symbols, AutoCAD requires a control code. The *control code sequence* for a symbol begins with two percent signs (%%). The next character you enter represents the symbol. These control codes are used for single-line text objects that are generated with the **TEXT** or **DTEXT** commands. The following list gives the most popular control code sequences:

Control Code	Description	Symbol
%%D	Degrees symbol	°
%%P	Plus/minus sign	±
%%C	Diameter symbol	Ø

In order to add the note Ø2.75, the control sequence %%C2.75 is used. See Figure 8-35A.

A single percent sign can be added normally. However, when a percent sign must precede another control sequence, %%% can be used to force a single percent sign. For example, suppose you want to type the note 25%±2%. You must enter 25%%%%P2%.

Drawing underscored or overscored text

Text can be underscored (underlined) or overscored by typing a control sequence in front of the line of text. The control sequences are:

%%O = overscore
%%U = underscore

For example, the note <u>UNDERSCORING TEXT</u> must be entered as %%UUNDER-SCORING TEXT. The resulting text is shown in Figure 8-35B. A line of text may require both underscoring and overscoring. For example, the control sequence %%O%%ULINE OF TEXT produces the note with both underscore and overscore.

The %%O and %%U control codes are toggles that turn overscoring and underscoring on and off. Type %%U preceding a word or phrase to turn underscoring on. Type %%U after the desired word or phrase to turn underscoring off. Any text following the second %%U then appears without underscoring. For example, <u>DETAIL A</u> HUB ASSEMBLY would be entered as %%UDETAIL A%%U HUB ASSEMBLY.

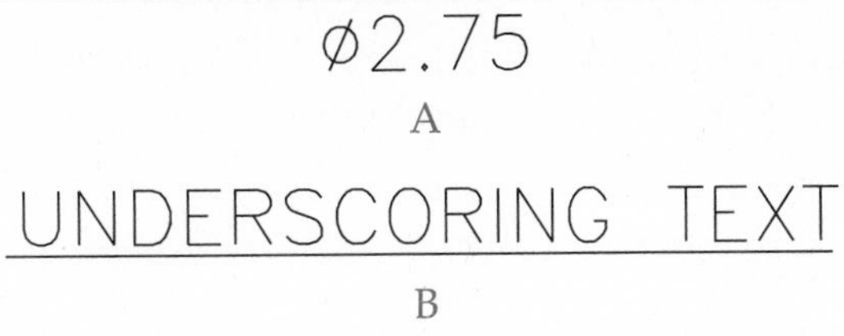

Figure 8-35.
A—The control sequence %%C creates the Ø (diameter) symbol.
B—The control sequence %%U underscores text.

$$\varnothing 2.75$$

A

<u>UNDERSCORING TEXT</u>

B

Entering special characters using the Unicode system

AutoCAD Release 14 supports the Unicode character encoding standard. A *Unicode* font can have up to 65,535 separate characters in a font file, with figures for many different languages. This standard provides support for these languages by allowing the use of characters that are not found on the keyboard. The Unicode standard is used for multiline text objects created with the **MTEXT** command (or the **LEADER** command discussed in Chapter 18), and with the **DTEXT** command.

The Unicode special characters are accessed by typing what is called an *escape sequence*. The prefix \U+ is followed by a four-digit hexadecimal number identifying the symbol. A *hexadecimal* number is a base 16 number, rather than base 10. For example, \U+2205 is the escape sequence for entering a diameter symbol. The following are some examples that are commonly used in drafting technology:

Unicode	Description	Symbol	Example
\U+2205	Diameter symbol	Ø	\U+2205.750 = Ø.750
\U+00B0	Degree symbol	°	45\U+00B0 = 45°
\U+00B1	Plus/minus symbol	±	2.625\U+00B1.005 = 2.625±.005

NOTE

When you type %%C in the **Multiline Text Editor**, it is immediately changed to \U+2205. The listing in the **Symbols** drop-down list provides **Diameter %%c**. This implies that the correct entry should actually be %%C. However, when you pick **Diameter %%c** from the **Symbols** list, \U+2205 is automatically displayed in the text window. It does not really matter, because the result in the final text is a diameter symbol. When using an external text editor, \U+2205 and %%C display the expected symbols.

EXERCISE 8-12

❑ Start AutoCAD and use the setup option of your choice.
❑ Use the **DTEXT** command and control codes to type the following:

    45°
    1.375±.005
    Ø3.875
    79%
    UNDERSCORING TEXT

❑ Save the drawing as EX8-12.

Redrawing Text Quickly

Text often requires a great deal of time to regenerate, redraw, and plot because each character is drawn with many individual vectors (line segments). The **Quick Text** mode makes text appear as rectangles equal to the height of each text string. This speeds regeneration and plotting time. The **Quick Text** mode is turned on and off with the **QTEXT** (quick text) command. Figure 8-36 shows a comparison between displays when **QTEXT** is on and off.

The **QTEXT** command is entered at the Command: prompt. If the last setting was off, the command line appears as follows:

```
Command: QTEXT↵
ON/OFF ⟨Off⟩:
```

Enter ON to quicken the redraw time. When quick text is on, text entities first appear as text so you can check them. The text converts to rectangles when the drawing is regenerated. If you want to review the text after **QTEXT** has been turned on, you need to turn **QTEXT** off. Follow this with the **REGEN** command to display the text in the normal format.

Figure 8-36.
Comparison of **QTEXT** turned on and off.

QTEXT on

THE QUICK TEXT MODE IS USED TO
SPEED REGENERATION TIME IN
COMPLEX DRAWINGS.

QTEXT off

PROFESSIONAL TIP   To save valuable drafting time, add text styles to your template drawings. If only a single text height is needed in the template, set the text height for the style.

Revising Text with DDEDIT

Text editing is accomplished using the **DDEDIT** command. **DDEDIT** is accessed by selecting the **Edit Text** button on the **Modify II** toolbar, picking **Text...** in the **Object** cascading menu of the **Modify** pull-down menu, or entering ED or DDEDIT at the Command: prompt.

When editing text, AutoCAD first asks you to select an annotation object—any text, leader, or dimension object. If you pick single-line text that was drawn with the **TEXT** or **DTEXT** commands, you get the **Edit Text** dialog box, Figure 8-37. If you pick text that was drawn with the **MTEXT** command, you get the **Multiline Text Editor**. Multiline text is also drawn with the **LEADER** command, which is explained in Chapter 18.

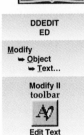

DDEDIT
ED

Modify
➡ Object
  ➡ Text...

Modify II
toolbar

Edit Text

Figure 8-37.
Selected text appears
in the **Edit Text**
dialog box.

When editing text in either dialog box, if you press [Delete] or [Backspace], the highlighted text disappears and you can enter new text. Pressing the key combination [Ctrl]+[V] to paste the contents of the Clipboard will replace the highlighted text with the new text. If you make a mistake, use the editing keys or press **Cancel** and pick the desired text again. Move the cursor arrow inside the **Text:** text box and pick to remove the highlight around the text. Use the left and right arrow keys to move through the entire line of text, and access the portion of the text that is hidden beyond the limits of the text box. Edit the line of text shown in Figure 8-38 following this procedure:

1. Notice the word inTERPRET should read INTERPRET. To see the beginning of the text, press [Home]. Use the cursor to highlight the letters in by picking and dragging the cursor through the text.
2. Type IN.
3. Notice the word DEMENSIONS is misspelled. Press [Ctrl]+[→] to move to the start of DEMENSIONS. Press [→] once and press [Delete] to delete the E. Now, type in an I, as shown in Figure 8-38B.
4. Pick **OK** or press [Enter] to accept the text changes. The revised text is then displayed on your drawing as shown in Figure 8-39.
5. Press [Enter] or **Cancel** to exit the **DDEDIT** command, or enter U to undo the editing if you made a mistake.

Figure 8-38.
Highlight the text
you want to replace.
Then, type the
revised text.

1. inTERPRET DEMENSIONS AND TOLERANCES PER ASME Y14.5−1994
2. REMOVE ALL BURRS AND SHARP EDGES
3. ALL FILLETS AND ROUNDS R.125

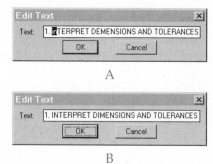

Figure 8-39.
The revised text is displayed on your screen.

1. INTERPRET DIMENSIONS AND TOLERANCES PER ASME Y14.5−1994
2. REMOVE ALL BURRS AND SHARP EDGES
3. ALL FILLETS AND ROUNDS R.125

 NOTE   The examples used in this discussion show how to use the **Edit Text** dialog box to make changes in your text. Spelling is conveniently checked with the AutoCAD **Spell Checker**, which is explained later in this chapter.

Editing techniques

Although it is recommended that you enter text as carefully as possible initially, there are times when you must revise text. The following techniques can be used to help edit text with the **DDEDIT** command:

- **Highlighting in the Text: text box.** Text can be highlighted by moving the cursor arrow to the desired text and picking. Hold the pick button down while you move the cursor across the text to be highlighted. Release the pick button when you have highlighted all of the intended text.
- **Removing highlighting in the Text: text box.** Press the [Spacebar], [Delete], or [Backspace] to remove highlighted text.
- **Moving around inside the Text: text box.** Move the cursor arrow inside the **Text:** text box and pick. Then use [←] to move the cursor to the left or [→] to move the cursor to the right.
- **Inserting text.** Type any desired text at the text cursor location. This inserts new text and shifts all existing text to the right.
- **[Backspace].** Pressing [Backspace] when text is not highlighted removes text to the left of the text cursor and moves the text at the right along with the text cursor.
- **[Spacebar].** Pressing [Spacebar] when text is not highlighted moves all of the text to the right of the text cursor.
- **[←] (left arrow).** Moves the text cursor to the left.
- **[→] (right arrow).** Moves the text cursor to the right.
- **[Ctrl]+[X].** Deletes the entire string of highlighted text.

PROFESSIONAL TIP

When using **DDEDIT** to edit single-line text (**TEXT** or **DTEXT**), the same code shows up in the editor that was originally used. For example, if you typed %%c for the diameter symbol, then %%c is displayed, rather than the diameter symbol. Be sure you edit the symbols properly to get the desired results.

When you use the **Multiline Text Editor** to edit text with a diameter symbol, the diameter symbol is displayed as a box. When you finish editing the text, a question mark appears where the diameter symbol should be. This is not good. Be sure to watch for these boxes and insert the proper character code for the desired symbol to avoid getting question marks on your drawing.

EXERCISE 8-13

❑ Start AutoCAD and use the setup option of your choice.
❑ Use the **DTEXT** command to place the following text:

    3068 SOLID CORE PANELED ENTRY DOOR SC306 ACME DOOR CO.

❑ Use the **DDEDIT** command to change the text to read:

    3'-0" × 6'-8" STEEL FRAME PANELED ENTRY DOOR ER44 CECO ENTRY SYSTEMS.

❑ Turn **QTEXT** on, then off. Observe the results. Do not forget to use **REGEN** to change the display.
❑ Save the drawing as EX8-13.

Changing Text with DDMODIFY

DDMODIFY
MO

Modify
  ↳ Properties...

Object Properties toolbar

Properties

The **DDMODIFY** command can be used to change text. **DDMODIFY** can be accessed by picking the **Properties** button on the **Object Properties** toolbar, selecting **Properties...** from the **Modify** pull-down menu, or entering MO or DDMODIFY at the Command: prompt as follows:

> Command: **MO** *or* **DDMODIFY**↵
> Select one object to modify: *(pick the line of text you want to edit)*

If you select text created with the **DTEXT** or **TEXT** command, the **Modify Text** dialog box is displayed. See Figure 8-40. The elements of the **Modify Text** dialog box are described below.

- **Properties area.** The **Color...** button opens the **Select Color** dialog box, where you can select a desired color. The **Layer...** button accesses the **Select Layer** dialog box, and the **Linetype...** button opens the **Select Linetype** dialog box. These two dialog boxes are discussed in Chapter 4. The **Thickness:** box is for 3D applications and is introduced in Chapter 27. The **Linetype Scale:** box is used to change the linetype scale and is explained in Chapter 4.

- **Text:.** This text box is where you edit the text. This works just like the **Text:** box in the **Edit Text** dialog box.

- **Origin area.** This area lets you change the X, Y, and Z coordinates of the text insertion point by changing the values in the **X:**, **Y:**, or **Z:** edit boxes. You can also choose the **Pick Point** ⟨ button to change the pick point with the screen cursor. Single-line text can also be relocated using the **CHANGE** command, which is covered later in this chapter.

- The lower-right corner of the **Modify Text** dialog box provides several convenient options for changing text. Use the **Height:**, **Rotation:**, **Width Factor:**, and **Obliquing:** text boxes to change the related text feature. The **Justify:** drop-down list has the available justification options if you want to change the format. The **Style:** drop-down list has the text styles that have been previously loaded. The **Upside Down** and **Backward** check boxes are off if there is no check.

The **DDMODIFY** command can also be used to change multiline text. When you enter the **DDMODIFY** command and select multiline text to change, the **Modify MText** dialog box is displayed, as shown in Figure 8-41. The **Modify MText** dialog box is almost the same as the **Modify Text** dialog box. The **Linetype...** button, **Thickness:** text box, and **Linetype Scale:** text box are inactive, because they cannot be assigned to an **MTEXT** object.

Figure 8-40.
The **Modify Text** dialog box shows the text and all of its properties.

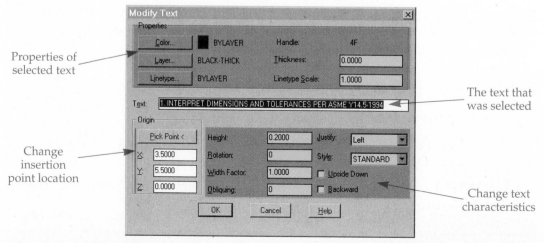

Properties of selected text

The text that was selected

Change insertion point location

Change text characteristics

AutoCAD and its Applications—Basics

Figure 8-41.
The **Modify MText** dialog box is used to change multiline text. It can be used to change the text insertion point.

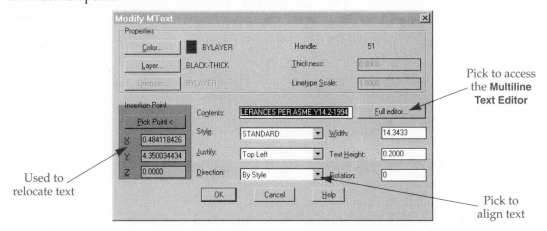

Used to
relocate text

Pick to access
the **Multiline
Text Editor**

Pick to
align text

The **Direction:** list is not included in the **Modify Text** dialog box. Pick the drop-down arrow to reveal the options:

- **By Style.** This option maintains the alignment to match the style
- **Horizontal.** This option makes vertical text horizontal
- **Vertical.** This option changes horizontal text to vertical.

Use the **Contents:** text box to edit the text as needed. Picking the **Full editor...** button opens the **Multiline Text Editor**, where text modifications can be made.

EXERCISE 8-14

❑ Start AutoCAD and use the setup option of your choice.
❑ Use the **MTEXT** command to place the following text on your drawing (incorrectly as shown) using ROMANS style and .125 text height. Insert the first boundary corner at 1,4 and the opposite corner at 9.5,2.5.

    1. INTERPRET DEMINSIONIN AND TOLERENCING PER ANSI Y14.5M–1982.
    2. MOVE ALL BURRS AND EDGES.
    3. ALL FILLETS AND ROUNDS ARE .125 R.
    4. FINISH ALL OVER.

❑ Use the **DDMODIFY** command to revise the above text as follows:

    1. INTERPRET DIMENSIONING AND TOLERANCING PER ASME
       Y14.5M–1994.
    2. REMOVE ALL BURRS AND SHARP EDGES.
    3. ALL FILLETS AND ROUNDS R.125.
    4. FINISH ALL OVER 62 MICROINCHES.

❑ Change the insertion point to 1.25,6.0.
❑ Save the drawing as EX8-14.

Changing Text with DDCHPROP

The **DDCHPROP** command can be used to make color, layer, linetype, linetype scale, and thickness changes to single-line text; and can be used to make color and layer changes to multiline text. The **DDCHPROP** command is accessed by entering CH or DDCHPROP at the Command: prompt and then selecting the text to change. After selecting the text, the **Change Properties** dialog box opens.

Once the **Change Properties** dialog box opens, you may change any one of the properties. Use the buttons or text boxes to make changes. See Figure 8-42.

Figure 8-42.
The **Change Properties** dialog box can be used to change the properties of text.

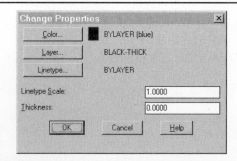

Changing Text with CHANGE

Text can be moved or modified using the **CHANGE** command. The **CHANGE** command is accessed by entering -CH or CHANGE at the Command: prompt. The command sequence is as follows:

> Command: **-CH** *or* **CHANGE**↵
> Select objects: *(pick text to be changed)*
> Select objects: ↵
> Properties/⟨Change point⟩: ↵
> Enter text insertion point: *(pick a new text location)*
> Text style: STANDARD
> New style or press ENTER for no change: *(type a new defined text style or press* [Enter] *to keep the same style)*
> New height ⟨0.2000⟩: *(type new height or press* [Enter] *to keep the same height)*
> New rotation angle ⟨0⟩: *(type new rotation angle or press* [Enter] *to keep the same angle)*
> New text ⟨selected text string⟩: *(type new text or press* [Enter] *to keep the same text)*
> Command:

Figure 8-43 shows text that has been relocated. The style, height, angle, and text also have been changed.

Figure 8-43.
Using the **CHANGE** command to relocate text, change text style, and rotation angle.

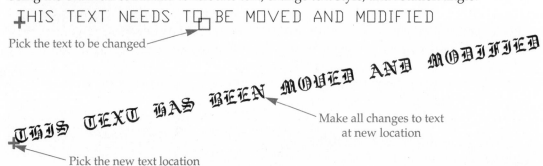

Pick the text to be changed

Make all changes to text at new location

Pick the new text location

NOTE   Text properties can also be changed with the **CHANGE** command. At the Properties/⟨Change point⟩: prompt, enter P for properties. You will receive the following prompt:

Change what property (Color/Elev/LAyer/LType/ltScale/Thickness) ?

Enter the property you wish to change.

NOTE The **CHANGE** command cannot be used to specify a new insertion point for text created with the **MTEXT** command. Also, the thickness and elevation of **MTEXT** objects cannot be changed with this command.

EXERCISE 8-15

❏ Start AutoCAD and use the setup option of your choice.
❏ Place the following text on your drawing using .25 (6mm) high letters: THIS IS THE ORIGINAL TEXT.
❏ Use the **CHANGE** command to move and change the above text to read: THIS IS THE REVISED TEXT IN A NEW LOCATION.
❏ Use the **CHANGE** command to move the previous text, change its style, and reword it as follows: THIS IS THE NEW TEXT WITH CHANGED STYLE AND LOCATION.
❏ Save the drawing as EX8-15.

Checking Your Spelling

You have been introduced to editing text on the drawing with the **DDEDIT** and **DDMODIFY** commands. You can use these commands to change lines of text and even correct spelling errors. However, AutoCAD has a powerful and convenient tool for checking the spelling on your drawing.

To check spelling enter SP or SPELL at the Command: prompt, pick **Spelling** from the **Tools** pull-down menu, or pick the **Spelling** button on the **Standard** toolbar. After entering the command, you are asked to select the text to be checked. You need to pick each line of single-line text or one pick on multiline text to select the entire paragraph. Enter the command and pick the text like this:

```
Command: SP or SPELL↵
Select objects: (pick the text)
Select objects: ↵
```

The **Check Spelling** dialog box is displayed. See Figure 8-44. The following describes the features found in the **Check Spelling** dialog box:

* **Current dictionary: American English.** The dictionary being used is identified at the top of the dialog box. You can change to a different dictionary by picking the **Change Dictionaries...** button.
* **Current word.** Displays a word that may be spelled incorrectly.

Figure 8-44.
The **Check Spelling** dialog box.

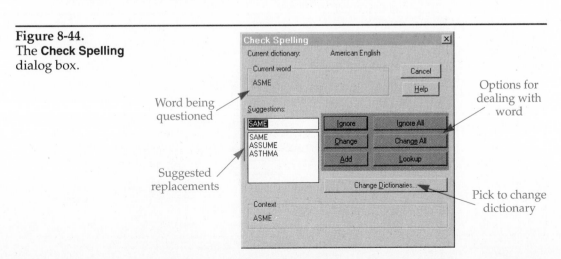

- **Suggestions:.** Gives you a list of possible correct spellings for the current word. The highlighted word in the first box is AutoCAD's best guess. Following the highlighted word is a list of other choices. If there are many choices, the scroll bar is available for you to use. If you do not like the word that AutoCAD has highlighted, move the cursor arrow to another word and pick it. The word you pick then becomes highlighted in the list and is shown in the **Suggestions:** text box.
- **Ignore.** Pick this button to skip the current word. In Figure 8-44, ASME is not a misspelled word, it just is not recognized by the dictionary. You would select the **Ignore** button and the spell check goes on to the next word.
- **Ignore All.** Pick this button if you want AutoCAD to ignore all of the words that match the current word.
- **Change.** Pick this button to replace the **Current word** with the word in the **Suggestions:** text box.
- **Change All.** Pick this button if you want to replace the **Current word** with the word in the **Suggestions:** text box throughout the entire selection set.
- **Add.** Pick this button to add the current word to the custom dictionary. You can add words with up to 63 characters.
- **Lookup.** This button asks AutoCAD to check the spelling of the word you enter in the **Suggestions:** text box.
- **Context.** At the bottom of the dialog box, AutoCAD displays the line of text where the current word was found.

Changing dictionaries

AutoCAD provides you with several dictionaries: one American English, two British English, and two French. There are also dictionaries available for 24 different languages. Pick the **Change Dictionaries...** button to access the **Change Dictionary** dialog box. See Figure 8-45.

The areas of the **Change Dictionary** dialog box are as follows:
- **Main dictionary area.** This is where you can select one of the many language dictionaries to use as the current dictionary. To change the main dictionary, pick the down arrow to access the drop-down list. Next, pick the desired language dictionary from the list. The main dictionary is protected and cannot be added to.
- **Custom dictionary area.** This displays the name of the current custom dictionary, sample.cus by default. You can create your own custom dictionary by entering a new file name with a .cus extension. Words can be added or deleted and dictionaries can be combined using any standard text editor. If you use a word processor such as MS Word or WordPerfect, be sure to save the file as *text only*, with no special text formatting or printer codes.

Figure 8-45.
The **Change Dictionaries** dialog box.

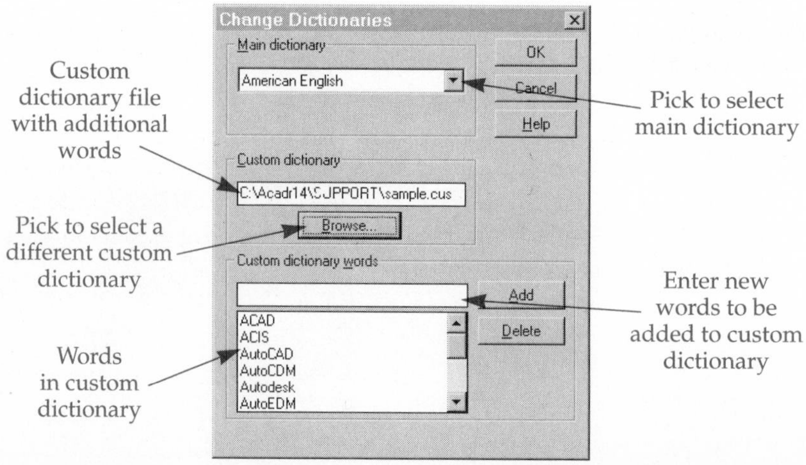

Custom dictionary file with additional words

Pick to select a different custom dictionary

Words in custom dictionary

Pick to select main dictionary

Enter new words to be added to custom dictionary

AutoCAD and its Applications—Basics

- **Browse....** Pick this button to get the **Select Custom Dictionary** dialog box.
- **Custom dictionary words.** Type a word in the text box that you either want to add or delete from the custom dictionary. For example, ASME Y14.5M is custom text used in engineering drafting. Pick the **Add** button to accept the custom word in the text box, or pick the **Delete** button to remove the word from the custom dictionary. Custom dictionary entries may be up to 32 characters in length. Pick **OK** when you are done, or pick **Cancel**. Use the **Help...** button as needed.

The current custom dictionary may be displayed at the prompt line by using the **DCTCUST** system variable:

Command: **DCTCUST**↵
New value for DCTCUST, or . for none ⟨*current*⟩:

Entering the **DCTMAIN** system variable at the Command: prompt displays the current main dictionary:

Command: **DCTMAIN**↵
New value for DCTMAIN, or . for none ⟨"enu"⟩:

The "enu" is the abbreviation for the American English main dictionary.

EXERCISE 8-16

❑ Start AutoCAD and use the setup option of your choice.
❑ Use the **MTEXT** command to type a short paragraph of your own choice with spelling errors.
❑ Check the spelling and correct the misspelled words.
❑ Save as EX8-16.

Additional Text Tips

Text presentation is important on any drawing. It is a good idea to plan your drawing using rough sketches to allow room for text and notes. Some things to consider when designing the drawing layout include:

✓ Placement of the views.
✓ Arrange text to avoid crowding.
✓ Place related notes in groups to make the drawing easy to read.
✓ Place all general notes in a common location. Locate notes in the lower-left corner or above the title block when using ANSI standards. Place notes in the upper-left corner when using military standards.
✓ Always use the spelling checker.

Chapter Test

Write your answers in the spaces provided.

1. Give the command and entities required to display the following: IT IS FAST AND EASY TO DRAW TEXT USING AUTOCAD. The text must be .375 units high, have the default txt font, and fit between two points:

   Command: _____

   Justify/Style/⟨Start point⟩: _____

   Align/Fit/Center/Middle/Right/TL/TC/TR/ML/MC/MR/BL/BC/BR: _____

   First text line point: _____

   Second text line point: _____

   Height ⟨.200⟩: _____

   Text: _____

2. Give the command and entries to underscore the following text and place it at a selected start point: VERIFY ALL DIMENSIONS DURING CONSTRUCTION.

   Command: _____

   Justify/Style/⟨Start point⟩: _____

   Height ⟨*current*⟩: _____

   Rotation angle ⟨0⟩: _____

   Text: _____

3. How do you turn on the **Quick Text** mode if it is currently off using the Command: prompt?

   Command: _____

   ON/OFF ⟨Off⟩: _____

4. What command is used to view text on the screen as it is typed? _____

5. Name three ways to access the **DTEXT** command. _____

   _____

   _____

   _____

6. Give the letter you must enter for the following justification options when using the **DTEXT** command:

   A. Left-justified text: _____

   B. Right-justified text: _____

   C. Text between two points without regard for text height: _____

   D. Center the text horizontally and vertically: _____

   E. Text between two points with a fixed height: _____

   F. Center text along a baseline: _____

   G. Top and Left horizontal: _____

   H. Middle and Right horizontal: _____

   I. Bottom and Center horizontal: _____

7. List the **DTEXT** command **Justify** options. _____

_____

_____

8. How would you specify a text style with a double width factor?

_____

_____

9. How would you specify a text style with a 15° angle? _____

_____

_____

10. How would you specify vertical text? _____

_____

_____

11. Give the control sequence required to draw the following symbols when using the **DTEXT** command:

A. 30° _____

B. 1.375 ±.005 _____

C. ∅24 _____

D. <u>NOT FOR CONSTRUCTION</u> _____

12. Why use the **Quick Text** mode rather than have the actual text displayed on the screen? _____

_____

_____

_____

_____

13. When setting text height in the **STYLE** command, what value do you enter so text height can be altered each time the **TEXT** or **DTEXT** commands are used? _____

_____

14. Give the command that lets you alter the location, style, height, and wording of existing single-line text. _____

_____

_____

15. Identify the command used to revise existing single-line text on the drawing by using the **Edit Text** dialog box. _____

16. When editing single-line text, how do you remove the character located in front of the text cursor? _____

_____

_____

17. When using the **Edit Text** dialog box, how do you move the text cursor to the left without removing text characters? _____

_____

_____

18. When using the **Edit Text** dialog box, how do you remove all of the text to the right of the text cursor? _____

_____

_____

19. When editing text in the **Text:** text box, the flashing vertical bar is called the

_____

20. Determine the AutoCAD text height for text to be plotted .188″ high using a half (1″ = 2″) scale. (Show your calculations.)_____

_____

21. Determine the AutoCAD text height for text to be plotted .188″ high using a scale of 1/4″ = 1′-0″. (Show your calculations.)_____

_____

22. What would you do if you just completed editing a line of text and discovered you made a mistake? Assume you are still in the **Edit Text** dialog box._____

_____

23. Identify two ways to move around inside the **Text:** text box of the **Edit Text** dialog box. _____

_____

_____

_____

24. What happens when you press the space bar or the [Backspace] key when the text inside the **Text:** text box is highlighted? _____

_____

25. What happens when you press [Ctrl]+[X] when the text within the **Text:** text box is highlighted? _____

_____

_____

_____

26. Name the command that lets you make multiline text objects. _____

27. How does the width of the multiline text boundary affect what you type? _____

_____

_____

_____

28. What happens if the multiline text that you are entering exceeds or is not as long as the boundary length that you initially establish? _____

_____

_____

29. What happens when you pick the first corner followed by the other corner of the multiline text boundary? _____

_____

_____

_____

30. Name the command that you enter if you want to enter multiline text at the prompt line rather than in a text editor. _____

31. Name two commands that allow you to edit multiline text. _____

32. How are fractions drawn when using the **TEXT** or **DTEXT** commands? _____

_____

_____

33. How do you draw stacked fractions when using the **MTEXT** command? _____

_____

_____

34. What is the keyboard shortcut for the **DTEXT** command? _____

35. What does a width factor of .5 do to the text when compared with the default width factor of 1? _____

_____

36. What do you get when using the **DDEDIT** command on multiline text? _____

_____

37. What is an annotation object? _____

_____

_____

38. What is the keyboard shortcut for the **MTEXT** command? _____

_____

_____

39. How do you move the text cursor down one line at a time in the **Multiline Text Editor**? _____

_____

40. What happens when you pick the **Other...** option in the **Symbol** list of the **Character** tab of the **Multiline Text Editor**? _____

_____

_____

41. Name the internal storage area that temporarily stores information that you copy or cut from a document. _____

42. When you are in the **Multiline Text Editor**, how do you open the **Edit text** cursor menu? _____

_____

_____

43. What is the purpose of the <u>**Width**</u> drop-down list found in the **Properties** tab of the **Multiline Text Editor**? _____

44. Describe how to find a word or words in a text object and have the word or words replaced with another word or words. _____

_____

_____

45. Describe how you would create a text style that has the name ROMANS-125_15, uses the romans.shx font, has a fixed height of .125, a text width of 1.25, and an obliquing angle of 15. _____

_____

_____

_____

46. Identify three ways to access the AutoCAD spell checker. _____

_____

_____

_____

47. What is the purpose of the word found in the **Current word** box of the **Check Spelling** dialog box? _____

_____

48. How do you change the **Current word** if you do not think the word that is displayed in the **Suggestions:** text box of the **Check Spelling** dialog box is the correct word, but one of the words in the list of suggestions is the correct word? _____

_____

_____

_____

49. What is the purpose of the **Add** button in the **Check Spelling** dialog box? _____

_____

_____

_____

50. How do you change the main dictionary for use in the **Check Spelling** dialog box?

_____

_____

_____

_____

Drawing Problems

1. Start AutoCAD, use the setup option of your choice, and create text styles as needed. Use the **TEXT** or **DTEXT** command to type the following information. Change the text style to represent each of the four fonts named. Use a .25 unit text height and 0° rotation angle. Save the drawing as P8-1.

   TXT–AUTOCAD'S DEFAULT TEXT FONT WHICH IS AVAILABLE FOR USE WHEN YOU BEGIN A DRAWING.
   ROMANS–SMOOTHER THAN TXT FONT AND CLOSELY DUPLICATES THE SINGLE-STROKE LETTERING THAT HAS BEEN THE STANDARD FOR DRAFTING.
   ROMANC–A MULTISTROKE DECORATIVE FONT THAT IS GOOD FOR USE IN DRAWING TITLES
   ITALICC–AN ORNAMENTAL FONT SLANTED TO THE RIGHT AND HAVING THE SAME LETTER DESIGN AS THE COMPLEX FONT.

2. Start AutoCAD and use the setup option of your choice and create text styles as needed. Change the options as noted in each line of text. Then use the **DTEXT** command to type the text, changing the text style to represent each of the four fonts named. Use a .25 unit text height. Save the drawing as P8-2.

   TXT–EXPAND THE WIDTH BY THREE.
   MONOTXT–SLANT TO THE LEFT –30°.
   ROMANS–SLANT TO THE RIGHT 30°.
   ROMAND–BACKWARDS.
   ROMANC–VERTICAL.
   ITALICC–UNDERSCORED AND OVERSCORED.
   ROMANS–USE 16d NAILS @ 10" OC.
   ROMANT–⌀32 (812.8).

3. Start AutoCAD and use the setup option of your choice. Create text styles with the following fonts to provide the information requested: Arial, BankGothic M & BT, City Blueprint, Stylus BBT, Swis 721 BdOul BT, Vineta BT, Wingdings.

   A. Use the **DTEXT** command to type the complete alphabet and numbers 1–10 for the text fonts, all symbols available on the keyboard, and the diameter, degree, and plus/minus symbol.

   B. Use .375 unit height with all other variables at default values.

   C. Save the drawing as P8-3.

---

4. Use the **MTEXT** command to type the following text using a text style with Romans font and .125 text height. The heading text height is .25. Check your spelling. Save the drawing as P8-4.

NOTES:
1. INTERPRET DIMENSIONS AND TOLERANCES PER ASME Y14.5M—1994.
2. REMOVE ALL BURRS AND SHARP EDGES.

CASTING NOTES UNLESS OTHERWISE SPECIFIED:
1. .31 WALL THICKNESS.
2. R.12 FILLETS.
3. R.06 ROUNDS.
4. 1.5°—3.0° DRAFT.
5. TOLERANCES:
    ±1° ANGULAR
    ±.03 TWO PLACE DIMENSIONS.
6. PROVIDE .12 THK MACHINING STOCK ON ALL MACHINE SURFACES.

5. Use the **MTEXT** command to type the following text using a text style with Stylus BT font and .125 text height. The heading text height is .188. After typing the text exactly as shown, edit the text with the following changes:

A. Change the \ in item 7 to 1/2.

B. Change the [in item 8 to 1.

C. Change the 1/2 in item 8 to 3/4.

D. Change the ^ in item 10 to a degree symbol.

E. Check your spelling on the text after making the change.

F. Save as drawing P8-5.

COMMON FRAMING NOTES:
1. ALL FRAMING LUMBER TO BE DFL #2 OR BETTER.
2. ALL HEATED WALLS @ HEATED LIVING AREAS TO BE
    2 X 6 @ 24" OC.
3. ALL EXTERIOR HEADERS TO BE 2—2 X 12 UNLESS
    NOTED, W/ 2" RIGID INSULATION BACKING UNLESS
    NOTED.
4. ALL SHEAR PANELS TO BE 1/2" CDX PLY W/ 8d
    @ 4" OC @ EDGE, HDRS, & BLOCKING AND 8d @
    8" OC @ FIELD UNLESS NOTED.
5. ALL METAL CONNECTORS TO BE SIMPSON CO. OR
    EQUAL.
6. ALL TRUSSES TO BE 24" OC. SUBMIT TRUSS
    CALCS TO BUILDING DEPT. PRIOR TO ERECTION.
7. PLYWOOD ROOF SHEATHING TO BE \ STD GRADE
    32/16 PLY LAID PERP TO RAFTERS. NAIL W/ 8d
    @ 6"OC @ EDGES AND 12" OC @ FIELD.
8. PROVIDE [1/2" STD GRADE T&G PLY FLOOR
    SHEATHING LAID PERP TO FLOOR JOISTS. NAIL W/
    10d @ 6" OC @ EDGES & BLOCKING AND 12" OC
    @ FIELD.
9. BLOCK ALL WALLS OVER 10'—0" HIGH AT MID.
10. LET—IN BRACES TO BE 1 X 4 DIAG BRACES @ 45^
    FOR ALL INTERIOR LOAD BEARING WALLS.

AutoCAD and its Applications—Basics

6. Open P4-7 and complete the window schedule by entering a text style with the Stylus BT font. Create a layer for the text. Draw the hexagonal symbols in the SYM column. Save the drawing as P8-6.

7. Open P4-8 and complete the door schedule by entering a text style with the Stylus BT font. Create a layer for the text. Draw the circle symbols in the SYM column. Save the drawing as P8-7.

8. Open P4-9 and complete the finish schedule by entering a text style with the Stylus BT font. Save the drawing as P8-8.

9. Open P4-11 and complete the schematic by entering a text style with the Romans font. Create a layer for the text. Save the drawing as P8-9.

10. Open P4-12 and complete the block diagram by entering a text style with the Romans font. Create a layer for the text. Save the drawing as P8-10.

11. Open P5-9 and add text to the circuit diagram. Use a text style with the Romans font. Create a layer for the text. Save the drawing as P8-11.

12. Open P5-10 and add text to the schematic. Use a text style with the Romans font. Create a layer for the text. Save the drawing as P8-12.

13. Add title blocks, borders, and text styles to the template drawings you created in earlier chapters. Create a Border layer for the border lines and thick title block lines. Create a Title block layer for thin title block lines and text. Make three template drawings with borders and title blocks for your future drawings. Use the following guidelines:

    A. Prototype 1 for A-size, 8 1/2 × 11 drawings, named TITLEA–MECH.

    B. Prototype 2 for B-size, 11 × 17 drawings, named TITLEB–MECH.

    C. Prototype 3 for C-size, 17 × 22 drawings, named TITLEC–MECH.

    D. Set the following values for the drawing aids:

       Units = three-place decimal

       Grid = .500

       Snap = .250

    E. Draw a border 1/2" from the drawing limits.

    F. Design a title block using created text styles. Place it in the lower-right corner of each drawing. The title block should contain the following information: company or school name, address, date, drawn by, approved by, scale, title, drawing number, material, revision number. See the example on the following page.

    G. Record the information about each template in a log.

R -	CHANGE		DATE	ECN

HYSTER COMPANY

THIS PRINT CONTAINS CONFIDENTIAL INFORMATION WHICH IS THE PROPERTY OF HYSTER COMPANY. BY ACCEPTING THIS INFORMATION THE BORROWER AGREES THAT IT WILL NOT BE USED FOR ANY PURPOSE OTHER THAN THAT FOR WHICH IT IS LOANED.

SPECIFICATIONS

UNLESS OTHERWISE SPECIFIED DIMENSIONS ARE IN
~~INCHES~~ MILLIMETERS AND TOLERANCES FOR :

____ PLACE DIMS± _____ :____ PLACE DIMS± _____

ANGLES ± _____ : WHOLE DIMS± _____

DR.	SCALE	DATE
CK. MAT'L.	CK. DESIGN	REL. ON ECN
NAME		

MODEL	DWG. FIRST USED	SIMILAR TO

DEPT.	PROJECT	LIST DIVISION	H	PART NO.	R

---

14. Draw a small parts list (similar to the one shown below) connected to your C-size prototype title block.

A. Enter PARTS LIST with a style containing a complex font.

B. Enter the other information using text and the **DTEXT** command. Do not exit the **DTEXT** command to start a new line of text.

C. Save the drawing as TITLEC-PARTS.

D. Record the information about the template in a log.

3	HOLDING PINS	12
2	SIDE COVERS	3
1	MAIN HOUSING	1
KEY	DESCRIPTION	QTY

PARTS LIST

UNLESS OTHERWISE SPECIFIED
ALL DIMENSIONS IN

INCHES

AND TOLERANCES FOR:

1	PLACE DIMS:	±.1
2	PLACE DIMS:	±.01
3	PLACE DIMS:	±.005
	ANGULAR:	±30'
	FRACTIONAL:	±.1/32
	FINISH:	125? in.

JANE'S
DESIGN

DR:	SCALE:	DATE:	APPD:
JANE	FULL	XX—XX—XX	

MATERIAL:

MILD STEEL

NAME:

XXX—XXXX

FIRST USED ON:	SIMILAR TO:	B	PART NO: 123—321	REV: 0

15. Draw an architectural template for a 17" × 22" or 22" × 34" sheet size with a title block along the right side similar to the one shown below. Use the same layout and layer instructions given for Problem 13. Save the drawing as ARCH. Record the information about the template in a log.

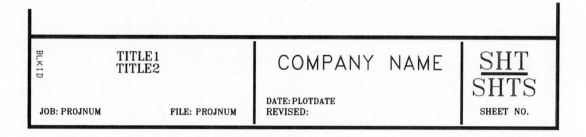

16. Draw title blocks with borders for your electrical, piping, and general drawings. Use the same instructions provided in Problem 13. The title block can be similar to the one displayed with Problem 13, but the area for mechanical drafting tolerances is not required. Research sample title blocks to come up with your design. Save the templates as ELEC A, ELEC B, PIPE A, PIPE B, or another name related to the drawing type and sheet size.

17. Draw the AND/OR schematic shown below. Save your drawing as P8-17.

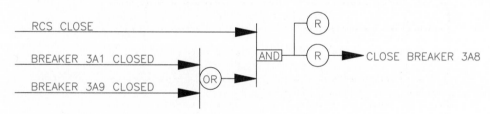

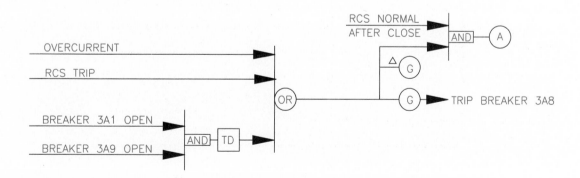

18. Draw the controller schematic shown below. Save your drawing as P8-18.

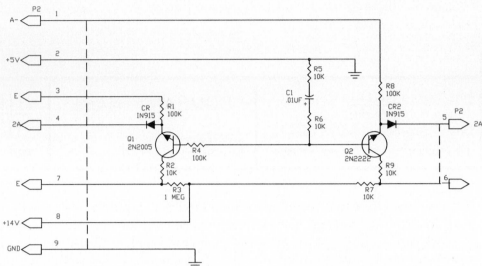

NOTES:

1. INTERPRET ELECTRICAL AND ELECTRONICS DIAGRAMS PER ANSI Y14.15.

2. UNLESS OTHERWISE SPECIFIED:

   RESISTANCE VALUES ARE IN OHMS.
   RESISTANCE TOLERANCE IS 5%.
   RESISTORS ARE 1/4 WATT.
   CAPACITANCE VALUES ARE IN MICROFARADS.
   CAPACITANCE TOLERANCE IS 10%.
   CAPACITOR VOLTAGE RATING IS 20V.
   INDUCTANCE VALUES ARE IN MICROHENRIES.

REFERENCE DESTINATIONS
LAST USED
R9
C1
CR2
Q2

Learning Objectives

After completing this chapter, you will be able to:
- Use realtime zoom and pan.
- Magnify a small part of the drawing to work on details.
- Move the display window to reveal portions of the drawing outside the boundaries of the monitor.
- Create named views that can be recalled instantly.
- Use the **Aerial View** window.
- Define the terms model space and paper space.
- Create multiple viewports in the graphics window.
- Explain the differences between the **REDRAW** command and the **REGEN** command.

You can view a specific portion of a drawing using the AutoCAD display commands. The **ZOOM** command allows you to enlarge or reduce the amount of the drawing displayed. The portion displayed can also be moved using the **PAN** command. Panning is like looking through a camera and moving the camera across the drawing. The **DSVIEWER** command enables the **Aerial View** window. Using this window, you can locate a particular area of the drawing to view. The **VIEW** command allows you to create and name specific views of the drawing. When further drawing or editing operations are required, the view can be quickly and easily recalled.

Display functions allow you to work in model space or paper space. *Model space* is used for drawing and designing, while *paper space* is used for plotting. The **MVIEW** command allows you to switch between the two drawing environments. Detailed information on the use of model space and paper space to prepare multiview drawings is provided in Chapter 3 and Chapter 10.

This chapter also discusses the differences between the **REDRAW** and **REGEN** commands. Additionally, using the **REGENAUTO** and **VIEWRES** commands to achieve optimum display speeds and quality is discussed.

Redrawing and Regenerating the Screen

AutoCAD
User's
Guide   1

A *blip* is a small cross displayed when a point is picked on the screen. See Figure 9-1. These blips are not part of your drawing; they simply stay on the screen until it is redrawn. The **REDRAW** command is used to clean the blips from the screen and refresh objects after editing operations.

Figure 9-1.
Tiny crosshairs, or blips, appear on the screen when a point is selected.

Blips

REDRAW
R

View
➡ Redraw

Standard toolbar

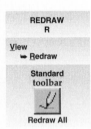

Redraw All

Redraw the screen by picking the **Redraw All** button in the **Standard** toolbar, selecting **Redraw** from the **View** pull-down menu, or by entering REDRAW or R at the Command: prompt.

PROFESSIONAL TIP

Using **REDRAW** every time blips appear will slow your drawing sessions. Redraw the screen only when the blips interfere with the drawing process.

The **REDRAW** command simply refreshes the current screen. To regenerate the screen, the **REGEN** command is used. This command recalculates all of the drawing object coordinates and regenerates the display based on the current zoom magnification. Therefore, if you have zoomed in on objects in your drawing and curved edges appear to be straight segments, using **REGEN** will smooth the curves. To access the **REGEN** command, pick **Regen** from the **View** pull-down menu or enter REGEN or RE at the Command: prompt. The screen is immediately regenerated.

REGEN
RE

View
➡ Regen

Working inside another command

To begin a new command, you usually need to complete or cancel the current command. Most menu picks automatically cancel the command in progress before initiating the new one. However, some commands function without canceling an active command.

A *transparent command* temporarily interrupts the active command. After the transparent command is completed, the command that was interrupted is resumed. Therefore, it is not necessary to cancel the initial command. Many display commands can be used transparently, including **REDRAW**, **PAN**, **VIEW**, **HELP**, **AV**, and several **ZOOM** options.

When entering a transparent command from the command line, precede the command name by an apostrophe. For example, the following command sequence shows the **REDRAW** command entered transparently during the **LINE** command.

```
Command: LINE↵
From point: (select the first point)
To point: 'R or 'REDRAW.↵
```

This clears all blips so you can see the drawing better.

```
Resuming LINE command.
To point: (select the second point)
To point: 'GRID ↵
>>Grid spacing(X) or ON/OFF/Snap/Aspect ⟨current⟩: .25↵
Resuming LINE command.
To point:
```

PROFESSIONAL TIP

A transparent redraw is executed when **Redraw** is picked from the **View** pull-down menu. Settings such as **GRID**, **SNAP**, and **ORTHO** can be used transparently, but it is quicker to activate these with the appropriate function keys.

All of the commands discussed in this chapter, with the exception of **DSVIEWER**, **REGEN**, **VIEWRES**, and **VPORTS**, can be used transparently. A detailed discussion of transparent commands and how they are used is given later in the chapter.

Using blips

Blips are often turned off to eliminate the need for redraws. To turn blips off, select **Drawing Aids...** from the **Tools** pull-down menu. This opens the **Drawing Aids** dialog box. Pick the check mark in the **Blips** check box (or type B). See Figure 9-2. Blips can also be turned off using the **BLIPMODE** command at the Command: prompt.

BLIPMODE

Tools
→ Drawing Aids...

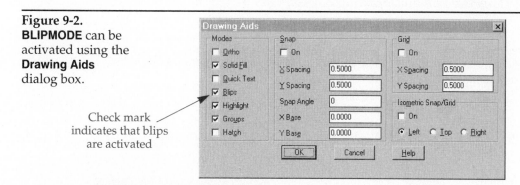

Figure 9-2.
BLIPMODE can be activated using the **Drawing Aids** dialog box.

Check mark indicates that blips are activated

PROFESSIONAL TIP

Turning **BLIPMODE** off affects the current drawing only. If you want blips to be off in new drawings, turn off **BLIPMODE** in the template drawing.

Getting Close to Your Work

AutoCAD User's Guide 6

The ability to *zoom in* (magnify) a drawing allows designers to create extremely small items, such as the electronic circuits found in a computer. The **ZOOM** command is a helpful tool that you will use often. It also can be used as a transparent command. The different options of the **ZOOM** command are discussed in the next sections.

The ZOOM options

ZOOM
Z

View
→ Zoom ⟩

Each of the **ZOOM** options can be accessed by its corresponding **Zoom** flyout button in the **Standard** toolbar, or by selecting the **Zoom** cascading menu from the **View** pull-down menu. See Figure 9-3. Also, entering ZOOM or Z at the Command: prompt lists the options as follows:

Command: **Z** *or* **ZOOM**↲
All/Center/Dynamic/Extents/Previous/Scale(X/XP)/Window/⟨Realtime⟩:

Brief explanations of the **ZOOM** options are provided below.

- **In.** This option is available only on the toolbar and the pull-down menu. It automatically executes a 2X zoom scale factor.
- **Out.** This option is available only on the toolbar and the pull-down menu. It automatically executes a .5X zoom scale factor.
- **All.** Zooms to display drawing limits. If objects are drawn beyond the limits, a **Zoom Extents** is performed. Always use the **All** option after you change the drawing limits.
- **Center.** Pick the center and height of the next screen display. Rather than a height, a magnification factor can be entered by typing a number followed by an X, such as 4X. The current value represents the height of the screen in drawing units. Entering a smaller number enlarges the image size, while a larger number reduces it. The command sequence is as follows:

All/Center/Dynamic/Extents/Previous/Scale(X/XP)/Window/Realtime: **C**↲
Center point: *(pick a center point)*
Magnification or Height ⟨*current*⟩: **4X**↲
Command:

- **Dynamic.** Allows for a graphic pan and zoom with the use of a view box that represents the screen. This option is discussed in detail later in the chapter.
- **Extents.** Zooms to the extents of the drawing. This is the portion of the drawing area that contains drawing objects.

Figure 9-3.
ZOOM command options. A—The **ZOOM** flyout button on the **Standard** toolbar. B—The **Zoom** cascading menu.

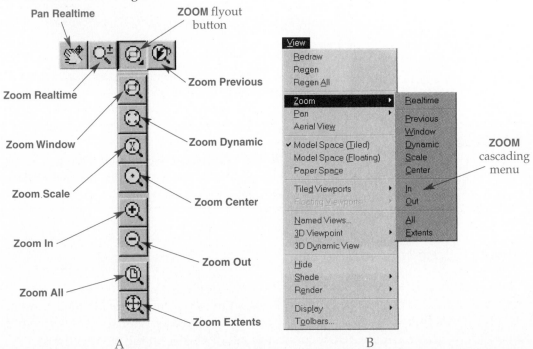

A   B

- **Window.** Pick opposite corners of a box. Objects in the box enlarge to fill the display. The **Window** option is the default if you pick a point on the screen.
- **Scale(X).** A positive number is required here to indicate the magnification factor of the original display. You can enlarge or reduce relative to the current display by typing an X after the scale. Type 2X if you want the image enlarged two times. Type .5X if you want the image reduced by half. Typing a number without the X zooms relative to the original drawing.
- **Scale(XP).** This option is used in conjunction with model space and paper space. It scales a drawing in model space relative to paper space and is used primarily in the layout of scaled multiview drawings. A detailed discussion of this option is given in Chapter 10.
- **Previous.** Returns to the previous display. You can go back ten displays, one at a time.

Performing realtime zoom

When using the command line, the default option of the **ZOOM** command is **Realtime**. A *realtime zoom* can be viewed as it is performed. From the keyboard, it is activated by pressing [Enter] at the **ZOOM** command prompt line, or by entering RTZOOM at the Command: prompt. It can also be selected by picking the **Zoom Realtime** button in the **Standard** toolbar, or by picking **Realtime** in the **Zoom** cascading menu in the **View** pull-down menu.

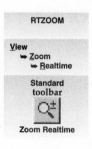

The **RTZOOM** command allows you to see the model move on the screen as you zoom. It is the quickest and easiest method for adjusting the magnification of drawings on the screen. The command sequence is as follows:

Command: **Z** *or* **ZOOM.**↵
All/Center/Dynamic/Extents/Previous/Scale(X/XP)/Window/⟨Realtime⟩:↵
Press Esc or Enter to exit, or right-click to activate pop-up menu.

The magnifying glass icon with a plus and minus is displayed when **Zoom Realtime** is executed. Press and hold the left mouse button (pick button) and move the pointer up to enlarge and down to reduce. When you have achieved the display you want, release the button. If the display needs further adjustment after the initial zoom, press and hold the left mouse button again and move the pointer to get the desired display. Once you are done, press the [Esc] key or the [Enter] key to exit.

If you press the right mouse button (the enter button), a pop-up cursor menu is displayed. See Figure 9-4. This menu appears at the cursor location and contains five viewing options.

- **Pan.** Activates the **Pan Realtime** command. This allows you to adjust the placement of the drawing on the screen. If additional zooming is required, right-click again to display the pop-up menu and pick **Zoom**. In this manner you can toggle back and forth between **Pan** and **Zoom Realtime** to accurately adjust the view. A detailed explanation of **Pan** is given later in the chapter.
- **Zoom.** A check appears to the left of this option if it is active.
- **Zoom Window.** Activates the **Zoom Window** option and changes the cursor display. See Figure 9-5. You can pick opposite corners of a window but you must press and hold the pick button and drag the window box to the opposite corner, then release the pick button.

Figure 9-4.
The cursor pop-up menu appears at the cursor location and contains five viewing options.

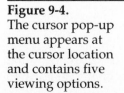

Figure 9-5.
The cursor changes
when **Zoom Window** is
selected from the cursor
pop-up menu.

- **Zoom Previous.** Restores the previous display. This is a handy function if the current display is not to your liking and it would be easier to start over rather than to make further adjustments.
- **Zoom Extents.** Zooms to the extents of the drawing.

Enlarging with a window

The **ZOOM Window** option requires that you pick opposite corners of a rectangular window enclosing the area to be zoomed. The first point you pick is automatically accepted as the first corner of the zoom window. After this corner is picked, a box appears attached to the crosshairs. It grows and shrinks as you move the pointing device. When the second corner is picked, the center of the window becomes the center of the new screen display. If you wish to return to the previous display, select **ZOOM** and use the **Previous** option. If you want to see the entire drawing, use the **All** option. Figure 9-6 shows **ZOOM Window** and **ZOOM Previous** used on a drawing.

Figure 9-6.
A—When using the **ZOOM Window** command, select the corners of a window (shown here highlighted). B—The selected window will fill the drawing screen. To return to the original view, use the **ZOOM Previous** command.

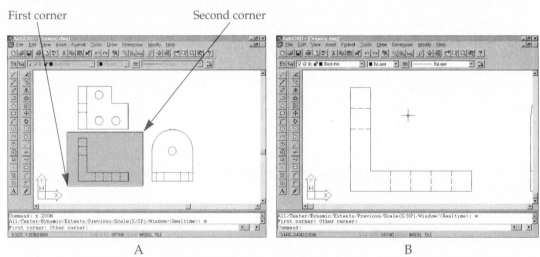

First corner   Second corner

A   B

Accurate displays with a dynamic zoom

The **ZOOM Dynamic** option allows you to accurately specify the portion of the drawing you want displayed. This is done by constructing a *view box*. This view box is proportional to the size of the display area. If you are looking at a zoomed view when **ZOOM Dynamic** is selected, the entire drawing is displayed on the screen. To practice with this command, load any drawing into AutoCAD. Then, select the **Zoom Dynamic** command.

The screen is now occupied by three boxes. See Figure 9-7. A fourth box is displayed later. Each box has a specific function:

- **Drawing extents.** (blue dotted line) This box shows the area of the drawing that is occupied by drawing entities. It is the same area that is displayed with **ZOOM Extents**.

Figure 9-7.
Features of the **ZOOM Dynamic** command.

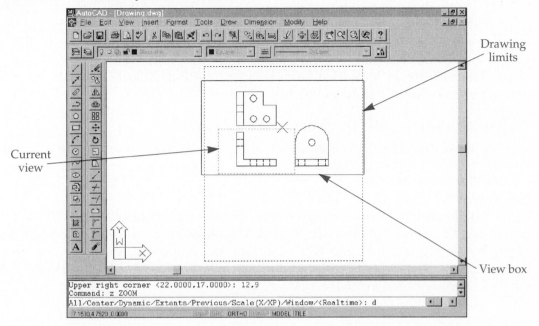

- **Current view.** (green dotted line) This is the view that was displayed before you selected **ZOOM Dynamic**.
- **Panning view box.** (X in the center) Move the pointing device to find the center point of the desired zoomed display. When you press the pick button, the zooming view box appears.
- **Zooming view box.** (arrow on right side) This box allows you to decrease or increase the area that you wish to zoom. Move the pointer to the right and the box increases in size. Move the pointer to the left and the box shrinks. You can also pan up or down with the zooming view box. The only restriction is that you cannot move the box to the left.

The **ZOOM Dynamic** command is not complete until you press [Enter]. If you press the pick button to select the zooming view box, the panning view box reappears. Then, the box can be repositioned. In this manner, you can fine-tune the exact display needed. This is also helpful in defining permanent views, which is discussed later in this chapter.

EXERCISE 9-1

❏ Start AutoCAD and load a drawing from a previous exercise or drawing problem.
    ❏ Enlarge and reduce the drawing using **Zoom Realtime**.
    ❏ Move around the drawing using **Pan Realtime**.
    ❏ Select **ZOOM Window** and enlarge a portion of the drawing.
    ❏ Select **ZOOM Window** again, to move in closer to a detail.
    ❏ Use **ZOOM Previous** to return to the last display.
    ❏ Select **ZOOM Extents** to show only the drawing entities.
    ❏ Select **ZOOM All** to display the entire drawing limits.
    ❏ Select **ZOOM Dynamic**. Maneuver the view box to select a portion of the drawing.
    ❏ Use **ZOOM Dynamic** to enlarge the display.
❏ Save the drawing as EX9-1, then quit the drawing session.

On a large drawing that involves a number of separate details, using the **ZOOM** command can be time-consuming. Being able to quickly specify a certain part of the drawing would be much easier. This is possible with the **VIEW** command. It allows you to create named views. A view can be a portion of the drawing, such as the upper-left quadrant, or it can denote an enlarged portion. After the view is created, you can instruct AutoCAD to display it at any time.

Creating views with the View dialog box

The **VIEW** command can be accessed by picking the **Named Views** button in the **Viewpoint** toolbar, selecting **Named Views...** from the **View** pull-down menu, or entering DDVIEW or V at the Command: prompt. This activates the **View Control** dialog box. See Figure 9-8.

A list of currently defined views is shown in the **View Control** dialog box. If you want to save the current display as a view, pick the **New...** button. The **Define New View** dialog box is displayed, Figure 9-9. Now, type the desired view name in the **New Name:** edit box. The **Current Display** option button is the default; click **Save View**, and the view name is added to the list.

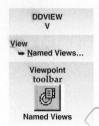

DDVIEW
V

View
→ Named Views...

Viewpoint
toolbar

Named Views

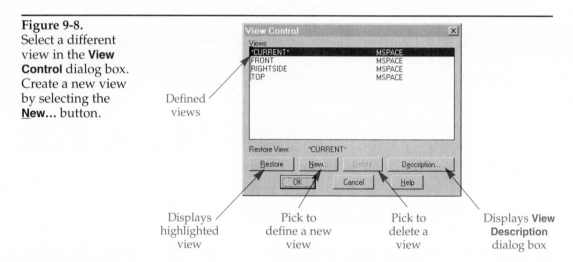

Figure 9-8.
Select a different view in the **View Control** dialog box. Create a new view by selecting the **New...** button.

Defined views

Displays highlighted view

Pick to define a new view

Pick to delete a view

Displays **View Description** dialog box

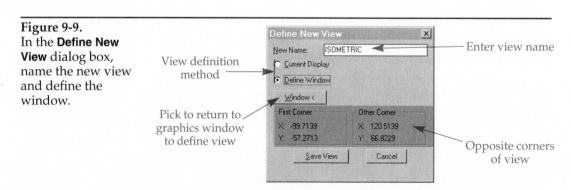

Figure 9-9.
In the **Define New View** dialog box, name the new view and define the window.

View definition method

Pick to return to graphics window to define view

Enter view name

Opposite corners of view

If you want to use a window to define the view, pick the **Define Window** radio button, and then pick the **Window** ⟨ button. You are prompted for the first corner. Select the window. After you pick the second corner, the **Define New View** dialog box reappears. Pick the **Save View** button and the **View Control** dialog box is updated to reflect the new view.

NOTE

The crosshairs in a 3D view remain on the 3D axis until you pick the first window point, then the window is displayed. After entering a name in the **New Name:** text box, you must pick the **Save View** button, rather than pressing [Enter].

To display listed views, simply pick its name from the file list and pick the **Restore** button. The name of the view appears in the **Restore View:** label. Now, pick the **OK** button and the screen displays the selected view.

To delete a view displayed in the dialog box, first pick the view name in the list to highlight it, then pick **Delete**. Notice that the view name is immediately removed from the list. If no view name is highlighted, the **Delete** button is grayed-out.

You can get a detailed description of the selected view by picking the **Description...** button. This opens the **View Description** dialog box, which provides a variety of information about the view. See Figure 9-10. A discussion of these values related to 3D drawings is given in *AutoCAD and its Applications—Advanced, Release 14*.

Figure 9-10.
The **View Description** dialog box provides information about a view.

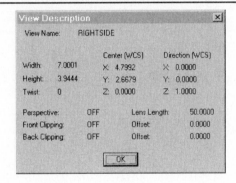

Creating views at the **Command:** prompt

When VIEW or -V is entered at the Command: prompt, you are presented with the following five options:

```
Command: -V or VIEW.↵
?/Delete/Restore/Save/Window:
```

- **?.** This option lists currently defined view names. You are prompted for which views to list. Responding with [Enter] accepts the default and displays all currently defined view names.

```
?/Delete/Restore/Save/Window: ?↵
View(s) to list ⟨*⟩: ↵
Saved views:
View name              Space
FRONT                  M
RIGHT SIDE             M
TOP                    M
Command:
```

- **Delete (D).** This option removes unneeded views. After selecting this option, you are prompted to enter the name of the view to be deleted. Type the name and press [Enter].
- **Restore (R).** A saved view can be displayed on the screen using this option. Simply enter the name of the view you want to display at the View name to restore: prompt. The view is then immediately displayed.

- **Save (S).** This option creates a new view. Enter the new view name at the View name to save: prompt. The current display becomes the new view.
- **Window (W).** This option also creates a new view. After entering the view name, you define the view with a window. The following command sequence appears:

> Command: **-V** *or* **VIEW**↵
> ?/Delete/Restore/Save/Window: **W**↵
> View name to save: *(enter the view name and press* [Enter]*)*
> First corner: *(pick one window corner)*
> Other corner: *(pick the second corner)*
> Command:

PROFESSIONAL TIP    Part of your project planning should include view names. A consistent naming system guarantees that all users will know the view names without having to list them. The views can be set as part of the template drawings. Then, view names can be placed in a custom screen menu as discussed in *AutoCAD and its Applications—Advanced, Release 14*.

---

6 Moving around the Display Screen

The **PAN** command allows you to move your view point around the drawing without changing the magnification factor. You can then view objects that lie just outside the edges of the display screen.

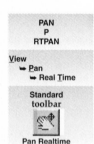

PAN
P
RTPAN

View
↳ Pan
  ↳ Real Time

Standard
toolbar

Pan Realtime

Performing realtime pan

A *realtime pan* allows you to see the drawing move on the screen as you pan. It is the quickest and easiest method for adjusting the location of drawings on the screen. Both the **PAN** and **RTPAN** commands activate realtime pan. You can pick **Real Time** from the **Pan** cascading menu in the **View** pull-down menu, pick the **Pan Realtime** button on the **Standard** toolbar, or enter PAN, P, or RTPAN at the Command: prompt.

After executing the command, press and hold the pick button and move the pointing device in the direction you wish to pan. The pan icon of the hand is displayed when a realtime pan is executed. A right-click displays the cursor pop-up menu shown back in Figure 9-4.

If you pan to the edge of your drawing, a bar is displayed on one side of the hand cursor. The bar correlates to the side of the drawing. For example, if you reach the left side of the drawing, a bar and arrow appear on the left side of the hand. These icons are shown in Figure 9-11.

Figure 9-11.
A bar and arrow appear by the hand cursor when you pan to the edge of the drawing.

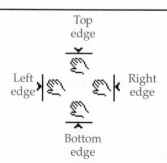

Top edge

Left edge   Right edge

Bottom edge

Picking the pan displacement

The *pan displacement* is the distance the drawing is moved on the screen. You can visually pick the displacement by selecting **Point** from the **Pan** cascading menu in the **View** pull-down menu or entering -PAN or -P at the Command: prompt. AutoCAD prompts for the base point of displacement. Then, you must pick where you want the first point to appear in the next display. The display window is moved the distance between the two points. See Figure 9-12.

Command: **-P** *or* **-PAN**↵
Displacement: *(pick the point to drag)*
Second point: *(pick the final location of the first point)*
Command:

Figure 9-12.
PAN moves the drawing around the screen. A—Panning to the left. B—Panning up. C—Complete pan.

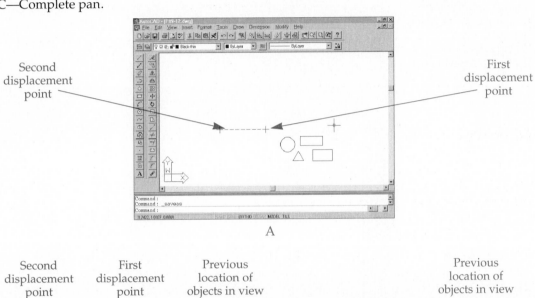

Second displacement point

First displacement point

A

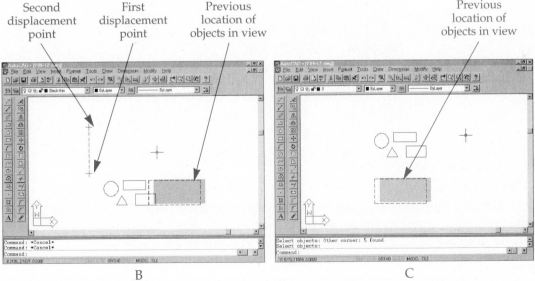

Second displacement point

First displacement point

Previous location of objects in view

Previous location of objects in view

B

C

You can also enter the displacement, or the distance the display window is to be moved, by giving coordinates. See Figure 9-13. The coordinates can be either relative or absolute. The following command sequence performs a relative displacement 8 units to the right and 3 units up:

Command: **-P** *or* **-PAN**↵
Displacement: **8,3**↵
Second point: ↵
Command:

Suppose the coordinate location of the point you referenced was 4,5. Then, the relative displacement for the above movement is calculated as 4,5 + 8,3 = 12,8 for the second point. The absolute coordinates can also be used:

Command: **-P** *or* **-PAN**↵
Displacement: **4,5**↵
Second point: **12,8**↵
Command:

Figure 9-13.
Relative coordinates can be used to pan across a drawing.

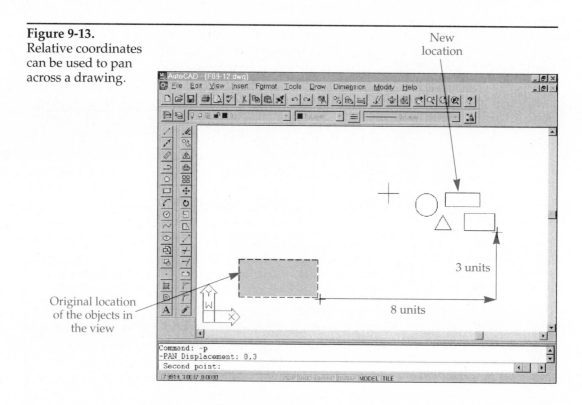

Using pan presets

You can automatically pan from the center of your current drawing display to one of the four edges by using one of the pan presets provided in the **View** pull-down menu. The four available options are shown in Figure 9-14.

Figure 9-14.
The **PAN** options can be found in the **Pan** cascading menu of the **View** pull-down menu.

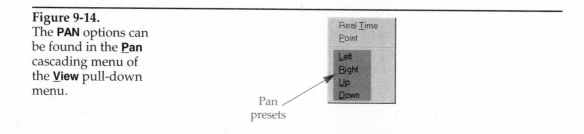

AutoCAD
User's
Guide

14

AutoCAD can save you time on zooming and panning at the expense of display accuracy. Or, AutoCAD can provide a highly accurate display at the expense of zoom and pan speed. The main factor is the view resolution.

The *view resolution* refers to the number of lines used to draw circles and arcs. High resolution values display smooth circles and arcs. Low resolution values display segmented circles and arcs. You can control the view resolution of circles and arcs with the **VIEWRES** command:

    Command: **VIEWRES**↵
    Do you want fast zooms? ⟨Y⟩ ↵
    Enter circle zoom percent (1-20000) ⟨*current*⟩:

If your response to the first prompt is Yes, AutoCAD uses fast zooms. When a **ZOOM**, **PAN**, or **VIEW Restore** command is used, AutoCAD *refreshes* the screen as if the **REDRAW** command was used. The redraw speed can only be used if you do not reduce or enlarge outside of the generated areas. After zooming in, a circle will appear less smooth.

If speed is not a concern, then answer No to the first prompt. This causes AutoCAD to perform a regeneration (**REGEN**) when a display command is issued. Circles and arcs will always appear to have the same smoothness.

The actual smoothness of circles and arcs is controlled by the circle zoom percent. It can vary between 1 and 20000. The default is 100, which produces a relatively smooth circle. A number smaller than 100 causes circles and arcs to be drawn with fewer vectors (straight lines). A number larger than 100 causes more vectors to be included in the circles, as shown in Figure 9-15.

The circle zoom percent is only used when AutoCAD is forced to do a regeneration. This is why a circle may appear to be composed of several straight sides after you zoom in on it. If you want a smooth circle, use the **REGEN** command.

The view resolution can be set in a dialog box by picking **Preferences...** from the **Tools** pull-down menu. This accesses the **Preferences** dialog box. Now, pick the **Performance** tab. The **Arc and circle smoothness:** text box contains the current **VIEWRES** setting. See Figure 9-16. Changing this number changes the resolution as previously discussed.

The **VIEWRES** command is a display function only and has no effect on the plotted drawing. A drawing is plotted using an optimum number of vectors for the size of circles and arcs. See Chapter 10 of this text for detailed information on plotting.

PROFESSIONAL TIP
    If you are concerned with speed, set **VIEWRES** for fast zooms and set the circle zoom percent to 100 or less. Circles may look like they have straight line sides, but drawing regeneration takes less time.

Figure 9-15.
The higher the **VIEWRES** value, the smoother a circle will appear.

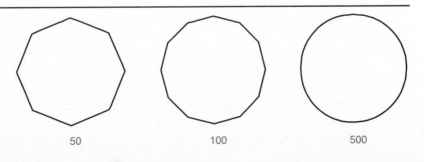

50   100   500

Figure 9-16.
The view resolution
(**VIEWRES**) variable
can be set in the
Preferences
dialog box.

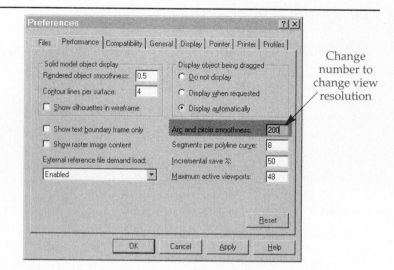

Change
number to
change view
resolution

❑ Begin a new drawing or use one of your templates.
❑ Draw three circles and three arcs of different sizes.
❑ Zoom in on the smallest circle using the **Dynamic** option. Notice the straight line segments that make up the circle.
❑ Keep zooming in on the circle edge (with **ZOOM Window**) until you force a regeneration.
❑ Set the **VIEWRES** command for fast zooms and a 10% circle zoom. **ZOOM All** and notice the shape of the circles and arcs after a regeneration.
❑ Select the **VIEWRES** command and answer No for fast zooms. Set circle zoom to 20%. Zoom in on a circle three times. Notice when a regeneration is performed.
❑ Save the drawing as EX9-2 and quit the drawing session.

The View Pull-Down Menu

Often-used display commands can be accessed from the **View** pull-down menu, Figure 9-17. This menu provides access to most of AutoCAD's display and viewing commands. Eight of the selections lead to cascading menus, which provide additional options and other commands.

- **Redraw.** Redraws the current viewport.
- **Regen.** Regenerates the current viewport.
- **Regen All.** Regenerates all the viewports in model space or paper space.
- **Zoom.** Provides access to all **ZOOM** command options.
- **Pan.** Provides access to all **PAN** command options.
- **Aerial View.** Displays the entire drawing in the aerial view window. Allows you to zoom, pan, and locate details quickly. This is explained in detail later in the chapter.
- **Model Space (Tiled).** This is the default display setting. A check mark indicates that the current setting of the **TILEMODE** system variable is 1. A **TILEMODE** setting of 1 means that model space is current and only *tiled viewports* can be created. Therefore, when this item has a check mark by it, the **Floating Viewports** selection is grayed-out and unselectable.
- **Model Space (Floating).** Picking this option sets **TILEMODE** to 0, activating paper space. If no *floating viewports* currently exist in paper space, the **MVIEW** command is entered so the necessary viewports can be created.

Figure 9-17.
The **View** pull-down
menu.

- **Paper Space.** Switches **TILEMODE** to 0 and activates paper space. If floating viewports have been created, the crosshairs appear to be laying over the top of them. Paper space is a 2D environment, so when this item has a check mark by it, the 3D selections are grayed-out.
- **Tiled Viewports.** Displays a cascading menu for viewport layout and construction. Enables you to create tiled viewports with the **VPORTS** command. This selection is available only when there is a check mark by **Model Space (Tiled)** because the **VPORTS** command is only available when **TILEMODE** is set to 1.
- **Floating Viewports.** Displays a cascading menu for paper space viewport layout and construction. Enables you to create floating viewports with the **MVIEW** command. This selection is available only when there is a check mark by **Model Space (Floating)** or **Paper Space**, because the **MVIEW** command is only available when **TILEMODE** is set to 0.
- **Named Views….** Displays the **View Control** dialog box, enabling you to work with named views.
- **3D Viewpoint.** Provides access to fifteen different preset 3D viewing options.
- **3D Dynamic View.** Activates the **DVIEW** command, providing total control over the creation of a 3D viewpoint and display.
- **Hide.** Executes the **HIDE** command to remove hidden lines from 3D objects.
- **Shade.** Executes the **SHADE** command that displays the 3D model as a shaded rendering. Displays a cascading menu of four different shading options.
- **Render.** Activates the AutoCAD render module that enables you to add lights.
- **Display.** Provides access via a cascading menu to UCS icon display, attribute display, and the AutoCAD text window.
- **Toolbars….** Enables users to display and customize toolbars. See *AutoCAD and its Applications—Advanced, Release 14*.

NOTE   The **Hide, Shade, Render**, and **Toolbars...** selections are used in 3D modeling and menu customizing. They are covered in detail in *AutoCAD and its Applications—Advanced, Release 14*.

Using Transparent Display Commands

Certain commands can be used while you are inside another command. These commands are said to be *transparent* to the current command. The display commands **ZOOM**, **PAN**, and **VIEW** can be used transparently. AutoCAD system variables can also be used in the transparent mode.

Suppose that while drawing a line, you need to place a point somewhere off the screen. One option is to cancel the **LINE** command. Then zoom out to see more of the drawing and select **LINE** again. A more efficient method is to use **PAN** or **ZOOM** while still in the **LINE** command. An example of drawing a line to a point off the screen is as follows:

Command: **L** *or* **LINE**↵
From point: *(pick a point)*
To point: *(pick the* **Pan** *button from the* **Standard** *toolbar, or type* **'PAN** *and press* [Enter]*)*
≫Press Esc or Enter to exit, or right-click to activate pop-up menu. *(pan to the location desired then press* [Enter]*)*
Resuming LINE command.
To point: *(pick a point)*
To point: ↵
Command:

The double prompt (≫) indicates that a command has been put *on hold* while you use a transparent command. The transparent command must be completed before the original command is returned. At that time, the double prompt disappears.

The above procedure is similar when using the **ZOOM** and **VIEW** commands. When typed at the keyboard, an apostrophe (') is entered before the command. To connect a line to a small feature, enter **'ZOOM** at the To point: prompt. To perform a drawing or editing function across views, use **'VIEW**.

PROFESSIONAL TIP

Both the **Pan** button and **Zoom** button activate commands transparently, but the **Named Views** button does not. To execute a transparent **VIEW** command, you must type **'VIEW** at the Command: prompt and enter the appropriate option.

When trying to perform a transparent display, you may receive the following message:

∗∗Requires a regen, cannot be transparent.
Resuming *current* command.

In this situation, you might try a less dramatic **ZOOM**, **PAN**, or **VIEW** that does not require AutoCAD to regenerate the display.

EXERCISE 9-3

❏ Begin a new drawing or use one of your templates.
❏ Set the drawing limits at 12,9, grid spacing at .5, and snap spacing at .25.
❏ Construct the two arcs shown on the following page.
❏ Window a view of the left arc and name it 1. Restore view 1.
❏ Select the **LINE** command and snap to the top of the arc.
❏ Select **ZOOM Realtime** or **ZOOM Dynamic** transparently. Increase the zooming view box to include both arcs, but do not cause a regeneration.

❏ Extend the line to the top of the other arc. Begin a second line at the bottom of the right arc.

❏ Select **VIEW** transparently and restore view 1. Attach the line to the bottom of the left arc.

❏ Use **ZOOM Realtime** or **ZOOM Dynamic** to show the completed object.

❏ Save the drawing as EX9-3 and quit the drawing session.

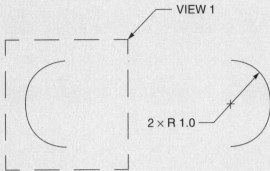

Using the Aerial View

AutoCAD
User's
Guide   6

When you work on a large drawing, you can spend a lot of time zooming and panning the graphics window trying to locate a particular detail or feature. One of the most powerful display change features in AutoCAD is the **Aerial View** window. **Aerial View** is a navigation tool that lets you see the entire drawing in a separate window, locate the detail or feature you want, and move to it quickly. You can zoom in on an area, change the magnification, and match the view in the graphics window to the one in the **Aerial View** window (or vice versa).

DSVIEWER

View
→Aerial View

Standard
toolbar

Aerial View

To open the **Aerial View** window, pick the **Aerial View** button on the **Standard** toolbar, pick **Aerial View** from the **View** pull-down menu, or enter DSVIEWER at the Command: prompt. The entire drawing is then displayed in the **Aerial View** window. See Figure 9-18.

Figure 9-18.
The **Aerial View** window (shown here highlighted) is initially in the lower-right corner of the screen.

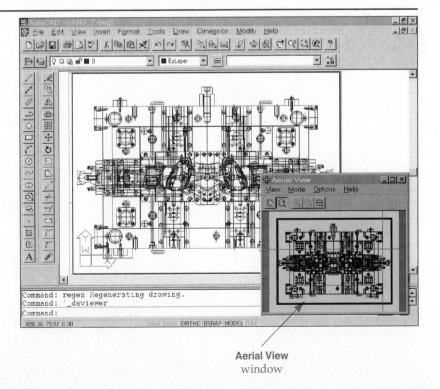

Aerial View
window

The **Aerial View** window initially appears at the lower-right of the graphics window, but can be moved to any convenient location on the screen. To do so, pick the title bar of the **Aerial View** window, hold down the left mouse button, and drag the window to a new location.

NOTE

Aerial View cannot be used in paper space mode or if a perspective view is displayed using the **Distance** option to the **DVIEW** command. The **DVIEW** command and its options are covered later in this chapter and in *AutoCAD and its Applications—Advanced, Release 14*.

The menu bar in the **Aerial View** window contains three pull-down menus and five buttons. See Figure 9-19. The menus and buttons are described as follows:
- **View pull-down menu.** Controls viewing commands.
    - **Zoom In**—Increases the magnification of the image in the **Aerial View** window.
    - **Zoom Out**—Decreases the magnification of the image in the **Aerial View** window.
    - **Global**—Displays the entire generated drawing area in the **Aerial View** window.
- **Mode pull-down menu.** Sets **Zoom** or **Pan** mode. A black dot indicates the active mode.
    - **Pan**—Switches the aerial viewer into **Pan** mode, maintaining the current zoom display size and allowing you to reposition it in a new location.
    - **Zoom**—Switches the aerial viewer into **Zoom** mode, where you can draw a window anywhere in the generated area of the drawing.
- **Options pull-down menu.** Contains aerial viewer options.
    - **Auto Viewport**—When on, switching to a different tiled viewport automatically causes the new viewport to be displayed in the aerial view window.
    - **Dynamic Update**—This causes the **Aerial View** window to update its display after each change in the drawing. Enable this only if your display system is very fast.
- **Toolbar buttons.**
    - **Pan**—Switches the aerial viewer into **Pan** mode.
    - **Zoom**—Switches the aerial viewer into **Zoom** mode.
    - **Zoom In**—Increases the magnification of the image in the **Aerial View** window.
    - **Zoom Out**—Decreases the magnification of the image in the **Aerial View** window.
    - **Global**—Displays the entire generated area of the drawing in the **Aerial View** window.

Figure 9-19.
The **Aerial View** window has pull-down menus and a toolbar. These contain options for working with the window.

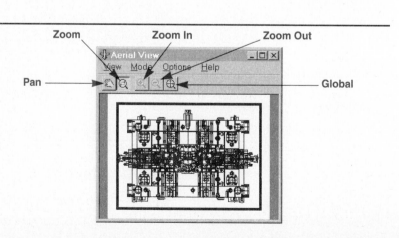

AutoCAD and its Applications—Basics

Using the AutoCAD graphics window scroll bars

The scroll bars allow a quick and easy way to pan the drawing display. Picking the arrow buttons at the end of the scroll bar moves the display a small amount. Picking the scroll bar itself pans the drawing by its current height or width, depending on the direction of the pan. The elevator button can be picked and dragged as needed to move a desired amount. The scroll bars can be used to move the display anywhere within the generated area of the drawing.

PROFESSIONAL TIP

Although regeneration has been virtually eliminated with Release 14, it is still possible. You should try to avoid regeneration because it slows your work and thought processes. Try the following tips for all your new drawings:

✓ Set your drawing limits to include a little extra for a border.
✓ **ZOOM All**.
✓ Create a view named ALL (or a name of your choice) of the entire drawing area.
✓ Avoid using **ZOOM All**, **ZOOM Extents**, or **REGEN** again.
✓ Create additional views as you need them.
✓ Use **Aerial View** whenever possible in place of other display commands. To redisplay the entire drawing without causing a regeneration, restore the view named ALL.
✓ Use **ZOOM Realtime** or **ZOOM Dynamic** instead of the other display commands.

EXERCISE 9-4

❏ Start AutoCAD and open the elev1.dwg drawing in the AutoCAD R14\Help folder.
  ❏ Activate the **Aerial View** and zoom to the spire and chimney in the upper-right corner of the drawing. Use the **Zoom** button in the **Aerial View** window.
  ❏ Pick the **Pan** button in the **Aerial View** window. Move the zoom box in the **Aerial View** to the lower-left corner of the building and pick so that the portico (carport extension) is displayed in the drawing window.
  ❏ Zoom out to view the entire building using the **Zoom Out** button in the **Aerial View**.
  ❏ Resize your **Aerial View** window so it occupies at least one-quarter of your display screen.
  ❏ Pick the **Zoom** button in the **Aerial View** window and create a zoom box just large enough to view one window of the house.
  ❏ Pick the **Pan** button and move the zoom box around the **Aerial View**, picking different locations to look at as you go.
❏ When you are finished experimenting with the **Aerial View**, quit the session without saving.

Model space can be thought of as the *space* where you draw and design in AutoCAD. The term *model* has more meaning when working in 3D, but you can consider any drawing or design a model, even if it is two-dimensional.

The best way to tell if you are in model space is to look at the UCS (User Coordinate System) icon. Located in the lower-left corner of the screen, this icon represents the current directions of the X and Y coordinates. See Figure 9-20. A detailed discussion of User Coordinate Systems and the UCS icon is given in *AutoCAD and its Applications—Advanced, Release 14*.

Figure 9-20.
The UCS icon for model space and paper space.

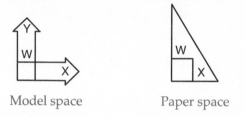

Model space   Paper space

Paper space, on the other hand, is a *space* you create when you are ready to lay out a drawing or model to be plotted. Basically, it is as if you place a sheet of paper on the screen, then insert, or *reference*, one or more drawings to the paper. In order to create this plotting layout, you must first enter paper space by using the **TILEMODE** system variable. The function of tiled viewports is discussed later in this chapter. For now, in order to enter paper space you must either pick **Paper Space** from the **View** pull-down menu or use the **TILEMODE** variable as follows:

Command: **TILEMODE**↵
New value for TILEMODE ⟨1⟩: **0**↵
Entering Paper space. Use Mview to insert Model space viewports.
Regenerating drawing.
Command:

After **TILEMODE** is set to 0 you are automatically placed in paper space. Notice on the status bar that the **MODEL** indicator tile has changed to **PAPER**, and the paper space icon is now displayed in the lower-left corner of the screen. See Figure 9-21.

Remember that you should create all your drawings and designs in model space, not in paper space. Only paper layouts for plotting purposes should be created in paper space. Therefore, return to model space by picking **Model Space (Tiled)** from the **View** pull-down menu, or set the **TILEMODE** variable to 1.

There are two quick ways to switch back and forth between model space and paper space. You can switch using the **View** pull-down menu, or double-click on the space indicator button found on the status bar. This toggles the space and updates the button to display the name of the current space.

Figure 9-21.
The paper space button is located in the status bar at the bottom of the screen.

Indicates
paper space

Do not be confused by **TILEMODE**, model space, and paper space. The discussion in Chapter 10 will provide you a better understanding. Right now, think of these terms in the following manner:

Activity	Space	TILEMODE
Drawing and design	Model	1
Plotting and printing layout	Paper	0

Creating Tiled Viewports in Model Space

Tiled model space viewports are created with the **VPORTS** command. The AutoCAD graphics window can be divided into *tiled viewports,* of which only 48 can be active at one time. You can check this number using the **MAXACTVP** (maximum active viewports) system variable at the Command: prompt.

The edges of tiled viewports butt against one another like floor tile. The **TILEMODE** variable must be set to 1 (on) to display tiled viewports. The arrangement of the viewports can vary, as indicated by the options of the **VPORTS** command. The default arrangement contains three viewports and is shown in Figure 9-22. To set this arrangement, pick **3 Viewports** from the **Tiled Viewports** cascading menu in the **View** pull-down menu, or enter **VPORTS** as follows:

Command: **VPORTS**↵
Save/Restore/Delete/Join/SIngle/?/2/⟨3⟩/4: ↵
Horizontal/Vertical/Above/Below/Left/⟨Right⟩: ↵
Regenerating drawing.
Command:

When you accept the defaults, AutoCAD displays an arrangement of two viewports on the left side of the screen, and a large viewport on the right. The other possible combinations of three viewports are shown in Figure 9-23.

Figure 9-22.
The default arrangement of viewports.

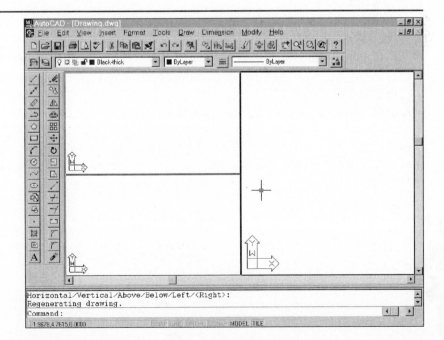

Figure 9-23.

A variety of viewport arrangements is possible with the **VPORTS** command and the **3** option.

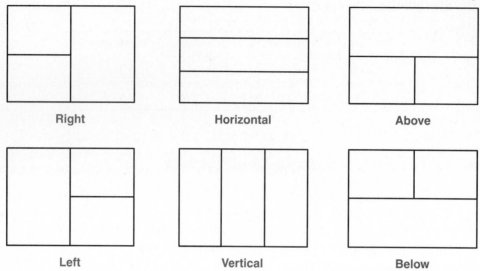

Right   Horizontal   Above

Left   Vertical   Below

Move the pointing device around and notice that only one viewport contains crosshairs. This is called the *active viewport*. The pointer is represented by an arrow in the others. To make a different viewport active, move the pointer into it and press the pick button. As you draw in one viewport, the image is displayed in all of them. Try drawing lines and other shapes and notice how the viewports are affected. Then use a display command, such as **ZOOM**, in the current viewport and notice the results. Only the current viewport reflects the use of the **ZOOM** command.

Preset tiled viewport layouts can be selected from an image tile menu. Pick **Layout...** in the **Tiled Viewports** cascading menu of the **View** pull-down menu. This displays the **Tiled Viewport Layout** dialog box. See Figure 9-24. You can select a pre-arranged layout by either picking the image on the right or by picking the written description from the list on the left. After you select a layout, the image and description are highlighted. If this is the desired layout, pick **OK** and the screen changes to the new configuration.

Notice in Figure 9-24 that there are several additional image tiles. You can create custom viewport layouts and add them to this dialog box. Menu customization techniques is covered in *AutoCAD and its Applications—Advanced, Release 14*.

Figure 9-24.

Select the image or name of the viewport arrangement.

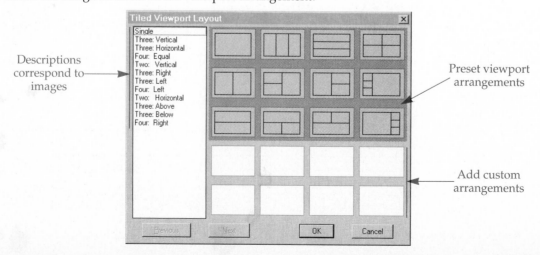

Descriptions correspond to images

Preset viewport arrangements

Add custom arrangements

Uses of tiled viewports

Viewports in model space can be used for both 2D and 3D drawings. They are limited only by your imagination and need. See *AutoCAD and its Applications—Advanced, Release 14* for examples of the **VPORTS** command in 3D. The nature of 2D drawings, whether mechanical multiview, architectural construction details, or unscaled schematic drawings, lend themselves well to viewports.

NOTE
Several sample drawings are included with the AutoCAD software. If AutoCAD was installed using default settings, the sample drawings should be located in the AutoCAD R14\Sample folder. Check with your instructor or supervisor to locate these drawings, or browse through the folders to determine their locations. The sample drawings include a variety of drawing and design disciplines and are excellent for testing and practice. You should use these drawings, especially when learning the display commands.

EXERCISE 9-5

❑ Start AutoCAD and open the wilhome.dwg drawing from the AutoCAD R14\Sample folder. (wilhome.dwg will reside in this folder if AutoCAD was installed according to suggestions in the *Installation Guide*.)
❑ When the drawing is displayed on the screen, you should see a house floor plan and several elevations. Zoom into various locations to get familiar with the drawing.
❑ Use the **VPORTS** command to create the default arrangement of three viewports. (Make sure **TILEMODE** is set to 1.) The large viewport should be on the right.
❑ Use **PAN Realtime** to center the drawing in the large viewport. Use **ZOOM Realtime** to enlarge the drawing to fill the viewport.
❑ In the upper-left viewport, use **ZOOM Window** to find aquarium elevation in the upper-left corner of the drawing.
❑ Pick the lower-left viewport and zoom in on the Grand Room at the upper-right of the house. Use **ZOOM** and **PAN Realtime** to locate the entertainment center.
❑ Quit without saving the drawing.

Creating Multiple Floating Viewports in Paper Space

Floating model space viewports are created with the **MVIEW** command when **TILEMODE** is set to 0. These *floating viewports* are actually holes that are cut into the paper of paper space so that the model space drawing can be seen. These viewports are separate objects and can overlap. As you will see in Chapter 10, several different size floating viewports can be constructed.

The viewports created by the **MVIEW** command are used when laying out a multiview drawing for plotting or printing. Since these viewports are created in paper space, the **TILEMODE** system variable must be set to 0. Think of the relationship of **TILEMODE** and viewports as follows:

Activity	Space	TILEMODE	Command
Drawing and design	Model	1	**VPORTS** (tiled)
Plotting and printing layout	Paper	0	**MVIEW** (entities)

The options of the **MVIEW** command are discussed in detail in Chapter 10.

Introduction to 3D Display Commands

The commands **DVIEW** (dynamic view) and **VPOINT** (viewpoint) are used in 3D drawing. An introduction to the basics of 3D drawing is provided in Chapter 27. However, these two display commands are introduced in the next sections.

Establishing a dynamic view

When using the **DVIEW** command to view a 3D drawing, you can see the object move as you perform viewing commands such as **ROTATE** and **PAN**. Follow the given example for a brief overview of the **DVIEW** command. First, open the campus.dwg drawing. This drawing should be in the AutoCAD R14\Sample folder. The drawing that appears is a 3D model of campus buildings, and is displayed at an angle appropriate for 3D viewing.

Now use the **PLAN** command to see the plan, or top, view of the model. After the following command sequence, your display should look like Figure 9-25.

        Command: **PLAN**↵
        ⟨Current UCS⟩/Ucs/World: ↵
        Regenerating drawing.
        Command:

Now, use the following commands to create viewports, with a dynamic view in the large viewport:

        Command: **VPORTS**↵
        Save/Restore/Delete/Join/SIngle/?/2/⟨3⟩/4: ↵
        Horizontal/Vertical/Above/Below/Left/⟨Right⟩: ↵
        Command:

Your screen should now look like Figure 9-26.

Next, use the **DVIEW** command to create a 3D view of the campus in the large viewport. First, make the large viewport active by picking anywhere inside it. Now, proceed as follows:

        Command: **DVIEW**↵
        Select objects: ↵

Figure 9-25.
The campus drawing displayed in a single viewport.

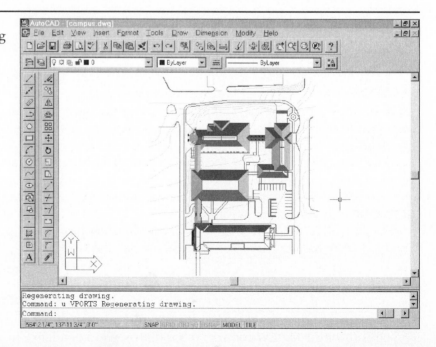

AutoCAD and its Applications—Basics

Figure 9-26.
The **VPORTS**
command is used
to display three
viewports.

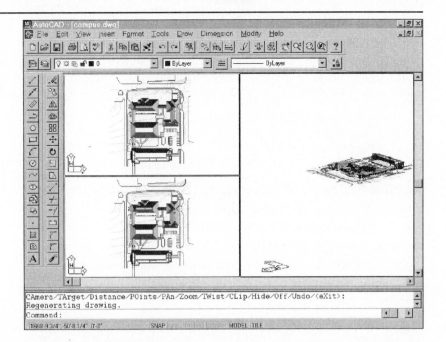

NOTE

The **DVIEW** command can also be selected by picking **3D Dynamic View** in the **View** pull-down menu.

In order to speed up the **DVIEW** process, press [Enter] at the Select objects: prompt. This displays a house that requires less regeneration time. Your drawing returns to the screen at the completion of the **DVIEW** command. If you want to work with objects in your drawing on the screen using the **DVIEW** options, use any of the selection methods to select them.

> CAmera/TArget/Distance/POints/PAn/Zoom/TWist/CLip/Hide/Off/Undo/⟨eXit⟩: **TA**↵
> Toggle angle in/Enter angle from XY plane ⟨–90.00⟩: **–15**↵
> Toggle angle from/Enter angle in XY plane from X axis ⟨90.00⟩: **–40**↵
> CAmera/TArget/Distance/POints/PAn/Zoom/TWist/CLip/Hide/Off/Undo/⟨eXit⟩: ↵
> Command:

PROFESSIONAL TIP

When working in large drawings, it is best to use the small house for **DVIEW** by pressing [Enter] at the Select objects: prompt. If your drawing is complex, the computer may slow down because it is constantly regenerating the highlighted display as the drawing is dynamically moved on the screen.

Try to determine the direction from which you are viewing the campus. Notice in the small viewports that the small parking lot is toward the bottom-right of the screen. Now look at the UCS icon in the large viewport. If it appears that the small parking lot is on the other side of the buildings, that is correct.

There are several other options and possibilities with the **DVIEW** command. You can create a true perspective view by specifying the distance from camera to target. In addition, you can zoom in or away from the object, or clip the front or rear of the screen image. Additional information regarding these options is found in *AutoCAD and its Applications—Advanced, Release 14.*

Creating a 3D viewpoint

The **VPOINT** command allows you to specify the direction that you will view the object from. You can enter XYZ coordinates, or you can visually determine your viewpoint using an *XYZ tripod*. This example uses coordinate entry to determine both viewpoints. Make the upper-left viewport active and enter the following commands:

Command: **VPOINT** *or* **-VP**↵
Rotate/⟨View point⟩ ⟨*current*⟩:**-1,-1,1**↵
Regenerating drawing.
Command:

Activate the lower-left viewport and enter the following:

Command: **VPOINT** *or* **-VP**↵
Rotate/⟨View point⟩ ⟨*current*⟩: **1,-1,1**↵
Regenerating drawing.
Command:

The screen should now resemble Figure 9-27.

Figure 9-27.
The **VPOINT** command is used to create two different views in the small viewports.

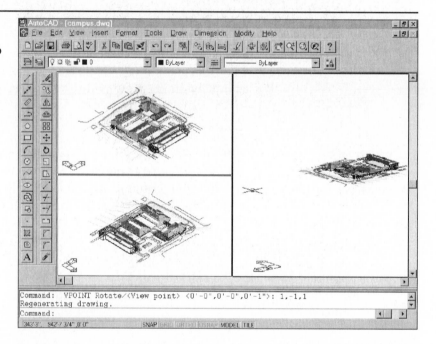

One advantage of multiple viewports is that each viewport is a separate screen. Therefore, you can display any view of the drawing you wish in each screen. In addition, 3D drawings can appear as either wireframe or solid. A *wireframe* is an object that shows all lines, including those at the back of the object. The views currently on your screen show wireframes. To make an object look more realistic, use the **HIDE** command to represent a solid object.

Make the lower-left viewport active and zoom in on the entrance way along the right face of the campus area. See Figure 9-28A. Now, use the **HIDE** command to remove hidden lines. The **HIDE** command is accessed by picking **Hide** from the **View** pull-down menu, or entering HIDE or HI at the Command: prompt. This process may take a few minutes depending on the speed of your computer.

Command: **HIDE** *or* **HI**↵
Regenerating drawing.
Hiding lines 100% done
Command:

The hidden lines are removed from the active viewport. See Figure 9-28B.

Figure 9-28.
A—Section of building shown as a wireframe. B—Details are clear when hidden lines are removed.

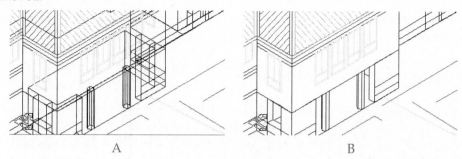

A   B

| **NOTE** | Entering SHADE at the Command: prompt colors 3D solid faces. The **SHADE** command is covered in detail in *AutoCAD and its Applications–Advanced, Release 14*. |

Redrawing and Regenerating Viewports

Since each viewport is a separate screen, you can redraw or regenerate a single viewport at a time without affecting the others. The **REGEN** (regenerate) command instructs AutoCAD to recalculate all of the entities in the drawing. This takes considerably longer than a **REDRAW**, especially if the drawing is large. However, **REGEN** can clarify a drawing by smoothing out circles, arcs, ellipses, and splines.

To redraw all of the viewports, use the **REDRAWALL** command or pick **Redraw** from the **View** pull-down menu. If you need to regenerate all of the viewports, use the **REGENALL** command or pick **Regen All** from the **View** pull-down menu.

EXERCISE 9-6

❑ Use the display of the campus drawing that is currently on your screen. If the display is not on your screen, refer to the previous section of this text and follow the example to this point.
❑ Make the upper-left viewport active and draw some lines in the parking lot. The lines should be displayed in all viewports.
❑ Make the lower-left viewport active and draw some lines.
❑ Use the **REDRAW** command while the lower-left viewport is active. Notice that only the lower-left viewport is redrawn.
❑ Use the **REDRAWALL** command, or pick **Redraw** from the **View** pull-down menu.
❑ Pick the large viewport and use the **REGEN** command.
❑ Use the **REGENALL** command. Notice how much longer it takes to perform this command than the **REDRAWALL** command.
❑ Quit the drawing session.

Controlling automatic regeneration

When developing a drawing, you may use a command that changes certain aspects of the entities. When this occurs, AutoCAD does an automatic regeneration to update the entities. This may not be of concern to you when working on small drawings, but this regeneration may take considerable time on large and complex drawings. In addition, it may not be necessary to have a regeneration of the drawing at all times. If this is the case, set the **REGENAUTO** command to off.

```
Command: REGENAUTO↵
ON/OFF ⟨current⟩: OFF↵
Command:
```

Some of the commands that may automatically cause a regeneration are **ZOOM**, **PAN**, **PLAN**, **HIDE**, and **VIEW Restore**.

Controlling the Order of Display

AutoCAD has the ability to display both raster and vector images in the graphics window. A *raster image* is composed of dots, or *pixels*, and is also referred to as *bit map*. Raster images contain no XYZ coordinate values. Objects in a *vector image* (drawing), such as those created in AutoCAD, are given XYZ coordinate values. So, all these objects are composed of points, or *vectors*, connected by straight lines.

Drawings containing both raster and vector images can have objects that overlap each other. For example, in Figure 9-29A the raster image of the **Zoom Previous** button is imported into AutoCAD and overlays the vector image of the text label. In this case the text label should be displayed on top of the raster image. To do this, use the **DRAWORDER** command by picking **Bring Above Object** in the **Display Order** cascading menu of the **Tools** pull-down menu, or enter DRAWORDER or DR at the Command: prompt as follows:

```
Command: DR or DRAWORDER
Select objects:
Select objects:
Above object/Under object/Top/⟨Bottom⟩: A↵
Select reference object: (pick the outline of the raster image)
Regenerating drawing.
Command:
```

The drawing will now be displayed and plotted as shown in Figure 9-29B.

The drawing order is the order in which objects are displayed and/or plotted. If an object is moved to the top of the drawing order, it is displayed and plotted first. If one object is moved above another object, it is displayed on top—the text in Figure 9-29B. These order and arrangement functions are handled by the following **DRAWORDER** options:

- **Above object.** The selected object is moved above the reference object. The **Bring Above Object** option in the cascading menu does the same.
- **Under object.** The selected object is moved below the reference object. The **Send Under Object** option in the cascading menu does the same.
- **Top.** The selected object is placed at the top of the drawing order. The **Bring to Top** option in the cascading menu does the same.
- **Bottom.** The selected object is placed at the bottom of the drawing order. The **Send to Bottom** option in the cascading menu does the same.

See *AutoCAD and its Applications–Advanced, Release 14* for more detailed information on the use of raster drawings in AutoCAD.

Figure 9-29.
A—An imported raster image obscures part of a vector drawing. B—The **DRAWORDER** command is used to bring the vector drawing above the raster image.

Zoo[m Prev]ious   Zoom Previous

A   B

Chapter Test

Write your answers in the spaces provided.

1. What is the difference between the **REDRAW** and **'REDRAW** commands? _____

   _____

   _____

2. What are *blips* and how does **REDRAW** affect them?_____

   _____

   _____

3. Which command allows you to change the display of blips? _____

   _____

4. Give the proper command option and value to automatically zoom to a 2X scale
   factor. _____

5. What is the difference between **ZOOM Extents** and **ZOOM All**? _____

   _____

6. During the drawing process, when should you use **ZOOM**? _____

   _____

   _____

7. How many different boxes are displayed during the **ZOOM Dynamic** command?

   _____

8. What is a *pan displacement*? _____

   _____

   _____

9. When using the **ZOOM Dynamic** option, what represents the current view? _____

   _____

10. Which command option allows you to create a view of the current screen display?

    _____

11. What option would you choose to display an existing view?_____

12. How would you obtain a listing of existing views? _____

    _____

13. What is the purpose of the **PAN** command?_____

    _____

14. How does **PAN** work? _____

    _____

15. How do you access the **PAN** command presets? _____

    _____

16. What is *view resolution*? _____

    _____

17. What is the purpose of the **VIEWRES** command? _____

    _____

    _____

18. If you answer No to the prompt Do you want fast zooms, what does AutoCAD do when you issue any display command? _____

19. What does the **VIEWRES** zoom percentage refer to? _____

_____

20. What is the difference between **Model Space (Tiled)** and **Model Space (Floating)**?

_____

_____

_____

21. What is the affect of picking **Global** from the <u>V</u>**iew** pull-down menu in the **Aerial View** window? _____

_____

22. How is a transparent display command entered at the keyboard? _____

_____

23. When will AutoCAD not execute a transparent display command? _____

_____

24. What is the function of the **Auto** <u>V</u>**iewport** option of **Aerial View** window? _____

_____

_____

25. List two ways to enable the **Aerial View** window. _____

_____

_____

26. Cite several advantages of **Aerial View** over other display commands. _____

_____

_____

27. Explain the difference between model space and paper space. _____

_____

_____

28. What is the purpose of the **TILEMODE** system variable? _____

_____

_____

29. Describe the default viewport layout for the **VPORTS** command. _____

_____

30. What type of object does the **DVIEW** command use to initially establish a 3D view?

_____

31. How do the **DVIEW** and **VPOINT** commands differ? _____

_____

_____

32. Which command regenerates all of the viewports? _____

33. What is the function of **REGENAUTO**? _____

_____

_____

Drawing Problems

1. Open the drawing named elev1 found in the AutoCAD R14\Help folder. Perform the following display functions on the drawing:

   A. **ZOOM All.**

   B. Create a view named All.

   C. Zoom in to display the right side of the house.

   D. Create a view of this new window named Rightside.

   E. **ZOOM Previous**.

   F. Use **Zoom** and **Pan Realtime** to create a display of the third level of the house containing the three dormer windows, the chimney, and the spire.

   G. Create a view of this new window named Peak.

   H. Display the view named All.

   I. Save the drawing as P9-1.

2. Load one of your own mechanical template drawings that contains a border and title block. Do the following:

   A. Zoom into the title block area. Create and save a view named Title.

   B. Zoom to the extents of the drawing and create and save a view named All.

   C. Determine the area of the drawing that will contain notes, parts list, or revisions. Zoom into these areas and create views with appropriate names such as Notes, Partlist, Revisions, etc.

   D. Divide the drawing area into commonly used multiview sections. Save the views with descriptive names such as Top, Front, Rightside, Leftside, etc.

   E. Restore the view named All.

   F. Save the drawing as P9-2, or as a template.

3. Load one of your own prototype drawings used for architectural layout that contains a border and title block. Do the following:

   A. Zoom into the title block area. Create and save a view named Title.

   B. Zoom to the extents of the drawing and create and save a view named All.

   C. Determine the area of the drawing that will contain notes, schedules, or revisions. Zoom into these areas and create views with appropriate names such as Notes, Partlist, Revisions, etc.

   D. Restore the view named All.

   E. Save the drawing as P9-3, or as a template.

4. Open the drawing named tower.dwg. This drawing should be in the AutoCAD R14\Sample folder. Then perform the following:

A. Make sure the **MODEL** setting on the status bar is highlighted. Make the large viewport active. Pick **Model Space (Tiled)** in the **View** pull-down menu.

B. Type **DVIEW** or pick **3D Dynamic View** in the **View** pull-down menu. Press [Enter] at the Select objects: prompt. Type OFF and press [Enter] twice to turn off the perspective view and to exit **DVIEW**.

C. Create named views of different parts of the tower, such as Roof, Side, Front, etc.

D. **ZOOM All** and create a view named All.

E. Return to the floating model space viewports.

F. Restore the view named All in the large viewport. Use **Pan** and **Zoom Realtime** to center and enlarge the view. Restore two of the additional views in the upper-left and upper-right viewport.

G. Activate the lower-left viewport and execute the **PLAN** command. Use **Pan** and **Zoom Realtime** to center and enlarge the view.

H. Pick the center-left viewport and execute the **VPOINT** command. Enter the values of –1,–2,2 for the view point. Use **Pan** and **Zoom Realtime** to center and enlarge the view.

I. Save the drawing as P9-4 only if required by your instructor.

Multiview Layouts, Plotting and Printing

Learning Objectives

After completing this chapter, you will be able to:
- ○ Describe the techniques of paper space and multiview layout.
- ○ Use standard borders and title block formats provided by AutoCAD.
- ○ Customize the standard title block for your school or company.
- ○ Identify options and variables found in the **PLOT** command.
- ○ Use the **Print/Plot Configuration** dialog box to prepare a drawing for plotting.
- ○ Determine the scale factor of a drawing.
- ○ Print and plot a drawing.
- ○ Configure a new plotting device.
- ○ Use the **Batch Plot** utility to plot a group of drawings without loading AutoCAD.

Paper space and model space are used to simplify drawing creation and plotting layout. Drawings created in model space are arranged in paper space using setup wizards, the **MVIEW** command, and the **MVSETUP** command. These tools have over-lapping functions, but slightly different capabilities. The goal of using each is to lay out your drawing to be plotted on a sheet of paper. This chapter also discusses the **Print/Plot Configuration** dialog box functions in detail. In addition, suggestions for improving the quality and efficiency of your plots are given.

Using paper space and model space will simplify your plotting procedure. This chapter will explain these concepts.

What is Paper Space?

Paper space is a state or mode in which you create a finished layout to be printed or plotted. The actual drawing is not created in paper space. Paper space is like a sheet of paper on which the final drawing layout is produced. *Model space* is the state or mode in which the actual drawing or model is constructed.

AutoCAD provides a means for switching between model space and paper space in the **TILEMODE** system variable. A **TILEMODE** setting of 1 is the default setting and places you in model space. A **TILEMODE** setting of 0 activates paper space. This is discussed in detail later.

When paper space is active (**TILEMODE** = 0), AutoCAD inserts a piece of "paper" over the drawing on your screen. This hides the drawing; the only way you can see the objects is to either return to model space or cut "holes" in the paper. These holes are called *viewports*.

Viewports are cut using a "cutting tool," such as the **MVIEW** command. As soon as a hole is cut in the paper, the drawing shows through. See Figure 10-1.

Figure 10-1.
Paper space and model space. A—When paper space is activated, a piece of "paper" hides the drawing on the screen. B—When a hole is cut in the paper with the **MVIEW** command, the drawing shows through.

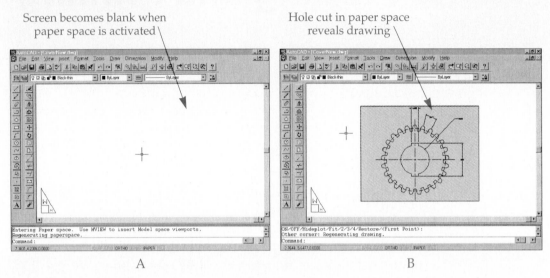

Why should you use paper space?

A paper space layout enables you to see the position and scale of the drawing on the sheet of paper. While in paper space, viewports can be activated, allowing the drawing (in model space) to be edited. When the drawing is completed, it can be scaled to fit properly within the viewport.

More than one viewport can be cut into the paper. The drawings within different viewports can have different scales, and viewports can overlap. A variety of drawings, details, and views can be placed inside the viewports. This is illustrated in a detailed example in Chapter 24.

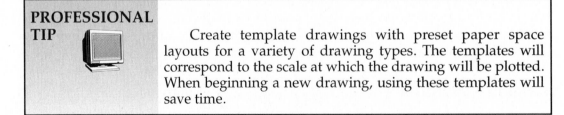

PROFESSIONAL TIP

Create template drawings with preset paper space layouts for a variety of drawing types. The templates will correspond to the scale at which the drawing will be plotted. When beginning a new drawing, using these templates will save time.

After the drawing is completed and arranged in the paper space layout, it can be plotted. There is no need to calculate a plot scale based on the drawing scale; the drawing is simply plotted at a scale of 1:1 in paper space. To make matters even easier, you can recall a set of preestablished plot settings from a file and plot the drawing without setting a single plot parameter. This powerful technique is discussed later in this chapter.

Paper Space Commands and Functions

There are several ways to create and edit paper space and multiview layouts in AutoCAD. The quickest method is to use a wizard when you create a new drawing. A second method is to use a template drawing. These techniques were discussed thoroughly in Chapter 2. A third method is to insert floating model space viewports into a paper space layout with the **MVIEW** command. The use of this command is covered in Chapter 24, but is introduced in this chapter. The fourth method for creating a paper space layout is with the **MVSETUP** command. This process is more involved than using wizards, templates, and **MVIEW**, but contains a wider variety of options.

NOTE Functions introduced in Release 14 have taken away some of the tasks from **MVSETUP**. Future releases of AutoCAD may eliminate this command and incorporate its options into easier-to-use operations. While the **MVSETUP** command is complex, it still has value as an all-inclusive tool for drawing template setup, viewport creation, and viewport manipulation. Therefore, it is discussed in detail later in this chapter. As you read, try to identify the aspects of **MVSETUP** that can be accomplished using other AutoCAD functions.

Using a wizard

When you load AutoCAD or use the **NEW** command, the **Create New Drawing** dialog box is displayed. From this dialog box, you can use a wizard to set up the drawing. Wizards were discussed in Chapter 2, but let's take a moment to review the advanced setup wizard. See Figure 10-2. The **Step 7: Layout** tab contains the question "Do you want to use advanced paper space layout capabilities?" If you select **Yes**, you are given three additional options:

- **Work on my drawing while viewing the layout.** This displays a template drawing layout on your screen in paper space and places the cursor inside a single active floating model space viewport.
- **Work on my drawing without the layout visible.** This presents a blank screen in model space. If you then select **Paper Space** from the **View** pull-down menu, **TILEMODE** is set to 0 and the paper space template drawing containing a single floating model space viewport is displayed.

Figure 10-2.
The advanced setup wizard provides advanced paper space layout capabilities.

Template will have one model space viewport

Options for starting conditions

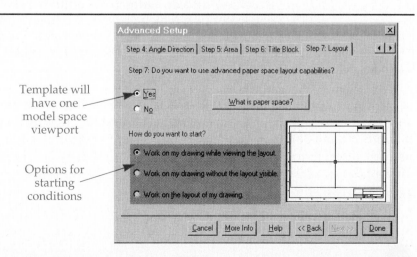

- **Work on the layout of my drawing.** This displays the template drawing in paper space. The floating model space viewport is not active. The border, title block, and viewport object can be edited. You must switch to model space to edit the drawing or model.

In all three options, only one floating model space viewport is cut into the paper space layout. Other methods must be used to add and edit viewports.

Using a template drawing

Once a wizard has been used to create a prototype drawing, you should save it as a template drawing. Use the **SAVEAS** command and select the .dwt file type. If you save it in the same folder that contains all of the standard template drawings, it will be displayed in the list of templates the next time you begin a new drawing.

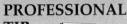

> **PROFESSIONAL TIP**
>
> Template drawings can contain all of the settings, features, and parameters that are defined using wizards, **MVSETUP**, and **MVIEW**. Therefore, a well-planned development of template drawings can eliminate future time spent using the other commands and functions.

> **CAUTION**
>
> If you select the **Use a Template** button at startup, all of the standard templates supplied with AutoCAD will be displayed with the floating model space viewport active. This viewport is the same size as the drawing border and overlaps the title block.

Using the MVIEW command

The function of **MVIEW** is to construct floating model space viewports in a paper space layout. Consider it the "knife" of paper space. Using its options, you can cut any number of openings (viewports) into the paper space layout. After using a wizard, you may need to use **MVIEW** to cut additional viewports in the paper.

> **NOTE**
>
> Remember that a viewport created with **MVIEW** is an AutoCAD object and can be edited. It is a "hole" in your paper through which you can see the drawing or model you are creating. Since the viewport can be moved to a new location on the paper or resized, it is called a *floating viewport*.

The quickest way to use **MVIEW** is to pick **Floating Viewports** in the **View** pull-down menu. See Figure 10-3. This feature is useful for creating a variety of viewports for both 2D and 3D drawings and for the layout of several different types of views, such as those found on drawings of architectural details. The following example shows how an additional viewport can eliminate the need to draw another enlarged detail view. Refer to Figure 10-4.

Figure 10-3.
Pick **Floating**
Viewports in the
View pull-down
menu to construct a
variety of paper
space viewports.

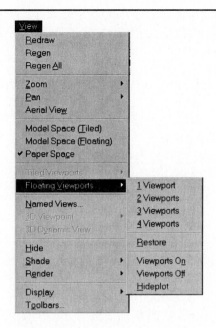

Figure 10-4.
Using viewports in
a mechanical
drawing. Steps
correspond to
procedure on
page 396.

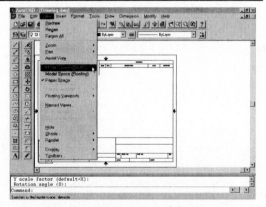

Step 1— Activate model space.

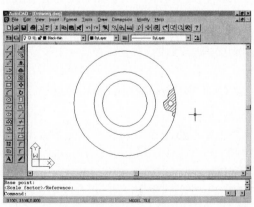

Step 2— Create drawing.

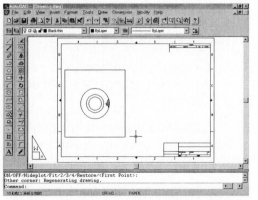

Step 3— Resize viewport in paper space.

(continued)

Step 4— Scale the drawing.

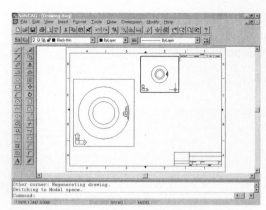

Step 5— Add second viewport.

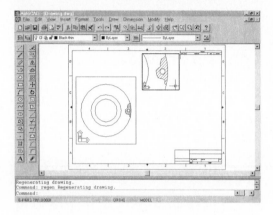

Step 6— Enlarge drawing in
second viewport.

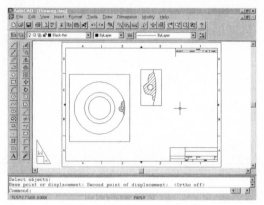

Step 7— Resize viewport.

1. Begin a new drawing using a wizard or template. Set **TILEMODE** to 1 by picking **Model Space (Tiled)** in the **View** pull-down menu in order to work on the drawing without seeing the border and title block.
2. Construct the drawing.
3. Select **Paper Space** from the **View** pull-down menu. Select the outline of the viewport and resize it using grips.
4. Select **Model Space (Floating)** from the **View** pull-down menu. Use the **ZOOM** command and the **XP** option to scale the drawing inside the viewport. For example, the drawing in Figure 10-4 was scaled so it will be plotted at 2:1 when the drawing is plotted in paper space at the scale of 1:1:

   Command: **Z** *or* **ZOOM**↵
   All/Center/Dynamic/Extents/Previous/Scale(X/XP)/Window/<Realtime>: **2XP**↵
   Command:

5. Pick **Floating Viewports** from the **View** pull-down menu and pick the **1 Viewport** option. Pick opposite corners to create a new viewport. The drawing appears in the new viewport, which is active. The active viewport is indicated by a thick border. This viewport will be used to display a detail of the part at a larger scale.
6. Use **ZOOM** and enter the appropriate scale for the detail. If the new detail is to be shown four times its actual size, enter 4XP at the prompt.
7. Switch to paper space by double-clicking on the **MODEL** button in the status bar or by typing PS at the Command: prompt. Use grips to adjust the size and location of the new viewport. Resize the viewport so that it is filled with the detail.

This example shows how a paper space layout can be used to increase drawing productivity and reduce the need to redraw parts of an object. The views inside the viewports are scaled correctly and arranged in paper space. The drawing can now be plotted at full scale in paper space.

> **NOTE**
>
> In Chapters 23 and 24 you will see how details and drawings can be inserted into and referenced from other drawings. When using these techniques with multiple viewports, you must carefully control which layers are displayed in each viewport. This task is handled by the **VPLAYER** command, and by using options in the **Layer & Linetype Properties** dialog box. This is covered in the detailed discussion of **MVIEW** in Chapter 24.

Review of paper space commands and functions

The following list provides definitions of commands and variables related to paper space.

- **Setup wizards.** Wizards can be used to set up new drawings. They allow you to establish parameters, select a template drawing, and choose the space in which to work. See Chapter 2 for more information on wizards.
- **TILEMODE = 1.** Model space is active. This is the state in which you construct the drawing or model.
- **TILEMODE = 0.** Paper space is active. This is the state in which you lay out the drawing or model prior to plotting.
- **MS.** Switches from paper space to model space.
- **PS.** Switches from model space to paper space.
- **VPORTS.** Allows you to create a tiled viewport configuration in model space.
- **VPLAYER.** Controls the display of viewport layers in paper space. This is an advanced function that is best applied to drawings that contain several different views.
- **MVIEW.** Allows you to cut floating model space viewports into the paper space layout.
- **MVSETUP.** Enables the user to insert a template drawing on the screen and create a layout of multiple viewports. In addition, viewports can be added and scaled and the objects inside the viewports can be aligned and rotated.

Using MVSETUP to Construct Paper Space Layout

The **MVSETUP** (multiview setup) command is an AutoLISP routine that can be customized to insert any type of border and title block. AutoLISP is discussed in *AutoCAD and its Applications—Advanced, Release 14*.

To use **MVSETUP**, first open a drawing or model that you want to display. This command is not available in any of AutoCAD's menus, so it must by typed at the Command: prompt. After the first use of **MVSETUP**, you can enter MVS as the command name. The following is the command sequence for using **MVSETUP** the first time:

        Command: **MVSETUP**↵
        Initializing…
        Enable paper space?(No/⟨Yes⟩):↵

Pressing [Enter] to accept the default automatically turns off the **TILEMODE** system variable. Notice the paper space UCS icon is displayed and your drawing has disappeared. If you turn **TILEMODE** off before entering **MVSETUP**, the Enable paper space? prompt does not appear.

The **Title block** option of the **MVSETUP** command lets you establish a drawing border and title block. The title block is created on the current layer with the current linetype and color. Therefore, it is a good idea to create a layer specifically for the drawing border and title block and set it as the current layer *before* using the **MVSETUP** command. If you forget to set the layer current before entering the command, use the **Options** choice of the **MVSETUP** command. This allows you to set a different layer current, change your drawing limits, or change drawing units before the drawing border and title block are drawn.

```
Align/Create/Scale viewports/Options/Title block/Undo: T↵
Delete objects/Origin/Undo/〈Insert title block〉:↵
```

The default suboption of the **Title block** option allows you to insert a title block. The following suboptions are also available:
- **Delete objects.** Allows you to select objects to delete from paper space, such as unused viewports. Model space objects cannot be deleted here.
- **Origin.** Permits you to relocate the sheet origin.
- **Undo.** Undoes the previous operation.
- **Insert title block.** This is the default. When selected, the following is displayed in the text window:

```
Available title block options:
  0:       None
  1:       ISO A4 Size(mm)
  2:       ISO A3 Size(mm)
  3:       ISO A2 Size(mm)
  4:       ISO A1 Size(mm)
  5:       ISO A0 Size(mm)
  6:       ANSI-V Size(in) (this is the vertical A-size format)
  7:       ANSI-A Size(in) (this is the horizontal A-size format)
  8:       ANSI-B Size(in)
  9:       ANSI-C Size(in)
 10:       ANSI-D Size(in)
 11:       ANSI-E Size(in)
 12:       Arch/Engineering (24 × 36 in)
 13:       Generic D size Sheet (24 × 36 in)
Add/Delete/Redisplay/〈Number of entry to load〉: (type the desired sheet size format,
    such as 7, and press [Enter])
```

Next, you are asked if you want to create a drawing with the sheet size specifications you selected. If you select number 7 and a file named ansi-a.dwg is not in your AutoCAD folder, pressing [Enter] at this prompt creates a drawing file with the name shown to be used as a prototype in the future. AutoCAD automatically draws the border and title block shown in Figure 10-5.

NOTE   **MVSETUP** inserts template drawings that are stored in the AutoCAD R14\Support folder. If you create a drawing, it is automatically placed in the current folder, which by default is AutoCAD R14. Instead, you may wish to create a template file as discussed later in the "Saving a drawing template file" section.

Figure 10-5.
One of the border
and title block
arrangements
available with the
MVSETUP
command.

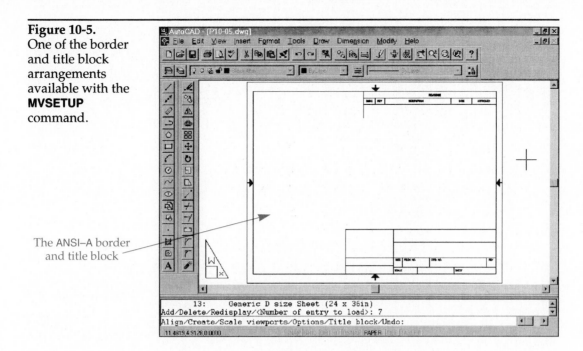

The ANSI–A border
and title block

 NOTE Using a template when starting a new drawing is another way of inserting a title block into paper space. This procedure was discussed in Chapter 2. The templates available are the same as those offered by the **MVSETUP** command.

The **Create** option is used to establish the viewports once the border and title block are inserted. The command sequence follows:

Align/Create/Scale viewports/Options/Title block/Undo: **C**↵
Delete objects/Undo/⟨Create viewports⟩:↵

Press [Enter] and a list of the viewport layout options is displayed:

Available Mview viewport layout options:
0:      None
1:      Single
2:      Std. Engineering
3:      Array of Viewports
Redisplay/⟨Number of entry to load⟩: **1**↵

A single viewport works best for the A-size sheet. The next prompt asks you to identify the boundary for the viewport by picking the opposite corners. This is similar to forming a window.

Bounding area for viewports. ⟨First point⟩: *(pick a point)*
Other point: *(move the cursor and pick the second point)*

The model space drawing that you started with is now displayed inside the paper space viewport, Figure 10-6.

 NOTE Option number two of the available **Mview** viewport layout options is the standard engineering option. It is used to construct multiview engineering layouts from a 3D drawing. This powerful function is discussed in Chapter 27.

Figure 10-6.
Opening a floating viewport in paper space allows the model space drawing to be visible.

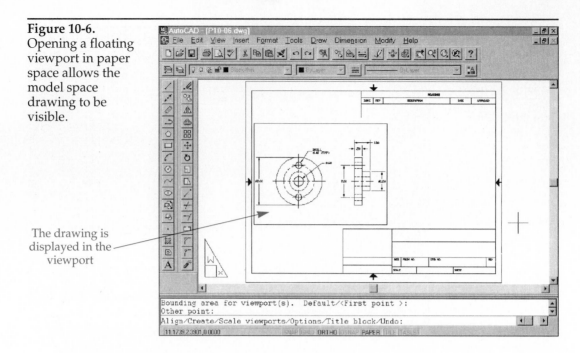

The drawing is displayed in the viewport

Notice in Figure 10-6 that the drawing has been scaled to extents within the viewport. The drawing scale can be adjusted easily.

The **Scale viewports** option of the **MVSETUP** command is used to scale the drawing. This option uses a ratio of paper space units to model space units. For example, 1:1 is one paper space unit for one model space unit, or a full scale, as shown in Figure 10-7. The default is full scale, or 1:1. The drawing may not change much in size, depending on the size of the viewports. The following command sequence is used:

Align/Create/Scale viewports/Options/Title block/Undo: **S**↵
Select the viewports to scale...
Select objects: *(pick the viewport outline, not the drawing)*
Select objects:↵
Enter the ratio of paper space units to model space units...
Number of paper space units. ⟨1.0⟩:↵
Number of model space units. ⟨1.0⟩: ↵
Align/Create/Scale viewports/Options/Title block/Undo:↵

Figure 10-7.
Viewports are scaled with the **Scale Viewports** option of the **MVSETUP** command.

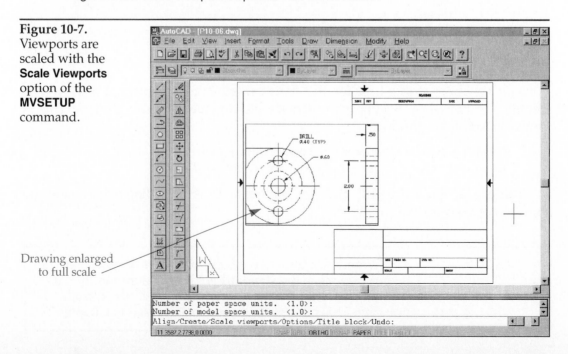

Drawing enlarged to full scale

The **Scale** option of **MVSETUP** executes **ZOOM XP**, which scales the viewport by the ratio of the scale factor. For example, if the drawing is to be plotted at a scale of 1/4″ = 1″, the ratio is 1:4. If the drawing is to be plotted at 1/4″ = 1′-0″, the ratio is 1:48. This would be the same as entering 1/4XP or 1/48XP at the **ZOOM** command prompt.

A viewport is an entity that can be altered in paper space using **MOVE**, **STRETCH**, or grips. After using the **Scale viewports** option, part of your drawing may extend past the edge of the viewport. Simply use grips to stretch the viewport. Figure 10-8A shows the results of using grips to resize the viewport shown in Figure 10-7.

The drawing inside the viewport can also be adjusted using **PAN** and **ZOOM**. Double-click on the **PAPER** button in the status bar to enter model space, then pick either the **Pan** or **Zoom** button in the **Standard** toolbar. Adjust the image until it is located properly. This only affects the view inside the viewport, not the paper space drawing. See Figure 10-8B.

Figure 10-8.
A—You can move, stretch, or scale a viewport using commands or grips. B—Switch to model space to pan and zoom the drawing inside the viewport.

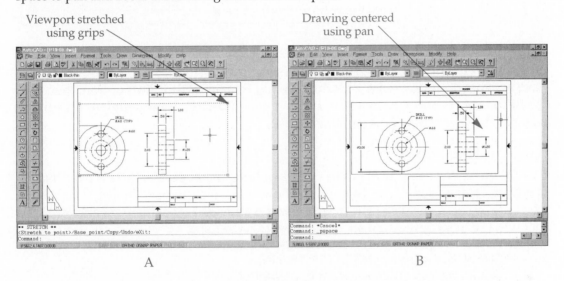

Viewport stretched using grips

Drawing centered using pan

A   B

Creating your own title block format

When you insert a title block using **MVSETUP**, you have the option of creating a new drawing based on the selected template by responding to the following prompt:

Create a drawing named ansi-a.dwg? ⟨Y⟩: ↵

The ansi-a.dwg is now available to be edited and customized for your own applications. Figure 10-9 shows a customized ANSI-A title block. Once the title block is customized, you can use the **SAVEAS** command to save the ansi-a.dwg as a drawing template file.

Saving a drawing template file

A *drawing template file* is a blank drawing sheet that contains a border and title block. It is also known as a *prototype drawing*. Template files are listed with a .dwt file extension. Modified title block formats can be saved as template files, which can be quickly called up for future use.

Figure 10-9.
A customized
ANSI-A title block
with border.

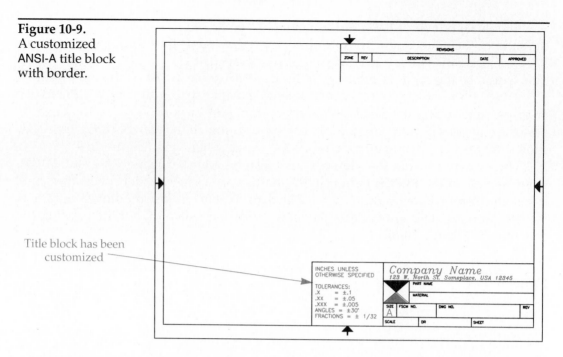

Title block has been
customized

To save the current border and title block as a template file, use the **SAVEAS** command. Provide an appropriate name (such as MECH-A) for the file, then pick the **Save as type:** drop-down list. Pick the **Drawing Template File (*.dwt)** option, then pick the **Save** button. The next time you begin a new drawing, your template file will be listed in the **Create New Drawing** dialog box.

Adding title blocks to the MVSETUP list

Following the list of available title block options is the Add/Delete/Redisplay/⟨Number of entry to load⟩: prompt. The **Add** option allows you to customize the list of prototype drawings by inserting a specific drawing and naming the drawing type and size. The following sequence gives you an idea of how this works:

Add/Delete/Redisplay/⟨Number of entry to load⟩: **A.**⏎
Title block description: **MECH (11 X 8.5 IN).**⏎
Drawing to insert (without extension): **SAMPLE.**⏎
Specify default usable area? ⟨Y⟩: **N.**⏎

If you press [Enter] to accept the default Y to this prompt, AutoCAD asks you to pick two points that define the usable area. However, the N response shown above is more convenient and works well in most situations. If you do define the usable area, it is a good idea to locate the lower-left of the title block at 0,0. You are then prompted to locate the upper-right corner of the title block. You may enter coordinates or pick a diagonal corner at this second prompt.

A new Available title block options: list is displayed. The new border and title block design you specified appears in the revised list as one of the options:

14. MECH (11 X 8.5 IN)
    Add/Delete/Redisplay/⟨Number of entry to load⟩: *(enter a desired sheet format, such as 14, and press [Enter])*

If you press [Enter] at this prompt without typing a number, the **MVSETUP** command option line is redisplayed. Select another option or press [Enter] to exit **MVSETUP**.

AutoCAD and its Applications—Basics

Additional MVSETUP options

The following descriptions outline the remaining **MVSETUP** options:

- **Align.** This option is used to align views in multiple viewports. You get this prompt when you use the **Align** option:

    Angled/Horizontal/Vertical alignment/Rotate view/Undo:

- **Angled**—This suboption is used to pan a drawing in a viewport at a desired angle. The following prompts are displayed:

    Base point: (*pick a point as an origin*)
    Other point: (*pick a point in the viewport to be panned*)
    Distance from base point: (*enter a distance or pick two points to establish a distance from the base point*)
    Angle from base point: (*enter an angular value or pick two points representing an angle where the second point is to be positioned from the base point*)

- **Horizontal**—This suboption allows you to align views in horizontal viewports:

    Base point: (*pick a point as an origin*)
    Other point: (*pick a point in the viewport to be aligned*)

- **Vertical alignment**—This suboption allows you to align entities in vertical viewports. It is similar to the **Horizontal** option.

- **Rotate view**—This suboption allows you to rotate a drawing in a viewport around a selected base point:

    Specify in which viewport the view is to be rotated...
    Base point: (*pick a point as the pivot point for the rotation*)
    Angle from base point: (*enter an angle and press* [Enter], *or pick two points representing the angle*)

- **Options.** This option lets you establish several different functions that are associated with your layout. The prompt appears:

    Choose option to set — Layer/LImits/Units/Xref:

- **Layer**—This suboption allows you to specify an existing layer or create a new layer for your border and title block. It is a good idea to put your border and title block on a separate layer, perhaps BORDER. This gives you the flexibility to freeze, thaw, and manipulate the layer as needed. Enter L for layer to get this prompt:

    Layer name for title block or . for current layer: **BORDER.**↵

- **LImits**—This suboption instructs AutoCAD to reset the drawing limits equal to the extents when the border is inserted. The prompt has a No default:

    Set drawing limits? ⟨N⟩: ↵

- **Units**—This suboption allows you to specify the units in which the drawing information is presented. Inch units are the default. You can also enter F for feet, ME for meters, or M for millimeters:

    Paper space units are in Feet/Inches/MEters/Millimeters? ⟨in⟩:

- **Xref**—This suboption determines if the border and title block are to be inserted in the drawing or referenced to a master drawing. A referenced drawing is not added to the current drawing file but is displayed. A referenced drawing is also referred to as *attached*. This helps to keep the file smaller. Referencing drawings is discussed in detail in Chapter 24. The default is **Insert**, or you can type A and press [Enter] for **Attach**:

> Xref Attach or Insert title block? ⟨Insert⟩: ↵

Working with the TILEMODE system variable

The **TILEMODE** system variable is set to 1 when it is on. **TILEMODE** must be turned off to have AutoCAD provide you with the standard border and title block formats. **TILEMODE** can be set at the Command: prompt by typing TILEMODE and then entering a 1 (on) or a 0 (off) at the prompt. The variable can also be set when you initially enter the **MVSETUP** command:

> Command: **MVSETUP**↵
> Enable paper space?(No/⟨Yes⟩): **N**↵

Answering no to the above prompt gives you the opportunity to establish your own model space drawing units, scale, and paper size. The prompts continue:

> Units type (Scientific/Decimal/Engineering/Architectural/Metric): *(enter the desired units, D for example.)*

The text screen is displayed with several scale options to choose from. Each of the **Units type** options has a corresponding selection list. This is the **Decimal** list:

> Decimal Scales
> (4.0)   4 TIMES
> (2.0)   2 TIMES
> (1.0)   FULL
> (0.5)   HALF
> (0.25)   QUARTER
> Enter the scale factor: *(enter the desired scale, such as 1)*
> Enter the paper width: *(enter the paper width, such as 11)*
> Enter the paper height: *(enter the paper height, such as 8.5)*
> Command:

EXERCISE 10-1

❏ Begin a new drawing and name it EX10-1.
❏ Draw a rectangle 4 units by 3 units. Place a 1 unit diameter circle in the center of the rectangle.
❏ Use the **MVSETUP** command to insert a standard ANSI-A border and title block format.
❏ Adjust the scale and orientation as needed.
❏ Save the drawing as EX10-1 and quit the drawing session.

Using the PLOT Command

PLOT

File
↳ Print...

Standard
toolbar

Print

Before printing or plotting, make sure that your output device is configured properly, as described in the *AutoCAD Installation Guide.* The **PLOT** command can be entered in several ways. Select **Print...** from the **File** pull-down menu, pick the **Print** button in the **Standard** toolbar, or enter PLOT at the Command: prompt. The **Print/Plot Configuration** dialog box appears, Figure 10-10. This dialog box allows you to define and preview each one of the parameters you specify for the final printing or plotting of your drawing.

Figure 10-10.
Plot parameters are specified in the **Print/Plot Configuration** dialog box.

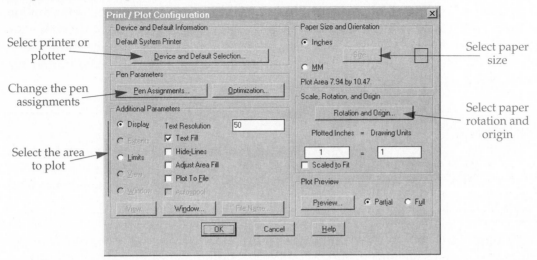

Dialog boxes are usually controlled with the **FILEDIA** system variable. However, this dialog box is controlled with the **CMDDIA** system variable. By default, **CMDDIA** is set to 1 (on). This displays the **Print/Plot Configuration** dialog box. When **CMDDIA** is set to 0 (off), all printing and plotting parameters must be entered on the command line. This is useful when creating automatic plotting script files (see Chapter 28), or when customizing AutoCAD. See *AutoCAD and its Applications—Advanced, Release 14* for detailed discussions on customizing techniques.

Device and default selection

As you look at the **Print/Plot Configuration** dialog box, notice the **Device and Default Information** area in the upper-left corner. This is where AutoCAD displays information about the currently configured printer or plotter.

Pick the **Device and Default Selection...** button to access the **Device and Default Selection** dialog box shown in Figure 10-11. You can use this dialog box to change any of the printer or plotter specifications. The current device is highlighted in the **Select a Device Configuration** area. When additional devices are shown, you can make a different one current by picking it from the list. Add printers and plotters to the list by selecting **Printer Setup...** in the **File** pull-down menu. This displays the **Preferences** dialog box, in which the **Printer** tab is used to add, modify, and remove printing and plotting devices. See *Appendix C* for information on configuring devices for AutoCAD.

Figure 10-11.
Available printers and plotters are listed in the **Device and Default Selection** dialog box.

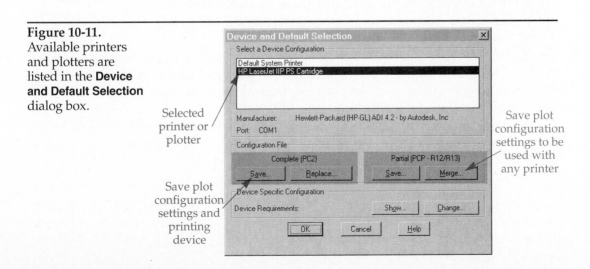

The **Configuration File** area of the **Device and Default Selection** dialog box provides access to two different kinds of files. These files, called *plot configuration* (PC) files, contain all of the parameters that are set in the **Print/Plot Configuration** dialog box. The .pc2 file is new to Release 14 and contains complete information about all of the plot/print settings, plus the specific device that is used to generate the plot. The .pcp file is an AutoCAD Release 12 and 13 file that contains information about the plot/print settings. This file is referred to as a *partial* configuration file because it is not specific to any device.

PROFESSIONAL TIP

The only difference between a .pc2 and a .pcp file is that the currently selected printing device is saved in the .pc2 file along with the plot configuration parameters. Remember the differences between these two files.

Complete (.PC2) file. Save this file if you want to preserve all of the plot configuration parameters plus the currently selected printing device by picking the **Save...** button. Use a file name that is the same as the drawing name in order to avoid future confusion. The next time you wish to plot the drawing, simply pick the **Replace...** button to load the file. When the .pc2 file is loaded, it automatically replaces all current plot configuration settings and the current plotting device.

Partial (.PCP) file. Save this file if you want to preserve all of the plot configuration parameters by picking the **Save...** button. The next time you wish to plot the drawing simply pick the **Merge...** button to load the file. The saved settings in the .pcp file are loaded and merged with the currently selected plotting device. Therefore, the .pcp file can be used with any plotting device that is selected.

PROFESSIONAL TIP

If you create a drawing or design that must be printed with a specific device, save the configuration as a complete (.pc2) configuration file. If your drawing can be plotted on any number of different devices and you wish to preserve only the plot settings, save it as a partial (.pcp) configuration file.

PC files are used for the following tasks:
- Making changes to plot specifications before plotting.
- Making plot files for different drawing types or for template drawings.
- Making a plot file for each configured plotter or printer.
- Setting up a drawing to be plotted in a variety of formats.
- Giving a plot file to another person or company.

Each of the values you set in the **Print/Plot Configuration** dialog box can be saved in a PC file. This means that you can set values for individual prototype drawings. Then, when a prototype is used to construct a new drawing, you only need to retrieve a PC file and plot the drawing without making any additional changes to the plotting parameters.

Normally, the PC file is saved to the AutoCAD R14 folder and defaults to the current drawing name, but you may want to provide a name that is more descriptive if the drawing is to be used as a template for other projects.

Use the buttons in the **Device Specific Configuration** area to review or change your printer or plotter settings. The **Show...** button opens the **Show Device Requirements** dialog box, Figure 10-12. The device requirements for the system printer are shown. In the Windows environment, the system printer is the output device specified in the Printers folder. Pick the **Change...** button to make any changes. If your currently configured device is the Windows system printer, the Windows Print Setup dialog box is displayed. See Figure 10-13A. In this dialog box you can select any other configured system printer, the paper size and source, and the orientation of the paper. Pick the **Properties** button to change any of the detailed aspects of the current printer. This displays a device-specific dialog box related to the system printer. See Figure 10-13B. Pick **OK** to dismiss all dialog boxes.

Figure 10-12.
The **Show Device Requirements** dialog box lists requirements for the current printer.

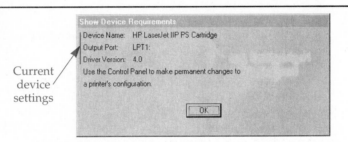

Current device settings

Figure 10-13.
A—The Windows Print Setup dialog box. B—The dialog box used to view and change printer properties contains options for the specific printer being used.

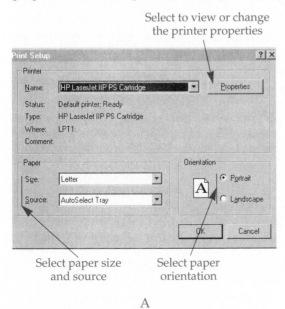

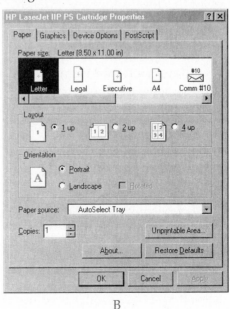

Select to view or change the printer properties

Select paper size and source

Select paper orientation

A

B

> **NOTE**
>
> The changes that you make to the system printer only affect printed AutoCAD drawings. If you want the changes to be in effect for all printed Windows applications, make the changes using the Printers icon in Windows.

Pen parameters

The **Pen Parameters** area in the **Print/Plot Configuration** dialog box allows you to set pen parameters based on your drawing standards or the type of printer/plotter you are using. Pick the **Pen Assignments...** button to get the **Pen Assignments** dialog box, Figure 10-14. When you highlight a pen assignment by selecting it, the values for the selected pen are displayed in the **Modify Values** area. The values that can be changed include the pen number, linetype, speed, and width.

Figure 10-14.
The **Pen Assignments** dialog box enables you to set the plotter pen selection.

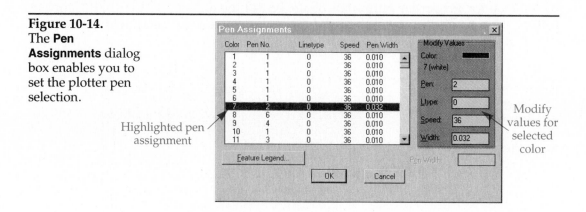

Highlighted pen assignment

Modify values for selected color

When you plot a drawing on a pen plotter, you must assign the color numbers used for your on-screen objects to the correct pen numbers in the plotter. For example, suppose you create a drawing using the first seven colors available in AutoCAD. Those colors—red, yellow, green, cyan, blue, magenta, and white (or black)—are mapped to color numbers 1 through 7. By default, these color numbers are automatically assigned to matching pen numbers. In other words, all red entities on-screen are plotted with pen number 1, all yellow entities with pen number 2, all green entities with pen number 3, and so on. If you did nothing to change this convention, you would need a separate pen for every color used in your drawing!

It is more efficient and cost-effective to map the various colors used in your drawing to only a few pens. Look at the **Pen Assignments** dialog box shown in Figure 10-14. In this example, colors 1 through 6 are assigned to pen number 1. The entities drawn with these colors will be plotted with a thin pen. These entities include dimensions, text, hatching, and centerlines. The object lines in the drawing were drawn with color number 7. Since object lines should be drawn thick, color number 7 is assigned to pen number 2. The line weight, or thickness, of pen number 2 is also set to .032 inches to conform to the ANSI standard for object lines. Therefore, only two pens are required to accurately plot all the drawing entities.

Fortunately, most pen plotters are capable of using various pen sizes. These pens, which are similar to ink pens used for inking plastic film, are available in a range of tip sizes. If your pen plotter is compatible with these types of pens, you need not set the pen width in the **Pen Assignments** dialog box. Simply insert the correct pen size in the appropriate pen position on your plotter.

Other types of output devices, such as laser printers or ink jet plotters, do not use pens. However, you can still produce finished plots with the proper line weights by assigning the desired pen widths to the color numbers used in your drawing.

You will also note that **Linetype** and **Speed** values can be changed in the **Pen Assignments** dialog box. For most pen plotters, the linetype, pen speed, and pen force values are controlled by the plotter itself or the installed plotter driver. It is very unlikely that you will need to change these values. Also, notice the **Feature Legend...** button at the lower-left of the **Pen Assignments** dialog box. Pick this button to display the **Feature Legend** dialog box shown in Figure 10-15. The linetypes shown in this dialog box reflect the linetypes that are generated by your plotter. These linetypes are different than the linetypes created in your drawing. Therefore, entities drawn in linetypes other than Continuous will plot correctly as a function of the plotter itself. It is usually unnecessary to adjust the linetypes in the **Pen Assignments** dialog box.

Figure 10-15.
The **Feature Legend** dialog box displays the linetypes generated by the plotter.

Plotter linetypes

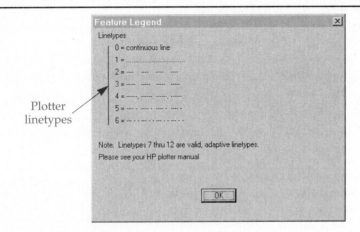

PROFESSIONAL TIP

In the unlikely event that you do need to adjust pen speeds, they should be set according to the type of paper or film you are using. In addition, you should consider the type of pen, such as liquid ink, fiber tip, or roller ball, and the lines or text to be plotted. A fast pen speed may not draw quality lines or text. Set a slower pen speed to improve the plot quality.

Also, since most pen plotters generate the required linetypes for AutoCAD drawings, leave the linetypes set to Continuous (0) in the **Pen Assignments** dialog box. Doing so ensures that the lines in your drawing are properly plotted.

The **Optimization...** button in the **Plot Configuration** dialog box displays the **Optimizing Pen Motion** dialog box. This dialog box contains check boxes that let you control the efficiency of pen movement. By default, AutoCAD minimizes wasted pen motion with the settings shown in Figure 10-16. With the exception of the **No optimization** check box, each consecutive check increases optimization. Picking a higher level option automatically checks all previous options. The options available in this dialog box will vary depending on the type of printer or plotter that you are using. For nonpen plotters, like dot matrix printers, these options may not be available at all since they have no effect on these output devices.

Figure 10-16.
The **Optimizing Pen Motion** dialog box. Each checked box increases optimization.

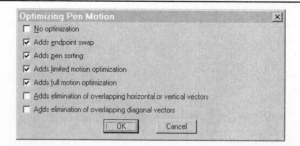

PROFESSIONAL TIP

You may need to experiment with your plotter to be sure that optimization is an asset. In most cases, it reduces plot time but may also cause problems, such as unnecessary pen changes.

Additional parameters—choosing what and how to plot

After selecting the desired output device and making the necessary pen assignments, you must decide what part of the drawing you want to plot. Look at the **Additional Parameters** area of the **Print/Plot Configuration** dialog box, Figure 10-17.

Figure 10-17.
The **Additional Parameters** area of the **Print/Plot Configuration** dialog box.

Select the portion of the drawing to plot

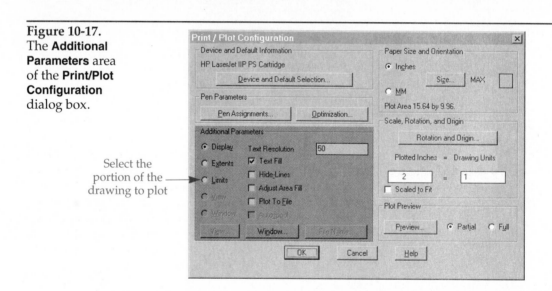

This section allows you to choose the portion of the drawing to be plotted, and how it is to be plotted. The five radio-button options are described below:

- **Display.** This option plots the current screen display.
- **Extents.** The **Extents** option plots only the area of the drawing in which objects (entities) are drawn. Before using this option, zoom the extents to include all drawn entities to verify exactly what will be plotted. Be aware that border lines around your drawing (like the title block) may be clipped off if they are at the extreme edge of the screen. This often happens because you are requesting the plotter to plot at the extreme edge of its active area.
- **Limits.** This option plots everything inside the defined drawing limits.

- **View.** Views saved with the **VIEW** command are plotted using this option. Until a view name has been given, this option is not available. To specify a view name, pick the **View...** button to display the **View Name** dialog box. Select the name of the view you want plotted and pick **OK**. The view name you select does not need to be displayed on the screen, but the **TILEMODE** system variable must be off (0) to plot any saved view from either model space or paper space.
- **Window.** This option appears grayed-out until you pick the **Window...** button to display the **Window Selection** dialog box, Figure 10-18. This option requires that you define two opposite corners of a window around the portion of the drawing to be plotted. Enter the coordinates of the desired window in the appropriate **X:** and **Y:** text boxes. If you want to define the window with your pointing device, pick the **Pick ⟨** button at the upper-left of the dialog box. This clears the dialog boxes and redisplays the graphics window. You are then prompted at the command line to pick the window corners that surround the part of the drawing you want plotted. After you have picked the corners, the **Window Selection** dialog box is redisplayed. Pick **OK** to return to the **Print/Plot Configuration** dialog box.

Figure 10-18.
Specify a plot window using the **Window Selection** dialog box. Enter coordinates or pick a new window.

Slect a new window

Coordinates of current window

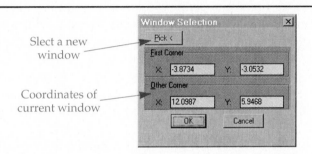

NOTE

If the window you define is too close to an entity, some portion of that entity may be clipped off in your plot. If this happens, simply adjust the window size the next time you plot. You can prevent these errors by using the **Preview** dialog box.

- **Text Resolution.** Text fonts such as Bitstream, TrueType, and Adobe Type 1 are affected by the value in this text box. A high value increases resolution but decreases plotting speed and screen display time. Faster plotting speed and screen display time are achieved with lower values.
- **Text Fill.** Filled text fonts will be filled if this box is checked.
- **Hide Lines.** Enables you to plot a 3D drawing with hidden lines removed. This function works the same as the **HIDE** command does with the display. Note that plotting takes a little longer when removing hidden lines because AutoCAD must calculate the lines to be removed. Do not check this box when plotting 2D drawings.
- **Adjust Area Fill.** Check this box if you want entities such as wide polylines, traces, doughnuts, and solids filled completely. Precise plots result because the pen is adjusted inside the boundary of the object by one-half the pen width. When this check box is turned off, the pen plots at the center of the boundary. This is fine for most applications, but may be poor for printed circuit board artwork.

You may work with paper space to create drawing layouts containing multiple views of varying scales. These layouts may contain 3D views inside paper space viewports in which the hidden lines must be removed for ease of visualization. The **Hide_Lines** check box in the **Print/Plot Configuration** dialog box will not automatically remove the hidden lines from a 3D object in a paper space viewport. You must turn on the **Hideplot** option of the **MVIEW** command before plotting. The **MVIEW** command and the use of paper space multiview layouts are discussed in Chapter 24.

Creating a plot file

Some computer operating systems allow you to continue working on a drawing while other instructions are being handled by the computer. This capability is called *multitasking* and is a standard feature of the Windows 95, Windows NT, and Unix operating systems. For those operating systems capable of true multitasking, it can be extremely handy to redirect plot output to an external file. This plot file can then be sent directly to a configured plotter while you continue working on a drawing.

Redirecting plot output to a .plt file is good practice if you have only one office or class computer connected to a printer or plotter. This is also the case if your office or school uses a plot spooler. A plot spooler is connected to a plotter and is basically a "smart" disk drive with memory. It reads the .plt file from disk and sends the drawing data to the plotter. A plot spooler removes the need of having a computer connected to the plotter.

Additionally, plot files can be stored in a plot queue on the file server in a networked computer environment. A *plot queue* is a lineup, or list of files, waiting to be plotted. The .plt files can be loaded in the queue and started while users on the network continue doing other work. The **Batch Plot** utility can also be used to plot a group of .plt files.

If you want to redirect plot output to a file, pick the **Plot To File** check box. This activates the **File Name...** button, which is normally grayed-out. Picking this button displays the **Create Plot File** dialog box, Figure 10-19. Observe that saved plot files are automatically given the extension .plt, and that the plot file name defaults to the current drawing name. If you have not yet provided a name for the current drawing, the plot file is saved with a file name of drawing.plt. To provide a different name for the plot file, enter the name in the **File name:** text box and pick **OK**. The **Print/Plot Configuration** dialog box reappears. Pick **OK** once more to close the dialog box and create the plot file. When the plot file is complete, you are notified on the command line.

Creating an autospool file

AutoCAD has the capability to save raster files in a variety of formats. To do so, you must first establish a printer configuration for raster file export using an Autodesk Device Interface (ADI) driver. See *Appendix C* for configuration information. If a raster export configuration has already been established, it will be listed in the **Device and Default Selection** dialog box. See Figure 10-20.

Figure 10-19.
The **Create Plot File** dialog box. Select the destination and the name of the file.

Folder in which file will be saved

File name

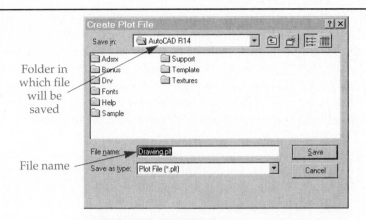

Figure 10-20.
Raster export configurations are listed with printer and plotter selections.

Configuration for saving raster files

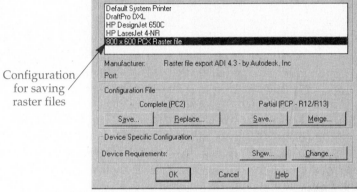

In this example, the ADI device has been configured for export to a .pcx file. When this device is selected, the **Autospool** check box in the **Print/Plot Configuration** dialog box is available. Pick this check box, then pick **File Name...** to display the **Create Plot File** dialog box. The default file name (autospool.pcx) can be changed. Once this file is saved, it can be used in any application that accepts that specific type of file.

Paper size and orientation

The upper-right area of the **Print/Plot Configuration** dialog box controls the paper size and orientation, Figure 10-21. Pick either the **Inches** or **MM** radio button to set the units for the paper size specification.

Figure 10-21.
The **Paper Size and Orientation** area of the **Plot Configuration** dialog box is highlighted.

Select the paper size

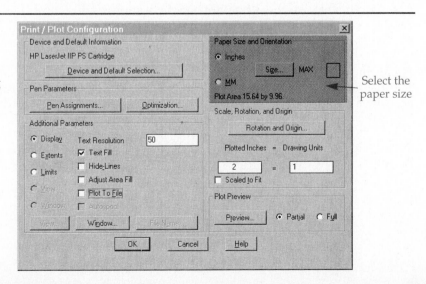

Pick the **Size...** button to access the **Paper Size** dialog box. Select the desired standard paper (or film) size, such as the D-size entry shown in Figure 10-22. You can also enter your own size specifications in one of the **USER Width** and **Height** text boxes. If you enter your own size specifications, make sure the values you enter do not exceed the maximum size indicated in the list. The maximum listed size is the largest plot media your plotter can handle. Therefore, the sizes listed in the **Paper Size** dialog box will vary according to the printer or plotter you are using.

Figure 10-22.
All available sheet sizes are listed in the **Paper Size** dialog box. Select the size you want to use.

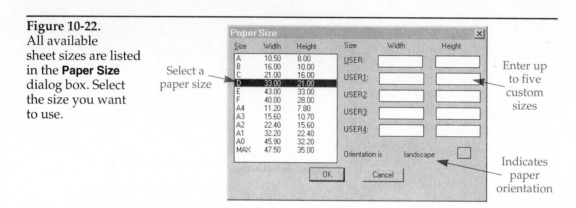

All pen plotters require margins around the edges of the plot media. This space allows for the plotter's grip wheels, clamps, and other holding devices. As a result, the available size may be smaller than the ANSI standard sizes. The following table shows standard paper sizes and the available plotting areas for each.

Designation	Paper size	Plotting area
A	8 ½ × 11	8 × 10 ½
B	11 × 17	10 × 16
C	17 × 22	16 × 21
D	22 × 34	21 × 33
E	34 × 44	33 × 43

Whether you select a standard size or enter your own size, the available plotting area is reported in the **Paper Size and Orientation** area of the **Print/Plot Configuration** dialog box.

Plot rotation and origin

Options to control the plot rotation and origin are located in the **Scale, Rotation, and Origin** area of the **Print/Plot Configuration** dialog box. Pick the **Rotation and Origin...** button to access the **Plot Rotation and Origin** dialog box shown in Figure 10-23.

Figure 10-23.
The **Plot Rotation and Origin** dialog box is used to change the origin and rotation of the plot.

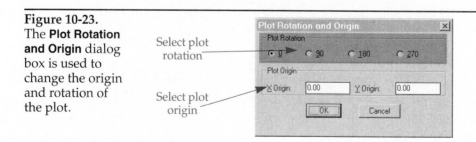

In AutoCAD, the horizontal screen measurement relates to the long side of the paper. This orientation is known as *landscape* format. However, you might create a drawing, form, or chart in *portrait* format. This format orients the long side of the plot vertically. AutoCAD rotates plots in 90° clockwise increments, and **0**, **90**, **180**, and **270** options for degree rotation settings appear in the **Plot Rotation** area. Figure 10-24 illustrates the result of a 90° plot rotation.

Figure 10-24.
Plot rotation. A—Standard plot with no rotation. Long side of paper is horizontal. B—Plot with a 90° clockwise rotation. Long side of paper is vertical.

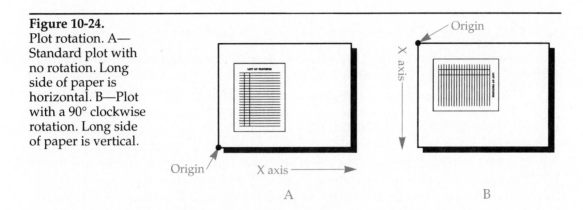

A   B

The origin of a pen plotter is the lower-left corner of the plot media. To begin plotting a drawing at that point, leave the values shown in the **Plot Origin** text boxes at 0.00. If you want to move the drawing away from the default origin, change the required values in the text boxes. For example, to move the drawing four units to the right and three units above the plotter origin, enter a 4 in the **X Origin:** text box, and a 3 in the **Y Origin:** text box. For printers, the origin is the upper-left corner of the paper. The coordinates of 4,3 will move the print origin four units to the right and three units down. Remember that the units you enter should be consistent with the units specified in the **Paper Size and Orientation** area of the **Print/Plot Configuration** dialog box.

Determining drawing scale factors

The proper scale factor is vitally important because it makes sure that text, dimension values, and dimensioning entities (such as arrowheads and tick marks) are plotted at the proper size. The scale factor of the drawing should already be established by the time you are ready to plot and should be an integral part of your template and prototype drawings. To obtain the correct text height, the desired plotted text height is multiplied by the scale factor. The scale factor is also used in the **DIMSCALE** dimension variable.

NOTE   Determine the plot scale and scale factor when you begin the drawing. If you find the drawing scale factor does not correspond to the plotting scale, you will need to update dimensions and text.

The scale factor is always the reciprocal of the drawing scale. For example, if you wish to plot a mechanical drawing at a scale of 1/2″ = 1″, calculate the scale factor as follows:

1/2″ = 1″
.5″ = 1″
1 ÷ .5 = 2 *(The scale factor is 2 and* **DIMSCALE** *= 2)*

An architectural drawing to be plotted at a scale of 1/4″ = 1′-0″ has a scale factor calculated as follows:

> 1/4″ = 1′-0″
> .25″ = 12″
> 12 ÷ .25 = 48 *(The scale factor is 48 and* **DIMSCALE** = 48)

The scale factor of a civil engineering drawing that has a scale of 1″ = 60′ is calculated as:

> 1″ = 60′
> 1″ = 60 × 12 = 720″ *(The scale factor is 720 and* **DIMSCALE** = 720)

Once the scale factor of the drawing has been determined, calculate the height of the text in AutoCAD. If text height is to be plotted at 1/8″, it should not be drawn at that height. Remember, all geometry created in AutoCAD should be drawn at full scale.

For example, if you are working on a civil engineering drawing with a scale of 1″ = 60′, the scale factor and **DIMSCALE** both equal 720. Text drawn 1/8″ high appears as a dot. The full-size civil engineering drawing in AutoCAD is 720 times larger than it will be when plotted at the proper scale. Therefore, you must multiply the text height by 720 in order to get text that appears in correct proportion on the screen. For 1/8″ high text to appear correctly on-screen, calculate the AutoCAD text height as follows:

> 1/8″ × 720
> .125 × 720 = 90 *(The proper height of the text is 90)*

Remember, scale factors, text heights, and **DIMSCALE** values should be determined before beginning a drawing. The best method is to incorporate these as values within your template and prototype drawing files.

Scaling the plot

AutoCAD drawing geometry is created at full scale, and the drawing is scaled at the plotter to fit on the sheet size. The **Plotted Inches = Drawing Units** section in the **Scale, Rotation, and Origin** area of the **Print/Plot Configuration** dialog box is used to specify the plot scale. The **Plotted Inches = Drawing Units** text boxes (or **Plotted MM. = Drawing Units** text boxes) allow you to specify the plot scale as a ratio of plotted units to drawing units. An architectural drawing to be plotted at 1/4″ = 1′-0″ can be entered in the text boxes as:

> 1/4″ = 1′ *or* .25 = 12 *or* 1 = 48

A mechanical drawing to be plotted at a scale of 1/2″ = 1″ can be entered in the text boxes as:

> 1/2″ = 1″ *or* .5 = 1 *or* 1 = 2

Pick the **Scaled to Fit** check box if you want AutoCAD to automatically adjust your drawing to fit on the paper. This is useful if you have a C-size pen plotter but need to plot a D-size or E-size drawing. However, keep in mind that you may have considerable blank space left on the paper, depending on the size and proportions of your drawing.

The **Scaled to Fit** feature is also useful if you are printing a large drawing on a dot matrix or laser printer that can only use A-size sheets. The drawing is automatically scaled down to fit the size of printer paper.

Calculating the drawing area and limits

To calculate the available area on a sheet of paper at a specific scale, use this formula:

(Unit ÷ Scale) × Media size = Limits

For example, to find the limits of a B-size (17″ × 11″) sheet of paper at 1/2″ = 1″ scale:

(1 ÷ .50) × 17 = 2 × 17 = 34 (X distance)
(1 ÷ .50) × 11 = 2 × 11 = 22 (Y distance)

Thus, the limits of a B-size sheet at the scale of 1/2″ = 1″ are 34,22. The same formula applies to architectural scales. The limits of a C-size architectural sheet (24″ × 18″) at a scale of 1/4″ = 1″-0″ can be determined like this:

(1′-0″ ÷ 1/4″) × 24 = (12″ ÷ .25″) × 24 = 48 × 24 = 1152″ ÷ 12 = 96′ (X distance)

Use the same formula to calculate the Y distance for the 18″ side of the paper. The charts in Figure 10-25 provide limits for common scales on various paper sizes for each drafting field. The charts also list text height, scale factors, and linetype scales for the best linetype quality. The approximate drawing area reflects an average border allowed for plotter gripping mechanisms. The approximate drawing limits reflect this approximate drawing area.

Figure 10-25.
Common scales and their drawing limits, text height, scale factors, and linetype scales.

Architectural Sheet Size and Settings								
Paper size (in)	Approx. drawing area	Scale	Actual sheet limits	Approx. drawing limits	Text height		Scale factor	Ltscale
					1/8″	1/4″		
A 12 × 9	10 × 7.5	1″ = 1′-0″	12′ × 9′	10′ × 7.5′	1.5	3.0	12	6
		1/2″ = 1′-0″	24′ × 18′	20′ × 15′	3.0	6.0	24	12
		1/4″ = 1′-0″	48′ × 36′	40′ × 30′	6.0	12.0	48	24
		1/8″ = 1′-0″	96′ × 72′	80′ × 60′	12.0	24.0	96	48
B 18 × 12	16 × 11	1″ = 1′-0″	18′ × 12′	16′ × 11′				
		1/2″ = 1′-0″	36′ × 24′	32′ × 20′				
		1/4″ = 1′-0″	72′ × 48′	64′ × 40′				
		1/8″ = 1′-0″	144′ × 96′	128′ × 80′				
C 24 × 18	22 × 16	1″ = 1′-0″	24′ × 18′	22′ × 16′				
		1/2″ = 1′-0″	48′ × 36′	44′ × 32′				
		1/4″ = 1′-0″	96′ × 72′	88′ × 64′				
		1/8″ = 1′-0″	192′ × 144′	176′ × 28′				
D 36 × 24	34 × 22	1″ = 1′-0″	36′ × 24′	34′ × 22′				
		1/2″ = 1′-0″	72′ × 48′	68′ × 44′				
		1/4″ = 1′-0″	144′ × 96′	136′ × 88′				
		1/8″ = 1′-0″	288′ × 192′	272′ × 176′				
E 48 × 36	46 × 34	1″ = 1′-0″	48′ × 36′	46′ × 34′				
		1/2″ = 1′-0″	96′ × 72′	92′ × 68′				
		1/4″ = 1′-0″	192′ × 144′	184′ × 136′				
		1/8″ = 1′-0″	384′ × 288′	368′ × 272′				

(continued)

Mechanical Sheet Size and Settings

Paper size (in)	Approx. drawing area	Scale	Actual sheet limits	Approx. drawing limits	Text height 1/8″	Text height 1/4″	Scale factor	Ltscale
A 11 × 8.5	9 × 7	2″ = 1″ 3/4″ = 1″ 1/2″ = 1″ 1/4″ = 1″	5.5 × 4.25 14.67 × 11.33 22 × 17 44 × 34	4.5″ × 3.5″ 12″ × 9.33″ 18″ × 14″ 36″ × 28″	.0625 .167 .25 .5	.125 .33 .5 1.0	.5 1.33 2 4	.25 .67 1 2
B 17 × 11	15 × 10	2″ = 1″ 3/4″ = 1″ 1/2″ = 1″ 1/4″ = 1″	8.5 × 5.5 22.67 × 14.67 34 × 22 68 × 44	7.5″ × 5″ 20″ × 13.33″ 30″ × 20″ 60″ × 40″				
C 22 × 17	20 × 15	2″ = 1″ 3/4″ = 1″ 1/2″ = 1″ 1/4″ = 1″	11 × 8.5 29.33 × 14.67 44 × 34 88 × 68	10″ × 7.5″ 26.67″ × 20″ 40″ × 30″ 80″ × 60″				
D 34 × 22	32 × 20	2″ = 1″ 3/4″ = 1″ 1/2″ = 1″ 1/4″ = 1″	17 × 11 45.33 × 29.33 68 × 44 136 × 88	16″ × 10″ 42.67″ × 26.67″ 64″ × 40″ 128″ × 80″				
E 44 × 34	42 × 32	2″ = 1″ 3/4″ = 1″ 1/2″ = 1″ 1/4″ = 1″	22 × 17 58.67 × 45.33 88 × 68 176 × 136	21″ × 16″ 56″ × 42.67″ 84″ × 64″ 168″ × 128″				

Civil Sheet Size and Settings

Paper size (in)	Approx. drawing area	Scale	Actual sheet limits	Approx. drawing limits	Text height 1/8″	Text height 1/4″	Scale factor	Ltscale
A 11 × 8.5	9 × 7	1″ = 10′ 1″ = 20′ 1″ = 30′ 1″ = 50′	110′ × 85′ 220′ × 170′ 330′ × 255′ 550′ × 425′	90′ × 70′ 180′ × 140′ 270′ × 210′ 450′ × 350′	15 30 45 75	30 60 90 150	120 240 360 600	60 120 180 300
B 17 × 11	15 × 10	1″ = 10′ 1″ = 20′ 1″ = 30′ 1″ = 50′	170′ × 110′ 340′ × 220′ 510′ × 330′ 850′ × 550′	150′ × 100′ 300′ × 200′ 450′ × 300′ 750′ × 500′				
C 22 × 17	20 × 15	1″ = 10′ 1″ = 20′ 1″ = 30′ 1″ = 50′	220′ × 170′ 440′ × 340′ 660′ × 510′ 1100′ × 850′	200′ × 150′ 400′ × 300′ 600′ × 450′ 1000′ × 750′				
D 34 × 22	32 × 20	1″ = 10′ 1″ = 20′ 1″ = 30′ 1″ = 50′	340′ × 220′ 680′ × 440′ 1020′ × 660′ 1700′ × 1100′	320′ × 200′ 640′ × 400′ 960′ × 600′ 1600′ × 1000′				
E 44 × 34	42 × 32	1″ = 10′ 1″ = 20′ 1″ = 30′ 1″ = 50′	440′ × 340′ 880′ × 680′ 1320′ × 1020′ 2200′ × 1700′	420′ × 320′ 840′ × 640′ 1260′ × 960′ 2100′ × 1600′				

(continued)

Metric Sheet Size and Settings								
Paper size (mm)	Approx. drawing area	Scale	Actual paper limits (mm)	Approx. drawing limits (mm)	Text height		Scale factor	Ltscale
					1/8"	1/4"		
A4 297 × 210	277 × 190	1 = 2	594 × 420	554 × 380	.25	.5	50.8	1
		1 = 5	1485 × 1050	1385 × 950	.625	1.25	127	2
		1 = 10	2970 × 2100	2770 × 1900	1.25	2.5	254	5
		1 = 20	5940 × 4200	5540 × 3800	2.5	5	508	10
		1 = 50	14850 × 10500	13850 × 9500	6.25	12.5	1270	25
		1 = 100	29700 × 21000	27700 × 19000	12.5	25	2540	50
A3 420 × 297	400 × 277	1 = 2	820 × 594	780 × 554				
		1 = 5	2100 × 1485	2000 × 1385				
		1 = 10	4200 × 2970	4000 × 2770				
		1 = 20	8400 × 5940	8000 × 5540				
		1 = 50	21000 × 14850	20000 × 13850				
		1 = 100	42000 × 29700	40000 × 27700				
A2 594 × 420	577 × 400	1 = 2	1188 × 840	1148 × 800				
		1 = 5	2970 × 2100	2870 × 2000				
		1 = 10	5940 × 4200	5740 × 4000				
		1 = 20	11880 × 8400	11480 × 8000				
		1 = 50	29700 × 21000	28700 × 20000				
		1 = 100	59400 × 42000	57400 × 40000				
A1 841 × 594	801 × 554	1 = 2	1682 × 1188	1642 × 1148				
		1 = 5	4205 × 2970	4105 × 2870				
		1 = 10	8410 × 5940	8210 × 5740				
		1 = 20	16820 × 11880	16420 × 11480				
		1 = 50	42050 × 29700	41050 × 28700				
		1 = 100	84100 × 59400	82100 × 57400				
A0 1189 × 841	1149 × 801	1 = 2	2378 × 1682	2338 × 1642				
		1 = 5	5945 × 4205	5845 × 4105				
		1 = 10	11890 × 8410	11690 × 8210				
		1 = 20	23780 × 16820	23380 × 16420				
		1 = 50	59450 × 42050	58450 × 41050				
		1 = 100	118900 × 84100	116900 × 82100				

Previewing the plot

The size and complexity of some drawings often require long plotting times. By previewing a plot before it is sent to the output device, you can catch errors, saving material and valuable plot time. This feature is found in the **Plot Preview** area at the lower-right of the **Plot Configuration** dialog box, Figure 10-26. Either the **Partial** or **Full** preview option is selected.

If the **Partial** option is selected and you pick the **Preview...** button, AutoCAD quickly displays the **Preview Effective Plotting Area** dialog box shown in Figure 10-27. The outline is the paper size, and the paper dimensions are given below for reference. The area the image occupies is called the *effective area*. The effective area dimensions are noted and the outline of this area is provided within the paper size. AutoCAD displays a dashed line when the effective area and the paper size are the same. While this shows you how the drawing compares to the paper size, the final plot depends on how the printer or plotter is set up.

Figure 10-26.
The **Plot Preview** area of the **Print/Plot Configuration** dialog box is shown here highlighted. Select **Partial** or **Full** and the **Preview...** button to preview the plot.

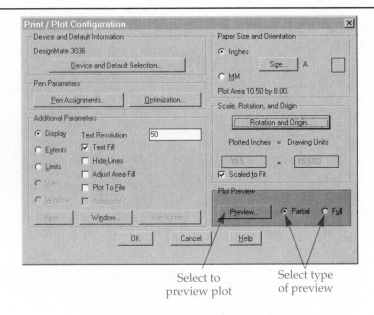

Select to preview plot

Select type of preview

Figure 10-27.
Selecting the **Preview...** button when **Partial** is checked displays the **Preview Effective Plotting Area** dialog box.

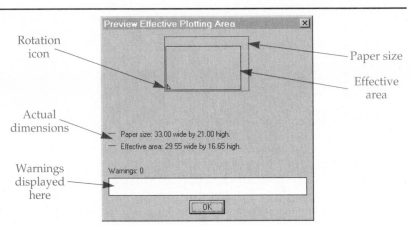

Rotation icon

Paper size

Effective area

Actual dimensions

Warnings displayed here

If there is something wrong with the relationship of the display and the paper, AutoCAD gives you messages in the **Warnings:** text box. These warnings give you an opportunity to make corrections and then preview the plot again. You may encounter the following warnings:

- Effective area too small to display.
- Origin forced effective area off display.
- Plotting area exceeds paper maximum.

Notice the small symbol in the lower-left corner of the effective area in Figure 10-27. This is called the *rotation icon*. When the rotation icon appears in the lower-left corner, it indicates the 0° default rotation angle. The icon is in the upper-left corner when the rotation is 90°, the upper-right corner for a 180° rotation, and in the lower-right corner for a 270° rotation. See Figure 10-28.

Figure 10-28.
The rotation icon as it appears in each rotation angle selection.

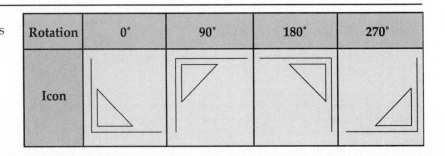

Rotation	0°	90°	180°	270°
Icon				

Set the **Full** option and pick the **Preview...** button if you want a full preview. The full preview displays the drawing in the graphics window as it will actually appear on the plotted hard copy. This takes the same amount of time as a drawing regeneration. Therefore, the drawing size determines how quickly the image is produced.

The drawing is displayed inside a paper outline. The cursor assumes the shape of the zoom icon. Press and hold the pick button as you move the cursor up to enlarge, and down to reduce. Right-click to display the zoom pop-up menu, as shown in Figure 10-29. This is the same menu that is activated when you use the **PAN** and **ZOOM** commands. It provides several display options and an exit option. The pop-up menu is handy because it allows you to closely examine the drawing before you commit to plotting. You can also press [Esc] or [Enter] to exit to the **Print/Plot Configuration** dialog box.

Figure 10-29.
The zoom pop-up menu can be displayed when a full preview is selected.

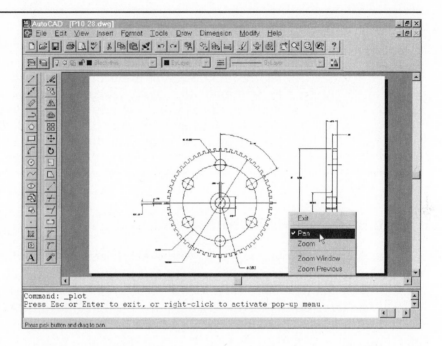

A full preview is also displayed by picking **Print Preview** in the **File** pull-down menu. This selection bypasses the **Print/Plot Configuration** dialog box.

Before you pick **OK** in the **Print/Plot Configuration** dialog box, there are several items you should check:

✓ The printer or plotter is plugged in and turned on.
✓ The parallel or serial cable to the computer is secure.
✓ The pen carousel is loaded and secure, or the pen is in the plotter arm.
✓ Pens of proper color and thickness are in correct locations in pen carousel or rack.
✓ The plot media is properly loaded in the plotter and paper grips or clamps are in place.
✓ The printer or plotter area is clear for unblocked paper movement.

Once you are satisfied with all plotter parameters and are ready to plot, pick the **OK** button to exit the **Print/Plot Configuration** dialog box. AutoCAD then displays the following message on the command line:

Effective plotting area: *(xx)* wide by *(yy)* high

These are the actual dimensions of the current plotting area. A dialog box is also displayed that indicates the name of the drawing being printed, and a meter shows the percentage of the file that has been regenerated and sent to the printer. See Figure 10-30.

Figure 10-30.
When you send a drawing to a printer or plotter, a progress meter allows you to gauge how long the plot will take.

```
Printing   P10-28.dwg

┌─Regeneration Progress──────┐
│           100%              │
└────────────────────────────┘

        ┌──────────┐
        │  Cancel  │
        └──────────┘
```

PROFESSIONAL TIP   You can stop a plot in progress at any time by pressing [Esc] or picking the **Cancel** button in the dialog box shown in Figure 10-30. Keep in mind that it may take several seconds to terminate the plot, depending on the amount of the drawing file that has already been sent to the plotter. You may also find it necessary to turn the plotter off and then turn it back on after canceling. This action removes any remaining plot data from the plotter's internal buffer.

Using the Batch Plot Utility

The **Batch Plot** utility is new to AutoCAD Release 14 and adds a powerful new dimension to printing and plotting. Using this utility, you can create a list of drawings to be printed and then instruct AutoCAD to begin plotting while you return to work on other projects. **Batch Plot** opens a temporary session of AutoCAD for its purposes, but does not allow you to edit drawings or adjust plot parameters in any way. **Batch Plot** must be selected by picking Programs from the Windows Start menu, then selecting Batch Plot Utility from the AutoCAD menu.

CAUTION   Use **Batch Plot** only if you have previously created all required plot files and .pcp or .pc2 files. Always preview your plots to check for accuracy before saving any of the above files. Valuable time may be wasted if you do not plan your plots accurately.

Batch Plot checklist

Before you use **Batch Plot**, be sure you have completed the following tasks. Following these guidelines is important if the utility is to run successfully.

✓ Check each drawing to be plotted for accuracy and completeness. If you are plotting a view, display the named view to be plotted before saving the drawing. The default view is plotted by **Batch Plot**.

✓ Conduct a full preview of the drawing to check for the accuracy of plot parameters.

✓ Create a .pcp file if a single plotter is to be used, and carefully check the plot parameters before creating the file.
✓ If more than one drawing is to be plotted using the same plotter, but having different plot parameters, create a .pcp file for each drawing.
✓ If batch drawings will use different devices, carefully check the plot parameters of each and save them as .pc2 files.

The **Batch Plot** dialog box

The **AutoCAD Extended Batch Plot Utility** dialog box is displayed after Batch Plot Utility is selected from the Start menu. This dialog box contains five tabs. Each of these tabs is explained in detail later.

- **File.** Create a list of drawings to plot.
- **Layers.** Select drawing layers to turn on or off during plotting.
- **Plot Area.** Select the area of the drawing to plot. This includes views, viewports, model space, or paper space.
- **Logging.** If enabled, creates an ASCII text file that contains a record of all batch plotting activities.
- **Plot Stamping.** Allows a text string of up to 50 characters to be placed in one corner of the drawing.

Creating a new batch plot list

The first step in using the **Batch Plot** utility is to make a list of the drawings to be plotted. Activate the **File** tab and use the following steps (see Figure 10-31):

1. Pick the **Add Drawing...** button to add a drawing to the **Drawing File** list. This displays the **Add Drawing File** dialog box, which is a standard file dialog box. Select the desired drawing and pick **OK**.
2. Pick the drawing name in the **Drawing File** list to highlight it then pick the **Associate PCP/PC2...** button. This displays the **Associate PCP/PC2 File** dialog box, Figure 10-32A. Select the desired file and pick the **Open** button. The PC file is displayed in the file list next to its drawing file. See Figure 10-32B.
3. Follow the procedure in steps 1 and 2 for all files to be added to the batch plot list.
4. Pick the **Save List As...** button to save the completed batch plot list. The **Save Batch Plot List File** dialog box is displayed. Provide a name for the file and pick **Save**. This saves the file with a .bp2 file extension. This file is used by **Batch Plot** to plot your drawings.

Figure 10-31.
The **Batch Plot Utility** dialog box.

Drawings listed here

Pick to add a drawing to the list

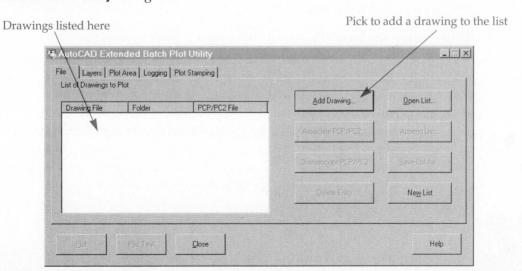

Figure 10-32.
A—PC files are selected in the **Associate PCP/PC2 File** dialog box. B—The PC file is displayed in the file list next to its drawing file.

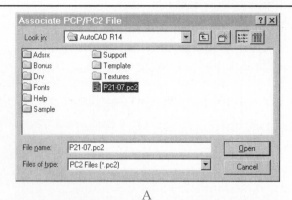

A

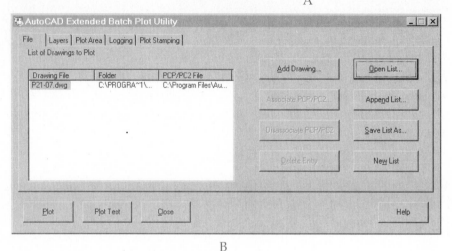

B

Editing a batch plot list file

You can open an existing batch plot list file and add or delete files. In addition, you can attach (append) another .bp2 file to the current one. All of these functions are done in the **AutoCAD Extended Batch Plot Utility** dialog box.

- **Add a drawing to the list.** Pick the **Add Drawing...** button and follow steps 1 and 2 as described in the last section.
- **Delete a file from the list.** To delete a file from the current list, highlight the file name and pick the **Delete Entry** button.
- **Append a list to the current one.** Pick the **Append List...** button to display the **Append Batch Plot List File** dialog box. Select the desired .bp2 file and pick **Open**. The selected file is appended to the end of the current one, and all files are displayed in the list box.

Plotting specific layers

The **Layers** tab allows you to specify which layers you wish to turn off during plotting. Use the following procedure:

1. Highlight the drawing file name to display its layers.
2. Select all layers you do not want plotted and pick the **Off** button. See Figure 10-33.
3. If you turn off layers that should be plotted, select them and then pick the **On** button.
4. If you want to delete any changes made to the on/off settings, pick the **Refresh** button. The warning Refreshing the Layer List will reload all the layers from the current drawing. Do you wish to proceed? is displayed. Pick **OK** to continue.

Figure 10-33.
The **Layers** tab enables layers to be turned off during plotting.

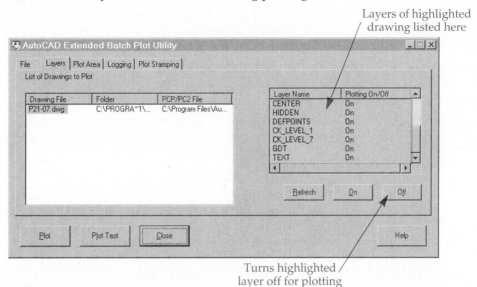

Layers of highlighted
drawing listed here

Turns highlighted
layer off for plotting

Selecting the area to plot

The **Plot Area** tab enables you to control the area of the drawing you wish to plot. Three areas in this tab allow you to control what is plotted. See Figure 10-34.

- **Plot Area.** Radio buttons provide the selections of **Display**, **Extents**, **Limits**, and **View**. When active, the **View** drop-down list shows all named views in the drawing file.
- **Plot Space.** Select either the **Model Space** or **Paper Space** radio button. In addition, a viewport can be selected from the **Viewport** drop-down list.
- **Plot Scale.** Change the plot scale here if necessary. If a PC file has not been associated with the selected drawing file, then the plot scale area will reflect the most recent setting in the **Print/Plot Configuration** dialog box. If a PC file has been associated to the selected drawing file, then the **Plot Scale** area displays the settings specified in plot parameters file. Make it a habit to check this area carefully to ensure that the drawing is plotted at the proper scale.

Figure 10-34.
The **Plot Area** tab allows you to select the area, space, and scale of drawing to be plotted.

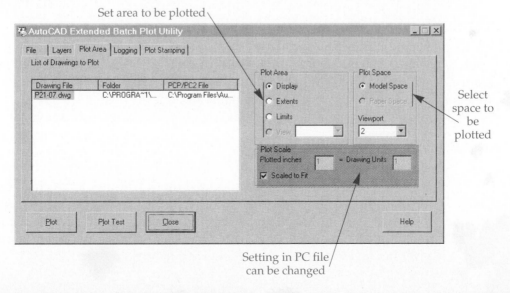

Set area to be plotted

Select
space to
be
plotted

Setting in PC file
can be changed

Logging the batch plot process

Logging creates a text file record of the batch file process. Pick the **Logging** tab to display these options. See Figure 10-35. Logging is enabled by default, but can be disabled by picking the **Enable Logging** check box. The ebatchp.log file is saved in the AutoCAD R14\Support\Ebatchp folder. You can change the name and location of the log file by entering a new name in the **Log File name** text box, or by picking the **Browse...** button to display the **Batch Log File** dialog box. This is a standard files dialog box for specifying the name and location of a file.

Figure 10-35.
The **Logging** tab provides control over the batch plot log file.

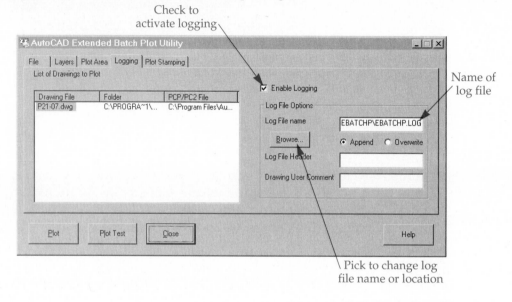

A record of each batch plot is added (appended) to the ebatchp.log file by default. If keeping a record of batch plotting is important, do not disable this feature, and be sure that the **Append** radio button is selected. Pick the **Overwrite** radio button if you want only the last batch plotted file to be kept on record.

Two options allow you to add lines of text to the log file.
- **Log File Header.** The first line of text printed in the current log file.
- **Drawing User Comment.** The first line of text printed in the log for a specific drawing. A different line of text can be entered for each drawing.

Placing a plot stamp on the drawing

A plot stamp is a line of text up to 50 characters that is located in one of the four corners of the drawing. Pick the **Plot Stamping** tab, and refer to Figure 10-36. Plot stamping is enabled by default but can be disabled by picking the **Enable Plot Stamping** check box. The following plot stamp options are available:
- **Corner.** Select one of the four drawing corners in the drop-down list for the stamp location.
- **Orientation.** Select either horizontal or vertical text alignment from the **Orientation** drop-down list.
- **Stamp Gap.** The plot stamp can be located up to 1″ from the specified corner.
- **Text Style.** Displays the text style to be used for the stamp. The Standard text style is displayed here until you select a new one using the **Change...** button.
- **Layer.** Displays the layer to be used for the stamp. Layer 0 is set by default, but a new one can be specified by picking the **Change...** button.

Figure 10-36.
The **Plot Stamping** tab enables you to place a line of text up to 50 characters in one corner of the drawing.

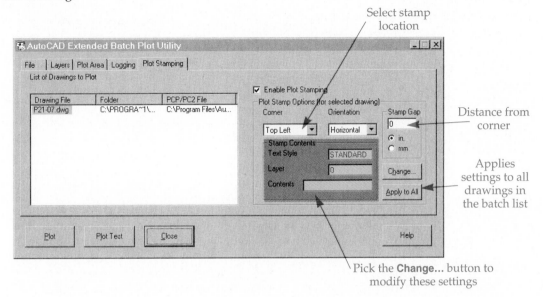

Select stamp location

Distance from corner

Applies settings to all drawings in the batch list

Pick the **Change...** button to modify these settings

- **Contents.** Displays the text contents to be used for the stamp. This is blank by default but new text can be entered by picking the **Change...** button.
- **Change... button.** Displays the **Plot Stamp Contents** dialog box, Figure 10-37A. Select the appropriate text style and layer for the stamp by using the respective drop-down list. The contents of the stamp can be imported from a text file by picking the **File...** button, or up to 50 characters of text can be entered in the **Contents** text box. In addition, a pre-defined field, such as file name or time and date, can be used for the stamp. First pick the **Pre-defined Fields** drop-down list then pick the field you wish to use. Pick the **Insert** button and the field is displayed in the text box. See Figure 10-37B.
- **Apply to All.** The options in the **Plot Stamping** tab are applied to all drawings in the batch plot. AutoCAD defaults to the Standard text style and layer 0 if some drawings do not contain the specified text styles and layers.

Figure 10-37.
A—The **Plot Stamp Contents** dialog box allows you to specify the text style, layer, and contents of the plot stamp. B—The **Time/Date Plotted** field is selected from the drop-down list.

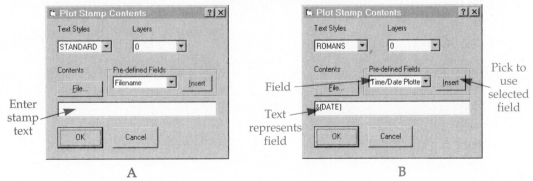

Enter stamp text

Field

Text represents field

Pick to use selected field

A   B

Before you use one of the specified fields, be sure that you have specified a value for that field in the AutoCAD drawing. For example, enter a value for **PROJECTNAME** in AutoCAD prior to using **Batch Plot** if you want that field to be the plot stamp.

Command: **PROJECTNAME.**↵
New value for PROJECTNAME, or . for none <"">:
  SteelFab-230-411-B.↵

Any AutoCAD system variable can be used as text for the plot stamp. For example, if you wished to display, for client information and billing purposes, the total editing time spent on a drawing, enter the **TDINDWG** variable in the **Contents** text box as &(TDINDWG).

Testing the batch plot

The **Plot Test** button provides a quick test for your batch plot file without actually plotting the drawings. The results of the test, including any problems that are found, are displayed in the **Plot Test Results** dialog box. A variety of problems can occur, especially if the drawing is being plotted on a different computer than the one it was drawn on. This is common with drawings that contain xref files (see Chapter 24), special fonts, and symbols. Always try to remedy these problems before performing a batch plot.

The **PACK** command copies all files associated with a drawing to a selected location. This is a bonus tool and is available if a full install of AutoCAD was performed. See Appendix C for information on this command.

Plotting a batch plot list

After the list is complete you can choose to close the current session without plotting by picking the **Close** button. Be sure to save the current list first.

Pick the **Plot** button to begin plotting the list. The **Batch Plot Progress** dialog box displays the status of the plotting. Pick the **Cancel Remaining Drawings** button if you wish to stop the plotting.

When the plotting begins you can open AutoCAD and continue working on other projects, or open any other application while **Batch Plot** works in the background. Minimize the **AutoCAD Batch Plot Utility** dialog box to remove it from the screen.

Plotting Hints

Plotting can slow down productivity in an office or a classroom if not done efficiently. Establish and follow a procedure for using the plotter. For a company, this might involve adding a special night shift to plot drawings when computer operators are not working. In a school, a student may be assigned to plot drawings, or specific times can be set aside for the task. In any situation, instruct all drafters, engineers, and other plotter users of the proper operating procedures. Post these in strategic locations.

Planning your plots

Planning is again the key word when dealing with plots. In the same way you planned the drawing, you must plan the plot. The following items need to be considered when planning:

✓ Size and type of plotting media, such as bond paper, vellum, or polyester film.

✓ Type of title block.

✓ Location and scale of multiple views.

✓ Origin location.

✓ Scale of the drawing.

✓ Color, thickness, and types of pens to be used.

✓ Speed of pens.

✓ Orientation of 3D views.

✓ Portion to be plotted: view, window, display, limits, or extents.

This is only a sample of decisions that should be made before you begin plotting. Remember, the plotter is the funnel that all drawings must go through before they are evaluated, approved, and sent to production or the client. When a bottleneck develops at the plotter, the time savings of a CAD system can be drastically reduced.

Both schools and businesses can make use of plotting request forms. The example shown in Figure 10-38 is used in a school's CAD lab. Its purpose is to require AutoCAD users to prepare as much as possible before plotting. Use this form or develop one of your own to increase your plotting efficiency.

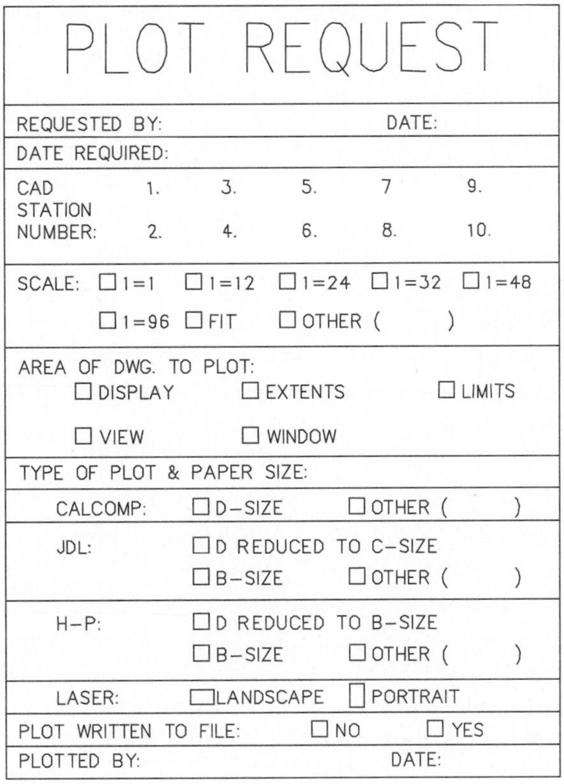

Figure 10-38.
An example of a plotting request form.

```
PLOT REQUEST

REQUESTED BY:                          DATE:
DATE REQUIRED:
CAD          1.     3.     5.     7      9.
STATION
NUMBER:      2.     4.     6.     8.     10.

SCALE:  □1=1   □1=12   □1=24   □1=32   □1=48
        □1=96  □FIT    □OTHER (        )

AREA OF DWG. TO PLOT:
        □DISPLAY       □EXTENTS        □LIMITS
        □VIEW          □WINDOW
TYPE OF PLOT & PAPER SIZE:
   CALCOMP:   □D-SIZE        □OTHER (      )
   JDL:       □D REDUCED TO C-SIZE
              □B-SIZE        □OTHER (      )
   H-P:       □D REDUCED TO B-SIZE
              □B-SIZE        □OTHER (      )
   LASER:     □LANDSCAPE    □PORTRAIT
PLOT WRITTEN TO FILE:      □NO      □YES
PLOTTED BY:                          DATE:
```

Eliminate unnecessary plots

One goal of using computers for design and manufacturing is to reduce or eliminate paper drawings. This is a difficult concept for many people to grasp because there is nothing to hold in their hands. When design data proceeds directly to manufacturing, there is no paper drawing to approve, touch, mark on, or keep lying around. Therefore, many plots are unnecessary.

The easiest way to eliminate the problems associated with plotting is to eliminate plotting. Make plots *only* when absolutely necessary. This results in time and money savings. A few additional suggestions include the following:

✓ Obtain approvals of designs while the drawings are on the screen. This procedure is good in theory, but for most people it is still easier to check a paper print of a drawing for errors.

✓ Transfer files or disks for the checker's comments.

✓ Create a special layer with a unique color for mark-ups. Freeze or erase this layer when finally making a plot.

✓ Use a "redlining" software package, such as Autodesk View, that enables the checker to review the drawing and apply markups to it without using AutoCAD.

✓ Classroom instructors should check drawings on disk. Use a special layer for instructor comments.

✓ Use a printer when check prints are sufficient.

✓ Avoid making plots for backups. Rather, save your drawing files in three different locations, such as hard disk, flexible disk at workstation, and flexible disk at another location. These may also be supplemented with a backup on tape cartridges, optical disks, or other external storage devices.

If you must plot...

Industry still exists on a paper-based system. Therefore, it is important that plotters are used efficiently. That means using the plotter only for what is required. Here are a few hints for doing just that.

✓ Ask yourself, "Do I *really* need a plot?" If the answer is an unqualified *yes*, then proceed.

✓ Plan your plot!

✓ Pick the least busy time to make the plot.

✓ If more than one plotter is available, use the smallest, least complex model.

✓ Select the smallest piece of paper possible.

✓ Use the lowest quality paper possible. Select bond for check plots and vellum or polyester film for final plots.

✓ Decide on only one color and thickness of pen to make the plot.

✓ Use the most inexpensive pen possible. Obtain a fiber tip or disposable pen for check plots. Choose a wet ink, steel, jewel, or ceramic tip pen only for final plots on vellum or polyester film.

✓ Enter the fastest pen speed that will still achieve quality without the pen skipping.

✓ Use a continuous linetype when possible. Hidden and center linetypes increase plot time significantly and cause pen wear. This is not as much of a factor with penless plotters, such as laser and inkjet.

✓ Create batch plot files and use batch plotting at times when plotter and printer use is light.

Producing quality plots

The time comes when you must plot the highest quality drawing for reproduction, evaluation, or client use. Then, use your plotter in a manner that does the job right the first time. Keep in mind these points before making that final plot.

✓ If you have several plotters, choose the one that will produce the quality of print you need. Select the right tool for the job.

✓ Choose the paper size appropriate for the drawing.

✓ Set pen speeds slow enough to produce good lines without skipping.

✓ Use the proper ink for your climate.

Chapter Test

Write your answers in the spaces provided.

1. What is paper space? _____

   _____

   _____

2. What is the "hole" cut into paper space with the **MVIEW** command? _____

   _____

   _____

3. What is the quickest way to display a paper space border and title block that contains a single floating model space viewport? _____

   _____

   _____

4. Give the values of the **TILEMODE** variable for the following settings.

   A. Paper space: **TILEMODE** = _____

   B. Model space: **TILEMODE** = _____

5. What command allows you to cut viewports into paper space? _____

6. What command enables the user to insert a template drawing on the screen and create a layout of multiple viewports? _____

7. What option of the command in Question 6 allows the user to insert viewports?

   _____

8. What command is used to generate paper copies of your drawings? _____

   _____

9. What **CMDDIA** value is needed to issue plot prompts at the Command: line? _____

   _____

10. List the different displays of a drawing you can select to plot using the **Print/Plot Configuration** dialog box. _____

_____

_____

11. Define a "plot file" and explain how it is used._____

_____

_____

12. Define a "plot queue."_____

_____

_____

13. Explain when you would rotate a plot 90° clockwise. _____

_____

_____

14. What do you enter in the dialog box to make the plotted drawing twice the size of the soft copy drawing? _____

_____

15. What do you enter to specify a scale of 1/4″ = 1′-0″? _____

_____

16. Name the system variable that controls the display of the **Print/Plot Configuration** dialog box._____

17. How do you stop a plot in progress? _____

_____

18. Name the pull-down menu where the **Print...** command is found. _____

19. How do you add several printers or plotters to the **Select Device** area of the **Device and Default Selection** dialog box? _____

_____

_____

20. What is the difference between a .pc2 file and a .pcp file? _____

_____

_____

21. How do you save a plot file named PLOT1 to a 3.5″ disk?_____

_____

_____

_____

22. How do you set pen assignments in a dialog box?_____

_____

_____

_____

23. Identify the two types of paper orientation. _____

_____

AutoCAD and its Applications—Basics

24. Specify the option button that is picked to make millimeters the units for all plot specifications. _____

25. List an advantage of the **Partial** plot preview format._____
_____
_____

26. Cite two advantages of the **Full** plot preview format. _____
_____
_____

27. Identify at least one disadvantage of the **Full** plot preview format._____
_____

28. What option is set in the **Print/Plot Configuration** dialog box when you want to export a raster file via an ADI device? _____

29. Explain why you should plan your plots. _____
_____
_____

30. Provide the best method to speed up the plotting process in a classroom or company. _____
_____
_____

31. Check prints are best generated on a(n) _____.

32. What type of paper and pens should be used for a check plot? _____
_____

33. What type of paper and pens should be used for a final plot? _____
_____

Drawing Problems

1. Create a new B-size decimal template drawing for use with mechanical (machine) parts. Use the following guidelines:
   A. Use a wizard to set up the border and title block, or use one of your own paper space drawings.
   B. Establish the appropriate settings to make this a half-scale (1"=2") drawing.
   C. Create three different text styles. One to plot at 1/8" high, another at 3/16" high, and a third at 1/4" high. Set the text heights and **LTSCALE** according to the values given in the chart in this chapter.
   D. Save the drawing template as MECH-B-HALF.DWT.

2. Create a new C-size architectural template drawing. Use the following guidelines:
   A. Use a wizard to set up the border and title block, or use one of your own paper space drawings. Set units to architectural and set the area to 160' × 120'. Select to work on the drawing without the layout visible.

B. Establish the appropriate settings to make this a 1/8"=1′ scale drawing.

C. Create three different text styles. One to plot at 1/8" high, another at 3/16" high, and a third at 1/4" high. Set the text heights and **LTSCALE** according to the values given in the chart in this chapter.

D. Save the drawing as ARCH-C-EIGHTH.DWT.

3. Create a new C-size civil engineering template drawing. Use the following guidelines:

A. Use a wizard to set up the border and title block, or use one of your own paper space drawings. Set units to engineering, angle to surveyor, angle measure to east, angle direction to counterclockwise, and set the area to 1000′ × 750′. Select to work on the drawing while viewing the layout.

B. Establish the appropriate settings to make this a 1"=50′ scale drawing.

C. Create three different text styles. One to plot at 1/8" high, another at 3/16" high, and a third at 1/4" high. Set the text heights and **LTSCALE** according to the values given in the chart in this chapter.

D. Save the drawing as CIVIL-C-1=50.DWT.

4. Open one of your drawings from Chapter 8. Plot the drawing on B-size paper using the **Limits** option. Use different color pens for each color in the drawing.

5. Zoom in on a portion of the drawing used for Problem 4 and select the **Display** plotting option. Rotate the plot 90° and fit it on the paper.

6. Using the same drawing used in Problem 4, select **PLOT** and use the **Window** option. Window a detailed area of the drawing. Plot the drawing to fit the paper size chosen.

*For problems 7–9, draw the views needed to describe each object completely. Set up appropriate layers, colors, linetypes, and use a template drawing to begin each problem. Do not dimension the drawings. Plot the drawings in paper space using a scale of 1:1. Save the problem as **P10-(problem number)**.*

7.

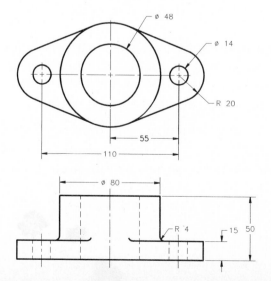

8.

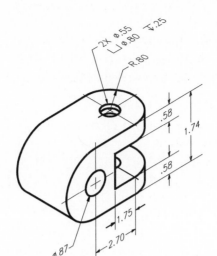

2X ⌀.55 ⍱.25
⌴ ⌀.80
R.80
.58
1.74
.58
1.75
2.70
⌀.87

9.

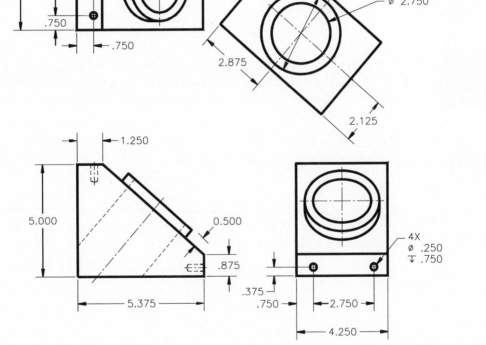

4.250 2.750
.750
.750

⌀ 3.750
⌀ 2.750
2.875
2.125

1.250
5.000
0.500
.875
5.375

4X
⌀ .250
⍱ .750
.375
.750 2.750
4.250

10. Draw the schematic shown on an A-size sheet at full scale. Use a template drawing with a single floating model space viewport. The size of the components is not important, but keep the same proportions as shown. Plotted text height should be 1/8". Save the drawing as P10-10. Plot in paper space at 1:1.

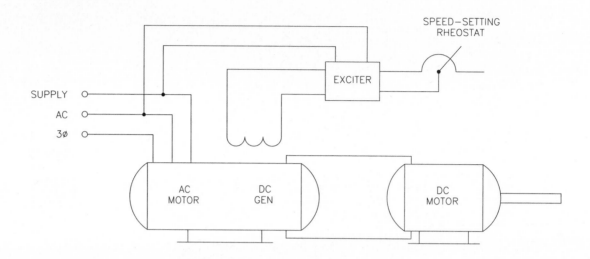

11. Draw the schematic shown on a B-size sheet at full scale. Use a template drawing with a single floating model space viewport. The size of the components is not important, but keep the same proportions as shown. Plotted text height should be 1/8". Save the drawing as P10-11. Plot in paper space at 1:1.

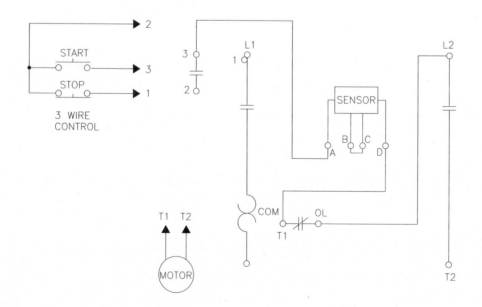

12. Draw the stainless steel stud shown on a B-size sheet at a scale of 2:1 (2 times actual size). Use a template drawing with a single floating model space viewport. Do not dimension the drawing. Be sure that paper space is active before using the **PLOT** command. Create a .pcp file for this drawing. Save the drawing as P10-12. Set the plot scale at 1:1.

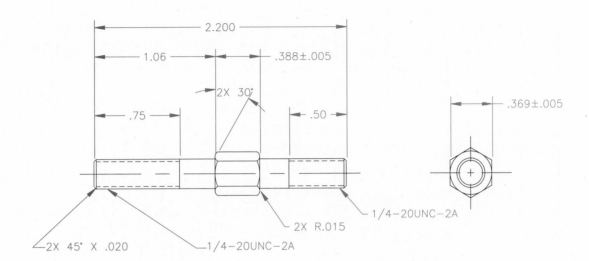

Roof framing details. (Mark Hartman)

Chapter 11

Basic Editing Commands

Learning Objectives

After completing this chapter, you will be able to:

- Draw chamfers and angled corners with the **CHAMFER** command.
- Use the **FILLET** command to draw fillets, rounds, and other rounded corners.
- Remove a portion of a line, circle, or arc using the **BREAK** command.
- Relocate an object using the **MOVE** command.
- Use the **TRIM**, **EXTEND**, and **LENGTHEN** commands to edit an object.
- Use the **CHANGE** command to revise an existing object.
- Make single and multiple copies of existing objects using the **COPY** command.
- Draw a mirror image of an object.
- Change the angular position of an object using the **ROTATE** command.
- Use the **ALIGN** command to move and rotate an object simultaneously.
- Change the size of an object using the **SCALE** command.
- Modify the length and height of an object using the **STRETCH** command.
- Set the **PICKAUTO**, **PICKFIRST**, and **GRIPS** system variables to vary selection techniques.
- Create selection sets and object groups.

This chapter explains commands and methods for changing a drawing. With manual drafting techniques, editing and modifying a drawing can take hours or even days. AutoCAD, however, makes the same editing tasks simpler and quicker. In Chapter 4 you learned how to draw and erase lines. The **ERASE** command is one of the most commonly used editing commands. You also learned how to select objects by picking with the cursor or using a window box, crossing box, window polygon, crossing polygon, or fence. The items selected are referred to as a *selection set*.

Many of the same selection methods and techniques can be used for the editing commands discussed in this chapter. You will learn how to draw angled and rounded corners. You will also learn how to move, copy, rotate, scale, and create a mirror image of an existing object. These features are found in the **Modify** toolbar and **Modify** pull-down menus. The editing commands discussed in this chapter are basically divided into two general groups—editing individual features of a drawing and editing major portions of a drawing. Commands typically used to edit individual features of a drawing include the following:

- **CHAMFER**
- **FILLET**
- **BREAK**
- **TRIM**
- **EXTEND**
- **LENGTHEN**

The following commands are used to edit entire drawings or major portions of a drawing, though they can be used to edit individual features:

- **MOVE**
- **COPY**
- **ROTATE**
- **MIRROR**
- **SCALE**
- **STRETCH**
- **CHANGE**
- **GROUP**

Drawing Chamfers

A *chamfer* in mechanical drafting is a small angled surface used to relieve a sharp corner. AutoCAD defines a chamfer as "any angled corner on the drawing." The size of a chamfer is determined by its distance from the corner. A 45° chamfer is the same distance from the corner in each direction, Figure 11-1. Chamfers were introduced in Chapter 5.

Figure 11-1.
Examples of different chamfers.

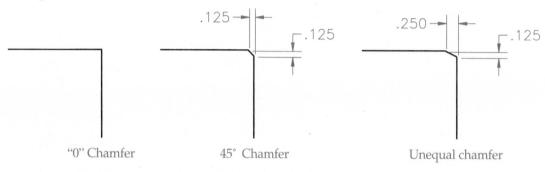

"0" Chamfer   45° Chamfer   Unequal chamfer

CHAMFER
CHA

Modify
 ↪ **Chamfer**

Modify
toolbar

Chamfer

Chamfers are drawn between two lines that may, or may not, intersect. Chamfers can also connect polylines, xlines, and rays. The **CHAMFER** command can be accessed by selecting the **Chamfer** button in the **Modify** toolbar, by picking **Chamfer** from the **Modify** pull-down menu, or by typing CHA or CHAMFER at the Command: prompt. The following shows the default values and the options that are available when you enter the **CHAMFER** command:

> Command: **CHA** *or* **CHAMFER.**⌐
> (TRIM mode) Current chamfer Dist1 = 0.5, Dist2 = 0.5
> Polyline/Distance/Angle/Trim/Method/⟨Select first line⟩:

The current settings are displayed for your reference. Chamfers are established with two distances, or a distance and angle. The default value is 0.5 for both distances. This produces a 45° × 0.5 chamfered corner. The following is a brief description of each **CHAMFER** option:

- **Polyline.** Use this option if you want to chamfer all of the eligible corners on a polyline. The term "eligible" means that the chamfer distance is small enough to work on the corner.
- **Distance.** This option lets you set the chamfer distance for each line from the corner.
- **Angle.** This option uses a chamfer distance on the first selected line and applies a chamfer angle to determine the second line chamfer.
- **Trim.** Enter this to set the **Trim** mode. If **Trim** is on, the selected lines are trimmed or extended as required from the corner before creating the chamfer line. If **No trim** is active, the **Trim** mode is off. In this case, the selected lines are not trimmed or extended and only the chamfer line is added.
- **Method.** This is a toggle that sets the chamfer method to either **Distance** or **Angle**. **Distance** and **Angle** values can be set without affecting each other.

Setting the chamfer distance

The chamfer distance must be set before you can draw chamfers. The distances that you set remain in effect until changed. Most drafters set the chamfer distance as exact values, but you can also pick two points to set the distance. The following procedure is used to set the chamfer distance:

Command: **CHA** *or* **CHAMFER**↵
(TRIM mode) Current chamfer Dist1 = 0.5, Dist2 = 0.5
Polyline/Distance/Angle/Trim/Method/⟨Select first line⟩: **D**↵
Enter first chamfer distance ⟨0⟩: *(specify a distance, such as .25)*
Enter second chamfer distance ⟨0.25⟩: *(press [Enter] for the current distance, or type a new value)*
Command:

Now you are ready to draw chamfers. Enter the **CHAMFER** command and select the first and second lines:

Command: **CHA** *or* **CHAMFER**↵
(TRIM mode) Current chamfer Dist1 = 0.25, Dist2 = 0.25
Polyline/Distance/Angle/Trim/Method/⟨Select first line⟩: *(pick the first line)*
Select second line: *(pick the second line)*

After the lines are picked, AutoCAD automatically chamfers the corner. Objects can be chamfered even when the corners do not meet. AutoCAD extends the lines as required to generate the specified chamfer and complete the corner if **TRIMMODE** is on. If **TRIMMODE** is off, AutoCAD does not extend the lines to complete the corner. This is discussed later.

If the specified chamfer distance is so large that the chamfered objects disappear, AutoCAD does not perform the chamfer. Instead, a message such as 2 lines were too short is given. If you want to chamfer additional corners, press [Enter] to repeat the **CHAMFER** command. The results of several chamfering operations are shown in Figure 11-2.

Figure 11-2.
Using the **CHAMFER** command.

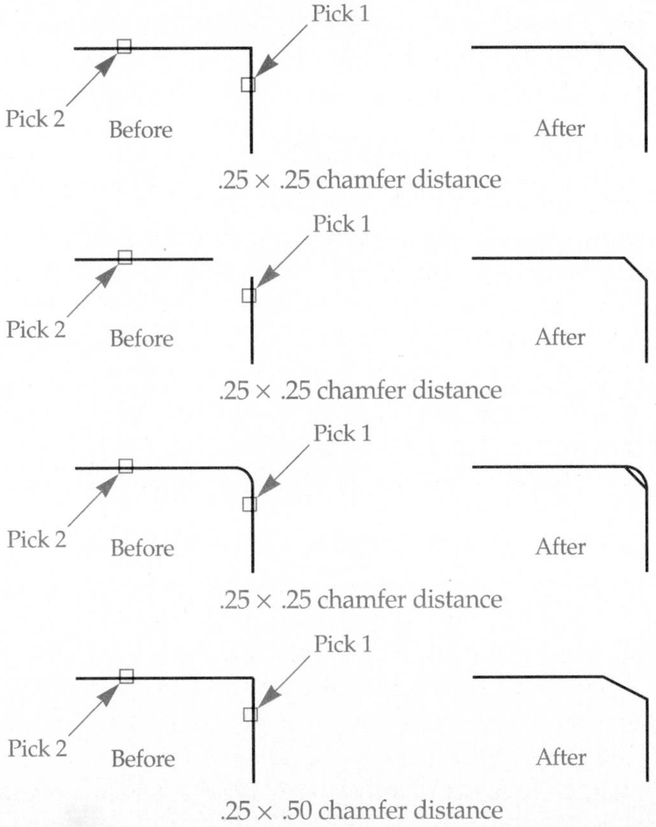

Pick 1 / Pick 2 / Before / After — .25 × .25 chamfer distance

Pick 1 / Pick 2 / Before / After — .25 × .25 chamfer distance

Pick 1 / Pick 2 / Before / After — .25 × .25 chamfer distance

Pick 1 / Pick 2 / Before / After — .25 × .50 chamfer distance

Chamfering the corners of a polyline

Polylines are objects that can be made up of many different widths and shapes. Polylines are drawn and edited in Chapters 16 and 17. All corners of a closed polyline can be chamfered at one time. Enter the **CHAMFER** command, select the **Polyline** option, and then select the polyline. The corners of the polyline are chamfered to the distance values set. If the polyline was drawn without using the **Close** option, the beginning corner is not chamfered, as shown in Figure 11-3.

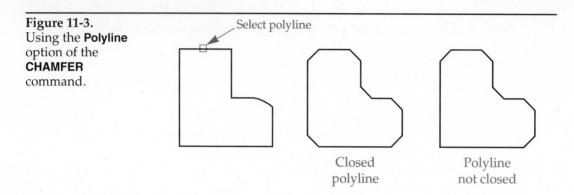

Figure 11-3.
Using the **Polyline** option of the **CHAMFER** command.

Select polyline

Closed polyline

Polyline not closed

Setting the chamfer angle

Instead of setting two chamfer distances, you can set the chamfer distance for one line and an angle to determine the chamfer to the second line. To do this, use the **Angle** option:

Command: **CHA** *or* **CHAMFER.**⏎
Polyline/Distance/Angle/Trim/Method/⟨Select first line⟩: **A.**⏎
Enter chamfer length on the first line ⟨0⟩: *(enter a chamfer distance, .5 for example)*
Enter chamfer angle from the first line ⟨0⟩: *(enter an angle, 45 for example)*
Command:

Now, you are ready to enter the **CHAMFER** command again and draw a chamfer with the **Angle** option, as shown in Figure 11-4. You can see in the following command sequence that distance and angle are now the defaults:

Command: **CHA** *or* **CHAMFER.**⏎
(TRIM mode) Current chamfer Length = 0.5, Angle = 45.0
Polyline/Distance/Angle/Trim/Method/⟨Select first line⟩: *(pick line 1)*
Select second line: *(pick line 2)*
Command:

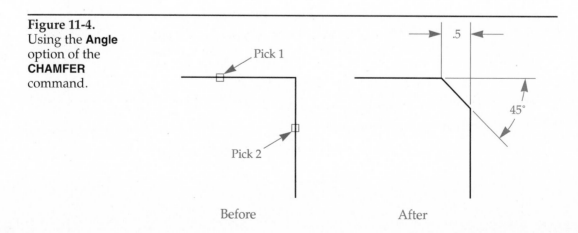

Figure 11-4.
Using the **Angle** option of the **CHAMFER** command.

Pick 1

Pick 2

.5

45°

Before

After

Setting the chamfer method

When you set chamfer distances or distance and angle, AutoCAD maintains the setting until you change it. You can set the values for each method without affecting the other. Use the **Method** option if you want to toggle between drawing chamfers by **Distance** and by **Angle**. The default option contains the values that you previously set:

> Command: **CHA** *or* **CHAMFER**↵
> (TRIM mode) Current chamfer Length = 0.5, Angle = 45.0
> Polyline/Distance/Angle/Trim/Method/⟨Select first line⟩: **M**↵
> Distance/Angle ⟨Angle⟩: **D**↵
> Polyline/Distance/Angle/Trim/Method/⟨Select first line⟩: *(pick line 1)*
> Select second line: *(pick line 2)*
> Command:

Setting the chamfer Trim mode

You can have the selected lines automatically trimmed with the chamfer, or you can have the selected lines remain in the drawing after the chamfer, as shown in Figure 11-5. To set this, enter the **Trim** option and then select either T for **Trim** or N for **No trim**:

> Command: **CHA** *or* **CHAMFER**↵
> Polyline/Distance/Angle/Trim/Method/⟨Select first line⟩: **T**↵
> Trim/No trim ⟨Trim⟩: **N**↵
> Polyline/Distance/Angle/Trim/Method/⟨Select first line⟩: *(pick line 1)*
> Select second line: *(pick line 2)*
> Command:

You can also use the **TRIMMODE** system variable to set **Trim** or **No trim** by typing TRIMMODE at the Command: prompt. A 1 setting trims the lines before chamfering, while a 0 setting does not trim the lines.

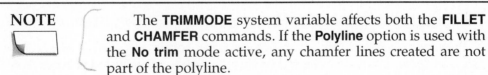

NOTE   The **TRIMMODE** system variable affects both the **FILLET** and **CHAMFER** commands. If the **Polyline** option is used with the **No trim** mode active, any chamfer lines created are not part of the polyline.

Figure 11-5.
Using the **Trim** option of the **CHAMFER** command. A—With trim. B—With no trim.
C—The result when the lines do not extend to the corners.

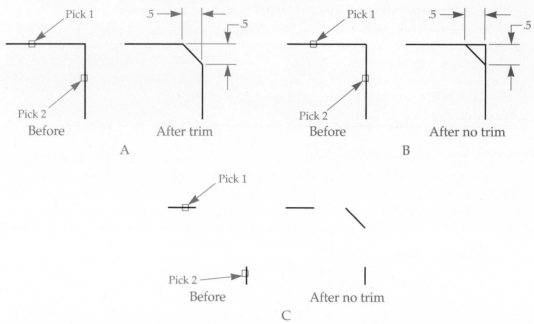

PROFESSIONAL TIP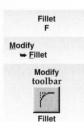

When the **CHAMFER** or **FILLET** command is set to **Trim**, lines that do not connect at a corner are automatically extended and the chamfer or fillet is applied. However, when the **No trim** option is used, these lines are not extended, but the chamfer or fillet is drawn anyway. If you have lines that are drawn short of a corner and want them to connect to the chamfer or fillet, you need to extend them if you draw in the **No trim** mode.

EXERCISE 11-2

❑ Begin a new drawing or use one of your templates.
❑ Draw the "Before" object shown in Figure 11-5 and then use the **Trim** mode as needed to create the "After" object.
❑ Save the drawing as EX11-2.

Drawing Rounded Corners

In mechanical drafting, an inside rounded corner is called a *fillet*. An outside rounded corner is called a *round*. AutoCAD refers to all rounded corners as fillets.

Fillets were introduced in Chapter 5 when drawing filleted corners on rectangles with the **RECTANGF** command. The **FILLET** command draws a rounded corner between intersecting and nonintersecting lines, circles, and arcs. To access the **FILLET** command, pick the **Fillet** button on the **Modify** toolbar, select **Fillet** from the **Modify** pull-down menu, or type F or FILLET at the Command: prompt.

Fillet
F

Modify
⟿ Fillet

Modify
toolbar

Fillet

Fillets are sized by radius. The default radius is 0.5. A new radius is specified first by typing R on the prompt line for the **Radius** option as follows:

Command: **F** *or* **FILLET**↲
(TRIM mode) Current fillet radius = 0.5
Polyline/Radius/Trim/⟨Select first object⟩: **R**↲
Enter fillet radius ⟨*current*⟩: (*type the fillet radius, .25 for example, and press* [Enter]*, or press* [Enter] *to accept the current value*)

Once the fillet radius has been given, repeat the **FILLET** command to fillet the objects. The command sequence shown in Figure 11-6 is as follows:

Command: **F** *or* **FILLET**↲
(TRIM mode) Current fillet radius = 0.25
Polyline/Radius/Trim/⟨Select first object⟩: (*pick the first object to be filleted*)
Select second object: (*pick the other object to be filleted*)
Command:

Figure 11-6.
Using the **FILLET** command.

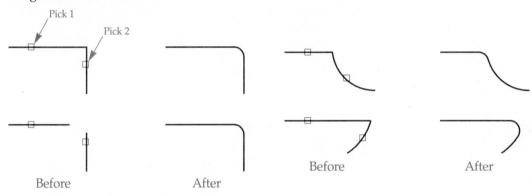

EXERCISE 11-3

☐ Begin a new drawing or use one of your templates.
☐ Draw the "Before" objects shown in Figure 11-6. Use the **FILLET** command as needed to create the "After" objects.
☐ Save the drawing as EX11-3.

Rounding the corners of a polyline

Fillets can be drawn at all corners of a closed polyline by selecting the **Polyline** option. The current fillet radius is used with this option. Polylines are fully explained in Chapters 16 and 17. The command sequence shown in Figure 11-7 is as follows:

Command: **F** *or* **FILLET**↲
(TRIM mode) Current fillet radius = 0.25
Polyline/Radius/Trim/⟨Select first object⟩: **P**↲
Select 2D polyline: (*pick the polyline*)
n lines were filleted
Command:

AutoCAD tells you how many lines were filleted. Then the Command: prompt returns. If the polyline was drawn without using the **Close** option, the beginning corner is not filleted.

Figure 11-7.
Using the **Polyline**
option of the **FILLET**
command.

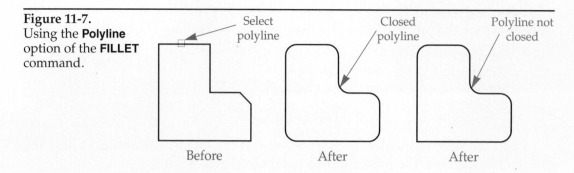

Setting the fillet Trim mode

The **TRIMMODE** system variable and the **Trim** option controls whether or not the **FILLET** command trims off object segments that extend beyond the fillet radius point. When the **Trim** mode is active, objects are trimmed. When the **Trim** mode is inactive, the filleted objects are not changed after the fillet is inserted, as shown in Figure 11-8. Use the **Trim** option like this:

```
Command: F or FILLET↵
(TRIM mode) Current fillet radius = 0.25
Polyline/Radius/Trim/〈Select first object〉: T↵
Trim/No trim 〈Trim〉: N↵
Polyline/Radius/Trim/〈Select first object〉: (pick the first object)
Select second object: (pick the second object)
Command:
```

Figure 11-8.
Using the **Trim** option of the **FILLET** command. A—With trim. B—With no trim.

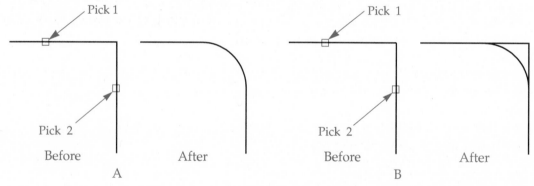

If the lines to be filleted do not connect at the corner, they are automatically extended when the **Trim** mode is on. However, they are not extended when using **No trim**. If you do not want a separation between the line and the filleted corner, extend the lines to the corner before filleting.

Filleting parallel lines

You can also draw a fillet between parallel lines. When parallel lines are selected, a radius is placed between the two lines. In **Trim** mode, a longer line is trimmed to match the length of a shorter line. The radius of a fillet between parallel lines is always half of the distance between the two lines, regardless of the **FILLETRAD** setting. The **FILLETRAD** setting does not change to this radius.

Chamfering and filleting objects together

Line objects (lines, arcs, and circles) can be filleted and chamfered to other line objects or to polyline objects. When the **Trim** option is active and a line object is connected to a polyline, the separate entities (the line, polyline, and filleted corner) become a single polyline. When the **No Trim** option is active, the entities retain their original properties and the fillet or chamfer is a line object. Polylines are discussed in Chapters 16 and 17.

All corners of a single polyline can be edited using the **Polyline** option of the **CHAMFER** or **FILLET** command. A single corner of a polyline can be filleted or chamfered by selecting the polyline on both sides of the corner. However, two separate polylines cannot be chamfered or filleted together. If you attempt this, AutoCAD will respond with a message at the Command: prompt: Cannot chamfer (fillet) polyline segments from different polylines.

Presetting the chamfer distance and the fillet radius

AutoCAD lets you set the chamfer distance and fillet radius to a designated value. This application was introduced in Chapter 5, with chamfering and filleting rectangles. Using this feature saves time when the chamfer distance and fillet radius remain constant on your drawing.

To set these values, use the **CHAMFERA**, **CHAMFERB**, **CHAMFERC**, **CHAMFERD**, and **FILLETRAD** system variables. The initial default of **CHAMFERA**, **CHAMFERB**, and **FILLETRAD** is 0.5. The initial default of **CHAMFERC** is 1.0, and **CHAMFERD** is 0.0. The values you set become the defaults until they are changed again.

The **CHAMFERA** and **CHAMFERB** variables are used for presetting the chamfer values for use with the **Distance** option. For example, if you want .125 for both chamfer distances, type the following:

    Command: **CHAMFERA**↵
    New value for CHAMFERA ⟨0.5⟩: **.125**↵
    Command: **CHAMFERB**↵
    New value for CHAMFERB ⟨0.5⟩: **.125**↵
    Command:

The next time the **CHAMFER** command is used, the default values displayed at the Command: prompt will be Current chamfer Dist1 = 0.125, Dist2 = 0.125.

The **CHAMFERC** and **CHAMFERD** system variables are related to the **Angle** option. **CHAMFERC** is the chamfer distance value, and **CHAMFERD** is the chamfer angle. These variables are set in the same way that **CHAMFERA** and **CHAMFERB** are set.

When you change the values of **CHAMFERC** and **CHAMFERD**, the new settings will be the default when you use the **Angle** option of the **CHAMFER** command. You can accept the defaults by pressing [Enter], or enter new values as desired.

When presetting the fillet radius, first enter FILLETRAD at the Command: prompt. You are then asked to enter a new value. For example, if you want .25 radius, type the following:

    Command: **FILLETRAD**↵
    New value for FILLETRAD ⟨0.5⟩: **.25**↵
    Command:

The FILLETRAD setting determines the default radius available when using the **FILLET** command. If you do not use the default radius, you must select the **Radius** option to reset the **FILLETRAD** variable.

> **PROFESSIONAL TIP** Using the **FILLET** or **CHAMFER** command with a 0 fillet radius or 0 chamfer distances is a quick and convenient way to create square corners.

EXERCISE 11-4

❏ Begin a new drawing or use one of your templates.
❏ Preset the chamfer and fillet values before drawing the following exercises.
❏ Draw the objects shown in Figure 11-1.
❏ Draw the "Before" objects shown in Figure 11-2 and use the **CHAMFER** command as needed to create the "After" objects.
❏ Draw the "Before" object shown in Figure 11-4 and use the **CHAMFER** command as needed to create the "After" object.
❏ Draw the "Before" objects shown in Figure 11-6 and use the **FILLET** command as needed to create the "After" objects.
❏ Save the drawing as EX11-4.

> **PROFESSIONAL TIP** The **CHAMFER** and **FILLET** commands can be used in any drafting field. For example, angled or rounded corners are frequently used in architectural drafting. If you are working in architectural drafting, be sure to set the chamfer or fillet distances in the proper units.

Removing a Section from an Object

BREAK
BR

Modify
↳ Break

Modify
toolbar

Break

The **BREAK** command is used to remove a portion of a line, circle, arc, trace, or polyline. The **BREAK** command can be accessed by picking the **Break** button in the **Modify** toolbar, by picking **Break** in the **Modify** pull-down menu, or by typing BR or BREAK at the Command: prompt.

The **BREAK** command can be used four different ways, depending on what you want to achieve. The following explains each of these applications:

* **1 point.** This sequence is used to split an object in two without removing a portion. For example, if you pick a line with this option, the line becomes two lines. There is no visible break, and both lines have an endpoint at the break point, as shown in Figure 11-9. The prompt line looks like this:

> Command: **BR** *or* **BREAK**↵
> Select object: *(pick the desired point on the object)*
> Enter second point (or F for first point): **@**↵
> Command:

The @ symbol means that the second break point is exactly where you picked the first break point.

Figure 11-9.
Using the **BREAK**
command to break
an object at a single
point, without
removing any of the
object.

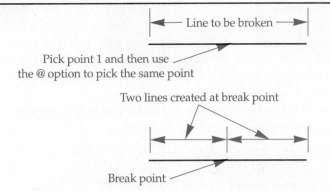

- **1 point select.** This sequence is used to split an object in two without removing a portion and allows you to select the location for the break. The previous **1 Point** sequence uses your Select object: pick point as the location of the break. The **1 Point Select** method allows you to use the **F** option to place the break point more accurately after selecting the object. The **F** option is used by typing F and pressing [Enter] to get a new first point prompt. The prompts look like this:

    Command: **BR** *or* **BREAK**↲
    Select object: *(pick the object)*
    Enter second point *(or F for first point)*: **F**↲
    Enter first point: *(pick the first break point)*
    Enter second point: **@**↲
    Command:

- **2 Points.** When you enter the **BREAK** command and pick an object at the Select object: prompt, the point you pick on the object becomes the first break point. AutoCAD then asks you to enter the second point. After you pick the second point, the object is broken between the two points, as shown in Figure 11-10. This is the command sequence:

    Command: **BR** *or* **BREAK**↲
    Select object: *(pick the object at the first break point)*
    Enter second point (or F for first point): *(pick the second break point)*
    Command:

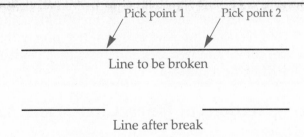

- **2 Point Select.** This sequence is used to split an object in two and remove a portion, just like the previous **2 Points** method. However, this application allows you to select a new first point by using the **F** option. First you select the object to break, then place the new location of the break by using the **F** option like this:

    Command: **BR** *or* **BREAK**↲
    Select object: *(pick the object)*
    Enter second point *(or F for first point)*: **F**↲
    Enter first point: *(pick the first break point)*
    Enter second point: *(pick the second break point)*
    Command:

When breaking arcs or circles, always work in a counterclockwise direction. Otherwise, you may break the portion of the arc or circle that you want to keep. If you want to break off the end of a line or arc, pick the first point on the object. Then pick the second point slightly beyond the end to be cut off, Figure 11-11. When you pick a second point that is not on the object, AutoCAD selects the nearest point on the object to the point you picked.

If you want to break a line from the point of intersection with another line, use the object snap **Intersect** mode as follows:

Command: **BR** *or* **BREAK**⏎
Select object: *(pick the line)*
Enter second point (or F for first point): **INT**⏎
of *(move the aperture to the intersection and pick)*
Command:

The line is now broken between the first point and the point of intersection.

Figure 11-11.
Using the **BREAK** command on circles and arcs.

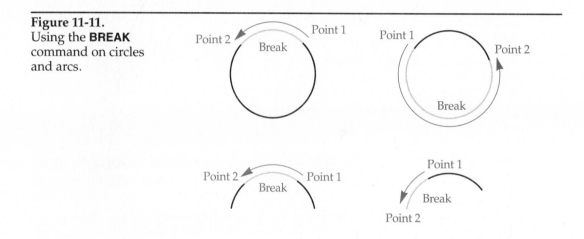

Trimming Sections of Lines, Circles, and Arcs

TRIM
TR

Modify
➥ Trim

Modify
toolbar

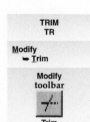

Trim

The **TRIM** command cuts lines, polylines, circles, arcs, ellipses, splines, xlines, and rays that extend beyond a desired point of intersection. To access the **TRIM** command, pick the **Trim** button in the **Modify** toolbar, pick **Trim** from the **Modify** pull-down menu, or type TR or TRIM at the Command: prompt.

The command requires that you pick a "cutting edge" and the object(s) to trim. The *cutting edge* can be an object that defines the point where the object you are trimming will be cut. A cutting edge can be an object such as a line, arc, or text. If two corners of an object overrun, select two cutting edges and two objects. Refer to Figure 11-12 as you go through the following sequence:

```
Command: TR or TRIM↵
Select cutting edges: (Projmode = UCS, Edgemode = No extend)
Select objects: (pick first cutting edge)
Select objects: (pick second cutting edge)
Select objects: ↵
⟨Select object to trim⟩/Project/Edge/Undo: (pick the first object to trim)
⟨Select object to trim⟩/Project/Edge/Undo: (pick the second object to trim)
⟨Select object to trim⟩/Project/Edge/Undo: ↵
Command:
```

Figure 11-12.
Using the **TRIM** command. Note the cutting edges.

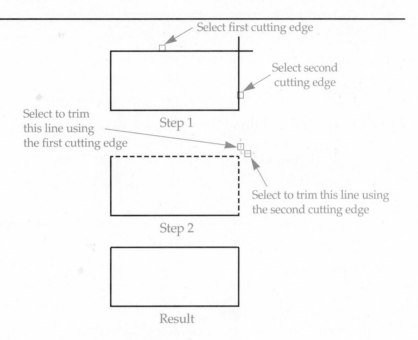

Select first cutting edge

Select second cutting edge

Step 1

Select to trim this line using the first cutting edge

Select to trim this line using the second cutting edge

Step 2

Result

Trimming to an implied intersection

An *implied intersection* is the point where two or more objects would meet if extended. Trimming to an implied intersection is possible using the **Edge** option of the **TRIM** command. When you enter the **Edge** option, the choices are **Extend** and **No extend**. When **Extend** is active, AutoCAD checks to see if the cutting edge object will extend to intersect the object to be trimmed. If so, the implied intersection point can be used to trim the object. This does not change the cutting edge object at all. The command sequence for the **TRIM** operation shown in Figure 11-13 is as follows:

```
Command: TR or TRIM↵
Select cutting edges: (Projmode = UCS, Edgemode = No extend)
Select objects: (pick the cutting edge)
Select objects: ↵
⟨Select object to trim⟩/Project/Edge/Undo: E↵
Extend/No extend ⟨No extend⟩: E↵
⟨Select object to trim⟩/Project/Edge/Undo: (pick the object to trim)
⟨Select object to trim⟩/Project/Edge/Undo: ↵
Command:
```

The **Edge** option can also be set using the **EDGEMODE** system variable. **Extend** is active when the **EDGEMODE** is 1. With this setting, the cutting edge object is checked to see if it will extend to intersect the object to be trimmed. Set the **EDGEMODE** system variable by typing EDGEMODE at the Command: prompt and entering the new value. The **EDGEMODE** variable is not stored within the drawing and always returns to the 0 default when opening a file.

Figure 11-13.
Trimming to an implied intersection.

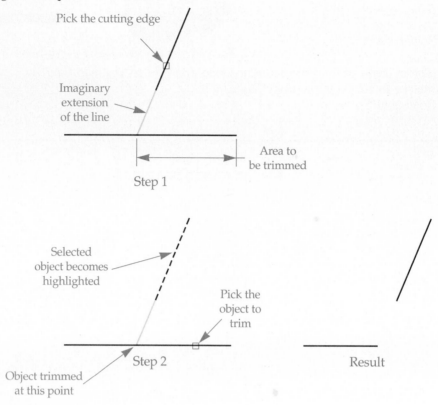

Using the Undo option

The **TRIM** command has an **Undo** option that allows you to cancel the previous trimming without leaving the command. This is useful when the result of a trim is not what you expected. To undo the previous trim, simply type U immediately after performing an unwanted trim. The trimmed portion returns and you can continue trimming other objects:

Command: **TR** *or* **TRIM**↵
Select cutting edges: (Projmode = UCS, Edgemode = No extend)
Select objects: *(pick the first cutting edge)*
Select objects: ↵
⟨Select object to trim⟩/Project/Edge/Undo: *(pick the object to trim)*
⟨Select object to trim⟩/Project/Edge/Undo: **U**↵
Command has been completely undone.
⟨Select object to trim⟩/Project/Edge/Undo: *(pick the object to trim)*
⟨Select object to trim⟩/Project/Edge/Undo: ↵
Command:

An introduction to the Project mode

In a 3D drawing environment, some lines may appear to intersect, but may not actually intersect. In such a case, using the **Project** option of the **TRIM** command can allow trimming operations. This option is also controlled by the **PROJMODE** system variable. Using AutoCAD for 3D drawing is explained in *AutoCAD and its Applications—Advanced, Release 14*.

Extending Lines

The **EXTEND** command is the opposite of the **TRIM** command. The **EXTEND** command is used to lengthen lines, elliptical arcs, rays, open polylines, and arcs to meet other objects. **EXTEND** does not work on closed polylines because an unconnected endpoint does not exist.

To use the **EXTEND** command, pick the **Extend** button in the **Modify** toolbar, select **Extend** from the **Modify** pull-down menu, or type EX or EXTEND at the Command: prompt. The command format is similar to **TRIM**. You are asked to select boundary edges, as opposed to cutting edges. *Boundary edges* are objects such as lines, arcs, or text to which the selected objects are extended. The command sequence is shown below and illustrated in Figure 11-14:

> Command: **EX** *or* **EXTEND**↵
> Select boundary edges: (Projmode = UCS, Edgemode = No extend)
> Select objects: *(pick the boundary edge)*
> Select objects: ↵
> ⟨Select object to extend⟩/Project/Edge/Undo: *(pick the object to extend)*
> ⟨Select object to extend⟩/Project/Edge/Undo: ↵
> Command:

If there is nothing for the selected line to meet, AutoCAD gives the message No edge in that direction or Entity does not intersect an edge.

Figure 11-14.
Using the **EXTEND** command. Note the boundary edges.

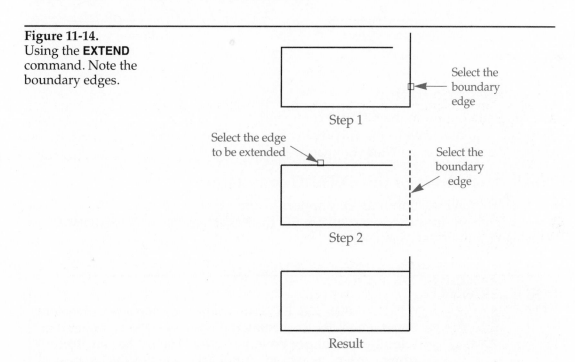

Select the boundary edge

Step 1

Select the edge to be extended

Select the boundary edge

Step 2

Result

Extending to an implied intersection

You can extend an object to an implied intersection using the **Edge** option in the **EXTEND** command. When you enter the **Edge** option, the choices are **Extend** and **No extend**, just as with the **TRIM** command. When **Extend** is active, the boundary edge object is checked to see if it intersects when extended. If so, the implied intersection point can be used as the boundary for the object to be extended, as shown in Figure 11-15. This does not change the boundary edge object at all.

Command: **EX** *or* **EXTEND**↵
Select boundary edges: (Projmode = UCS, Edgemode = No extend)
Select objects: *(pick the boundary edge)*
Select objects: ↵
⟨Select object to extend⟩/Project/Edge/Undo: **E**↵
Extend/No extend ⟨No extend⟩: **E**↵
⟨Select object to extend⟩/Project/Edge/Undo: *(pick the object to extend)*
⟨Select object to extend⟩/Project/Edge/Undo: ↵
Command:

The **Edge** option can also be set using the **EDGEMODE** system variable as previously discussed with the **TRIM** command.

Figure 11-15.
Extending to an implied intersection.

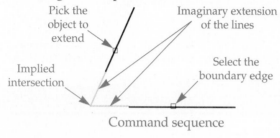
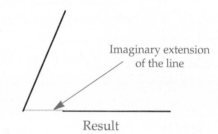

Command sequence   Result

Using the Undo option

The **Undo** option in the **EXTEND** command can be used to reverse the previous operation without leaving the **EXTEND** command. The command sequence is the same as discussed for the **TRIM** command.

The Project mode of the EXTEND command

In a 3D drawing, some lines may appear to intersect in a given view, but may not actually intersect. In such a case, you can use the **Project** option or the **PROJMODE** as explained for the **TRIM** command.

PROFESSIONAL TIP

The **TRIM** and **EXTEND** commands have a convenient **Smart** mode. To use the **Smart** mode, press [Enter] rather than selecting a cutting or boundary edge. Then, when an object to trim or extend is picked, AutoCAD searches for the nearest intersecting object or implied intersection in the direction of your pick (depending on the **EDGEMODE** setting). AutoCAD then uses this object as the cutting or boundary edge. The object must be visible on the screen, and cannot be a block or xref object. Also, trimming can be done between two actual or implied intersections, but not between a combination of one actual and one implied intersection.

Changing Lines and Circles

The endpoint location of a line or the radius of a circle can be altered using the **CHANGE** command. The endpoint of one or more lines can be moved by picking a new point. This new point is called the *change point*.

To access the **CHANGE** command, or type -CH or CHANGE at the Command: prompt. The keyboard shortcut is a hyphen (-) typed before CH. You are then prompted to select the objects to change. After the objects are selected, AutoCAD prompts for the change point.

For example, suppose a corner where two lines meet is not correct. Enter the **CHANGE** command and select the two lines. At the Properties/⟨Change point⟩: prompt, pick the new point or enter a coordinate. AutoCAD automatically relocates the endpoints of the selected lines, Figure 11-16. The command sequence is as follows:

> Command: **-CH** *or* **CHANGE.**↵
> Select objects: *(pick the lines individually or with a crossing box)*
> Select objects: ↵
> Properties/⟨Change point⟩: *(pick the new point)*
> Command:

Figure 11-16.
Using the **CHANGE** command to relocate a corner.

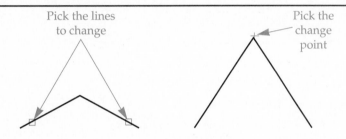

Pick the lines to change

Pick the change point

NOTE

If **ORTHO** is on when **CHANGE** is used, lines are disconnected and extended parallel to each other up to the new point.

The **CHANGE** command can also be used to revise the radius of a circle. You can pick a change point that the new circle is to be drawn through, or press [Enter] to specify a new radius, Figure 11-17. The command sequence is as follows:

> Command: **-CH** *or* **CHANGE.**↵
> Select objects: *(pick the circle to change)*
> Select objects: ↵
> Properties/⟨Change point⟩: *(pick a change point through which the new circle is to be drawn or press [Enter] to specify a new radius)*
> Enter circle radius: *(enter a radius value and press [Enter])*
> Command:

Figure 11-17.
Using the **CHANGE** command to revise the radius of a circle.

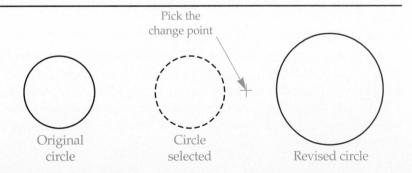

Pick the change point

Original circle

Circle selected

Revised circle

Using the **CHANGE** command to move text is discussed in Chapter 8. Changing common properties such as layer, linetype, and color is explained in Chapter 4. The 3D applications are discussed in *AutoCAD and its Applications—Advanced, Release 14.*

Moving an Object

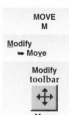

MOVE
M

<u>Modify</u>
➥ Mo<u>v</u>e

Modify toolbar

Move

In many situations, you may find that the location of a view or feature is not where you want it. This problem is easy to fix using the **MOVE** command. You can access the **MOVE** command by picking the **Move** button in the **Modify** toolbar, picking **Mo<u>v</u>e** from the **<u>M</u>odify** pull-down menu, or typing M or MOVE at the Command: prompt.

After the **MOVE** command is accessed, AutoCAD asks you to select the objects to be moved. Use any of the selection set options to select the objects. Once all of the items are selected, the next prompt requests the base point. The *base point* provides a reference point. Most drafters select a point on an object, the corner of a view, or the center of a circle. The next prompt asks for the second point of displacement. This is the new position. All selected entities are moved the distance from the base point to the displacement point.

The following **MOVE** operation relates to the object shown in Figure 11-18. As the base point is picked, the object is automatically dragged into position if the **DRAGMODE** variable is set to **Auto**. This is the command sequence:

Command: **M** *or* **MOVE**↵
Select objects: *(pick individual entities or window the object to be moved)*
Select objects: ↵
Base point or displacement: *(enter coordinates or pick a point on-screen)*
Second point of displacement: *(establish the new position by typing coordinates or picking a second point on-screen)*
Command:

Figure 11-18.
Using the **MOVE** command. When you select the object to be moved, it becomes highlighted.

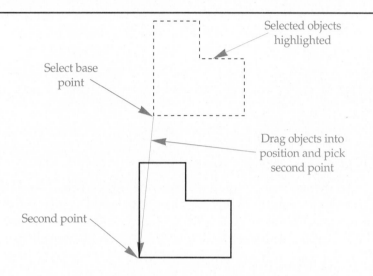

Selected objects highlighted

Select base point

Drag objects into position and pick second point

Second point

PROFESSIONAL TIP

Always use object snap to your best advantage with editing commands. For example, suppose you want to move an object to the center point of a circle. Use the **OSNAP Center** option to select the center of the circle as the second point of displacement.

Copying Objects

The **COPY** command is used to make a copy of an existing object or objects. To access the **COPY** command, pick the **Copy** button in the **Modify** toolbar, select **Copy** from the **Modify** pull-down menu, or type CO or COPY at the Command: prompt. The command prompts are the same as the **MOVE** command. However, when a second point of displacement is picked, the original object remains and a copy is drawn. The following command sequence is illustrated in Figure 11-19:

Command: **CO** *or* **COPY**↵
Select objects: *(pick individual entities or window the object to be copied)*
Select objects: ↵
〈Base point or displacement〉/Multiple: *(enter coordinates and press [Enter], or pick with the pointing device)*
Second point of displacement: *(establish the new position by typing coordinates and pressing [Enter], or pick a point on the screen)*
Command:

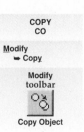

COPY
CO

Modify
➡ Copy

Modify toolbar

Copy Object

Figure 11-19.
Using the **COPY**
command.

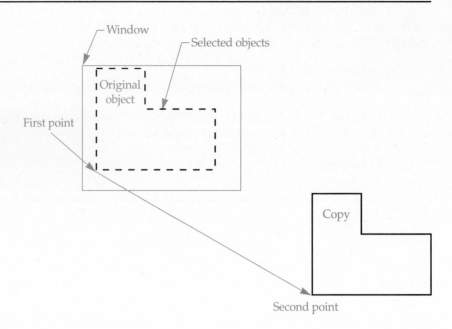

Making multiple copies

To make several copies of the same object, select the **Multiple** option of the **COPY** command by typing M at the ⟨Base point or displacement⟩/Multiple: prompt. The prompt for a second point repeats. When you have made all the copies needed, press [Enter]. The command sequence is as follows. The results are shown in Figure 11-20.

Command: **CO** *or* **COPY**⏎
Select objects: *(pick individual entities or window the object to be copied)*
Select objects: ⏎
⟨Base point or displacement⟩/Multiple: **M**⏎
Base point: *(pick a location on-screen)*
Second point of displacement: *(pick a location on-screen)*
Second point of displacement: *(pick the second position)*
Second point of displacement: *(pick the third position)*
Second point of displacement: ⏎
Command:

Figure 11-20.
Using the **Multiple**
option of the **COPY**
command.

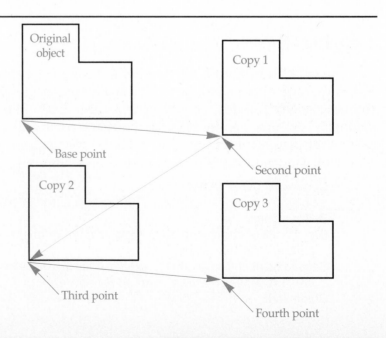

AutoCAD and its Applications—Basics

❑ Begin a new drawing or use one of your templates.
❑ Draw a square and an equilateral triangle (equal sides and angles) using the **POLYGON** command.
❑ Move the square to a new location.
❑ Copy the triangle next to the new square position. Leave a small space between the two objects.
❑ Move all features to a new position in the upper-left corner of the screen.
❑ Make four copies of the square anywhere on the screen. The new copies should not touch other objects.
❑ Save the drawing as EX11-7.

Drawing a Mirror Image of an Object

It is often necessary to draw an object in a reflected, or mirrored, position. The **MIRROR** command performs this task. Mirroring an entire drawing is common in architectural drafting when a client wants a plan drawn in reverse.

The **MIRROR** command is accessed by picking the **Mirror** button in the **Modify** toolbar, by selecting **Mi̲rror** in the **Mo̲dify** pull-down menu, or by typing MI or MIRROR at the Command: prompt.

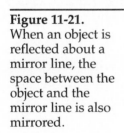

MIRROR
MI

Modify
↳ Mirror

Modify
toolbar

Mirror

Selecting the mirror line

When you enter the **MIRROR** command, you select the objects to mirror and then select a mirror line. The *mirror line* is the hinge about which objects are reflected. The objects and any space between the objects and the mirror line are reflected, Figure 11-21.

Figure 11-21.
When an object is reflected about a mirror line, the space between the object and the mirror line is also mirrored.

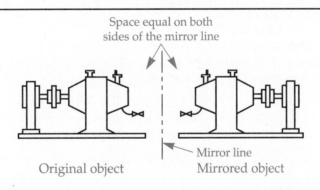

Space equal on both sides of the mirror line

Original object

Mirror line
Mirrored object

The mirror line can be placed at any angle. Once you pick the first endpoint, a mirrored image appears and moves with the cursor. Once you select the second mirror line endpoint, you have the option to delete the original objects. The command sequence shown in Figure 11-22 is as follows:

> Command: **MI** *or* **MIRROR**⏎
> Select objects: *(use any selection method—a window is common)*
> Select objects: ⏎
> First point of mirror line: *(pick the first point on the mirror line on or away from the object)*
> Second point: *(pick the second point on the mirror)*
> Delete old objects? ⟨N⟩ *(type Y and press [Enter] to delete the old objects, or press [Enter] to accept the default)*
> Command:

Figure 11-22.
Using the **MIRROR** command. You have the option to delete the old objects.

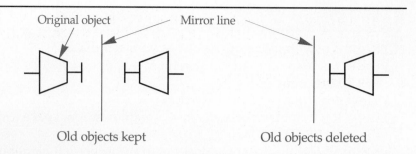

Original object   Mirror line

Old objects kept   Old objects deleted

❏ Begin a new drawing or use one of your templates.
❏ Draw the half object shown below. Then, complete the entire object using the **MIRROR** command. Do not dimension.
❏ Save the drawing as EX11-8 and quit.

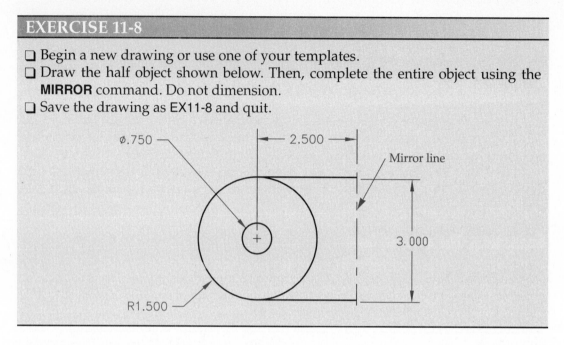

ø.750

2.500

Mirror line

3.000

R1.500

Mirroring text

Normally, the **MIRROR** command reverses any text associated with the selected object. Backwards text is generally not acceptable, although it is used for reverse imaging. To keep the text readable, the **MIRRTEXT** system variable must be zero. There are two values for **MIRRTEXT**, as shown in Figure 11-23.

- **1.** Text is mirrored in relation to the original object. This is the default value.
- **0.** Prevents text from being reversed.

Figure 11-23.
The **MIRRTEXT** system variable options.

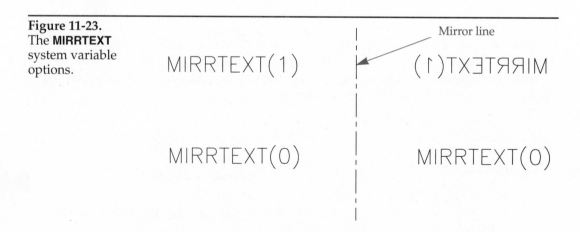

Mirror line

MIRRTEXT(1)   MIRRTEXT(1)

MIRRTEXT(0)   MIRRTEXT(0)

To draw a mirror image of an existing object and leave the text readable, set the **MIRRTEXT** variable to 0. Then, proceed to the **MIRROR** command. The entire command sequence is as follows:

Command: **MIRRTEXT**↵
New value for MIRRTEXT ⟨1⟩: **0**↵
Command: **MIRROR**↵
Select objects: *(select objects to mirror)*
Select objects: ↵
First point of mirror line: *(pick the first mirror line point)*
Second point: *(pick the second mirror line point)*
Delete old objects? ⟨N⟩ *(type Y and press [Enter], or press [Enter])*
Command:

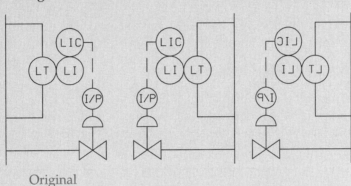
Rotating Existing Objects

Design changes often require that an object, feature, or view be rotated. For example, the office furniture layout may have to be moved, copied, or rotated for an interior design. AutoCAD allows you to easily revise the layout to obtain the final design.

To rotate selected objects, pick the **Rotate** button on the **Modify** toolbar, pick **Rotate** from the **Modify** pull-down menu, or type RO or ROTATE at the Command: prompt. Objects can be selected using any of the selection set options. Once the objects are selected, pick a base point and enter a rotation angle. A negative rotation angle revolves the object clockwise. A positive rotation angle revolves the object counterclockwise. See Figure 11-24. The **ROTATE** command sequence appears as follows:

ROTATE
RO

Modify
➥ Rotate

Modify
toolbar

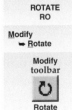

Rotate

Command: **RO** *or* **ROTATE**↵
Select objects: *(pick the objects using any of the selection methods)*
Select objects: ↵
Base point: *(pick the base point on or near the object, or enter coordinates and press [Enter])*
⟨Rotation angle⟩/Reference: *(type a positive or negative rotation angle and press [Enter], or pick a point on-screen)*
Command:

Figure 11-24.
Rotation angles.

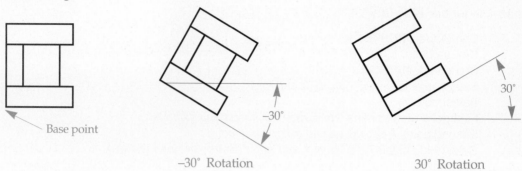

Base point

−30° Rotation

30° Rotation

If an object is already rotated and you want a different angle, you can do this in two ways. Both ways involve using the **Reference** option after selecting the object for rotation. The first way is to specify the existing angle and then the new angle, Figure 11-25A:

⟨Rotation angle⟩/Reference: **R**↵
Reference angle ⟨0⟩: **135**↵
New angle: **180**↵

The other method is to pick a reference line on the object and rotate the object in relationship to the reference line, Figure 11-25B:

⟨Rotation angle⟩/Reference: **R**↵
Reference angle ⟨0⟩: *(pick an endpoint of a reference line that forms the existing angle)*
Second point: *(pick the other point of the reference line that forms the existing angle)*
New angle: *(specify a new angle, such as **180**, and press* **[Enter]***)*

Figure 11-25.
Using the **Reference** option of the **ROTATE** command. A—Entering reference angles. B—Selecting points on a reference line.

135°

Pick two endpoints of a reference line

Base point

Original position 135°

Original position

180°

180°

Rotated from original position

Rotated from reference line

A

B

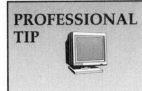

PROFESSIONAL TIP

Always use the **OSNAP** modes to your best advantage when editing. For example, suppose you want to rotate an object. It may be difficult to find an exact corner without using **OSNAP** modes. To select the base point, use the **Endpoint** or **Intersect** option.

Moving and Rotating an Object at the Same Time

The **ALIGN** command is primarily used for 3D applications, but it has 2D applications when you want to move and rotate an object. The command sequence asks you to select objects, and then asks for three source points and three destination points. For 2D applications, you only need two source and two destination points. Press [Enter] when the prompt requests the third source and destination points.

The *source points* define a line related to the object's original position. The *destination points* define the location of this line relative to the object's new location.

To access the **ALIGN** command, pick **Align** in the **3D Operation** cascading menu of the **Modify** pull-down menu, or type AL or ALIGN at the Command: prompt. The command sequence is as follows. Refer to Figure 11-26:

> Command: **AL** *or* **ALIGN**↵
> Select objects: *(select the objects)*
> Select objects: ↵
> Specify 1st source point: *(pick the first source point)*
> Specify 1st destination point: *(pick the first destination point)*
> Specify 2nd source point: *(pick the second source point)*
> Specify 2nd destination point: *(pick the second destination point)*
> Specify 3rd source point or ⟨continue⟩: ↵
> Scale objects to align points? [Yes/No] ⟨No⟩: *(if the distance between the source points is different than the distance between the destination points)*
> Command:

ALIGN **AL**
Modify ↳ **3D Operation**   ↳ **Align**

Figure 11-26.
Using the **ALIGN** command to move and rotate a kitchen cabinet layout against a wall.

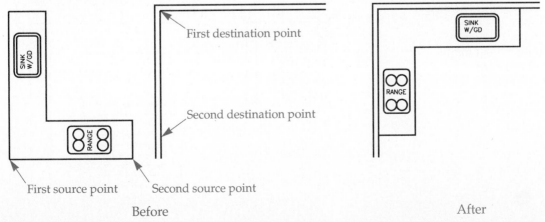

First destination point

Second destination point

First source point

Second source point

Before

After

❑ Begin a new drawing or use one of your templates.
❑ Make a drawing similar to the one shown below. Do not add text or leaders.
❑ Use the **ALIGN** command to move and rotate part A into position with part B. S1 is the first source point and S2 is the second source point. D1 is the first destination point and D2 is the second destination point.
❑ Save the drawing as EX11-11.

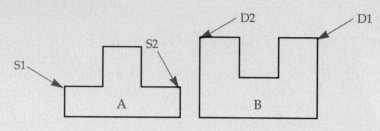

Changing the Size of an Object

A convenient editing command that saves hours of drafting time is the **SCALE** command. This command lets you change the size of an object or the complete drawing. The **SCALE** command enlarges or reduces the entire object proportionately. If associative dimensioning is used, the dimensions also change to reflect the new size. This is discussed in Chapter 19.

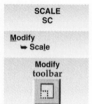

SCALE
SC

Modify
➥ Scale

Modify
toolbar

Scale

To scale objects, pick the **Scale** button in the **Modify** toolbar, pick **Scale** from the **Modify** pull-down menu, or type SC or SCALE at the Command: prompt. The command sequence is as follows:

Command: **SC** or **SCALE**↵
Select objects: (use any selection technique to select objects)
Select objects: ↵
Base point: (select the base point)
⟨Scale factor⟩/Reference:

Using scale factors

Specifying the scale factor is the default option. Enter a number to indicate the amount of enlargement or reduction. For example, if you want to double the scale, type 2 at the ⟨Scale factor⟩/Reference: prompt, as shown in Figure 11-27. The chart in Figure 11-28 shows sample scale factors.

Figure 11-27.
Using the **SCALE** command. The base point does not move, but every other point in the object does.

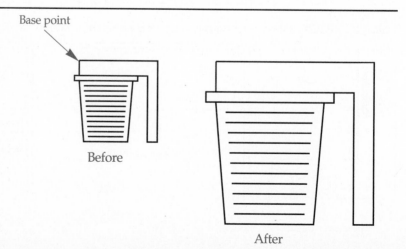

Base point

Before

After

Figure 11-28.
Different scale
factors and the
resulting sizes.

Scale Factor	Resulting Size
10	10 × bigger
5	5 × bigger
2	2 × bigger
1	Equal to existing size
.75	3/4 of original size
.50	1/2 of original size
.25	1/4 of original size

Using the Reference option

An object can also be scaled by specifying a new size in relation to an existing dimension. For example, suppose you have a shaft that is 2.50" long and you want to make it 3.00" long. To do so, use the **Reference** option as follows, as shown in Figure 11-29:

〈Scale factor〉/Reference: **R**↵
Reference length 〈1〉: **2.5**↵
New length: **3**↵
Command:

Figure 11-29.
Using the **Reference** option of the **SCALE** command.

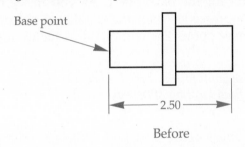
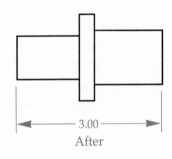

Base point

2.50

Before

3.00

After

NOTE

The **SCALE** command changes all dimensions of an object proportionately. If you want to change only the width or length of an object, use the **STRETCH** or **LENGTHEN** command.

EXERCISE 11-12

❏ Begin a new drawing or use one of your templates.
❏ Draw two 2.25" squares so that two sides are horizontal.
❏ Double the size of one square.
❏ Use the **Reference** option to make the other square 3.25" long on one side.
❏ Save the drawing as EX11-12.

Stretching an Object

The **SCALE** command changes the length and width of an object proportionately. The **STRETCH** command changes only one dimension of an object. In mechanical drafting, it is common to increase the length of a part while leaving the diameter or width the same. In architectural design, room sizes may be stretched to increase the square footage.

When using the **STRETCH** command, you can select objects with a crossing window or crossing polygon. To use a crossing window, type C at the Select objects: prompt or drag your selection window from right to left.

To access the **STRETCH** command, pick the **Stretch** button in the **Modify** toolbar, pick **Stretch** from the **Modify** pull-down menu, or type S or STRETCH at the Command: prompt. The command sequence is as follows:

Command: **S** *or* **STRETCH.⏎**
Select objects to stretch by crossing-window or crossing-polygon...
Select objects: *(select the first corner of a crossing window)*
Other corner: *(pick the second corner)*
Select objects: *(pick additional objects or press [Enter])*

Select only the portion of the object to be stretched, as shown in Figure 11-30. If you select the entire object, the **STRETCH** command works like the **MOVE** command.

Next, you are asked to pick the base point. This is the point from which the object will be stretched. Then, pick a new position for the base point. As you move the screen cursor, the object is stretched or compressed. When the displayed object is stretched to the desired position, pick the new point. The command sequence after selecting objects is as follows:

Base point or displacement: *(pick the base point for the stretch to begin)*
Second point of displacement: *(pick the final location of the base point)*
Command:

The example in Figure 11-30 shows the object being stretched. This is a common use of the **STRETCH** command. You can also use the **STRETCH** command to reduce the size of an object.

STRETCH
S

Modify
↪ Stretch

Modify
toolbar

Stretch

Figure 11-30.
Using the **STRETCH** command.

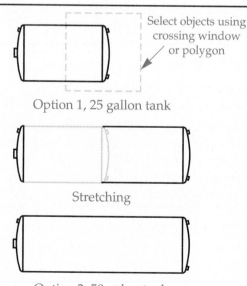

Select objects using crossing window or polygon

Option 1, 25 gallon tank

Stretching

Option 2, 50 galon tank

Using the Displacement option

The **Displacement** option works the same with the **STRETCH** command as with the **MOVE** and **COPY** commands.

> Command: **STRETCH**↵
> Select objects to stretch by crossing-window or crossing-polygon...
> Select objects: *(pick the first corner of a crossing-window, or crossing-polygon option)*
> Other corner: *(pick the second corner)*
> Select objects: ↵
> Base point or displacement: *(enter an X and Y displacement value such as 2,3)*
> Second point of displacement: ↵
> Command:

When you press [Enter] at the Second point of displacement: prompt, the object is automatically stretched as you specified with the X and Y coordinates at the Base point or displacement: prompt. In this case, the object is stretched 2 units in the X direction and 3 units in the Y direction.

PROFESSIONAL TIP

It may not be common to have objects lined up in a convenient manner for using the **Crossing** selection method with the **STRETCH** command. You should consider using the **Crossing-polygon** selection option to make selecting the objects easier. Also, make sure the **DRAGMODE** variable is turned on so you can watch the object stretch to its new size. If the stretched object is not what you expected, cancel the command with the [Esc] key. The **STRETCH** command and other editing commands discussed in this chapter work well with **ORTHO** on. This restricts the object movement to only horizontal and vertical directions.

EXERCISE 11-13

❏ Begin a new drawing or use one of your templates.
❏ Design and draw a cylindrical-shaped object similar to the tank in Figure 11-30.
❏ Stretch the object to approximately twice its original length.
❏ Stretch the object to about twice its original height.
❏ Save the drawing as EX11-13 and quit.

Changing the Length of an Object

The **LENGTHEN** command can be used to change the length of objects and the included angle of an arc. Objects can only be lengthened one at a time. The **LENGTHEN** command does not affect closed objects. For example, you can lengthen a line, polyline, arc, elliptical arc, or spline but you cannot lengthen a closed polygon.

To access the **LENGTHEN** command, pick the **Lengthen** button in the **Modify** toolbar, pick **Lengthen** from the **Modify** pull-down menu, or type LEN or LENGTHEN at the Command: prompt. When you select an object, AutoCAD gives you the current length if the object is linear, or the included angle if the object is an arc:

> Command: **LEN** *or* **LENGTHEN**↵
> DElta/Percent/Total/DYnamic/⟨Select object⟩: *(pick an object)*
> Current length: 1.500, included angle: 75.000
> DElta/Percent/Total/DYnamic/⟨Select object⟩:

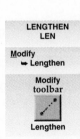

LENGTHEN
LEN

Modify
↳ Lengthen

Modify
toolbar

Lengthen

Each option is described below:

- **Delta.** The **Delta** option allows you to specify a positive or negative change in length measured from the endpoint of the selected object. The lengthening or shortening happens closest to the selection point and changes the length by the amount entered. See Figure 11-31.

> Command: **LEN** *or* **LENGTHEN.**↵
> DElta/Percent/Total/DYnamic/⟨Select object⟩: **DE.**↵
> Angle/⟨Enter delta length (0.000)⟩: *(enter the desired length, .75 for example)*
> ⟨Select object to change⟩/Undo: *(pick the object)*
> ⟨Select object to change⟩/Undo: (press [Enter] *to make the change or type* U *to undo the change)*
> Command:

Figure 11-31.
Using the **Delta** option of the **LENGTHEN** command.

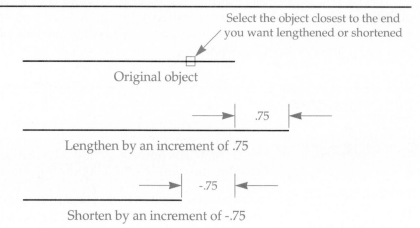

Select the object closest to the end you want lengthened or shortened

Original object

Lengthen by an increment of .75

Shorten by an increment of -.75

The **Delta** option has an **Angle** suboption that lets you change the included angle of an arc by a specified angle. The command sequence is as follows, as shown in Figure 11-32:

> Command: **LEN** *or* **LENGTHEN.**↵
> DElta/Percent/Total/DYnamic/⟨Select object⟩: **DE.**↵
> Angle/⟨Enter delta length (0.000)⟩: **A.**↵
> Enter delta angle ⟨0.000⟩: *(enter an angle such as* 45*)*
> ⟨Select object to change⟩/Undo: *(pick the arc)*
> ⟨Select object to change⟩/Undo: ↵
> Command:

- **Percent.** The **Percent** option allows you to change the length of an object or the angle of an arc by a specified percentage. If you consider the original length 100%, then you can make the object shorter by specifying less than 100% or longer by specifying more than 100%. Look at Figure 11-33 and follow this command sequence:

> Command: **LEN** *or* **LENGTHEN.**↵
> DElta/Percent/Total/DYnamic/⟨Select object⟩: **P.**↵
> Enter percent length ⟨100.0⟩: **125.**↵
> ⟨Select object to change⟩/Undo: *(pick the object)*
> ⟨Select object to change⟩/Undo: ↵
> Command:

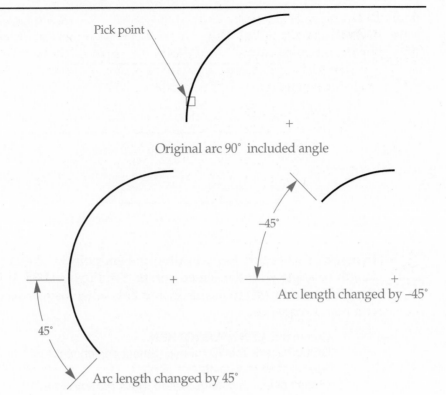

Figure 11-32.
Using the **Angle** suboption of the **LENGTHEN** command's **Delta** option.

Pick point

Original arc 90° included angle

−45°

Arc length changed by −45°

45°

Arc length changed by 45°

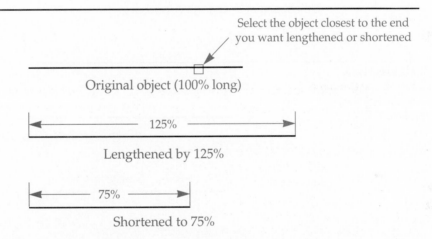

Figure 11-33.
Using the **Percent** option of the **LENGTHEN** command.

Select the object closest to the end you want lengthened or shortened

Original object (100% long)

125%

Lengthened by 125%

75%

Shortened to 75%

- **Total.** The **Total** option allows you to set the total length or angle by the value that you specify. You do not have to select the object before entering one of the options, but doing so lets you know the current length and, if an arc, angle of the object. See Figure 11-34:

> Command: **LEN** *or* **LENGTHEN**↵
> DElta/Percent/Total/DYnamic/⟨Select object⟩: *(pick an object)*
> Current length: 3.000
> DElta/Percent/Total/DYnamic/⟨Select object⟩: **T.**↵
> Angle/⟨Enter delta length (1.000)⟩: *(enter a new length such as 3.75 or A if it is an angle)*
> ⟨Select object to change⟩/Undo: *(pick the object)*
> ⟨Select object to change⟩/Undo: ↵
> Command:

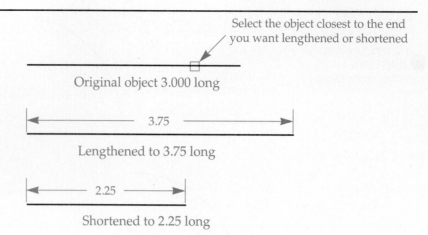

Figure 11-34.
Using the **Total** option of the **LENGTHEN** command.

Select the object closest to the end you want lengthened or shortened

Original object 3.000 long

3.75

Lengthened to 3.75 long

2.25

Shortened to 2.25 long

- **Dynamic.** This option lets you drag the endpoint of the object to the desired length or angle with the screen cursor. See Figure 11-35. It is helpful to have the grid and snap set to usable increments when using this option. This is the command sequence:

> Command: **LEN** *or* **LENGTHEN.**↵
> DElta/Percent/Total/DYnamic/⟨Select object⟩: **DY**↵
> Specify new end point.
> ⟨Select object to change⟩/Undo: *(pick the object and move the cursor to the desired length)*
> ⟨Select object to change⟩/Undo: ↵
> Command:

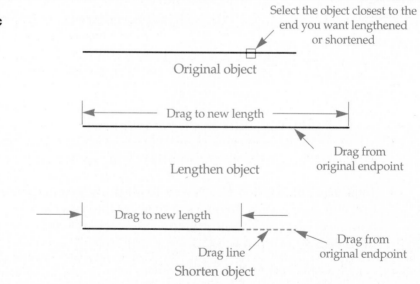

Figure 11-35.
Using the **Dynamic** option of the **LENGTHEN** command.

Select the object closest to the end you want lengthened or shortened

Original object

Drag to new length

Lengthen object

Drag from original endpoint

Drag to new length

Drag line

Drag from original endpoint

Shorten object

❏ Begin a new drawing or use one of your templates.
❏ Use the **LENGTHEN** command and the following options to draw objects similar to the ones specified in the given figure numbers. (Note: Use the **COPY** command to make two copies of each original object, one for lengthening and one for shortening.)
　❏ **Delta**—Figure 11-31 and Figure 11-32.
　❏ **Percent**—Figure 11-33.
　❏ **Total**—Figure 11-34.
　❏ **Dynamic**—Figure 11-35.
❏ Save the drawing as EX11-14.

NOTE　　　　Only lines and arcs can be lengthened dynamically. A spline's length can only be decreased. Splines are discussed in Chapter 17.

Selecting Objects before Editing

Throughout this chapter, you have worked with the basic editing commands by entering the command and then selecting the object to be edited. You can also set up AutoCAD to let you select the object first and then enter the desired editing command. The system variables that affect this procedure are **PICKAUTO**, **PICKFIRST**, and **GRIPS**. They should be set as follows:

- **PICKAUTO = 1 (on).** This allows you to automatically pick objects by the method used to pick and move the cursor.
- **PICKFIRST = 1 (on).** This system variable lets you pick the object before entering the editing command. When **PICKFIRST** is set to 0 (off), you must enter the command name before selecting the object. Notice the difference in the appearance of the crosshairs when **PICKFIRST** is on and off, and when **GRIPS** is off.
- **GRIPS = 0 (off).** Grips are used for automatic editing, and are discussed in detail in Chapter 12. For **PICKFIRST** to have its best performance, turn **GRIPS** off. If you are following along with this text while working at your computer, be sure to turn the **GRIPS** system variable back on when working in Chapter 12.

With these variable settings, you now have the flexibility of entering the command and then selecting the object, or selecting the object and then entering the command. The editing commands work the same either way.

❏ Open EX11-7 or start a new drawing and draw a square and triangle of any size.
❏ Set the following system variables to the settings given:
　❏ **PICKAUTO** = 1
　❏ **PICKFIRST** = 1
　❏ **GRIPS** = 0
❏ Select the square. Then, enter the **MOVE** command to move it to a new position.
❏ Select the triangle. Then, enter the **COPY** command to make a copy of it.
❏ Experiment with selecting the objects and then entering an editing command, such as **ROTATE** or **SCALE**.
❏ Erase an object by selecting the object before entering the **ERASE** command.
❏ Save the drawing as EX11-15.

Selecting Objects for Future Editing

The **SELECT** command is used to preselect an object or group of objects for future editing. It is designed to increase your productivity. Often you are working with the same set of objects, moving, copying, or scaling them. Set these aside as a selection set with the **SELECT** command. Then continue to perform another drawing task. To return to those objects set aside, enter P for **Previous** at the Select objects: prompt. Only the last selection set you make can be modified. The command sequences for creating a selection set and then moving it are as follows:

Command: **SELECT**⏎
Select objects: *(use any method to select an individual object or group of objects)*
Select objects: *(select additional objects or press* [Enter]*)*
Command:

This creates a selection set. Later, when you want to move these objects, use the **Previous** option as follows:

Command: **M** *or* **MOVE**⏎
Select objects: **P**⏎ *(this selects the object or group of objects previously selected using the **SELECT** command)*
Select objects: ⏎
Base point or displacement: *(pick the base point)*
Second point of displacement: *(pick the new location of the base point)*
Command:

EXERCISE 11-16

❑ Begin a new drawing or use one of your templates.
❑ Draw two circles with 1.5″ (38.1mm) radii spaced .25″ (6.35mm) apart.
❑ Use the **SELECT** command to select both circles for future editing.
❑ Draw at least three other small objects.
❑ Use the **COPY** command and the **Previous** option to copy the original two circles to a new location.
❑ Save the drawing as EX11-16 and quit.

Creating Object Groups

A group is a named selection set. These selection sets are saved with the drawing and, therefore, exist between multiple drawing sessions. Objects can be members of more than one group and groups can be nested. *Nesting* means placing one group inside of another group.

An object existing in multiple groups creates an interesting situation. For example, if a line and an arc are grouped and then the arc is grouped with a circle, moving the first group moves the line and arc, and moving the second group moves the arc and circle. Nesting can be used to place smaller groups into larger groups for easier editing.

The **PICKSTYLE** system variable is used to determine whether selecting a grouped object selects the individual object or the entire group. **PICKSTYLE** has the following settings:

- **0.** No group selection or associative hatch selection. Hatch is used in sectioning and is discussed in Chapter 22. Associative hatch means that the hatch pattern is associated with the object. So, when the object is changed, the hatch pattern changes with it.
- **1.** Group selection is the default.
- **2.** Associative hatch selection.
- **3.** Group selection and associative hatch selection.

Change the **PICKSTYLE** setting like this:

Command: **PICKSTYLE**↵
New value for PICKSTYLE ⟨1⟩: *(enter a new value)*

The **GROUP** command can be accessed by picking **Object Group...** from the **Tools** pull-down menu or by typing G or GROUP at the Command: prompt. Any of these entry methods displays the **Object Grouping** dialog box shown in Figure 11-36.

GROUP
G

Tools
➥ Object
    Group...

Figure 11-36.
The **Object Grouping** dialog box. The different elements are shown here highlighted.

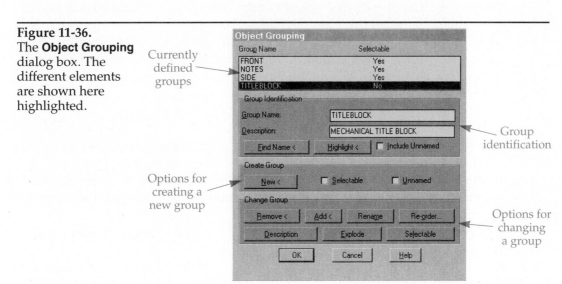

There are many elements found in the **Object Grouping** dialog box. The text box displays the **Group Name** and lists whether or not the group is **Selectable**. If a group is selectable, picking any object in it selects the entire group. Making a group nonselectable allows individual objects within the group to be edited.

The **Group Identification** area has several components:

- **Find Name ⟨.** This button displays a dialog list of all groups with which an object is associated. When you pick this button, a Pick a member of a group: prompt appears. Once you pick an object, the **Group Member List** dialog box lists any groups with which the object is associated.

- **Highlight ⟨.** This button allows a group name to be specified, then highlights all its members in the drawing editor. This allows you to see the parts of the drawing that are identified as the members of that group. Then pick the **Continue** button or press [Enter] to return to the **Object Grouping** dialog box.

- **Include Unnamed.** This is a check box that causes unnamed groups to be listed with named groups. Unnamed groups are given a default name by AutoCAD in the format: *Ax, where x is an integer value that increases with each new group, such as *A6. Unnamed groups can be named later using the **Rename** option.

The **Create Group** area contains the options for creating a new group:

- **New ⟨.** This button creates a new group from the selected objects using the name entered in the **Group Name:** text box. AutoCAD issues a Select objects for grouping: prompt after you enter a new name in the **Group Name:** text box.

- **Selectable.** A check in this box sets the initial status of the **Selectable** value as Yes for the new group. This is indicated in the **Selectable** list described earlier. No check here specifies No in the **Selectable** list. This can be changed later.

- **Unnamed.** This indicates whether the new group will be named. If this box is checked, AutoCAD assigns its own default name as detailed previously.

The **Change Group** area of the **Object Grouping** dialog box shows the options for changing a group:

- **Remove** ⟨. Pick this button to remove objects from a group definition.
- **Add** ⟨. This button allows objects to be added to a group definition.
- **Rename.** Pick this button to change the name of an existing group. Unnamed groups can be renamed.
- **Re-order....** Objects are numbered in the order that they are selected when defining the group. The first object is numbered 0, not 1. This button allows objects to be re-ordered within the group. For example, if a group contains a set of instructions, you can re-order the instructions to suit the typical steps that are used. The **Order Group** dialog box is displayed when you pick this button. The elements of this dialog box are briefly described as follows:
  - **Group Name**—Displays the name of the selected group.
  - **Description**—Displays the description for the selected group.
  - **Remove from position (0-*n*):**—Position number of the object to re-order, where *n* is the total number of objects found in the group. You place the desired order in the text box to the right of this and the next two features.
  - **Replace at position (0-*n*):**—Position to which the number is being moved.
  - **Number of objects (1-*n*):**—Displays the number of objects or the range to re-order.
  - **Reverse Order**—Pick this button to have the order of all members in the group reversed.
- **Description.** Updates the group with the new description entered in the **Description:** text box.
- **Explode.** Pick this button to delete the selected group definition, but not the group's objects. The group name is removed and the original group is exploded. Copies of the group become unnamed groups. By selecting the **Include Unnamed** check box, these unnamed groups are displayed and can then be exploded, if needed.
- **Selectable.** Toggles the selectable value of a group. This is where you can change the value in the **Selectable** list.

EXERCISE 11-17

❑ Load AutoCAD and open one of your previous, more complex drawings.
❑ Use the **GROUP** command to name and describe several different elements of the drawing as groups. For example, for views use FRONT, TOP, SIDE, TITLEBLOCK, or NOTES.
❑ Use each element of the **Object Grouping** dialog box to see the effect on the groups that you have named.
❑ Save as EX11-17.

PROFESSIONAL TIP   The **Bonus Standard** toolbar includes three advanced editing tools: **Multiple Entity Stretch**, **Move Copy Rotate**, and **Extended Trim**. These tools are available if a full installation of AutoCAD was performed. See Appendix A for bonus menu information.

Chapter Test

Write your answers in the spaces provided.

1. Give the command and entries used to draw a 45° × .125 chamfer:

   Command: _____

   Polyline/Distance/Angle/Trim/Method/⟨Select first line⟩: _____

   Enter first chamfer distance ⟨*current*⟩: _____

   Enter second chamfer distance ⟨*previous*⟩: _____

   Command: _____

   Polyline/Distance/Angle/Trim/Method/⟨Select first line⟩: _____

   Select second line: _____

2. Give the command and entries required to produce .50 radius fillets on all corners of a closed polyline:

   Command: _____

   Polyline/Radius/⟨Select first object⟩: _____

   Enter fillet radius ⟨*current*⟩: _____

   Command: _____

   Polyline/Radius/Trim/⟨Select first object⟩: _____

   Select 2D polyline: _____

3. Give the command, entries, and actions required to move an object from position A to position B:

   Command: _____

   Select objects: _____

   Select objects: _____

   Base point or displacement: _____

   Second point of displacement: _____

4. Give the command and entries needed to make two copies of the same object:

   Command: _____

   Select objects: _____

   Select objects: _____

   ⟨Base point or displacement⟩/Multiple: _____

   Base point: _____

   Second point of displacement: _____

   Second point of displacement: _____

5. Give the command and entries necessary to draw a reverse image of an existing object and remove the existing object:

   Command: _____

   Select objects: _____

   Select objects: _____

   First point of mirror line: _____

   Second point: _____

   Delete old objects? ⟨N⟩: _____

6. Give the command and entries needed to rotate an object 45° clockwise:

Command: _____

Select objects: _____

Select objects: _____

Base point: _____

⟨Rotation angle⟩/Reference: _____

7. Give the command and entries required to reduce the size of an entire drawing by one-half:

Command: _____

Select objects: _____

Select objects: _____

Base point: _____

⟨Scale factor⟩/Reference: _____

8. Give the command and entries needed to change the first break point picked to the intersection of two other lines:

Command: _____

Select object: _____

Enter second point (or F for first point): _____

Enter first point: _____

Enter second point: _____

of: _____

_____

9. Give the command sequence that revises the radius of a circle:

Command: _____

Select objects: _____

Select objects: _____

Properties/⟨Change point⟩: _____

10. Define the term "displacement" as it relates to the **MOVE** and **COPY** commands.

_____

_____

11. Explain the difference between the **MOVE** and **COPY** commands. _____

_____

_____

12. List two locations you normally choose as the base point when using the **MOVE** or **COPY** commands. _____

_____

13. Describe the purpose of the **SELECT** command. _____

_____

_____

14. What is a selection set? _____
    _____
    _____

15. How do you select objects for editing that have previously been picked using the **SELECT** command? _____
    _____

16. How is the size of a fillet specified? _____
    _____

17. Identify the selection method or methods issued by AutoCAD when using the **STRETCH** command. _____
    _____

18. List two ways to cancel the **STRETCH** command. _____
    _____

19. The **EXTEND** command is the opposite of the _____ command.
    _____

20. Name the system variable used to preset the fillet radius. _____

21. In what direction should you pick points to break a portion out of a circle or arc?
    _____

22. Name the command that trims an object to a cutting edge. _____

23. Name the command associated with boundary edges. _____

24. The **MOVE, COPY, TRIM, EXTEND,** and **STRETCH** commands are located in the _____ pull-down menu.

25. Name the command that can be used to move and rotate an object simultaneously.
    _____
    _____

26. Describe the purpose of the **PICKFIRST** system variable. _____
    _____

27. Describe the difference between **Trim** and **No trim** when using the **CHAMFER** and **FILLET** commands. _____
    _____
    _____
    _____
    _____

28. What is the purpose of the **Method** option in the **CHAMFER** command? _____
    _____
    _____

29. How can you split an object in two without removing a portion? _____
    _____
    _____
    _____

30. Name the option in the **TRIM** and **EXTEND** commands that allows you to trim or extend to an implied intersection. _____

31. How do you use the **Smart** mode? _____

_____

32. Identify the **LENGTHEN** command option with its descriptions by placing the letter of the command option in the blank in front of its description.

_____ Change a length or arc angle by a percentage of the total. A. **Delta**

_____ Drag the endpoint of the object to the desired length   B. **Percent**
or angle.   C. **Total**

_____ Allows a positive or negative change in length from the   D. **Dynamic**
endpoint.

_____ Set the total length or angle to the value specified.

33. Define a group. _____

_____

34. How do you access the **Object Grouping** dialog box? _____

_____

_____

35. Describe how you create a new group. _____

_____

_____

_____

36. Give the keyboard shortcut for the following commands:

CHAMFER _____

FILLET _____

BREAK _____

TRIM _____

EXTEND _____

CHANGE _____

MOVE _____

COPY _____

MIRROR _____

ROTATE _____

ALIGN _____

SCALE _____

LENGTHEN _____

Drawing Problems

Use your templates as appropriate for each of the following problems. Start a new drawing for each problem, unless indicated otherwise.

1. Draw the object shown as view A. Change the angle of the object to 45° as shown in view B. Then rotate it to a 90° rotation angle as shown in view C. Save the drawing as P11-1.

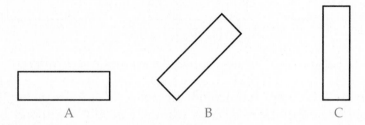

A   B   C

2. Draw the object shown below. Scale it down to 1/4 size. Then scale the object 10 times. Save the drawing as P11-2.

3. Draw object A using the **LINE** command, making sure that the corners overrun. Then trim the lines all at the same time. Select all four lines when asked to select cutting edges. Pick all overruns when asked to select object to trim. The object should appear as shown in view B. Save the drawing as P11-3.

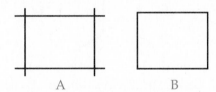

A   B

4. Draw object A using the **LINE** and **ARC** commands. Make sure that the corners overrun and the arc is centered, but does not touch the lines. Then use the **TRIM, EXTEND,** and **MOVE** commands to make the object look like the example shown in view B. Save the drawing as P11-4.

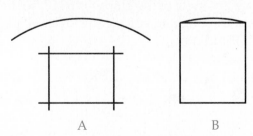

A   B

5. Open drawing P11-4 for further editing. Using the **STRETCH** command, change the shape to that shown in view B. Make a copy of the new revision. Change the copy to represent the example shown in view C. Save the drawing as P11-5.

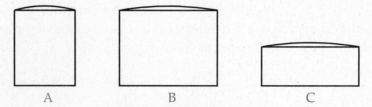

A   B   C

6. Refer to Figure 11-30 in this chapter. Draw and make three copies of the object shown in Option 1. Stretch the first copy to twice its length as shown as Option 2. Stretch the second copy to twice its height. Double the size of the third copy using the **SCALE** command. Save the drawing as P11-6.

7. Draw objects A, B, and C shown below without dimensions. Then, move objects A, B, and C to new positions. Select a corner of object A and the center of objects B and C as the base points. Save the drawing as P11-7.

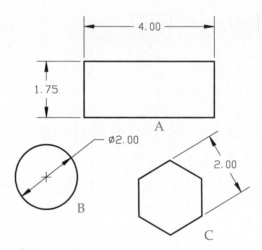

8. Draw objects A, B, and C shown in Problem 11-7 at the left side of the screen. Make a copy of object A two units to the right. Make four copies of object B three units, center-to-center, to the right using the **Multiple** option. Make three copies of object C three units, center-to-center, to the right. Save the drawing as P11-8.

9. Draw the object shown using the **ELLIPSE, COPY,** and **LINE** commands. The rotation angle of the ellipse is 60°. Use the **BREAK** or **TRIM** command when drawing and editing the lower ellipse. Save the drawing as P11-9 and quit.

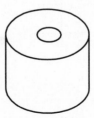

10. Open drawing P11-9 for further editing. Shorten the height of the object using the **STRETCH** command as shown below. Next, add to the object as indicated. Save the drawing as P11-10 and quit.

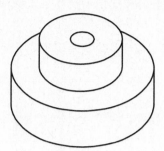

11. Draw the object shown as view A. Use the **TRIM** command to help change the object to the example shown as view B. Save the drawing as P11-11.

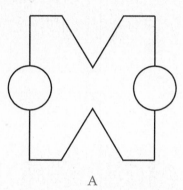 

A   B

12. Draw view A, without dimensions. Use the **CHAMFER** and **FILLET** commands to your best advantage. Then draw a mirror image of it as shown in view B. Now, remove the original view and move the new view so that point 2 is at the original point 1 location. Save the drawing as P11-12.

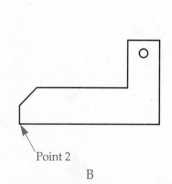

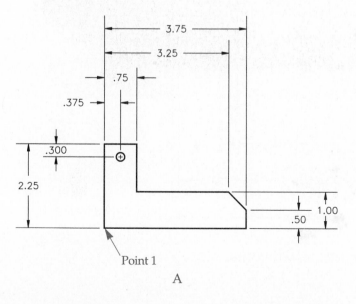

A   B

13. Draw the object shown below, without dimensions. The object is symmetrical; therefore, draw only the right half. Then mirror the left half into place. Use the **CHAMFER** and **FILLET** commands to your best advantage. Save the drawing as P11-13.

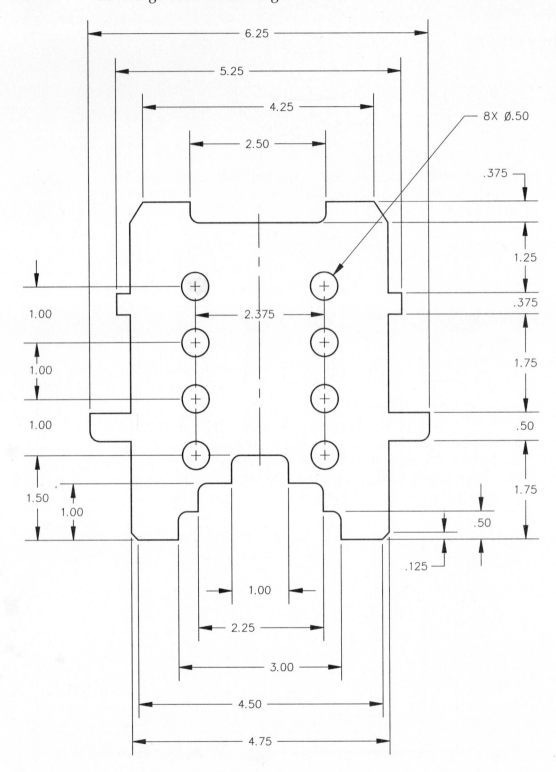

NOTE: ALL FILLETS AND ROUNDS R.125.

14. Refer to the view shown below for this problem. Plan to use the **TRIM**, **OSNAP**, and **OFFSET** commands to assist you in drawing the view. Do not draw centerlines or dimensions. Save the completed drawing as P11-14.

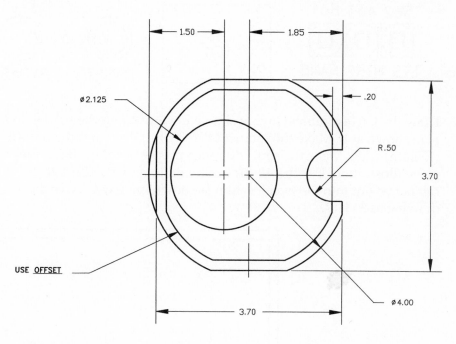

15. Draw the object shown below, without dimensions. Then mirror the right half into place. Use the **CHAMFER** and **FILLET** commands to your best advantage. Save the drawing as P11-15.

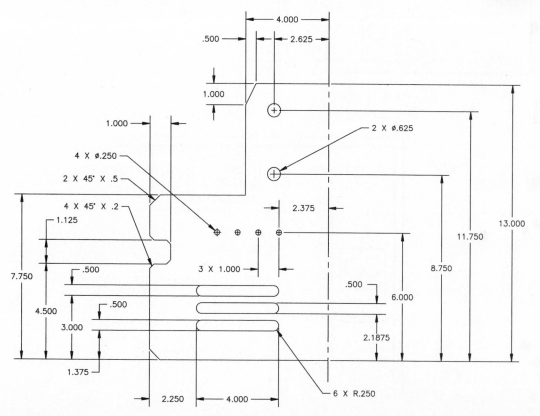

16. Redraw the objects shown below. Then mirror the drawing, but have the text remain readable. Delete the original image during the mirroring process. Save the drawing as P11-16.

2b1

TRANSFER

5a2 4a1 8a1

LTS. HTRS. FANS

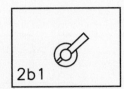

2b1

1b1

RESET

11b1

BYPASS

17. Draw the kitchen cabinet layout shown in view A and the partial floor plan shown at B. Make the cabinet 24″ (600mm) deep and the walls 6″ (150mm) wide. Make the sink and range proportional in size to the given illustration. Use the **ALIGN** command to move and rotate the cabinet layout into the wall location as shown in view C. Save the drawing as P11-17.

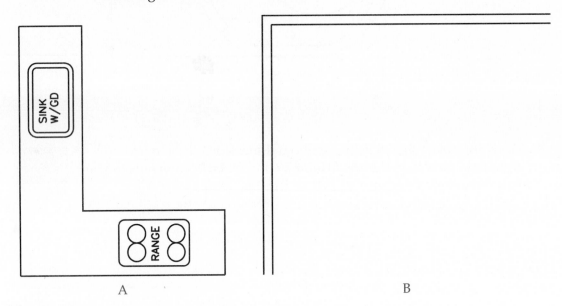

A

B

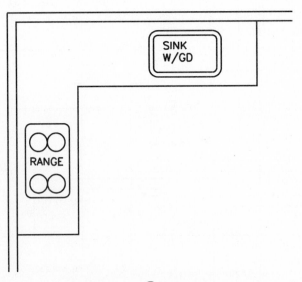

C

18. Draw the objects shown at the left using the dimensions given, but do not draw the dimensions. Copy all of the objects to a position to the right and perform the specified **TRIM** and **EXTEND** operations. Save the drawing as P11-18.

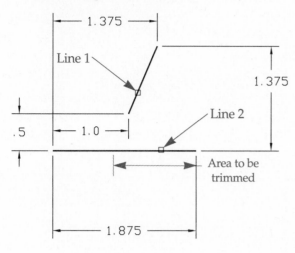

Trim line 2 back to the implied intersection with line 1

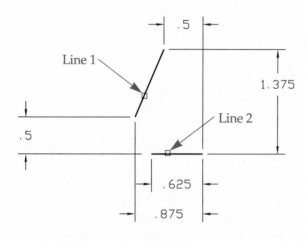

Extend line 2 to the implied intersection with line 1

19. Draw the objects shown at the left using the dimensions given, but do not draw the dimensions. Copy all of the objects to a position to the right and perform the specified **LENGTHEN** operations from the right end of the copied lines. Save the drawing as P11-19.

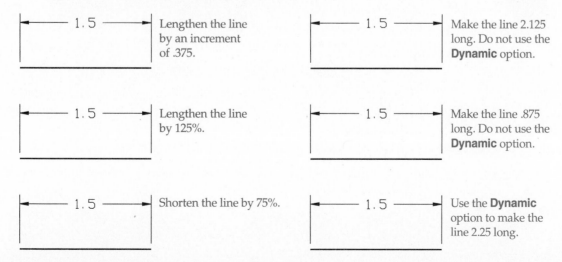

20. Draw the objects shown at the left using the dimensions given, but do not draw the dimensions. Copy all of the objects to a position to the right and perform the specified **LENGTHEN** operations. Perform all operations from the bottom-left end of the copied arcs. Save the drawing as P11-20.

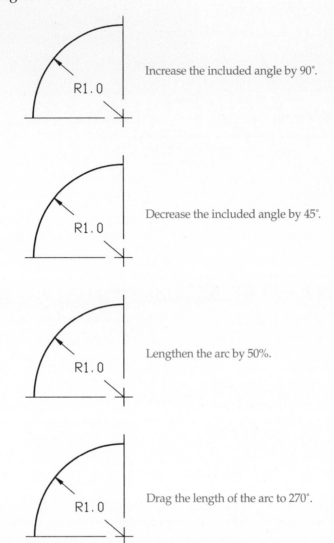

Increase the included angle by 90°.

Decrease the included angle by 45°.

Lengthen the arc by 50%.

Drag the length of the arc to 270°.

21. Draw the following object without dimensions. Use the **TRIMMODE** to your advantage. Save the drawing as P11-21.

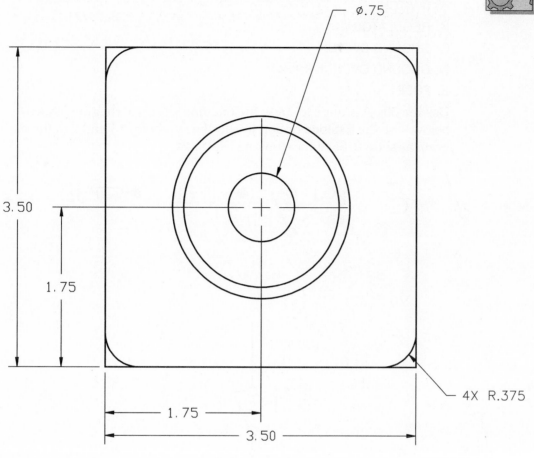

ø.75

3.50

1.75

1.75

3.50

4X R.375

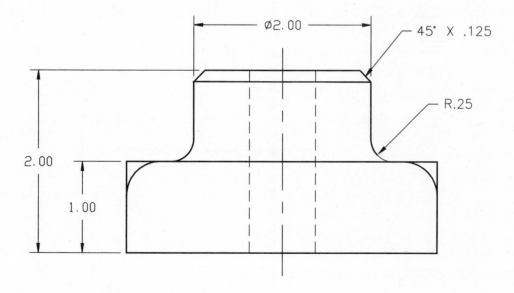

ø2.00

45° X .125

R.25

2.00

1.00

22. Draw the objects shown at A, B, C, D, and E below. Use the **GROUP** command to name each of the drawings as follows:

    A. SWITCH

    B. REGULATOR

    C. GROUND-SWITCH

    D. GROUND-OVERCURRENT

    E. FUSE

Use the object groups to draw the one-line electrical diagram shown below. Use the **Explode** option to edit the symbols at 1 and 2 in the diagram as shown. Save the drawing as P11-22.

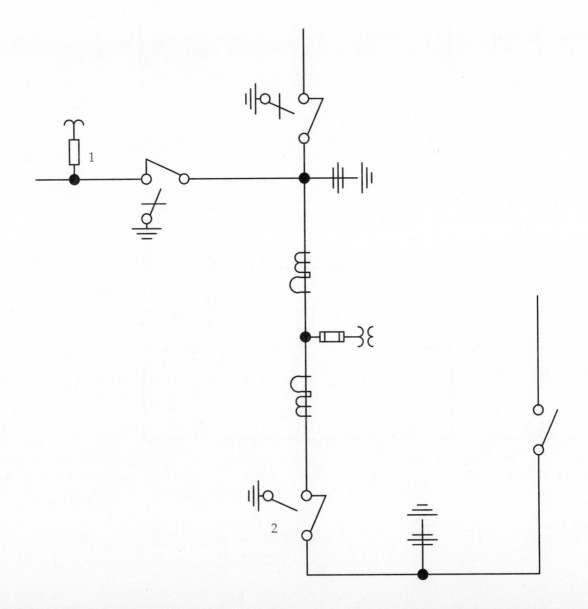

23. Draw the following bracket. Do not include dimensions in your drawing. Use the **FILLET** command where appropriate. Save the drawing as P11-23.

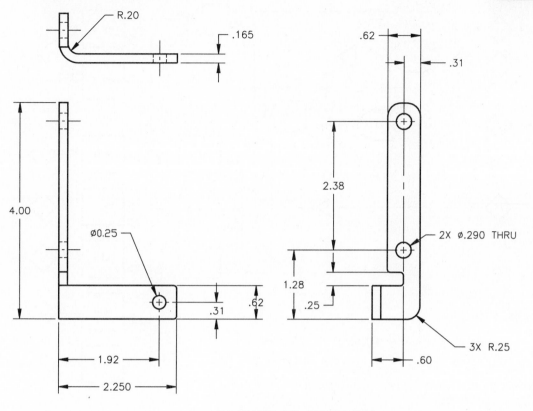

ALL FILLETS AND ROUNDS R.06

24. Draw this refrigeration system schematic. Save the drawing as P11-24.

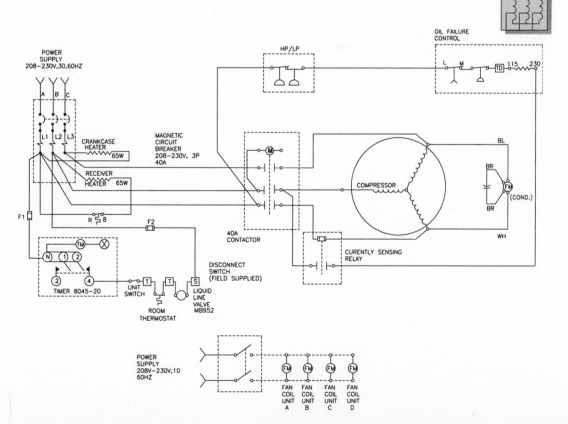

25. Draw this timer schematic. Save the drawing as P11-25.

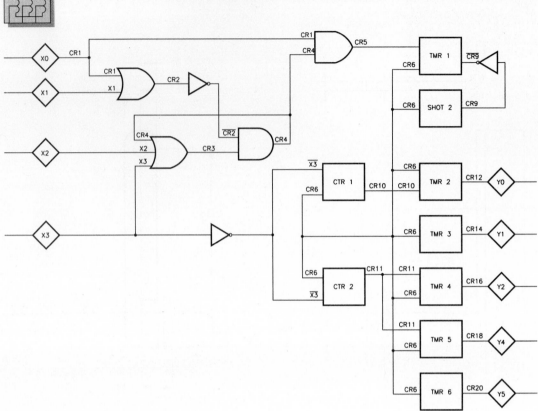

Chapter 12

Automatic Editing

Learning Objectives

After completing this chapter, you will be able to:
○ Use grips to do automatic editing with the **STRETCH**, **COPY**, **MOVE**, **ROTATE**, **SCALE**, and **MIRROR** commands.
○ Identify the system variables used for automatic editing.
○ Perform automatic editing through the **Modify** dialog box.
○ Change the properties of an object.

In Chapter 11, you learned how to use commands that let you do a variety of drawing and editing activities with AutoCAD. These editing commands give you maximum flexibility and increase productivity. However, this chapter takes editing a step further by allowing you to first select an object and then automatically perform editing operations.

Automatic Editing with Grips

"Hold," "grab," and "grasp" are all words that are synonymous with grip. In AutoCAD, *grips* are features on an entity that are highlighted with a small box. For example, the grips on a straight line are the endpoints and midpoint. When grips are used for editing, you can select an object to automatically activate the grips. Then, pick any of the small boxes to perform stretch, copy, move, rotate, scale, or mirror operations. In order for grips to work the **GRIPS** system variable must be on.

> Command: **GRIPS**↵
> New value for GRIPS ⟨0⟩: **1**↵
> Command:

When **GRIPS** is on and there is no command active, a pickbox is located at the intersection of the screen crosshairs. You can pick any object to activate the grips. Figure 12-1 shows what grips look like on several different entities. For text, the grip box is located at the insertion point.

Figure 12-1.
Grips are placed at
strategic locations
on objects.

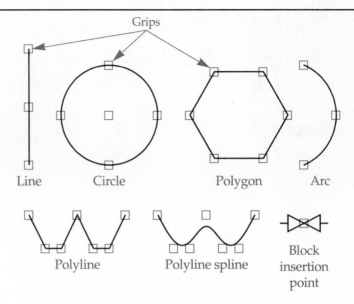

You can control grips settings by picking **Grips...** in the **Tools** pull-down menu or by typing GR or DDGRIPS at the Command: prompt. The **Grips** dialog box shown in Figure 12-2 is then displayed.

Notice the **Select Settings** area in the **Grips** dialog box. Pick the **Enable Grips** check box to turn grips on or off. Pick the **Enable Grips Within Blocks** check box to have grips displayed on every subentity of a block. A *block* is a special symbol designed for multiple use. Blocks are discussed in detail in Chapter 23. When this check box is off, the grip location for a block is at the insertion point, as shown in Figure 12-1. Grips in blocks can also be controlled with the **GRIPBLOCK** system variable. The default for **GRIPBLOCK** is 0. Change this setting to 1 to turn on grips within blocks.

Figure 12-2.
The **Grips** dialog
box.

Turn grips
on or off

Change the
color of grips

Change the
size of grips

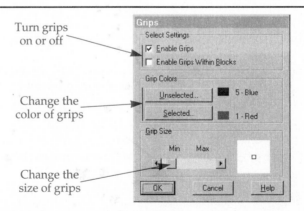

The **Grip Colors** area allows you to change the color of grips. The grips displayed when you first pick an entity are referred to as *unselected grips* because you have not yet picked a grip to perform an operation. An unselected grip is a square with a color outline. Unselected grips are blue by default and are called "warm."

After you pick a grip it is called a *selected grip*. A selected grip appears as a filled-in square, as shown in Figure 12-3. Selected grips are red by default and are called "hot." If more than one entity is selected and they have warm grips, then they are all affected by what you do with the hot grips. Entities that have warm and hot grips are highlighted and are part of the selection set.

Figure 12-3.
Selected (hot) grips
are filled-in squares.
Unselected (warm)
grips are colored
outlines.

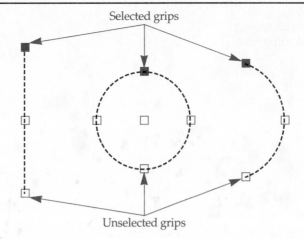

Selected grips

Unselected grips

You can remove highlighted entities from the selection set by holding down the [Shift] key and picking the entity to be removed. The highlighting goes away, but the grips remain. These are called "cold" grips. Entities with cold grips are not affected by what you do to entities with warm grips. Return the entity with cold grips to the selection set by picking it again.

You can also control grip color with the **GRIPCOLOR** and **GRIPHOT** system variables. **GRIPCOLOR** controls the color of unselected (warm) grips, while **GRIPHOT** regulates the color of selected (hot) grips. When you enter one of these variables, simply set the color number as desired.

The **Grip Size** scroll bar in the **Grips** dialog box lets you graphically change the size of the grip box. Change the grip size to whatever works best for your drawing. Very small grip boxes may be difficult to pick. However, the grips may overlap if they are too large.

The grip size can be given a numerical value at the command line using the **GRIPSIZE** system variable. To change the default of 3, enter GRIPSIZE at the Command: prompt and then type a desired size in pixels.

Using grips

To activate grips, move the pick box to the desired entity and pick. The object is highlighted and the unselected grips are displayed. To select a grip, move the pick box to the desired grip and pick it. Notice that the crosshairs snap to a grip. When you pick a grip the command line changes to:

** STRETCH **
⟨Stretch to point⟩/Base point/Copy/Undo/eXit:

This activates the **STRETCH** command. All you have to do is move the cursor to make the selected object stretch, as shown in Figure 12-4. If you pick the middle grip of a line or arc, or the center grip of a circle, the object moves. These are the other options:

- **Base point.** Type B and press [Enter] to select a new base point.
- **Copy.** Type C and press [Enter] if you want to make one or more copies of the selected object.
- **Undo.** Type U and press [Enter] to undo the previous operation.
- **eXit.** Type X and press [Enter] to exit the command. The selected grip is gone, but the unselected grips remain. You can also use [Esc] key to cancel the command. Canceling twice removes the selected and the unselected grips and returns the Command: prompt.

Figure 12-4.
Using the automatic
STRETCH command.
Note the selected
grip. A—Stretching a
line. B—Stretching a
circle. C—Stretching
an arc.

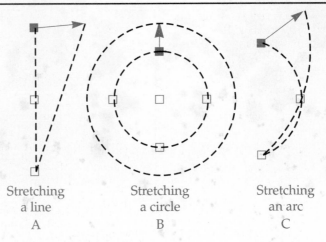

Stretching
a line
A

Stretching
a circle
B

Stretching
an arc
C

You can pick entities individually, or use a window or crossing box. Figure 12-5 shows how you can stretch features of an object after selecting all of the entities. Step 1 in Figure 12-5A stretches the first corner and Step 2 stretches the second corner. You can also make more than one grip hot at the same time by holding down the [Shift] key as you pick the grips, as shown in Figure 12-5B. Here are some general rules and guidelines that can help make grips work for you:

✓ Be sure the **GRIPS** system variable is on.
✓ Pick an entity or group of entities to activate grips.
✓ Entities in the selection set are highlighted.
✓ Pick a warm grip to make it hot.
✓ Make multiple grips hot by holding the [Shift] key while picking warm grips.
✓ If more than one entity has hot grips, they are all affected by the editing commands.
✓ Remove entities from the selection set by holding down the [Shift] key and picking them, thus making the grips cold.
✓ Return entities to the selection set by picking them again.
✓ Remove hot grips from the selection set by pressing [Esc] key to cancel. Cancel again to remove all grips from the selection set. If you have not yet picked a hot grip, cancel twice at the keyboard.

Figure 12-5.
Stretching an object. A—Select corners to stretch individually. B—Select several hot grips by holding down the [Shift] key.

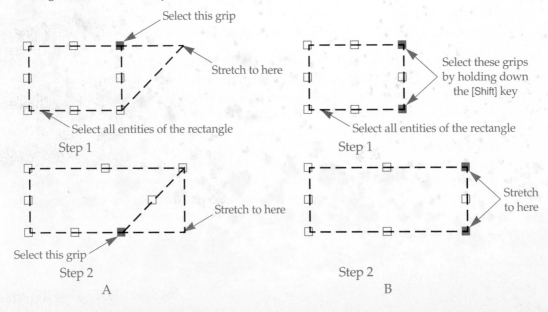

Select this grip

Stretch to here

Select all entities of the rectangle

Step 1

Select these grips
by holding down
the [Shift] key

Select all entities of the rectangle

Step 1

Stretch to here

Select this grip

Step 2

A

Stretch
to here

Step 2

B

EXERCISE 12-1

❏ Start a new drawing or use one of your templates.
❏ Draw a line with coordinates X = 2, Y = 4 and X = 2, Y = 7. Draw a circle with the center at X = 5.5, Y = 5.5, with a radius of 1.5. Finally, draw an arc with its center at X = 8.5, Y = 5.5, a start point of X = 9.5, Y = 4, and an endpoint of X = 9.5, Y = 7.
❏ In the space at the lower-left of the screen, draw a polyline similar to the one in Figure 12-1.
❏ Make sure **GRIPS** is on.
❏ Experiment with the **STRETCH** command using grips by picking the points as follows:
  ❏ Line—Pick the ends first and then the middle to see what happens.
  ❏ Circle—Pick one of the quadrants, and then the center.
  ❏ Arc—Pick the ends and the middle.
  ❏ Polyline—Pick various grips.
❏ Save the drawing as EX12-1.

You can also use the **MOVE, ROTATE, SCALE,** and **MIRROR** commands to automatically edit entities. All you have to do is pick the object and then select one of the grips. When you see the ** STRETCH ** command, press [Enter] to cycle through the command options:

```
** STRETCH **
⟨Stretch to point⟩/Base point/Copy/Undo/eXit: ↵
** MOVE **
⟨Move to point⟩/Base point/Copy/Undo/eXit: ↵
** ROTATE **
⟨Rotation angle⟩/Base point/Copy/Undo/Reference/eXit: ↵
** SCALE **
⟨Scale factor⟩/Base point/Copy/Undo/Reference/eXit: ↵
** MIRROR **
⟨Second point⟩/Base point/Copy/Undo/eXit:
```

As an alternative to pressing [Enter], you can enter the first two characters of the desired command from the keyboard. Type **MO** for move, **MI** for mirror, **RO** for rotate, **SC** for scale, and **ST** for stretch.

AutoCAD also allows you to click the right mouse button and open a grips cursor menu, as shown in Figure 12-6. This menu is only available after a grip has been activated (hot).

The cursor menu allows you to access the five grip editing options without using the keyboard. All you do is pick either **Move, Mirror, Rotate, Scale,** or **Stretch** as needed. Another option in the cursor menu is **Base Point**. This also allows you to select another base point. The cursor menu also provides direct access to the **Copy** option, which is explained later in this chapter. The **Undo** option lets you close the cursor menu and return to the current grip activity.

Figure 12-6.
The grip cursor
menu appears when
a grip is selected
and you pick the
right mouse button.

<u>E</u>nter
<u>M</u>ove
Mi<u>r</u>ror
<u>R</u>otate
Sca<u>l</u>e
<u>S</u>tretch
<u>B</u>ase Point
<u>C</u>opy
Reference
<u>U</u>ndo
<u>P</u>roperties...
<u>G</u>o to URL...
E<u>x</u>it

An added bonus in the grips cursor menu is the **Properties...** option. Selecting this opens a dialog box where you can change characteristics of the objects being edited. If one object is selected, it activates the **DDMODIFY** command. The **DDMODIFY** command was introduced in Chapter 4, and is used later in this chapter. If multiple objects are selected, the **Properties...** option accesses the **DDCHPROP** command. This command is used to change object characteristics using the **Change Properties** dialog box. This dialog box was introduced in Chapter 4 and is discussed again later in this chapter. Selecting the **Exit** option in the grips cursor menu closes the menu and removes the hot grip.

NOTE

When AutoCAD is configured to display a screen menu, the **Move**, **Mirror**, **Rotate**, **Scale**, and **Stretch** automatic editing commands appear in a separate screen menu whenever a grip is selected. See *AutoCAD and its Applications— Advanced, Release 14.*

PROFESSIONAL TIP

Many of the conventional AutoCAD editing operations can be performed when warm grips are displayed on-screen and the **PICKFIRST** variable is set to 1 (its default value). The editing commands can be selected from the pull-down menus, toolbars, or entered at the Command: prompt. For example, the **ERASE** command can be used to clear the screen of all entities displayed with warm grips by first picking the entities and then selecting the **ERASE** command.

Moving an object automatically

If you want to move an object with grips, select the object, pick a grip to use as the base point, and then cycle through the commands until you get to this prompt:

```
** MOVE **
⟨Move to point⟩/Base point/Copy/Undo/eXit:
```

The selected grip becomes the base point. Then, move the object to a new point and pick. The **MOVE** operation is complete, as shown in Figure 12-7. If you accidentally pick the wrong grip or decide to change the grip base point, enter B and press [Enter] for the **Base point** option and pick a new one.

Figure 12-7.
The automatic
MOVE command.
The selected grip
becomes the base
point for the move.

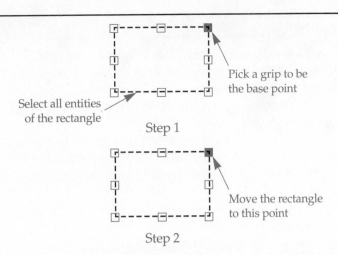

Pick a grip to be
the base point

Select all entities
of the rectangle

Step 1

Move the rectangle
to this point

Step 2

EXERCISE 12-2

❏ Start a new drawing or use one of your templates.
❏ Draw a 1.5″ (38mm) diameter circle with its center at X = 2, Y = 3.
❏ Use grips to move the circle 2″ (50mm) to the right.
❏ Save the drawing as EX12-2.

Copying an object automatically

The **Copy** option is found in each of the editing commands. When using the **STRETCH** command, the **Copy** option allows you to make multiple copies of the entity you are stretching. Holding down the [Shift] key while performing the first **STRETCH** operation accesses the **Multiple** mode. The prompt looks like this:

```
** STRETCH (multiple) **
⟨Stretch to point⟩/Base point/Copy/Undo/eXit: ↵
```

The **Copy** option in the **MOVE** command is the true form of the **COPY** command. You can activate the **Copy** option by entering C as follows:

```
** MOVE **
⟨Move to point⟩/Base point/Copy/Undo/eXit: C↵
** MOVE (multiple) **
⟨Move to point⟩/Base point/Copy/Undo/eXit: (make as many copies as desired and
    enter X to exit, or press [Esc])
```

Holding down the [Shift] key while performing the first **MOVE** operation also puts you in the **Copy** mode. The **Copy** option works similarly in each of the editing commands. Try it with each to see what happens. When you are in the **STRETCH** or **MOVE** commands, you can also access the **Copy** option directly by picking the right mouse button to open the grips cursor menu. Pick the **Copy** option in the cursor menu to perform the same copy activities that were previously explained.

PROFESSIONAL TIP

When in the **Copy** option of the **MOVE** command, if you make the first copy followed by holding the [Shift] key, the distance of the first copy automatically becomes the snap spacing for additional copies.

❏ Start a new drawing or use one of your templates.
❏ Use the **RECTANG** command to draw the objects shown at A, B, C, and D below. Do not draw dimensions.
❏ Use the **Copy** option of the **STRETCH** command to make object A look similar to the example at the right.
❏ Use the **Copy** option of the **STRETCH** command to make object B look similar to the example at the right. Make two grips hot for this to work.
❏ Use the **Copy** option of the **MOVE** command to make multiple copies to the right of object C.
❏ Use the **MOVE** command to make multiple copies to the right of object D while holding down the [Shift] key.
❏ Save the drawing as EX12-3 and quit.

Rotating an object automatically

To automatically rotate an object, select the object, pick a grip to use as the base point, and press [Enter] until you see this prompt:

```
** ROTATE **
⟨Rotation angle⟩/Base point/Copy/Undo/Reference/eXit:
```

Now, move your pointing device to rotate the object. Pick the desired rotation point, or enter a rotation angle like this:

```
⟨Rotation angle⟩/Base point/Copy/Undo/Reference/eXit: 45↵
```

Enter R and press [Enter] if you want to use the **Reference** option: The **Reference** option may be used when the object is already rotated at a known angle and you want to rotate it to a new angle. The reference angle is the current angle and the new angle is the desired angle. Figure 12-8 shows the **Rotation** options.

```
⟨Rotation angle⟩/Base point/Copy/Undo/Reference/eXit: R↵
Reference angle ⟨0⟩: 45↵
** ROTATE **
⟨New angle⟩/Base point/Copy/Undo/Reference/eXit: 10↵
```

Figure 12-8.
The **Rotation angle** option and **Reference** option of the **ROTATE** command.

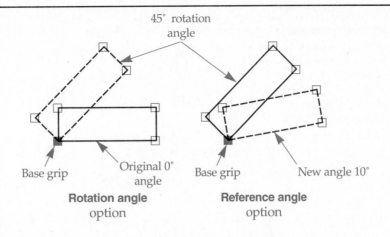

Rotation angle
option

Reference angle
option

Base grip

Original 0° angle

Base grip

New angle 10°

45° rotation angle

EXERCISE 12-4

❏ Start a new drawing or use one of your templates.
❏ Use the **RECTANG** command to draw a rectangle similar to the one shown at the left of Figure 12-8. Orient the long sides so they are at 0°.
❏ Use grips to rotate the object 45°.
❏ Rotate the object again to 20° using the **Reference** option.
❏ Save the drawing as EX12-4.

Scaling an object automatically

If you want to scale an object with grips, cycle through the editing options until you get this prompt:

```
** SCALE **
⟨Scale factor⟩/Base point/Copy/Undo/Reference/eXit:
```

Move the screen cursor and pick when the object is dragged to the desired size. You can also enter a scale factor to automatically increase or decrease the scale of the original object. Refer to Chapter 11 for a review of scale factors. You can use the **Reference** option if you know a current length and a desired length. Enter R for the **Reference** option:

```
⟨Scale factor⟩/Base point/Copy/Undo/Reference/eXit: R↵
Reference length ⟨current⟩: 3.0↵
** SCALE **
⟨New length⟩/Base point/Copy/Undo/Reference/eXit: 5.25↵
```

The selected base point remains in the same place when the object is scaled. Figure 12-9 shows the two **Scale** options.

Figure 12-9.
The options for the automatic **SCALE** command include the **Scale factor** option and the **Reference length** option.

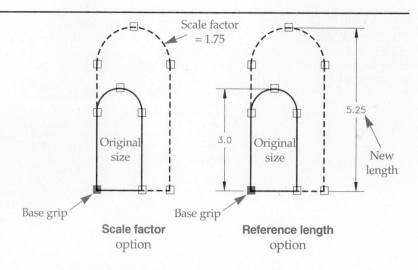

Scale factor = 1.75

Original size

Base grip

Scale factor option

3.0

5.25

Original size

New length

Base grip

Reference length option

Mirroring an object automatically

If you want to mirror an object using grips, the selected grip becomes the first point of the mirror line. Use the **Base point** option to reselect the first point of the mirror line. Then press [Enter] to cycle through the editing commands until you get this prompt:

```
** MIRROR **
⟨Second point⟩/Base point/Copy/Undo/eXit:
```

Pick another grip or any point on the screen as the second point of the mirror line, Figure 12-10. Unlike the standard **MIRROR** command, the automatic **MIRROR** command does not give you the option to delete the old objects. The old objects are deleted automatically. If you want to keep the original object while mirroring, use the **Copy** option in the **MIRROR** command.

Figure 12-10.
When using the automatic **MIRROR** command, the selected grip becomes the first point of the mirror line and the original object is automatically deleted.

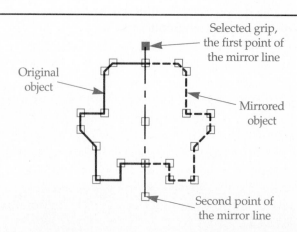

Selected grip, the first point of the mirror line

Original object

Mirrored object

Second point of the mirror line

❑ Start a new drawing or use one of your templates.
❑ Draw a shape similar to the original object in Figure 12-10.
❑ Use grips to mirror the object along the centerline.
❑ Save the drawing as EX12-6.

Basic Editing vs. Automatic Editing

In Chapter 11 you were introduced to basic editing. Basic editing allows you to first enter a command and then select the desired object to be edited. You can also set system variables to first select the desired objects and then enter the desired command. The automatic editing features discussed in this chapter use grips and related editing commands to edit an object automatically, after first selecting the object.

The **Object Selection Settings** dialog box allows you to control the way that you use editing commands. This dialog box is displayed by picking **Selection...** from the **Tools** pull-down menu, or by typing SE or DDSELECT at the Command: prompt. See Figure 12-11. These are the items found in the **Object Selection Settings** dialog box:

- **Noun/Verb Selection.** When you first select objects and then enter a command, it is referred to as the *noun/verb* format. This technique is used throughout most of this book. The pick box is displayed at the screen crosshairs. A "✓" in the **Noun/Verb Selection** check box means that the noun/verb method is active. The **PICKFIRST** system variable can also be used to set the noun/verb selection. When using the *verb/noun* format, you enter the command before selecting the object. In this text, the verb/noun method is used primarily in Chapter 11. Remove the "✓" from the **Noun/Verb Selection** check box to enter the command before making a selection. Some editing commands, such as **FILLET, CHAMFER, DIVIDE, MEASURE, OFFSET, EXTEND, TRIM,** and **BREAK** require that you enter the command before you select the object.

- **Use Shift to Add.** When this check box is off, every entity or group of entities you select is highlighted and added to the selection set. If you pick this check box, it changes the way AutoCAD accepts entities you pick. For example, if you pick an entity, it is highlighted and added to the selection set. However, if you pick another entity, it is highlighted and the first one is removed from the selection set. This means that you can only include one entity by picking, or one group of entities with a selection window. If you want to add more items to the selection set, you must hold down the [Shift] key as you pick them. Turning on the **PICKADD** system variable does the same thing as turning on this feature. Pressing the [Ctrl]+[K] key combination also turns the **PICKADD** system variable on and off.

- **Press and Drag.** This is the same as turning on the **PICKDRAG** system variable. With **Press and Drag** on, you create a selection window by picking the first corner, then moving the puck while holding down the pick button. Release the pick button when you have the desired selection window. By default, **Press and Drag** is off. This means that you need to pick both the first and second corner of the desired selection window.

- **Implied Windowing.** By default, this option is on. This means that you can automatically create a window by picking the first point and moving the cursor to the right to pick the second point, or make a crossing box by picking the first point and moving the cursor to the left to pick the second point. This is the same as turning on the **PICKAUTO** system variable. This does not work if **PICKDRAG** is on.

DDSELECT
SE

Tools
↪ Selection...

- **Object Grouping.** This option controls whether or not AutoCAD recognizes grouped objects as singular entities. When off, the individual elements of a group can be selected for separate editing without having to first explode the group.
- **Associative Hatch.** The default is off, which means that if an associative hatch is moved, the hatch boundary does not move with it. Select this toggle if you want the boundary of an associative hatch to move when you move the hatch pattern. It is a good idea to have this on for most applications. Hatches and hatch boundaries are fully explained in Chapter 22.
- **Default.** Picking this button sets the selection methods to the AutoCAD defaults, as shown in Figure 12-11.

Figure 12-11.
The **Object Selection Settings** dialog box.

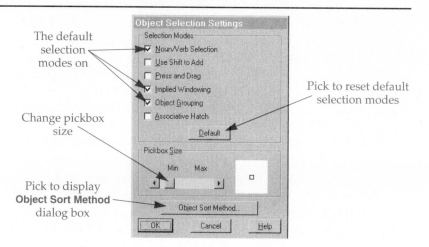

- **Pickbox Size.** This scroll bar lets you adjust the size of the pick box. The sample in the image tile will get smaller or larger as you move the scroll bar. Stop when you have the desired size. The pick box size is also controlled by the **PICKBOX** system variable.
- **Object Sort Method....** The **Object Sort Method** dialog box shown in Figure 12-12 appears when you pick this button. The check boxes in the **Object Sort Method** dialog box allow you to control the order that entities are displayed or plotted in. The check boxes are explained as follows:
  - **Object Selection**—Objects selected using a windowing method are placed in the selection set in the order they occur in the drawing database.
  - **Object Snap**—Object snap modes find objects in the order they occur in the drawing database.
  - **Redraws**—Objects are displayed by a **REDRAW** command in the order they occur in the drawing database.
  - **Regens**—Objects are displayed by a drawing regeneration in the order they occur in the drawing database.

Figure 12-12.
This dialog box can be accessed by picking **Object Sort Method...** from the **Object Selection Settings** dialog box.

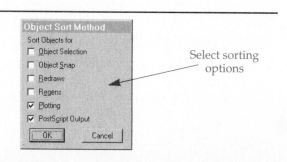

AutoCAD and its Applications—Basics

- **P̲lotting**—Objects are plotted in the order they occur in the drawing database.
- **PostS̲cript Output**—**PSOUT** processes objects in the order they occur in the drawing database. PostScript is a copyrighted page description language that is used in the desktop publishing industry. This is discussed further in *AutoCAD and its Applications—Advanced, Release 14*. The **PSOUT** command converts any AutoCAD drawing to a PostScript file.

Entity sorting is also controlled by the **SORTENTS** system variable. The following values duplicate the check boxes in the dialog box:

- **0.** Sorting is turned off.
- **1.** Object selection sorting.
- **2.** Object snap sorting.
- **4.** Sorts entities in a redraw.
- **8.** Slide creation sorting.
- **16.** Regeneration sorting.
- **32.** Plot sorting.
- **64.** Sort for PostScript output.

The default, 96, specifies sorting for plotting and PostScript output. This is because the numeric values for each setting are *bit* values. Bit values allow you to add together the individual setting values to indicate each of the set values. Since the values 64 + 32 = 96, this **SORTENTS** setting sorts both for **P̲lotting** and for **PostScript** output. If you wanted to set the object sort method to include **O̲bject Selection** (1), **Object S̲nap** (2), and **R̲edraws** (4), the **SORTENTS** value should be 7 (1 + 2 + 4 = 7).

PROFESSIONAL TIP

Notice in Figure 12-12 that only two of the check boxes are checked. Entity sorting takes time and should only be used if the drawing or application software you are using requires entity sorting. Turn the **O̲bject Selection** sorting on if you want AutoCAD to find the last object drawn when selecting overlapping entities.

EXERCISE 12-7

- ❏ Start a new drawing, use one of your templates, or open a previous exercise.
- ❏ Enter the **DDSELECT** command to open the **Object Selection Settings** dialog box.
- ❏ Adjust the pick box size and observe the image tile.
- ❏ Pick **Object Sort Method...** to open the **Object Sort Method** dialog box.
- ❏ Cancel both dialog boxes.
- ❏ Quit the drawing session without saving or keep it open for the next exercise.

Automatic Editing in a Dialog Box

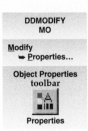

DDMODIFY
MO

Modify
 ➥ Properties...

Object Properties toolbar

Properties

To edit an entity using the **Modify** dialog box, pick the **Properties** button from the **Object Properties** toolbar, pick **P̲roperties...** from the **M̲odify** pull-down menu or type MO or DDMODIFY at the Command: prompt. You are first asked to select an object to modify:

    Command: **MO** *or* **DDMODIFY**↵
    Select one object to modify: *(pick a single object to modify)*

If you pick a line, you get the **Modify Line** dialog box. If you pick a circle, you get the **Modify Circle** dialog box shown in Figure 12-13. Each of the **Modify** dialog boxes is

Figure 12-13.
Modify dialog boxes, such as the **Modify Circle** dialog box, can be used to edit entities.

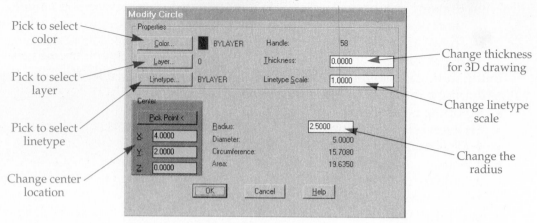

Pick to select color

Pick to select layer

Pick to select linetype

Change center location

Change thickness for 3D drawing

Change linetype scale

Change the radius

slightly different. For example, the **Modify Line** dialog box contains text boxes to change the endpoint coordinates. If you pick an entity such as a polygon, you get the **Modify Polyline** dialog box. This dialog box contains items that allow you to automatically edit various aspects of a polyline. Remember that polygons and rectangles are polylines.

The **Modify Text** dialog box is an excellent way to quickly edit text. To get the **Modify Text** dialog box shown in Figure 12-14, enter the **DDMODIFY** command and pick the single-line text to be modified. The **Properties** area allows you to change the color, linetype, layer, linetype scale, and thickness. Use the **Text:** edit box to remove, add, or change the text as needed. Change the text origin by selecting the **Pick Point ⟨** button and picking a new point on the screen, or enter new X,Y coordinates. Automatically change the text height in the **Height:** text box, or change the rotation angle, width factor, or obliquing angle by altering the values in these text boxes. Pick the arrow at the right of the **Justify** box to get the justification drop-down list. Pick the desired justification from this list. Select a text style from the **Style** drop-down list. Check either the **Upside Down** or the **Backward** boxes if you want these conditions to be in effect.

You get the **Modify MText** dialog box when you select multiline text to edit. This dialog box has features similar to the **Modify Text** dialog box, except there is also a **Full editor...** button, which opens the **Multiline Text Editor**.

Figure 12-14.
Text can be edited easily using the **Modify Text** dialog box.

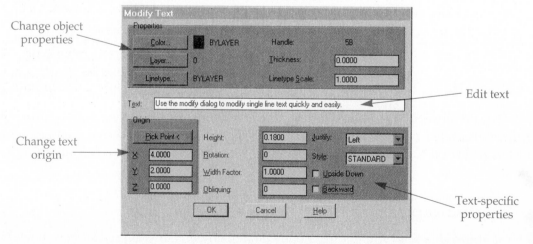

Change object properties

Change text origin

Edit text

Text-specific properties

The next sections discuss features found in **Modify** dialog boxes. These features are common to all of the **Modify** dialog boxes.

Properties

The **Properties** section of all **Modify** dialog boxes contains several common elements:

- **Color....** Pick this button to get the **Select Color** dialog box, which displays the available colors. Simply pick a desired color for the entity, or enter a color name or number in the **Color:** text box.
- **Layer....** Picking this button displays the **Select Layer** dialog box, where you can set the selected entity to a desired layer. Layers are discussed in Chapter 4.
- **Linetype....** Pick this button to see the **Select Linetype** dialog box. Here you can change the entity linetype by selecting one of the linetypes that has already been loaded.
- **Thickness:.** This text box lets you change the thickness of a 3D entity. This is discussed in Chapter 27.
- **Linetype Scale:.** This text box allows you to change the individual object linetype scale as a multiplier of the **LTSCALE** system variable.

Changing the center point

When an object such as a circle or an arc is selected using **DDMODIFY**, the following information is provided:

- **Pick Point ⟨.** Pick this button to establish a new center point. The dialog box disappears, the graphics window returns, and you see this prompt:

> Center point: *(pick a new center point, or enter the coordinates for a new center location and press* [Enter]*)*

- **X:, Y:, Z:.** Use these text boxes to change the values of the X, Y, and Z coordinates. The Z coordinate is for 3D drawings. The center location automatically changes when you enter new values and pick the **OK** button.

When modifying a circle, related information for the diameter, circumference, and area appear near the center of the **Modify** dialog box. The radius is also given in a text box. If you want to change the radius, double-click on the **Radius:** text box and enter a new value. The circle automatically changes to the new radius.

NOTE   Changing an object's properties by picking the **Properties** button on the **Object Properties** toolbar or **Properties...** from the **Modify** pull-down menu will display different dialog boxes, depending on how many objects are selected. Only single objects can be modified using a **Modify** dialog box, so when more than one object is selected, the **Change Properties** dialog is displayed just as if you had used the **DDCHPROP** command. **DDCHPROP** and the **Change Properties** dialog are discussed in the next section of this chapter. If you type the **DDMODIFY** command, then AutoCAD allows you to select only one object.

❏ Start a new drawing, use one of your templates, or open a previous exercise.
❏ Draw a line with endpoint coordinates X = 2, Y = 3, and X = 2, Y = 6.
❏ Draw a circle with a radius of 1.250 and a center location of X = 6, Y = 4.5.
❏ Use the **DTEXT** command with .25″ text height to position the word LINE below the line and CIRCLE below the circle.
❏ Use the **Modify Line** dialog box to edit the line as follows:
   ❏ Change the "from point" to X = 6.750, Y = 3.770.
   ❏ Change the "to point" to X = 6.750, Y = 6.750.
❏ Use the **Modify Circle** dialog box to edit the circle as follows:
   ❏ Change the center location to X = 7.125, Y = 5.25.
   ❏ Change the radius to .375.
❏ Change the LINE label to .125″ height and place it above the line.
❏ Change the CIRCLE label to read Circle and justify the middle of it with the center of the circle. Modify the text height to be .375″.
❏ Save the drawing as EX12-8.

PROFESSIONAL TIP

If you are trying to pick an entity that is on top of another, AutoCAD may not pick the one you want. However, AutoCAD picks the last thing you drew if **Object Selection** is on in the **Object Sort Method** dialog box.

Changing the Properties of an Object

In Chapter 11 you learned how to make changes to an object using the **CHANGE** command. This is a popular command because it is easy to use and allows you to change either the location of an object or properties related to the object. You used the default, **Change point**, to change the location of an object. You can also change properties of the feature by typing P for the **Properties** option. The **CHANGE** command is accessed by typing -CH or CHANGE. The keyboard shortcut is a hyphen (-) typed before CH:

```
Command: -CH or CHANGE↵
Select objects: (pick the object)
Select objects: ↵
Properties/⟨Change point⟩: P↵
Change what property (Color/Elev/LAyer/LType/ltScale/Thickness) ?
```

The following properties can be changed with the **CHANGE** command:
- **Color.** Changes the color of the selected object.
- **Elev.** Used to change the elevation in 3D drawing.
- **Layer.** Changes the layer designation.
- **LType.** Changes the current linetype of a selected object to a linetype that has been loaded using the **LINETYPE** command.
- **ltScale.** Changes the individual object linetype scale.
- **Thickness.** Used to change the thickness in 3D drawing.

The **CHPROP** (change property) command lets you change only properties of an object. It does not allow for a point change, as in the **CHANGE** command. This is the command sequence for **CHPROP**:

> Command: **CHPROP**↵
> Select objects: *(pick the object)*
> Select objects: ↵
> Change what property (Color/LAyer/LType/ltScale/Thickness) ?

Except for **Elevation**, the **CHPROP** options are the same as those discussed for the **CHANGE** command.

If you prefer to use a dialog box, you can change properties by picking the **Properties** button on the **Object Properties** toolbar, or by picking **Properties...** in the **Modify** pull-down menu, or by entering **CH** or **DDCHPROP** at the Command: prompt. When using the **Properties** button on the **Object Properties** toolbar, picking a single object opens the object-specific modify dialog box, such as **Modify Line** and **Modify Circle**. Picking more than one object opens the **Change Properties** dialog box shown in Figure 12-15.

DDCHPROP
CH

Modify
↳ **P**roperties...

Object Properties
toolbar

Properties

Figure 12-15.
The **Change Properties** dialog box is accessed with the **DDCHPROP** command.

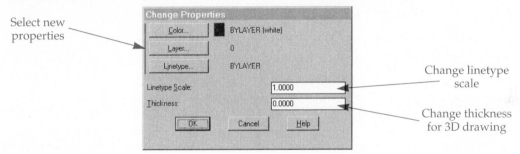

Select new properties

Change linetype scale

Change thickness for 3D drawing

As you look at the **Change Properties** dialog box, you can see some of the items discussed earlier. You can pick **Color...** to change the entity color, pick **Layer...** to change the layer, or pick **Linetype...** to change the linetype. The thickness or linetype scale of an object can be changed using edit boxes.

EXERCISE 12-9

❏ Start a new drawing or use one of your templates.
❏ Draw a vertical line on the left side of the screen, a circle in the middle, and a hexagon on the right side.
❏ Load the CENTER, HIDDEN, and PHANTOM linetypes.
❏ Use the **CHANGE** command to change the line's linetype to CENTER.
❏ Use the **CHPROP** command to change the circle's linetype to HIDDEN and the color to red.
❏ Enter the **Change Properties** dialog box and change the linetype of the hexagon to PHANTOM and the color to yellow.
❏ Save the drawing as EX12-9 and quit.

PROFESSIONAL TIP The **Extended Change Properties** tool is available in the **Bonus Standard** toolbar. This tool is available if a full installation was performed. See Appendix A for bonus menu information.

Chapter Test

Write your answers in the spaces provided.

1. Give the command and entries required to turn on grips:
   Command: _____
   New value for GRIPS ⟨ ⟩: _____

2. Give the prompts needed to rotate an object from an existing 60° angle to a new 25° angle:
   ⟨Rotation angle⟩/Base point/Copy/Undo/Reference/eXit: _____
   Reference angle ⟨ ⟩: _____
   ⟨New angle⟩/Base point/Copy/Undo/Reference/eXit: _____

3. Give the prompts required to scale an object to become three-quarters of its original size:
   ⟨Scale factor⟩/Base point/Copy/Undo/Reference/eXit: _____

4. Name the two system variables that control the color of grips. _____
   _____
   _____

5. Name the six editing commands that can be accessed automatically using grips.
   _____
   _____
   _____

6. Explain the difference between "noun/verb selection" and "verb/noun selection."
   _____
   _____
   _____

7. Name the system variable that allows you to set the "noun/verb selection." _____

8. What does **Use Shift to Add** mean? _____
   _____
   _____
   _____

9. Describe how **Press and Drag** works. _____
   _____
   _____
   _____

10. Name the system variable that is used to turn on **Press and Drag**. _____

11. Name the system variable that turns on **Implied Windowing**. _____

12. Identify two ways to access the **Object Selection Settings** dialog box. _____
    _____

13. Explain two ways to change the pick box size. _____
    _____

14. Give the command sequence and explain how you would change the radius of a circle from 1.375 to 1.875 using a dialog box. _____

_____

_____

_____

_____

_____

15. Identify the pull-down menu and the item you pick from this menu to access the dialog box described in Question 14. _____

_____

16. How would you change the linetype of an entity using the dialog box described in Question 14? _____

_____

_____

_____

17. Name three commands that allow you to change the properties of an object. ____

_____

18. Which of the commands in Question 17 accesses the **Change Properties** dialog box?

_____

19. How do you access the **Change Properties** dialog box through a pull-down menu?

_____

20. How do you change the color of an entity using the **Change Properties** dialog box?

_____

_____

21. How do you open the grips cursor menu? _____

_____

22. What is the purpose of the **Base Point** option in the grips cursor menu? _____

_____

23. Explain the function of the **Undo** option in the grips cursor menu. _____

_____

24. Describe the purpose of the **Properties...** option in the grips cursor menu. _____

_____

25. What happens when you choose the **Exit** option in the grips cursor menu? _____

_____

26. What is the function of using the [Ctrl]+[K] key combination? _____

_____

Drawing Problems

Use templates as appropriate for each of the following problems. Use grips and the associated editing commands or other editing techniques discussed in this chapter.

1. Draw the objects shown at A below and then use the **STRETCH** command to make them look like the objects at B. Do not include dimensions. Save the drawing as P12-1.

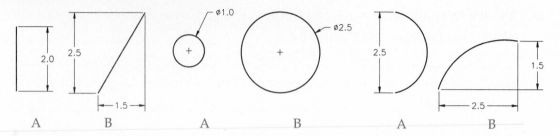

2. Draw the object shown at A below. Then using the **Copy** option of the **MOVE** command, copy the object to the position shown at B. Edit object A so that it resembles example C. Edit object B so that it looks like D. Do not include dimensions. Save the drawing as P12-2.

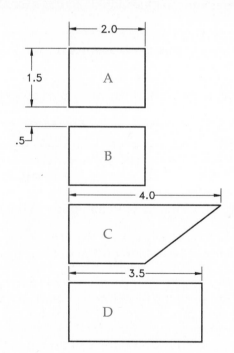

3. Draw the object shown at A below. Then copy the object, without rotating it, to a position below as indicated by the dashed lines. Then, rotate the object 45°. Copy the rotated object at B to a position below as indicated by the dashed lines. Use the **Reference** option to rotate the object at C to 25° as shown. Do not include dimensions. Save the drawing as P12-3.

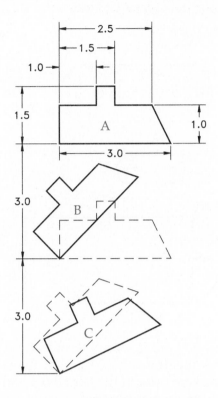

4. Draw the individual entities (vertical line, horizontal line, circle, arc, and "C" shape) at A below using the dimensions given. Then, use grips and the editing commands to create the object shown at B. Do not include dimensions. Save the drawing as P12-4.

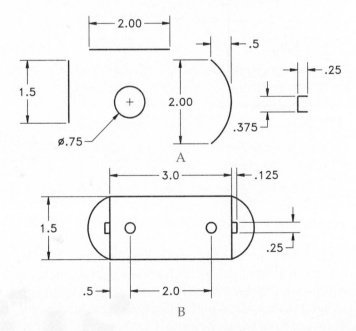

5. Use the completed drawing from Problem 12-4. Erase everything except the completed object and move it to a position similar to A below. Copy the object two times to positions B and C. Use the **SCALE** command to scale the object at B to fifty percent of its original size. Use the **Reference** option of the **SCALE** command to enlarge the object at C from the existing 3.0 length to a 4.5 length as shown in C. Do not include dimensions. Save as P12-5.

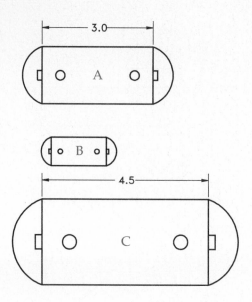

6. Draw the dimensioned partial object shown at A. Do not include dimensions. Mirror the drawing to complete the four quadrants as shown at B. Change the color of the horizontal and vertical parting lines to red and the linetype to Center. Save the drawing as P12-6.

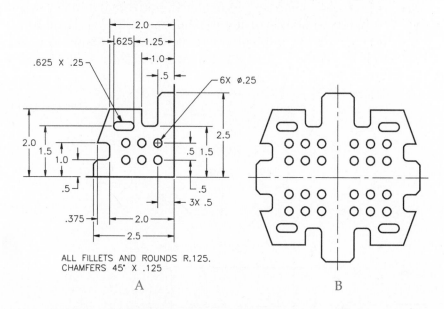

7. Load the final drawing you created in Problem 12-6. Use the **Modify Circle** dialog box to change the circles from a .25 diameter to a .125 diameter. Use the **Change Properties** dialog box to change the linetype of the slots to Phantom. Be sure the linetype scale allows the linetypes to be displayed. Save the drawing as P12-7.

AutoCAD and its Applications—Basics

8. Use the editing commands discussed in this chapter to assist you in drawing the following object. Draw the object within the boundaries of the given dimensions. All other dimensions are flexible. Do not include dimensions in the drawing. Save the drawing as P12-8.

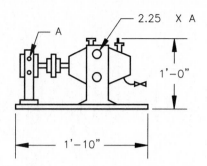

9. Draw the following object within the boundaries of the given dimensions. All other dimensions are flexible. Do not include dimensions. After drawing the object, create a page for a vendor catalog as follows:

- All labels should be ROMAND text centered directly below the view. Use a text height of .125.
- Label the drawing ONE-GALLON TANK WITH HORIZONTAL VALVE.
- Keep the valve the same scale as the original drawing in each copy.
- Copy the original tank to a new location and scale it so that it is two times its original size. Rotate the valve 45°. Label this tank TWO-GALLON TANK WITH 45° VALVE.
- Copy the original tank to another location and scale it so that it is 2.5 times the size of the original. Rotate the valve 90°. Label this tank TWO- AND ONE-HALF GALLON TANK WITH 90° VALVE.
- Copy the two-gallon tank to a new position and scale it so that it is two times this size. Rotate the valve to 22°30′. Label this tank FOUR-GALLON TANK WITH 22°30′ VALVE.
- Left-justify this note at the bottom of the page: Combinations of tank size and valve orientation are available upon request.
- Use the **Modify Text** dialog box to change all tank labels to ROMANC, .25″ high.
- Use the **Modify Text** dialog box to change the note at the bottom of the sheet to ROMANS, centered on the sheet using uppercase letters.
- Save the drawing as P12-9.

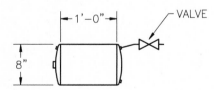

10. Open Problem 11-14 if you have already drawn it. If you have not yet drawn this object, refer to that problem and draw it now. Do not include dimensions. Use the **DDMODIFY** command and other editing commands to edit the drawing as follows:

- Change the Ø2.125 circle to Ø1.50.
- Change the R.50 dimension to R.375.
- Change the 2.7750 length to 4.80.
- Save the drawing as P12-10.

11. Draw this integrated circuit schematic. Save the drawing as P12-11.

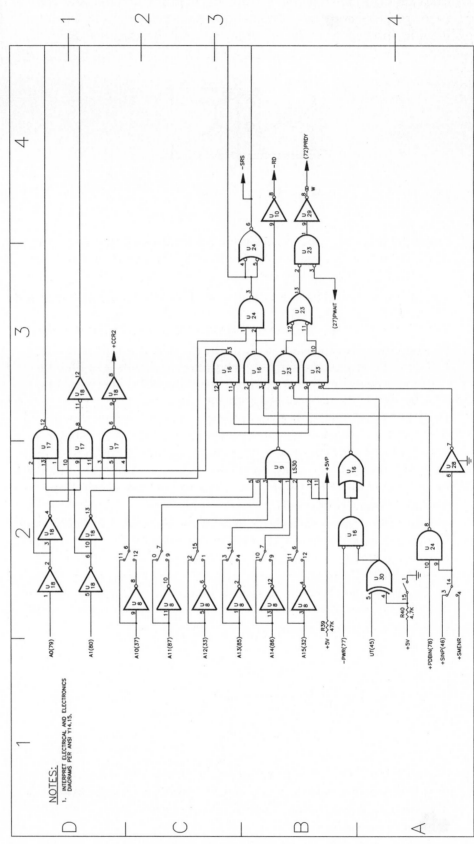

Creating Multiple Objects with Array

Learning Objectives

After completing this chapter, you will be able to:
- ○ Create an arrangement of objects in a rectangular pattern.
- ○ Create an arrangement of any objects in a circular pattern.

Some designs require a rectangular or circular pattern of the same object. For example, office desks are often arranged in rows. Suppose your design calls for five rows, each having four desks. You can create this design by drawing one desk and copying it 19 times. You can also save the desk as a block and insert it 20 times. However, both of these options are time-consuming. A quicker method is to use AutoCAD's **ARRAY** command. Using **ARRAY**, you first select the object(s) to be copied. Then, enter the type of arrangement (rectangular or polar).

A *rectangular array* creates rows and columns of the selected items, and you must provide the spacing. A *polar array* constructs a circular arrangement. For a circular array, you must specify the number of items to array, the angle between items, and the center point of the array. Some examples are shown in Figure 13-1.

Figure 13-1.
Example arrays created with the **ARRAY** command.

A   B   C   D

Rectangular arrays

A   B   C   D

Polar arrays

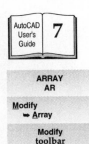
In this chapter, you will experiment with the **ARRAY** command on a .5 unit square. You may want to draw this object now to use as you study the chapter.

The **ARRAY** command is accessed by typing AR or ARRAY at the Command: prompt. It can also be accessed by picking the **Array** button on the **Modify** toolbar or selecting **Array** from the **Modify** pull-down menu. After you issue the **ARRAY** command, AutoCAD asks you to select objects. All of the selection set methods, such as window and crossing, are valid. After you select the desired objects, you must specify whether you want a rectangular or polar array. The command sequence is as follows:

> Command: **AR** *or* **ARRAY**↵
> Select objects: *(select the objects)*
> 1 found
> Select objects: ↵
> Rectangular or Polar array (R/P) ⟨*current*⟩: *(type* R *or* P *and press* [Enter]*)*

Rectangular Placement of Objects

A rectangular array places objects in line along the X and Y axes. You can specify a single row, a single column, or multiple rows and columns. *Rows* are horizontal and *columns* are vertical. AutoCAD reminds you of this by indicating the direction in parentheses: (– – –) for rows and (⁞ ⁞ ⁞) for columns. The following sequence creates a pattern having 3 rows, 3 columns, and .5 spacing between objects. Remember, the object is a .5 unit square.

> Rectangular or Polar array (R/P) ⟨*current*⟩: **R**↵
> Number of rows (– – –) ⟨1⟩: **3**↵
> Number of columns (⁞ ⁞ ⁞) ⟨1⟩: **3**↵
> Unit cell or distance between rows (– – –): **1**↵
> Distance between columns (⁞ ⁞ ⁞): **1**↵
> Command:

The original object and resulting array are shown in Figure 13-2. When giving the distance between rows and columns, be sure to include the width and height of the object. Figure 13-2 shows how to calculate the distance between objects in a rectangular array.

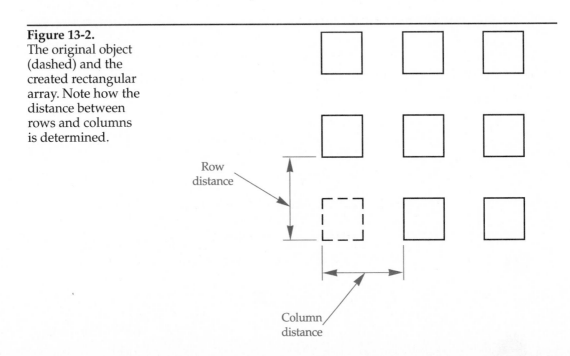

Figure 13-2.
The original object (dashed) and the created rectangular array. Note how the distance between rows and columns is determined.

Row distance

Column distance

AutoCAD allows you to point to the distance separating objects. This is called the *unit cell*. The unit cell distance is the same as the distance between rows and columns. However, it is entered with the pointing device, just like selecting a window. See Figure 13-3. The second point's distance and direction from the first point determines the X and Y spacing for the array.

Unit cell or distance between rows (– – –): *(pick corner)*
Other corner: *(pick second corner)*

Figure 13-3.
The unit cell spacing box is the same as the distance between rows and columns.

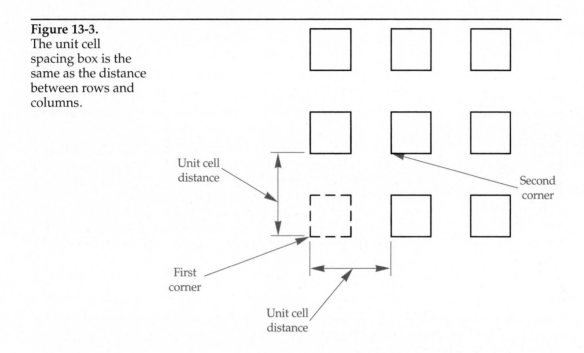

Figure 13-4 shows how you can place arrays in four directions by entering either positive or negative row and column distance values. The dashed box is the original object. The row and column distance is one unit and the box is .5 units square.

Specifying the unit cell distance can create a quick row and column arrangement in any direction. For example, in Figure 13-5 the second unit cell corner is picked to the left and below the first corner.

Figure 13-4.
Placing arrays in one of four directions by giving positive or negative row and column distance values. The original object is shown highlighted.

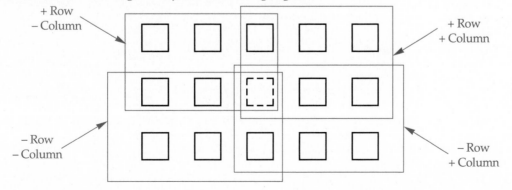

Figure 13-5.
Creating a
rectangular array by
picking a negative
unit cell distance.

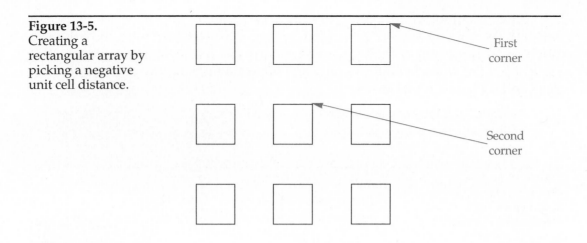

First
corner

Second
corner

EXERCISE 13-1

❏ Start a new drawing or use one of your templates.
❏ Construct the Bill of Materials form shown below using the **LINE** and **ARRAY** commands. Line A is arrayed in nine rows and one column. The distance between rows is given. Line B is arrayed in one row and three columns. The distance between the columns is provided.
❏ Complete the headings using the **DTEXT** command with middle justification.
❏ Save the drawing as EX13-1 and quit.

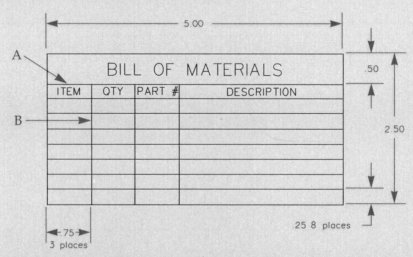

Arranging Objects around a Center Point

Use the **Polar** option of the **ARRAY** command to create a polar array. First, erase everything on your screen except for one .5 unit square. Enter the following command sequence:

> Command: **ARRAY**↵
> Select objects: *(select the object)*
> 1 found
> Select objects: ↵
> Rectangular or Polar array (R/P) ⟨*current*⟩: **P**↵
> Base/⟨Specify center point of array⟩: *(pick the center point)*

Next, AutoCAD requests the number of objects you want in the array. If you know the exact number needed, enter that value. If you would rather specify an angle between items, just press [Enter]. In the example below, [Enter] is pressed.

> Number of items: ↵
> Angle to fill (+ =ccw, – =cw) ⟨360⟩:

Notice the letters +=ccw and –=cw in parentheses. You can array the object in a counterclockwise direction by entering a positive angle value. Numbers entered without the plus sign are positive. Objects can be arrayed clockwise by entering the minus sign before the angle value. Pressing [Enter] at this prompt without entering a value copies the object through 360°. This is the default value.

The final value needed is the angular spacing between the arrayed objects.

> Angle between items: **45**↵

A number entered at this prompt is assumed to be the angle. This prompt is only displayed if you pressed [Enter] at the Number of items: prompt. If you specify the number of items, AutoCAD calculates the angle for you. The last prompt is:

> Rotate objects as they are copied? ⟨Y⟩ **N**↵
> Command:

You can have the objects rotated as they are copied around the pivot point. This keeps the same face of the object always pointing toward the pivot point. If objects are not rotated as they are copied, they remain in the same orientation as the original object. See Figure 13-6.

Figure 13-6.
Using the **Polar** option of the **ARRAY** command to rotate a box. A—The box is rotated as it is arrayed. B—The box is not rotated as it is arrayed.

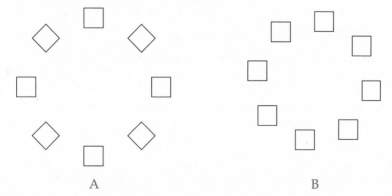

A   B

EXERCISE 13-2

❏ Start a new drawing or use one of your templates.
❏ Create a 360° polar array of five circles.
❏ Copy one of the circles to the side of the polar array.
❏ Create an array with the copied circle. Each circle should be 30° apart and go through 270°.
❏ Save the drawing as EX13-2 and quit.

Chapter Test

Write your answers in the spaces provided.

1. What is the difference between polar and rectangular arrays? _____

    _____

    _____

2. What four values should you know before you create a rectangular array? _____

    _____

    _____

3. Define "unit cell." _____

    _____

4. Suppose an object is 1.5" (38mm) wide and you want a rectangular array with .75" (19mm) spacing between objects. What should you specify for the distance between columns? _____

5. How do you create a rectangular array that is rotated? _____

    _____

6. What values should you know before you execute a polar array? _____

    _____

    _____

7. Suppose you enter a value for the Number of items: prompt in a polar array. Which of the following values are you not required to give? Circle one.

    A. Angle to fill.

    B. Angle between items.

    C. Center point.

    D. Rotate objects as they are copied.

8. What happens to an object when it is not rotated as it is arrayed? _____

    _____

    _____

9. How do you specify a clockwise array rotation? _____

    _____

Drawing Problems

1. Draw the following object views using the dimensions given. Use **ARRAY** to construct the hole and tooth arrangements. Place the drawing on one of your template drawings. Do not add dimensions. Save the drawing as P13-1.

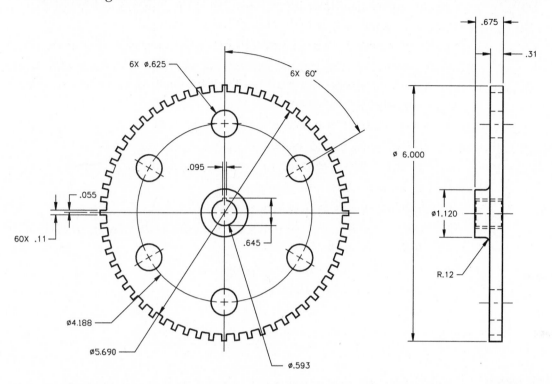

2. Draw the electrical schematic shown below using the same layout. Carefully study the drawing and determine the least number of lines and components that you need to draw, then decide how best to use **ARRAY** and other editing commands to complete the drawing. Use a B-size template. Text should be 1/8" high. Save the drawing as P13-2.

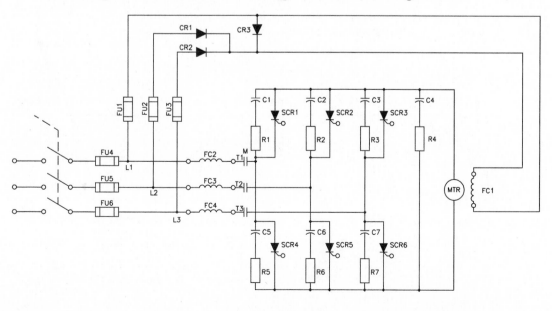

3. The following engineering sketch shows a steel column arrangement on a concrete floor slab for a new building. The steel columns are represented by I-shaped symbols. The columns are arranged in "bay lines" and "column lines." The column lines are numbered 1, 2, and 3. The bay lines are labeled A through G. The width of a bay is 20'-0". Line balloons, or tags, identify bay and column lines. Draw the arrangement using **ARRAY** for the steel column symbols and for the tags. The following guidelines will help you.

A. Begin a new drawing named P13-3 or use an architectural template.

B. Select architectural units and 36 × 24 sheet size. Determine the scale required for this floor plan to fit on this sheet size, and determine your limits accordingly.

C. Set the grid spacing at 2'-0" (24").

D. Set the snap spacing at 12".

E. Use the **PLINE** command to draw the steel column symbol.

F. Do not dimension the drawing.

G. Draw all objects to dimensions given.

H. Place text inside the tag balloons. Set **OSNAP** to **Center**, use **DTEXT Middle**, text height 6".

I. Place a title block on the drawing.

J. Save the drawing as P13-3.

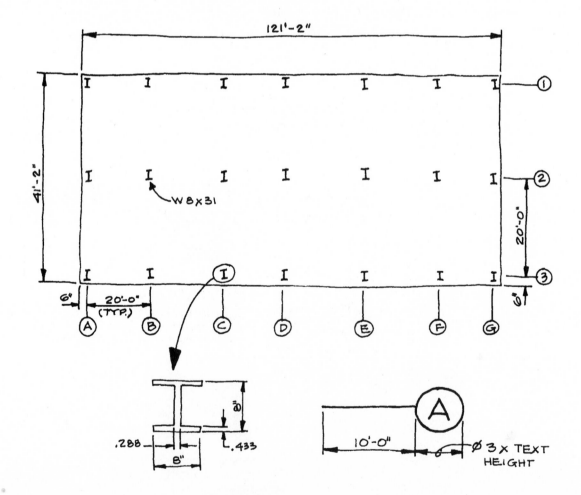

AutoCAD and its Applications—Basics

4. The engineering sketch given is a proposed office layout of desks and chairs. One desk has been shown with the layout of chair, keyboard, monitor, and tower-mounted computer (dotted lines). All of the desk workstations should have the same configuration. Exact size and locations of doors and windows is not important for this problem. Set the **SAVETIME** variable to save your drawing every ten minutes. Use the following guidelines to complete this problem.

A. Begin a new drawing called P13-4.

B. Choose architectural units.

C. Select C–size template drawing and be sure to create this drawing in model space. Use the **ZOOM XP** option to display the drawing at a scale that fits the C-size layout.

D. Use the appropriate drawing and editing commands to complete this problem quickly and efficiently.

E. Draw the desk and computer hardware to the dimensions given.

F. Do not dimension the drawing. Plot in paper space at a 1:1 scale.

G. Save the drawing as P13-4.

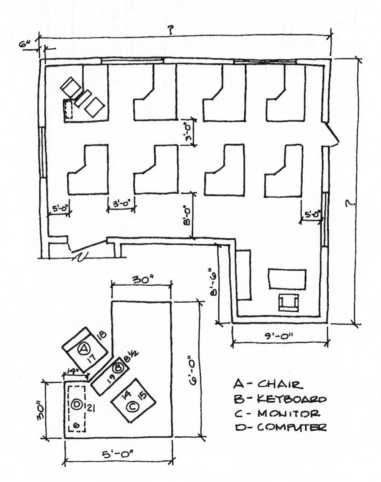

A - CHAIR
B - KEYBOARD
C - MONITOR
D - COMPUTER

5. You have been given an engineer's sketches and notes, and are asked to construct a drawing of a sprocket. Create a front and side view of the sprocket using the **ARRAY** command. Place the drawing on one of your template drawings. Do not add dimensions. Save the drawing as P13-5.

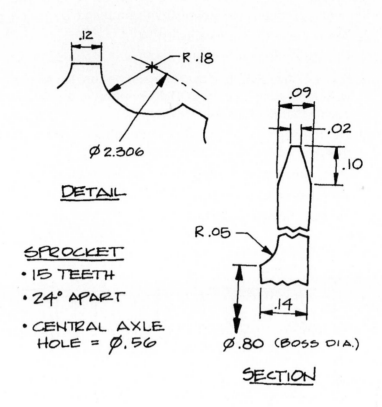

.12

R .18

Ø 2.306

DETAIL

SPROCKET
• 15 TEETH
• 24° APART
• CENTRAL AXLE
  HOLE = Ø.56

.09

.02

.10

R .05

.14

Ø.80 (BOSS DIA.)

SECTION

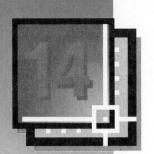

Chapter 14

Obtaining Information about the Drawing

Learning Objectives

After completing this chapter, you will be able to:
- ○ Use AutoCAD to calculate the area of an object by adding and subtracting entities.
- ○ List data related to a single point, entity, group of entities, or an entire drawing.
- ○ Find the distance between two points.
- ○ Identify a point location.
- ○ Determine the amount of time spent in a drawing session.

When working on a drawing, you may need to ask AutoCAD for information about the drawing, such as distances and areas. You can also ask AutoCAD how much time you have spent on a drawing. The commands that allow you to do this include **AREA**, **DBLIST** (database list), **DIST** (distance), **ID** (identification), **LIST**, **STATUS**, and **TIME**. The **STATUS** command was discussed in Chapter 3 of this text.

These commands are accessed from the **Inquiry** flyout button in the **Standard** toolbar and the **Inquiry** cascading menu in the **Tools** pull-down menu. See Figure 14-1. The **Mass Properties** command provides data related to the properties of a region or 3D object created with solids. This topic is discussed in *AutoCAD and its Applications—Advanced, Release 14.*

Figure 14-1.
The inquiry commands are grouped together in both the toolbar and pull-down menu.
A—The **Inquiry** flyout button in the **Standard** toolbar.
B—The **Inquiry** cascading menu in the **Tools** pull-down menu.

Finding the Area of Shapes and Objects

AREA

Tools
➡ Inquiry
  ➡ Area

Standard toolbar

Area

The most basic function of the **AREA** command is to find the area of any object, circle, polyline, or spline. To select an entity, use the **Object** option as follows:

Command: **AREA.**⏎
⟨First point⟩/Object/Add/Subtract: **O.**⏎
Select objects: *(pick object)*
Area = *(n.nn)*, Circumference = *(n.nn)*
Command:

The *n* given above represents the numeric values of the area and circumference of the object. The second value returned by the **AREA** command varies depending on the type of object selected.

Object	Value returned
Line	Perimeter
Pline	Perimeter
Circle	Circumference
Spline	Length
Rectangle	Length

PROFESSIONAL TIP

AutoCAD gives you the area between three or more points picked on the screen, even if the three points are not connected by lines. The perimeter of the selected points is also given.

Shapes drawn with lines or polylines do not need to be closed for AutoCAD to calculate their area. AutoCAD calculates the area as if a line connects the first and last points.

To find the area of a shape created with the **LINE** command, pick all the vertices of that shape. See Figure 14-2. This is the default mode of the **AREA** command. Set a running object snap such as **Endpoint** or **Intersection** to help you pick the vertices.

Command: **AREA.**⏎
⟨First point⟩/Object/Add/Subtract: *(pick point 1)*
Next point: *(pick point 2)*
Next point: *(continue picking points until all corners of the object have been selected; then press [Enter])*
Next point: ⏎
Area = *(n.nn)*, Perimeter = *(n.nn)*
Command:

Figure 14-2.
Pick all corners to find the area of an object drawn with the **LINE** command.

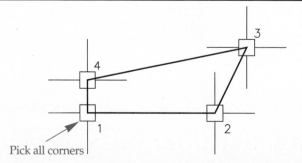

Adding and subtracting areas

If you select the **Add** option, you can pick objects drawn with the **PLINE** command. They are then automatically added to calculate the total area. After entities have been added, the **Subtract** option allows you to remove selected areas. Once either of these options is entered, the **AREA** command remains in effect until canceled. You can continue to add or subtract objects and shapes using the **Add** and **Subtract** options.

The next example uses both the **Add** and **Subtract** options. It also shows how entities drawn with the **PLINE** command are easier to pick. Refer to Figure 14-3 as you go through the following sequence:

> Command: **AREA**↵
> ⟨First point⟩/Object/Add/Subtract: **A**↵
> ⟨First point⟩/Object/Subtract: **O**↵
> (ADD mode) Select object: *(pick the polyline)*
> Area = 16.85, Length = 22.43
> Total area = 16.85
> (ADD mode) Select object: ↵
> ⟨First point⟩/Object/Subtract: **S**↵
> ⟨First point⟩/Object/Add: **O**↵
> (SUBTRACT mode) Select objects: *(pick the first circle)*
> Area = 0.79, Circumference = 3.14
> Total area = 16.07
> (SUBTRACT mode) Select objects: *(pick the second circle)*
> Area = 0.79, Circumference = 3.14
> Total area = 15.28
> (SUBTRACT mode) Select objects: ↵
> ⟨First point⟩/Object/Add: ↵

The total area of the object in Figure 14-3, subtracting the area of the two holes, is 15.28. Lengths and circumferences are given for each object as it is selected. These are not affected by the adding or subtracting functions.

Figure 14-3.
First select the outer boundary of the object using the **AREA** command **Add** option.
Then, select the inner boundaries (the circles) using the **AREA** command **Subtract** option.
This will calculate the area of the object.

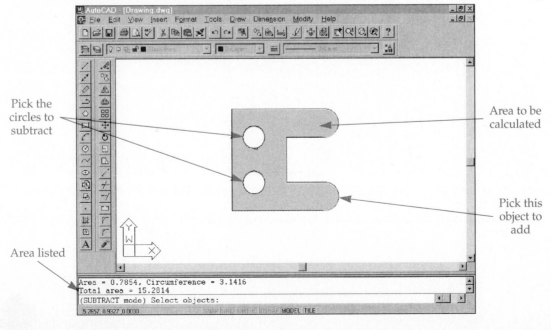

Notice in the previous command sequence that if you are finished adding and wish to subtract, you must press [Enter] at the (ADD mode) Select objects: prompt. The same is true if you have completed subtracting and wish to add.

PROFESSIONAL TIP

Calculating area, circumference, and perimeter of shapes made with the **LINE** command can be time-consuming. You must pick each vertex on the object. If you need to calculate areas, it is best to create lines and arcs with the **PLINE** or **SPLINE** command. Then choose the **Object** option when adding or subtracting entities.

EXERCISE 14-1

❏ Start a new drawing or use one of your templates.
❏ Draw the objects shown below. Use the size dimensions given. The exact locations of the cutout and holes are not important.
❏ Use the **AREA** command to calculate the area of the entire object.
❏ Use the **AREA** command to subtract the areas of the rectangle and two circles.
❏ List the following information:
  ❏ Area of large rectangle _____
  ❏ Perimeter of large rectangle _____
  ❏ Perimeter of small rectangle _____
  ❏ Circumference of one circle _____
  ❏ Area of large rectangle minus the areas of the three shapes _____
❏ Save the drawing as EX14-1. This drawing is used for the next exercise.

6.50

3.00

4.25

1.00

2 X ⌀.75

Listing Drawing Data

LIST
L

Tools
→ Inquiry
  → List

Standard
toolbar

List

The **LIST** command displays data about any AutoCAD object. Line length, circle or arc locations and radii, polyline widths, and object layers are just a few of the items AutoCAD gives you with the **LIST** command. You can select several objects to list.

Command: **LI** *or* **LIST** ↵
Select objects: *(pick objects using any selection option)*
Select objects: ↵

When you press [Enter], the data for each of the objects picked is displayed in the text window. The following data is given for a line:

```
LINE        Layer:          (layer name)
            Space:          Model space
    Handle  = (nn)
from point,  X = (nn.nn)      Y = (nn.nn)       Z = (nn.nn)
  to point,  X = (nn.nn)      Y = (nn.nn)       Z = (nn.nn)
Length = (nn.nn)      Angle in XY Plane = (nn.nn)
            Delta X = (nn.nn)      Delta Y = (nn.nn)      Delta Z = (nn.nnn)
```

The Delta X and Y numbers show the horizontal and vertical distance between the *from point* and *to point* of the line. These two numbers, the length, and angle provide you with four measurements for a single line. An example of the data provided for two-dimensional lines is shown in Figure 14-4. If a line is three-dimensional, the **LIST** command displays an additional line of information as follows:

3D Length = *(nn.nn)* Angle from XY Plane = *(nn.nn)*

Figure 14-4.
Measurements of a line provided by the **LIST** command.

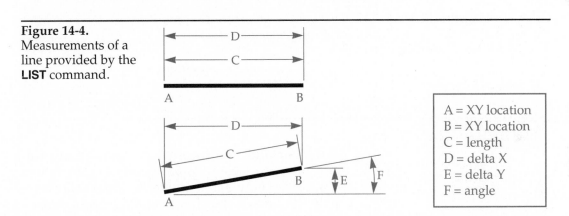

A = XY location
B = XY location
C = length
D = delta X
E = delta Y
F = angle

The data given by the **LIST** command for text, multiline text, circles, and splines are as follows:

```
        TEXT      Layer:   (layer name)
                  Space:   Model space
        Handle =  (nn)
  Style = (name)      Font file = (name)
  start  point,   X = (n.nn)      Y = (n.nn)      Z = (n.nn)
 height (n.nn)
   text (text label)
 rotation angle        (nn)
   width scale factor  (n.nn)
obliquing angle        (nn)
generation normal
```

```
      MTEXT   Layer:   (layer name)
                Space:  Model space
               Handle = (nn)
Location:      X = (n.nn)      Y = (n.nn)      Z = (n.nn)
Width:         (n.nn)
Normal:        X = (n.nn)      Y = (n.nn)      Z = (n.nn)
Rotation:      (n.nn)
Text style:    (style name)
Text height:   (n.nn)
Attachment:    (corner of multiline text insertion point)
Flow direction: (direction text is read based on language)
Contents:      (multiline text contents)


       CIRCLE   Layer: (layer name)
                 Space: Model space
        Handle = (nn)
   center point, X = (n.nn)       Y = (n.nn)   Z = (n.nn)
      radius     (n.nn)
 circumference   (n.nn)
        area     (n.nn)


       SPLINE   Layer:       (layer name)
                 Space:       Model space
        Handle = (nn)
        Length:  (n.nn)
         Order:  (n.nn)
     Properties: Planar, Non-Rational, Non-Periodic
Parametric Range: Start (n.nn)
                  End (n.nn)
  Control Points: X = (n.nn) ,   Y = (n.nn) ,   Z = (n.nn)
                  (All XYZ control points listed)
      User Data: Fit Points
                  X = (n.nn) ,   Y = (n.nn) ,   Z = (n.nn)
                  (All XYZ fit points listed)
```

PROFESSIONAL TIP

The **LIST** command is probably the most powerful inquiry command in AutoCAD. It provides all of the information you need to know about a selected object. Practice listing as many different objects as possible in your drawings. This exercise will help you to gain a greater understanding of the different kinds of data stored with each AutoCAD object.

Listing all the drawing data

The **DBLIST** (database list) command lists all of the data for every entity in the current drawing. The information provided is in the same format as the **LIST** command. As soon as you enter **DBLIST**, the data begins to quickly scroll up the screen. The scrolling stops when a complete page (screen) is filled with database information. Press [Enter] to scroll to the end of the next page. Use the scroll buttons to move forward and backward through the listing.

If you find the data you need, press the [Esc] key to exit the **DBLIST** command. The **DBLIST** command is initiated by typing DBLIST at the Command: prompt.

DIST
DI

Tools
➡ Inquiry
➡ Distance

Standard
toolbar

Distance

Finding the Distance between Two Points

The **DIST** command finds the distance between two points. Use object snap modes to accurately pick locations. See Figure 14-5. The **DIST** command provides distance and angle of the line. It also gives delta X, Y, and Z dimensions.

Command: **DI** *or* **DIST**↵
First point: *(select point)* Second point: *(select point)*
Distance = 2.85, Angle in XY Plane = 353, Angle from XY Plane = 0
Delta X = 2.83, Delta Y = –0.37, Delta Z = 0.0000
Command:

Figure 14-5.
Use the running object snap **Endpoint** and the **DIST** command to find the distance between two endpoints of a line.

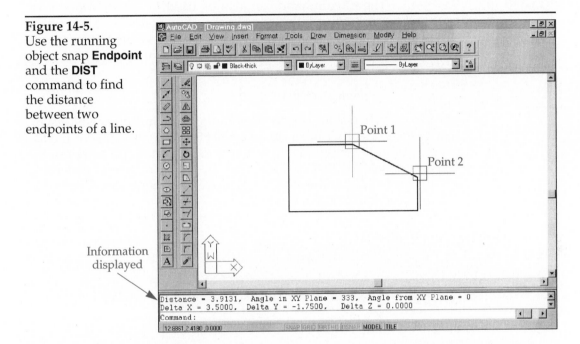

Information displayed

If you pick the **Distance** button in the **Standard** toolbar, notice the syntax that is displayed at the Command: prompt.

Command: '__dist First point:

The apostrophe that appears before dist indicates that this is a transparent command. Transparent commands can be used while you are working inside of another command. The **ID** command, discussed in the next section, is transparent if selected from **Standard** toolbar or the pull-down menu.

Identifying a Point Location

ID

Tools
➡ Inquiry
➡ ID Point

Standard
toolbar

Locate Point

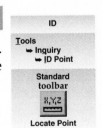

The **ID** command gives the coordinate location of a single point on the screen. This can be used to find the endpoint of a line or the center of a circle. Simply pick the point to be identified. Use the object snap modes for accuracy.

Command: **ID**↵
Point: *(select the point)*
X = *(nn.nn)* Y = *(nn.nn)* Z = *(nn.nn)*
Command:

The **ID** command can also help you identify a coordinate location on the screen. Suppose you want to see where the point X = 8.75, Y = 6.44 is located. Enter these numbers at the Point: prompt. AutoCAD responds by placing a blip (marker) at that exact location. In order to use this feature, the **BLIPMODE** variable must be on.

> Command: **ID**↵
> Point: **8.75,6.44**↵
> X = 8.75 Y = 6.44 Z = 0.00
> Command:

PROFESSIONAL TIP

The **ID** command can also be used to specify a point as the origin for relative coordinates. For example, if you wish to begin drawing a line 10'-6" on the X axis from the corner of a building, select **ID** and pick the corner. Next, select **LINE** and enter the following at the From point: prompt:

> From point: **@10' 6" ,0**↵

When you use the **ID** command, it automatically resets the system variable called **LASTPOINT** to the value of the **ID** point. When you include the @ sign, AutoCAD works from the **LASTPOINT** value. The Tracking function provides similar capabilities with added enhancements. See Chapter 6 for a discussion of Tracking.

EXERCISE 14-2

❑ Load AutoCAD and open EX14-1 if it is not currently on the screen.
❑ Use the **LIST** command to display information about one circle and one line on the drawing.
❑ Select the **DBLIST** command to display information about your drawing.
❑ Select **DBLIST** again and press [Esc] to end the listing.
❑ Use object snap options to find the following information:
  ❑ Distance between the two circle center points. _____
  ❑ Distance between the lower circle center point and the left edge of the large rectangle. _____
  ❑ Distance between the lower-left and upper-right corners of the large rectangle. _____
  ❑ **ID** of the center point of the upper circle. _____
  ❑ **ID** of the lower-left corner of the small rectangle. _____
  ❑ **ID** of the midpoint of the large rectangle's right side. _____
  ❑ **ID** of point (6,4) on your screen. _____
❑ Save the drawing as EX14-2 and quit.

Checking the Time

The **TIME** command displays the current time, the time related to your drawing, and the time related to the current drawing session. The display for the **TIME** command is as follows:

```
Command: TIME↵
Current time: Wednesday, February 14, 19XX at 13:39:22:210 PM
Times for this drawing:
    Created:    Monday, February 12, 19XX at 10:24:48:130 AM
    Last updated:   Monday, February 12, 19XX at 14:36:23:46 PM
    Total editing time:   0 days 01:23:57:930
    Elapsed timer (on):   0 days 00:35:28:650
    Next automatic save in:    0 days 01:35:26:680
Display/ON/OFF/Reset:
```

There are a few things to keep in mind when checking the **TIME** display. First, the drawing creation time starts when you "OK" a new drawing with the **NEW** command, or by using the **BLOCK** command discussed in Chapter 23. Second, the **SAVE** command affects the Last updated: time. However, when **QUIT** is used to end a drawing session and you do not save the drawing, all time in that session is discarded. Finally, you can time a specific drawing task by using the **Reset** option to reset the elapsed timer.

While the **TIME** display is on the screen, it is static. That means that none of the times are being updated. You can request an update by choosing the **Display** option as follows:

```
Display/ON/OFF/Reset: D↵
```

When you enter the drawing editor, the timer is on by default. If you want to stop the timer, just enter OFF at the prompt. If the timer is off, enter ON to start it again.

If the date and time are incorrect, they can be reset from the Windows Control Panel. Control Panel is located in the Start menu by picking Settings, Figure 14-6. The Control Panel allows you to modify certain aspects of your system, such as screen colors and system time. Double-click on the Date/Time icon, Figure 14-7. This displays the Date/Time Properties dialog box, in which you can change your system's date and time. See Figure 14-8.

Figure 14-6.
The Control Panel is found by picking Settings in the Start menu.

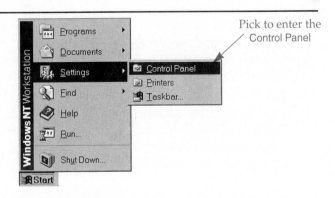

Pick to enter the Control Panel

Figure 14-7.
Select the Date/Time icon to change the system clock settings.

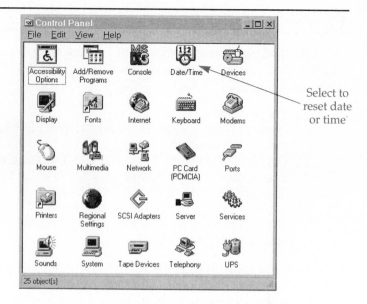

Select to reset date or time

Figure 14-8.
Highlight the item to change and enter the new setting.

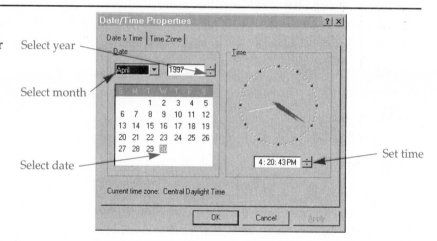

Select year

Select month

Select date

Set time

It is important that your system date and time are always accurate. Date and time changes are recognized by other Windows applications that use the system clock, such as Windows Explorer and Clock. Windows Explorer functions are covered in Chapter 30 of this text.

To change the system date and time, do the following:
1. Select Settings from the Start menu.
2. Pick the Control Panel icon to activate the Control Panel window.
3. In the Control Panel window, double-click on the Date/Time icon.
4. Pick the Date/Time tab if it is not active.
5. Set the date by picking the month drop-down list and selecting the proper month. Set the year using the up or down arrows. Pick on the day shown in the calendar. Pick and drag to highlight the hour, minutes, seconds, or AM/PM, and type the correct time. Use the up and down arrows to change the value of the highlighted item.
6. Pick the OK button and select Close from the File pull-down menu in the Control Panel.

❑ Open any one of your previous drawings.
❑ Select the **TIME** command and study the information that is displayed.
❑ If the current date and time are incorrect, inform your instructor or supervisor. Then, use the Windows Control Panel to set the correct date and time.
❑ Update the **TIME** display.
❑ Reset the elapsed timer.
❑ Exit AutoCAD without saving.

Chapter Test

Write your answers in the spaces provided.

1. To add entity areas, when do you select the **Add** option? _____
   _____

2. When using the **AREA** command, explain how picking a polyline is different than picking an object drawn with the **LINE** command. _____
   _____

3. What information is provided by the **AREA** command? _____
   _____

4. What is the **LIST** command used for? _____
   _____

5. Describe the meaning of delta X and delta Y. _____
   _____
   _____

6. What is the function of the **DBLIST** command? _____
   _____

7. How do you cancel the **DBLIST** command? _____

8. What are the two purposes of the **ID** command? _____
   _____
   _____

9. What information is provided by the **TIME** command? _____
   _____

10. When does the drawing time start?_____
    _____

11. It is necessary to exit AutoCAD to reset the date and time. (True/False) _____

Drawing Problems

*Load AutoCAD for windows and start a new drawing for each of the following problems. Insert your floppy disk and name the drawing as **P16**-(problem number).*

1. Draw the object shown below using the dimensions given. Draw all of the features using **PLINE** and **CIRCLE** commands. Follow these instructions as you proceed:

   A. Check the time when you enter the drawing editor.

   B. Use the default units and limits.

   C. Set the grid spacing to .5 and snap spacing to .25.

   D. Measure the area of object A and subtract the areas of the other three features.

   E. Write the areas and perimeters in the chart provided.

   F. Use the **Add, Subtract**, and **Object** options of **AREA** to find the measurements. Do not exit the **AREA** command. Complete all of the following calculations in one selection of **AREA**.

   G. Select **TIME** and note your time in the drawing editor.

   H. Save the drawing as P16-1.

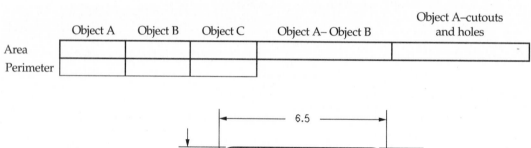

	Object A	Object B	Object C	Object A– Object B	Object A–cutouts and holes
Area					
Perimeter					

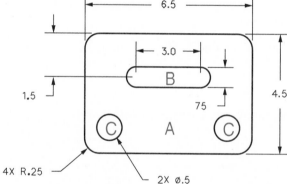

AutoCAD and its Applications—Basics

2. Draw the deck shown below using the **PLINE** command. Draw the hexagon using the **POLYGON** command. Use the following settings and provide all measurements listed.

   A. Set architectural units. Use 1/2" fractions and decimal degrees. Leave remaining units settings at default values.

   B. Set the limits to 100',80' and **ZOOM All**.

   C. Set the grid spacing to 2' and snap spacing to 1'.

   D. Calculate the measurements requested in the charts below.

   E. Select the **DBLIST** command.

   F. Select **TIME** and note the time in the drawing editor.

   G. Save the drawing as P16-2.

	Object A	Object B	Object A–Object B
Area			
Perimeter			

	Line CD	Distance EC
Distance		

	Point C	Point D	Point F
ID			

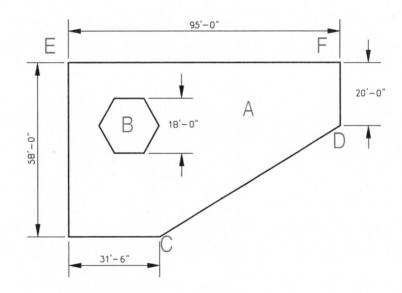

3. The drawing shown below is a view of the gable end of a portion of a house. Draw the house using the dimensions given. Use the following instructions and provide all the measurements listed. Draw windows as single line only. Spacing between second floor windows is 3". Height of the windows is not important for this problem. The width of this end of the house is 16'-6". The length of the roof is 40'. Use AutoCAD to create all necessary constructions. You may want to use **PLINE** to assist in creating specific shapes in this drawing. Calculate the following:

A. Total area of the roof. _____

B. Diagonal distance from one corner of the roof to the other. _____

C. Area of first floor window. _____

D. Total area of all second floor windows, including 3" space between them._____

E. Siding will cover the house. What is the total area of siding for this end? _____

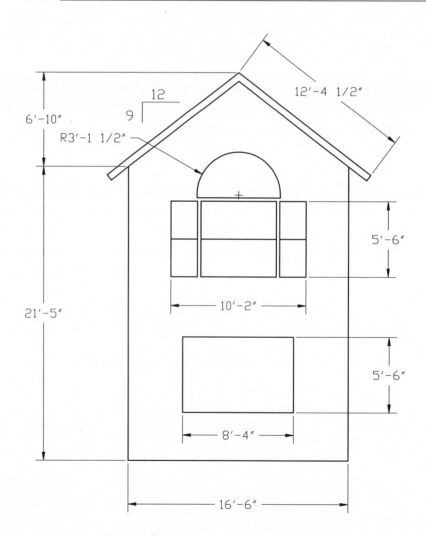

AutoCAD and its Applications—Basics

4. The drawing shown below is a side view of a pyramid. The pyramid has four sides. Using AutoCAD construction and inquiry techniques, calculate the following:

   A. Area of one side. _____

   B. Perimeter of one side. _____

   C. Area of all four sides. _____

   D. Area of the base. _____

   E. True length distance from the midpoint of the base on one side to the apex.

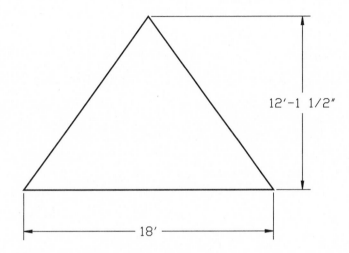

5. Draw the property plat shown below. Label property line bearings and distances only if required by your instructor. Calculate the area of the property plat in square feet and convert to acres. Save the drawing as P14-5.

   A. Square feet: _____

   B. Acres: _____

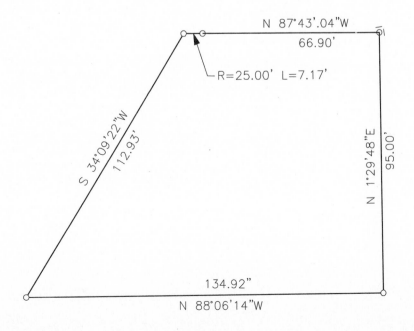

6. Draw the subdivision plat shown below. Label the drawing as shown. Calculate the acreage of each lot and record that value as a label inside the lot as follows: 2.49 AC. Save the drawing as P14-6.

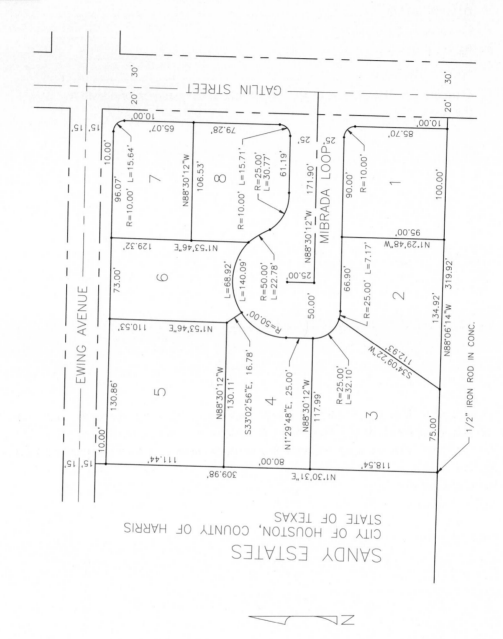

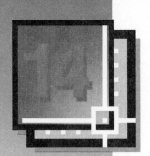

Chapter 15

Working with AutoCAD Files

Learning Objectives

After completing this chapter, you will be able to:
- ○ Explain the meaning and use of DOS file extensions.
- ○ List files using Windows Explorer.
- ○ Copy, move, delete, and rename files using Windows Explorer.
- ○ Manage critical files using the **Preferences** dialog box.
- ○ Create user profiles using the **Preferences** dialog box.
- ○ Import and export a variety of file types in AutoCAD.
- ○ Define DOS file extensions.

AutoCAD works with several types of computer files. The files are identified by a three-letter file extension at the end of the file name.

The AutoCAD drawing file format is compatible with a variety of other software applications. You can export the industry standard .dxf file for use with other CAD packages, or specific applications. Files can also be exported for use in the design and animation software 3D Studio, or for use in the stereolithography process. In addition, you can import several different file types into AutoCAD. Working with files in this fashion is easier than using the Windows Explorer, discussed in Chapter 30.

Types of File Names

Drawing file names can be up to 255 characters long. They can contain letters, numbers, spaces, dollar signs ($), hyphens (-), and underscores (_). When you begin a new drawing, AutoCAD adds a file extension to the end of the file name. This extension is .dwg. If you name a drawing Building 340, AutoCAD creates the file as Building 340.dwg. When you open the drawing to edit, you only have to type Building 340. AutoCAD knows to look for that file, plus the .dwg extension. File names are not case-sensitive. This means that you can name a drawing PROBLEM 20-12, but Windows interprets Problem 20-12 as the same file name. See Figure 15-1.

Figure 15-1.
File names are not case sensitive. This alert box appears when you attempt to save as an already existing file.

After you edit the Building 340.dwg file and save it again, the original is converted to a backup file. Its file extension is automatically changed to .bak (backup). AutoCAD maintains a current .dwg file and one .bak file. If you revise the Building 340 drawing again, the .bak file is erased and the previous .dwg copy becomes the backup. Only a newly revised drawing is given the .dwg file extension.

Some common file extensions used by AutoCAD and Windows include the following:

AutoCAD	
.bak	Backup copy of a drawing file.
.dcl	Dialog control language description file.
.dwg	Drawing file.
.dwt	Drawing template file.
.lin	File containing the linetypes used by AutoCAD.
.mnu	Menu source file.
.pat	Hatch patterns file.
.plt	Plot file.
Windows	
.bmp	Bitmap file.
.clp	Windows Clipboard file.
.com	Command file.
.dll	Dynamic-link library file.
.exe	Executable file.
.ini	Initialization file.
.wmf	Windows metafile.

Introduction to Windows Explorer

The Windows Explorer is a program that allows you to manage and display folders and files. It is activated by picking Programs from the Start menu, then selecting Windows Explorer. This chapter discusses how to list, select, copy, move, delete, and rename files. If you need detailed information on the features of Windows Explorer, see Chapter 30.

Listing folders and files

The Windows Explorer window is labeled Exploring - C:\ in the title bar. The directory label C:\ reflects the name of the currently selected storage device and folder. See Figure 15-2. The window is composed of the title bar, a menu bar of five pull-down menus, the All Folders list box, the Contents list box, and a status bar at the bottom of the window.

Figure 15-2.
The Windows Explorer window is labeled with the name of the currently selected storage device and folder.

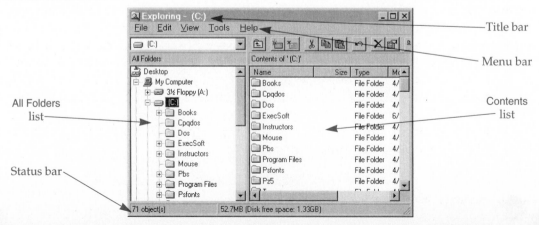

Folder and device icons in the All Folders list box may be preceded by a small box containing a "+" or a "−" symbol. The + indicates that the folder contains additional folders, or **subdirectories**. Picking the + symbol expands the tree to display the next level of folders. You can collapse or hide the display by picking the "−" symbol.

Folders in the All Folders list box can be opened with a single pick on the icon. The folder contents are displayed in the Contents list box. Folders in the Contents list box must be double-clicked to open. The open folder is automatically closed when a new one is selected and opened. See Figure 15-3.

Figure 15-3.
Pick a folder to display its contents in the Contents list box.

Contents of "open" folder displayed in the Contents list box

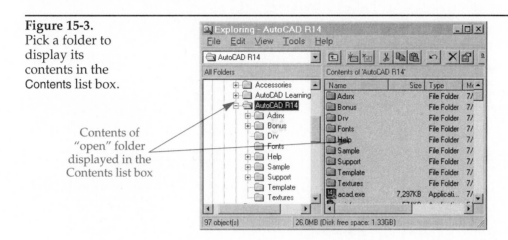

The contents of a folder can be viewed in four different ways. These are found in the View pull-down menu.

- **Large icons.** Displays each file's icon in a large format with the file name below it. See Figure 15-4A.
- **Small icons.** Displays each file's icon in a small format with the file name to the right side. See Figure 15-4B.
- **List.** Displays a small icon list of file names that fills the height of the list box with multiple columns. Files that do not fit in the box are listed in additional columns to the right. Use the horizontal scroll bar to display them. See Figure 15-4C.
- **Details.** Displays a single column of file names, size, type, and last date and time modified. See Figure 15-4D.

The Explorer window can be resized, maximized, minimized, and closed just like any other window.

Selecting files

When performing functions such as copying, moving, renaming, and deleting, it is first necessary to select the file(s). When files have been selected, they are highlighted. They can be selected five different ways.

- Pick the file to select it.
- To select a group of files that are listed together, pick a point that doesn't highlight a file and hold and drag the pointer to display a dashed selection box. As the dashed box touches the file name, it is highlighted. The selection box should touch all files required. Release the pick button to complete the selection. See Figure 15-5.
- Pick the first file in the list, hold the [Shift] key, then pick the last file in the list. All files between are highlighted.

Figure 15-4.
There are four different ways to have files listed in the Contents list box. A—Large icons.
B—Small icons. C—List. D—Details.

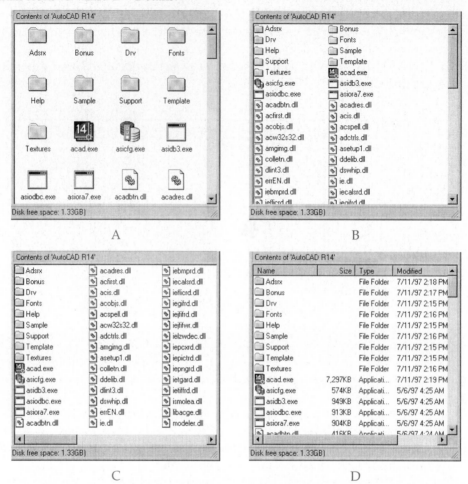

A

B

C

D

Figure 15-5.
A group of files that
are listed together can
be selected by clicking
and dragging the
dashed box so that all
files are highlighted.

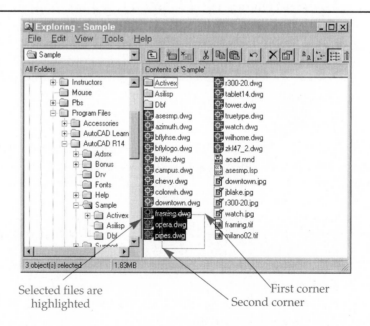

Selected files are
highlighted

First corner
Second corner

- Pick the first file, hold the [Ctrl] key, then pick other files that are scattered throughout the list.
- Press the [Tab] key to activate the Contents list box, then use the arrow keys to locate and highlight a single file.

Once files have been selected by one of the above methods, you can perform the required function.

Copying folders and files

Copying folders and files is quick and easy, and can be done using menu selections or accelerator keys.

1. Open the folder you wish to copy from.
2. Pick (highlight) the file to be copied, then pick Copy from the Edit pull-down menu, or press [Ctrl]+[C] to copy to the Clipboard. See Figure 15-6.
3. Open the folder or drive you wish to copy to.
4. Pick Paste from the Edit pull-down menu, or press [Ctrl]+[V] to paste from the Clipboard.

The same steps can be used to copy a folder or a group of files. Use one of the selection methods previously mentioned to highlight the group.

Figure 15-6.
Files can be copied by using Copy and Paste from the Edit pull-down menu.

Highlighted file is copied

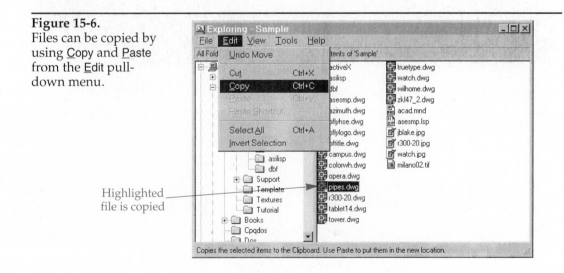

Moving folders and files

Folders and files can be moved quickly by using the *drag and drop* method. First select the files that are to be moved, then pick and hold as you drag the files to the new folder or drive. An outline of the files is attached to the pointer as they are dragged. See Figure 15-7. The destination folder or drive is highlighted as the pointer touches it. When the correct destination is highlighted, release the pick button.

Figure 15-7.
An outline of the files is attached to the pointer as they are dragged.

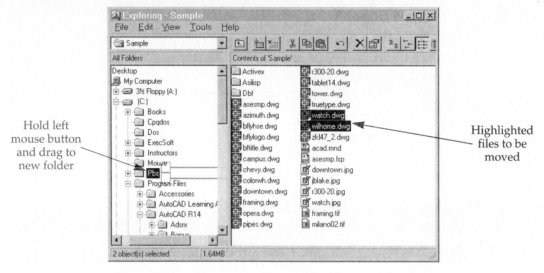

Hold left mouse button and drag to new folder

Highlighted files to be moved

Renaming folders and files

Before a folder or file can be renamed it must first be selected. Then proceed using one of the two following methods:

1. Pick Rename from the File pull-down menu. See Figure 15-8.
2. Type the new name. Be sure to include the three-letter file extension if it is displayed.
3. Press [Enter] or pick anywhere on the screen.

Figure 15-8.
Pick Rename from the File pull-down menu to rename a file or folder.

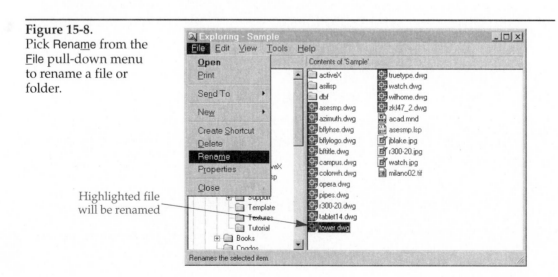

Highlighted file will be renamed

You can quickly rename a folder or file without using the Rename command as follows:

1. Pick the file or folder to select it.
2. Pick it again and a blinking cursor appears at the end of the name.
3. Type the new name and press [Enter] or pick anywhere on the screen.

PROFESSIONAL TIP

If the files in the Contents list box are displayed with the three-letter file extension, you must type it when renaming a file. If you omit the extension, a Windows alert informs you that the file may be unusable if the extension is changed. You can avoid this problem by doing the following:

1. Pick Options in the View pull-down menu.
2. Pick the View tab in the Options dialog box.
3. Pick Hide file extensions for known file types.
4. Pick OK to exit.

By performing this operation, files in the Contents list box are displayed without the three-letter extension. Therefore, when you rename a file, Windows automatically retains the file extension. This provides you with a fail-safe manner for renaming files.

Deleting folders and files

The act of deleting folders and files is not the drastic action that it was with Windows 3.x and MS-DOS. Windows 95 and Windows NT store all deleted items in the Recycle Bin. Delete folders and files as follows:

1. Select the folder or file(s) to be deleted.
2. Pick Delete from the File pull-down menu, or press the [Delete] key.
3. The Confirm File Delete dialog box asks if you are sure you want to send the file(s) to the Recycle Bin. Pick Yes.

The Recycle Bin is a repository for all deleted files. See Figure 15-9. If for any reason you feel that a file has been deleted by mistake, open the Recycle Bin and remove the file as follows:

1. Display the Windows Desktop.
2. Double-click on the Recycle Bin to open it.
3. Select the files you wish to restore.
4. Pick Restore from the File pull-down menu. The files are removed from the Recycle Bin and returned to their original location prior to the deletion.

Figure 15-9.
The Recycle Bin is a repository for all deleted files.

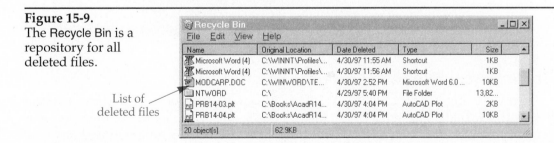

List of deleted files

CAUTION

Empty the Recycle Bin only when you are sure that its contents are no longer needed. Once the Recycle Bin has been emptied you cannot recover the files.

Viewing the properties of a file

You can quickly display detailed information, called *properties*, about any file as follows:
1. Select the file.
2. Pick P̲roperties from the E̲dit pull-down menu. The Properties dialog box is displayed. See Figure 15-10.

Or use the right-click method:
1. Right-click on the file name. This displays the Edit cursor menu.
2. Pick P̲roperties from the E̲dit cursor menu. See Figure 15-11.

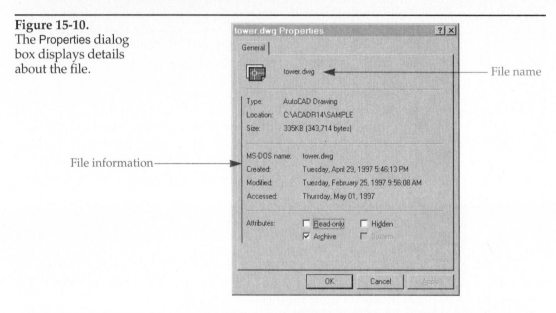

Figure 15-10.
The Properties dialog box displays details about the file.

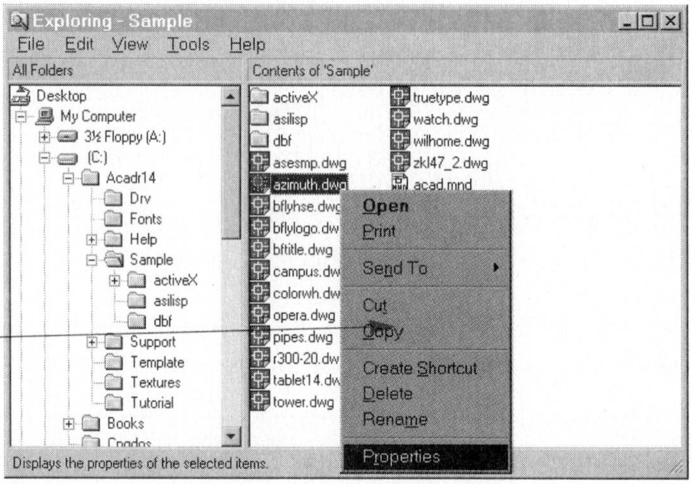

File name

File information

Figure 15-11.
Right-click on a file to access the Edit cursor menu.

Edit cursor menu

Create a new folder

Avoid saving your files in the AutoCAD program directories or folders. It is best to create new folders for your work. Always check with your instructor or supervisor before creating new folders or performing any disk management function. New folders are created as follows using Windows Explorer:
1. Open Windows Explorer, then select the drive, directory, or folder in which you wish to create a new folder.
2. Pick New̲ from the F̲ile pull-down menu, then pick Folder.
3. A new highlighted folder appears in the Contents list box with the name New Folder. Type the name of the folder and press [Enter].

Recovering a Damaged Drawing

A damaged drawing file is one that has been corrupted and cannot be loaded into the AutoCAD drawing editor with the **OPEN** command. Drawings can be corrupted in the following ways:

- A bad or corrupted floppy disk.
- Running out of disk space during a drawing session.
- Power failures.
- Hardware or software problems.

AutoCAD provides a method for recovering most damaged files. You can type RECOVER at the Command: prompt, or select **Recover...** in the **Drawing Utilities** cascading menu from the **File** pull-down menu. This displays the **Select File** dialog box. Select the proper folder and file and AutoCAD attempts to recover the damaged drawing.

RECOVER

File
↳ Drawing
   Utilities
↳ Recover...

For example, if the bad file is named \AutoCAD R14\Struct\Foundation Slab, pick the \Struct folder. Then, pick the Foundation Slab drawing name. AutoCAD then tries to recover the damaged file. If it is successful, the file is loaded into the drawing editor, and it can be worked on normally. If you do not save the file before exiting AutoCAD, the recovered drawing is lost.

Using the AUDIT Command

You can perform a diagnostic check on your drawing files with the **AUDIT** command. This checks for, and corrects, errors. You have the option of fixing errors or leaving them.

```
Command: AUDIT↵
Fix any errors detected? ⟨N⟩ ↵
1                        Blocks audited
Pass 1      145          objects audited
Pass 2      145          objects audited
Total errors found 0            fixed 0
Command:
```

If you answer no, as in the above example, any errors are listed for your reference, but they are not fixed. To fix errors in the transferred drawing, type Y at the Fix any errors detected? prompt.

AutoCAD displays the errors and notifies you that they are fixed like this:

```
3 Blocks audited
Pass 29                  objects audited
Pass 14                  objects audited

total errors found 2 fixed 2
```

If the system variable **AUDITCTL** is set to 1 (on), AutoCAD automatically creates an audit report that lists the corrections made. This report is given the same name as the drawing, but has an .adt file extension. The file is placed in the same directory as the drawing. This is an ASCII text file (American Standard Code for Information Interchange). You can open this file and read the information using any ASCII text editor, such as Windows Notepad or WordPad.

Listing the audit report

It is not necessary to leave AutoCAD and exit Windows to display the audit report. Pick Start from the Taskbar, then pick Programs, Accessories, and Notepad.

To list the audit report, first select Open... from the File menu. Then, change to the folder where the audit report is, select All Files (*.*) for the type of file, and select the audit file. Pick OK and the contents of the file are then displayed on the screen. After reviewing the file, you can exit Notepad.

Understanding AutoCAD's Temporary Files

AutoCAD maintains several temporary files while you are working on a drawing. You might consider these as "worksheets" that AutoCAD opens, much like the notes, references, sketches, and calculations you may have scattered around your desk. These files are created automatically to store portions of the AutoCAD program not currently in use, and for information related to the current drawing file. These files are critical to AutoCAD's operation, and must be maintained and safeguarded properly.

Program swap files

AutoCAD uses a virtual memory system. *Virtual memory* is a combination of RAM and hard disk space. The main program file for AutoCAD is named acad.exe. It is a very large file—over 7.1MB. If there is not enough room in your computer's physical memory (RAM) to store the program, AutoCAD creates *pages* of the program in free space on your hard disk drive.

A virtual memory system keeps only the part of the program that is currently being used in physical memory. If additional portions of the program are needed, AutoCAD creates a page on the hard disk and writes the least-used portion of the program to that page. The new portion of the program that is requested is written to physical memory. Thus, AutoCAD creates a *paging* system using virtual memory. The least-used pages are written to a page called a *swap file*, and are held there until needed again.

When required, AutoCAD's paging system creates a swap file in the root directory of the current disk drive, and gives it a .swr extension. These files are critical to AutoCAD, and must never be deleted while you are in a drawing session. Should you experience an improper termination of AutoCAD, and the drawing file is not saved properly, these swap files may be left open. In that case the files are no longer of use and can be deleted, but only *after* you have exited AutoCAD.

| CAUTION | If you feel that swap files have been left behind after an abnormal exit from AutoCAD, you may delete all files that have an .swr extension, or that have names such as aobcgffe and have no extension. Never delete any of these temporary files while you are working in AutoCAD. Doing so may damage the current drawing and cause AutoCAD to terminate improperly. |

Temporary files

The second piece of AutoCAD's virtual memory system is called the *pager*. This works similar to the swap file system, but creates temporary storage space for drawing file information. The entire contents of a small drawing may fit into your computer's physical memory, but as the drawing grows larger, portions of it must be temporarily removed. AutoCAD creates a *page file* for the least-used portion of your drawing, and opens the physical memory for new drawing data. When the drawing data contained in the page file is needed, it is *paged* back into memory. These temporary files are given the file extension of .ac$. These are vital files and must never be deleted while working in AutoCAD.

If AutoCAD should terminate improperly, these page files are left open in the current drawing directory. The .ac$ files that are left behind are no longer of any use, and can be deleted. Always delete these files with Explorer, and never while you are working in AutoCAD.

Create a workspace for temporary files

The default workspace for AutoCAD's temporary files is \Windows\Temp. You can create a directory on your hard drive and tell AutoCAD to always use that directory for storage of temporary files. Use the following procedure to allocate space for these files.

1. Pick **Preferences...** in the **Tools** pull-down menu.
2. Pick the **Files** tab.
3. Pick the **+** symbol to the left of **Temporary Drawing File Location**. The current location is display. The default is \Windows\Temp in Windows 95, and \Temp in Windows NT.
4. Pick the current directory (folders) path to select it.
5. Pick the **Browse...** button to display the **Browse for Folder** dialog box.
6. Find the folder you want to use for temporary files and select it. Pick **OK** to exit.

NOTE

After you complete step 3 above you can type in a new location if you know the exact path. Be sure to specify the drive letter and complete path. For example, if you created a folder on the C: drive in the \AutoCAD R14 directory named Tempfile, the proper path to type is C:\AutoCAD R14\Tempfile. See Figure 15-12.

Figure 15-12.
The location of temporary drawing files can be specified in the **Preferences** dialog box.

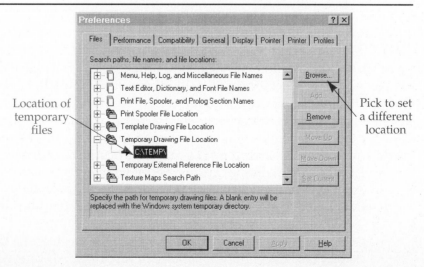

Location of temporary files

Pick to set a different location

Automatically saved drawing files

The **SAVETIME** system variable allows you to specify the time interval that AutoCAD uses to automatically save the current drawing file. This becomes your first line of backup, and is also considered a temporary file. Should you encounter a problem in AutoCAD and find your drawing file is corrupted as a result of an improper termination or system crash, this file may be a valuable backup. As a default setting, AutoCAD names the automatically saved file auto1.sv$ and saves it in the \Windows\Temp folder in Windows 95, and C:\Temp in Windows NT. If you ever need to use this drawing because the original is corrupt, you must rename it as a .dwg file. To rename the drawing, follow the procedure described earlier and simply type a .dwg extension at the end of the file name.

Remember, any time you wish to change the interval between automatic saves, just use the **SAVETIME** system variable at the AutoCAD Command: prompt. You can also change the **SAVETIME** variable by picking **Preferences...** from the **Tools** pull-down menu. Pick the **General** tab. **Automatic save** is listed at the upper left. Change the value in the **Minutes between saves:** text box and pick **OK** to exit.

Creating Multiple-User Preference Files (Profiles)

Prior releases of AutoCAD used the **CONFIG** command to change values and settings for display, plotting, and pointing devices. These settings were saved in the acad.cfg file. Release 14 employs the **PREFERENCES** command for these functions. If you type CONFIG, the **Preferences** dialog box is displayed.

A *preference* is something you prefer or favor. Therefore, the **Preferences** dialog box allows you to change the settings and values for a variety of devices and functions to match what you prefer. All of your preferences can be saved in a *user profile*. Multiple profiles can be saved by a single user for different applications, and several users can create individual profiles to avoid conflict.

PROFESSIONAL TIP

The use of profiles should be emphasized in a school setting or in a company where more than one person will be using the same computer. The intention is that each user can establish the settings to their liking, and then save those settings in a file. Then, regardless of who used the computer previously, and how they may have changed the preferences, it is simply a matter of importing your profile to reset all the preferences.

Preferences dialog box definitions

PREFERENCES
PR

Tools
↳ Preferences...

Pick **Preferences** from the **Tools** pull-down menu to display the **Preferences** dialog box, or type PR or PREFERENCES at the Command: prompt. Refer again to Figure 15-12.

The **Preferences** dialog box contains eight tabs. They enable you to control the manner in which AutoCAD functions, how it looks, and how it addresses other devices. Some of these preferences you will not need to change, and others are introduced as needed in this text and in *AutoCAD and its Applications—Advanced, Release 14*.

- **Files tab.** Displays the directories (folders) and files used by AutoCAD.
- **Performance tab.** AutoCAD performance values can be set here.
- **Compatibility tab.** Enables you to retain compatibility with previous AutoCAD releases.
- **General tab.** General preferences are set here, such as the **SAVETIME** variable.
- **Display tab.** Alters the appearance of the AutoCAD screen.

- **Pointer tab.** Sets the current pointing device.
- **Printer tab.** Sets the current printing and plotting device, and provides the ability to select new devices and modify existing ones.
- **Profiles tab.** Provides the ability to create and manage multiple user configurations (profiles).

What is a user profile?

A user profile should not be confused with settings found in a drawing. Template files and prototype drawings are used to save settings relating to a drawing session, such as units, limits, object snap settings, drawing aids, grip settings, dimension styles, and text styles. A profile is used to save settings related to the performance and appearance of the software and hardware. A profile can be composed of, but is not limited to, the following settings and values:

- Temporary drawing file location
- Template drawing file location
- Text display format
- Arc and circle smoothness
- Start-up dialog box display
- Minutes between automatic saves
- File extension for temporary files
- AutoCAD screen menu display
- Colors and fonts for AutoCAD screen
- Type of pointer and length of crosshairs
- Type of printer or plotter

Creating a user profile

A profile can be created and then modified as you determine certain settings and values that work best for you. For example, say you decide you like the pointer crosshairs to extend to the edges of the graphics window, you often use the **Inquiry** toolbar, and you prefer the graphics window background color to be gray. Use the following steps to first establish the settings.

1. Pick **Toolbars...** in the **View** pull-down menu to display the **Toolbars** dialog box.
2. Pick the **Inquiry** check box. The **Inquiry** toolbar is displayed. Pick **OK** to exit. See Figure 15-13.
3. Pick **Preferences...** from the **Tools** pull-down menu to display the **Preferences** dialog box.
4. Pick the **Pointer** tab and set the **Percentage of screen size** to 100.
5. Pick the **Display** tab, then pick the **Colors** button.
6. In the **Window Element** drop-down list, pick **Graphics window background**.
7. In the **Basic Colors** palette, pick gray. Pick **OK** to exit.

Figure 15-13.
The **Inquiry** toolbar is selected from the **Toolbars** dialog box.

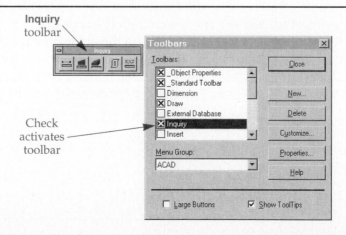

Inquiry toolbar

Check activates toolbar

All of your preferences have now been set. Next, these settings must be saved in a profile or else they will be lost when AutoCAD is closed. Use the following steps to save the settings to a file.

1. Pick the **Profiles** tab in the **Preferences** dialog box. See Figure 15-14.
2. Pick the **Export...** button, then select a folder location for the new file, enter a file name, and pick **Save**. Note that the file is given a .reg extension. The profile becomes a registry file.
3. In order to apply the profile the next time you run AutoCAD, it must be imported and displayed in the profile list box. Pick the **Import...** button, select the proper .reg file, and then pick **Open**.
4. The imported file is displayed in the list. Select the file to highlight it, then pick the **Set Current** button.

Figure 15-14.
The **Profiles** tab of the **Preferences** dialog box allows you to create and manage user profiles

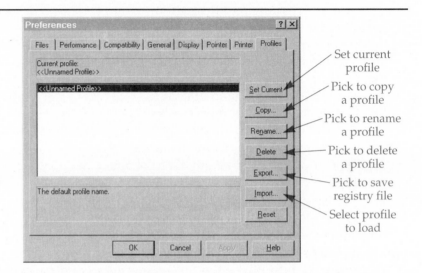

All of the settings in your profile are applied while the **Preferences** dialog box is still open. Therefore you can select any of the profiles and set them current to see what the settings look like. Of course, all preference settings are not visible, such as temporary file locations and current printer. Additional buttons in the **Profiles** tab are described here.

- **Copy....** Displays the **Copy Profile As** dialog box. Select the profile you wish to copy first, then enter a new name in the **Profile name:** text box. See Figure 15-15. You can also enter a description of the profile if desired. After picking **OK**, the name of the copy is shown in the list box of the **Profiles** tab.
- **Rename....** Displays the **Change Profile To** dialog box. Select the profile you wish to rename first, then enter a new name in the **Profile name:** text box.
- **Delete.** Displays an AutoCAD alert box asking if you want to delete the profile. Pick **Yes** and the selected profile is deleted.
- **Reset.** Resets the selected profile to the default AutoCAD settings.

Figure 15-15.
An existing profile can be copied with a new name using the **Copy Profile As** dialog box.

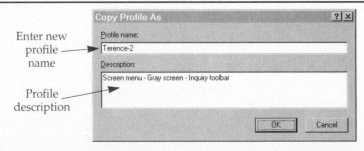

AutoCAD's .dxf File Format

AutoCAD users may need to exchange files with other programs, or import other software files into AutoCAD. The .dxf (drawing interchange file) file format is used for this purpose. This format has become an accepted standard for microcomputer CAD programs.

Files prepared using the .dxf format are standard ASCII code. The information contained in the file can be read by any computer that "understands" the ASCII format.

Binary .dxf file

The standard .dxf file is in ASCII format, but you also have the option of creating a binary form of the .dxf file. A *binary code* is composed of data in the form of bits having a value of either 1 or 0. This type of file can be up to 25% smaller than an ASCII file, and it is just as accurate. The binary file is given the same extension of .dxf. It can be read quicker than an ASCII file, and AutoCAD can create it and load it using the **DXFOUT** and **DXFIN** commands. Since .dxf files are so much smaller than drawing files, and binary files are even smaller, using the **Binary** option of the **DXFOUT** command may be a good practice if you must provide interchange files to a coworker or client who works with Release 10 or newer versions of AutoCAD.

Contents of an ASCII .dxf file

You do not need to understand the contents of a .dxf file to successfully translate drawings. Yet, when customizing or programming AutoCAD and using AutoLISP, you will use information like that found in a .dxf file. The contents of a .dxf file is arranged into four sections.

*   **Header.** Every drawing variable and its value is listed in this section.
*   **Tables.** Named items, such as layers, linetypes, styles, and views, are found in this section.
*   **Blocks.** All entities and their values that are part of blocks are listed in this section.
*   **Entities.** Objects in the drawing are located here.

A quick method of displaying and examining a .dxf file is to open it using your favorite text editor or word processing program, or the Windows Notepad program.

Once in Notepad, open the .dxf file. The file is long, and contains a list of all the variables and settings used by AutoCAD. If you plan to study menu customization or programming, you should become familiar with the components of .dxf files and the syntax used. Refer to the *AutoCAD Customization Guide* for detailed information on this type of file.

Exporting a .dxf file

The **DXFOUT** command creates a .dxf ASCII drawing file from an AutoCAD drawing. To test the **DXFOUT** command, begin a new drawing and name it dxftest. Draw a single line on your screen using the **LINE** command. The .dxf file is created by picking **Export...** in the **File** pull-down menu. This displays the **Export Data** dialog box. Use this method only if you want to create an ASCII .dxf file. This is a general files dialog box and is used for creating export files of a variety of types. It is described later in this chapter. The **DXFOUT** command allows you to create ASCII or binary .dxf files. Enter the **DXFOUT** command at the Command: prompt as follows:

    Command: **DXFOUT**↵

The **Create DXF File** dialog box is displayed, Figure 15-16A. The file name default is the same as the drawing name, but with a .dxf extension. The **Save as type:** drop-down list provides three different versions of .dxf files. Select the version that you require, enter a new file name if necessary, and pick **OK** to accept the file name.

The **Options...** button displays the **Export Options** dialog box. Here you can specify decimal accuracy, choose the file format, and create a file of selected objects. See Figure 15-16B. The degree of accuracy can range from 0 to 16 decimal places.

The **Select Objects** check box allows you to select specific shapes or objects to include in the .dxf file. If you use this option, only the objects that you pick are placed in the file. You are prompted to select objects only after the **Save** button is picked in the **Create DXF File** dialog box.

A binary .dxf file can be created by picking the **BINARY** radio button. When binary is selected the decimal accuracy is set at 6 decimal places and cannot be changed. See Figure 15-16B.

You can quickly check to be sure the .dxf file was created by executing the **DXFOUT** command again. The file should appear in the file list box.

Figure 15-16.
The **DXFOUT** command displays the **Create DXF File** dialog box. Enter a file name and select a folder for the file. B—A binary .dxf file is created by clicking the **BINARY** option button in the **Export Options** dialog box.

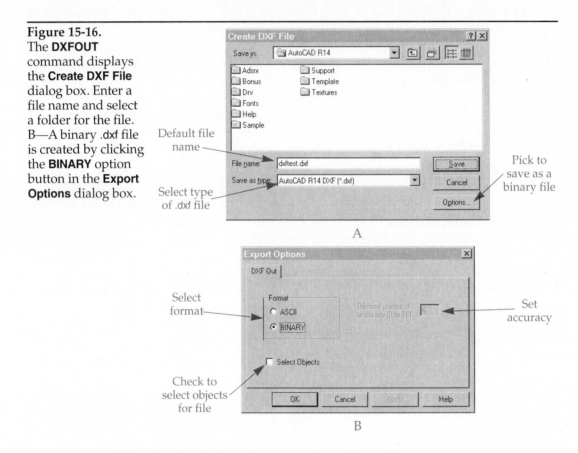

When using the **DXFOUT** command, you can specify a file name other than the default. If the file name you provide already exists, AutoCAD informs you accordingly and displays the **Create DXF File** alert box shown in Figure 15-17. Pick the **Yes** button to replace the file or pick the **No** button to cancel.

After using the **DXFOUT** command to create the .dxf file, use the **SAVEAS** command to save your drawing file.

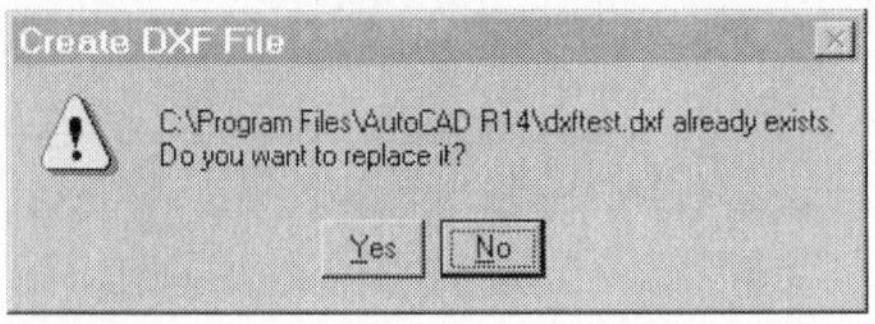

Figure 15-17.
The **Create DXF File** alert box warns you if a file with the same name already exists.

Importing a .dxf file

To import a .dxf file directly into AutoCAD, first select **Open...** from the **File** pull-down menu. In the **Select File** dialog box, pick **DXF (*.dxf)** in the **Files of type** drop-down list, then select the .dxf file and pick **Open**. This opens the .dxf file just as if it were a drawing file.

The **DXFIN** command can also be used to import a .dxf file into AutoCAD. First, begin a new drawing. Do not add entities or make setup steps. If you use an old drawing, only the entities of the .dxf file are inserted. The layers, blocks, and other drawing definitions of the old drawing will override those of the .dxf file.

For example, if you created the dfxtest.dxf file earlier, begin a new drawing called dxftest1. Now import the .dxf file by typing DXFIN at the Command: prompt. When the **Select DXF File** dialog box appears, select dxftest.dxf from the file list box or enter the file name DXFTEST in the **File Name:** text box, Figure 15-18. Then, pick the **Open** button or press [Enter]. The dialog box disappears and the drawing is regenerated.

The line should appear on the screen as it was in the original dxftest drawing. The new drawing dxftest1 with the inserted .dxf file is not given the .dwg extension until you save it.

Figure 15-18.
The **DXFIN** command displays the **Select DXF File** dialog box. Enter a file name or select it from the list.

Select file to be opened →

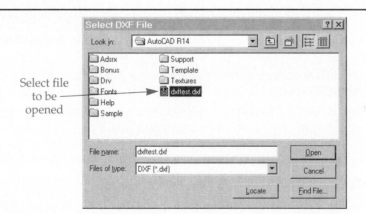

DXF applications

There are several applications where you will want to convert an AutoCAD file to .dxf format. The most common application is sharing drawings with CAM systems or other CAD systems. Numerical control (NC) programs also use .dxf files. The file is used to translate the shape and features of a machine part to code that can be used for lathes, milling machines, and drill presses. In addition, desktop publishing programs like Quark XPress®, Ventura Publisher®, and Pagemaker™ use .dxf files to translate drawings into images that can be inserted into a page layout. Also, programs that perform stress analysis and calculations often rely on .dxf drawings.

Importing a scanned file

Scanning is the process of creating an electronic file from a hard copy. Scanners reflect light off the hard copy and translate this data into an electronic file. Many scanning programs create a .dxb (drawing interchange binary) file after scanning an existing paper drawing with a camera or plotter-mounted scanner. A plotter-mounted scanner is shown in Figure 15-19. The file created is a binary code. The **DXBIN** command converts this code into drawing data. This drawing data becomes an AutoCAD drawing file with a .dwg extension. Pick **Drawing Exchange Binary...** from the **Insert** pull-down menu, or use the command as follows:

Command: **DXBIN**↵

Figure 15-19.
This scanner is attached to a large format plotter and is capable of detecting lines as fine as 0.007 inch. (Houston Instrument, A Summagraphics Company)

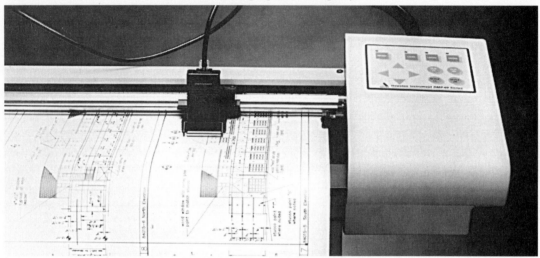

The **FILEDIA** system variable determines what you see on the screen. If **FILEDIA** is 1, the **Select DXB File** dialog box appears. Accept the default file name, or enter the file name of a specific scanned drawing, and pick the **Open** button. You can then edit the drawing using typical AutoCAD commands.

If **FILEDIA** is 0, the file dialog box is replaced with a file name prompt. The following prompt appears after you enter DXBIN at the Command: prompt:

DXB file: *(enter file name and press* [Enter]*)*

After you enter a file name, it can then be edited and saved as a drawing file.

Locating Errors in a Transferred File

AutoCAD generally does not check a .dxf file for errors, but you can do this if you need to. To do so, instruct AutoCAD to automatically list errors in the file before you transfer a .dxf file. Use the following steps:

1. Pick **Preferences** from the **Tools** pull-down menu to display the **Preferences** dialog box.
2. Pick the **General** tab.
3. Activate the **Audit after each DXFIN or DXBIN** check box. See Figure 15-20.

Make this setting part of your user profile if you work with these types of files often.

The automatic auditing process does not correct errors in the file. Errors must be corrected by editing the .dxf file or by using the **AUDIT** command while working on the drawing. See the section earlier in this chapter titled *Using the Audit Command* for a discussion on the use of this command.

Figure 15-20.
The **General** tab of the **Preferences** dialog box provides for auditing .dxf and .dxb files when opened in AutoCAD.

AutoCAD will check imported files

Exporting and Inserting Files

AutoCAD provides you with the ability to work with files other than .dxf files. You can export the current drawing to files that can be used in other programs for rendering, animation, desktop publishing, presentations, stereolithography, and solids modeling. This section provides a brief overview of AutoCAD's capabilities in exporting and inserting a variety of different files. All of these options can be selected from the **File** pull-down menu by picking **Export...**, or from the **Insert** pull-down menu.

Figure 15-21 illustrates the **Export Data** dialog box and the **Insert** pull-down menu. These two methods display a standard files dialog box. The **Export Data** dialog box requires that you first pick the type of file you wish to work with in the **Save As Type:** drop-down list. Next, enter the file name, or select it from the files displayed in the file list.

Selecting any of the five options in the **Insert** pull-down menu highlighted in Figure 15-21B will display the standard files dialog box, with titles indicating the type of file selected. The next sections cover the different importing and exporting commands.

Figure 15-21.
A—A variety of file types can be exported from AutoCAD for use in other software with the **Export Data** dialog box. B—The **Insert** pull-down menu provides another means of importing other files into the AutoCAD drawing.

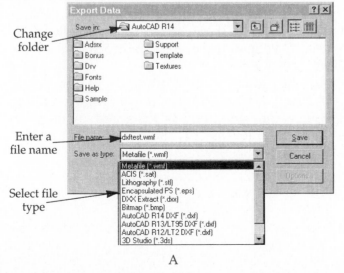

Change folder

Enter a file name

Select file type

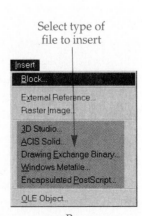

Select type of file to insert

A

B

AutoCAD Release 12 and 13 files

The **SAVEAS** command allows you to export an AutoCAD Release 14 drawing file in Release 12 and 13 format. Pick **Save As...** in the **File** pull-down menu to display the **Save Drawing As** dialog box. Pick the **Save as type:** drop-down list to see the types of .dwg files that can be saved. See Figure 15-22. You can save the current drawing as Release 12 or 13, or you can select any drawing from the file list to save as a previous version.

Figure 15-22.
The **Save Drawing As** dialog box displays the types of .dwg files that can be saved.

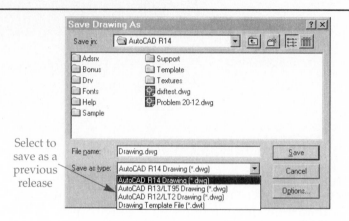

Select to save as a previous release

3D Studio files

The program 3D Studio is an Autodesk product that allows you to design, render, and animate 3D models. You can export or import 3D Studio files with AutoCAD Release 14. When you type 3DSOUT at the Command: prompt to export a 3D Studio file, you are prompted to select objects. Select all of the 3D objects you wish to export and press [Enter]. The **3D Studio Output File** dialog box is displayed. Enter the file name in the **File name:** text box. Press [Enter] or pick **Save** when you are finished. Exporting a 3D Studio file can also be executed by picking the **3D Studio (*.3ds)** file type in the **Export Data** dialog box.

You can also import an existing 3D Studio file into AutoCAD by selecting **3D Studio...** from the **Insert** pull-down menu. The **3D Studio File Import** dialog box is displayed. Select the appropriate .3ds file from the list and press [Enter]. You can also import a 3D Studio file by typing 3DSIN at the Command: prompt.

Solid model files

A *solid* is a 3D object that is composed of a specific material and possesses unique characteristics related to its shape and composition. These characteristics are called *mass properties*. Solids are created in AutoCAD with one of several commands found in the **Solids** cascading menu of the **Draw** pull-down menu.

The term *solid modeling* refers to the process of constructing a part from one or more 3D solid shapes called *primitives*, and performing any necessary editing functions to create the final product. This procedure is discussed in detail in *AutoCAD and its Applications—Advanced, Release 14,* and in *AutoCAD AME—Solid Modeling for Mechanical Design* by Ted Saufley.

A solid model is frequently used with analyzing and testing software, or in the manufacturing of the part. AutoCAD drawings can be converted into a file that can be used for these purposes. To do so, use the **ACISOUT** command. Choose **Export...** from the **File** pull-down menu. Pick **ACIS (*.sat)** in the file type drop-down list of the **Export Data** dialog box. When you pick **OK**, you are prompted to select objects. Use any of the standard selection methods to choose the solid objects, then press [Enter]. If ACISOUT is typed at the Command: prompt, the **Create ACIS File** dialog box is displayed instead of the **Export Data** dialog box. Notice that the .sat extension is the default setting. Do not change this. Type the file name in the **File name:** text box and press [Enter] or pick **Save**. The .sat file is stored in ASCII format.

Solid model data that is stored in the .sat file can be read back into AutoCAD using the **ACISIN** command. When you enter this command, the **Select ACIS File** dialog box is displayed. Pick the file from the list, then pick **Open** or press [Enter]. The **ACISIN** command is also activated by picking **ACIS Solid...** in the **Insert** pull-down menu.

PROFESSIONAL TIP

The ASCII file created by the **ACISOUT** command may be from three to four times smaller than the .dwg drawing file. For this reason, it may be efficient to store 3D solid models as .sat files instead of drawings. When you need to work with the model for any purpose in AutoCAD, simply use the **ACISIN** command. This command creates solid objects from the model data stored in the ASCII file.

Stereolithography files

Stereolithography is a technology where a plastic prototype 3D model is created using a computer-generated solid model, a laser, and a vat of liquid polymer. This technology is also referred to as *rapid prototyping* because a prototype 3D model can be designed and formed in a short amount of time, without using standard manufacturing processes. Most software used to create a stereolithograph can read an .stl file. AutoCAD can export a drawing file to the .stl format, but *cannot* import an .stl file.

After entering the **STLOUT** command, you are prompted to select a single object as follows:

    Command: **STLOUT**↵
    Select a single solid for STL output:
    Select objects:

If you select more than one object AutoCAD prompts you:

    Only one solid per file permitted.

Select one object and press [Enter]. You are then asked if you want to create a binary .stl file. If you answer no to this prompt, an ASCII file is created. Keep in mind that a binary .stl file may be at least five times smaller than the ASCII .stl file. After you choose the type of file to create, the **Create STL File** dialog box is displayed. Type the file name in the **File name:** text box and pick **Save** or press [Enter].

PostScript files

PostScript is a copyrighted page description language developed by Adobe Systems. This language is widely used in the desktop publishing industry. AutoCAD drawing files can be exported to the .eps PostScript file format by typing PSOUT at the Command: prompt. The **Create PostScript File** dialog box is displayed. You can also pick **Export...** from the **File** pull-down menu to display the **Export Data** dialog box. Then, pick **Encapsulated PS (*.eps)** in the files type drop-down list. Type the file name in the **File name:** text box and pick **Save** or press [Enter].

When a PostScript file is selected for export, the **Options...** button is activated. Pick this to view the **Export Options** dialog box. This allows you to fine-tune the content and appearance of the exported .eps file. The use of PostScript files is discussed in detail in *AutoCAD and its Applications—Advanced, Release 14*.

PostScript files can be imported into AutoCAD by picking **Encapsulated Postscript...** from the **Insert** pull-down menu. The **Select Postscript File** dialog box is displayed. Then, pick **Encapsulated PS (*.eps)**. Type the file name in the **File Name:** text box and pick **Open** or press [Enter].

Additional files

Four additional files are listed in the **Export Data** dialog box and are defined here.

- **Metafile (.wmf).** A Windows file that contains vector information. It can be scaled and retain its resolution. See *AutoCAD and its Applications—Advanced, Release 14* for a detailed discussion of metafiles.
- **DXX Extract (.dxx).** An extract file of attribute information contained in a block. This file is created by using the **ATTEXT** command, and is explained thoroughly in Chapter 25 of this text.
- **Bitmap (.bmp).** A *bitmap* is a digital image composed of bits or screen pixels. Also referred to as a *raster image*. It contains no vector information, as does the metafile. Bitmaps are discussed in *AutoCAD and its Applications—Advanced, Release 14*.
- **Drawing Web Format (.dwf).** A compressed 2D file format that can be published on the World Wide Web for others to view. See *AutoCAD and its Applications—Advanced, Release 14* for a discussion of the Internet capabilities of AutoCAD Release 14.

Chapter Test

Write your answers in the spaces provided.

1. What is a file type extension? _____
   _____

2. What do the following file extension types mean?
   A. .BAK _____
   _____

   B. .LIN _____
   _____

   C. .MNU _____
   _____

   D. .PLT _____
   _____

E. .BMP _____

_____

F. .EXE _____

_____

3. How do you launch Windows Explorer? _____

_____

4. How do you list all files on the floppy disk in the A: drive? _____

_____

_____

5. In the Windows Explorer, how do you open a folder in the All Folders list box to view its files in the Contents list box? _____

_____

6. Using Windows Explorer, how do you select several files that are scattered randomly throughout the file list?_____

_____

7. What is the procedure for changing a file name? _____

_____

_____

8. How can a file be moved to a new location? _____

_____

_____

9. How are files initially deleted? _____

_____

_____

10. How are files removed from the Recycle Bin to prevent being permanently deleted? _____

_____

_____

11. How can a damaged file be recovered? _____

_____

12. What command allows you to run a diagnostic check of a drawing file? _____

_____

13. What type of memory system does AutoCAD use to create pages of the program on the hard disk? _____

_____

14. What file type is created by the system in Question 13, and what is its three-letter file extension? _____

_____

15. What is AutoCAD's pager system, and what is the three-letter file extension that it creates? _____

16. What is the name of the backup drawing file that AutoCAD creates automatically based on the value of the **SAVETIME** variable? _____

17. Explain why drawing file translations are needed. _____

_____

_____

_____

18. Define the following abbreviations.
    DXF _____

    DXB _____

19. What is the purpose of the **DXFOUT** command? _____

_____

20. When would you use the **DXFIN** command? _____

_____

21. List the four sections contained in a .dxf file. _____

22. Suppose you plan to import a .dxf file. What setup steps must you perform to the new drawing before importing the .dxf file? _____

_____

23. List some of the programs that can use .dxf files. _____

_____

24. When would you use the **DXBIN** command? _____

25. Is the .dwg, .dxf, or .dxb file type typically the largest? _____

26. What **FILEDIA** system variable value must be used to ensure that a file dialog box appears when needed? _____

27. Does AutoCAD automatically list errors in a transferred .dxf file? _____

28. Does the automatic auditing process correct errors in a file? _____

29. Describe the function of the **AUDIT** command when used to correct errors in a transferred file. _____

_____

_____

30. Name five types of files, other than .dxf, that can be imported into AutoCAD. ___

_____

31. Why might it be more efficient to store solid models in the form of .sat files rather than as drawing files? _____

_____

_____

32. What is an .stl file and what is it used for? _____

_____

_____

Drawing Problems

1. Make backup copies of all your diskettes. Use the Copy command in Windows Explorer. Copy the files in two different ways.

   A. Copy all files with a .dwg extension to the new disk. Then copy all .bak files to the new disk.

   B. Copy a second disk, or recopy the first disk.

   C. List the files on your backup disk. Be sure that files with both .dwg and .bak extensions have been copied. Then rename all files with the .bak extension to have an .old extension.

2. Get a printed listing of the files contained on one disk. Ask your instructor or supervisor for assistance if you are not familiar with the printer.

3. Load one of your simple drawings into the AutoCAD graphics window. Create a .dxf file of the drawing. Generate a printed copy of the contents of the .dxf file.

4. The purpose of this drawing is to create entities and generate a .dxf file. Then, edit the .dxf file with a text editor and use the **DXFIN** command to view the revised drawing. You must refer to Appendix C of the *AutoCAD Customization Guide* to complete this problem. Use the following steps:

   A. Begin a new drawing and name it P15-4.

   B. Draw circle A at 4,4 with a 1″ radius.

   C. Draw circle B at a distance of 3,0 from circle A with radius of .5″.

   D. Save the drawing.

   E. Make a .dxf file of the drawing using the name of the drawing.

   F. Load the .dxf file into your text editor and change the radius of circle A to 2 and the location of circle B to 4,2. The circle information is listed in the ENTITIES section of the .dxf file. Use a search function of your text editor to find this section.

   I. Save the .dxf file.

   J. Begin a new drawing named P15-4A. Use the **DXFIN** command to load the P15-4.dxf file. Do you notice any changes? Save the drawing.

5. Create a disk that you use for storage of only .dxf files. Open your drawing files and save them as .dxf files to the disk. Keep this disk for backup purposes.

6. If you have access to a scanner, create a .dxb file from an old, hand-drawn print. Import the .dxb file using the **DXBIN** command. Compare the new AutoCAD drawing with the original.

7. Use one of the previous problems to fix errors that may exist in the transferred file using the **AUDIT** command.

Problems 8 and 9 require that you have access to another microCAD program or a program that is designed to work with AutoCAD output. Another school or company in your area may have one such program that you can use to exchange files.

8. Load one of your drawings that contains layers, blocks, and a variety of entities into AutoCAD. Create a .dxf file of the drawing. Import the file into another program that can accept .dxf file translations. Compare the new drawings with the AutoCAD version. Look especially at layers, block definitions, and entities such as polylines.

9. Obtain a .dxf file from another microCAD or CAD/CAM program. Use the **DXFIN** command to convert it to an AutoCAD drawing file. Compare the new AutoCAD drawing with the original version.

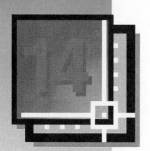

Introduction to Polylines and Multilines

Learning Objectives

After completing this chapter, you will be able to:

- ○ Use the **PLINE** command to draw objects.
- ○ Compare the results of using **FILL** on and off.
- ○ Explain the function of the **REDRAW** command.
- ○ Draw objects using the **TRACE** command.
- ○ Use the **MLINE** command to draw features.
- ○ Create your own multiline styles with the **MLSTYLE** command.
- ○ Sketch with AutoCAD.

Two AutoCAD features that provide you with endless possibilities for design and drafting applications are polylines and multilines. This chapter introduces you to the use of polylines and fully explains how to create drawing features with multilines. You will also see how to freehand sketch with AutoCAD. A complete discussion of editing polylines is given in Chapter 17 of this text.

The term *polyline* is composed of the words "poly" and "line." *Poly* means many, and a polyline is a single object that can be made up of one or more varied-width line segments. Polylines are drawn with the **PLINE** command and its options. Another command that works similar to the **PLINE** command is the **TRACE** command.

Multilines are combinations of parallel lines consisting of between 1 and 16 individual lines called *elements.* You can offset the elements as needed to create any desired pattern for any field of drafting, including architectural, schematic, or mechanical. Multilines are drawn using the **MLINE** command and related options.

Introduction to Drawing Polylines

The **PLINE** (polyline) command is used to draw polylines. Polylines have advantages over normal lines because of the following possible uses:

- • Making thick or tapered lines.
- • Much more flexibility than lines drawn with the **TRACE** command (discussed later in the chapter).
- • Can be used with any linetype.
- • Can be used to draw a filled circle or doughnut shape using the **DONUT** command.

- Can be edited using advanced editing features.
- Closed polygons can be drawn.
- The area or perimeter of a polyline feature can be determined without extra effort.
- Arcs and straight lines of varying thickness can be joined as a single entity.

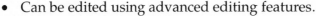

The **PLINE** command basically functions like the **LINE** command. However, there are additional options, and all segments of a polyline are a single entity. To draw a polyline, you can pick the **Polyline** button from the **Draw** toolbar, pick **P**olyline from the **D**raw pull-down menu, or type PL or PLINE at the Command: prompt:

> Command: **PL** *or* **PLINE**.⏎
> From point: *(select a point)*
> Current line-width is 0.0000

A line width of 0.0000 produces a line of minimum width. If this line width is acceptable, you may begin by selecting the endpoint of a line when the following prompt appears:

> Arc/Close/Halfwidth/Length/Undo/Width/⟨Endpoint of line⟩: *(select a point)*

If additional line segments are added to the first line, the endpoint of the first line automatically becomes the starting point of the next line.

Setting the polyline width

If it is necessary to change the line width, type W (for width) at the following prompt:

> Arc/Close/Halfwidth/Length/Undo/Width/⟨Endpoint of line⟩: **W**.⏎

When the **Width** option is selected, you are asked for the starting and ending widths. If a tapered line is desired, enter different values for the starting and ending widths at the following prompts:

> Starting width ⟨0.0000⟩: *(enter a width and press* [Enter]*)*
> Ending width ⟨starting width⟩: *(enter a different width and press* [Enter]*)*

The starting width that you select becomes the default for the ending width. Therefore, to keep the line the same width, press [Enter] at the Ending width: prompt. The following command sequence draws the line shown in Figure 16-1. Notice that the start and endpoints of the line are located at the center of the line.

> Command: **PL** *or* **PLINE**.⏎
> From point: **4,4**.⏎
> Current line-width is 0.0000
> Arc/Close/Halfwidth/Length/Undo/Width/⟨Endpoint of line⟩: **W**.⏎
> Starting width is ⟨0.0000⟩: **.25**.⏎
> Ending width ⟨.2500⟩: .⏎
> Arc/Close/Halfwidth/Length/Undo/Width/⟨Endpoint of line⟩: **8,4**.⏎

Figure 16-1.
A thick polyline drawn using the **Width** option of the **PLINE** command.

Drawing a tapered polyline

Enter different starting and ending widths if you want to draw a tapered polyline, Figure 16-2. In the following example, the starting width is .25 units and the ending width is .5 units.

```
Command: PL or PLINE↵
From point: 4,4↵
Current line-width is 0.0000
Arc/Close/Halfwidth/Length/Undo/Width/⟨Endpoint of line⟩: W↵
Starting width is ⟨0.0000⟩: .25↵
Ending width ⟨.25⟩: .5↵
Arc/Close/Halfwidth/Length/Undo/Width/⟨Endpoint of line⟩: 8,4↵
```

If you want to draw an arrowhead, give 0 as the starting width and then use any desired ending width.

Figure 16-2.
Using **PLINE** to draw a wide tapered line.

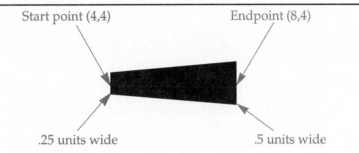

Start point (4,4)   Endpoint (8,4)

.25 units wide   .5 units wide

Using the Halfwidth option

The **Halfwidth** option allows you to specify the width from the center to one side. This is done by selecting the **Halfwidth** option of the **PLINE** command and specifying the widths. Notice that the line in Figure 16-3 is twice as wide as the line in Figure 16-2.

```
Arc/Close/Halfwidth/Length/Undo/Width/⟨Endpoint of line⟩: H↵
Starting half-width ⟨0.0000⟩: .25↵
Ending half-width ⟨.2500⟩: .5↵
```

Figure 16-3.
Using the **Halfwidth** option of the **PLINE** command. Notice that a starting value of .25 produces a width of .5 units, and an ending value of .5 produces a width of 1 unit.

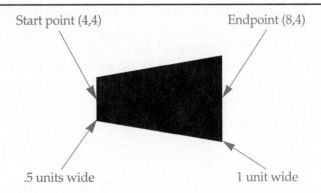

Start point (4,4)   Endpoint (8,4)

.5 units wide   1 unit wide

Using the Length option

The **Length** option allows you to draw another polyline at the same angle as the previous polyline. To use this option, type L and give the desired length. For example:

```
Command: PL or PLINE↵
From point: (pick a starting point for polyline number 1)
Current line-width is 0.0000
Arc/Close/Halfwidth/Length/Undo/Width/⟨Endpoint of line⟩: (pick the endpoint for
    polyline number 1)
Arc/Close/Halfwidth/Length/Undo/Width/⟨Endpoint of line⟩: ↵
Command: ↵
PLINE
From point: (pick a starting point for polyline number 2)
Current line-width is 0.0000
Arc/Close/Halfwidth/Length/Undo/Width/⟨Endpoint of line⟩: L↵
Length of line: (enter any desired length for polyline number 2)
Arc/Close/Halfwidth/Length/Undo/Width/⟨Endpoint of line⟩: ↵
Command:
```

The second polyline is drawn at the same angle as the previous polyline, and at the length you specify.

Undoing previously drawn polylines

While using the **PLINE** command, you may pick the **Undo** button in the **Standard** toolbar, pick **Undo** in the **Edit** pull-down menu, press the [Ctrl]+[Z] key combination, or type U at the prompt line and press [Enter] to erase the last polyline segment drawn. Each time you pick undo, another polyline segment is erased. A quick way to go back and correct the polyline while you remain in the **PLINE** command is as follows:

```
Arc/Close/Halfwidth/Length/Undo/Width/⟨Endpoint of line⟩: U↵
```

After you type U followed by [Enter], the last polyline segment drawn is automatically removed. However, the rubber band cursor remains attached to the end of the polyline segment drawn previous to the last one. You can now continue drawing additional polyline segments, or type U again to undo more polyline segments. You can keep using the **Undo** option to remove all of the polyline segments up to the first point of the polyline. The polyline segments are removed in reverse from the order that they were drawn.

U
[Ctrl]+[Z]

Edit
↪ Undo

Standard
toolbar

Undo

The **U** command (*not* the **Undo** option of the **PLINE** command) works in much the same way. However, the **U** command can be used to undo any previous commands. This is done after the command has been completed by picking the **Undo** button from the **Standard** toolbar, by picking **Undo** in the **Edit** pull-down menu, by pressing the [Ctrl]+[Z] key combination, or typing U at the Command: prompt. AutoCAD gives you a message telling you which command was undone:

```
Command: U↵
PLINE
Command:
```

In this example, the **PLINE** command was the last command undone. The **UNDO** command, which has many options when compared with the **U** command, is discussed later in this chapter.

Drawing Thick Lines Using the TRACE Command

When it is necessary to draw wide lines, the **TRACE** command can be used instead of the **PLINE** command. To use the **TRACE** command, type TRACE at the Command: prompt. All of the **LINE** command procedures apply to **TRACE** except that the line width is set first, and it cannot be closed.

The current trace width is specified in brackets. If you want to specify a trace width equal to .125, type .125 at the Trace width: prompt. The following command and prompts produce a six-sided object. Try using the **TRACE** command while responding to the prompts as follows:

```
Command: TRACE↵
Trace width 〈0.05〉: .125↵
From point: 2,2↵
To point: @6,0↵
To point: @2,2↵
To point: @0,3↵
To point: @−2,2↵
To point: @−6,0↵
To point: @0,−7↵
To point: 2,2↵
To point: ↵
Command:
```

When you use the **TRACE** command, the lines are made up of *trace segments*. The previous trace segment is not drawn until the next endpoint is specified. This is because trace segment ends are mitered to fit the next segment.

The default trace width is 0.05. When you change the trace width, this value becomes the new default until changed again. The trace width is also controlled by the **TRACEWID** system variable. The initial default is 0.05, but you can change it by typing TRACEWID at the Command: prompt and entering a new value.

The **UNDO** command works differently than the **U** command. The **UNDO** command can be used to undo any previous command. When you type the **UNDO** command, the following options appear:

```
Command: UNDO↵
Auto/Control/BEgin/End/Mark/Back/〈Number〉:
```

The default option is **Number**. You designate the number of previous command sequences you want removed. For example, if you enter 1, the previous command sequence is removed. If you enter 2, the previous two command sequences are removed. When using this command, AutoCAD tells you which previous commands were undone with a message after you press [Enter]:

```
Command: UNDO↵
Auto/Control/BEgin/End/Mark/Back/〈Number〉: 2↵
PLINE LINE
Command:
```

The **Auto** option can be turned on or off. When **Auto** is on, any group of commands that are used to insert an item are removed together. For example, when a command contains other commands, all of the commands in that group are removed as one single command. If **UNDO Auto** is off, each command in a group of commands is treated individually. This following prompt is displayed:

```
Auto/Control/BEgin/End/Mark/Back/<Number>: A↵
ON/OFF <On>: (type ON or OFF or press [Enter] to accept default)
```

The **Control** option allows you to select how many of the **UNDO** suboptions you want active. You can even disable the **UNDO** command altogether. When you enter C, you get the following prompt:

```
Auto/Control/BEgin/End/Mark/Back/<Number>: C↵
All/None/One 〈All〉: (Select control option and press [Enter])
```

Selecting the **All** suboption keeps the full range of **UNDO** options active. This is the default setting. The **None** suboption disables the **U** and **UNDO** commands. When the **U** command is entered, the following prompt appears:

```
Command: U↵
U command disabled: Use UNDO command to turn it on
```

If you type UNDO at the Command: prompt, the following appears:

```
Command: UNDO↵
All/None/One 〈All〉:
```

You must activate the **UNDO** options by pressing [Enter] for **All** or entering O for the **One** mode. The **One** suboption limits **UNDO** to one operation only:

```
Auto/Control/BEgin/End/Mark/Back/〈Number〉: C↵
All/None/One 〈All〉: O↵
```

Now, when you enter the **UNDO** command, you get the following prompt:

```
Command: UNDO↵
Control/〈1〉:
```

You can press [Enter] to undo only the previous command, or type C to return to the **Control** options. With **One** active, you can remove only those items drawn with the previous command. AutoCAD acknowledges this with the message:

Command: **UNDO**↵
Control/⟨1⟩: ↵
LINE
Everything has been undone
Command:

The **Begin** and **End** options of the **UNDO** command work together to cause a group of commands to be treated as a single command. Entering the **U** command removes commands that follow the **Begin** option but precede the **End** option. These options can be used if you can anticipate the possible removal of a consecutive group of commands. For example, if you think you may want to undo the next three commands altogether, then do the following:

Command: **UNDO**↵
Auto/Control/BEgin/End/Mark/Back/⟨Number⟩: **BE**↵
Command: **LINE**↵
From point: (*pick a point*)
To point: (*pick other endpoint*)
To point: ↵
Command: **PLINE**↵
From point: (*pick one endpoint*)
Current line-width is 0.0000
Arc/Close/Halfwidth/Length/Undo/Width/⟨Endpoint of line⟩: (*pick the other endpoint of the polyline*)
Arc/Close/Halfwidth/Length/Undo/Width/⟨Endpoint of line⟩: ↵
Command: **LINE**↵
From point: (*pick a point*)
To point: (*pick other endpoint*)
To point: ↵
Command: **UNDO**↵
Auto/Control/BEgin/End/Mark/Back/⟨Number⟩: **E**↵
Command: **U**↵

The **U** command in the last line undoes the three commands that you executed between **UNDO BEgin** and **UNDO End**.

PROFESSIONAL TIP

When you use the **UNDO** command, AutoCAD maintains an "undo" file. This file saves previously used **UNDO** commands. All **UNDO** entries saved before disabling **UNDO** with the **Control None** option are discarded. This frees up some disk space, and may be valuable information for you to keep in mind if you ever get close to a full disk situation. If you want to continue using **U** or **UNDO** to some extent, then you might consider using the **UNDO Control One** suboption. This allows you to keep using **U** and **UNDO** to a limited extent while freeing disk space holding current **UNDO** information.

The **UNDO Mark** option inserts a marker in the undo file. The **Back** option allows you to delete commands "back" to the marker. For example, if you do not want any work to be undone by the **UNDO Back** option, then enter the **Mark** option following the work:

Auto/Control/BEgin/End/Mark/Back/⟨Number⟩: **M**↵
Command:

Then, use the **UNDO Back** option to undo everything back to the marker.

> Command: **UNDO**↵
> Auto/Control/BEgin/End/Mark/Back/⟨Number⟩: **B**↵

If no marks have been entered, this will undo everything in the entire drawing. AutoCAD questions your choice with the following message:

> This will undo everything: OK? ⟨Y⟩:

If you want everything that you have drawn and edited to be undone, press [Enter]. If not, type N or NO followed by [Enter], or use [Esc].

CAUTION

Be very careful when using the **Back** option. This undoes everything in the entire drawing. You can bring it back if you type REDO and press [Enter] *immediately* after using **UNDO Back.** If you use any other command, even **REDRAW**, after using **UNDO Back**, the drawing is gone forever. The **REDO** command is explained here.

PROFESSIONAL TIP

The **UNDO Mark** option can be used to assist in the design process. For example, if you are working on a project and have completed the design on a portion of the structure, you can mark the spot with the **Mark** option and then begin work on the next design phase. If anything goes wrong with this part of the design, you can simply use **UNDO Back** to remove everything back to the mark.

| AutoCAD User's Guide | **1** |

REDO
[Ctrl]+[Y]

Edit
➥ Redo

Standard toolbar

Redo

Redoing the Undone

The **REDO** command is used to bring back objects that were erased using the **UNDO** and **U** commands. Type REDO, pick **Redo** from the **Edit** pull-down menu, press the [Ctrl]+[Y] key combination, or pick the **Redo** button from the **Standard** toolbar to activate the command.

REDO only works immediately after undoing something. **REDO** does *not* bring back polyline segments that were removed using the **Undo** option within the **PLINE** command.

EXERCISE 16-3

❑ Start a new drawing or use one of your templates.
❑ Use the **PLINE** command to draw the following:
    ❑ A rectangle 2 units by 4 units, 0 width.
    ❑ A rectangle 2 units by 4 units, .125 width.
    ❑ A line 6 units long with a .125 starting width and .250 ending width.
    ❑ A line 6 units long using the **Halfwidth** option. Starting width is .125 and ending width is .250.
❑ Use the **UNDO** command to remove the last three polylines.
❑ Use **REDO** to bring back the last removed polyline.
❑ Save the drawing as EX16-3.

Filling Polylines and Traces

In the discussion of the **PLINE** and **TRACE** commands, the results were shown as if they were solid, or filled in. You can leave traces and polylines filled in or show an outline. This is controlled by the **FILL** command, Figure 16-4. The **FILL** command only has **ON** and **OFF** options.

      Command: **FILL**⏎
      ON/OFF ⟨*current*⟩:

The value specified in brackets is the default, or previous setting. **FILL** may be turned on or off in the prototype drawing. When **FILL** is off, traces and polylines appear as outlines and the corners are mitered. After turning **FILL** off, type RE or REGEN to have the fill removed.

Figure 16-4.
Examples of **FILL**
when it is turned on
and off.

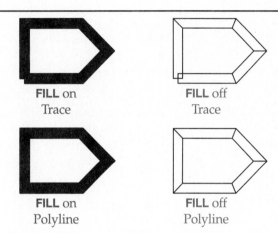

     FILL on   **FILL** off
      Trace   Trace

     FILL on   **FILL** off
     Polyline   Polyline

PROFESSIONAL TIP

When there are many wide polylines or traces on a drawing, it is best to have the **FILL** mode turned off. This saves time when redrawing, regenerating, or plotting a check copy. Turn the **FILL** mode on for the final drawing.

EXERCISE 16-4

❑ Start a new drawing or use one of your templates
❑ Use the **TRACE** command to draw a 2 unit by 4 unit rectangle with a .125 line width. Draw another with .25 line width.
❑ Use the **PLINE** command to draw a rectangle 2 units by 4 units with .125 line width. Draw another with .25 line width.
❑ Turn **FILL** off and on and observe the difference.
❑ Use the **REGEN** command with **FILL** on and off, and notice the regeneration speed in each situation. There may not be much difference with a fast computer unless the file begins to get large.
❑ Save the drawing as EX16-4.

Drawing Multilines

A multiline consists of between 1 and 16 parallel lines. The lines in a set of multi-lines are called *elements*. The multiline function has two related commands: **MLINE** and **MLSTYLE**. The **MLINE** command draws the multiline. The **MLSTYLE** command allows configuration, or style, of the multiline to be set. The AutoCAD default style has two elements and is called STANDARD.

The **MLINE** command is accessed by picking the **Multiline** button from the **Draw** toolbar, by picking **Multiline** in the **Draw** pull-down menu, or by typing ML or MLINE at the Command: prompt as follows:

```
Command: ML or MLINE↵
Justification = Top, Scale = 1.00, Style = STANDARD
Justification/Scale/STyle/⟨From point⟩: 2,2↵
⟨To point⟩: 6,2↵
Undo/⟨To point⟩: 6,6↵
Close/Undo/⟨To point⟩: 2,6↵
Close/Undo/⟨To point⟩: C↵
Command:
```

Notice the familiar ⟨From point⟩: and ⟨To point⟩: prompts, plus some other options found in the **MLINE** command. These prompts work just as they did in the **LINE** command. The other options are **Close** and **Undo**. Use the **Close** option by typing C at the last prompt to close a polygon. Enter U during the command sequence to undo the previously drawn multiline segment. The object created in the previous command sequence is shown in Figure 16-5. Two lines are drawn because this is the STANDARD AutoCAD multiline style.

Figure 16-5.
This multiline object was created with the command sequence given in the text.

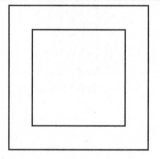

Multiline justification

Multiline justification determines how the resulting lines are offset, based on the definition points provided. The *definition points* are the points you enter when drawing the multilines. Justification can be specified only once during a single **MLINE** command sequence and is based on a counterclockwise rotation direction. The justification value is stored in the AutoCAD system variable **CMLJUST**. The justification options are **Top**, **Zero**, and **Bottom**.

Top justification is the AutoCAD default, but the current value remains in effect until changed. To change the justification, enter J at the first prompt followed by the first letter of the desired justification format (T, Z, or B). Figure 16-6 shows the results of the three different justification options using the same point entries, as given in the following command sequence:

Command: **ML** *or* **MLINE**↵
Justification = Top, Scale = 1.00, Style = STANDARD
Justification/Scale/STyle/⟨From point⟩: **J**↵
Top/Zero/Bottom ⟨top⟩:*(type* T, Z, *or* B, *and press* [Enter]*)*
Justification = *(as specified)*, Scale = 1.00, Style = STANDARD
Justification/Scale/STyle/⟨From point⟩: **2,2**↵
⟨To point⟩: **6,2**↵
Undo/⟨To point⟩: **6,6**↵
Close/Undo/⟨To point⟩: **2,6**↵
Close/Undo/⟨To point⟩: **C**↵
Command:

Figure 16-6.
Multiline justification options.

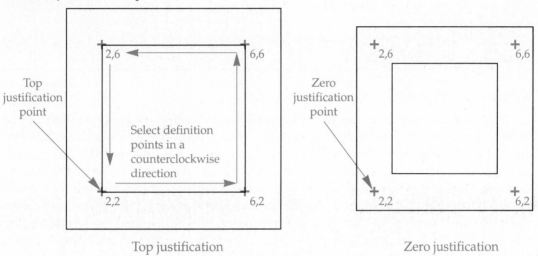

Top justification   Zero justification

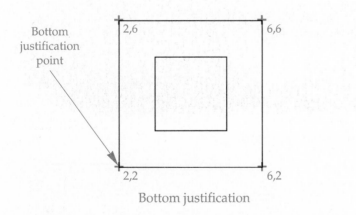

Bottom justification

+ This symbol represents the justification definition points

    The multiline justification can be set using the **CMLJUST** system variable by entering 0 for **Top**, 1 for **Zero**, and 2 for the **Bottom** option. For example, change to the **Zero** option like this:

Command: **CMLJUST**↵
New value for CMLJUST <0>: **1**↵
Command:

As shown in Figure 16-6, the justification options control the direction of the offsets for multiline elements of the current style. These examples draw the multiline segments in a counterclockwise direction. Unexpected results can often occur, depending on the justification and drawing direction.

EXERCISE 16-5

❏ Start a new drawing or use one of your templates.
❏ Use the **MLINE** command and justification options to draw three objects similar to the ones shown in Figure 16-6.
❏ Use your own point input that results in a layout that is similar to the illustration in Figure 16-6.
❏ Observe the difference between the justification options.
❏ Save the drawing as EX16-5.

Adjusting the multiline scale

The **Scale** option controls the multiplier for the offset values specified in the **MLSTYLE** command. The multiplier is stored in the **CMLSCALE** system variable. For the command sequence given in the previous section, the scale is 1.00. This means that the distance between multiline elements is 1 unit. In the case of **Zero** justification, the lines are offset 0.5 units on either side of the definition points picked. If the scale value is 2, the result is 2 units offset for the **Top** and **Bottom** justification, and a **Zero** offset of 1 and –1 on each side of the definition points. Change the offset **Scale** to 2 by typing S and 2 at the appropriate prompts, as given below. Figure 16-7 shows a comparison between multilines drawn at several different offset **Scale** values.

```
Command: ML or MLINE↵
Justification = Top, Scale = 1.00, Style = STANDARD
Justification/Scale/STyle/⟨From point⟩: S↵
Set Mline scale ⟨1.00⟩: 2↵
```

Figure 16-7.
Multiline scales.

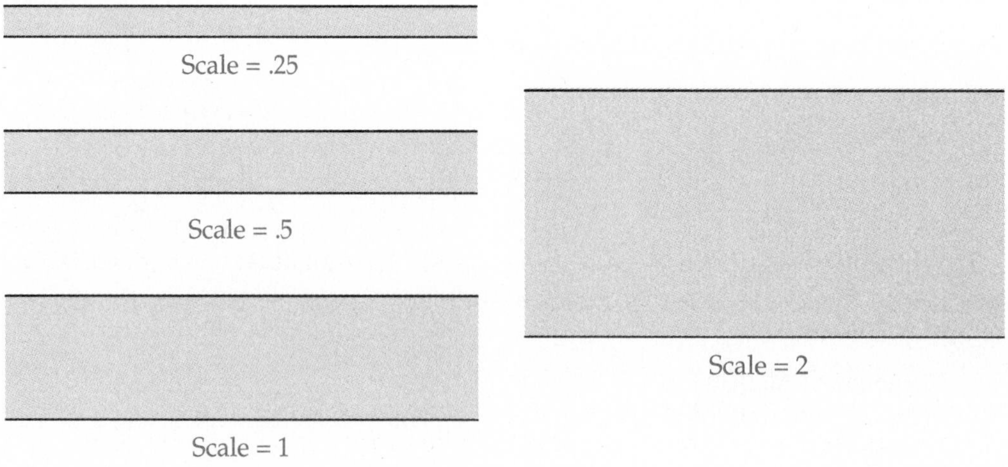

Scale = .25

Scale = .5

Scale = 1

Scale = 2

❏ Start a new drawing or use one of your templates.
❏ Use the **MLINE** command and the **Scale** option to draw three objects at scales similar to the ones shown in Figure 16-7.
❏ Use your own point input that results in a layout that is similar to the illustration in Figure 16-7.
❏ Observe the difference between the scales.
❏ Save the drawing as EX16-6.

Setting your own multiline style

The **STyle** option in the **MLINE** command allows you to specify the current multi-line style. However, the multiline style must be saved using the **MLSTYLE** command before it can be accessed. To use multiline styles that have been saved in the **MLSTYLE** command, type ST to access the style option and then type the known multiline style name as follows:

Command: **ML** *or* **MLINE**⏎
Justification = Top, Scale = 1.00, Style = STANDARD
Justification/Scale/STyle/⟨From point⟩: **ST**⏎
Mstyle name (or ?): **ROAD1**⏎
Justification = Zero, Scale = 1.00, Style = ROAD1

If you forget the name of the desired multiline style, you can type ? to get the text screen shown in Figure 16-8.

Figure 16-8.
The **AutoCAD Text Window** showing the loaded multiline styles.

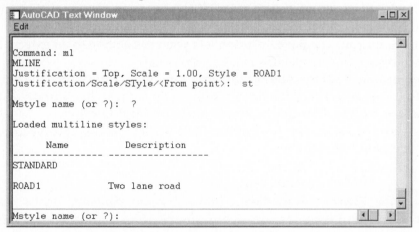

```
Command: ml
MLINE
Justification = Top, Scale = 1.00, Style = ROAD1
Justification/Scale/STyle/<From point>:  st

Mstyle name (or ?):  ?

Loaded multiline styles:

     Name            Description
---------------  ------------------
STANDARD

ROAD1            Two lane road


Mstyle name (or ?):
```

Introduction to the Multiline Styles

Styles are defined using the **MLSTYLE** command and stored in the **CMLSTYLE** system variable. The **MLSTYLE** command can be accessed by picking the **Multiline Style...** entry in the **Format** pull-down menu, or MLSTYLE can be typed at the Command: prompt.

MLSTYLE
Format
 ➥ Multiline
      Style...

The **MLSTYLE** command displays the **Multiline Styles** dialog box. This is where multiline styles can be defined, edited, and saved. See Figure 16-9. Styles can be saved either to the drawing's symbol table, or externally in a file so they can be used in other drawings.

Figure 16-9.
The **Multiline Styles** dialog box is used to define, edit, and save multiline styles.

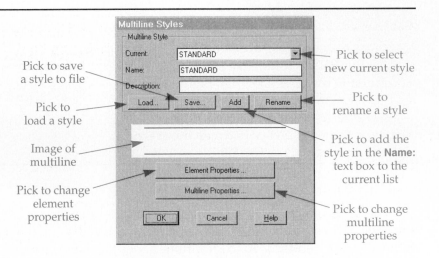

The options found in the **Multiline Style** part of the dialog box are described as follows:

- **Current: text box.** The **Current:** text box makes the identified multiline style current. This adjusts the value of the AutoCAD system variable **CMLSTYLE**. The use of this option provides a list box showing currently defined multiline styles. Use the down arrow to show the list and to pick the style that you want to make current. Until you create styles, the only style available is STANDARD.
- **Name: text box.** This is where you enter the name for a new style. Creating a new style is discussed later in the chapter.
- **Description: text box.** An optional description of your multiline style may be entered here. This is discussed later in this chapter.
- **Load... button.** The **Load...** button allows you to load a multiline style contained in an external multiline definition file or from the symbol table of the current drawing.
- **Save... button.** The **Save...** button lets you save a style to an external file. The style is saved to an .mln file.
- **Add button.** Pick the **Add** button after entering a multiline style name in the **Name:** text box. This adds the multiline style name to the **Current:** list.
- **Rename button.** Pick this button to rename a multiline style.

The image tile in the center of the **Multiline Style** dialog box displays a representation of the current multiline elements.

Using the Element Properties dialog box

Picking the **Element Properties...** button in the **Multiline Styles** dialog box accesses the **Element Properties** dialog box, Figure 16-10. You can create new multiline styles using this dialog box. The following items are contained in the **Element Properties** dialog box:

- **Elements: section.** This part of the dialog box displays the current **Offset** values, **Color**, and **Linetype**. Picking a set of elements highlights the items for further definition in this dialog box.
- **Add button.** Pick this button to add a new element to the multiline definition. Doing this adds an element with these settings: **Offset** = 0.0, **Color** = BYLAYER, and **Ltype** = BYLAYER. This allows you to draw a multiline element between the two existing elements.
- **Delete button.** Pick this button to delete the highlighted items in the **Elements:** list.
- **Offset text box.** Type either a positive or negative offset value for the highlighted offset in the **Elements:** list. Press [Enter] to accept what you type.

Figure 16-10.
The **Element Properties** dialog box is used to create multiline styles.

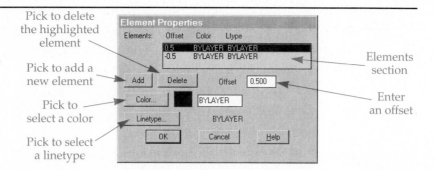

- **Color... button.** The **Color...** button accesses the **Select Color** dialog box. Pick the desired color to change the color of the highlighted item in the **Elements:** list. The new color is displayed in an image tile next to the **Color...** button.
- **Linetype... button.** Pick this button to get the **Select Linetype** dialog box. Pick the desired linetype from the **Loaded Linetypes** list. Linetypes must be loaded before they can be used. The selected linetype is displayed in the **Elements:** list.

For example, if you add a new set of elements to the **Elements:** list, leave the color BYLAYER, and change the linetype to CENTER2, you get the display shown in Figure 16-11. Pick **OK** to leave the **Element Properties** dialog box. The current status of the multiline is displayed in the **Multiline Style** image tile. You can continue in this manner to add up to 16 different color and linetype elements to the custom multiline style.

Figure 16-11.
Adding a new element to a multiline style.

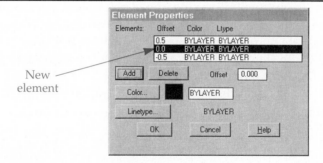

Using the Multiline Properties dialog box

You can continue to customize the multiline style by adding various end caps, segment joints, and background color by picking the **Multiline Properties...** button in the **Multiline Styles** dialog box. Doing this displays the **Multiline Properties** dialog box shown in Figure 16-12. The following explains the options for you to use in the **Multiline Properties** dialog box:

Figure 16-12.
The **Multiline Properties** dialog box is used to customize a multiline style.

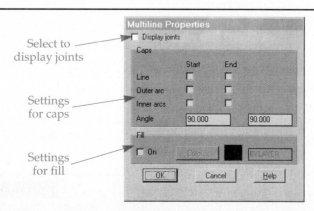

- **Display joints.** This check box is an on/off toggle for the display of joints. *Joints* are lines that connect the vertices between adjacent multiline elements. Joints are also referred to as *miters*. Figure 16-13 displays a multiline drawn with joints on and with joints off.

Figure 16-13.
How an object appears with multiline joints on and off.

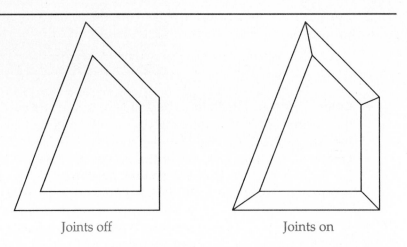

Joints off   Joints on

- **Caps area.** These settings control the placement of end caps on the multilines. End caps are lines drawn between the corresponding vertices of the beginning or ending points of the elements of the multiline. Caps can be set at the start point, endpoint, or both using the check boxes. Arcs may also be specified. Arcs can be set to connect the ends of the outermost lines only, between pairs of interior elements, or both the outer and interior lines. These arcs are drawn tangent to the elements they connect. Drawing outermost arcs requires at least two multiline elements.

  You can also change the angle of the cap relative to the direction of the last drawn line segment by placing new values in the **Angle** text boxes. Figure 16-14 shows examples of several different end cap options.

Figure 16-14.
Several different multiline end cap options.

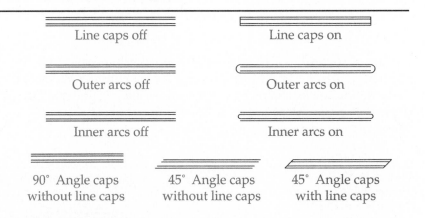

Line caps off   Line caps on

Outer arcs off   Outer arcs on

Inner arcs off   Inner arcs on

90° Angle caps   45° Angle caps   45° Angle caps
without line caps   without line caps   with line caps

- **Fill area.** If turned on, the multiline is filled with a solid fill pattern in the color specified using the fill color option. Pick the **On** switch to activate the **Color...** button. You can leave the color set BYLAYER or change it by picking the **Color...** button. Figure 16-15 shows multilines drawn with **Fill** turned on and off.

Figure 16-15.
Multiline Fill on and off.

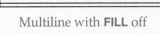

Multiline with **FILL** off   Multiline with **FILL** on

Steps in creating and drawing a multiline

Now that you have seen how the **MLINE** and **MLSTYLE** commands work, you can put it all together by creating and drawing your own multiline style. Suppose you need to draw a multiline for a two lane road to be used on a mapping project. The following procedure is used to draw the multiline:

1. Access the **Multiline Styles** dialog box, pick **Element Properties...** and set the following elements:

Offset	Color	Ltype
0.25	BYLAYER	BYLAYER
0.0	BYLAYER	CENTER2
–0.25	BYLAYER	BYLAYER

2. Pick **OK**.
3. Pick the **Multiline Properties...** button in the **Multiline Styles** dialog box. Be sure the **Display joints**, **Caps**, and **Fill** toggles are turned off, and the **Caps Angle** is 90°.
4. Pick **OK**.
5. Type ROAD1 in the **Name:** text box in the **Multiline Style** area of the **Multiline Styles** dialog box.
6. In the **Description:** text box, type TWO LANE ROAD WITH CENTERLINE. See Figure 16-16.
7. Pick the **Save...** button in the **Multiline Styles** dialog box to get the **Save Multiline Style** dialog box.
8. The acad.mln file is highlighted as shown in Figure 16-17. Pick the **Save** button.

Figure 16-16.
The **Multiline Styles** dialog box with the new style named ROAD1 entered in the **Name:** box and its description typed in the **Description:** box.

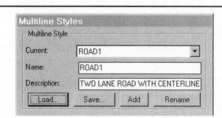

Figure 16-17.
The **Save Multiline Style** dialog box.

Folder where acad.mln is located

Default file name

Default extension

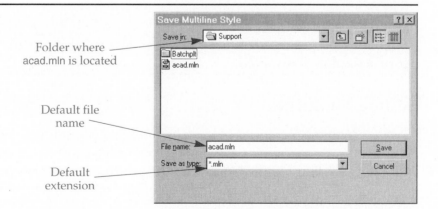

9. Pick the **Load...** button in the **Multiline Styles** dialog box to access the **Load Multiline Styles** dialog box.
10. Pick the ROAD1 multiline style as shown in Figure 16-18 and then pick **OK.**

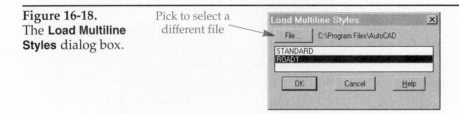

Figure 16-18.
The **Load Multiline Styles** dialog box.

Pick to select a different file

11. Pick **OK** to exit the **Multiline Style** dialog box.
12. Enter the **MLINE** command to draw the ROAD1 multiline.

If the ROAD1 multiline style was not loaded in the **Multiline Style** dialog box, use the **STyle** option to access it. Then, draw the multiline shown in Figure 16-19 using the following command sequence:

```
Justification/Scale/STyle/⟨From point⟩: ST↵
Mstyle name (or ?): ROAD1↵
Justification = Zero, Scale = 1.00, Style = ROAD1
Justification/Scale/STyle/⟨From point⟩: 2,2↵
⟨To point⟩: 6,2↵
Undo/⟨To point⟩: ↵
Command:
```

Figure 16-19.
Drawing the ROAD1 multiline style.

EXERCISE 16-7

❏ Start a new drawing or use one of your templates.
❏ Use the **MLSTYLE** and the **MLINE** commands to create and draw the following:
  ❏ A multiline with joints similar to Figure 16-13.
  ❏ Multilines with several end cap options similar to Figure 16-14.
  ❏ A multiline with **Fill** on.
  ❏ A multiline with a different linetype similar to Figure 16-19.
❏ Save the drawing as EX16-7.

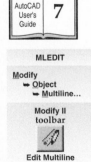

AutoCAD User's Guide 7

MLEDIT

Modify
→ Object
  → Multiline...

Modify II toolbar

Edit Multiline

Editing Multilines

The **MLEDIT** command allows limited editing of multiline objects. The **MLEDIT** command can be accessed by picking the **Edit Multiline** button in the **Modify II** toolbar, by picking **Multiline...** in the **Object** cascading menu of the **Modify** pull-down menu, or by typing MLEDIT at the Command: prompt. This displays the **Multiline Edit Tools** dialog box shown in Figure 16-20. The image buttons in this dialog box show you an example of what to expect when using each option.

Figure 16-20.
The **Multiline Edit Tools** dialog box has twelve different options. Refer to the text for an explanation of each option.

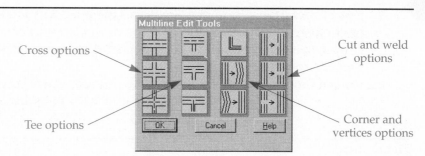

Cross options

Tee options

Cut and weld options

Corner and vertices options

Editing the crossing

The **Multiline Edit Tools** dialog box has four columns, each with three image buttons. The first (left) column displays three different types of intersections. Picking a button allows you to create the type of intersection shown. The name of the **MLEDIT** option is displayed in the lower-left corner of the dialog box when you pick an image button. The buttons in the first column are described below:

- **Closed Cross.** This option lets you create what is referred to as a *closed cross*. This is where the first multiline, called the foreground, remains unchanged while the second multiline is trimmed to intersect with the foreground multiline as shown in Figure 16-21. Note that the trimming is apparent, not actual. This means that the line visibility is changed, but it is still one multiline element. The command sequence is like this:

  Command: **MLEDIT** ↵ *(pick the **Closed Cross** image button and pick **OK**)*
  Select first mline: *(pick the foreground multiline)*
  Select second mline: *(pick the intersecting multiline)*

Figure 16-21.
The **Closed Cross** option of the **MLEDIT** command.

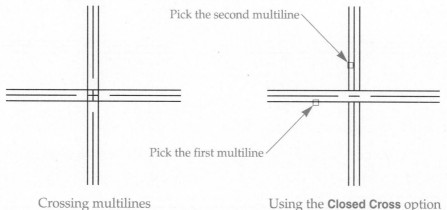

Pick the second multiline

Pick the first multiline

Crossing multilines

Using the **Closed Cross** option

The closed cross intersection is drawn. AutoCAD also issues a prompt to let you pick additional multilines for intersection, or type U to undo the intersection you just made. If you undo, AutoCAD gives the Select first mline: prompt again:

  Select first mline (or Undo): **U** ↵
  Select first mline: *(pick the foreground multiline)*
  Select second mline: *(pick the intersecting multiline)*
  Select first mline (or Undo): ↵
  Command:

- **Open Cross.** Select the **Open Cross** image button to trim all of the elements of the first picked multiline and only the outer elements of the second multiline, as shown in Figure 16-22. The command sequence is the same as for the **Closed Cross**.
- **Merged Cross.** The **Merged Cross** image button allows you to trim all outer elements while all interior elements remain the same, as shown in Figure 16-23.

Figure 16-22.
The **Open Cross** option of the **MLEDIT** command.

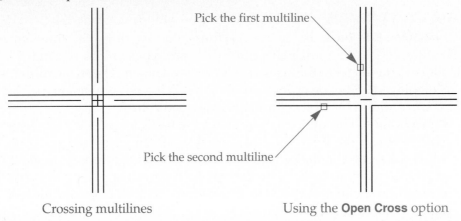

Crossing multilines — Using the **Open Cross** option

Figure 16-23.
The **Merged Cross** option of the **MLEDIT** command.

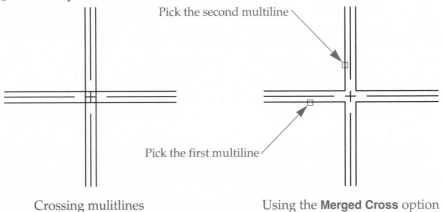

Crossing mulitlines — Using the **Merged Cross** option

Editing the tees

The second column of the **Multiline Edit Tools** dialog box is for editing tees. The **MLEDIT** tee options are illustrated in Figure 16-24. The options are described as follows:

- **Closed Tee.** Pick the **Closed Tee** option to have AutoCAD trim or extend the first selected multiline to its intersection with the second multiline.
- **Open Tee.** The first pick of the **Open Tee** option is the multiline to trim or extend and the second is the intersecting multiline. The intersecting multiline is trimmed and left open where the first multiline joins.
- **Merged Tee.** The **Merged Tee** option trims or extends the intersecting multiline by creating an open appearance with the outer elements and joining the interior elements.

Figure 16-24.
The **Tee** options of the **MLEDIT** command.

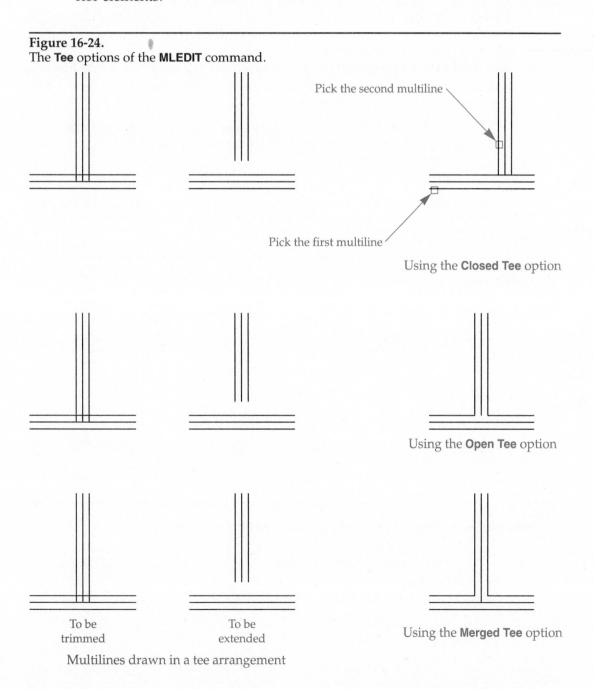

Pick the second multiline

Pick the first multiline

Using the **Closed Tee** option

Using the **Open Tee** option

To be trimmed

To be extended

Using the **Merged Tee** option

Multilines drawn in a tee arrangement

Editing the corner joint and multiline vertices

The third column of the **Multiline Edit Tools** dialog box has a corner joint option and vertex control options. These options are described below:

- **Corner Joint.** This option creates a corner joint between two multilines. The first multiline is trimmed or extended to its intersection with the second multiline, as shown in Figure 16-25.

- **Add Vertex.** This option adds a vertex to an existing multiline at the location where you pick, as shown in Figure 16-26. The command sequence is a little different than the previous options:

  Command: **MLEDIT**↵ (*pick the* **Add Vertex** *image button and pick* **OK**)
  Select mline: (*pick the place on the mline for the new vertex*)
  Select mline (or Undo): ↵
  Command:

- **Delete Vertex.** The **Delete Vertex** option removes a vertex from an existing multiline nearest to the location where you pick, as shown in Figure 16-26.

Figure 16-25.
The **Corner Joint** option of the **MLEDIT** command.

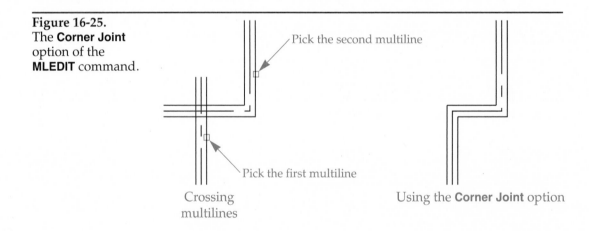

Pick the second multiline

Pick the first multiline

Crossing multilines

Using the **Corner Joint** option

Figure 16-26.
The **Add Vertices** and **Delete Vertices** options of the **MLEDIT** command.

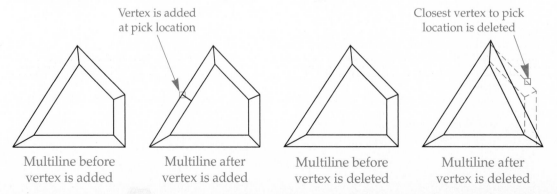

Vertex is added at pick location

Closest vertex to pick location is deleted

Multiline before vertex is added

Multiline after vertex is added

Multiline before vertex is deleted

Multiline after vertex is deleted

Cutting and welding multilines

The fourth column of image buttons in the **Multiline Edit Tools** dialog box is for *cutting* a portion out of a single multiline element or the entire multiline, or connecting a space between multiline ends. AutoCAD refers to the connecting operation as *welding*. The options are illustrated in Figure 16-27.

Figure 16-27.
The **Cut Single**, **Cut All**, and **Weld** options of the **MLEDIT** command.

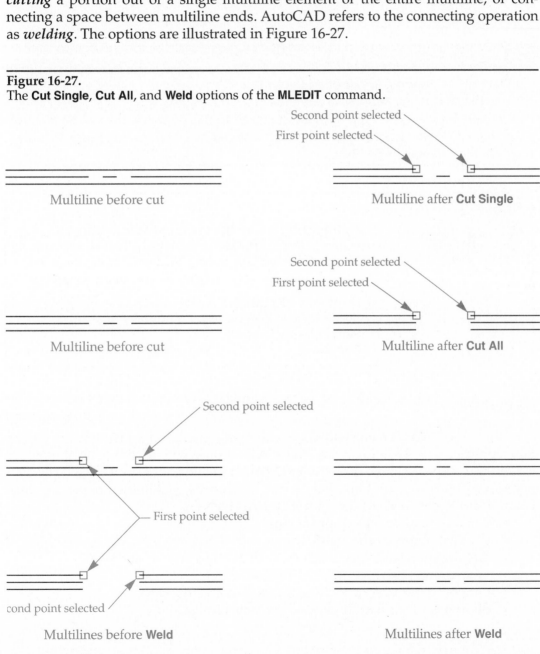

- **Cut Single.** This option allows you to cut a single element between two specified points. Cutting only affects visibility of elements, and does not separate a multiline object. The multiline is still a single object. The command sequence is as follows:

> Command: **MLEDIT** ↵ *(pick the **Cut Single** image button and pick **OK**)*
> Select mline: *(pick the place for the first cut point on the mline)*
> Select second point: *(pick the place for the second cut point)*
> Select mline (or Undo): ↵
> Command:

- **Cut All.** This **MLEDIT** option cuts all the elements of a multiline between specified points. The multiline is still a single object, even though it appears to be separated.
- **Weld All.** This option repairs all cuts in a multiline between two selected points.

EXERCISE 16-11

❏ Start a new drawing or use one of your templates.
❏ Use the **MLINE** and **MLEDIT** commands to do the following:
  ❏ Draw multilines similar to those in Figure 16-27. Then, use the **Cut Single**, **Cut All**, and **Weld** options to edit the multilines similar to those in Figure 16-27.
❏ Save the drawing as EX16-11.

PROFESSIONAL TIP

Multiline objects can be converted to individual line segments using the **EXPLODE** command. This command is explained in Chapter 17, Chapter 20, and Chapter 23. The following is a brief look at the **EXPLODE** command sequence:

> Command: **EXPLODE** ↵
> Select objects: *(pick the object to explode)*
> Select objects: ↵
> Command:

Sketching with AutoCAD

While the **SKETCH** command is not commonly used, it does have value for certain applications. Sketching with AutoCAD allows you to draw as if you are sketching with pencil and paper. The **SKETCH** command is sometimes used when it is necessary to draw a contour that is not defined by geometric shapes or lines. Examples of freehand sketching with AutoCAD include:

- Contour lines on topographic maps.
- Maps of countries and states.
- Architectural landscape symbols, such as trees, bushes, and plants.
- Graphs and charts.
- Graphic designs, such as those found on a greeting card.
- Short breaks, such as those used in mechanical drafting.

Using the SKETCH Command

Before using the **SKETCH** command, it is best to turn **SNAP** and **ORTHO** modes off, because they limit the cursor's movement. Normally, you want total control over the cursor when sketching. The **SKETCH** command can be accessed from the keyboard When you enter **SKETCH**, AutoCAD responds with the following:

Command: **SKETCH.**⏎
Record increment ⟨0.1000⟩:

The Record increment is the length of each sketch line element generated as you move the cursor. For example, if the record increment is 0.1 (default value), sketched images consist of 0.1 long lines. An increment setting of 1 creates sketched line segments 1 unit long. Reducing the record increment increases the accuracy of your sketched image. However, record increments less than .1 consume great amounts of computer storage.

To view the chosen record increment, turn the **ORTHO** mode on and draw stair steps. Each horizontal and vertical element is the length of the record increment. If the **SNAP** mode is also on, the record increment automatically equals the snap increment. Figure 16-28 shows a comparison of .1 and 1 record increments. To set a .1 record increment, type .1 and press [Enter], or press [Enter] to accept the default value.

Record increment ⟨0.1000⟩: ⏎

AutoCAD then issues the following prompt:

Sketch. Pen eXit Quit Record Erase Connect .

Once you see this prompt, the buttons on your puck activate the **SKETCH** subcommands. The subcommands may also be entered at the keyboard by typing the capitalized letter in each option. The normal puck buttons for **SNAP** (4) and **ORTHO** (5) modes remain disabled as long as the **SKETCH** command is active. The following list shows the puck button and keyboard letters used to access each subcommand.

Keyboard Entry	Puck Button	Subcommand Function
Pen (P)	0	Pen up, pen down.
"." (period)	1	To draw a line from the endpoint of a sketched line.
Record (R)	2	Records sketched lines as permanent.
eXit (X, space bar, or [Enter])	3	Records sketched lines and exits **SKETCH** command.
Quit (Q, [Esc])	4	Removes all entities created before R or X.
Erase (E)	5	Erases all entities created before R or X.
Connect (C)	6	Connects to endpoint of sketched line after a pen up has been issued.

Figure 16-28.
Sketching record increments.

.1 Record increment
(actual size)

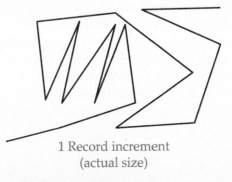

1 Record increment
(actual size)

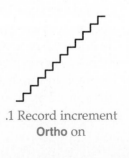

.1 Record increment
Ortho on

The sketched line segments are line objects by default. You can use the **SKPOLY** system variable to create sketched lines that are polyline objects. **SKPOLY** is 0 for line objects or 1 for polyline objects. This setting is changed by typing SKPOLY at the Command: prompt and entering the new value.

Drawing sketched lines

Sketching is done with the **Pen** subcommand. It is similar to sketching with paper and pencil. When the pencil is "down," you are ready to draw. When the pencil is "up," you are thinking about what to draw next or moving to the next location. Type P to select "pen down," and sketch. You can also press your left mouse button to move the pen "up" and "down." Move your cursor around to create a line. Type P again to select pen up to stop sketching. When you type P or use puck button 0, the prompt line reads:

Sketch. Pen eXit Quit Record Erase Connect . ⟨Pen down⟩ ⟨Pen up⟩

PROFESSIONAL TIP   If you don't consider yourself an artist, trace an existing design. Tape it to a digitizer and move the cursor along the outline of the shape with the pen down. Don't forget to select "pen up" when moving to a new sketching location.

Using the **Period** (.) subcommand

To draw a straight line from the endpoint of the last sketched line to a selected point, do the following:
1. Complete drawing the segment you are working on and make sure the pen is up.
2. Move the screen cursor to the desired point.
3. Type a period (.) or press puck button 1. A straight line is automatically drawn. If **ORTHO** is turned on, only vertical or horizontal lines are drawn.

Using the **Erase** subcommand

You can erase while sketching. If you make a mistake, type E for the **Erase** command, or press puck button 5. The "pen" may be up or down. If the pen is down, it is automatically raised. AutoCAD responds with the message:

Erase: Select end of delete. ⟨Pen up⟩

Move the cursor to erase any portion of the sketch, beginning from the last point. When finished, type P or press pick button 0. If you decide not to erase, type E or press button 5. AutoCAD returns to the **SKETCH** command after issuing the message Erase aborted.

Recording sketched lines

As you sketch, the lines are displayed in color and are referred to as *temporary lines*. Temporary lines become *permanent lines*, and are displayed in their final color, after they are *recorded*. You can record the lines and remain in the **SKETCH** command by typing R or pressing puck button 2. You can also record and exit the **SKETCH** command by typing X and pressing the right mouse button, the space bar, the [Enter] key, or puck button 3. AutoCAD responds with a message indicating the number of lines recorded. For example, if you created 32 lines, the message reads 32 lines recorded.

Quitting the SKETCH command

To quit the **SKETCH** command without recording temporary lines, type Q, press [Esc], or press puck button 4. This removes all temporary lines and returns the Command: prompt.

Connecting the endpoint of the line

It is not uncommon to select "pen up" to pause or to make a menu selection. When the pen is up, return to the last sketched point and resume sketching by typing C or pressing puck button 6. AutoCAD responds with this message:

Connect: Move to the endpoint of line.

Move the cursor to the end of the previously sketched temporary line. As soon as the crosshairs touch the previously drawn line, the pen automatically goes down and you can resume sketching.

Consuming storage space with the SKETCH command

Sketching rapidly consumes computer storage space. A drawing with fine detail will quickly fill your floppy disk. Therefore, the **SKETCH** command should be used only when necessary. The record increment should be set as large as possible, yet still appear pleasing. In commercial applications, such as topographical maps, the storage capacity is designed to accept the required input. Figure 16-29 shows a sketch of a rose. This drawing nearly filled one high-density 3.5" floppy disk (1,440,000 bytes).

Figure 16-29.
A rose drawn using the **SKETCH** command.
(Courtesy of Susan Waterman)

EXERCISE 16-12

❑ Start a new drawing or use one of your templates.
❑ Use the **SKETCH** command to sketch a bush, tree, or houseplant in plan (top) view.
❑ Save the drawing as EX16-12.

Chapter Test

Write your answers in the spaces provided.

1. Give the commands to draw a polyline from point A to point B with a beginning width of .500 and an ending width of 0. Then, undo the polyline as if you made a mistake. Finally, bring it back as if you realized you did not make a mistake:

   Command: _____

   From point: _____

   Current line-width is 0.0000 _____

   Arc/Close/Halfwidth/Length/Undo/Width/⟨Endpoint of line⟩:_____

   Starting width ⟨0.0000⟩: _____

   Ending width ⟨.500⟩: _____

   Arc/Close/Halfwidth/Length/Undo/Width/⟨Endpoint of line⟩:_____

   Arc/Close/Halfwidth/Length/Undo/Width/⟨Endpoint of line⟩:_____

   Command: _____

   Auto/Control/BEgin/End/Mark/Back/⟨Number⟩: _____

   Command: _____

2. Give the command and entries needed to draw two parallel lines, with a centerline between, with center justification, and end line caps, and the style is already saved as ROAD1:

   Command: _____

   Justification = Top, Scale = 1.00, Style = STANDARD _____

   Justification/Scale/STyle/⟨From point⟩: _____

   Mstyle name (or ?): _____

   Justification = Top, Scale = 1.00, Style = ROAD1 _____

   Justification/Scale/STyle/⟨From point⟩: _____

   Top/Zero/Bottom ⟨top⟩: _____

   Justification = Zero, Scale = 1.00, Style = ROAD1_____

   Justification/Scale/STyle/⟨From point⟩: _____

   ⟨To point⟩: _____

   Undo/⟨To point⟩: _____

3. How do you draw a filled arrow using the **PLINE** command? _____

   _____

   _____

4. Name two commands that can be used to draw wide lines._____

   _____

5. Which **PLINE** option allows you to specify the width from the center to one side?

   _____

   _____

6. What is an advantage of leaving the **FILL** mode turned off?_____

   _____

7. What is the difference between picking **Undo** from the **Edit** pull-down menu and entering the **UNDO** command? _____

_____

_____

_____

8. Name the command that is used to bring back an object that was previously removed using **UNDO**. _____

9. Name the **MLINE** command option that establishes how the resulting lines are offset based on the definition points provided. _____

_____

10. Name the option that controls the multiplier for the offset values specified in the **MLINE** command. _____

11. How do you access the **Multiline Style** dialog box? _____

_____

12. Describe the function of the **Add** button in the **Element Properties** dialog box. ___

_____

_____

13. Describe the function of the **Linetype...** button in the **Element Properties** dialog box. _____

_____

_____

_____

_____

14. Define "end caps." _____

_____

_____

15. Name the **Multiline Properties Caps** options. _____

_____

16. Define "joints." _____

_____

17. What do you get when you enter the **MLEDIT** command? _____

_____

18. How do you access one of the **MLEDIT** options? _____

_____

19. List the three options that are used for editing crossings in the **MLEDIT** command.

_____

_____

20. Name the **MLEDIT** option where the intersecting multiline is trimmed or extended and left open where the first multiline joins. _____

21. Name the **MLEDIT** option that allows you to remove a vertex from a multiline.

_____

22. Name the **MLEDIT** option that lets you remove a portion from an individual multiline element. _____

23. Name the **MLEDIT** option that removes all of the elements of a multiline between two specified points. _____

24. Name the **MLEDIT** option that repairs all cuts in a multiline. _____

25. Explain why the **SNAP** and **ORTHO** modes should be turned off for most sketching applications. _____

_____

_____

Drawing Problems

1. Use the **PLINE** command to draw the following object with a .032 line width. Do not draw dimensions. Save the drawing as P16-1.

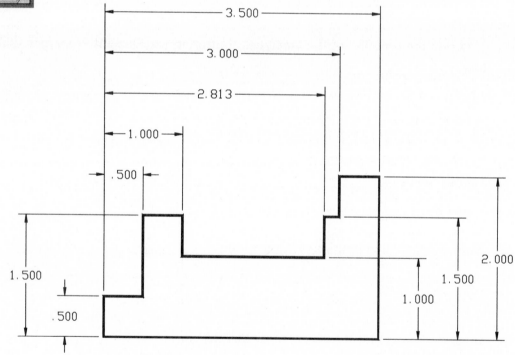

2. Use the **PLINE** command to draw the following object with a .032 line width. Do not draw dimensions. Save the drawing as P16-2.

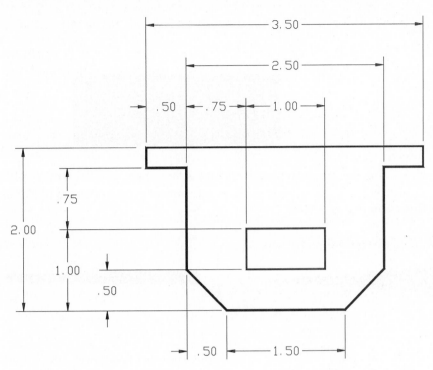

3. Use the **TRACE** command to draw the following object with a .032 line width. Do not draw dimensions.

   A. Turn off the **FILL** mode and use the **REGEN** command. Then, turn on **FILL** and do **REGEN** again.

   B. Observe the difference with **FILL** on and off.

   C. Save the drawing as P16-3.

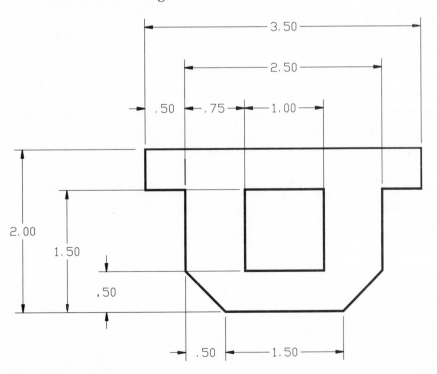

4. Use the **PLINE** command to draw the filled rectangle shown below. Do not draw dimensions. Save the drawing as P16-4.

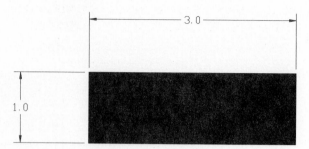

5. Draw the objects shown at A and B below. Then, use the **Undo** option to remove object B. Use the **REDO** command to get object B back. Save this drawing as P16-5.

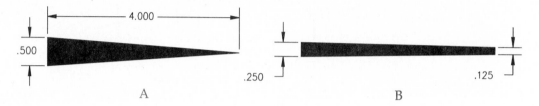

A   B

6. Draw the object shown below. Set decimal units, .25 grid, .0625 snap, and limits at 11,8.5. Save your drawing as P16-6.

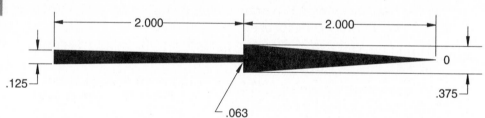

7. Open P4-13 and add the arrowheads. Draw one using the **PLINE** command and then use editing commands to place the rest. Refer to the original problem. Save the drawing as P16-7.

8. Open P5-8 and add the arrowheads using the **PLINE** command to draw the first and then using editing commands to place the rest. Refer to the original problem. Save the drawing as P16-8.

9. Open P12-11 and fill in the diodes (solid-filled triangles) using the **PLINE** command. Refer to the original problem. Save the drawing as P16-9.

10. Draw the following objects using the **Multiline** command. Use the options indicated with each illustration. Set limits to 11,8.5, **Grid** at .50, and **Snap** at .25. Set the line offset to .125. Do not add text or dimensions to the drawings. Save the drawings as P16-10.

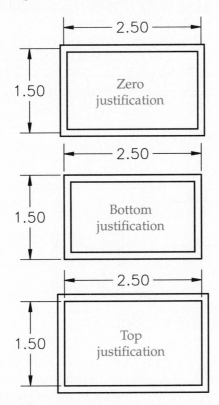

11. Draw the following objects using the multiline commands. Establish a line offset proportional to the given objects. Do not draw the dimensions or text. Save the drawing as P16-11.

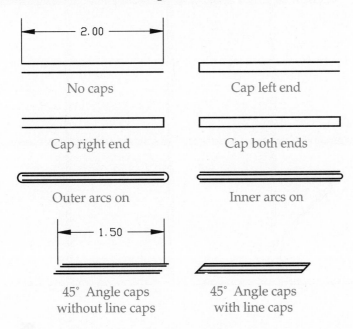

12. Draw the partial floor plan using the **MLINE** command. Carefully observe how the dimensions correlate with the double lines to determine your **Justification** settings. Also, use the **Cap** and **Break** options appropriately. Set limits to 88',68', **Grid** to 24, **Snap** to 12, and use architectural units. Make all walls 6″ thick. Do not add text or dimensions to the drawing. Save the drawing as P16-12.

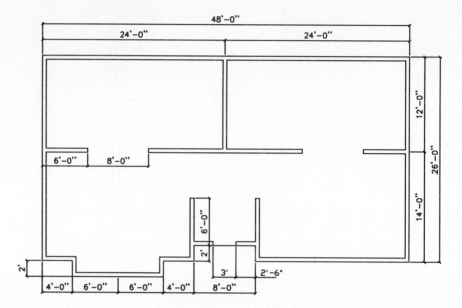

13. Draw the following proposed subdivision map using the multiline commands. Establish a line offset proportional to the given map. Use a centerline for the linetype at the center of the roads. The absolute coordinates are given at the road end and intersection centerlines. Do not draw the text. Save the drawing as P16-13.

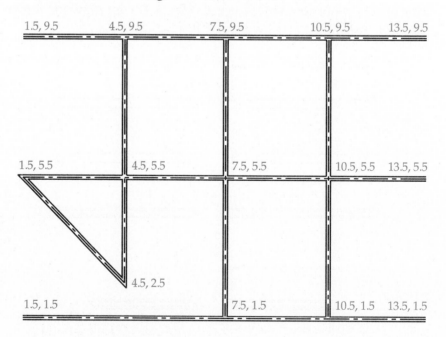

14. Draw the partial floor plan using multilines for the walls. Draw the window schedule. Do not dimension. Save the drawing as P16-14.

WINDOW SCHEDULE

SYMBOL	MANUFACTURER	MODEL #	UNIT DIMENSION	ROUGH OPENING SIZE
Ⓐ	ANDERSON	C135	2'-0 x 3'-4⅞"	2'-0" x 3'-5"
Ⓑ	ANDERSON	C235	4'-0" x 3'-4⅞"	4'-0" x 3'-5"
Ⓒ	ANDERSON	CW24	4'-8" x 4'-0"	4'-9" x 4'-0"
Ⓓ	ANDERSON	C26	4'-0" x 5'-11"	4'-0 x 6'-0"
Ⓔ	ANDERSON	CW14-3	7'-1" x 4'-0"	7'-1" x 4'-0"
Ⓕ	ANDERSON	A31 FIXED	2'-11¹⁵⁄₁₆"x 2'-0⅛"	3'-0" x 2'-0"
Ⓖ	ANDERSON	2820	2'-8⅝"x 1'-11"	2'-8" x 1'-11"

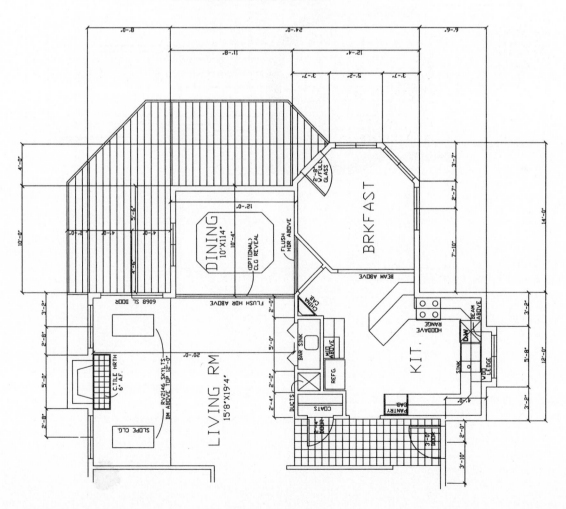

15. Draw this floor plan using multilines for the straight walls and arcs and offsets for the curved walls. Do not dimension. Save the drawing as P16-15.

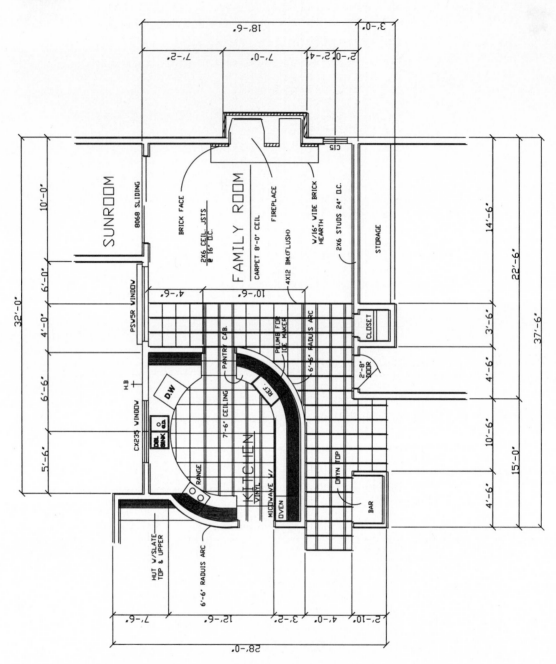

16. Draw the following proposed electrical circuit using the multiline commands. Establish a line offset proportional to the given layout. Use a phantom line for the linetype at the center of the runs. The absolute coordinates are given at the connections. Do not draw the text. You can establish any drawing features that are not defined by coordinates. Save the drawing as P16-16.

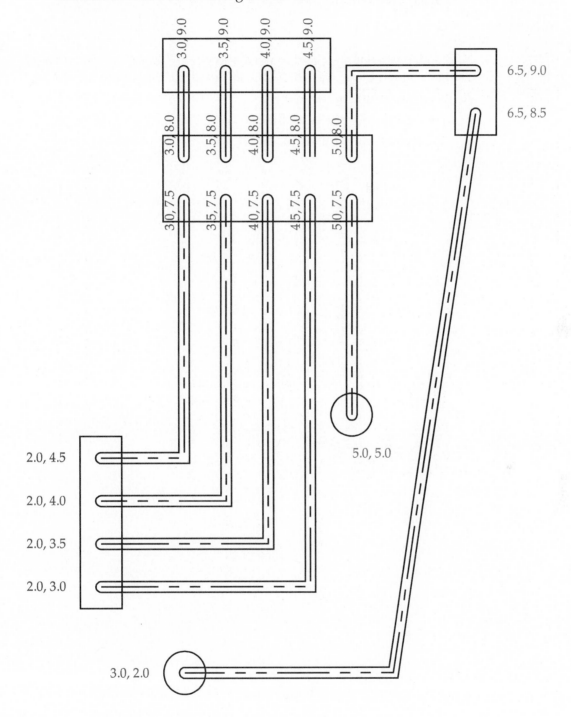

17. Use the **SKETCH** command to sign your name. Save the drawing as P16-17.

18. Use the **SKETCH** command to design the cover of a greeting card. Save the design as P16-18.

19. Find a map of your state and make a photocopy. Tape the copy to your digitizer tablet. Using the **SKETCH** command, do the following:

    A. Trace the outline of the map.

    B. Include all major rivers and lakes.

    C. Save the drawing as P16-19.

Drawing and Editing Polylines and Splines

Learning Objectives

After completing this chapter, you will be able to:
- ○ Use the **PLINE** command to draw polylines and polyarcs.
- ○ Preset the polyline width.
- ○ Use the **PEDIT** command to make changes to existing polylines.
- ○ Identify the **PEDIT** options.
- ○ Use the **EXPLODE** command to remove all polyline width characteristics.
- ○ Make a polyline boundary.
- ○ Draw and edit spline curves.

The **PLINE** command was introduced in Chapter 16 as a way to draw thick lines. As you will find, the **PLINE** command also draws a variety of special shapes, limited only by your imagination. The section on **PLINE** in Chapter 16 focused on line-related options, such as **Width**, **Halfwidth**, and **Length**. The editing functions were limited to the **ERASE** and **UNDO** commands. This chapter covers using **PLINE** to make polyline arcs and advanced editing commands for polylines.

You can access the **PLINE** command by picking the **Polyline** button in the **Draw** toolbar, selecting **Polyline** from the **Draw** pull-down menu, or typing PL or PLINE at the Command: prompt.

PLINE
PL

Draw
➥ Polyline

Draw
toolbar
↩
Polyline

AutoCAD
User's   4
Guide

Drawing Polyline Arcs

The **Arc** option of the **PLINE** command functions like the **ARC** command, except that **PLINE** options include **Width** and **Halfwidth**. The arc width can range from 0 up to the radius of the arc. A polyline arc with different end widths is drawn by changing the **Width**. The arc shown in Figure 17-1 was drawn with the following command sequence:

```
Command: PL or PLINE↵
From point: (pick the first point)
Current line-width is (status specified)
Arc/Close/Halfwidth/Length/Undo/Width/⟨Endpoint of line⟩: W↵
Starting width ⟨current⟩: .1↵
Ending width ⟨current⟩: .4↵
Arc/Close/Halfwidth/Length/Undo/Width/⟨Endpoint of line⟩: A↵
Angle/CEnter/CLose/Direction/Halfwidth/Line/Radius/Second
   pt/Undo/Width/⟨Endpoint of arc⟩: (pick the arc endpoint)
Angle/CEnter/CLose/Direction/Halfwidth/Line/Radius/Second
   pt/Undo/Width/⟨Endpoint of arc⟩: ↵
Command:
```

Figure 17-1.
A polyline arc with
different starting
and ending widths.

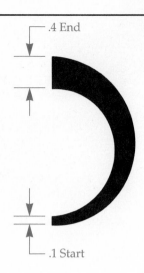

.4 End

.1 Start

Drawing a continuous polyline arc

A polyline arc continued from a previous line or polyline is tangent at the last point entered. The arc's center is determined automatically, but you can pick a new center. If a polyline arc is drawn before a straight polyline, the arc's direction is the same as the previous line, arc, or polyline. This may not be what you want. In this case, it may be necessary to set one of the **PLINE Arc** options. These include **Angle**, **CEnter**, **Direction**, **Radius**, and **Second pt** (second point). They work much like the **ARC** command options.

Specifying the included angle

The following command sequence is used to enter the **Angle** option for a polyline arc, as shown in Figure 17-2:

> Arc/Close/Halfwidth/Length/Undo/Width/⟨Endpoint of line⟩: **A**↵
> Angle/CEnter/CLose/Direction/Halfwidth/Line/Radius/Second
>   pt/Undo/Width/⟨Endpoint of arc⟩: **A**↵
> Included angle: *(specify the included angle, such as* 60, *and press* [Enter]*)*
> Center/Radius/⟨Endpoint⟩: *(select the arc endpoint)*
> Angle/CEnter/CLose/Direction/Halfwidth/Line/Radius/Second
>   pt/Undo/Width/⟨Endpoint of arc⟩: ↵
> Command:

Figure 17-2.
Drawing a polyline
arc with a specified
angle.

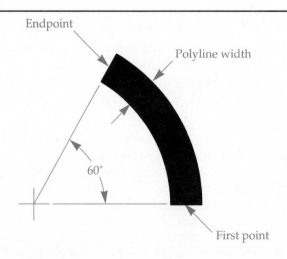

Endpoint

Polyline width

60°

First point

Selecting the CEnter option

When a polyline arc continues from a drawn item, the center point is calculated automatically. You may want to pick a new center point when the polyline arc does not continue from another item or if the one calculated is not suitable. The **CEnter** option is used as follows:

Arc/Close/Halfwidth/Length/Undo/Width/⟨Endpoint of line⟩: **A.**⏎

Angle/CEnter/CLose/Direction/Halfwidth/Line/Radius/Second
    pt/Undo/Width/⟨Endpoint of arc⟩: **CE.**⏎ *(notice that two letters, CE, are required for this option)*

Center point: *(select the arc center point)*

Angle/Length/⟨Endpoint⟩: *(select the arc endpoint, or type A or L and press [Enter])*

If A is entered at this prompt, the next prompt is:

Included angle: *(select an included angle and press [Enter])*

If L is entered, the next prompt is:

Length of chord: *(select a chord length and press [Enter])*

The Command: prompt then returns.

Using the Direction option

The **Direction** option alters the bearing of the arc. It changes the default option of placing the polyline arc tangent to the last polyline, arc, or line. This option can also be entered when you are drawing an unconnected polyline arc. The **Direction** option functions much like the **Direction** option of the **ARC** command.

Angle/CEnter/CLose/Direction/Halfwidth/Line/Radius/Second
    pt/Undo/Width/⟨Endpoint of arc⟩: **D.**⏎

Direction from start point: *(enter a direction in positive or negative degrees, or specify a point on either side of the start point)*

End point: *(select the endpoint of the arc)*

Drawing a polyline arc by radius

Polyline arcs can be drawn by giving the arc's radius. This is done by typing R. Then, respond to these prompts:

Angle/CEnter/CLose/Direction/Halfwidth/Line/Radius/Second
    pt/Undo/Width/⟨Endpoint of arc⟩: **R.**⏎

Radius: *(type the arc radius and press [Enter])*

Angle/⟨End point⟩: *(pick the arc endpoint)*

Specifying a three-point polyline arc

A three-point arc can be drawn by typing S for **Second pt**. The prompts are as follows:

Angle/CEnter/CLose/Direction/Halfwidth/Line/Radius/Second
    pt/Undo/Width/⟨Endpoint of arc⟩: **S.**⏎

Second point: *(pick the second point on the arc)*

End point: *(pick the endpoint to complete the arc)*

Using the CLose option

The **CLose** option saves drafting time by automatically adding the last segment to close a polygonal shape. The **PLINE Arc** option will close the shape with a polyline arc segment, rather than a straight polyline. Notice that CL is typed at the prompt line to distinguish this option from the **CEnter** option. You can also close a shape by selecting **Close** from the **Assist** pull-down menu. Figure 17-3 shows how the command sequence below closes a shape.

Angle/CEnter/CLose/Direction/Halfwidth/Line/Radius/Second
pt/Undo/Width/⟨Endpoint of arc⟩: **CL**↵

Figure 17-3.
Using the **CLose** option of the **PLINE** command.

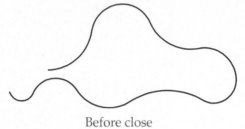 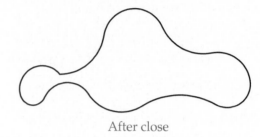

Before close   After close

Presetting polyline widths

You can preset the constant width of polylines and rectangles with the AutoCAD system variable **PLINEWID**. This can save you valuable drafting time. Set the **PLINEWID** system variable by typing PLINEWID at the Command: prompt and entering a new value.

Although polygon objects are constructed with polylines, they are not affected by the **PLINEWID** variable. When you are done drawing wide polylines or rectangles, be sure to set the value of **PLINEWID** to 0 (zero).

Revising Polylines Using the **PEDIT** Command

Polylines are drawn as single segments. A polyline joined to another polyline might then be joined to a polyline arc. Even though you draw connecting segments, AutoCAD puts them all together. The result is one polyline. When editing a polyline, you must edit it as one entity or divide it into its single segments. These changes are made with the **PEDIT** and **EXPLODE** commands.

The **PEDIT** command is accessed by picking the **Edit Polyline** button in the **Modify II** toolbar or by entering PE or PEDIT at the Command: prompt. The **PEDIT** command is also found by selecting **Polyline** in the **Object** cascading menu of the **Modify** pull-down menu. The following prompt appears:

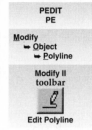

> Command: **PE** *or* **PEDIT**↵
> Select polyline: *(use one of the selection set options and press* [Enter] *when completed)*

Move the cursor and pick the polyline to be changed using any selection option. If you are using a pickbox on a wide polyline, you must place the pickbox on an edge, rather than in the center. If the polyline you want to change was the last object drawn, simply type L for **Last**.

If the object you select is a line or arc entity, this message is displayed:

> Object selected is not a polyline.
> Do you want to turn it into one? ⟨Y⟩

A Y response, or [Enter], turns the selected object into a polyline. Type N to leave the object as is. Note that if the selection set contains more than one object, only the first object found in the drawing database will be converted to a polyline. The rest of the objects are ignored.

PROFESSIONAL TIP A group of connected lines and arcs can be turned into a continuous polyline using the **Join** option. The **Join** option is discussed later in this chapter.

Revising a Polyline as One Unit

A polyline can be edited as a single entity, or it can be divided to revise each individual segment. This section shows you the options for changing the entire polyline. Notice the number of options given in the prompt:

> Command: **PE** *or* **PEDIT**↵
> Select polyline: *(pick a polyline)*
> Close/Join/Width/Edit vertex/Fit/Spline/Decurve/Ltype gen/Undo/eXit ⟨X⟩:

The default option in brackets is X for **eXit**. Pressing [Enter] returns you to the Command: prompt.

Opening and closing a polyline

You may decide that you need to close an open polyline, or you may need to reopen a closed polyline. Both of these functions are done with the **Close** option of the **PEDIT** command. Type C at the prompt line.

If you select **Close** for a polyline that is already closed, AutoCAD converts the request to **Open**. Also, typing O opens a closed polyline. Picking an open polyline and the **Close** option returns the **Close** prompt. The **Open** option will *not* work on a polyline that was closed by manually drawing the final segment. The polygon must have been closed with the **Close** option. Figure 17-4 shows open and closed polylines.

Figure 17-4.
Open and closed polylines.

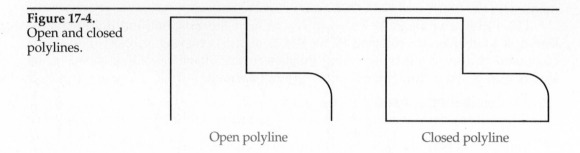

Open polyline   Closed polyline

Joining polylines to other polylines, lines, and arcs

Polylines, lines, and arcs can be joined to create a single polyline. The **Join** option works only if the polyline and other entities meet exactly. They cannot cross, nor can there be spaces or breaks within the entities. Refer to Figure 17-5. The command sequence to join objects is as follows:

Command: **PE** *or* **PEDIT**↵
Select polyline: *(select the original polyline)*
Close/Join/Width/Edit vertex/Fit/Spline/Decurve/Ltype gen/Undo/eXit ⟨X⟩: **J**↵
Select objects: *(select all of the objects to be joined)*
Select objects: ↵
nn segments added to polyline
Close/Join/Width/Edit vertex/Fit/Spline/Decurve/Ltype gen/Undo/eXit ⟨X⟩: ↵
Command:

Figure 17-5.
Enlarged views of features that are joined and not joined.

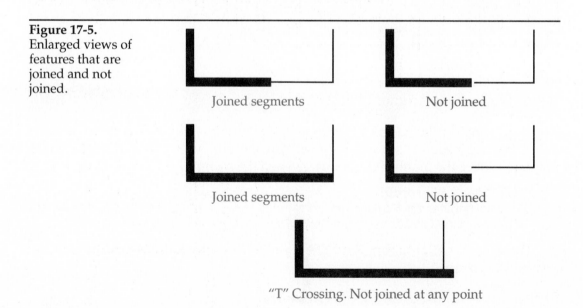

Joined segments   Not joined

Joined segments   Not joined

"T" Crossing. Not joined at any point

Select each object to be joined or group them with one of the selection options. The original polyline can be included in the selection set, but it does not need to be. See Figure 17-6.

Figure 17-6.
Joining a polyline to other connected lines and arcs.

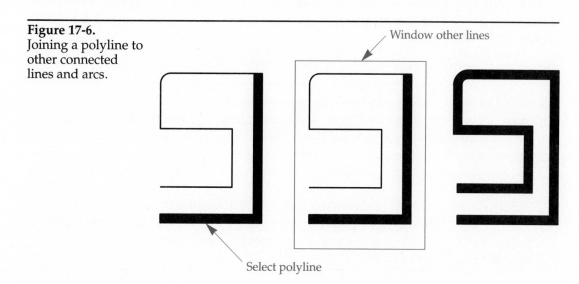

Window other lines

Select polyline

PROFESSIONAL TIP

Once items have been joined into a continuous polyline, the polyline can be closed using the **Close** option.

Changing the width of a polyline

The **Width** option of the **PEDIT** command changes a polyline width to a new width. The width of the original polyline can be constant or it can vary. To change a polyline from a .06 width to a .1 width, follow these steps:

```
Command: PE or PEDIT↵
Select polyline: (pick the polyline)
Close/Join/Width/Edit vertex/Fit/Spline/Decurve/Ltype gen/Undo/eXit ⟨X⟩: W↵
Enter new width for all segments: .1↵
Close/Join/Width/Edit vertex/Fit/Spline/Decurve/Ltype gen/Undo/eXit ⟨X⟩: ↵
Command:
```

Figure 17-7 shows an existing polyline and a new polyline using the **PEDIT Width** option.

Figure 17-7.
Changing the width of a polyline.

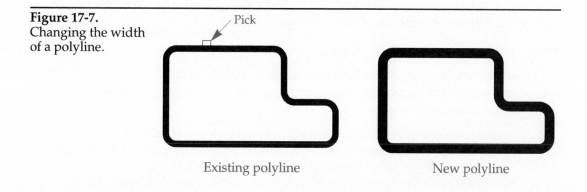

Pick

Existing polyline   New polyline

Circles drawn with the **CIRCLE** command cannot be changed to polylines. Polyline circles can be produced using the **PLINE Arc** option and drawing two 180° arcs, or by using the **DONUT** command. Change the width of doughnuts by individually picking each using the **PEDIT** command and **Width** option previously discussed. A **Window**, **Crossing**, or **Fence** selection will not change all doughnut widths at the same time.

EXERCISE 17-2

❑ Start a new drawing or use one of your templates.
❑ Draw a series of connected lines and arcs. Then, use the **PEDIT** command to change these items to a single polyline. Finally, change the width of the polyline.
❑ Draw a closed polyline. Use the **Close** option to draw the final segment.
❑ Use the **Open** option of the **PEDIT** command to open the polyline, and use **Close** to close it again.
❑ Connect a series of lines and arcs to a polyline. Then join all items as one polyline.
❑ Draw two doughnuts, each with a .5 unit inside diameter and 1.0 unit outside diameter. Change the width of the doughnuts to .1 using the **PEDIT** command.
❑ Save the drawing as EX17-2.

Changing a polyline corner or point of tangency

Another **PEDIT** option is **Edit vertex**. When you enter E for this option, an "X" appears on screen at the first vertex or point of tangency. This **PEDIT** option has nine suboptions, as shown in the following prompts:

Close/Join/Width/Edit vertex/Fit/Spline/Decurve/Ltype gen/Undo/eXit ⟨X⟩: **E**↵
Next/Previous/Break/Insert/Move/Regen/Straighten/Tangent/Width/eXit ⟨N or P⟩:

The suboptions of the **Edit vertex** option are defined as follows:
- **Next (N).** Moves the screen "X" to the next vertex or point of tangency on the polyline.
- **Previous (P).** Moves the "X" to the previous vertex or tangency on the polyline.
- **Break (B).** Breaks a portion out of the polyline.
- **Insert (I).** Adds a new polyline vertex.
- **Move (M).** Moves a polyline vertex to a new location.
- **Regen (R).** Generates the revised version of the polyline.
- **Straighten (S).** Straightens polyline segments.
- **Tangent (T).** Specifies tangent direction for curve fitting.
- **Width (W).** Changes a polyline width.
- **eXit (X).** Returns to the **PEDIT** prompt.

Only the current point is affected by editing functions, Figure 17-8. If you edit the vertices of a polyline and nothing appears to happen, use the **Regen** option to regenerate the revised edition of the polyline.

Making breaks in a polyline

The **Break** suboption of the **Edit vertex** option breaks out a portion of a polyline. Select the **Next** or **Previous** suboptions to move the "X" to the correct vertex. Then, follow this command sequence:

Close/Join/Width/Edit vertex/Fit/Spline/Decurve/Ltype gen/Undo/eXit ⟨X⟩: **E**↵
Next/Previous/Break/Insert/Move/Regen/Straighten/Tangent/Width/eXit ⟨N⟩: *(move the screen "X" to the position where you want the break to begin)*
Next/Previous/Break/Insert/Move/Regen/Straighten/Tangent/Width/eXit ⟨N⟩: **B**↵

AutoCAD and its Applications—Basics

Figure 17-8.
Using the **Next** and **Previous** suboptions of the **Edit vertex** option. Note the position of the "X".

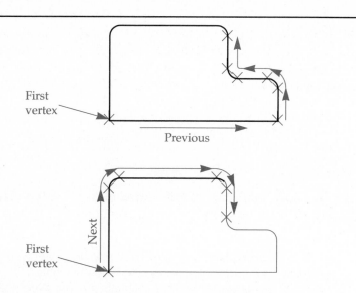

AutoCAD enters the point shown with an "X" as the first point to break.

> Next/Previous/Go/eXit ⟨N⟩: *(move the screen "X" to the next or previous position)*

Move the screen "X" to the vertex you want as the second break point. Then, enter G for **Go**. This instructs AutoCAD to remove the portion of the polyline between the two selected points. The steps below are illustrated in Figure 17-9.

> Next/Previous/Break/Insert/Move/Regen/Straighten/Tangent/Width/eXit ⟨N or P⟩: **B**↵
> Next/Previous/Go/eXit ⟨N⟩: **P**↵ *(this is point 1)*
> Next/Previous/Go/eXit ⟨P⟩: ↵ *(this is point 2)*
> Next/Previous/Go/eXit ⟨P⟩: ↵ *(this is point 3)*
> Next/Previous/Go/eXit ⟨P⟩: **G**↵ *(this is point 4)*

Figure 17-9.
Using **Edit vertex** to break out a portion of a polyline.

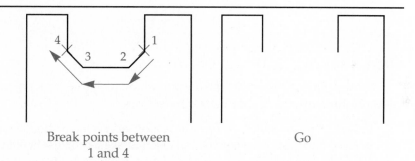

Break points between 1 and 4

Go

Insert a new vertex in a polyline

A new vertex can be added to a polyline using the **Insert** suboption. Use the **Next** or **Previous** suboptions to locate the vertex next to where you want the new vertex. Refer to the following command sequence and Figure 17-10:

> Close/Join/Width/Edit vertex/Fit/Spline/Decurve/Ltype gen/Undo/eXit ⟨X⟩: **E**↵
> Next/Previous/Break/Insert/Move/Regen/Straighten/Tangent/Width/eXit ⟨N⟩: *(move the "X" cursor to the desired location using **Next** or **Previous**)*
> Next/Previous/Break/Insert/Move/Regen/Straighten/Tangent/Width/eXit ⟨N⟩: **I**↵
> Enter location of new vertex: *(move the screen crosshairs to the new vertex location using your pointing device and pick or type the coordinates)*

Figure 17-10.
Using the **Insert** suboption of the **Edit vertex** option to insert a new vertex.

New vertex location   New vertex inserted

Moving a polyline vertex

The **Move** suboption of **Edit vertex** moves a vertex. The screen "X" cursor must be placed on the point to move before you enter M. The following sequence is shown in Figure 17-11:

Close/Join/Width/Edit vertex/Fit/Spline/Decurve/Ltype gen/Undo/eXit ⟨X⟩: **E**↵
Next/Previous/Break/Insert/Move/Regen/Straighten/Tangent/Width/eXit ⟨N⟩: *(move the "X" cursor to the vertex to be moved using* **Next** *or* **Previous***)*
Next/Previous/Break/Insert/Move/Regen/Straighten/Tangent/Width/eXit ⟨N⟩: **M**↵
Enter new location: *(pick the new point with your pointing device or type the coordinates)*

Figure 17-11.
Using the **Move** suboption **Edit vertex** option to place a vertex in a new location.

Existing vertex location

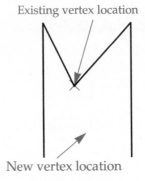
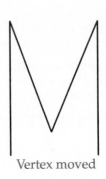

New vertex location   Vertex moved

Straightening polyline segments or arcs

You can straighten polyline segments or polyline arcs between two points. Use the **Straighten** option of **Edit vertex** as follows:

Close/Join/Width/Edit vertex/Fit/Spline/Decurve/Ltype gen/Undo/eXit ⟨X⟩: **E**↵
Next/Previous/Break/Insert/Move/Regen/Straighten/Tangent/Width/eXit ⟨N⟩: *(move the "X" cursor to the first point of the segments to be straightened)*
Next/Previous/Break/Insert/Move/Regen/Straighten/Tangent/Width/eXit ⟨N⟩: **S**↵
Next/Previous/Go/eXit ⟨N⟩: *(move the "X" to the last point)*
Next/Previous/Go/eXit ⟨N⟩: **G**↵

If the "X" is not moved before G is entered, AutoCAD straightens the segment to the next vertex. This option provides a quick way to straighten an arc, Figure 17-12.

PROFESSIONAL TIP  Two bonus tools can be used when editing polylines. The **Multiple Pedit** tool is available in the **Bonus Standard** toolbar, and the **Pline Converter** tool is in the **Tools** cascading menu of the **Bonus** pull-down menu. The bonus tools are only available if a full installation of AutoCAD was performed. See Appendix A for bonus menu information.

Figure 17-12.
Straightening
polylines.

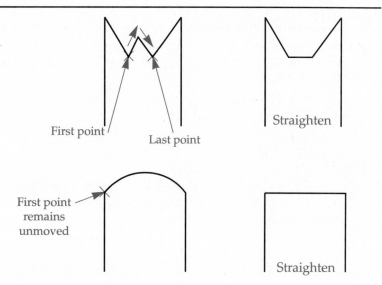

Changing polyline segment widths

The **Width** option of **Edit vertex** is the only command that changes the starting and ending widths of an existing polyline segment. Move the screen "X" to the segment before the one to be altered. The command sequence is as follows:

Close/Join/Width/Edit vertex/Fit/Spline/Decurve/Ltype gen/Undo/eXit ⟨X⟩: **E**↵
Next/Previous/Break/Insert/Move/Regen/Straighten/Tangent/Width/eXit ⟨N⟩: *(move the "X" cursor to the segment prior to the one to be changed)*
Next/Previous/Break/Insert/Move/Regen/Straighten/Tangent/Width/eXit ⟨N⟩: **W**↵
Enter starting width ⟨current⟩: *(enter the revised starting width and press* [Enter]*)*
Enter ending width ⟨revised start width⟩: *(enter the revised ending width and press* [Enter]*, or press* [Enter] *to keep the width the same as the starting width)*
Next/Previous/Break/Insert/Move/Regen/Straighten/Tangent/Width/eXit ⟨N⟩: **R**↵

Notice that the starting width default is the current setting. The ending width default is the same as the revised starting width. When you press [Enter] to complete this command, nothing happens. You must select the **Regen** option to have AutoCAD draw the revised polyline. See Figure 17-13.

Figure 17-13.
Changing the starting and ending widths of existing polylines. Use the **Regen** option to display the change.

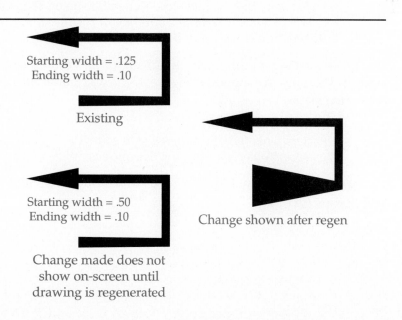

Starting width = .125
Ending width = .10

Existing

Starting width = .50
Ending width = .10

Change made does not show on-screen until drawing is regenerated

Change shown after regen

EXERCISE 17-3

❏ Start a new drawing or use one of your templates.
❏ Draw a polyline with a series of segments. Have at least eight corners and three arcs.
❏ Enter the **Edit vertex** option and move the screen "X" cursor around using the **Next** and **Previous** suboptions.
❏ Break the polyline between any three points. Then, undo the breaks.
❏ Insert a new vertex in the polyline.
❏ Move one vertex of the polyline.
❏ Straighten one arc segment or at least three line segments.
❏ Change the starting and ending widths of one segment.
❏ Save the drawing as EX17-3.

Making a smooth curve out of polyline corners

In some situations, you may need to convert a polyline into a series of smooth curves. One example is a graph. A graph may show a series of plotted points as a smooth curve rather than straight segments. This process is called *curve fitting* and is done using the **Fit** suboption of **Edit vertex**.

The **Fit** suboption constructs pairs of arcs passing through control points. You can specify control points, or you can use the vertices of the polyline's corners. Closely spaced control points produce a smooth curve.

Prior to curve fitting, each vertex can be given a tangent direction. AutoCAD then fits the curve based on the tangent directions that you set. However, you do not need to enter tangent directions. Specifying a tangent direction is used to edit vertices when **Fit** does not produce the best results.

To edit tangent directions, enter the **Edit vertex** option of the **PEDIT** command. Move the screen "X" to each vertex to be changed. Enter the **Tangent** option and specify a tangent direction in degrees or pick a point in the expected direction. The direction you choose is indicated by an arrow placed at the vertex.

Close/Join/Width/Edit vertex/Fit/Spline/Decurve/Ltype gen/Undo/eXit ⟨X⟩: **E**↵
Next/Previous/Break/Insert/Move/Regen/Straighten/Tangent/Width/eXit ⟨N⟩: *(move the screen "X" to the desired vertex)*
Next/Previous/Break/Insert/Move/Regen/Straighten/Tangent/Width/eXit ⟨N⟩: **T**↵
Direction of tangent: *(specify a direction in positive or negative degrees and press [Enter], or pick a point in the desired direction)*

Once the tangent directions are given for all vertices to be changed, select the **Fit** option. The polyline shown in Figure 17-14 was made into a smooth curve with the following steps:

Command: **PE** *or* **PEDIT**↵
Select polyline: *(pick the polyline to be edited)*
Close/Join/Width/Edit vertex/Fit/Spline/Decurve/Ltype gen/Undo/eXit ⟨X⟩: **F**↵

If the result does not look like the curve you anticipated, return to the **Edit vertex** suboption. Then, make changes using **PEDIT** options.

Figure 17-14.
Using the **Fit** option
of the **PEDIT**
command.

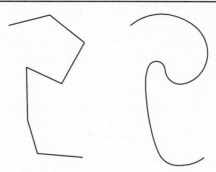

Using the Spline option

With the **Fit** option, the curve passes through polyline vertices. The **Spline** option also smoothes the corners of a straight-segment polyline. However, this option produces a different result. The curve passes through the first and last control points or vertices. However, the curve *pulls* toward the other vertices but does not pass through them. The **Spline** option is used as follows:

    Command: **PE** *or* **PEDIT**↵
    Select polyline: *(pick the polyline to be edited)*
    Close/Join/Width/Edit vertex/Fit/Spline/Decurve/Ltype gen/Undo/eXit ⟨X⟩: **S**↵

A comparison of the **Fit** and **Spline** options is shown in Figure 17-15.

Figure 17-15.
A comparison of **Fit**
and **Spline** options.

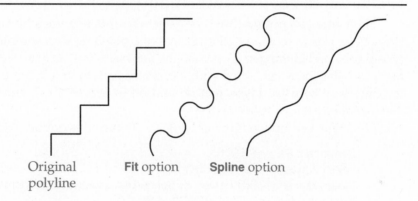

Original   **Fit** option   **Spline** option
polyline

Straightening all segments of a polyline

The **Decurve** option returns a polyline edited with the **Fit** or **Spline** options to its original form. However, the information entered for tangent direction is kept for future reference. The following **Decurve** option steps are shown in Figure 17-16.

    Command: **PE** *or* **PEDIT**↵
    Select polyline: *(pick the polyline to be edited)*
    Close/Join/Width/Edit vertex/Fit/Spline/Decurve/Ltype gen/Undo/eXit ⟨X⟩: **D**↵

Figure 17-16.
Using the **Decurve**
option.

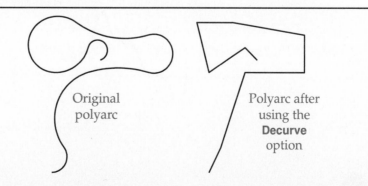

Original   Polyarc after
polyarc   using the
                  Decurve
                  option

EXERCISE 17-4

❑ Start a new drawing or use one of your templates.
❑ Draw a polyline with at least five vertices. Smooth the polyline using the **Fit** option of the **PEDIT** command.
❑ Decurve the new polyline.
❑ Practice with **Undo** by first drawing a series of polyline segments. After using **PEDIT** to make some changes, select **Undo** to return to the original polyline. Finally, use the **REDO** command to work on the edited polyline again.
❑ Save the drawing as EX17-4.

Changing the appearance of polyline linetypes

The **Ltype gen** option (linetype generation) determines how linetypes other than Continuous look in relation to the vertices of a polyline. For example, when a Center linetype is used and **Ltype gen** is off, then the line has a long dash at each vertex. When **Ltype gen** is on, the line is generated with a constant pattern in relation to the vertices. Look at the difference between **Ltype gen** on and off in Figure 17-17, and also notice the effect these settings have on spline curves.

The **Ltype gen** option is either on or off. To turn this option on, follow these steps:

Command: **PE** *or* **PEDIT**↵
Select polyline: *(pick the polyline)*
Close/Join/Width/Edit vertex/Fit/Spline/Decurve/Ltype gen/Undo/eXit ⟨X⟩: **L**↵
Full PLINE linetype ON/OFF ⟨Off⟩: **ON**↵

Figure 17-17.
Comparison of
Ltype gen on and off.

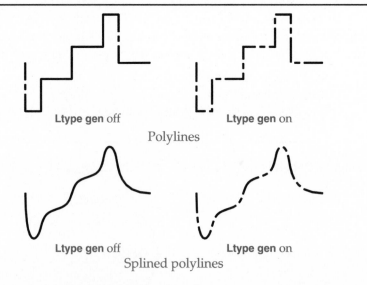

Ltype gen off   Ltype gen on
Polylines

Ltype gen off   Ltype gen on
Splined polylines

You can also change the **Ltype gen** value using the **PLINEGEN** system variable. This variable must be set before the desired polyline is drawn. **PLINEGEN** does not affect previously drawn polylines. The options are 0 for off or 1 for on. The setting is changed by typing PLINEGEN at the Command: prompt.

Converting a Polyline into Individual Line and Arc Segments

A polyline is a single entity composed of polyline and polyline arc segments. The **EXPLODE** command changes the polyline to a series of lines and arcs.

To explode an object, pick the **Explode** button in the **Modify** toolbar or type X or EXPLODE at the Command: prompt or pick **Explode** from the **Modify** pull-down menu. When a wide polyline is exploded, the resulting line or arc is redrawn along the centerline of the original polyline, Figure 17-18. When the **EXPLODE** command is accessed, you are asked to select objects:

EXPLODE
X

Modify
➥ Explode

Modify
toolbar

Explode

> Command: **X** *or* **EXPLODE**↵
> Select objects: *(pick the polyline to be exploded)*
> Select objects: ↵

The **EXPLODE** command removes all width characteristics and tangent information. However, AutoCAD gives you a chance to change your mind by offering this message:

> Exploding this polyline has lost width information.
> The UNDO command will restore it.

Figure 17-18.
Exploding a wide
polyarc.

Polyarc before   Polyarc after

Additional Methods for Smoothing Polyline Corners

Earlier in this chapter, the **Fit** and **Spline** options of the **PEDIT** command were discussed. With the **Fit** option, the resulting curve passes through the polyline vertices. The **Spline** option creates a curve that passes through the first and last control points, or vertices. The curve then *pulls* toward the other vertices but does not pass through them.

There are also two spline curve options—**Cubic** and **Quadratic**. These options create B-spline curves. The *cubic curve* is extremely smooth. The *quadratic curve* is not as smooth as the cubic curve, but it is smoother than a curve made with the **Fit** option. Like a cubic curve, a quadratic curve passes through the first and last control points. The remainder of the curve is tangent to the polyline segments between intermediate control points, Figure 17-19.

Figure 17-19.
A comparison of the **Fit**, **Quadratic** spline curve, and **Cubic** spline curve options.

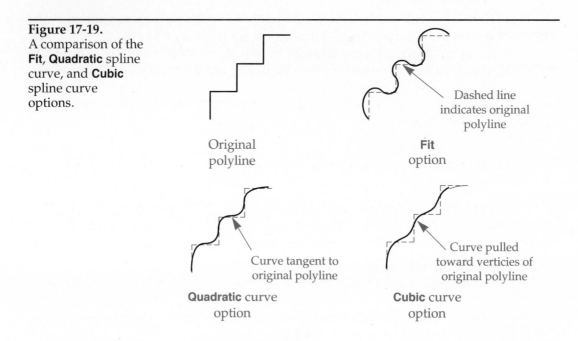

Original polyline

Dashed line indicates original polyline

Fit option

Curve tangent to original polyline

Quadratic curve option

Curve pulled toward verticies of original polyline

Cubic curve option

The system variable **SPLINETYPE** determines whether AutoCAD draws cubic or quadratic curves. The default setting is 6. This draws a cubic curve when using the **Spline** option of the **PEDIT** command. If you set **SPLINETYPE** to 5, a quadratic curve is generated. Set the **SPLINETYPE** variable by typing SPLINETYPE at the Command: prompt and entering the numeric value for the spline. The values 5 and 6 are the only valid values for **SPLINETYPE**.

EXERCISE 17-6

❑ Draw a polyline similar to the original polyline shown in Figure 17-19.
❑ Use the **COPY** command to make three copies of the original polyline.
❑ Use the **Fit** option of the **PEDIT** command to smooth the first copy.
❑ Set **SPLINETYPE** to 5 for a quadratic curve.
❑ Use the **Spline** option of the **PEDIT** command to smooth the second copy.
❑ Set **SPLINETYPE** to 6 for a cubic curve.
❑ Use the **Spline** option again to smooth the third copy.
❑ Compare the original polyline with the three new curves.
❑ Save the drawing as EX17-6.

The **SPLINESEGS** system variable controls the number of line segments used to construct spline curves. The **SPLINESEGS** default value is 8. This setting creates a fairly smooth spline curve with moderate regeneration time. If you decrease the value, the spline curve is less smooth. If you increase the value, the spline curve is smoother. Although increasing the value above 8 creates a more precise spline curve, it also increases regeneration time and drawing file size. Change the **SPLINESEGS** variable by typing SPLINESEGS at the Command: prompt and entering a new value. Figure 17-20 shows the relationship between several **SPLINESEGS** values.

AutoCAD and its Applications—Basics

Figure 17-20.
A comparison of **SPLINESEGS** values.

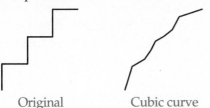

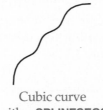

Original
polyline

Cubic curve
with a **SPLINESEGS**
value of 2

Cubic curve
with a **SPLINESEGS**
value of 8 (default)

Cubic curve
with a **SPLINESEGS**
value of 20

NOTE When AutoCAD is configured to display screen menus and you select a polyline to edit, the first **PEDIT** screen menu changes to display some of the **PEDIT** options. Also displayed near the bottom of this screen menu is **PolyVars** (polyline variables). Selecting **PolyVars** accesses the **Set Spline Fit Variables** dialog box displaying five options, including **Quadratic**, **Cubic**, and **Bezier**.

EXERCISE 17-7

❑ Draw a polyline similar to the original polyline shown in Figure 17-20.
❑ Use the **COPY** command to make three copies of the original polyline.
❑ Set **SPLINETYPE** to 6 for a cubic curve.
❑ Set the **SPLINESEGS** system variable to 2.
❑ Use the **Spline** option of the **PEDIT** command to smooth the first copy.
❑ Set **SPLINESEGS** to 8.
❑ Use the **Spline** option to smooth the second copy.
❑ Set **SPLINESEGS** to 20.
❑ Use the **Spline** option to smooth the third copy.
❑ Compare the original polyline and the smoothness of the three new curves.
❑ Save the drawing as EX17-7.

Making Curves Using the SPLINE Command

You can use the **SPLINE** command to create NURBS curves. A NURBS curve (non-uniform rational B-spline) is considered to be a true spline. The spline created by fitting a spline curve to a polyline is merely a linear approximation of a true spline and is not as accurate. An additional advantage of spline objects over smoothed polylines is that splines use less memory and disk space.

To access the **SPLINE** command, pick the **Spline** button in the **Draw** toolbar, pick **Spline** in the **Draw** pull-down menu, or type SPL or SPLINE at the Command: prompt. A spline is created by specifying the control points along the curve using any standard coordinate entry method:

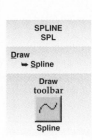

SPLINE
SPL

Draw
↳ Spline

Draw
toolbar

Spline

```
Command: SPL or SPLINE↵
Object/⟨Enter first point⟩: 2,2↵
Enter point: 4,4↵
Close/Fit Tolerance/⟨Enter point⟩: 6,2↵
Close/Fit Tolerance/⟨Enter point⟩: ↵
Enter start tangent: ↵
Enter end tangent: ↵
Command:
```

Chapter 17 Drawing and Editing Polylines and Splines

When you have given all of the necessary points along the spline, pressing [Enter] ends the point specification process and allows the start tangency and end tangency to be entered. Specifying the tangents changes the direction at which the spline curve begins and ends. Pressing [Enter] at these prompts accepts the default direction, as calculated by AutoCAD, for the specified curve. The results of the previous command sequence is shown in Figure 17-21.

Figure 17-21.
Using the **SPLINE** command with the AutoCAD defaults for start and end tangents.

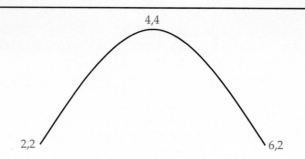

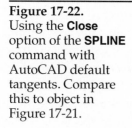
NOTE   If only two points are specified along the spline curve, an object that looks like a line is created, but the actual object is still a spline.

Drawing closed splines

The **Close** option can be used to draw closed splines. The following command sequence is used. Refer to Figure 17-22.

```
Command: SPL or SPLINE↵
Object/⟨Enter first point⟩: 2,2↵
Enter point: 4,4↵
Close/Fit Tolerance/⟨Enter point⟩: 6,2↵
Close/Fit Tolerance/⟨Enter point⟩: C↵
Enter tangent: ↵
Command:
```

After closing a spline, you are prompted to specify a tangent direction for the start/end point of the spline. Pressing [Enter] accepts the AutoCAD default.

Figure 17-22.
Using the **Close** option of the **SPLINE** command with AutoCAD default tangents. Compare this to object in Figure 17-21.

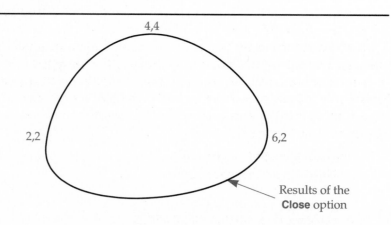

Results of the **Close** option

AutoCAD and its Applications—Basics

Altering the **Fit Tolerance** specifications

Different results can be achieved by altering the **Fit Tolerance** specifications. The outcomes of different settings vary, depending on the configuration of the individual spline object. The setting specifies a tolerance within which the spline curve passes through the fit points.

Figure 17-23 displays the **Fit Tolerance** for six test cases. The following is the command sequence for the example shown in color:

```
Command: SPL or SPLINE↵
Object/⟨Enter first point⟩: 0,0↵
Enter point: 2,2↵
Close/Fit Tolerance/⟨Enter point⟩: 4,0↵
Close/Fit Tolerance/⟨Enter point⟩: 5,5.5↵
Close/Fit Tolerance/⟨Enter point⟩: 6,0↵
Close/Fit Tolerance/⟨Enter point⟩: F↵
Enter Fit Tolerance ⟨0.00⟩: 3↵
Enter start tangent: ↵
Enter end tangent: ↵
Command:
```

Figure 17-23.
The effect of different **Fit Tolerance** values on a spline. The line in color correlates to the command sequence given in the text.

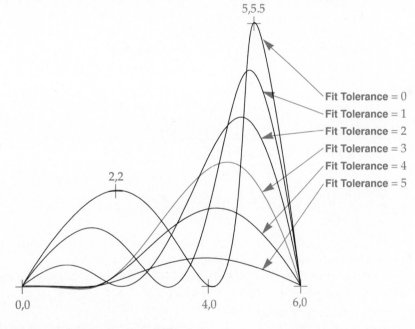

Specifying the start and end tangents

The previous examples used AutoCAD's default start and end tangents. You can also specify a start and end tangency using the **Tangent** or **Perpendicular** object snap modes. The tangency direction is in the direction of the selected point. An illustration showing the results of the **Tangent** and **Perpendicular** object snaps on two splines with the same point entries is given in Figure 17-24. This is the command sequence for the **Perpendicular** selection:

```
Command: SPL or SPLINE↵
Object/⟨Enter first point⟩: 2,2↵
Enter point: 4,4↵
Close/Fit Tolerance/⟨Enter point⟩: 6,2↵
Close/Fit Tolerance/⟨Enter point⟩: ↵
Enter start tangent: _per to (pick the line)
Enter end tangent: _per to (pick the line)
Command:
```

Figure 17-24.
Examples of start
and end tangents
perpendicular to
a line and tangent
to a line.

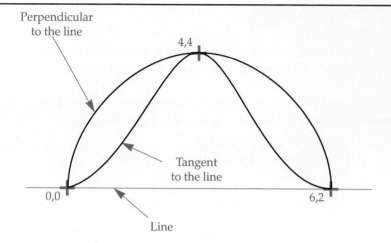

Converting a spline-fitted polyline to a spline

A spline-fitted polyline object can be converted to a spline object using the **Object** option of the **SPLINE** command. This option works for either 2D or 3D objects. The command sequence is as follows:

```
Command: SPL or SPLINE↵
Object/⟨Enter first point⟩: O↵
Select object to convert to splines.
Select objects: (pick the spline-fitted polyline)
Select objects: ↵
Command:
```

EXERCISE 17-8

❏ Start a new drawing or use one of your templates.
❏ Draw a spline with control points similar to Figure 17-21. Use the AutoCAD default tangents.
❏ Draw a similar spline to the right of the first one using the **Close** option and default tangents.
❏ Draw three splines each with the same control points, similar to Figure 17-23. Set the **Fit Tolerance** for the splines at 0, 3, and 4 respectively.
❏ Draw a line and two splines similar to Figure 17-24. Use the **Perpendicular** object snap mode for the start and end tangents on one spline. Use the **Tangent** object snap mode on the other.
❏ Save as EX17-8.

AutoCAD User's Guide **7**

SPLINEDIT SPE

Modify
➥ Edit Spline

Modify II toolbar

Edit Spline

Editing Splines

The **SPLINEDIT** command allows you to edit spline objects. Fit points can be added or moved to alter the shape of a curve. The spline can be opened, closed, or joined. Start and endpoint tangents can also be changed.

To access the **SPLINEDIT** command, pick the **Edit Spline** button on the **Modify II** toolbar, pick **Spline** in the **Object** cascading menu of the **Modify** pull-down menu, or type SPE or SPLINEDIT at the Command: prompt. The command sequence is as follows:

```
Command: SPE or SPLINEDIT↵
Select spline: (pick a spline)
```

When you pick a spline, the control points and fit tolerance data are displayed in the grip color, as shown in Figure 17-25. The command continues with this prompt:

Fit Data/Close/Move Vertex/Refine/rEverse/Undo/eXit ⟨X⟩:

The **SPLINEDIT** command options are described in the following sections.

Figure 17-25.
The control points
on a spline when
using the **SPLINEDIT**
command.

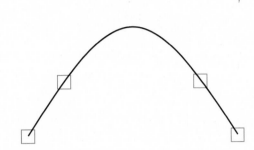

Editing fit data

The **Fit Data** option of the **SPLINEDIT** command allows spline control points to be edited. These control points are called *fit points*. Entering the **Fit Data** option gives you the suboptions shown in the following command sequence:

```
Command: SPE or SPLINEDIT↵
Select spline: (pick a spline)
Fit Data/Close/Move Vertex/Refine/rEverse/Undo/eXit ⟨X⟩: F↵
Add/Close/Delete/Move/Purge/Tangents/toLerance/eXit ⟨X⟩:
```

The purpose of these suboptions is described in the following section. Also, refer to Figure 17-26 for examples.

- **Add.** This allows new fit points to be added to the spline definition. When adding, a fit point must be located with the cursor, or you can type the X,Y location of the fit point. Fit points appear as unhighlighted grip boxes. When one is selected, it becomes highlighted along with the next fit point in the spline. The added fit point occurs between the two highlighted fit points. If the start or end of the spline is selected, a prompt is issued asking whether to insert the new fit point before or after the existing one. Respond with B or F accordingly. When a fit point is added, the spline curve is refit through the added point. See Figure 17-26.

    The **Add** option functions in a running mode. This means that you can continue to add points as needed. By pressing [Enter] at an Enter new point: prompt, you can continue to select existing fit points. Therefore, points can be added anywhere on the spline. The command sequence looks like this:

```
Command: SPE or SPLINEDIT↵
Select spline: (pick a spline)
Fit Data/Close/Move Vertex/Refine/rEverse/Undo/eXit ⟨X⟩: F↵
Add/Close/Delete/Move/Purge/Tangents/toLerance/eXit ⟨X⟩: A↵
Select point: (pick a fit point)
Enter new point: (pick a location to add a point)
Enter new point: (pick a location to add a point)
Enter new point: ↵
Select point: ↵
Add/Close/Delete/Move/Purge/Tangents/toLerance/eXit ⟨X⟩: ↵
Fit Data/Close/Move Vertex/Refine/rEverse/Undo/eXit ⟨X⟩: ↵
Command:
```

Figure 17-26.
Demonstrations of
using the **SPLINEDIT**
command **Fit Data**
suboptions.
Compare the
original spline to
edited objects.

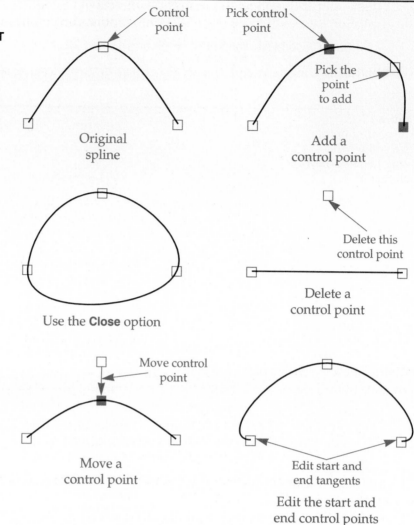

Original spline

Add a control point

Use the **Close** option

Delete a control point

Move a control point

Edit the start and end control points

- **Close/Open.** If the selected spline is open, the option is **Close**. If the spline is closed, the option is **Open**. Using this option lets you open a closed spline or close an open spline, as shown in Figure 17-26.
- **Delete.** The **Delete** option allows fit points to be deleted as needed. However, at least two fit points must remain. Even when only two points remain, the object is still listed as a spline and not a line. See Figure 17-26. This also operates in the running mode, allowing as many deletions as needed. The spline curve is refit through the remaining fit points. The prompts work like this:

Command: **SPE** *or* **SPLINEDIT** ⏎
Select spline: *(pick a spline)*
Fit Data/Close/Move Vertex/Refine/rEverse/Undo/eXit ⟨X⟩: **F**⏎
Add/Close/Delete/Move/Purge/Tangents/toLerance/eXit ⟨X⟩: **D**⏎
Select point: *(pick a fit point)*
Select point: *(pick a fit point)*
Select point: ⏎
Add/Close/Delete/Move/Purge/Tangents/toLerance/eXit ⟨X⟩: ⏎
Fit Data/Close/Move Vertex/Refine/rEverse/Undo/eXit ⟨X⟩: ⏎
Command:

AutoCAD and its Applications—Basics

- **Move.** This option allows fit points to be moved as necessary. See Figure 17-26. When **Move** is specified, the following options are available:
  - **Next**—Highlights the next fit point.
  - **Previous**—Highlights the previous fit point.
  - **Select Point**—Allows you to pick a different point to move rather than using the **Next** or **Previous** options.
  - **eXit**—Returns you to the **Fit Data** option prompt.
  - 〈**Enter new location**〉—Moves the currently highlighted point to the specified location.

> Command: **SPE** *or* **SPLINEDIT**↵
> Select spline: *(pick a spline)*
> Fit Data/Close/Move Vertex/Refine/rEverse/Undo/eXit 〈X〉: **F**↵
> Add/Close/Delete/Move/Purge/Tangents/toLerance/eXit 〈X〉: **M**↵
> Next/Previous/Select Point/eXit/〈Enter new location〉 〈N〉: **S**↵
> Next/Previous/Select Point/eXit/〈Enter new location〉 〈N〉: **X**↵
> Add/Close/Delete/Move/Purge/Tangents/toLerance/eXit 〈X〉: ↵
> Fit Data/Close/Move Vertex/Refine/rEverse/Undo/eXit 〈X〉: ↵
> Command:

- **Purge.** This option removes fit point data from a spline. After doing this, the spline is not as easy to edit. In very complex drawings, such as Geographical Information Systems (GIS), where many very complex splines are created, purging them reduces the file size by simplifying the definition. Once purged, the **Fit Data** option is no longer presented by the **SPLINE** command for the purged spline.
- **Tangents.** This option allows editing of the start and end tangents for an open spline and editing of the tangent for a closed spline. Tangency is set in the direction of the selected point. See Figure 17-26. The **System Default** option sets the tangency values to the AutoCAD defaults. This is how you use the **Tangents** option to set the **System Defaults**:

> Command: **SPE** *or* **SPLINEDIT**↵
> Select spline: *(pick a spline)*
> Fit Data/Close/Move Vertex/Refine/rEverse/Undo/eXit 〈X〉: **F**↵
> Add/Close/Delete/Move/Purge/Tangents/toLerance/eXit 〈X〉: **T**↵
> System Default/〈Enter start tangent〉: **S**↵
> System Default/〈Enter end tangent〉: **S**↵
> Add/Close/Delete/Move/Purge/Tangents/toLerance/eXit 〈X〉: ↵
> Fit Data/Close/Move Vertex/Refine/rEverse/Undo/eXit 〈X〉: ↵
> Command:

- **Tolerance.** The **Fit Tolerance** values can be adjusted using this option. The results are immediate, so the fit tolerance can be adjusted as necessary to produce different results.
- **eXit.** Returns you to the **SPLINEDIT** option line.

Opening or closing a spline

This option depends on the status of the spline object currently being edited. Using this option lets you open a closed spline or close an open spline. If the spline is open, the option is **Close**, if the spline is closed, the option is **Open**.

Moving a vertex

This **SPLINEDIT** option allows the control points for the spline to be moved. When you access this option, you get a series of suboptions, as shown in the following prompts:

```
Command: SPE or SPLINEDIT↵
Select spline: (pick a spline)
Fit Data/Close/Move Vertex/Refine/rEverse/Undo/eXit ⟨X⟩: M↵
Next/Previous/Select Point/eXit/⟨Enter new location⟩ ⟨N⟩: ↵
```

Each of the **Move Vertex** options are explained below:
* **Next.** Highlights the next fit point.
* **Previous.** Highlights the previous fit point.
* **Select Point.** Allows you to pick a different point to move, rather than using the **Next** or **Previous** options.
* **eXit.** Returns you to the **Fit Data** option prompt.
* ⟨**Enter new location**⟩. Moves the currently highlighted point to the specified location.

EXERCISE 17-9

❑ Start a new drawing or use one of your templates.
❑ Draw a spline with control points similar to the ORIGINAL SPLINE in Figure 17-26. Use the AutoCAD default tangents.
❑ Copy the original spline to five locations similar to the layout of Figure 17-26.
❑ Use the **SPLINEDIT** command on the upper-right spline to add a control point similar to Figure 17-26.
❑ Use the **SPLINEDIT** command to close the middle-left spline similar to Figure 17-26.
❑ Use the **SPLINEDIT** command on the middle-right spline to delete the top control point similar to Figure 17-26.
❑ Use the **SPLINEDIT** command on the lower-left spline to move the top control point similar to Figure 17-26.
❑ Use the **SPLINEDIT** command on the lower-right spline to edit the start and end tangents with the **Tangent** object snap similar to Figure 17-26.
❑ Save as EX17-9.

Smoothing or reshaping a section of the spline

The **Refine** option allows fine tuning of the spline shape. Control points can be added to help smooth or reshape a section of the spline. Using **Refine** removes the fit point data from the spline. Entering the **Refine** option gives you these suboptions:

```
Command: SPLINEDIT↵
Select spline: (pick a spline)
Fit Data/Close/Move Vertex/Refine/rEverse/Undo/eXit ⟨X⟩: R↵
Add control point/Elevate Order/Weight/eXit ⟨X⟩:
```

The following gives a description of each **Refine** suboption:
* **Add control point.** This allows new control points to be specified on a spline as needed.
* **Elevate Order.** The order of a spline is the degree of the spline polynomial +1. For example, a cubic spline has an order of 4. Elevating the order of a spline causes more control points to appear on the spline for greater control. The spline in Figure 17-27 has the control point order elevated from 5 to 9. The setting can be between 4 and 26, but cannot be adjusted downward. For example, once set to 24, the only remaining settings are 25 and 26.

Figure 17-27.
The effects of elevating the order of control points and increasing the weight of a control point.

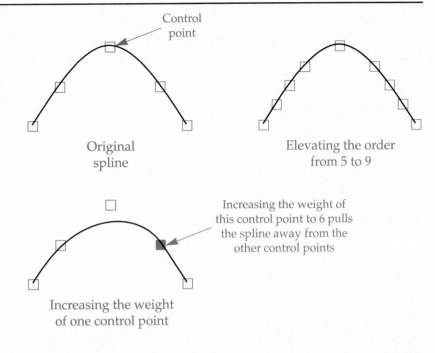

Original spline

Elevating the order from 5 to 9

Increasing the weight of one control point

Increasing the weight of this control point to 6 pulls the spline away from the other control points

- **Weight.** The default value of 1.0 can be adjusted higher or lower. This controls the weight of individual control points. When all of the control points have the same weight factor, they all exert the same amount of "pull" on the resulting spline. When a weight value is lessened, that control point is not able to pull the spline as close to it as before. Likewise, when the weight is increased, the control point pulls harder and brings the spline closer to it, as shown in Figure 17-27. The only valid settings for this are positive numbers. The control point selection options of this subcommand are the same as those discussed with **Move Vertex**, except the request to change weight is ⟨New weight data⟩:

Add control point/Elevate Order/Weight/eXit ⟨X⟩: **W**↵
Next/Previous/Select Point/eXit/⟨Enter weight⟩ ⟨*current*⟩: *(enter a positive number)*

Reversing the order of spline control points

The **rEverse** option of the **SPLINEDIT** command reverses the listed order of the spline control points. This makes the previous start point the new endpoint, and the previous endpoint the new start point. This affects the various selection options.

Undoing SPLINEDIT changes

The **Undo** option undoes the previous change. You can also use this option to undo to the beginning of the current **SPLINEDIT** command.

Exiting the SPLINEDIT command

Using the **eXit** option in the **SPLINEDIT** command returns you to the Command: prompt. You can press the [Enter] key, since X (for exit) is the default.

Making a Polyline Boundary

BOUNDRY
BO

Draw
➥ Boundry...

When you draw an object with the **LINE** command, each line segment is a single entity. You can create a polyline boundary of an area made up of closed line segments. To do this, pick **Boundary...** from the **Draw** pull-down menu, or type BO or BOUNDARY at the Command: prompt.

Now, the **Boundary Creation** dialog box shown in Figure 17-28 is displayed. The **Object Type:** text box can be set to either **Polyline** or **Region**. If set to **Polyline**, AutoCAD creates a polyline around the area. If set to **Region**, AutoCAD creates a closed 2D area. A region may be used for area analysis, shading, or other purposes. The features in the **Define Boundary Set** area are discussed in Chapter 22.

Figure 17-28.
The **Boundary Creation** dialog box.

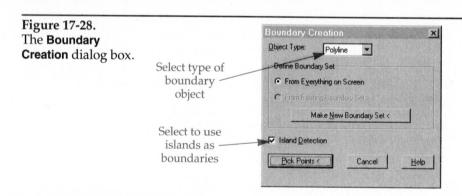

The **Island Detection** check box causes all objects within the outermost boundary to be used as boundary objects. Objects inside of a boundary are called *islands*, as shown in Figure 17-29.

When you select the **Pick Points** ⟨ button, the following prompts appear:

Select internal point: (*pick a point inside a closed polygon*)
Selecting everything...
Selecting everything visible...
Analyzing the selected data...
Select internal point: (*pick a point inside another closed polygon*)
Select internal point: ↵
Command:

Figure 17-29.
An example showing a boundary and islands.

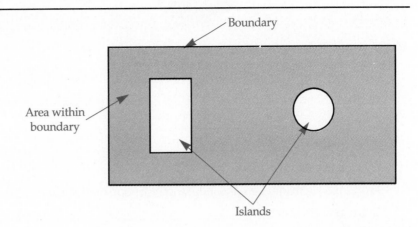

If the point you pick is inside a closed polygon, then the boundary is highlighted, as shown in Figure 17-30. If the area you want does not close, as in the lower-right example in Figure 17-30, then the **Boundary Definition Error** alert box appears. Pick **OK**, close the area, and try again.

Figure 17-30.
When you select an internal point, the boundary becomes highlighted. Boundaries must be closed objects.

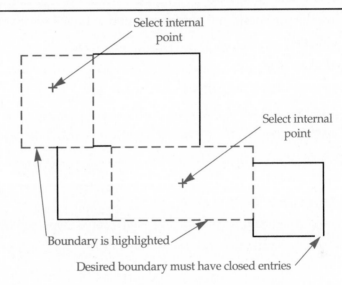

Unlike the **PEDIT Join** option, the polyline boundary created with the **BOUNDARY** command does not replace the original objects used to create it. The polyline simply *traces* over the defining entities with a polyline. Thus, the separate entities still exist and are *underneath* the newly created boundary. To avoid duplicate geometry, move the boundary to another screen location, erase the original defining entities, and then move the boundary back to its original position.

PROFESSIONAL TIP

Area calculations can be simplified by first using the **BOUNDARY** command, or by joining entities with the **PEDIT Join** option, before issuing the **AREA** command. Then, use the **AREA Entity** option to perform the area calculation. If you want to retain the original separate entities and **PEDIT Join** was used, explode the joined polyline. If **BOUNDARY** was used, simply erase the polyline boundary.

Chapter Test

Write your answers in the spaces provided.

1. Give the command and entries required to make a polyline arc with a starting width of 0 and ending width of .25. Draw it from a known center to an endpoint.

   Command: _____

   From point: _____

   Current line-width is (*status*)

   Arc/Close/Halfwidth/Length/Undo/Width/⟨Endpoint of line⟩:_____

   Starting width ⟨*current*⟩: _____

   Ending width: _____

   Arc/Close/Halfwidth/Length/Undo/Width/⟨Endpoint of line⟩:_____

   Angle/CEnter/CLose/Direction/Halfwidth/Line/Radius/Second pt/Undo/Width/⟨Endpoint of arc⟩: _____

   Angle/Length/⟨Endpoint⟩: _____

2. Give the command and entries required to turn three connected lines into a polyline:

   Command: _____

   Select polyline: _____

   Entity selected is not a polyline.

   Do you want to turn it into one? ⟨Y⟩:_____

   Close/Join/Width/Edit vertex/Fit/Spline/Decurve/Ltype gen/Undo/eXit ⟨X⟩: _____

   Select objects: _____

   Select objects: _____

   2 segments added to polyline

   Close/Join/Width/Edit vertex/Fit/Spline/Decurve/Ltype gen/Undo/eXit ⟨X⟩: _____

3. Give the command and entries needed to change the width of a polyline from .1 to .25:

   Command: _____

   Select polyline:_____

   Close/Join/Width/Edit vertex/Fit/Spline/Decurve/Ltype gen/Undo/eXit ⟨X⟩: _____

   Enter new width for all segments: _____

   Close/Join/Width/Edit vertex/Fit/Spline/Decurve/Ltype gen/Undo/eXit ⟨X⟩: _____

*For Questions 4 through 10, give the **PEDIT Edit vertex** option that relates to the definition given.*

4. Moves the screen X to the next position._____

5. Moves a polyline vertex to a new location. _____

6. Breaks a portion out of a polyline._____

7. Required for AutoCAD to redraw the revised edition of a polyline. _____

8. Specifies tangent direction._____

9. Adds a new polyline vertex._____

10. Returns you to the **PEDIT** options._____

11. Which **PEDIT** option and suboption allow you to change the starting and ending widths of a polyline? _____

12. Why does it appear that nothing happens after you change the starting and ending widths of a polyline? _____
_____

13. How do you change the width of a doughnut? _____

14. Which command will remove all width characteristics and tangency information from a polyline? _____
_____

15. What happens to the screen cursor after you select the **PEDIT** command? _____
_____

16. What happens if you select **Close** for a polyline that is already closed? _____
_____

17. When you select the **Edit vertex** option of the **PEDIT** command, where is the screen cursor X placed by AutoCAD? _____

18. How do you move the screen X to edit a different vertex? _____
_____

19. Can you use the **Fit** option of the **PEDIT** command without using the **Tangent** option first? _____

20. Explain the difference between a fit curve and spline curve. _____
_____
_____

21. Explain the relationship between the quadratic curve, cubic curve, and **Fit** options. _____
_____
_____

22. Discuss the construction of a quadratic curve. _____
_____
_____
_____

23. What **SPLINETYPE** setting allows you to draw a quadratic curve? _____

24. What **SPLINETYPE** setting allows you to draw a cubic curve? _____

25. Name the system variable that adjusts the smoothness of a spline curve. _____

26. Name the pull-down menu and the selections in that menu for accessing the polyline editing options. _____

27. Explain how you can adjust the way polyline linetypes are generated with the **PLINE** command. _____
_____
_____

28. Name the system variable that allows you to alter the way polyline linetypes are generated. _____

---

29. Name the command used to create a polyline boundary. _____

30. Name the command that can be used to create a true spline. _____

31. How do you accept the AutoCAD defaults for the start and end tangents of a spline?
_____

32. Name the option that allows you to turn a spline-fitted polyline into a true spline.
_____

33. Name the command that allows you to edit splines. _____

34. What is the purpose of the **Add** suboption in the **Fit Data** option? _____
_____
_____

35. What happens to the spline if you use the **Delete** option and only two control points remain? _____
_____

36. Name the options that let you move fit points in a spline. _____
_____

37. What is the purpose of the **Redefine** option in the **SPLINEDIT** command? _____
_____
_____

38. Identify the **SPLINEDIT** option that lets you increase the number of control points that appear on a spline for greater control. _____

39. This option in the **SPLINEDIT** command controls the pull that a control point exerts on the spline. _____

40. How many changes can you undo in the **SPLINEDIT** command when using the **Undo** option? _____
_____

Drawing Problems

Start a new drawing for the following problems. Set up your own units, limits, and other variables to suit each problem.

1. Draw the polyline shown below. Use the **Line**, **Arc**, **Width**, and **Close** options to complete the shape. The polyline width will be 0, except at those points indicated. Save the drawing as P17-1.

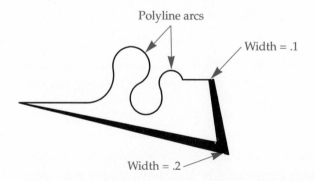

Polyline arcs

Width = .1

Width = .2

2. Draw the two curved arrows below using the **PLINE Arc** and **Width** options. The arrowhead should have a starting width of 1.4 and ending width of 0. The arrow body should have a beginning width of .8 and ending width of .4. Save the drawing as P17-2.

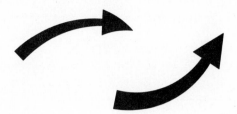

3. Change the object from Problem 17-1 into a rectangle. Use the **PEDIT** options **Decurve, Straighten, Width, Insert**, and **Move**. First, open P17-1, then make a second copy of the object to edit. Save the completed drawing as P17-3.

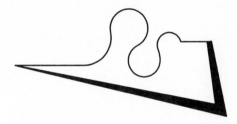

4. Open P17-2 and make the following changes. Then, save the drawing as P17-4.

A. Combine the two polylines using the **Join** option.

B. Change the beginning width of the left arrow to 1.0 and the ending width to .2.

C. Draw a polyline .062 wide similar to line A below.

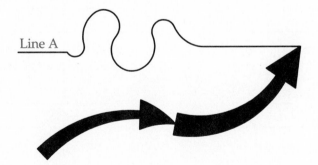

Line A

5. Draw the object shown below using the **LINE** command. Do not dimension the object. Then, change the object to a polyline, making the polyline .032 wide. Save the drawing as P17-5.

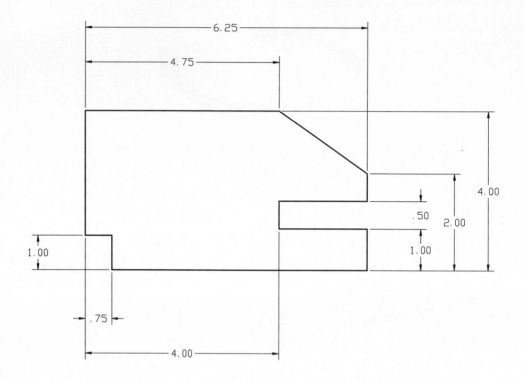

6. Use the **PLINE** command to draw object A below. Copy object A and use the **PEDIT** command to create object B as shown. Save the drawing as P17-6.

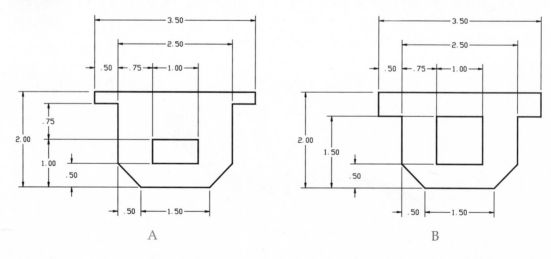

A

B

7. Open drawing P17-1. Explode the polyline and observe the results. Restore the original polyline using the **UNDO** command. Save the drawing as P17-7 and quit.

8. Draw a polyline .032 wide using the following absolute coordinates:

Point	Coordinates	Point	Coordinates	Point	Coordinates
1	1,1	5	3,3	9	5,5
2	2,1	6	4,3	10	6,5
3	2,2	7	4,4	11	6,6
4	3,2	8	5,4	12	7,6

Copy the polyline three times. Use the **PEDIT Fit** option to smooth the first copy. Use the **PEDIT Spline** option to create a quadratic curve in the second copy. Make the third copy into a cubic curve. Use the **PEDIT Decurve** option to return one polyline to its original form. Save the drawing as P17-8.

9. Draw a patio plan similar to the example shown at A below. Draw the house walls 6″ wide. Copy the A drawing to the positions shown at B, C, and D. Your client wants to see at least four different designs. Use the **Fit** option at B, a cubic spline at C, and a quadratic spline at D. Change the **SPLINETYPE** variable as required. Save the drawing as P17-9.

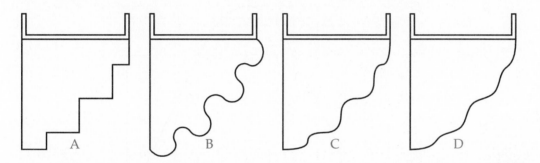

10. Open drawing P17-9 and make some new designs since your client is not satisfied with the first four proposals. This time, use the grips to edit the patio designs similar to the examples shown at A, B, C, and D below. Save the drawing as P17-10.

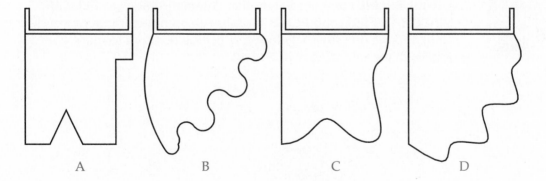

11. Use the **SPLINE** command to draw the curve for the cam displacement diagram below. Use the following instructions and the given drawing to complete this problem:

   A. Total rise = 2.000

   B. Total displacement can be any length.

   C. Divide the total displacement into 30° increments.

   D. Draw a half circle on one end divided into 6 equal parts.

   E. Draw a horizontal line from each part of the half circle into the cam displacement diagram.

   F. Draw the displacement curve with the **SPLINE** command by picking points where horizontal and vertical lines cross.

   G. Label the degree increments along the horizontal scale. Save as P17-11.

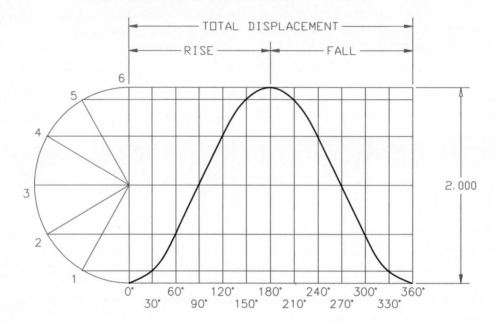

12. Use the **SPLINE** command and other commands such as **ELLIPSE**, **MIRROR**, **OFFSET**, and **PLINE** to design an architectural door knocker similar to the one shown below. Use gothice text font to place your initials in the center. Save as P17-12.

AutoCAD and its Applications—Basics

13. Draw a spline similar to the original spline shown below. Copy the original spline to seven locations similar to the layout shown below. Perform the **SPLINEDIT** operation identified under each of the seven splines. Save as P17-13.

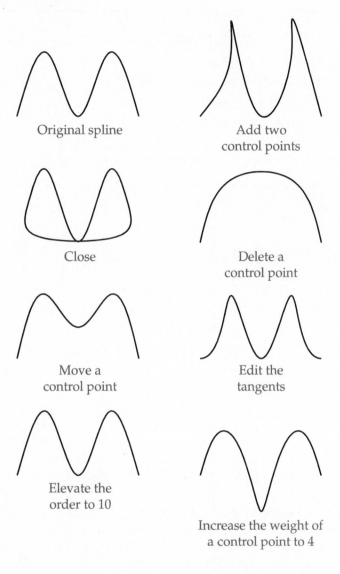

Original spline

Add two
control points

Close

Delete a
control point

Move a
control point

Edit the
tangents

Elevate the
order to 10

Increase the weight of
a control point to 4

14. Open P17-5 and remove the polyline width. Plot the drawing with pen assignment that results in the lines set to ANSI standards (.032 for object lines). Save the drawing as P17-14.

15. Open P17-6 and remove the polyline width. Plot the drawing with pen assignment that results in the lines set to ANSI standards (.032 for object lines). Save the drawing as P17-15.

Foundation Plan. (Steve D. Bloedel)

Chapter 18

Basic Dimensioning Practices

Learning Objectives

After completing this chapter, you will be able to:
- ○ Use the dimensioning commands to dimension given objects to ASME and other drafting standards.
- ○ Identify and set variables that affect the appearance of dimensions.
- ○ Add linear, angular, diameter, and radius dimensions to a drawing.
- ○ Set the appropriate units and decimal places for dimension numbers.
- ○ Use text size and style consistent with ASME and other professional standards.
- ○ Use the proper character codes to display symbols with dimension text.
- ○ Add dimensions to a separate layer.
- ○ Place general notes on drawings.
- ○ Draw datum and chain dimensions.
- ○ Dimension curves.
- ○ Draw oblique dimensions.
- ○ Use the **LEADER** command to draw specific notes with leader lines.
- ○ Dimension objects with arrowless tabular dimensions.
- ○ Prepare thread symbols and notes.
- ○ Create and use dimension styles.
- ○ Override existing dimension variables.

Dimensions are given to describe the size, shape, and location of features on an object or structure. The dimension may consist of numerical values, lines, symbols, and notes. Typical AutoCAD dimensioning features and characterics are shown in Figure 18-1.

Each drafting field (such as mechanical, architectural, civil, and electronics) uses a different type of dimensioning technique. It is important for a drafter to place dimensions in accordance with company and industry standards. The standard emphasized in this text is ASME Y14.5M-1994 *Dimensioning and Tolerancing*. The *M* in Y14.5M means the standard is written with metric numeric values. ASME Y14.5M-1994 is published by The American Society of Mechanical Engineers (ASME). The standard can be ordered directly from ASME, 345 E. 47th Street, New York, NY 10017. It can also be obtained from the American National Standards Institute (ANSI), 1430 Broadway, New York, NY 10018. This text discusses the correct application of both inch and metric dimensioning.

AutoCAD's dimensioning functions provide you with unlimited flexibility. Available commands allow you to dimension linear distances, circles, and arcs. You can also place a note with an arrow and leader line pointing to the feature. In addition to these commands, AutoCAD includes a number of variables that allow you to

Figure 18-1.
Dimensions describe size and location. Follow accepted conventions when dimensioning.

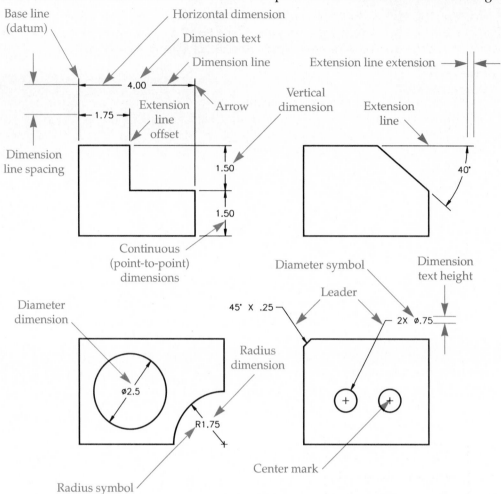

modify the appearance of dimensions. These affect the height, width, style, and spacing of individual components of a dimension.

This text covers the comprehensive elements of AutoCAD dimensioning in four chapters: this chapter covers fundamental standards and practices for dimensioning; Chapter 19, *Editing Dimensions*, covers editing procedures for dimensions; Chapter 20, *Dimensioning with Tolerances*, covers dimensioning applications with tolerances; and Chapter 21, *Geometric Dimensioning and Tolerancing*, covers geometric dimensioning and tolerancing practices. If you use AutoCAD for mechanical drafting in the manufacturing industry, you may want to study all four dimensioning chapters. If your business is in another field, such as architectural design, you may want to learn the basics covered in Chapters 18 and 19, and skip Chapters 20 and 21.

This chapter will get you started dimensioning immediately with AutoCAD. As you progress, you will learn about dimensioning variables that can be set to control the way dimensions are presented. You can control things such as the space between dimension lines, the arrowhead size and type, and the text style, height, and position. You will also learn how to create dimension styles that have settings used on the types of drawings done at your company or school.

When you dimension objects with AutoCAD, the objects are automatically measured exactly as you have them drawn. This makes it important for you to draw accurate original objects and features. Use the object snaps to your best advantage when dimensioning.

Dimension Arrangement

Dimensions are meant to communicate information about the drawing. Different industries and companies apply similar techniques for presenting dimensions. The two most accepted arrangements of text are unidirectional and aligned.

Unidirectional dimensioning

Unidirectional dimensioning is typically used in the mechanical drafting field. The term *unidirectional* means one direction. This system has all dimension numbers and notes placed horizontally on the drawing. They are read from the bottom of the sheet.

Unidirectional dimensions normally have arrowheads on the ends of dimension lines. The dimension number is usually centered in a break near the center of the dimension line. See Figure 18-2.

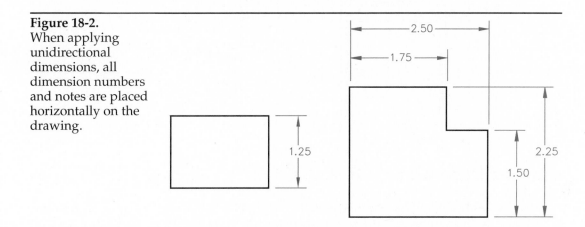

Figure 18-2. When applying unidirectional dimensions, all dimension numbers and notes are placed horizontally on the drawing.

Aligned dimensioning

Aligned dimensions are typically placed on architectural or structural drawings. The term *aligned* means the dimension numbers are lined up with the dimension lines. The dimension numbers for horizontal dimensions read horizontally. Dimension numbers for vertical dimensions are placed so they are read from the right side of the sheet. See Figure 18-3. Numbers for dimensions placed at an angle read at the same angle as the dimension line. Notes are usually placed so they read horizontally.

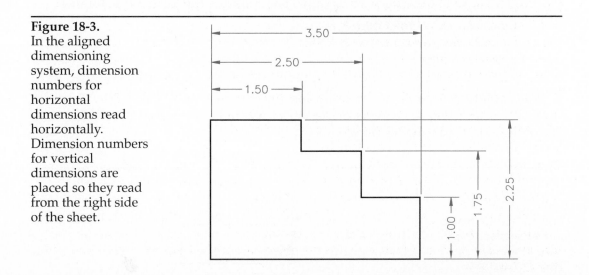

Figure 18-3. In the aligned dimensioning system, dimension numbers for horizontal dimensions read horizontally. Dimension numbers for vertical dimensions are placed so they read from the right side of the sheet.

When using the aligned system, terminate dimension lines with tick marks, dots, or arrowheads. In architectural drafting, the dimension number is generally placed above the dimension line and tick marks are used. See Figure 18-4.

Figure 18-4.
An example of aligned dimensioning in architectural drafting. Notice the tick marks used in place of the arrowheads and the placement of the dimensions above the dimension line.

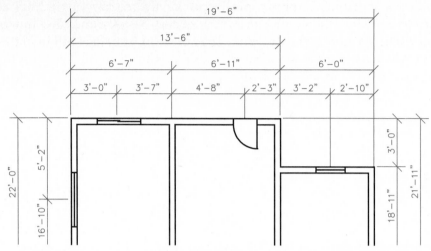

Drawing Dimensions with AutoCAD

AutoCAD has a variety of dimensioning applications that fall into five fundamental categories: linear, angular, diameter, radius, and ordinate. These applications allow you to perform nearly every type of dimensioning practice needed for your discipline.

Drawing Linear Dimensions

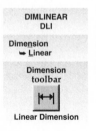

DIMLINEAR
DLI

Dimension
↳ Linear

Dimension
toolbar

Linear Dimension

Linear means straight. In most cases, dimensions measure straight distances, such as horizontal, vertical, or slanted surfaces. The **DIMLINEAR** command allows you to measure the length of an object and place extension lines, dimension lines, dimension text, and arrowheads automatically. To do this, pick the **Linear Dimension** button in the **Dimension** toolbar, pick **Linear** from the **Dimension** pull-down menu, or enter DLI or DIMLINEAR at the Command: prompt. The command sequence is as follows:

> Command: **DLI** or **DIMLINEAR**↵
> First extension line origin or press ENTER to select: *(pick the origin of the first extension line)*
> Second extension line origin: *(pick the origin of the second extension line)*

The points you pick are the extension line origins. See Figure 18-5. Place the crosshairs directly on the corners of the object where the extension lines begin. Use one of the object snap modes for accuracy.

Figure 18-5.
Establishing extension line origins. The **Endpoint** or **Intersection** object snap modes are useful in accurately locating the origins.

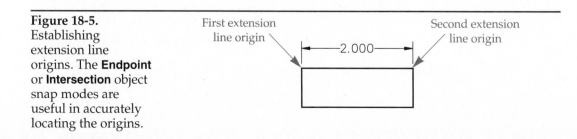

First extension line origin

Second extension line origin

The **DIMLINEAR** command allows you to generate horizontal, vertical, aligned, or rotated dimensions. After selecting the object or points of origin for dimensioning, the following prompt appears:

Dimension line location (Mtext/Text/Angle/Horizontal/Vertical/Rotated):

These options are outlined as follows:
- **Dimension line location.** This is the default. Simply drag the dimension line to a desired location and pick. See Figure 18-6. This is where preliminary plan sheets and sketches help you determine proper distances to avoid crowding. The extension lines, dimension line, dimension text, and arrowheads are automatically drawn, and the Command: prompt returns:

  Dimension line location (Mtext/Text/Angle/Horizontal/Vertical/Rotated):
     (pick the dimension line location)
  Dimension text = 2.000
  Command:

- **Mtext.** This option accesses the **Multiline Text Editor**, Figure 18-7. Here you can provide a specific measurement or text format for the dimension. See Chapter 8 for a complete description of the **Multiline Text Editor**. The chevrons (⟨ ⟩) represent the current dimension value. Edit the dimension text and pick **OK**. For example, the ASME standard recommends that a reference dimension be displayed enclosed in parenthesis. Type an open and closed parenthesis around the chevrons to create a reference dimension. If you want the current dimension value changed, delete the chevrons and type the new value. If you want the chevrons to be part of the dimension text, type the new value inside or next to the chevrons. While this is not an ASME standard, it may be needed for some applications.

Figure 18-6.
Establishing the dimension line's location.

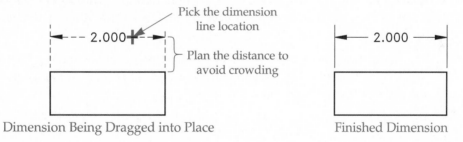

Dimension Being Dragged into Place   Finished Dimension

Figure 18-7.
When you enter M for the **Mtext** option, the **Multiline Text Editor** appears. The chevrons (⟨ ⟩) represent the dimension value that AutoCAD has calculated.

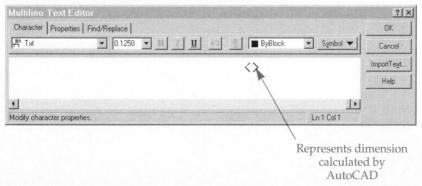

Represents dimension
calculated by
AutoCAD

- **Text.** This option uses the command line to change dimension text. This is convenient if you prefer to type the desired text rather than using the **Multiline Text Editor**. The **Text** and **Mtext** options both create multiline text objects. The **Text** option displays the current dimension value in brackets and allows you to accept this value by pressing [Enter], or type a new value. The command sequence works like this:

    Dimension line location (Mtext/Text/Angle/Horizontal/Vertical/Rotated):**T**↵
    Dimension text ⟨2.875⟩: ↵

    Pressing [Enter] at the previous prompt accepts the current value. Type a new value, such as a reference dimension (which is displayed in parentheses), as follows:

    Dimension text ⟨2.875⟩: **(2.875)**↵

- **Angle.** This option allows you to change the dimension text angle. This option can be used when creating aligned dimensions or for adjusting the dimension text to a desired angle. The sequence is as follows:

    Dimension line location (Mtext/Text/Angle/Horizontal/Vertical/Rotated): **A**↵
    Enter text angle: **90**↵

- **Horizontal.** This option sets the dimension to a horizontal distance only. This may be helpful when dimensioning the horizontal distance of a slanted surface. The **Mtext**, **Text**, and **Angle** options are available again in case you want to change the dimension text value or angle.
- **Vertical.** This option sets the dimension being created to a vertical distance only. This option may be helpful when dimensioning the vertical distance of a slanted surface. Like the **Horizontal** option, the **Mtext**, **Text**, and **Angle** options are available.
- **Rotated.** This option allows an angle to be specified for the dimension line. A practical application is dimensioning to angled surfaces and auxiliary views. This technique is different from other dimensioning commands because you are asked to provide a dimension line angle. See Figure 18-8. The command sequence looks like this:

    Dimension line location (Mtext/Text/Angle/Horizontal/Vertical/Rotated): **R**↵
    Dimension line angle ⟨0⟩: *(enter a value, such as* 45, *or pick two points on the line to be dimensioned)*

Figure 18-8.
Rotating a dimension for an angled view.

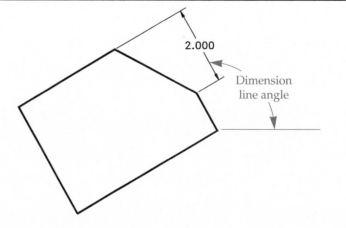

2.000

Dimension line angle

Selecting an object to dimension

In the previous discussion, the extension line origins were picked in order to establish the extents of the dimension. Another powerful AutoCAD option allows you to pick a single line, circle, or arc to dimension. This works when you are using the **DIMLINEAR** command and the **DIMALIGNED** command, which is discussed later. You can use this AutoCAD feature any time you see the First extension line origin or press ENTER to select: prompt. Press [Enter] and select the object being dimensioned. When you select a line or arc, AutoCAD automatically begins the extension lines from the endpoints. If you pick a circle, the extension lines are drawn from the closest quadrant and its opposite quadrant. If the **Rotated** option is used with a circle, you are asked for the dimension line angle. Then, the extension lines are drawn tangent to the circle from the dimension line location. See Figure 18-9.

Figure 18-9.
AutoCAD can automatically determine the extension line origins if you select a line, arc, or circle.

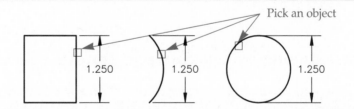

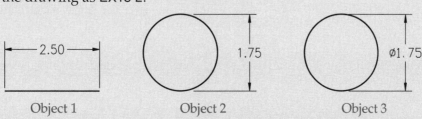

Dimensioning in AutoCAD, like dimensioning on a conventional drafting board, should be performed as accurately and neatly as possible. You can achieve consistently professional results by using the following guidelines:

- Always construct drawing geometry accurately. Never truncate, or round-off, decimal values when entering locations, distances, or angles. For example, enter .4375 for 7/16, rather than .44.
- Set the system variable **DIMDEC** to the desired precision level before beginning your dimensioning. Most drawings have varying levels of precision for specific drawing features, so select the most common precision level to start with, and adjust the precision as needed for each dimension. Setting the dimension precision is explained later in this chapter.
- Always use the precision drawing aids to ensure the accuracy of the dimensions. If the point being dimensioned does not coincide with a snap point or a known coordinate, use an appropriate object snap override.
- *Never* type a different dimension value than what appears in the brackets. If a dimension needs to change, revise the drawing or dimensioning variables accordingly. The ability to change the dimension in the brackets is provided by AutoCAD so that a different text format can be specified for the dimension. Prefixes and suffixes can also be added to the dimension in the brackets. A typical example of a prefix might be to specify the number of times a dimension occurs, such as 4X 1.750. Other examples of this capability appear later in this chapter.

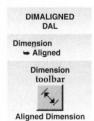
AutoCAD User's Guide 10

Dimensioning Angled Surfaces and Auxiliary Views

When dimensioning a surface drawn at an angle, it may be necessary to align the dimension line with the surface. For example, auxiliary views are normally placed at an angle. In order to properly dimension these features, the **DIMALIGNED** or the **Rotated** option of **DIMLINEAR** can be used.

Using the DIMALIGNED command

DIMALIGNED
DAL

Dimension
↳ Aligned

Dimension
toolbar

Aligned Dimension

The **DIMALIGNED** command can be accessed by picking the **Aligned Dimension** button on the **Dimension** toolbar, picking **Aligned** in the **Dimension** pull-down menu, or typing DAL or DIMALIGNED at the Command: prompt. The results of the **DIMALIGNED** command are displayed in Figure 18-10. The following shows the command sequence:

Command: **DAL** *or* **DIMALIGNED**↵
First extension line origin or press ENTER to select: *(pick first extension line origin)*
Second extension line origin: *(pick second extension line origin)*
Dimension line location (Mtext/Text/Angle): *(pick the dimension line location)*
Dimension text = 2.250
Command:

Figure 18-10.
The **DIMALIGNED** dimensioning command allows you to place dimension lines parallel to angled features.

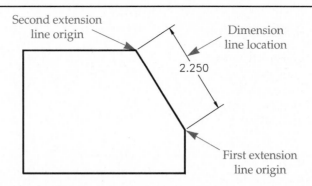

EXERCISE 18-3

❑ Start AutoCAD and use one of your templates.
❑ Set up the appropriate layers for your drawing elements, including a layer for dimensions.
❑ Use the proper dimensioning techniques and commands to dimension the objects exactly as shown.
❑ Save the drawing as EX18-3.

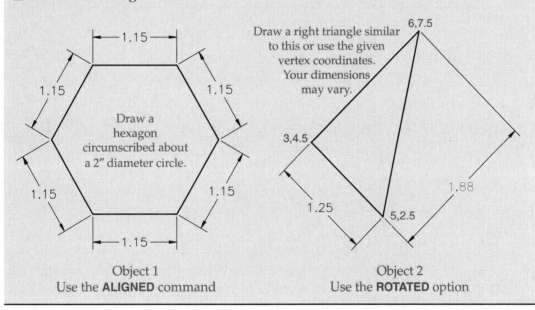

Object 1
Use the **ALIGNED** command

Object 2
Use the **ROTATED** option

Dimensioning Angles

Coordinate and angular dimensioning are both accepted for dimensioning angles. *Coordinate dimensioning* of angles can be accomplished with the **DIMLINEAR** command. These dimensions locate the corner of the angle, as shown in Figure 18-11.

Angular dimensioning locates one corner with a dimension and provides the value of the angle in degrees. See Figure 18-12. You can dimension the angle between any two nonparallel lines. The intersection of the lines is the angle's vertex. AutoCAD automatically draws extension lines if they are needed.

The type of angular unit depends on the **DIMAUNIT** setting. The **DIMANGULAR** command is used for the angular method. The **DIMANGULAR** command is accessed by picking the **Angular Dimension** button in the **Dimension** toolbar, picking **Angular** in the **Dimension** pull-down menu, or by entering DAN or DIMANGULAR at the Command: prompt. Refer to Figure 18-12A as you read the following sequence:

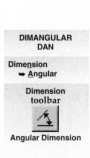

DIMANGULAR
DAN

Dimension
↳ Angular

Dimension
toolbar

Angular Dimension

Command: **DAN** *or* **DIMANGULAR.**⏎
Select arc, circle, line, or press ENTER: *(pick the first leg of the angle to be dimensioned)*
Second line: *(pick the second leg of the angle to be dimensioned)*
Dimension arc line location (Mtext/Text/Angle): *(pick the desired location of the dimension line arc)*
Dimension text = 30
Command:

Figure 18-11.
Coordinate dimensioning of angles.

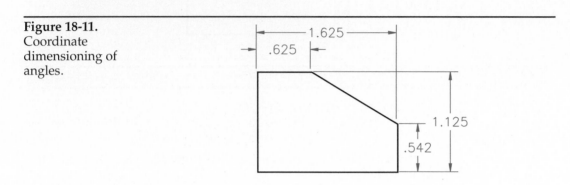

Figure 18-12.
Two examples of drawing angular dimensions.

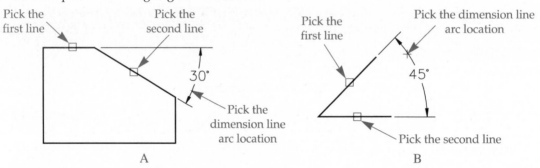

The last prompt asks you to pick the dimension line arc location. If there is enough space, AutoCAD places the dimension text, dimension line arc, and arrowheads inside the extension lines. If there is not enough room between extension lines for the arrowheads and numbers, AutoCAD automatically places the arrowheads outside and the number inside the extension lines. If space is very tight, AutoCAD may place the dimension line arc and arrowheads inside and the text outside, or place everything outside of the extension lines. See Figure 18-13.

Figure 18-13.
Manually locating the dimension number for an angle.

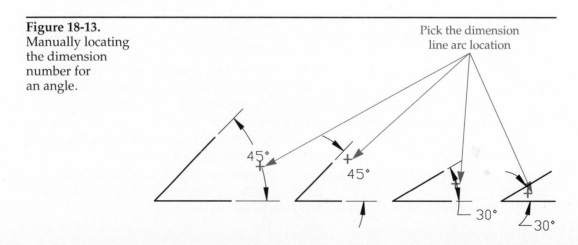

Placing angular dimensions on arcs

The **DIMANGULAR** command can be used to dimension the included angle of an arc. The arc's center point becomes the angle vertex and the two arc endpoints are the origin points for the extension lines. See Figure 18-14. The command sequence is as follows:

Command: **DAN** *or* **DIMANGULAR.**↵
Select arc, circle, line, or press ENTER: *(pick the arc)*
Dimension arc line location (Mtext/Text/Angle): *(pick the desired dimension line location)*
Dimension text = 128
Command:

Figure 18-14.
Placing angular
dimensions on arcs.

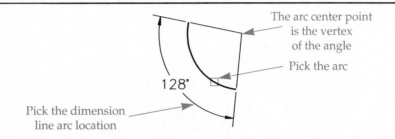

The arc center point
is the vertex
of the angle

Pick the arc

128°

Pick the dimension
line arc location

Placing angular dimensions on circles

The **DIMANGULAR** command can also be used to dimension a portion of a circle. The circle's center point becomes the angle vertex and two picked points are the origin points for the extension lines. See Figure 18-15. The command sequence is as follows:

Command: **DAN** *or* **DIMANGULAR.**↵
Select arc, circle, line, or press ENTER: *(pick the circle)*

The point you pick on the circle becomes the endpoint of the first extension line. You are then asked for the second angle endpoint. This becomes the endpoint of the second extension line:

Second angle endpoint: *(pick the second point)*
Dimension arc line location (Mtext/Text/Angle): *(pick the desired dimension line location)*
Dimension text = 85
Command:

Figure 18-15.
Placing angular
dimensions on
circles.

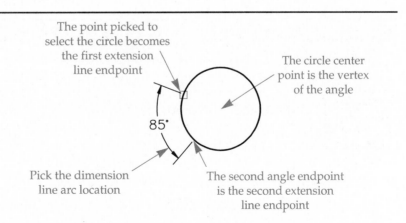

The point picked to
select the circle becomes
the first extension
line endpoint

The circle center
point is the vertex
of the angle

85°

Pick the dimension
line arc location

The second angle endpoint
is the second extension
line endpoint

Angular dimensioning through three points

You can also establish an angular dimension through three points. The points are the angle vertex and the two angle line endpoints. See Figure 18-16. To do this, press [Enter] after the first prompt:

Command: **DAN** or **DIMANGULAR**.↵
Select arc, circle, line, or press ENTER: ↵
Angle vertex: *(pick a vertex point and a "rubberband" connects between the vertex and the cursor to help locate the first point)*
First angle endpoint: *(pick the first endpoint)*
Second angle endpoint: *(pick the second endpoint)*
Dimension arc line location (Mtext/Text/Angle): *(pick the desired dimension line location)*
Dimension text = 60

This method also dimensions angles over 180°.

Figure 18-16.
Angular dimensions using three points.

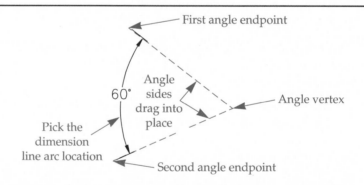

❑ Start AutoCAD and use one of your templates.
❑ Set up the appropriate layers for your drawing elements, including a layer for dimensions.
❑ Use the **LINEAR** and **ANGULAR** dimensioning commands to dimension the object exactly as shown.
❑ Save the drawing as EX18-4.

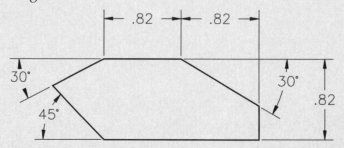

Dimensioning Practices

Dimensioning practices often depend on product requirements, manufacturing accuracy, standards, and tradition. Dimensional information includes size dimensions, location dimensions, and notes. Two techniques that identify size and location are chain and datum dimensioning. The method used depends on the accuracy of the product and the drafting field.

Size dimensions and notes

Size dimensions provide the size of physical features. They include lines, notes, or dimension lines and numbers. Size dimensioning practices depend on the techniques used to dimension different geometric features. See Figure 18-17. A *feature* is considered any physical portion of a part or object, such as a surface, hole, window, or door. Dimensioning standards are used so an object designed in one place can be manufactured or built somewhere else.

Specific notes and general notes are the two types of notes on a drawing. *Specific notes* relate to individual or specific features on the drawing. They are attached to the feature being dimensioned using a leader line. *General notes* apply to the entire drawing and are placed in the lower-left corner, upper-left corner, or above or next to the title block. Where they are placed depends on company or school practice.

Figure 18-17.
Size dimensions and specific notes.

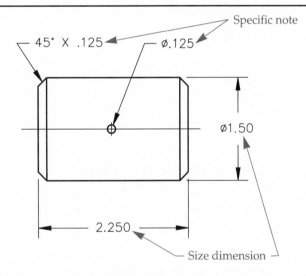

Dimensioning flat surfaces and architectural features

In mechanical drafting, flat surfaces are dimensioned by giving measurements for each feature. If there is an overall dimension provided, you can omit one of the dimensions. The overall dimension controls the omitted dimension. In architectural drafting, it is common to place all dimensions without omitting any of them. The idea is that all dimensions should be shown to help make construction easier. See Figure 18-18.

Figure 18-18.
Dimensioning flat surfaces and architectural features.

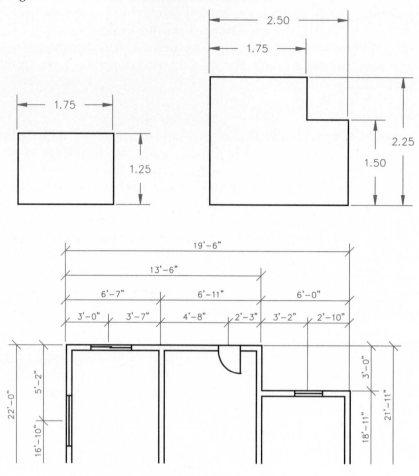

Dimensioning cylindrical shapes

Both the diameter and length of a cylindrical shape can be dimensioned in the view where the cylinder appears rectangular. See Figure 18-19. This allows the view where the cylinder appears as a circle to be omitted.

Figure 18-19.
Dimensioning cylindrical shapes.

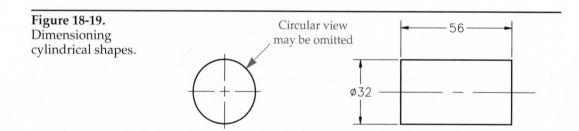

Dimensioning square and rectangular features

Square and rectangular features are usually dimensioned in the views where the length and height are shown. The square symbol can be used preceding the dimension for the square feature. See Figure 18-20. The square symbol must be created as a block and inserted. Blocks are discussed in Chapter 23 of this text.

Figure 18-20.
Dimensioning square and rectangular features.

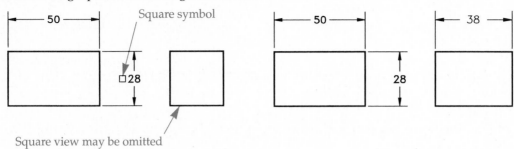

Dimensioning cones and hexagonal shapes

There are two ways to dimension a conical shape. One method is by giving the diameters at both ends and the length. See Figure 18-21. Another method is to give the taper angle and length. Hexagonal shapes are dimensioned by giving the distance across the flats and the length. See Figure 18-22.

Figure 18-21.
Dimensioning conical shapes. These shapes can also be dimensioned with an angle and length.

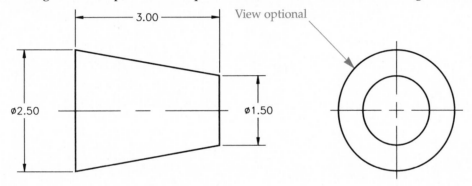

Figure 18-22.
Hexagons are dimensioned across their flats with a length given.

❏ Start AutoCAD and use one of your templates.
❏ Set up the appropriate layers for your drawing elements, including a layer for dimensions.
❏ Hint: To orient the hexagon as shown, use a six-sided circumscribed polygon. When prompted to enter the radius value, type @.625⟨0. Use X and Y filters with the appropriate object snap modes and construction lines to assist you in drawing the side view of the hexagon.
❏ Dimension the objects exactly as shown using the proper dimensioning commands and techniques.
❏ Save the drawing as EX18-5.

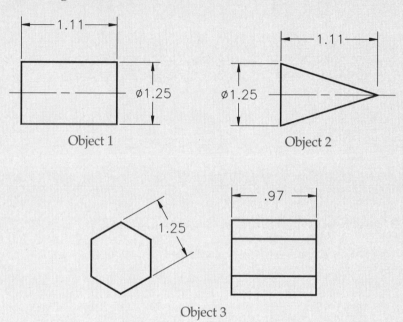

Object 1

Object 2

Object 3

Location Dimensions

Location dimensions are used to locate features on an object. They do not provide the size. Holes and arcs are dimensioned to their centers in the view where they appear circular. Rectangular features are dimensioned to their edges. See Figure 18-23. In architectural drafting, windows and doors are dimensioned to their centers on the floor plan.

Rectangular coordinates and polar coordinates are the two basic location dimensioning systems. *Rectangular coordinates* are linear dimensions used to locate features from surfaces, centerlines, or center planes. AutoCAD performs this type of dimensioning using a variety of dimensioning subcommands. The most frequently used dimensioning command is **DIMLINEAR** and its options. See Figure 18-24.

The *polar coordinate system* uses angular dimensions to locate features from surfaces, centerlines, or center planes. The angular dimensions in the polar coordinate system are drawn using AutoCAD's **DIMANGULAR** command. See Figure 18-25.

Figure 18-23.
Locating circular and rectangular features.

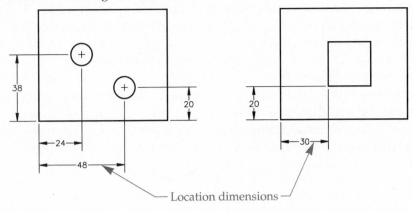

Location dimensions

Figure 18-24.
Rectangular coordinate location dimensions.

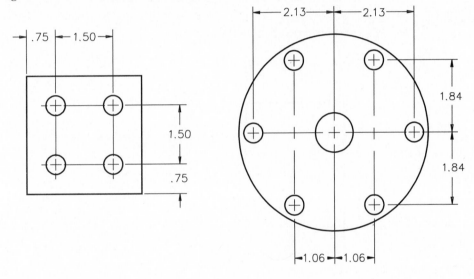

Figure 18-25.
Polar coordinate location dimensions.

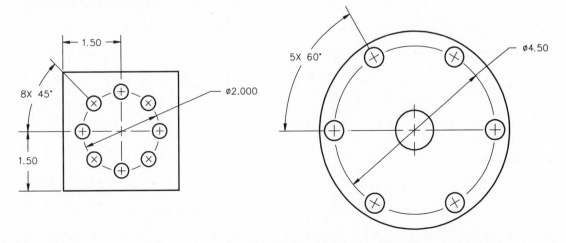

Datum and Chain Dimensioning

With *datum*, or *baseline dimensioning*, dimensions on an object originate from common surfaces, centerlines, or center planes. Datum dimensioning is commonly used in mechanical drafting because each dimension is independent of the others. This achieves more accuracy in manufacturing. Figure 18-26 shows an object dimensioned with surface datums.

Chain dimensioning, also called *point-to-point dimensioning*, places dimensions in a line from one feature to the next. Chain dimensioning is sometimes used in mechanical drafting. However, there is less accuracy than with datum dimensioning since each dimension is dependent on other dimensions in the chain. Architectural drafting uses chain dimensioning in most applications. Figure 18-27 shows an example of chain dimensioning. In mechanical drafting, it is common to leave one dimension blank and provide an overall dimension. Architectural drafting practices usually show dimensions all the way across, plus an overall dimension.

Figure 18-26.
Datum dimensioning.

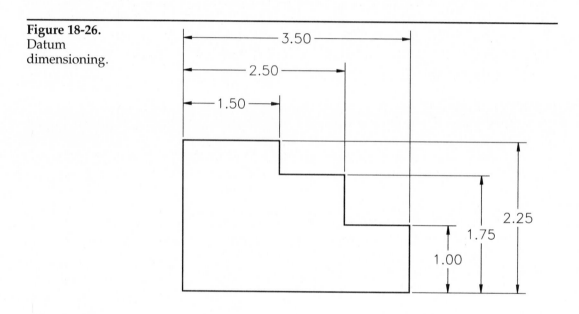

Figure 18-27.
Chain dimensioning.

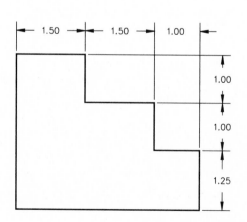
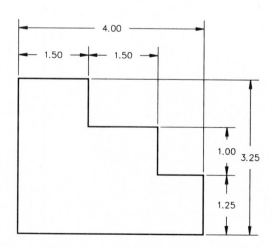

Making datum and chain dimensioning easy

AutoCAD refers to datum dimensioning as *baseline* and chain dimensioning as *continue*. Datum dimensioning is controlled by the **DIMBASELINE** command, and chain dimensioning is controlled by the **DIMCONTINUE** command. The **DIMBASELINE** and **DIMCONTINUE** commands are used in the same manner. The prompts and options are the same. Use the **Undo** option in the **DIMBASELINE** or **DIMCONTINUE** commands to undo previously drawn dimensions.

Datum dimensions

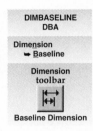

DIMBASELINE
DBA

Dimension
➥ **Baseline**

Dimension
toolbar

Baseline Dimension

Datum dimensions are created by picking the **Baseline Dimension** button in the **Dimension** toolbar, picking **Baseline** in the **Dimension** pull-down menu, or by entering either DBA or DIMBASELINE at the Command: prompt. Baseline dimensions can be created with linear, ordinate, and angular dimensions. Ordinate dimensions are discussed later in this chapter.

When you begin a new drawing and enter the **DIMBASELINE** command, AutoCAD asks you to Select base dimension:. Therefore, a dimension must exist before using **Baseline**. AutoCAD will use the most recently drawn dimension as the base dimension, unless you specify a different one. You can add additional datum dimensions to the previous dimension. AutoCAD automatically spaces and places the extension lines, dimension lines, arrowheads, and numbers. For example, to dimension the series of horizontal baseline dimensions shown in Figure 18-28, use the following procedure:

```
Command: DLI or DIMLINEAR↵
First extension line origin or press ENTER to select: (pick the first extension line origin)
Second extension line origin: (pick the second extension line origin)
Dimension line location (Mtext/Text/Angle/Horizontal/Vertical/Rotated): (pick the
    dimension line location)
Dimension text = 2.000
Command:
Command: DBA or DIMBASELINE↵
Specify a second extension line origin or (⟨select⟩/Undo): (pick the next second
    extension line origin)
Dimension text = 3.250
Specify a second extension line origin or (⟨select⟩/Undo): (pick the next second
    extension line origin)
Dimension text = 4.375
Specify a second extension line origin or (⟨select⟩/Undo): ↵
Select base dimension: ↵
Command:
```

Figure 18-28.
Using **DIMBASELINE** command. AutoCAD automatically spaces and places the extension lines, dimension lines, arrowheads, and numbers.

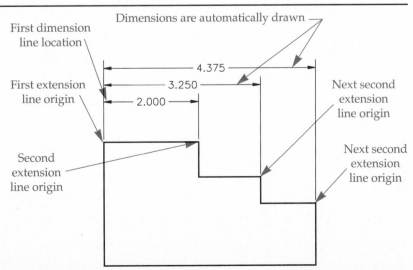

You can continue to add baseline dimensions until you press [Enter] twice to return to the Command: prompt.

If you want to come back later and add datum dimensions to an existing dimension other than the most recently drawn dimension, you can use the select option by pressing [Enter] at the first prompt to get the Select base dimension: prompt like this:

Command: **DBA** *or* **DIMBASELINE**↵
Specify a second extension line origin or (〈select〉/Undo): ↵
Select base dimension: *(pick the base dimension)*
Specify a second extension line origin or (〈select〉/Undo): *(pick the next second extension line origin)*
Dimension text = 4.375
Specify a second extension line origin or (〈select〉/Undo): ↵
Select base dimension: ↵
Command:

When picking an existing dimension to use as the baseline, the extension line nearest the point where you select the dimension is used as the baseline point.

You can also draw baseline dimensions to angular features. First, draw an angular dimension and enter the **DIMBASE** command, or enter the command and pick an existing angular dimension. Figure 18-29 shows the result of the following command sequence:

Command: **DBA** *or* **DIMBASELINE** ↵
Specify a point on an object or (〈select〉/Undo): *(pick the next second extension line origin)*
Specify a point on an object or (〈select〉/Undo): *(pick the next second extension line origin)*
Select base dimension: ↵
Command:

Figure 18-29.
Using **DIMBASE** command to datum dimension angular features.

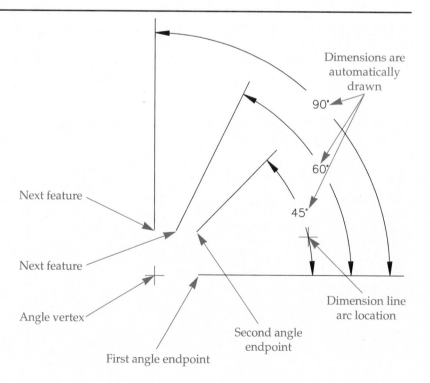

Chain dimensions

As previously mentioned, when creating chain dimensions you will receive the same prompts and options received while creating datum dimensions. Chain dimensioning is shown in Figure 18-30. Chain dimensions (continue dimensions) are created by picking the **Continue Dimension** button in the **Dimension** toolbar, picking **Continue** in the **Dimension** pull-down menu, or by entering DCO or DIMCONTINUE at the Command: prompt. Continue dimensions can be created with linear, ordinate, and angular dimensions. Ordinate dimensions are discussed later in this chapter.

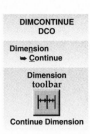

DIMCONTINUE
DCO

Dimension
➥ Continue

Dimension
toolbar

Continue Dimension

Figure 18-30.
Using the
DIMCONTINUE
command.

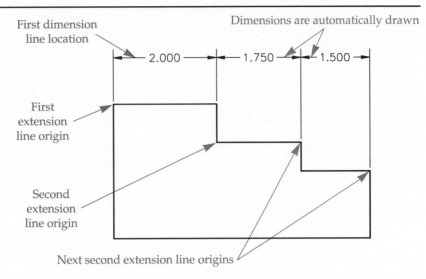

First dimension line location

Dimensions are automatically drawn

2.000   1.750   1.500

First extension line origin

Second extension line origin

Next second extension line origins

PROFESSIONAL TIP

You do not have to use **DIMBASELINE** or **DIMCONTINUE** immediately after a dimension that is to be used as a base or chain with other dimensions. You can come back later and do it by pressing the [Enter] key to use the select option as previously discussed. Then, select the dimension you want to use and draw the datum or chain dimensions that you need.

EXERCISE 18-6

❑ Begin a new drawing or start a drawing with one of your templates.
❑ Set up the appropriate layers for your drawing elements, including dimensions.
❑ Draw and dimension an object similar to Figure 18-28.
❑ Draw angle datum dimensions similar to Figure 18-29.
❑ Draw and dimension an object similar to Figure 18-30.
❑ Save the drawing as EX18-6.

Including Symbols with Dimension Text

AutoCAD User's Guide 10

After you select a feature to dimension, AutoCAD responds with the measurement, or dimensioning number. In some cases, such as dimensioning radii and diameters, AutoCAD automatically places the radius (R) or diameter (∅) symbol before the dimension number. However, in other cases related to linear dimensioning this is not automatic. The recommended ASME standard for a diameter dimension is to place the diameter symbol (∅) before the number. This can be done using the **Mtext** option of the dimensioning commands. Notice that when the **Multiline Text Editor** appears, the chevrons are already in place. Place the text cursor in the location where you want the symbol placed, such as in front of the chevrons. Then, open the **Symbol** drop-down list and pick the **Diameter** option followed by **OK**. The graphics cursor returns and you are asked to pick the dimension line location. Other symbols are also available in the **Symbol** drop-down list. You can also use the character codes or the Unicode entries to place symbols. The **Multiline Text Editor** and drawing special symbols are covered in Chapter 8 of this text.

Additional symbols are used in dimensions to point out certain features on the drawing. The diameter symbol (∅) for circles and the radius symbol (R) for arcs are easily drawn. Additional symbols, such as □ for a square feature, can be drawn individually. However, this can be time-consuming. Instead, save the symbol as a block and insert it in the drawing before the dimension text. Storing and inserting blocks is discussed in Chapter 23 of this text. Often used ASME symbols are shown in Figure 18-31.

Figure 18-31.
Common dimensioning symbols and how to draw them.

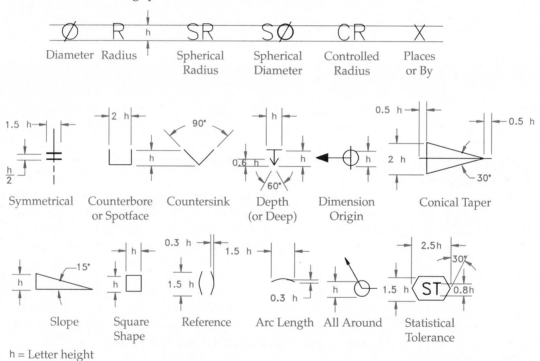

h = Letter height

DIMCENTER
DCE

Dimension
↪Center Mark

Dimension
toolbar

⊕

Center Mark

Drawing Center Dashes or Centerlines in a Circle or Arc

When small circles or arcs are dimensioned, the **DIMDIAMETER** and **DIMRADIUS** commands leave center dashes. If the dimension of a large circle crosses through the center, the dashes are left out. Center dashes and centerlines are drawn by picking the **Center Mark** button in the **Dimension** toolbar, picking **Center Mark** in the **Dimension** pull-down menu, or entering DCE or DIMCENTER at the Command: prompt. The command sequence is as follows:

Command: **DCE** *or* **DIMCENTER**↵
Select arc or circle: *(pick the arc or circle)*
Command:

When the circle or arc is picked, center dashes are automatically drawn. The size of the center dashes, or the amount that the centerlines extend outside the circle or arc, is controlled by the **DIMCEN** (dimension centerline) variable. The default provides center dashes 0.09 units long. If **DIMCEN** is set to 0, center dashes or centerlines are not drawn. A positive value gives center dashes. For example, the value .125 displays center dashes that are .125 units long. When decimal-inch units are used, this is the recommended length. A negative **DIMCEN** value draws complete centerlines in addition to center dashes. With a negative value, centerlines extend beyond the circle or arc by the value entered. For example, a –.125 value extends centerlines .125 units beyond the circle or arc. Figure 18-32 shows the application of positive and negative **DIMCEN** values. The command sequence is as follows:

Command: **DIMCEN**⏎
New value for DIMCEN ⟨0.09⟩: **–.125**⏎
Command:

Figure 18-32.
Using the **DIMCEN** variable. A positive value draws center dashes. A negative value draws complete centerlines. A value of 0 will not draw any center marks.

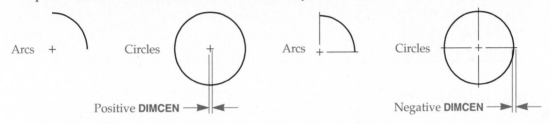

Arcs   +   Circles   Arcs   +   Circles

Positive **DIMCEN** ⟶⏐◀—   Negative **DIMCEN** ⟶⏐◀—

PROFESSIONAL TIP
     A negative **DIMCEN** value for small circles may result in placement of center dashes only. This is because AutoCAD needs room for the center dash and a space before the rest of the centerline is placed. If this occurs, try a smaller negative **DIMCEN** value or accept the results with the value you have set.

NOTE
     Later in this chapter you will see how to visually set up the center marks using the **Geometry** dialog box.

Dimensioning variables can be entered transparently while in another command. For example:

Command: **DDI** *or* **DIMDIAMETER**⏎
Select arc or circle: **'DIMCEN**⏎

While dimensioning, if you are not at a point or object selection prompt, there is no need for the apostrophe. Variable names cannot be changed at a Dimension text: prompt because the entry is interpreted as an actual text value. At most dimensioning prompts, the variable name can be entered without the DIM prefix. The exception to this is **DIMCEN**, which is interpreted as a **CEN** object snap override if not preceded by DIM.

Transparent changes to variable settings can be very helpful. In the following sequence, last minute changes are made to the **DIMCEN** variable while creating a diameter dimension:

Command: **DDI** or **DIMDIAMETER**.↵
Select arc or circle: (*select a circle*)
Dimension line location (Mtext/Text/Angle): **DIMCEN**.↵
Current value ⟨0.0900⟩ New value: **-.09**.↵
Dimension line location (Mtext/Text/Angle): (*complete your dimension*)

When dimension variables are set transparently, the setting is temporary for some, such as **DIMFIT** and **DIMUPT**. Others, such as **DIMCEN** and **DIMDEC**, retain the transparent setting. Temporary settings are only in effect during the dimensioning operation that they were set in. The variable is immediately reset to the previous value upon completion or cancellation of the current dimensioning command.

EXERCISE 18-7

❏ Start AutoCAD and use one of your templates.
❏ Set up the appropriate layers for your drawing elements, including dimensions.
❏ Draw circles and arcs similar to those shown in Figure 18-32.
❏ Set the **DIMCEN** value to add center dashes as shown. Use positive and negative values of .125.
❏ Save the drawing as EX18-7.

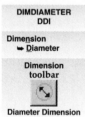

AutoCAD User's Guide **10**

DIMDIAMETER
DDI

Dimension
➥ Diameter

Dimension
toolbar

Diameter Dimension

Dimensioning Circles

Circles are normally dimensioned by giving the diameter. The ASME standard for dimensioning arcs is to give the radius. However, AutoCAD allows you to dimension either a circle or arc with a diameter dimension. Diameter dimensions are produced by picking the **Diameter Dimension** button on the **Dimension** toolbar, picking **Diameter** in the **Dimension** pull-down menu, or entering DDI or DIMDIAMETER at the Command: prompt. You are then asked to select the arc or circle.

When using the **DIMDIAMETER** command, a leader line and diameter dimension value are attached to the cursor when you pick the desired circle or arc. You can drag the leader to any desired location and length before picking where you want it. The resulting leader points to the center of the circle or arc just as recommended by the ASME standard. See Figure 18-33. The command sequence is as follows:

Command: **DDI** or **DIMDIAMETER**.↵
Select arc or circle: (*pick the circle*)
Dimension text = 1.250
Dimension line location (Mtext/Text/Angle): (*pick the dimension line location*)
Command:

Figure 18-33.
Using the **DIMDIA** command with the AutoCAD dimensioning variable defaults.

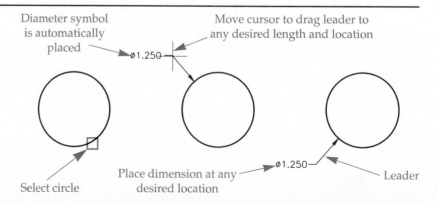

Diameter symbol is automatically placed

Move cursor to drag leader to any desired length and location

ø1.250

Select circle

Place dimension at any desired location

ø1.250

Leader

You also have the **Mtext**, **Text**, and **Angle** options that were introduced earlier. Use the **Mtext** or **Text** option if you want to change the text value or the **Angle** option if you want to change the angle of the text. The **Mtext** or **Text** option might be used if you are dimensioning an arc, because an R should precede the dimension number rather than a diameter symbol. Remember, in these cases you also need to divide the given diameter by 2 to get the radius. When you enter M for the **Mtext** option, the **Multiline Text Editor** appears. Delete the chevrons (⟨ ⟩) and then type R plus the dimension value. Then pick **OK** and the dimension text is placed.

Dimensioning holes

Holes are dimensioned in the view where they appear as circles. Give location dimensions to the center and a leader showing the diameter. Leader lines can be drawn using the **DIMDIAMETER** command as previously discussed. Set the **DIMCEN** variable to produce center marks. Multiple holes of the same size can be noted with one hole dimension, such as 2X ⌀.50. See Figure 18-34. Use the **Mtext** or **Text** option to create this dimension. The **Angle** option can be used to change the angle of the text numbers.

Figure 18-34.
Dimensioning
holes.

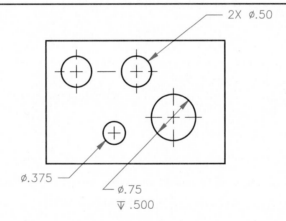

Dimensioning for manufacturing processes

A *counterbore* is a larger diameter hole machined at one end of a smaller hole. It provides a place for the head of a bolt. A *spotface* is similar to a counterbore except that it is not as deep. The spotface provides a smooth recessed surface for a washer. A *countersink* is a cone-shaped recess at one end of a hole. It provides a mating surface for a screw head of the same shape. A note for these features is provided using symbols. First, locate the centers in the circular view. Then, place a leader providing machining information in a note. See Figure 18-35. Symbols for this type of application must be customized and are discussed in Chapter 23. These symbols are displayed in Figure 18-31. Turn **DIMUPT** on to give you the maximum flexibility using the **DIMDIAMETER** command. **DIMDIAMETER** gives you multiline text to use during the creation of the dimension. Additional text can be added by editing the dimension text, since it is actually an **MTEXT** object.

Figure 18-35.
Dimension notes for
machining
processes.

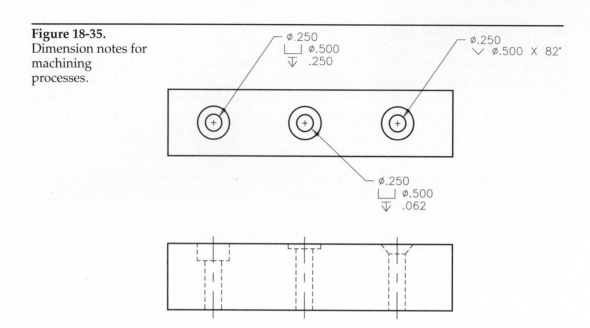

Counterbore   Spotface   Countersink

**PROFESSIONAL
TIP**   After creating any dimension, the dimension text can be
directly edited using the **DDEDIT** command. This allows you
to enter multiline text and special notations. Editing dimensions is covered in Chapter 19 of this text.

Dimensioning repetitive features

Repetitive features refer to many features having the same shape and size. When
this occurs, the number of repetitions is followed by an X, a space, and the size dimension. The dimension is then connected to the feature with a leader. See Figure 18-36.

Figure 18-36.
Dimensioning repetitive features (shown in color).

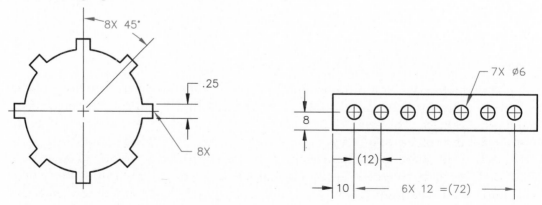

The ASME standard recommends a small space between the object and the extension line. See Figure 18-1. This happens when the **DIMEXO** variable is set to its default or some other desired positive value. This is very useful *except* when providing dimensions to centerlines for the location of holes. When the endpoint of the centerline is picked, a positive **DIMEXO** value leaves a space between the centerline and the beginning of the extension line. This is not a preferred practice. Change **DIMEXO** to 0 to remove the gap. Be sure to change **DIMEXO** back to its positive setting for dimensioning to other objects.

Use of **DIMEXO** and other dimensioning variables is fully explained later in this chapter when using the **Dimension Styles** dialog box.

Another way to avoid the unwanted gap between the centerline and the extension line is to use the **Intersection** object snap to pick where the centerline and the circle meet or use the **Quadrant** object snap to select the desired quadrant of the circle. This way, if **DIMEXE** is greater than or equal to **DIMEXO**, there is no gap created.

EXERCISE 18-9

❏ Start AutoCAD and use one of your templates.
❏ Set up the appropriate layers for your drawing elements, including dimensions.
❏ Use the proper dimensioning techniques and commands to dimension the objects exactly as shown.
❏ Save the drawing as EX18-9.

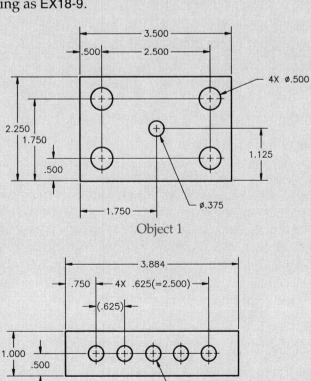

Object 1

Object 2

AutoCAD User's Guide **10**

DIMRADIUS
DRA

Dime**n**sion
➡ **R**adius

Dimension
toolbar

Radius Dimension

Dimensioning Arcs

The standard for dimensioning arcs is a radius dimension. A radius dimension is placed with the **DIMRADIUS** command. Access this command by picking the **Radius Dimension** button on the **Dimension** toolbar, by picking **R**adius in the **Dime**n**sion** pull-down menu, or by entering either DRA or DIMRADIUS at the Command: prompt.

When using the **DIMRADIUS** command, you get the Select arc or circle: prompt. A leader line and radius dimension value is attached to the cursor when you pick the desired arc or circle. You can drag the leader to any desired location and length before picking where you want it. The resulting leader points to the center of the arc or circle just as recommended by the ASME standard. See Figure 18-37. The command sequence is as follows:

Command: **DRA** *or* **DIMRADIUS.**⏎
Select arc or circle: *(pick an arc)*
Dimension line location (Mtext/Text/Angle): *(drag the leader to a desired location and pick)*
Dimension text = 0.750
Command:

As with the previous dimensioning commands, you can use the **Mtext** or **Text** option to change the dimension text or use the **Angle** option to change the angle of the text numbers.

Figure 18-37.
Using the **DIMRAD** command to dimension arcs with AutoCAD dimensioning variable defaults.

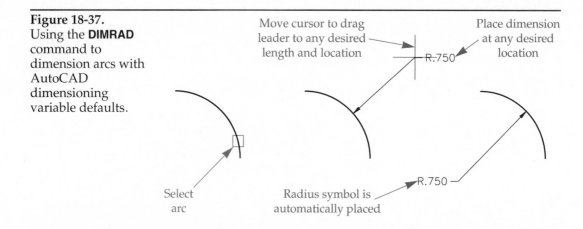

Dimensioning fillets and rounds

Small inside arcs are called *fillets.* Small arcs on outside corners are called *rounds.* Fillets are designed to strengthen inside corners. Rounds are used to relieve sharp corners. Fillets and rounds can be dimensioned individually as arcs or in a general note. The general note is ALL FILLETS AND ROUNDS R.125 UNLESS OTHERWISE SPECIFIED and is usually placed near the title block. See Figure 18-38.

Figure 18-38.
Dimensioning fillets and rounds.

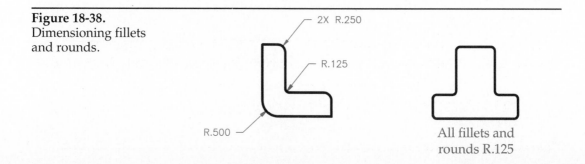

❏ Start AutoCAD and use one of your templates.
❏ Set up the appropriate layers for your drawing elements, including dimensions.
❏ Draw and dimension an object similar to Figure 18-37.
❏ Draw and dimension an object similar to Figure 18-38.
❏ Save the drawing as EX18-10.

Dimensioning Curves

When possible, curves are dimensioned as arcs. When they are not in the shape of a constant-radius arc, they should be dimensioned to points along the curve using the **DIMLINEAR** command. See Figure 18-39.

Figure 18-39.
Dimensioning curves that are not a constant radius.

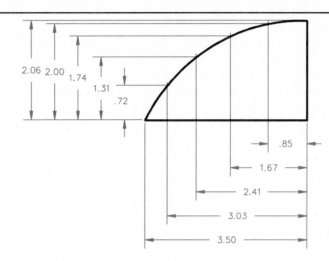

Dimensioning curves with oblique extension lines

The curve shown in Figure 18-39 is dimensioned using the normal practice, but in some cases, spaces may be limited and oblique extension lines are used. First, dimension the object using the **DIMLINEAR** command as appropriate, even if dimensions are crowded or overlap. See Figure 18-40A.

The .150 and .340 dimensions are to be placed at an oblique angle above the view. The **Oblique** option is accessed by picking **Oblique** in the **Dimension** pull-down menu. Oblique is one of the options found in the **DIMEDIT** command which is explained in detail later in this chapter.

After selecting the command, you are asked to select the objects. Pick the dimensions to be redrawn at an oblique angle. In this case, the .150 and .340 dimensions are selected.

    Command: _dimedit Dimension Edit (Home/New/Rotate/Oblique) ⟨Home⟩:_o
    Select objects: *(pick the .150 and .340 dimensions)*
    Select objects: ↵

Next, you are asked for the obliquing angle. Careful planning is needed to make sure the correct obliquing angle is selected. Obliquing angles originate from 0° East and revolve counterclockwise:

    Enter obliquing angle (press ENTER for none): **135.**↵
    Command:

The result is shown in Figure 18-40B.

Figure 18-40.
Drawing
dimensions with
oblique extension
lines.

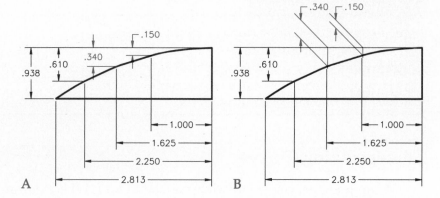

Drawing Leader Lines

The **DIMDIAMETER** and **DIMRADIUS** commands automatically place leaders on the drawing. The **LEADER** command allows you to begin and end a leader line where you desire. You can also place single or multiple lines of text with the leader. This command is ideal for the following situations:

- Adding specific notes to the drawing.
- When a leader line must be staggered to go around other drawing features. Keep in mind that staggering leader lines is not a recommended ASME standard.
- Where a double leader is required. Drawing two leaders from one note is not a recommended ASME standard.
- When making custom leader lines.
- When drawing curved leaders for architectural applications.

AutoCAD's **LEADER** command creates leader lines and related notes that are considered complex objects. This command provides you with the flexibility to place tolerances and multiple lines of text with the leader. The leader line characteristics, such as arrowhead size and text positioning, are controlled by the dimension variable settings. Other features, such as the leader format and annotation style, are controlled by options in the **LEADER** command. *Annotation* means the addition of notes or text and is commonly used in computer-aided drafting.

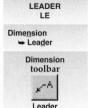

LEADER
LE

Dimension
↳ Leader

Dimension
toolbar

Leader

The **LEADER** command is accessed by picking the **Leader** button in the **Dimension** toolbar, selecting **Leader** in the **Dimension** pull-down menu, or by entering LE or LEADER at the Command: prompt. The initial prompts look like the **LINE** command, with the From point: and To point: prompts. This allows you to pick where the leader starts and ends. In mechanical drafting, properly drawn leaders have one straight segment extending from the feature to a horizontal shoulder, which is 1/4″ (6mm) long. While most other fields also use straight leaders, AutoCAD provides the option of drawing curved leaders. Examples are shown in Figure 18-41. The command sequence begins like this:

Command: **LE** *or* **LEADER.**↵
From point: *(pick the leader start point)*
To point: *(pick the second leader point, which is the start of the leader shoulder)*
To point (Format/Annotation/Undo) 〈Annotation):↵

AutoCAD automatically draws a leader shoulder unless the leader line is 15° or less off horizontal. While the ASME standard does not recommend a leader line that is less than 15° or greater than 75° from horizontal, it is sometimes necessary. If you need to create a shoulder, pick the endpoint of the leader shoulder like this:

Command: **LE** *or* **LEADER.**↵
From point: *(pick the leader start point)*
To point: *(pick the second leader point, which is the start of the leader shoulder)*
To point (Format/Annotation/Undo) 〈Annotation): *(pick the end of the leader shoulder)*
To point (Format/Annotation/Undo) 〈Annotation):

Figure 18-41.
Using the **LEADER** command to draw a curved leader and a straight leader, and identification of the leader elements.

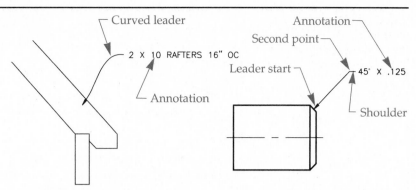

Annotation option is the default, and is accessed by pressing [Enter]. Type the desired note at the next prompt and then press [Enter] to get the MText: prompt. Press [Enter] to get back to the Command: prompt, or type as many lines of text as you want and press the [Enter] key after each line of text. The prompts continue like this for placing one line of text:

> Annotation (or press ENTER for options): **2 X 6 STUDS 16" OC.**↵
> MText: ↵
> Command:

If you wanted to place more than one line of text, the prompts would have continued like this:

> Annotation (or press ENTER for options): **2 X 6 STUDS 16" OC.**↵
> MText: **W/ 5 1/2" BATTS R-19 MIN.**↵
> MText: **FOIL FACE 1 SIDE**
> MText: ↵
> Command:

The results of using the previous leader commands are shown in Figure 18-42. Text placed using the **LEADER** command is a multiline text object (all of the lines of text are one object). You may want to review the **MTEXT** command in Chapter 8 of this text. When there is more than one line of text, the lines are justified on the left side if the leader is on the left, and justified on the right if the leader is on the right. If text is moved to the other side of the leader point, it is rejustified. The leader shoulder is centered on the multiple lines of text. See Figure 18-42.

Figure 18-42.
Placing annotations with a leader.

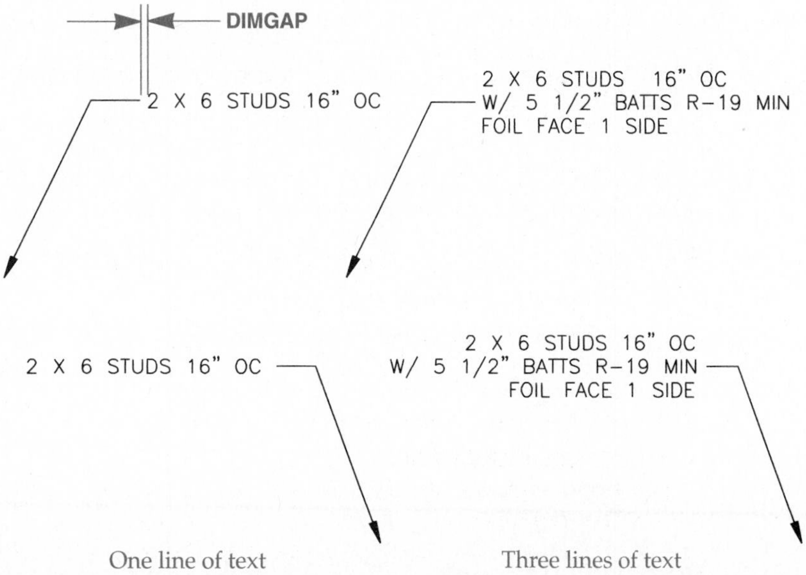

One line of text

Three lines of text

ASME Y14.5M-1994 recommends the leader shoulder be centered at the start of the first line of text or at the end of the last line of text. After using the **LEADER** command and placing the desired text, use grips and cycle to the **MOVE** command. Quickly move the text to the preferred position.

The text of a leader is locationally associated with the leader object. If you move the text, the leader follows. However, you can grip edit the leader and have the text remain in position. Once you have done this, the associativity of the leader to the text now uses the new relative positions. This is true if text has been entered or if a block object is used.

Using the Annotation suboptions

The **Annotation** option can be accessed by pressing the [Enter] key as previously described. Typing A and pressing the [Enter] key will also access the option. If you press [Enter] again, you get the options within **Annotation**:

> To point (Format/Annotation/Undo) ⟨Annotation⟩:↵
> Annotation (or RETURN for options):↵
> Tolerance/Copy/Block/None/⟨MText⟩:

Now, you can press [Enter] to accept the **Mtext** default and access the **Multiline Text Editor**. In the text editor, you can type paragraph text and pick **OK** when done. The other **Annotation** suboptions are as follows:

- **Tolerance.** Enter T to use the **Tolerance** option. This displays the **Geometric Tolerance** dialog box for creation of a feature control frame. See Figure 18-43A. Geometric tolerancing is explained in detail in Chapter 21 of this text.
- **Copy.** This option copies text, mtext, feature control frame, or a block, and connects the new object to the leader being created. The option begins with the Select object: prompt. All you have to do is pick a single object feature and it is automatically copied to a position at the leader shoulder. See Figure 18-43B. The command sequence is as follows:

> Annotation (or RETURN for options): ↵
> Tolerance/Copy/Block/None/⟨MText⟩: **C**↵
> Select object: *(pick the object)*
> Command:

- **Block.** This option inserts a specified block at the end of the leader. A *block* is a symbol that was previously created and saved. Blocks can be inserted into other drawings. These multiple-use symbols are explained in detail in Chapter 23 of this text. Blocks can be scaled during the insertion process. A special symbol block called TARGET is inserted in Figure 18-43C. The command to insert the block at the default scale of 1:1 and 0° rotation angle is:

> Annotation (or RETURN for options): ↵
> Tolerance/Copy/Block/None/⟨MText⟩: **B**↵
> Block name (or ?): **TARGET**↵
> Insertion point: *(pick an insertion point)*
> X scale factor ⟨1⟩/Corner/XYZ: ↵
> Y scale factor (default=X): ↵
> Rotation angle ⟨0⟩: ↵
> Command:

Additional information about these prompts is provided in Chapter 23.

- **None.** This option ends the leader with no annotation of any kind. See Figure 18-43D.

> Annotation (or RETURN for options): ↵
> Tolerance/Copy/Block/None/⟨MText⟩: **N**↵
> Command:

Figure 18-43.
Examples of using the **LEADER** command **Annotation** options.

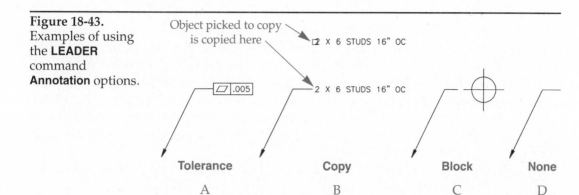

Object picked to copy is copied here

⊡ 2 X 6 STUDS 16" OC

⟨ .005

2 X 6 STUDS 16" OC

Tolerance — A

Copy — B

Block — C

None — D

Using the LEADER command Format options

The **LEADER** command also allows you to modify the way a leader line is presented. This is done by accessing the **Format** option:

> Command: **LE** *or* **LEADER**↵
> From point: *(pick the leader start point)*
> To point: *(pick the second leader point, which is the start of the leader shoulder)*
> To point (Format/Annotation/Undo) ⟨Annotation⟩: **F**↵
> Spline/STraight/Arrow/None/⟨Exit⟩:

The **Format** options are explained as follows:
- **Spline.** Enter S for the **Spline** option. This lets you draw leader lines using a spline object rather than straight segments. This practice is commonly used in architectural drafting. See Figure 18-44A.
- **STraight.** If you are inside the **LEADER** command and previously set **Format** to draw **Spline** leaders, then enter ST to change back to straight segments. AutoCAD automatically defaults back to drawing straight segment leaders when you leave the **LEADER** command. See Figure 18-44B.
- **Arrow.** Use the **Arrow** option if you selected the **None** (no arrow) option and then decided to change back to using an arrow while in the **LEADER** command. AutoCAD automatically defaults back to using an arrow when you leave the **LEADER** command. See Figure 18-44C.
- **None.** This allows you to draw a leader without an arrow. See Figure 18-44D.
- **Exit.** Exit is the default here. Press the [Enter] key or enter E to exit the **Format** options and return to the To point: prompt.

Figure 18-44.
Examples of using the **LEADER** command **Format** options.

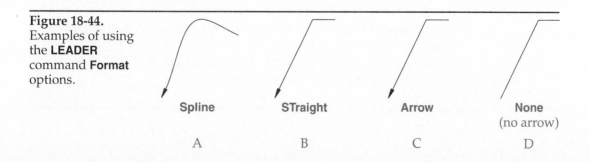

Spline — A

STraight — B

Arrow — C

None (no arrow) — D

Using the Undo option

The **Undo** option removes the last leader segment that you drew. This is handy if you accidentally draw an extra leader shoulder or segment and want to remove it. You can use the **Undo** option by entering U at the To point (Format/Annotation/Undo) ⟨Annotation⟩: prompt.

Using multiple leaders

The **LEADER** command can be used to connect notes to various features on a drawing. While a single leader line is the preferred ASME standard, some companies allow multiple leaders. See Figure 18-45. In order to draw multiple leader lines to the same note, use the **LEADER** command to place the first leader and the note. Then enter the **LEADER** command again and pick the beginning of the previous leader shoulder as the second point. Use the **Annotation None** option to terminate the command. The welding symbol shown in Figure 18-45B was created as a block and then inserted using the **Annotation Block** option.

Figure 18-45.
Alternate application of the **LEADER** command.

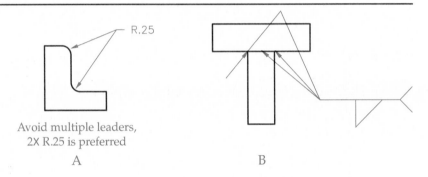

Avoid multiple leaders, 2X R.25 is preferred

A   B

PROFESSIONAL TIP   A **Quick Leader** tool is available in the **Bonus Standard** toolbar. This toolbar is available if a full installation of AutoCAD was performed. See Appendix A for bonus menu information.

EXERCISE 18-11

❑ Start AutoCAD and use one of your templates.
❑ Set up the appropriate layers for your drawing elements, including dimensions. Use the **LEADER** command to draw the following:
  ❑ Draw and dimension objects similar to Figure 18-45.
  ❑ Place one line of text with a straight leader and three lines of text with another leader as shown in Figure 18-44.
  ❑ Use the **Annotation Copy** and **None** options to place leaders similar to Figure 18-43. The **Tolerance** and **Block** options are not suggested at this time because these topics have not yet been explained.
  ❑ Use the **Format** options **Spline**, **STraight**, **Arrow**, and **None** to draw leaders similar to Figure 18-44. Annotation can be placed, if you wish.
❑ Save the drawing as EX18-11.

AutoCAD and its Applications—Basics

Dimensioning chamfers

A *chamfer* is an angled surface used to relieve sharp corners. The ends of bolts are commonly chamfered to allow them to engage the threaded hole better. Chamfers of 45° are dimensioned with a leader giving the angle and linear dimension, or with two linear dimensions. This can be accomplished using the **LEADER** command. See Figure 18-46.

Chamfers other than 45° must have either the angle and a linear dimension or two linear dimensions placed on the view. See Figure 18-47. The **DIMLINEAR** and **DIMANGULAR** commands are used for this purpose.

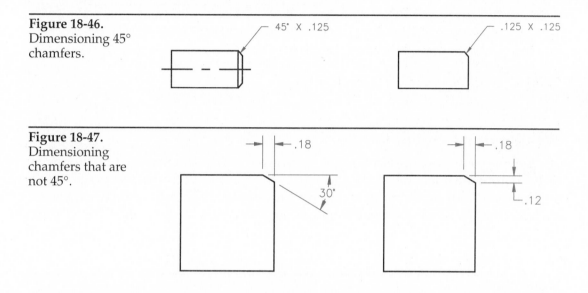

Figure 18-46.
Dimensioning 45° chamfers.

Figure 18-47.
Dimensioning chamfers that are not 45°.

❏ Start AutoCAD and use one of your templates.
❏ Set up the appropriate layers for your drawing elements, including dimensions.
❏ Draw and dimension objects similar to Figure 18-46.
❏ Draw and dimension objects similar to Figure 18-47.
❏ Save the drawing as EX18-12.

Alternate Dimensioning Practices

In industries where computer-controlled machining processes are used, it is becoming common to omit dimension lines. Arrowless and tabular dimensioning are two types of dimensioning that omit dimension lines. Another type, chart dimensioning, involves changing values of a product, and the dimensions are shown in a chart.

Arrowless dimensioning

Arrowless dimensioning is becoming popular in mechanical drafting. It is also used in electronics drafting, especially for chassis layout. This type of dimensioning has only extension lines and numbers. Dimension lines and arrowheads are omitted. Dimension numbers are aligned with the extension lines. Each dimension number represents a dimension originating from a common point. This starting, or 0, dimension is typically known as a *datum*, or *baseline*. Holes or other features are labeled with identification letters. Sizes are given in a table placed on the drawing. See Figure 18-48.

Figure 18-48.
Arrowless
dimensioning.

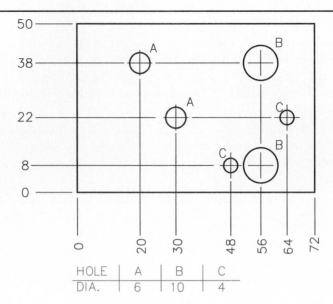

Tabular dimensioning

Tabular dimensioning is a form of arrowless dimensioning where dimensions to features are shown in a table. The table gives the location of features from the X-axis and Y-axis. It also provides the depth of features from a Z-axis, when appropriate. Each feature is labeled with a letter or number that correlates to the table. See Figure 18-49.

Figure 18-49.
Tabular dimensioning. (Doug Major)

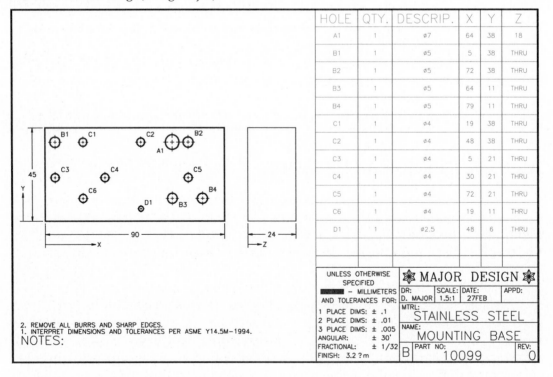

HOLE	QTY.	DESCRIP.	X	Y	Z
A1	1	⌀7	64	38	18
B1	1	⌀5	5	38	THRU
B2	1	⌀5	72	38	THRU
B3	1	⌀5	64	11	THRU
B4	1	⌀5	79	11	THRU
C1	1	⌀4	19	38	THRU
C2	1	⌀4	48	38	THRU
C3	1	⌀4	5	21	THRU
C4	1	⌀4	30	21	THRU
C5	1	⌀4	72	21	THRU
C6	1	⌀4	19	11	THRU
D1	1	⌀2.5	48	6	THRU

Chart dimensioning

Chart dimensioning may take the form of unidirectional, aligned, arrowless, or tabular dimensioning. It provides flexibility in situations where dimensions change as requirements of the product change. The views of the product are drawn and variable dimensions are shown with letters. The letters correlate to a chart where the different options are shown. See Figure 18-50.

Figure 18-50.
Chart dimensioning.

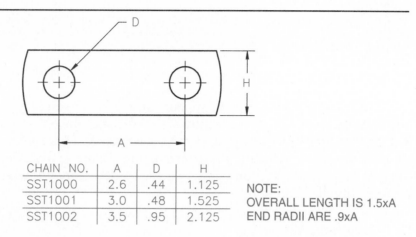

CHAIN NO.	A	D	H
SST1000	2.6	.44	1.125
SST1001	3.0	.48	1.525
SST1002	3.5	.95	2.125

NOTE:
OVERALL LENGTH IS 1.5xA
END RADII ARE .9xA

Drawing arrowless dimensions

AutoCAD refers to arrowless dimensioning as *ordinate dimensioning.* These dimensions are done using the **DIMORDINATE** command. This command is accessed by picking the **Ordinate Dimension** button in the **Dimension** toolbar, by picking **Ordinate** in the **Dimension** pull-down menu, or by entering DOR or DIMORDINATE at the Command: prompt. When using this command, AutoCAD automatically places an extension line and number along X and Y coordinates. Since you are working in the X-Y axes, it is often best to have **ORTHO** on.

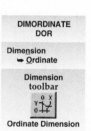

DIMORDINATE
DOR

Dimension
➥ Ordinate

Dimension
toolbar

Ordinate Dimension

The World Coordinate System (WCS) 0,0 coordinate has been in the lower-left corner of the screen for the drawings you have already completed. In most cases, this is fine. However, when doing ordinate dimensioning, it is best to have the dimensions originate from a primary datum, which is often a corner of the object. The WCS is fixed; the User Coordinate System (UCS), on the other hand, can be moved to any orientation desired.

All of the ordinate dimensions originate from the current UCS origin. The UCS is discussed in detail in Chapter 3 of *AutoCAD and its Applications—Advanced, Release 14*. In general, UCS allows you to set your own coordinate system. If you do this, all of the Dimension text: prompts display the actual dimensions from the X-Y coordinates on the object. Move the UCS origin to the corner of the object or the appropriate datum feature using the following command sequence:

> Command: **UCS**↵
> Origin/ZAxis/3point/Object/View/X/Y/Z/Prev/Restore/Save/Del/?/⟨World⟩: **O**↵
> Origin point ⟨0,0,0⟩: *(pick the origin point at the corner of the object to be dimensioned as shown in Figure 18-51A)*

Next, if there are circles on your drawing, use the **DIMCENTER** command to place center marks in the circles, as shown in Figure 18-51B. This makes your drawing conform to ASME standards and provides something to pick when dimensioning the circle locations. Now, you are ready to start placing the ordinate dimensions. Enter the **DIMORDINATE** command as follows:

> Command: **DOR** *or* **DIMORDINATE**↵
> Select Feature: *(pick the feature to be dimensioned)*

Figure 18-51.
A—Draw the object and move the UCS origin to the X–Y corner. B–Add the center marks to the circular features using the **CENTER** command.

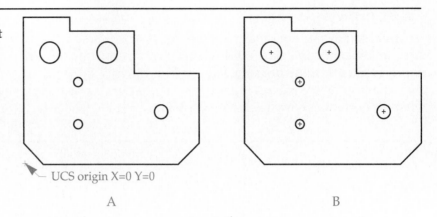

UCS origin X=0 Y=0

A   B

When the Select Feature: prompt appears, move the screen cursor to the point or feature to be dimensioned. If the feature is the corner of the object, pick the corner. If the feature is a circle, pick the end of the center mark. This leaves the required space between the center mark and the extension line. Zoom in if needed and use the object snaps to help. The next prompt asks for the leader endpoint, which actually refers to the extension line endpoint.

> Leader endpoint (Xdatum/Ydatum/Mtext/Text): *(pick the endpoint of the extension line)*
> Dimension text = 0.500

If the X-axis or Y-axis distance between the feature and the extension line endpoint is large, the default axis may not be the desired axis for the dimension. When this happens, use the **Xdatum** or **Ydatum** option to tell AutoCAD which axis originates the dimension:

> Leader endpoint (Xdatum/Ydatum/Mtext/Text): **X**↵
> Leader endpoint: *(pick the endpoint of the extension line)*

Use the **Mtext** option to open the **Multiline Text Editor** and type the desired text followed by picking **OK**. The Leader endpoint (Xdatum/Ydatum/Mtext/Text): prompt returns. Pick the leader endpoint to complete the command.

Figure 18-52 shows the ordinate dimensions placed on the object. Notice the dimension text is aligned with the extension lines. Aligned dimensioning is standard with ordinate dimensioning. Finally, complete the drawing by adding any missing lines, such as centerlines or fold lines. Identify the holes with letters and correlate a dimensioning table. See Figure 18-53.

Figure 18-52.
Placing the ordinate dimensions.

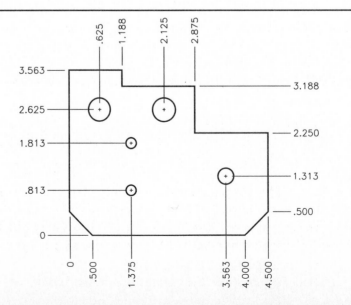

AutoCAD and its Applications—Basics

Figure 18-53.
Completing the drawing.

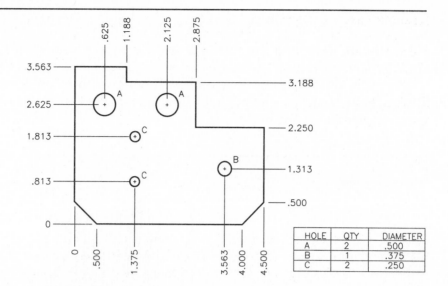

You can leave the UCS origin at the corner of the object, or move it back to the corner of the screen (WCS) by pressing [Enter] for the **World** default:

    Command: **UCS.**↵
    Origin/ZAxis/3point/Entity/View/X/Y/Z/Prev/Restore/Save/Del/?/〈World〉: ↵

PROFESSIONAL TIP

Most ordinate dimensioning tasks work best with **ORTHO** on. However, when the extension line is too close to an adjacent dimension number, it is best to stagger the extension line as shown in the following illustration. With **ORTHO** off, the extension line is automatically staggered when you pick the offset second extension line point as demonstrated.

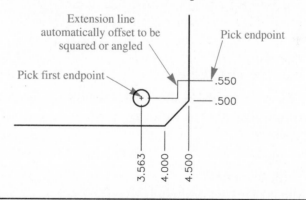

EXERCISE 18-13

❑ Start AutoCAD and use one of your templates.
❑ Set up the appropriate layers for your drawing elements, including dimensions.
❑ Draw and use ordinate dimensioning to dimension the object shown in Figure 18-48.
❑ Save the drawing as EX18-13.

Thread Drawings and Notes

There are many different thread forms. The most common forms are the Unified and metric screw threads. The parts of a screw thread are shown in Figure 18-54.

Threads are commonly shown on a drawing with a simplified representation. Thread depth is shown with a hidden line. This method is used for both external and internal threads. See Figure 18-55.

Figure 18-54.
Parts of a screw thread.

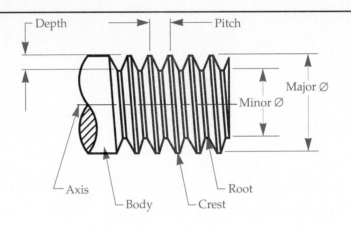

Figure 18-55.
Simplified thread representations.

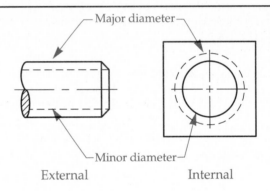

External   Internal

Showing the thread note

The view shows the reader that a thread exists, but the thread note gives exact specifications. The thread note for Unified screw threads must be given in the following order:

3/4 - 10UNC - 2A
(1)   (2) (3)   (4) (5)
(1) Major diameter of thread, given as fraction or decimal inch.
(2) Number of threads per inch.
(3) Thread series. UNC = Unified National Course. UNF = Unified National Fine.
(4) Class of fit. 1 = large tolerance. 2 = general purpose tolerance. 3 = tight tolerance.
(5) A = external thread. B = internal thread.

The thread note for metric threads is displayed in the following order:

M 14 X 2
(1) (2) (3)
(1) M = metric thread.
(2) Major diameter in millimeters.
(3) Pitch in millimeters.

There are too many Unified and metric screw threads to discuss here. Refer to the *Machinery's Handbook* or a comprehensive drafting text for more information.

The thread note is typically connected to the thread view with a leader. See Figure 18-56. A chamfer is often placed on the external thread. This makes it easier to engage the mating thread.

Figure 18-56.
Displaying the thread note with a leader.

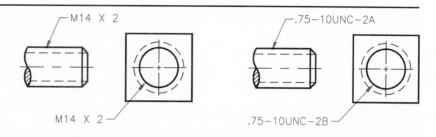

EXERCISE 18-14

❑ Start AutoCAD and use one of your templates.
❑ Set up the appropriate layers for your drawing elements, including dimensions.
❑ Draw a simplified representation of an external and internal Unified screw thread. Do the same for a metric screw thread.
❑ Use the **LEADER** command to label each view. Label the Unified screw thread as 3/4-10UNC-2A and the metric screw thread as M14 X 2.
❑ Your drawing should look similar to Figure 18-56.
❑ Save the drawing as EX18-14.

Dimension Styles

AutoCAD User's Guide 10

Dimension styles are saved sets of dimension variable settings that determine the appearance of the dimensions. *Dimension variables* are AutoCAD system variables that help you control the way dimensions look. So far in this chapter, you have used only a few of the many dimensioning variables. The dimensioning variables that you used where introduced to help you perform specific tasks. A dimension style is created by changing the dimension variables as needed to achieve the desired dimension appearance for your drafting application. For example, the dimension style for mechanical drafting probably has ROMANS text font placed in a break in the dimension line, and the dimension lines are capped with arrowheads. See Figure 18-3. The dimension style for architectural drafting may use CIBT text font placed above the dimension line, and dimension lines are terminated with slashes. See Figure 18-4. The dimension style can have dimensions based on national or international standards, or set up to match company or school applications and standards. Dimension styles can also have a family of settings that allow you to have different settings for each specific type of dimension. The dimensioning practice that you have been doing in this chapter was based on the AutoCAD STANDARD dimension style. This is a dimension style that uses all of the AutoCAD default settings and variables.

Creating Dimension Styles

You might think of dimension styles as the dimensioning standards you use. Dimension styles are usually established for a specific type of drafting field or application. You can customize dimension styles to correspond to drafting standards such as ASME/ANSI, ISO (International Organization for Standardization), MIL (military), architectural, structural, civil, or your own school or corporate standards. Dimension styles are created using the **Dimension Styles** dialog box. See Figure 18-57.

Figure 18-57.
The **Dimension
Styles** dialog box.
The STANDARD
dimension style is
the AutoCAD
default.

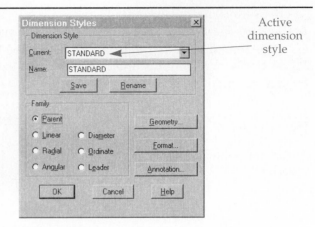

Active
dimension
style

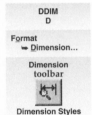

DDIM
D

Format
➥ Dimension...

Dimension
toolbar

Dimension Styles

This dialog box is accessed by picking the **Dimension Styles** button in the **Dimension** tool bar, by picking **Dimension Style...** in the **Format** pull-down menu, or by entering D or DDIM at the Command: prompt.

The **Dimension Style** area of the **Dimension Style** dialog box displays STANDARD in the **Current:** text box. The **Current:** text box is where the active dimension style name is displayed. If additional text styles exist, they are accessed in the drop-down list. Pick a name from the list to make another dimension style current. The standard dimension style is the AutoCAD default. If you begin a drawing with a wizard, the default dimension style is STANDARD_WIZARDSCALED. This means the dimension style features are scaled to the settings and units you set up in the **Quick** or **Advanced** wizard. If you change any of the AutoCAD default dimension variables, the changes are automatically stored in a dimension style named +STANDARD. See Figure 18-58.

The **Name:** text box is where you display a dimension style to be saved or renamed. When the dimension variables are changed to match your drafting practice, the dimension style name is entered in the **Name:** text box. You then pick the **Save** button to save the dimension style. If you change the dimensioning variables to match your architectural applications, then you might enter a dimension style named ARCHITECTURAL in the **Name:** text box and pick **Save**. This makes ARCHITECTURAL the current style. See Figure 18-59A. Follow this same procedure for establishing all of the dimension style names you need, such as one for mechanical drawing. Figure 18-59B shows the dimension styles list with the two new styles ARCHITECTURAL and MECHANICAL added to the STANDARD and +STANDARD.

If you want to rename a dimension style, open the **Current:** drop-down list and pick the style for display in the text box. Then enter the new name in the **Name:** text box followed by picking the **Rename** button.

Figure 18-58.
Changes to the
AutoCAD default
dimension style
STANDARD result in
a new dimension
style named
+STANDARD.

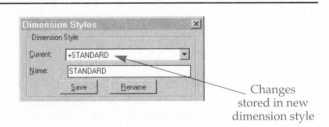

Changes
stored in new
dimension style

Figure 18-59.
A—A dimension style is named ARCHITECTURAL to match dimension variable options used for architectural drafting applications. B—The **Current:** drop-down list shows the new dimension styles named ARCHITECTURAL and MECHANICAL along with STANDARD and +STANDARD.

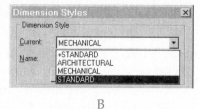

A   B

Creating your own dimension style families

Look at the **Family** area of the **Dimension Styles** dialog box in Figure 18-57. In a family, many family members share specific qualities or features, yet each member has certain qualities or features all their own. If you compare this to a human family, the sons and daughters share the name. This is the same as the dimension style name. The children share some of the general tendencies and features of the parent (parent setting). Yet, each child looks and acts different than the parent (individual family member setting).

In technical terms, a *parent style* is a general style that applies to all of the family members, or each type of dimension. A *family member* is one of the specific dimension types, including linear, radial, angular, diameter, ordinate and leaders. Dimension style families allow you to create a dimension style that has variations depending on the type of dimensioning you are doing. For example, you may want diameter dimensions to be created with centerlines in the circle and radius dimensions to have only a center mark; or you might want filled arrowheads on your linear dimensions and dots placed at the end of leaders. Dimension style families offer this kind of flexibility. Another example might be the display of linear dimensions with the text above the dimension line and using tick marks at the ends of the dimension lines, but have the text placed in the center of radial dimensions and use arrowheads. Rather than create a dimension style for each one of these different characteristics, you can create a dimension style name and have the parent settings that match most applications. Then, set family member, such as the radial, to their own unique characteristics. Thus, dimension families are divided into two categories, parent styles and family members.

To create a parent style, first pick the **Parent** radio button in the **Dimension Styles** dialog box. Then using the **Geometry...**, **Format...**, and **Annotation...** buttons, set the dimension variables to match the general features of your dimensions. You will learn how to use these button and set the dimension variables in the next section. These settings include features such as text styles, placement and sizes, and arrowheads. Next, in the **Dimension Style** area, save the parent style with the desired name.

To set specific variations for family members, select the appropriate radio button, make the desired changes to the variables, and then pick **Save**. Each time you select a different family member after making changes, a message such as Saved to Architectural is given in the lower-left corner of the **Dimension Styles** dialog box. Changes to parent styles are not applied to family members after the style has been created, named, and saved. You should always create the parent style first and then modify each of the desired family members, saving your changes as you go.

The **Geometry...**, **Format...**, and **Annotation...** buttons access dialog boxes used for setting and changing dimension variables. The dialog boxes are used to make changes, because they are convenient and eliminate the need to memorize the dimensioning variable names needed to make the same changes at the Command: prompt.

Using the Geometry dialog box

Pick the **Geometry...** button in the **Dimension Styles** dialog box to open the **Geometry** dialog box. See Figure 18-60. This dialog box is used to change dimension features related to the dimension line, extension line, arrowheads, center mark, and scale. The following discussion explains how each of these adjustments work:

- **Dimension Line**. This area is used to change the format of the dimension line with the following dimension variables:

  - **Suppress:**—This option has two toggles that keep either the first, second, or both dimensions lines and their arrowheads from being displayed. The **1st** and **2nd** refer to the first and second points picked when the dimension was created. Dimension lines are displayed by default. The Command: prompt equivalent for these dimension variables are **DIMSD1** and **DIMSD2** (suppress dimension line) and the result of using these is shown in Figure 18-61.

  - **Extension**—This text box is inactive unless you are using tick marks instead of arrowheads. Architectural tick marks, or oblique arrowheads, are often used when dimensioning architectural drawings. The different settings for arrowhead styles are explained later. In this style of dimensioning, the dimension lines often cross over the extension lines. The extension represents how far the dimension line extends beyond the extension line. See Figure 18-62. The 0.00 default is used to draw dimensions that are not extended past the extension lines. The Command: prompt dimension variable is **DIMDLE** (dimension line extension).

Figure 18-60.
The **Geometry**
dialog box.

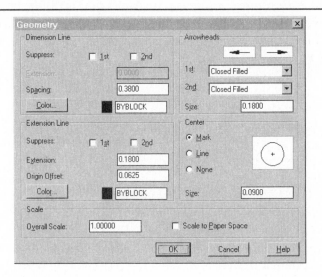

Figure 18-61.
Using the **DIMSD1** and **DIMSD2** dimensioning variables.

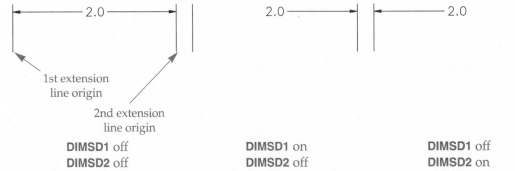

Figure 18-62.
Using the **DIMDLE** variable to allow the dimension line to extend past the extension line. With the default value of 0, the dimension line does not extend.

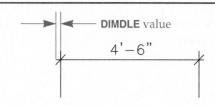

- **Spacing**—This text box allows you to change the spacing between the dimension lines of baseline dimensions. The default spacing is .38 units. AutoCAD automatically spaces the dimension lines this distance when you use the **DIMBASELINE** command. The default value is generally too close for most drawings. Try other values to help make the drawing easy to read. Figure 18-63 shows the dimension line spacing. The Command: prompt equivalent is **DIMDLI** (dimension line increment).
- **Color**—Picking this button opens the **Select Color** dialog box where you can assign a color to the dimension lines. The color is normally assigned the default of ByBlock, which indicates that the dimension line assumes the currently active color setting of all elements within the dimension object. The ByBlock color setting means that the color assigned to the created block is used for the component objects of the block. All associative dimensions are created as block objects. Blocks are symbols designed for multiple use and are explained in Chapter 23. Associative dimensions are discussed in this chapter and in Chapter 19. This setting is subject to the current **CECOLOR** variable. If the current entity color is set to **BYLAYER** when the dimension block is created, then it comes in with a bylayer setting. The component objects of the block then take on the color of the layer where the dimensions are created. If the current entity color is an absolute color, then the component objects of the block take on that specific color regardless of the layer where the dimension was created. Different color settings are normally only used for pen width considerations when plotting the drawing. The Command: prompt equivalent is **DIMCLRD** (color of dimension line).

Figure 18-63.
The **DIMDLI** variable controls the spacing between dimension baselines.

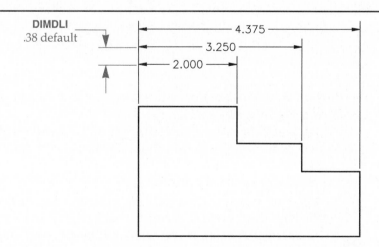

- **Extension Line**. The **Extension Line** area of the **Geometry** dialog box is used to change the format of the extension lines with the following dimension variables:
  - **Suppress**—This option is used to suppress either the first, second, or both extension lines. Extension lines are displayed by default. An extension line might be suppressed, for example, if it coincides with an object line. See Figure 18-64. The Command: prompt entries are **DIMSE1** and **DIMSE2** (suppress extension line).
  - **Extension**—This text box is used to set the extension line extension which is the distance the extension line runs past the last dimension line. See Figure 18-65. The default is .18 and the Command: prompt equivalent is **DIMEXE** (extension line extension). An extension line extension of .125 is common on most drawings.
  - **Origin Offset**—This text box is used to change the distance between the object and the beginning of the extension line. See Figure 18-65. Most applications require this small offset. The default is .0625. It is recommended that a 0.0 setting be used when an extension line meets a centerline. The Command: prompt equivalent is **DIMEXO** (extension line offset).
  - **Color...**—The color button is used to change the extension line color. The default is ByBlock and the Command: prompt equivalent is **DIMCLRE** (color of extension line).

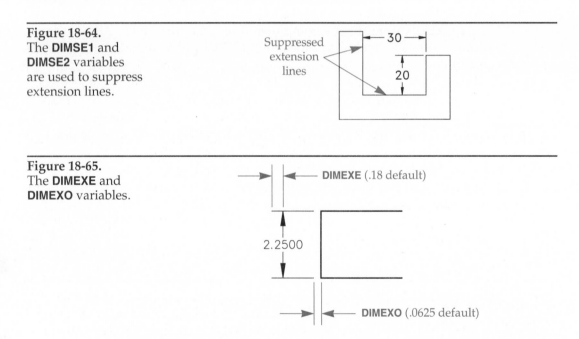

Figure 18-64.
The **DIMSE1** and **DIMSE2** variables are used to suppress extension lines.

Suppressed extension lines

Figure 18-65.
The **DIMEXE** and **DIMEXO** variables.

DIMEXE (.18 default)

2.2500

DIMEXO (.0625 default)

- **Arrowheads**. This area provides several different arrowhead options and controls the arrowhead size.
  - **1st: and 2nd:**—The default arrowhead is Closed Filled as displayed in the **1st:** and **2nd:** drop-down lists and in the image tiles above the lists. Open the list to access the arrowhead options. See Figure 18-66. Use the scroll bar to access the complete list of arrowhead options. If you pick a new arrowhead in the **1st:** drop-down list, AutoCAD automatically makes the same selection for the **2nd:** drop-down list and the representation in the image tiles change to match the selection. If you want a different arrowhead for the **1st:** and **2nd:**, pick the desired **1st:** arrowhead and then open the **2nd:** list and pick another. Figure 18-67 shows an example of each of the optional arrowheads. AutoCAD provides you with a wide variety of arrowhead options. Check your drafting standards before selecting the appropriate arrowhead.

Figure 18-66.
The default
arrowhead is **Closed
Filled**.

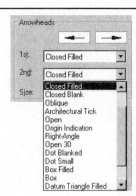

Figure 18-67.
Shown are examples of the **Arrowheads** options in the drop-down list.

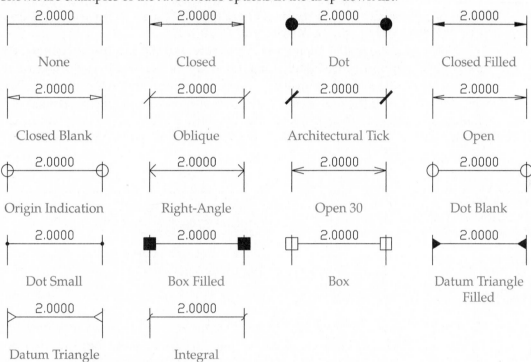

- **Size**—This text box allows you to change the size of arrowheads. The default value is .18. An arrowhead size of .125″ is common on mechanical drawings. The arrowhead size can also be changed at the Command: prompt with the **DIMASZ** (arrowhead size) dimension variable. Figure 18-68 shows arrowhead size value.

Figure 18-68.
The **DIMASZ**
variable can be
used to change the
arrowhead size. The
default values is .18.

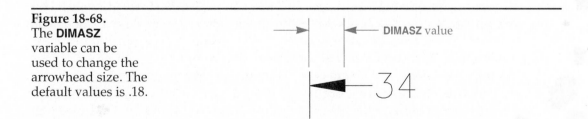

You can also access the arrowheads by picking on the left image tile to have the image automatically changed in both tiles. Each time you pick the image tile, the next arrowhead option in the list is displayed. Pick on the right image tile to make the second arrowhead different from the first.

Notice in Figure 18-67 there is no example of the **User Arrow...** option. This option is used to access an arrowhead of your own design. For this to work, you must first design an arrowhead and save it as a block. Blocks are discussed in Chapter 23 of this text. When you pick the **User Arrow...** option in the **Arrowheads** list, you get the **User Arrow** dialog box. See Figure 18-69. Type the name of your custom arrow block in the **Arrow Name:** text box and then pick **OK** to have the arrow used on the drawing.

Change arrowheads at the Command: prompt with the **DIMBLK**, **DIMBLK1**, **DIMBLK2**, and **DIMSAH**. Use the **DIMBLK** (block) variable if both arrowheads are the same. The **DIMBLK** variable accepts the name of the arrowhead style you want to use. To set up separate arrowheads, first set **DIMSAH** (separate arrowheads) ON. The arrowheads that are used by the first and second dimension lines are set by using **DIMBLK1** and **DIMBLK2**.

When you access the **Oblique** or **Architectural Tick** arrowhead options, the **Extension:** text box in the **Dimension Line** area is activated. This allows you to enter a value for a dimension line projection beyond the extension line. The default value is zero, but some architectural companies like to project the dimension line past the extension line by setting this to a desired value. See Figure 18-62. This is controlled at the Command: prompt with the **DIMDLE** dimension variable.

Figure 18-69.
The **User Arrow** dialog box is opened when you pick the **User Arrow...** option in the drop-down list.

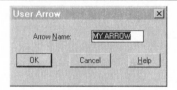

- **Center**. This area of the **Geometry** dialog box allows you to select the way center marks are placed in circles and arcs. There are three radio buttons that are identified as **Mark**, **Line**, and **None**. The image tile at the right of the radio buttons shows a representation of the currently selected radio button. You can also change the center mark option by picking directly on the image tile.
    - **None**—This is the default that provides for no center marks to be placed in circles and arcs.
    - **Mark**—The **Mark** option is used to place only center marks without lines.
    - **Line**—This option places center marks and centerlines.
    After selecting either the **Mark** or **Line** center mark option, you can place center marks on circles and arcs by using the **DIMCENTER** command. This command is accessed by picking the **Center Mark** button in the **Dimension** toolbar, by picking **Center Mark** in the **Dimension** pull-down menu, or by entering DIMCENTER or DCE at the Command: prompt.
    - **Size**—The **Size:** text box is used to change the size of the center mark and center line. The default size is .09. The size specification controls the **Mark** and **Line** options in different ways as shown in Figure 18-32. The center mark size is changed at the Command: prompt with the **DIMCEN** dimension variable as discussed earlier in this chapter.

AutoCAD and its Applications—Basics

- **Scale**. This area of the **Geometry** dialog box allows you to set the scale factor for all dimension features in the entire drawing.
  - **Overall Scale**—AutoCAD automatically sets a scale factor based on the setup option. If the scale factor is 1, then the dimension variables are equal to their designated settings. If the scale factor is 2, then the values of the dimension variables are doubled. For example, if the arrowhead size is .125, then a scale factor of 2 makes the arrowheads .250. This value can also be set at the Command: prompt by using the **DIMSCALE** dimensioning variable.
  - **Scale to Paper Space**—This check box is used if you want the geometry scale factor to be related to paper space settings. The **Overall Scale** is disabled when **Scale to Paper Space** is checked. This is also done at the Command: prompt with the **DIMSCALE** variable set to 0.

EXERCISE 18-15

- ❏ Start AutoCAD and use one of your templates.
- ❏ Open the **Dimension Styles** dialog box and notice STANDARD as the current dimension style.
- ❏ Access the **Geometry** dialog box.
- ❏ Look at the **Dimension Line** area as you refer to Figure 18-63.
- ❏ Look at the **Extension Line** area as you refer to Figure 18-65.
- ❏ Look at the **Arrowheads** area and pick each of the arrowhead options as you see the representation in the image tiles change. Try picking on the image tile to see the results. Try making the first and second arrowheads the same and different. Notice when you pick the **Oblique** and **Architectural Tick** arrowheads that the **Extension:** text box in the **Dimension Line** area becomes active.
- ❏ Look at the **Center** area as you pick each of the radio buttons and see how the image tile changes to match the selection. Pick on the image tile to see what happens.
- ❏ Use the **Geometry** dialog box to make the following settings based on your preferred drafting field:

Setting	Architectural	Mechanical
Dimension line spacing	.75	.50
Extension line extension	.18	.125
Extension line offset	.08	.0625
Arrowheads	Dot, Oblique, or Architectural Tick	Closed Filled, Closed Blank, or Open
Arrowhead size	.18	.125
Center	Mark	Line
Center size	.25	.125

- ❏ Pick the **OK** button.
- ❏ You are now back in the **Dimension Style** dialog box. Notice the +STANDARD dimension style added to the list.
- ❏ Type MECHANICAL or ARCHITECTURAL in the **Name:** text box depending on the drafting field for which you made settings.
- ❏ Pick the **Save** button. The dimension style you created should now be in the list.
- ❏ Pick **OK**.
- ❏ Save the drawing as EX18-15.

Using the Format dialog box

The **Format** dialog box is used to establish the way dimension text appears on the drawing, and the way dimension lines and arrowheads are placed. The **Format** dialog box is opened by picking the **Format...** button in the **Dimension Styles** dialog box. The **Format** dialog box is shown in Figure 18-70 with default settings.

Figure 18-70.
The **Format** dialog
box.

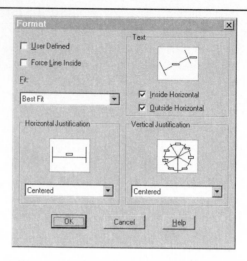

- **User Defined**. This check box allows you to control the location of the dimension text. With **User Defined** off (the default) AutoCAD centers the text within the dimension line, or places the text outside the second extension line on small space dimensions. Checking the **User Defined** box gives you control over text placement and dimension line length outside of extension lines. Figure 18-71 shows the flexibility that can be gained with **User Defined** on. The text can be placed where you want it, such as moved to the side within the extension lines, or placed outside of the extension lines. The **DIMUPT** (user positioned text) variable controls this application at the Command: prompt.
- **Force Line Inside**. This check box forces AutoCAD to place the dimension line inside the extension lines, even when the text and arrowheads are outside. The default application is with the dimension line and arrowheads outside the extension lines. Figure 18-72 shows the difference between **Force Line Inside** on and off. Forcing the dimension line inside the extension lines is not an ASME standard, but it may be preferred by some companies. The dimension variable for this application is **DIMTOFL** (text outside, force line inside).
- **Fit:**. This drop-down list provides several options that control the way the dimension line, text, and arrowheads are formatted. Figure 18-73 shows the complete list. The **DIMFIT** variable is used at the Command: prompt with settings 0 through 4. The results of each setting are shown in Figure 18-74.
  - **Best Fit**—This is the **Fit:** default and allows AutoCAD to place text and dimension lines with arrowheads inside of extension lines if space is available. Dimension lines with arrowheads are placed outside of extension lines if space is limited. Everything is placed outside of extension lines if there is not enough space between extension lines. The **Best Fit** option is the same as setting **DIMFIT** to 3 when typed at the Command: prompt.
  - **Text and Arrows**—When this option is used, AutoCAD places the text, dimension line and arrowheads inside the extension lines if there is enough space, or everything is placed outside the extensions if there is not enough space. This is controlled by the **DIMFIT** variable set at 0.

Figure 18-71.
Dimension text placement flexibility is gained when using the **User Defined** option in the **Format** dialog box.

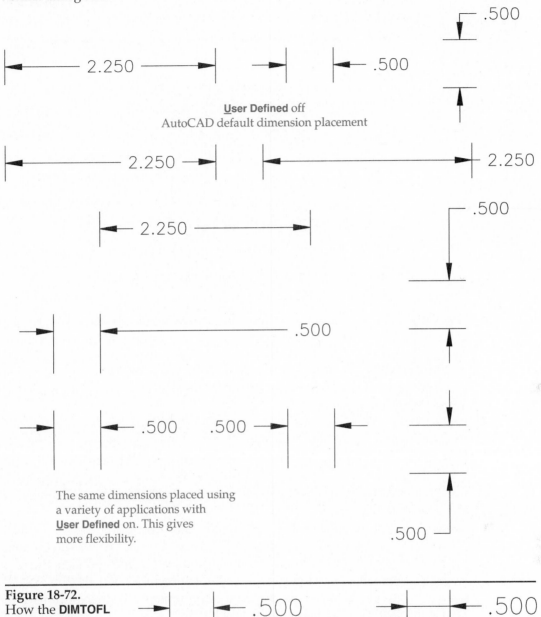

User Defined off
AutoCAD default dimension placement

The same dimensions placed using a variety of applications with **User Defined** on. This gives more flexibility.

Figure 18-72.
How the **DIMTOFL** variable affects dimensions.

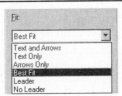

DIMTOFL = off

DIMTOFL = on

Figure 18-73.
The **Fit:** box provides several options for the way the dimension line, text, and arrowheads are formatted.

Fit:

Best Fit

Text and Arrows
Text Only
Arrows Only
Best Fit
Leader
No Leader

Figure 18-74.
How the **DIMFIT** variable affects dimensions with limited space.

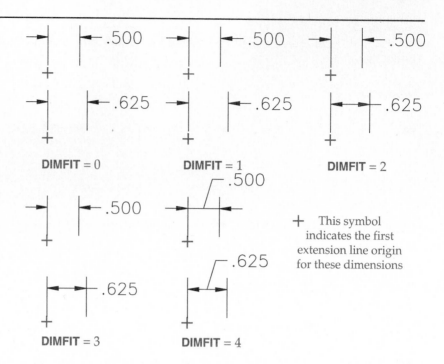

- **Text Only**—The text, dimension line, and arrowheads are placed inside the extension lines if there is enough space for everything. If there is enough space for only the text inside the extension lines, then the dimension lines and arrowheads are placed outside. Everything is outside if there is not enough room for the text inside. **DIMFIT** is set at 1 when this option is used at the Command: prompt.

- **Arrows Only**—The text, dimension line, and arrowheads are placed inside the extension lines if there is enough space for everything. The text is placed outside if there is enough space for only the arrowheads and dimension line inside the extension lines. Everything is outside if there is not enough room for anything inside. This is a **DIMFIT** setting of 2 when set at the Command: prompt.

- **Leader**—AutoCAD places the text inside and the dimension line and arrowheads outside if space permits. If the text does not fit inside, the text is placed away from the dimension line and a leader line connects the text to the dimension line. This practice is not recommended by the ASME standard, but can be used in crowded situations if all other options fail. This is the **DIMFIT** dimension variable set at 4.

- **No Leader**—This is similar to the **Leader** option except the text is placed away from the dimension line with no leader connecting the dimension line. This is even more unconventional than using the **Leader** option. The **DIMFIT** setting for this option is 5 when performed at the Command: prompt.

- **Horizontal Justification**. This area of the **Format** dialog box is used to align the placement of the dimension text horizontally with the dimension line or extension lines. The image tile provides a representation of the currently selected option. The rectangle in the image tile represents the dimension text. Pick the down arrow to access the drop-down list. See Figure 18-75. You can select the options by picking the desired name in the list or you can pick on the image tile to cycle through the options. The horizontal justification is controlled at the Command: prompt by using the **DIMJUST** (justification) variable. The **DIMJUST** variable has settings 0 through 4 that match the options in the **Format** dialog box. The results of these options are displayed in Figure 18-76.

Figure 18-75.
The **Horizontal Justification** image tile showing the **Centered** default option. The drop-down list shows the other **Horizontal Justification** options.

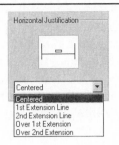

Figure 18-76.
How the **DIMJUST** variable affects dimension text.

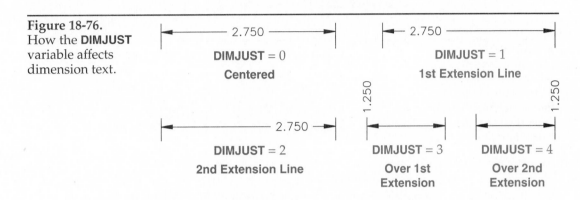

The following explains each of these options as related to the choices in the **Horizontal Justification** list.

- **Centered**—This option is the AutoCAD default which places dimension text centered on the dimension line as shown by the image tile in Figure 18-75.
- **1st Extension Line**—This option locates the text next to the extension line that is placed first. The **DIMJUST** setting is 1.
- **2nd Extension Line**—This option locates the text next to the extension line that is placed second. The **DIMJUST** setting is 2.
- **Over 1st Extension**—This option places the text aligned with and over the first extension line. This practice is not commonly used. The **DIMJUST** setting is 3.
- **Over 2nd Extension**—This option places the text aligned with and over the second extension line. This practice is also not commonly used. The **DIMJUST** setting is 4.

PROFESSIONAL TIP

Each of the **Horizontal Justification** options provide you with the ability to set the dimension text in a single fixed position for all future dimension placement until you change to a different option. If these fixed settings do not give you enough flexibility, you might consider leaving horizontal justification at the **Centered** option and check the **User Defined** check box to give you total flexibility when placing each dimension.

- **Text**. This area of the **Format** dialog box allows you to control the alignment of dimension text inside and outside of the extension lines. This area is used when you want to draw unidirectional dimensions or aligned dimensions which were discussed early in this chapter. See Figures 18-2 and 18-3.
  - **Inside Horizontal and Outside Horizontal**—The default has the **Inside Horizontal** and **Outside Horizontal** check boxes on. This draws unidirectional dimensions that are commonly used for mechanical manufacturing drafting applications. A combination can also be used, but normally these

check boxes are either on or off. The image tile represents the status of these check boxes. You can change the settings by picking the check boxes or on the image tile at the dimension number images. **Inside Horizontal** and **Outside Horizontal** are turned off for making aligned dimensions which are typically used for architectural dimensioning. Figure 18-77 shows a comparison of when the image tile representation for **Inside Horizontal** and **Outside Horizontal** are turned on and off and a drawing displayed for each application. **Inside Horizontal** is controlled at the Command: prompt by the **DIMTIH** (text inside is horizontal) variable, and **Outside Horizontal** is controlled by the **DIMTOH** (text outside is horizontal) variable.

Figure 18-77.
A comparison of when the image tile representation for **Inside Horizontal** and **Outside Horizontal** are turned on and off.

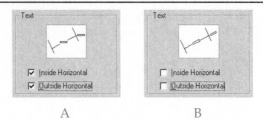

A   B

- **Vertical Justification**. This area of the **Format** dialog box is used to set the vertical alignment of dimension text in relation to the dimension line. To change the vertical justification, pick on the image tile to cycle through the options or pick one of the options found in the drop-down list. See Figure 18-78.
  - **Centered**—This option is the default which places dimension text centered in a gap provided in the dimension line. This is the dimensioning practice that is commonly used in mechanical drafting and many other fields. The **DIMTAD** (text above dimension line) variable is turned off when controlling this application at the Command: prompt. See Figure 18-79.
  - **Above**—This is the option that is generally used for architectural drafting and building construction where the dimension text is placed above the dimension line. This places the dimension text horizontally and above horizontal dimension lines and in a gap provided in vertical and angled dimension lines. Architectural drafting commonly uses *aligned dimensioning* where the dimension text is aligned with the dimension lines and all text either reads from the bottom or right side of the sheet. In order for the dimension text to be placed above and aligned with vertical and angled dimension lines, the **Inside Horizontal** and **Outside Horizontal** check boxes must be off. The **Above** option and its related image tile is shown in Figure 18-78A. When entered at the Command: prompt, the **DIMTAD** setting is on. See Figure 18-79.

Figure 18-78.
The **Vertical Justification** image tile for the **Centered** default option. Also shown are the other **Vertical Justification** options and the image tile representation for each.

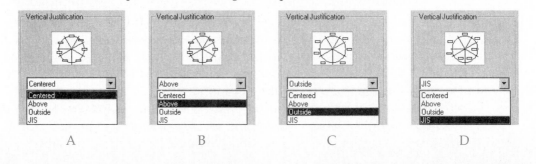

A   B   C   D

Figure 18-79.
Using the **DIMTAD** variable.

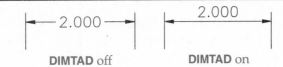

DIMTAD off   DIMTAD on

- **Outside**—This option places the dimension text outside the dimension line and either above or below a horizontal dimension line or to the right or left of a vertical dimension line depending on which way you move the cursor. Figure 18-78C shows the related image tile.
- **JIS**—This is the option for use when dimensioning for the *Japanese Industrial Standards*. The related image tile is shown in Figure 18-78D.

PROFESSIONAL TIP

When dimensioning mechanical drawings, it is common to have **User Defined** on, **Horizontal** and **Vertical Justification Centered**, and **Inside Horizontal** and **Outside Horizontal** on.

For architectural drafting, it is typical to have **User Defined** on, **Force Line Inside** on, **Horizontal Justification Centered**, **Vertical Justification Above**, and **Inside Horizontal** and **Outside Horizontal** off. Figure 18-4 shows an example of a partial architectural floor plan with aligned dimensioning and text above the dimension line.

EXERCISE 18-16

❑ Start AutoCAD and use one of your templates.
❑ Open the **Dimension Styles** dialog box and access the **Format** dialog box.
❑ Set the **User Defined**, **Force Line Inside**, and **Fit** options as needed to draw and dimension objects or place dimensions similar to Figures 18-71, 18-72, and 18-74.
❑ Pick each of the **Horizontal Justification** options as you watch how the image tile changes with each selection.
❑ Pick each of the **Vertical Justification** options as you watch how the image tile changes with each selection.
❑ Set the **Horizontal** and **Vertical Justification** options as needed to place dimensions similar to Figures 18-76 and 18-79.
❑ Turn **Inside Horizontal** and **Outside Horizontal** on and off as you observe how the image tile changes.
❑ Save the drawing as EX18-16.

Using the Annotation dialog box

Changes can be made to dimension text by picking the **Annotation...** button in the **Dimension Styles** dialog box. This opens the **Annotation** dialog box. See Figure 18-80. *Annotation* is anything that has to do with text such as dimension text and drawing notes. Each of the **Annotation** dialog box features are explained in the following:

- **Primary Units**. Primary units are defined by AutoCAD as the part of the dimension from which tolerances or other units are calculated or related. The options in the **Primary Units** area are discussed in the next section. Tolerances are discussed in Chapters 20 and 21 of this text.
- **Tolerance**. The **Tolerance** area of the **Annotation** dialog box is discussed in Chapter 20 of this text.

Figure 18-80.
The **Annotation**
dialog box.

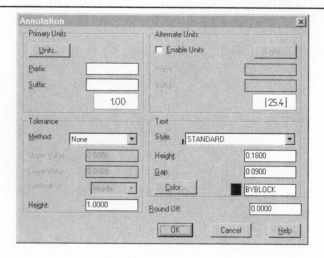

- **Alternate Units**. This area is used to set alternate units. *Alternate units*, or *dual dimensioning*, have inch measurements followed by millimeters in brackets or millimeters followed by inches in brackets. Dual dimensioning practices are no longer a recommended ASME standard. ASME recommends that drawings be dimensioned using inch or metric units only. However, the use of alternate units can be used in many other applications.

  - **Enable Units**—Pick this check box to activate the alternate units. See Figure 18-81. Alternate units are set at the Command: prompt with the **DIMALT** (alternate) variable.

  - **Units...**—This button accesses the **Alternate Units** dialog box. This dialog box looks similar to, and its features work in the same manner as, those found in the **Primary Units** dialog box, which is discussed in the next section. The **Angles:** area of the **Alternate Units** dialog box is disabled, because there are no alternate unit options for angular measurements. The related dimension variables when entered at the Command: prompt are **DIMALTU** for **Units**, **DIMALTD** for **Dimension Precision:**, **DIMALTZ** for **Dimension Zero Suppression**, **DIMALTTD** for **Tolerance Precision:**, **DIMALTTZ** for **Tolerance Zero Suppression**, and **DIMALTF** for **Scale**.

  - **Prefix: and Suffix:**—You can also set **Alternate Units** prefix and suffix as needed when the alternate units are enabled. These are controlled at the Command: prompt with the **DIMAPOST** variable.

- **Text**. This area of the **Annotation** dialog box is used to set the dimension text style, height, gap, and color. The following explains each of the options.

  - **Style:**—The dimension text style uses the STANDARD text style by default. Text styles must be loaded using the **STYLE** command, in the current drawing, before they are available for use in dimension text. In Figure 18-82 there are two additional text styles in the **Style:** list. Pick the desired text style for use in dimensions. Dimension text styles are changed at the Command: prompt by using the **DIMTXSTY** (text style) variable.

Figure 18-81.
The **Alternate Units**
area of the
Annotation dialog
box.

Pick to access
alternate units

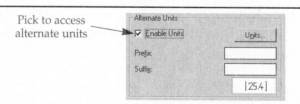

Figure 18-82.
The **Style:** drop-down
list in the **Text** area of
the **Annotation** dialog
box. A text style must
have been loaded using
the **STYLE** command
before it can be
displayed in this list.

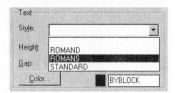

- **Height:**—The dimension text height is set by entering the desired value in this text box. Dimension text height is commonly the same as the text height found on the rest of the drawing, except for titles which are higher. The text height for other drawing text is set using the **STYLE** command, or in one of the text commands. The default dimension text height is .18, which is an acceptable standard. Many companies use a text height of .125". The ASME standard recommends text height between .125" and .188". The text height for titles and labels is usually between .18 or .25. Dimension text height can be set at the Command: prompt with the **DIMTXT** (text) variable.
- **Gap:**—This text box is used to set the gap between the dimension line and the dimension text. This setting also controls the distance between the leader shoulder and the text and the space between the basic dimension box and the text. Basic dimensions are used in geometric tolerancing and are explained in Chapter 20. The default gap is .09. Figure 18-83 shows the gap in a linear and leader dimension. The gap is changed at the Command: prompt by using the **DIMGAP** dimension variable.
- **Color...**—Pick this button to open the **Select Color** dialog box for changing the color of dimension text. The dimension color default is ByBlock. The dimension text color is changed at the Command: prompt with the **DIMCLRT** (color of text) command.
- **Rounding Off:**. This text box in the **Annotation** dialog box is used to have AutoCAD round off all numbers to a specified value. The default is zero, which means that no rounding takes place and all dimensions are placed exactly as measured. If you enter a value of .1, all dimensions are rounded to the closest .1 unit. For example, an actual measurement of 1.188 is rounded to 1.2. This variable is controlled at the Command: prompt with **DIMRND** (round).

Figure 18-83.
The gap displayed
in a linear and
leader dimension.

Using the Primary Units area

The following section explains the function of each of the options in the **Primary Units** area of the **Annotation** dialog box. The **Units...** button accesses the **Primary Units** dialog box. See Figure 18-84. The elements of the **Primary Units** dialog box are explained in the following:

- **Units**. This area is where you select the type of units for use as dimension text. The default is Decimal units. See Figure 18-86. A definition and examples of the different units are provided in Chapter 2 of this text. The **Architectural** and

Figure 18-84.
The **Primary Units**
dialog box.

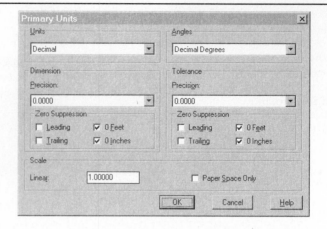

Fractional options place dimension fractions in line, such as 3/4. The **Architectural (stacked)** and **Fractional (stacked)** options place dimension fractions stacked, such as $\frac{3}{4}$. The Windows Desktop units are decimal format units using Control Panel settings for decimal separator and number grouping symbols. To find this setting, go to Control Panel and select Regional Settings. Then pick the Number tab. Here is where the Windows Desktop settings are made. Dimension units are controlled at the Command: prompt with the **DIMUNIT** variable. This variable has eight settings that correspond to the options in the **Units** list. These settings are shown in the following table:

Value	Units	Example
1	Scientific	155E+01
2	Decimal	12.50
3	Engineering	1'-3.50"
4	Architectural (stacked)	$1'-3\frac{1}{2}''$
5	Fractional (stacked)	$12\frac{1}{2}''$
6	Architectural	1'-3 1/2"
7	Fractional	12 1/2"
8	Windows Desktop	See previous discussion

- **Dimension**. The **Dimension** area controls the decimal place precision and the placement of leading and trailing zeros in dimension numerals.

    The **Precision:** drop-down list allows you to decide how many zeros follow the decimal place when decimal related units are selected. The default is 0.0000, while 0.00 and 0.000 settings are common in inch mechanical drafting depending on the desired tolerance. When fractional related units are selected, the precision values are related to the smallest desired fractional denominator. The default is 1/16", but you can choose other options ranging from 1/256" to 1/2" or 0" if you want no fractional values displayed. A variety of dimension precision can be found on the same drawing. Dimension unit precision is controlled at the Command: prompt with the **DIMDEC** variable.

The **Zero Suppression:** area provides four check boxes. These options are used to suppress or keep leading and trailing zeros in the primary units.

The **Leading** check box is off by default which leaves a zero on dimension numerals less than one, such as 0.50. This option is used when doing metric dimensioning as recommended by the ASME standard. Check this box to remove the 0 on decimal units less than one, as recommended by ASME if you are doing inch dimensioning.

The **Trailing** check box is off by default which leaves zeros after the decimal point based on the precision setting. This is usually off for inch dimensioning, because the trailing zeros often control tighter tolerances for manufacturing processes. Check this box when doing metric dimensioning, because the ASME standard recommends that zeros be removed following decimal metric dimensions.

The **0 Feet** check box is on by default which removes the zero in feet and inch dimensions when there are zero inches. For example, when **0 Feet** is on, a measurement reads 12'. If **0 Feet** is off, the same dimension reads 12'-0".

The **0 Inches** check box is on by default which removes the zero when the inch part of feet and inch dimensions is less than one inch, such as 12'-7/8". If this check box is off, the same dimension reads 12'-0 7/8".

Zero suppression is set at the Command: prompt with the **DIMZIN** (zero inch display) variable. **DIMZIN** has settings 0 through 3, 4, 8, and 15 which are identified in the following chart:

Architectural Applications					
Value	**Results**	**Inches**		**Feet and Inches**	
0	Removes 0' and 0"	1/2"	4"	2'	1'-0 1/2"
1	Includes 0' and 0"	0'-0 1/2"	0'-4"	2'-0"	1'-0 1/2"
2	Includes 0' omits 0"	0'-0 1/2"	0'-4"	2'	1'-0 1/2"
3	Includes 0" omits 0'	1/2"	4"	2'-0"	1'-0 1/2"
Mechanical Applications					
Value	**Results**	**Example and Recomendations**			
0	Includes leading 0 and trailing 0's	0.500, not recommended for inches			
4	Omits leading 0, includes trailing 0's	0.500 becomes .500, not recommended for metric			
8	Includes leading 0, omits trailing 0's	0.500 becomes 0.5, not recommended for inches			
12	Omits leading and trailing 0's	0.500 becomes .5, not recommended for metric and has limited use in inches			

PROFESSIONAL TIP — Any settings you make during the **Quick** or **Advanced** setup or when using the **UNITS** command are not altered by changes made in the **Primary Units** dialog box or with the **DIMDEC**, **DIMUNIT**, or **DIMAUNIT** dimension variables.

- **Angles**. This area of the **Primary Units** dialog box is used to set the desired type of angular units for dimensioning. Angular units were discussed in the section in Chapter 2 on AutoCAD setup and with the **UNITS** command. The setup options and **UNITS** command do not control the type of units used for dimensioning. These must be set here or by using the dimension variable at the Command: prompt. The default is **Decimal Degrees** and the other options are **Deg/Min/Sec**, **Grads**, **Radians**, and **Surveyor**. See Figure 18-85. Angular units for dimensions are set at the Command: prompt with the **DIMAUNIT** (angular units) variable.

Figure 18-85.
The **Units** and the **Angles** drop-down lists in the **Primary Units** dialog box.

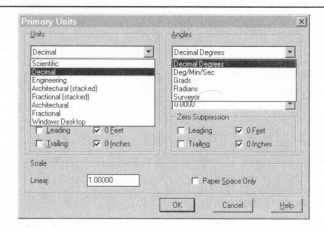

- **Tolerance**. This area of the **Primary Units** dialog box is discussed in Chapter 20 of this text.
- **Scale**. This area of the **Primary Units** dialog box is used to set the scale factor of linear dimensions. If the scale factor in the **Linear** text box is 1, then dimension values are displayed the same as they are measured. If the setting is 2, then dimension values are twice as much as the measured amount. For example, an actual measurement of 2 inches is displayed as 2 with a linear scale of 1, but the same measurement is displayed as 4 when the linear scale is 2. The Command: prompt control uses the **DIMLFAC** (linear units scale factor) dimensioning variable.

  The **Paper Space Only** check box is off by default. Placing a check in this box makes the linear scale factor active only when dimensioning in paper space. To do this at the Command: prompt, set **DIMLFAC** to a negative value that represents the desired scale factor.

Prefixes are special notes or applications that are placed in front of the dimension text. *Suffixes* are special notes or applications that are placed after the dimension text. A typical prefix might be SR3.5 where SR means spherical radius. A typical suffix might be 3.5 MAX, where MAX is the abbreviation for maximum, or 3.5 MIN where MIN is the abbreviation for minimum. The abbreviation IN. can also be used when one or more inch dimensions are placed on a metric dimensioned drawing, or a suffix of MM on one or more millimeter dimensions on an inch drawing.

When a prefix is used on a diameter or radius dimension, the prefix replaces the ∅ or R symbol.

The desired prefix and suffix is entered in the **Prefix:** or **Suffix:** edit box. Figure 18-86A shows SR entered as a prefix and MIN entered as a suffix. Figure 18-86B shows a dimension drawn with the SR prefix and MIN suffix. The **Primary Units** prefix and suffix is controlled at the Command: prompt with the **DIMPOST** variable.

Figure 18-86.
A—SR is entered as a prefix and MIN is entered as a suffix in the **Primary Units** area of the **Annotation** dialog box.
B—A dimension drawn with the SR prefix and MIN suffix set in A.

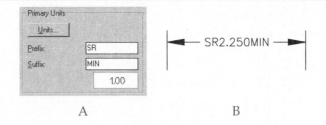

A   B

EXERCISE 18-17

❏ Start AutoCAD and use one of your templates.
❏ Open the **Dimension Styles** dialog box and open the **Annotation** dialog box.
❏ Set the primary units to three place decimal.
❏ Load the ROMANS and CIBT text fonts. Open the **Annotation** dialog box and notice the options in the **Style:** drop-down list in the **Text** area.
❏ Set text height at .125 and the gap at .05.
❏ Draw a dimension 5.625 using ROMANS font with the dimension text centered in a gap provided in the dimension line.
❏ Draw another dimension 5.625 using CIBT font with the dimension text above the dimension line.
❏ Set the prefix, suffix, and other variables needed to draw the dimension shown in Figure 18-86B. Remove the prefix and suffix from the dialog box when finished.
❏ Save the drawing as EX18-17.

Making Your Own Dimension Styles

Creating and recording dimension styles is part of your AutoCAD management responsibility. You should carefully evaluate the items that are contained in the dimensions for the type of drawings you do. During this process, be sure to carefully check company or national standards to verify the accuracy of your plan. Then make a list of features and values for the dimensioning variable you use based on what you have learned in this chapter. When you are ready, use the **Dimension Styles** dialog box options to establish dimension style families and family members that are named to suit your drafting practices. The following provides two lists of possible dimension style settings. One list is for mechanical manufacturing and the other is for architectural drafting applications. The other settings are AutoCAD defaults. The meanings and methods for making these settings is explained through the rest of this chapter.

Setting	Mechanical	Architectural
Dimension line spacing	.50	.75
Extension line extension	.125	.18
Extension line offset	.0625	.08
Arrowheads	Closed, Closed Filled, or Open	Dot, Closed Filled, Oblique, Architectural Tick, or Right Angle
Arrowhead size	.125	.18
Center	Line	Mark
Center size	.25	.25
User Defined	On	On
Vertical Justification	Centered (default)	Above
Inside Horizontal	On (default)	Off
Outside Horizontal	On (default)	Off
Primary Units	Decimal (default)	Architectural or Architectural (stacked)
Dimension Precision	0.000	1/16"
Zero Suppression Metric	Leading Off / Trailing On	Leading Off / Trailing On
Zero Suppression Inch	Leading On / Trailing Off	Leading On / Trailing Off
Angles	Decimal Degrees (default)	Deg/Min/Sec
Tolerances	By application	None
Text Style	ROMANS	CIBT
Text Height	.125	.188
Text Gap	.05	.1

EXERCISE 18-18

❏ Create your own dimension style prototype list for the type of drafting you perform.
❏ Open the **Dimension Styles** dialog box and change the settings as needed to match the list you created.
❏ Save the dimension style with a name that describes the list you made.
❏ Save as EX18-18.

Creating and Controlling Dimensioning Styles at the **Command:** Prompt

The **DIMSTYLE** command allows you to identify and create dimensioning styles at the Command: prompt. The command sequence is as follows:

```
Command: DST or DIMSTYLE.↵
dimension style: STANDARD
Dimension Style Edit (Save/Restore/STatus/Variables/Apply/?) ⟨Restore⟩:
```

After you enter the **DIMSTYLE** command, AutoCAD gives you a message identifying the current dimension style. The dimension style identified in the above command sequence is STANDARD. This is the AutoCAD default dimension style.

Use the **Save** option of the **DIMSTYLE** command to enter the dimension style name. The following command sequence is used to save a dimension style named ARCHFL for architectural floor plan drawings:

Command: **DST** *or* **DIMSTYLE**↵
dimension style: STANDARD
Dimension Style Edit (Save/Restore/STatus/Variables/Apply/?) 〈Restore〉: **S**↵
?/Name for new dimension style: **ARCHFL**↵
Command:

Proceed in the same manner to change the dimensioning variables reflecting your proposed ASME inch and ASME millimeters styles for mechanical drawings. Use the **Save** command for each of the created styles. Do this for any dimensioning style that you want created in your prototype drawing.

Listing the dimension styles

Enter ? to list the dimension styles created for the current drawing. List the name or names of styles you want listed to help you remember if they have been created, or press [Enter] to accept the wild card 〈*〉 for all dimension styles:

Command: **DST** *or* **DIMSTYLE**↵
dimension style: STANDARD
Dimension Style Edit (Save/Restore/STatus/Variables/Apply/?) 〈Restore〉: **?**↵
Dimension style(s) to list 〈*〉: ↵

The **AutoCAD Text Window** is displayed showing the list of available dimension styles. Press the [F2] key to toggle between the **AutoCAD Text Window** and the graphics window, or double-click the **AutoCAD Text Window** control menu to close.

Using the Restore option

The **Restore** option lets you change dimensioning variable settings by reading new settings from an existing dimension style. You can access **Restore** at the keyboard. The current style is listed when you enter the **DIMSTYLE** command. Change to a different dimension style by entering that dimension style name as follows:

Command: **DST** *or* **DIMSTYLE**↵
dimension style: STANDARD
Dimension Style Edit (Save/Restore/STatus/Variables/Apply/?) 〈Restore〉: ↵
?/Enter dimension style name or press ENTER to select dimension: **ARCHFL**↵
Command:

You can also press [Enter] and pick any existing dimension to determine the style. **Restore** is the default in the **DIMSTYLE** command, so you can type R and press [Enter] or just press the [Enter] key:

Command: **DST** *or* **DIMSTYLE**↵
dimension style: ARCHFL
Dimension Style Edit (Save/Restore/STatus/Variables/Apply/?) 〈Restore〉: ↵
?/Enter dimension style name or press ENTER to select dimension: ↵
Select dimension: *(pick a dimension on the drawing)*
dimension style: ARCHFL
Command:

Now you know that the dimension you picked was drawn using the ARCHFL style, which is the current style.

The **Restore** option lets you list the dimension styles in the current drawing. To do so, enter ? in the same manner as described with the **Save** option. If you want to display the difference between one of your dimension styles and the current style, enter the tilde character (~) and the style to compare:

?/Enter dimension style name or ENTER to select dimension: **~ASME–IN**↵

When you press [Enter], AutoCAD shows you the difference between styles in the **AutoCAD Text Window.** Keep in mind that the **AutoCAD Text Window** only displays the dimension variable settings that are *different* between the current style and the style name that you entered.

Using the STatus option

The **STatus** option of the **DIMSTYLE** command is used to display the settings of all dimension variables for the current dimension style. Enter ST as follows:

> Command: **DST** *or* **DIMSTYLE**↵
> dimension style: ARCHFL
> Dimension Style Edit (Save/Restore/STatus/Variables/Apply/?) ⟨Restore⟩: **ST**↵

The **AutoCAD Text Window** displays all the dimension variable names, the settings, and a descriptive statement about each variable.

Using the Variables option

Another way to list the current dimension style and variable settings of a dimension style without changing the current settings is with the **Variable** option. You can name a dimension style to list the variables, or pick a dimension on the screen just as with the **Restore** option:

> Command: **DST** *or* **DIMSTYLE**↵
> dimension style: ARCHFL
> Dimension Style Edit (Save/Restore/STatus/Variables/Apply/?) ⟨Restore⟩: **V**↵
> ?/Enter dimension style name or press ENTER to select dimension: ↵
> Select dimension: *(pick a dimension on the drawing)*

The screen changes to the AutoCAD **Text Window** listing the current dimensioning variable settings for the dimension you picked.

Use the **?** option if you want to look at the dimensioning variables used in the current drawing. You can compare the current dimension style with another style by entering ~ and the style name to compare as follows:

> Command: **DST** *or* **DIMSTYLE**↵
> dimension style: ARCHFL
> Dimension Style Edit (Save/Restore/STatus/Variables/Apply/?) ⟨Restore⟩: **V**↵
> ?/Enter dimension style name or press ENTER to select dimension: **~ASME–IN**↵
> Differences between ASME-IN and current settings:
>   ASME-IN   Current Setting
> DIMSCALE   1.0000   48.000

The **AutoCAD Text Window** then displays only the dimension variables that are different between the current style and the ASME–IN style.

Using the Apply option

Use the **Apply** option in the **DIMSTYLE** command if you want to select a dimension and have it applied to the current dimension style settings. The command sequence is as follows:

> Command: **DST** *or* **DIMSTYLE**↵
> Dimension Style Edit (Save/Restore/STatus/Variables/Apply/?) ⟨Restore⟩: **A**↵
> Select objects: *(select the dimension or dimensions that you want to have applied to the current dimension style)*
> Select objects: ↵
> Command:

AutoCAD and its Applications—Basics

❏ Start AutoCAD and open an existing drawing or use one of your templates.
❏ Design dimensioning variables that can be used for two different dimension styles. Name one ARCHFL for drawing architectural floor plans and name the other ASME-IN for inch dimensioned ASME standard drawings. Design a few dimension variable variations for each style based on the content of this chapter.
❏ Save these dimension styles under the name identified with each.
❏ Use the **Restore** option to restore the dimension style that is not currently set.
❏ Use the tilde (~) to have AutoCAD show you the difference between the styles.
❏ Use the **?** option to list the available dimension styles.
❏ Use the **STatus** option to display the dimension variable names of the current dimension style.
❏ Access the dimension variable status screen with the **Variable** option.
❏ Restore the ASME-IN dimension style if it is not current. Use the **Apply** option and select the dimensions on the drawing to convert to the current dimension style.
❏ Save as EX18-19.

PROFESSIONAL TIP   The **Bonus** pull-down menu includes tools that allow you to import and export dimension style settings. This menu is available if a full installation of AutoCAD was performed. See Appendix A for additional information on the **Dimstyle Export** and **Dimstyle Import** tools.

Overriding Existing Dimensioning Variables

Generally, it is appropriate to have one or more dimensioning variables set to perform specific tasks that relate to your dimensioning practices. However, situations may arise where it is necessary to alter dimensioning variables to modify one or more specific dimensions on the final drawing. For example, assume you have the **DIMEXO** (dimension extension line offset) variable set at .062, which conforms to ASME standards. However, in your final drawing there are three specific dimensions that require a 0 extension line offset. You can pick these three dimensions and alter the **DIMEXO** variable exclusively using the **DIMOVERRIDE** command. The command works like this:

Command: **DOV** *or* **DIMOVERRIDE**↵
Dimension variable to override (or Clear to remove overrides): **DIMEXO**↵
Current value ⟨.062⟩ New value: **0**↵
Dimension variable to override: *(type another variable name to override or press* [Enter]*)*
Select objects: *(select the dimension or dimensions to override)*
Select objects: ↵
Command:

The **DIMEXO** variable automatically changes from .062 to 0 on the three selected dimensions. You can also clear any previous overrides by using the **Clear** option like this:

Command: **DOV** *or* **DIMOVERRIDE**↵
Dimension variable to override (or Clear to remove overrides): **C**↵
Select objects: *(select the dimension or dimensions to clear an override)*
Select objects: ↵
Command:

EXERCISE 18-20

❏ Start AutoCAD and use one of your templates.
❏ Make a drawing similar to Figure 18-39 with dimensioning variables set as follows:

> **DIMASZ** = .1
> **DIMGAP** = .05
> **DIMDLE** = .12
> **DIMDLI** = .5
> **DIMEXO** = .06

❏ Use datum (baseline) dimensioning to make your job easier.
❏ After completing the entire drawing, with the dimensioning variables set as required, use the **DIMOVERRIDE** command to change only the **DIMEXO** variable to 0 on all dimensions except the overall dimensions.
❏ Save the drawing as EX18-20.

Using the Dimensioning Mode

Throughout this chapter, you have been introduced to performing dimensioning tasks by using toolbar buttons, pull-down menus, or by typing commands directly at the Command: prompt. AutoCAD provides you maximum flexibility by providing access to many dialog boxes. These dialog boxes offer you to the most visual communication with AutoCAD. The dimensioning practices that have been discussed throughout this chapter can also be accessed at the Command: prompt by putting AutoCAD into the dimensioning mode. Most of the commands that have been introduced can be entered while in the dimensioning mode. The dimensioning mode is used by entering either **DIM** or **DIM1** at the Command: prompt. The **DIM** command allows you to enter as many consecutive dimensioning commands as you want until you decide to exit the command. The **DIM1** command allows you to use only one dimensioning command before automatically returning you to the Command: prompt. When you enter the **DIM** or **DIM1** command you are in the dimensioning mode and you get the Dim: prompt:

Command: **DIM** *or* **DIM1**↵
Dim:

If you want to leave the dimensioning mode, enter E or EXIT or press the [Esc] key. Dimensioning commands, with names that are different from what you have already learned, are used at the Dim: prompt while you are in the dimensioning mode. Generally, dimensioning commands are entered at the Command: prompt with the **DIM** prefix. However, the **DIM** prefix is not used when at the Dim: prompt in the dimensioning mode. The following is a list that shows the AutoCAD commands and their related dimensioning mode commands:

AutoCAD command	Dimensioning mode command	AutoCAD command	Dimensioning mode command
DIMALIGNED	ALIGNED	DIMOVERRIDE	OVERRIDE
DIMANGULAR	ANGULAR	DIMRADIUS	RADIUS
DIMBASELINE	BASELINE	DIMSTYLE (Restore)	RESTORE
DIMCENTER	CENTER	DIMLINEAR (Rotated)	ROTATED
DIMCONTINUE	CONTINUE	DIMSTYLE (Save)	SAVE
DIMDIAMETER	DIAMETER	DIMSTYLE (Status)	STATUS
DIMEDIT (Home)	HOMETEXT	DIMEDIT	TEDIT
DIMLINEAR (Horizontal)	HORIZONTAL	DIMEDIT (Rotate)	TROTATE
LEADER	LEADER	DIMSTYLE (Apply)	UPDATE
DIMEDIT (Text)	NEWTEXT	DIMSTYLE (Variables)	VARIABLES
DIMEDIT (Oblique)	OBLIQUE	DIMLINEAR (Vertical)	VERTICAL
DIMORDINATE	ORDINATE		

To give you an example of how the **DIM** command works, try drawing a horizontal linear dimension and a couple of datum dimensions similar to Figure 18-28 like this:

    Command: **DIM**↵
    Dim: **HOR** *or* **HORIZONTAL**↵
    First extension line origin or press ENTER to select: *(pick the first extension line origin)*
    Second extension line origin: *(pick the second extension line origin)*
    Dimension line location (Mtext/Text/Angle): *(pick the dimension line location)*
    Dimension text ⟨2.000⟩: ↵
    Dim: **BASELINE**↵
    Second extension line origin or RETURN to select: *(pick the origin of the next dimension's second extension line)*
    Dimension text ⟨2.75⟩: ↵
    Dim: **BASE** *or* **BASELINE**↵
    Second extension line origin or (⟨select⟩/Undo): *(pick the origin of the next dimension's second extension line)*
    Dimension text ⟨3.250⟩: ↵
    Dim: **BASE** *or* **BASELINE**↵
    Second extension line origin or (⟨select⟩/Undo): *(pick the origin of the next dimension's second extension line)*
    Dimension text ⟨4.375⟩: ↵
    Dim: **E** *or* **EXIT**↵
    Command:

EXERCISE 18-21

❑ Begin a new drawing or use one of your prototypes.
❑ Use the **DIM1** command to draw an object with dimensions similar to Figure 18-6.
❑ Use the **DIM** command to draw an object with dimensions similar to Figure 18-3.
❑ Save the drawing as EX18-21.

Chapter Test

Write your answers in the spaces provided.

1. Describe the function of dimension variables._____

   _____

   _____

   _____

2. What are the recommended standard units of measure on engineering drawings and related documents? _____

   _____

3. Name the units of measure commonly used in architectural and structural drafting, and show an example. _____

4. What is the recommended height for dimension numbers and notes on drawings?

   _____

5. Name the pull-down menu where the **Linear**, **Aligned**, and **Radius** dimensioning commands are found. _____

6. Name the two dimensioning commands that provide linear dimensions for angled surfaces. _____

   _____

7. Name the command used to dimension angles in degrees. _____

8. What are the two types of notes found on a drawing? _____

   _____

9. AutoCAD refers to chain dimensioning as _____.

10. AutoCAD refers to datum dimensioning as _____.

11. The command used to provide diameter dimensions for circles is _____.

12. The command used to provide radius dimensions for arcs is _____.

13. What does the M mean in the title of the standard ASME Y14.5M-1994?_____

   _____

   _____

14. Does a text style have to be loaded using the **STYLE** command before it can be accessed for use in dimension text?_____

   _____

15. How do you access the **DIMRADIUS** and **DIMDIAMETER** in a pull-down menu? __

   _____

   _____

16. How do you place a datum dimension from the origin of the previously drawn dimension? _____

   _____

   _____

17. How do you place a datum dimension from the origin of a dimension that was drawn during a previous drawing session? _____
_____
_____
_____
_____

18. Oblique extension lines are drawn using the _____ command and by accessing the _____ option.

19. Define annotation. _____
_____
_____

20. Identify how to access the leader command using the following methods:
Toolbar— _____
Pull-down menu— _____
At the Command: prompt— _____

21. Text placed using the **LEADER** command is a _____ text object.

22. Describe the purpose of the **Annotation Copy** option of the **LEADER** command.
_____
_____
_____

23. Name and briefly describe the five **Format** options of the **LEADER** command.
_____
_____
_____
_____
_____
_____

24. Which **LEADER** command option removes the last leader segment that you drew?
_____

25. Define arrowless dimensioning. _____
_____
_____

26. AutoCAD refers to arrowless dimensioning as _____ dimensioning.

27. Name the pull-down menu selection that allows you to draw arrowless dimensions.
_____

28. What is the importance of the User Coordinate System (UCS) when doing arrowless dimensioning? _____
_____
_____
_____

29. Identify the elements of this Unified screw thread note: 1/2-13 UNC-2B.

1/2— _____

13—_____

UNC— _____

2—_____

B— _____

30. Identify the elements of this metric screw thread: M 14 X 2.

M—_____

14—_____

2—_____

31. Name the dialog box that is used to control dimensioning variables._____
_____

32. Identify at least three ways to access the dialog box identified in Question 31.

_____

_____

_____

33. Define an AutoCAD dimension style._____

_____

_____

_____

34. If you change any of the standard dimensioning variables, AutoCAD stores the changes in another style named _____.

35. Provide a general description of dimension style family members. _____

_____

_____

_____

_____

_____

36. Identify the parent family member._____

_____

_____

37. Name the dialog box that is used to control the appearance of dimension lines, extension lines, arrowheads, center marks, and dimension scale. _____

_____

38. Name the dialog box that is used to control dimensioning variables that adjust the location of dimension lines, dimension text, arrowheads, and leader lines.

_____

39. Name the dialog box that is used to control the dimensioning variables that display the dimension text. _____

40. Name the **DIMLINEAR** option that opens the **Multiline Text Editor** for changing the dimension text. _____

41. Name the **DIMLINEAR** option that allows you to change dimension text at the prompt line._____

42. How do you quickly cycle through the **DIMLINEAR** command options at the keyboard without typing the option character and pressing [Enter]? _____
_____

43. When cycling through the **DIMLINEAR** options identified in question number 42, what is the purpose of the **DLI** option? _____
_____

44. What is the keyboard shortcut for the **DIMBASELINE** command? _____

45. Name at least four arrowhead types that are available in the **Geometry** dialog box for common use on architectural drawings._____
_____
_____
_____

46. Identify the **Format** dialog box option that allows you to control the dimension text location as you place the dimension._____

47. Name the option in the **Format** dialog box that provides vertical justification of text that is commonly used in architectural drafting._____

48. Name the option in the **Format** dialog box that provides vertical justification of text that is commonly used in mechanical drafting._____
_____

49. Define primary units._____
_____

50. Given the following dimension text examples, identify if the application is for inch decimal drawings, metric decimal drawings, or architectural drawings:
    12'-6"—_____
    0.5— _____
    .500— _____

Drawing Problems

Use the startup option of your choice or use one of your templates. Set limits, units, dimension variables, and other parameters as needed. Use the following general guidelines.

A. Draw the needed views to exact size. Mechanical drafting problems presented in 3D require you to select the proper multiviews. Architectural and other problems are drawn as given. Use dimension styles that match the type of drawing as discussed in this chapter. Use ROMANS font for mechanical drawings and CIBT font for architectural drawings.

B. Use grids, object snap options, and the **OSNAP** command to your best advantage.

C. Apply dimensions accurately using ASME or other related industry/architectural standards. Dimensions are in inches, or feet and inches unless otherwise specified.

D. Set dimension styles to suit the drawing.

E. Use your own judgment to establish and place missing dimensions, if any exist.

F. Set separate layers for views, dimensions, and other features.

G. Plot drawings with proper line weights.

H. Place general notes for mechanical drawings only 1/2″ from lower-left corner:

    3. UNLESS OTHERWISE SPECIFIED, ALL DIMENSIONS ARE IN INCHES *(or* MILLIMETERS *as applicable).*

    2. REMOVE ALL BURRS AND SHARP EDGES.

    1. INTERPRET DIMENSIONS AND TOLERANCES PER ASME Y14.5M-1994.

    NOTES:

I. Save each drawing as **P18**-*(problem number).*

 1.

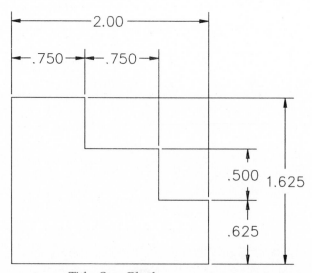

Title: Step Block

2.

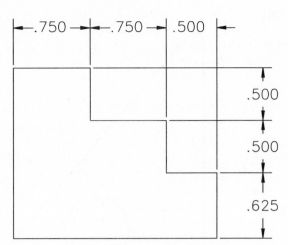

Title: Step Block

3.

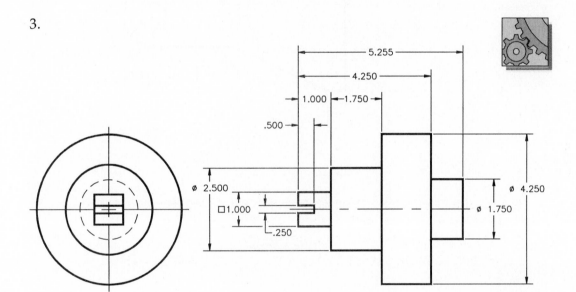

Title: Shaft
Material: SAE 1030

4.

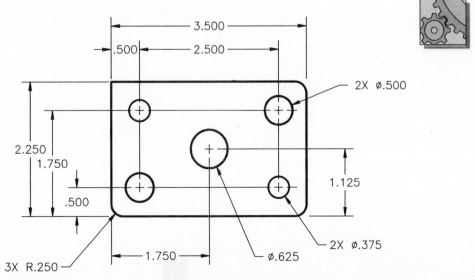

Title: Gasket

5.

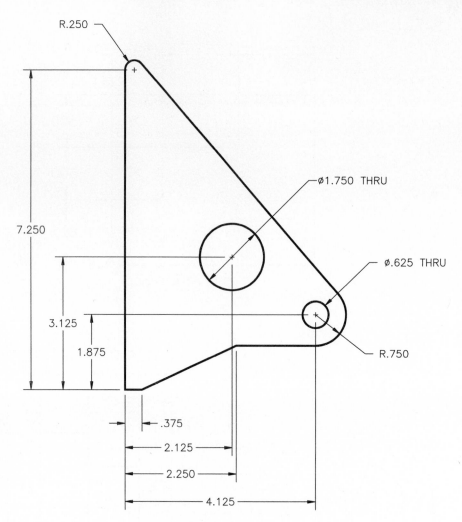

R.250

Ø1.750 THRU

Ø.625 THRU

R.750

7.250

3.125

1.875

.375

2.125

2.250

4.125

Title: Gasket

6.

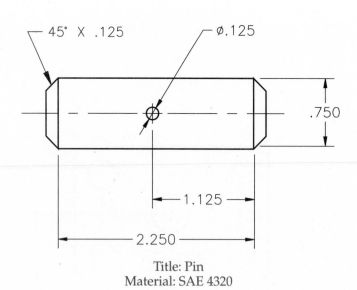

45° X .125

Ø.125

.750

1.125

2.250

Title: Pin
Material: SAE 4320

7.

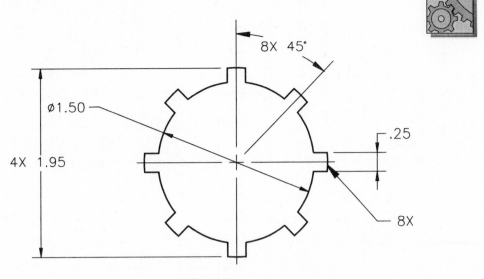

8X 45°

⌀1.50

4X 1.95

.25

8X

Title: Spline
Material: MS .125 THK

8.

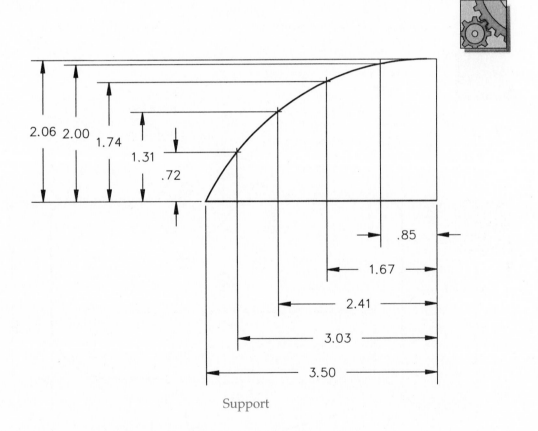

2.06 2.00 1.74 1.31 .72

.85

1.67

2.41

3.03

3.50

Support

9.

Draw this object.

A

Modify the dimensions as shown here.

B

Title: Shim

10.

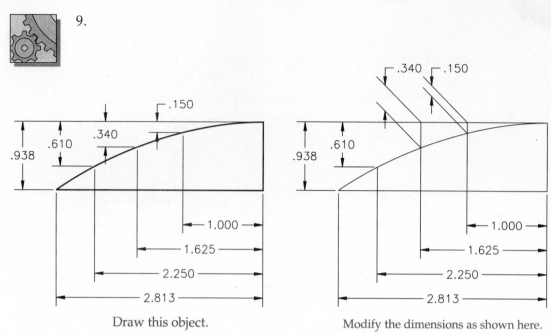

11.

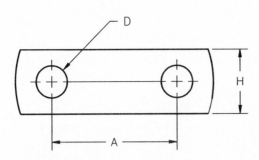

CHAIN NO.	A	D	H
SST1000	2.6	.44	1.125
SST1001	3.0	.48	1.525
SST1002	3.5	.95	2.125

Note:
Overall Length is 1.5xA
end radii are .9xA

Title: Chain Link
Material: Steel

12. Convert the given drawing to a drawing with the holes located using arrowless dimensioning based on the X and Y coordinates given in the table. Place a table above your title block with Hole (identification), Quantity, Description, and Depth (Z-axis).

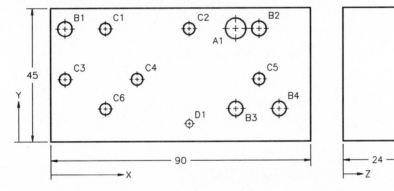

HOLE	QTY.	DESCRIP.	X	Y	Z
A1	1	⌀7	64	38	18
B1	1	⌀5	5	38	THRU
B2	1	⌀5	72	38	THRU
B3	1	⌀5	64	11	THRU
B4	1	⌀5	79	11	THRU
C1	1	⌀4	19	38	THRU
C2	1	⌀4	48	38	THRU
C3	1	⌀4	5	21	THRU
C4	1	⌀4	30	21	THRU
C5	1	⌀4	72	21	THRU
C6	1	⌀4	19	11	THRU
D1	1	⌀2.5	48	6	THRU

Title: Base
Material: Bronze

13.

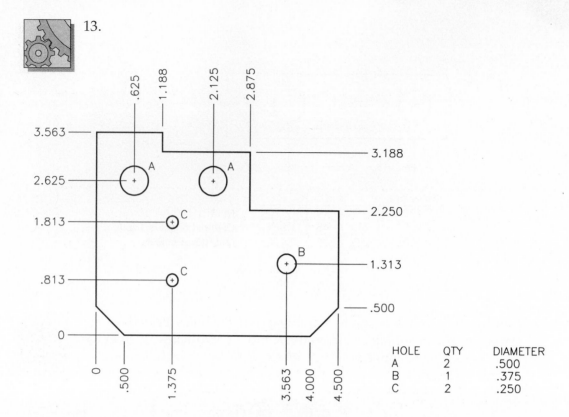

HOLE	QTY	DIAMETER
A	2	.500
B	1	.375
C	2	.250

Title: Chassis
Material: Aluminum .100 THK

14.

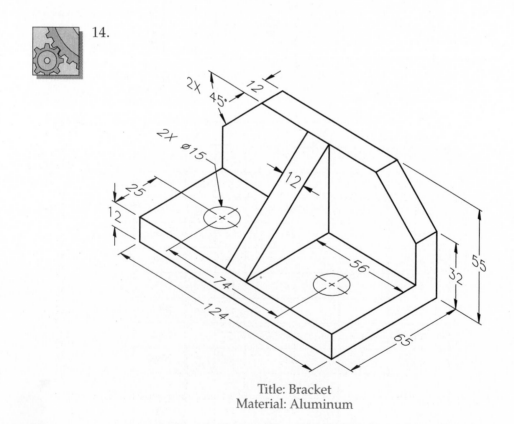

Title: Bracket
Material: Aluminum

15.

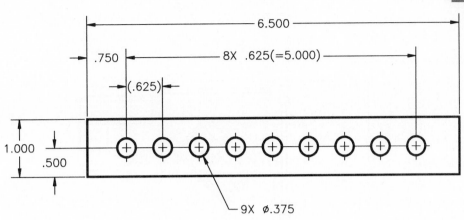

16.

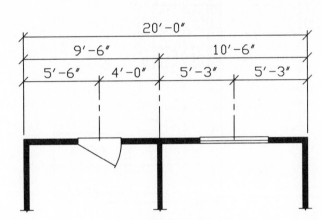

Door and Window

17.

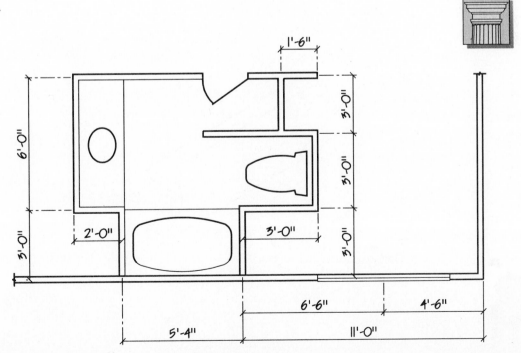

Title: Bathroom Area

18. The overall dimensions are given on the following kitchen drawing. Establish the rest of the dimensions using your own design.

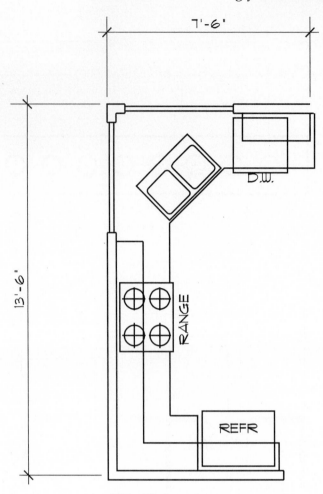

Title: Kitchen Area

19.

Title: Shim MS
Metric 10 THK

20. Half of the object is removed for clarity. The entire object should be drawn.

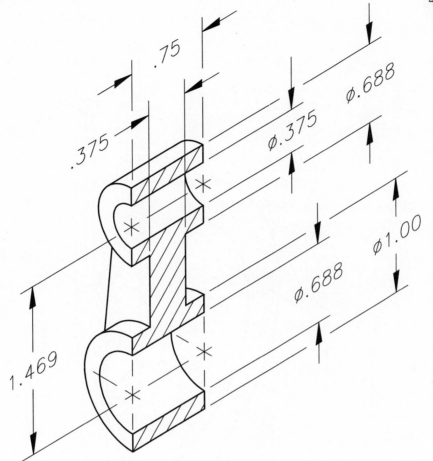

Title: Shaft Support
Material: Cast Iron (CI)

21. Half of the object is removed for clarity. The entire object should be drawn.

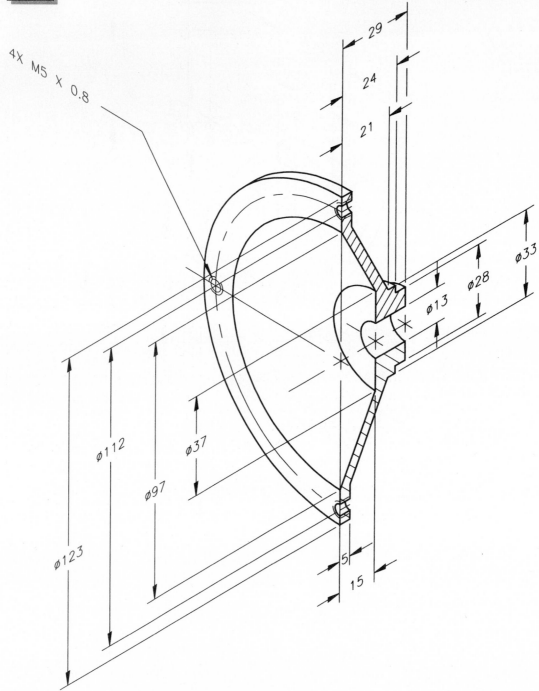

Title: Transmission Cover
Material: Cast Iron (CI)
Metric

22. Draw this floor plan. Size windows and doors to your own specifications.

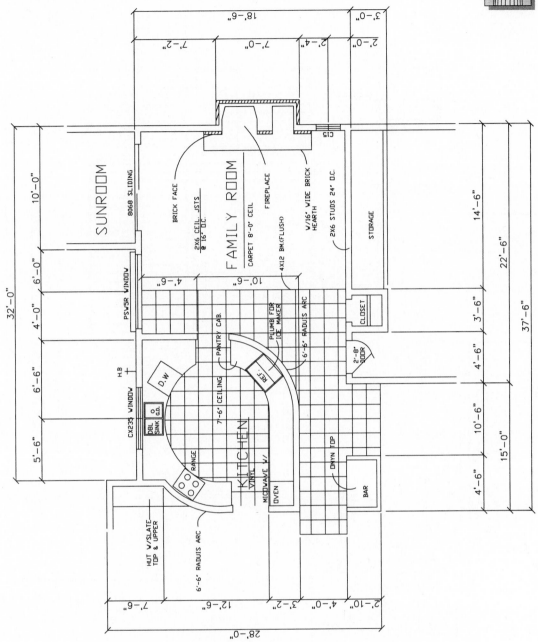

Title: Kitchen Floor Plan

23. Draw this floor plan. Size windows and doors to your own specifications.

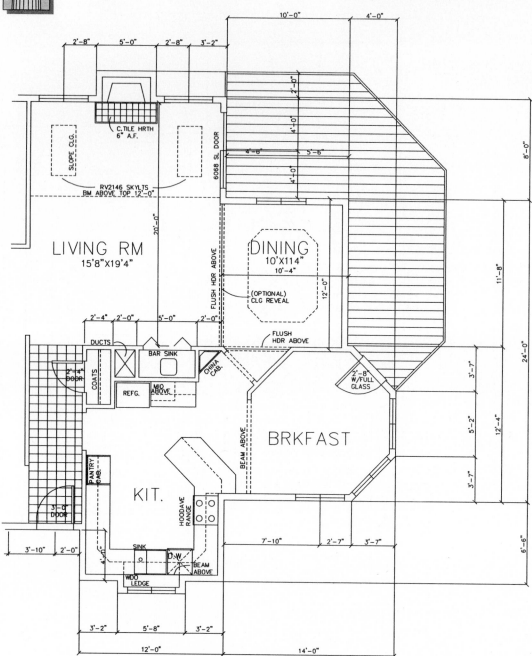

Title: Kitchen, Breakfast, Dining, Living Room

24.

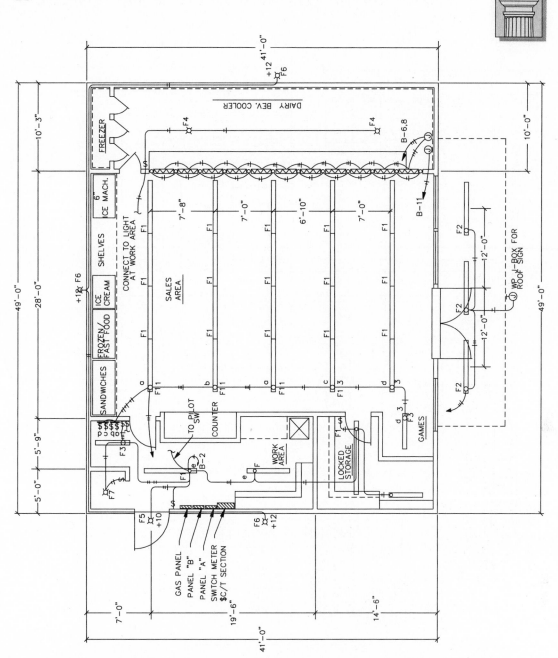

Title: Store Electrical Floor Plan

25.

HOLE LAYOUT			
KEY	SIZE	DEPTH	NO. REQD
A	⌀.250	THRU	6
B	⌀.125	THRU	4
C	⌀.375	THRU	4
D	R.125	THRU	2

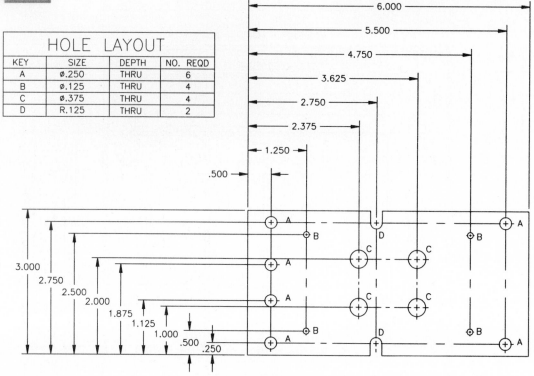

Title: Chassis Base (datum dimensioning)
Material: 12 gage Aluminum

26.

HOLE LAYOUT			
KEY	SIZE	DEPTH	NO. REQD
A	⌀.250	THRU	6
B	⌀.125	THRU	4
C	⌀.375	THRU	4
D	R.125	THRU	2

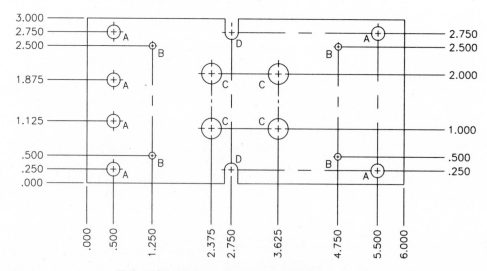

Title: Chassis Base (arrowless dimensioning)
Material: 12 gage Aluminum

27.

HOLE LAYOUT

KEY	X	Y	SIZE	TOL
A1	.500	2.750	⌀.250	±.002
A2	.500	1.875	⌀.250	±.002
A3	.500	1.125	⌀.250	±.002
A4	.500	.250	⌀.250	±.002
A5	5.500	2.750	⌀.250	±.002
A6	5.500	.250	⌀.250	±.002
B1	1.250	2.500	⌀.125	±.001
B2	1.250	.500	⌀.125	±.001
B3	4.750	2.500	⌀.125	±.001
B4	4.750	.500	⌀.125	±.001
C1	2.375	2.000	⌀.375	±.005
C2	2.375	1.000	⌀.375	±.005
C3	3.626	2.000	⌀.375	±.005
C4	3.625	1.000	⌀.375	±.005
D1	2.750	.375	R.125	±.002
D2	2.750	2.625	R.125	±.002

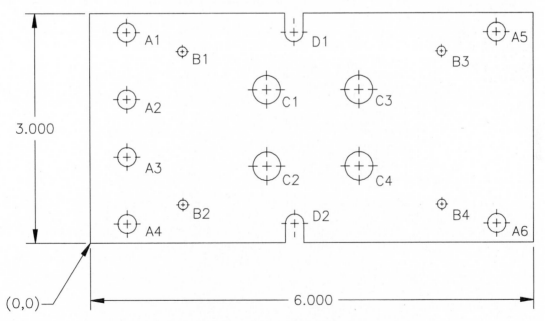

Title: Chassis Base (arrowless tabular dimensioning)
Material: 12 gage Aluminum

28.

HOLE LEGEND

KEY	DIAMETER	DEPTH
A	SEE VIEW A	THRU
B	.500	THRU
C	.594	THRU
D	1.625	THRU
E	.813	THRU
F	SEE VIEW B	THRU
G	.141	THRU

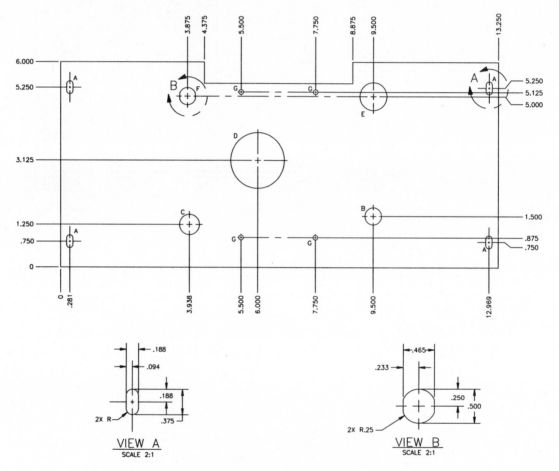

VIEW A
SCALE 2:1

VIEW B
SCALE 2:1

Title: Mounting Bracket
Material: 12 gage steel

29.

HOLE LAYOUT

KEY	DIAMETER	DEPTH
A	.218	THRU
B	.250	THRU
C	.281	THRU
D	.625	THRU
E	.313	THRU

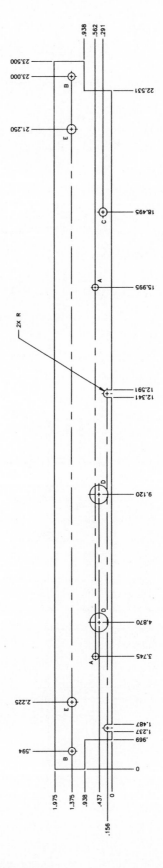

Title: Chassis Divider
Material: 16 gage aluminum

30.

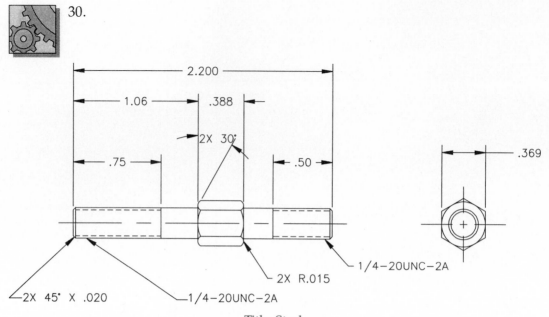

Title: Stud
Material: Stainless Steel

31.

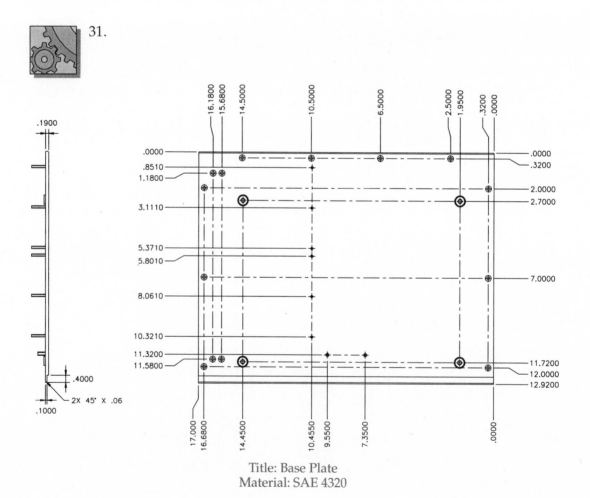

Title: Base Plate
Material: SAE 4320

32.

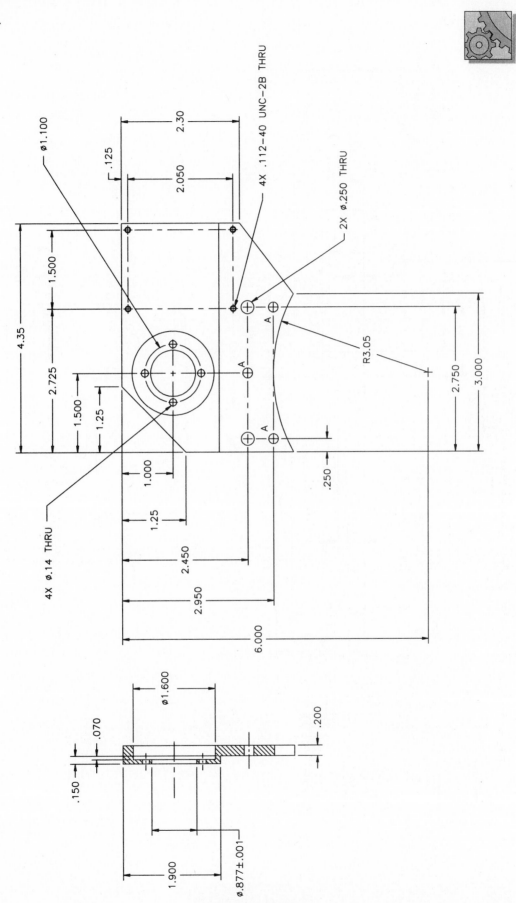

Title: Bracket
Material: SAE 1040

33.

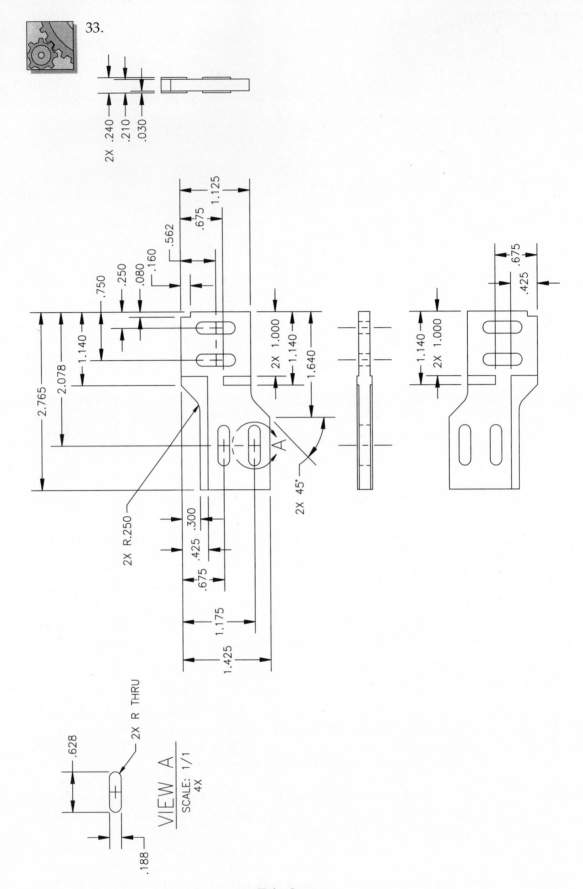

Title: Support
Material: Aluminum

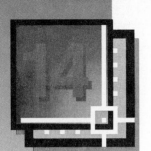

Chapter 19

Editing Dimensions

Learning Objectives

After completing this chapter, you will be able to:
- Make changes to existing dimensions.
- Edit associative dimensions.

The tools used to edit dimensions vary from simple erasing techniques to object editing commands. Often, the object is edited and the dimensions are automatically updated to reflect the changes. This chapter provides you with a variety of useful techniques for editing dimensions.

Erasing Dimensions

In Chapter 4 you were introduced to the **ERASE** command. There are many selection options: **Last**, **Previous**, **Window**, **Crossing**, **WPolygon**, **CPolygon**, and **Fence**.

Erasing features such as large groups of dimensions often becomes difficult. The objects may be very close to other parts of the drawing. It is time-consuming to erase each object individually. When this situation occurs, the **Crossing**, **CPolygon**, and **Fence** selection options are useful. Figure 19-1 shows a comparison of using **ERASE Window** and **ERASE Crossing** on a group of dimensions. For a review of these techniques, refer to Chapter 4.

Editing Dimension Text Position

In addition to the dimensioning variables that control the dimension text placement, the **DIMTEDIT** command controls the placement and orientation of an existing associative dimension. Remember, an associative dimension is a dimension drawn with **DIMASO** on, and all elements of the dimension act as one object.

Good dimensioning practice requires that adjacent dimension numbers be staggered rather than stacked. See Figure 19-2. The **DIMJUST** system variable can be used to stagger dimensions if it is set before the dimension is placed. Use the **DIMTEDIT** command to stagger the text after a dimension has been placed.

Access this command by entering DIMTEDIT at the Command: prompt, by picking the **Dimension Text Edit** button on the **Dimension** toolbar, by picking an option from the **Align Text** cascading menu in the **Dimension** pull-down menu, or by entering TEDIT at the Dim: prompt. The **DIMTEDIT** command sequence is as follows:

Command: **DIMTEDIT**↵
Select dimension: *(pick the dimension to be altered)*

DIMTEDIT

Dimension
↳ Align Text

Dimension
toolbar

Dimension Text Edit

Figure 19-1.
Using the **Window**
and **Crossing**
options of the
ERASE command.

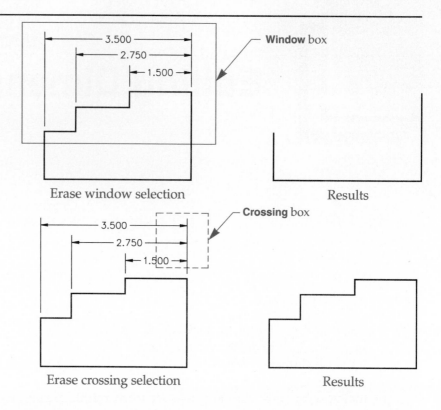

Erase window selection

Results

Erase crossing selection

Results

Figure 19-2.
Using the **DIMTEDIT**
command to stagger
dimensions.

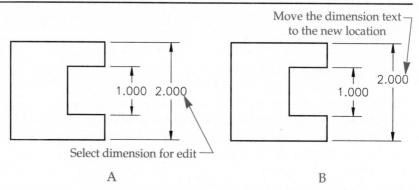

A

B

If **DIMASO** was on when the dimension was created, the text of the selected dimension automatically drags with the screen cursor. This allows you to see where to place the text at the next prompt:

Enter text location (Left/Right/Home/Angle): *(pick the desired text location)*

AutoCAD automatically moves the text and reestablishes the break in the dimension line. See Figure 19-2B.

The **DIMTEDIT** command also allows you to automatically move the dimension text to the left or right, place it at an angle, or move it back to the original position. The following options are used:

- **Left (L).** Moves horizontal text to the left and vertical text down.
- **Right (R).** Moves horizontal text to the right and vertical text up.
- **Home (H).** Moves text that had been changed back to its original position.
- **Angle (A).** Allows you to place dimension text at an angle. This works similar to the **TROTATE** command, which is mentioned later in this chapter. The text rotates around its middle point. The angle can be entered numerically or by selecting two points:

Enter text location (Left/Right/Home/Angle): **A.⏎**
Text angle: **45.⏎**

AutoCAD and its Applications—Basics

Figure 19-3 shows the effects of the **DIMTEDIT** options.

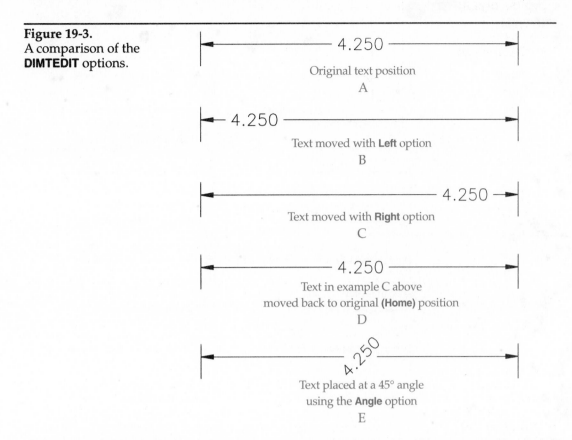

Figure 19-3.
A comparison of the
DIMTEDIT options.

Original text position
A

Text moved with **Left** option
B

Text moved with **Right** option
C

Text in example C above
moved back to original **(Home)** position
D

Text placed at a 45° angle
using the **Angle** option
E

Using the DIMEDIT command

The **DIMEDIT** command can be used to change the text or extension lines of an existing dimension. Access the **DIMEDIT** command by picking the **Dimension Edit** button in the **Dimension** toolbar or entering DED or DIMEDIT at the Command: prompt:

DIMEDIT
DED

Dimension
toolbar

Dimension Edit

> Command: **DED** *or* **DIMEDIT**↵
> Dimension Edit (Home/New/Rotate/Oblique) ⟨Home⟩:

This command has four options that can be used to edit individual or multiple dimensions. The options are shown in Figure 19-4 and described as follows:

- **Home (H).** This default option is identical to the **Home** option of the **DIMTEDIT** command.
- **New (N).** This option allows specification of new dimension text. After selecting this option, the **Multiline Text Editor** is displayed. Enter the new text and select the **OK** button. The Select objects: prompt then appears, and the selected dimensions assume the new text.
- **Rotate.** This option rotates dimension text similar to the **Angle** option of the **DIMTEDIT** command.
- **Oblique.** Changes the extension line angle. This has the same effect as using the **OBLIQUE** command at the Dim: prompt.

> Dimension Edit (Home/New/Rotate/Oblique) ⟨Home⟩: **O**↵
> Select objects: *(select the dimension or dimensions)*
> Select objects: ↵
> Enter obliquing angle (press ENTER for none): *(press [Enter] for no*
> *obliquing angle or type an angle such as* 45)

The oblique option can also be accessed directly by picking **Oblique** from the **Dimension** pull-down menu.

Figure 19-4.
Using the **DIMEDIT**
command.

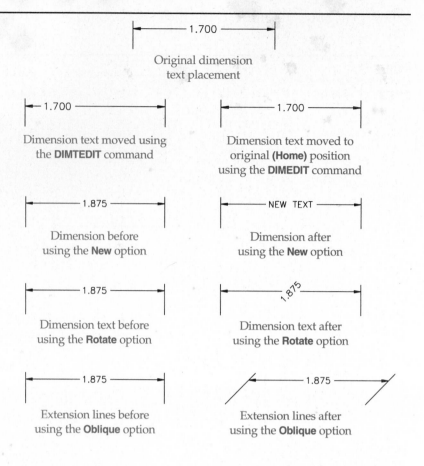

Original dimension
text placement

Dimension text moved using
the **DIMTEDIT** command

Dimension text moved to
original (**Home**) position
using the **DIMEDIT** command

Dimension before
using the **New** option

Dimension after
using the **New** option

Dimension text before
using the **Rotate** option

Dimension text after
using the **Rotate** option

Extension lines before
using the **Oblique** option

Extension lines after
using the **Oblique** option

NOTE

Dimension text can also be rotated using the **TROTATE** command. This command can only be accessed by entering TR or TROTATE at the Dim: prompt. Then enter the new text angle and select the dimension to be changed.

EXERCISE 19-1

❑ Begin a new drawing or use one of your templates.
❑ Using Figure 19-3 as an example, draw an original dimension similar to A. Copy the original dimension to four places represented by B, C, D, and E. Use the **DIMTEDIT** command to perform the following:
  ❑ Use the **Left** option to edit the dimension at B.
  ❑ Use the **Right** option to edit the dimension at C.
  ❑ Use the **Left** option to edit the dimension at D. Then use the **Home** option to move the text back to the original position.
❑ Use the **Angle** option to edit the dimension at E and place the text at a 45° angle.
❑ Using Figure 19-4 as an example, draw the original dimensions located on the left.
  ❑ Copy the original dimensions to the positions at the right.
  ❑ Perform the **DIMTEDIT** function on the middle top dimension.
  ❑ Use the **DIMEDIT** options on the rest of the dimensions as indicated in the caption for each example.
❑ Save the drawing as EX19-1.

AutoCAD and its Applications—Basics

Using the UPDATE Command

Dimension
➡ Update

Dimension
toolbar

Dimension Update

The **UPDATE** command changes existing dimensions to reflect the current settings for dimensioning variables. The only dimensions not affected by **UPDATE** are those drawn using the **DIMBASELINE** or **DIMCONTINUE** commands. For example, suppose you change the **DIMDLI** variable, which changes the dimension string spacing. All new dimensions drawn with the **DIMBASELINE** or **DIMCONTINUE** commands reflect the revised dimension line spacing. However, the **UPDATE** command would not alter the existing dimension line spacing. Although, if you use the **DIMASZ** variable to change the arrowhead size, then any dimensions picked with the **UPDATE** command are automatically changed to reflect the new arrowhead size.

Access this command by picking the **Dimension Update** button on the **Dimension** toolbar, or by picking **Update** in the **Dimension** pull-down menu. While in the **DIM** command, type UP or UPDATE at the Dim: prompt.

Using the DIMOVERRIDE Command

The **DIMOVERRIDE** command overrides dimensioning variables associated with an individual dimension or a group of dimensions. This command is accessed by entering either DOV or DIMOVERRIDE at the Command: prompt.

This command does not affect the current dimension variable settings on the rest of the drawing. For example, if you wanted to change the extension line offset (**DIMEXO**) from .0625 to 0, use the following procedure (see Figure 19-5):

Command: **DOV** *or* **DIMOVERRIDE**↵
Dimension variable to override (or Clear to remove overrides): **DIMEXO**↵
Current value ⟨0.0625⟩ New value: **0**↵
Dimension variable to override: ↵
Select objects: *(select the dimension or dimensions to override)*
Select objects: ↵
Command:

Figure 19-5.
Using the **DIMOVERRIDE** command. Notice that the offset is removed in B.

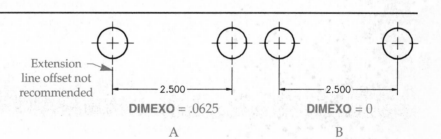

Extension line offset not recommended

DIMEXO = .0625   DIMEXO = 0

A   B

EXERCISE 19-2

❑ With **DIMEXO** set to .0625, draw and dimension the objects in Figure 19-5A.
❑ Use the **DIMOVERRIDE** command to change **DIMEXO** to 0 as in Figure 19-5B.
❑ Save the drawing as EX19-2.

Editing Associative Dimensioned Objects

Associative dimensioning permits dimensions to change as an object is edited. This means that when a dimension object is edited, the dimension value automatically changes to match the edit. The automatic update is only applied when you accept the default value or keep the chevrons (⟨ ⟩) as part of the text during the original dimension placement. This provides you with an important advantage when editing an AutoCAD drawing. Any changes to the object are automatically transferred to the dimensions.

The dimensioning variable that controls associative dimensioning is **DIMASO** (associative). **DIMASO** is on by default. With the **DIMASO** variable turned on, stretching, trimming, or extending an object also changes the dimensions associated with the object. With the **DIMASO** variable turned off, elements of the dimension are considered separately. Thus, you can edit the dimension line, arrowheads, extension lines, and dimension numbers as individual items. With **DIMASO** turned on, these items act together as one entity. You can then erase the entire dimension by picking any part of the dimension.

The **DIMALIGNED**, **DIMANGULAR**, **DIMDIAMETER**, **DIMLINEAR**, **DIMORDINATE**, and **DIMRADIUS** commands are influenced by associative dimensioning. The marks placed by the **DIMCENTER** command remain as unique items and are not affected.

Another variable that works with associative dimensioning is **DIMSHO**. If **DIMASO** and **DIMSHO** are both on, the dimension for an object being stretched (for example) shows the new dimension text while it is being stretched. Both **DIMASO** and **DIMSHO** are on by default.

When a drawing is changed using **GRIPS**, **MIRROR**, **ROTATE**, and **SCALE** commands, the dimensions are also changed when **DIMASO** is on. **Linear** and **Angular** dimensioning options are altered by the **STRETCH** command. Only linear dimensions are affected by the **EXTEND** and **TRIM** commands. Refer to Chapters 11 and 12 of this text if you need to review the editing commands.

Stretching an object and its dimensions

When stretching an object, select the object and dimension using the crossing-window or crossing-polygon option. The **STRETCH** command produces a pick box and you must either specify the selection option or create an implied window. The command sequence shown in Figure 19-6 is as follows:

Command: **S** *or* **STRETCH**↵
Select objects to be stretched by crossing-window or crossing-polygon...
Select objects: **C**↵
First corner: *(pick the first corner of the crossing box)*
Other corner: *(pick the second crossing box corner)*
Select objects: ↵
Base point or displacement: *(pick the base point on the object to be stretched)*
Second point of displacement: *(pick the new point to where the object is to be stretched and observe the object being dragged into position)*
Command:

EXERCISE 19-3

❑ Draw objects similar to the original objects in Figure 19-6 and then use the **STRETCH** command to edit the objects similar to the revised objects in Figure 19-6.
❑ Save the drawing as EX19-3.

Figure 19-6.
When you stretch an object and an associative dimension, the dimension text is
automatically changed to reflect the new value.

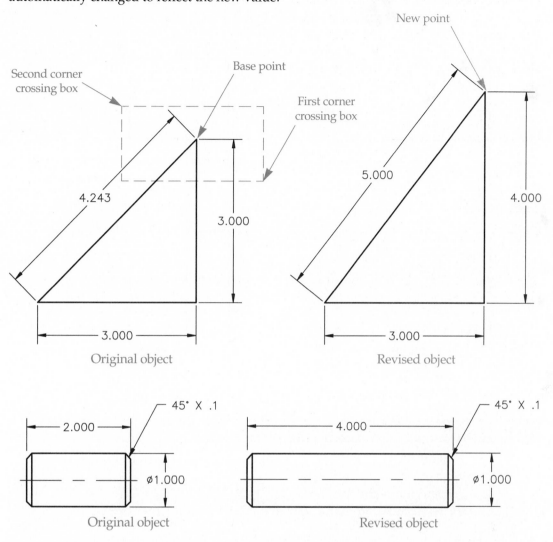

Moving dimension text

ASME standards advise that adjacent dimensions be staggered. However,
AutoCAD centers all dimension text unless **DIMUPT** is on. Using grips is the fastest
way to adjust text position, requiring only quick picks and no command entry.
Simply pick the dimension, pick the dimension text grip, and then drag it to the new
location. See Figure 19-7A. The **STRETCH** command can also be used to move
dimension text within the dimension line. See Figure 19-7B.

The **DIMTEDIT** and **DIMEDIT** commands (discussed earlier in this chapter) can also
be used to move dimension text.

PROFESSIONAL TIP The **DIMUPT** variable allows you to position the text as
desired during the dimensioning process. The default for this
variable is off, but you can turn it on if you want this
flexibility. **DIMUPT** is controlled by the **User Defined** check
box in the **Format** dialog box. This dialog box and the
DIMUPT variable were explained in Chapter 18.

Figure 19-7.
A—Using grips to stretch text to a different location. B—Using the **STRETCH** command to stretch text to a different location

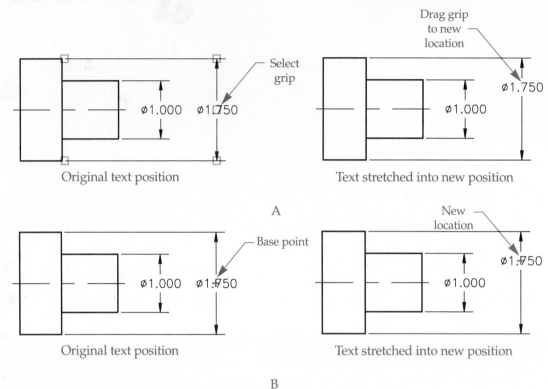

A

B

Extending dimensions

EXTEND
EX

Modify
↳ Extend

Modify
toolbar

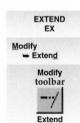

Extend

With the **EXTEND** command, it is possible to extend an object and related dimensions to meet another object. The command sequence is as follows:

```
Command: EX or EXTEND↵
Select boundary edges (Projmode = UCS, Edgemode = No extend)
Select objects: (pick the boundary edge)
Select objects: ↵
```

The boundary edge is the line that the desired object will extend to. See Figure 19-8A. Then pick the dimension and lines to extend.

```
⟨Select object to extend⟩/Project/Edge/Undo: (pick the dimension to be extended)
⟨Select object to extend⟩/Project/Edge/Undo: ↵
Command:
```

Notice in Figure 19-8C that one line of the original object remains. This line can be removed using the **ERASE** command.

Figure 19-8.
When you extend an associative dimension, the dimension text is automatically updated to reflect the new value.

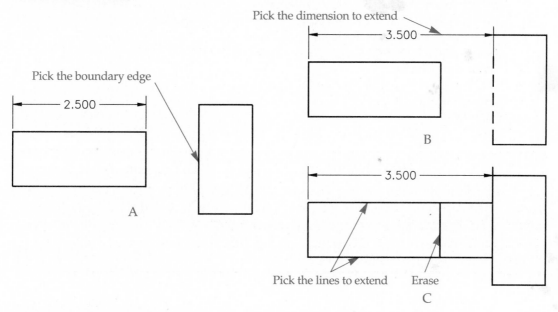

Trimming dimensions

The **TRIM** command is the opposite of the **EXTEND** command. See Figure 19-9. First, draw a line on the original object to trim to. Then, follow this **TRIM** command sequence:

Command: **TR** *or* **TRIM**↵
Select cutting edges (Projmode = UCS, Edgemode = No extend)
Select objects: *(pick cutting edges that lines and dimensions will be shortened to)*
Select objects: ↵

TRIM
TR

Modify
➥ **Trim**

Modify toolbar

Trim

Figure 19-9.
When you trim an associative dimension, the dimension text is automatically updated to reflect the new value.

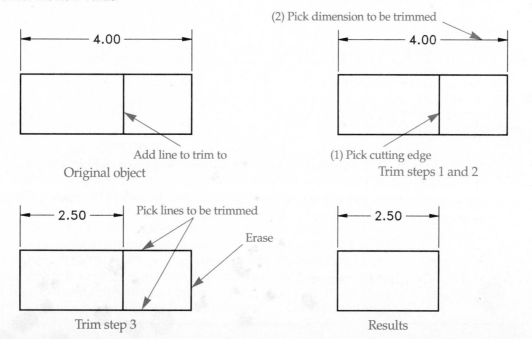

The location where you pick the dimension establishes the trim position for the dimension.

⟨Select object to extend⟩/Project/Edge/Undo: *(pick the dimension to be trimmed)*
⟨Select object to extend⟩/Project/Edge/Undo: *(pick the line to be trimmed)*
⟨Select object to extend⟩/Project/Edge/Undo: *(pick the line to be trimmed)*
⟨Select object to extend⟩/Project/Edge/Undo: ↵
Command: **ERASE**↵
Select objects: *(select the line on the right)*
Select objects: ↵
Command:

EXERCISE 19-5

❏ Draw objects similar to the originals at A in Figure 19-8.
❏ Use the **EXTEND** command to edit the objects similar to B and C in Figure 19-8.
❏ Draw an object similar to the original object in Figure 19-9.
❏ Use the **TRIM** command to edit the object similar the results in Figure 19-9.
❏ Save the drawing as EX19-5.

Making Changes to Dimensions

The component parts of a dimension can be edited after using the **EXPLODE** command. Dimensions also can be changed individually or in groups using the **UPDATE**, **HOMETEXT**, and **NEWTEXT** commands.

Exploding an associative dimension

An associative dimension is treated as one entity even though it consists of extension lines, a dimension line, arrowheads, and numbers. At times, it is necessary to work with the individual parts so you can select parts to edit. For example, you can erase the text without erasing the dimension line, arrowheads, or extension lines. To do this, you must break the dimension into its individual parts with the **EXPLODE** command. Be careful when exploding dimensions because they may lose their layer assignment. The command sequence is as follows:

EXPLODE
EX

Modify
➥ Explode

Modify
toolbar

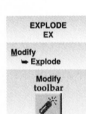

Explode

Command: **EX** *or* **EXPLODE**↵
Select objects: *(pick the dimension to be exploded)*
Select objects: ↵
Command:

PROFESSIONAL TIP

Exercise caution when using the **EXPLODE** command on dimensions: they loose their layer and color definitions. Once exploded, the dimension is placed on layer 0. This is normally not acceptable. You may want to use the **CHPROP** command to put the exploded dimension elements back to the dimensioning layer and color, and set them to Bylayer. An easier way to remove the associative dimension feature from a dimension is to use the **DIMOVERRIDE** command or the **UPDATE** option discussed next. If you know in advance that you need to work with the individual elements of the dimensions, then turn the **DIMASO** variable off before starting the drawing.

AutoCAD and its Applications—Basics

Changing variables or text of existing dimensions at the Dim: prompt

You can change the text or variables of individual dimensions or all dimensions on the drawing. The **UPDATE**, **HOMETEXT**, and **NEWTEXT** commands can be used to perform these tasks when you are inside the **DIM** command. The **HOMETEXT** and **NEWTEXT** commands work just like the **DIMEDIT** command.

The **UPDATE** command updates existing dimensions with the current dimensioning variables, units, and text style. For example, the **DIMASZ** (dimension arrowhead size) default value is .18. Suppose that after completing a drawing you learn the company standard requires .25 arrowheads. This is easy to fix. Select **DIMASZ** and enter the new value as .25. At the Dim: prompt, enter UP or UPDATE. Then select the items to be changed by picking them individually or windowing. It is common to change the entire drawing using the window selection process. The steps are as follows:

Command: **DIM**↵
Dim: **UP** *or* **UPDATE**↵
Select objects: *(pick individual dimensions, a group of dimensions, or window the entire drawing)*

The selected objects are now automatically updated with the new current variables. See Figure 19-10.

Figure 19-10. The **UPDATE** command can be used to change all objects (such as arrowheads) on a drawing to a new value, once the new setting is entered.

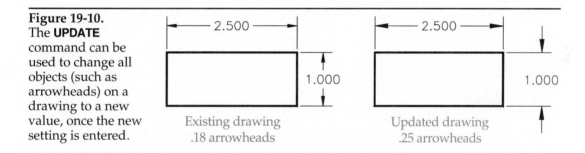

Existing drawing .18 arrowheads

Updated drawing .25 arrowheads

The **HOMETEXT** command changes the position of dimension text to its original location. For example, suppose the **STRETCH** or **TEDIT** command is used to move a dimension number to a new location. The **HOMETEXT** command moves the number back to the center. See Figure 19-11.

Command: **DIM**↵
Dim: **HOM** *or* **HOMETEXT**↵
Select objects: *(pick the dimension to be changed)*
Select objects: ↵
Dim:

Figure 19-11. The **HOMETEXT** command can be used to return a dimension to the center.

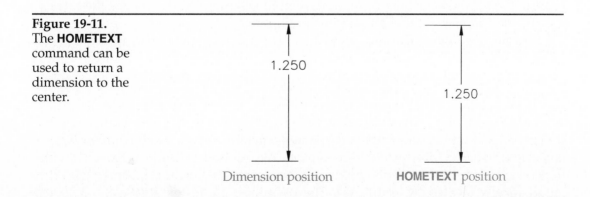

Dimension position

HOMETEXT position

The **NEWTEXT** command can be used to add a prefix or suffix or edit the text format of existing dimensions. Suppose you find that a diameter symbol was left off a linear dimension. Issue the **NEWTEXT** command to change the dimension text format. See Figure 19-12.

Command: **DIM**⏎
Dim: **N** *or* **NEWTEXT**⏎
Dimension text ⟨0.0000⟩: **%%C ⟨⟩**
Select objects: *(pick the dimension to be edited)*
Select objects: *(press* [Enter] *to close the selection set)*
Dim:

Notice the chevrons entered after the %%C code. This allows you to add the diameter symbol and keep the existing dimension.

Figure 19-12.
The **NEWTEXT** command can be used to change the value, add a prefix, or add a suffix to an existing dimension.

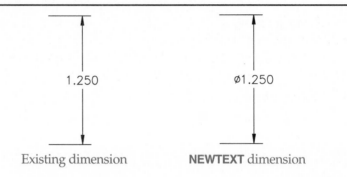

Existing dimension   **NEWTEXT** dimension

PROFESSIONAL TIP

Never use the **NEWTEXT** command to type in a different dimensional value than appears in the brackets. Doing so destroys the associativity between the dimension and the associated feature. If the dimensioned object is stretched, trimmed, or extended, the dimension *will not* update. If a dimension needs to change, revise the drawing accordingly. Only use **NEWTEXT** to change the existing dimension text format or add a prefix or suffix to a dimension.

EXERCISE 19-6

❑ Draw the object on the left in Figure 19-10.
❑ Update the arrowheads to .25 as shown on the right in Figure 19-10.
❑ Draw a dimension similar to the left example in Figure 19-11, and then move the dimension text back home as shown at the right.
❑ Use the dimension from the previous item in this exercise and change the text to new text similar to the right example in Figure 19-12.
❑ Save the drawing as EX19-6.

Dimension Definition Points

When you draw an associative dimension, the points used to specify the dimension and the middle point of the dimension text are called *definition points*, or *defpoints*. When a dimension is redefined, the revised position is based on the definition points. The definition points are located on the Defpoints layer. This layer is automatically created by AutoCAD. The definition points are displayed with the dimension.

Normally, the Defpoints layer does not plot. The definition points are plotted only if the Defpoints layer is renamed. The definition points are displayed when the dimensioning layer is on, even if the Defpoints layer is off.

If you select an object for editing and wish to include the dimensions in the edit, then you must include the definition points of the dimension in the selection set. If you need to snap to a definition point only, use the **Node** object snap.

Paper Space Dimensioning

Be cautious when placing associative dimensions on a drawing created in model space when you are currently in the paper space mode. These dimensions remain unchanged when you use editing commands like **STRETCH**, **TRIM**, or **EXTEND**, or display commands such as **ZOOM** or **PAN** in a model space viewport. To make sure that AutoCAD calculates a scale factor that is compatible between model and paper space, check the **Scale to Paperspace** check box in the **Geometry** dialog box accessed through the **Dimension Styles** dialog box. This dialog box is covered in Chapter 18 of this text.

When you draw dimensions in paper space that describe something from your model space drawing, first set the **Viewport** option in the **DIMLFAC** variable while in paper space like this:

> Command: **DIM**↵
> Dim: **LFAC**↵
> Current value ⟨1.000⟩ New value (Viewport): **V**↵
> Select viewport to set scale: *(pick the desired viewport)*

When using the **Viewport** option, AutoCAD automatically calculates the scaling of model space to paper space with the current zoom factor and assigns this value to **DIMLFAC** as a negative number. This does not work when dimensioning with the **ORDINATE** command.

PROFESSIONAL TIP

Dimensions should normally be created in model space. Use caution when dimensioning in paper space. Linear dimensions of model space objects can be created in paper space, but radius and diameter dimensions of model space objects cannot be created in paper space. This means that some of your dimensions are in model space and others in paper space. This situation would require a lot of dimension variable juggling and space swapping. However, there are valid reasons to place notes in paper space when they are part of the drawing format.

Chapter Test

Write your answers in the spaces provided.

1. Name at least three selection options that can be used to easily erase a group of dimensions surrounding an object without erasing any part of the objects.

   _____

   _____

   _____

2. Define *associative dimension*. _____

_____

_____

3. This command allows you to control the placement and orientation of an existing associative dimension._____

4. Identify where and how to access the command in Question 3, given the following general locations:

   Toolbar: _____

   Command: prompt: _____

5. Name the command to use if you want to change the text or extension lines of an existing dimension. _____

6. Identify where and how to access the command in Question 5, given the following general locations:

   Toolbar: _____

   Keyboard shortcut at the Command: prompt:_____

7. What happens when you use the **New** option of the **DIMEDIT** command?

_____

_____

_____

8. Name the **DIMEDIT** option that is used to change extension lines to an angle of your choice. _____

9. What is the purpose of the **UPDATE** command? _____

_____

_____

10. Identify where and how to access the **UPDATE** command, given the following general locations:

    Toolbar: _____

    Pull-down menu: _____

    Command: prompt: _____

11. What is the purpose of the **DIMOVERRIDE** command?_____

_____

_____

12. Give the keyboard shortcut for the **DIMOVERRIDE** command. _____

13. Identify two selection options that can be used when selecting an object and its associated dimension for stretching._____

_____

_____

14. Why is it important to have associative dimensions for editing objects? _____

_____

_____

15. Name four commands that can be used to move dimension text within the dimension line. _____

_____

16. Name the command that can be used to lengthen an object and its dimension to meet another object. _____

17. Name the command that can be used to trim an object and its dimension to meet another object. _____

18. What are definition points? _____

_____

_____

19. On which layer are definition points automatically located by AutoCAD? _____

_____

20. Should dimensions normally be created in paper space or model space? _____

_____

Drawing Problems

1. Open P18-1 and edit as follows:
   A. Stretch the total length to 2.250 and stretch the total height to 1.750.
   B. Save the drawing as P19-1.

2. Open P18-2 and edit as follows:
   A. Add an overall height and length dimension.
   B. Edit the overall dimensions that you just placed by using the **DIMEDIT New** option to place parenthesis around the dimension text. This makes the dimension comply with the ASME standard as reference dimensions.
   C. Save the drawing as P19-2.

3. Open P18-3 and edit as follows:
   A. Erase the left side view.
   B. Stretch the vertical dimensions to provide more space between dimension lines. Be sure the space you create is the same between all vertical dimensions.
   C. Stagger the existing vertical dimension numerals if they are not staggered as shown in the original problem.
   D. Erase the 1.750 horizontal dimension and then stretch the 5.255 and 4.250 dimensions to make room for a new datum dimension from the baseline to where the 1.750 dimension was located. This should result in a new baseline dimension that equals 2.750. Be sure all horizontal dimension lines are equally spaced.
   E. Save the drawing as P19-3.

4. Open P18-6 and edit as follows:
   A. Use the existing drawing as the model and make four copies.
   B. Leave the original drawing as it is, and edit the other four pins in the following manner, keeping the Ø.125 hole exactly in the center of each pin.

C. Make one pin with a total length of 1.500.

D. Create the next pin with a total length of 2.000.

E. Edit the third pin with a length of 2.500.

F. Change the last pin to a length of 3.000.

G. Organize the pins on your drawing in a vertical row ranging in length from the smallest to the largest. You may need to change the drawing limits.

H. Save the drawing as P19-4.

5. Open P18-15 and edit as follows:

A. Stretch the total length from 6.500 to 7.750.

B. Add two more holes that continue the equally spaced pattern of .625 apart.

C. Change the 8X .625(=5.00) dimension to read 10X .625(=6.250).

D. Save the drawing as P19-5.

6. Open P18-17 and edit as follows:

A. Make the Bathroom 8'-0" wide by stretching the walls and vanity that are currently 6'-0" wide. Do this without increasing the size of the water closet compartment. Provide two equally spaced oval sinks where there is currently one.

B. Save the drawing as P19-6.

7. Open P18-18 and edit as follows:

A. Make the Kitchen 15'-0" deep where it is currently 13'-6".

B. Stretch the 7'-6" dimension (counter and wall) to 9'-0" and make the wall and cabinet at the refrigerator the same dimension.

C. Save the drawing as P19-7.

8. Open P18-22 and edit as follows:

A. Move the right fireplace wall at the Family Room and Sunroom so the width of the sunroom is 14'-0'.

B. Remove the Bar in the lower left corner of the floor plan.

C. Widen the Closet at the lower center of the plan from 3'-6' to 6'-0' to the left without changing the 4'-6' dimension at the adjacent door.

D. Add floor tile where the Bar was removed and edit the floor tile around the expanded Closet and doorway area.

E. Save the drawing as P19-8.

9. Open P18-24 and edit as follows:

A. Make the building 52'-0' long by adding the additional square footage to the Locked Storage and Work Area.

B. Make the building 44'-0' deep by adding the square footage equally to each side of the structure.

C. Save the drawing as P19-9.

10. Open P18-25 and edit as follows:

A. Lengthen the part .250 on each side for a new overall dimension of 6.500.

B. Change the width of the part from 3.000 to 3.500 by widening an equal amount on each side.

C. Save the drawing as P19-10.

11. Open P18-26 and edit as follows:

   A. Lengthen the part .250 on each side for a new overall dimension of 6.500.

   B. Change the width of the part from 3.000 to 3.500 by widening an equal amount on each side.

   C. This problem requires that you change the UCS origin to keep the datum located at the lower left corner of the object.

   D. Save the drawing as P19-11.

12. Open P18-28 and edit as follows:

   A. Lengthen the mounting bracket equally on both sides to a new overall dimension of 13.500.

   B. Lengthen the A slots from .375 to .500, and lengthen the B lots from .500 to .750 equally on both sides for all slots.

   C. Save the drawing as P19-12.

13. Open P18-30 and edit as follows:

   A. Shorten the .75 thread on the left side to .50.

   B. Shorten the .388 hexagon length to .300.

   C. Save the drawing as P19-13.

14. Draw and completely dimension the 12 gage stainless steel cam. Save the drawing as P19-14.

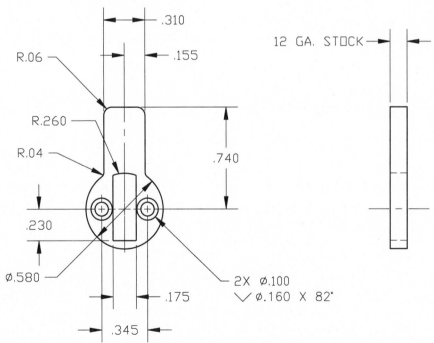

15. Open P19-14 and edit the drawing to match the cam shown below. Save the drawing as P19-15.

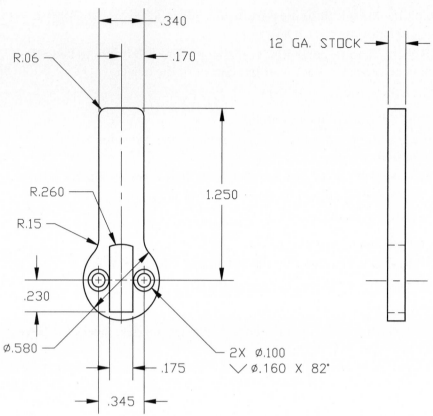

AutoCAD and its Applications—Basics

Chapter 20

Dimensioning with Tolerances

Learning Objectives

- ○ Define and use dimensioning and tolerancing terminology.
- ○ Prepare drawings with dimensions and tolerances from engineering designs, sketches and layouts.

This chapter explains the basics of tolerancing and how to prepare dimensions with tolerances for mechanical manufacturing drawings. Chapter 18 introduced you to the creation of dimension styles and how to set the dimension geometry, format, primary units, alternate units, and dimension text specifications. Dimensioning for mechanical drafting usually uses the following AutoCAD settings, depending on company practices:

Geometry

- Objects are dimensioned in inches or millimeters.
- Dimension line spacing is usually more than the .38 default.
- The extension line extension is .125 and the extension line offset is .0625.
- Arrowheads are closed filled, closed blank, closed, or open.
- The small dot is used on a leader pointing to a surface.
- The centerline option is used for circles and located arcs. Fillets and rounds generally have no center marks.

Format

- The user defined format is convenient for flexible text placement.
- Best fit is common but other format options work better for some applications.
- Horizontal and vertical justification is usually centered.
- Text placement is normally inside and outside horizontal for unidirectional dimensioning.

Annotation

- Primary units are typically decimal, with the number of decimal places controlled by the feature tolerance.
- Alternate units for dual dimensioning is not a recommended ASME/ANSI standard.
- The text is usually Romans font, .125 high, and with a gap of .0625.
- The tolerance method depends on the application.

Tolerancing Fundamentals

A *tolerance* is the total amount that a specific dimension is permitted to vary. A tolerance is not given to values that are identified as reference, maximum, minimum, or stock sizes. The tolerance may be applied directly to the dimension, indicated by a general note, or identified in the drawing title block. See Figure 20-1.

Figure 20-1.
Specifying the tolerance on the dimension, in a general note, or in the drawing title block.

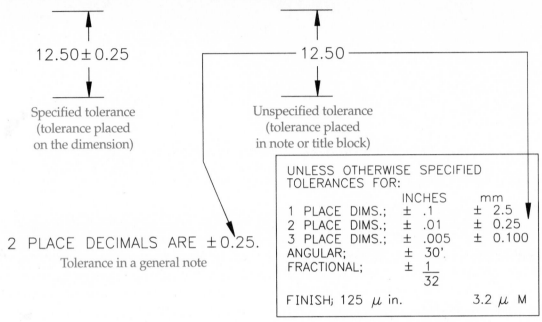

The *limits* of a dimension are the largest and smallest numerical value that the feature can be. In Figure 20-2A, the dimension is stated as 12.50±.25. This is referred to as *plus-minus dimensioning*. The tolerance of this dimension is the difference between the maximum and minimum limits. The upper limit is 12.50 + .25 = 12.75, and the lower limit is 12.50 – .25 = 12.25. So, if you take the upper limit and subtract the lower limit, you have the tolerance of .50.

The specified dimension is the part of the dimension where the limits are calculated from. The specified dimension of the feature shown in Figure 20-2 is 12.50. A dimension on a drawing may be displayed with plus-minus dimensioning, or the limits may be calculated and shown as in Figure 20-2B. Many schools and companies prefer the second method, *limits dimensioning*, because the limits are given and calculations are not required.

Figure 20-2.
Plus-minus dimensioning and limits dimensioning.

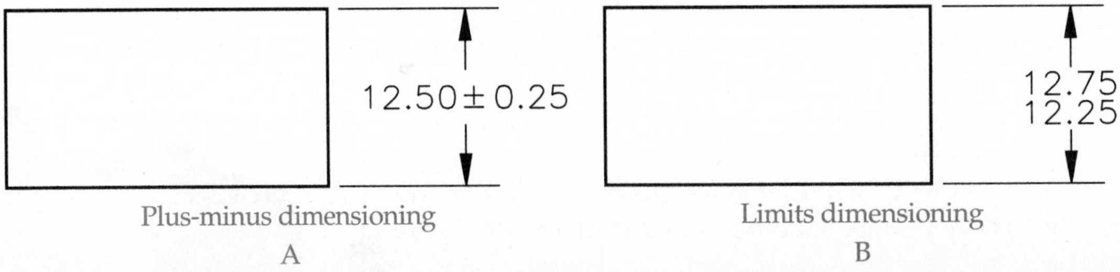

12.50±0.25

12.75
12.25

Plus-minus dimensioning

A

Limits dimensioning

B

A *bilateral tolerance* is permitted to vary in both + and – directions from the specified dimension. An *equal bilateral tolerance* has the same variation in both directions. An *unequal bilateral tolerance* is where the variation from the specified dimension is not the same in both directions. See Figure 20-3.

A *unilateral tolerance* is permitted to increase or decrease in only one direction from the specified dimension. See Figure 20-4.

Figure 20-3.
Bilateral tolerances.

$$24\,^{+0.08}_{-0.20} \qquad .750\,^{+.002}_{-.003}$$

Metric   Inch

Unequal bilateral tolerance

$$24\pm0.1 \qquad\qquad .750\pm.005$$

Metric   Inch

Equal bilateral tolerance

Figure 20-4.
Unilateral tolerances.

$$24\,^{0}_{-0.2} \qquad\qquad .625\,^{+.000}_{-.004}$$

$$24\,^{+0.2}_{0} \qquad\qquad .625\,^{+.004}_{-.000}$$

Metric   Inch

Dimension and Tolerance Decimal Places

The ASME Y14.5M-1994, *Dimensioning and Tolerancing* standard has separate recommendations for the way the number of decimal places is displayed for inch and metric dimensions. Examples of inch and metric decimal dimension numbers are shown in Figure 20-3 and 20-4. The following are some general rules:

Inch

- A specified inch dimension is expressed to the same number of decimal places as its tolerance. Zeros are added to the right of the decimal point if needed. For example, the inch dimension .250±.005 has an additional zero added to the .25 to match the three-decimal tolerance. The dimensions 2.000±.005 and 2.500±.005 both have zeros added to match the tolerance.
- Both plus and minus values of an inch tolerance have the same number of decimal places. Zeros are added to fill in where needed. For example:

$$^{+.005}_{-.010} \quad not \quad ^{+.005}_{-.01}$$

Metric

- The decimal point and zeros are omitted when the metric dimension is a whole number. For example, the metric dimension 12 has no decimal point followed by a zero. This rule is true unless tolerance values are displayed.
- When a metric dimension includes a decimal portion, the last digit to the right of the decimal point is not followed by a zero. For example, the metric dimension 12.5 has no zero to the right of the five. This rule is true unless tolerance values are displayed.
- Both plus and minus values of a metric tolerance have the same number of decimal places. Zeros are added to fill in where needed.

- Zeros are not added after the specified dimension to match the tolerance. For example, both 24±0.25 and 24.5±0.25 are correct. However, some companies prefer to add zeros after the specified dimension to match the tolerance, as in 24.00±0.25 or 24.50±0.25.

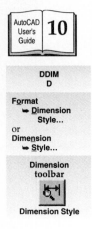

AutoCAD User's Guide **10**

DDIM
D

F**o**rmat
➥ **D**imension Style...
or
Dimension
➥ **S**tyle...

Dimension toolbar

Dimension Style

Setting Primary Units

Dimension variables are quickly changed and dimension styles are conveniently created in the **Dimension Styles** dialog box. See Figure 20-5. This dialog box is accessed by picking the **Dimension Style** button in the **Dimension** toolbar, by picking **Dimension Style...** in the **F**o**rmat** pull-down menu, or by entering D or DDIM at the Command: prompt. Once in the **Dimension Styles** dialog box, pick the **Annotation...** button to open the **Annotation** dialog box. See Figure 20-6. The **Primary Units** area is used to set the type of units and the precision of dimension and tolerance values.

Figure 20-5.
The **Dimension Styles** dialog box

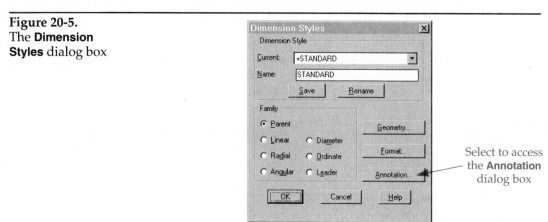

Select to access the **Annotation** dialog box

Figure 20-6.
The **Annotation** dialog box.

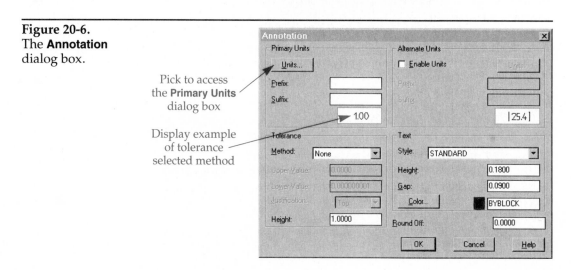

Pick to access the **Primary Units** dialog box

Display example of tolerance selected method

Primary units are the type of units to be used for the dimension style. Pick the **Units...** button in the **Primary Units** area. This accesses the **Primary Units** dialog box. See Figure 20-7. The **Units**, **Angles**, and **Scale** areas of this dialog box are discussed in Chapter 18 of this text.

In the **Primary Units** dialog box, the **Tolerance** and **Dimension** areas have the same settings. The **Precision:** list allows you to set the number of zeros displayed after the tolerance decimal point. The ASME standard recommends that the precision for the tolerance and the dimension be the same for inch dimensions but may be different for metric values as previously shown. You must set the precision for **Primary Units** and

Figure 20-7.
The **Primary Units**
dialog box.

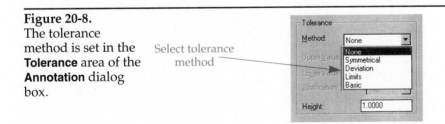

These areas should
have settings that
match the desired
values.

the **Tolerance** separately, even if you want them to be the same. AutoCAD does not automatically set this for you. The dimension variable used at the Command: prompt for this setting is **DIMTDEC** (tolerance decimal).

The **Zero Suppression** options have the same effect in the **Tolerance** area as they do in the **Dimension** area. These options and the **Dimension** area were explained in Chapter 18.

The settings in the **Dimension** area should match the settings in the **Tolerance** area. For example, **Leading** should be off and **Trailing** should be on for metric dimensions, and **Leading** should be on and **Trailing** should be off for inch dimensions. Zero suppression is controlled at the Command: prompt with the **DIMTZIN** (tolerance zero inch display) variable. This variable uses the same settings as the **DIMZIN** variable, which was discussed in Chapter 18.

Setting Tolerance Methods

The **Tolerance** area of the **Annotation** dialog box is where tolerance methods can be applied to your drawing. See Figure 20-6. The **Method:** list provides **None** as the default. This means that no tolerance method is used with your dimensions and the options in this area are disabled. The image shown in the **Primary Units** area reflects the tolerance method selected. Pick the down arrow to see the other options in the **Method:** list. See Figure 20-8.

Figure 20-8.
The tolerance
method is set in the
Tolerance area of the
Annotation dialog
box.

Select tolerance
method

Symmetrical tolerance method

The **Symmetrical** option is used to draw dimension text displaying an equal bilateral tolerance in the plus/minus format. When the **Symmetrical** option is selected, the **Upper Value:** text box, **Justification:** list, and **Height:** text box are active and the image tile in the **Primary Units** area displays an equal bilateral tolerance. Enter a tolerance value in the **Upper Value:** text box. See Figure 20-9. The **Symmetrical** option can be set at the Command: prompt by turning the **DIMTOL** (tolerance) variable on, turning the **DIMLIM** (limits) variable off, and setting the **DIMTP** (tolerance plus) and **DIMTM** (tolerance minus) variables to the same numerical value.

Figure 20-9.
Setting the
Symmetrical
tolerance method
and a resulting
dimension with a
bilateral
plus/minus
tolerance.

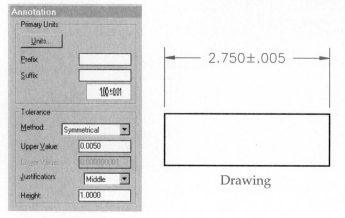

Setting

2.750±.005

Drawing

EXERCISE 20-1

❏ Begin a new drawing or use one of your prototypes.
❏ Set the units, precision, zero suppression, and tolerance method as needed to draw the object with a bilateral tolerance dimension like Figure 20-9.
❏ Save the drawing as EX20-1.

Deviation tolerance method

AutoCAD refers to an unequal bilateral tolerance as *deviation*. This means that the tolerance deviates (departs) from the specified dimension with two different values. When you select **Deviation**, the **Upper Value:** and **Lower Value:** text boxes are available to enter the desired upper and lower tolerance values. See Figure 20-10. The image tile in the **Primary Units** area changes to match a representation for an unequal bilateral tolerance.

Figure 20-10.
Setting the **Deviation**
tolerance method
and a resulting
dimension with an
unequal bilateral
tolerance.

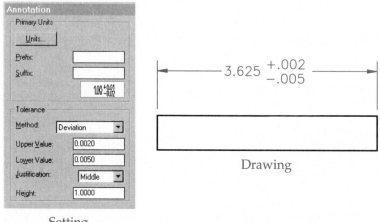

Setting

$3.625 \begin{smallmatrix} +.002 \\ -.005 \end{smallmatrix}$

Drawing

The **Deviation** option can also be used to draw a unilateral tolerance by entering zero as either the **Upper Value** or the **Lower Value**. If you are using English units, AutoCAD includes the sign before the zero tolerance. When metric units are used, the sign is omitted. See Figure 20-11.

Figure 20-11.
AutoCAD automatically places the plus (+) or minus (–) symbol in front of the zero part of a unilateral tolerance when English units are used. The sign is omitted with metric units.

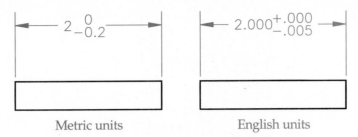

Metric units   English units

> **NOTE**
> The **MEASUREMENT** system variable is used to change between English units and metric units. If the variable is set to 0, English units are active. A setting of 1 corresponds to metric units.

The **Deviation** option can be set at the Command: prompt by turning the **DIMTOL** variable on, turning the **DIMLIM** variable off, and setting the **DIMTP** and **DIMTM** variables to different numerical values. When you turn **DIMTOL** on, **DIMLIM** is automatically turned off. When you turn **DIMLIM** on, the **DIMTOL** variable is automatically turned off.

EXERCISE 20-2

❑ Begin a new drawing or use one of your prototypes.
❑ Set the units, precision, zero suppression, and tolerance method as needed to draw the following:
  ❑ An object with an unequal bilateral tolerance dimension like Figure 20-10.
  ❑ An object with a unilateral tolerance dimension, like the English units example in Figure 20-11.
  ❑ Change the **MEASUREMENT** system variable to 1 and draw another dimension using the same unilateral set for the previous object. Note the differences.
❑ Save the drawing as EX20-2.

Limits tolerance method

The difference between plus/minus dimensioning and limits dimensioning is shown in Figure 20-2. When you pick the **Limits** option, the **Upper Value:** and **Lower Value:** text boxes are available to enter the desired amount you want added and subtracted from the specified dimension to create the limits. The values you enter can be the same or different. See Figure 20-12.

The **Limits** option can be set at the Command: prompt by turning the **DIMTOL** variable off, turning the **DIMLIM** variable on, and setting the **DIMTP** and **DIMTM** variables to the desired numerical values.

EXERCISE 20-3

❑ Begin a new drawing or use one of your prototypes.
❑ Set the units, precision, zero suppression, and tolerance method as needed to draw the object with a limits tolerance dimension like Figure 20-12.
❑ Save the drawing as EX20-3.

Figure 20-12.
Setting the **Limits**
tolerance method
and a resulting
dimension with
limits tolerance.

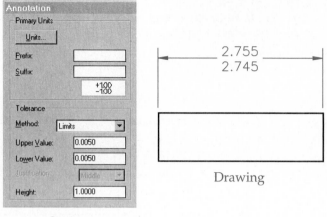

Setting

Drawing

Basic tolerance method

The basic tolerance method is used to draw basic dimensions. A *basic dimension* is used in geometric dimensioning and tolerancing, which is covered in Chapter 21. When you pick the **Basic** option, all other options in the **Tolerance** area are disabled because a basic dimension has no tolerance. A basic dimension has a box around it, as shown in the **Primary Units** area image tile. See Figure 20-13.

Figure 20-13.
The **Basic** tolerance
method.

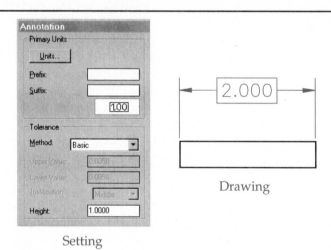

Setting

Drawing

Tolerance method review

✓ If your dimension tolerances do not reflect the level of precision you want, set precision using the **Precision:** drop-down list in the **Tolerance** area of the **Primary Units** dialog box. You can also use the **DIMTDEC** variable to set the desired value.

✓ Each tolerance method option you pick is represented in the **Primary Units** image tile in the **Annotation** dialog box. You can also pick on the image tile to automatically cycle through the tolerance method options.

✓ Inch tolerance dimensions should have a check in the **Leading Zero Suppression** check box in the **Dimension** and **Tolerance** areas of the **Primary Units** dialog box. This allows you to properly place inch tolerance dimensions based on ASME standards without the zero before the decimal point, such as .625±.005.

✓ Metric tolerance dimensions should not have a check in the **Leading Zero Suppression** box in the **Dimension** and **Tolerance** areas of the **Primary Units** dialog box. This allows you to properly place metric tolerance dimensions based on ASME standards with the zero before the decimal point, such as 12±0.2.

Tolerance justification

How the tolerance value is placed in alignment with the specified dimension is controlled with the **Justification:** drop-down list in the **Tolerance** area of the **Annotation** dialog box. This list is active when the **Symmetrical** and **Deviation** options are used. **Middle** justification centers the tolerance with the specified dimension, and is the default. This is also the ASME recommended practice. The other options are **Top** and **Bottom**. Dimensions displaying each of the justification options is provided in Figure 20-14. Tolerance justification is controlled at the Command: prompt with the **DIMTOLJ** variable.

Figure 20-14.
The tolerance justification options.

$2.625^{+.002}_{-.005}$	$2.625+.002$ $-.005$	$+.002$ $2.625-.005$
Middle	Top	Bottom

Tolerance height

The text height of the tolerance in relationship to the text height of the specified dimension is set using the **Height:** text box in the **Tolerance** area of the **Annotation** dialog box. The default is 1.00, which makes the tolerance text the same height as the specified dimension text. This is the recommended ASME standard. If you want the tolerance height three-quarters as high as the specified dimension height, enter .75 in the **Height:** box. Some companies prefer this practice to keep the tolerance part of the dimension from taking up additional space. Figure 20-15 shows an example of dimensions with different tolerance text heights. The tolerance height is set at the Command: prompt with the **DIMTFAC** variable.

Figure 20-15.
Various tolerance height settings.

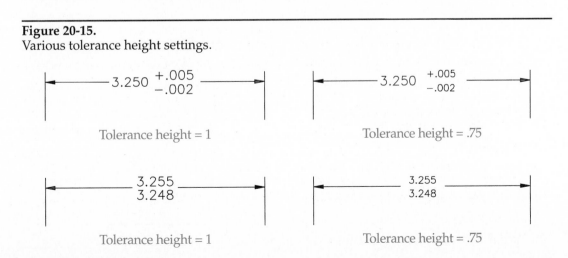

$3.250\ ^{+.005}_{-.002}$	$3.250\ ^{+.005}_{-.002}$
Tolerance height = 1	Tolerance height = .75
3.255 3.248	3.255 3.248
Tolerance height = 1	Tolerance height = .75

❏ Begin a new drawing or use one of your templates.
❏ Set the units, precision, zero suppression, tolerance method, justification, and height as needed to draw the following:
    ❏ Objects with dimensions like Figure 20-14.
    ❏ Objects with dimensions like Figure 20-15.
❏ Save the drawing as EX20-4.

Chapter Test

Write your answer in the spaces provided

1. Define *tolerance*. _____
_____

2. Give an example of an equal bilateral tolerance in inches. _____
_____

3. Give an example of an unequal bilateral tolerance in inches. _____
_____

4. Give an example of an equal bilateral tolerance in metric. _____
_____

5. Give an example of an unequal bilateral tolerance in metric. _____
_____

6. What are the limits of the dimension: 3.625±.005? _____
_____

7. Give an example of a unilateral tolerance in inches. _____
_____

8. Give an example of a unilateral tolerance in metric. _____
_____

9. Name the dialog box where dimension variables are changed and dimension styles are created. _____

10. List the ways to open the dialog box specified in Question 9. _____
_____
_____
_____

11. How do you open the **Annotation** dialog box? _____
_____

12. How do you set the number of zeros after the decimal place in the dimension tolerance? _____
_____

13. What zero suppression settings should you use for metric dimensions? _____
_____

14. What zero suppression settings should you use for inch dimensions? _____
_____

15. What is the purpose of the **None** option in the **Tolerance Method:** list? _____
_____

16. What is the purpose of the **Symmetrical** option in the **Tolerance Method:** list?____
_____

17. What is the purpose of the **Deviation** option in the **Tolerance Method:** list? _____
_____

18. What is the purpose of the **Limits** option in the **Tolerance Method:** list? _____
_____

19. What happens to the image tile in the **Primary Units** area of the **Annotation** dialog box when you pick the **Limits** option in the **Tolerance Method:** list? _____
_____

20. Name the tolerance justification option recommended by the ASME standard. __
_____

21. What is the result of a tolerance height setting of 1? _____
_____

22. What tolerance height setting is recommended by the ASME standard? _____
_____

23. What setting do you use if you want the tolerance height to be three-quarters of the specified dimension?_____
_____

Drawing Problems

Set limits, units, dimensioning variables, and other parameters as needed. Follow these guidelines.

    A. *Draw the needed multiviews to exact size. You must select the proper multiview for the problems presented in 3D.*
    B. *Use grids, object snap options, and the* **OSNAP** *command to your best advantage.*
    C. *Apply dimensions accurately using ASME standards.*
    D. *Set dimensioning variables to suit the drawing.*
    E. *Set separate layers for views and dimensions.*
    F. *Plot drawings with 0.6mm object lines and 0.3mm thin lines.*
    G. *Place the following general notes 1/2″ from lower-left corner:*

        3. UNLESS OTHERWISE SPECIFIED, ALL DIMENSIONS ARE IN MILLIMETERS.
          (or INCHES *as applicable*)
        2. REMOVE ALL BURRS AND SHARP EDGES.
        1. INTERPRET PER ASME Y14.5M-1994.
        NOTES:

H. Create dimension styles with family members that suit the specific needs of each drawing. For example, save dimension styles for metric or inch drawings as appropriate.

I. Save the drawings as P20-(problem number).

1.

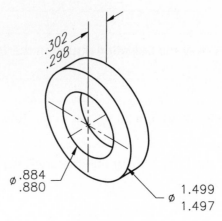

Title: Washer
Material: SAE 1020
Inch

2.

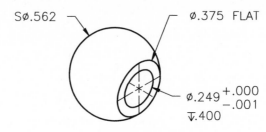

Title: Handle
Material: Bronze
Inch

3.

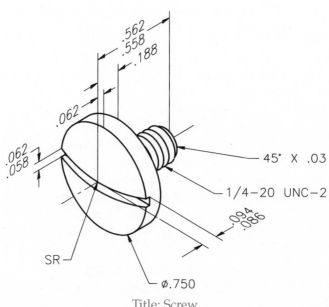

Title: Screw
Material: SAE 4320
Inch

AutoCAD and its Applications—Basics

4.

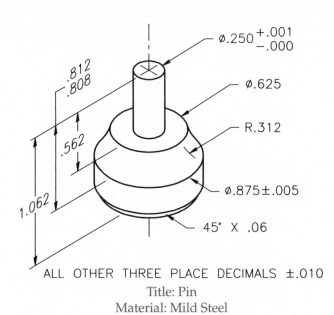

Ø.250 +.001 / -.000

.812 / .808

Ø.625

R.312

.562

Ø.875±.005

1.062

45° X .06

ALL OTHER THREE PLACE DECIMALS ±.010
Title: Pin
Material: Mild Steel
Inch

5. *This object is shown as a section for clarity. Do not draw a section.*

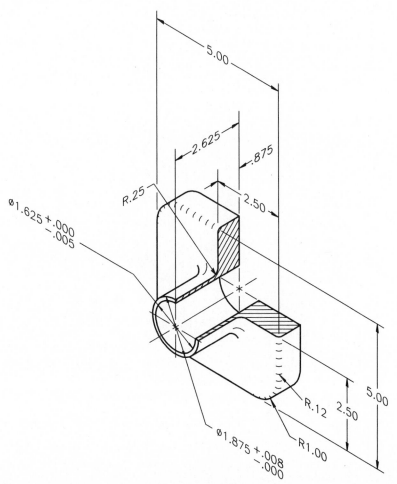

5.00

2.625

.875

2.50

R.25

Ø1.625 +.000 / -.005

5.00

2.50

R.12

Ø1.875 +.008 / -.000

R1.00

Title: Thrust Washer
Material: SAE 5150
Inch

6.

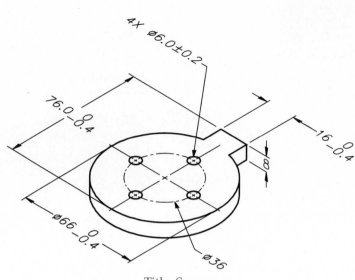

4X ⌀6.0±0.2

76.0 −0.4 0

16 −0.4 0

8

⌀66 −0.4 0

⌀36

Title: Spacer
Material: Cold Rolled Steel
Metric

7.

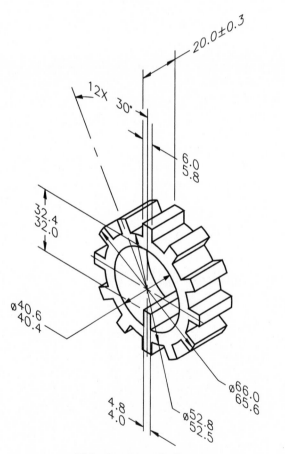

20.0±0.3

12X 30°

6.0
5.8

32.4
32.0

⌀40.6
40.4

⌀66.0
65.6

4.8
4.0

⌀52.8
52.5

Title: Locking Collar
Material: SAE 1080
Metric

Geometric Dimensioning and Tolerancing

Learning Objectives

After completing this chapter, you will be able to:
- ○ Identify geometric tolerancing symbols.
- ○ Use the **TOLERANCE** and **LEADER** commands.
- ○ Draw feature control frames.
- ○ Edit feature control frames.
- ○ Place basic dimensions on a drawing.
- ○ Draw datum feature symbols.
- ○ Identify how to draw projected tolerance zone symbols.

This chapter is an introduction to geometric dimensioning and tolerancing (GD&T) as adopted by the American National Standards Institute (ANSI) and published by the American Society of Mechanical Engineers (ASME) for engineering and related document practices. The standard is titled ASME Y14.5M-1994, *Dimensioning and Tolerancing*. **Geometric tolerancing** is a general term that refers to tolerances used to control form, profile, orientation, runout, and location of features on an object.

The drafting applications identified in this chapter use the AutoCAD geometric tolerancing capabilities and additional recommendations to comply with the ASME Y14.5M-1994 standard. This chapter is only an introduction to geometric dimensioning and tolerancing (GD&T). For complete coverage of GD&T, refer to *Geometric Dimensioning and Tolerancing*, also published by Goodheart-Willcox. Before beginning this chapter, it is recommended that you have a solid understanding of dimensioning and tolerancing standards and AutoCAD applications. This introductory material is presented in Chapters 18 through 20 of this text.

The discussion in this chapter divides the dimensioning and geometric tolerancing symbols into the following five basic types:
- Dimensioning symbols.
- Geometric characteristic symbols.
- Material condition symbols.
- Feature control frame.
- Datum feature and datum target symbols.

When you draw GD&T symbols, it is recommended that you use a dimensioning layer so the symbols and text can be plotted as lines that are the same thickness as extension and dimension lines (.01" or .3mm). The suggested text font is Romans. These practices correspond with ASME Y14.2M-1992 *Line Conventions and Lettering*.

Dimensioning Symbols

Symbols represent specific information that would be difficult and time-consuming to duplicate in note form. Symbols must be clearly drawn to the required size and shape so they communicate the desired information uniformly. Symbols are recommended by ASME Y14.5M because symbols are an international language, read the same way in any country. In an international economy, it is important to have effective communication on engineering drawings. Symbols make this communication process uniform. ASME Y14.5M also states that the adoption of dimensioning symbols does not prevent the use of equivalent terms or abbreviations in situations where symbols are considered inappropriate.

Symbols aid in clarity, ease of drawing presentation, and reducing drawing time. Creating and using AutoCAD symbols is covered later in this chapter and in Chapter 23 of this text. Figure 21-1 shows recommended dimensioning symbols.

Figure 21-1.
Dimensioning symbols recommended by ASME Y14.5M-1994.

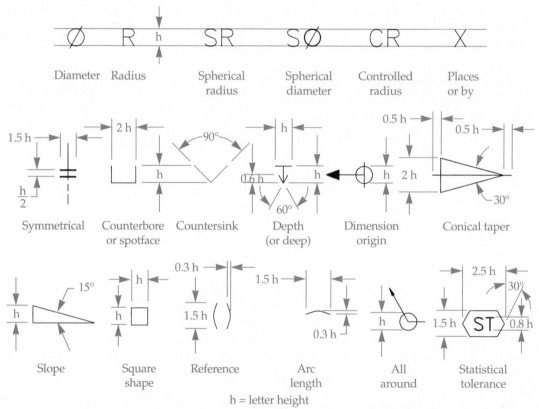

Geometric Characteristic Symbols

In GD&T, symbols are used to provide specific controls related to the form of an object, the orientation of features, the outlines of features, the relationship of features to an axis, or the location of features. These are known as *geometric characteristic* symbols. Geometric characteristic symbols are separated into five types: form, profile, orientation, location, and runout, as shown in Figure 21-2. The symbols in Figure 21-2 are drawn to the actual size and shape recommended by ASME Y14.5M, based on .125"(3mm) high lettering.

Figure 21-2.
Geometric
characteristic
symbols
recommended by
ASME Y14.5M-1994.

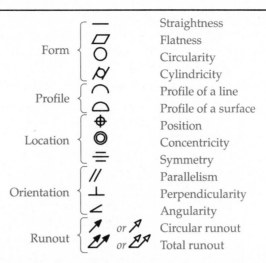

Form		Straightness
		Flatness
		Circularity
		Cylindricity
Profile		Profile of a line
		Profile of a surface
Location		Position
		Concentricity
		Symmetry
Orientation		Parallelism
		Perpendicularity
		Angularity
Runout		Circular runout
		Total runout

Material Condition Symbols

Material condition symbols are often referred to as *modifying symbols* because they modify the geometric tolerance in relation to the produced size or location of the feature. Material condition symbols are only used in geometric dimensioning applications. The symbols used in the feature control frame to indicate *maximum material condition (MMC)* or *least material condition (LMC)* are shown in Figure 21-3. Regardless of feature size (RFS) is also a material condition. However, there is no symbol for RFS because it is assumed for all geometric tolerances and datum references unless MMC or LMC is specified.

Figure 21-3.
Material condition
symbols. In ASME
Y14.5M-1994, there
is no symbol for
RFS, since it is
assumed unless
otherwise specified.

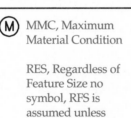

(M) MMC, Maximum
Material Condition

RES, Regardless of
Feature Size no
symbol, RFS is
assumed unless
otherwise specified

(L) LMC, Least Material
Condition

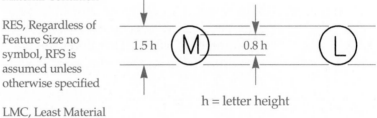

1.5 h (M) 0.8 h (L)

h = letter height

Surface control regardless of feature size

Regardless of feature size is assumed when there is no material condition symbol following the geometric tolerance in the feature control frame. *Regardless of feature size* means that the geometric tolerances remain the same regardless of the actual produced size. The term *produced size*, when used here, means the actual size of the feature when measured after manufacture.

When the feature control frame is connected to a feature surface with a leader or an extension line, it is referred to as *surface control*. See Figure 21-4. The geometric characteristic symbol shown is straightness, but the applications are the same for any characteristic.

Figure 21-4.
The drawing specifies surface control regardless of feature size. The related meaning is also shown.

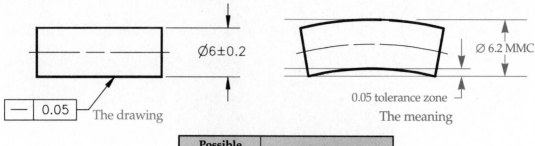

	Possible produced sizes	Maximum out-of-straightness
MMC	6.20	* 0
	6.10	0.05
	6.00	0.05
	5.90	0.05
LMC	5.80	0.05

* Perfect form required

Look at the chart in Figure 21-4 and notice the possible sizes range from 6.20 (MMC) to 5.80 (LMC). With surface control, perfect form is required at MMC. *Perfect form* means that the object cannot exceed a true geometric form boundary established at maximum material condition. The geometric tolerance at MMC is zero, as shown in the chart. As the produced size goes away from MMC, the geometric tolerance increases until it equals the amount specified in the feature control frame.

Axis control regardless of feature size

Axis control is used when the feature control frame is shown with the diameter dimension. See Figure 21-5. Regardless of feature size is assumed. With axis control, perfect form is not required at MMC. Therefore, the specified geometric tolerance stays the same at every produced size. See the chart in Figure 21-5.

Figure 21-5.
The drawing specifies axis control regardless of feature size. The related meaning is also shown.

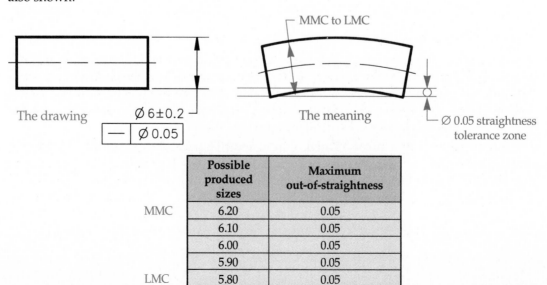

	Possible produced sizes	Maximum out-of-straightness
MMC	6.20	0.05
	6.10	0.05
	6.00	0.05
	5.90	0.05
LMC	5.80	0.05

Maximum material condition control

If the material condition control is maximum material condition, then the symbol for MMC must be placed in the feature control frame. See Figure 21-6. When this application is used, the specified geometric tolerance is held at the maximum material condition-produced size. See the chart in Figure 21-6. Then, as the produced size goes away from MMC, the geometric tolerance increases equal to the change. The maximum geometric tolerance is at the LMC-produced size.

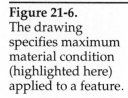

Figure 21-6. The drawing specifies maximum material condition (highlighted here) applied to a feature.

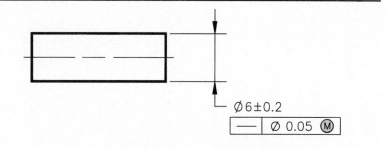

Ø6±0.2

	Possible produced sizes	Maximum out-of-straightness
MMC	6.20	0.05
	6.10	0.15
	6.00	0.25
	5.90	0.35
LMC	5.80	0.45

Least material condition control

If the material condition control is least material condition, then the symbol for LMC must be placed in the feature control frame. When this application is used, the specified geometric tolerance is held at the least material condition-produced size. Then, as the produced size goes away from LMC, the geometric tolerance increases equal to the change. The maximum geometric tolerance is at the MMC produced size.

Feature Control Frame

A geometric characteristic, geometric tolerance, material condition, and datum reference (if any) for an individual feature are specified by means of a feature control frame. The *feature control frame* is divided into compartments containing the geometric characteristic symbol in the first compartment followed by the geometric tolerance. Where applicable, the geometric tolerance is preceded by the diameter symbol, which describes the shape of the tolerance zone, and followed by a material condition symbol, if other than RFS. See Figure 21-7.

When a geometric tolerance is related to one or more datums, the datum reference letters are placed in compartments following the geometric tolerance. When there is a multiple datum reference, both datum reference letters, separated by a dash, are placed in a single compartment after the geometric tolerance. A *multiple datum reference* is established by two datum features, such as an axis established by two datum diameters. Figure 21-8 shows several feature control frames with datum references.

Figure 21-7.
Feature control frames with geometric characteristic symbol, geometric tolerance, and diameter symbol. The material condition symbol is left off for RFS, since it is assumed. Note that the geometric tolerance is total, not plus/minus.

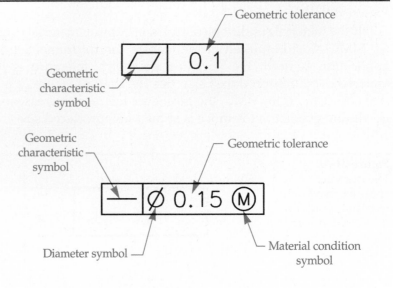

Figure 21-8.
Feature control frames with datum references.

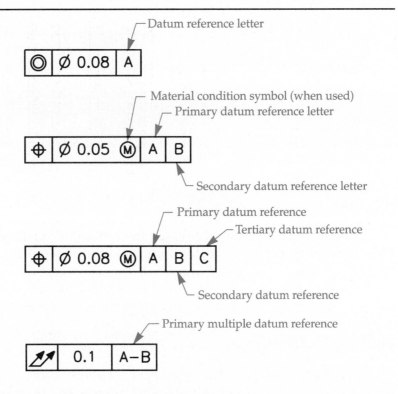

There is a specific order of elements in a feature control frame. See Figure 21-9. Notice that the datum reference letters can be followed by a material condition symbol where applicable.

Basic Dimensions

A basic dimension is considered a theoretically perfect dimension. Basic dimensions are used to describe the theoretically exact size, profile, orientation, and location of a feature. These dimensions provide the basis from which permissible variations are established by tolerances on other dimensions, in notes, or in feature control frames. In simple terms, a basic dimension tells you where the geometric tolerance zone or datum target is located.

Figure 21-9.
Order of elements in
a feature control
frame.

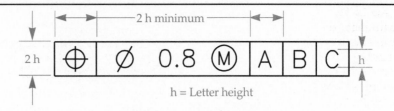

h = Letter height

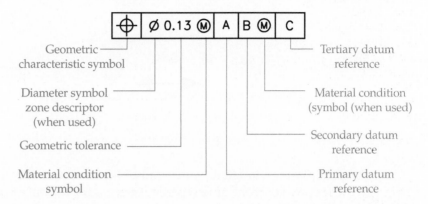

Geometric
characteristic symbol

Diameter symbol
zone descriptor
(when used)

Geometric tolerance

Material condition
symbol

Tertiary datum
reference

Material condition
(symbol (when used)

Secondary datum
reference

Primary datum
reference

Basic dimensions are shown on a drawing by placing a rectangle around the dimension, as shown in Figure 21-10. A general note can also be used to identify basic dimensions in some applications. For example, the note UNTOLERANCED DIMENSIONS LOCATING TRUE POSITION ARE BASIC indicates the dimensions that are basic. The basic dimension symbol around a dimension is a signal to the reader to look for a geometric tolerance in a feature control frame related to the features being dimensioned.

Figure 21-10.
Basic dimensions.

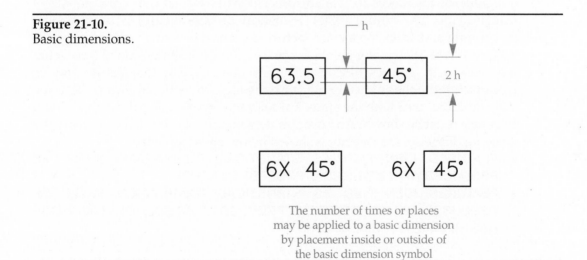

The number of times or places
may be applied to a basic dimension
by placement inside or outside of
the basic dimension symbol

h = Letter height

Additional Symbols

Other symbols used in geometric dimensioning and tolerancing are shown in Figure 21-11. These symbols are used for specific applications, and are identified as follows:

- **Free state.** Free state describes distortion of a part after the removal of forces applied during manufacture. The free state symbol is placed in the feature control frame after the geometric tolerance and the material condition (if any), if the feature must meet the tolerance specified while in free state.

Figure 21-11.
Additional
dimensioning
symbols.

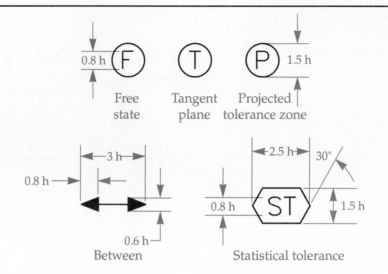

- **Tangent plane.** A tangent plane symbol is placed after the geometric tolerance in the feature control frame when it is necessary to control a feature surface by contacting points of tangency.
- **Projected tolerance zone.** A projected tolerance zone symbol is placed in the feature control frame to inform the reader that the geometric tolerance zone is projected away from the primary datum.
- **Between.** The between symbol is used with profile geometric tolerances to identify where the profile tolerance is applied.
- **Statistical tolerance.** The statistical tolerance symbol is used to indicate that a tolerance is based on statistical tolerancing. *Statistical tolerancing* is the assigning of tolerances to related dimensions based on the requirements of statistical process control (SPC). Statistical process control is a method of monitoring and adjusting a manufacturing process by using statistical signals. The statistical tolerancing symbol is placed after the dimension or geometric tolerance that requires SPC. See Figure 21-12. When the feature can be manufactured either by using SPC or by using conventional means, both the statistical tolerance with the statistical tolerance symbol and the conventional tolerance must be shown. An appropriate general note should accompany the drawing. Either of the two notes shown below are acceptable:
  - FEATURES IDENTIFIED AS STATISTICAL TOLERANCED SHALL BE PRODUCED WITH STATISTICAL PROCESS CONTROL.
  - FEATURES IDENTIFIED AS STATISTICAL TOLERANCED SHALL BE PRODUCED WITH STATISTICAL PROCESS CONTROL, OR THE MORE RESTRICTIVE ARITHMETIC LIMITS.

Figure 21-12.
Different ways to
apply a statistical
tolerance. The
statistical tolerance
symbol is shown
here highlighted.

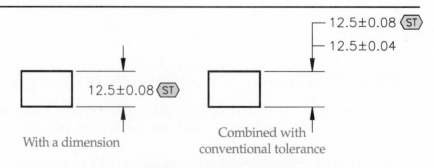

Datum Feature Symbol

Datums are considered theoretically perfect surfaces, planes, points, or axes. In this introduction to datum-related symbols, the datum is assumed. In geometric dimensioning and tolerancing, the datums are identified with a *datum feature symbol*.

Each datum feature requiring identification must have its own identification letter. Any letter of the alphabet can be used to identify a datum except for *I, O,* or *Q.* These letters can be confused with the numbers 1 or 0. On drawings where the number of datums exceed the letters in the alphabet, double letters are used, starting with *AA* through *AZ,* and then *BA* through *BZ.* Datum feature symbols can be repeated only as necessary for clarity. Figure 21-13 shows the datum feature symbol recommended by ASME Y14.5M-1994.

The datum feature used in drawings prior to the release of ASME Y14.5M-1994 is distinctively different. Figure 21-14 shows the previous datum feature.

Figure 21-13.
Datum feature symbol based on ASME Y14.5M-1994.

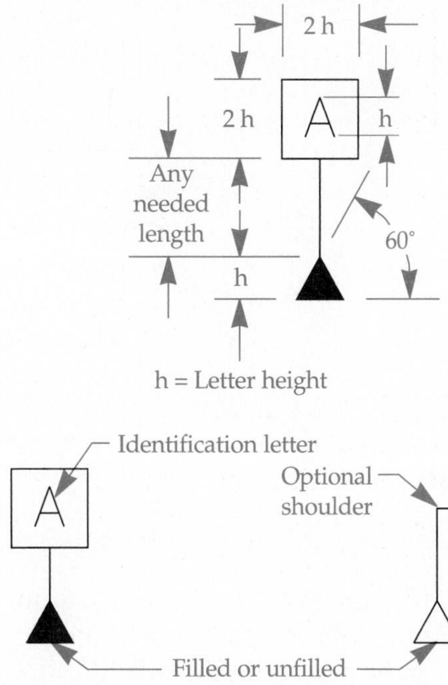

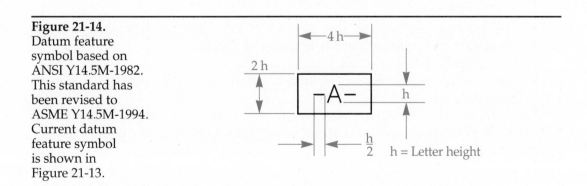

Figure 21-14.
Datum feature symbol based on ANSI Y14.5M-1982. This standard has been revised to ASME Y14.5M-1994. Current datum feature symbol is shown in Figure 21-13.

Applications of the datum feature symbol

When a surface is used to establish a datum plane on a part, the datum feature symbol is placed on the edge view of the surface or on an extension line in the view where the surface appears as a line. See Figure 21-15. A leader line can also be used to connect the datum feature symbol to the view.

Figure 21-15.
The datum feature symbol is placed on the edge view or on an extension line in the view where the surface appears as a line.

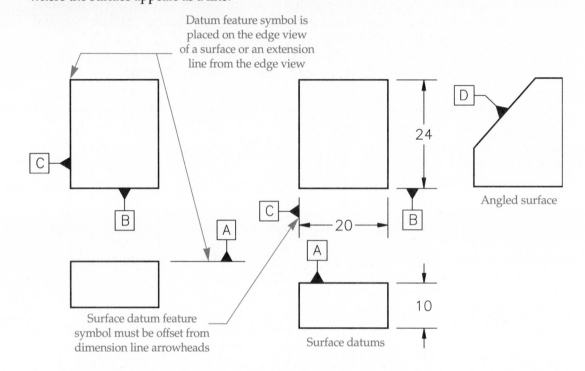

When the datum is an axis, the datum feature symbol can be placed on the drawing using one of the following methods. See Figure 21-16.
- The symbol can be placed on the outside surface of a cylindrical feature.
- The symbol can be centered on the opposite side of the dimension line arrowhead.
- The symbol can replace the dimension line and arrowhead when the dimension line is placed outside of the extension lines.
- The symbol can be placed on a leader line shoulder.
- The symbol can be placed below, and attached to, the center of a feature control frame.

Elements on a rectangular symmetrical part or feature can be located and dimensioned in relationship to a datum center plane. Datum center plane symbols are shown in Figure 21-17.

Geometric Dimensioning and Tolerancing with AutoCAD

The previous section gave a brief introduction to the appearance and use of geometric dimensioning and tolerancing symbols. AutoCAD has provided you with the ability to add GD&T symbols to your drawings. The feature control frame and related GD&T symbols can be created using the **TOLERANCE** and **LEADER** commands.

AutoCAD and its Applications—Basics

Figure 21-16.
Methods of representing the datum axis.

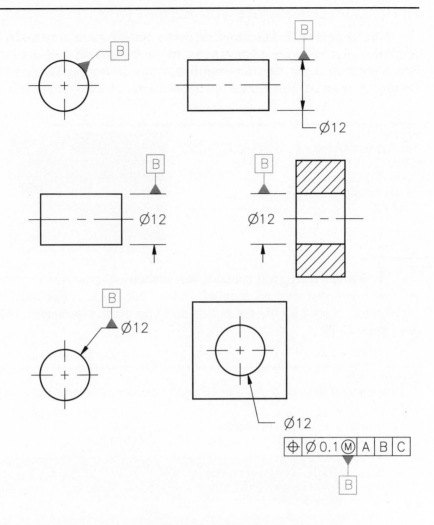

Figure 21-17.
Placement of center datum feature symbols. Axis and center plane datum feature symbols must align with, or replace, the dimension line arrowhead. Or, the datum must be placed on the feature, leader shoulder, or feature control frame.

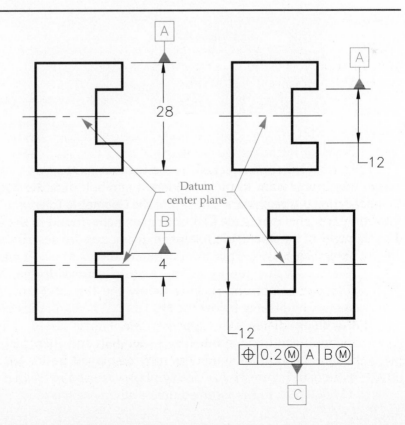

Using the TOLERANCE command

The **TOLERANCE** command provides tools for creating GD&T symbols. Access this command by picking **Tolerance...** in the **Dimension** pull-down menu, picking the **Tolerance** button on the **Dimension** toolbar, or typing TOL or TOLERANCE at the Command: prompt. This command accesses the **Symbol** dialog box. See Figure 21-18.

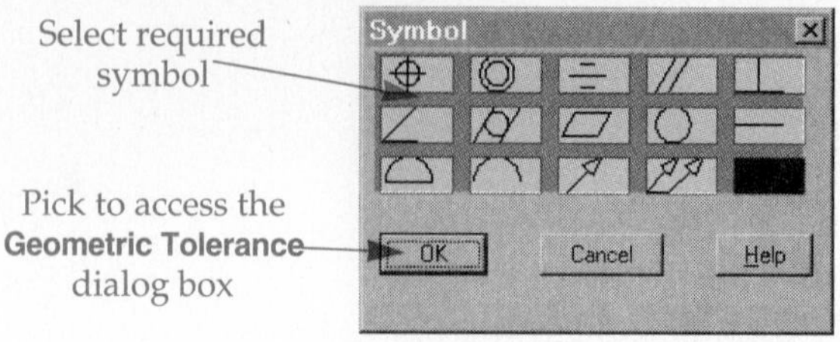

Figure 21-18.
The **Symbol** dialog box. Pick the desired geometric characteristic symbol.

Select required symbol

Pick to access the **Geometric Tolerance** dialog box

The **Symbol** dialog box contains the geometric characteristic symbols. The last option is blank and displays no symbol. When you pick a desired symbol, it becomes highlighted. Next, pick the **OK** button and you get the **Geometric Tolerance** dialog box. See Figure 21-19.

Figure 21-19.
The **Geometric Tolerance** dialog box is used to build a feature control frame to desired specifications.

The symbol selected in the **Symbol** dialog box. Pick here to access that dialog box.

Tolerance compartments

Datum reference compartments

Enter a datum identifier

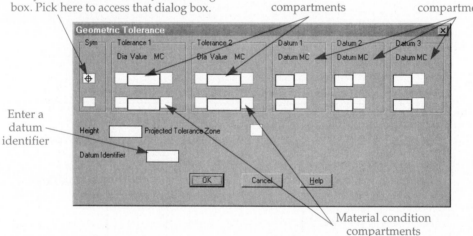

Material condition compartments

The symbol that you picked in the **Symbol** dialog box is displayed in the **Sym** image tile. If you want to pick a different symbol, pick the **Sym** image tile and the **Symbol** dialog box reappears. The rest of the **Geometric Tolerance** dialog box is divided into compartments that relate to the compartments found in the feature control frame. The elements of the **Geometric Tolerance** dialog box are described as follows:

- **Tolerance 1 area.** This compartment allows you to enter the first geometric tolerance value found in the feature control frame. You can also add a diameter symbol by picking below the **Dia** label and a material condition symbol by picking below the **MC** label. When you pick below **MC**, the **Material Condition** dialog box appears. See Figure 21-20. Highlight the desired material condition symbol by picking it, and then pick the **OK** button. The material condition symbol is now displayed under **MC**. Notice the old RFS symbol in Figure 21-20. This symbol was used in ANSI Y14.5M-1982. In ASME Y14.5M-1994, RFS is assumed unless otherwise specified.

Figure 21-20.
The **Material Condition** dialog box. Pick the desired material condition symbol for the geometric tolerance and datum reference as needed. Notice the symbol for RFS appears here. This symbol is not used in ASME Y14.5M-1994, but may be needed when editing older drawings.

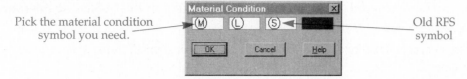

Pick the material condition symbol you need.

Old RFS symbol

There are two edit boxes in each compartment. The edit boxes are located below the **Value** label. The top edit box is for the information found in a single feature control frame, while the bottom edit box is for information needed for a double-feature control frame. Double-feature control frames are used for applications such as unit straightness, unit flatness, composite profile tolerance, composite positional tolerance, and coaxial positional tolerance. Figure 21-21 shows 0.5 entered in the **Tolerance 1** top text box, preceded by a diameter symbol and followed by an MMC symbol. Remember that a zero precedes metric decimals and there is no zero in front of inch decimals.

Figure 21-21.
The **Geometric Tolerance** dialog box with a diameter symbol, geometric tolerance, and MMC material condition symbol added to the **Tolerance 1** area (shown here highlighted).

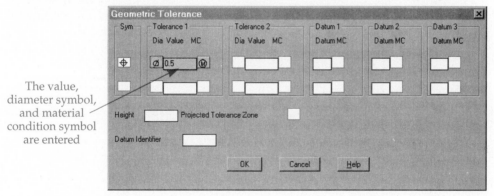

The value, diameter symbol, and material condition symbol are entered

- **Tolerance 2 area.** This compartment is used for the addition of a second geometric tolerance to the feature control frame. This is not a common application, but it may be used in some cases where there are restrictions placed on the geometric tolerance specified in the first compartment. For example, 0.8 MAX, which means that the specification given in the first compartment is maintained but cannot exceed 0.8 maximum.
- **Datum 1 area.** This is used to establish the information needed in the primary datum reference compartment. You can also enter a material condition symbol by picking **MC**.
- **Datum 2 and Datum 3 areas.** These work the same as **Datum 1**, but are for setting the secondary and tertiary datum reference information. Look back at Figure 21-9 to see how the datum reference and related material condition symbols are placed in the feature control frame.
- **Height.** Enter the height of a projected tolerance zone and pick to the right of **Projected Tolerance Zone** to access the symbol. This topic is discussed later in this chapter.

- **Datum Identifier.** If working in accordance with the ANSI Y14.5M-1982 standard, you can specify a datum feature symbol here. If you want to comply with ASME Y14.5M-1994, you need to design a datum feature symbol and save it as a block. Creating your own dimensioning symbols is discussed later in this chapter and in Chapter 23.

When you have entered all of the desired information in the **Geometric Tolerance** dialog box, pick the **OK** button. See Figure 21-22. Now the following prompt is issued:

Enter tolerance location: *(pick the place for the feature control frame to be drawn)*
Command:

The feature control frame from the previous command sequence is shown in Figure 21-23.

Figure 21-22.
The **Geometric Tolerance** dialog box with a diameter symbol, geometric tolerance, and MMC material condition symbol added to the **Tolerance 1** area. Identifiers A at **Datum 1**, B and the MMC symbol at **Datum 2**, and C at **Datum 3** are also added. (These items are shown here highlighted.)

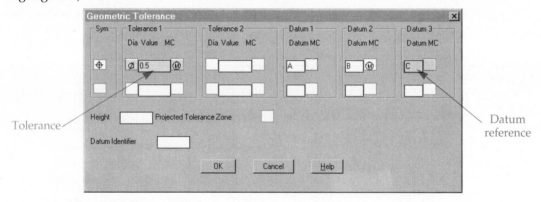

Figure 21-23.
The feature control frame created by the sequence displayed in Figure 21-22.

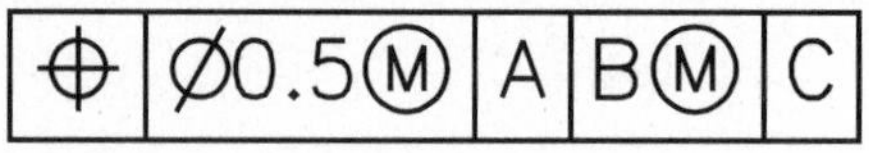

$\bigoplus$ | $\emptyset$0.5Ⓜ | A | BⓂ | C

- ❏ Begin a new drawing or use one of your prototypes. These settings are suggested:
  - ❏ Limits: 8.5,11
  - ❏ Grid: .25
  - ❏ Romans text font for dimensioning
  - ❏ Snap: .125
- ❏ Draw the same feature control frames that are displayed in Figure 21-7 and Figure 21-8.
- ❏ Save the drawing as EX21-1.

Using the LEADER command to place GD&T symbols

You can also use the **LEADER** command to access the same dialog boxes and draw a feature control frame connected to a leader line. Refer to Chapter 18 for a complete review of using the **LEADER** command. This can be accomplished by using the following command sequence:

> Command: **LE** *or* **LEADER**↵
> From point: *(pick the leader starting point)*
> To point (Format/Annotation/Undo) ⟨Annotation⟩: *(pick the end of the shoulder)*
> To point (Format/Annotation/Undo) ⟨Annotation⟩: *(press* [Enter] *for the default)*

Annotation means notes. The **Annotation** option allows you to enter a single line of text to go with the leader, or you can press the [Enter] key to get a list of **Annotation** options:

> Annotation (or press ENTER for options): ↵
> Tolerance/Copy/Block/None/⟨MText⟩: **T**↵

Enter T to access the **Tolerance** option. This activates the **Symbol** dialog box and the **Geometric Tolerance** dialog box. Establish the feature control frame information and pick **OK**. The feature control frame is connected to the leader shoulder. See Figure 21-24.

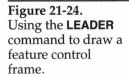

Figure 21-24.
Using the **LEADER** command to draw a feature control frame.

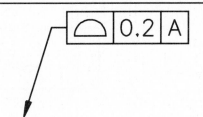

EXERCISE 21-2

❑ Load AutoCAD and open EX21-1.
❑ Draw the same feature control frame with a leader that is displayed in Figure 21-24.
❑ Save the drawing as EX21-2.

Projected Tolerance Zone Introduction

In some situations where positional tolerance is used entirely in out-of-squareness, it may be necessary to control perpendicularity and position next to the part. The use of a *projected tolerance zone* is recommended when variations in perpendicularity of threaded or press-fit holes could cause the fastener to interfere with the mating part. A projected tolerance zone is usually specified for a fixed fastener, such as the threaded hole for a bolt or the press-fit hole for a pin. The length of a projected tolerance zone can be specified as the distance the fastener extends into the mating part, the thickness of the part, or the height of a press-fit stud. The normal positional tolerance extends through the thickness of the part.

However, this application can cause an interference between the location of a thread or press-fit object and its mating part. This is because the attitude of a fixed fastener is controlled by the actual angle of the threaded hole. There is no clearance available to provide flexibility. For this reason, the projected tolerance zone is established at true position and extends away from the primary datum at the threaded feature. The projected tolerance zone provides a bigger tolerance because it is projected away from the primary datum, rather than within the thread. The projected tolerance is also easier to inspect than the tolerance applied to the pitch diameter of the thread, because a thread gauge with a post projecting above the threaded hole can be used to easily verify the projected tolerance zone with a coordinate measuring machine (CMM).

One method for displaying the projected tolerance zone is by placing the projected tolerance zone symbol and height in the feature control frame after the geometric tolerance and related material condition symbol. The related thread specification is then connected to the sectional view of the thread symbol. With this method, the projected tolerance zone is assumed to extend away from the threaded hole at the primary datum. See Figure 21-25.

Feature 21-25.
Projected tolerance zone representation with the length of the projected tolerance zone given in the feature control zone. The projected tolerance zone symbol is shown here highlighted.

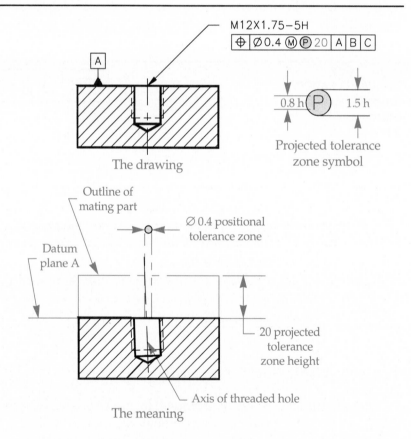

The drawing

The meaning

To provide additional clarification, the projected tolerance zone can be shown using a chain line in the view where the related datum appears as an edge and the minimum height of the projection is dimensioned. See Figure 21-26. The projected tolerance zone symbol is shown alone in the feature control frame after the geometric tolerance and material condition symbol (if any). The meaning is the same as previously discussed.

Figure 21-26.
Projected tolerance zone representation with the length of the projected tolerance zone shown with a chain line and a minimum dimension in the adjacent view. The projected tolerance zone symbol is shown here highlighted.

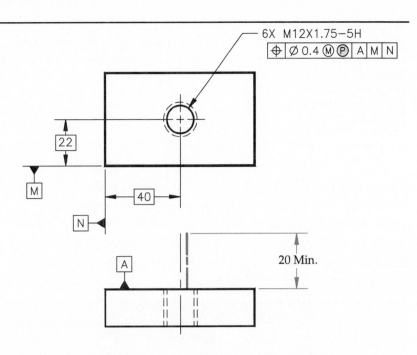

Drawing the projected tolerance zone with AutoCAD

You can add projected tolerance zone specifications to the feature control frame by using the **Geometric Tolerance** dialog box. Type the desired geometric tolerance, diameter symbol, material condition symbol, and datum reference as previously discussed. Type the projected tolerance zone height in the **Height** text box. Notice that 24 is entered in the **Height** text box in Figure 21-27. Pick the **Projected Tolerance Zone** image tile to insert the projected tolerance zone symbol. Pick the **OK** button when ready.

Figure 21-27.
Entering the projected tolerance zone height and symbol in the **Geometric Tolerance** dialog box.

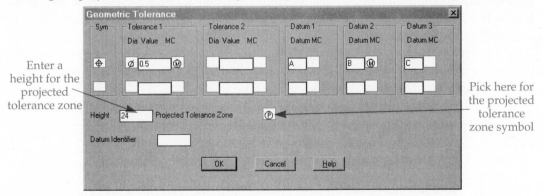

Now follow the screen prompts and place the feature control frame in the desired location. Notice in Figure 21-28 that AutoCAD displays the projected tolerance zone height in a separate compartment below the feature control frame. This representation is in accordance with ANSI Y14.5M-1982. The ASME Y14.5M-1994 convention has no lower compartment, as shown in Figure 21-25.

Figure 21-28.
The AutoCAD
feature control
frame with
projected tolerance
zone compartment
conforms to ANSI
Y14.5M-1982
standards.

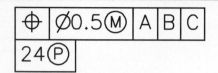

If you want to dimension the projected tolerance zone height with a chain line, then omit the **Height** in the **Geometric Tolerance** dialog box and only pick the projected tolerance zone symbol. This adds a compartment below the feature control frame with only the projected tolerance zone symbol. This representation is in accordance with ANSI Y14.5M-1982, but does not match the ASME Y14.5M-1994 convention illustrated in Figure 21-26.

EXERCISE 21-3

❑ Start AutoCAD and open EX21-1.
❑ Draw the feature control frame and projected tolerance zone compartment shown in Figure 21-28.
❑ Save the drawing as EX21-3.

Drawing a Double-Feature Control Frame

Several GD&T applications require that the feature control frame be doubled in height, with two sets of geometric tolerancing information provided. These applications include unit straightness and flatness, composite positional tolerance, and coaxial positional tolerance. Use the **TOLERANCE** or **LEADER** command and pick the desired geometric characteristic symbol from the **Symbol** dialog box. When the **Geometric Tolerance** dialog box is displayed, pick the bottom **Sym** image tile. The **Symbol** dialog box is displayed again. Pick another geometric characteristic symbol. This results in two symbols displayed in the **Sym** area. See Figure 21-29. Continue picking and typing the needed information in both sets of tolerance and datum compartments.

Figure 21-29.
Double-feature control frame information displayed in the **Geometric Tolerance** dialog box.

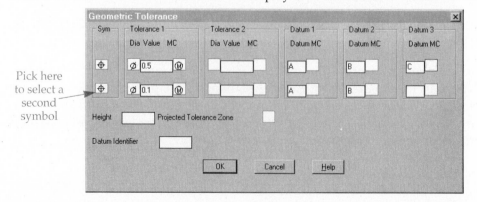

AutoCAD and its Applications—Basics

If the two symbols in the **Sym** image tiles are the same, then the double-feature control frame is drawn with one geometric characteristic symbol displayed in the first compartment. See Figure 21-30A. If you are drawing a double-feature control frame with different geometric characteristic symbols for a combination control, then the feature control frame has two separate compartments. See Figure 21-30B.

Figure 21-30.
A—If the same symbol is entered in the **Sym** image tiles of the **Geometric Tolerance** dialog box, it will be displayed once in the first compartment of the feature control frame. B—If two different symbols are used, they are displayed in two separate compartments.

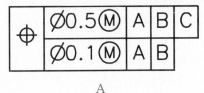

A

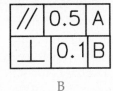

B

EXERCISE 21-4

❑ Start AutoCAD and open EX21-1.
❑ Draw the feature control frames shown in Figure 21-30.
❑ Save the drawing as EX21-4.

Drawing the Datum Feature Symbol

To draw the datum feature symbol with AutoCAD, use the **TOLERANCE** or **LEADER** command. When you get the **Symbol** dialog box, pick the blank option and then pick **OK**. This accesses the **Geometric Tolerance** dialog box without any geometric characteristic symbol displayed. Type the desired datum identification (–A–) in the **Datum Identifier** text box. See Figure 21-31.

Pick the **OK** button and then place the datum feature symbol in the desired position on the drawing. The resulting datum feature symbol correlates with ANSI Y14.5M-1982. See Figure 21-32A. You can also draw an ANSI Y14.5M-1982 datum feature symbol connected to a feature control frame by selecting the desired geometric characteristic symbol and entering the needed information in the **Geometric Tolerance** dialog box. See Figure 21-32B.

Figure 21-31.
Enter a datum identifier in the text box found in the **Geometric Tolerance** dialog box. This creates a datum feature symbol based or ANSI Y14.5M-1982 standards.

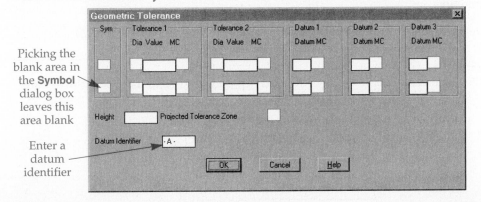

Picking the blank area in the **Symbol** dialog box leaves this area blank

Enter a datum identifier

Figure 21-32.
A—A datum feature symbol drawn without a feature control frame. B—A datum feature symbol drawn with a feature control frame. Note that these datum feature symbols are drawn to the ANSI Y14.5M-1982 standards.

A   B

PROFESSIONAL TIP

Chapter 23 of this text gives you a detailed discussion on how to create your own custom symbol libraries. It is recommended that you design dimensioning symbols that are not available in AutoCAD. Dimensioning symbols might include the counterbore, countersink, depth, and other symbols displayed in Figure 21-1. Geometric tolerancing symbols can include the datum feature symbol that is currently recognized by ASME Y14.5M-1994. See Figure 21-13.

Controlling the Height of the Feature Control Frame

Figure 21-9 shows the height of the feature control frame as being twice the height of the text. Text on engineering drawings is generally .125" (3mm). This makes the feature control frame height equal to .25" (6mm). The distance from the text to the feature control frame is controlled by the **DIMGAP** dimension variable. The **DIMGAP** default is .09". If the drawing text is .125", then the space between the text and the feature control frame should be .0625" to get a .25" high frame. Change **DIMGAP** by entering a new value in the **Gap:** text box in the text area of the **Annotation** dialog box. Remember that the **Annotation** dialog box is opened by picking the **Annotation...** button in the **Dimension** styles dialog box. Change the **DIMGAP** at the Command: prompt as follows:

        Command: **DIMGAP**↵
        New value for DIMGAP ⟨0.09⟩: **.0625**↵
        Command:

The results of this setting is shown in the feature control frame in Figure 21-33.

Figure 21-33.
The **DIMGAP** dimension variable controls the distance from the text to the box in the feature control frame and the basic and the basic dimension. Note: This value applies to both sides of the text.

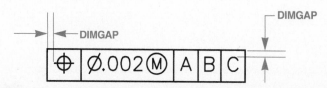

Drawing Basic Dimensions

You can have AutoCAD automatically draw basic dimensions using the **Dimension Styles** dialog box. Remember, access this dialog box by picking the **Dimension Styles** button on the **Dimension** toolbar, by picking **Dimension Style...** in the **Format** pull-down menu, or by typing D or DDIM at the Command: prompt.

When inside the **Dimension Styles** dialog box, pick the **Annotation...** button to get the **Annotation** dialog box. To access the basic dimension feature, pick **Basic** in the **Method:** drop-down list in the **Tolerance** area. See Figure 21-34. Notice that the image tile in the **Primary Units** area displays a basic dimension example.

Figure 21-34.
Use the **DDIM** command to access the **Dimension Styles** dialog box. Then, pick **Basic** in the **Annotation** dialog box to draw basic dimensions. You can also pick on the image tile to cycle through the options.

The image tile adjusts to basic dimensions

Select **Basic** from the list

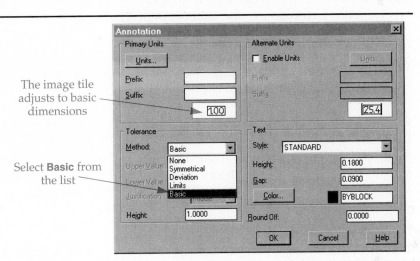

You can also activate the basic dimension feature by picking the image tile and cycling through the options until you get the basic dimension example. Pick the **OK** button in the **Annotation** dialog box and the **Dimension Styles** dialog boxes to return to the drawing editor and begin drawing basic dimensions. See Figure 21-35. The **DIMGAP** variable also controls the space between the basic dimension text and the box around the dimension.

Figure 21-35.
An AutoCAD basic dimension.

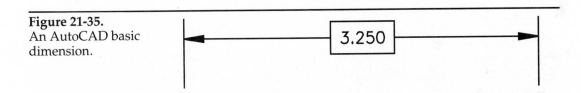

3.250

EXERCISE 21-6

- ❏ Load the AutoCAD and open EX21-1.
- ❏ The dimension text height was set to .125″ in EX21-1. Set the **DIMGAP** dimension variable so the feature control frame height is two times the text height. (**DIMGAP** = .0625)
- ❏ Draw the feature control frame shown in Figure 21-33.
- ❏ Draw the basic dimension shown in Figure 21-35.
- ❏ Save the drawing as EX21-6.

Editing the Feature Control Frame

A feature control frame acts as one object. When you pick any place on the frame, the entire object is selected. You can edit feature control frames using **ERASE**, **COPY**, **MOVE**, **ROTATE**, and **SCALE**. The **STRETCH** command and **GRIPS** only move the feature control frame, similar to when they are used with text objects.

You can edit the information inside of a feature control frame by using the **DDEDIT** command. When you enter **DDEDIT** and select the desired feature control frame, the **Geometric Tolerance** dialog box is displayed with all of the current values displayed. Make any desired changes and pick the **OK** button. The feature control frame is now revised as needed. You can also use the **DDEDIT** command to edit basic dimensions. This displays the **Edit Multiline Text** dialog box, where you can edit the basic dimension as any other dimension.

Sample GD&T Applications

This chapter is intended to give you a general overview of GD&T applications and basic instruction on how to draw GD&T symbols using AutoCAD. If you are in the manufacturing industry, you may have considerable use for geometric dimensioning and tolerancing. The support information may be a review or it may inspire you to learn more about this topic. The drawings in Figure 21-36 are intended to show you some common GD&T applications using the available geometric characteristics.

Figure 21-36.
Examples of typical geometric dimensioning and tolerancing applications using various geometric characteristics.

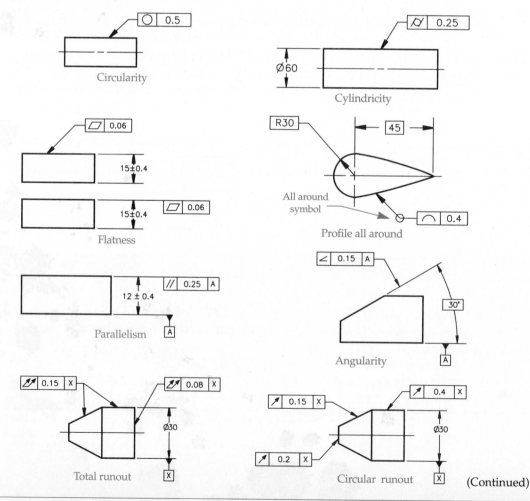

(Continued)

Figure 21-36.
(Continued)

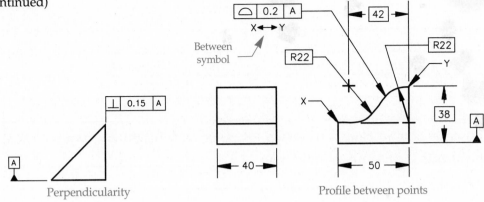

Between symbol

Perpendicularity

Profile between points

Chapter Test

Write your answers in the spaces provided:

1. Name each of the following geometric characteristic symbols:

A. _____   H. _____

B. _____   I. _____

C. _____   J. _____

D. _____   K. _____

E. _____   L. _____

F. _____   M. _____

G. _____   N. _____

2. Label the parts of the following feature control frame:

A. _____

B. _____

C. _____

D. _____

E. _____

F. _____

G. _____

⊕ ⌀ 0.05 Ⓜ A B Ⓜ C

3. Name two commands that can be used to draw a feature control frame. _____

_____

4. Identify the dialog box that contains the geometric characteristic symbols.

_____

5. What appears after you pick a geometric characteristic symbol followed by picking OK in the dialog box identified in Question 4? _____

_____

6. Identify the procedure used to draw a feature control frame connected to a leader. _____

_____

_____

_____

_____

_____

7. Describe how to place a projected tolerance zone height and symbol compartment with the feature control frame. _____

_____

_____

_____

_____

8. How do you get one symbol in the first compartment of a double-feature control frame? _____

_____

_____

_____

_____

_____

9. How do you get two different geometric characteristic symbols in the first compartments of a double-feature control frame? _____

_____

_____

_____

_____

10. Describe how to draw a basic dimension with AutoCAD. _____

_____

_____

_____

_____

11. Identify the dimension variable that controls the space between the text in a feature control frame and basic dimension and the box surrounding these items.

_____

12. Describe how to draw a datum feature symbol with AutoCAD, without drawing an attached feature control frame. _____

_____

_____

_____

13. Name the command that can be used to change the information in an existing feature control frame. _____

14. How do you get a **Geometric Tolerance** dialog box without any symbol shown in the **Sym** image tiles?_____

_____

_____

_____

15. Name the current standard for dimensioning and tolerancing that is adopted by the American National Standards Institute and published by the American Society of Mechanical Engineers._____

_____

Drawing Problems

Create dimension styles that will assist you in the solution of these problems. Draw fully dimensioned multiview drawings. The required number of views depends upon the problem and is to be determined by you. Apply geometric tolerancing as discussed in this chapter. Use ANSI Y14.5M-1982 standards as applied by AutoCAD, or modify the available applications to use ASME Y14.5M-1994 standards. The problems are presented with ASME Y14.5M-1994 standards.

1. Open P20-5 and edit by adding the geometric tolerancing shown below. If you did not draw P20-5, then open a new drawing and draw the problem now. Untoleranced dimensions are ±0.5. Save as P21-1.

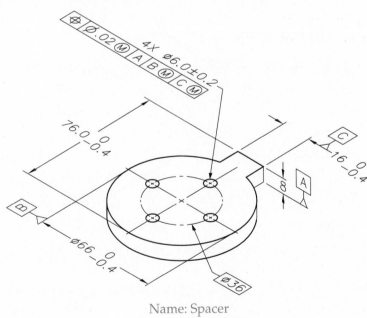

Name: Spacer
Material: SAE 1085
Metric

2. Open P20-6 and edit by adding the geometric tolerancing shown
   below. If you did not draw P20-6, then open a new drawing and draw
   the problem now. Note: The problem is shown with a cutaway for
   clarity. You do not need to draw a section. Untoleranced dimensions
   XX = ±.02 and XXX = ±.005. Save as P21-2.

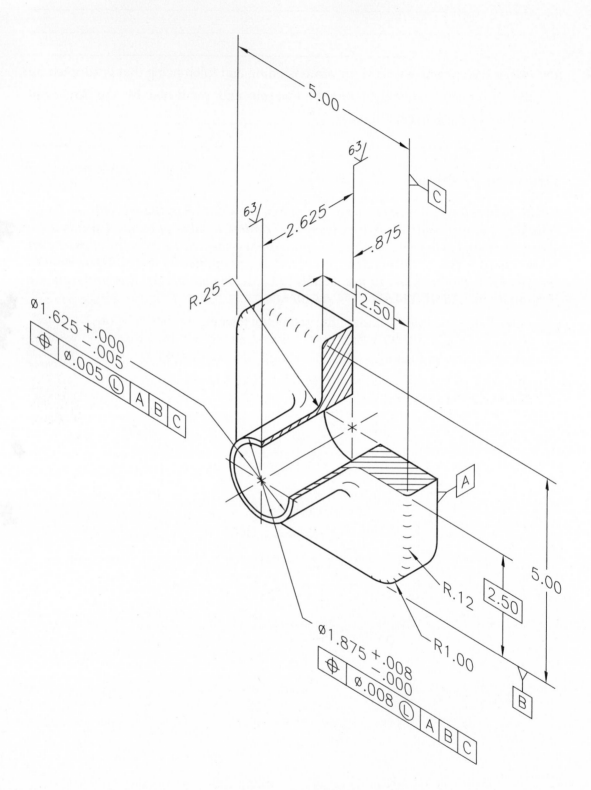

Name: Thrust Washer
Material: SAE 5150
Inch

3. Open P20-7 and edit by adding the geometric tolerancing shown below. If you did not draw P20-7, then open a new drawing and draw the problem now. Save as P21-3.

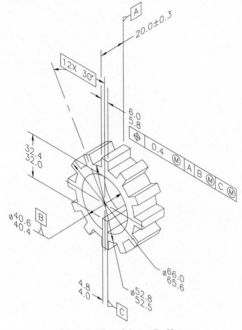

Name: Locking Collar
Material: SAE 1080
Metric

4. Draw the following object as previously instructed. Untoleranced dimensions are ±0.3. Save as P21-4.

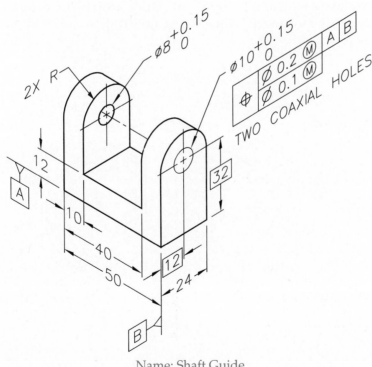

Name: Shaft Guide
Material: Cast Iron
Metric

---

5. Draw the following object as previously instructed. Note: The problem is shown with a full section for clarity. You do not need to draw a section. Untoleranced dimensions are ±.010. Save as P21-5.

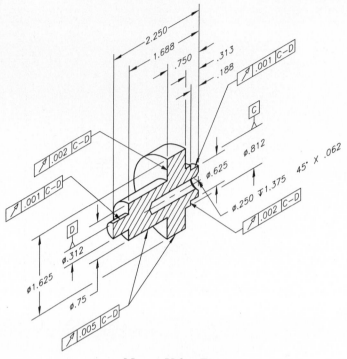

Name: Valve Pin
Material: Phosphor Bronze
Inch

6. Draw the following object as previously instructed. Note: The problem is shown with a half section for clarity. You do not need to draw a section. Untoleranced dimensions are ±.010. Save as P21-6.

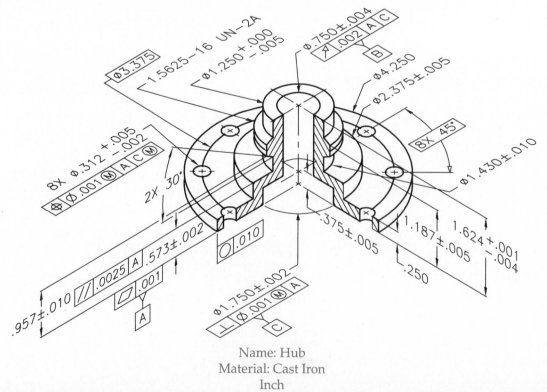

Name: Hub
Material: Cast Iron
Inch

7. Open P18-31 and edit by adding the geometric tolerancing shown below. If you did not draw P18-31, then open a new drawing and draw the problem now. Save as P21-7.

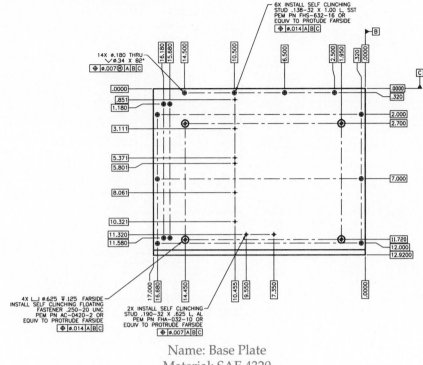

Name: Base Plate
Material: SAE 4320
Inch

8. Open P18-32 and edit by adding the geometric tolerancing shown below. If you did not draw P18-32, then open a new drawing and draw the problem now. Save as P21-8.

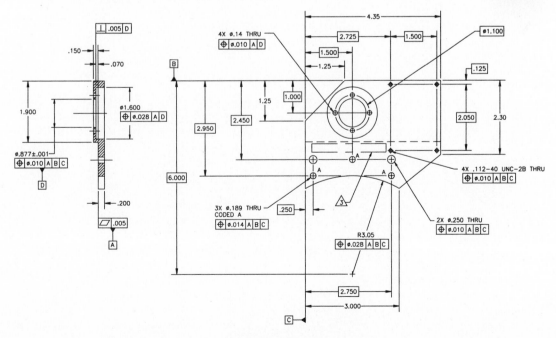

Name: Bracket
Material: SAE 1040
Inch

9. Open P18-33 and edit by adding the geometric tolerancing shown below. If you did not draw P18-33, then open a new drawing and draw the problem now. Save as P21-9.

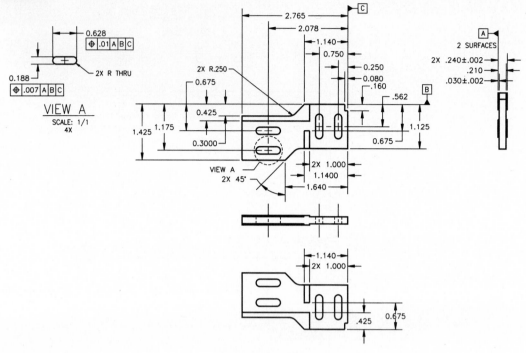

Name: Support
Material: Aluminum
Inch

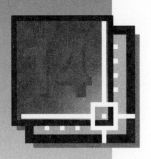

Drawing Section Views and Graphic Patterns

Learning Objectives

After completing this chapter, you will be able to:
- ○ Identify sectioning techniques.
- ○ Use sections and dimensioning practices to draw objects given in engineering sketches.
- ○ Draw section material using the **HATCH**, **BHATCH**, and **SOLID** commands.
- ○ Prepare graphic displays, such as graphs and logos, using the **HATCH** and **SOLID** commands.
- ○ Interpret a hatch pattern definition and create your own custom hatch pattern using the Windows Notepad.
- ○ Edit existing associative hatch patterns using **HATCHEDIT**.

In mechanical drafting, internal features in multiviews appear as hidden lines. These features must be dimensioned. However, it is poor practice to dimension to hidden lines. Therefore, section views are used to clarify the hidden features.

Section views show internal features as if a portion of the object is cut away. They are used in conjunction with multiviews to completely describe the exterior and interior features of an object.

When sections are drawn, a *cutting-plane line* is placed in one of the views to show where the cut was made. The cutting-plane line is the *saw* that cuts through the object to expose internal features. It is drawn with a thick dashed or phantom line in accordance with ANSI Y14.2M. The arrows on the cutting-plane line indicate the line of sight when looking at the section view.

The cutting-plane lines are often labeled with letters that relate to the proper section view. A title, such as SECTION A-A, is placed under the view. When more than one section view is drawn, labels continue with B-B through Z-Z. The letters I, O, and Q are not used because they may be confused with numbers.

Labeling multiple section views is necessary for drawings with multiple sections. When only one section view is present and its location is obvious, a label is not needed. Section lines are used in the section view to show where the material has been cut away. See Figure 22-1.

Sectioning is also used in other drafting fields, such as architectural and structural drafting. Cross sections through buildings show the construction methods and materials. See Figure 22-2. The cutting-plane lines used in these fields are often composed of letter and number symbols. This helps coordinate the large number of sections found in a set of architectural drawings.

Figure 22-1.
A three-view
multiview drawing
with a section view.

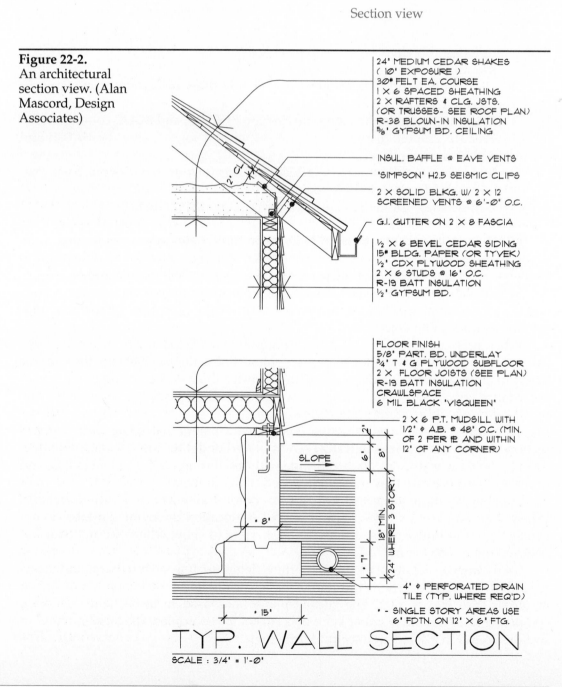

Direction
of sight

Cutting–plane label

Cutting–
plane line

Regular
multiviews

Section
lines

SECTION A–A

Section–view label

Section view

Figure 22-2.
An architectural
section view. (Alan
Mascord, Design
Associates)

24" MEDIUM CEDAR SHAKES
(10" EXPOSURE)
30# FELT EA. COURSE
1 X 6 SPACED SHEATHING
2 X RAFTERS & CLG. JSTS.
(OR TRUSSES- SEE ROOF PLAN)
R-38 BLOWN-IN INSULATION
⅜" GYPSUM BD. CEILING

INSUL. BAFFLE @ EAVE VENTS

'SIMPSON' H2.5 SEISMIC CLIPS

2 X SOLID BLKG. W/ 2 X 12
SCREENED VENTS @ 6'-0" O.C.

G.I. GUTTER ON 2 X 8 FASCIA

½ X 6 BEVEL CEDAR SIDING
15# BLDG. PAPER (OR TYVEK)
½" CDX PLYWOOD SHEATHING
2 X 6 STUDS @ 16' O.C.
R-19 BATT INSULATION
½" GYPSUM BD.

FLOOR FINISH
5/8" PART. BD. UNDERLAY
¾" T & G PLYWOOD SUBFLOOR
2 X FLOOR JOISTS (SEE PLAN)
R-19 BATT INSULATION
CRAWLSPACE
6 MIL BLACK 'VISQUEEN'

2 X 6 P.T. MUDSILL WITH
1/2" ⌀ A.B. @ 48" O.C. (MIN.
OF 2 PER 12 AND WITHIN
12' OF ANY CORNER)

SLOPE

4" ⌀ PERFORATED DRAIN
TILE (TYP. WHERE REQ'D)

* - SINGLE STORY AREAS USE
6' FDTN. ON 12" X 6" FTG.

TYP. WALL SECTION

SCALE : 3/4' = 1'-0'

AutoCAD and its Applications—Basics

Types of Sections

There are many types of sections available for the drafter to use. The section used depends on the detail to be sectioned. For example, one object may require the section be taken completely through the object. Another may only need to remove a small portion to expose the interior features.

Full sections remove half of the object. See Figure 22-1. In this type of section, the cutting-plane line passes completely through the object along a center plane.

Offset sections are the same as full sections, except that the cutting-plane line is staggered. This allows you to cut through features that are not in a straight line. See Figure 22-3.

Figure 22-3.
An offset section.

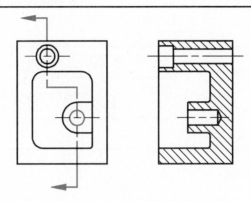

Half sections show one-quarter of the object removed. The term *half* is used because half of the view appears in section and the other half is shown as an exterior view. Half sections are commonly used on symmetrical objects. A centerline is used to separate the sectioned part of the view from the unsectioned portion. Hidden lines are normally omitted from the unsectioned side. See Figure 22-4.

Figure 22-4.
A half section.

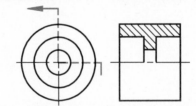

Aligned sections are used when a feature is out of alignment with the center plane. In this case, an offset section will distort the image. The cutting-plane line cuts through the feature to be sectioned. It is then rotated to align with the center plane before projecting into the section view. See Figure 22-5.

Revolved sections clarify the contour of objects that have the same shape throughout their length. The section is revolved in place within the object, or part of the view may be broken away. See Figure 22-6. This section makes dimensioning easier.

Removed sections serve much the same function as revolved sections. The section view is removed from the regular view. A cutting-plane line shows where the section was taken. When multiple removed sections are taken, the cutting planes and related views are labeled. The section views are placed in alphabetical order. The letters *I*, *O*, and *Q* are not used because they may be mistaken for numbers. Drawing only the ends of the cutting-plane lines simplifies the views. See Figure 22-7.

Broken-out sections show only a small portion of the object removed. This section is used to clarify a hidden feature. See Figure 22-8.

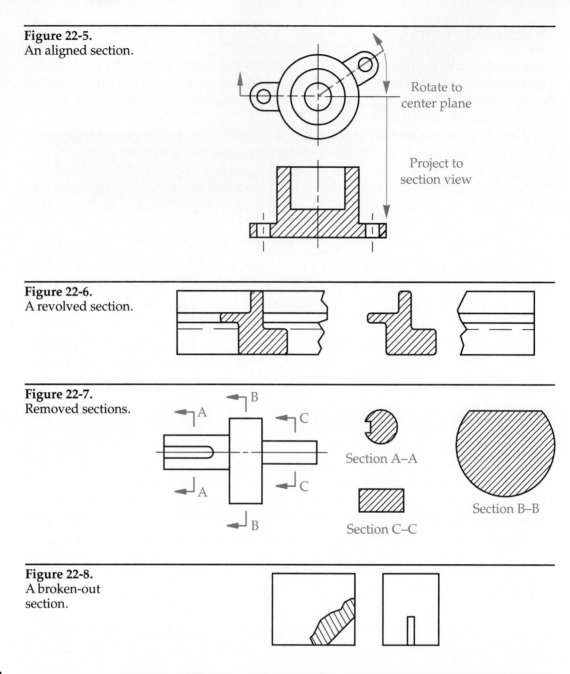

Figure 22-5.
An aligned section.

Rotate to center plane

Project to section view

Figure 22-6.
A revolved section.

Figure 22-7.
Removed sections.

Section A–A

Section C–C

Section B–B

Figure 22-8.
A broken-out section.

AutoCAD User's Guide **4**

Section Line Symbols

Section lines are placed in the section view to show where material has been cut away. The following rules govern section line usage:

- Section lines are placed at 45° unless another angle is required to satisfy the next two rules.
- Section lines should not be drawn parallel or perpendicular to any other adjacent lines on the drawing.
- Section lines should not cross object lines.
- Avoid section lines placed at angles greater than 75° or less than 15° from horizontal.

Section lines may be drawn using different patterns to represent the specific type of material. Equally-spaced section lines represent a general application. This is adequate in most situations. Additional patterns are not necessary if the type of material is clearly indicated in the title block. Different section line material symbols are needed when connected parts of different materials are sectioned.

AutoCAD has standard section line symbols available. These are referred to as *hatch patterns*. These symbols are located in the acad.pat file. The AutoCAD pattern labeled ANSI31 is the general section line symbol and is the default pattern in a new drawing. It is also used for cast iron. The ANSI32 symbol is used for sectioning steel. Other standard AutoCAD hatch patterns are shown in Figure 22-9.

Figure 22-9.
Standard AutoCAD hatch patterns. (Autodesk, Inc.)

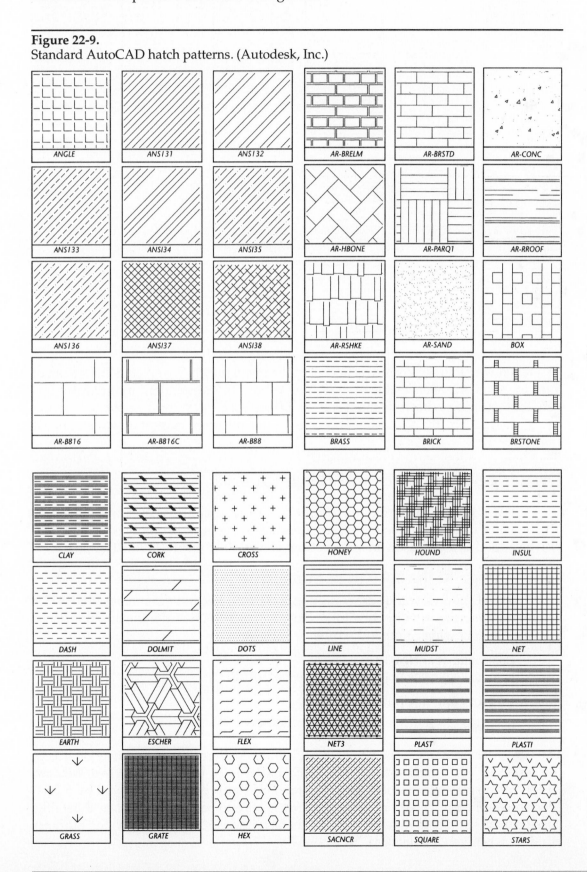

Figure 22-9.
(Continued)

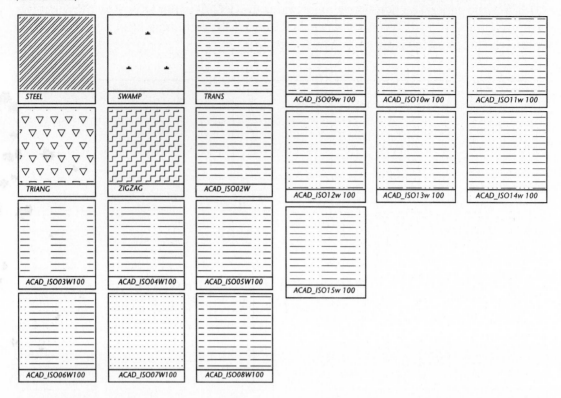

When very thin objects are sectioned, the material may be completely blackened or filled in. AutoCAD refers to this as *solid*. The ASME Y14.2 M standard recommends that very thin sections be drawn without section lines or solid fill. When you change to a different hatch pattern, the new pattern becomes the default in the current drawing until it is changed.

Drawing Section Lines and Hatch Patterns

AutoCAD hatch patterns are not limited to sectioning. They can be used as artistic patterns in a graphic layout for an advertisement or promotion. They might also be added as shading on an architectural elevation or technical illustration.

Introduction to the HATCH command

HATCH
-H

AutoCAD allows you to draw section lines or other patterns using the **HATCH** command. Entering -H (a hyphen followed by H) or HATCH at the Command: prompt displays the following command sequence options:

> Command: **-H** *or* **HATCH**↵
> Enter pattern name or [?/Solid/User defined] ⟨ANSI31⟩:

Entering ? gives you this prompt:

> Pattern(s) to list ⟨*⟩:

You can enter the name or names of specific hatch patterns, or press [Enter] to accept the wildcard (*), which lists all the hatch patterns in the **AutoCAD Text Window**. AutoCAD displays the names of all the standard hatch patterns followed by a brief description of each. The list of pattern names is several pages long, so use [Enter], the space bar, or scroll bars to scroll through the list. Press [F2] to go back to the graphics window when you are finished.

To draw a hatch pattern, press [Enter] at the Enter pattern name or [?/Solid/User defined] ⟨ANSI31⟩: prompt to accept the ANSI31 default pattern, or enter a different pattern name. You are then asked to define the pattern scale and angle.

Enter pattern name or [?/Solid/User defined] ⟨ANSI31⟩: ↵
Scale for pattern ⟨1.0000⟩: ↵
Angle for pattern ⟨0⟩: ↵

Press [Enter] after each prompt to use the default value shown in brackets. The pattern scale default is 1 (full scale). If the drawn pattern is too tight or too wide, type a new scale. Figure 22-10 shows different scale factors.

Figure 22-10.
Hatch pattern scale factors.

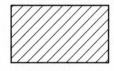
Scale = 1

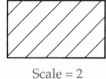
Scale = 2

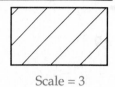
Scale = 3

The relationship between the hatch scale in model space and paper space is controlled by the scale factor. The default scale factor of 1 specifies one drawing unit. Respond to the scale prompt with the desired size of the pattern in model space or paper space.

The hatch scale can be specified referencing model space, if desired. However, it is much simpler to reference the scale to paper space. This allows the scale factor to be based on the plotted scale of the drawing. To do this, enter XP after the scale. The XP indicates "relative to paper space units". Therefore, entering 1XP as the scale factor causes AutoCAD to automatically calculate the actual scale required within model space to match the specified value of 1 in paper space:

Scale for pattern ⟨1.0000⟩: **1XP**↵

When you do this, notice that the next use of the **HATCH** command offers the actual pattern scale calculated by AutoCAD as the default. It is not necessary to enter 1XP again since the default value shown is the model space equivalent. Model space and paper space are discussed in detail in Chapter 10 of this text.

An alternative method of entering values for this prompt is by picking two points in the drawing. AutoCAD then measures the distance and uses it as the scale factor. This method does not allow the **XP** option to be used.

The pattern default angle is 0. This gives you the same pattern angle shown in Figure 22-9. To alter the pattern angle, type a new value.

PROFESSIONAL TIP

When you start AutoCAD with a Wizard, the hatch pattern scale factor is automatically set based on the information you provide. The adjusted settings are related to the full scale of the objects you draw. You can leave the settings as established by AutoCAD or you can change them. If you are using a template or starting AutoCAD from scratch, you can set the hatch pattern scale factor to match the drawing size.

Enter a larger scale factor when hatching large areas. This makes your section lines look neater and saves regeneration and plot time. For metric drawings, set the hatch scale to 25.4, because 1″ = 25.4mm.

Selecting objects to be hatched

It is important to consider the boundary of the area you plan to hatch. It is easy to hatch within a circle or square. When the Select objects: prompt appears, pick the circle, or window the square. If the square was drawn as one closed polyline, then pick it as one entity. The circumference of the circle and the perimeter of the square automatically become the hatch boundary. See Figure 22-11.

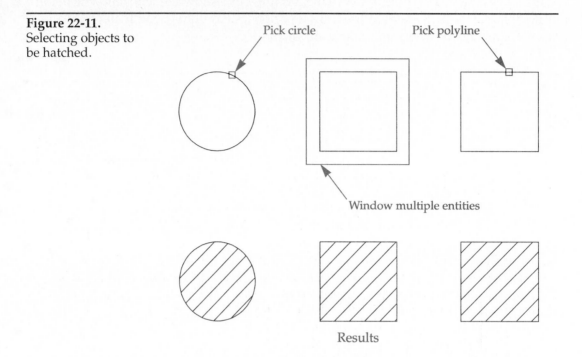

Figure 22-11.
Selecting objects to be hatched.

Pick circle

Pick polyline

Window multiple entities

Results

Drawing a hatch without selecting objects

A problem may arise when you try to hatch an object that is composed of more than one enclosed area. If adjacent areas are drawn with interconnecting lines, the hatching may not be what you expect. Only the right side of each pair of blocks in Figure 22-12 is to be hatched. Notice the possible results using **Window** selection and picking the lines of the right side.

To overcome the problems that can occur (as were shown in Figure 22-12), AutoCAD provides a feature called *direct hatching*, which allows you to define a boundary without selecting any objects. So, if you want to successfully hatch the right side of Figure 22-12, use the direct hatching option to place a polyline boundary around the area to be hatched. You can keep the polyline or delete it. When you see the Retain polyline? ⟨N⟩: prompt, press [Enter] to accept the default to have the polyline boundary removed after the hatch is drawn. Type Y and press [Enter] to keep the polyline boundary. If you type Y to keep the polyline boundary, then the ⟨Y⟩ option becomes the default for the next **HATCH** operation until changed again. When you pick the first point of the polyline boundary, you get options that are just like the **PLINE** command:

        Command: **-H** *or* **HATCH**↵
        Enter pattern name or [?/Solid/User defined] ⟨ANSI31⟩: ↵
        Scale for pattern ⟨1.0000⟩: ↵
        Angle for pattern ⟨0⟩: ↵
        Select hatch boundaries or press ENTER for direct hatch option,
        Select objects: ↵
        Retain polyline? ⟨N⟩ ↵

Figure 22-12.
When selecting an area made up of interconnecting lines, the results may be undesirable. A—AutoCAD would not hatch the area and gave the error message: Unable to hatch the boundary. B—The hatch extends into the adjacent area.

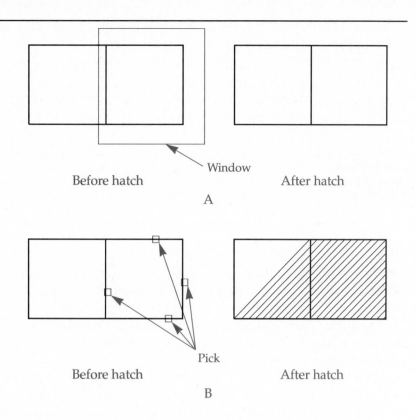

Before hatch   Window   After hatch

A

Before hatch   Pick   After hatch

B

From point: *(pick the first point at a corner of the right square in Figure 22-13)*
Arc/Close/Length/Undo/⟨Next point⟩: *(pick point 2)*
Arc/Close/Length/Undo/⟨Next point⟩: *(pick point 3)*
Arc/Close/Length/Undo/⟨Next point⟩: *(pick point 4)*
Arc/Close/Length/Undo/⟨Next point⟩: **C**↵

Figure 22-13.
Using direct hatching.

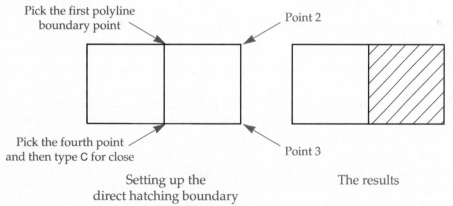

Pick the first polyline boundary point

Point 2

Pick the fourth point and then type C for close

Point 3

Setting up the direct hatching boundary

The results

You can draw another polyline boundary or you can press [Enter] to have the hatch drawn in the boundary that you just finished:

From point or press ENTER to apply hatch: ↵
Command:

You do not have to draw a hatch pattern in a predefined area. You can draw a hatch pattern anyplace using the direct hatching method. The hatch pattern can be drawn with or without the polyline boundary. See Figure 22-14.

Figure 22-14.
You can draw a hatch pattern with or without the polyline boundary defined.

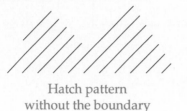

Hatch pattern
without the boundary

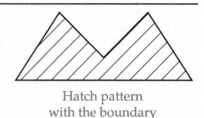

Hatch pattern
with the boundary

The hatch pattern is nonassociative

An associative pattern is a hatch pattern that is automatically updated when an object is edited. Patterns drawn with the **HATCH** command are nonassociative. This means that if you pick only the hatch boundary to edit, the hatch pattern does not change with it. For example, if you pick a hatch boundary to scale, only the boundary is scaled while the pattern remains the same. You need to select both the boundary and the pattern before editing.

The **HATCH** command creates a true hatch object. This means that the appearance of the hatch pattern can be modified with the **HATCHEDIT** command, which is covered later in this chapter. If the **HATCH** command is used to create a hatch with the ANSI31 pattern, it can be modified to any pattern defined in the acad.pat file.

Making individual line hatch patterns

When you use the **HATCH** command and draw a hatch pattern using any of the designated hatch names, the pattern is drawn as a block. This means that the entire hatch pattern acts as one object. For example, if you pick one line of the pattern to erase, the entire hatch pattern is erased. You can make each line of the hatch pattern an individual object by typing an asterisk (*) before the hatch pattern name:

> Command: **-H** *or* **HATCH**↵
> Enter pattern name or [?/Solid/User defined] 〈*current*〉 ***ANSI31**↵

The rest of the command sequence works as previously discussed. Now, each line in the hatch pattern is a single object. This allows you to edit the lines individually. Include all of the lines in a selection set if you want to edit them together. The individual line hatch pattern remains as default until changed. Be sure to change it if you want to draw the next hatch pattern as a block. A hatch pattern can also be exploded to create individual lines.

EXERCISE 22-1

❑ Start AutoCAD and use one of your templates.
❑ Draw object lines on the Object layer or other appropriately named layer.
❑ Create a new layer for hatch lines and set the color as desired. Name the layer Hatch. Save this to update your template.
❑ Use the **?** option of the **HATCH** command to look at the list of hatch patterns in the **AutoCAD Text Window**. Return to the Command: prompt.
❑ Practice using the **HATCH** command by drawing the objects from the following figures with the specified patterns:
  ❑ Figure 22-10. Set the scale as shown. Use ANSI31 and angle 0.

❑ Figure 22-11. The first object is a circle. The second object is a square drawn using the **LINE** command and the last line closed. The third object is a square drawn using the **PLINE** command and the last polyline segment closed. Use ANSI31, scale 1, and angle 0.

❑ Figure 22-13. Draw the figure shown on the left using any combination of interconnecting lines. Hatch only the right side using the direct hatching option. Use ANSI31, scale 1, and angle 0.

❑ Figure 22-14. Use the direct hatching option to draw shapes that are similar to the examples. Draw one with the polyline boundary deleted and the other with the polyline boundary kept. Use ANSI31, scale 1, and angle 0.

❑ Save the drawing as EX22-1.

Hatching around text

AutoCAD automatically places an imaginary box around the text in a hatch boundary. Hatch patterns are not placed inside of these imaginary boxes. The text must also be selected as an element of the hatch boundary for this to work properly. An example is the bar graph shown in Figure 22-15. Always place the text before hatching the area. Be sure you pick the object and the text:

Command: **-H** *or* **HATCH**↵
Enter pattern name or [?/Solid/User defined] 〈*current*〉: ↵
Scale for pattern 〈1.0000〉: ↵
Angle for pattern 〈0〉: ↵
Select hatch boundaries or press ENTER for direct hatch option,
Select objects: *(pick the object to be hatched)*
n found
Select objects: *(pick the text to be hatched around)*
Select objects: ↵
Command:

In the previous example, the object and the text were picked individually. You can also window both for this to work.

Figure 22-15.
Hatching around text.

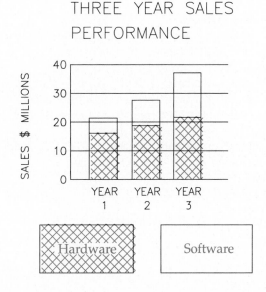

THREE YEAR SALES PERFORMANCE

Hatching objects solid

The **HATCH** command can also be used to make objects solid by using the **Solid** option. The **Solid** option is accessed by entering S for the hatch pattern name. As with any hatch pattern that you use, the SOLID pattern becomes the default until you change it again. See Figure 22-16.

Figure 22-16.
Using the **Solid** option of the **HATCH** command to make solid objects.

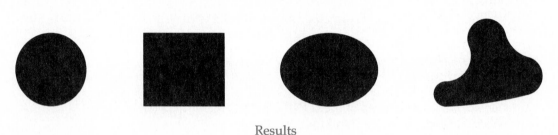

Select Objects to
be Made Solid

Results

Drawing your own simple hatch patterns

When you enter HATCH at the Command: prompt, one of the options is **User defined**. This allows you to provide angle, spacing, and single or double specifications for a very simple hatch pattern. See Figure 22-17. The command sequence is as follows:

> Command: **HATCH**↵
> Enter pattern name or [?/Solid/User defined] ⟨*current*⟩: **U**↵
> Angle for crosshatch lines ⟨0⟩: (*specify an angle, or pick two points on the screen and press* [Enter] *to accept the default angle*)
> Spacing between lines ⟨1.0000⟩: (*type in the spacing desired, or pick two points on the screen to define the spacing and press* [Enter] *to accept the default spacing*)
> Double hatch area? ⟨N⟩ (*type* Y *and press* [Enter] *for double hatch lines, or press* [Enter] *for the single hatch default*)
> Select hatch boundaries or press ENTER for direct hatch option,
> Select objects: (*pick the object to be hatched*)
> *n* found
> Select objects: ↵
> Command:

Figure 22-17.
Using the **User defined** option of the **HATCH** command.

0 Angle
.125 single hatch

45° .125 Space
single hatch

45° .125 Space
double hatch

45° .25 Space
double hatch

The relationship between the hatch line spacing in model space and paper space is controlled by the scale factor. If you are planning to plot a drawing at 1/2″ = 1″ (half scale), then the scale factor is 2. This means that one model space unit is equal to 2 paper space units. AutoCAD automatically controls this line spacing when you enter a line spacing of 2XP:

> Spacing between lines ⟨1.00⟩: **2XP**↵

This was discussed earlier in this chapter. Model space and paper space are explained in Chapter 10 of this text.

PROFESSIONAL TIP

Sometimes the hatch spacing is too wide or too close. Select **ERASE Last** or **Undo** to remove the pattern. Try a smaller or larger value.

Using the HATCH Style option

An object may have several areas enclosed within each other. See Figure 22-18. The **Style** option of the **HATCH** command allows you to choose the features to be hatched. The three style options are:
- **N.** Normal style. This hatches every other feature.
- **O.** Hatches outermost feature area only.
- **I.** Ignores all interior features and hatches the entire object.

Any one of the options can be used by typing the desired pattern followed by a comma and the option. The command sequence for this is as follows:

> Command: **-H** *or* **HATCH**↵
> Enter pattern name or [?/Solid/User defined] ⟨*current*⟩: **NET3,N**↵
> Scale for pattern ⟨1.0000⟩: (*for example, type* 2 *and press* [Enter]*)*
> Angle for pattern ⟨0⟩: ↵
> Select hatch boundaries or press ENTER for direct hatch option,
> Select objects: **W**↵
> First corner: (*pick first corner*)
> Other corner: (*pick second corner*)
> *n* found
> Select objects: ↵
> Command:

Figure 22-19 shows the results of using each **HATCH** style option on the object in Figure 22-18.

Figure 22-18.
The outer object has three enclosed features.

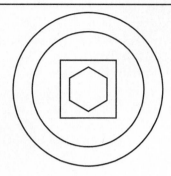

Figure 22-19.
The **Style** option of the **HATCH** command allows you to hatch enclosed features differently.

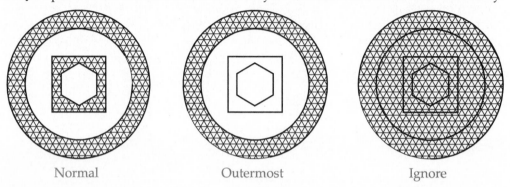

Normal　　　　　　　　　Outermost　　　　　　　　　Ignore

EXERCISE 22-2

❑ Start AutoCAD and use the template that you modified in Exercise 22-1, or use another template and modify it in the following manner.
❑ Create a new layer for hatch lines. Set the color as magenta. Name the layer Hatch-Magenta.
❑ Practice using the **HATCH** command by drawing the objects from the following figures with the patterns as shown. Draw all object lines on the Object layer or other appropriately named layer.
　❑ Figure 22-15. Draw the HARDWARE and SOFTWARE legend boxes to practice hatching around text.
　❑ Figure 22-16. Using the **Solid** option. Change the pattern from Solid as you continue with the next part of this exercise.
　❑ Figure 22-17. Set the pattern, space, and angle the same as examples.
　❑ Figure 22-19. Set the pattern, scale, and angle the same as examples.
❑ Save the drawing as EX22-2.

AutoCAD
User's
Guide

4

Automatic Boundary Hatching

So far you have seen how the **HATCH** command is used to place hatch patterns inside defined areas. In addition, you were cautioned about hatching adjacent areas. It is important that the hatch boundary be clearly defined, otherwise strange things could happen.

The **BHATCH** command simplifies the hatching process by automatically hatching any enclosed area. Simply pick inside an enclosed area, rather than picking the entities or drawing a polyline to be hatched as with the **HATCH** command. The **BHATCH** command creates associative hatch patterns by default, but can be set to create nonassociative patterns.

Associative hatch patterns update automatically when the boundary is edited. If the boundary is stretched, scaled, or otherwise edited, the hatch pattern automatically fills the new area with the original hatch pattern. Associative hatch patterns can be edited using the **HATCHEDIT** command, which is discussed later in this chapter.

The **BHATCH** command is accessed by picking the **Hatch** button on the **Draw** toolbar, by picking **Hatch...** in the **Draw** pull-down, or by entering H or BHATCH at the Command: prompt. Entering the **BHATCH** command displays the **Boundary Hatch** dialog box. See Figure 22-20.

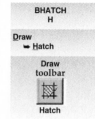

Figure 22-20.
The **Boundary Hatch** dialog box.

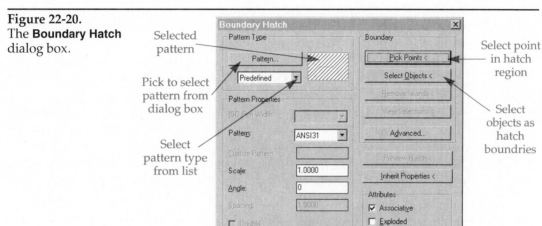

The **Boundary Hatch** dialog box contains the following elements:
- **Pattern... button.** Pick the **Pattern...** button or type [Alt]+[R] to access the **Hatch pattern palette** dialog box. See Figure 22-21. This dialog box displays a list of the hatch patterns at the left and an image of each pattern that allows you to see what the patterns look like. Pick a pattern name and have the corresponding pattern image highlighted, or pick a pattern image and have the name highlighted. Pick the **Next** button to continue looking at more pattern names and images. When the **Previous** button is active, pick it to look at the previous listings and images. Pick **Cancel** to get out of the dialog box without making a selection. After selecting a pattern, pick **OK** to return to the **Boundary Hatch** dialog box. The selected pattern is displayed in the image tile and listed in the **Pattern:** text box.

Figure 22-21.
The **Hatch pattern pallette** dialog box.

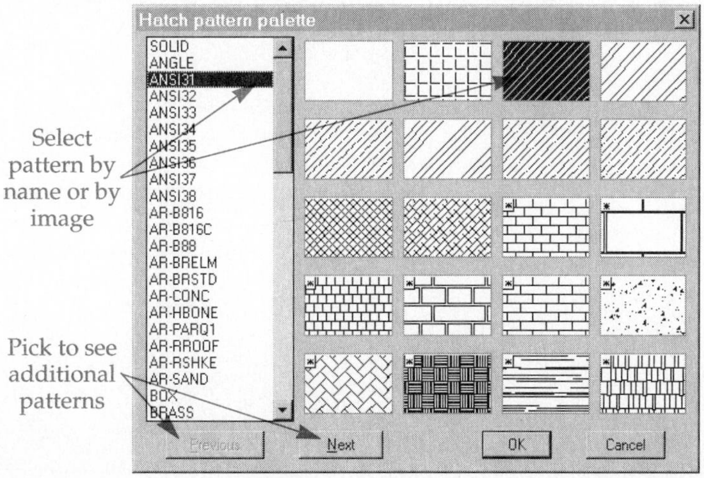

- **Pattern Type drop-down list.** This list has following options:
  - **Predefined**—This is AutoCAD's standard hatch patterns, which are stored in the acad.pat file. A predefined pattern is displayed in the image tile. When the predefined patterns are active, picking on the image tile at the right allows you to scroll through the available AutoCAD hatch patterns. This is a convenient way to see and select a hatch pattern.
  - **User-defined**—When you pick this option, the image tile is removed. This selection allows you to draw a user-style pattern using the current linetype.
  - **Custom**—This allows you to access a custom pattern defined in a pattern file other than the acad.pat file.
- **Pattern Properties area.** This is the area where you set the properties related to the selected hatch pattern. The features are:
  - **ISO Pen Width:**—This is a drop-down list available when a predefined ISO pattern is selected. This drop-down list (shown in Figure 22-22) allows you to pick a pen width for ISO pattern scaling.
  - **Pattern:**—This list provides an easy way to access predefined patterns. When you pick a pattern name from this list, the image tile automatically displays the pattern, as shown in Figure 22-23.
  - **Custom Pattern:**—This allows you to enter a custom pattern name in the text box. This is available only if **Custom** is selected as the pattern type.

Figure 22-22.
Pick the desired pen width for ISO pattern scaling list. (List shown here highlighted.)

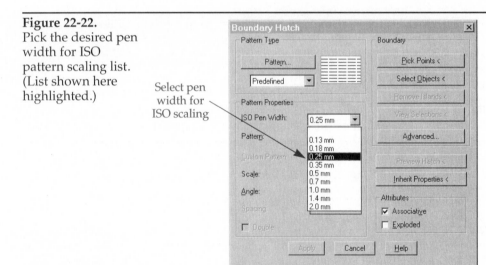

Figure 22-23.
The image tile automatically displays a representation of the pattern selected from the **Pattern:** list. (The list and the image tile are shown here highlighted.)

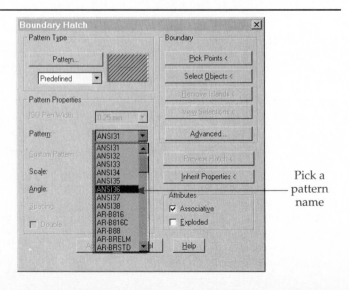

- **Scale:**—This text box allows you to set the pattern scale. AutoCAD stores the hatch pattern scale in the **HPSCALE** system variable.
- **Angle:**—This text box allows you to set the pattern angle, as discussed earlier in this chapter. AutoCAD stores the hatch pattern angle in the **HPANG** system variable.
- **Spacing:**—This text box is available if **User-defined** is selected. It allows you to set user-defined hatch spacing, as explained earlier. AutoCAD stores the hatch pattern spacing in the **HSPACE** system variable.
- **Double**—Pick this check box to activate double hatch lines for a user-defined hatch pattern. AutoCAD stores this setting in the **HPDOUBLE** system variable.
- **Boundary area.** This area of the **Boundary Hatch** dialog box controls the way you hatch objects. The features are described as follows:
  - **Pick Points ⟨ button**—Using this button is the easiest method of defining an area to be hatched. When you pick the button, the drawing returns. Pick a point within the region to be hatched, and AutoCAD automatically defines the boundary around the selected point. The following prompts are displayed:

    Select internal point: (*pick a point inside the area to be hatched*)
    Analyzing the selected data…
    Analyzing internal islands…
    Select internal point: (*pick an internal point of another object or* [Enter] *if you are done selecting objects*)

    More than one internal point can be selected. When you are finished selecting points, press [Enter] and the **Boundary Hatch** dialog box returns. Then pick the **Apply** button, and the feature is automatically hatched, as shown in Figure 22-24.

Figure 22-24.
Applying a hatch to a feature.

Move the screen cursor and pick a point inside the area to be hatched

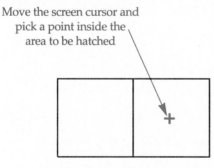

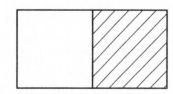

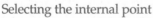
Selecting the internal point   The results

NOTE   When you are at the Select internal point: prompt, you can enter U or UNDO to undo the last selection, in case you picked the wrong area. You can also undo the hatch pattern by entering U at the Command: prompt after the pattern is drawn. However, you can preview the hatch before applying it to save time.

- **Select <u>O</u>bjects ⟨ button**—This button is used if you have items that you want to hatch by picking the object, rather than picking inside the object. These items can be circles, polygons, or closed polylines. This method works especially well if the object to be hatched is crossed by other objects, such as the graph lines that cross the bars in Figure 22-25. Picking a point inside the bar results in the hatch displayed in Figure 22-25A. You can pick inside each individual area of each bar, but this can be time-consuming. If the bars were drawn using a closed polyline, all you have to do is use the **Select <u>O</u>bjects ⟨** button to pick each bar. See Figure 22-25B.

  The **Select <u>O</u>bjects ⟨** button can also be used to pick an object inside an area to be hatched to exclude it from the hatch pattern. An example of this is the text shown inside the hatch area of Figure 22-26.

Figure 22-25.
A—Applying a hatch pattern to objects that cross each other using the **<u>P</u>ick Points ⟨** button.
B—Applying a hatch pattern to a closed polygon using the **Select <u>O</u>bjects ⟨** button.

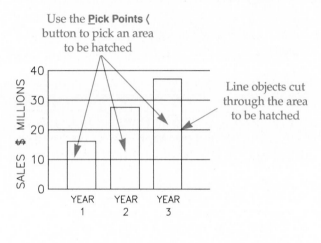

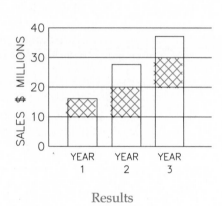

Results

A

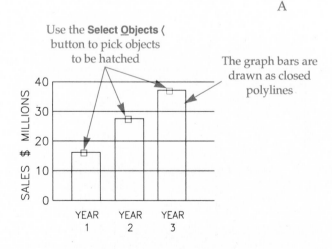

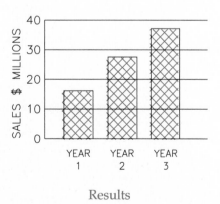

Results

B

AutoCAD and its Applications—Basics

Figure 22-26.
Using the **Select Objects** ⟨ button to exclude an object from the hatch pattern.

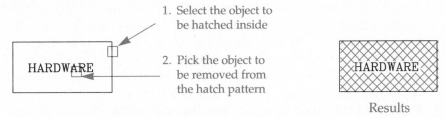

1. Select the object to be hatched inside

2. Pick the object to be removed from the hatch pattern

Results

- **Remove Islands** ⟨ button—An *island* is a closed area inside of a hatch area. When you use the **Pick Points** ⟨ button to hatch an internal area, islands are automatically left unhatched, as shown in Figure 22-27A. However, if you want islands to be hatched, use the **Remove Islands** ⟨ button after selecting the internal point. The graphics window returns with the following prompts:

  Select island to remove: *(pick the islands to remove)*
  ⟨Select island to remove⟩/Undo: ↵

  Select the islands to remove and press [Enter] to return to the dialog box. The island objects are now removed from the hatch boundary. See Figure 22-27B.

Figure 22-27.
A—Using the **Pick Points** ⟨ button to hatch an internal area leaves islands unhatched.
B—After picking an internal point, use the **Remove Islands** ⟨ button to pick an island.
This allows the island to be hatched.

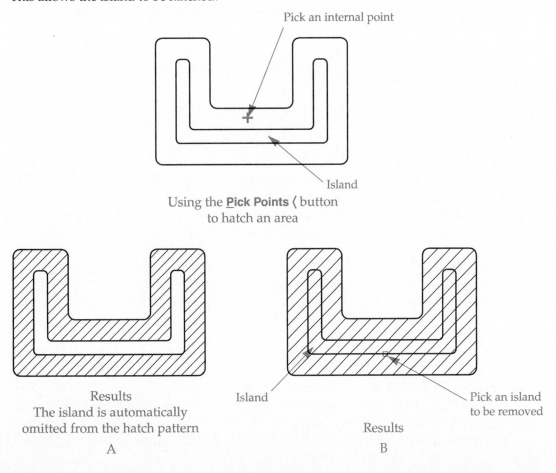

Pick an internal point

Island

Using the **Pick Points** ⟨ button
to hatch an area

Results
The island is automatically
omitted from the hatch pattern

A

Island

Pick an island
to be removed

Results

B

- **View Selection ⟨ button**—You can instruct AutoCAD to let you see the boundaries of selected objects. The **View Selections ⟨** button is available after picking objects to be hatched. Pick this button to have the drawing displayed with the hatch boundaries highlighted. Look at the highlighted boundary and then pick the **Continue** button to return to the **Boundary Hatch** dialog box.
- **Advanced... button**—Picking the **Advanced...** button accesses the **Advanced Options** dialog box, explained later in this chapter.
- **Preview Hatch ⟨ button**—Pick the **Preview Hatch ⟨** button if you want to look at the hatch pattern before you apply it to the drawing. This allows you to see if any changes need to be made before the hatch is drawn. When using this option, AutoCAD temporarily places the hatch pattern on your drawing and displays the **Boundary Hatch Continue** dialog box. When finished with the preview, press [Enter] or pick **Continue**. The **Boundary Hatch** dialog box is displayed again. Change the hatch pattern as needed, preview the hatch again, and pick the **Apply** button to have the hatch pattern drawn.
- **Inherit Properties ⟨ button**—This button allows you to select a previously drawn hatch pattern and use it as the current hatch pattern settings. The prompt looks like this:

  Select hatch object: *(pick the desired hatch pattern)*

  The **Boundary Hatch** dialog box is displayed with the settings of the selected pattern.
- **Attributes area.** The **Attributes** area of the **Boundary Hatch** dialog box has the **Associative** and the **Exploded** check boxes, which work as follows:
  - **Associative**—This check box is on by default. As discussed earlier, an associative hatch pattern is automatically updated to match any changes to the boundary area. When this box is empty, the hatch drawn is not associative.
  - **Exploded**—Pick this check box if you want the hatch pattern to be drawn with individual line objects rather than as a block pattern. When this box is checked, an asterisk is placed in front of the pattern name in the **HPNAME** system variable.

EXERCISE 22-3

- ❏ Start AutoCAD and use one of your templates with a Hatch layer.
- ❏ Open the **Boundary Hatch** dialog box and pick the **Pattern...** button to view the pattern lists and images. Select several different images and pattern names to see what happens.
- ❏ Use the **LINE** command to draw an object similar to the ones on the top of the next page. The exact dimensions are up to you. Be sure each area of the object is closed.
- ❏ Use the **BHATCH** command to make a full section of the object, as shown in the right object on the top of the next page. Use the ANSI31 hatch pattern.
- ❏ Draw the bar graph shown in Figure 22-25 without text. Use a closed polyline to draw the graph bars. Use the **BHATCH Select Objects** option to select the bars for hatching.
- ❏ Draw the HARDWARE box shown in Figure 22-26. Hatch the area inside the box without hatching the text.
- ❏ Use closed polylines to draw the object at the top of Figure 22-27. Copy the object to a position directly below the original. Use the **Pick Points** option to hatch the top object as shown in Figure 22-27A. Use the **Pick Points** button and the **Remove Islands** button to hatch the bottom object, as shown in Figure 22-27B.

AutoCAD and its Applications—Basics

- ❏ Preview each hatch pattern before you apply it, to be sure the results are what you expect.
- ❏ Enter the **BHATCH** command and pick the **Inherit Properties** 〈 button. Pick a hatch pattern on your drawing that is different from the current hatch pattern settings. Notice that the name and settings of the selected pattern becomes current.
- ❏ Save the drawing as EX22-3.

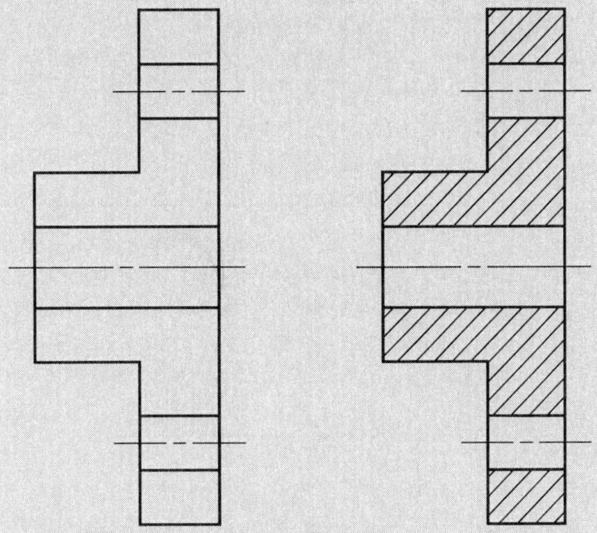

Object to be hatched   Applied hatch

Correcting errors in the boundary

The **BHATCH** command works well unless you have an error in the hatch boundary. The most common error is a gap in the boundary. This can be very small and difficult to detect, and happens when you do not close the geometry or use object snaps for accuracy. However, AutoCAD is quick to let you know by displaying the **Boundary Definition Error** alert box. See Figure 22-28. Pick the **OK** button and then return to the drawing to find and correct the problem. Figure 22-29 shows an object where the corner does not close. The error is too small to see on the screen, but using the **ZOOM** command reveals the problem.

Another error message occurs when you pick a point outside the boundary area. When this happens, you also get the **Boundary Definition Error** alert. All you have to do is pick **OK** and select a new point that is inside the boundary you want hatched.

Figure 22-28.
A **Boundary Definition Error** alert box is displayed if problems occur in your hatching operation.

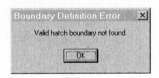

Boundary Definition Error

Valid hatch boundary not found.

OK

Figure 22-29.
Using the **ZOOM** command to find the source of the hatching error.

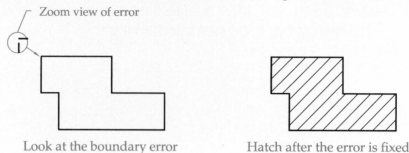

Look at the boundary error   Hatch after the error is fixed

PROFESSIONAL TIP

When creating an associative hatch, it is best to specify only one internal point per hatch block placement. Specifying more than one internal point for the same hatch pattern can produce unexpected results when you edit the hatch boundary.

Improving boundary hatching speed using the **Advanced** option

In most situations, boundary hatching works with satisfactory speed. Normally the **BHATCH** command evaluates the entire drawing that is visible on the screen to establish the boundary. This process can take some time on a large drawing.

You can improve the hatching speed and resolve other problems by picking the **Advanced...** button in the **Boundary Hatch** dialog box. This displays the **Advanced Options** dialog box. See Figure 22-30. Notice in the **Define Boundary Set** area that the **From Everything on Screen** option button is active. This evaluates everything on screen for hatching.

Figure 22-30.
The **Advanced Options** dialog box.

Pick to be able to define the boundary area

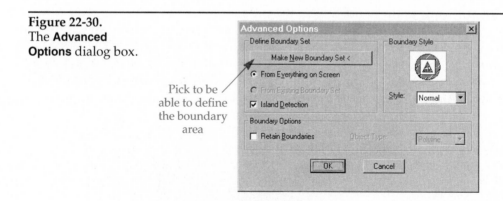

If you want to limit what AutoCAD evaluates when hatching, you can define the boundary area so the **BHATCH** command only considers a specified portion of the drawing. To do this, pick the **Make New Boundary Set** ⟨ button. Then at the Select objects: prompt, use a window to select the features of the object to be hatched. This is demonstrated in Figure 22-31 by using the following command sequence:

Select objects: *(pick the first window corner)*

Figure 22-31.
The boundary set limits the area that AutoCAD evaluates during a boundary hatching operation.

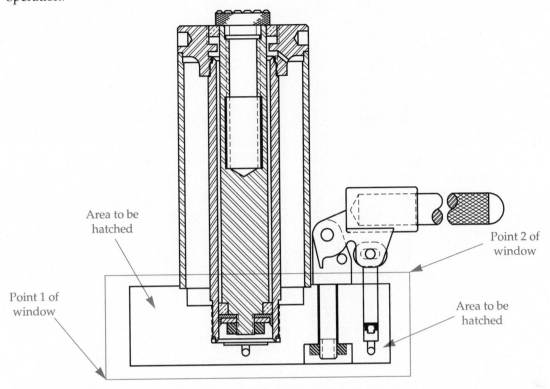

Notice if you move the box to the right of the first pick point, the selection window is automatic. If you move the box to the left of the first pick point, the selection is a crossing option.

Other corner: *(pick the second corner of the window)*
n found
Select objects: ↵
Analyzing the selected data...

Now the **Advanced Options** dialog box returns and the **From Existing Boundary Set** option button is active. See Figure 22-32. Pick the **OK** button and the **Boundary Hatch** dialog box appears. Use the **Pick Points** ⟨ button to pick the areas to be hatched. The results are shown in Figure 22-33.

Figure 22-32.
When the **From Existing Boundary Set** option is selected, AutoCAD only evaluates objects in the boundary for the hatch.

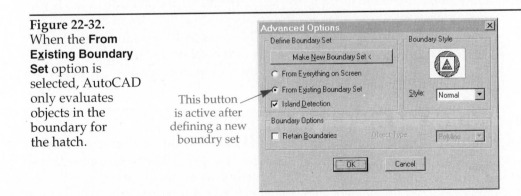

Figure 22-33.
Results of hatching the drawing in Figure 22-31 after selecting a boundary set.

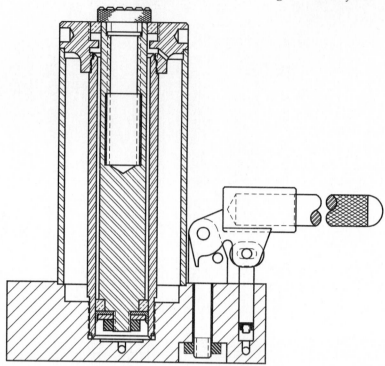

You can make as many boundary sets as you wish. However, the last one made remains current until another is created. The **Retain Boundaries** check box can be selected as soon as a boundary set is made. Checking this box allows you to keep the boundary of a hatched area as a polyline, and continues to save these as polylines every time you create a boundary area. The default is no check in this box, so the hatched boundaries are not saved as polylines.

Accessing the Hatch Style options through the Hatch Boundary dialog box

Earlier in this chapter, you learned about using the **Style** option in the **HATCH** command. This feature allows you to decide which features are to be hatched and which are not.

You can create the same hatch styles through the **Boundary Hatch** dialog box. To do this, pick the **Advanced...** button to display the **Advanced Options** dialog box. Look at the **Boundary Style** area shown in Figure 22-32. **Normal** is the default in the **Style:** text box and its representative image is shown above. Pick the down arrow in the **Style:** drop-down list to get the other options. When you pick one of the options, the image tile displays the expected results. You can also click on the image tile to cycle through the options. The image tiles for the **Outer** and **Ignore** options are shown in Figure 22-34.

Island detection and retaining the boundaries

Earlier in this chapter (Figure 22-27) you were introduced to hatching around or through islands. Look at Figure 22-32, which displays the **Advance Options** dialog box. Notice that the **Island Detection** check box is active by default. This setting leaves internal objects (islands) unhatched. Pick the check box to remove the check if you want to hatch through islands.

Figure 22-34.
Shown are the **Outer** and **Ignore** options for hatch style. Notice how the image tile (shown here highlighted) changes to reflect how the hatch will appear on the drawing. The **Normal** style is shown in Figure 22-32.

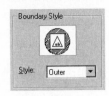

Outer

Ignore

Notice also in Figure 22-32 that the **Retain Boundaries** check box is not checked by default. When you use the **BHATCH** command and pick an internal area to be hatched, AutoCAD automatically creates a temporary boundary around the area. If the **Retain Boundaries** check box is unchecked, the temporary boundaries are automatically removed when the hatch is complete. However, if you check the **Retain Boundaries** check box, the hatch boundaries are kept when the hatch is completed.

Also, when the **Retain Boundaries** check box is checked, the **Object Type** list at the right is activated, as shown in Figure 22-35. Notice in Figure 22-35 that the **Object Type:** drop-down list has two options: **Polyline** and **Region**. **Polyline** is the default. This means that the boundary is a polyline object around the hatch area. If you select the **Region** option, then the hatch boundary is the hatched region. A *region* is a closed two-dimensional area.

Figure 22-35.
There are two object type options for the boundary. These options are only available if **Retain Boundaries** is checked.

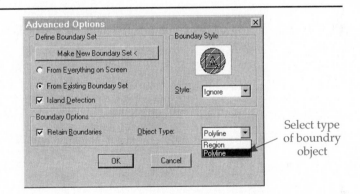

Select type of boundry object

PROFESSIONAL TIP

There are a number of techniques that can help save you time when hatching, especially with large and complex drawings. These include the following:

✓ Zoom in on the area to be hatched to make it easier for you to define the boundary. When you zoom into an area to be hatched, the hatch process is much faster because AutoCAD doesn't have to search the entire drawing to find the hatch boundaries.

✓ Preview the hatch before you apply it. This allows you to easily make last minute adjustments.

✓ Turn off layers where there are lines or text that might interfere with your ability to accurately define hatch boundaries.

✓ Create boundary sets of small areas within a complex drawing to help save time.

Editing Hatch Patterns

HATCHEDIT
HE

Modify
➥ Object
  ➥ Hatch...

Modify II
toolbar

Edit Hatch

You can edit hatch boundaries and hatch patterns with grips and editing commands such as **ERASE**, **COPY**, **MOVE**, **ROTATE**, and **SCALE**. If a hatch pattern is associative, whatever you do to the hatch boundary is automatically done to the associated hatch pattern. As explained earlier, a hatch pattern is associative if the **Associati̲ve** check box in the **Boundary Hatch** dialog box is active.

A convenient way to edit a hatch pattern is by using the **HATCHEDIT** command. You can access this command by picking **Hatch...** in the **Object** cascading menu of the **Modify** pull-down menu, picking the **Edit Hatch** button on the **Modify II** toolbar, or entering HE or HATCHEDIT at the Command: prompt. The command sequence is as follows:

> Command: **HE** *or* **HATCHEDIT**.↵
> Select hatch object: *(pick the hatch pattern to edit)*

When you select a hatch pattern or patterns to edit, the **Hatchedit** dialog box is displayed. See Figure 22-36. The **Hatchedit** dialog box has the same features as the **Boundary Hatch** dialog box, except that only the items that control hatch pattern characteristics are available.

Figure 22-36.
The **Hatchedit** dialog box is used to edit hatch patterns. Notice that only the options related to hatch characteristics are available.

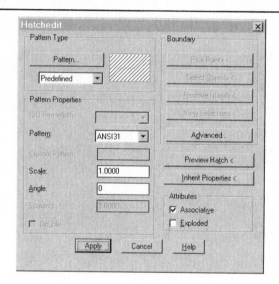

The available features work just like they do in the **Boundary Hatch** dialog box. You can change the pattern type, scale, or angle; explode the pattern; remove the associative qualities; set the inherit properties of an existing hatch pattern; or use the **Advanced Options** dialog box to edit the hatch pattern. You can also preview the edited hatch before applying it to your drawing.

EXERCISE 22-4

❏ Start AutoCAD and use one of your templates that has a Hatch layer.
❏ Draw each of the objects displayed at each of the A positions shown on the following page.
❏ Be sure the hatch pattern is associative.
❏ Copy the objects at the A positions to B and C positions.
❏ Use the **HATCHEDIT** command to change the hatch pattern of the A objects to the representation found at B and C positions.
❏ Adjust the hatch pattern, scale, angle, and style to obtain the figure shown on the following page.
❏ Save as EX22-4.

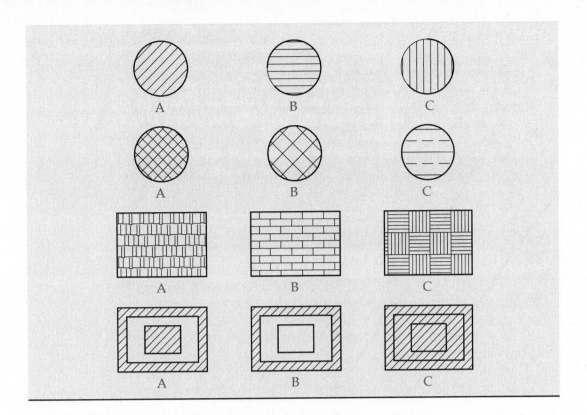

Editing associative hatch patterns

When you edit an object with an associative hatch pattern, the hatch pattern changes to match the edit. For example, the object in Figure 22-37A is stretched and the hatch pattern matches the new object. When the island in Figure 22-37B is erased, the hatch pattern is automatically revised to fill the area where the island was located.

Figure 22-37.
Editing objects with associative hatch patterns. The hatch pattern changes to match the edit.

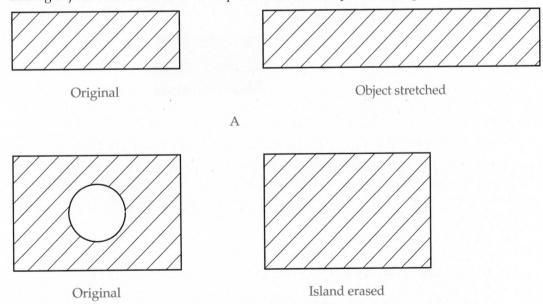

Original

Object stretched

A

Original

Island erased

B

❏ Start AutoCAD and use one of your templates.
❏ Use the **BHATCH** command to create associative hatch patterns during this exercise.
❏ Draw the original hatched object shown in Figure 22-37A. Copy the object to the right of the original and then use the **STRETCH** command to stretch the copied object into the edited object.
❏ Draw the original hatched object with the island shown in Figure 22-37B. Copy the object to the right of the original. Erase the island from the copied object to see what happens.
❏ Save the drawing as EX22-5.

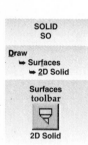

SOLID
SO

Draw
➥ Surfaces
  ➥ 2D Solid

Surfaces
toolbar

2D Solid

Drawing Objects with Solid Fills

In previous chapters you have learned that polylines, polyarcs, trace segments, and doughnuts may be filled in solid when **FILL** mode is on. When **FILL** is off, these objects are drawn as outlines only. The **SOLID** command works in much the same manner except that it fills objects or shapes that are already drawn and fills areas that are simply defined by picking points.

The **SOLID** command is accessed by picking the **2D Solid** button from the **Surfaces** toolbar, picking **2D Solid** from the **Surfaces** cascading menu in the **Draw** pull-down menu, or entering SO or SOLID at the Command: prompt. You are then prompted to select points. If the object to fill solid is rectangular, pick the corners in the numbered sequence shown in Figure 22-38. The command sequence is as follows:

```
Command: SO or SOLID.↵
First point: (pick point 1)
Second point: (pick point 2)
Third point: (pick point 3)
Fourth point: (pick point 4)
Third point:
```

Figure 22-38.
Using the **SOLID**
command. Select
the points in the
order shown.

Notice that AutoCAD prompts you for another third point after the first four. This prompt allows you to fill in additional parts of the same object, if needed. The subsequent points you select fill in the object in a triangular fashion. Continue picking points, or press [Enter] to stop. The following sequence draws the object shown in Figure 22-39.

```
Command: SO or SOLID.↵
First point: (pick point 1)
Second point: (pick point 2)
Third point: (pick point 3)
Fourth point: (pick point 4 and the rectangular portion is drawn)
Third point: (pick point 5)
Fourth point: ↵
Third point: ↵
```

Figure 22-39.
The **SOLID**
command allows
you to enter a
second *third point*
(point 5 here) after
entering the fourth
point.

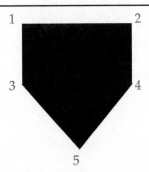

Different types of solid arrangements can be drawn by altering the numbering sequence. See Figure 22-40. Also, the **SOLID** command can be used to draw filled shapes without prior use of the **LINE**, **PLINE**, or **RECTANG** commands; simply pick the points. Consider using various object snap modes when picking the points.

Figure 22-40.
Using a different
numbering
sequence for the
SOLID command
will give you
different results.

 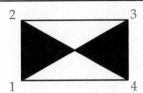

**PROFESSIONAL
TIP**

Using the Solid pattern of the **HATCH** or **BHATCH** commands is an excellent way to create solid objects, as shown in Figure 22-16. To fill a circle, use the **DONUT** command and set a 0 (zero) inside diameter, or hatch the circle with the Solid pattern.

Keep in mind that many solids and dense hatches require extensive regeneration. On a complex drawing, create filled solids and hatching on a separate layer and keep the layer frozen until you are ready to plot the drawing. Many solids and dense hatch patterns also adversely affect plot time. Save plotting time by making check plots with **FILL** mode off.

EXERCISE 22-6

❏ Start AutoCAD and use one of your templates.
❏ Create a new layer named Solid-Magenta and draw all solids on this layer.
❏ Practice using the **SOLID** command by drawing the objects shown in Figures 22-38, 22-39, and 22-40.
❏ Save the drawing as EX22-6.

Chapter Test

Write your answers in the spaces provided.

1. Give the command and entries required to use the ANSI37 hatch pattern with double scale to hatch the inside of a given circle:

   Command: _____

   Enter pattern name or [?/Solid/User defined] ⟨*current*⟩: _____

   Scale for pattern ⟨1.0000⟩: _____

   Angle for pattern ⟨0⟩: _____

   Select hatch boundaries or press ENTER for direct hatch options,

   Select objects: _____

   Select objects: _____

2. Give the command and entries needed to draw your own hatch pattern. Set a 30° hatch angle, 1.5 spacing, and single hatch lines pattern to hatch the inside of a rectangle drawn with polylines:

   Command: _____

   Enter pattern name or [?/Solid/User defined] ⟨*current*⟩: _____

   Angle of crosshatch lines ⟨0⟩: _____

   Spacing between lines ⟨1.0000⟩: _____

   Double hatch area? ⟨N⟩: _____

   Select hatch boundaries or press ENTER for direct hatch options,

   Select objects: _____

   Select objects: _____

3. Given a square within a square, provide the command and entries used to hatch between the two squares (the outermost area). Use the default values of the ANSI31 hatch pattern:

   Command: _____

   Enter pattern name or [?/Solid/User defined] ⟨*current*⟩: _____

   Scale for pattern ⟨1.0000⟩: _____

   Angle for pattern ⟨0⟩: _____

   Select hatch boundaries or press ENTER for direct hatch options,

   Select objects: _____

   First corner: _____

   Other corner: _____

   Select objects: _____

4. Give the command and entries needed to fill in a rectangular area. Identify specific corners on the rectangle as you give the prompts. For example, specify the upper-right corner.

Command: _____

First point: _____

Second point: _____

Third point: _____

Fourth point: _____

Third point: _____

5. Give the command and responses to show a list and description of all the hatch patterns:

Command: _____

Enter pattern name or [?/Solid/User defined] ⟨*current*⟩: _____

Pattern(s) to list ⟨*⟩: _____

6. Give the command and responses used to hatch an object while providing an imaginary box around text located inside the hatch area.

Command: _____

Enter pattern name or [?/Solid/User defined] ⟨*current*⟩: _____

Scale for pattern ⟨1.0000⟩: _____

Angle for pattern ⟨0⟩: _____

Select objects: _____

Select objects: _____

Select objects: _____

For Questions 7–12, name the type of section identified in each of the following statements:

7. Half of the object is removed; the cutting-plane line generally cuts completely through along the center plane. _____

8. Used primarily on symmetrical objects; the cutting-plane line cuts through one-quarter of the object. _____

9. The cutting-plane line is staggered through features that do not lie in a straight line.

_____

10. The section is turned in place to clarify the contour of the object. _____

_____

11. This section is rotated and located from the object. The location of the section is normally identified with a cutting-plane line. _____

12. Remove a small portion of the view to clarify an internal feature. _____

_____

13. AutoCAD's standard section line symbols are called _____.

14. Give the code and results of using the three **HATCH Style** options. _____

_____

_____

15. In which pull-down menu is <u>H</u>atch... located? _____

16. Name the command that lets you automatically hatch an enclosed area just by picking a point inside the area. _____

17. Explain the purpose and function of the **Patte<u>r</u>n...** button in the **Boundary Hatch** dialog box. _____

_____

_____

_____

18. In addition to the method in Question 17, identify at least two ways to select a predefined hatch pattern in the **Boundary Hatch** dialog box. _____

_____

_____

_____

19. Explain how you set a hatch scale in the **Boundary Hatch** dialog box. _____

_____

20. Identify two ways to change a hatch pattern (where all elements of the hatch are one unit) so that each element is an individual entity. _____

_____

21. Explain how to use an existing hatch pattern on a drawing as the current pattern for your next hatch. _____

_____

_____

22. Describe the purpose of the **Preview Ha<u>t</u>ch** ⟨ button found in the **Boundary Hatch** dialog box. _____

_____

_____

23. What happens if you try to hatch an area where there is a gap in the boundary?

_____

_____

24. How do you limit AutoCAD hatch evaluation to a specific area of the drawing?

_____

_____ _____

_____

25. Define associative hatch pattern. _____

_____

_____

_____

26. How do you change the hatch angle in the **Boundary Hatch** dialog box?

_____

_____

_____

27. Describe the fundamental difference between using the **Pick Points** ⟨ and the **Select Objects** ⟨ buttons in the **Boundary Hatch** dialog box. _____

_____

_____

_____

_____

28. If you use the **Pick Points** ⟨ button inside the **Boundary Hatch** dialog box to hatch an area, how do you hatch around an island inside the area to be hatched? _____

_____

_____

_____

_____

29. How do you use the **BHATCH** command to hatch an object with text inside without hatching the text? _____

_____

_____

_____

_____

30. How do you access the hatch style options through the **Boundary Hatch** dialog box? _____

_____

_____

_____

_____

_____

31. Name the command that may be used to edit existing associative hatch patterns.

_____

32. What do you get when you enter the command identified in Question 31? _____

_____

33. How does the item identified in Question 32 compare to what you get when you enter the **BHATCH** command?_____

_____

_____

_____

34. What would you do if you want an existing hatch pattern on a drawing to take on the same characteristics as another hatch pattern on the same drawing? _____

_____

_____

_____

_____

35. What happens if you erase an island inside an associated hatch pattern? _____

_____

_____

_____

_____

36. What is the result of stretching an object that is hatched with an associative hatch pattern? _____

_____

_____

_____

37. Identify two ways to create a solid circle. _____

_____

_____

38. How do you draw a hatch pattern without displaying the boundary? _____

_____

_____

39. How do you access the Solid pattern when using the **HATCH** command? _____

_____

_____

_____

Drawing Problems

*Name each of the drawings **P22-**(problem number). Follow these guidelines for all of the problems. Use the appropriate template with mechanical drawing title blocks.*

1–4. Draw the full sections as indicated.

    A. Draw the views to full size.

    B. Set grid, snap, limits, and units values as needed. Use object snaps.

    C. Apply dimensions accurately following ASME standards.

    D. Set dimensioning variables to suit the drawing.

    E. Use the **LAYER** command to set separate layers for views, dimensions, and section lines.

    F. Place the following general notes 1/2″ from the lower-left corner.

        2.   REMOVE ALL BURRS AND SHARP EDGES

        1.   INTERPRET PER ASME Y14.5M-1994

        NOTES:

1.

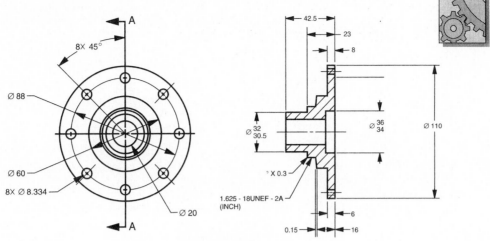

Name: Hub
Material: Cast Iron

2. Draw the half section. Add the additional notes: OIL QUENCH 40-45C,
CASE HARDEN .020 DEEP, and 59-60 ROCKWELL C SCALE.

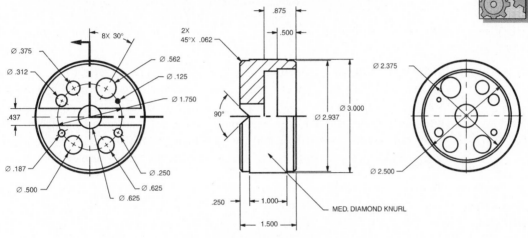

Name: Diffuser
Material: AISI 1018

3. Draw the aligned sections as indicated. Add the additional notes:
FINISH ALL OVER 1.63mm UNLESS OTHERWISE SPECIFIED and ALL
DIMENSIONS ARE IN MILLIMETERS.

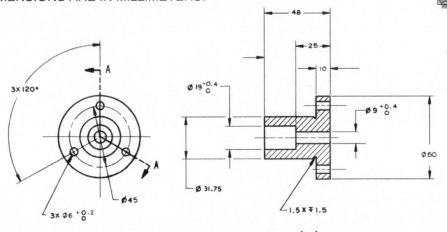

SECTION A-A

Name: Bushing
Material: SAE 1030

4. Draw the aligned sections as indicated. Add the additional notes: FINISH ALL OVER 1.63mm UNLESS OTHERWISE SPECIFIED and ALL DIMENSIONS ARE IN MILLIMETERS.

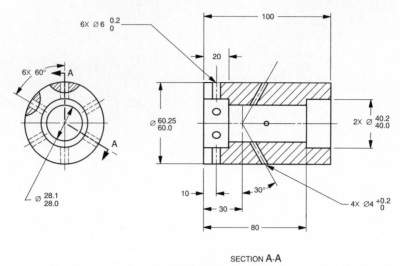

SECTION A-A

Name: Nozzle
Material: Phosphor Bronze

5–15. Draw the following problems using commands discussed in this chapter and in previous chapters. Use templates that are appropriate for the specific problems. Use text styles that correlate with the problem content. Place dimensions and notes when needed. Make your drawings proportional to the given problems when dimensions are not given. Save each of the drawings as P22-(problem number).

5.

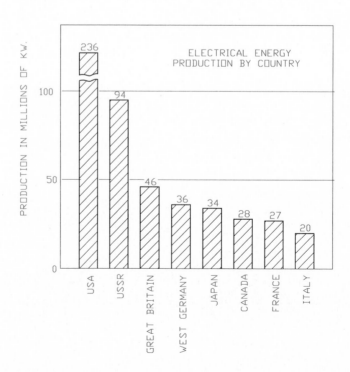

6.

COMPONENT LAYOUT

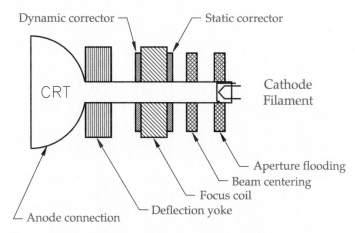

Dynamic corrector — Static corrector

CRT

Cathode
Filament

Aperture flooding

Beam centering

Focus coil

Deflection yoke

Anode connection

7.

SOLOMAN SHOE COMPANY

PERCENT OF TOTAL SALES EACH DIVISION

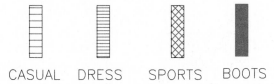

CASUAL   DRESS   SPORTS   BOOTS

42.2   39.5
        22.4   23.9   21.1   29.8 25.4
  14.6   16.8   15.5   23.1   21.7
                                                            35.9 36.7
                                                              21
                                                          6.4

JAN—MAR   APR—JUN   JUL—SEP   OCT—DEC

8.

DIAL TECHNOLOGIES
EXPENSE BUDGET
FISCAL YEAR

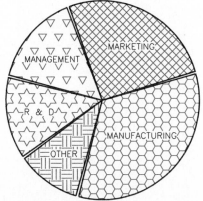

9.

SALES HISTORY

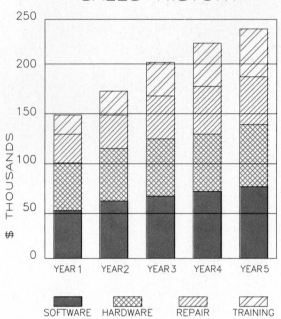

 10.

RAY

 11.

Architectural
Design
Consultants

AutoCAD and its Applications—Basics

12.

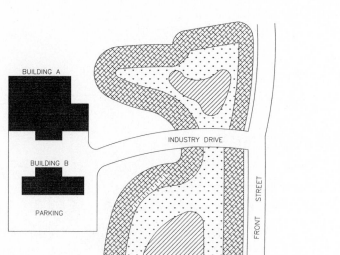

13.

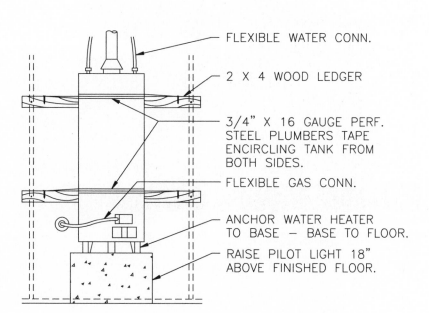

14.

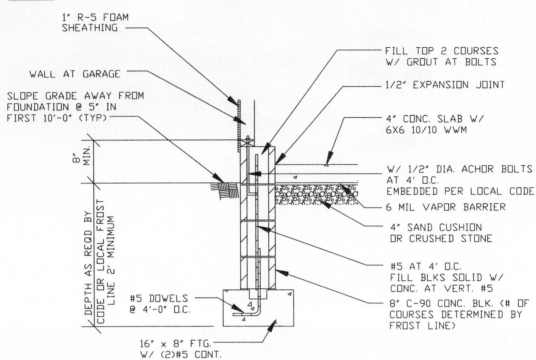

1" R-5 FOAM
SHEATHING

WALL AT GARAGE

SLOPE GRADE AWAY FROM
FOUNDATION @ 5" IN
FIRST 10'-0" (TYP)

8" MIN.

DEPTH AS REQD BY
CODE OR LOCAL FROST
LINE 2' MINIMUM

#5 DOWELS
@ 4'-0" O.C.

16" × 8" FTG.
W/ (2)#5 CONT.

FILL TOP 2 COURSES
W/ GROUT AT BOLTS

1/2" EXPANSION JOINT

4" CONC. SLAB W/
6X6 10/10 WWM

W/ 1/2" DIA. ACHOR BOLTS
AT 4' O.C.
EMBEDDED PER LOCAL CODE

6 MIL VAPOR BARRIER

4" SAND CUSHION
OR CRUSHED STONE

#5 AT 4' O.C.
FILL BLKS SOLID W/
CONC. AT VERT. #5

8" C-90 CONC. BLK. (# OF
COURSES DETERMINED BY
FROST LINE)

Chapter 23

Creating Symbols for Multiple Use

Learning Objectives

After completing this chapter, you will be able to:
- ○ Create and save blocks.
- ○ Insert blocks into a drawing.
- ○ Edit a block and update it in a drawing.
- ○ Create blocks that are saved independent of the drawing.
- ○ Construct and use a symbol library of blocks.

One of the greatest benefits of AutoCAD is its ability to store symbols for future use. These symbols, or *blocks*, can be inserted into a drawing scaled and rotated. If a block is edited, drawings having the block can be updated to include the new version. The term *wblock* refers to the command **WBLOCK**, which is used to write a block description as a separate drawing file. Since any AutoCAD drawing can be inserted into another drawing, this provides *global* access (any drawing), as opposed to *local* access (current drawing). Therefore, a block can be used only in the drawing in which it was created. Both types can be used to create a *symbol library*, which is a related group of symbols.

When a drawing is inserted or referenced, it becomes part of the drawing on the screen, but its content is not added to the current drawing file. Any named entities, such as blocks and layers, are referred to as *dependent symbols*. When a dependent symbol is revised, a drawing that references it is automatically updated the next time it is loaded into AutoCAD.

Creating Symbols as Blocks

The ability to draw and store symbols is one of the greatest time-saving features of CAD. AutoCAD provides the **BLOCK** command to create a symbol and keep it with a specific drawing file. The predrawn block can be inserted as many times as needed into any drawing. Upon insertion, the block can be scaled and rotated to meet the drawing requirements.

Constructing blocks

A block can be any shape, symbol, view, or drawing that you use more than once. Before constructing a block, review the drawing you are working on. (This is where a sketch of your drawing is convenient.) Look for shapes, components, notes, and assemblies that are used more than once. These can be drawn once and then saved as blocks.

Existing drawings can also be used as blocks. This can be done two different ways:
- Use the **BASE** command on the drawing to assign an insertion point.
- Insert the existing drawing into the drawing you are working on.

These two methods are discussed later in this chapter.

Drawing the block components

Draw a block as you would any other drawing geometry. Use any AutoCAD commands you need. If you want the block to have the color and linetype of the layer it will be inserted on, be sure to set layer 0 current before you begin drawing the block. If you forget to do this and draw the objects on another layer, simply use the **CHPROP** or **DDCHPROP** command to place all the objects on layer 0 before using the **BLOCK** command.

When you finish drawing the object, decide what is the best place on the symbol to use as an insertion point. When you insert the block into a drawing, the symbol is placed with its insertion point on the screen cursor. Figure 23-1 illustrates some common blocks and their insertion points (shown as dots).

Figure 23-1.
Common symbols and their insertion points for placement on drawings. The insertion points are shown here as colored dots.

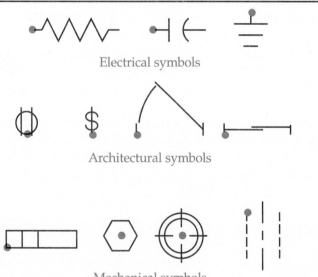

Electrical symbols

Architectural symbols

Mechanical symbols

If it is important that the block maintains a specific color and linetype regardless of the layer it is to be used on, be sure to set the color and linetype before drawing the objects. On the other hand, if the block can assume the current color and linetype when the block is inserted into the drawing, use the ByBlock options of the **COLOR** and **LINETYPE** commands.

To set the color to ByBlock, enter COLOR at the Command: prompt and then enter BYBLOCK at the New object color: prompt, pick ByBlock in the **Color Control** drop-down list of the **Object Properties** toolbar; or pick **Color...** from the **Format** pull-down menu to access the **Select Color** dialog box. See Figure 23-2.

Figure 23-2.
Pick **Color** from the **Format** pull-down menu, then pick the **BYBLOCK** button to have the block assume the current color when inserted into a drawing.

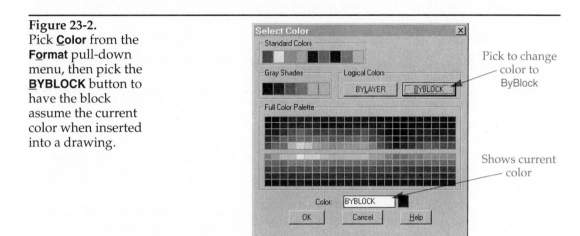

To set the linetype to ByBlock, pick ByBlock in the **Linetype Control** drop-down list of the **Object Properties** toolbar. Another method is to pick **Linetype...** from the **Format** pull-down menu, which displays the **Layer & Linetype Properties** dialog box. Pick ByBlock in the **Linetype** list and then pick the **Current** button. See Figure 23-3. This dialog box is also accessed by entering LINETYPE or LT at the Command: prompt.

Figure 23-3.
Pick ByBlock in the **Linetype** list of the **Layer & Linetype Properties** dialog box. Then pick the **Current** button.

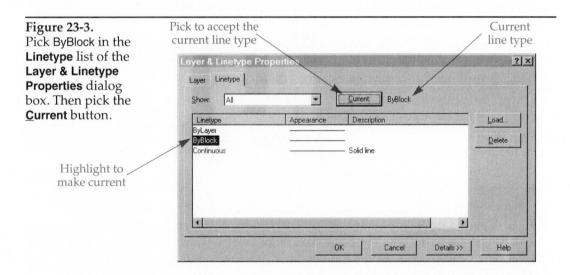

Once both color and linetype are set to ByBlock, the **Object Properties** toolbar should look like Figure 23-4. Now you can use any AutoCAD commands to create your block shapes. Whenever a block created with these ByBlock settings is inserted into a drawing, it will assume the current color and linetype, regardless of the current layer values.

Figure 23-4.
ByBlock appears in the **Color Control** and **Linetype Control** drop-down lists of the **Object Properties** toolbar.

BMAKE
B

Draw
→ Block
→ Make...

Draw
toolbar

Make Block

Creating blocks

When you draw a shape, you have not yet created a block. To save your object as a block, pick the **Make Block** button in the **Draw** toolbar, pick **Make...** from the **Block** cascading menu in the **Draw** pull-down menu, or enter B or BMAKE at the Command: prompt. Either of these methods displays the **Block Definition** dialog box. See Figure 23-5. The process for creating a block is as follows:

1. In the **Block name:** text box, enter a name, such as PUMP. The name cannot exceed 31 characters and can include numbers, letters, the dollar sign ($), hyphen (-), and underscore(_).

2. Pick the **Select Objects** ⟨ button. The graphics screen returns and you are prompted to select objects. Select all of the objects that will compose the block. The number of objects selected is shown below the **Select Objects** ⟨ button.

3. Locate the insertion point of the block by either entering XYZ coordinates in the **Base Point** area of the dialog box, or pick the **Select Point** ⟨ button. The graphics screen returns and you are prompted for the insertion base point. Pick a point using object snaps and the dialog box is redisplayed.

4. If the objects chosen for the block should remain in the drawing, be sure a check mark appears in the **Retain Objects** check box. Pick **OK** to save the block.

If you forget to check the **Retain Objects** check box, the objects selected for the block will be erased. This is normal. If you want to keep them in the drawing, just enter OOPS at the Command: prompt to return them to the screen. This action retains the block, whereas entering U at the Command: prompt, or picking the **Undo** button, removes the block from the drawing.

Figure 23-5.
Blocks are created using the **Block Definition** dialog box.

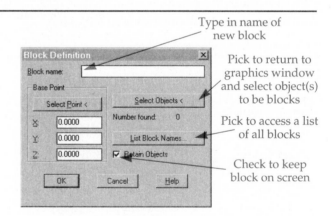

Type in name of new block

Pick to return to graphics window and select object(s) to be blocks

Pick to access a list of all blocks

Check to keep block on screen

> **NOTE**
>
> Remember that a block can only be used in the drawing in which it was created.

To verify that the block was saved properly, access the **Block Definition** dialog box. Pick the **List Block Names...** button and a list of all blocks are displayed in the **Block Names In This Drawing** dialog box. See Figure 23-6.

Figure 23-6.
A—The asterisk in the **Pattern:** text box of the **Block Names In This Drawing** dialog box shows all blocks. B—The DOS wildcard characters can be used to limit blocks listed.

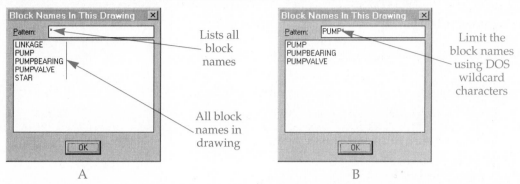

You can limit the block names that are displayed by using the **Pattern:** text box. For example, if your drawing contains a large number of blocks and you just want to list all blocks that begin with PUMP, type PUMP* in the **Pattern:** text box and press [Enter]. The DOS wildcard characters, asterisk (*) and question mark (?) are valid. The asterisk is a substitute for any and all characters, whereas the question mark is a substitute for a single character. Note the following examples:

Entry	Displays
PUMP*	All names that begin with PUMP and end with any number of characters.
*PUMP	All names that end with PUMP and are preceded by any number of characters.
DOOR???	All names that begin with DOOR and end with any three characters.
???DOOR	All names that begin with any three characters and end with DOOR.
*DOOR??	All names that contain DOOR preceded by any number of characters, and ending with any two characters.

When the **BLOCK** command is entered at the Command: prompt, the options in the **Block Definition** dialog box are presented as prompts. To display a list of block names, use the **?** option as follows:

Command: **BLOCK**↵
Block name (or ?): **?**↵
Block(s) to list ⟨*⟩:

Press [Enter] to list all of the blocks in the current drawing. The following information is then displayed in the **AutoCAD Text Window:**

Defined blocks.
PUMP

User Blocks	External Reference	Dependent Blocks	Unnamed Blocks
1	0	0	0

This **AutoCAD Text Window** reports the name and number of blocks. When you create a block, you have actually created a *block definition*. Therefore, the first entry in the block listing is that of *defined* blocks. *User blocks* are those created by you. *External references* are drawings referenced with the **XREF** command. (**XREF** is discussed in Chapter 24.) Blocks that reside in a referenced drawing are called *dependent blocks*. *Unnamed blocks* are entities such as associative dimensions and hatch patterns.

Step through the process of drawing a block again. Draw a one unit square and name it PLATE. See Figure 23-7. Select the **BLOCK** command. Name the block PLATE. Pick the insertion point at the lower-left corner. Select the object using the **Window** option. Select **BLOCK** again and use the **?** option to see that it was saved.

Figure 23-7.
The procedure for drawing a one unit square block.
A—Draw the block.
B—Pick the insertion point.
C—Select the box using a window or other select option.

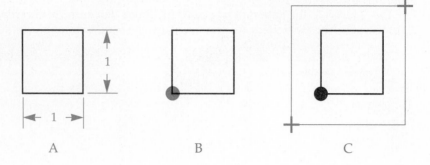

A   B   C

EXERCISE 23-1

❑ Start AutoCAD and open one of your templates with decimal units.
❑ Draw a circle with a one unit diameter and add centerlines on layer 0.
❑ Make a block of the circle and centerlines and name it CIRCLE.
❑ Pick the center of the circle as the insertion point.
❑ Save the drawing as EX23-1.

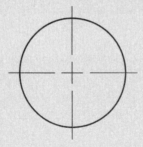

AutoCAD User's Guide 11

Using Blocks in a Drawing

Once a block has been created, it is easy to insert it into a drawing. Before inserting a block, give some thought to the size the block should be and the rotation angle needed. Blocks are normally inserted on specific layers. Set the proper layer *before* inserting the block. Once a block has been inserted into a drawing it is referred to as a **block reference**.

Inserting blocks

Blocks are placed on your drawing with the **DDINSERT** command. Type DDINSERT or I at the Command: prompt, pick the **Insert Block** button in the **Draw** toolbar, or pick **Block...** in the **Insert** pull-down menu. This accesses the **Insert** dialog box, Figure 23-8A.

In the **Insert** dialog box, pick the **Block...** button to access the **Defined Blocks** dialog box, Figure 23-8B. Highlight the name of the block you wish to insert. If the list of block names is long, use the scroll bar to view additional blocks. You may also enter the name in the **Selection:** text box. Pick **OK** once the desired block name is in the **Selection:** text box. The **Insert** dialog box returns and the selected name is displayed in the **Block...** text box.

DDINSERT
I

Insert
➡ Block

Draw
toolbar

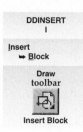

Insert Block

To specify the other values in this dialog box, remove the check from **Specify Parameters on Screen** check box. To specify the other values on screen using the Command: line, leave the check and pick **OK**. The following describes the buttons and other features of the **Insert** dialog box:

Figure 23-8.
A—The **Insert** dialog box allows you to select and prepare a block for insertion. B—Select the block you wish to insert from the list in the **Defined Blocks** dialog box and pick **OK**.

Pick to access the **Defined Blocks** dialog box

Pick to access the **Select Drawing File** dialog box

Select to have block exploded

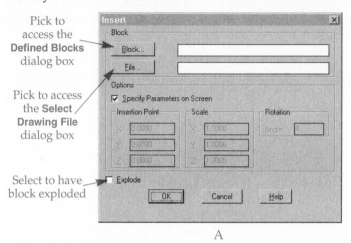

List of blocks in drawing

A   B

- **File button.** Allows you to select a drawing file for insertion into the current drawing.
- **Options area.** If there is a check in **Specify Parameters on Screen**, then the **Insertion Point, Scale,** and **Rotation** values cannot be selected. If you wish to enter these values here, remove the check to enable the three text boxes. Enter values for XYZ insertion point and scale, and block rotation. If preset values are used, the block is immediately inserted when you pick **OK**. If presets are not used, the block appears attached to the crosshairs.
- **Explode check box.** When a block is created it is saved as a single entity, therefore it is a single entity when inserted in the drawing. Check this box if you wish to explode the block into its original objects for editing purposes.

When the **INSERT** command is entered at the Command: prompt, the options in the **Insert** dialog box are presented as prompts. When prompted for a block name, enter a name, press [Enter] to accept the current name, or use the **?** option to display a list of block names:

> Command: **INSERT**↵
> Block name (or ?) ⟨*current*⟩: **?**↵
> Block(s) to list ⟨*⟩:

Press [Enter] to list all of the blocks in the **AutoCAD Text Window**. Whether entering a block name using the **INSERT** command at the Command: prompt or completing the insertion on screen from the **Insert** dialog box, the command sequence is as follows:

> Insertion point: (*pick the point*)
> X scale factor ⟨1⟩ / Corner / XYZ: (*pick a point, type a number and press* [Enter], *or press* [Enter] *to accept the default*)

Moving the cursor scales the block dynamically as it is dragged. If you want to scale the block visually, pick a point when the object appears correct.

> Y scale factor (default=X): *(type a number and press* [Enter], *or press* [Enter] *to accept the default)*
> Rotation angle ⟨0⟩: *(pick a point, or type a number and press* [Enter]*)*

The X and Y scale factors allow you to stretch or compress the block to suit your needs. This is why it is a good idea to draw blocks to fit inside a one unit square. It makes the block easy to scale because you can type the exact number of units for the X and Y dimensions. If you want the block to be three units long and two units high, respond:

> X scale factor ⟨1⟩ / Corner / XYZ: **3**↵
> Y scale factor (default=X): **2**↵

Notice that the Y prompt allows you to accept the X value for Y by just pressing [Enter]. The object shown in Figure 23-9 was given several different X and Y scale factors during the **INSERT** command.

Figure 23-9.
Shown is a comparison of the PLATE block inserted using different X and Y scale factors.

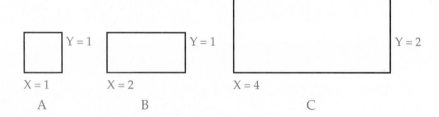

A   B   C

PROFESSIONAL TIP

> A block's rotation angle can also be based on the current UCS. Should you wish to insert a block at a specific angle based on the current or an existing UCS, first be sure the proper UCS is restored. Then insert the block and use a zero rotation angle. If you subsequently change the UCS, the inserted blocks retain their original angle.

Block insertion options

It is possible to obtain a mirror image of a block just by typing a negative value for the scale factor. For example, a –1,–1 scale factor mirrors the block to the opposite quadrant of the coordinate system and retains the original size. Figure 23-10 illustrates mirroring techniques. The insertion point is indicated with a dot.

An approximate dynamic scaling technique is achieved using the **Corner** option. You can see the block change size as you move the cursor if **DRAGMODE** is set to **Auto**. Select the **Corner** option at the X scale factor prompt as follows:

> X scale factor ⟨1⟩ / Corner / XYZ: **C**↵
> Other corner: *(move cursor to change size and pick a point)*

Figure 23-10.
Negative and positive scale factors have different effects when inserting a block.

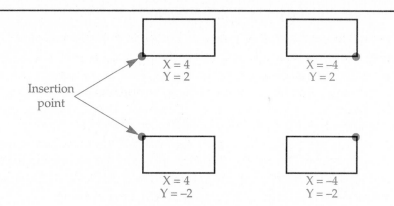

Insertion point

X = 4
Y = 2

X = –4
Y = 2

X = 4
Y = –2

X = –4
Y = –2

A coordinate value can be typed or a point can be picked. Be sure to pick a point above and to the right of the insertion point to insert the block as drawn. Picking corner points to the left or below the insertion points will generate mirror images such as those in Figure 23-10.

NOTE

Before a block can be edited, it must be returned to its original objects with the **EXPLODE** command. Block editing and redefinition is covered later in this chapter.

EXERCISE 23-2

❑ Open EX23-1 if it is not currently on your screen.
❑ Draw a 1 × 1 square on layer 0 and make it a block named PLATE.
❑ Insert the PLATE block into the drawing. Enter an X scale factor of 6 and a Y scale factor of 4.
❑ Insert the CIRCLE block twice into the PLATE block as shown. The small circle is one unit in diameter and the large circle is 1.5 units in diameter.
❑ Make a block of the entire drawing and name it PLATE-1. Pick the lower-left corner as the insertion point.
❑ Insert the PLATE-1 block on your drawing and enter a scale of –1, –1. Also rotate the object 45°.
❑ Save the drawing as EX23-2.

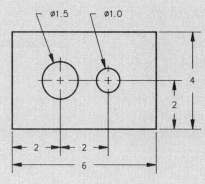

Ø1.5   Ø1.0

4

2

2   2

6

The effects of layers on blocks

Blocks retain the property characteristics of the layer on which they were drawn. From Chapter 4, you learned that all objects in AutoCAD are created in ByLayer mode by default. This means that the object color and linetype are dictated by the layer on which they are created. For example, suppose the CIRCLE block was drawn on layer 1 having the color red and a dashed linetype. When inserted, the block appears red and dashed, no matter what layer it is inserted on. If different colors, linetypes, or even layers are used in a block, they also remain the same when the block is inserted on a different layer. Therefore, a block defined in ByLayer mode retains its properties when inserted into another drawing. If the layers included in the inserted block do not exist in the drawing, AutoCAD automatically creates them.

For a block to assume the property characteristics of the layer it is inserted on, it must be created on layer 0. Suppose you create the CIRCLE block on layer 0 and insert it on layer 1. The block becomes part of layer 1 and thus assumes the color and linetype of that layer. Exploding the CIRCLE block returns the objects back to layer 0 and to the original color and linetype assigned to layer 0.

An exception occurs if entities within the block are drawn using an explicit color or linetype; in other words, not using the default ByLayer mode. In this case, the exploded CIRCLE block objects would retain their original properties.

Changing the layer, color, and linetype of a block

If you insert a block on the wrong layer, use the **DDCHPROP** command (change properties) by entering CH or DDCHPROP at the Command: prompt. The command sequence is as follows:

Command: **CH** *or* **DDCHPROP**↵
Select objects: *(pick the block to change)*
Select objects: ↵

The **Change Properties** dialog box is displayed. See Figure 23-11A. Pick the **Layer...** button then pick the new layer in the **Select Layer** dialog box. See Figure 23-11B. Pick **OK** to exit both dialog boxes.

Figure 23-11.
A—The **Change Properties** dialog box allows you to change an object's color, layer, and linetype. B—Pick the new layer in the **Select Layer** dialog box.

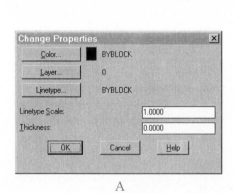

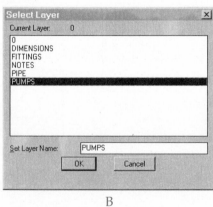

A   B

The block is now changed to the proper layer. If the block was originally created on layer 0, it will assume the color and linetype of the new layer. If it was created on another layer, it will retain its original color and linetype.

To prevent a block from assuming a different color than the assigned layer color, set the current color to ByLayer before creating blocks by picking ByLayer in the **Color Control** drop-down list. Now any entities or blocks that are drawn assume the color of the current layer. The same is true of the linetype of an entity. In order to avoid problems, the linetype should be set as a function of the layer rather than using the **LINETYPE** command. Check to be sure the linetype is set to ByLayer by picking ByLayer in the **Linetype Control** drop-down list.

The layer, color, and linetype of a block can also be changed in the **Properties** area of the **Modify Block Insertion** dialog box. See Figure 23-12. To access this dialog box pick **Properties...** in the **Modify** pull-down menu, or pick the **Properties** button in the **Object Properties** toolbar. Then select the object to be changed. The button selection and command sequence at this point are the same as previously presented.

Figure 23-12.
An object's color, layer, and linetype can be changed in the **Properties** area of the **Modify Block Insertion** dialog box.

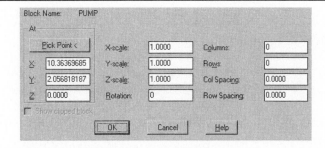

Inserting Multiple Copies of a Block

The **INSERT** and **ARRAY** features are combined in the **MINSERT** (multiple insert) command. This method of inserting and arraying not only saves time, but also disk space. To access the **MINSERT** command, enter MINSERT at the Command: prompt.

An example of an application using **MINSERT** is to place an arrangement of desks on a drawing. Suppose you want to draw the layout shown in Figure 23-13. Change to architectural units and set the limits to 30',22'. Draw a rectangle 4' by 3' and save it as a block called DESK. The arrangement is to be three rows and four columns. Spacing between desks should be two feet horizontally and four feet vertically. Follow this sequence:

```
Command: MINSERT↵
Block name (or ?): DESK↵
    Insertion point: (pick a point)
    X scale factor ⟨1⟩/Corner/XYZ: ↵
    Y scale factor ⟨default=X⟩: ↵
    Rotation angle ⟨0⟩: ↵
    Number of rows (—) ⟨1⟩: 3↵
    Number of columns (|||) ⟨1⟩: 4↵
    Unit of cell or distance between rows (—): 7'↵
    Distance between columns (|||): 6'↵
```

The resulting arrangement is shown in Figure 23-13. The total pattern takes on the characteristics of a block, except that a **MINSERT** array cannot be exploded. If the initial block is rotated, all arrayed objects are also rotated about their insertion points. If the minserted object is rotated about the insertion point, all objects are aligned on that point.

Figure 23-13.
To create an
arrangement of
desks using
MINSERT, first
create a block
called DESK.

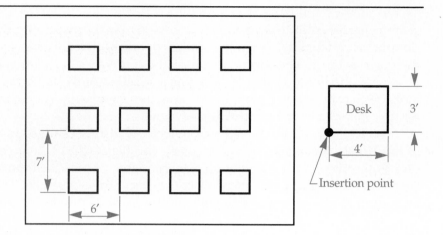

PROFESSIONAL TIP

In the previous example, if you were working with different desk sizes, a one unit square may serve your purposes better than an exact size block. To create a 5′ × 3′-6″ (60″ × 42″) desk, insert a one unit square block using **INSERT** or **MINSERT**, and enter the following for the X and Y values:

X scale factor ⟨1⟩/Corner/XYZ: **60.**↵
Y scale factor ⟨default = X⟩: **42.**↵

A one unit square block can be used in this manner for a variety of objects.

EXERCISE 23-3

❑ Start AutoCAD and start a new drawing with architectural units and 80′,60′ limits. Then, **ZOOM All**.
❑ Draw the chair shown below and save it as a block named **CHAIR**.
❑ Use the **MINSERT** command twice to create the theater arrangement. The sides of the chairs should touch. Each row on either side of the aisle should have 10 chairs. The spacing between rows is 4 feet. The width of the center aisle is 5 feet.
❑ Consider where you should insert the first chair to obtain the pattern.
❑ Save the drawing as EX23-3.

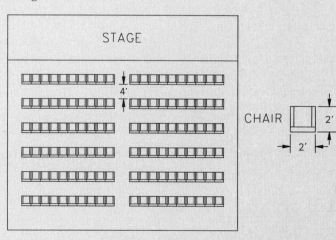

Inserting entire drawings

The **INSERT** command can be used to insert an entire drawing into the current drawing. When one drawing is inserted into another, the inserted drawing becomes a block reference. As a block, it may be moved to a new location with a single pick. The drawing is inserted on the current layer, but does not inherit the color, linetype, or thickness properties of that layer. You can explode the inserted drawing back to its original objects if desired. Once exploded, the drawing objects revert to their original layers.

By default, every inserted drawing has a base insertion point of 0,0,0. If necessary, you can change the insertion point using the **BASE** command. Pick **B**ase from the **Block** cascading menu in the **D**raw pull-down menu, or enter BASE at the Command: prompt as follows:

BASE

Draw
↳ **B**lock
  ↳ **B**ase

> Command: **BASE**↵
> Base point ⟨0.0000,0.0000,0.0000⟩: *(pick a point or enter a new coordinate)*

The new base point now becomes the insertion point.

PROFESSIONAL TIP

When working on a drawing, it is common practice in industry to refer to other drawings to check features or dimensions. In many instances, the prints are not available and must be produced. You can avoid such delays by using the **INSERT** command. When you need to reference another drawing, simply insert it into your current drawing. When you are done checking the features or dimensions you need, simply **UNDO** the **INSERT** operation or erase the inserted drawing.

EXERCISE 23-4

☐ Open drawing EX23-2 if it is not already on your screen.

☐ If your drawing does not have a RED layer, make one and set it as current.

☐ Draw a 6 × 4 unit rectangle. Insert two CIRCLE blocks into the rectangle, both one unit in diameter. Make a new block of this drawing and name it PLATE-2.

☐ Erase the screen. Set the current layer to 0. Insert both the PLATE-1 and PLATE-2 blocks.

☐ The PLATE-2 block should appear red because it was created on the red layer. PLATE-1 should be black.

☐ Make sure RED is the current layer. Insert the PLATE-1 block into your drawing. It should appear red because it was created on layer 0 and assumes the color of the layer on which it is inserted.

☐ Enter the **BASE** command. Choose an insertion point below and to the left of the objects on the screen.

☐ Save the drawing as EX23-4.

☐ Start a new drawing named PLATES.

☐ Insert drawing EX23-4 into your new drawing. The insertion point you pick is the one established using the **BASE** command.

☐ Pick any editing command and select a line of one of the plates. The entire drawing should be highlighted since the drawing is actually one large block.

☐ Save the drawing again as EX23-4.

Presetting block insertion variables

You can speed up the insertion of blocks by presetting the scale or rotation angle. These preset options are available by typing them at the Insertion point: prompt of the **INSERT** command, or when using the **Insert** dialog box. The preset options not only save time, but also allow you to see the scaled size and rotation angle before you pick the insertion point. This helps you determine if the scale and rotation angle are correct.

Preset options can be used two ways. If the **S** option is entered at the Insertion point: prompt, you are asked for the scale factor, then the insertion point and rotation angle. If you enter PS, a prompt requests the scale factor for insertion display purposes only. After you pick the insertion point, the normal **INSERT** prompts are displayed. This second method is a *temporary* preset. The difference is illustrated in the following examples. The first example inserts the block PLATE at a preset scale factor of 2.

```
Command: INSERT↵
Block name (or ?) ⟨current⟩: PLATE↵
   Insertion point: S↵
   Scale factor: 2↵
   Insertion point: (pick an insertion point)
   Rotation angle ⟨0⟩: ↵
```

The next example illustrates a temporary preset of the scale factor.

```
Command: INSERT↵
Block name (or ?) ⟨current⟩: PLATE↵
   Insertion point: PS↵
   Scale factor: 2↵
   Insertion point: (pick an insertion point)
   X scale factor ⟨1⟩ / Corner / XYZ: ↵
   Y scale factor (default=X): ↵
   Rotation angle ⟨0⟩: ↵
```

The temporary preset allows you to see the preset scale or rotation angle as you drag the block. You can also change the scale and rotation angle by entering a value at the normal prompts. Remember, to use temporary preset, enter P followed by the option you wish to preset at the Insertion point: prompt. For example, to temporarily set the rotation angle, enter PR at the Insertion point: prompt. The following list describes the functions of the preset options.

- **S.** Affects the overall scale of X, Y, and Z axes. Rotation angle is also requested.
- **X.** Affects only the X scale. Rotation angle is also requested.
- **Y.** Affects only the Y scale. Rotation angle is also requested.
- **Z.** Affects only the Z scale. Rotation angle is also requested.
- **R.** Sets the rotation angle. The normal **INSERT** scaling options are presented.

In addition, the AutoCAD system variable **INSNAME** (insert name) can be used to store the name of a block you wish to insert. For example, if you will be inserting several copies of the DESK block, you can use **INSNAME** as follows:

```
Command: INSNAME↵
New value of INSNAME, or . for none ⟨""⟩: DESK↵
```

Now when you use the **INSERT** command, the name DESK appears as the default for the block name.

> Command: **INSERT**↵
> Block name (or ?) ⟨DESK⟩: *(press [Enter] to accept this block name, or provide another block name and press [Enter])*

As shown here, you may provide another block name at the **INSERT** prompt, such as CHAIR, regardless of the **INSNAME** setting. The name CHAIR is then stored in the **INSNAME** variable. To specify no default block name, enter a period (.) at the **INSNAME** prompt.

Editing Blocks

Blocks must first be broken into their original components before they can be edited. This is especially important when an entire view or drawing has been inserted. Two methods can be used to break blocks apart. The first method, asterisk insertion, is done at the time of insertion. The second, the **EXPLODE** command, can be done at any time.

Breaking a block apart with asterisk insertions

A block is a single object. Individual objects that make up the block, such as lines, arcs, and circles, cannot be edited. The **MOVE**, **COPY**, **ROTATE**, and **SCALE** commands affect the block as a single item.

If you plan to edit the individual items upon insertion, you can insert a block exploded into its original components. This is easily done by picking the **Explode** check box in the **Insert** dialog box. See Figure 23-8A. When using **INSERT** at the Command: prompt, type an asterisk before the block name:

> Command: **INSERT**↵
> Block name (or ?): ***PLATE–1**↵
>   Insertion point: *(pick a point)*
>   Scale factor ⟨1⟩: ↵
>   Rotation angle ⟨0⟩: ↵

The inserted geometry is not part of a block. It consists of individual objects, which can be edited.

Exploding the block

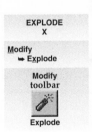

EXPLODE
X

Modify
→ E**x**plode

Modify
toolbar

Explode

The **EXPLODE** command is used to break apart any existing block, polyline, or dimension. To access this command, select the **Explode** button on the **Modify** toolbar, pick **Explode** in the **Modify** pull-down menu, or enter EXPLODE or X at the Command: prompt as follows:

> Command: **X** *or* **EXPLODE**↵
> Select objects: *(pick the block)*
> Select objects: ↵

When the block is exploded, the component objects are quickly redrawn. The exploded block is now composed of objects that can be changed individually. To see if **EXPLODE** worked properly, select any object formerly part of the block. Only that entity should be highlighted. If so, the block was exploded properly.

NOTE You can explode a block that was scaled using different X, Y, and Z values when it was inserted into the drawing. This is technically called a *nonuniformly* scaled block. Versions of AutoCAD prior to Release 13 did not allow exploding these blocks.

Redefining existing blocks

A situation can arise where you discover that a block must be edited. This is an easy process, even if you have placed the block on a drawing many times. To redefine an existing block, follow this procedure:

1. Insert the block to be redefined anywhere on screen.
2. Explode the block you just inserted using the **EXPLODE** command.
3. Edit the block as needed.
4. Recreate the block using the **BLOCK** command.
5. Give the block the same name it had before. Answer Yes to redefine the block.
6. Give the block the same insertion point as the original.
7. All insertions of the block are updated when the **BLOCK** command is complete.

A common mistake is to forget to use the **EXPLODE** command. When you try to create the block again with the same name, the following error message is displayed and the command is aborted:

    Block ⟨name⟩ references itself
    Regenerating drawing.
    Invalid

This means you are trying to create a block that already exists. Enter the **EXPLODE** command and try again.

NOTE You can also redefine existing blocks using the **Block Definition** dialog box instead of the **BLOCK** command. This dialog box was covered earlier in this chapter. After the block has been inserted and exploded, access the **Block Definition** dialog box. Enter the same block name, select the objects, pick the same insertion point, pick **OK**, and select the **Redefine** button in the **Warning** dialog box.

Understanding the circular reference error

The concept of a block *referencing itself* may be a little difficult to understand at first, so let's take a closer look at how AutoCAD works with blocks. A block can be composed of any AutoCAD objects, including other blocks. When using the **BLOCK** command to incorporate an existing block into the new block, AutoCAD must make a list of all the objects that compose the new block. This means that AutoCAD must refer to any existing block definitions that are selected to be part of the new block. But if you select an instance (reference) of the block being redefined as a component object for the new definition, a problem occurs. You are trying to redefine a block name using a previous version of the block with the same name. In other words, the new block refers to a block of the same name, or *references itself*.

For example, use a block called BOX that is composed of four line objects. The block should be changed so that it contains a small circle in the lower-left corner. If the original block BOX is exploded, all that is left are the four line objects. After drawing the required circle, the block command is activated and the block named BOX can be redefined by selecting the four lines and the circle as the component objects. Redefining a block destroys the old definition and creates a new one. See Figure 23-14A.

Alternately, if you do not explode the block, but still draw the circle and try to redefine the block, the objects selected to define the revised block BOX would now be a block reference of the block BOX and a circle. The old definition of BOX has not been destroyed, but a new definition has been attempted. Thus AutoCAD is trying to define the block BOX by using an instance of the block BOX. This is referred to as a *circular reference*, and is what is meant by a block referencing itself. See Figure 23-14B.

Figure 23-14.
A—The correct procedure for redefining a block. B—Redefining a block that has not first been exploded creates an invalid circular reference.

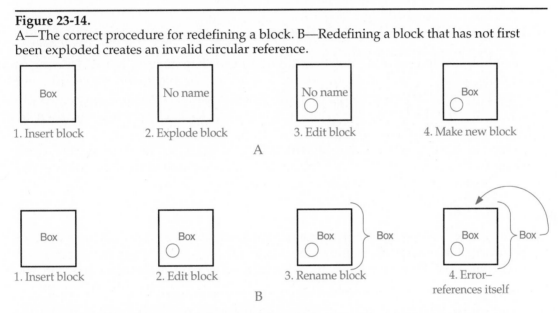

Creating a block from a drawing file

You can create a block from any existing drawing. This allows you to avoid redrawing the object as a block, thus saving time. Remember, if something has already been drawn, try to use it as a block rather than redrawing it. Use the **INSERT** command in the following manner to define a block named BOLT from an existing drawing file named fastener.dwg.

> Command: **INSERT**↵
> Block name (or ?): **BOLT=FASTENER**↵
> Insertion point: (*press the* [Esc] *key*)

The drawing is not inserted on screen because the command is canceled. However, a block named BOLT is added to the drawing file and can be used like any other block.

The same procedure is possible using the **Insert** dialog box. Select the fastener file using the **File...** button. The selected file is then displayed in both the **Block...** and **File...** text boxes. Change the name from FASTENER to BOLT in the **Block...** text box and pick **OK**. In this case the file is inserted into the drawing, but is given a block name of BOLT.

Making Permanent Global Blocks

Symbols created with the **BLOCK** command can only be used in the drawing in which they were made. However, you may want to use blocks on many different drawings without having to redraw them. The **WBLOCK** command allows you to create a drawing file (.dwg extension) out of a block. This drawing can then be inserted as a block in any drawing.

There are several ways to use the **WBLOCK** command. To illustrate the first, open drawing EX23-1. Convert your CIRCLE block to a permanent symbol by making it a separate drawing file using the following procedure:

Command: **W** *or* **WBLOCK**↵

The **Create Drawing File** dialog box appears, displaying a listing of all drawing files in the current folder. Type the name of the wblock, HOLE, in the **File name:** text box and press [Enter]. Each time you select the **WBLOCK** command, the **Create Drawing File** dialog box appears, unless the **FILEDIA** system variable is set to the value of zero (0).

Block name: **CIRCLE**↵

The above sequence wrote a new block, HOLE, to a drawing file on disk. The prompt asked for the name of an existing block. Type CIRCLE to convert it into a separate drawing file named HOLE.

> **NOTE** When another drawing is inserted into the current drawing it acts like a block. It is a single object and cannot be edited unless broken into its original components.

To assign the new drawing name to the same name as the block, type an equal symbol (=) for the block name as follows:

Command: **W** *or* **WBLOCK**↵

Enter CIRCLE in the **File name:** text box in the **Create Drawing File** dialog box. Now, proceed as follows:

Block name: =↵

Making a new wblock

Suppose you want to create a separate file from a shape you just drew, but have not yet made a block. Enter the **WBLOCK** command, but do not supply a block name. Press [Enter] instead. Then select the insertion point and the objects to be included in the new drawing.

Command: **W** *or* **WBLOCK.**↵

Enter DESK in the **File name:** text box in the **Create Drawing File** dialog box. Now, proceed as follows:

Block Name: ↵
Insertion base point: *(pick a point)*
Select objects: *(select objects to be in the new drawing)*
Select objects: ↵

This sequence is exactly like that of the **BLOCK** command. Remember that this drawing is saved to disk as a drawing file, *not* as a block in the current drawing. Be sure to select the proper folder for the file. A drawing file that is to be saved into the blocks folder on the C: hard drive would be named c:\blocks\desk. If you want to save the drawing file on a disk in the A: drive, type the file name as A:desk in the **File name:** text box, or pick the drive in the **Save in:** drop-down list.

Preparing a drawing for use as a symbol

An entire drawing can also be stored as a wblock. Type an asterisk (*) for the block name.

Command: **W** *or* **WBLOCK.**↵

Enter a file name in the **File name:** text box in the **Create Drawing File** dialog box. Now, proceed as follows:
Block Name: *↵

In this case, the whole drawing is saved to disk as if you used the **SAVE** command. The difference is that all unused blocks are deleted from the drawing. If the drawing contains any unused blocks, this method reduces the size of a drawing considerably.

PROFESSIONAL TIP    The wblock-asterisk method is a good technique to clean your drawing of unused named objects to reduce the file size. Use this routine when you have completed a drawing and know that the unused blocks, layers, styles, and objects are no longer needed. The **PURGE** command can also be used to remove any unused layers, linetypes, text styles, dimension styles, multiline styles, blocks, and shapes. But the process is slower than using the wblock-asterisk method. **PURGE** is discussed later in this chapter.

Inserting a separate drawing file with the Select Drawing File dialog box

When you use the **DDINSERT** command, you have the option to insert a block or a wblock. Picking the **File...** button activates the **Select Drawing File** dialog box. You can now scroll through listings in any folder, or on another drive, and pick the file name you need.

If you type INSERT at the Command: prompt, you can access the **Select Drawing File** dialog box by entering a tilde (~) at the Block name (or ?): prompt as follows:

Command: **INSERT**↵
Block name (or ?): ~↵

You can use the tilde character whenever any AutoCAD command prompt requests a file name. One of several dialog boxes is then displayed, regardless of the **FILEDIA** system variable setting.

EXERCISE 23-6

❏ Open drawing EX23-2. If you have not done this exercise, do so now.
❏ Create a drawing file called PLATE-1 using the existing block of the same name.
❏ Use Windows Explorer to list your drawing files. Be sure plate-1.dwg is listed.
❏ Start a new drawing.
❏ Insert the PLATE-1 drawing into the current drawing.
❏ Save the drawing as EX23-6.

Revising an inserted drawing

You may find that you need to revise a drawing file that has been used in other drawings. If this happens, you can quickly update any drawing in which the revised drawing is used. For example, if the drawing file named pump was used several times in a drawing, simply use the **INSERT** command, and place an equal sign (=) after the block name to update all the pump symbols:

Command: **INSERT** ↵
Block name (or ?): **PUMP=**↵
Block PUMP redefined
Regenerating drawing.
   Insertion point: *(press* [Esc]*)*

All of the pump symbols are automatically updated, and by canceling the command, no new symbols are added to the drawing.

Suppose you had inserted a drawing file named fastener into your current drawing, but gave it the block name of screw. Now you have decided to revise the fastener drawing. The screw block can be updated using the **INSERT** command as follows:

Command: **INSERT**↵
Block name (or ?): **SCREW=FASTENER**↵
Block SCREW redefined
Regenerating drawing.
   Insertion point: *(press* [Esc]*)*

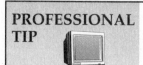

PROFESSIONAL TIP   If you work on projects in which inserted drawings may be revised, it may be more productive to use reference drawings instead of inserted drawing files. Reference drawings are used with the **XREF** command, discussed in Chapter 24. All referenced drawings are automatically updated when a drawing file that contains the xrefed material is loaded into AutoCAD.

Creating a Symbol Library

As you become proficient with AutoCAD, begin to construct symbol libraries. A *symbol library* is a collection of related shapes, views, and symbols that are used repeatedly. You may eventually want to incorporate symbols into your screen and tablet menus. This is discussed in detail in *AutoCAD and its Applications— Advanced, Release 14*. First, you need to know where symbols (blocks and drawing files) are stored and how they can be inserted into different drawings.

Blocks vs. separate drawing files

As discussed earlier, the principal difference between the **BLOCK** and **WBLOCK** commands is that a block is saved with the drawing in which it is created and can only be used in that drawing. The **WBLOCK** command saves a separate drawing file that can be used in any drawing. A complete drawing file occupies considerably more disk space than a block.

If you decide to use blocks, each person in the office or class must have a copy of the drawing that contains the blocks. This is often done by creating the blocks in a template or separate drawing file. If drawing files are used, each student or employee must have access to the files.

Using 3.5″ disks

Disks are good for temporarily storing backup copies of drawing and data files. They also allow you to transport files from one workstation to another in the absence of a network or modem. However, avoid making disks the primary means for storage of symbols, especially if you have sufficient room on the hard disk drive, optical drive, or network server drives. Inserting and removing disks from a disk drive is tedious and time-consuming, because it takes more time for the computer to access the disks. If you must adopt this method, follow these guidelines.

- Create all symbols as separate drawing files.
- Assign one person to initially create the symbols for each specialty.
- Follow class or company symbol standards.
- Create a symbol library listing using a printer or plotter. Include a picture of the symbol, its insertion point, necessary information, and where it is located. A sample is shown in Figure 23-15. Provide all persons who use the symbols with a copy of the listing.
- Save one group of symbols per disk. For example, individual disks may contain the following types of symbols:
  - ✓ Electronic
  - ✓ Electrical
  - ✓ Piping
  - ✓ Mechanical
  - ✓ Structural
  - ✓ Architectural
  - ✓ Landscaping
  - ✓ Mapping
- These are methods of labeling disks:
  - ✓ In the Windows Explorer, right click on the 3½ Floppy (A:) icon. This activates the pop-up menu. Select Properties to access the 3½ Floppy (A:) Properties dialog box. Type a label in the Label: text box of the General tab, and press OK.
  - ✓ Use the DOS LABEL command to assign a name to each disk in the following manner:
    1. Pick Programs ⟩ from the Start menu, then pick Command Prompt.
    2. Enter C:\⟩ LABEL A:STRUCTURAL

Figure 23-15.
Piping flow diagram blocks used for template drawings in the symbol library listing. The colored dot indicates the insertion point, and is not part of the block.

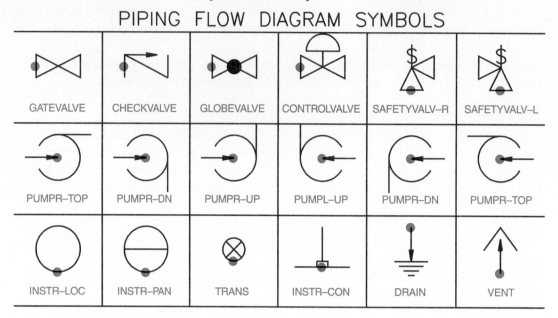

PIPING FLOW DIAGRAM SYMBOLS

GATEVALVE	CHECKVALVE	GLOBEVALVE	CONTROLVALVE	SAFETYVALV–R	SAFETYVALV–L
PUMPR–TOP	PUMPR–DN	PUMPR–UP	PUMPL–UP	PUMPR–DN	PUMPR–TOP
INSTR–LOC	INSTR–PAN	TRANS	INSTR–CON	DRAIN	VENT

This gives the disk in the A: drive the name STRUCTURAL. Eleven characters can be used for a label. Use the DOS VOL command to find out the label of a disk.

    C:\\) **VOL A:**↵

DOS responds:

Volume in drive A is STRUCTURAL
Volume Serial Number is 2309-OCFA

   ✓ Use stick-on disk labels on all disks. Write on the label before attaching it to the disk. Use the same name as the volume label.
- Copy symbol disks and provide a copy for each workstation in the class or office.
- Keep backup copies of all symbol disks in a secure place.
- When symbols are revised, update all copies of diskettes containing the edited symbols.
- Inform all users of any changes to symbols.

Using the hard disk drive

The local or network hard disk drive is one of the best places to store a symbol library. It is easily accessible, quick, and more convenient to use than disks. Symbols should be created with the **WBLOCK** command, as they were with disks. The drawing files can be saved in the current folder (usually AutoCAD R14) or another folder. If drawing files are stored in the AutoCAD R14 folder they are easier to find. However, storing symbols in separate folders keeps the AutoCAD folder uncluttered and easy to manage.

If a symbol is saved as a file, you must search for its folder the first time the symbol is used. After its initial insertion, the drawing file is saved as a block definition in the current drawing, and can be accessed by entering its file name.

Drawing files are saved on the hard disk drive using the same systematic approach as with disks. These additional guidelines also apply:

- All workstations in the class or office should have folders with the same names.
- One person should be assigned to update and copy symbol libraries to all workstation hard drives.
- Drawing files should be copied onto each workstation's hard drive from a master disk or network server.
- The master disks and backup disks of the symbol libraries should be kept in separate locations.

Copying a symbol library into a new drawing

A symbol library of blocks that is part of a drawing can be copied into a new drawing file. The incoming blocks are not displayed, only included in the drawing file. It enables you to use blocks created on one drawing without also having to use the drawing. The process is simple. If the drawing pipeflow.dwg on the disk in the A: drive contains the needed blocks, enter the following at the Command: prompt.

Command: **INSERT**↵
Block name (or ?) ⟨*current*⟩: **A:PIPEFLOW**↵
   Insertion point: *(press* [Esc] *to cancel)*

The blocks are now included with your drawing. Check this by selecting **BLOCK** and the **?** option.

NOTE   If a symbol library is saved as a template, it cannot be inserted into another drawing. However, a symbol library template is beneficial when starting a new drawing in which those symbols are to be used. For example, when starting a new mechanical drawing, a mechanical template that contains a mechanical symbol library would be helpful.

Create a symbol library listing

After deciding which method of using symbols is best for you, create a symbol library listing. Distribute it to all persons who will be using the symbols. The list can be a pen or printer plot of the symbol libraries on each drawing. These lists should be updated when revisions are made to symbols. A copy on 8.5″ × 11″ paper should be given to all AutoCAD users. A larger copy should be placed on a wall or bulletin board. Examples of symbol library lists used in engineering offices are shown in Figure 23-16 and Figure 23-17.

Renaming Blocks

Block names can be changed with the **RENAME** command. To change the name of the CIRCLE block to HOLE, enter the **RENAME** command as follows:

Command: **RENAME**↵
Block/Dimstyle/LAyer/LType/Style/Ucs/VIew/VPort: **B**↵
Old block name: **CIRCLE**↵
New block name: **HOLE**↵

Figure 23-16.
Shown are instrumentation loop diagram symbols. (Willamette Industries, Inc.)

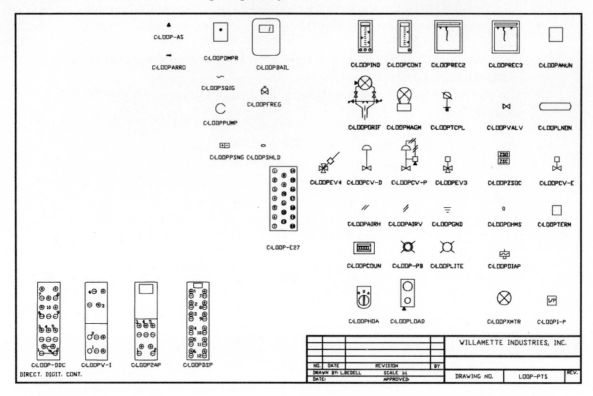

Figure 23-17.
Shown are isometric piping symbols. (Willamette Industries, Inc.)

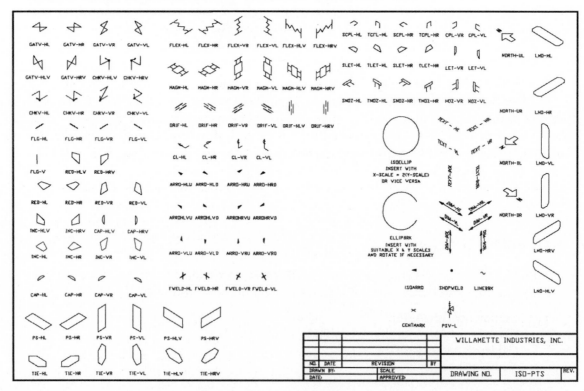

The block name is changed. To check that the name was changed, select the **BLOCK** or **INSERT** command. Use the **?** option to get a listing. The following information will appear in the **AutoCAD Text Window**:

```
Define blocks
PLATE
HOLE
PLATE-1
User        External     Dependent     Unnamed
Blocks      Reference    Blocks        Blocks
3           0            0             0
```

The **RENAME** command only works for blocks, not wblocks. To change the name of a wblock, use the Windows Explorer file renaming procedure explained in Chapter 15 of this text.

Renaming blocks using a dialog box

Blocks may also be renamed from a dialog box. As with the **RENAME** command, you may rename dimension styles, layers, linetypes, text styles, UCS's, named views, and saved viewport configurations. Enter DDRENAME at the Command: prompt to activate the **Rename** dialog box. See Figure 23-18.

Figure 23-18.
The **Rename** dialog box allows you to change the name of a block.

Select objects to rename

Select block to rename

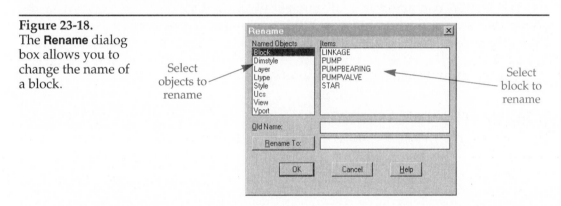

To rename the CIRCLE block for example, select Block from the **Named Objects** list. A list of block names defined in the current drawing appears in the **Items** list. Pick CIRCLE to highlight it in the list. CIRCLE then appears in the **Old Name:** text box. Enter the new block name, HOLE, in the **Rename To:** text box. Pick the **Rename To:** button and the new block name HOLE appears in the **Items** list. Pick **OK** to exit the **Rename** dialog box.

>
> **NOTE**
> Since AutoCAD does not permit the renaming of layer 0 to a different layer name or the renaming of the Continuous linetype, these two named entities do not appear in the **Items** list in the **Rename** dialog box.

> **PROFESSIONAL TIP**
> Several block-related tools are available in the Bonus material. The **Extended Clip**, **Copy Nested Entities**, **Trim to Block Entities**, **Extend to Block Entities**, and **List Xref/Block Entities** tools are found in the **Bonus Standard** toolbar. These tools are only available if a full installation was performed. See Appendix A for bonus menu information.

Deleting Named Entities

A block is a *named entity*, or *object*. Other such named objects are dimension styles (dimstyles), layers, linetypes, shapes, text styles, and multiline styles. In many drawing sessions, not all of the named entities in a drawing are used. For example, your drawing may contain several layers, text styles, and blocks that are not used. Since these entities occupy drawing file space, it is good practice to delete, or *purge* the unused objects using the **PURGE** command.

PURGE
PU

File
➥ Drawing
Utilities
➥ Purge

To access this command pick **Purge** 〉 in the **Drawing Utilities** cascading menu of the **File** pull-down menu, or enter PU or PURGE at the Command: prompt. The **All** option displays each of the unused named objects one at a time and gives you an opportunity to delete or save them. You can also select the specific named object you wish to purge. Use **PURGE** in the following manner to delete a block named LINESPEC:

      Command: **PU** *or* **PURGE**↵
      Purge unused Blocks/Dimstyles/LAyers/LTypes/SHapes/STyles/Mlinestyles/All: **B**↵
      Names to purge ⟨*⟩↵
      Verify each name to be purged? ⟨Y⟩↵
      Purge block LINESPEC? ⟨N⟩ **Y**↵

The **PURGE** command lists all unused blocks individually and gives you the option to answer yes or no. Use the **PURGE** command in the same manner to delete any of the unused entities listed above. The **All** option can be used to delete all unused named objects. This is a good procedure to clean up a drawing after it is completed, but is slower than the wblock-asterisk method.

Chapter Test

Write your answers in the spaces provided.

1. Define *symbol library*. _____

   _____

   _____

   _____

2. Which option of the **COLOR** and **LINETYPE** commands should be set, and what is the quickest way to set them, if you want the block to assume the current color and linetype when it is inserted into a drawing?_____

   _____

   _____

3. When should blocks be drawn to fit inside a one unit square?_____

   _____

4. A block name can be _____ characters long.

5. How do you obtain a listing of all blocks in the current drawing? _____

   _____

   _____

   _____

6. Describe block nesting. _____

   _____

7. How do you preset block insertion variables using a dialog box? _____
_____
_____

8. Describe the effect of entering negative scale factors when inserting a block.
_____
_____

9. Why would the **Corner** option be used when scaling a block during insertion?
_____
_____
_____

10. What properties do blocks drawn on a layer other than 0 assume when inserted?
_____
_____

11. Why would you draw blocks on layer 0? _____
_____

12. What are the limitations of the **MINSERT** command? _____
_____

13. What is the purpose of the **BASE** command? _____
_____

14. What is the purpose of the **INSNAME** system variable? _____
_____

15. Explain why you would choose to use preset options when inserting a block.
_____

16. Explain the difference between **PS** and **S** as preset options. _____
_____
_____

17. Name the two methods that break a block into its individual entities for editing.
_____
_____

18. Suppose you have found that a block was incorrectly drawn. Unfortunately, you have already inserted the block 30 times. How can you edit all of the blocks quickly? _____
_____
_____

19. What is the primary difference between **BLOCK** and **WBLOCK**? _____
_____
_____
_____

20. The **WBLOCK** command asks for block name. What would you enter at the Block name: prompt to make a drawing file out of an existing block? _____

21. What would you enter at the Block name: prompt to remove all unused blocks from a drawing? _____

_____

22. Suppose you revise a drawing named desk. However, the desk drawing had been inserted several times into another drawing as wblocks named DESK2. How would you update the DESK2 insertions? _____

_____

_____

23. Why is it best to put symbol libraries on the hard disk drive rather than disks?

_____

_____

_____

24. What advantage is offered by having a symbol library of blocks in a separate drawing, rather than using wblocks? _____

_____

25. Give the command and entries needed to insert all of the blocks from a drawing named a:struct-1 into the current drawing.

Command: _____

Block name (or ?) ⟨current⟩: _____

Insertion point: _____

26. What is the purpose of the **PURGE** command? _____

_____

Drawing Problems

1. Create a symbol library for one of the drafting disciplines listed below, and then save it as a template or a drawing file. Then, after checking with your instructor, draw one problem using the library. If you saved the symbol library as a template, start the problem with the template. If you saved it as a drawing file, start a new drawing and insert the symbol library into it.

Specialty areas you might create symbols for include:
   • Mechanical (machine features, fasteners, tolerance symbols).
   • Architectural (doors, windows, fixtures).
   • Structural (steel shapes, bolts, standard footings).
   • Industrial piping (fittings, valves).
   • Piping flow diagrams (tanks, valves, pumps).
   • Electrical schematic (resistors, capacitors, switches).
   • Electrical one-line (transformers, switches).
   • Electronics (IC chips, test points, components).
   • Logic diagrams (and gates, nand gates, buffers).
   • Mapping, civil (survey markers, piping).
   • Geometric tolerancing (feature control frames).

Save the drawing as P23-1, or choose an appropriate name, such as ARCH-PRO or ELEC-PRO.

2. Display the symbol library created in Problem 1 on the screen and make a print with your printer. Put the printed copy of the symbol library in your notebook as a reference.

3. Open Problem 3 from Chapter 13 (P13-3). The sketch for this drawing is shown below. Erase all copies of the symbols that were made, leaving the original intact. This includes steel column symbols and the bay and column line tags. Then follow these steps:

A. Make a block of each of the remaining steel column and tag symbols.

B. Use the **MINSERT** or **ARRAY** commands to place the symbols in the drawing.

C. Dimension the drawing as shown in the problem drawing in Chapter 13. Set the proper dimension variables for this type of drawing. Dimensions should be given in feet and inches. Show zero inches as follows: 20'-0".

D. Save the drawing as P23-3.

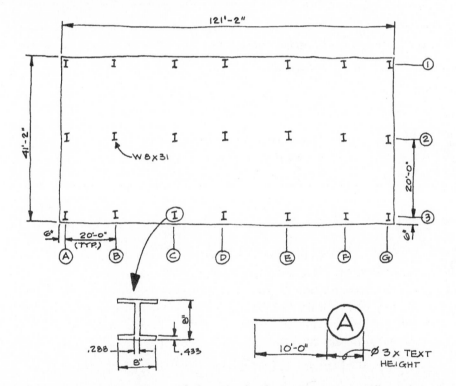

*Problems 4–8 represent a variety of electrical schematics, piping flow diagrams, and logic diagrams. They are all not-to-scale drawings created using symbols (blocks). The symbols should first be drawn as blocks or wblock drawings and then saved in a symbol library using one of the methods discussed in this chapter. Create each drawing as shown and place a border and title block on each drawing. Save the drawings as **P23-4**, **P23-5**, and so on.*

4.

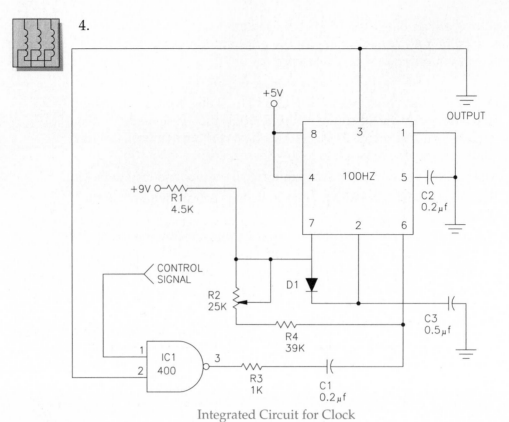

+5V

8	3	1
4	100HZ	5
7	2	6

OUTPUT

+9V R1
     4.5K

C2
0.2μf

CONTROL
SIGNAL

D1

R2
25K

C3
0.5μf

R4
39K

1
IC1   3
2   400

R3   C1
1K   0.2μf

Integrated Circuit for Clock

5.

TV-2
RESERVE
FEED
TANK

LR

TI

PI
52

PI
51

P-10

Piping Flow Diagram

6.

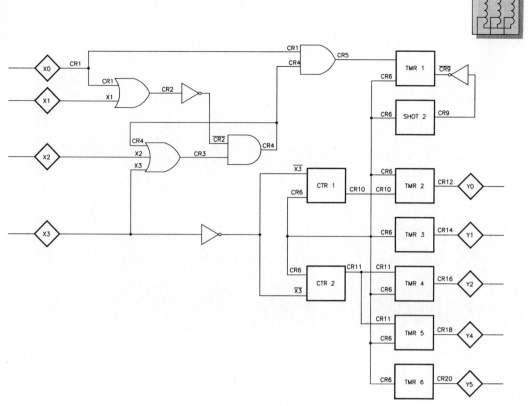

Logic Diagram of Marking System

7.

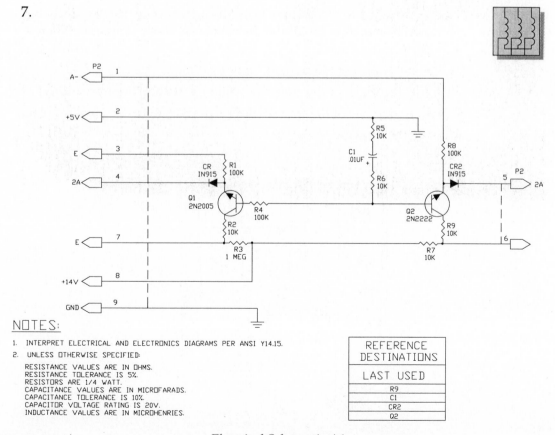

NOTES:

1. INTERPRET ELECTRICAL AND ELECTRONICS DIAGRAMS PER ANSI Y14.15.
2. UNLESS OTHERWISE SPECIFIED:

RESISTANCE VALUES ARE IN OHMS.
RESISTANCE TOLERANCE IS 5%.
RESISTORS ARE 1/4 WATT.
CAPACITANCE VALUES ARE IN MICROFARADS.
CAPACITANCE TOLERANCE IS 10%.
CAPACITOR VOLTAGE RATING IS 20V.
INDUCTANCE VALUES ARE IN MICROHENRIES.

REFERENCE DESTINATIONS	
LAST USED	
R9	
C1	
CR2	
Q2	

Electrical Schematic A1

8.

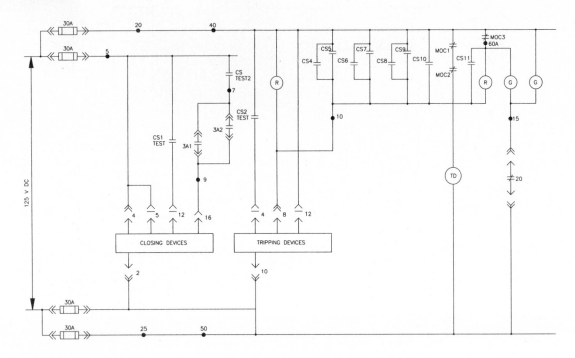

Electrical Schematic B1

9. Open Problem 4 from Chapter 13 (P13-4). The sketch for this drawing is shown below. Erase all of the desk workstations except one. Then follow these directions:

A. Create a block of the remaining workstation.

B. Insert the block in the drawing using the **MINSERT** command.

C. Dimension one of the workstations as shown in the original problem.

D. Save the drawing as P23-9.

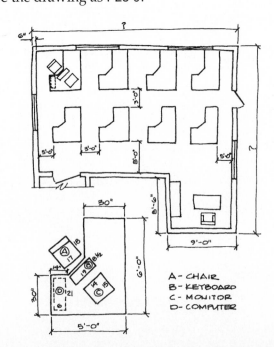

A - CHAIR
B - KEYBOARD
C - MONITOR
D - COMPUTER

Problems 10–14 are presented as engineering sketches. They are not-to-scale, schematic drawings made using symbols. The symbols should first be drawn as blocks and then saved in a symbol library. Place a border and title block on each of the drawings.

10. This is a logic diagram of a portion of a computer's internal components. Create the drawing on a C-size sheet. Save the drawing as P23-10.

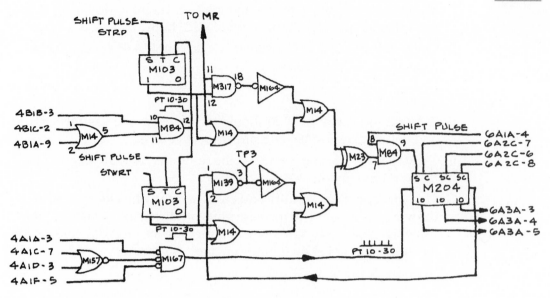

11. Draw the piping flow diagram of a cooling water system on a B-size sheet. Look closely at this drawing. Using editing commands, it may be easier than you think. Draw thick flow lines with polylines. Save the drawing as P23-11.

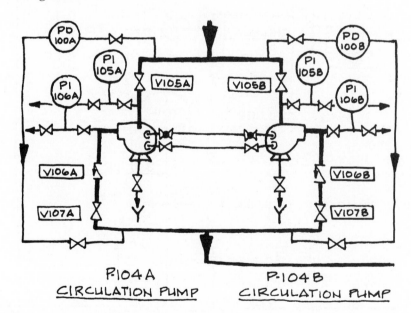

12. The general arrangement of a basement floor plan for a new building is shown. The engineer has shown one example of each type of equipment. Use the following instructions to complete the drawing:

A. The drawing should fit on C-size sheet.

B. All text should appear 1/8″ high, except bay and column line tags, which are 3/16″ high. The text balloons for bay and column lines should be twice the diameter of the text height.

C. The column and bay line steel symbols represent wide-flange structural shapes, and should be 8″ wide × 12″ high.

D. The PUMP and CHILLER installations (except PUMP #5) should be located per the dimensions given for PUMP #1 and CHILLER #1. Use the dimensions shown on the sketch for other PUMP and CHILLER units.

E. TANK #2 and PUMP #5 (P-5) should be located exactly as TANK #1 and P-4, and should be the same respective sizes.

F. Tanks T-3, T-4, T-5, and T-6 are all the same size, and are aligned 12′ from column line A.

G. Plan this drawing carefully and create as many blocks or wblock drawings as possible to increase your productivity. Dimension the drawing completely as shown, and provide location dimensions for all equipment not shown in the engineer's sketch.

H. Save the drawing as P23-12.

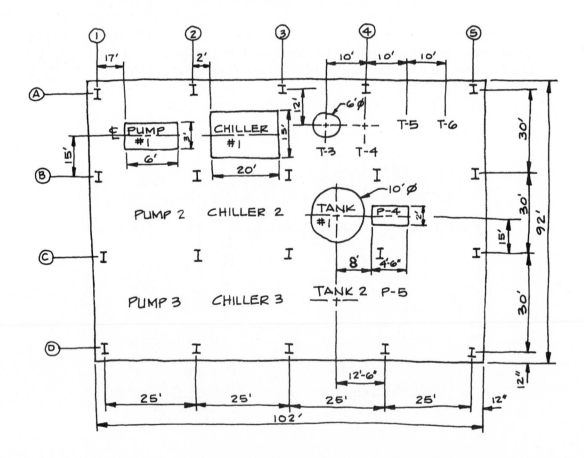

AutoCAD and its Applications—Basics

13. The drawing in Problem 12 (P23-12) must be revised. The engineer has provided you with a sketch of the necessary revisions. It is up to you to alter the drawing as quickly and efficiently as possible. The dimensions shown on the sketch *do not* need to be added to the drawing; they are provided for construction purposes only. Revise P23-12 so that all CHILLERS, and TANKS #3, #4, #5, and #6 reflect the changes. Save your drawing as P23-13.

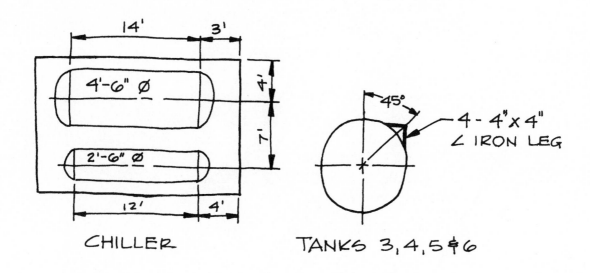

CHILLER   TANKS 3,4,5&6

14. This piping flow diagram is part of an industrial effluent treatment system. Draw it on a C-size sheet. Eliminate as many bends in the flow lines as possible. Place arrowheads at all flow line intersections and bends. Flow lines should not run through valves or equipment. Use polylines for thick flow lines. Save the drawing as P23-14.

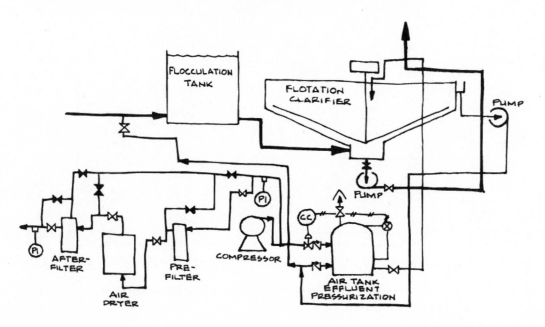

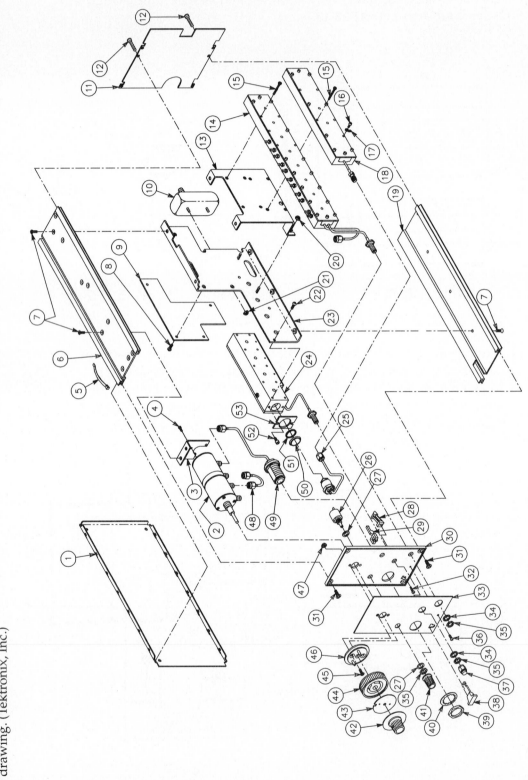

Assembly drawing. (Tektronix, Inc.)

External References and Multiview Layouts

Learning Objectives

After completing this chapter, you will be able to:
- ○ Define the function of external references.
- ○ Reference an existing drawing into the current drawing using the **XREF** command.
- ○ Overlay an existing drawing onto the current drawing.
- ○ Change the path of external references.
- ○ Bind dependent symbols to a drawing.
- ○ Construct multiple viewports in a paper space drawing.
- ○ Construct a multiview drawing using external references of different scales.
- ○ Control the display of layers using the **VPLAYER** command.

As you create multiple objects in a drawing by copying, the drawing file grows in size. This is because AutoCAD must maintain a complete description of the geometry of each one of the copied objects. On the other hand, when you use a block to represent repetitive objects, AutoCAD maintains only one description of the block's geometry. All the other instances of the block are recorded as X, Y, Z coordinates, and AutoCAD refers to the original *block definition* to obtain the block's data. The size of a drawing is decreased considerably if many blocks are used.

AutoCAD enables you to go even further in your efforts to control the size of drawing files with the use of the **XREF** command. This command allows you to incorporate, or "reference," one or more existing drawings into the current drawing without adding them to the contents of the current file. This procedure is excellent for applications in which existing base drawings or complex symbols and details must be shared by several users, or used often. This chapter explores the use of the **XREF** command, and illustrates how it can be used to create a paper space multiview architectural layout with a variety of scales.

Using Reference Drawings

Any machine or electrical appliance contains a variety of subassemblies and components. These components are assembled to create the final product. The final product occupies a greater amount of space and weighs more than any of the individual parts. In the same way, a drawing composed of a variety of blocks and inserted drawings grows much larger and occupies more disk space than the individual symbols and components.

Imagine creating a design model of an automobile by projecting numerous holograms (laser-generated 3D pictures) onto a viewing area. The design occupies perceived space, yet weighs nothing. When the lasers are turned off, the image of the car vanishes. Yet, the individual components that were projected still exist in computer storage and can be displayed again if needed. That is the principle behind the AutoCAD reference drawing concept.

AutoCAD allows you to *reference* existing drawings to the master drawing you are currently working on. When you externally reference (xref) a drawing, its geometry is not added to the current drawing (as are inserted drawing files), but is displayed on the screen. This makes for much smaller files. It also allows several people in a class or office to reference the same drawing file, and always be assured that any revisions to the reference drawing (master) will be displayed in any drawing where it is used.

To display the **External Reference** dialog box, pick **E̲xternal Reference...** from the **I̲nsert** pull-down menu, pick the **External Reference** button from either the **Reference** or the **Insert** toolbar, or enter XREF or XR at the Command: prompt. The **External Reference** dialog box is a complete management tool for your external references. See Figure 24-1.

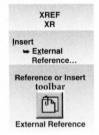

XREF
XR

Insert
 ↳ External
   Reference...

Reference or Insert
toolbar

External Reference

Figure 24-1.
The **External Reference** dialog box provides access to all of the options for externally referenced files.

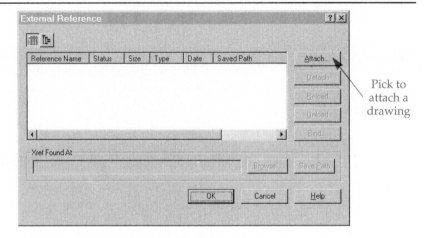

Reference drawings can be used in two basic forms:
- Constructing a drawing using predrawn symbols or details (similar to the use of blocks).
- Laying out a drawing to be plotted that is composed of multiple views or details, using existing drawings. This technique is discussed in detail later in the chapter.

Benefits of external references

An important benefit of using xrefs is that whenever the master drawing is loaded into AutoCAD, the latest version of the xrefs are displayed. If the xrefs are modified between the time you revise the master and the time you plot it, all of the revisions are automatically reflected. This is because AutoCAD reloads each xref whenever the master drawing is loaded.

Other significant aspects of xrefs is that they can be nested, and you can use as many xrefs as needed for the drawing. This means that a detail referenced to the master drawing can be composed of smaller details that are themselves xrefs. You can also use object snap options to attach entities or other xrefs to the referenced drawing.

Attaching an external reference to the current drawing

Using the **XREF** command is similar to using the **INSERT** command. Suppose, for example, that you want to add the geometry for a standard title block to the current drawing. In this example, a reference to a file in the AutoCAD R14\Sample directory named bftitle.dwg is attached. To attach the reference, start the **XREF** command and pick the **Attach...** button in the **External Reference** dialog box. Selecting the **Attach...** button when no external references currently exist displays the **Select File to Attach** dialog box. This is a standard file dialog box with a drawing preview area and a **Find File...** option. Use this dialog box to go to the appropriate folder and select the desired drawing file to attach.

Once a file to attach has been specified, the **Attach Xref** dialog box is displayed, Figure 24-2. This dialog box is used to indicate how and where the reference is placed in the current drawing. The **Xref Name** area shows the name and path of the current xref. To change the drawing name to be attached, pick the **Browse...** button and select the new drawing. When attaching an xref, the **Attachment** option in the **Reference Type** area is selected. Working with the **Xref Overlay** option is discussed later.

Figure 24-2. The **Attach Xref** dialog box is used to indicate how and where an external reference is placed in the current drawing.

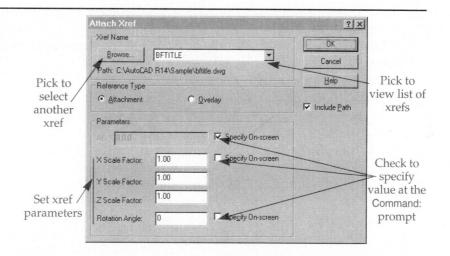

Pick to select another xref

Pick to view list of xrefs

Set xref parameters

Check to specify value at the Command: prompt

Note that when one or more external references already exist in the current drawing, picking the **Attach...** button in the **External Reference** dialog box skips the file dialog and goes right to the **Attach Xref** dialog box. To select a new file to attach, use the **Browse...** button. To insert another copy of an existing xref, use the drop-down list in the **Xref Name** area to select from the currently referenced files.

The **Parameters** area contains the controls for location, scaling, and rotation. The **At:** text box allows you to enter a 2D or 3D coordinate location for insertion of the external reference. By default, the X,Y, and Z scale factors are set to 1 and the rotation angle is 0. Each of these fields provides the option to either enter the data directly in the dialog box, or toggle the **Specify On-screen** check box so you are prompted at the command line.

The **Include Path** check box offers the option of saving the directory path location with the external reference. When the path is not included, AutoCAD looks only in the Support File Search Path specified in the **Files** tab of the **Preferences** dialog box to find the referenced file. This can be helpful when exchanging drawings with other sites that use different directory structures.

In the example in Figure 24-2, the file AutoCAD R14\Sample\bftitle.dwg is selected for attachment. Because the **Specify On-screen** toggle is checked, when you pick **OK** the dialog box is dismissed. The xref is attached to your cursor and you are given the Insertion point: prompt. To specify the insertion point, you can use any valid point specification option, including object snap.

NOTE

The drawing bflylogo.dwg is an xref for bftitle.dwg. Therefore, in order to attach bftitle.dwg, AutoCAD must be able to locate and attach bflylogo.dwg. If the AutoCAD R14\Sample folder is not included in the Support File Search Path specified in the **Files** tab of the **Preferences** dialog box, bftitle.dwg cannot be attached.

As you can see, the options for attaching an xref are essentially the same as when inserting a block. Both of the commands function in a similar manner, yet it is the internal workings of the commands that are different. Remember that externally referenced files are not added to the current drawing file's database as are inserted drawings. Therefore, using external references helps to keep your drawing file size to a minimum.

The **External Reference** dialog box also provides access to additional information about the referenced files. The **External Reference** listing can be displayed either in list view or in tree view. To view your xrefs in a list, pick the **List View** button at the top-left corner of the listing or press [F3]. The list view displays statistical information about each xref. See Figure 24-3. To see all of the data available in this dialog box, highlight an xref name. The data fields saved in the **External Reference** dialog box are described as follows:

- **Reference Name.** Lists the names of the external references.
- **Status.** Shows the current characteristic of xref.
  - **Loaded**—The xref is displayed and regenerated.
  - **Unloaded**—The xref is not displayed or regenerated.
  - **Unreferenced**—The xref has nested xrefs that are not found or are unresolved. An unreferenced xref is not displayed.
  - **Not Found**—The xref file was not found.
  - **Unresolved**—The file is missing or cannot be found.
  - **Orphaned**—The parent of the nested xref was unloaded.
  - **Reload**—Marked to be reloaded. Loading and unloading happens after the dialog session is over.
  - **Unload**—Marked to be unloaded.
- **Size.** Shows the file size for each xref.
- **Type.** Indicates whether the **Attach** or **Overlay** option was used.
- **Date.** Shows the last modification date for the file being referenced.
- **Saved Path.** The path saved in the xref data. If only a file name appears here, then no directory path data is saved.

Figure 24-3.
The **External Reference** dialog box provides access to additional information on referenced files.

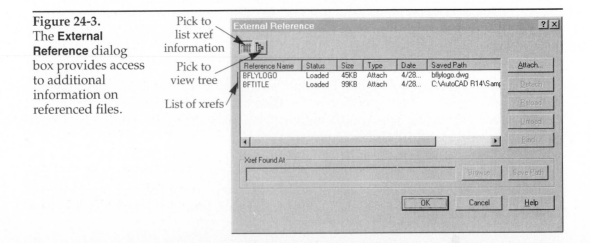

To quickly see a listing of your externally referenced files that shows nesting levels, pick the **Tree View** button or press the [F4] key. See Figure 24-4. *Nesting* is when an externally referenced file is referenced by an xref in the current drawing. In the tree view, the drawing is indicated using the standard AutoCAD R14 drawing file icon, and xrefs appear as a sheet of paper with a paper clip. Nesting levels are shown in a format similar to directory folders. The icon appears differently, depending on the current status of the drawing. A drawing whose status is *unloaded* will be grayed-out. A question mark indicates that the file was *not found*, an up arrow means *reload*, and a down arrow is *unload*.

Figure 24-4.
The tree view shows nested xref levels and the status of each xref.

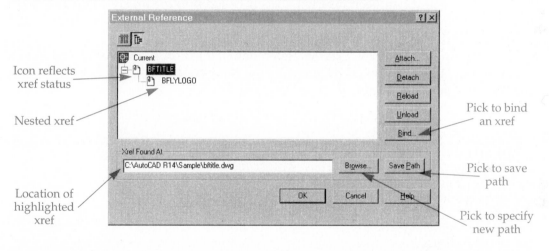

Overlaying the current drawing with an external reference

As you have learned in the previous discussion, you can attach an xref to the current, or master drawing. Then, each time you open the master drawing in AutoCAD, the xref is also loaded and appears on the screen. This attachment remains permanent until you remove it by highlighting it and picking the **Detach...** button in the **External Reference** dialog box. When you detach an externally referenced file, all xrefs nested within the detached file are also removed. Detached references are no longer displayed in the list or the tree, but the actual detachment does not occur until the dialog session is over. This is helpful if you accidentally detach an xref, because you can simply cancel the dialog box to prevent the detachment and restart the dialog session if necessary.

There are many situations in which you may want to see what your drawing looks like with another drawing overlaid on it. This is called *overlay drafting* in manual drafting terms. *Overlay drafting* involves the use of a pin bar and registered holes punched along the top of all the drawings used in the overlay.

The difference between an overlaid and an attached xref is in the way that nested xrefs are handled. An overlaid xref displays nested xrefs that it contains if the xrefs were *attached*, but not if they were *overlaid*. Overlays are commonly used when it is necessary to view another drawing's geometry, but you do not want that geometry to be carried into the master drawing.

Updating the xref path

If an externally referenced file is not found in the **Saved Path** location, AutoCAD searches along the *library* path, which includes the current drawing folder and the Support File Search Path set in the **Preferences** dialog box. If a file with a matching name is found, it is resolved. In such a case, the **Saved Path** differs from where the file was actually found. You can check this by highlighting an xref name and then comparing the path listed in the **Saved Path** column with the listing in the **Xref Found At:** area. To update the **Saved Path**, pick the **Save Path** button.

When a drawing has been moved and the new location is not on the library path, its status is indicated as **Not Found**. You can update the path to refer to the new location by selecting the **Browse...** button in the **Xref Found At:** area. Using the **Select New Path** dialog box, go to the new folder and select the desired file. When the path is updated, the xref is automatically reloaded when you pick **OK**, so it is not necessary to specify that the xref is to be reloaded.

Binding the external reference

An externally referenced file can be made a permanent part of the master drawing just as if it had been inserted. This is called *binding* an xref. This is a useful tool when you need to send the full drawing file on disk to a plotting service, or give a copy of the drawing file to a client.

To bind an xref using the **External Reference** dialog box, highlight the xref to bind and select the **Bind...** button. This displays the **Bind Xrefs** dialog box, which contains the **Bind** and **Insert** radio buttons. See Figure 24-5.

Figure 24-5.
The **Bind Xrefs**
dialog box allows
you to specify how
the xref is
incorporated into
the master drawing.

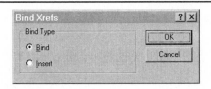

The **Insert** option brings the xref in as if you used the **INSERT** command. All instances of the xref are converted to normal block objects Also, the drawing is entered into the block definition table, and all named objects such as layers, blocks, and styles are incorporated into the master drawing as named in the xref. This method provides the best results for most purposes.

PROFESSIONAL TIP Try the bonus tool named **PACKNGO** to save all files associated with a drawing to a location of your choice. The bonus tools are available if a full installation of AutoCAD was performed. See *Appendix A* of this text for more information on this command.

Selecting the **Bind** option also brings the xref in as a native part of the master drawing and converts all instances of the xref to blocks. However, the xref name is incorporated into the names of all the named objects. For example, prior to the xref being bound, a layer named Notes within an externally referenced drawing file named Title shows up as Title|Notes. When you bind the xref using the **Bind** option, the vertical line in each of the named objects is replaced with 0. This means that the Notes layer is subsequently named Title0Notes. Any of these named objects can be renamed as desired using the **RENAME** command.

In some cases, you may need to incorporate specific named objects from an xref into the master drawing. If you only need select items, it can be counterproductive to bind an entire drawing. In this case, you can bind only the named objects you select. This technique is covered later in this chapter.

Clipping the external reference

A frequent need with externally referenced files is to display only a specific portion of a drawing. AutoCAD allows you to create a boundary that displays a subregion of an external reference. All geometry occurring outside the border is invisible. Objects that are partially within the subregion appear to be trimmed at the boundary. Although these objects appear trimmed, the referenced file is not changed in any way. Clipping is applied to selected instances of an xref, and not to the actual xref definition.

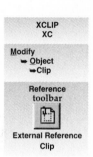

XCLIP
XC

Modify
➡ Object
➡Clip

Reference
toolbar

External Reference
Clip

The command used to create and modify clipping boundaries is **XCLIP**. To access the **XCLIP** command, pick **Clip** from the **Object** cascading menu in the **Modify** pull-down menu, pick the **External Reference Clip** button from the **Reference** toolbar, or enter XC or XCLIP at the Command: prompt. The prompt sequence for creating a rectangular boundary is as follows:

    Command: **XC** *or* **XCLIP**↵
    Select objects: *(select any number of xref objects)*
    n found
    Select objects: ↵
    ON/OFF/Clipdepth/Delete/generate Polyline/⟨New boundary⟩: ↵

A Select objects: prompt allows you to select any number of xrefs to be clipped. Then press [Enter] to accept the default **New boundary** option. This option allows you to select the clipping boundary. The other options of the **XREF** command include the following:

- **ON and OFF.** The clipping feature can be turned on or off as needed by using these options.
- **Clipdepth.** Allows a front and back clipping plane to be defined. The front and back clipping planes define what portion of a 3D drawing is displayed. An introduction to 3D drawing techniques is given in Chapter 27 of this text. Clipping of 3D models is discussed in *AutoCAD and its Applications—Advanced, Release 14*.
- **Delete.** To remove a clipping boundary completely, use this option.
- **generate Polyline.** Creates a polyline object to represent the clipping border of the selected xref.

The **XCLIP** command continues as follows:

    Specify clipping boundary:
    Select polyline/Polygonal/⟨Rectangular⟩: *(pick* [Enter] *to select a rectangular boundary)*
    First corner: *(pick first corner)*
    Other corner: *(pick other corner)*

The results of the previous example are illustrated in Figure 24-6. Note that the geometry outside of the clipping boundary is no longer displayed. A clipped xref can be edited just like an unclipped xref. The clipping boundary moves with the xref. Note also that nested xrefs are clipped according to the clipping boundary for the parent xref.

Figure 24-6.
A clipping boundary limits the area of an xref that is displayed. A—The rectangular boundary selection option. B—The result of the selection.

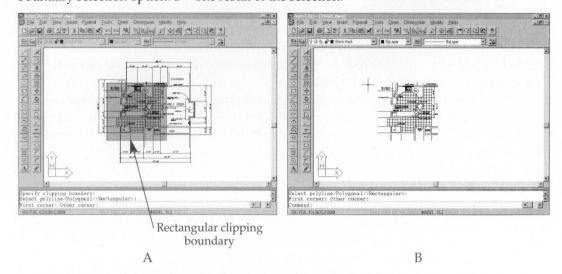

Rectangular clipping
boundary

A   B

There are two other options for defining a clipping boundary.

- **Select polyline.** Allows you to select an existing polyline object as a boundary definition. The border can be composed only of straight line segments, so any arc segments in the selected polyline are treated as straight line segments. If the polyline is not closed, the start and end of the boundary are connected.
- **Polygonal.** Allows an irregular polygon to be drawn as a boundary. This option is similar to a Window-Polygon selection, and allows a fairly flexible boundary definition.

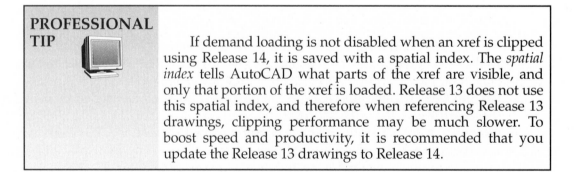

PROFESSIONAL TIP

If demand loading is not disabled when an xref is clipped using Release 14, it is saved with a spatial index. The *spatial index* tells AutoCAD what parts of the xref are visible, and only that portion of the xref is loaded. Release 13 does not use this spatial index, and therefore when referencing Release 13 drawings, clipping performance may be much slower. To boost speed and productivity, it is recommended that you update the Release 13 drawings to Release 14.

Demand loading is enabled by default. To check or change the demand load settings, use the **External reference file demand load:** option under the **Performance** tab of the **Preferences** dialog box.

External Reference dialog box options

The **External Reference** dialog box provides all of the necessary management tools for xrefs. See Figure 24-3. As discussed previously, the **Attach...** option button allows xrefs to be attached or overlaid. When an attached or overlaid xref is no longer needed, it can be detached using the **Detach** button. When the **Detach** button is picked, all highlighted xrefs are marked for detachment, and are immediately removed from the listing. The xref is detached after you pick **OK** to close the dialog box. When an xref is detached, all instances of the xref are erased, and all referenced data is removed from the current drawing.

If an externally referenced file is edited while the master drawing is open, the version on disk may be different than the version currently displayed. To update the xref, use the **Reload** button. This forces AutoCAD to read and display the most recently saved version of the drawing.

When you need to temporarily remove an xref without actually detaching it, the **Unload** button is used. When an xref is unloaded, it is not displayed or regenerated, so the working speed of your drawing is increased. To display the xref again, pick the **Reload** button.

The **Bind...** button displays the **Bind Xrefs** dialog box shown in Figure 24-5. It converts xref definitions to standard local block definitions. The two methods of binding xrefs to the current drawing are **Bind** and **Insert**. These methods are radio buttons in the **Bind Xrefs** dialog box and are explained as follows:

- **Bind.** This method binds the selected xref definition to the current drawing. Xref-dependent symbol table names are changed from blockname|symbolname to blockname$n$symbolname syntax. For example, if you had an xref named RED containing a layer named BLUE, after binding the xref-dependent layer, RED|BLUE would become a locally defined layer named RED0BLUE. The number in n is automatically incremented if a local symbol table definition with the same name already exists. In this example, if RED0BLUE already existed in the drawing, the xref-dependent layer RED|BLUE would be renamed RED1BLUE. In this manner, unique symbol table names are created for all xref-dependent symbol table definitions bound to the current drawing.

- **Insert.** This method binds the xref to the current drawing in a way similar to detaching and inserting the reference drawing. Rather than being renamed using blockname$n$symbolname syntax, xref-dependent symbol table names are stripped of the xref name. For example, if you had an xref named RED containing a layer named BLUE, after an insert-like bind, the xref-dependent layer RED|BLUE would become the locally defined layer BLUE. As with inserting drawings, no symbol table name incrementing occurs if a local symbol table shares the same name as a bound xref-dependent symbol. The bound xref-dependent symbol would assume the properties of the locally defined symbol table name.

Binding Dependent Symbols to a Drawing

AutoCAD refers to *dependent symbols* as named items such as blocks, dimension styles, layers, linetypes, and text styles. If you reference a drawing, you cannot directly use any of its dependent symbols. For example, a layer that exists only on a referenced drawing cannot be made current in the master drawing in order to draw on it. It is the same for text styles. If one of the dependent symbols, such as a dimension style or linetype, is one that you would like to use on the master drawing, you can permanently *bind* or affix any of these symbols to the master drawing. After a permanent bind is created, the dependent symbol, such as the text style, can be used on the master drawing.

When a drawing is referenced to the master, the layer names of the xref are given the name of the referenced drawing, followed by the piping symbol (|), and then the name of the layer. This naming convention enables you to quickly identify which layers belong to a specific referenced drawing. Figure 24-7A illustrates referenced drawing layer names as they appear in the **Layer & Linetype Properties** dialog box. These layer names appear grayed-out in the **Layer Control** drop-down list. See Figure 24-7B.

Remember, you are not allowed to draw on any layer that belongs to an externally referenced file. Likewise, you cannot insert a block or reference a text style or dimension style that belongs to an xref. To use any of these named objects, you must bind them to the master drawing. When you do not wish to bind the entire drawing using the **XREF Bind** option, you can use the **XBIND** command to select which items to bind.

Figure 24-7.
Layer names on a reference drawing are preceded by the xref drawing name. A—The **Layer & Linetype Properties** dialog box. B—The **Layer Control** drop-down list.

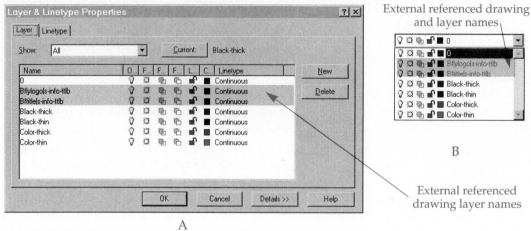

External referenced drawing and layer names

B

External referenced drawing layer names

A

XBIND
XB

Modify
➥ Object
  ➥ External
     Reference
     ➥ Bind...

Reference
toolbar

External Reference
Bind

To access the **XBIND** command, pick the **External Reference Bind** button from the **Reference** toolbar, pick the **Bind...** option from the **External Reference** cascading menu that is found in the **Object** cascading menu in the **Modify** pull-down menu, or enter XB or XBIND at the Command: prompt. The **Xbind** dialog box is shown in Figure 24-8.

Figure 24-8.
The **Xbind** dialog box is used to bind individual xref dependent symbols into the master drawing.

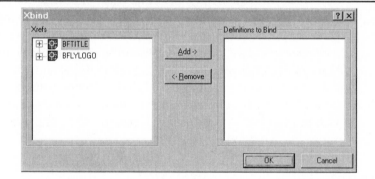

In Figure 24-8, two xrefs are shown to exist in the master drawing. These are indicated by the AutoCAD Release 14 drawing icons. Notice that a plus sign (+) is shown in the box to the left of the icon. This indicates that double-clicking the icon will expand the listing to show the contents of the drawing. Figure 24-9 shows the BFTITLE external reference expanded one level to show the named object groups.

To select an individually named object from a category, you must first expand its branch by double-clicking on its icon. Figure 24-10 shows the **Xbind** dialog box displaying the text styles defined in the BFTITLE external reference.

Figure 24-9.
Double-clicking on an xref expands the branch to show the symbols groups to select from.

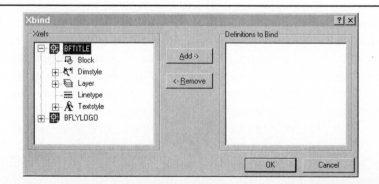

Figure 24-10.
Double-click on the symbol group icon to display the dependent symbols.

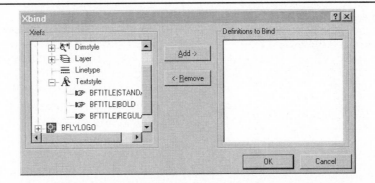

To select a symbol for binding, highlight it and pick the **Add -⟩** button. The names of all symbols selected for binding are displayed in the list on the right, labeled **Definitions to Bind**. The name appears with the xref name prefix and the vertical bar. When all desired symbols have been selected, pick the **OK** button. A report is displayed at the command line indicating how many of each type of object was bound.

When a dependent symbol has been bound to the master drawing, it is automatically renamed. The renaming consists of replacing the vertical bar with two dollar signs and a number, typically 0. For example, a bound layer named a-new-door belonging to the xref named XREF1 would be named xref1$0$a-new-door.

In addition to the naming scheme for the bound layers, a bound layer can also have a linetype previously not defined in the master drawing. An automatic binding is performed so that the required linetype definition can be referenced by the new layer. The linetype name such as Xref1$0$hidden is listed. Similarly, a bound block may result in the automatic binding of layers, linetypes, or nested blocks.

Bound symbol names can be renamed as desired. You can remove the prefix, or rename the symbol entirely. Use either the **DDRENAME** or the **RENAME** command to rename any named object.

NOTE

You can instruct AutoCAD to create and maintain a log file of the **Attach**, **Detach**, and **Reload** functions used on any drawing containing xrefs. Simply set the **XREFCTL** system variable to 1. AutoCAD creates an .xlg file having the same name as the current drawing, and locates it in the same directory. Each time you load a drawing that contains xrefs, or use the **Attach**, **Detach**, and **Reload** options of the **XREF** command, AutoCAD appends information to the log file. A new heading, or title block, is added to the log file each time the related drawing file is opened. The log file provides the following information:

- Drawing name, date, time, and type of xref operation.
- Nesting level of all xrefs affected by the operation.
- A list of the symbol tables affected by the operation, and the names of the symbols added to the drawing. A few examples of symbol tables are blocks, styles, linetypes, and layers.

You can also create a general log file of all activity while in AutoCAD. Select **Preferences...** from the **Tools** pull-down menu. This displays the **Preferences** dialog box. Pick the **General** tab, then select the **Maintain a Log File** check box in the **Drawing session safety precautions** area on the lower-left side of the panel. A log file will be created in the directory that is specified under the **Files** tab of the **Preferences** dialog box. After exiting AutoCAD, you can view this ASCII file using Windows Notepad or any text editor.

When an xref is loaded, a write lock is placed on the file to prevent other users from changing the xref. This is because demand loading is enabled by default. *Demand loading* means the only portion of the xref file loaded is the part necessary to regenerate the master drawing. Data on frozen layers and data outside of the clipping region is not loaded. The file is, however, kept open in case you thaw a layer or change the clipping and therefore need to access more of the xref drawing data. Because the file is kept open, it is locked and cannot be edited by anyone else.

Demand loading speeds the process of resolving xrefs, and in most cases is best left on. However, if you disable demand loading, the xref file is loaded entirely into the master drawing and can be opened or edited as desired by other users on the network. To update an xref after the source file has been changed, use the **Reload** option of the **XREF** command.

Demand loading can be disabled or enabled using the **External reference file demand load:** drop-down list in the **Performance** tab of the **Preferences** dialog box.

Creating Multiple Viewports in Paper Space

Multiview mechanical drawings and architectural construction drawings often contain sections and details drawn at different scales. AutoCAD allows you to lay out a multiview drawing with views of different scales and plot at full scale.

Imagine that you have manually developed three separate drawings of a house floor plan and construction details. Assume that you lay a C-size piece of vellum (with preprinted border and title block) on a table. Take the three drawings, each at a different scale, and arrange them on the sheet of vellum. Take a full-size photograph of the entire drawing. The photo contains all drawings at the proper scale, including the border and title block. Finally, remove the views from the original sheet of vellum and return them to storage. That's the concept behind creating multiple viewports in paper space.

One of the reasons for creating multiple viewport layouts in paper space using different scales is the ability to plot the layout at the scale of 1:1. This means that scales do not have to be calculated prior to plotting, but they must be considered during the planning stages of your drawing.

Understanding model space and paper space

Creating a multiple viewport layout requires a basic understanding of two concepts—model space and paper space. Model space is the *space* that you draw and design in. It is the default space you enter when AutoCAD is loaded. All of your drawings and models should be created here. Paper space is the mode that you select when you wish to create a layout of your drawing prior to plotting. The powerful aspect of using paper space is that you can create a layout of several different drawings and views, each with different scales. You can even mix 2D and 3D views in the same paper space layout.

As mentioned in Chapter 10, four commands govern how you work with model space and paper space. The material provided in this chapter will guide you through the use of these commands, but a short preview here will help you understand their functions.

AutoCAD and its Applications—Basics

- **TILEMODE = 1.** Represents model space, and the **VPORTS** command is used to establish multiple *tiled* viewports. This is the default setting when you enter AutoCAD.
- **TILEMODE = 0.** Represents paper space, and the **MVIEW** command is used to create multiple floating viewports in paper space.
- **MSPACE.** Command used when **TILEMODE** is set to 0, to move from paper space to one of the floating model space viewports.
- **PSPACE.** Command used when **TILEMODE** is set to 0, to move from one of the floating model space viewports to paper space.
- **MVIEW.** Enables you to *cut* model space viewports into the *paper* of paper space. Can only be used when **TILEMODE** is set to 0. You might even call this command the AutoCAD knife. Using it, you can cut any number and size of rectangular viewports at any location on your paper. A viewport created with **MVIEW** is an AutoCAD object, and can be moved, copied, or resized.

> **NOTE**
>
> The **Create** option of the **MVSETUP** command can also be used to construct an arrangement of viewports in paper space.

If this seems a bit confusing to you, try using the information in the following chart to help you understand the relationship between model and paper space.

Activity	Space	TILEMODE	Command
Drawing and design	Model	1	**VPORTS** (tiled)
Plotting and printing layout	Paper	0	**MVIEW** (objects)

After you use these commands and procedures a few times, you will begin to see how easy they are to understand. Everything you draw is constructed in model space. When preparing a drawing or model for plotting, the necessary views are created in paper space.

Drawing in model space

When you begin a new drawing in AutoCAD, you are automatically in model space. This is the default setting in the acad.dwg file, in all the templates, and when using the **Quick Setup** or **Advanced Setup** wizard. The standard UCS icon is displayed in the lower-left corner of the screen when you are in model space. In addition, a system variable called **TILEMODE** controls the setting of model space and paper space. The model space default setting of **TILEMODE** is 1, and the paper space setting is 0. Enter the following to change the paper space:

```
Command: TI or TILEMODE.↵
New value for TILEMODE ⟨1⟩: 0↵
Entering Paper space. Use MVIEW to insert Model space viewports.
Regenerating paperspace.
Command:
```

Note the special paper space UCS icon resembling a triangle is displayed. See Figure 24-11. The **TILEMODE** variable can also be set using the **View** pull-down menu. Take note of the function of the following three selections in the **View** pull-down menu:

- **Model Space (Tiled).** Sets **TILEMODE** to 1 (model space). Use the **VPORTS** command to created tile viewports.
- **Model Space (Floating).** Executes the **MSPACE** command and activates the crosshairs in the current viewport. If there are no viewports in paper space, the **MVIEW** command is executed.
- **Paper Space.** Sets **TILEMODE** to 0 (paper space). Use the **MVIEW** command to create viewports in paper space.

Figure 24-11.
The paper space
UCS icon resembles
a triangle.

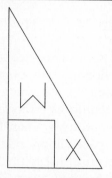

Multiple Viewport Creation

An overview of creating multiple viewports for plotting will first be discussed to introduce the commands and options before detailing the creation of a multiview plot. The most important visualization aspect involved in creating a multiview layout is to imagine that the sheet of paper you are creating will contain several cutouts *(viewports)*, through which you can see other drawings *(models)*. See Figure 24-12.

Figure 24-12.
Views of other
drawings can be
seen through
viewports *cut into*
paper space.

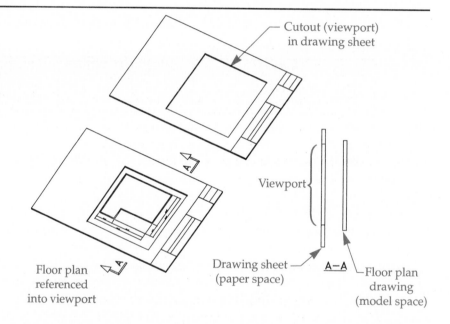

As you know, objects and designs should be created at full-size in model space. If you are designing a machine part, you are probably using decimal units. If you are designing a house, you are using architectural units.

Now, imagine the C-size paper is hanging up in front of you, and the first viewport is cut 12″ wide and 10″ high. You want to display the floor plan of a house inside the opening. If you then place the full-size model of the floor plan directly behind the C-size paper, the house will extend many feet beyond the edges of the paper. How can you place the drawing within the viewport? You know the floor plan should be displayed inside the viewport at a scale of 1/4″ = 1′-0″. The scale factor of 1/4″ = 1′-0″ is 48. Therefore, you need to move the floor plan model away from the C-size paper until it is 1/48 (reciprocal of 48) the size it is now. When you do that, the entire floor plan fits inside the viewport you cut. This is accomplished with the **XP** (times paper space) option of the **ZOOM** command discussed later. See Figure 24-13.

Figure 24-13.
The floor plan is placed inside a viewport.

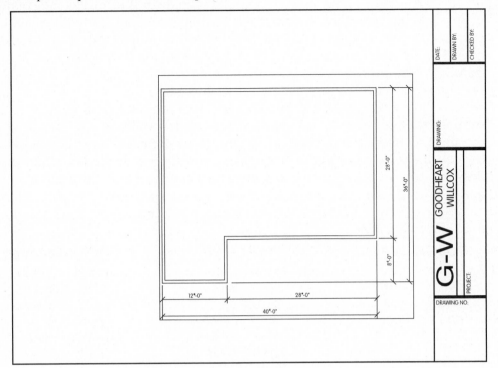

Zoom to the appropriate scale after *referencing* (inserting) a drawing into a viewport. Review the following procedure for constructing multiview plots. The first six steps can be omitted if your prototype drawing or template contains these settings and entities.

1. Set **TILEMODE** to 0 to enter paper space.
2. Set **UNITS** to match the type of drawing you are creating.
3. Set **LIMITS** to match paper size and plotter limits.
4. Make a layer for referenced drawings.
5. Create a border layer or reference a drawing that has a border and title block.
6. Make a layer for viewport entities, and set this as the current layer.
7. Enter MVIEW and make the size viewport needed.
8. Change to model space.
9. Use the **XREF** command to reference an existing drawing. Insert the drawing at 0,0 and use the remaining defaults.
10. Zoom to the extents of the drawing.
11. Set the scale to the appropriate value using the **XP** option of the **ZOOM** command.
12. Use **VPLAYER** (viewport layer) and either the **Vpvisdflt** (viewport visibility default) or **Freeze** options to freeze layers of this referenced drawing in selected viewports.
13. Return to paper space.
14. Repeat the process using the **MVIEW** command.

Constructing a Multiview Drawing for Plotting

Now that you have a good idea of the multiview plotting process, the following example leads you through the details of the procedure. This example uses a house floor plan, a stair detail, and a footing detail. This drawing is *not* among the sample drawings furnished with AutoCAD. Instead, the drawing is based on Exercise 24-1. Complete Exercise 24-1 before working through the example. It is composed of three simple architectural drawings.

❑ If you wish to work along at your computer with the following example of multiview drawing construction, complete this exercise before reading further. It is not necessary to complete this exercise in order to understand the process discussed in the following example, but it may assist you in quickly grasping the concepts of the procedure.

❑ The three drawings shown below—the floor plan, stair detail, and footing detail—should be created for this exercise. They are highly simplified for the purpose of this exercise and explanation, and should not be regarded as complete representations of actual designs. Exact dimensions are not necessary, because the purpose of this exercise is to illustrate the creation of a multiview drawing. You may simplify the drawings further to speed up the exercise.

❑ Each drawing should be created, named, and stored separately with different names. Do not put a border or title block on the drawings. The names are shown in the following table:

FLOOR.DWG		STAIR.DWG		FOOTING.DWG	
Layer	**Color**	**Layer**	**Color**	**Layer**	**Color**
Wall	White	Wall	Yellow	Floor	Green
Dimen	Cyan	Floor	White	Foot	White
Notes	Red	Stair	Green	Dimen	Cyan
		Foot	White	Notes	Red
		Dimen	Cyan	Earth	Yellow
		Notes	Red		

❑ Use the following scales and scale factors when constructing each of the drawings.
FLOOR.DWG: 1/4" = 1'-0" (Scale factor = 48)
STAIR.DWG: 3/8" = 1'-0" (Scale factor = 32)
FOOTING.DWG: 3/4" = 1'-0" (Scale factor = 16)

The scale factors are important when setting the **DIMSCALE** dimensioning variable, and when establishing text height. Remember to multiply the plotted text height, such as .125, by the scale factor, such as 48, to get the text height to use in AutoCAD ($.125 \times 48 = 6$). The scale factor is also used with the **ZOOM XP** command discussed later in the text.

❑ Save the drawings to a hard disk folder, preferably not in the \AutoCAD R14 directory. Check with your instructor or supervisor before creating or using hard disk space. Save backup copies on a floppy disk.

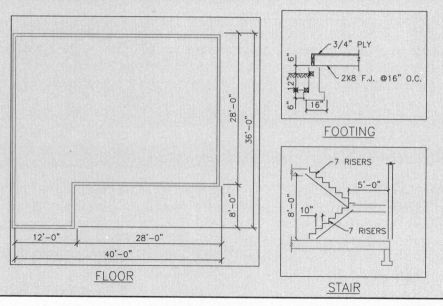

FLOOR

FOOTING

STAIR

Initial drawing setup

The first aspect of drawing setup is to place a border and title block on the screen. It should be the proper size for the plot you wish to make. This can be accomplished in one of several ways, depending on the depth of your preparation. First, set **TILEMODE** to 0, then do one of the following:

- Draw a border on a separate layer, then draw a title block.
- Draw a border and insert a predrawn title block.
- Open or insert a predrawn standard border and title block template containing all constant text and attributes for variable information.

The method you use is not of primary importance for this example, but it is always best to use existing borders and title blocks for reasons that are discussed later.

PROFESSIONAL TIP   This initial setup phase is unnecessary if your school or company uses preprinted border and title block sheets. You might use a *phantom* border and title block sheet on the screen for layout purposes, and to add additional information to the title block. This phantom information can be frozen before plotting.

When setting up a drawing, first enter paper space, then set the units and limits to match the type of drawing you are creating. Be sure that the extents of your border and title block match the maximum active plotting area, or *clip limits* of your plotter. This example uses a standard architectural C-size sheet (18" × 24"), and assumes that the plotter's active area is .75" less on all sides, for a total plotting area of 16.5" × 22.5".

```
Command: TI or TILEMODE↵
New value for TILEMODE ⟨1⟩: 0↵
Entering Paper space. Use MVIEW to insert Model space viewports.
Regenerating paperspace.
Command: UNITS↵
```

Use the following **UNITS** settings and then reply to the Command: prompts.

- Architectural units.
- Units precision = 1/2".
- Systems of angle measure = Decimal degrees.
- Angles precision = 0.
- Direction for angle 0 = East (0).
- Angles measured counterclockwise.

```
Command: LIMITS↵
Reset Paper space limits:
ON/OFF/⟨Lower left corner⟩ ⟨0'-0",0'-0"⟩: ↵
Upper right corner ⟨1'-0",0'-9"⟩: 26,20↵
```

The upper-right corner limit of 26,20 provides additional space on the screen outside the paper limits.

```
Command: Z or ZOOM↵
All/Center/Dynamic/Extents/Previous/Scale(X/XP)/Window/⟨Realtime⟩: A↵
Command:
```

Creating new layers

The border and title block should be on a separate layer, so you may want to create a new layer, called Border or Title, and assign it a separate color. Be sure to make this new layer current before you draw the border.

At this point you can set an appropriate snap grid and visible grid values. If you wish to use an existing border and title block, insert it now. The prototype drawing should include proper grid and snap settings.

One of the principle functions of this example is to use existing drawings of the house floor plan, stairs, and footing. These drawings will not become a part of our new drawing, but they will be *referenced* with the **XREF** command in order to save drawing file space. Therefore, you should also create a new layer for these drawings and name it Xref. Assign the Xref layer the color of 7.

The referenced drawings will fit inside viewports that are made with the **MVIEW** command. These viewports are rectangles and are given the entity name of Viewport. Therefore, they can be edited like any other AutoCAD entity. Create a layer called Viewports or Vport for these entities and assign it a color.

The layers of any existing drawings that you reference (xref) into your new drawing remain intact. Therefore, you do not have to create additional layers unless you want to add information to your drawing.

If you do not have an existing C-size architectural border and title block, you can draw a border at this time. Make the Border layer current and draw a polyline border using the **RECTANG** command at the dimensions of 16.5″ × 22.5″. Draw a title block if you wish. Your screen should look similar to Figure 24-14.

Figure 24-14.
The border and title block in paper space.

Creating a viewport in paper space

The process of creating viewports is completed in paper space because viewports are *cut* out of the paper. When creating a drawing in paper space, your screen represents a sheet of paper. You must now create an opening, called a *viewport*, through which you can view a model, design, or drawing. In this case, the model is a floor plan. First, cut an opening in the paper so you can see the floor plan that is behind it. Keep in mind that the sheet of paper measures 18″ × 24″ and the first viewport to be cut measures 11.5″ × 12″.

The **MVIEW** command is used to create the viewports. Since viewports are entities, make the Viewports layer current, so they reside on their own layer. This allows them to be frozen later to avoid being plotted. The first viewport can be located from the lower-left corner of the border by using the **From** object snap mode. Enter the following:

```
Command: MV or MVIEW↵
ON/OFF/Hideplot/Fit/2/3/4/Restore/⟨First Point⟩: FROM↵
Base point: INT↵
of (pick lower-left corner of border)
⟨Offset⟩: @7,3↵
Other corner: @12,11.5↵
Regenerating drawing.
Command:
```

Your screen should now look like Figure 24-15.

Figure 24-15.
A viewport added to the border and title block in paper space.

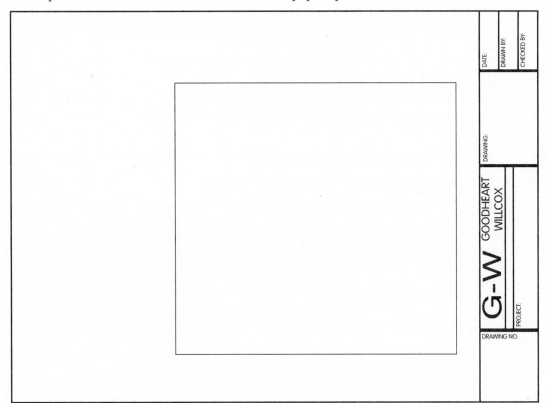

At this point, you can continue creating as many viewports as required. However, this example continues the process, and references a drawing into the new viewport. The other options of the **MVIEW** command are discussed in detail later in this chapter.

NOTE   Throughout this material, the command line versions of the **LAYER** and **XREF** commands are used. This helps maintain the step-by-step approach of the procedure, and will ensure that the process is clear and easy to follow. The command line versions of these commands are accessed by prefixing the command entry with a hyphen. For example, instead of LA or LAYER, you will enter -LAYER.

Placing views in the drawing

A viewport has now been created into which you can insert a view of the 2D or 3D model (drawing) that has been previously created. In this case, we will reference the drawing of the floor plan named FLOOR. Instead of using the **INSERT** command, which combines an existing drawing with the new one, use the **XREF** command so that AutoCAD creates a *reference* to the FLOOR drawing. This allows the size of the new drawing to remain small because the FLOOR drawing has not been combined with it.

The following procedure allows you to enter model space, reference an existing drawing to the new one, and **ZOOM** to see the referenced drawing.

Command: **MS** *or* **MSPACE**↵
Command: **-LAYER**↵
?/Make/Set/New/ON/OFF/Color/Ltype/Freeze/Thaw/LOck/Unlock: **S**↵
New current layer ⟨VIEWPORTS⟩: **-XREF**↵
?/Make/Set/New/ON/OFF/Color/Ltype/Freeze/Thaw/LOck/Unlock: ↵
Command: **-XREF**↵
?/Bind/Detach/Path/Unload/Reload/Overlay/⟨Attach⟩: ↵

The **Select file to attach** dialog box is displayed. See Figure 24-16.

Figure 24-16.
The **Select file to attach** dialog box.

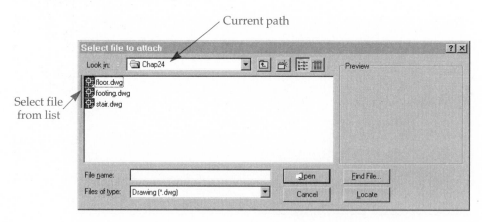

Select floor.dwg in the dialog box, or enter the drawing name FLOOR at the Xref to Attach: prompt. The following messages and prompts are then displayed:

```
Attach Xref FLOOR: FLOOR.DWG
FLOOR loaded.
Insertion point: 0,0↵
    X scale factor ⟨1⟩ / Corner / XYZ: ↵
    Y scale factor (default = X): ↵
    Rotation angle ⟨0⟩: ↵
Command: Z or ZOOM↵
All/Center/Dynamic/Extents/Previous/Scale(X/XP)/Window/⟨Realtime⟩: E↵
Command:
```

Your drawing should now resemble the one shown in Figure 24-17.

Figure 24-17.
The floor plan is referenced into the first viewport.

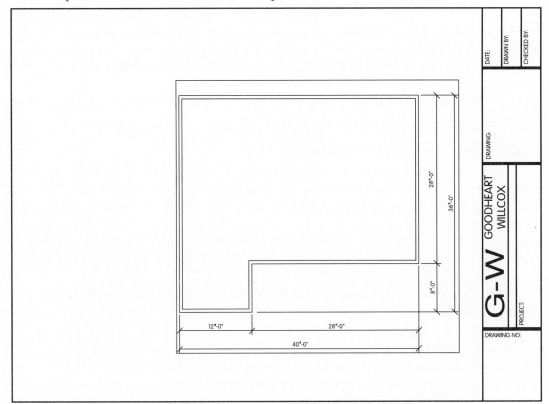

All of the layers on the referenced drawing are added to the new drawing. These layers can be distinguished from existing layers because the drawing name is automatically placed in front of the layer name and separated by a piping symbol (¦). This naming convention is shown in the **Layer Control** drop-down list on the **Object Properties** toolbar and in the **Layer & Linetype Properties** dialog box.

To display the **Layer Control** drop-down list, click on the down arrow to the right of the **Layer Control** text box. To access the **Layer Control** dialog box, click the **Layers** button at the far left of the **Object Properties** toolbar, select **Layer...** from the **Format** pull-down menu, or enter LA or LAYER at the Command: prompt.

Scaling a drawing in a viewport

When a drawing has been referenced and placed in a viewport, it is ready to be scaled. After using the **Extents** option of the **ZOOM** command, the referenced drawing fills the viewport. However, this does not imply that the drawing is displayed at the correct scale.

The scale factor of each view of the multiview drawing is an important number to remember; it is the number you use to size your drawing in the viewport. The scale factor is used in conjunction with the **XP** option of the **ZOOM** command. Since the intended final scale of the floor plan on the plotted drawing is to be 1/4″ = 1′-0″, the scale factor is 48, or 1/48 of full size. A detailed discussion of determining scale factors is given in Chapter 10. Be sure you are still in model space, and that the crosshairs are present in the viewport where you are working. Enter the following:

```
Command: Z or ZOOM↵
All/Center/Dynamic/Extents/Previous/Scale(X/XP)/Window/⟨Realtime⟩: 1/48XP↵
```

The drawing may not change much in size, depending on the size of the viewport. Also, keep in mind that the viewport itself is an entity that can be moved or stretched if needed. Remember to change to paper space when editing the size of the viewport. If part of your drawing extends beyond the edge of the viewport after using the **ZOOM XP** command, simply use grips or the **STRETCH** command to change the size of the viewport.

Controlling viewport layer visibility

If you create another viewport using **MVIEW**, the floor plan will immediately fill it. This is because a viewport is just a window through which you can view a drawing or 3D model that has been referenced to the current drawing. One way to control what is visible in subsequent viewports is to freeze all layers of the FLOOR drawing in any new viewports that are created. The **VPLAYER** (viewport layer) command controls the display of layers in specific viewports, whereas the **LAYER** command controls layers in all viewports.

The following example uses the **VPLAYER** command and the **Vpvisdflt** option to control the display of layers in new viewports.

```
Command: VPLAYER↵
?/Freeze/Thaw/Reset/Newfrz/Vpvisdflt: V↵
Layer name(s) to change default viewport visibility⟨⟩: FLOOR*↵
Change default viewport visibility to Frozen/⟨Thawed⟩: F↵
?/Freeze/Thaw/Reset/Newfrz/Vpvisdflt: ↵
```

The asterisk (*) after the name FLOOR instructs AutoCAD to freeze all the layers on the FLOOR drawing in subsequent viewports. Look at the **Layer & Linetype Properties** dialog box in Figure 24-18 and note the image of a snowflake and a rectangle. Unless the column is expanded it simply reads **F....** If you use your cursor to widen the column you can see that the heading actually reads **Freeze in New Viewports**. This indicates that in any newly created viewports, those layers will be frozen by default. Any layer's frozen or thawed status in new viewports can be controlled by picking on the icon to toggle between frozen and thawed. The frozen or thawed status in the current viewport is controlled by the icons in the column directly to the left of the **Freeze in New Viewports** column, labeled **Freeze in Current Viewport**. Select one of the **Floor** layers, then pick the **Freeze in New Viewports** icon. Notice that the snowflake is replaced with a sun, indicating that the layer is thawed in any newly created viewports. These options are the same as using the **VPLAYER** command. The remaining options of the **VPLAYER** command are discussed later in this chapter.

Figure 24-18.
The snowflake and rectangle icon indicates a frozen layer in a viewport. The sun replaces the snowflake when the layer is thawed.

Layers frozen in new viewports

PROFESSIONAL TIP

Use the [Shift] and [Ctrl] keys in combination with picking to select multiple layer names. When multiple layers are selected, toggling one setting makes the same new setting apply to all highlighted layer names.

Creating additional viewports

The previous example of creating a viewport and referencing a drawing to it is the same process that is used to create the additional two viewports in our example. In this case, two viewports are created before using the **XREF** command. If you know the number, size, and location of all viewports needed on a multiview drawing, it may save time to create them all at once.

PROFESSIONAL TIP

Viewports can always be added, deleted, or resized on a drawing. So, if your class or company uses standard sheet layouts containing several views, create and save templates that contain viewports. You can also create prototype drawings that contain viewports. Custom prototype drawings with viewports can be added to the list in the **MVSETUP** command.

The following command sequence resets paper space, changes the current layer to VIEWPORT, and uses the **MVIEW** command and grips to create new viewports. It then returns to model space to reference new drawings, and uses the **ZOOM** command to size the drawing in the viewport. The **VPLAYER** command is also used to control layer visibility in new viewports.

Command: **PS** *or* **PSPACE**↵
Command: **-LAYER**↵
?/Make/Set/New/ON/OFF/Color/Ltype/Freeze/Thaw/LOck/Unlock: **S**↵
New current layer ⟨*current*⟩: **VIEWPORTS**↵
?/Make/Set/New/ON/OFF/Color/Ltype/Freeze/Thaw/LOck/Unlock: ↵
Command: **MV** *or* **MVIEW**↵
ON/OFF/Hideplot/Fit/2/3/4/Restore/⟨First Point⟩: **.5,3**↵ *(this is the location relative to the lower-left corner of the border)*
Other corner: **6.5,9**↵

Be sure grips are on and pick the viewport you just drew. Copy the viewport to a position directly above the first. Next, use the grips and **STRETCH** command to change the height of the top viewport to 5″ while keeping the width the same. The final arrangement of the three viewports is shown in Figure 24-19.

Figure 24-19.
Two additional viewports are placed and sized on the drawing.

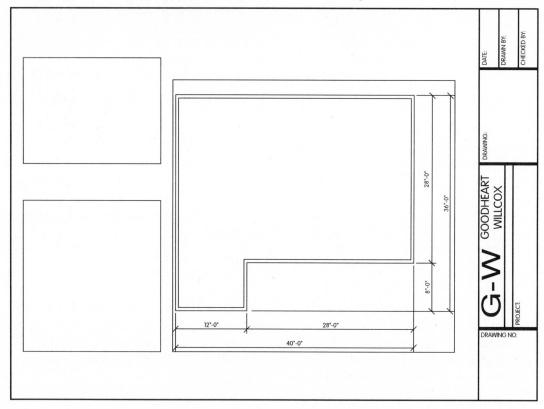

Now that the viewports are complete, you can begin referencing the remaining two drawings. Change to model space, set the current layer to Xref, and pick the lower-left viewport to make it active. The stair drawing can now be referenced.

Command: **-XREF**↵
?/Bind/Detach/Path/Reload/Overlay/⟨Attach⟩: ↵
Xref to Attach ⟨FLOOR⟩: **STAIR**↵

AutoCAD and its Applications—Basics

Insert the drawing at 0,0 and accept the defaults for scale and rotation. Notice in Figure 24-20 that the stair drawing is shown in all three viewports. The **VPLAYER** command must be used to freeze the stair layers in selected viewports.

```
Command: VPLAYER↵
?/Freeze/Thaw/Reset/Newfrz/Vpvisdflt: F↵
Layer(s) to Freeze: STAIR*↵
All/Select/⟨current⟩: S↵
Switching to Paper space.
Select objects: (pick the outline of the large and upper-left viewports)
Select objects: ↵
Switching to Model space.
?/Freeze/Thaw/Reset/Newfrz/Vpvisdflt: ↵
Command:
```

Figure 24-20.
The reference drawing stair is displayed in all viewports. **VPLAYER** must be used to restrict its visibility.

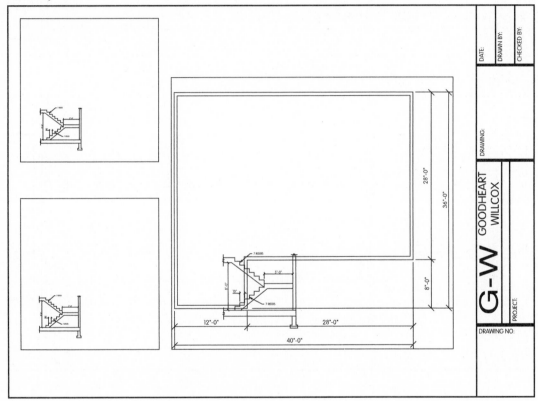

Use the **ZOOM Extents** command to display the drawing completely in the lower-left viewport, then scale the drawing with **ZOOM XP**.

NOTE

If you do not use **ZOOM Extents** first, your drawing may disappear after using **ZOOM XP**. This may occur if you pick the insertion point when using the **XREF** command, rather than entering 0,0 for the insertion point.

The plotted scale of the stair detail should be 3/8″ = 1′-0″. The scale factor is calculated as follows:

$$3/8″ = 1′-0″$$
$$.375″ = 12″$$
$$12/.375 = 32$$

The scale factor is 32, but you must use the reciprocal (1/32) for the **ZOOM XP** command.

> Command: **Z** *or* **ZOOM**↵
> All/Center/Dynamic/Extents/Previous/Scale(X/XP)/Window/⟨Realtime⟩: **1/32XP**↵

Your drawing should now resemble the one shown in Figure 24-21.

Figure 24-21.
The scaled stair drawing in the second viewport.

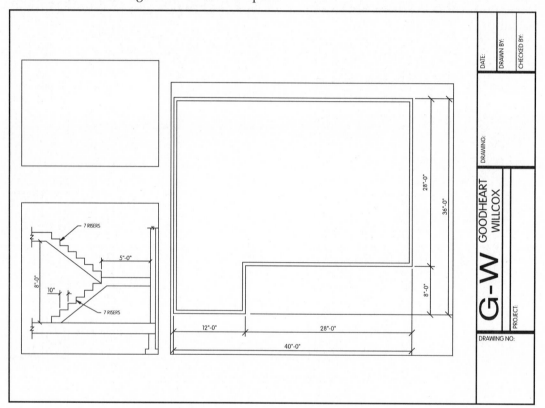

The final drawing can now be inserted into the last viewport. Pick the top viewport with your pointing device to make it active. Notice that the current viewport is surrounded by a white line. Crosshairs should now be displayed in the active viewport. Try to prepare the third view by following these steps.

1. Model space should be active.
2. The Xref layer should be current.
3. **XREF Attach** the footing drawing.
4. Freeze the Footing layers in the other two viewports with **VPLAYER**.
5. **ZOOM Extents**, then **ZOOM XP** for proper scale. Plotted scale is to be 3/4″ = 1′-0″.

When the final drawing has been referenced and scaled, your screen should look like Figure 24-22.

AutoCAD and its Applications—Basics

Figure 24-22.
The new drawing is completed by referencing the footing.

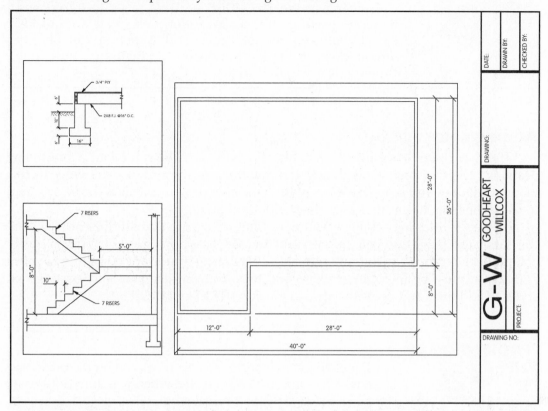

PROFESSIONAL TIP

You can use any display command inside a viewport. If a drawing is not centered after using **ZOOM XP**, simply use **PAN** to move it around. If lines of a drawing touch a viewport edge, those lines will not be visible if the viewport layer is frozen or turned off.

NOTE

Be sure to set the current layer to Xref when referencing a drawing so that the inserted drawing is not placed on another layer, such as Viewports.

Adjusting viewport display, size, and location

If you need to adjust a drawing within a viewport, first be sure that you are in model space. Then, pick the desired viewport to make it active, and use an appropriate display command, such as **ZOOM** or **PAN**.

The entire viewport can be moved to another location, but you must first be in paper space. Pick the viewport border and its grips appear. An object inside the viewport is not selected when picked because those objects are in model space. After selection, adjust the location of the viewports. Remember the following when adjusting viewports:

- **Model space.** Adjust the display of a drawing or model inside a specific viewport.
- **Paper space.** Adjust the size or location of a viewport.

Adding notes and titles

There are two ways in which titles and notes can be added to a multiview drawing. The first method is to add the notations to the original drawing. In this manner, all titles and notes are referenced to the new drawing. This is the best system to use if the titles, scale label, and notes will not change.

However, titles may change. You may want to be sure that all titles of views are the same text style, or you might want to add a special symbol. This is easily completed after the drawings are referenced. The most important thing to remember is that you must be in paper space to add text. You can use new and existing text styles to add titles and notes to a drawing using **DTEXT** or **MTEXT**.

Removing viewport outlines

The viewport outlines can be turned off for plotting purposes, as shown in Figure 24-23. Turn off or freeze the VIEWPORTS layer as follows:

```
Command: -LAYER↵
?/Make/Set/New/ON/OFF/Color/Ltype/Freeze/Thaw/LOck/Unlock: F↵
Layer name(s) to Freeze: VIEWPORTS↵
?/Make/Set/New/ON/OFF/Color/Ltype/Freeze/Thaw/LOck/Unlock: ↵
```

Plotting a Multiview Drawing

You have already taken care of scaling the views when you referenced them and used the **ZOOM XP** command. The drawing that now appears on your screen in paper space can be plotted at full scale, 1=1, with the **PLOT** command.

Figure 24-23.
The completed drawing with titles added and viewport outlines turned off.

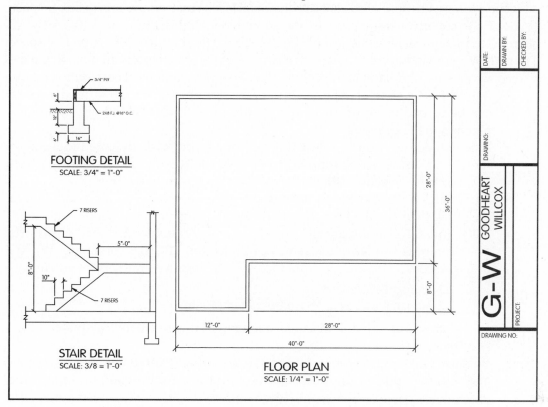

Using the **PLOT** command in this manner is a simple procedure, but only if you planned your drawing(s) at the start of the project. The process of creating a properly-scaled multiview layout will go smoothly if you have planned the project. Review the following items, and keep them in mind when starting any drawing or design project—especially one that involves the creation of a multiview paper space layout.
- Determine the size of paper to be used.
- Determine the type of title block, notes, revision blocks, parts lists, etc., that will appear on the drawing.
- Prepare a quick sketch of the view layouts and their plotted scales.
- Determine the scales to be used for each viewport.
- Establish proper text styles and heights based on the drawing scale factors.
- Set the **DIMSCALE** variable using the proper scale factor when creating drawings in model space.

There is no substitute for planning a project before you begin. It may seem like an unnecessary expense of time, but it will save time later in the project, and may help you become more productive in all your work.

PROFESSIONAL TIP

You may never have to specify a scale other than full (1=1) when plotting. Any object or design, whether 2D or 3D, can be referenced into a border and title block drawing, scaled with **ZOOM XP**, and then plotted. Try using the paper space layout procedure for all your drawings, even if they are just a single view. You will find that you need fewer border and title block prototype drawings, and the process will become quicker.

AutoCAD
User's
Guide
12

MVIEW Command Options

The primary purpose of the **MVIEW** command is to create viewports in paper space. If you use the **MVIEW** command in model space when **TILEMODE** is set to 0, AutoCAD changes to paper space for the rest of the command, then returns you to model space. The **MVIEW** command also allows you to change the size of viewports, fit them in the displayed screen area, or default to a specific value. Brief descriptions of each option follow:

- **ON/OFF.** The contents of a viewport (the drawing or design in model space) can be turned on or off. If viewports are turned off, less time is required to regenerate the drawing.
- **Hideplot.** Allows you to select the viewports you wish to have hidden lines removed from when plotting in paper space. Hidden lines are removed from 3D objects by selecting **ON**, and are shown by selecting **OFF**.
- **Fit.** Creates a viewport to fit the current screen display. You can zoom into an area first, then use the **Fit** option to create a viewport in the windowed area.
- **2/3/4.** AutoCAD automatically creates a configuration of 2, 3, or 4 viewports. The prompt is similar to the same option for the **VPORTS** command. When 2 or 3 is selected, you are prompted for specific locations and arrangements.

        2–Horizontal/⟨Vertical⟩:
        3–Horizontal/Vertical/Above/Below/Left/⟨Right⟩:

    When 4 is selected, four equal size viewports are created within a specified area.
- **Restore.** This option works if you have used the **VPORTS** command to create and save viewport configurations. AutoCAD asks for the configuration name, then allows you to either specify the locations and size of the viewports, or fit it into the current display.

        ?/Name of window configuration to insert ⟨*ACTIVE⟩: *(enter the name and press* [Enter]*)*
        Fit/⟨First Point⟩:

    If you accept the default, you can position and size the new viewports by selecting two points to window an area in paper space. If you select Fit, the restored viewports are scaled to fit the graphics area.
- **⟨First Point⟩.** The default option allows you to select or enter the coordinates of the first corner of the viewport. Then, you are prompted for the other corner and a window is attached to the crosshairs. Pick the opposite corner and the viewport is drawn.

EXERCISE 24-2

- ❑ Use the prototype method to recall the border and title block drawing you used in Exercise 24-1. Name the drawing EX24-2.
- ❑ Create layers for referenced drawings (Xref) and viewports (Viewport).
- ❑ Use the **MVIEW 2/3/4** option to create an arrangement of three viewports on the **VIEWPORT** layer. Leave space in the upper-right corner for an additional viewport.
- ❑ Use the **ZOOM Window** command to display the open area in the upper-right corner of the drawing.
- ❑ Select the **Fit** option of the **MVIEW** command to create a viewport in the current screen display.
- ❑ Reference the floor drawing used in Exercise 24-1 into one of the viewports in the group of three viewports. Be sure the Xref layer is current.
- ❑ Turn off the contents of that viewport with the **OFF** option of the **MVIEW** command.
- ❑ Save the drawing as EX24-2, then quit the drawing session.

VPLAYER Command Options

The **VPLAYER** (viewport layer) command controls the visibility of layers within selected viewports. This function differs from the **LAYER** command, which controls the visibility of all layers in the drawing. The following list describes the function of each of the **VPLAYER** command options.

- **?.** After entering a question mark, AutoCAD prompts you to select a viewport. If you selected the upper-left viewport in Figure 24-22, the following display appears in the text window:

> Layers currently frozen in viewport 4:
> FLOOR|WALL
> FLOOR|DIMEN
> FLOOR|NOTES
> STAIR|DIMEN
> STAIR|FLOOR
> STAIR|NOTES
> STAIR|STAIR
> STAIR|WALL
> Switching to Model space:
> ?/Freeze/Thaw/Reset/Newfrz/Vpvisdflt:

- **Freeze.** Enables you to selectively freeze one or more layers in any selected viewport(s).
- **Thaw.** This option allows you to thaw layers that were frozen with the **Freeze** option. As with the **Freeze** option, you can selectively thaw one or more layers in any viewport(s).
- **Reset.** Removes any viewport visibility default settings that were established with the **Vpvisdflt** option, and resets it to the default setting for a layer in a given viewport. This means that if you reset layers in a selected viewport, they become visible.
- **Newfrz.** Enables you to create a new frozen layer in all viewports, then it can be thawed in the viewport in which it is to be displayed. The prompt for this option is:

> ?/Freeze/Thaw/Reset/Newfrz/Vpvisdflt: **N**↵
> New Viewport frozen layer name(s): **WALLS**↵
> ?/Freeze/Thaw/Reset/Newfrz/Vpvisdflt: **T**↵

After entering the **Thaw** option, you can select the viewport(s) in which you want the new layer named WALLS to be visible.

- **Vpvisdflt (viewport visibility default).** This option enables you to control the visibility of layers in new viewports. Use this option if you do not want existing layers to be visible in new viewports.

> ?/Freeze/Thaw/Reset/Newfrz/Vpvisdflt: **V**↵
> Layer name(s) to change default viewport visibility: *(enter layer name)*

The **VPLAYER** command options are accessed by entering VPLAYER at the Command: prompt, or using the **Layer & Linetype Properties** dialog box. The **MVIEW** command options are accessed by entering MV or MVIEW at the Command: prompt, or by using the **Floating Viewports** cascading menu on the **View** menu. See Figure 24-24.

Figure 24-24.
The **MVIEW** command options are found by selecting **Floating Viewports** in the **View** pull-down menu.

Chapter Test

Write your answers in the spaces provided.

1. How does the **XREF Overlay** option differ from the **Attach** option? _____

_____

_____

2. What command enables you to construct a paper space viewport, attach an external reference, and zoom to a specific portion of the drawing? _____

_____

3. What effect does the use of referenced drawings have on drawing file size? _____

_____

4. When are xrefs updated in the master drawing? _____
   _____

5. Why would you want to bind a dependent symbol to a master drawing? _____
   _____
   _____

6. What does the layer name WALL0NOTES mean? _____
   _____
   _____
   _____

7. Name the system variable that controls the creation of the xref log file. _____
   _____

8. Your drawings should be created in what *space*? _____

9. Which system variable allows you to switch from model space to paper space?
   _____

10. What value should the variable mentioned in Question 9 be set to in order to
    draw in the space mentioned in Question 8? _____

11. What value should the variable mentioned in Question 9 be set to in order to use
    the **MVIEW** command? _____

12. What is the function of the **MVIEW** command? _____
    _____

13. Why would you want to reference one drawing to another rather than insert it?
    _____
    _____
    _____

14. Indicate the command, option, and value you would use to specify a 1/2″ = 1′-0″
    scale inside a viewport. _____

15. Name the command and option you would use to freeze all layers of drawings
    inside any new viewports. _____

16. Do you need to be in paper space or model space in order to resize a viewport?
    _____

17. Why would you plot a multiview drawing at full scale (1=1) if it was created with
    MVIEW and contained several views at different scales? _____
    _____

18. Explain why you should plan your plots. _____
    _____
    _____

Drawing Problems

1. Open one of your dimensioned drawings from Chapter 19. Construct a multiview layout and generate a plot on C-size paper.

   A. Set **TILEMODE** to 0 and create four viewports of equal size, but separated by 1″ of empty space.

   B. Select each viewport and display a different view of the drawing.

   C. Plot the drawing and be sure to use the scale of 1 = 1.

   D. Save the drawing as P24-1.

2. Open one of your dimensioned drawings from Chapter 19. Construct a multiview layout and generate a plot on C-size or B-size paper. Create a single viewport and plot at the scale of 1:1.

3. Open one of your dimensioned drawings from Chapter 20. Construct a multiview layout and generate a plot on C-size or B-size paper. Create a single viewport and plot at the scale of 1:1.

4. Open one of your dimensioned drawings from Chapter 21. Construct a multiview layout and generate a plot on C-size or B-size paper. Create a single viewport and plot at the scale of 1:1.

5. Open one of your drawings from Chapter 22. Construct a multiview layout and generate a plot on C-size or B-size paper. Create a single viewport and plot at the scale of 1:1.

6. Open one of your drawings from Chapter 23. Construct a multiview layout and generate a plot on C-size or B-size paper. Create a single viewport and plot at the scale of 1:1.

Chapter 25

Assigning Attributes and Generating a Bill of Materials

Learning Objectives

After completing this chapter, you will be able to:
- ○ Assign visible or hidden values (attributes) to blocks.
- ○ Edit attributes in existing blocks.
- ○ Create a template file for the collection of block attributes.
- ○ Collect attribute values in a bill of materials.

Blocks become more useful when written information is given with them. It is even more helpful to assign information that is visible (displayed) and information that is hidden. From this data, a list much like a bill of materials can be requested and printed.

Written or numerical values assigned to blocks are called *attributes* by AutoCAD. Attribute information can be extracted from the drawing, rather than used only as text labels. Examples of blocks with attributes are shown in Figure 25-1. The creation, editing, and extraction of attributes can also be handled with dialog boxes that are displayed with the **DDATTDEF**, **DDATTE**, **DDMODIFY**, and **DDATTEXT** commands.

Working with attributes can also be done from the command line using the **ATTDEF**, **ATTDISP**, and **ATTEXT** commands. The **ATTDEF** (attribute define) command allows you to specify attribute text and specify how it is displayed. The **ATTDISP** (attribute display) command governs which attributes are displayed. You can selectively or collectively edit attributes using the **ATTEDIT**(attribute edit) command. Using the **ATTEXT** (attribute extract) command, you can extract attributes from a drawing in a list or report form.

Assigning Attributes to Blocks

The first step in defining block attributes is to decide what information about the block is needed. Then decide how the computer should ask you for the attribute. What is the size? might be such a prompt. The name of the object should be your first attribute. This is followed by items such as manufacturer, type, size, price, and weight.

Suppose you are drawing a valve symbol for a piping flow diagram. You might want to list all product-related data. The number of attributes needed are limited only by the project requirements.

Figure 25-1.
Examples of blocks with attributes.

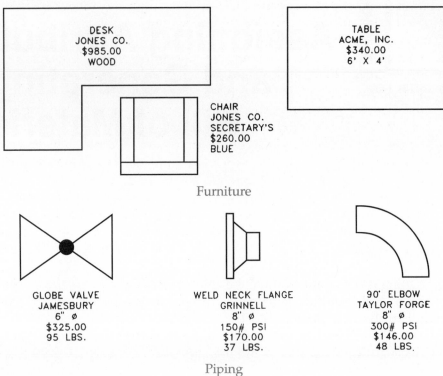

Furniture

Piping

Once the symbol is completed and shown on the screen, select the **DDATTDEF** command. All of the aspects of an attribute can be assigned on the screen in a dialog box by using the **DDATTDEF** command. This command activates the **Attribute Definition** dialog box. See Figure 25-2. To access this dialog box, pick **Define Attributes...** from the **Block** cascading menu in the **Draw** pull-down menu or enter AT or DDATTDEF at the Command: prompt.

DDATTDEF
AT

Draw
→ Block
  → Define
    Attributes

Figure 25-2.
Attributes can be assigned in the **Attribute Definition** dialog box.

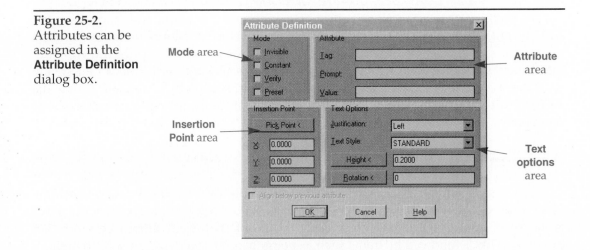

The **Attribute Definition** dialog box is divided into four areas. Each of these areas allows you to set the specific aspects of the attribute. The **Mode**, **Attribute**, **Text Options**, and **Insertion Point** areas and their components are as follows:

- **Mode.** In this area, pick any of the mode check boxes you wish to set. The modes are described as follows:
  - **Invisible**—Should the attribute be visible? Enter I to make the attribute invisible. It will not be displayed when the block is inserted.
  - **Constant**—Should the attribute always be the same? Entering C to turn on the **Constant** option means that all future uses of the block display the same value for the attribute. You will not be prompted for a new value.
  - **Verify**—Do you want a prompt to remind you about the value you entered? When creating an attribute, you enter the attribute value at the prompt. To check that the value you entered is correct, turn **Verify** on.
  - **Preset**—Should all attributes assume preset values and not display prompts? The **Preset** option creates variable attributes, but disables all attribute prompts during the insertion of a block. Default values are used instead. This works only with normal attributes. The setting does not affect dialog box entry discussed later.

    If you do not turn on any of these options, the display shows **Normal**. A normal display means that you will be prompted for all attributes and they will be visible.
- **Attribute.** This area lets you assign a tag, a prompt, and a value to the attribute.
  - **Tag:**—Enter the name of the attribute here. You must give a name or number. There can be any character in the tag, but blanks are not allowed.
  - **Prompt:**—Enter the statement you want the computer to ask when this block is inserted. For example, What is the valve size? or Enter valve size: are good prompts if size is the attribute tag. If **Constant** mode is set, this option is inactive.
  - **Value:**—The entry you type here is placed in the drawing as a *default* when the block is inserted unless you change it at the prompt. You do not have to enter anything here. You might type a message regarding the type of information needed. The default is displayed in chevrons (⟨ ⟩). You might have a message, such as 10 SPACES MAX or NUMBERS ONLY. **Value:** and **Tag:** are active if the **Constant** mode is set.

    Once these are set, if you need to change any one of these values, simply double-click on the current entry and type the new value. If you click once in the edit box, you can use any of the cursor keys to edit the text. Each of these edit boxes displays only a limited number of characters. The boxes can contain up to 256 characters. If you type more than the maximum displayable characters, the text scrolls off the left side of the edit box. If you need to view the first part of the text, use the arrow keys to move to that position.
- **Text Options.** Since attributes are text, the justification, style, height, and rotation are needed. Notice in Figure 25-2 that two drop-down lists enable you to select the text justification and the text style. Below those lists are text boxes for entering height and rotation.
  - **Justification:**—If you wish to select centered text, pick the arrow or anywhere inside this text box, and a list of text alignment options is displayed. When you pick **Center**, the list closes and the word Center appears in the text box.
  - **Text Style:**—Pick the arrow or anywhere inside this text box, and a list of all text styles in the current drawing is displayed. Pick the style you need, and it is displayed in the text box.

- **He̲ight** ⟨—A height value may be entered at this text box. Selecting the button temporarily returns you to the graphics screen and allows you to indicate to AutoCAD the value on the screen by picking points. Once the point is picked, the dialog box returns and the new height value is highlighted in the text box.
  - **R̲otation** ⟨—This button and text box work in the same manner as the **He̲ight** ⟨ button and text box.
- **Insertion Point.** This area is used to select the location, or the insertion point, for the attribute.
  - **Pic̲k Point** ⟨— Selecting the button temporarily returns you to the graphics screen and allows you to indicate to AutoCAD the value on the screen by picking points. Once the point is picked, the dialog box returns and the insertion point is shown in the **X̲:**, **Y̲:**, and **Z̲:** text boxes.
  - **X̲:**, **Y̲:**, and **Z̲:**—An insertion point can be entered at these text boxes.
- **A̲lign below previous attribute.** If you want to create another attribute, press [Enter] to start the **DDATTDEF** command. If you want the next attribute to be placed below the first with the same justification, pick this check box. When you do this, the **Text Options** and **Insertion Point** areas are inactive.

If everything is correct, pick **OK** and the attribute label is placed on the screen. This is the attribute tag. Do not be dismayed; this is the only time the tag appears. When the block is inserted, you are asked for the information that takes the place of the tag.

When you finish creating attributes, use the **BMAKE**, **BLOCK**, or **WBLOCK** commands as discussed in Chapter 23. When creating the block, be sure to select the objects and all of the attributes that go with that block. If you are using **BMAKE**, it is recommended that you toggle the **Retain Objects** check box is off. When the block is created, it should disappear, as should all of the attributes. If attributes remain on the screen, undo and try again, making sure that all attributes are selected.

Assigning attributes using the Command: prompt

All of the aspects of an attribute can be assigned at the Command: prompt using the **ATTDEF** command. To access this command enter **ATTDEF** or **-AT** and the Command: prompt as follows:

```
Command: -AT or ATTDEF↵
Attribute modes – – Invisible:N Constant:N Verify:N Preset:N
Enter (ICVP) to change, or press ENTER when done:
```

This prompt offers the same option found in the **Mode** area of the **Attribute Definition** dialog box. In this case all are toggle switches, and the default option is **N** for no, or normal. If you do not turn on any of these options, the display shows **Normal**. A normal display means that you will be prompted for all attributes and they will be visible. Request the **Normal** option by pressing [Enter]. The next three prompts let you assign a value to the attribute.

```
Attribute tag: TYPE↵
Attribute prompt: Enter valve type:↵
Default attribute value: GATE↵
```

These prompts are asking for the same information needed for the **Attribute** area of the **Attribute Definition** dialog box.

The remainder of the **ATTDEF** command is the same series of prompts found in the **Text Options** and **Insertion Point** areas in the **Attribute Definition** dialog box. Since attributes are text, they need to be positioned and sized. The current text style is assigned unless a new one is selected. When you complete the **ATTDEF** command, press [Enter] and the attribute tag appears on screen. This is the only time the tag name appears, because when the block is inserted, the inserted information that takes its place.

When you define a second attribute and reach the text positioning prompt, the previous text is highlighted. This indicates that if you press [Enter], the new text assumes the same justification and is positioned directly below the highlighted text. If you prefer a different position, enter new values or pick a new point.

Now, use the **BMAKE**, **BLOCK**, or **WBLOCK** commands as previously discussed.

Editing Attribute Definitions

Occasionally you may need to change certain aspects of text attributes *before* they are included in a block or wblock. If you only want to change the tag, prompt, or default value assigned to a text attribute, you may do so quickly using the **DDEDIT** command. To access the **DDEDIT** command, pick the **Edit Text** button on the **Modify II** toolbar, select **Text...** from the **Object** cascading menu in the **Modify** pull-down menu, or enter ED or DDEDIT at the Command: prompt. **DDEDIT** only allows you to select one attribute definition at a time. The command sequence is as follows:

Command: **ED** *or* **DDEDIT**↵
⟨Select an annotation object⟩/Undo: *(select one attribute definition to change)*

DDEDIT
ED

Modify
➡ Object
  ➡ Text...

Modify II
toolbar

Edit Text

The **Edit Attribute Definition** dialog box is now displayed, as shown in Figure 25-3. Revise the **Tag:**, **Prompt:**, or **Default:** values as required in the corresponding text boxes. If necessary, refer to Chapter 8 to review the editing techniques available in this type of dialog box. When you are done making changes, click the **OK** button and the dialog box is closed. The **DDEDIT** prompt remains on the command line should you want to select another entity or undo the changes you made. When you are finished, press [Enter] to end the command.

Figure 25-3.
The **Edit Attribute Definition** dialog box is used to change the tag, prompt, and default value of an attribute.

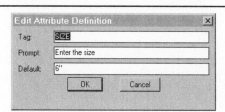

Using the Modify Attribute Definition dialog box

The **Modify Attribute Definition** dialog box provides expanded editing capabilities for text attributes. To activate this dialog box, pick the **Properties** button on the **Object Properties** toolbar, pick **Properties...** from the **Modify** pull-down menu, or enter MO or DDMODIFY at the Command: prompt.

DDMODIFY
MO

Modify
➡ Properties...

Object Properties
toolbar

Properties

NOTE   If you use the toolbar or pull-down menu to access the **Modify Attribute Definition** dialog box, you must either select the text attribute to be edited before the dialog box is activated, or select one attribute and press [Enter] at the second Select object: prompt. If you attempt to select more than one attribute, you will receive the **Change Properties** dialog box instead of the **Modify Attribute Definition** dialog box.

As shown in Figure 25-4, you can change the color, linetype, layer, or thickness of the selected attribute in the **Properties** area at the top of the dialog box. Just below the **Properties** section are the **Tag:**, **Prompt:**, and **Default:** text boxes. These edit boxes provide the same capabilities as the **DDEDIT** command described previously.

Figure 25-4.
The **Modify Attribute Definition** dialog box allows all aspects of the attribute's text to be changed.

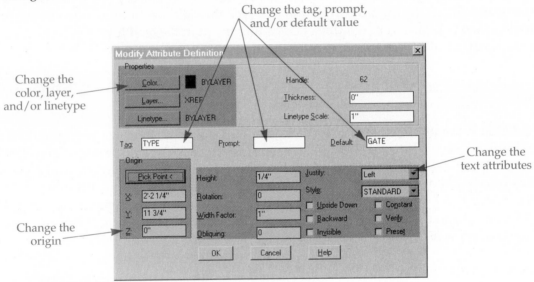

You can change the origin of the text attribute by selecting the **Pick Point ⟩** button and picking a new point on the screen, or entering new X, Y, or Z coordinates in the appropriate text boxes. You will also note the options to change the text height, rotation angle, width factor, and obliquing angle.

Picking the arrow or anywhere in the **Justify:** text box activates a drop-down list from which you may select a new text justification. To change the attribute's text style, pick the arrow or anywhere in the **Style:** text box. If another text style is defined in the current drawing, it appears in this drop-down list. Pick the **Upside Down** or **Backward** check boxes if you want these conditions applied to your text attribute.

Perhaps the most powerful feature of the **Modify Attribute Definition** dialog box is the ability to change the attribute modes originally defined for a text attribute. You may recall that an attribute may be defined with **Invisible, Constant, Verify,** or **Preset** modes. Remember the **Constant** mode assumes the values of an attribute will remain unchanged. Therefore, no prompt is defined for the attribute and no prompt is presented when the attribute is inserted.

The example shown in Figure 25-4 illustrates this restriction. Observe that since the **Constant** box is checked, no prompt appears in the **Prompt:** text box. To revise the attribute definition for normal prompting, pick the **Constant** check box to remove the check mark and enter a prompt in the **Prompt:** text box. If you want to turn on the **Verify** or **Preset** modes, or change an attribute from visible to invisible, pick the appropriate check box.

Editing attribute definitions at the Command: prompt

Similar to the options available when editing normal text, the **CHANGE** command may be used to change the attribute text insertion point, text style, height, and rotation angle of selected attribute definitions. The **CHANGE** command also permits you to revise the attribute tag, prompt, and default value (if a default value was initially provided). However, unlike the **DDEDIT** command, **CHANGE** allows you to select more than one attribute definition at a time to edit. To access the **CHANGE** command, enter C or CHANGE at the Command: prompt. The command sequence and options appear as follows:

> Command: **C** *or* **CHANGE**↵
> Select objects: *(select the attribute definition[s] to change)*
> Select objects: *(press [Enter] to close the selection set)*
> Properties/⟨Change point⟩: ↵
> Enter text insertion point: *(pick a new insertion point or press [Enter])*
> Text style: STANDARD
> New style or press ENTER for no change: *(enter an existing style name or press [Enter])*
> New height ⟨0.2000⟩: *(enter a new height or press [Enter])*
> New rotation angle ⟨0⟩: *(enter a new angle or press [Enter])*
> New tag ⟨SIZE⟩: *(provide a new tag and press [Enter], or press [Enter] to accept the tag)*
> New prompt ⟨ENTER THE SIZE⟩: *(enter a new prompt and press [Enter], or press [Enter] to accept the prompt)*
> New default value ⟨6"⟩: *(provide a new default value and press [Enter], or press [Enter] to accept the default value)*

Inserting Blocks with Attributes

When you use the **INSERT** command to place a block with attributes in your drawing, you are prompted for additional information after the insertion point, scale factors, and rotation angle are specified. The prompt that you entered in the **DDATTDEF** or **ATTDEF** command appears, and the default attribute value appears in brackets. Accept the default by pressing [Enter], or provide a new value. Then the attribute is displayed.

Attribute prompts may be answered using a dialog box if the **ATTDIA** system variable is set to a value of 1 (on). After entering the location, size, and orientation using **DDINSERT** or **INSERT**, the **Enter Attributes** dialog box appears. See Figure 25-5. This dialog box can list up to eight attributes. If a block has more than eight attributes, you can display the next page of attributes by clicking the **Next** button.

Responding to attribute prompts in a dialog box has distinct advantages over answering the prompts on the command line. With the dialog box, you can see at a glance whether all the attribute values are correct. To change a value, simply move to the incorrect value and enter a new one. You can quickly move forward through the attributes and buttons in this dialog box by using the [Tab] key. Using the [Shift]+[Tab] key combination cycles through the attributes and buttons in reverse order. When you are finished, pick **OK** to close the dialog box. The inserted block with attributes then appears on screen.

Figure 25-5.
The **Enter Attributes** dialog box allows you to enter or change attributes when a block is inserted. If the block has more than eight attributes, pick the **Next** button to see the next *page*. The button is grayed-out here since there are only three attributes.

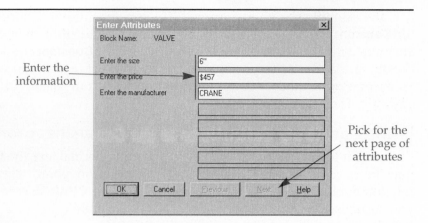

Enter the information →

Pick for the next page of attributes

PROFESSIONAL TIP

Set the value of **ATTDIA** to 1 in your template drawings to automatically activate the **Enter Attributes** dialog box whenever you insert a block with attributes.

EXERCISE 25-1

❏ Start AutoCAD and use your A-size or B-size architectural template.
❏ Draw the valve symbol shown.

GATE
CRANE
6"
$457

❏ Assign the attributes using the **DDATTDEF** or **ATTDEF** command.

Tag	Prompt	Value	Mode
Type	(None)	Gate	Constant
Mfgr.	Enter the valve manufacturer:	Crane	Invisible
Size	Enter the size:	6"	Normal and Preset
Price	Enter the price:	$457	Invisible

❏ Create a block using the **BMAKE, BLOCK,** or **WBLOCK** command. Include the valve and all of the attributes in the block and name it VALVE.
❏ Use the **DDINSERT** or **INSERT** command to place a copy of the VALVE block on your screen. Enter new values for the attributes if you wish. You should be prompted twice for the price if the **Verify** option was set properly.
❏ Save the drawing as EX25-1.

Attribute prompt suppression

Some drawings may use blocks with attributes that always retain their default values. In this case, there is no need to be prompted for the attribute values. You can turn off the attribute prompts by entering 0 for the **ATTREQ** system variable.

    Command: **ATTREQ**↵
    New value for ATTREQ ⟨1⟩: **0**↵

Try inserting the VALVE block. Notice that none of the attribute prompts appear. The **ATTREQ** value is saved with the drawing. To display attribute prompts again, change the value of **ATTREQ** back to 1.

PROFESSIONAL TIP   Part of your project and drawing planning should involve system variable settings such as **ATTREQ**. Setting **ATTREQ** to 0 before using blocks can save time in the drawing process. Always remember to set **ATTREQ** back to 1 when you want to use the prompts instead of accepting defaults. When anticipated attribute prompts are not issued, you should check the current **ATTREQ** setting and adjust it if necessary.

Controlling the Attribute Display

Attributes are meant to contain valuable information about the blocks in your drawings. This information is normally not displayed on the screen or during plotting. Its principal function is to generate materials lists and to speed accounting. Use the **DTEXT** and **MTEXT** commands for specific labels. You can control the display of attributes on the screen using the **ATTDISP** command.

Command: **ATTDISP**↵
Normal/ON/OFF ⟨Normal⟩:

The options are as follows:
- **Normal.** This mode displays attributes exactly as you created them. This is the default mode.
- **ON.** This mode displays *all* attributes.
- **OFF.** This mode suppresses *all* attributes.

PROFESSIONAL TIP   After attributes have been drawn, added to blocks, and checked for correctness, hide them by turning off **ATTDISP**. If left on, they clutter the screen and lengthen regeneration time. In a drawing where attributes should be visible but are not, check the current setting of **ATTDISP** and adjust it if necessary.

Changing Attribute Values

As mentioned earlier, you can freely edit attribute definitions with the **DDEDIT**, **DDMODIFY**, or **CHANGE** commands before they are included in a block. However, once the block is created the attributes are part of it and must be changed using the **ATTEDIT** command. To access the **ATTEDIT** command, pick **Global** from the **Attribute** cascading menu of the **Object** cascading menu in the **Modify** pull-down menu, or enter -ATE or ATTEDIT at the Command: prompt. The **ATTEDIT** command sequence is as follows:

ATTEDIT
-ATE

Modify
↪ Object
  ↪ Attribute
    ↪ Gobal

Command: **-ATE** *or* **ATTEDIT**↵
Edit attributes one at a time? ⟨Y⟩

This prompt asks if you want to edit attributes individually. It is possible to change the same attribute on several insertions of the same block. Pressing [Enter] at this prompt allows you to select any number of different attributes. AutoCAD lets you edit them all, one at a time, without leaving the **ATTEDIT** command. If you respond with *no*, you may change specific letters, words, and values of a single attribute. This can affect all insertions of the same block. For example, suppose a block named RESISTOR was inserted on a drawing in 12 places. However, you misspelled the attribute as RESISTER. Answer N to the Edit attributes one at a time? prompt. This is a *global* attribute editing method.

Each **ATTEDIT** technique allows you to determine the exact block and attribute specifications to edit. These prompts appear:

Block name specification 〈*〉:
Attribute tag specification 〈*〉:
Attribute value specification 〈*〉:

To selectively edit attribute values, respond to the prompt with a name or value. Suppose you enter an attribute and receive the following message:

0 attributes selected. *Invalid*

You have picked an attribute that was not specified. It is often quicker to press [Enter] for the three specification prompts and then *pick* the attribute you need to edit.

Editing several insertions of the same attribute

A situation may occur when a block having a wrong or misspelled attribute is inserted several times. For example, in Figure 25-6 the VALVE block was inserted three times with the manufacturer's name as CRANE. Unfortunately, the name was supposed to be POWELL. Enter **ATTEDIT** and respond in the following manner:

Command: **ATTEDIT**⏎
Edit attributes one at a time? 〈Y〉 **N**⏎
Global edit of attribute values.
Edit only attributes visible on screen? 〈Y〉: ⏎
Block name specification 〈*〉: ⏎
Attribute tag specification 〈*〉: ⏎
Attribute value specification 〈*〉: ⏎
Select attributes: *(pick* CRANE *on all* VALVE *blocks and press* [Enter] *when completed)*
(n) attributes selected. *(n equals the number of attributes picked)*
String to change: **CRANE**⏎ *(words or characters to change)*
New string: **POWELL**⏎

Figure 25-6.
Global editing changes the same attribute on several block insertions.

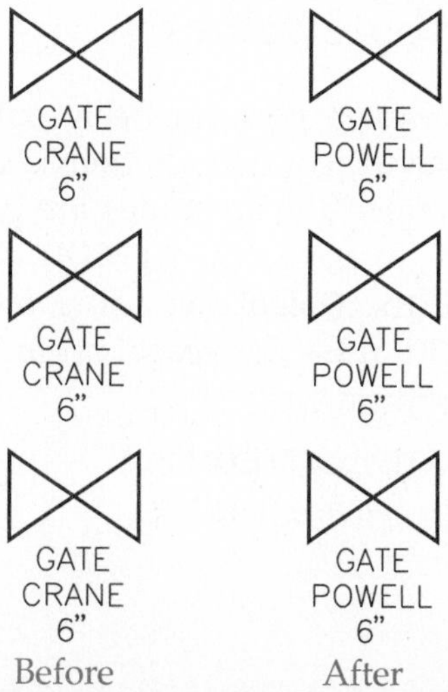

GATE
CRANE
6"

GATE
POWELL
6"

GATE
CRANE
6"

GATE
POWELL
6"

GATE
CRANE
6"

GATE
POWELL
6"

Before

After

After pressing [Enter], CRANE attributes on the blocks selected are changed to read POWELL.

PROFESSIONAL TIP

Use care when assigning the **Constant** mode option to attribute definitions. The **ATTEDIT** command displays the following error message if you attempt to edit an inserted block attribute with a **Constant** setting:

0 attributes selected. *Invalid*

The inserted block must then be exploded and redefined. Assign **Constant** to only those attributes you know will not change.

Editing different attributes one at a time

Global editing is a more precise method of changing specific attributes and text strings. On the other hand, individual editing allows you to change any value on any attribute. Several attributes and text strings can be changed without leaving the **ATTEDIT** command. After you answer Y to the Edit attributes one at a time? prompt, and press [Enter] for the three *specification* options, select the attributes. Press [Enter] when you are finished; then this prompt appears:

(*n*) attributes selected.
Value/Position/Height/Angle/Style/Layer/Color/Next 〈N〉:

With this prompt, a small X appears at the first attribute selected. The X indicates the attribute that is being edited. The order that AutoCAD picks attributes to edit is the same order in which you selected them. The **Next** option is the default. Pressing [Enter] causes the X to jump to the next attribute in sequence. The X does not jump to the next attribute automatically after you make a change. It remains in case you want to make more than one change to the attribute. Prompts for all attribute editing options are as follows:

- **Value.** Change or Replace? ⟨R⟩: Pressing [Enter] here indicates you want to replace the attribute. AutoCAD requests a new attribute value. You can change any part of the attribute by typing C for **Change**. AutoCAD responds with String to change and New string prompts. A *string* is any sequence of consecutive characters.
- **Position.** Enter text insertion point:
- **Height.** New height ⟨*current*⟩:
- **Angle.** New rotation angle ⟨0⟩:
- **Style.** Text style: (*current*)
      New style or press ENTER:
- **Layer.** New layer ⟨*current*⟩:
- **Color.** New color ⟨BYLAYER⟩:

Individual editing of attributes can be used to correct misspelled words, replace words, or change attribute information. Look at the attributes attached to the block in Figure 25-7. The manufacturer was changed from POWELL to CRANE. The price was changed from $565.00 to $556.00. Suppose these are the only two attributes to be edited. The entire command sequence looks like this:

Command: **ATTEDIT**↵
Edit attributes one at a time? ⟨Y⟩ ↵
Block name specification ⟨*⟩:↵
Attribute tag specification ⟨*⟩:↵
Attribute value specification ⟨*⟩:↵
Select Attributes: *(select the two attributes)*
2 attributes selected. *(the X appears at* POWELL, *the first attribute selected)*
Value/Position/Height/Angle/Style/Layer/Color/Next ⟨N⟩: **V**↵
Change or Replace? ⟨R⟩: **R**↵
New attribute value: **CRANE**↵
Value/Position/Height/Angle/Style/Layer/Color/Next ⟨N⟩: ↵ *(pressing* [Enter] *moves the*
      X to the next attribute, $565.00*)*
Value/Position/Height/Angle/Style/Layer/Color/Next ⟨N⟩: **V**↵
Change or Replace? ⟨R⟩: **C**↵
String to change: **65**↵
New string: **56**↵
Value/Position/Height/Angle/Style/Layer/Color/Next ⟨N⟩: *(press* [Enter] *at this prompt*
      to get out of the **ATTEDIT** *command and see the final change take place)*

The completed attribute edit is shown in Figure 25-7C.

Figure 25-7.
The attributes to be changed are indicated with an X.

GATE
XPOWELL
6"
$565

A

GATE
CRANE
6"
X$565

B

GATE
CRANE
6"
$556

C

When making blocks that contain attributes, add as many attributes as will be needed. If you do not have values for some of them, just enter TO COME as the value, or enter something to remind you that information is needed. Adding an attribute to a block is much more time-consuming than changing an attribute using the **ATTEDIT** command.

Editing Attributes Using a Dialog Box

The **DDATTE** (dynamic dialog attribute editing) command allows you to edit attributes in a dialog box. You can edit as many block attributes as desired one at a time. To access the **DDATTE** command, pick the **Edit Attribute** button on the **Modify II** toolbar, pick **Single...** from the **Attribute** cascading menu of the **Object** cascading menu in the **Modify** pull-down menu, or enter ATE or DDATTE at the Command: prompt. After using one of these methods to access **DDATTE**, you are then prompted to select the attribute to be edited. When an attribute is selected, the **Edit Attributes** dialog box is then activated.

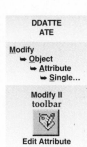

DDATTE
ATE

Modify
➡ Object
➡ Attribute
➡ Single...

Modify II
toolbar

Edit Attribute

Editing attributes in a single block

If attributes in one block need editing, enter DDATTE and select the block as follows:

Command: **ATE** *or* **DDATTE**⏎
Select block: *(select block)*

The **Edit Attributes** dialog box appears on-screen. See Figure 25-8. The attributes of the selected block are listed on the left. Their current values are shown in the edit boxes on the right. Move the cursor to the value to be edited and double-click so the box is highlighted, and enter the new value. Remember that if you pick the box, you can move the cursor to the incorrect letter, then use the delete key to remove a letter, type to insert characters, or use [Backspace] to delete. You can then pick **Cancel** or **OK**, or you can press [Enter] to move to the next attribute. When finished, pick **OK** at the bottom of the dialog box. The attribute associated with the block is changed. If **Cancel** is picked, no changes are made and the drawing is redisplayed.

Figure 25-8.
The **Edit Attributes** dialog box displays all of the attributes assigned to the selected block. You can change any of these attributes.

Attribute prompts

Current values

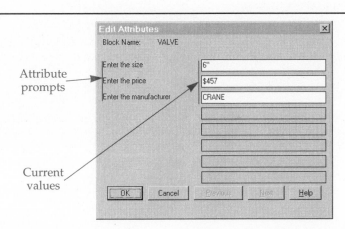

EXERCISE 25-3

❏ Start AutoCAD; open drawing EX25-2 if it is not already on screen.
❏ Be sure there are three insertions of the VALVE block. Align them as shown in the diagram below.
❏ Set **ATTDISP** to *on* to display all attributes.
❏ Use the **ATTEDIT** or **DDATTE** command and choose the individual edit option.
❏ Assuming the blocks are numbered 1 to 3, top to bottom, change the individual attributes to the following values:

	1	2	3
Type	Gate	Gate	Gate
Mfgr.	Crane	Powell	Jenkins
Size	4"	8"	10"
Price	$376.00	$563.00	$837.00

❏ Connect the valves with straight lines as shown.
❏ Save the drawing as EX25-3.

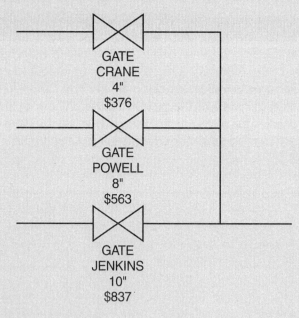

Redefining a block and its attributes

You may encounter a situation in which an existing block and its associated attributes must be revised. You may need to delete existing attributes, or add new ones, in addition to revising the geometry of the block itself. This could normally be a time-consuming function, but is made easy with the **ATTREDEF** command. To access the **ATTREDEF** command type AT or ATTREDEF at the Command: prompt. The **ATTREDEF** command then prompts you to select the attribute to be redefined.

When redefining a block and its attributes, a copy of the existing block that is being redefined must be exploded prior to using **ATTREDEF** or completely new geometry must be used. If it is not, you will get a Block *nnn* references itself error. The prompts for this command are as follows:

> Command: **AT** *or* **ATTREDEF**↵
> Name of Block you wish to redefine: *(enter block name and press* [Enter]*)*
> Select objects for new Block...
> Select objects: *(select the block geometry and all new and existing attributes and press* [Enter]*)*
> Insertion base point of new block: *(pick insertion base point)*
> Command:

All existing instances of the redefined block and attributes will be immediately updated. If any of the old attributes were omitted from the redefined block, they will not be included in the new version.

Using Attributes to Automate Drafting Documentation

So far you have seen that attributes are extremely powerful tools for assigning textual information to drawing symbols. However, attributes may also be used to automate any detailing or documentation task that requires a great deal of text. Such tasks include title block information, revision block data, and parts list or list of materials generation.

Attributes and title blocks

After a drawing is completely drawn and dimensioned, it is then necessary to fill out the information in the drawing title block. This is usually one of the more time-consuming tasks associated with drafting documentation. Using the following suggested guidelines, this task can be efficiently automated.

1. The title block format is first drawn using the correct layer(s) and in accordance with industry or company standards. You can use one of the title block formats provided by the **MVSETUP** command discussed in Chapters 10 & 24, or create your own. Be sure to include your company or school logo within the title block. If you work in an industry that produces items for the federal government, also include the applicable FSCM code in the title block. A typical A-size title block drawn in accordance with the ANSI Y14.1, *Drawing Sheet Size and Format* standard is illustrated in Figure 25-9.

 NOTE   The FSCM (Federal Supply Code for Manufacturers) is a five-digit numeric code identifier applicable to any organization that produces items used by the federal government. It also applies to government activities that control design, or are responsible for the development of certain specifications, drawings, or standards that control the design of items.

Figure 25-9.
A title block sheet must adhere to applicable standards. This title block is for an A-size sheet and adheres to ANSI Y14.1, *Drawing Sheet Size and Format.*

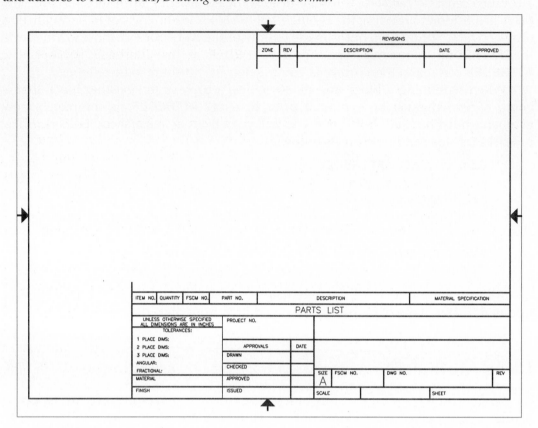

2. After drawing the title block, create a separate layer for the title block attributes. By placing the attributes on a separate layer, you can easily suppress the title block information by freezing the layer that contains the attributes. This can greatly reduce redraw and regeneration times. When you are ready to plot the finished drawing, simply thaw the frozen layer.

3. Define attributes for each area of the title block. As you create the attributes, determine the appropriate text height and justification modes for each. The attributes should include the drawing title, drawing number, drafter, checker, dates, scale, sheet size, material, finish, revision letter, and tolerance information. See Figure 25-10. Include any other information that may be specific to your organization or application.

Figure 25-10.
This shows attributes that have been defined for each field of a title block.

ITEM NO.	QUANTITY	FSCM NO.	PART NO.		DESCRIPTION		MATERIAL SPECIFICATION
					PARTS LIST		

UNLESS OTHERWISE SPECIFIED ALL DIMENSIONS ARE IN INCHES TOLERANCES:		PROJECT NO. PROJECT				
1 PLACE DIMS: TOL1						
2 PLACE DIMS: TOL2		APPROVALS	DATE		TITLE	
3 PLACE DIMS: TOL3		DRAWN DRAWN	DATE			
ANGULAR: ANGL						
FRACTIONAL: FRAC		CHECKED CHECKED	DATE	SIZE A	FSCM NO.	DWG NO. NUMBER	REV REV
MATERIAL MATERIAL		APPROVED APPROVED	DATE			
FINISH FINISH		ISSUED ISSUED	DATE	SCALE SCALE		SHEET SHEET

Insertion point

AutoCAD and its Applications—Basics

4. Assign default values to attributes wherever possible. As an example, if your organization consistently specifies the same overall tolerances on drawing dimensions, the tolerance attributes can be assigned default values.

5. Once you have defined each attribute, **WBLOCK** the entire drawing to disk with a descriptive file name. Some examples of names for an A-size title block are TITLEA or FORMATA. Be sure to use 0,0 as the insertion point for the title block.

PROFESSIONAL TIP

The size of each title block area imposes limits on the number of characters you can have in a line of text. You can provide a handy cue to yourself by including a reminder in the attribute. When defining an attribute in which you wish to place a reminder, include the information in the attribute prompt:

Attribute prompt: **Enter drawing name (15 characters max):**

Each time the block or prototype drawing is used that contains this attribute, the prompt will display the reminder shown above.

After all of the attributes have been defined, the **WBLOCK** command can be used to create a prototype drawing that can be inserted into a new drawing, or the **BLOCK** command can be used to create a block of defined attributes within the current prototype drawing file. Either method is acceptable, and the uses of both are explained in the following descriptions.

- **WBLOCK method.** The **WBLOCK** command saves a drawing file to disk, so it can be inserted into any other drawing. Prototype drawings used in this manner should be given descriptive names such as TITLE-A or TITLBLKA. The name should provide some indication of the drawing size. To utilize the prototype file, begin a new drawing and insert the prototype. After locating and scaling the drawing, the attribute prompts are displayed. As you enter the requested information, it is placed in the title block. This method requires that you begin with a blank drawing, and that you know the information requested by the attribute prompts when you begin. Remember, should you enter information that is incorrect, it can be altered using the **DDATTE** (**ATE**) command.

- **BLOCK method.** The **BLOCK** command prompts you to select objects. Be sure to select *only* the defined attributes you just created. Do not select the headings of title block areas, or any of the geometry in the title block. When prompted to pick the insertion base point, select a corner of the title block that will be convenient to use each time this block is inserted into a drawing. The *X* in Figure 25-10 shows an appropriate location for the insertion base point. The current prototype drawing now contains a block of defined attributes for use in the title block. To begin a new drawing you must open this prototype and give it a new name to protect the integrity of the prototype. The title block data can be entered at any time during the creation of the new drawing. To do so, use the **INSERT** command, and pick the proper insertion base point. The attribute prompts are then either displayed on the command line or in a dialog box, depending on the value of the **ATTDIA** variable. If **ATTDIA** is set to 1, all of the attributes can be entered in a dialog box such as the one shown in Figure 25-11. The **WBLOCK** command can be used to save the defined attributes to disk as a file if you wish to have the ability to use the attributes on any drawing.

Figure 25-11.
Attributes can be
entered in a dialog
box when **ATTDIA** is
set to 1. If there are
more than eight
attributes, pick the
Next button to see
the next *page*. Pick
OK when the final
page of attributes is
completed.

Enter the
appropriate
information

Pick to see
the next page

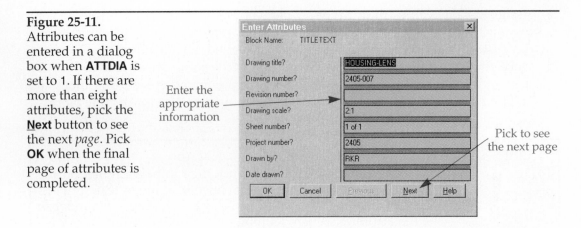

Regardless of the method used, title block data can be entered quickly and accurately without the use of text commands. If the attributes are entered in a dialog box, all of the information can be seen at one time, and mistakes can be corrected quickly. Attributes can be easily edited at a later date if necessary. Attribute text height or position can be changed with the **ATTEDIT** command, and the content of the attribute is changed with the **DDATTE** command. The completed title block after insertion of the attribute block is shown in Figure 25-12.

Figure 25-12.
The title block after insertion of the attributes. When the drawing is complete, dates and approvals can be added with the **DDATE** command.

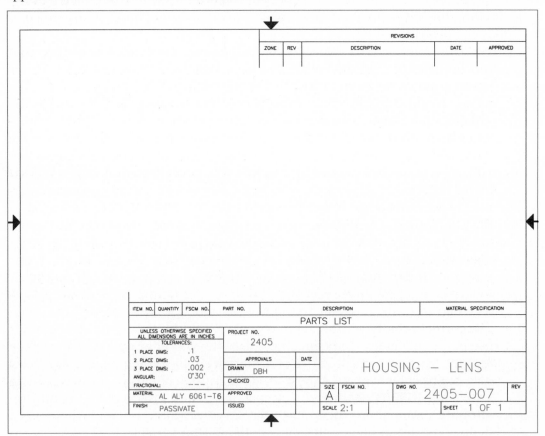

Attributes and revision blocks

It is almost certain that a detail drawing will require revision at some time in the life cycle of a product. Typical changes that occur include design improvements and the correction of drafting errors. The first time that a drawing is revised, it is usually assigned the revision letter A. If necessary, revision letters continue with B through Z, but the letters I, O, and Q are not used, because they might be confused with numbers.

Title block formats include an area specifically designated to record all drawing changes. This area is normally located at the upper-right of the title block sheet, and is commonly called the *revision block*. The revision block provides space for the revision letter, description of the change, date, and approvals. The zone column is optional, and need only be added if applicable. Zones appear in the margins of a title block sheet and are indicated by alphabetical and numeric entries. They are used for reference purposes the same way as reference letters and numbers are used to identify a street or feature on a road map. Although A-size and B-size title blocks may include zones, they are rarely needed.

Block attributes provide a handy means of completing the necessary information in a revision block. Refer to Figure 25-13 as you follow these guidelines:

- First, create a revision block in the appropriate drawing layer(s).
- Define attributes that describe the zone (optional), revision letter, description of change, and change approval on a separate layer.
- Use left-justified text for the change description attribute, and middle-justified text for the remainder.
- **WBLOCK** the lines and attributes to disk, or **BLOCK** them into the current prototype drawing. Use a descriptive name such as REVBLK or REV. Keep in mind that each line of the parts list or revision block comes with its own border lines, therefore the borders must be saved with the attributes. Use the upper-left endpoint of the revision block as the insertion point.

Figure 25-13.
The revision block is comprised of lines, attributes, and an insertion point. The border lines must be drawn as part of the block.

Now, after a drawing has been revised, simply insert the revision block at the correct location into the edited drawing. If the **ATTDIA** system variable is set to 1, you can answer the attribute prompts in the **Enter Attributes** dialog box. See Figure 25-14. After providing the change information, click the **OK** button and the completed revision block is automatically added to the title block sheet. See Figure 25-15.

Attributes and parts lists

Assembly drawings require a parts list, or list of materials, which includes the quantity, FSCM code (optional), part number, description, and item number for each component of the assembly or subassembly. In some organizations, the parts list is generated as a separate document; usually in an 8 1/2" × 11" format. In other companies, it is common practice to include the parts list on the face of the assembly drawing. Whether as a separate document or as part of the assembly drawing itself, parts lists provide another example of how attributes may be used to automate the documentation process.

Figure 25-14.
Drawing revisions are entered in the **Enter Attributes** dialog box when **ATTDIA** is set to 1.

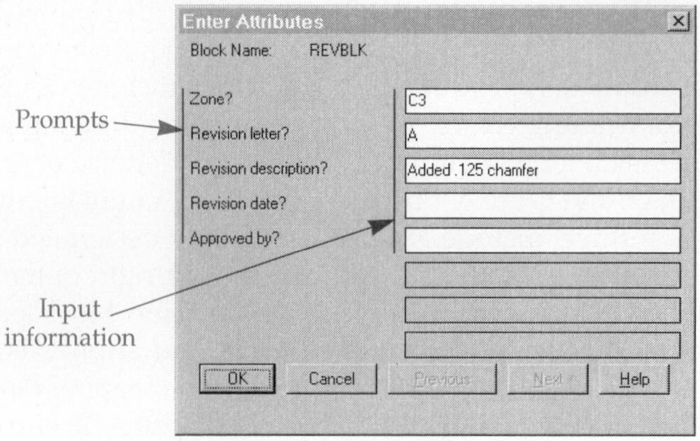

Prompts ──→

Input information ──→

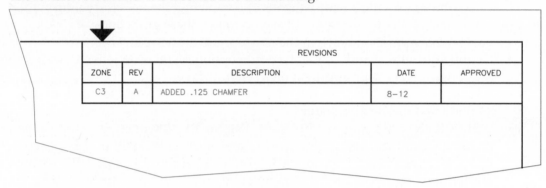

Figure 25-15.
The revision block after it is inserted into the drawing.

		REVISIONS			
ZONE	REV	DESCRIPTION		DATE	APPROVED
C3	A	ADDED .125 CHAMFER		8–12	

Refer once again to the title block in Figure 25-9. You will observe a section specifically designated for a parts list located just above the title block area. Now, consider the example illustrated in Figure 25-16 as you follow the guidelines:

- First, create a parts list block in the appropriate drawing layer(s).
- Define attributes on a separate layer that describe the quantity, zone (optional), part number, item description, material specification, and item number for the components of an assembly drawing.
- Use left-justified text for the item description attribute and middle-justified text for the remainder.
- **WBLOCK** the parts list block to disk with a descriptive name like PL for parts list, or BOM for bill of materials. Use the lower-left endpoint of the parts list block as the insertion point as shown in Figure 25-16.

Figure 25-16.
Attributes and an insertion point are defined for a parts list block.

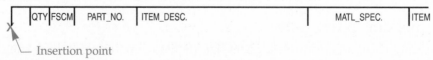

| QTY | FSCM | PART_NO. | ITEM_DESC. | MATL_SPEC. | ITEM |

└─ Insertion point

Now, after an assembly drawing has been completed, simply insert the parts list block at the correct location into the drawing. If the **ATTDIA** system variable is set to 1, you can answer the attribute prompts in the **Enter Attributes** dialog box, as illustrated in Figure 25-17.

Figure 25-17.
The parts list information is entered in the **Enter Attributes** dialog box when **ATTDIA** is set to 1.

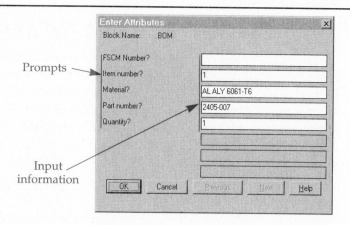

Prompts →

Input information →

After providing the parts list information, click the **OK** button and the completed parts list block is automatically added to the title block sheet. See Figure 25-18. Repeat the procedure as many times as required for each component of the assembly drawing.

From the preceding examples, you can see that block attributes are powerful entities. Their applications are virtually endless. Can you think of any other drafting procedures that could be similarly automated?

Figure 25-18.
The parts list block after it is inserted into a drawing.

QTY REQD	FSCM NO.	PART OR IDENTIFYING NO.	NOMENCLATURE OR DESCRIPTION	MATERIAL SPECIFICATION	ITEM NO.
1		2405-007	PLATE, MOUNTING	AL ALY 6061-T6	1

PARTS LIST

PROFESSIONAL TIP

A truly integrated CAD environment continually seeks out new methods to automate the drafting and design process. In such organizations, the *electronic geometry* embodied in a CAD file is the original, or master, document. If you work in a supervisory capacity, you are probably authorized to *sign-off* completed drawings, or to approve revised drawings. How can you *electronically* add your signature to an AutoCAD drawing? Consider using the following procedure.

• Set the **SKPOLY** system variable to use polylines when you use the **SKETCH** command. Use the **SKETCH** command to reproduce your signature. Sketching your name is a little difficult with a pointing device, but it can be reasonably accomplished with a bit of practice.

• Use the **PEDIT** command to *tweak* the signature into a more acceptable representation of your handwriting.

• **WBLOCK** your signature to a floppy disk. Keep the floppy in your briefcase or locked away in a secure location. Do not store your signature block on the hard drive or on the network drive where anyone can access it.

• When you need to approve a drawing, simply insert and scale your signature block as required in the correct location.

Collecting Attribute Information

AutoCAD provides a method for listing attributes associated with any specified block. It is helpful for tabulating block information. Creating a special *template file* is part of this method. This file is a list of attributes that can be used in a bill of materials by third-party packages, or in databases. It is used with drawings that contain specific blocks and attributes you wish to list. The **ATTEXT** command creates an *extract file* that allows AutoCAD to find and list the attributes specified in the template file. This extract file can display the attributes on the screen or send them to a printer.

Creating a template file

You often need to be selective in the blocks and attributes that are listed. This requires guidelines for AutoCAD to use when sorting through a drawing. To pick out specific block attributes, these guidelines are in the form of a *template file*. The AutoCAD template file allows you to pick out specific items from blocks and list them. The template file, a simple text file, can be made using database, word processing, or text editor programs.

In addition to listing attributes, the template file can be designed to extract block properties. Those include:

- **Name.** Block name.
- **Level.** Block nesting level.
- **X.** X coordinate of insertion point.
- **Y.** Y coordinate of insertion point.
- **Z.** Z coordinate of insertion point.
- **Layer.** Name of layer block is inserted on.
- **Orient.** Rotation angle of block.
- **Number.** Counts number of insertions.
- **Handle.** A unique identifier for the block.
- **XSCALE.** X insertion scale factor.
- **YSCALE.** Y insertion scale factor.
- **ZSCALE.** Z insertion scale factor.
- **XEXTRUDE.** X extrusion direction.
- **YEXTRUDE.** Y extrusion direction.
- **ZEXTRUDE.** Z extrusion direction.

PROFESSIONAL TIP

Your application determines which properties need to be included in the template file. Template files can be created for different groups or departments of a company. The following chart lists possible attributes for a desk in the left column. Across the top are several different departments in a company. An **X** indicates which item is to be included in that department's template file.

Attribute	Shipping	Purchasing	Accounting	Engineering
Manufacturer		X	X	
Size	X	X		X
Price		X	X	
Weight	X			X
Color		X		X
Material	X	X		X

AutoCAD and its Applications—Basics

The example template file shown below could be used to extract information from the piping flow diagram in Exercise 25-3.

BL:NAME	C010000
BL:LAYER	C005000
BL:X	N008002
BL:Y	N008002
BLANK	C004000
MFGR	C010000
SIZE	C008000
PRICE	C010000

You would write this file using database or text editing programs such as the Windows Notepad. Notice that the items that are block characteristics begin with BL:. The items that are block attributes are given the name used at the Attribute tag: prompt of the **ATTDEF** command. The item BLANK is placed in the file to provide spacing between the Y coordinate and MFGR. There would be no line space between those two items if this had been omitted.

The numbers in the right column all begin with either C or N. The C indicates that character information is to be extracted and N represents numeric information. If a character other than a number is included in an attribute, use C instead of N. Notice that the PRICE attribute uses C. That is because the dollar symbol ($) is used in front of the price in the attribute.

The first three numbers after the C or N character indicate the number of spaces allotted for the attribute. There are ten spaces allotted for MFGR. The following three digits specify the number of decimal places in the attribute. The X and Y locations have been assigned two decimal places. This is detailed in Figure 25-19.

Figure 25-19.
The template file shows numeric and character entries.

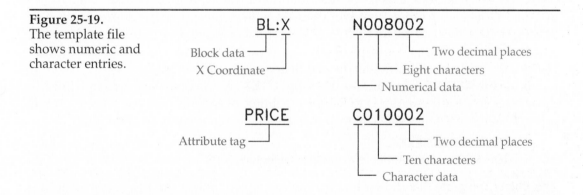

❑ This exercise guides you through the construction of a template file for the drawing EX25-3. Use the Windows Notepad to create the file.

❑ Open drawing EX25-3 if it is not already on your screen.

❑ Open the start menu on your Windows task bar.

❑ Pick Programs ❭, then Accessories ❭, and then pick the Notepad icon to launch the Windows Notepad.

❑ Begin entering the following text at the flashing vertical cursor located at the top left of the Notepad window. You may place either a [Tab] or spaces between the columns:

BL:NAME	C010000
BL:LAYER	C005000
BL:X	N008002

BL:Y	N008002
BLANK	C004000
MFGR	C010000
SIZE	C008000
PRICE	C010000

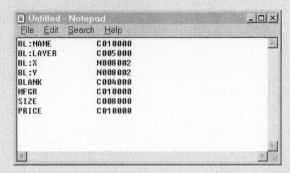

❏ When you are through entering text, your screen should appear as shown below.
❏ Select Save As… from the File pull-down menu, and save the file with the name EX25-3. Notepad automatically adds the .TXT extension to the file name.
❏ Select Exit from the File pull-down menu to exit Notepad and return to AutoCAD.

Listing block attributes

AutoCAD provides three different formats for listing extracted information. The DXF format is related to programming and is the most complex. See Appendix C, *AutoCAD Customization Guide,* for information on the DXF format. The other two— SDF and CDF—are formats that can be used with a variety of other programs. The *SDF (Space Delimited Format)* is the easiest for the average user to interpret. It means that the different *fields,* or groups of data are separated by spaces. The *CDF (Comma Delimited Format)* uses commas instead of spaces to separate fields.

Issue the **ATTEXT** command by entering ATTEXT at the Command: prompt. Specify the format you want or enter O to list the attributes of specific selected objects. At this point, select the SDF format. The response here needs to be only the first letter.

Command: **ATTEXT**↵
CDF, SDF, or DXF Attribute extract (or Objects)?⟨C⟩: **S**↵

The **Select Template File** dialog box is then displayed. Select the file you wish to use from the box showing folders and files. Note in Figure 25-20 that the file named ex22-3.txt is selected. Pick **OK**, and the **Create extract file** dialog box appears. If you wish to have the extracted attributes saved in an existing file, select the extract file from the box of folders and files. To save the extracted attributes to a new file, enter a new file name in the **File Name:** text box. The current drawing name is the default. Be sure the extract file name you enter is slightly different than the template file name— for example, EX25-3A.

AutoCAD automatically appends a .txt to the file name you enter. See Figure 25-21. If you use the same name, your original template file will be deleted. Pick **OK** after entering the file name. If all goes well, AutoCAD reports that you have *n* records in extract file. The number of records listed in the file is based on the number of blocks that contain the attributes you were searching for.

Figure 25-20.
The **Select Template File** dialog box allows you to choose a file.

Correct path

Select a file

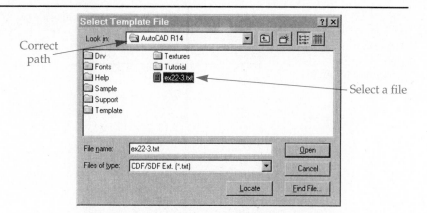

Figure 25-21.
The **Create extract file** dialog box allows you to select an existing extract file name, or enter a new extract file name.

Enter a file name

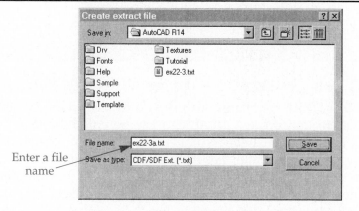

The extract file can be displayed on the screen by opening the file in the Windows Notepad. An example of the extract file in SDF format is shown in Figure 25-22. The same file in CDF format appears in Figure 25-23. Of the three formats discussed, the CDF format appears the most cumbersome. However, it (as well as the SDF format) may be used with specific database programs, such as dBASE. Decide which format is most suitable for your application. Regardless of the extract file format chosen, you may print the file from the Windows Notepad by selecting Print from the File pull-down menu.

Figure 25-22.
An extract file displayed in SDF format in the Windows Notepad.

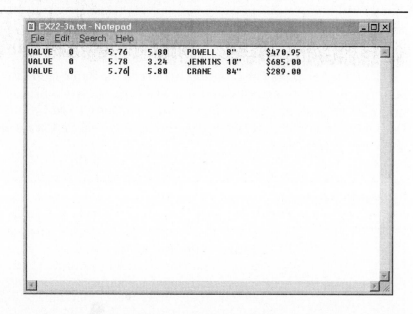

Figure 25-23.
An extract file displayed in CDF format in the Windows Notepad.

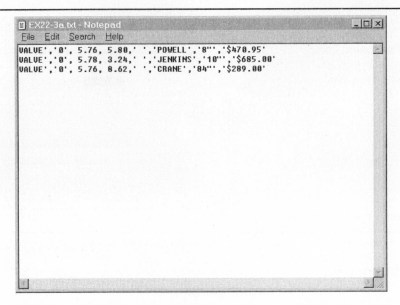

Listing block attributes with the DDATTEXT command

The **DDATTEXT** command enables you to use dialog boxes for all steps in the attribute extraction process. DDATTEXT can be entered at the Command: prompt to activate the **Attribute Extraction** dialog box. See Figure 25-24. Select the desired file format, such as SDF, by clicking the appropriate option button. If you want specific blocks in the extract file, click the **Select Objects >** button, and use any selection method to pick the blocks. If you do not select objects, all blocks in the drawing (specified by the template file) will be used.

Figure 25-24.
The **DAATTEXT** command activates the **Attribute Extraction** dialog box.

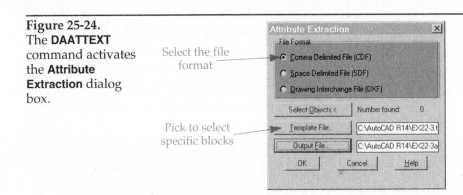

Select the file format

Pick to select specific blocks

Pick the **Template File...** button to select a file name from the **Template File** dialog box. This dialog box is exactly the same as the one shown in Figure 25-20. The output file, or extract file, can be selected by clicking the **Output File...** button. This displays the **Output File** dialog box, which is exactly the same as the **Create extract file** dialog box shown in Figure 25-21.

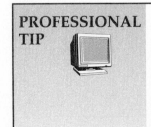

PROFESSIONAL TIP

The bill of materials listing discussed in this chapter is a basic list of each block's selected attributes. As you become familiar with AutoCAD, customize it to meet your needs. Study magazines devoted to AutoCAD and read the *AutoCAD User's Guide*. You will find numerous software packages that generate specialized bills of material containing quantities and totals, rather than just a list of blocks.

❏ Open EX25-4 if it is not already on your screen.
❏ Select the **ATTEXT** command and enter SDF format.
❏ Enter the template file name as EX25-4. Enter EX25-4A for the extract file name.
❏ Select **ATTEXT** again and display the bill of materials on the screen.

Chapter Test

Write your answers in the spaces provided.

1. Define an *attribute*. _____

2. Explain the purpose of the **ATTDEF** command. _____
_____

3. Define the function of the following four **ATTDEF** modes:
    A. Invisible— _____
    B. Constant— _____
    C. Verify—_____
    D. Preset— _____

4. What attribute information does the **ATTDEF** command request? _____
_____
_____

5. Identify the three commands that may be used to edit attributes before they are included within a block. _____
_____
_____

6. Which command allows you to change an existing attribute from **Visible** to **Invisible**?_____
_____

7. List the three options for the **ATTDISP** command._____
_____

8. What is meant by *global* attribute editing? _____
_____

9. How does individual attribute editing differ from global editing? _____
_____
_____
_____

10. Identify the purpose of the following two prompts in the global attribute editing routine.
    String to change:_____
    New string: _____

11. List the different aspects of the attribute that you can change when you edit attributes one at a time. _____

12. Which command allows you to use a dialog box to create attributes? _____

    _____

13. Explain the function of the **DDATTE** command._____

    _____

14. How does editing an attribute with **DDEDIT** differ from using **DDMODIFY**?_____

    _____

15. What purpose does the **ATTREQ** system variable serve? _____

    _____

16. To enter attributes using the dialog box, you must set the **ATTDIA** system variable

    to _____.

17. When created, a drawing extract file is given this file extension._____

18. The command that allows you to create the file type mentioned in Question 17

    is _____.

19. How is character and numerical data specified in a template file? _____

    _____

20. How many characters are allowed for an attribute name in the template file? ___

    _____

21. How do you create a template file? _____

    _____

22. Define all of the aspects of each of the following template file entries.

    BL:X_____

    N006002 _____

    PRICE _____

    C010003 _____

23. Describe the difference between CDF and SDF attribute extract formats._____

    _____

24. The first time you create a file using the **ATTEXT** command, it is given a

    _____ extension.

Drawing Problems

1. Start AutoCAD and start a new drawing. Draw the structural steel wide flange shape shown on the following page using the dimensions given. Do not dimension the drawing. Create attributes for the drawing using the information given. Make a block of the drawing and name it W12X40. Insert the block once to test the attributes. Save the drawing as P25-1.

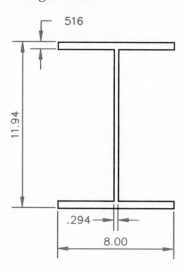

Attributes			
	Steel	W12 × 40	Visible
	Mfgr	Ryerson	Invisible
	Price	$.30/lb	Invisible
	Weight	40 lbs/ft	Invisible
	Length	10'	Invisible
	Code	03116WF	Invisible

2. Load the drawing in Problem 1 (P25-1) and construct the floor plan shown using the dimensions given at a scale of 1/4"=1'-0". Dimension the drawing. Insert the block W12X40 six times as shown. Required attribute data is given in the chart below the drawing. Enter the appropriate information for the attributes as you are prompted for it. Note the steel columns labeled 3 and 6 require slightly different attribute data. You can speed the drawing process by using **ARRAY** or **COPY**. Save the drawing as P25-2.

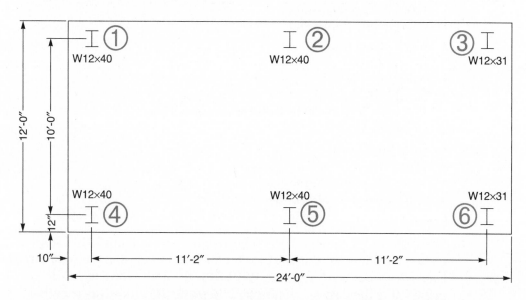

	Steel	Mfgr	Price	Weight	Length	Code
Blocks ①, ②, ④, & ⑤	W12×40	RYERSON	$.30/lb	40 lbs/ft	10'	03116WF
Blocks ③ & ⑥	W12×31	RYERSON	$.30/lb	31 lbs/ft	8.5'	03125WF

3. Load Problem 2 (P25-2) into the drawing editor. Create a template file for use in extracting the data from structural steel blocks inserted in Problem 2. Use the following information in your template file:

Item	Characters	Decimal Places
Block name	8	0
Tag	8	0
Mfgr	20	0
Price	12	0
Weight	8	0
Length	6	1
Code	8	0

Use the **ATTEXT** command to create a listing of the attribute information. When using **ATTEXT**, give the extract file a slightly different name than the template file. If not, your template file will be converted into the extract file. The extract file that is created from Problem 2 should appear as follows:

```
W12X40    RYERSON    $.30/LB    40LB/FT    10FT     03116WF
W12X40    RYERSON    $.30/LB    40LB/FT    10FT     03116WF
W12X40    RYERSON    $.30/LB    40LB/FT    10FT     03116WF
W12X40    RYERSON    $.30/LB    40LB/FT    10FT     03116WF
W12X31    RYERSON    $.29/LB    31LB/FT    8.5FT    03125WF
W12X31    RYERSON    $.29/LB    31LB/FT    8.5FT    03125WF
```

4. Select a drawing from Chapter 23 and create a bill of materials for it using the template file method and the **ATTEXT** command. The template file should list all of the attributes of each block in the drawing. Use the SDF format to display the file. Display the file in the Windows Notepad.

5. Create a drawing of the computer workstation layout in the classroom or office in which you are working. Provide attribute definitions for all of the items listed here.
   - Workstation ID number
   - Computer brand name
   - Model number
   - Processor chip
   - Amount of RAM
   - Hard disk capacity
   - Video graphics card brand and model
   - CD ROM speed
   - Date purchased
   - Price
   - Vendor's phone number
   - Add other data as you see fit

   Generate an extract file for all of the computers in the drawing.

6. Open one of the template drawings created for Problem 13 of Chapter 8. Define attributes for the title block information, revision block, and parts list as described in this chapter. **WBLOCK** the entire drawing to disk using 0,0 as the insertion base point. Repeat the procedure for other templates.

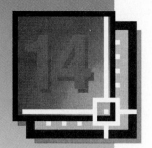

Isometric Drawing

Learning Objectives

After completing this chapter, you will be able to:
- ○ Describe the nature of isometric and oblique views.
- ○ Set an isometric grid.
- ○ Construct isometric objects.
- ○ Create isometric text styles.
- ○ Demonstrate isometric and oblique dimensioning techniques.

Being able to visualize and draw three-dimensional shapes is a skill that every drafter, designer, and engineer should possess. This is especially important with CAD systems that support 3D modeling. However, there is a distinct difference between drawing a view that *looks* three-dimensional and a *true* 3D model.

A 3D model can be rotated on the display screen to view from any angle. The computer calculates the points, lines, and surfaces of the object in space. Three-dimensional models are introduced in Chapter 27. This chapter focuses on creating views that *look* three-dimensional, using some special AutoCAD functions and two-dimensional coordinates and objects.

Pictorial Drawing Overview

The word *pictorial* means "like a picture." It refers to any realistic form of drawing. Pictorial drawings show height, width, and depth. Several forms of pictorial drawings are used in industry today. The least realistic is *oblique*. However, this is the simplest type. The most realistic, but also the most complex, is *perspective*. *Isometric* drawing falls midway between the two as far as realism and complexity are concerned.

Oblique drawings

An oblique drawing shows objects with one or more parallel faces having true shape and size. A scale is selected for the orthographic, or front faces. Then, an angle for the depth (receding axis) is chosen. Three types of oblique drawings are used: *cavalier*, *cabinet*, and *general*, Figure 26-1. These vary in the angle and scale of the receding axis. Both cavalier and cabinet drawings use an angle of 45°. The receding axis is drawn at half scale for a cabinet view and at full scale for a cavalier. The general oblique is normally drawn at an angle other than 45° and at 3/4 scale for the receding axis.

Figure 26-1.
The three types of oblique drawings differ in the scale and angle of the receding axis.

Cavalier   Cabinet   General

Isometric drawings

Isometric drawings are more realistic than oblique drawings. The entire object appears as if it is tilted toward the viewer. The word *isometric* means equal measure. This equal measure refers to the angle between the three axes (120°) after the object has been tilted. The tilt angle is 35°16′. This is shown in Figure 26-2. The 120° angle corresponds to an angle of 30° from horizontal.

Figure 26-2.
An object is tilted 35°16′ to achieve an isometric view having 120° between the three axes. Notice how the highlighted face corresponds to each view.

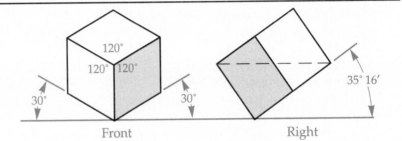

Front   Right

 NOTE   When constructing isometric drawings, remember that lines parallel in the orthogonal views must be parallel in the isometric view.

The most appealing aspect of isometric drawing is that all three axis lines can be measured using the same scale. This saves time, while still producing a pleasing pictorial representation of the object. This type of drawing is produced when you use the **Isometric** option of the **SNAP** command, discussed later.

Closely related to isometric drawing is *dimetric* and *trimetric*. These forms of pictorial drawing differ from isometric in the scales used to measure the three axes. Dimetric drawing uses two different scales, and trimetric uses three scales. Using different scales is an attempt to create *foreshortening*. This means the lengths of the sides appear to recede. The relationship between isometric, dimetric, and trimetric drawings is illustrated in Figure 26-3.

Figure 26-3.
Isometric, dimetric, and trimetric differ in the scales used to draw the three axes. The isometric shown here has the scales represented as one. You can see how the dimetric and trimetric scales vary.

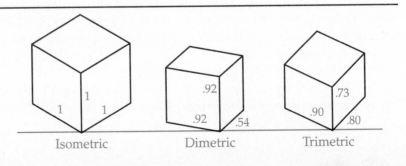

Isometric   Dimetric   Trimetric

Perspective drawing

The most realistic form of pictorial drawing is perspective. The eye naturally sees objects in perspective. Look down a long hall and notice that the wall and floor lines seem to converge in the distance at an imaginary point. That point is called the *vanishing point*. The most common types of perspective drawing are *one-point* and *two-point*. These forms of pictorial drawing are often used in architecture. They are also used in the automotive and aircraft industries. Examples of one-point and two-point perspectives are shown in Figure 26-4. A perspective of a 3D model can be produced in AutoCAD using the **DVIEW** command. See *AutoCAD and its Applications— Advanced, Release 14* for complete coverage of the **DVIEW** command.

Figure 26-4.
An example of one-point and two-point perspective.

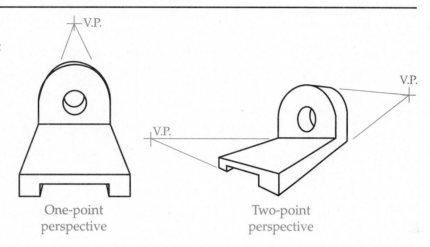

One-point perspective

Two-point perspective

Isometric Drawing

The most common method of pictorial drawing used in industry is isometric. These drawings provide a single view showing three sides that can be measured using the same scale. An isometric view has no perspective and may appear somewhat distorted. Isometric axes are drawn at 30° to horizontal, as shown in Figure 26-5.

The three axes shown in Figure 26-5 represent the width, height, and depth of the object. Lines that appear horizontal in an orthographic view are placed at a 30° angle. Lines that are vertical in an orthographic view are placed vertically. These lines are parallel to the axes. Any line parallel to an axis can be measured and is called an *isometric line*. Lines not parallel to the axes cannot be measured and are called *nonisometric lines*. Note the two nonisometric lines in Figure 26-5.

Figure 26-5.
Isometric axes layout. Lines not parallel to any of the three axes are called nonisometric lines.

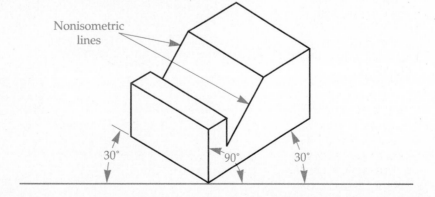

Nonisometric lines

30°   90°   30°

Circular features shown on isometric objects must be oriented properly or they will appear distorted. Figure 26-6 shows the correct orientation of isometric circles on the three principle planes. These circles appear as ellipses on the isometric object. The small diameter (minor axis) of the ellipse must always align on the axis of the circular feature. Notice that the centerline axes of the holes in Figure 26-6 are parallel to one of the isometric planes.

A good basic rule to remember about isometric drawing is that lines parallel in an orthogonal view must be parallel in the isometric view. AutoCAD's **ISOPLANE** feature makes that task, and the positioning of ellipses, easy.

Figure 26-6.
Proper isometric circle (ellipse) orientation on isometric planes. The minor axis always aligns with the axis centerline.

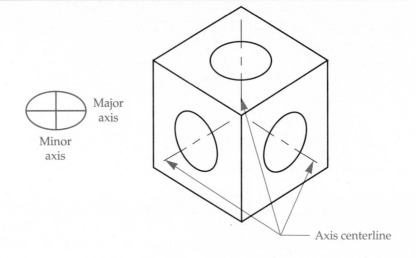

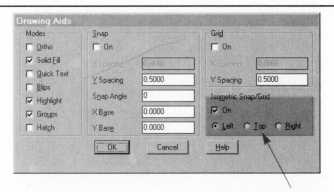

PROFESSIONAL TIP

If you are ever in doubt about the proper orientation of an ellipse in an isometric drawing, remember that the minor axis of the ellipse must always be aligned on the centerline axis of the circular feature. This is shown clearly in Figure 26-6.

Setting isometric variables with a dialog box

You can quickly pick your isometric variables from the **Drawing Aids** dialog box. To access this dialog box, type DDRMODES or RM at the Command: prompt, or select **Drawing Aids...** from the **Tools** pull-down menu. This dialog box contains options for isometric drawing. See Figure 26-7.

Figure 26-7.
The **Drawing Aids** dialog box allows you to pick settings needed for isometric drawing.

Set isometric snap and grid

AutoCAD and its Applications—Basics

To activate the isometric snap grid, pick the **On** check box. Notice that the **X spacing** edit boxes in the **Gri̲d** and **S̲nap** areas are grayed-out. Since X spacing relates to horizontal measurements, it is not used in the isometric mode. You can only set the Y spacing for grid and snap in isometric.

Three option buttons at the lower right of the dialog box allow you to select the isoplane orientation. Be sure to pick the **On** check boxes if you want **Snap** and **Grid** to be activated.

To turn off the **Isometric** mode, simply pick the **On** check box in the **Iso̲metric Snap/Grid** area so that the "✓" disappears. The **Isometric** mode is turned off and you are returned to the drawing editor when you pick the **OK** button.

Setting the isometric snap at the Command: prompt

When the grid is turned on, horizontal and vertical lines of dots are displayed. To begin drawing an isometric object, it is helpful to have the grid dots at an angle. The angle represents the three axis lines of the isometric layout. This is easy using the **SNAP** command. Select the **Style** option, then the **Isometric** option. Finally, enter the vertical spacing.

> Command: **SNAP**↵
> Snap spacing or ON/OFF/Aspect/Rotate/Style ⟨*current*⟩: **S.**↵
> Standard/Isometric ⟨S⟩: **I.**↵
> Vertical spacing ⟨*current*⟩: **.25.**↵

The grid dots on the screen change to the isometric orientation, as shown in Figure 26-8. If your grid dots are not visible, turn the grid on.

Notice the crosshairs also change and appear angled. This aids you in drawing lines at the proper angles. Try drawing a four-sided surface using the **LINE** command. Draw it so that it appears to be the left side of a box in an isometric layout. See Figure 26-9. To draw nonparallel surfaces, you can change the angle of the crosshairs to make your task easier.

Figure 26-8.
An example of an isometric grid setup in AutoCAD.

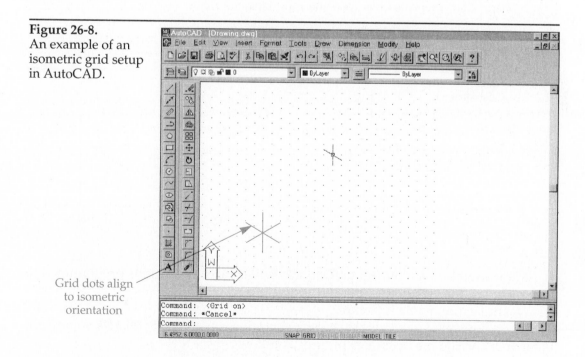

Grid dots align to isometric orientation

Figure 26-9.
A four-sided object drawn with the **LINE** command can be used as the left side of an isometric box.

Draw the left side of an isometric box

<Select object to trim>/Project/Edge/Undo:
<Select object to trim>/Project/Edge/Undo:
Command:

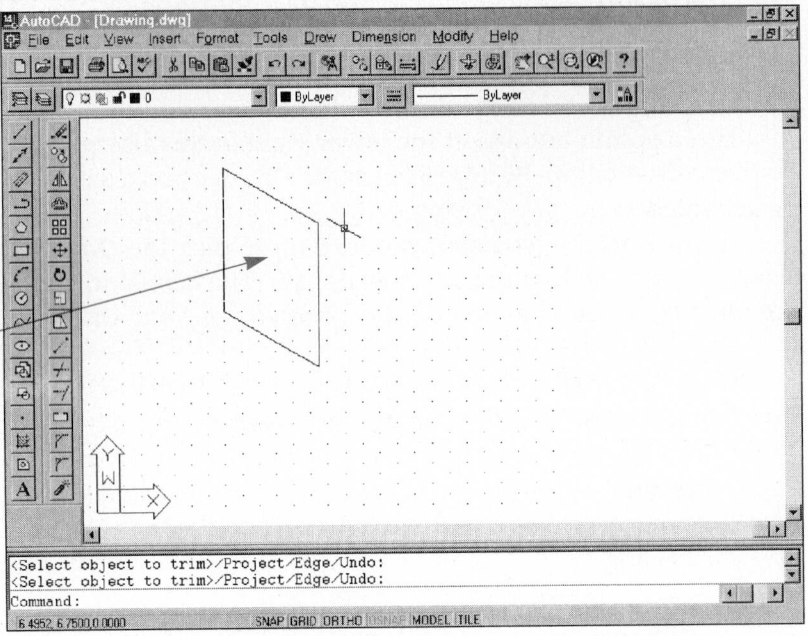

Changing the crosshairs orientation at the Command: prompt

Drawing an isometric shape is possible without ever changing the angle of the crosshairs. However, the drawing process is easier and quicker if the angles of the crosshairs align with the isometric axes.

Whenever the isometric snap style is enabled, simply press the [F5] key or the [Ctrl]+[E] key combination and the crosshairs immediately change to the next plane. AutoCAD refers to the isometric positions as *isoplanes*. The isoplanes are displayed on the prompt line as a reference.

Command: ⟨Isoplane Left⟩ ⟨Isoplane Top⟩ ⟨Isoplane Right⟩

The three crosshair orientations are shown in Figure 26-10.

Figure 26-10.
The three isometric crosshair positions are set with the **ISOPLANE** command.

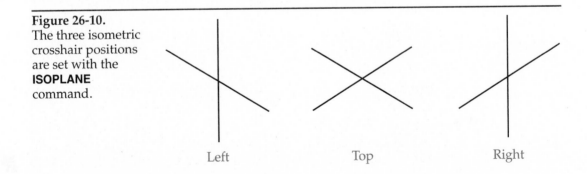

Left   Top   Right

Many multibutton digitizer tablet pucks have one of the buttons programmed to toggle the isoplane when the isometric snap style is active. The specific button varies from manufacturer to manufacturer.

Another method to toggle the crosshair position is with the **ISOPLANE** command. Enter ISOPLANE at the Command: prompt as follows:

Command: **ISOPLANE**↵
Left/Top/Right/⟨Toggle⟩: ↵

Press [Enter] to toggle the crosshairs to the next position. The command line displays the new isoplane setting with the following message:

Current Isometric plane is: Right

You can toggle immediately to the next position by pressing [Enter] at the Command: prompt to repeat the **ISOPLANE** command and pressing [Enter] again. To specify the plane of orientation, type the first letter of that position:

Left/Top/Right/⟨Toggle⟩: **R**↵
Current Isometric plane is: Right

The **ISOPLANE** command can also be used transparently while in another command to toggle between isoplanes. For example, suppose that you start to draw a line and then realize you are in the left isoplane and need to be in the top isoplane. The procedure to use is as follows:

Command: **LINE**↵
From point: **'ISOPLANE**↵
⟩⟩Left/Top/Right/⟨Toggle⟩: **T**↵
Current Isometric plane is: Top
Resuming LINE command.
From point: *(pick the start point for the line)*

The crosshairs are always in one of the isoplane positions when the isometric snap style is in effect. An exception occurs during a display or editing command when a multiple selection set method (such as a window) is used. In these cases, the crosshairs then change to the normal vertical and horizontal positions. At the completion of the display or editing command, the crosshairs automatically revert to their former isoplane orientation.

EXERCISE 26-1

❑ Use one of your templates to begin a new drawing.
❑ Set the grid spacing at .5.
❑ Set the snap style to the **Isometric** option. Specify .25 vertical spacing.
❑ Use the **LINE** command to draw the objects shown. Do not dimension the objects.
❑ Change the **ISOPLANE** orientation as needed.
❑ Save the drawing as EX26-1.

Isometric ellipses

Placing an isometric ellipse on an object is made easy using AutoCAD. An ellipse is positioned automatically to the current isoplane setting. Use the **ELLIPSE** command by picking the **Ellipse** button on the **Draw** toolbar or typing EL or ELLIPSE at the Command: prompt. You can also select **Axis, End** from the **Ellipse** cascading menu in the **Draw** pull-down menu. The following prompt appears:

Command: **EL** *or* **ELLIPSE**↵
Arc/Center/Isocircle/⟨Axis endpoint 1⟩: **I**↵
Center of circle: *(pick a point)*
⟨Circle radius⟩/Diameter:

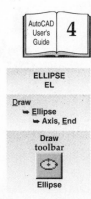

AutoCAD
User's
Guide **4**

ELLIPSE
EL

Draw
➥ Ellipse
➥ Axis, End

Draw
toolbar

Ellipse

Do not select the **Center** option; this method does not allow you to create isocircles. Instead, select **Isocircle**, and then pick the center point and diameter. Three options are available for determining the size of the ellipse at this last prompt.

- When **DRAGMODE** is on, the ellipse changes size as the cursor moves. Set the radius by picking a point.
- Enter a numeric value and press [Enter] to have AutoCAD draw the ellipse at a specific radius.
- Type D and you are asked for the circle diameter. Enter a number, press [Enter], and the ellipse appears.

Always check the isoplane position before locating an ellipse on your drawing. You can dynamically view the three positions that an ellipse can take. Enter the **ELLIPSE** command, pick the **Isocircle** option, and then toggle the crosshair orientation. See Figure 26-11. The ellipse rotates each time you toggle the crosshairs.

The isometric ellipse is a true ellipse. If selected, grips are displayed at the center and four quadrant points. This simplifies the editing process. See Figure 26-12.

PROFESSIONAL TIP

Prior to drawing isometric ellipses, it is good practice to first place a marker at the ellipse center point. A good technique is to set **PDMODE** to 3 and use **POINT** to place an X at the center. This is especially useful if the ellipse does not fall on grid or snap points.

Figure 26-11.
The orientation of an isometric ellipse is determined by the crosshair orientation.

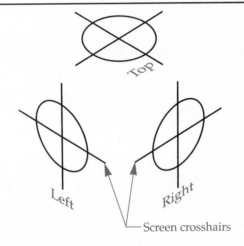

Figure 26-12.
An isometric ellipse has grips at its four quadrant points and its center.

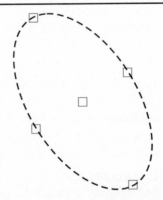

AutoCAD and its Applications—Basics

CAUTION	It may be tempting to resize or otherwise adjust an isometric ellipse or arc by selecting one of the grips. Keep in mind that as soon as you resize an isometric ellipse in this manner, its angular value has changed and it is no longer isometric. If you rotate an isometric ellipse while **ORTHO** is on, it will not appear in a proper isometric plane. You *can* rotate an isometric ellipse, but be sure to enter a value of 120° if you want it to rotate from one of the isometric planes to another.

EXERCISE 26-2

❏ Open EX26-1 if this drawing is not already on your screen.
❏ Select the **ELLIPSE** command to place an ellipse on the three sides of the object.
❏ Draw the numbered ellipses in the following manner:
   1. Pick a radius of .5 using the cursor.
   2. Enter a radius of .75 at the keyboard.
   3. Type D and enter a diameter of .6 at the keyboard.
❏ The finished drawing should look like the example given below.
❏ Save the drawing as EX26-2.

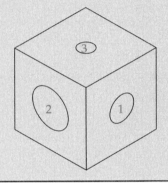

Constructing isometric arcs

The **ELLIPSE** command can also be used to draw an isometric arc of any included angle. Select the **Arc** option of the **ELLIPSE** command or pick **Arc** from the **Ellipse** cascading menu in the **Draw** pull-down menu. Use the following steps to construct an isometric arc:

   Command: **EL** *or* **ELLIPSE.**↵
   Arc/Center/Isocircle/⟨Axis endpoint 1⟩: **A**↵
   ⟨Axis endpoint 1⟩/Center/Isocircle: **I**↵
   Center of circle: *(pick the center of the arc)*
   ⟨Circle radius⟩/Diameter: *(pick the radius or type a value and press* [Enter]*)*
   Parameter/⟨start angle⟩: *(pick a start angle or type a value and press* [Enter]*)*
   Parameter/Included/⟨end angle⟩: *(pick an end angle or type an included angle value and press* [Enter]*)*
   Command:

A common application of isometric arcs is drawing fillets or rounds. Once a round is created isometrically, the edge (corner) of the object sits back from its original, unfilleted position. See Figure 26-13A. You can draw the complete object first, then trim away the excess after locating the fillets. You can also draw the isometric arcs and then the connecting lines. Either way, the center point of the ellipse is a critical feature, and should be located first. In Figure 26-13, the arc at the upper left was drawn first, then copied to the upper back position using grips. Use **ORTHO** to help quickly draw 90° arcs.

The next step is to move the original edge to its new position. This is tangent to the isometric arcs. You can do this by snapping the line to the quadrant point of the arc. See Figure 26-13B. Notice the grips on the line and on the arc. The endpoint of the line is snapped to the quadrant grip on the arc. The final step is to trim away the excess lines and upper right arc. The completed feature is shown in Figure 26-13C.

Rounded edges, when viewed straight on, cannot be shown as complete-edge lines that extend to the ends of the object. Instead, a good technique to use is a broken line in the original location of the edge. This is clearly shown in the figure in Exercise 26-3.

EXERCISE 26-3

❑ Load AutoCAD and begin a new drawing named EX26-3.
❑ Set the grid spacing at .5.
❑ Set the snap style to the **Isometric** option, and specify a .25 vertical spacing.
❑ Use the **LINE** command and draw the object shown below. Do not dimension the object.
❑ Fillets and rounds are all .25 radius.
❑ Change the isoplane as needed, and use the **ELLIPSE** command and **Arc** option to complete the object.
❑ Save the drawing as EX26-3.

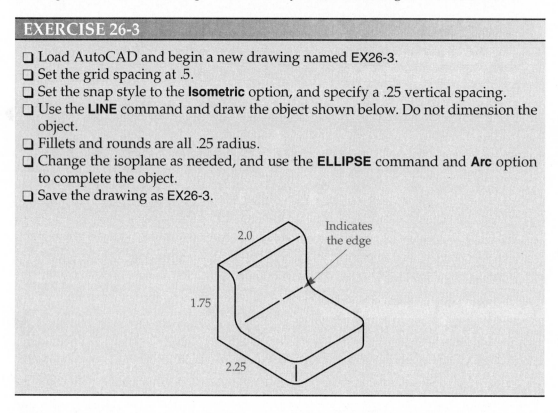

Figure 26-13.
Rounds can be drawn with the **Arc** option of the **ELLIPSE** command.

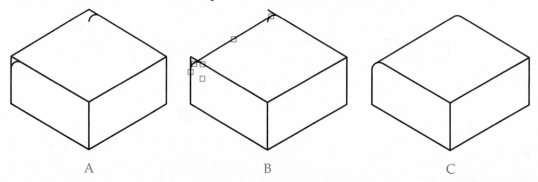

A   B   C

Creating isometric text styles

Isometric text should appear to lie in one of the isometric planes. Text should not look like it was added at the last minute. Drafters and artists occasionally neglect this aspect of pictorial drawing and it shows on the final product. Text should align with the plane that it applies to. This involves creating new text styles.

Figure 26-14 illustrates possible orientation of text on an isometric drawing. Text may be located on the object or positioned away from it as a note. These examples were created using only two text styles.

The text styles in Figure 26-14 are based on styles that use an obliquing angle of either 30° or –30°. The labels refer to the style numbers given in the chart below. The angle indicates the rotation angle entered when using one of the **TEXT** commands. For example, ISO-2 90 means that the ISO-2 style was used and the text was rotated 90°. This technique can be applied to any font.

Name	Font	Obliquing Angle
ISO-1	Romans	30°
ISO-2	Romans	–30°

Figure 26-14.
Isometric text applications. The text shown here indicates the ISO style used and the angle used.

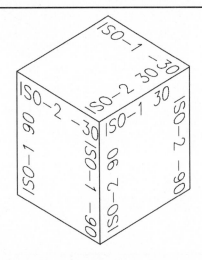

❏ Use one of your templates to begin a new drawing.
❏ Create one text style to label the angled (nonisometric) surface of the wedge. See the illustration below.
❏ Create a second style to label the front of the wedge.
❏ Save the drawing as EX26-4.

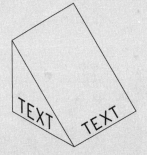

Isometric Dimensioning

An important aspect of isometric dimensioning is to place dimension lines, text, and arrowheads in the proper plane. Remember these guidelines:

✓ The extension lines should always extend the plane being dimensioned.
✓ The heel of the arrowhead should always be parallel to the extension line.
✓ The strokes of the text that would normally be vertical should always be parallel with the extension lines or dimension lines.

These techniques, as well as a dimensioned isometric part, are shown in Figure 26-15. AutoCAD does not automatically dimension isometric objects. You must first create isometric arrowheads and text styles. Then, manually draw the dimension lines and text as they should appear in each of the three isometric planes. This is time-consuming when compared to dimensioning normal 2D drawings.

You have already learned how to create isometric text styles. These can be set up in an isometric prototype drawing if you draw isometrics often. Examples of arrows for the three isometric planes are shown in Figure 26-16.

Figure 26-15.
A dimensioned isometric part. Note the text and arrowhead orientation in relation to the extension lines.

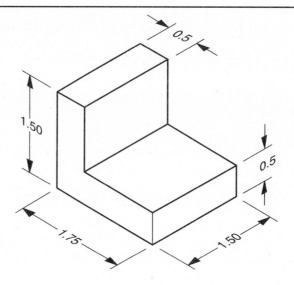

Figure 26-16.
Examples of arrowheads in each of the three isometric planes.

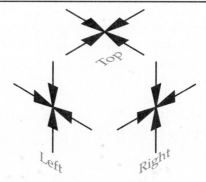

Arrowheads can be drawn with the **PLINE** or **LINE** commands or filled-in with the **SOLID** command. Every arrowhead does not need to be drawn individually. First, draw two isometric axes, as shown in Figure 26-17A. Then, draw one arrowhead like the one shown in Figure 26-18B. Use the **MIRROR** command to create additional arrows. As you create new arrows, move them to their proper plane. Save each arrowhead as a block in your isometric template or prototype. Use names that are easy to remember.

AutoCAD and its Applications—Basics

Figure 26-17.
Creating isometric arrowheads. A—Draw the two isometric axes for arrowhead placement.
B—Draw the first arrowhead on one of the axis lines. Then, mirror the arrowhead
to create others.

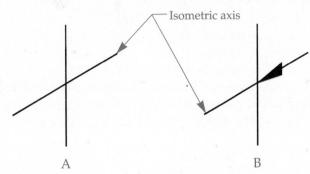

A   B

Oblique dimensioning

AutoCAD has a way to semi-automatically dimension isometric and oblique lines.
First, the dimensions must be drawn using any of the linear dimensioning commands.
Figure 26-18A illustrates an object that has been dimensioned using the **DIMALIGNED**
and **DIMLINEAR** commands. Then, use the **Oblique** option of the **DIMEDIT** command to
rotate the extension lines. See Figure 26-18B.

To access the **Oblique** option, type DIMEDIT at the Command: prompt and enter O.
You can also select **Oblique** from the **Dimension** pull-down menu. Select the dimension
and enter the obliquing angle:

    Command: **DIMEDIT**↵
    Dimension Edit (Home/New/Rotate/Oblique) ⟨Home⟩: **O**↵
    Select objects: *(pick dimension number 1)*
    Select objects: ↵
    Enter obliquing angle (press ENTER for none): **30**↵
    Command:

Figure 26-18A shows numbers by each dimension. The following list gives the
obliquing angle required for each numbered dimension in order to achieve the finished drawing shown in Figure 26-18B.

Figure 26-18.
The **OBLIQUE** dimensioning command requires that you select an existing dimension and
enter the desired obliquing angle. Refer to the text for the angles represented by the
circled numbers.

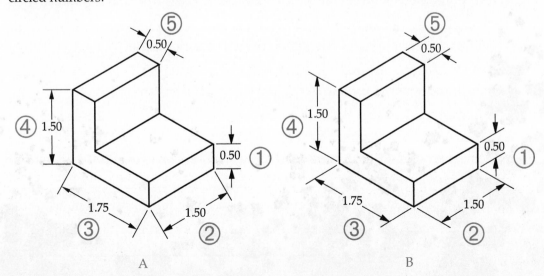

A   B

Dimension	Obliquing Angle
1	30°
2	−30°
3	30°
4	−30°
5	30°

This technique creates suitable dimensions for an isometric drawing and is quicker than the previous method discussed. Keep in mind that the oblique method does not rotate the arrows so that the arrowhead heels are aligned with the extension lines. It also does not draw the dimension text aligned in the plane of the dimension.

Chapter Test

Write your answers in the spaces provided.

1. The simplest form of pictorial drawing is _____.

2. How does isometric drawing differ from oblique drawing? _____
   _____
   _____

3. How do dimetric and trimetric drawings differ from isometric drawings? _____
   _____
   _____

4. The most realistic form of pictorial drawing is_____.

5. Provide the correct entries at the following prompts to set an isometric snap with a spacing of 0.2.
   Command: _____
   Snap spacing or ON/OFF/Aspect/Rotate/Style ⟨*current*⟩:_____
   Standard/Isometric ⟨S⟩: _____
   Vertical spacing ⟨*current*⟩:_____

6. What function does the **ISOPLANE** command perform? _____
   _____
   _____

7. Which pull-down menu contains the command to access the **Drawing Aids** dialog box? _____

8. What factor determines the orientation of an isometric ellipse?_____
   _____

9. List the three methods used to define the size of an isometric ellipse. _____
   _____
   _____

10. Which aspect of the **STYLE** command allows you to create text that can be used on an isometric drawing? _____

11. What command and two options must you select in order to draw isometric arcs?
    _____
    _____

12. On what parts of an isometric circle are grips located? _____
_____
_____

13. Can grips be used to correctly resize an isometric circle? Explain your answer.
_____
_____

14. What technique does AutoCAD provide for dimensioning isometric objects? ___
_____
_____

Drawing Problems

Create an isometric template drawing. Use the template to construct the iso-metric drawings in Problems 1–10. Items that should be set in the template include grid spacing, snap spacing, ortho setting, and text size. Save the template as **isoproto.dwt.** *Save the drawing problems as* **P26-**(*problem number*).

1.

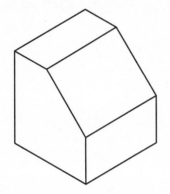

2.

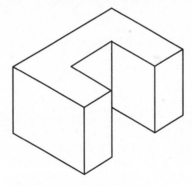

3.

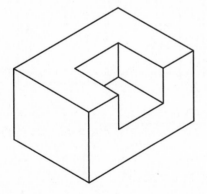

4.

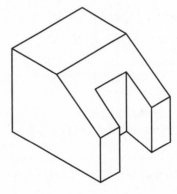

5.

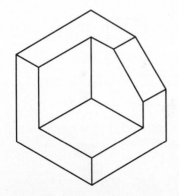

6.

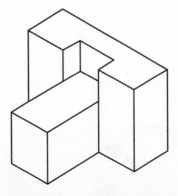

7.

8.

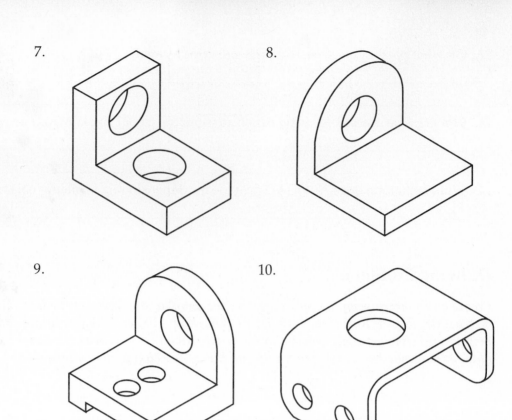

9.

10.

For Problems 11–14, create isometric drawings using the views shown.

11.

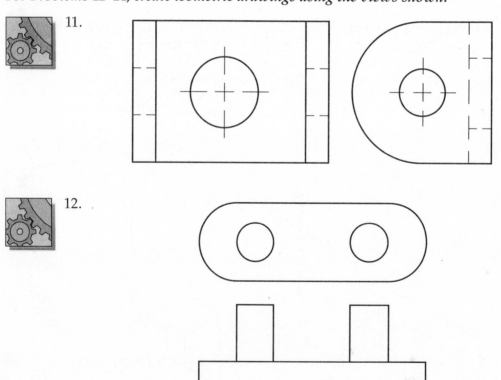

12.

13.

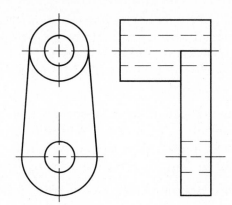

14.

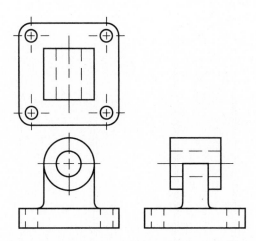

15. Construct a set of isometric arrowheads to use when dimensioning isometric drawings. Load your isometric template drawing. Create arrowheads for each of the three isometric planes. Save each arrowhead as a block. Name them with the first letter indicating the plane: T for top, L for left, and R for right. Also number them clockwise from the top. See the example for the right isometric plane. Save the template again when finished.

16. Create a set of isometric text styles like those shown in Figure 26-14. Load your template drawing and make a complete set in one font. Make additional sets in other fonts if you wish. Enter a text height of 0 so that you can specify the height when placing the text. Save the template again when finished.

17. Begin a new drawing named P26-17 using your template. Select one of the following problems to dimension: Problem 5, 7, 8, or 9. When adding dimensions, be sure to use the proper arrowhead and text style for the plane that you are working in. Save the drawing when completed.

18. Create an isometric drawing of the switch plate. Select a view that displays the features of the object. Do not include dimensions. Save the drawing as P26-18.

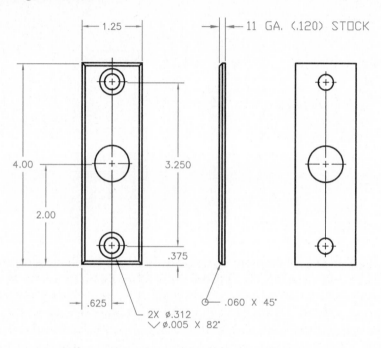

19. Create an isometric drawing of the retainer. Select a view that displays the features of the object. Do not include dimensions. Save the drawing as P26-19.

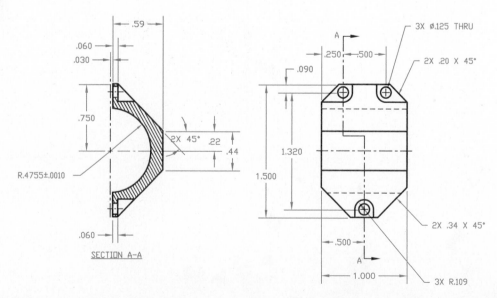

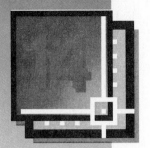

Introduction to Three-Dimensional Drawing

Learning Objectives

After completing this chapter, you will be able to:
- ○ Describe the nature and function of rectangular, spherical, and cylindrical 3D coordinate systems.
- ○ Use the "right-hand rule" of 3D visualization.
- ○ Construct extruded and wireframe 3D objects.
- ○ Display 3D objects at any desired viewpoint.

Computers are especially suited to handle information about points in space. However, in order for computer software to accept and use this information, the drafter or designer must first have good 3D visualization skills. These skills include the ability to see an object in three dimensions and to visualize it rotating in space. These skills can be obtained by using 3D techniques to construct objects, and by trying to picture two-dimensional sketches and drawings as 3D models.

This chapter provides an introduction to several aspects of 3D drawing and visualization. A thorough discussion of 3D drawing, visualization, and display techniques is provided in *AutoCAD and its Applications—Advanced, Release 14*.

Rectangular 3D Coordinates

AutoCAD User's Guide | 13

A computer can draw lines because it knows the X and Y values of the endpoints. The line does not really exist in the computer, only the points do. When drawing in 3D, you define the third dimension with a third coordinate measured along the Z axis. A computer can only draw lines in 3D if it knows the X, Y, and Z coordinate values of each point on the object.

Compare the 2D coordinate system to the 3D system in Figure 27-1. Note that the positive values of Z in the 3D system come up from the X-Y plane of a 2D drawing.

Figure 27-1.
A comparison of 2D and 3D coordinate systems.

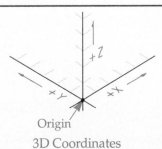

2D Coordinates   3D Coordinates

Consider the surface of your screen as the new Z plane. Anything behind the screen is negative Z and anything in front of the screen is positive Z.

The object in Figure 27-2A is a 2D drawing showing the top view of an object. The XY coordinate values of each point are shown. To convert this object to its three-dimensional form, Z values are given to each vertex, or corner. Figure 27-2B shows the object pictorially with the XYZ values of each point listed.

Figure 27-2.
Each vertex of a 3D object must have an X, Y, and Z value.

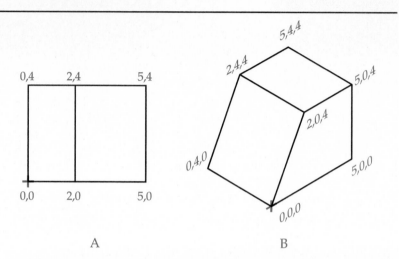

A

B

This same object could have been drawn using negative Z coordinates. It would extend behind the screen. Although the sign of the Z value makes no difference to AutoCAD, it is easier to work with positive values.

Study the nature of the 3D coordinate system. Be sure you understand Z values before you begin constructing 3D objects. It is important that you visualize and plan your design when working with 3D constructions.

Three-dimensional objects can be drawn in AutoCAD using two additional coordinate systems—spherical and cylindrical. These two systems enable you to work with point locations using distances and angles in order to draw a variety of shapes. For a complete discussion of spherical and cylindrical coordinate systems, please refer to *AutoCAD and its Applications—Advanced, Release 14.*

EXERCISE 27-1

❏ Study the multiview sketch below.
❏ Given the 3D coordinate axes, freehand sketch the object pictorially. Each tick mark is one unit. Use correct dimensions as given in the multiview drawing.
❏ When you complete the freehand sketch, draw the object in AutoCAD with the **LINE** command by entering XYZ coordinates for each point.
❏ Save the drawing as EX27-1 and quit.

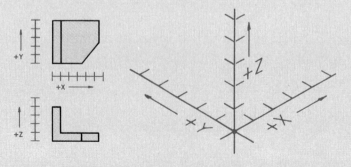

Creating Extruded 3D Shapes

Most shapes drawn with AutoCAD are extruded shapes. *Extruded* means that a 2D shape is given a base elevation and a thickness. The object then rises up, or "extrudes" to its given thickness. The **ELEV** command controls the base elevation and thickness. **ELEV** does not draw, it merely sets the base elevation and thickness for the next objects drawn.

> **NOTE**
>
> The current elevation is the level on which the next objects will be drawn. Therefore, if you set the elevation at 2.0, then draw the bottom of a machine part, the bottom of that part is now sitting at 2.0 units above the zero elevation. On the other hand, the *thickness* setting is the value that determines the height of the next object you draw. Therefore, if you want to draw a part 2.0 units high, with the bottom of the part resting on the zero elevation plane, set elevation to 0.0 and thickness to 2.0.

The process of drawing a rectangular box four units long by three units wide by two units high begins with the **ELEV** command:

```
Command: ELEV↵
New current elevation ⟨0.0000⟩: ↵
New current thickness ⟨0.0000⟩: 2↵
Command:
```

Nothing happens on-screen. Now use the **LINE** command to draw the top view of the rectangular box. Although it appears that you are drawing four lines, you are actually drawing planes. Each plane has a thickness that you cannot see.

Before you display the 3D construction, use the following instructions to add a hexagon and a circle, as shown in Figure 27-3. The hexagon should sit on top of the rectangle and extend three units above. The circle should appear to be a hole through the rectangle. Since the circle and rectangle have the same elevation, there is no need to use the **ELEV** command.

Figure 27-3.
A hexagon and a circle added to the rectangle for the command sequence given in the text.

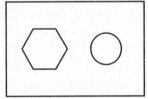

Before drawing the hexagon, set the base elevation to the top surface of the rectangle and thickness (height) of the hexagon feature using the **ELEV** command as follows:

```
Command: ELEV↵
New current elevation ⟨0.0000⟩: 2↵
New current thickness ⟨2.0000⟩: 3↵
Command:
```

Now, draw the hexagon. The bracketed numbers after each prompt reflect the current values. A "2" is entered for the elevation because the hexagon sits on top of the rectangle, which is two units thick. This is where the hexagon starts. The "3" is the thickness (height) of the hexagon above its starting point.

Next, set the elevation and thickness for the circle:

    Command: **ELEV**↵
    New current elevation ⟨2.0000⟩: **0**↵
    New current thickness ⟨3.0000⟩: **2**↵
    Command:

Now, draw the circle to the right of the hexagon. The object is now ready to be viewed in 3D.

PROFESSIONAL TIP

Keep in mind that a "hole" drawn using **ELEV** and **CIRCLE** is not really a hole to AutoCAD. It is a cylinder with solid ends. This becomes clear when you display the objects in a 3D view with hidden lines removed.

Some 3D drawing hints

✓ Erasing a line drawn with the **ELEV** thickness set to a value other than zero erases an entire plane.
✓ Shapes drawn using the **LINE** and **ELEV** commands are open at the top and bottom.
✓ Circles drawn with **ELEV** are closed at the ends.
✓ The **PLINE** and **TRACE** commands give thickness to lines and make them appear as walls in the 3D view.

AutoCAD User's Guide **11**

The Right-Hand Rule

Before we discuss viewing the 3D drawing, it is worthwhile to review a good technique for 3D visualization. Once you understand the following procedure, viewing a 3D object oriented in AutoCAD's rectangular coordinate system should be relatively easy.

The *right-hand rule* is a graphic representation of positive coordinate values in the three axis directions of a coordinate system. The UCS (User Coordinate System) is based on this concept of visualization. This requires that you use the thumb, index finger, and middle finger of your right hand and hold them open in front of you, as shown in Figure 27-4.

Although this may seem a bit unusual to do (especially if you are sitting in the middle of a school library or computer lab), it can do wonders for your understanding of the nature of the three axes. It can also help in understanding how the UCS can be rotated about each of the axis lines, or fingers.

Imagine that your thumb represents the X axis, your index finger is the Y axis, and your middle finger is the Z axis. Hold your hand in front of you and bend your middle finger so it is pointing directly at you. Now you see the plan view. The positive X axis is pointing to the right and the positive Y axis is pointing up. The positive Z axis comes toward you, and the origin of this system is the palm of your hand.

This concept can be visualized even better if you are sitting at a computer and the AutoCAD graphics screen is displayed. If the UCS icon is not displayed in the lower-left corner of the screen, turn it on as follows:

    Command: **UCSICON**↵
    ON/OFF/All/Noorigin/ORigin ⟨ON⟩: **ON**↵

Figure 27-4.
Try positioning
your hand like this
to understand the
relationship of the
X, Y, and Z axes.

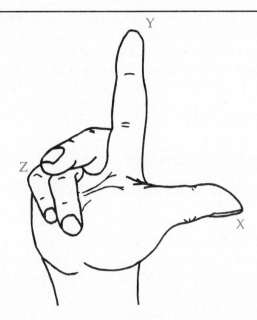

Now orient your right hand as shown in Figure 27-4 and position it next to the UCS icon on the screen. Your index finger and thumb should point in the same directions as Y and X, respectively, on the UCS icon. Your middle finger will be pointing out of the screen. This technique can also be used to eliminate confusion when the UCS is rotated to odd angles.

When you use the **VPOINT** command (discussed later in this chapter), a tripod appears on the screen. It is composed of three axis lines, which are X, Y, and Z. When you see the tripod, you should be able to make the comparison with the right-hand rule. See Figure 27-5.

Figure 27-5.
Compare the UCS icon with the use of three fingers on the right hand and the tripod used by AutoCAD for 3D viewing.

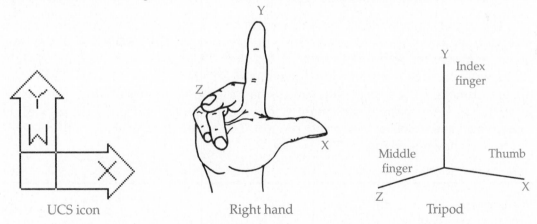

The UCS can be rotated to any position. The coordinate system rotates on one of the three axis lines, just like a wheel rotates on an axle. Therefore, if you want to rotate the X plane, keep your thumb stationary, and turn your hand toward or away from you. If you wish to rotate the Y plane, keep your index finger stationary and turn your hand to the left or right. When rotating the Z plane, you must keep your middle finger stationary and rotate your entire arm.

If you discover that your 3D visualization skills are weak or that you are having trouble with the UCS method, don't be afraid to use the right-hand rule. It is a useful technique for improving your 3D visualization skills.

The ability to rotate the UCS around one or more of the three axes can become confusing if proper techniques are not used to visualize the rotation angles. A complete discussion of these techniques is provided in *AutoCAD and its Applications—Advanced, Release 14*.

Displaying 3D Drawings

Once you have drawn a 3D object in plan view, you should change your point of view so that the object can be seen in three dimensions. The **VPOINT** command allows you to display the current drawing at any angle. It may be easier to understand the function of this command as establishing your position relative to the object.

Imagine that you can position yourself at a coordinate location in 3D space in relation to the object. The **VPOINT** command provides AutoCAD with the XYZ coordinates of your eyes, so the object can be positioned properly. **VPOINT** can be selected from the **View** pull-down menu by picking the **3D Viewpoint** cascading menu and then **Tripod**. Several preset viewpoints can also be selected by picking the appropriate button in the **Viewpoint** toolbar. See Figure 27-6.

Figure 27-6.
The **Viewpoint** toolbar contains several preset viewpoints that can be selected by picking the appropriate button. These are shown here highlighted.

Accesses the **View Control** dialog box

Preset views

Use the **VPOINT** command to establish your position relative to the object by entering VPOINT at the Command: prompt as follows:

    Command: **VPOINT.⏎**
    Rotate/⟨View point⟩ ⟨0.0000,0.0000,1.0000⟩:

The three numbers reflect the XYZ coordinates of the current viewpoint. You can change these coordinates to select different viewpoints. The **VPOINT** values shown above represent the coordinates for the plan view. This means that your line of sight is along the positive Z axis looking down on the XY plane. Since it is difficult to visualize a numerical viewpoint, you can display a graphic representation of the XYZ axes and pick the desired viewpoint with your pointing device. To do so, simply press [Enter] at the Rotate/⟨View point⟩: prompt. The screen display changes to one similar to that shown in Figure 27-7.

Figure 27-7.
The **VPOINT** axes display enables you to position your point of sight in relation to the object.

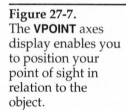 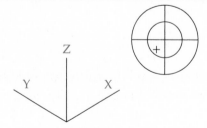

As you move the pointing device, notice what happens on screen. The XYZ coordinate tripod moves and the small crosshairs near the concentric circles also move. The concentric circles represent a compass. When the small crosshairs are inside the small circle, you are viewing the object from above. When the crosshairs are located between the two circles, you are viewing the object from below.

The easiest way to locate the viewpoint is to move the cursor while observing the XYZ axes tripod movement. Pick the location where you are satisfied with the appearance of the axes. It may take some practice. Remember that in the top, or plan view, the X axis is horizontal, Y axis is vertical, and Z axis comes out of the screen. As you move the tripod, keep track of where the crosshairs are located inside the compass. Compare their position to that of the tripod.

Move the tripod until it is positioned like the one given in Figure 27-8. Press the pick button. The display should then resemble that figure.

Figure 27-8.
The three axes and a
3D view display.

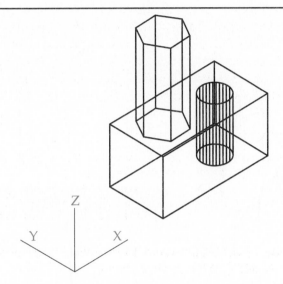

The number of viewpoints you can select is endless. To get an idea of how the axes tripod and compass relate to the viewpoint, see the examples in Figure 27-9. It can be hard to distinguish top from bottom in wireframe views. Therefore, the viewpoints shown in Figure 27-9 are all from above the object and the **HIDE** command has been used to clarify the views. Use the **VPOINT** command to try each of these 3D positions on your computer.

When you are ready to return to the World Coordinate System plan view, use the **PLAN** command. To access the **PLAN** command, type PLAN at the Command: prompt, or select the **3D Viewpoint** from the **View** pull-down menu, select **Plan View**, and then **World** as shown in Figure 27-10. The command sequence is as follows:

    Command: **PLAN**↵
    ⟨Current UCS⟩/Ucs/World: **W**↵
    Regenerating drawing.
    Command:

As an alternative to the **PLAN** command, you can also type the XYZ coordinates for the plan view using the **VPOINT** command.

    Command: **VPOINT**↵
    Rotate/⟨View point⟩ ⟨*current*⟩: **0,0,1**↵
    Regenerating drawing.
    Command:

Figure 27-9.
Examples of viewpoint locations and their related axes positions.

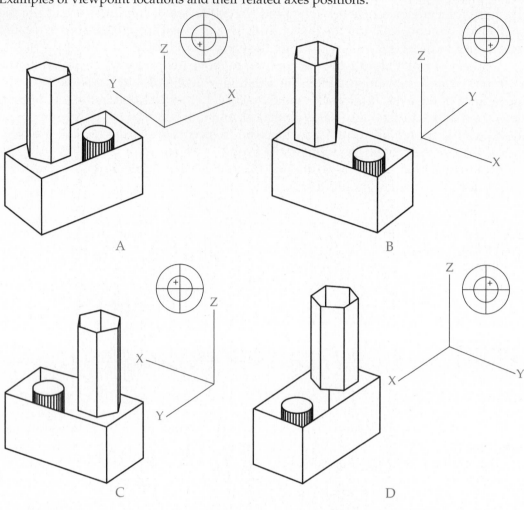

A

B

C

D

Figure 27-10.
The **PLAN** command can be accessed through the **View** pull-down menu.

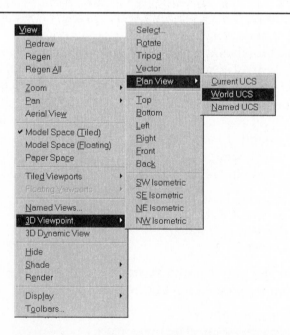

Either method automatically performs a **ZOOM Extents** operation that fills the graphics window with your original top view. You can use the **ZOOM All** option to redisplay the original drawing limits.

AutoCAD and its Applications—Basics

❏ Set the grid spacing to .5 and snap spacing to .25.
❏ Set the elevation at 0 and the thickness at 2.
❏ Using the **RECTANG** command, draw a 2 × 3 unit rectangle.
❏ Add a 180° arc to each end of the rectangle.
❏ Set the elevation at 2 and the thickness at 3.
❏ Draw a 1 unit diameter circle in the center of the rectangle.
❏ Use the **VPOINT** command to display the 3D view of your drawing. Display it from three viewpoints using the axes tripod.
❏ Save the drawing as EX27-2.

Creating extruded 3D text

Text added on the plan view is displayed in 3D when you use the **VPOINT** command. However, the displayed text has no thickness, and rests on the zero elevation plane. You can give text thickness and change the elevation with the **DDCHPROP** or **DDMODIFY** command. Select the text to change, pick the **Thickness:** option, and enter a value. See Figure 27-11. Examples of 3D text before and after using the **HIDE** command are shown in Figure 27-12.

Figure 27-11.
The **Change Properties** dialog box can be used to give text thickness. Thickness can also be set in a **Modify** dialog box.

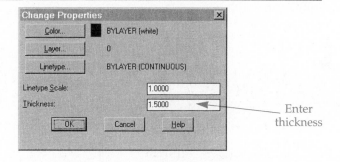

Enter thickness

Figure 27-12.
Thickness applied to 3D text with and without the **HIDE** option.

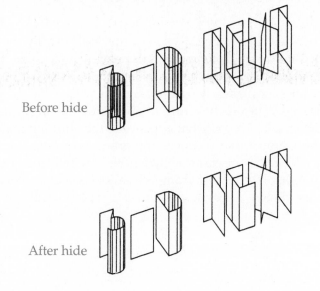

Before hide

After hide

Removing hidden lines in 3D displays

HIDE
HI

View
↳ Hide

Render
toolbar

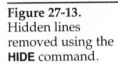

Hide

The displays shown in Figure 27-8 and Figure 27-12 are wireframe representations, where all edges and vertices are visible. A wireframe view can be confusing because features that are normally hidden from view are fully displayed. The best way to mask all features that would normally be hidden is to use the **HIDE** command.

Use **HIDE** only after you have selected a 3D viewing angle. Enter HIDE or HI at the Command: prompt, pick the **Hide** button in the **Render** toolbar, or select **Hide** from the **View** pull-down menu. The command sequence is as follows:

```
Command: HI or HIDE.↵
Regenerating drawing.
Hiding lines 100% done.
Command:
```

The size and complexity of the drawing and the speed of your computer determines how long you must wait for the lines to be hidden. The final display of the object in Figure 27-8 is shown in Figure 27-13 with hidden lines removed.

Figure 27-13.
Hidden lines removed using the **HIDE** command.

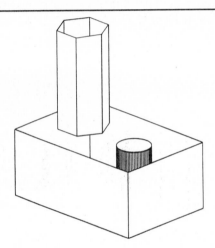

The view in Figure 27-13 may not look exactly as you expected. You probably expected the rectangle to appear solid with a circle in the top representing a hole. Think back to the initial construction of the rectangle. When drawn in the plan view, it consisted of four lines, or planes. It was not drawn with a top or bottom, just four sides. Then you placed a hexagon sitting at the same elevation as the top of the box, and a cylinder inside. That is what appears in the "hidden lines removed" display.

The features that compose the object in Figure 27-13 are shown individually in Figure 27-14. The objects are shown both as wireframes and with hidden lines removed.

To redisplay the wireframe view, just select another viewpoint or enter REGEN and press [Enter]. A regeneration displays all lines of the objects.

Figure 27-14.
Individual features of the object in Figure 27-13 in wireframe and with hidden lines removed.

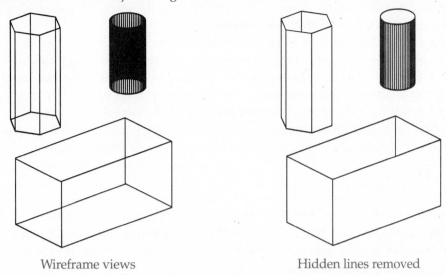

Wireframe views   Hidden lines removed

3D Construction Techniques

Three-dimensional objects can be drawn in three basic forms—wireframe, surface models, and solid models. The following section discusses the construction of wireframes, and the use of 3D faces to apply a surface to the wireframe. A *wireframe construction* is just that; an object that looks like it was made of wire. You can see through it.

There are not a lot of practical applications for wireframe models unless you are an artist designing a new object using coat hangers. Wireframe models are hard to visualize because it is difficult to determine the angle of view and the nature of the surfaces. For example, compare the two objects in Figure 27-15.

Surface modeling, on the other hand, is more easily visualized. It looks more like the real object. Surface models can be used to imitate solid models, and most importantly, can be used for shading and rendering models. These shaded and rendered models can then be used in any number of presentation formats, including slide shows, black and white or color prints, walk-through animation, or animation recorded to videotape.

Figure 27-15.
A wireframe object is harder to visualize than the surface model. (Autodesk, Inc.)

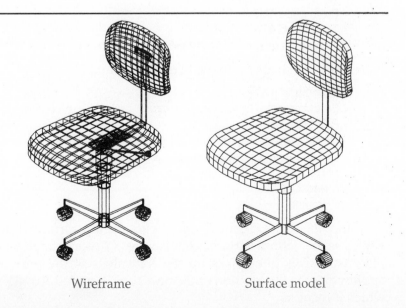

Wireframe   Surface model

A surface model can also be exported from AutoCAD for use in animation and rendering software, such as Autodesk's 3D Studio. In addition, surface models are the basis for the construction of composite 3D models, often called *virtual worlds*, which are used in the field of virtual reality.

On the other hand, *solid modeling* more closely represents designing an object using the materials from which it is to be made. This type of 3D design involves using primitive solid shapes, such as boxes, cylinders, spheres, and cones to construct an object. These shapes are added together and subtracted from each other to create a finished product. The solid model can then be shaded, rendered, and more importantly, analyzed to determine mass, volume, moments of inertia, and centroid location. Some third-party programs allow you to perform finite element analysis on the model.

Before constructing a 3D model, you should determine the purpose of your design. What will the model be used for—presentation, analysis, or manufacturing? This helps you determine which tools you should use to construct the model. The discussions and examples in this chapter provide an introductory view of the uses of wireframe, 3D faces, and basic surfaced objects in order to create 3D constructions. Further study of surface and solids modeling techniques is covered in *AutoCAD and its Applications—Advanced, Release 14*.

Constructing Wireframes and 3D Faces

Wireframes can be constructed using the **LINE**, **PLINE**, **SPLINE**, and **3DPOLY** commands. AutoCAD provides a number of methods to use, but one particularly useful method is called filters. A *filter* is an existing point, or vector, in your drawing file. When using a filter, you instruct AutoCAD to find the coordinate values of a selected point. Then, you supply the missing value, which can be X, Y, Z, or a combination. Filters can be used when working in two-dimensional space or when using a pictorial projection resulting from the **VPOINT** command.

Using filters to create 3D wireframe objects

When using **LINE**, you must know the XYZ coordinate values of each corner on the object. To draw an object, first decide the easiest and quickest method using the **LINE** command. One technique is to draw the bottom surface. Then, make a copy at the height of the object. Finally, connect the upper and lower corners with lines. The filters can be used with the **COPY** command, or by using grips to copy. From the plan view, step through the process in this manner:

```
Command: LINE↵
From point: 3,3↵
To point: @4,0↵
To point: (continue picking points to construct the box)
```

Next, copy the shape up to the height of 3 units.

```
Command: COPY↵
Select objects: (select the box using a window or crossing box)
Select objects: ↵
⟨Base point or displacement⟩/Multiple: (pick a corner of the box)
Second point of displacement: .XY↵
of (pick the same corner)
(need Z): 3↵
Command:
```

Since the shape is copied straight up, the top surface of the cube has the same XY values as the bottom surface. That is why .XY was entered as the second point of displacement. This filter picks up the XY values of the previous point specified and applies them to the location of the new copy. Now, all AutoCAD needs is the Z value, which it requests.

Check your progress by looking at the object using the **VPOINT** command. Enter the coordinates given below. Your display should look like that in Figure 27-16.

Command: **VPOINT**↵
Rotate/⟨View point⟩/⟨*current*⟩: **1,–2,.5**↵
Regenerating drawing.
Command:

Finish the object in the pictorial view using the **LINE** command and object snaps. Your drawing should look like Figure 27-17.

Figure 27-16.
A partially constructed box using the **LINE** command and filters.

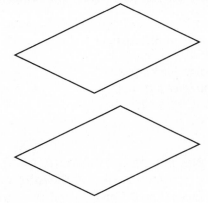

Figure 27-17.
A completed box using the **LINE** command.

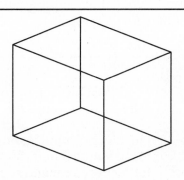

EXERCISE 27-3

❑ Set the grid spacing at .5, snap spacing at .25, and elevation at 0.
❑ Draw the object below to the dimensions indicated.
❑ Use the **LINE** and **COPY** commands to construct the object.
❑ Construct the top and bottom planes in the plan view. Connect the vertical lines in a 3D view.
❑ Save the drawing as EX27-3.

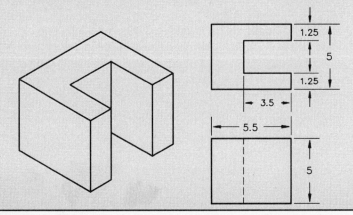

3DFACE
3F

Draw
➥ Surfaces
➥ 3D Face

Surfaces
toolbar

3D Face

Constructing 3D faces

Surfaces that appear solid are called *3D faces*. They can be made with the **3DFACE** command. Its prompt structure is similar to that of the **SOLID** command, but you can specify points in either a clockwise or counterclockwise manner. A 3D face must have at least three corners, but cannot have any more than four corners. To access the **3DFACE** command, enter 3F or 3DFACE at the Command: prompt, pick the **3D Face** button in the **Surfaces** toolbar, or pick **3D Face** from the **Surfaces** cascading menu in the **Draw** pull-down menu.

Draw the familiar box again, beginning with the bottom face, with the elevation set at 0. Then draw the top face. Draw the bottom face using the following command sequence:

    Command: **3F** *or* **3DFACE**⏎
    First point: *(pick a point)*
    Second point: *(pick a point)*
    Third point: *(pick a point)*
    Fourth point: *(pick a point)*
    Third point: ⏎
    Command:

Notice that after you placed the fourth point, a line automatically connected it to the first point. A prompt then asks for the third point again if you want to continue to draw additional faces. Press [Enter] to end the command.

The 3D face can be copied using the similar steps taken to copy the line surface. Remember to use filters for copying.

PROFESSIONAL TIP

When moving or copying objects in 3D space, it can simplify matters to use the displacement option to specify positioning data. This allows you to specify the X, Y, and Z movement simultaneously. For example, to copy the 3D face to a position 3 units above the original on the Z axis, use the following command sequence:

    Command: **COPY**⏎
    Select objects: *(pick the 3D face)*
    Select objects: ⏎
    ⟨Base point or displacement⟩/Multiple: **0,0,3.**⏎
    ⟨Second point of displacement⟩: ⏎

Because [Enter] was pressed at the Second point of displacement: prompt, the X,Y,Z values entered are used as a relative displacement instead of a base point. In this example, the object is copied to a position that differs from the original by 0 on the X axis, 0 on the Y axis, and +3 on the Z axis. To move an object +1 on the X, –4 on the Y, and +2 on the Z axis, the displacement value would be 1,–4,2.

Finally, the four sides of the box are drawn. First, set a viewpoint to display both 3D faces:

    Command: **VPOINT.**⏎
    Rotate/⟨View point⟩/⟨*current*⟩: **–1,–1,.75.**⏎
    Command:

The drawing should look like Figure 27-18. Zoom in if the view is too small. Complete the box using the **3DFACE** command and pick the points as numbered in Figure 27-18.

> Command: **3F** *or* **3DFACE**↵
> First point: *(pick point 1)*
> Second point: *(pick point 2)*
> Third point: *(pick point 3)*
> Fourth point: *(pick point 4)*
> Third point: ↵
> Command:

The first face is complete. Now draw the remaining faces in the same manner. The finished box should appear similar to that in Figure 27-19.

How does a 3D face object differ from ones drawn using the **ELEV** and **LINE** commands? For comparison, Figure 27-20 shows boxes drawn using the **ELEV**, **LINE**, and **3DFACE** commands with hidden lines removed by **HIDE**.

Figure 27-18. Top and bottom 3D faces of a box. The numbers indicate the order to pick points when using the **3DFACE** command to draw the sides.

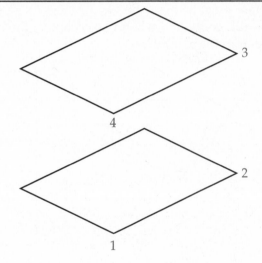

Figure 27-19. A completed **3DFACE** appears to be a wireframe construction before using **HIDE**.

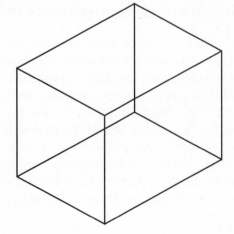

Figure 27-20.
Comparison of boxes drawn with **ELEV**, **LINE**, and **3DFACE** after **HIDE** command is selected.

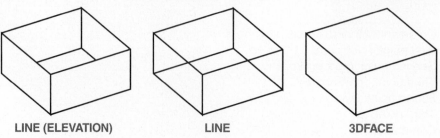

LINE (ELEVATION)   LINE   3DFACE

EXERCISE 27-4

❑ Set the grid spacing at .5, snap spacing at .25, and elevation at 0.
❑ Use the **3DFACE** command to construct the object to the dimensions given.
❑ Draw the bottom, two end faces, and the two top angled surfaces in the plan view. Draw the front and rear V-shaped surfaces in a 3D view. Each V-shaped end surface must be made of two 3D faces.
❑ Use the **HIDE** command when you complete the object.
❑ Save the drawing as EX27-4.

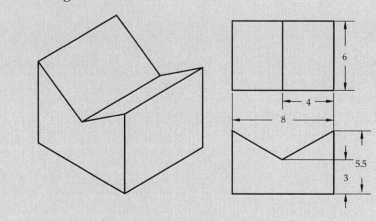

Constructing 3D Surface Modeled Objects

3D

Draw
➥ Surfaces
➥ 3D Surfaces

AutoCAD provides several predrawn 3D objects. These can be quickly placed in your drawing by providing a location and basic dimensions. Many of these 3D objects can be selected from the **Surfaces** toolbar. They can also be selected from the **3D Objects** dialog box, which is accessed by selecting **3D Surfaces...** from the **Surfaces** cascading menu of the **Draw** pull-down menu. See Figure 27-21.

Notice the list box to the left of the dialog box. These are the names of all the objects shown. An object can be selected by picking either the name or the image. When selected, the image and the name are highlighted.

The **3D** command can also be accessed by typing 3D at the Command: prompt. The available objects are then listed at the following prompt:

    Command: **3D**↵
    Box/Cone/DIsh/DOme/Mesh/Pyramid/Sphere/Torus/Wedge: (select the desired object)

Figure 27-21.
A—The **3D Objects** dialog box displays a group of 3D surface modeled objects. B—The same objects can be drawn using **Surfaces** toolbar.

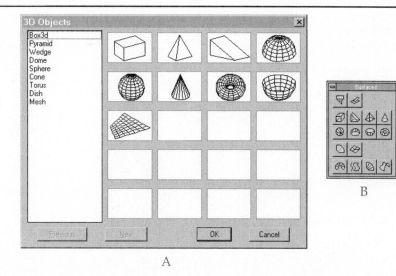

Regardless how a 3D object is selected, the first prompt requests a location point for the object. The remaining prompts request sizes in the form of length, width, height, diameter, radius, or number of longitudinal and latitudinal segments. For example, select **Dome** and the command sequence is as follows:

> Command: **3D**↵
> Box/Cone/DIsh/DOme/Mesh/Pyramid/Sphere/Torus/Wedge: **DO**↵
> Center of dome: *(pick a point)*
> Diameter/⟨radius⟩: *(enter a radius or pick on the screen)*
> Number of longitudinal segments ⟨16⟩: ↵
> Number of latitudinal segments ⟨8⟩: ↵

The object is drawn in the plan view, as shown in Figure 27-22A. Use the **VPOINT** command to produce a 3D view of the object, and use **HIDE** to remove hidden lines. The illustration in Figure 27-22B provides an explanation of longitudinal and latitudinal segments. Longitudinal refers to an east-west measurement, and latitudinal means north-south.

Figure 27-22.
A—The plan view of a dome. B—Longitudinal segments are measured east-west, and latitudinal segments are measured north-south.

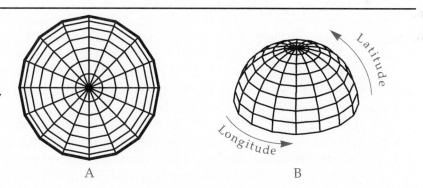

The group of objects provided in the **3D Objects** dialog box are easy to draw and fun to work with. Remember that if the current display is a plan view and you draw 3D objects, you must use the **VPOINT** command in order to see a 3D view. The illustrations in Figure 27-23 show all of the dimensions required to construct the pre-drawn 3D objects provided by AutoCAD.

Figure 27-23.
These dimensions are required to draw AutoCAD's surfaced objects.

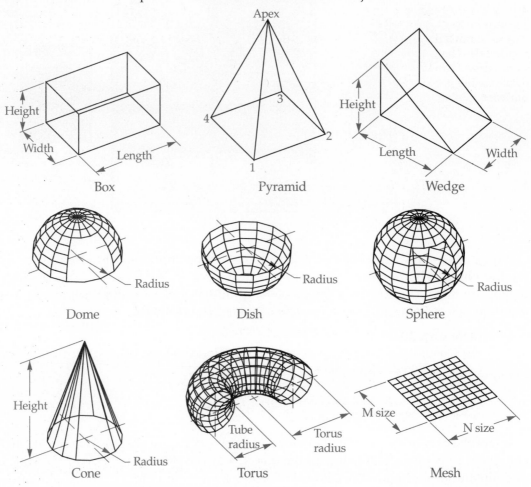

Introduction to Engineering Layouts

The **MVSETUP** command can be used to create a paper space layout of four floating model space viewports of any 3D model. The standard engineering drawing views top, front, and right side are automatically created. In addition, a pictorial view is placed in the upper right corner. This view appears in isometric format.

MVSETUP is actually an AutoLISP routine that provides you with a variety of useful options for constructing paper space layouts. The use of **MVSETUP** with 2D drawing layout was discussed in Chapter 10.

When **MVSETUP** is used to create a standard engineering layout from a 3D model, a step-by-step procedure must be followed in order to achieve properly aligned views. The following list is a general outline of the required steps. It is assumed that the 3D model has already been constructed in model space.

1. Use **MVSETUP** options to establish drawing limits and layers. Create a paper space border and title block layout with the **Title block** option.
2. Establish paper space viewports with the **Create** option of **MVSETUP** using the **Standard Engineering** option.
3. The **Scale** and **Align** options must be used to adjust the size and placement of each view within its viewport.
4. Complete the views by adding dimensions and notes, and revise any solid lines that should appear as hidden lines.

A detailed discussion of **MVSETUP** and the creation of a standard engineering drawing layout is provided in *AutoCAD and its Applications—Advanced, Release 14*.

Chapter Test

Write your answers in the spaces provided.

1. When looking at the screen, in which direction does the Z coordinate project? __

2. Which command allows you to give objects thickness?_____

3. If you draw a line after setting a thickness, what have you actually drawn?_____

4. What is the purpose of the right-hand rule? _____

5. According to the right-hand rule, name the coordinate axes represented by the following fingers:
   A. Thumb— _____
   B. Middle finger—_____
   C. Index finger— _____

6. What is the purpose of the **VPOINT** command?_____

7. When the **VPOINT** command's tripod is displayed, what do the concentric circles in the upper right represent? _____

8. How are you viewing an object when the little crosshairs are inside the small circle in the **VPOINT** command display? _____

9. How do you create 3D extruded text? _____

10. What is the function of the **HIDE** command? _____

11. Define "point filters." _____

12. How do you select one of AutoCAD's predrawn 3D shapes? _____

Drawing Problems

1. Draw Problem 9 from Chapter 26 using the **ELEV** command. Display the object in two different views. Use **HIDE** on one view. Save the drawing as P27-1.

2. Draw the object shown below using the **ELEV** command. Display the object in two different views. Use **HIDE** on one view. Save the drawing as P27-2.

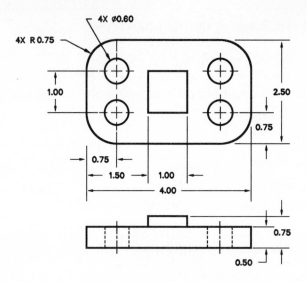

3. Choose Problem 4, 5, or 6 from Chapter 26 and draw it as a wireframe using the **LINE** command. Display the drawing with **VPOINT** in four different views. Save the drawing as P27-3.

4. Open drawing P27-3. Use the **3DFACE** command to create faces on the entire part. Display the part in four different views. Save the revised drawing as P27-4.

*For Problems 5-7, draw the objects in 3D form. Use the **LINE** and **3DFACE** commands. Can you create 3D blocks for use in these drawings? Display the drawings from three different viewpoints. Select the **HIDE** command for one of the views. Save the drawings as **P27-5**, **P27-6**, and **P27-7**.*

5.

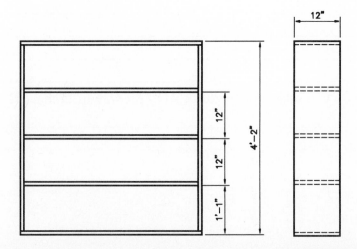

6.

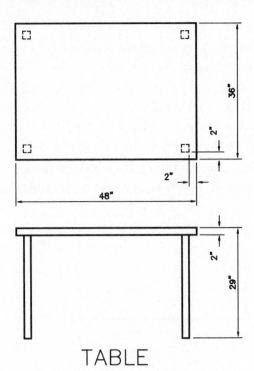

TABLE

7.

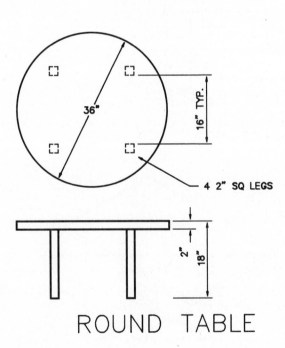

ROUND TABLE

8. Construct a 3D model of the table shown.

   A. Use any 3D construction techniques required.

   B. Use the dimensions given.

   C. Alter the design of the table to include rounded table top corners or rounded feet. Try replacing the rectangular feet shown with spheres.

   D. Use the **DVIEW** command to display the model.

   E. Use the **HIDE** command to remove hidden lines.

   F. Plot the table both in wireframe and with hidden lines removed.

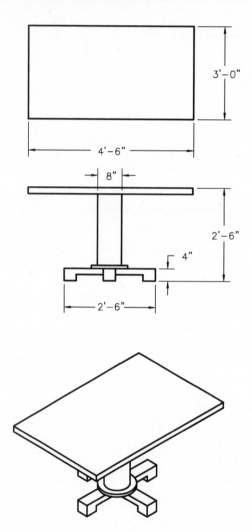

External Commands, Script Files, and Slide Shows

Learning Objectives

After completing this chapter, you will be able to:
- ○ Edit the acad.pgp file.
- ○ Use a text editor to create script files.
- ○ Create a continuous slide show of existing drawings.
- ○ Use the **SLIDELIB** command to create a slide library.

This chapter introduces you to the use of scripts. A *script* is a series of commands and variables listed in a text file. When the script file is activated by AutoCAD, the entire list of commands is performed without additional input from the user. One useful script is a continuous slide show. It is excellent for client presentations, demonstrations, and grading drawings.

Word processing or text editor programs can be used to write scripts. There are three tools available under the Windows 95 and NT operating systems for writing ASCII (American Standard Code for Information Interchange) text files: the MS-DOS EDIT text editor, Windows Notepad, and Windows WordPad.

Using Text Editors

The more experienced you become with AutoCAD, the more you will want to alter the program to suit your specific needs. Most of these alterations are done with a text editor program. While the Windows-supplied Notepad editor is quite capable of performing many of the text editing tasks appropriate for AutoCAD, it cannot accommodate files that exceed 50K (50,000 bytes) in size. However, Notepad, along with MS-DOS EDIT, are satisfactory for creating simple text files.

Word processors

Many AutoCAD users rely on full-fledged word processing programs to create their text files. These word processing files should be saved in ASCII format so they are readable by AutoCAD. There are dozens of word processing programs commercially available. The Windows WordPad program is a word processor that is included with Microsoft Windows. Like Notepad, WordPad may be accessed by picking Accessories in the Program menu, Figure 28-1.

Figure 28-1.
Both the Notepad text editor and Windows WordPad word processor can be accessed from the Accessories menu.

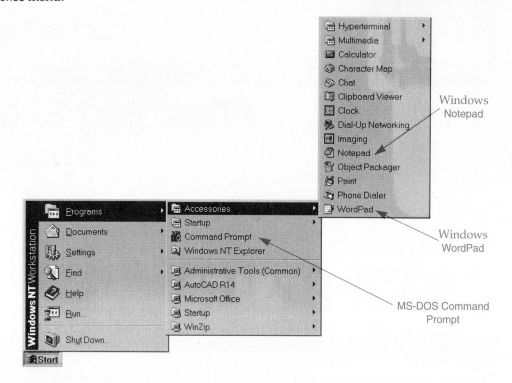

Other Windows-compatible programs you might be familiar with include Ami Pro, WordPerfect, and Microsoft Word. All are excellent tools for producing written documentation, but exceed what is needed to create text files for AutoCAD. If you choose to use a word processor, save the document as a text file. This prevents the inclusion of special formatting codes.

Programmer's text editors

The best type of text editor, however, is a programmer's editor. There are a wide variety of inexpensive yet powerful text editors. These programs are designed for creating the type of file needed to customize AutoCAD. The Norton Editor is one example of an excellent programmer's editor.

Programmer's editors are recommended over word processors because of their design, size, function, ease of use, and price. The MS-DOS EDIT text editor is excellent for many of the custom files you will write for AutoCAD.

PROFESSIONAL TIP
When working in Windows, use the Notepad to create or edit text files smaller than 50,000 bytes. If the file you are working with exceeds this size, use the EDIT text editor.

External Commands—The MS-DOS Prompt

One of the greatest advantages in using Microsoft Windows is the ability to have an application open in one window, while working in another window. This capability allows you to edit a text file with Notepad (or another Windows-based text editor) without exiting AutoCAD. Since many of the text files you create will be designed while running AutoCAD, this is a particularly handy feature.

AutoCAD and its Applications—Basics

However, there are times when it may be convenient to run a non-Windows application without exiting AutoCAD. This capability is provided with the Windows application called MS-DOS Command Prompt. You can access MS-DOS Command Prompt in the Programs menu, Figure 28-1. This selection opens the Command Prompt window, Figure 28-2.

Figure 28-2.
Pressing [Alt]+[Enter] toggles Command Prompt between a window and a full-screen display.

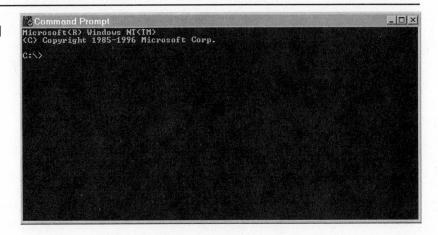

Even though MS-DOS Command Prompt is a Windows application, you may now issue a DOS command or run a non-Windows application at the DOS prompt. You can verify for yourself that MS-DOS Command Prompt is a Windows application by pressing the [Alt]+[Tab] key combination to activate the Windows Task List, Figure 28-3. Also, observe that MS-DOS Command Prompt exits to the C:\ directory. If necessary, change to the appropriate directory or drive to run your application. You have the option to display the DOS prompt in a window by pressing [Alt]+[Enter].

Figure 28-3.
As with other open Windows applications, the MS-DOS Command Prompt appears in the Windows Task List box.

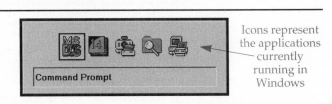

Icons represent the applications currently running in Windows

You can leave the Command Prompt window open or minimize it for later use. By pressing the [Alt]+[Tab] key combination, you can switch back to the Windows application you were running before you invoked MS-DOS Command Prompt. This action does not close MS-DOS Command Prompt. When you are ready to exit MS-DOS Command Prompt, simply type EXIT and press [Enter] or pick the close button.

AutoCAD Custom Guide **1**

External Commands–The ACAD.PGP File

External commands invoke functions that are not part of AutoCAD. Each of these external commands are defined in a file called acad.pgp (program parameters). This file is placed in the AutoCAD R14\Support folder during the AutoCAD installation procedure. A portion of the acad.pgp file is shown in the Notepad in Figure 28-4.

Figure 28-4.
The acad.pgp file opened in Notepad.

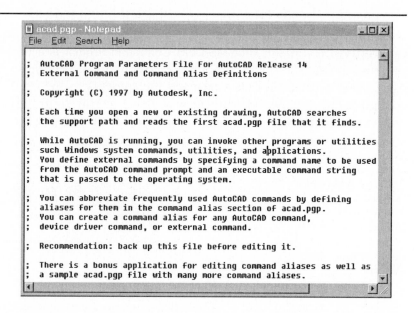

```
; AutoCAD Program Parameters File For AutoCAD Release 14
; External Command and Command Alias Definitions

; Copyright (C) 1997 by Autodesk, Inc.

; Each time you open a new or existing drawing, AutoCAD searches
; the support path and reads the first acad.pgp file that it finds.

; While AutoCAD is running, you can invoke other programs or utilities
; such Windows system commands, utilities, and applications.
; You define external commands by specifying a command name to be used
; from the AutoCAD command prompt and an executable command string
; that is passed to the operating system.

; You can abbreviate frequently used AutoCAD commands by defining
; aliases for them in the command alias section of acad.pgp.
; You can create a command alias for any AutoCAD command,
; device driver command, or external command.

; Recommendation: back up this file before editing it.

; There is a bonus application for editing command aliases as well as
; a sample acad.pgp file with many more command aliases.
```

The Windows Notepad can be initiated directly from AutoCAD. Enter the following to open acad.pgp in Notepad:

Command: **NOTEPAD.**↵
File to edit: **\AUTOCAD R14\SUPPORT\ACAD.PGP**↵

The directory folder path of AutoCAD R14\Support is the default name location used when AutoCAD is installed. If the name of the AutoCAD directory was changed, be sure to enter the correct directory name at the prompt above. The Windows Notepad is then opened and the acad.pgp file is displayed.

NOTE
You can also display any text file in a DOS shell window by using the **TYPE** external command as follows:

Command: **TYPE**↵
File to list: **\AUTOCAD R14\SUPPORT\ACAD.PGP | MORE**↵

This lists the contents of a text file one page at a time in the DOS window. You cannot edit the file. Press any key to view the next page. Press [Ctrl]+[C] to cancel the display and return to AutoCAD.

AutoCAD contains 11 external commands in the acad.pgp file, beginning with **CATALOG**. See Figure 28-5. The first word on each line is the command name that should be typed at AutoCAD's Command: prompt to execute the external command. The second word represents the DOS command or program to be executed. Notice that typing EDIT at the Command: prompt runs the MS-DOS EDIT text editor. Each field in the EDIT entry is separated by a comma and is defined as follows:

- **EDIT.** The command typed at the AutoCAD Command: prompt.
- **START EDIT.** The command or program name executed after the external command name is typed. This is the name that would normally be entered at the DOS prompt or Windows command line to run the text editor. Instructions on how to edit the acad.pgp file for purposes of running your favorite text editor are provided later in this chapter.
- **1.** This bit flag value specifies the way the program starts. This value begins the application but does not wait for it to finish. Other settings can be used to wait for the application to finish or to minimize the application.
- **File to edit:.** This is the prompt that appears after the command is typed.

Figure 28-5.
The external commands are defined in the acad.pgp file.

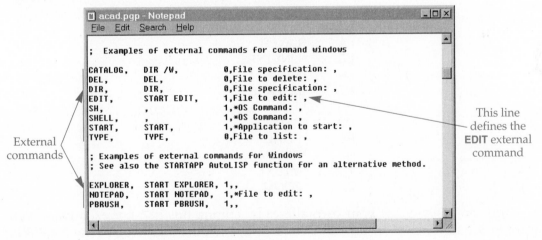

The **SH** and **SHELL** commands

The **SH** and **SHELL** entries in the acad.pgp file perform a function similar to the MS-DOS Command Prompt application discussed earlier in this chapter. When you enter SH or SHELL on the AutoCAD command line, the following prompt appears:

OS Command: *(enter an external command or press* [Enter]*)*

You may enter only one external command at the OS Command: prompt. When the command is completed, you are automatically returned to the AutoCAD graphics window. If you press [Enter] at the OS Command: prompt, you are presented with the DOS prompt in an MS-DOS shell window. Thus, pressing [Enter] performs much the same function as MS-DOS Command Prompt. As with MS-DOS Command Prompt, when you are ready to exit the AutoCAD shell, type EXIT and press [Enter].

PROFESSIONAL TIP

The **SH** or **SHELL** command is a handy way to delete a file or do a directory listing from within AutoCAD. If you choose to perform a directory listing, use the command form DIR/P to scroll the directory one page at a time. As with MS-DOS Command Prompt, be careful using certain DOS commands, and exit Windows before using any hard disk utility programs.

Command aliases

AutoCAD allows you to abbreviate command names. This feature was introduced with AutoCAD Release 11 and is called *command aliasing*. A list of predefined aliases furnished with AutoCAD can be displayed by viewing the contents of the acad.pgp file. You can do this by using the **TYPE** command as explained earlier in this chapter, or by loading the file into Notepad or another text editor. Scroll down past the list of external commands and you will see the list of command aliases. This is an extensive list containing over 160 aliases. An example of some command aliases is provided here. See Appendix F for the complete listing.

```
A,      *ARC
C,      *CIRCLE
CO,     *COPY
DV,     *DVIEW
E,      *ERASE
L,      *LINE
LA,     *LAYER
LT,     *LINETYPE
M,      *MOVE
MS,     *MSPACE
P,      *PAN
PS,     *PSPACE
PL,     *PLINE
R,      *REDRAW
T,      *MTEXT
Z,      *ZOOM
```

You can easily create your own aliases by editing this file. For example, if you want to add an alias **PP** for the **PLOT** command, enter the following below the **PLINE** command in the acad.pgp file:

```
PP,     *PLOT
```

Be sure to include the asterisk since it indicates to AutoCAD that this is an alias. Save the Notepad file. The revised .pgp file will not work until you open a new drawing, which reloads the acad.pgp file. You can also reload the acad.pgp file by entering the **REINIT** command. This displays the **Re-initialization** dialog box shown in Figure 28-6. Pick the **PGP File** check box in this dialog box, and then pick **OK** to re-initialize the acad.pgp file so that your new command alias will work.

AutoCAD and its Applications—Basics

Figure 28-6.
The **Re-initialization**
dialog box.

Check to reload the
acad.pgp file

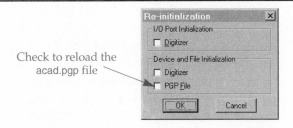

NOTE   The **Re-initialization** dialog box can also be used if you have one of your serial ports, such as COM1, configured for both a plotter and a digitizer. If you change the cable from plotter to digitizer, pick the **Digitizer** check boxes in both areas of the dialog box to reinitiate the digitizer.

Editing the ACAD.PGP file

There are several tools available to edit the acad.pgp file. The Windows Notepad, DOS EDIT, or another text editor may be used. Probably the easiest editing method is with the Windows Notepad.

PROFESSIONAL TIP   Always make backup copies of AutoCAD text files before editing them. Should you "corrupt" one of these files through incorrect editing techniques, simply delete that file and restore the original.

The DOS editor is executed by the acad.pgp file when EDIT is entered at the AutoCAD Command: prompt. The EDIT program is easy to use and efficient. This is because EDIT, like Notepad, is a full-screen editor that allows you to move the text cursor around the screen easily.

The acad.pgp file can be easily altered to specify your personal text editor instead of EDIT. For this example, we will use an editor called TE. If you are currently running AutoCAD, use the **NOTEPAD** external command to open the acad.pgp file in Windows Notepad.

        Command: **NOTEPAD**↵
        File to edit: **\AUTOCAD R14\SUPPORT\ACAD.PGP**↵

The acad.pgp file is displayed in Notepad. You may use any of the text editing keys to move the flashing text cursor around the screen. These keys include the left, right, up, and down arrows, as well as the [Home], [Page Up], [Page Down], [Insert], [Delete], and [End] keys. You can also move the text cursor with your pointing device. Use the down arrow key or your pointing device to move the text cursor to the line labeled

        EDIT,   START EDIT,   1,File to edit: ,

Remove the word EDIT in both places using the [Backspace] or [Delete] keys, and replace it with the word TE. When you are done, the acad.pgp file should appear as shown in Figure 28-7. Entering TE at the AutoCAD Command: prompt now initiates the text editor TE.

To save the edited file, activate the pull-down menus at the top of the screen. Select Save from the File pull-down menu, Figure 28-8.

Figure 28-7.
The word EDIT is replaced with TE to specify a different external text editor.

Name of text editor

Typed at Command: prompt

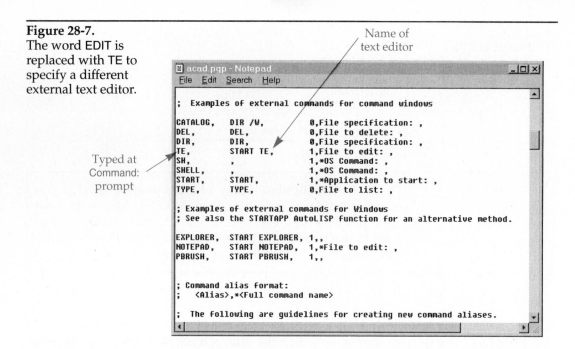

```
; Examples of external commands for command windows

CATALOG,    DIR /W,        0,File specification: ,
DEL,        DEL,           0,File to delete: ,
DIR,        DIR,           0,File specification: ,
TE,         START TE,      1,File to edit: ,
SH,         ,              1,*OS Command: ,
SHELL,      ,              1,*OS Command: ,
START,      START,         1,*Application to start: ,
TYPE,       TYPE,          0,File to list: ,

; Examples of external commands for Windows
; See also the STARTAPP AutoLISP function for an alternative method.

EXPLORER,   START EXPLORER, 1,,
NOTEPAD,    START NOTEPAD,  1,*File to edit: ,
PBRUSH,     START PBRUSH,   1,,

; Command alias format:
;    <Alias>,*<Full command name>

;  The following are guidelines for creating new command aliases.
```

Figure 28-8.
Select **Save** from the **File** pull-down menu to save the edited acad.pgp file.

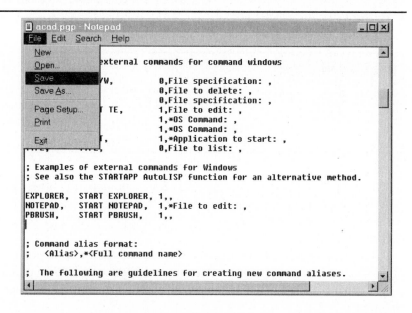

```
File  Edit  Search  Help
New
Open...          external commands for command windows
Save        /W,        0,File specification: ,
Save As...             0,File to delete: ,
                       0,File specification: ,
Page Setup...  TE,     1,File to edit: ,
Print                  1,*OS Command: ,
                       1,*OS Command: ,
Exit        ,          1,*Application to start: ,
                       0,File to list: ,

; Examples of external commands for Windows
; See also the STARTAPP AutoLISP function for an alternative method.

EXPLORER,   START EXPLORER, 1,,
NOTEPAD,    START NOTEPAD,  1,*File to edit: ,
PBRUSH,     START PBRUSH,   1,,

; Command alias format:
;    <Alias>,*<Full command name>

;  The following are guidelines for creating new command aliases.
```

To return to AutoCAD press [Alt]+[Tab] to display the Task List, then tab through the icons to highlight AutoCAD and release the [Alt] key.

If you try using the new text editor command in AutoCAD now, it will not work. This is because AutoCAD is still using the original version of the acad.pgp file. You must re-initialize the .pgp file with the **REINIT** command before the **TE** command can function properly.

PROFESSIONAL TIP

Command aliases can be added to or deleted from the acad.pgp file using the **acad.pgp–AutoCAD Alias Editor** dialog box. This is a bonus tool and is available only if a full installation was performed.

Creating Script Files to Automate AutoCAD

A *script file* is a list of commands that AutoCAD executes in sequence without input from the user. Scripts enable nonprogrammers to automate AutoCAD functions. Scripts can be used for specific functions, such as plotting a drawing with the correct **PLOT** command values and settings, or creating a slide show. A good working knowledge of AutoCAD commands is needed before you can confidently create a script file.

When writing a script file, use one command or option per line in the text file. This makes the file easier to fix if the script does not work properly. A return is specified by pressing [Enter] after typing a command. If the next option of a command is a default value to be accepted, press [Enter] again. This leaves a blank line in the script file, which represents pressing [Enter].

The following example shows how a script file can be used to plot a drawing. At your computer, enter these files with Notepad, EDIT, or another text editor. The file extension of the script name must be .scr. Also, place the file in the AutoCAD R14 folder. This occurs automatically if you enter EDIT at the Command: prompt to run the text editor.

Creating a plotting script

In Chapter 10, you learned that you can save plotter settings for a specific drawing in the form of a .pcp file. This eliminates setting all of the plot values each time you plot the same drawing. You can automate this process by including all of the plot values in a script file. If you have drawings that will always be plotted with the same settings, use script files to plot them.

PROFESSIONAL TIP
If a script file is used in the manner discussed here, you can simply execute the script file, then continue your work without having to go through the **Print/Plot Configuration** dialog box.

CAUTION
A single incorrect entry in a script file can cause it to malfunction. Test the keystrokes at the keyboard as you write the script file and record them for future reference. When writing a script for plotting purposes, this is an important step. Plotters and printers have different settings, and thus have different prompts in the **PLOT** command. Always step through the **PLOT** command and specify the plotter or printer you wish to use before writing the script file.

The following script file plots a C-size drawing. The contents of the script file are shown in the left column, and a description of each line is given to the right. This script file is named arch24-c.scr. The "arch" indicates an architectural drawing, the "24" is the scale factor, and "c" is the paper size.

cmddia	(executes **CMDDIA** system variable)
0	(disables the **Plot Configuration** dialog box)
plot	(executes **PLOT** command)
E	(what to plot—extents)
Y	(Y to change plot settings)
Y	(Y to change plotters)
3	(description =3 for HP DraftPro)
E	(what to plot—extents)
Y	(Y to change plot settings)
N	(N to not change plotters)
60	(number of seconds to wait for plotter port)
Y	(Y to request hard clip limits)
Y	(Y to change plot parameters)
C1	(specify color number 1)
1	(pen 1 for color 1)
0	(linetype 0 for color 1)
15	(pen speed for color 1)
0.010	(pen width for color 1)
C2	(specify color 2)
2	(pen 2 for color 2)
0	(linetype 0 for color 2)
15	(pen speed for color 2)
0.010	(pen width for color 2)
C3	(specify color 3)
3	(pen 3 for color 3)
0	(linetype 0 for color 3)
15	(pen speed for color 3)
0.010	(pen width for color 3)
C4	(specify color 4)
4	(pen 4 for color 4)
0	(linetype 0 for color 4)
15	(pen speed for color 4)
0.010	(pen width for color 4)
X	(exit parameter settings)
N	(do not write plot file)
I	(size units in inches)
0,0	(plot origin)
C	(paper size)
0	(plot rotation angle)
N	(do not adjust for pen width)
N	(do not remove hidden lines)
1=24	(drawing scale)

PROFESSIONAL TIP

Avoid pressing the space bar at the end of a line in the script file. This adds a space, and can cause the script to crash. Plus, finding spaces in a script file can be tedious work.

To run the script, select **Run Script...** from the **Tools** pull-down menu or type SCR or SCRIPT at the Command: prompt and then select the file name arch24-c.scr from the **Select Script File** dialog box. See Figure 28-9. Then sit back and watch the script run.

SCRIPT
SCR

Tools
  ↳ Run Script...

Figure 28-9.
The **Select Script File** dialog box.

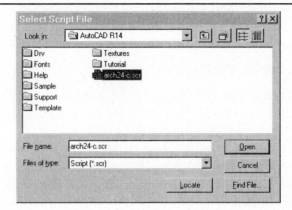

All the commands, options, and text screens associated with the commands in the script are displayed in rapid succession on the screen. If the script stops before completion, a problem has occurred. Flip the screen to the text window ([F2]) to determine the last command executed. Return to your text editor and correct the problem. Most often, there are too many or too few returns. Another problem is spaces at the end of a line. If you suspect these errors, retype the line.

EXERCISE 28-2

❑ Use one of your templates and create a new drawing named scrptest.
❑ Use the **DTEXT** command to write your name in the lower-right corner.
❑ Save the drawing, but do not exit AutoCAD.
❑ Use Notepad or DOS EDIT and write a script file named test.scr. The script file should do the following:
  ❑ Draw a circle at coordinates 4,4 with a radius of 1.
  ❑ Change the current color to green.
  ❑ Draw a doughnut centered on the circle with an inside diameter of 2.5 and an outside diameter of 2.8.
❑ Switch back to AutoCAD and use the **SCRIPT** command to run test.scr.
❑ If the script file does not run to completion, use Notepad to correct it. Run the script file again until it works.

Slides and Slide Shows

AutoCAD Custom Guide 6

A *slide* in AutoCAD, similar to a slide in photography, is a snapshot of the graphics screen display. Because of its nature, it cannot be edited or plotted. Slides can be viewed one at a time or as a continuous show. This is why slides are excellent for demonstrations, presentations, displays, and grading procedures.

Students and prospective employees can create an impressive portfolio using a slide show. A *slide show* is a group of slides that are displayed at preset intervals. The slide show is controlled by a script file—a list of commands similar to the previous script examples. Each slide is displayed for a specific length of time. The show can be continuous or a single pass.

Making and viewing slides

Creating slides is easy. First display the drawing for which you need a slide. You might display the entire drawing or zoom to a specific area or feature. AutoCAD creates a slide of the current screen display. Make as many slides of one drawing as you want. For each, select the **MSLIDE** command and provide a file name for the slide. Do not enter a file type, as AutoCAD automatically attaches an .sld file extension. If **FILEDIA** is set to 1, a dialog box appears. Use **MSLIDE** at the Command: prompt as follows:

> Command: **MSLIDE.**⏎

The **Create Slide File** dialog box is displayed. This is the standard file dialog box. Pick the drive and folder in which the file is to be stored, enter the name in the **File name:** text box, and pick the **Save** button.

Slide names should follow a pattern. Suppose you are making slides for a class called cad1. File names such as cad1sld1 and cad1sld2 are appropriate. If working on project #4305 for the Weyerhauser Company, you might name the slide to reflect the client name or project number, such as weyersl1 or 4305sld1.

PROFESSIONAL TIP

To create a slide file at the highest resolution, set **VIEWRES** to its maximum value of 20000 and execute a regeneration before using the **MSLIDE** command. After making the slide, restore **VIEWRES** to its previous value.

Viewing a slide is as simple as making one. Type VSLIDE at the Command: prompt to initiate the **VSLIDE** command.

> Command: **VSLIDE.**⏎

The **Select Slide File** dialog box appears. Pick the slide you want to display and pick **OK**. The slide is displayed in the graphics window.

PROFESSIONAL TIP

Keep the AutoCAD R14 directory free of drawing, slides, and AutoLISP files. This speeds the computer's access to AutoCAD files. Create a separate folder for slides or save slides on a floppy disk. If using floppy disks, be sure to give the appropriate file name when creating slides. A file name of A:cad1sld1 is entered to place a slide on a floppy disk in the A: disk drive.

EXERCISE 28-3

❑ Load any one of your drawings into the drawing editor.
❑ Create a slide of the entire drawing, using an appropriate file name.
❑ Make slides of two more drawings. Use similar naming techniques.
❑ View each of the slides as they are created.
❑ These slides are required to complete the next exercise.

Writing a slide show script file

A slide show script file contains only two or three commands. This depends on whether it is a single pass or continuous show. A slide show script file typically by contains the following commands:

- **VSLIDE.** This command is used to display a slide. The name of the slide follows the command. If the slide name is preceded by an asterisk (*), the slide is pre-loaded and displayed at the following **VSLIDE** command. This second command is not followed by a slide name, since the slide is already preloaded.
- **RSCRIPT.** This command is used at the end of a continuous script file. It causes the script to repeat.
- **DELAY.** Any slide file can be displayed for up to approximately 33 seconds using this command. Delays are given in milliseconds. A delay of four seconds is written as DELAY 4000.

A slide show begins with the creation of a script file using a text editor. The following script uses four slides. Each appears for three seconds and the script repeats. Notice that the next slide is preloaded while the previous one is viewed.

The show.scr script file is shown as it would be entered in the Windows Notepad, Figure 28-10. Also, do not forget that when using slide files on diskettes, include the disk drive letter and path in front of the file name, such as A:cad1sld2. Use this method with each **VSLIDE** command.

Figure 28-10.
The show.scr script file as it appears in the Windows Notepad.

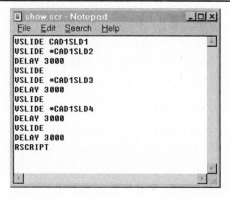

Viewing the slide show

The slide show is started by entering SCR or SCRIPT at the Command: prompt or by picking **Run Script...** from the **Tools** pull-down menu. Select the script file name show.scr from the **Select Script File** dialog box.

The show begins and the commands in the script file are displayed at the Command: prompt as the slides appear. To stop the show, press the [Backspace] key. You can then work on a drawing, use DOS commands, or work with a text editor on another script file. When finished, resume the slide show where it left off by typing RESUME. Any script file can be interrupted and restarted in this manner.

If your slide show encounters an error and fails to finish the first time through, do not panic. Take the following steps to "debug," or correct, problems in your script file.
1. Run the script to see where it crashes (quits working).
2. Check the command line for the last command that was executed.
3. Look for error messages, such as:
   - Can't open slide file *xxxxx* (Incorrect slide file name).
   - *xxxxx* Unknown command (Command spelled incorrectly or a space left at the end of the line).
   - Requires an integer value (Delay value not all numerical characters. Possibly a space at the end of the line).

4. Correct the problem in the script file and save the file.
5. Test the script.

The most common errors are misspelled commands and spaces at the end of lines. If you suspect there is a space at the end of a line, it is best to delete the line and retype it. If you use Notepad or EDIT, it is easy to see if a space exists. The flashing cursor, when placed at the end of a line, does not rest on the last character.

EXERCISE 28-4

❑ Create a script file named EX28-4. Use Notepad or your own text editor. It is not necessary to be in the AutoCAD drawing editor to create the script file.
❑ Include the three slides created in Exercise 28-3. If these slides have not been created, make slides of any three of your drawings.
❑ Delay each slide for two seconds.
❑ Make the show run continuously.
❑ Run the slide show. Correct any errors and run it again until it recycles without failing.

Creating and Using Slide Libraries

In addition to being displayed in slide shows, slide files are also used to create image tile menus. Image tile menus are groups of slides or vector images displayed in a dialog box. Examples are the geometric dimensioning and tolerancing symbols displayed after selecting **Tolerance...** in the **Dimensioning** pull-down menu. Constructing image tile menus is discussed in *AutoCAD and its Applications— Advanced, Release 14.*

Creating a slide library

To create a slide library, you must use a utility program called slidelib.exe, which operates from the DOS prompt. By default, the slidelib.exe utility program is installed in the AutoCAD R14\Support folder. Be sure to include this path when using the utility.

The slidelib.exe program can be used to create slide libraries in two ways. The first method involves listing the slides and their folder location after entering the **SLIDELIB** command. For example, suppose you have four slides of pipe fittings in the \Pipe subdirectory of the AutoCAD R14 folder. Compile these files in a slide library called PIPE in the following manner:

```
Command: SH↵
OS Command: SLIDELIB PIPE↵
SLIDELIB 1.2 (3/8/89)
(C) Copyright 1987-1989, 1994, 1995 Autodesk, Inc.
    All Rights Reserved
\AutoCAD R14\PIPE\90ELBOW↵
\AutoCAD R14\PIPE\45ELBOW↵
\AutoCAD R14\PIPE\TEE↵
\AutoCAD R14\PIPE\CAP↵
    ↵
    ↵
Command:
```

After entering the last slide, press [Enter] three times to end the **SLIDELIB** command. The new slide library file is saved as pipe.slb.

The second way to use **SLIDELIB** is to first create a list of the slides you will eventually want in the library. Do this with an ASCII text editor like Notepad or MS-DOS EDIT. This method allows you to accumulate slides over a period of time. Then, when you are ready to create the slide library, the list is prepared. For example, a list of those same pipe fittings is entered in a file called pipe.txt. The list appears in Notepad or EDIT as follows:

```
90ELBOW
45ELBOW
TEE
CAP
```

After completing the list of slides to include, use the **SLIDELIB** command. The **SLIDELIB** command needs to find the pipe.txt file and use it to create a slide library called pipe.slb. This can all be handled with one entry at the DOS prompt. First, you must shell out of AutoCAD for Windows:

```
Command: SH↵
OS Command: SLIDELIB PIPE ⟨ PIPE.TXT↵
SLIDELIB 1.2 (3/8/89)
(C) Copyright 1987-1989, 1994, 1995 Autodesk, Inc.
   All Rights Reserved
Command:
```

The screen flashes briefly and the AutoCAD graphic window is redisplayed. The less-than sign (⟨) instructs the **SLIDELIB** command to take input from the pipe.txt file to create a file called pipe.slb. To see the results, obtain a listing of all .slb files and look for pipe.slb.

Viewing slide library slides

The **VSLIDE** command also is used to view slides contained in a slide library. First change **FILEDIA** to 0. Then provide the library name plus the slide name in parentheses as follows:

```
Command: FILEDIA ↵
New value for FILEDIA ⟨1⟩: 0 ↵

Command: VSLIDE↵
Slide file: PIPE(90ELBOW)
```

Use the **REDRAW** command to remove the slide from the screen to display the previous drawing.

Making a slide show using the slide library

The advantage of using a slide library for a slide show is that you do not need to preload slides. A slide show of the four slides in the pipe.slb file would appear as follows:

```
VSLIDE PIPE(90ELBOW)
DELAY 1000
VSLIDE PIPE(45ELBOW)
DELAY 1000
VSLIDE PIPE(TEE)
DELAY 1000
VSLIDE PIPE(CAP)
DELAY 1000
REDRAW
```

The **REDRAW** command at the end of the slide show clears the screen and replaces the previous display. An **RSCRIPT** command instead of **REDRAW** repeats the show continuously.

Chapter Test

Write your answers in the spaces provided.

1. What precautions should you take when using a word processor to create text files for AutoCAD?_____

   _____

2. How do you activate Windows Notepad from the AutoCAD Command: prompt, and what is the name of the file that allows you to do it? _____

   _____

3. What is the maximum file size (in bytes) that can be handled by the Windows Notepad? _____

   _____

4. How do you open the MS-DOS Command Prompt? _____

   _____

5. What key combination is used to display the Windows Task List? _____

   _____

6. Name the two AutoCAD commands that perform a similar function to MS-DOS Prompt. _____

   _____

7. If you edit the acad.pgp file from within AutoCAD, what must you do for the new file definitions to take effect? _____

   _____

8. Describe external commands._____

   _____

9. Commands located in the acad.pgp file are executed by _____

   _____.

10. Name the parts of a command listing found in the acad.pgp file._____

    _____

    _____

11. What is a command alias, and how would you write one for the **POLYGON** command?_____

    _____

12. Define *script file.* _____

    _____

13. Why is it a good idea to put one command on each line of a script file?_____

    _____

14. List two common reasons why a script file might not work. _____

    _____

15. What two commands allow you to make and view slides?_____
_____

16. What file extension is assigned to slide files? _____

17. Explain why it is a good idea to keep slide files in a separate folder other than the AutoCAD R14 folder. _____
_____

18. List the three commands used when writing a slide show._____
_____
_____

19. To stop a slide show, press the _____ key.

20. How do you begin a slide show that has been stopped?_____
_____

21. Briefly explain the two methods used to create a **SLIDELIB** file._____
_____
_____

22. Suppose you want to view a slide named VIEW1, which is in a slide library file called VIEWS. How must you enter its name at the Slide file: prompt?
Slide file:_____

23. What is the principal difference between a slide show script file written for a slide library and one written for a group of slides? _____
_____

Problems

1. If you use a text editor or word processor other than MS-DOS EDIT or Notepad, create a new command in the acad.pgp file that loads the text editor.

2. Create a new command for the acad.pgp file that activates the Windows clock.

3. Write a script file called notes.scr that does the following:
   A. Executes the **TEXT** command.
   B. Selects the **Style** option.
   C. Enters a style name.
   D. Selects the last point using the "@" symbol.
   E. Enters a text height of .25.
   F. Enters a rotation angle of 0.
   G. Inserts the text: NOTES:.
   H. Selects the **TEXT** command again.
   I. Enters location coordinates for first note.
   J. Enters a text height of .125.
   K. Enters a rotation angle of 0.

L. Inserts the text: 1. INTERPRET DIMENSIONS AND TOLERANCES PER ANSI Y14.5.

M. Enters an [Enter] keystroke.

N. Inserts the text: 2. REMOVE ALL BURRS AND SHARP EDGES.

O. Enters [Enter] twice to exit the command.

Immediately before this script file is used, select the **ID** command and pick the point where you want the notes to begin. That point will be the "last point" used in the script file for the location of the word NOTES:. The script file, when executed, should draw the following:

NOTES:
1. INTERPRET DIMENSIONS AND TOLERANCES PER ASME Y14.5.
2. REMOVE ALL BURRS AND SHARP EDGES.

4. Create a slide show of your best AutoCAD drawings. This slide show should be considered as part of your portfolio for potential employers. Place all of the slides and the script file on a floppy disk. Make two copies of the portfolio disk on separate floppy disks. Keep the following guidelines in mind:

   A. Do not delay slides longer than 5 seconds. You can always press the [Backspace] key to view a slide longer.

   B. One view of a drawing is sufficient unless the drawing is complex. If so, make additional slides of the drawing's details.

   C. Create a cover slide or title page slide that gives your name.

   D. Create an ending slide that says THE END.

5. Create a slide show that illustrates specific types of drawings. For example, you might make a slide show for dimensioned mechanical drawings or for electrical drawings. These specialized slide shows in your portfolio are useful if you apply for a job in a specific discipline. Store all slide shows on the same disk. Identify slide shows by their content as follows:

   mech.scr—Mechanical
   arch.scr—Architectural
   pipe.scr—Piping
   struct.scr—Structural
   elect.scr—Electrical or Electronics
   map.scr—Mapping
   civil.scr—Civil

6. Create a script file to plot your most frequently used drawing. Use the following guidelines to write the script:

   A. Run a trial plot of the drawing first. Record all of the keystrokes required to plot the drawing correctly.

   B. Check the results of the trial plot to be sure that the use of pens and the location of the drawing on the paper is correct.

   C. Write the script file using the exact keystrokes you recorded.

   D. Test the script and note where problems occur.

   E. Fix the problems in the script file and test the script until it runs properly.

Digitizing Existing Drawings

Learning Objectives

After completing this chapter, you will be able to:
- ○ Describe the digitizer and the digitizing process.
- ○ Digitize existing drawings into AutoCAD.
- ○ Define scanning and discuss the advantages and disadvantages of scanning over manually digitizing a drawing.

Digitizing is the process of transferring information from a digitizing tablet into the computer. You can send commands to the computer by digitizing a command cell on the menu overlay. A *digitizing tablet*, or *digitizer*, is also used to convert existing paper drawings into AutoCAD drawing files. Digitizers range in size from 6″ square to 44″ × 60″. Many schools and industries use 12″ square digitizers to input commands from standard and custom tablet menus.

Most companies do not have the time to convert existing drawings to CAD because they rely on the CAD system for new product drawings. There are businesses that digitize existing drawings for other companies. These commercial operations use large format digitizers for D-size and E-size drawings.

Another way to convert existing drawings to CAD files is with a scanner. It sends a light or camera over the drawing to transfer the image to the computer. This technique is called *scanning*.

Digitizers

A digitizer consists of a plastic surface, called a *tablet*, and a pointing device for picking locations on the tablet. The digitizer provides extremely accurate location in the form of XY coordinates. Figure 29-1 shows a 12″ × 12″ digitizer and pointing device.

Digitizing an Existing Drawing

When a company begins converting to CAD, the normal procedure is to have a manual drafting group and a CAD group. Selected new drawings are done on the computer. This situation may continue until the full capabilities of CAD are realized. Manual drafters remain important because older drawings are often revised in the original format.

Figure 29-1.
A 12″ × 12″ digitizer
with pointing
device.

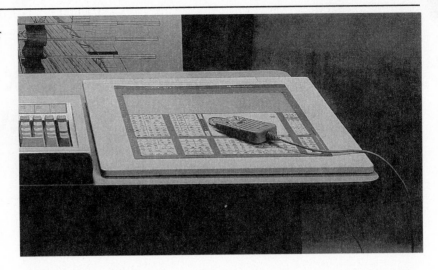

There comes a time when a company must make a decision to convert existing paper drawings to CAD drawing files. This problem is not confined to paper drawings. Sometimes it is necessary to convert one type of computer-generated drawing to another CAD system. This might be done with a translation program.

In some situations the only solution is to redraw the existing drawings with AutoCAD. Time is usually saved by digitizing the existing drawing, depending on the type of drawing. A digitizer large enough to accommodate the largest drawing is best, but large drawings can also be digitized on small digitizers, if necessary.

The digitizing process consists of a combination of digitized points and AutoCAD drawing and editing commands. Also plan to use **SNAP**, **ORTHO**, and object snap modes to your best advantage.

Installing and setting up the digitizer

Most systems are installed with a mouse to use as a pointing device. The digitizer and appropriate driver software must be installed. Once the digitizer has been installed, start AutoCAD and set the pointing device and its driver. To set the device and drive, pick **Preferences...** in the **Tools** pull-down menu, or enter PR or PREFERENCES at the Command: prompt. This accesses the **Preferences** dialog box. You can also access this dialog box by entering CONFIG at the Command: prompt.

Open the **Pointer** tab in this dialog box. In the **Pointer** tab you can select the current pointing device. If Windows NT or Windows 95 automatically set up the pointing device, then the Current System Pointing Device is highlighted and active. Follow these steps to make your digitizer and pointing device current:

1. Go through the device list and select the product that you have. For example, select and highlight:

   CalComp 2500, 3300, 3400 Series ADI 4.2 by Autodesk, Inc.

2. Pick the **Set Current** button. This opens the **AutoCAD Text Window** with the following series of instructions and options:

   Command: _preferences
   Supported models:
   1.   Model 25120 (obsolete)
   2.   Model 25180 (obsolete)
   3.   DrawingBoard II 33120 or 34120
   4.   DrawingBoard II 33180 or 34180
   5.   DrawingBoard II 33240 or 34240
   6.   DrawingBoard II 33360 or 34360
   7.   DrawingBoard II 33480 or 34480

AutoCAD
Installation
Guide **6**

PREFERENCES
PR
CONFIG

Tools
➥ Preferences...

Enter selection, 1-7 〈1〉: (type the number of your digitizer, such as 3, and press [Enter])

The digitizer can have the following types of cursor:

2   buttons
3   buttons
4   buttons
16   buttons

Enter the number of buttons on your cursor 〈16〉: (enter the number of buttons used)
Enter serial port name for digitizer or . for none 〈COM1〉: (press [Enter] to accept COM1 or type the name of another serial port, such as COM2, and press [Enter])

The **Preferences** dialog box returns and information about the selected digitizer and driver is displayed. See Figure 29-2. The **Accept input from:** area has two radio buttons, which are now active. You can select one of these buttons to use the **Digitizer only** or **Digitizer and mouse**. Pick the **OK** button when done.

Figure 29-2.
Using the **Preferences** dialog box to set a new current pointing device and its driver.

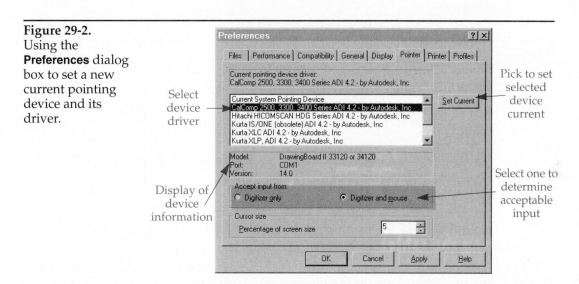

NOTE

For additional information, refer to the *Appendix* section for *Installing and Configuring AutoCAD* and *Configuring the Digitizer*.

Configuring the tablet

Before digitizing a drawing, you must configure the tablet, even if it was previously configured for another application. This is done to utilize the maximum area on the tablet. To configure the tablet, enter TA or TABLET at the Command: prompt, followed by entering CFG at the Option: prompt. The configure option is also available by picking **Configure** in the **Tablet** cascading menu of the **Tools** pull-down menu. The command sequence is as follows:

Command: **TA** or **TABLET**↵
Option (ON/OFF/CAL/CFG): **CFG**↵

Next, AutoCAD asks for the number of tablet menus. Since the entire tablet is used when digitizing an existing drawing, there are no menu areas. Type 0 and press [Enter]. When asked if you want to respecify the screen pointing area, answer Y. Then pick the lower-left corner followed by the upper-right corner. If your digitizer has proximity lights, watch them as you do this. One of the lights is on when the puck is in the screen pointing area and off when the puck leaves the area. Move the pointing device slowly to the extreme corners until you find the location where the light comes on. This helps you gain use of the entire screen pointing area when digitizing. See Figure 29-3. The prompt sequence is as follows:

Enter number of tablet menus desired (0-4) ⟨0⟩: ↵
Do you want to respecify the screen pointing area? ⟨N⟩: **Y**↵
Digitize lower left corner of screen pointing area: *(pick the lower-left corner of the pointing area)*
Digitize the upper right corner of screen pointing area: *(pick the upper-right corner of the pointing area)*
Command:

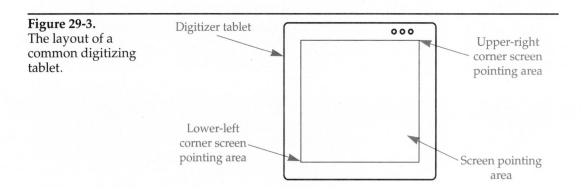

Figure 29-3.
The layout of a common digitizing tablet.

Calibrating the tablet

The next step, calibrating the tablet, aligns the drawing to be digitized with the tablet. Attach the drawing to the tablet using drafting tape. The drawing does not need to be exactly square on the screen pointing area, but it should be flat. Figure 29-4 shows a plot plan attached to the digitizer tablet.

The number of points that you digitize when calibrating the drawing to the tablet determines how accurately the existing drawing coordinates are transferred to the computer. This is called *transformation*. The following are the AutoCAD transformation options:

- **Orthogonal transformation.** AutoCAD allows you to enter two coordinates. Two points work well if the existing drawing is dimensionally accurate. A dimensionally accurate drawing normally has stable length and width measurements, and angles are not distorted.
- **Affine.** This is digitizing three points for calibration. This is necessary when lines are generally parallel, but the horizontal dimensions are stretched in relationship to the vertical dimensions. The calibration of three points provides accuracy by triangulation of three points.
- **Projective calibration.** This is the calibration of four points. When the existing drawing has stretched or has been distorted to the point where parallel lines tend to converge, then the calibration of four points may be necessary.
- **Multiple-point transformation.** This is the digitizing of more than four points. AutoCAD mathematically calculates the relationship between the points with accuracy proportional to the number of points digitized. However, nine points are usually the maximum number of points needed, since additional points tend to slow down the transformation process without improving the accuracy.

Figure 29-4.
A drawing to be digitized is placed on the tablet.

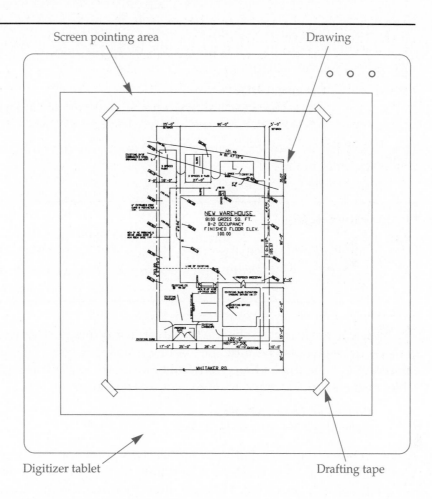

Screen pointing area   Drawing

NEW WAREHOUSE
8100 GROSS SQ. FT.
B-2 OCCUPANCY
FINISHED FLOOR ELEV.
100.00

WHITAKER RD.

Digitizer tablet   Drafting tape

PROFESSIONAL TIP

When selecting points for calibration, choose locations that are as accurate as possible. For example, in mapping applications, pick property corners or benchmarks. In mechanical drafting, use datums on the drawing. Select points that are distributed in a wide area around the drawing. In addition, the points should be in a triangular relationship rather than in a straight line.

Preparing the drawing

When attaching a drawing to the digitizer, use the following guidelines:

- Set the limits to correlate with the drawing dimensions. The limits for the drawing in Figure 29-4 should relate to the overall dimensions of the plot, plus space for notes. The plot is approximately 120′ × 200′. Allowing an additional 40′ in the horizontal and vertical directions for dimensions and notes makes the limits 160′ × 240′, or 1920″ × 2880″.
- Set the drawing units to correspond with the type of drawing you are transferring. The drawing in Figure 29-4 is a surveyed plot plan where engineering units are used, angles are measured in degrees/minutes/seconds, the direction of angle 0 is north 90°, and angles are measured clockwise.
- Set the grid and snap to a convenient value. A 20′ (240″) value works well for the plot plan.

- The property lines on the plot plan are based on a survey and are probably accurate. With this in mind, use the **UCS** command to set the origin to one of the property corners:

> Command: **UCS**↵
> Origin/ZAxis/3point/OBject/View/X/Y/Z/Prev/Restore/Save/Del/?/⟨World⟩: **O**↵
> Origin point: ⟨0,0,0⟩: *(pick the lower-left property line corner)*

This establishes the property corner at a 0,0 origin for convenience in locating other property corner points.

PROFESSIONAL TIP — Be sure to look straight down on the target point if you are digitizing points using a puck with crosshairs. Looking at an angle through the puck viewing glass results in inaccurate point selection.

Now you are ready to calibrate the tablet. The orthogonal, or two-point calibration, is used on the plot plan because the existing drawing is very accurate. To do this, enter the **TABLET** command and type CAL (calibrate) at the Option: prompt. At this point, the tablet mode is turned on and the screen cursor no longer appears.

> Command: **TA** *or* **TABLET**↵
> Option (ON/OFF/CAL/CFG): **CAL**↵

AutoCAD then requests that you digitize two points on the drawing and give the coordinates of each point. These two points may be anywhere, but usually are the endpoints of a vertical line. Drafters often pick two points on the left side of the object, such as the west property line on a plot plan. This begins the orientation of the digitizer in relation to the object as you work from left to right.

AutoCAD next asks for the exact coordinates of the two points. Look at the existing drawing in Figure 29-5 to be digitized as you follow these prompts:

> Digitize point #1: *(pick the lower-left property corner where you set the UCS origin)*
> Enter coordinates for point #1: *(enter 0,0 and press* [Enter] *to coincide with the UCS origin)*
> Digitize point #2: *(pick the north end of the west property line)*

Enter the length of the property line relative to the first point (X = 0, Y = 203.89′ or 2446.68″) when entering the coordinates for the second point:

> Enter coordinates for point #2: **0,2446.68**↵

Pressing [Enter] for the third point request automatically makes AutoCAD use the orthogonal transformation format:

> Digitize point #3 (or press ENTER to end): ↵

Enter the **TABLET** command and turn the tablet on now that the existing drawing has been calibrated to the digitizer:

> Command: **TA** *or* **TABLET**↵
> Option (ON/OFF/CAL/CFG): **ON**↵

Figure 29-5.
To calibrate the
tablet, carefully
select two points
and provide the
coordinates of those
points.

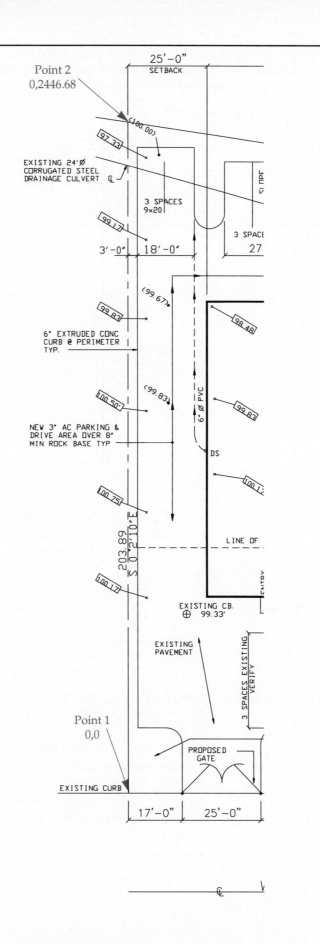

The screen cursor returns for you to use AutoCAD commands to draw lines and other features. Use the **LINE** command to draw the property boundaries by picking each property corner. Use the **Close** option for the last line. The resulting property boundaries are shown in Figure 29-6.

Figure 29-6.
Use the **LINE** command to construct the property boundaries.

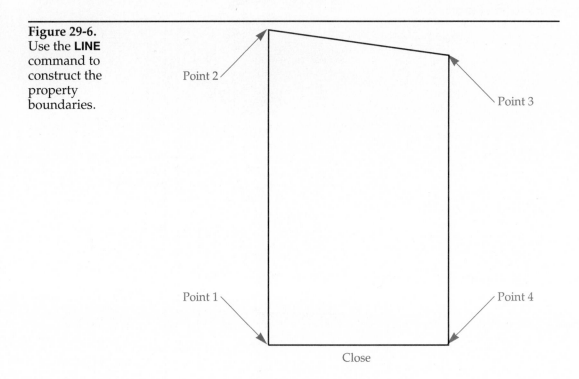

Point 2

Point 3

Point 1

Point 4

Close

Proceed by digitizing the buildings, roads, walkways, utilities, and other features using commands such as **LINE**, **PLINE**, **ARC**, and **CIRCLE**. Use the **DIM** command to dimension the plot plan, and use the **DTEXT** command to add notes. The finished drawing is shown in Figure 29-7.

> **NOTE**
>
> AutoCAD can be configured to display screen menus in addition to the toolbar and pull-down menus. This capability is discussed in *AutoCAD and its Applications—Advanced, Release 14*. When tablet mode is on, the displayed screen menus are disabled, but commands may still be entered from the keyboard, toolbars, and pull-down menus. To make selections from the screen menus, you must turn the tablet mode off by entering OFF at the Option: prompt of the **TABLET** command.
>
> Tablet mode may also be turned on or off with function key [F4], by pressing [Ctrl]+[T], or using the **TABMODE** system variable. When using **TABMODE**, 0 is off and 1 is on. Configuring the tablet to menu areas of the AutoCAD menu template overlay is discussed in *Appendix J* of this text.

Figure 29-7. The completed digitized drawing.

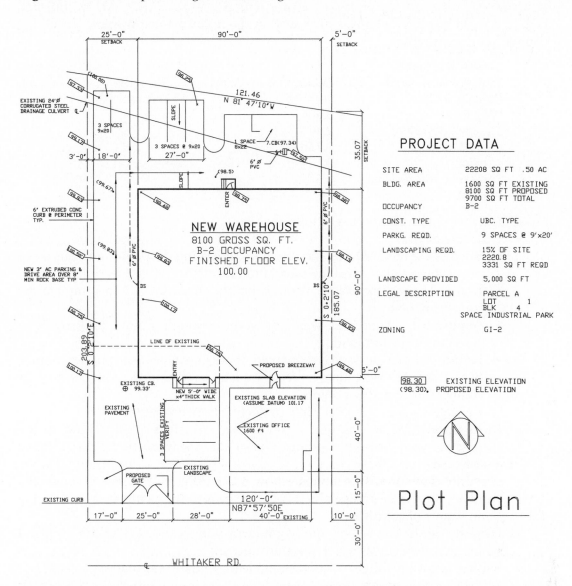

Plot Plan

PROJECT DATA

SITE AREA	22208 SQ FT .50 AC
BLDG. AREA	1600 SQ FT EXISTING 8100 SQ FT PROPOSED 9700 SQ FT TOTAL
OCCUPANCY	B-2
CONST. TYPE	UBC. TYPE
PARKG. REQD.	9 SPACES @ 9'x20'
LANDSCAPING REQD.	15% OF SITE 2220.8 3331 SQ FT REQD
LANDSCAPE PROVIDED	5,000 SQ FT
LEGAL DESCRIPTION	PARCEL A LOT 1 BLK 4 SPACE INDUSTRIAL PARK
ZONING	GI-2

98.30 EXISTING ELEVATION
(98.30). PROPOSED ELEVATION

PROFESSIONAL TIP

Remember, when digitizing an existing drawing, use the **SNAP** and **ORTHO** commands to your advantage. Also, be careful when you pick points on the existing drawing. Place the digitizing tablet at a convenient angle. Look directly into the crosshairs of the puck.

The plot plan example in the previous discussion used two calibration points. The existing drawing was very accurate, allowing two-point calibration to be successfully used. After entering two points, AutoCAD automatically calculated an orthogonal transformation.

Three or more points may be digitized to help provide greater accuracy. The same example could have been used to continue calibrating a third point. The third point would be another property line corner, forming a triangular relationship between the points. Press [Enter] when you have picked three calibration points.

When three points are digitized, AutoCAD calculates the relationship between orthogonal, affine, and projective transformations. When AutoCAD is finished making the calculations, a table is displayed in the **AutoCAD Text Window**, providing you with this information:

3 calibration points			
Transformation type:	Orthogonal	Affine	Projective
Outcome of fit:	success	exact	impossible
RMS Error:	6.324		
Standard deviation:	2.941		
Largest residual:	9.726		
At point:	2		
Second-largest residual:	8.975		
At point:	1		

These elements can be interpreted as follows:

- **Outcome of fit**.
  - **Success**—AutoCAD was successful in calibrating the points, and this is the only category that gives the calculation results.
  - **Exact**—There were exactly enough points for AutoCAD to complete the transformation.
  - **Impossible**—AutoCAD was not given enough points to provide a projective transformation.
  - **Failure**—If this message is displayed, there may have been enough points, but AutoCAD was unable to complete a transformation because of collinear or coincident points.
  - **Canceled**—This may occur in a projective transformation.
- **RMS Error.** *RMS* means root mean square, which is a calculation of the accuracy of your calibration points. The smaller the number, the closer it is to a perfect fit.
- **Standard deviation.** This indicates how much difference there is between the accuracy of points. If this value is near zero, then the points have nearly the same degree of accuracy.
- **Largest residual.** Estimates the worst error you might have in the digitized points, and tells you at which point this occurs.
- **Second largest residual.** Gives the next least accurate calculation.

When you pick more than three points, a successful calibration reports back to you in all three types of transformation with a table similar to this:

7 calibration points			
Transformation type:	Orthogonal	Affine	Projective
Outcome of fit:	success	success	success
RMS Error:	6.324	5.852	2.602
Standard deviation:	2.941	2.469	0.508
Largest residual:	9.726	8.984	4.7634
At point:	3	3	3
Second-largest residual:	8.975	8.233	4.012
At point:	5	5	5

Now, AutoCAD allows you to select the desired transformation type or repeat the table by pressing [Enter] at the following prompt:

Select transformation type…
Orthogonal/Affine/Projective?⟨Repeat table⟩: *(press* [Enter] *or type* O, A, *or* P *for the desired transformation type and press* [Enter]*)*
Command:

Digitizing large drawings

The drawing you plan to digitize may be too large for your tablet. Then you must divide the drawing into sections that fit the tablet area. For example, a large drawing can be divided into four sections. Establish the coordinates of the boundaries for each section. See Figure 29-8. The coordinates of each section are labeled and shown with dots for reference.

Next, tape the portion labeled as SECTION 1 to the tablet and calibrate the tablet to the coordinates 1,1 and 1,8. Digitize this section. See Figure 29-9.

Figure 29-8. Dividing a large drawing into sections for digitizing. Label the sections and the coordinates of the points defining the sections.

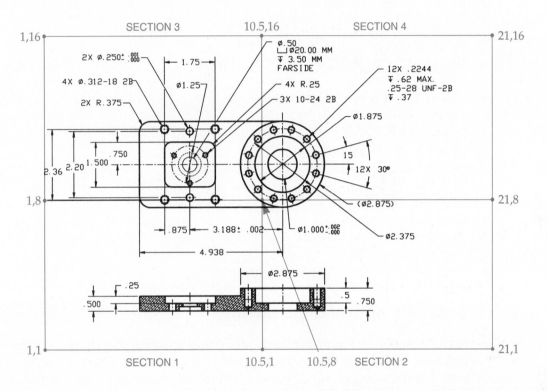

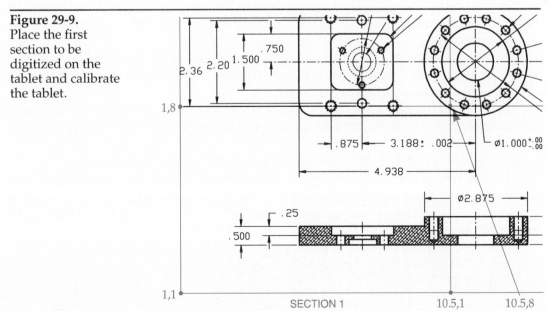

Figure 29-9. Place the first section to be digitized on the tablet and calibrate the tablet.

Proceed by placing the portion of the drawing labeled as SECTION 2 on the digitizer. Calibrate the tablet to the coordinates 10.5,1 and 10.5,8. Digitize the portion of the object shown as SECTION 2. See Figure 29-10.

Proceed by moving SECTION 3 of the drawing into place on the digitizer. Calibrate the tablet to the coordinates 1,8 and 1,16. Digitize the portion of the object shown as SECTION 3.

Proceed by moving SECTION 4 into place on the digitizer. Calibrate the tablet to the coordinates 10.5,8 and 10.5,16. Digitize the portion of the object shown as SECTION 4. The entire drawing has now been digitized.

Figure 29-10.
Place the second section to be digitized on the tablet and calibrate the tablet.

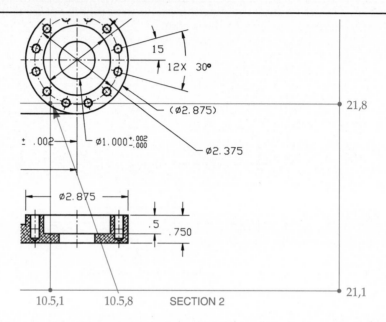

Optical Scanning of Existing Drawings

Scanning is a method of automatically digitizing existing drawings. Scanners work much the same way as taking a photograph of the drawing. One advantage of scanning over manually digitizing drawings is that the entire drawing—including dimensions, symbols, and text—is transferred to the computer. A disadvantage is that some drawings, when scanned, require much editing to make them presentable.

The scanning process picks up images from the drawing. What appears to be a dimension, for example, is only a graphic representation of the dimension, it is not an *entity*. If you want the dimensional information to be technically accurate, the dimensions must be edited and redrawn.

After the drawing is scanned, the image is sent to a raster converter that translates information to digital or vector format. A *raster* is an electron beam that generates a matrix of pixels. As you learned previously, pixels make up the drawing image on the display screen. A raster editor is then used to display the image for editing.

Companies using scanners can, in many cases, reproduce existing drawings more efficiently than companies that manually digitize drawings. When an existing drawing has been transferred to the computer, it becomes an AutoCAD drawing, which can be edited as necessary.

Scanners transfer drawings from paper, vellum, film, or blueline prints and convert the hardcopy image into a raster data file. An example of a scanner is shown in Figure 29-11.

Figure 29-11.
A 36″ wide large format grayscale scanner. (IDEAL Scanners and Systems)

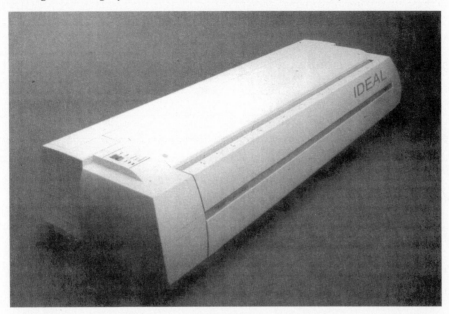

Chapter Test

Write your answers on a separate sheet of paper.

1. Give the command and related entries to configure the tablet so that the entire area is available as the screen pointing area:

   Command: _____

   Option (ON/OFF/CAL/CFG): _____

   Enter number of tablet menus desired (0-4) ⟨0⟩: _____

   Do you want to respecify the screen pointing area? ⟨N⟩: _____

   Digitize lower left corner of screen pointing area: _____

   _____

   Digitize upper right corner of screen pointing area: _____

   _____

2. Give the command and related entries needed to calibrate an existing drawing for digitizing using orthogonal transformation:

   Command: _____

   Option (ON/OFF/CAL/CFG): _____

   Digitize point #1:_____

   Enter coordinates for point #1: _____

   Digitize point #2:_____

   Enter coordinates for point #2: _____

   Digitize point #3 (or press ENTER to end): _____

3. List three methods used to turn the tablet mode on and off._____

   _____

   _____

4. Describe the function of a digitizer. _____
_____
_____
_____

5. List the four types of transformation and give the number of points required for each.
_____
_____
_____
_____
_____

6. Why is it generally unnecessary to digitize more than nine points? _____
_____
_____

7. List at least three things to consider when digitizing points for drawing transformation. _____
_____
_____

8. Explain the relationship of the limits, units, grid, and snap to digitizing an existing drawing. _____
_____
_____
_____
_____

9. Why is it important to look straight down into the puck crosshairs when digitizing points? _____
_____
_____

10. Define the following terms related to digitizing three or more points when transferring an existing drawing.
    A. Success— _____
    B. Exact— _____
    C. Impossible— _____
    D. Largest residual—_____

11. How are sections of a drawing coordinated when a large drawing is digitized?
_____
_____

12. Define *scanning*. _____
_____
_____

13. List an advantage and a disadvantage of scanning over digitizing drawings.

_____

_____

_____

_____

_____

_____

Drawing Problems

1. Make a photocopy of the drawing in Figure 29-7 or 29-8. Use the digitizing process to convert the drawing to AutoCAD. Save the drawing as P29-1.

2. Make a photocopy of the drawing below. Use the digitizing process to convert the drawing to AutoCAD. Save the drawing as P29-2.

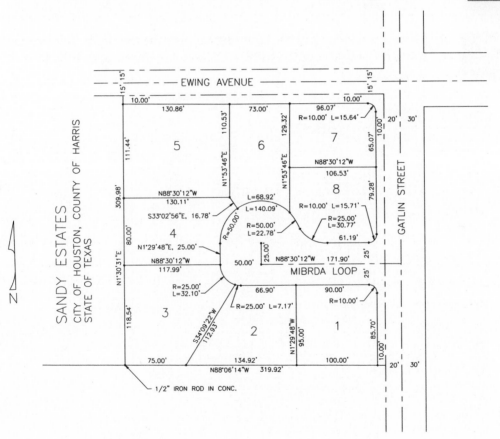

3. Make a photocopy of the drawing below. Use the digitizing process to convert the drawing to AutoCAD. Save the drawing as P29-3.

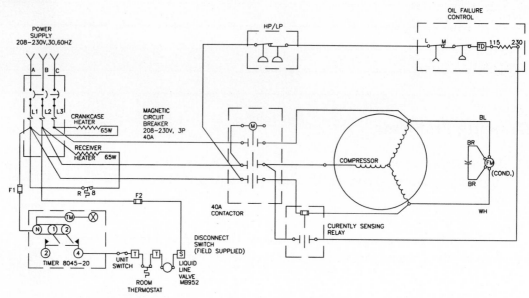

4. Make a photocopy of the drawing below. Use the digitizing process to convert the drawing to AutoCAD. Save the drawing as P29-4.

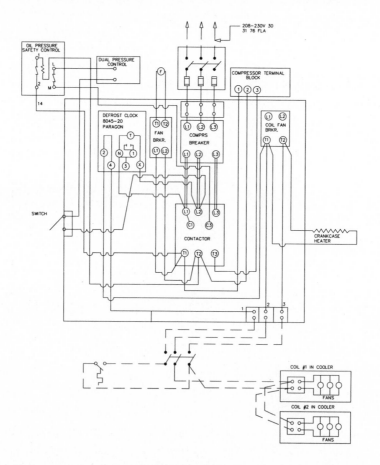

5. Obtain an existing industrial or class drawing that was created using manual techniques. Use the digitizing process to convert it to AutoCAD.

Learning Objectives

After completing this chapter, you will be able to:
- ○ Identify the various elements of Windows Explorer.
- ○ Start applications and print drawing files from Windows Explorer.
- ○ Drag and drop AutoCAD-related files into the AutoCAD graphics window.
- ○ Create and manage directory folders.
- ○ Format, label, and copy 3.5" disks.

Prudent file and disk management is of paramount importance to every computer user. This is particularly true in the case of AutoCAD. The loss of a large or complex drawing file through carelessness or negligence is a painful experience. Losing an entire directory of drawing files can be devastating.

A variety of suggestions and procedures for managing AutoCAD-related files have been offered throughout the preceding chapters. For example, Chapter 15 introduces Windows Explorer, in which files can be listed, moved, copied, renamed, and deleted.

In this chapter, you are introduced to additional methods of file and disk maintenance using the Microsoft Windows Explorer. Explorer can be used to simultaneously open a drawing file and start AutoCAD. Additionally, the *drag and drop* capability of Explorer is discussed as a means of inserting drawing files, AutoLISP routines, and text files into the AutoCAD drawing editor. For a complete description of Explorer, refer to the *Microsoft Windows NT or 95 User's Guide*.

NOTE	The discussion in this chapter is based primarily on the Windows NT operating system. In most respects, Windows 95 is identical or very similar to Windows NT. Where appropriate, the differences between the two systems are noted.

Introduction to Explorer

To launch Windows Explorer pick <u>P</u>rograms ⟩ in the Start menu, then pick Windows NT Explorer. See Figure 30-1. The Exploring window is displayed, similar to the one shown in Figure 30-2. This window is divided into two *panes*. The left pane displays storage devices and folders, and the right pane displays the contents of folders. If you are not familiar with the Windows terminology of folders and directories, read the next section carefully.

Figure 30-1.
To launch Windows
Explorer, pick
Programs ⟩ in the
Start menu, then
pick Windows NT
Explorer.

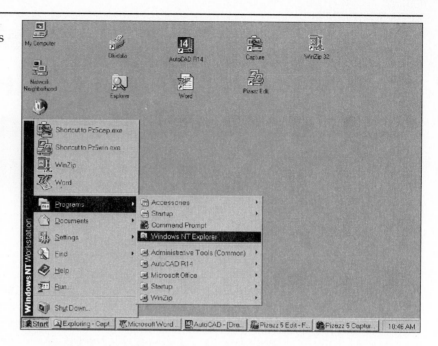

Figure 30-2.
The standard Exploring window.

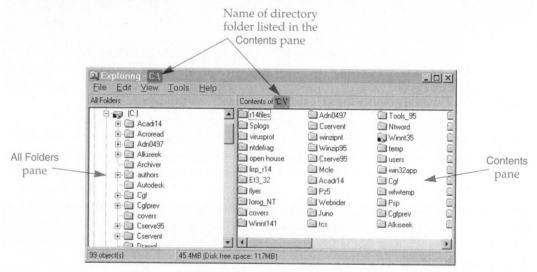

DOS directories or 95/NT folders

The purpose of the Windows Explorer is to enable you to navigate through the structure of your storage devices in order to manipulate and manage files. Files are arranged on your hard disk drive in the familiar DOS *tree structure*. In this structure, a main or *root directory* is the trunk of the tree. *Directories* form limbs from the tree trunk. Each directory can have smaller branches, called *subdirectories*. Files can be stored in any part of the tree.

Although the Windows engineers at Microsoft have softened the terminology from directories to *folders*, we are still dealing with the same old DOS tree structure introduced years ago. Using Windows NT and 95, we now should think of any kind of directory as a folder. Therefore a subdirectory is now a *subfolder*. Windows Explorer uses the file folder icon to represent a storage location and allows you to quickly create new folders in which to store program and data files.

Folder path names

In order to locate a file in a folder, you must literally "go out on a limb" of the Windows directory tree structure. Each limb and branch off the tree trunk is referred to as a ***path***. Notice the window title bar in Figure 30-2. It reflects the path name of the current location, or C:\. The current hard disk drive is named C:, and the main tree trunk, or root directory, is identified as C:\.

You can quickly expand the tree structure of the C:\ folder by picking on the plus sign (+) to the left of the hard drive icon. Now if you pick on the AutoCAD R14 folder icon or name, it opens to display its contents in the right pane. In addition, the path name in the window title bar changes to reflect the current path name. You are now venturing out on a tree limb. Pick the plus sign next to the AutoCAD R14 folder to expand the tree and notice the additional folders that appear. These are subfolders that are branches of the AutoCAD R14 limb. These subfolders branch down below and form the tree structure. Each of these subfolders is connected by a vertical line to the folder one level above it. See Figure 30-3.

Figure 30-3.
Picking the plus sign next to a folder expands the tree to display additional subfolders.

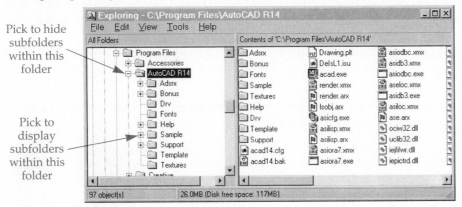

Elements of the Exploring window

When you use Explorer, all of your work is performed using a directory tree. This is a graphic representation of the directory structure and the folders and files it contains. When you start Explorer, the window displays the contents of the current drive. The window is divided in half with a *split bar*. The left half of the window displays the directory tree, and the right half lists the contents of the current folder. You can drag the split bar to the left or to the right to display more or less of the contents in each side of the window.

At the right of the window is a contents list of the subfolders and files contained in the selected folder. Each subfolder in this list is also represented with a folder icon. A *file icon* indicating the file type appears next to each file name. There are icons to represent program files (.exe and .bat files), document files (.txt and .wri files), and other types of files.

You must first select a file or folder in the Explorer window before you can work with it. When you want to select a file or folder, place the cursor over the desired file or folder icon and pick. More than one file or folder can be selected by pressing and holding the [Shift] key as you pick with your pointing device. The item(s) you select is then highlighted and you can proceed with the desired operation. More information about file and folder selection appears later in this chapter.

Drive icons represent each of the drives on your computer. These are located at the top of the list in the All Folders pane. A drive letter follows each icon. You can see that the floppy disk drive, A:, is represented with a different icon than those used for the hard disk, C:.

You can easily change to one of the available drives with a pick on the desired drive icon. If you are connected to a network or are using a RAM drive or CD-ROM device, appropriate icons are displayed.

Just below the Explorer window title bar are the five pull-down menus: File, Edit, View, Tools, and Help. Many of the commands located in these menus are explored later in this chapter.

Finally, as with all Microsoft Windows applications, the Explorer window can be moved, resized, closed, and reduced to the taskbar at any time. Standard methods are used to perform these activities.

Explorer toolbar buttons

Twelve toolbar buttons enable you to perform a variety of functions quickly. The toolbar is toggled on and off by picking Toolbar in the View pull-down menu. A checkmark next to Toolbar indicates that it is active.

Figure 30-4 provides quick identification of each toolbar button. The functions of these buttons are described later in this chapter.

Figure 30-4.
Toolbar buttons in the Exploring window.

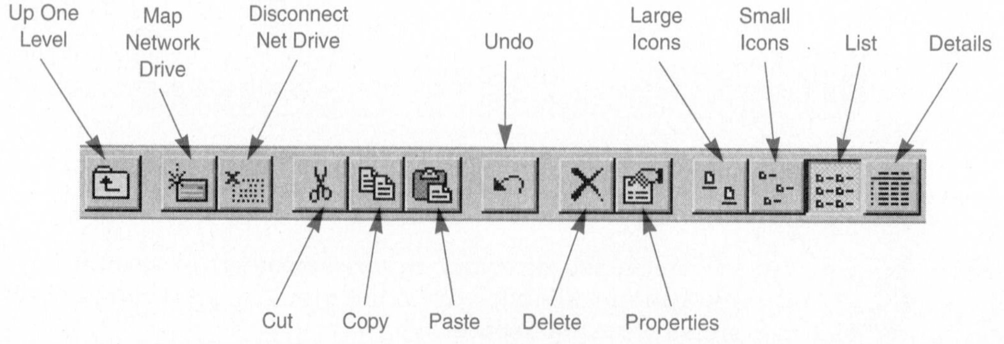

Basic Explorer Functions

Before using Explorer to manage your folders and files, it is best to have a good understanding of how these items are selected and what kinds of actions Explorer is capable of performing. See Chapter 15 for a discussion of the basic methods of selecting items in the Explorer window. Three additional methods of file and folder selection are provided here.

PROFESSIONAL TIP Windows NT and 95 have made extensive use of the right-click on the pointer. Practice using this feature inside windows and dialog boxes or when selecting folders and files. You will find that this method can speed up many operations normally performed by selecting items in the pull-down menus. Right-clicking is discussed where applicable in this chapter.

Selecting multiple folders and files

A consecutive group of items can be selected by picking the first item, then holding the [Shift] key and picking the last item in the group. Two or more consecutive groups can be selected as follows:
1. Pick the first item in a group. Hold the [Shift] key and pick the last item in the group.
2. Press the [Ctrl] key and select the first item in the second group.
3. Press the [Ctrl]+[Shift] keys and pick the last item in the group. This selects the second group.
4. Press the [Ctrl] key and select the first item in the third group.
5. Press the [Ctrl]+[Shift] keys and pick the last item in the group. This selects the third group.
6. Continue in this manner until all groups are selected.

If the number of files or folders you need to select far outnumber those that will remain unselected, use the following technique.
1. Pick Select All from the Edit pull-down menu. This selects all folders and files in the current drive or folder.
2. Deselect the items that you do not want to be part of the selected group.

A second method to use if only a few files or folders are to remain unselected is as follows:
1. Select only the files that are not to be acted on.
2. Pick Invert Selection from the Edit pull-down menu. This automatically deselects the items you picked and selects all remaining items.

The status bar at the bottom of the Exploring window displays the number of objects in the current folder, the total number of bytes in the selected items, and the disk free space if a folder in the left pane is selected. Check the status bar when selecting files to be copied to floppy disks. You can quickly see if the total file sizes can be accepted by the destination disk.

If you wish to hide the status bar to make more room to display folders and files, pick Status Bar from the View pull-down menu to toggle the status bar off.

Actions performed on selected files

The Windows Explorer is a powerful tool that can handle a wide variety of actions. In order for Explorer to act, the item must first be selected. A brief description of the actions that can be performed on selected items is given below.

- **Run.** Double-click on a program file (.exe) or document to launch that program.
- **Rename.** Pick File, then Rename to rename the selected item, or right-click and pick Rename in the cursor menu.
- **Copy.** Pick File, then Copy to copy the selected item(s), or right-click and pick Copy. Select the destination drive or folder, then pick Edit then Paste, or right-click and pick Paste. You can also press [Ctrl]+[C] to copy the selected items, then press [Ctrl]+[V] to paste the items.
- **Move.** Pick Cut from the Edit pull-down menu, then select the destination and pick Paste. It is quicker to drag and drop the items by selecting them, holding the pick button, and dragging the item to the destination. Be sure the destination drive or folder is highlighted before releasing the pick button.
- **Delete.** Pick File, then Delete; right-click and pick Delete; pick the Delete button on the toolbar; or press the [Delete] key to send the selected items to the Recycle Bin.
- **Properties.** Pick File, then Properties (or right-click and pick Properties) to display the general properties of the selected item. You can also press [Alt]+[Enter].
- **View.** View a file by picking File, then Quick View. Or right-click and pick Quick View in the cursor menu.
- **Print.** Pick File, then Print to print a file, or right-click and pick Print in the cursor menu.
- **Edit.** Pick File, then Edit to edit a batch (.bat) file, or right-click and pick Edit in the cursor menu.
- **Send.** A copy of the file can be sent to a floppy disk or to the My Briefcase icon by picking File, then Send To ⟩, or picking Send To ⟩ from the cursor menu.
- **New.** A new file, folder, or shortcut can be created by picking File, then New or right-click and pick New. Alternatively, pick File, then Create Shortcut.
- **Paste Shortcut.** Copy the item, then pick Edit and Paste Shortcut. You can also right-click and drag the item to the destination, then release the pick button.

Displaying folder and file icons

Icons representing folders and files can be displayed in the Contents pane by using one of four different buttons or menu selections. These options are found in the View pull-down menu. The current display method is indicated by a dot to the left of the name. The viewing options can also be selected by picking one of the four buttons at the right side of the toolbar. See Figure 30-5.

- **Large Icons.** Displays icons in a large format in rows and columns.
- **Small Icons.** Displays icons in a small format in rows and columns.
- **List.** Displays icons in a list on the left side of the pane. If the list is too long to fit the current size of the window, a second column is listed, and so on. The List option is only available in the small icon format.
- **Details.** Displays a single list of small icons, and provides columns for the folder or file name, size, type, date last modified, and attributes (i.e. hidden or archive).

PROFESSIONAL TIP

Viewing and arranging options can also be selected by right-clicking on any open area of the Contents pane.

Figure 30-5.
Viewing and
arranging options
are selected from
the <u>V</u>iew menu or
the toolbar.

Use the pull-down
menu or buttons
to select the
display method

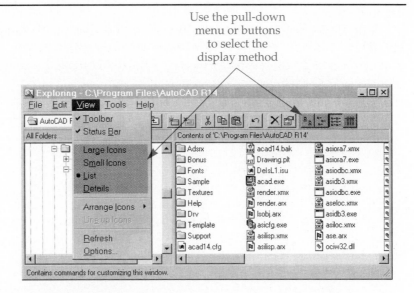

Arranging folder and file icons

Once you have selected the display that suits your needs, you can quickly arrange the icons by one of four methods. These are selected by picking Arrange <u>I</u>cons from the <u>V</u>iew pull-down menu.

- **by <u>N</u>ame.** Displays icons alphabetically. Folders are always listed first, then files. If a small or large icon view is set, the icons are arranged alphabetically in rows beginning at the upper-left and progressing to the right on each row.
- **by <u>T</u>ype.** Displays icons by file type. Folders are always displayed first, then files are listed alphabetically according to the three-letter file extension.
- **by Si<u>z</u>e.** Files are listed from smallest number of bytes to largest.
- **by <u>D</u>ate.** Displays icons by date last modified, most recent first. If small or large icon view is set, the icons are arranged in rows, with most recent on the left.

When icons are displayed in either small or large format, you can choose to move them around and arrange them to suit your needs, or let Explorer arrange them for you. The <u>A</u>uto Arrange option is the default, and icons are automatically arranged in rows and columns. Pick Arrange <u>I</u>cons in the <u>V</u>iew menu to see this option. A check mark means it is active. Turn this option off by selecting it to remove the check mark. Now you can freely pick and drag icons to new locations. See Figure 30-6A. If your arrangement gets too messy, you can align the icons into the nearest rows and columns by picking Lin<u>e</u> up Icons in the <u>V</u>iew menu. See Figure 30-6B. This option does not produce the compact arrangement that <u>A</u>uto Arrange provides, but merely moves icons to the nearest row and column. Gaps in the arrangement remain.

NOTE

When the <u>D</u>etails option is active, you can automatically reverse the order of listing by picking any one of the column headings in the Contents pane. For example, picking Size displays files first from largest to smallest, then folders. Pick size again to return to the default display of folders first, then files from largest to smallest. Test this feature by picking each of the column headings.

Figure 30-6.
A—Icons can be freely moved when <u>A</u>uto Arrange is turned off. B—Align the icons into the nearest rows and columns by picking Lin<u>e</u> up Icons in the <u>V</u>iew menu.

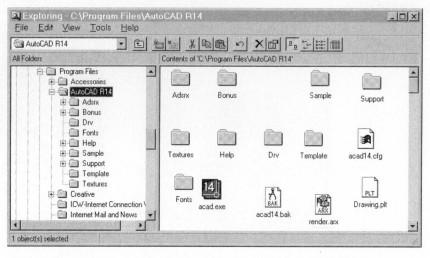

A

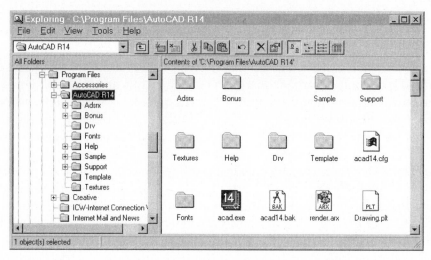

B

Launching Applications with Explorer

Many of the files that appear in the Exploring window are associated with application programs. By double-clicking on the file icon (or on the file name itself), you can load the file and simultaneously start the application with which it is associated. Consider the portion of the Exploring window shown in Figure 30-7. Double-clicking on the drawing file campus.dwg highlights the file name in the window. The Windows "hourglass" appears as AutoCAD is loaded and the campus drawing is opened.

AutoCAD and its Applications—Basics

Figure 30-7.
Double-clicking a
.dwg file in Explorer
starts AutoCAD and
loads the selected
file into the drawing
editor.

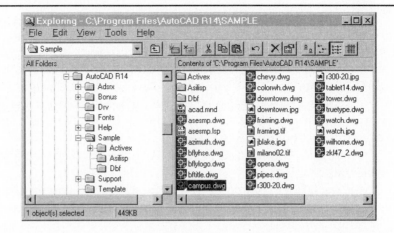

Drag and Drop Operations with Explorer

The Windows Explorer can also be used to dynamically "drag and drop" file icons
into the AutoCAD graphics window. This powerful capability allows you to insert
drawing files as blocks, insert text files as dynamic text, print or plot a drawing, and
import IGES, DXF, and PostScript files. Drag and drop can also be used to load menu,
font, linetype, shape, script, and slide files, as well as AutoLISP and ARX applications.
A file selected for drag and drop with AutoCAD must have one of the following file
extensions:

.arx	.dwg	.dxb	.dxf
.eps	.exe	.igs	.lin
.lsp	.mnu	.mnx	.ps
.scr	.shp	.sld	.txt

The following table lists the different kinds of drag and drop operations that can
be used in AutoCAD. Also listed are the required file name extensions, the related
AutoCAD commands, and the chapters in this text where additional command information can be found.

Operation	File Extension	Related Command	Related Chapter
Load a linetype file	.lin	**LINETYPE**	Chapter 4
Insert a text file	.txt	**DTEXT**	Chapter 8
Load a shape font	.shx	**STYLE**	Chapter 8
Insert a drawing file	.dwg	**INSERT**	Chapter 23
Print a drawing	.dwg	**PLOT**	Chapter 10
Load a slide file	.sld	**VSLIDE**	Chapter 28
Run a script file	.scr	**SCRIPT**	Chapter 28
Import a .dxf file	.dxf	**DXFIN**	Chapter 15
Load a .dxb file	.dxb	**DXBIN**	Chapter 15

Additional files that can be used with drag and drop are found in *AutoCAD and its
Applications, Advanced—Release 14.* The following table lists those files.

Operation	File Extension	Related Command
Load ADS and ARX applications	.exe, .arx	**XLOAD**
Import a PostScript image	.eps, .ps	**PSIN**
Load a menu file	.mnu	**MENU**
Insert an AutoLISP routine	.lsp	**LOAD**

Dragging and dropping a text file

You learned in Chapter 23 that AutoCAD entities, like text, can be saved to disk with the **WBLOCK** command and inserted into other drawing files. A text file created with a text editor outside of AutoCAD can also be inserted into a drawing file using the **MTEXT** command. This command was covered in Chapter 8.

External text files can also be inserted into a drawing using drag and drop. As an example, look at the notes.txt text file shown in the Windows Notepad in Figure 30-8. To drag this text file into AutoCAD, do the following:

1. Start both AutoCAD and Explorer. Arrange the display windows so that both are visible.
2. Issue the **DTEXT** command. Select the start point and justification for the text, and respond to the text height and rotation angle prompts. Stop when the Text: prompt appears.
3. Now, open the Explorer folder directory that contains the text file you want.
4. Drag the text file icon next to the desired file name into the AutoCAD graphics window, and then release the mouse (or puck) button, Figure 30-9. The text is inserted in the current text style and on the current layer. See Figure 30-10.

Figure 30-8.
An external text file with a .txt extension, like the one shown here in Notepad, can be dragged and dropped into the graphics window.

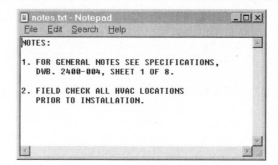

Figure 30-9.
After beginning the **DTEXT** command and answering the prompts for text height and rotation, drag the text file icon into the AutoCAD graphics window.

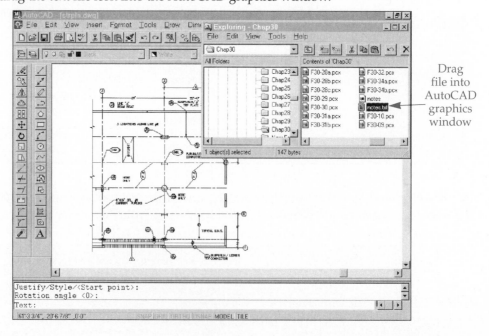

Figure 30-10.
The external text is inserted in the current text style, layer, and color.

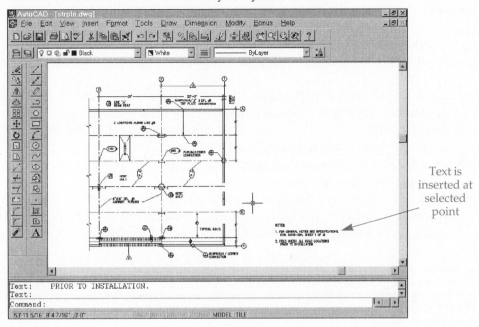

Text is inserted at selected point

External text files can be created with Notepad, WordPad, MS-DOS EDIT, or your own ASCII text editor. Remember that the text file must have a .txt extension. Without this extension, a text file has no association with an application. If you attempt to drag and drop a text file without a .txt extension, AutoCAD displays the alert box shown in Figure 30-11.

Figure 30-11.
The Drag and Drop alert box tells you that no association exists for a text file without a .txt extension.

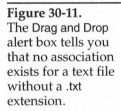 **NOTE**   Dragging and dropping text files works only with the **DTEXT** command. It does not work with the **TEXT** or **MTEXT** commands.

Using drag and drop to print a drawing

If you are using the system printer, you can drag a drawing file icon directly to the Printer icon. AutoCAD need not be loaded beforehand. Dragging and dropping a drawing file icon onto the printer icon automatically starts AutoCAD. The drawing file icon you select is inserted into the drawing editor using the **FILEOPEN** command. This command allows you to open a file without using a dialog box, regardless of the setting of the **FILEDIA** system variable. Once the drawing appears in the graphics window, the **Print/Plot Configuration** dialog box is displayed. You can then modify the printing parameters as required and print the drawing.

This drag and drop operation can be used when the Windows system printer is the desired output device, and is also valid if you want to plot a drawing on a pen or electrostatic plotter. To print a drawing on the system printer using drag and drop, do the following:

1. Launch Windows Explorer.
2. Display the Windows Desktop and double-click to open My Computer. See Figure 30-12A.
3. Double-click on the Printers folder to display the Printers window. See Figure 30-12B. Move the window so that it and Explorer are visible on your screen.
4. Select the file in Explorer you wish to print and drag it to the system printer icon in the Printers window and release.
5. AutoCAD is automatically started (unless it is already running), and the **Print/Plot Configuration** dialog box is displayed.
6. Make any necessary adjustments to the plotting parameters. If you wish to plot the drawing using a pen or electrostatic plotter, be sure to select the appropriate device in the **Device and Default Selection** dialog box. Pick **OK** to print the drawing.

Figure 30-12.
A—The My Computer window. B—Double-click on the Printers folder to display the Printers window.

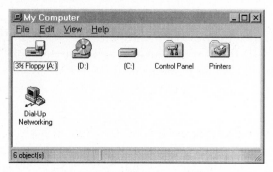

A

B

PROFESSIONAL TIP

You can place a system printer icon on the Windows Desktop and avoid having to open My Computer and the Printers folder. Simply create a Windows *shortcut* by pressing the [Ctrl] key, then pick and drag the system printer icon in the Printers window to a location on the Desktop. The label below this icon will change to "Shortcut to...". To change the label, pick the name to highlight it and then pick it again to edit. Type a new name, then press [Enter]. Now when you need to print a document, just drag the file name from Explorer and drop it on the new printer icon.

Using drag and drop to insert a drawing file

Drag and drop can also be used to insert any drawing into the current drawing session. This method is very similar to the **INSERT** command discussed in Chapter 23. Like **INSERT**, the drawing that you drag and drop becomes a block. Therefore, be sure to explode it after insertion, if necessary.

1. Start both AutoCAD and Explorer. Once again, arrange the display windows so that both are visible.

2. Make sure that the Command: prompt is displayed at the bottom of the AutoCAD graphics window.
3. Now, open the Explorer folder that contains the drawing file that you want to insert.
4. Drag the drawing file icon next to the file name into the AutoCAD graphics window and then release the mouse (or puck) button.
5. The **INSERT** command is echoed in the AutoCAD prompt area. Answer the prompts for the drawing insertion point, scale, and rotation angle.
6. If necessary, explode the inserted drawing.

EXERCISE 30-1

❑ Launch both Explorer and AutoCAD. Arrange the open display windows to resemble those shown in Figure 30-9.
❑ Open a directory containing one or more .dwg files. Using the method described on the previous page, drag a drawing file icon into the AutoCAD graphics window. Answer the prompts for insertion point, scale, and rotation angle, and then explode the inserted drawing.
❑ Use Notepad to create a simple text file like that shown in Figure 30-8. Make the notes specific to your particular application.
❑ Activate the AutoCAD graphics window and issue the **DTEXT** command. Pick a start point for the text, and accept the default text height and rotation angle values.
❑ Drag the text file you created with Notepad into the graphics window.
❑ If you are connected to a printer, try using drag and drop to print a drawing file with the printer icon as described earlier in this chapter.

Automatic Startup of Explorer

The drag and drop capabilities of Explorer make it an excellent companion application for AutoCAD. As such, you may want to have Explorer open and readily accessible whenever you are working with AutoCAD. Having both programs start together automatically is quite convenient, and simple to accomplish.

When Microsoft Windows is installed on a computer, a group window named StartUp is created, Figure 30-13A. As you can see from the illustration, the Windows installation program initially creates an empty menu. However, if you add a program item icon into the StartUp menu, the application represented by the program item icon is started automatically whenever Windows is loaded. As an example, consider the StartUp group window shown in Figure 30-13B. This menu contains the program item icons for three applications—AutoCAD, Explorer, and Notepad.

This is a reasonable selection of applications because these three programs work so well together. Now, whenever Microsoft Windows is started, the three items in the StartUp menu are automatically loaded and displayed simultaneously on the Windows desktop, Figure 30-14.

You can set up a StartUp menu like this one using the following procedure:
1. Right-click on the Start button, then pick Open. This opens the \Windows\Profiles \Administrator\Start Menu folder.
2. Double-click on the Programs icon. This opens the \Windows\Profiles\Administrator \Start Menu\Programs folder.
3. Press the [Ctrl] key while you pick and drag the Explorer icon to the Startup icon. Release the pointer button. This inserts a copy of Explorer in the Startup menu folder.
4. Double-click on the Startup folder icon, and notice that a copy of the Explorer icon is displayed. See Figure 30-15. If you want to change the name, just pick once on the label, then pick again. Do not double-click or you will launch Explorer. Now type a new name and press [Enter].

Figure 30-13.
A—The StartUp menu is created when Microsoft Windows is installed. B—Place any programs you want started every time Windows loads in the StartUp menu. Here, AutoCAD, Explorer, and Notepad programs are added to the StartUp menu.

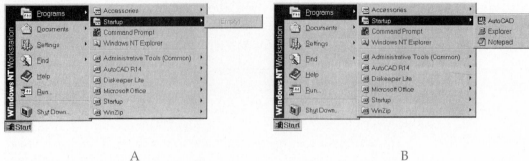

A   B

Figure 30-14.
Each of the applications in the StartUp window is loaded when Windows is started.

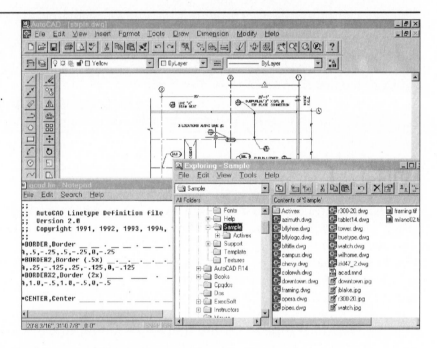

Figure 30-15.
Windows Explorer is added to the Startup menu by right-clicking on the Start button, then opening the Programs folder. A copy of the Explorer icon is then placed in the Startup folder.

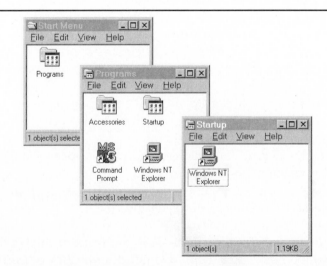

This procedure has placed a copy of Explorer in the Startup menu. Check this by restarting Windows, then picking Programs in the Start menu, then pick Startup in the top portion of the menu. Explorer should be listed. See Figure 30-16.

Figure 30-16.
Windows Explorer is added to the Startup menu.

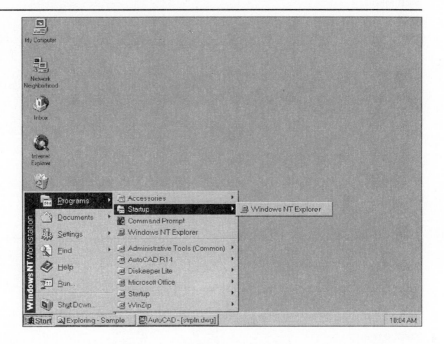

PROFESSIONAL TIP

Windows NT and 95 are document and folder-based operating systems. This means that you can perform a host of functions just by selecting and dragging files and folders. Therefore, almost anywhere you find a file name and its icon, it is possible to work with it. For example, when creating a Startup menu, you can run Explorer and scroll through its folders and files until you find the icon you need, then drag a copy of it to the \Windows\Profiles\Administrator\Start Menu\Programs folder.

A second method for adding programs to the Startup menu is described here for adding AutoCAD:

1. Pick Settings in the Start menu, then select the Taskbar... option. The Taskbar Properties dialog box is displayed.
2. Pick the Start Menu Programs tab. See Figure 30-17. Next pick the Add... button to display the Create Shortcut dialog box.
3. Pick the Browse... button, then double-click to open the AutoCAD R14 folder.
4. Pick the acad.exe icon and pick the Open button. See Figure 30-18.
5. Pick the Next ⟩ button to display the Select Program Folder dialog box. This dialog allows you to select the menu in which you wish to place the program.
6. Pick the Startup icon, then pick Next ⟩. See Figure 30-19.
7. Type the name you wish to appear in the Startup menu. For example, AutoCAD R14. Pick the Finish button when done. See Figure 30-20.
8. Pick OK in the Taskbar Properties dialog box. Check the Startup menu to see if the addition is listed.

Figure 30-17.
Pick the Start Menu
Programs tab to
customize the
Start Menu.

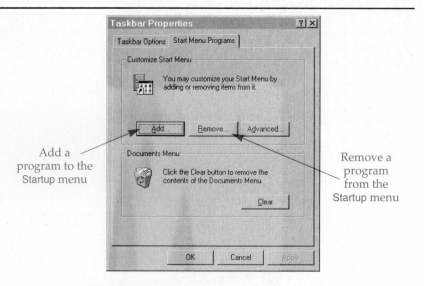

Add a
program to the
Startup menu

Remove a
program
from the
Startup menu

Figure 30-18.
Pick the acad.exe
icon in the Browse
window, then pick
Open to select it for
placement in the
Startup menu.

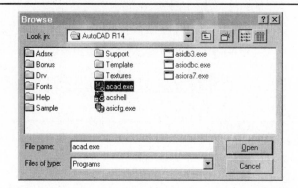

Figure 30-19.
Pick the Startup icon
to place AutoCAD
in the Startup menu
folder.

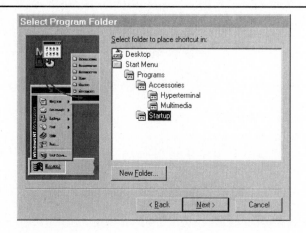

Figure 30-20.
Type the name you
wish to appear in
the Startup menu.

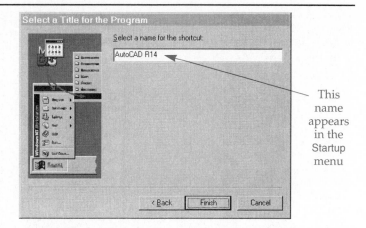

This
name
appears
in the
Startup
menu

Any other programs you wish to have launched automatically when Windows opens can be added in one of the ways just discussed. The next time Windows is loaded, the programs that are listed in the Startup menu will be automatically executed.

Items can be quickly deleted from the Startup menu using the following procedure:

1. When the Taskbar Properties dialog box is displayed, Figure 30-17, pick the Remove button.
2. Pick the plus sign to expand the Startup folder, Figure 30-21.
3. Pick the icon or file name you wish to delete, then pick the Remove button. Pick Yes to send the item to the Recycle Bin.
4. Pick Close then OK to complete the task.

Figure 30-21.
Pick the plus sign to
expand the Startup
folder.

Some additional startup considerations

If you like, you can choose to have an application load automatically at Windows startup and minimized to the taskbar. This saves desktop workspace. When you want to use the application, simply pick the button in the taskbar to open the minimized application.

As an example, suppose you use Notepad on a frequent basis, but do not want the Notepad window opened on screen when Windows is started. Use the following procedure to run Notepad minimized:

1. Right-click the Start button, then pick Open.
2. Double-click the Programs folder, then double-click the Startup folder.
3. Right-click on the Notepad shortcut icon, then pick Properties in the cursor menu. See Figure 30-22.

Figure 30-22.
Right-click on the
Notepad shortcut
icon, then pick
Properties in the
cursor menu.

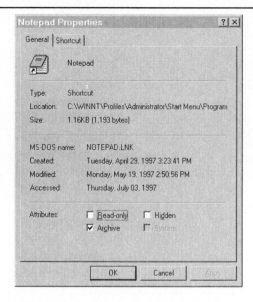

4. Pick the Shortcut tab in the Notepad Properties dialog box.
5. Pick on Minimized in the Run: drop-down list. See Figure 30-23.
6. Pick OK, then close the remaining windows. Restart Windows to ensure that your new settings have taken effect.

   The next time Windows is started, the minimized Notepad icon will appear in the taskbar. Pick on the icon when you want to work with Notepad.

Figure 30-23.
Pick Minimized in the
Run: drop-down list
to run Notepad
minimized at
startup.

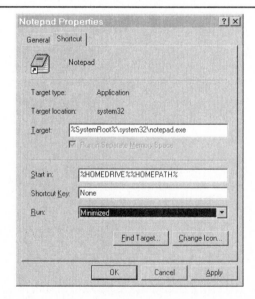

EXERCISE 30-2

❏ Check with your instructor or system administrator before performing this exercise.
❏ Create a Startup window using the techniques described in the preceding text. Be sure to include AutoCAD and Explorer in the Startup window.
❏ After you are satisfied with your Startup configuration, resize and position the windows to your personal taste. Minimize the applications on startup if desired.

Creating a New Folder

Organizing the files on your hard disk is a very important component of computer system maintenance. It is often desirable to keep block symbols, hatch patterns, and script files in separate subfolders. Once you have created a new folder, you can move and copy files and subfolders there from other locations on your hard disk. Creating folders is a simple task with Explorer. The same naming conventions used for file names apply to folder names. To create a folder, do the following:

1. Scroll the left pane of the Explorer window so that the drive or folder in which you wish to create a new folder is clearly visible.
2. Pick the drive or folder icon where you want the new folder to appear.
3. Pick New, then Folder from the File menu. Alternatively you can right-click in the Contents pane of Explorer, then pick New and Folder from the cursor menu. See Figure 30-24. A New Folder icon and label appear in the Contents list.
4. Type a new name and press [Enter]. The folder is ready to be used.

Figure 30-24.
Right-click in the Contents pane of Explorer, then pick New and Folder from the cursor menu to quickly create a new folder.

Searching for Files

Before you can work with files and folders you must find them. Windows provides a variety of options within Explorer to help you find the items you need. Pick Find, then Files or Folders... in the Tools menu, to begin a search. The Find: All Files dialog box appears. See Figure 30-25.

Figure 30-25.
Pick Find, then Files
or Folders... in the
Tools menu to begin
a search. The Find:
All Files dialog box
appears.

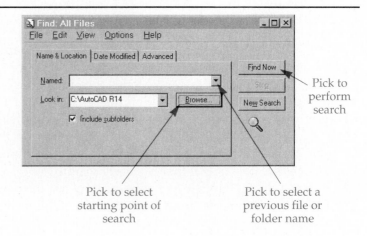

Pick to select
starting point of
search

Pick to select a
previous file or
folder name

Pick to
perform
search

Conducting a basic search

Pick the Name & Location tab if it is not active. This tab requires only two pieces of
search data; the file or folder name, and a location from which to begin the search.

1. Enter the item name in the Named: drop-down list. If prior searches have been
   conducted, pick the down arrow and select an existing name. Each item you
   search for is added to this list. If you wish to narrow the search to include the
   exact format of capital and lower-case characters, pick Case Sensitive from the
   Options menu.
2. Enter the drive or folder location of the item. Pick the Browse button to search for
   the location in a tree format. See Figure 30-26.
3. Pick the Include subfolders check box if you want the search to include all subfolders
   within the drive or folder location you have chosen.
4. Pick the Find Now button to begin the search. If the item you need is found and the
   search is still proceeding, pick the Stop button.
5. Pick the New Search button, then pick OK to clear the item name and begin a new
   search.

Figure 30-26.
Pick the Browse
button to search for
the location in a tree
format.

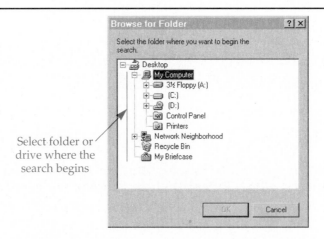

Select folder or
drive where the
search begins

Conducting a dated search

If you wish to look for items that were modified on a specific date or within a given time frame, pick the Date Modified tab of the Find: All Files dialog box. See Figure 30-27. Options selected in this tab are combined with the name and location criteria to focus the search. There are two basic options:

- **All files.** Locates all files based on the name and location criteria.
- **Find all files created or modified:.** Finds all files based on one of the following parameters:
  - **between (first date) and (second date)**—If you want the search limited to a single day, enter the same date in both text boxes.
  - **during the previous (select a number) month(s)**—Type a number or use the up and down arrows to select a value.
  - **during the previous (select a number) day(s)**—Type a number or use the up and down arrows to select a value.

Figure 30-27.
If you wish to look for items that were modified on a specific date or within a given time frame, pick the Date Modified tab of the Find: All Files dialog box.

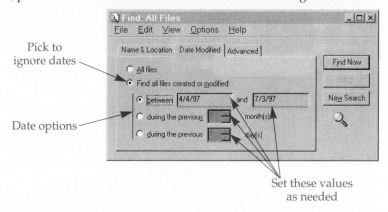

Pick to ignore dates

Date options

Set these values as needed

Advanced search options

Pick the Advanced tab to fine-tune the search even more. See Figure 30-28A. If you are not sure of the three-letter DOS file extension, pick the Of type drop-down list and select the descriptive name of the file type from the extensive list. See Figure 30-28B.

If you remember specific words, phrases, or short sentences (up to approximately 67 characters, including spaces), enter it in the Containing text: box.

NOTE When using the Containing text: search option, try to limit the search as much as possible using all other options previously mentioned, especially the location. In addition to searching for individual file names and types, Explorer must also examine the contents of individual files in order to find a match. This search can take a considerable amount of time if the search parameters are too general.

The final aspect of the advanced search is the file size, which is specified with the Size is: option. This is a maximum/minimum value and is set by picking either At least or At most in the drop-down list, then entering a value in the text box. See Figure 30-28C.

When a search is completed, the results are shown in a list box. See Figure 30-29.

Figure 30-28.
A—Pick the Of type drop-down list and select the descriptive name of the file type.
B—If you are not sure of the three-letter DOS file extension, pick the Of type drop-down list and select the descriptive name of the file type from the extensive list. C—To set the size option, pick either At least or At most in the drop-down list, then enter a value in the text box.

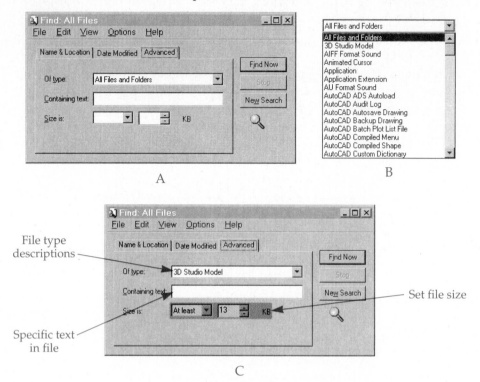

A

B

File type descriptions

Specific text in file

Set file size

C

Figure 30-29.
The search results.

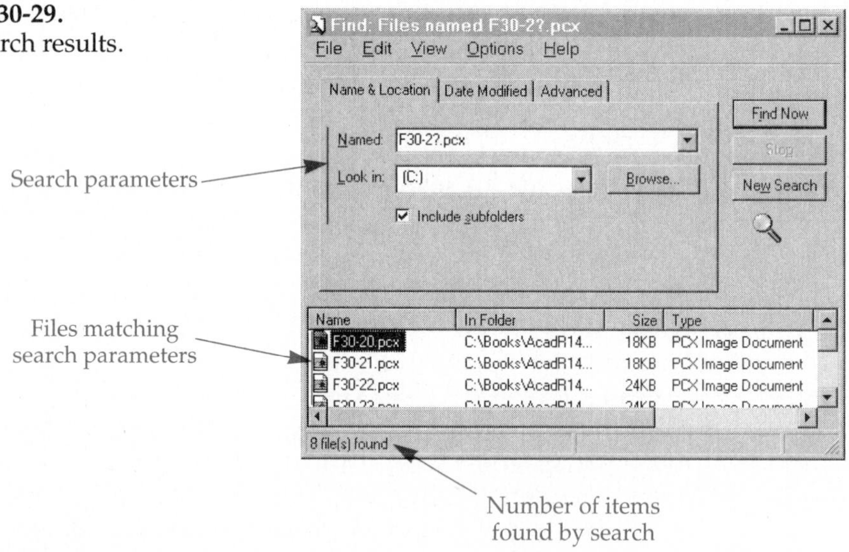

Search parameters

Files matching search parameters

Number of items found by search

PROFESSIONAL TIP

If you know which drive or folder a file is located in, you can quickly select it for a search. Just right-click on the folder or drive icon then pick Find... in the cursor menu. The folder name you picked is automatically placed in the Look in: text box.

❏ Insert one of your disks in the A: drive and select 3½ Floppy (A:) from the All Folders pane.

❏ Make a folder on the A: drive called CLASSES and another called PROJECTS.

❏ Make two subfolders in the CLASSES folder called CAD-I and CAD-II.

❏ Rename the two subfolders to CAD-1 and CAD-2.

❏ Make two subfolders in the PROJECTS folder called P-100 and P-200.

❏ Copy a group of drawing files from the hard disk to one of the subfolders under either CLASSES or PROJECTS. Extend your selection of drawing files as described in this chapter.

❏ Check the Contents pane to verify that the files were copied correctly. Now, delete the subfolder and all the files it contains.

❏ Delete all the folders created in this exercise.

Disk Operations Using Explorer

A variety of disk operations can also be performed with Explorer. These operations include formatting, labeling, and copying disks, along with managing files. Each of these functions is located in the cursor menu that appears after right-clicking on the disk drive icon, Figure 30-30.

Figure 30-30.
A cursor menu appears after right-clicking on the disk drive icon.

Formatting a 3.5" disk

You must format new floppy disks before they can be used. The formatting process prepares a floppy disk so that information can be copied to it. If the disk you intend to format has previously been used, Explorer detects this and informs you accordingly before it removes any existing data from the disk. To format a floppy disk, do the following:

1. Insert a floppy disk in the appropriate disk drive.
2. Select Format... from the cursor menu.
3. The Format dialog box then appears, Figure 30-31.
4. Specify the capacity of the disk to be formatted in the Capacity: list box, or use the drop-down to select the correct capacity.
5. If you want to provide a label for the disk, enter the desired label name in the text box. A label is an identifying name for the disk. The name is shown in the title bar of the directory window.
6. In the example shown in Figure 30-31A, a 1.44 MB disk is to be formatted in the A: drive. This disk will be used to store custom hatch patterns and the label Hatch_patterns is entered in the Volume Label: text box.
7. Once you have specified the appropriate drive, disk capacity, and entered a label (if desired), pick the Start button to begin formatting the disk.
8. When the formatting is complete, pick OK.

Figure 30-31.
A—The Windows NT Format dialog box. B—The Windows 95 Format dialog box.

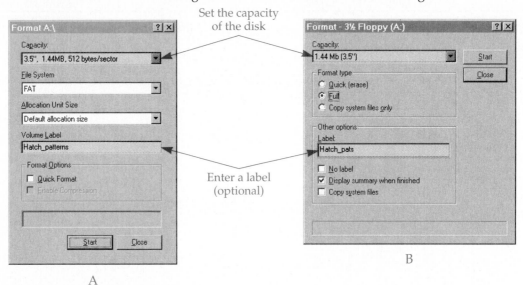

A

B

PROFESSIONAL TIP   Get in the habit of providing a volume label for each disk you format. Write the volume label name on the adhesive label that comes with the 3.5" disk before attaching it to the disk. Attempting to write on the label of a 5.25" disk after attaching it to the disk can cause damage.

CAUTION   Always use caution when formatting a disk. Remember that in addition to preparing a new disk, a full format erases any existing data on a previously formatted disk. Unless you are running a disk recovery utility program, you *cannot* recover information on a disk that is accidentally formatted.

Windows NT and 95 differ somewhat in the options provided in the Format dialog box. Note the differences in Figure 30-31 as you read the items here.

Windows NT

- **File system.** The FAT file system is the standard DOS, Windows 3.x, and Windows 95 File Allocation Table system. When Windows NT is installed, you have the option of partitioning part or all of the hard disk as the NT File System (NTFS). The NTFS option is only available when formatting a hard drive.
- **Allocation Unit Size.** The smallest part of a disk that is allocated to a file. The default setting is best for most uses.
- **Enable Compression.** Folders and files are compressed when saved to disk.

Windows 95

- **Full format.** A full format is the default in NT, but must be selected in 95. This executes a thorough check of the disk and marks bad sectors, but takes longer than a quick format.
- **Copy system files only.** Makes a bootable disk without formatting the disk.
- **No label.** Deletes current label from the disk.
- **Display summary when finished.** Displays a dialog box that provides detailed information about the disk when format is complete.
- **Copy system files.** Makes a bootable disk by copying system files, and formats the disk.

Copying a disk

Throughout this text you have been advised to always make a backup copy of your AutoCAD drawings on 3.5″ disks. It is also a good idea to have a second backup of your original backup. You can easily copy the contents of one 3.5″ disk to another using Explorer. To copy a disk, do the following:

1. Insert the source disk in the drive you want to copy from. If your computer has two drives, insert the destination disk in the second drive. The destination disk is called the *copy to* disk.
2. Right-click the drive icon for the source disk in the All Folders pane.
3. Select Copy Disk... from the cursor menu. The Copy Disk dialog box appears, Figure 30-32.
4. Labels and icons representing the disk formats are shown in the Copy Disk dialog box. Select the appropriate icons for the Copy from: and the Copy to: disks.
5. Pick the Start button. A Copy Disk alert asks you to insert the disk you want to copy from. Insert the proper disk and pick OK. If your computer has two disk drives, you'll be asked to insert both the source and destination disks. If using a single disk drive computer, you will have to switch disks.
6. At the next Copy Disk alert, insert the disk you want to copy to and pick OK.
7. The contents of the source disk are then copied to the destination disk.

Figure 30-32.
The Copy Disk dialog box.

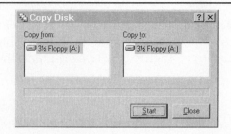

CAUTION

The Copy Disk command not only copies, it formats! Therefore, there is no need to spend time formatting a disk before making a copy. Be certain your destination disk is blank or only has unneeded files on it.

Protecting your disks

Dust, heat, cold, magnets, cigarette smoke, and coffee do great damage to your disks. Placing your disk on or near any other electrical or magnetic device can quickly ruin your files. This includes your digitizer tablet! A ringing telephone can even be a dangerous enemy of the disk because of its magnetic field. Beyond physical damage, you or someone else could write over the files on a disk, or put files on the wrong disk, making them difficult or impossible to find.

The easiest way to protect the data on your floppy disk from accidental erasure is to use the write-protect tab. A 3.5″ disk uses a small, sliding tab located on the bottom side of the disk. Notice that the write-protect tab is in effect when it is moved toward the edge of the disk. Use the point of a pen or your fingernail to slide the tab. For 5.25″ disks, the write-protect tab is a small, rectangular adhesive-backed piece that is placed over the write-protect notch. See Figure 30-33.

Figure 30-33.
A—On a 3.5″ disk, move the write-protect tab to the "Read Only" position.
B—Protect your 5.25″ disks by placing a write-protect tab over the notch on the disk.

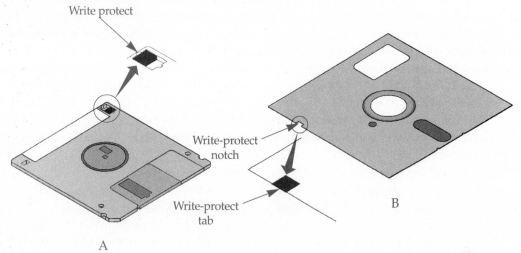

When the tab is moved to the write-protect position, you cannot format, save, or copy files to that disk. However, the files can be read from the disk. Explorer displays a dialog box with a write-protect error message if you attempt to format or save to a write-protected disk. If you must use the disk for writing or formatting purposes, simply remove the tab or move it to the appropriate position.

EXERCISE 30-4

❑ Insert one of your blank 3.5″ disks into the A: drive.
❑ Use the Format command to format the disk and label it PROBLEMS.
❑ Copy a drawing file from the \AutoCAD R14 folder on the hard disk to the floppy.
❑ Use the Copy Disk command to make a backup copy of the PROBLEMS disk.

Additional disk management functions

The cursor menu that is displayed by right-clicking on the floppy drive icon (Figure 30-30), provides several other functions for managing the contents of disks. The following list briefly describes these options:

- **Explore.** Changes the current Exploring window to reflect the contents of the disk.
- **Open.** Opens a separate window that displays all of the folders and files in the disk.
- **Find....** Opens the Find: All Files dialog box for the disk.
- **Create Shortcut.** Allows you to create a shortcut icon on the desktop. When you double-click on this icon, a 3.5″ disk window is opened, exactly like the Open command above.
- **Properties.** Opens the Properties dialog box for the disk. Provides a General tab, which displays general information about the disk, and provides a text box for naming the disk without formatting it. The Tools tab provides three tools that allow you to check the disk for errors, backup the disk to a tape drive, and defragment data stored on the disk. Check your *Windows NT* or *Windows 95 Users Guide*, or use the Windows online help for additional information on these tools.

Working with network drives

Two commands in the Explorer Tools pull-down menu and toolbar enable you to work with any network drives that are a part of your network system. These are Map Network Drive and Disconnect Network Drive. Once you have mapped your system to the other shared directories on the network, you will have access to any data and programs stored there.

Using this facility requires that you have prior knowledge of the workings of your network, and that you are aware of login names, passwords, procedures, and access rights to folders and files. Always consult your instructor, supervisor, or system administrator before connecting to or accessing networks with which you are not familiar. Consult your Windows documentation for detailed information on working with networks.

Running Windows 3.x File Manager in NT or 95

Many people are intimidated by change, especially if it means having to learn a new system just to continue doing the activities that must be done to continue our studies or do our jobs. If you are familiar with the workings of File Manager and wish to continue using it while learning the ins and outs of Explorer, it's easy to do. File Manager is actually hidden in NT and 95 and can be accessed quickly.

1. Pick Run... from the Start menu.
2. Type winfile in the Open text box and pick OK.

Figure 30-34.
A—The File Manager in Windows NT.
B—File Manager in Windows 95.

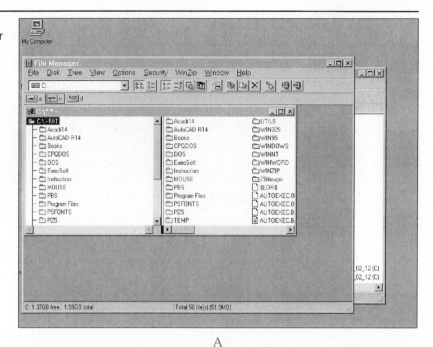

A

B

That's it! The File Manager appears as a window. The Windows NT version of File Manager has the addition of a Security pull-down menu and a toolbar similar to that in Explorer. See Figure 30-34A. The Windows 95 File Manager is a much closer duplicate of the old Windows 3.x version. See Figure 30-34B.

NOTE

This chapter has introduced you to only some of the features within Explorer. Become familiar with *all* of the functions offered by this useful tool. By making Explorer an integral part of your daily work, you can greatly increase your productivity.

Chapter Test

Write your answers in the spaces provided.

1. What two panes compose the Explorer window?_____
    _____

2. Directories and subdirectories are referred to as _____ and
    _____ in Windows.

3. Write the correct path name for a drawing file named houseplan located in the
    Architectural subfolder, which is a branch of the Projects folder on the C: hard disk
    drive. _____
    _____

4. How can you select a consecutive group of items? _____
    _____

5. How can you select a second consecutive group of items that are not adjacent to
    the first? _____
    _____

6. How do you run a program that is listed in Windows Explorer? _____
    _____

7. What size icons are displayed in Explorer when the List option is used? _____

8. Which AutoCAD command must be used when dragging and dropping an
    external text file? _____

9. What three-letter file extension is valid when using drag and drop to place text in
    an AutoCAD drawing? _____

10. What is the purpose of the Explorer window *split bar*? _____
    _____
    _____
    _____

11. What action should be performed after dragging and dropping a drawing file
    into the AutoCAD graphics window? _____
    _____

12. What menu can be customized to enable programs to be automatically launched
    when Windows is loaded? _____

13. Describe the right-clicking process for creating a new folder._____
    _____
    _____

14. Name the three categories in the Find: All Files dialog box that enable you to
    specify a variety of search parameters. _____
    _____
    _____

15. Which tab in the Find: All Files dialog box allows you to specify text contained in a
    file you are searching for? _____

16. How do you display the Format dialog box? _____

_____

17. How can a disk be labeled without formatting it? _____

_____

_____

18. How can 3.5" disks be protected to prevent data from being written to them accidentally? _____

_____

19. How can the Windows 3.x version of File Manager be run in Windows 95 or NT?

_____

_____

Problems

*Obtain the permission of your instructor or system administrator before creating or deleting folders, formatting or labeling disks, deleting files, or using any **Explorer** command that can alter the structure of the hard disk files and directories.*

1. This problem involves making new subfolders and copying drawing files to them.

   A. Make your own subfolder under the AutoCAD R14 folder. Name it using your initials.

   B. Make the new subfolder current.

   C. Copy all of your drawing files from one 3.5" disk to the subfolder.

   D. Make a subfolder within your new directory and name it Bak.

   E. Make the Bak subfolder current.

   F. Copy all of your .bak files into the Bak subfolder.

   G. Open a separate window for each of your subfolders.

2. Make a new subfolder of the folder you created in Problem 1. Name the new subfolder Test.

   A. Copy the contents of the Bak subfolder into Test.

   B. Open a new directory window for the Test subfolder.

   C. Rename one of the files in the Test subfolder to hey.you.

   D. Use the Search command and list all files with a .you file extension.

   E. Copy the hey.you file to the Bak subfolder and rename it who.me.

   F. Use the Search command and list all files with a .me file extension.

   G. Copy who.me to one of your 3.5" disks and name it yes.you.

   H. Delete the three files you just created.

   I. Activate the Bak subfolder and delete it and all the files it contains.

3. Format four disks in a row without exiting the Format dialog box. Provide volume labels for the disks as they are formatted. When all formatting is complete, change the names of each disk label without formatting the disks again.

4. Use the copy disk option of Windows to make backup copies of all your 3.5" disks that are used for drawing and data file storage. Label the disks that are copied with the same labels as the originals, but add a designation that indicates either "backup" or "copy".

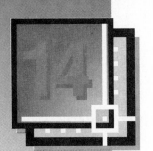

AutoCAD Release 14 Features

The following information has been condensed from the material in AutoCAD's **What's New** presentation. This is accessed by picking **What's New** in the **Help** pull-down menu.

Drawing Productivity

AutoCAD Release 14 features that address drawing productivity have been broken down into the following categories.

Overall product performance

- **File operations.** The time required to open drawing files, save drawings, and create blocks has been shortened significantly.
- **Display operations.** Zooms, pans, redraws, and regenerations have been speeded up.
- **Draw/edit operations.** Many editing operations take less time.

Reduced memory requirement

- **New graphics subsystem.** The AutoCAD ADI graphics pipeline has been replaced with a modern, more efficient HEIDI-based graphics system.
- **Lightweight polyline.** Polyline vertex data is stored as a single entity, thus requiring less memory.
- **Improved hatch object.** The Release 14 hatch object stores the calculated boundary of the hatch pattern along with a pointer to the hatch definition. This new hatch entity is not composed of individual lines and requires far less memory.
- **Application demand loading.** ARX (AutoCAD Runtime Extension) applications, such as the ACIS solid modeling feature, are loaded only as requested by the user, or when called by another application.

Paperspace performance

- **Regens not required.** Display operations in paper space no longer require a regen.
- **Real-time and transparent Pan and Zoom.** In Release 14, both real-time and transparent panning and zooming are supported in paper space.

Quick precision drawing

- **AutoSnap.** Users can visually preview and confirm snap point candidates before picking a point during drawing operations. Temporary markers are displayed at snap points, and a pop-up window displays a SnapTip with the name of the object snap mode.
- **Tracking.** Using tracking, users can visually locate points relative to other points.
- **Running object snap toggle.** Users can toggle any running object snaps *off* prior to selecting a point without losing the running object snap settings.
- **Coordinate entry priority.** This feature allows explicit coordinate entry to have precedence over any running object snaps.

Hybrid raster/vector drawings

Release 14 adds true support for combining a variety of raster images with standard AutoCAD vector drawings.

Layer and linetype management

- **Layer and Linetype Properties dialog box.** This dialog box has been extensively modified and enhanced to increase the accessibility and usability of drawing organization features and key object properties. Layer and Linetype tabs in the dialog box allow complete control over these features.
- **Make Layer Current command.** This new command allows users to set the current layer to match that of a selected drawing object.

Object property access

- **Display and edit object properties via toolbar.** The Release 14 **Object Properties** toolbar has been enhanced to list and set layer, color, and linetype, and to list and edit the properties of selected drawing objects as well.
- **Match properties.** A one-step interface for copying properties such as color and linetype from one object to another.
- **Improved property controls.** A drop-down list has been added to the color control of the **Object Properties** toolbar to allow selecting the active color. ToolTips are displayed for the icons in the layer control to clarify their meaning.

Windows UI integration

- **Explorer dialog support.** Release 14 utilizes the Explorer-style dialogs found in Windows 95 and NT 4.0, and the operation in AutoCAD is essentially the same in all dialogs.
- **Toolbars dialog.** Provides easy access and control of standard and custom toolbars in a more direct manner.
- **Right-button (shortcut) menus.** This feature increases productivity by offering a standard Windows method of direct object manipulation. Other shortcut menus are available for embedded objects, the command window and toolbars, and Explorer-style dialogs.
- **Menu modifications.** Pull-down menus and toolbars adhere more closely to Windows standards enabling improved learnability.
- **Online help.** Has been updated to use the latest Windows presentation and organization.

Command line editing

- **Command line recall.** Users have the ability to recall previous command line entries using the up and down arrow keys.
- **Command line editing.** Command line editing using standard Windows editing methods (such as insert, backspace, overwrite, end, etc.) is supported.

Interactive display improvements

- **Combined realtime Pan and Zoom tool.** Realtime **Pan** and **Zoom** are combined into a single command allowing the user to easily switch between **Pan** and **Zoom** modes.
- **Zoom extents improvements.** Zooming to the drawing extents no longer triggers a regen in most cases.
- **Adjustable cursor.** The size of the screen cursor is adjustable in Release 14.

Plot preview usability

An updated plot preview facility is now directly accessible from the **Standard** toolbar without going though the **Print** dialog box first.

Text usability

- **Text editor usability.** Release 14 provides a new method of specifying text placement that is easier to understand and more representative of final placement.
- **TrueType font support improvements.** Release 14 adds support for TrueType font families and additional character formatting including bold, italic, and underscore capabilities.
- **Find and Replace.** A find and replace feature is supported.

Modern learning tools

- **AutoCAD learning assistance.** This is an interactive, multimedia learning tool designed to assist users in increasing their productivity through a self-paced, as-needed tutorial facility.
- **Improved online documentation.** Online documentation is now integrated into the standard help system.
- **What's This Help.** Many of the dialogs in Release 14 feature a direct, on-demand link to the help system by utilizing a Windows standard **What's This** feature.
- **Direct access to AutoCAD web page.** A single **Standard** toolbar icon provides access to the AutoCAD web page via the user's configured web browser.

Start Up dialog box and new drawing wizards

- **Use a Wizard.** Wizards are intended for new or infrequent users who want to be guided through the basic steps of setting up a drawing.
- **Use a Template.** Selecting **Use a Template** from the **Start Up** dialog box displays a list of template drawing files (.dwt extension).
- **Start from Scratch.** Allows the user to choose either English or metric units and inserts some very basic default settings stored in the acad.dwt and acadiso.dwt drawing template files.
- **Open a Drawing.** Opens an existing drawing. The names of up to the last four opened drawings are displayed in the list box.

Bonus Material

When you select a full installation or Bonus and Batch Plotting in a custom installation, four additional Bonus toolbars and a **Bonus** pull-down menu are provided. See *Appendix C* for more details on how to install the Bonus material. The following section covers three of the toolbars and the pull-down menu. The **Internet Utilities** toolbar is discussed in *AutoCAD and its Applications—Advanced, Release 14.* The command shown in parenthesis is the command line entry equivalent.

Bonus Standard Toolbar

The buttons on the toolbar named **Bonus Standard Toolbar** are described as follows. See Figure A-1.

Figure A-1.
The **Bonus Standard** toolbar.

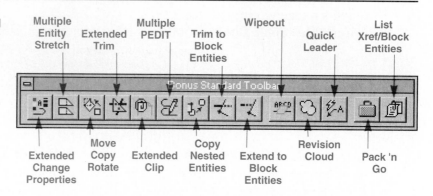

- **Extended Change Properties. (EXCHPROP)** A general editing feature for entities that enables you to change properties such as color, layer, linetype, linetype scale, thickness, polyline width, polyline elevation, text height, text style, **Mtext**, and attribute definitions.
- **Multiple Entity Stretch. (MSTRETCH)** Multiple entities can be selected using a crossing polygon or window. Pick a base point and the subsequent stretch affects all selected entities.
- **Move Copy Rotate. (MOCORO)** Multiple entities can be selected and then moved, copied, rotated, or scaled about a selected base point.
- **Extended Trim. (EXTRIM)** A powerful command that asks for a polyline, line, circle, or arc for a cutting edge. Next, pick the side to trim on and all lines are automatically trimmed on that side.
- **Extended Clip. (CLIPIT)** Enables you to select a polyline, wipeout, circle, or arc to use as a clipping edge, which then becomes the frame for a selected image, xref, or block. This allows you to create views and details that appear in circular or irregular-shaped frames.
- **Multiple Pedit. (MPEDIT)** Performs polyline edit functions on multiple polylines at the same time.
- **Copy Nested Entities. (NCOPY)** Copies entities that are nested inside a block or xref.
- **Trim to Block Entities. (BTRIM)** Blocks or xref objects can be used as cutting edges to trim intersecting entities.
- **Extend to Block Entities. (BEXTEND)** Blocks or xref objects can be used as boundary edges to which other entities can be extended.
- **Wipeout. (MPEDIT)** Fills an enclosed area, such as a polyline, with the background color.
- **Revision Cloud. (REVCLOUD)** Creates a series of connected polyline arcs to form a cloud-shaped entity used to surround a revised area on a drawing.
- **Quick Leader. (QLEADER)** A customizable leader command. To access the **Quick Leader Options** dialog box, press [Enter] at the first **QLEADER** prompt. Once the options have been set they remain in effect on subsequent uses of **QLEADER** until they are changed.
- **Pack 'n Go. (PACKNGO)** Copies all files that are associated with a drawing to any location that you choose. These files include xrefs, fonts, shapes, etc. A text file report is also copied to the location directory.
- **List Xref/Block Entities. (XLIST)** Pick a nested entity in a block or xref to list the object, block name, layer, color, and linetype.

Bonus Text Tools

The buttons on the **Bonus Text Tools** toolbar are described as follows. See Figure A-2.

Figure A-2.
The **Bonus Text Tools** toolbar.

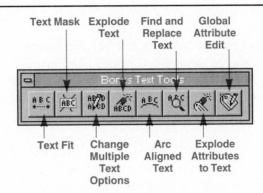

- **Text Fit. (TEXTFIT)** Changes existing text length to fit between new ending and starting points. Text height remains the same.
- **Text Mask. (TEXTMASK)** Hides (masks) all objects behind the selected text. Works with the **WIPEOUT** bonus routine to create a frame around the text that is selected or offset from the text a specified distance.
- **Change Multiple Text Items. (CHT)** Edit the height, justification, location, rotation, style, and text string of individual or global text strings.
- **Explode Text. (TXTEXP)** Explodes text or **Mtext** into lines and arcs. Thickness and elevation can then be assigned to the resulting entities.
- **Arc Aligned Text. (ARCTEXT)** Text can be placed along an arc.
- **Find and Replace Text. (FIND)** Displays the **Find and Replace** dialog box, which allows you to enter the text to find and the text to replace it with. It can be a case-sensitive replace, and can do a global change.
- **Explode Attributes to Text. (BURST)** Explodes selected block and converts attributes to text entities.
- **Global Attribute Edit. (GATTE)** Globally edits the selected block's attribute value to a new value that you provide.

Bonus Layer Tools

The buttons on the **Bonus Layer Tools** toolbar are described as follows. See Figure A-3.

Figure A-3.
The **Bonus Layer Tools** toolbar.

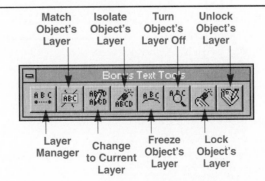

- **Layer Manager. (LMAN)** Layers can be frozen, thawed, on, or off. These are called *layer states,* and they can be saved in an .lay file, much the same as a viewport configuration file.

- **Match Object's Layer. (LAYMCH)** The layer of a selected object can be changed to match the layer of another selected entity.
- **Change to Current Layer. (LAYCUR)** The layers of one or more objects can be changed to the current layer.
- **Isolate Object's Layer. (LAYISO)** One or more selected layers can be isolated by turning all unselected layers off.
- **Freeze Object's Layer. (LAYFRZ)** The layer(s) of selected objects are frozen.
- **Turn Object's Layer Off. (LAYOFF)** The layer(s) of selected objects are turned off.
- **Lock Object's Layer. (LAYLCK)** The layer of a selected object is locked.
- **Unlock Object's Layer. (LAYULK)** The layer of a selected object is unlocked.

Bonus pull-down menu

The same commands listed in the previous **Bonus** toolbars sections are also located in the **Bonus** pull-down menu. See Figure A-4. Additional commands in the **Layers** cascading menu of the **Bonus** pull-down menu that are not found in the **Bonus Layer Tools** toolbar are as follows:

- **Turn All Layers On. (LAYON)** Turns all layers in the drawing on.
- **Thaw All Layers. (LAYTHW)** Thaws all layers in the drawing.

Figure A-4.
The **Bonus** pull-down contains five cascading menus.

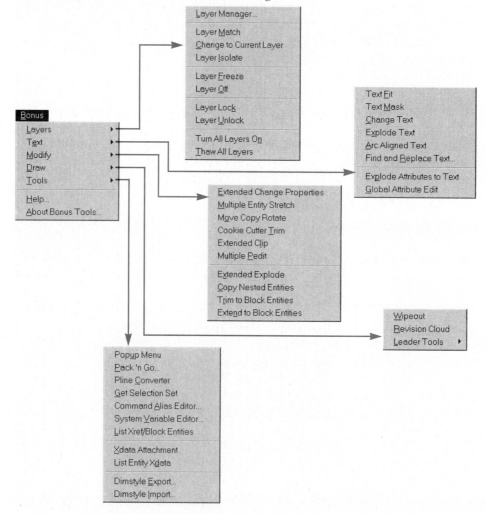

In addition to the commands that are found in both the **Bonus** toolbars and the **Bonus** pull-down menu, a **Tools** cascading menu is also provided in the pull-down. These command options are as follows:

- **Popup Menu. (BONUSPOP)** When toggled on, a check mark appears next to this item. Press [Ctrl] and right-click to display the **View** pop-up cursor menu.
- **Pack 'n Go... (PACK)** Displays the **Pack & Go** dialog box. See **Pack 'n Go** above in the *Bonus Standard Toolbar* section.
- **Pline Converter. (CONVERTPLINES)**
- **Get Selection Set. (GETSEL)** Creates a selection set of entities selected on one or more layers.
- **Command Alias Editor... (ALIASEDIT)** Displays the **acad.pgp – AutoCAD Alias Editor** dialog box. Two tabs allow you to add, remove, or edit command aliases or shell commands found in the acad.pgp file.
- **System Variable Editor... (SD)** Displays the **System Variables** dialog box that allows you to edit system variable settings and values while you work.
- **List Xref/Block Entities. (XLIST)** See above in the **Bonus Standard Toolbar** section.
- **Xdata Attachment. (XDATA)** Extended entity data (xdata) can be attached to a selected entity.
- **List Entity Xdata. (XDLIST)** Lists the xdata that is attached to an entity.
- **Dimstyle Export... (DIMEX)** All of the settings in a named dimension style can be exported to a file with a .dim file extension.
- **Dimstyle Import... (DIMIM)** Imports dimension styles saved in a .dim file.

Presentation-Quality Drawings

The following features address presentation-quality drawings:

- **Bitmap import.** Release 14 adds true support for importing a variety of image formats.
- **Solid fill.** The user can easily and quickly fill a boundary with a solid fill instead of a hatch pattern.
- **Display order control.** The **DRAWORDER** command allows the user to change the drawing and plotting order of many objects in the drawing database. This provides control over the display of geometry and hard copy output when two or more objects overlay each other.
- **Compound document support.** Provides improved control and output of objects inserted from other applications.
  - **Proportional scaling**—Dragging an object with its corner handles maintains the object's aspect ratio making it easier to match the object's scale to the drawing.
  - **Drawing order control**—Release 14 has the ability to control the display and print order of objects.
  - **Visibility control**—Users can quickly and easily toggle the display of embedded objects on and off with the **OLEHIDE** system variable.
  - **Selectability control**—Users can specify embedded objects to be selectable or not.
  - **Convert to raster during paste**—Embedded objects may be converted to raster objects during the paste operation.
  - **Compound document printing**—Embedded metafile objects may now be printed on nonstandard system printer devices.
- **Text Quality.** Improvements in both the display and output of TrueType fonts allows users to prepare higher quality drawings.
- **Photorealistic Rendering.** Release 14 supports photorealistic capabilities such as reflections and shadow-casting as well as the ability to apply realistic materials to models.

Communicate and Share Designs

AutoCAD Release 14 features that address communicate and share designs have been broken down into the following five categories.

External reference enhancements

- **Xref Manager.** Release 14 supports a new, intuitive dialog interface for managing Xrefs. The dialog provides the ability to display referenced drawings in either a tree-like, hierarchical view or as a sortable list of Xref file names and properties.
- **Clipping.** The display of Xref geometry may now be clipped with the **XCLIP** command.
- **Spatial and Layer Indices.** Spatial and layer indices can be created and saved with the reference drawing for use with demand loading.
- **Unload.** Users may now unload referenced drawings. This gives the equivalent performance gain of detaching the Xref but retains the Xref path information, layer settings, and name in the host drawing.

Raster image support

- **Image Support in Drawings.** Release 14 provides standardized support for a wide variety of raster image formats within AutoCAD drawings.
- **Image Manager.** The primary control of images is through the **IMAGE** command which calls the **Image** dialog box.
- **Image Clipping and Manipulation.** Imported images can be clipped to any closed polygonal boundary as well as scaled, moved, copied and rotated.
- **Display Controls.** Image brightness, contrast, fade, and transparency are fully adjustable.
- **Unload.** Users may temporarily hide the display of specified images while retaining the image file reference.

 NOTE For complete coverage of this material see *AutoCAD and its Applications—Advanced, Release 14.*

Internet tools

- **Drawing Web File (DWF) publishing.** Drawing Web Files (.dwf) files can be output directly from Release 14 using the **EXPORT** command. The DWF specification defines a simple, standard vector designed specifically for use on the World Wide Web.
- **Internet Utilities.** Provides users the ability to create and edit hotlinks in their drawings that are accessible when viewing .dwf files created from the drawing.
- **Browser Access.** Gives users an easy means as to launch their Internet web browser from within AutoCAD.

NOTE For complete coverage of this material see *AutoCAD and its Applications—Advanced, Release 14.*

File interoperability

- **AutoCAD R12/13 compatibility.** Release 14 reads Release 12 and Release 13 drawing format files automatically. In addition, Release 14 can save its drawing to both Release 12 and Release 13 formats.
- **Export.** Release 14 supports DWF, STL, and Release 12/LT 2 DXF, Release 13/LT 95 DXF, and Release 14 DXF file formats to its other export formats.
- **Save As dialog box.** The **Save As** dialog box in Release 14 supports saving drawing files in Release 12/LT 2, Release 13/LT 95, and Release 14 DWG and DWF file formats as well as the new .dwt (drawing template) format.

Template drawings

AutoCAD Release 14 introduces the use of template drawings. Using templates is similar to using a prototype drawing in previous releases of AutoCAD, as well as being similar to templates in Microsoft Office.

Customization Support

AutoCAD Release 14 features that address customization support have been broken down into the following five categories.

NOTE For complete coverage of this material see *AutoCAD and its Applications—Advanced, Release 14.*

ActiveX Automation support

AutoCAD Release 14 supports Active Automation, Microsoft's common, cross-application customization and integration facility. ActiveX Automation enables easy integration of AutoCAD with other Windows 95 applications.

Persistent AutoLISP

AutoLISP functions, routines and variables persist (i.e., remain loaded) if a new drawing is opened.

Object interoperability

Release 14 offers enhanced support for object interoperability for users who receive drawings containing custom objects, but who do not have the application that created them.

Application demand loading

In Release 14 an application is loaded only when one of its application-specific custom objects is encountered in a drawing, or when one of its application-specific commands is entered.

ARX API extensions

For application programmers, Release 14 allows an improved use of system MFC resources, access to new lightweight objects and selection mechanisms, and other enhancements.

Management Tools

AutoCAD Release 14 features that address management tools have been broken down into the following six categories.

Preferences control

- **Preferences dialog box.** The **PREFERENCES** and **CONFIG** commands of previous releases of AutoCAD are combined into a single, tabbed **Preferences** dialog box.
- **Project folders and path support.** Release 14 supports a new setting to specify the locations of Xref and raster image files referenced by a drawing in a project.
- **Profiles tab.** The **Profiles** tab of the new **Preferences** dialog permits saving and restoring a group of settings at one time.
- **Automatic configuration.** A default, usable configuration is automatically created if one is not found or specified.
- **System registry support.** Configuration settings are stored in the Windows system registry.

Network printing

- **Network print queue support.** Release 14 may be configured to plot directly to network print queues.
- **Plot spooling.** Support for the system print spooler is also available when using non-system ADI drivers.
- **Basic batch plotting.** Release 14 supports an external facility, **BATCHPLT**, to produce multiple plots in an unattended mode.

Autodesk license manager

Release 14 introduces an easy-to-administer and flexible tool that provides multiple-user software license management over TCP/IP networks.

Simplified installation

Release 14 provides a smooth, virtually hands-free, installation of the software.

- **Network installation wizard.** For users of the Autodesk License Manager, a network wizard guides the administrator step-by-step through installation of Release 14 across the network.
- **No personalization disk.** A separate personalization disk is no longer required during installation.

File sharing

In Release 14 protective file locking is handled by the Windows operating system instead of the proprietary DWK scheme found in previous AutoCAD releases.

Startup switch enhancement

Startup switches in Release 14 have been updated and extended to include support for the Release 14 profile settings and to provide enhanced support for Windows Long File Names (LFN).

System Requirements for AutoCAD and Hardware Overview

This appendix lists the system requirements for AutoCAD Release 14 and outlines the hardware, software, and data exchange options available for this latest AutoCAD release. It is intended to be used as a guide for configuring the AutoCAD system that best meets your needs. Your local authorized AutoCAD dealer will provide you with detailed information about system configuration options and assist you in selecting the platform, peripherals, and companion programs that are right for you. See the AutoCAD Release 14 *Installation Guide* for detailed information on peripheral configurations and settings.

Software and Hardware Requirements

The following software and hardware is required to run AutoCAD Release 14. Optional software and hardware is noted as such.

Software

- Windows NT version 3.51 or 4.0, or Windows 95

Memory

- 32MB of RAM (recommended)
- 50MB of hard disk space (minimum)
- 64MB of disk swap space (minimum)
- 10MB of RAM for each concurrent AutoCAD session (recommended)
- 2.5MB of free disk space during installation only (this space is used for temporary files that are removed when installation is complete)

 NOTE   An additional 8MB to 15MB of space may be required for files installed in the system folder. This need not be on the same drive as the program folder where you load AutoCAD.

Hardware

- Intel 486, Pentium (recommended), or better or compatible processor
- 640 by 480 VGA video display (1024 by 768 recommended)
- CD-ROM drive for initial installation only
- Windows-supported display adapter

- Mouse or other pointing device
- For international single-user and student locked versions only: IBM-compatible parallel port and hardware lock

Digitizers

Driver file	Company/model
dgcaln.dll	CalComp 3400 series
dgphitn.dll	Hitachi® HDG series
dgkur1n.dll	Kurta® IS/ONE*
dgkur23n.dll	Kurta XL, Kurta XLP
dgpsgn.dll	Summagraphics® MM series, Summagraphics MicroGrid series II & III
dgwintabn.dll	Wintab compatible digitizers

Printers and plotters

Driver file version	Company/model
plpcc.dll ADI 4.3	CalComp DrawingMaster plotter
plpcc.dll ADI 4.3	CalComp Electrostatic plotter
plpcc.dll ADI 4.3	CalComp pen plotter
plpcc.dll ADI 4.3	CalComp Solus plotter
plpcc.dll ADI 4.3	CalComp TechJET ink jet plotter
plphplp.dll ADI 4.3	Hewlett-Packard plotter (HP-GL)
plhpgl2.dll ADI 4.3	Hewlett-Packard ink-jet plotter (HPGL/2)
plhpgl2.dll ADI 4.3	Hewlett-Packard printer (HP-GL/2)
plhpgl2.dll ADI 4.3	Hewlett-Packard pen plotter (HP-GL/2)
plphip.dll ADI 4.2	Houston Instrument DMP plotter
plpoce.dll ADI 4.3	OCÉ plotter device
plppost.dll ADI 4.3	PostScript laser printer
plsys.dll ADI 4.3	Raster file export
ADI 4.3	System Printer

Hardware

The physical pieces of equipment used in computer-aided drafting and design are referred to as *hardware*. The microcomputer is the main component. It is accompanied by several other devices called *peripherals.* See Figure B-1. The specific components included in a CAD workstation are presented in the following discussion.

A typical microcomputer is a rectangular-shaped metal box containing the central processing unit (CPU), memory, floppy disk drives, and hard disk drive(s).

The heart of the computer—the CPU—is a chip that handles all the system's calculations. Several printed circuit boards, called *cards*, are found in the computer. These cards have a variety of integrated circuit chips and electronic components attached. Specific cards or *boards* are required for a video graphics display, the connection for a digitizer or mouse (called *serial ports*), and additional items such as extra memory for the computer.

Figure B-1.
Components of an
AutoCAD
workstation.

The computer has a group of blank chips (like empty storage boxes), called *memory*. Memory is also referred to as *random access memory (RAM)*. Random access memory refers to the ability of the computer to randomly store and search for data in this area of the memory. When the computer is turned on, the operating system is loaded into a small portion of the computer's memory. The operating system remains there because it can be accessed faster than if it was used directly from the hard disk drive.

When AutoCAD is loaded, it is placed into the computer's RAM. If your computer has a large amount of RAM, most of the AutoCAD program can be placed in the computer's memory. Then, when you work on a drawing, some (or all) of the drawing may also initially be placed in the computer's memory. If your drawing gets too big, some of it is removed from RAM, and copied, or *paged* to the hard disk. If the *page* of your drawing or AutoCAD is needed again, it is copied back into memory.

IBM compatible computers have 640K (640,000 bytes) of base memory. One byte is roughly equal to one character, such as a letter or number. Memory added to a computer above the basic 640K is called *extended memory*. In order to run AutoCAD Release 14, your computer must have a total of at least 32MB (32 million bytes) of memory, and 64MB is recommended. The more memory a computer has, the faster it can work. More memory allows the computer to load programs into memory and not have to work from the hard disk drive. Accessing the hard drive is much slower than accessing RAM.

Monitor

The *monitor* is the output display device that resembles a small TV. See Figure B-2. Common monitor sizes are 15", 17", and 21" (measured diagonally).

Display *resolution* determines how smooth or jagged text and objects appear on-screen. Resolution is measured in *pixels*. The word *pixel* means *picture element*. A pixel appears as a dot on the screen, but it is actually a tiny rectangle. The display of a monitor is composed of horizontal rows and vertical columns of pixels. A typical display resolution is 640 × 480, meaning there are 640 dots horizontally and 480 dots vertically. High-resolution monitors may display 1024 × 768 pixels, or more.

The resolution of your monitor is directly related to a component in the computer called a *graphics card*. This board is inserted in a slot inside the computer that allows the CPU to communicate with the graphics card and monitor.

Figure B-2. The monitor lets the drafter view the CAD drawings. Shown are two different size monitors. (NEC Technologies, Inc.)

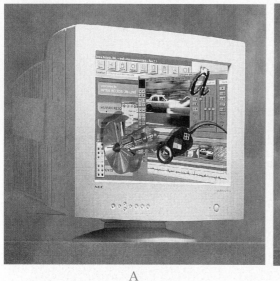

A

B

Graphics cards called *accelerator boards* may allow resolution of up to 1600 × 1200, and up to 16.7 million colors. Many industrial applications need high-end graphics accelerator boards because of the complexity of the models, renderings, and animations.

Keyboard

If you type well, you will soon discover that the keyboard is the most used input device at your workstation. It resembles a standard typewriter keyboard but has additional keys to the left, right, and top. See Figure B-3. The exact location and number of these keys varies from one model to another. In addition to typing commands, the keyboard can be used for entering precise coordinate values.

The keys labeled [F1]–[F10] (or [F1]–[F12]) are called *function keys*. These immediately perform commands that would otherwise have to be typed. AutoCAD uses function keys to control specific operations, many of which are discussed in Chapter 1 of this text.

Figure B-3.

A computer keyboard has many types of keys.

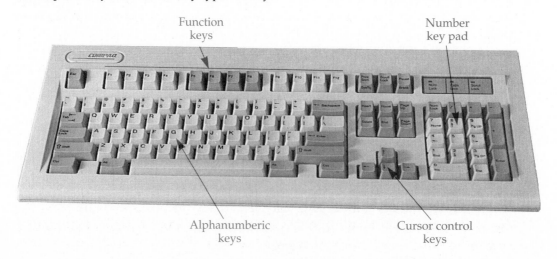

Function keys

Number key pad

Alphanumberic keys

Cursor control keys

Pointing devices

Another important input device is the pointer, or pointing device. A *pointing device* moves the cursor or crosshairs on the screen. With it, you can select point locations and commands from a screen or digitizer tablet menu. Commonly these pointing devices are a multibutton *puck* or a pen-shaped *stylus*. See Figure B-4. Pointing devices are connected to a *digitizer tablet*. Digitizer tablet layout and use is discussed in Chapter 29, Appendix E, and Appendix J of this text.

Figure B-4.
Digitizer pucks are available with different button arrangements. The stylus resembles a pen. (Kurta)

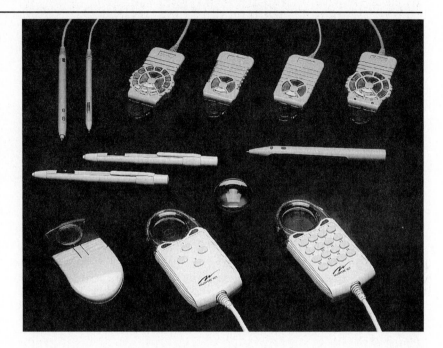

Other more commonly used pointing devices include the *mouse* and *trackball*. The mouse or trackball is often the best choice when cost and table space are concerns (since they do not require a digitizer). Each pointer functions differently, but all input information into the computer.

The digitizer tablet is the drawing board of the CAD workstation. Several examples are shown in Figure B-5. A plastic or paper *menu overlay* containing AutoCAD commands and drawing symbols can also be placed on the digitizer. Items can be selected directly from the menu without looking at the screen. Movement of the puck or stylus is recorded and displayed on the screen as the cursor position. Commands or menus can be picked on the screen by moving the pointing device to the desired item. Then press the pick button on the puck, or press down on the stylus.

The multibutton puck used with a digitizer tablet may have from 1 to 16 buttons. The bottom surface of the puck slides on the digitizer surface. A set of fine crosshairs mounted in the puck serve as the pick point for this device. When the display screen crosshairs move, they are showing the position of the puck's crosshairs on the tablet. One button—the pick button—enters points and selects menu commands. All the other buttons can be programmed to suit the user. See *AutoCAD and its Applications—Advanced, Release 14* for information on digitizer tablet and button customization.

The stylus, a pen-shaped pointer, attached to the digitizer with a cable, works in a different manner. The point of the stylus is pressed down on the surface of the digitizer. A slight click can be felt and heard. This indicates that a point or menu item at the cursor's position on the screen has been selected.

Figure B-5.
Digitizers are available in many different sizes. (CalComp)

The mouse is the most inexpensive pointing device because it does not require a digitizer tablet. A mouse needs only a small flat surface to operate. The mouse is available in two forms: mechanical and optical. See Figure B-6. An optical mouse uses a special reflective pad with grid lines. A light shines from the mouse to the pad. The location of the mouse is shown as the crosshairs location on the screen. The optical mouse must remain on the special pad in order to work.

Figure B-6.
A—An optical mouse. Note the reflective pad. (Summmagraphics)
B—A mechanical mouse can be used on almost any surface.

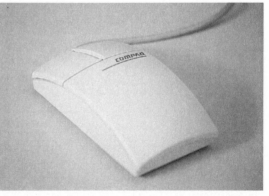

A   B

The mechanical mouse has a roller ball on the bottom. The movement of the roller on any flat surface is sent to the computer and displayed as the screen crosshairs movement. Unlike the stylus and puck, the mouse can be lifted and moved to another position without affecting the location of the screen crosshairs.

If you turn a mouse over, the roller ball is exposed. If this ball was increased in size, you would have a trackball. A trackball enables you to move the cursor on the screen by rolling a ball. A trackball requires only the amount of table space needed for it to sit on. The only part you move is the ball. There are a variety of trackballs available, but most have two or three buttons, much like a mouse. See Figure B-7

Figure B-7.
A trackball is a rotating device used to move the screen cursor or crosshairs.

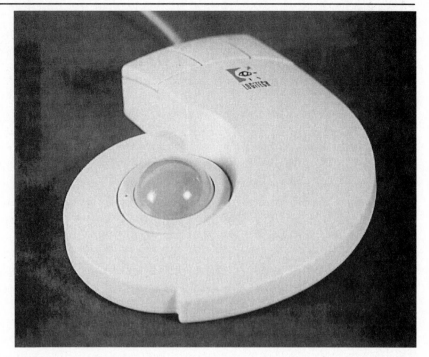

Storage devices and media

Your computer will have at least one floppy and one hard disk drive. Small lights on the front of the disk drives indicate when they are being accessed. These are the storage areas for AutoCAD and its drawings.

Nearly all computer users use 3.5″ flexible disks. They are enclosed in a hard plastic shell that protects them from damage. Originally designed to fit a shirt pocket, they are convenient to carry around. The 3.5″ disk can be formatted for either IBM/DOS compatible systems, or Apple Macintosh systems. The 3.5″ disk drive is the standard for new computers. See Figure B-8A. These disks hold up to 1.44MB of information.

Older systems use a 5.25″ floppy disk. These disks are rare today because they hold less information and are bulkier than the 3.5″ disks.

Figure B-8.
A—Floppy disk drives with a hard disk drive to the left. Note the extra compartment that has a CD-ROM drive. B—An external CD-ROM drive. (NEC Technologies, Inc.)

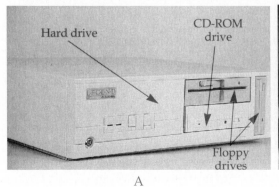

A   B

For those who need to use both sizes of diskette, the dual disk drive is available. This drive allows either size diskette to be placed in the same drive slot and used. If you are using an older computer with a low-density disk drive, you will not be able to use high-density disks.

Most new computers now come with a high-density compact optical digital disk drive (CD-ROM). The discs for CD-ROM drives are much like compact audio discs. The CD-ROM drive is found on most CAD workstations now. In fact, AutoCAD Release 14 is shipped on CD-ROM. An example of a CD-ROM drive is shown in Figure B-8B.

In addition to floppy disk drives, your computer also has a hard disk drive. The hard drive is a sealed unit that contains one or more metal disks, or "platters." These disks have a much greater storage capacity than floppy disks, and are measured in megabytes and gigabytes. Common hard disk sizes are 1 gigabyte (1GB) to over 10 gigabytes (10GB). A small light on the front of the computer indicates when the hard disk drive is being accessed. Before AutoCAD can be used, it must be installed onto the hard disk drive. (See *Appendix C* of this text for installation information.)

The need for greater storage capacity, and more reliable media has seen the increase in popularity of the readable/writable optical drive. The most popular of these drives uses optical disks that are about the same size as standard magnetic 3.5" floppy disks, except the optical disks are a little thicker. They typically store up to 256MB per disk (512MB compressed), however, optical drives that store over 4GB (gigabyte) of data are on the market. Optical drives provide the reliability of optical media without the cost or vulnerability of magnetic media. Optical disks can be rewritten with new data as required, just like magnetic floppies. They are also faster and more reliable for backups than magnetic tape drives.

Selecting floppy disks

Purchase packaged formatted or unformatted disks, keep them boxed, and store the box in a clean area. Keep disks away from extreme heat or cold and magnetic fields found around stereo speakers, telephones, and computer monitors.

A variety of disk drive configurations are now available for most new microcomputers. Therefore, be careful when purchasing floppy disks to make sure that you have the correct disks for your computer.

Even if you store most drawings on the hard disk drive, you will probably use floppy disks for temporary storage of your drawing files, and to share drawings with clients or other computer users. Before files can be stored on a disk, it must be properly prepared. This process is called *formatting*. Formatting is discussed in detail in Chapter 30 of this text. Disks can also be purchased preformatted.

Plotter

Paper and film drawings are most often output by a plotter. A plotter uses felt tip, ballpoint, or wet ink pens, ink jets, or pencils to put lines on paper. These devices can plot any size drawing, and are available in a variety of sizes. See Figure B-9. The plotting routine is covered in Chapter 10 of this text.

The *electrophotographic plotter* is increasing in popularity because of its speed and efficiency. A laser printer uses a single beam of light, however, an electrophotographic plotter uses an array of light-emitting diodes (LED) to draw the image. These tiny LEDs are packed 400 to the inch in the plotter shown in Figure B-10. This produces a plot resolution of 400 dpi (dots per inch). Electrophotographic plotters produce more accurate images than laser printers for large-format drawings.

Figure B-9.
Plotters are available in a variety of sizes and styles. (Hewlett-Packard Co.)

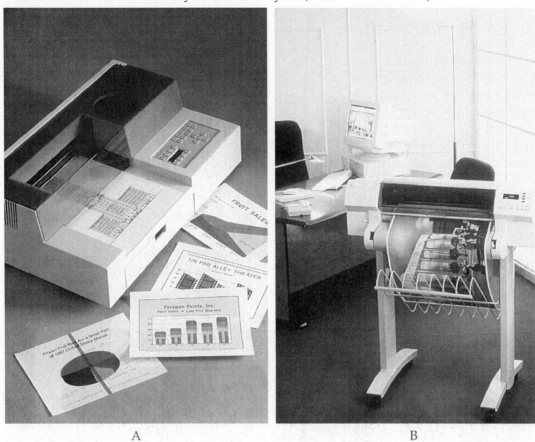

A   B

Figure B-10.
The electrophotographic plotter uses an array of LEDs to plot an image at 400 dpi. (CalComp)

A less expensive alternative to an electrophotographic plotter is an inkjet plotters. Inkjet plotters use a cartridge that shoots tiny drops of ink at the paper. The cartridge requires little maintenance, and may provide from 200 to 400 prints. Resolutions of 300 to 600 dpi are common. A typical inkjet plotter may be three to eight times faster than a pen plotter, depending on the drawing complexity and printing mode.

Plotters fall into two basic groups—vector and raster. Pen plotters are vector plotters because they draw lines using the XY coordinates of the drawing geometry. Although they are accurate and produce fine quality drawings, they are the slowest of the various plotter technologies. Raster plotters, on the other hand, convert CAD vectors into rows and columns of dots, often called a *bitmap*. Raster plotters, such as the inkjet, print an entire row at a time as the paper advances, whereas the pen plotter must constantly move around the paper, drawing each vector.

Printer

Large-format dot matrix printers can produce prints up to C-size (17″ × 22″). However, other more quiet printing devices—inkjet, laser, and electrophotographic devices—also create high-quality prints. Laser printers can plot up to 1200 dpi. Some inkjet printers can plot up to 720 dpi. An example of a laser printer is shown in Figure B-11.

Figure B-11.
This laser printer *paints* an image on a sensitized drum and prints up to 600 dpi resolution. (Hewlett-Packard Co.)

Network systems

There is an increasing need for drawing symbol consistency, accurate project time accounting, instant communication between coworkers, and data security. This has led to the popularity of *network systems*. A **network** is nothing more than several computers, connected by a cable, that communicate with each other. Complex networks have hundreds of computers or terminals working from a central computer called a **server**. Each workstation on the network still requires a CPU, input device, and display device. A diagram of a typical network system is shown in Figure B-12.

The hard disk drives in the server are normally large-capacity drives. They need to store a variety of software, and still have plenty of space for numerous files created by the computer users attached to the network. The network server can also store drawing files that may be needed by computer users in order to complete new drawings. For example, a base drawing of the walls of a structure can be stored on the server. When a student or employee needs to work on a new drawing of the plumbing or electrical layout of the structure, they simply load the base drawing from the server into their computer and begin working. In most cases, the base drawing is preserved in its original form and a different name is given to the new drawing. AutoCAD provides a facility that automatically locks a drawing when a person *checks it out* of the network. This means that only one person can work on a drawing at any given time, thus preventing several people from making different changes to the drawing.

Figure B-12.
Layout of a typical computer network system.

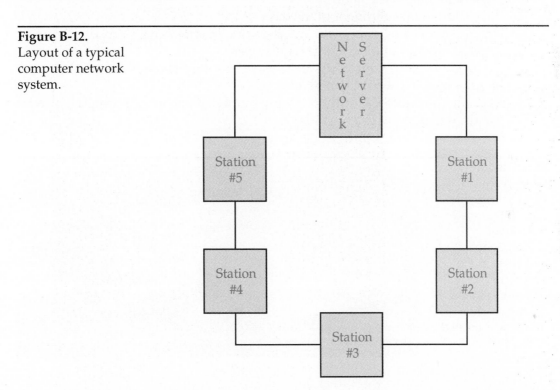

The Ergonomic Workstation

Ergonomics is the science of adapting the working environment to suit the needs of the worker. Since the advent of computers in the workplace in the early 1980s, an increasing number of work-related injuries and afflictions have been reported. By far, the most common of these are repetitive motion disorders. Carpal tunnel syndrome is probably the most well-known of these. Most injuries and disorders related to computer work are the result of the sedentary nature of the work, and the fast, repetitive motions of the hands and fingers on the keyboard and pointing devices.

Most disorders of this nature can be prevented to some extent by proper workstation configuration, good posture, and frequent exercises. Figure B-13 illustrates an example of ergonomic equipment for the computer workstation. Review the following checklist, and try to adhere to as many of the items as possible. As is often the case, a small adjustment of equipment, or the investment of a few extra dollars, can prevent unnecessary future injuries and lost productivity.

✓ Obtain a good chair with proper back support, height, and tilt adjustment.

✓ Use adaptive devices such as forearm supports, wrist and palm rests, and keyboard drawers to help maintain a level wrist position in relation to the keyboard and pointing device.

✓ Avoid resting your wrists on a table while typing, and use a light stroke on the keys.

✓ Investigate the variety of ergonomic keyboards on the market and test for comfort and efficiency.

✓ Position the equipment and supplies of your workstation for ease of use and access.

✓ The screen should be placed from 18" to 30" from the eyes and the top of the display screen should be at eye level.

✓ Lighting should not produce a glare on the screen.

✓ Provide under-desk space so that feet can be placed on a tilted footrest, or at minimum, flat on the floor.

✓ Take short breaks throughout the day.

✓ Practice refocusing your eyes, and engaging in stretching exercises for hands, arms, shoulders, and neck on a regular basis.

✓ Be aware of how your body feels, especially any changes you feel in your shoulders, arms, wrists, and hands.

✓ Consult your doctor if you notice any numbness, aching, or tingling in your hands, wrists, or arms.

Figure B-13.
The forearm supports provide relief from muscle tension for computer operators, and assist in the prevention of repetitive motion disorders. This design was created with AutoCAD. (MyoNetics Inc.)

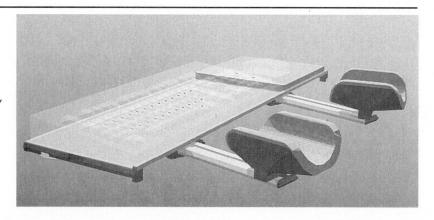

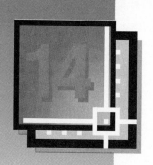

Installing and Configuring AutoCAD

Before you can use AutoCAD, it must be installed onto the hard disk and then configured to work with your specific hardware. The configuration procedure should be used only once, unless equipment is upgraded or new peripherals are added. To use two or more different menu systems, you can duplicate and alter AutoCAD's standard configuration file, acad14.cfg.

Before installing AutoCAD, follow these preparation and setup steps:

- Have Microsoft Windows NT 3.51 or 4.0, or Windows 95 installed and running.
- Determine the hard disk drive to install AutoCAD on.

These steps require only a few minutes and can prevent problems later.

Installing AutoCAD

Installing AutoCAD is a simple process, but it does require that you are somewhat prepared before beginning. First, be sure that you have enough hard disk space for the program files.

A typical installation of AutoCAD requires approximately 82MB of hard disk space and a full installation requires approximately 113MB. The setup process warns you if there is not enough disk space to install the files you have selected. Approximate hard disk storage areas required for some of the components are as follows:

Files	Disk Space
Full installation	113MB
Typical installation	82MB
Custom installation	varies
Program files	44.6MB
Fonts	1.5MB
Samples	17.2MB
Learning Tools	17.8MB
Bonus	4.5MB
Dictionaries	512KB
External Db	6.3MB
ADSRx	5.6MB
Batch plotting	768KB
Texture maps	13.4MB
Internet	352KB
OLE/ADI Plot	576KB

In an effort to run smoothly through the setup process, know the following information before starting.

- AutoCAD serial number_____.
- CD Key_____.
- Disk drive on which to install AutoCAD_____.
- Portion of the AutoCAD files to install_____.
- Dealer's name_____.
- Dealer's telephone number_____.

You are now ready to install the software. Insert the CD into the ROM drive and pick Run... from the Start menu. The Run dialog box is displayed. A blinking cursor appears in the Open: text box. Enter the name of the drive in which you inserted the CD followed by SETUP—for example, D:\SETUP. Substitute the appropriate letter for the disk drive you are using. See Figure C-1. Click the OK button, or press [Enter]. The AutoCAD setup program begins.

Figure C-1.
Access the Run dialog box and enter the name of the drive in which you inserted the installation CD.

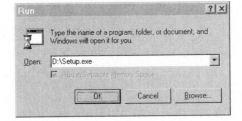

The next two screens provide installation information and ask if you accept or reject the license agreement. See Figures C-2 and C-3. If you accept you are asked to enter the serial number and CD key. See Figure C-4. These numbers are located on a label attached to the CD jewel box, and on the registration card sent with the product.

The next screen requests personal information. Enter the information requested, and use the [Tab] key to move between the text box fields. See Figure C-5. Errors in the personal information can be corrected by picking the 〈 **Back** button. Pick the **Next** 〉 button when you are finished. The same information is redisplayed, and you are given a chance to change your mind or correct anything you enter.

Figure C-2.
The first screen is a user welcome screen. It also provides copyright information for the program.

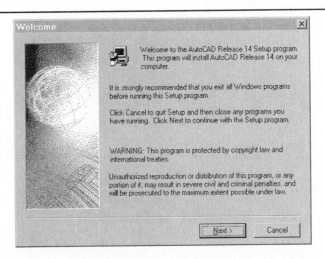

Figure C-3.
Pick **Accept** if you agree with the software license agreement in order to proceed with AutoCAD installation.

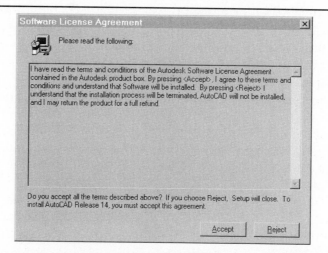

Figure C-4.
Provide the information needed for the **Serial Number:** and **CD Key:** text boxes.

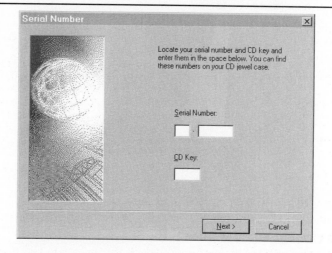

Figure C-5.
Pick **Next** ⟩ after personal information is entered.

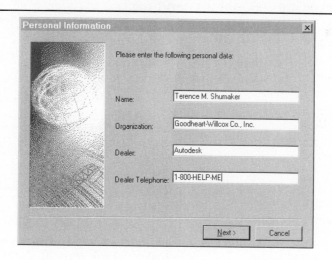

A default folder name is then displayed. This folder will contain all installed AutoCAD files. If you wish to change the folder name, pick the **Browse...** button and enter the name of the new folder. Pick the **Next〉** button if you accept the default name of Program Files\AutoCAD R14. See Figure C-6. If the folder does not exist you are asked if you want it created. Pick **Yes** to continue.

The next screen provides four choices for the amount of files that are installed onto your hard disk. See Figure C-7. If hard disk space is a concern to you, choose the **Compact** button. This installation requires 46MB of hard disk space. If you are unsure about which components to install, but have plenty of hard disk space, choose the **Typical** button. Since this button is the default, pressing [Enter] selects the typical installation.

Figure C-6.
Pick **Browse...** to select a different folder, or pick **Next〉** to accept the default folder.

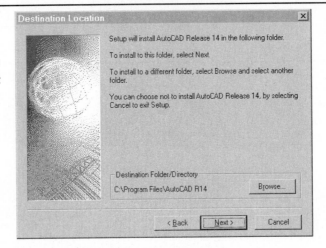

Figure C-7.
Pick the type of installation you prefer.

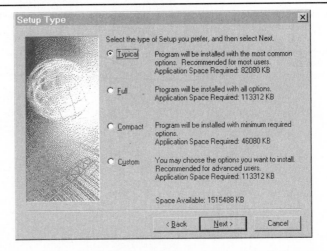

| NOTE | Regardless of the type of installation you select, you can always run the setup program again later and choose additional components to install. |

After selecting the installation type, the setup program informs you that it is checking for hard disk space. Then you are asked to select a folder name from a list, or accept the default name in the **Program Folders:** text box. See Figure C-8. Pick **Next** ⟩ to continue.

The final display indicates the components that you have selected for installation. See Figure C-9. If you wish to change this, pick the ⟨ **Back** button. Otherwise pick **Next** ⟩.

Figure C-8.
Select a folder name from a list, or accept the default name in the **Program Folders:** text box.

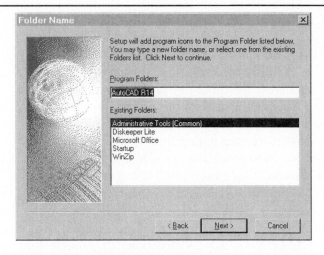

Figure C-9.
The final display indicates the components that you have selected for installation. This example shows a full installation.

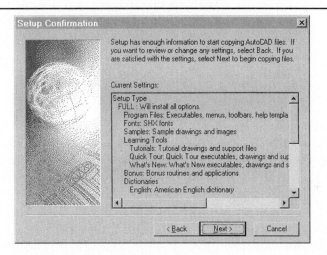

The installation begins, and may take between 5 to 15 minutes, depending on the components of the program you selected for installation. When the installation is complete you are asked if you want to restart the computer. See Figure C-10. If you wish to use AutoCAD right away, it is suggested that you pick the default button, **Yes, I want to restart my computer now**.

Figure C-10.
When the installation is complete you are asked if you want to restart the computer.

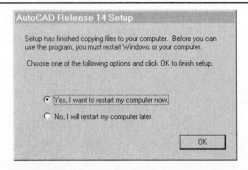

Configuring AutoCAD

Configuring AutoCAD for peripheral devices such as plotters, printers, display devices, and digitizers is a much simpler process than in previous releases. For example, upon installation, AutoCAD finds and uses the current pointing device and system printer. These become the default devices until they are changed.

If you wish to add a new plotter, use the following steps.

1. Pick **Preferences** from the **Tools** pull-down menu, then pick the **Printer** tab.
2. Pick the **New...** button to display a list of supported printing and plotting devices.
3. Select the appropriate device from the list and write your own description in the **Add a description:** text box. Pick the **OK** button.
4. Enter a number from the list of models displayed and press [Enter].
5. Enter a letter designation for a port and press [Enter].
6. Enter the port name, such as COM1, and press [Enter].
7. Press [Enter] to accept the default settings and the new printer is added to the list in the **Preferences** dialog box.

Use the same procedure to select a new pointing device. Pick the **Pointer** tab in the **Preferences** dialog box, select the appropriate device from the list and answer the remaining questions to configure the device.

NOTE

Video display boards (graphics cards), usually come with special drivers that are supplied on a diskette. Always consult the documentation provided with your video card for instructions to install special drivers.

Bonus Toolbars

When you select a full installation, four additional toolbars are displayed on your screen: **Internet Utilities**, **Bonus Standard**, **Bonus Text Tools**, and **Bonus Layer Tools**. They also appear if you select **Bonus** and **Batch Plotting** in a custom installation. In addition to the four toolbars, a **Bonus** pull-down menu is also provided. Refer to *Appendix A* of this text for detailed information about these toolbars and pull-down menu.

These bonus utilities are provided by Autodesk on an *as-is* basis, which means that they may contain bugs. These utilities are usually AutoLISP routines or ARX applications that may provide some measure of productivity, but are often new and not fully tested. They are provided for users to experiment with and may eventually, in future releases, become features of AutoCAD. You can access extensive, detailed help for the bonus tools by picking **Help...** from the **Bonus** pull-down menu.

If you uninstall AutoCAD and then reinstall it using a full or custom install, the bonus menus are not loaded automatically. That is because the original acadr14.cfg file is not removed during the uninstall procedure. This file is edited the first time AutoCAD is installed in order to alter the registries so that all subsequent sessions will load the bonus menus. To work around this, simply enter BONUSMENU at the AutoCAD Command: prompt to load the menus after you have reinstalled AutoCAD.

PROFESSIONAL TIP

Many of the bonus tools that are included in the toolbars and pull-down menu can provide the user with greater flexibility and productivity. Take the time to explore these tools as you work. Excellent on-line help including sample exercises is provided by picking **Help...** from the **Bonus** pull-down menu.

Hard Disk and System Management

Any business—be it a bakery or engineering firm—relies on structure, organization, and standard procedures. A business lacking in one of these areas does not operate efficiently.

Computer systems can be used within the company structure for organization and procedure, or computers can contain the structure and organize procedures. In either case, the method in which computer systems are managed greatly affects the operation of the entire company.

Effective management of an AutoCAD system in a school or business means paying careful attention to the following items:

- ✓ The structure and makeup of the hard disk and mass storage devices.
- ✓ The location of all files and drawings.
- ✓ Storage procedures for student/employee drawing files.
- ✓ Drawing file backup procedures.
- ✓ The kind of template drawings used for specific projects.
- ✓ The location and use of symbol libraries and reference drawings.
- ✓ The location and use of special screen and tablet menus.
- ✓ Drawing naming procedures.
- ✓ Drawing file creation procedures.
- ✓ Creation and distribution of new symbols and menus.
- ✓ Timely updating of software and hardware.
- ✓ Hardware maintenance.

Effective procedures and management techniques must be practiced by all students or employees. In addition, look for ways that standards can be improved and revised for greater efficiency. In this text, read the section in Chapter 1 on using drawing standards and the section in Chapter 23 on creating and using symbol libraries.

Hard Disk Structure

The hard disk drive is the heart of the AutoCAD computer system. It is the storage center for AutoCAD and other programs you use. In addition, it may hold hundreds of additional files, including drawings, menus, AutoLISP programs, slides, scripts, and text files. The manner in which you work with the hard disk and arrange its contents can affect your productivity and efficiency at the computer. Take some time to learn the nature of the hard disk drive.

The root directory folder and its contents

The root directory folder is the trunk of the hard disk tree from which every other folder, subfolder, and file branches. After your computer is set up, the root directory contains a Winnt or Windows folder. See Figure D-1. At this time, other programs may or may not be on the hard disk.

Figure D-1.
The root directory folder may contain only the Winnt directory when the computer is set up.

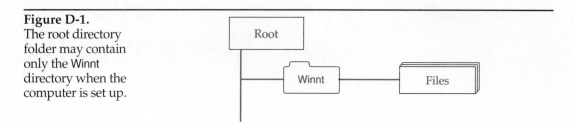

Before a program is installed on the hard disk, a directory folder should first be created. This is usually done automatically by the program's setup.exe file. The program files are copied into that directory. Program files should not be placed in the root directory folder. The default name for the AutoCAD folder is Program Files\AutoCAD R14, and all AutoCAD files reside in it and its subfolders. See Figure D-2.

Figure D-2.
AutoCAD files are stored in the AutoCAD R14 folder.

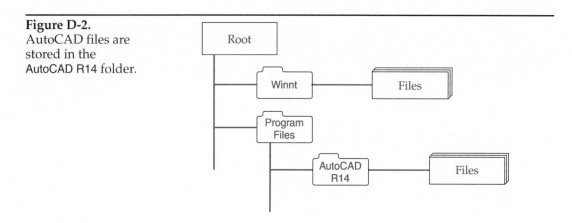

The files that reside in the AutoCAD R14 subfolders are the only ones required by AutoCAD. Any files that you create should be stored in either the appropriate subfolder, or in new subfolders. See Chapter 30 of this text for information on creating folders and subfolders. Additional information is provided in this appendix for creating and maintaining an efficient hard disk tree.

Designing and building a hard disk tree

When AutoCAD is installed, several subfolders are automatically created, depending on which files you instruct AutoCAD to install. These subfolders are created so that the AutoCAD R14 folder is not filled with files it does not need. Take some time to look at the contents of these subfolders and notice the files that are stored there.

After installing the software, you will be faced with other decisions about where to store new files that must go on the hard disk. Only you can decide which files should be saved on the hard disk and where they are to be saved. Regardless of the decisions you make, they should be based on careful consideration of the following:

Questions to ask

✓ Are the computers used for training or production?
✓ Will the computers be used for demonstrations?
✓ Will the system hardware be upgraded often?
✓ How often will drawings be saved to the hard disk?
✓ How many drawings, from how many users, are to be saved on the hard disk?
✓ Will custom menus, AutoLISP, and ADS programs be used?
✓ Will users have their own subfolders?

Points to consider

✓ Load new software in its own folder.
✓ Store nonessential files in subfolders of the parent software folder.
✓ If you have multiple hard drives, leave an empty buffer of at least five megabytes per hard drive for work space over and above the working space required by software such as AutoCAD.
✓ If users have their own subfolder, encourage them to work in it, not in the program directory.

When you answer these questions, and keep these points in mind, you can better estimate what to store on the hard disk and how it should be structured.

Regardless of what you store on the hard disk, have a plan for it. Drawings should not be saved in the AutoCAD R14 folder. Users should not be allowed to save files in the root directory. Decide on the nature of the hard disk structure and then stick to it. Make sure that all users are informed by documenting and distributing standard procedures to all who use the system. Place copies of procedures at each workstation.

Files to be used in conjunction with AutoCAD should be located in subfolders of the AutoCAD R14 folder. Possible subfolders include drawings, AutoLISP files, drivers, slides, and user folders. Within each of these subfolders reside the individual files. The subfolders of AutoCAD R14 in Figure D-3 are some of those that are automatically created when AutoCAD is installed. If you plan to store files within the AutoCAD directory tree, plan on creating new subfolders with names such as Drawings, Lisp, and Scripts. When specific types of files are kept in their own subfolders, file maintenance is easier.

Figure D-3.
Specific subfolders in the AutoCAD R14 folder are for files that are used with AutoCAD. These subfolders are automatically created when AutoCAD is installed.

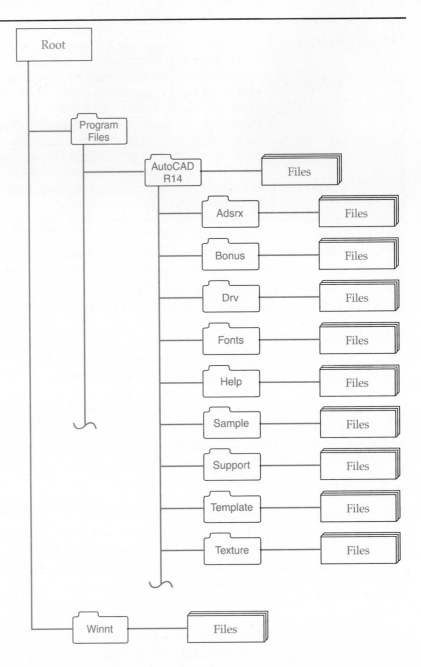

Your hard disk planning should take into account future software. New programs should be stored in their own directories on the hard disk, and managed in the same fashion as the AutoCAD files. The structure of a well-planned and closely managed hard disk should appear like that shown in Figure D-4.

Managing the AutoCAD System

One of your goals as an AutoCAD user should be to keep the computer system as efficient as possible. This means being organized and knowledgeable of school or company standards. Also know who has the authority to manage the system, and follow the system manager's guidelines.

If you are the system manager, develop standards and procedures, relay these to system users, and distribute up-to-date documentation, symbol libraries, menus, and standards. Revise standards as needed and distribute these to all users. In addition, handle software updates in a consistent and timely manner. Make the maintenance of hardware a priority.

Figure D-4.
The directory folder structure of a well-managed hard disk appears clean and organized.

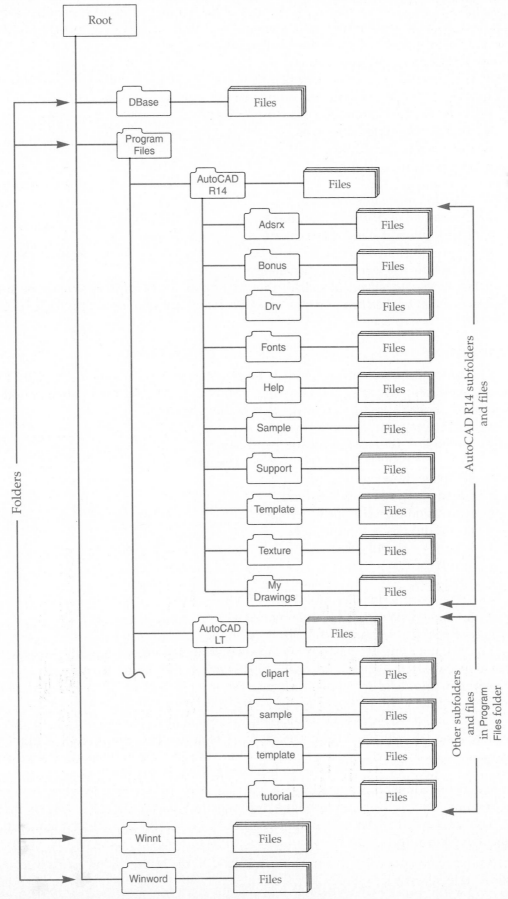

The system manager

One or two people, depending on the size of the department or company, should be assigned as system manager. The manager has control over all functions of the computer system, preventing inconsistencies in procedure, drawing format, and file storage. The manager is responsible for the following:

- Scheduling computer use.
- Structure of the hard disk directories.
- Administration of network server and user access to its files.
- Appearance and function of start-up menus.
- Drawing naming techniques.
- File storage procedures.
- File backup procedures.
- Drawing file access.
- Creation of symbol libraries.
- Development of written standards.
- Distribution of standards to users.
- Upgrading software and hardware.
- Hardware hygiene and maintenance.

When tasks are delegated, such as the creation of symbol library shapes, be sure to include accurate sketches or drawings. Check and approve final drawings before distributing them to users.

Developing operating standards and procedures

The basis of system management is that everyone performs their job using the same procedures, symbols, and drawing techniques. A department that operates smoothly is probably using standards such as the following:

- File naming conventions.
- Methods of file storage: location and name.
- Drawing sheet sizes and title blocks to be used.
- Template drawings.
- Creation of blocks and symbols.
- Dimensioning techniques.
- Use of dimensioning variables.
- Use of layers and colors.
- Text styles.
- Linetypes.
- Color schemes for plotting.
- Creation of screen and tablet menus.
- File backup methods and times.

Take the time initially to study the needs of your school or company. Meet with other department managers and users to determine the nature of their drawings. Always gain input from people who use the system and avoid making blanket decisions on your own.

Once needs have been established, develop a plan for implementing the required standards and procedures. Assign specific tasks to students or employees. Assemble the materials as they are completed and distribute the documentation and procedures to all users.

When developing procedures, begin with start-up procedures and work through the drawing process. Develop template drawings for specific types of projects first. The final aspects of system development should be screen and tablet menus and AutoLISP programs.

File maintenance

The integrity of files must be protected by all who work with the system. Procedures for file maintenance must be documented. Files of every type, including .dwg, .sld, .bat, .lsp, .mnu, and .bak must have a secure storage area. This can be hard disk directories, floppy disks, optical discs or magnetic tape storage areas, kept clean of nonessential files. File maintenance procedures should include the following:

- Location of essential AutoCAD files.
- Location of backup AutoCAD files.
- Print the contents of all hard disk directories for each workstation.
- Location and contents of all prototype drawings, supplemented with printed listings.
- Location and contents of all batch files and associated menus.
- Location of all user files, including drawings, slides, and text files.
- Proper creation of drawings using prototypes, layers, dimensioning techniques, linetypes, text styles, and symbols.
- Storage and backup methods for drawing files.
- Storage of printed or plotted copies of all drawing files.

Symbol libraries and menus

The development of symbol libraries and menus is a primary concern of managing an AutoCAD system. Symbols must be consistent and up-to-date. Menus must also be consistent throughout the department or company. A vital aspect of maintaining standards and consistency is a facility for updating symbol libraries and menus. This task should be given to certain students or employees and the results distributed to all users. Maintaining symbol libraries and menus includes the following:

- Standards for drawing symbols.
- System for naming symbols (blocks).
- System for block storage.
- Post a printed or plotted copy of all symbol libraries, their names, and locations.
- Creation and maintenance of custom screen and tablet menus.
- Use of custom menus by specific departments.
- Revisions to custom menus.
- Upgrading of menus on all hard disks.

Maintaining the software

Software upgrades and releases are issued regularly. If you purchase upgrades, converting to the new version should be smooth and have little, if any, effect on production. Establish a procedure for upgrading all computers in the classroom or office. Inform all users of changes by providing a printed listing of new features. If you work for a company, schedule professional upgrade training for managers and employees at an authorized *Autodesk Training Center (ATC)* or an authorized Autodesk Dealer. For information on the nearest ATC or AutoCAD dealer, call 1-800-964-6432. You can also get valuable training information on the World Wide Web at http://www.autodesk.com.

Maintain the management system

All systems require continuous maintenance to function efficiently. Enable users to contribute to the function of the system. Foster creativity by inviting suggestions from users. Meet with users and managers on a regular basis to learn what is functioning well and what is not. Remember, the system will function efficiently if a majority of those using it enjoy working with the system, and are encouraged to contribute to its growth and development.

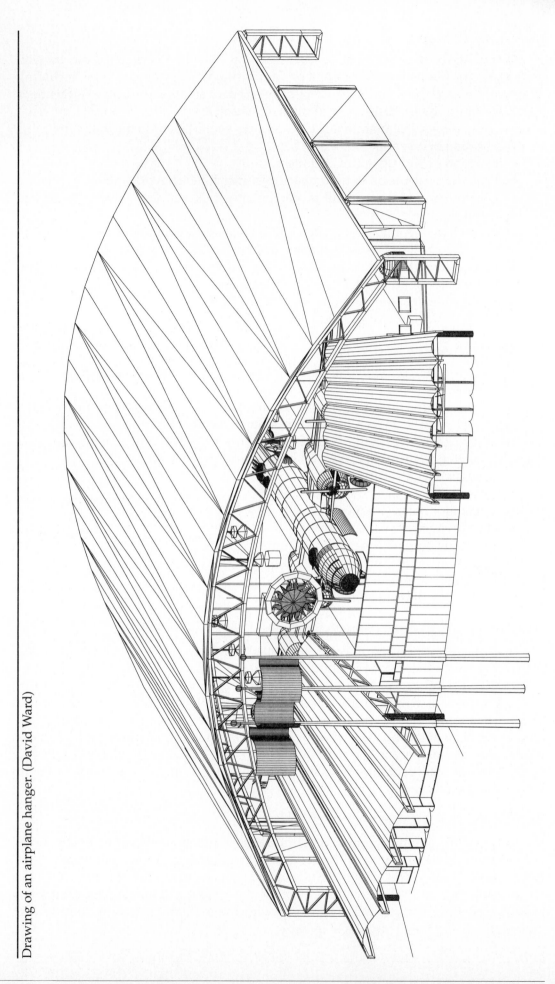

Drawing of an airplane hanger. (David Ward)

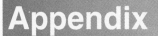

Appendix E

AutoCAD System Variables; Drawing Sheet Sizes and Scale Parameters

The following listing shows the AutoCAD system variables that can be stored within a prototype drawing file. The value of each of these variables is written into the drawing file when the drawing is saved, so that the next time the drawing is opened the values remain the same. Setting the values for most of these variables can be done by entering the associated command or by using the **SETVAR** command. Some variable values are derived by AutoCAD from the current condition of the drawing or the drawing environment, and cannot be directly set. These are referred to as *read-only*.

Each listing provides a brief description of the variable and the default setting when no prototype drawing is referenced. The symbol ↝ (eyeglasses) indicates that the variable is read-only.

Variable Name	Default Value	Description
ACISOUTVER	16	Controls version of files created using the **ACISOUT** command.
ANGBASE	0.0000	Direction for base angle 0 relative to current UCS.
ANGDIR	0	Counter-clockwise (0) or clockwise (1) angle measurement.
ATTDIA	0	Prompt on **Command:** line or use dialog box.
ATTMODE	1	Display mode for block attributes.
ATTREQ	1	Use attribute defaults or request values from user.
AUNITS	0	Format for angular units.
AUPREC	0	Precision of angular units.
BACKZ	↝	Back clipping plane offset from the target plane.
BLIPMODE	0	Controls display of marker blips.
CECOLOR	"BYLAYER"	Color of newly-created objects.
CELTSCALE	1.0000	Individual object linetype scaling for new objects.
CELTYPE	"BYLAYER"	Linetype for newly-created objects.
CHAMFERA	0.0000	First chamfer distance.
CHAMFERB	0.0000	Second chamfer distance.
CHAMFERC	0.0000	Chamfer length.
CHAMFERD	0.0000	Chamfer angle.
CLAYER	"0"	Currently active layer.
COORDS	1	Controls dynamic coordinate updating.
CVPORT	2	Identification number of current viewport.
DELOBJ	1	Controls deletion of objects used to create other objects.
DIMADEC	−1	Decimal places for angular dimensions.
DIMALT	off	Enables or disables alternate units dimensioning.
DIMALTD	2	Decimal places for alternate units dimensions.

(continued on next page)

(continued from previous page)

Variable Name	Default Value	Description
DIMALTF	25.4000	Alternate units dimension scale factor.
DIMALTTD	2	Decimal places for alternate units tolerance values.
DIMALTTZ	0	Zero suppression for alternate units tolerance values.
DIMALTU	2	Units format for alternate units dimensions.
DIMALTZ	0	Zero suppression for alternate units dimension values.
DIMAPOST	""	Prefix/suffix for alternate units dimensions.
DIMASO	on	Toggles associative dimensioning.
DIMASZ	0.1800	Dimension line and arrowhead size.
DIMAUNIT	0	Unit format for angular dimension values.
DIMBLK	""	Block name to use for both arrowheads.
DIMBLK1	""	Block name to use for first arrowhead.
DIMBLK2	""	Block name to use for second arrowhead.
DIMCEN	0.0900	Center mark size.
DIMCLRD	0	Dimension line, arrowhead and leader line color.
DIMCLRE	0	Dimension extension line color.
DIMCLRT	0	Dimension text color.
DIMDEC	4	Decimal places for dimension values.
DIMDLE	0.0000	Dimension line extension beyond extension lines.
DIMDLI	0.3800	Incremental spacing between baseline dimensions.
DIMEXE	0.1800	Extension line distance beyond dimension line.
DIMEXO	0.0625	Distance from origin to begin extension line.
DIMFIT	3	Controls placement of text and arrowheads.
DIMGAP	0.0900	Gap size between dimension line and dimension text.
DIMJUST	0	Horizontal justification of dimension text.
DIMLFAC	1.0000	Linear units scale factor for dimension values.
DIMLIM	off	Toggles creation of limits style dimensions.
DIMPOST	""	Prefix/suffix for primary units dimension values.
DIMRND	0.0000	Rounding value for dimensions.
DIMSAH	off	Toggles use of separate arrowhead blocks.
DIMSCALE	1.0000	Global dimension feature scale factor.
DIMSD1	off	Toggles suppression of first dimension line.
DIMSD2	off	Toggles suppression of second dimension line.
DIMSE1	off	Toggles suppression of first extension line.
DIMSE2	off	Toggles suppression of second extension line.
DIMSHO	on	Controls dynamic update of dimensions while dragging.
DIMSOXD	off	Suppress dimension lines outside of extension lines.
DIMSTYLE	↫	Name of current dimension style.
DIMTAD	0	Toggles placement of text above dimension line.
DIMTDEC	4	Decimal places for primary units tolerance values.
DIMTFAC	1.0000	Scale factor for tolerance text size relative to dimensions.
DIMTIH	on	Orientation of text inside extension lines.
DIMTIX	off	Toggles forced placement of text between extension lines.
DIMTM	0.0000	Lower tolerance value for limits or toleranced dimensions.
DIMTOFL	off	Toggles forced dimension line creation.
DIMTOH	on	Orientation of text outside extension lines.
DIMTOL	off	Toggles creation of tolerance style dimensions.
DIMTOLJ	1	Vertical justification for dimension tolerance text.
DIMTP	0.0000	Upper tolerance value for limits or toleranced dimensions.
DIMTSZ	0.0000	Size for dimension line tick marks instead of arrowheads.
DIMTVP	0.0000	Vertical position of text above/below dimension line.
DIMTXSTY	STANDARD	Text style used for dimension text.
DIMTXT	0.1800	Size of dimension text.

(continued on next page)

AutoCAD and its Applications—Basics

Variable Name	Default Value	Description
DIMTZIN	0	Zero suppression for primary units tolerance values.
DIMUNIT	2	Units format for primary dimension values.
DIMUPT	off	Controls user placement of dimension line/text.
DIMZIN	0	Zero suppression for primary units dimensions.
DISPSILH	0	Toggles display of wire frame curve silhouettes.
DRAGMODE	2	Controls object "dragging" feature.
DWGCODEPAGE	∽	**SYSCODEPAGE** value when drawing was created.
ELEVATION	0.0000	Current 3D elevation relative to current UCS.
EXPLMODE	1	**EXPLODE** support for nonuniformly scaled blocks.
EXTMAX	∽	Upper-right extents of drawing.
EXTMIN	∽	Lower-left extents of drawing.
FACETRES	0.5000	Smoothness of shaded and hidden line removed objects.
FILLETRAD	0.5000	Current fillet radius setting.
FILLMODE	1	Toggles fill for solid objects.
FRONTZ	∽	Front clipping plane offset from the target plane.
GRIDMODE	0	Toggles display of grid.
GRIDUNIT	0.5000, 0.5000	Current grid spacing in drawing units.
HANDLES	∽	Provides support for applications requiring handle access.
HPBOUND	1	Object type created by **BHATCH** and **BOUNDARY**.
INDEXCTL	0	Controls creation and saving of layer and spatial indexes.
INSBASE	0.0000, 0.0000, 0.0000	Insertion point set by **BASE** command.
ISOLINES	4	Number of isolines per surface on 3D objects.
LASTPOINT	0.0000, 0.0000, 0.0000	Last entered UCS coordinates for current space.
LENSLENGTH	∽	Length of lens in millimeters for perspective view.
LIMCHECK	0	Toggles active limit checking for object creation.
LIMMAX	12.0000, 9.0000	Upper-right limits.
LIMMIN	0.0000, 0.0000	Lower-left limits.
LTSCALE	1.0000	Current global linetype scale.
LUNITS	2	Current display format for linear units.
LUPREC	4	Current linear units precision value.
MEASUREMENT	0	Sets drawing units as English or metric.
MIRRTEXT	1	Toggles mirroring technique for text objects.
ORTHOMODE	0	Toggles orthogonal drawing control.
OSMODE	0	Current **Object Snap** mode bit value.
PDMODE	0	Current **POINT** object display mode.
PDSIZE	0.0000	Current **POINT** object display size.
PELLIPSE	0	Controls the object type created with **ELLIPSE**.
PICKSTYLE	1	Controls group and associative hatch selection.
PLINEGEN	0	Toggles linetype generation along a polyline.
PLINEWID	0.0000	Current polyline width value.
PLOTROTMODE	1	Controls the orientation of plots.
PROJECTNAME	""	Assigns a project name to the current drawing.
PROXYGRAPHICS	1	Specifies whether images of proxy objects are saved in the drawing.
PSLTSCALE	1	Paper space linetype scale factor.
PSQUALITY	75	Controls rendering quality and fill on postscript images.
QTEXTMODE	0	Toggles quick text display mode.
RASTERPREVIEW	1	Toggles drawing preview saving and sets format.
REGENMODE	1	Toggles automatic drawing regeneration.
SHADEDGE	3	Controls edge shading during rendering.
SHADEDIF	70	Sets ratio of diffuse reflective light to ambient light.
SKETCHINC	0.1000	Current **SKETCH** record increment value.

(continued on next page)

(continued from previous page)

Variable Name	Default Value	Description
SKPOLY	0	Toggles creation of polyline objects by **SKETCH**.
SNAPANG	0	Snap/grid rotation angle in current viewport.
SNAPBASE	0.0000, 0.0000	Snap/grid origin point in current viewport.
SNAPISOPAIR	0	Isometric plane for current viewport.
SNAPMODE	0	Toggles snap mode.
SNAPSTYL	0	Current snap style.
SNAPUNIT	0.5000, 0.5000	Snap spacing for current viewport.
SPLFRAME	0	Toggles display of frames for spline-fit polylines.
SPLINESEGS	8	Current number of segments generated for each spline.
SPLINETYPE	6	Current type of spline generation by **PEDIT**.
SURFTAB1	6	Tabulations generated for **RULESURF**/ **TABSURF**, and direction mesh density for **REVSURF**/ **EDGESURF**.
SURFTAB2	6	N direction mesh density for **REVSURF** and **EDGESURF**.
SURFTYPE	6	Surface fitting type performed by **PEDIT Smooth**.
SURFU	6	M direction surface density.
SURFV	6	N direction surface density.
SYSCODEPAGE	~	System code page specified in ACAD.XMF.
TARGET	~	Location of target point in current viewport.
TDCREATE	~	Time and date when the current drawing was created.
TDINDWG	~	Total editing time for the current drawing.
TDUPDATE	~	Time and date of last update and save.
TDUSRTIMER	~	User timer time elapsed.
TEXTFILL	1	Controls fill for Bitstream/TrueType/Adobe Type 1 fonts.
TEXTQLTY	50	Resolution for Bitstream/TrueType/Adobe Type 1 fonts.
TEXTSIZE	0.2000	Default height of text drawn in current style.
TEXTSTYLE	"STANDARD"	Current text style name.
THICKNESS	0.0000	Current 3D thickness.
TILEMODE	1	Controls access to paper space.
TRACEWID	0.0500	Current width for **TRACE** objects.
TREEDEPTH	3020	Maximum number of branches for tree-structured spatial index.
UCSFOLLOW	0	Toggles automatic change to plan view of current UCS.
UCSICON	1	Controls the display of the UCS icon.
UCSNAME	~	Name of the current UCS for the current space.
UCSORG	~	Origin point for the current UCS for the current space.
UCSXDIR	~	X direction for the current UCS for the current space.
UCSYDIR	~	Y direction for the current UCS for the current space.
UNITMODE	0	Current units display format.
VIEWCTR	~	Center point location for current view in current viewport.
VIEWDIR	~	Viewing direction of the current view in current viewport.
VIEWMODE	~	Current viewing mode for the current viewport.
VIEWSIZE	~	Height of the current view in the current viewport.
VIEWTWIST	~	View twist angle for current viewport.
VISRETAIN	1	Controls visibility of layers in xref files.
VSMAX	~	Upper-right corner of the current viewport virtual screen.
VSMIN	~	Lower-left corner of the current viewport virtual screen.
WORLDVIEW	1	Controls automatic change of UCS for **DVIEW**/**VPOINT**.
XCLIPFRAME	0	Controls visibility of xref clipping boundaries.

The following listing shows the AutoCAD system variables that are saved with the AutoCAD configuration. These variables are not associated with, or saved, in the drawing file. The values will be the same in the next drawing session as they are when you leave the current drawing. The default values shown here represent the values existing prior to AutoCAD's initial configuration. The symbol ⌒ indicates that the variable is read-only.

Variable Name	Default Value	Description
APBOX	1	Turns the **AutoSnap** aperture box on or off.
APERTURE	10	Object snap target aperture height.
AUDITCTL	0	Toggles AutoCAD's creation of an audit file (.ADT).
AUTOSNAP	7	Controls the display of the AutoSnap marker and SnapTip and turns the AutoSnap magnet on or off
CMDDIA	1	Enables/disables dialog boxes for a variety of commands.
CMLJUST	0	Current multiline justification.
CMLSCALE	1.0000	Scale factor for multiline features.
CMLSTYLE	"STANDARD"	Current multiline style name.
CURSORSIZE	5	Controls the size of the crosshairs as a percentage of screen size.
	full	
DCTCUST	""	Current custom dictionary filename and path.
DCTMAIN	(varies by country)	Main dictionary filename.
DEMANDLOAD		Specifies if and when AutoCAD demand loads a third-party application (if the drawing contains objects created in that application).
DRAGP1	10	Sets regen-drag input sampling rate.
DRAGP2	25	Sets fast-drag input sampling rate.
FILEDIA	1	Enables/disables file dialog boxes.
FONTALT	"simlex.shx"	Font file to be used when specified file is not found.
FONTMAP	"acad.fmp"	Font mapping file to be used when specified file is not found.
GRIPBLOCK	0	Controls assignment of grips within block objects.
GRIPCOLOR	5	Color of nonselected grips.
GRIPHOT	1	Color of selected grips.
GRIPS	1	Toggles availability of grip editing modes.
GRIPSIZE	3	Size of grip box in pixels.
HPBOUND	1	Controls object type created by **BHATCH** & **BOUNDARY.**
INETLOCATION	"www.autodesk. com/acaduser"	Internet location used by **BROWSER** command.
ISAVEBAK	1	Controls creation of a .bak file when saving.
ISAVEPERCENT	50	Determines amount of wasted space allowed in a drawing.
LISPINIT	1	Controls "persistent" AutoLISP.
LOGFILEMODE	0	Specifies whether text window contents are written to a log file.
LOGFILENAME	"C:\Program files\ AutoCAD R14\acad.log"	Specifies path and name for log file.
MAXSORT	200	Maximum number of symbols or filenames sorted by listing commands.
MENUCTL	1	Toggles screen menu switching in response to commands.
MTEXTED	"INTERNAL"	Name of text editor for editing **MTEXT** objects.
OLEHIDE	0	Controls the display of OLE objects in AutoCAD.
OSNAPCOORD	2	Controls whether typed coordinates override object snap settings.
PICKADD	1	Toggles additive selection of objects.
PICKAUTO	1	Toggles automatic windowing during selection process.
PICKBOX	3	Object selection pickbox height in pixels.

(continued on next page)

(continued from previous next page)

Variable Name	Default Value	Description
PICKDRAG	0	Controls selection window drawing method.
PICKFIRST	1	Controls selection and editing sequence.
PLINETYPE	2	Specifies whether AutoCAD uses light weight polylines.
PLOTID	""	Current default plotter description.
PLOTTER	0	Current default plotter identification.
PROJMODE	1	Controls projection mode for **TRIM/EXTEND**.
PROXYNOTICE	1	Controls display of notice when a proxy object is created.
PROXYSHOW	1	Controls display of proxy objects.
PSPROLOG	""	Name for prologue section read from acad.psf for **PSOUT**.
RTDISPLAY	1	Controls display of raster objects during real-time zoom or pan.
SAVEFILE	ᕂ	Current autosave destination filename.
SAVETIME	120	Autosave interval, in minutes.
SCREENBOXES	ᕂ	Number of available boxes in screen menu area.
SCREENMODE	ᕂ	Current graphics/text state of the AutoCAD display.
SORTENTS	96	Controls object sort order operations.
TEMPPREFIX	ᕂ	Directory name for placement of temporary files.
TOOLTIPS	1	Toggles display of toolbar ToolTips.
TREEMAX	10000000	Limits maximum number of nodes in spatial index tree.
XLOADCTL	1	Controls xref demand loading.
XLOADPATH	""	Path for storage of temporary copies of demand loaded xref files.
XREFCTL	0	Controls creation of .xlg.

The following listing shows the AutoCAD system variables that are not saved at all. These variables revert to default values when opening an existing drawing or starting a new one. Many of these variables are read-only, and reference drawing or operating system specific information. Other variables in this section are used to change standard features of AutoCAD, and are restored to default values in subsequent editing sessions to avoid unexpected results in common drafting procedures. Many of the variables shown here are commonly referenced or set when customizing. The symbol ᕂ indicates the variable is read-only.

Variable Name	Default Value	Description
ACADPREFIX	ᕂ	Current support directory search path.
ACADVER	ᕂ	Current AutoCAD version number, including patch level.
AFLAGS	0	Current attribute flags settings.
AREA	ᕂ	Stores the last area calculated by **AREA/LIST/DBLIST**.
CDATE	ᕂ	Current date and time presented as a real number.
CHAMMODE	0	Current chamfer method.
CIRCLERAD	0.0000	Radius of last circle drawn.
CMDACTIVE	ᕂ	Indicates what type of command is active.
CMDECHO	1	Controls echo of prompts and commands during the AutoLISP (command) function.
CMDNAMES	ᕂ	Name of the currently active command(s).
DATE	ᕂ	Current Julian date.
DBMOD	ᕂ	Drawing modification status.
DIASTAT	ᕂ	Exit method of last dialog session.
DISTANCE	ᕂ	Last distance calculated by **DIST**.
DONUTID	0.5000	Default ID for doughnuts.
DONUTOD	1.0000	Default OD for doughnuts.

(continued on next page)

(continued from previous page)

Variable Name	Default Value	Description
DWGNAME	∿	Name of current drawing.
DWGPREFIX	∿	Directory path for current drawing.
DWGTITLED	∿	Indicates if current drawing has been named.
EDGEMODE	0	Cutting and boundary edge determination method for **TRIM/EXTEND**.
EXPERT	0	Suppression level of warnings and double-checks.
HIGHLIGHT	1	Toggles highlighting of selected objects.
HPANG	0	Current default hatch pattern angle.
HPDOUBLE	0	Toggles double hatching for user-defined patterns.
HPNAME	"ANSI31"	Current default hatch pattern name.
HPSCALE	1.0000	Current default hatch pattern scale.
HPSPACE	1.0000	Current spacing for user-defined patterns.
INSNAME	""	Name of last block inserted.
LASTANGLE	∿	Last angle entered or drawn.
LASTPROMPT	""	Stores last text displayed at command line, including user input.
LOCALE	∿	ISO language code for running AutoCAD version.
LOGINNAME	∿	Currently configured user login name.
MAXACTVP	16	Maximum number of active model space viewports.
MAXOBJMEM	0	Specifies virtual memory parameters.
MENUECHO	0	Controls level of menu echo.
MENUNAME	∿	Currently loaded menu file and path names.
MODEMACRO	""	Displays text on status line—used in DIESEL.
OFFSETDIST	1.0000	Last entered offset distance.
PERIMETER	∿	Last perimeter value calculated by **AREA/LIST/DBLIST**.
PFACEVMAX	∿	Maximum number of vertices per face.
PLATFORM	∿	Current operating system.
POLYSIDES	4	Default number of polygon sides.
POPUPS	∿	Support level of display driver for pull-down menus.
RE-INIT	0	Reinitializes the digitizer, digitizer port, and acad.pgp file.
SAVENAME	∿	Default drawing save name.
SCREENSIZE	∿	Current viewport size in pixels.
SHPNAME	""	Default shape file name.
TABMODE	0	Enables/disables tablet mode.
TEXTEVAL	0	Controls evaluation method for text strings.
TRIMMODE	1	Controls object trimming for **FILLET** and **CHAMFER**.
UNDOCTL	∿	Current status of **UNDO** feature.
UNDOMARKS	∿	The number of **UNDO** marks that have been placed.
WORLDUCS	∿	Comparison of current UCS and World UCS.

Prototype Drawing Sheet Size Parameters			
Drawing Scale	D-size (34″ × 22″) Drawing Limits	C-size (22″ × 17″) Drawing Limits	B-size (17″ × 11″) Drawing Limits
1″ = 1″	34,22	22,17	17,11
1/2″ = 1″	68,44	44,34	34,22
1/4″ = 1″	136,88	88,68	68,44
1/8″ = 1″	272,176	176,136	136,88
1″ = 1′-0″	408,264	264,204	204,132
3/4″ = 1′-0″	544,352	352,272	272,176
1/2″ = 1′-0″	816,528	528,408	408,264
3/8″ = 1′-0″	1088,704	704,544	544,352
1/4″ = 1′-0″	1632,1056	1056,816	816,528
3/16″ = 1′-0″	2176,1408	1408,1088	1088,704
1/8″ = 1′-0″	3264,2112	2112,1632	1632,1056
3/32″ = 1′-0″	4352,2816	2816,2176	2176,1408
1/16″ = 1′-0″	6528,4224	4224,3264	3264,2112

Prototype Drawing Scale Parameters			
Drawing Scale	Dimension Scale (DIMSCALE)	Linetype Scale (LTSCALE)	Inversion Scale of Border & Parts List Blocks
1″ = 1″	.1	.5	1 = 1
1/2″ = 1″	2	1	1 = 2
1/4″ = 1″	4	2	1 = 4
1/8″ = 1″	8	4	1 = 8
1″ = 1′-0″	12	6	1 = 12
3/4″ = 1′-0″	16	8	1 = 16
1/2″ = 1′-0″	24	12	1 = 24
3/8″ = 1′-0″	32	16	1 = 32
1/4″ = 1′-0″	48	24	1 = 48
3/16″ = 1′-0″	64	32	1 = 64
1/8″ = 1′-0″	96	48	1 = 96
3/32″ = 1′-0″	128	64	1 = 128
1/16″ = 1′-0″	192	96	1 = 192

Command Aliases

These examples include most frequently used commands. These aliases are defined in the acad.pgp file in the AutoCAD R14\Support folder.

Command	Alias	Command	Alias
3DARRAY	3A	DDRENAME	REN
3DFACE	3F	DDRMODES	RM
3DPOLY	3P	DDSELECT	SE
ALIGN	AL	DDUCS	UC
APPLOAD	AP	DDUCSP	UCP
ARC	A	DDUNITS	UN
AREA	AA	DDVIEW	V
ARRAY	AR	DDVPOINT	VP
ASEADMIN	AAD	DIMALIGNED	DAL
ASEEXPORT	AEX	DIMANGULAR	DAN
ASELINKS	ALI	DIMBASELINE	DBA
ASEROWS	ARO	DIMCENTER	DCE
ASESELECT	ASE	DIMCONTINUE	DCO
ASESQLED	ASQ	DIMDIAMETER	DDI
-ATTDEF	-AT	DIMEDIT	DED
-ATTEDIT	-ATE	DIMLINEAR	DLI
BHATCH	BH	DIMORDINATE	DOR
BHATCH	H	DIMOVERRIDE	DOV
-BLOCK	-B	DIMRADIUS	DRA
BMAKE	B	DIMSTYLE	DST
-BOUNDARY	-BO	DIST	DI
BOUNDARY	BO	DIVIDE	DIV
BREAK	BR	DONUT	DO
CHAMFER	CHA	DRAWORDER	DR
-CHANGE	-CH	DTEXT	DT
CIRCLE	C	DVIEW	DV
COPY	CO	ELLIPSE	EL
DDATTDEF	AT	ERASE	E
DDATTE	ATE	EXPLODE	X
DDCHPROP	CH	EXPORT	EXP
DDCOLOR	COL	EXTEND	EX
DDEDIT	ED	EXTRUDE	EXT
DDGRIPS	GR	FILLET	F
DDIM	D	FILTER	FI
DDINSERT	I	-GROUP	-G
DDMODIFY	MO	GROUP	G
DDOSNAP	OS	-HATCH	-H

(continued on next page)

(continued from previous page)

Command	Alias
HATCHEDIT	HE
HIDE	HI
-IMAGE	-IM
IMAGE	IM
IMAGEADJUST	IAD
IMAGEATTACH	IAT
IMAGECLIP	ICL
IMPORT	IMP
-INSERT	-I
INSERTOBJ	IO
INTERFERE	INF
INTERSECT	IN
-LAYER	-LA
LAYER	LA
LEADER	LE
LENGTHEN	LEN
LINE	L
-LINETYPE	-LT
LINETYPE	LT
LIST	LI
LIST	LS
LTSCALE	LTS
MATCHPROP	MA
MEASURE	ME
MIRROR	MI
MLINE	ML
MOVE	M
MSPACE	MS
-MTEXT	-T
MTEXT	MT
MTEXT	T
MVIEW	MV
OFFSET	O
-OSNAP	-OS
-PAN	-P
PAN	P
PASTESPEC	PA
PEDIT	PE
PLINE	PL
PLOT	PRINT
POINT	PO
POLYGON	POL
PREFERENCES	PR
PREVIEW	PRE
PSPACE	PS
PURGE	PU
QUIT	EXIT

Command	Alias
RECTANGLE	REC
REDRAW	R
REDRAWALL	RA
REGEN	RE
REGENALL	REA
REGION	REG
-RENAME	-REN
RENDER	RR
REVOLVE	REV
ROTATE	RO
RPREF	RPR
SCALE	SC
SCRIPT	SCR
SECTION	SEC
SETVAR	SET
SHADE	SHA
SLICE	SL
SNAP	SN
SOLID	SO
SPELL	SP
SPLINE	SPL
SPLINEDIT	SPE
STRETCH	S
STYLE	ST
SUBTRACT	SU
TABLET	TA
THICKNESS	TH
TILEMODE	TI
TOLERANCE	TOL
TOOLBAR	TO
TORUS	TOR
TRIM	TR
UNION	UNI
-UNITS	-UN
-VIEW	-V
-VPOINT	-VP
WBLOCK	W
WEDGE	WE
XATTACH	XA
-XBIND	-XB
XBIND	XB
XCLIP	XC
XLINE	XL
-XREF	-XR
XREF	XR
ZOOM	Z

The following are alternative aliases and aliases as supplied in AutoCAD Release 13.

Command	Alias	Command	Alias	Command	Alias
COPY	CP	DIMEDIT	DIMED	DIMSTYLE	DIMSTY
DIMALIGNED	DIMALI	DIMLINEAR	DIMLIN	DIMTEDIT	DIMTED
DIMANGULAR	DIMANG	DIMORDINATE	DIMORD	DSVIEWER	AV
DIMBASELINE	DIMBASE	DIMOVERRIDE	DIMOVER	LEADER	LEAD
DIMCONTINUE	DIMCONT	DIMRADIUS	DIMRAD	TILEMODE	TM
DIMDIAMETER	DIMDIA				

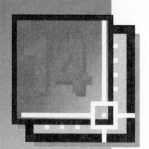

The tablet menu templates illustrated here show how the AutoCAD menu template can be altered to suit the needs of a company or individual. The menu shown in Figure G-1 is used for creating electrical loop and wiring diagrams. Look closely at some of the special commands. Also note that different menus can be called from this template.

Figure G-1.
Tablet menu for electrical loop and wiring diagrams. (Fitzgerald, Hagan & Hackathorn, Inc., Norwest Engineering)

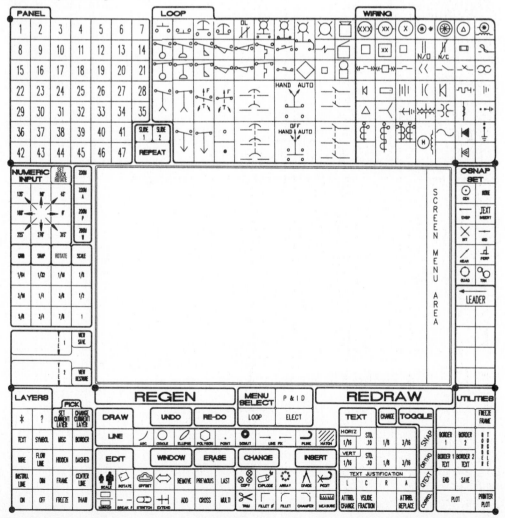

The tablet menu template shown in Figure G-2 was developed specifically for isometric piping drawings. All symbols are displayed in an orderly manner at the top of the menu. Note the section at the left of the screen area for isometric text.

Figure G-2.
Tablet menu template for isometric piping symbols. (Fitzgerald, Hagan & Hackathorn, Inc., Norwest Engineering)

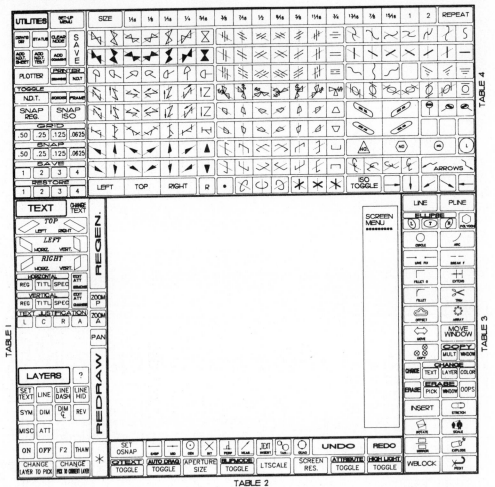

The tablet menu template shown in Figure G-3 was created for instrumentation loop diagrams. This menu does not have the detail as those shown earlier, but still reflects the needs of the individual using it. Notice the conversion chart on the right side of the template. Also note the cursor button references inside the screen area.

Figure G-3.
Tablet menu template for instrumentation loop diagrams. (Courtesy R. L. Dunn, Harris Group, Inc.)

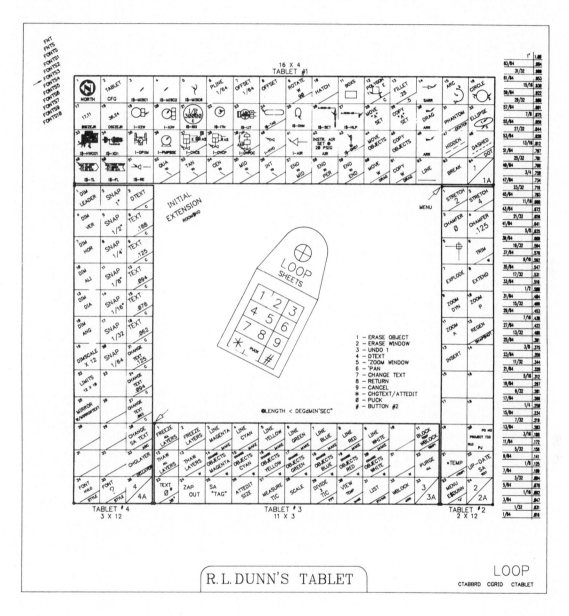

The AutoCAD tablet menu. (Autodesk, Inc.)

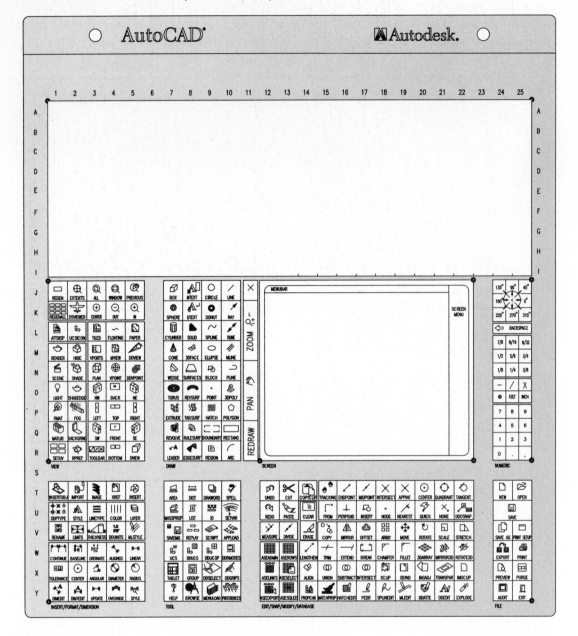

 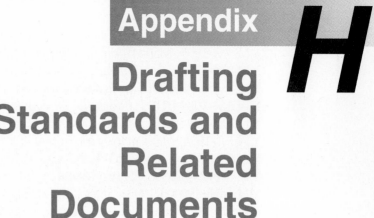
Drafting Standards and Related Documents

The following is a list of ANSI/ASME drafting standards or related documents. They are ANSI/ASME adopted, unless another standard developing organization, such as ANSI/NFPA, is indicated. The ANSI/ASME standards are available by contacting:

The American National Standards Institute
11 West 42nd Street
New York, NY 10036
or
The American Society of Mechanical Engineers
345 East 47th Street
New York, NY 10017

ABBREVIATIONS

Y1.1-1989, *Abbreviations for Use on Drawings and in Text*

CHARTS AND GRAPHS (Y15)

Y15.1M-1979 (R1993), *Illustrations for Publication and Projection*
Y15.2M-1979 (R1986), *Time-Series Charts*
Y15.3M-1979 (R1986), *Process Charts*

DIMENSIONS

B4.1-1967 (R1994), *Preferred Limits and Fits for Cylindrical Parts*
B4.2-1978 (R1994), *Preferred Metric Limits and Fits*
B4.3-1978 (R1994), *General Tolerances for Metric Dimensioned Products*
B4.4M-1981 (R1987), *Inspection of Workpieces*
B32.1-1952 (R1994), *Preferred Thickness for Uncoated, Thin, Flat Metals (Under 0.250/in.)*
B32.2-1969 (R1994), *Preferred Diameters for Round Wire-0.500 Inches and Under*
B32.3M-1984 (R1994), *Preferred Metric Sizes for Flat Metal Products*
B32.4M-1980 (R1994), *Preferred Metric Sizes for Round, Square, Rectangle, and Hexagon Metal Products*
B32.5-1977 (R1994), *Preferred Metric Sizes for Tubular Metal Products Other Than Pipe*
B32.6M-1984 (R1994), *Preferred Metric Equivalents of Inch Sizes for Tubular Metal Products Other Than Pipe*
B36.10M-1985, *Welded and Seamless Wrought Steel Pipe*
B36.19M-1985, *Stainless Steel Pipe*

DRAFTING STANDARDS

Y14.1-1995, *Decimal Inch Drawing Sheet Size and Format*

Y14.1M-1995, *Metric Drawing Sheet Size and Format*

Y14.2M-1992, *Line Conventions and Lettering*

Y14.3M-1994, *Multiview and Sectional View Drawings*

Y14.4M-1989 (R1994), *Pictorial Drawings*

Y14.5M-1994, *Dimensioning and Tolerancing*

Y14.5.1-1994, *Mathematical Definition of Y14.5*

Y14.5.2, *Certification of GD&T Professionals*

Y14.6-1978 (R1993), *Screw Thread Representation*

Y14.6aM-1981 (R1993), *Screw Thread Representation (Metric Supplement)*

Y14.7.1-1971 (R1993), *Gear Drawing Standards-Part 1-Spur, Helical, Double Helical, and Rack*

Y14.7.2-1978 (R1994), *Gear and Spline Drawing Standards-Part 2-Bevel and Hypoid Gears*

Y14.8M-1989 (R1993), *Castings and Forgings*

Y14.13M-1981 (R1992), *Mechanical Spring Representation*

Y14.18M-1986 (R1993) *Optical Parts*

Y14.24M-1989, *Types and Applications of Engineering Drawings*

Y14.32.1M-1994, *Chassis Frames Passenger Car and Light Truck—Ground Vehicle Practices*

Y14.34M-1989 (R1993), *Parts Lists, Data Lists, and Index Lists*

Y14.35M-1992, *Revision of Engineering Drawings and Associated Documents*

Y14.36-1978 (R1993), *Surface Texture Symbols*

Y14.36M-1996, *Surface Texture Symbols—Metric*

GRAPHIC SYMBOLS

Y32.2-1975, *Electrical and Electronic Diagrams*

Y32.2.3-1949 (R1994), *Pipe Fittings, Valves, and Piping*

Y32.2.4-1949 (R1993), *Heating, Ventilating, and Air Conditioning*

Y32.2.6-1950 (R1993), *Heat/Power Apparatus*

Y32.4-1977 (R1994), *Plumbing Fixture Diagrams Used in Architectural and Building Construction*

Y32.7-1972 (R1994), *Railroad Maps and Profiles*

Y32.9-1972 (R1989), *Electrical Wiring and Layout Diagrams Used in Architecture and Building*

Y32.10-1967 (R1994), *Fluid Power Diagrams*

Y32.11-1961 (R1993), *Process Flow Diagrams in the Petroleum and Chemical Industries*

Y32.18-1972 (R1993), *Mechanical and Acoustical Elements as Used in Schematic Diagrams*

ANSI/AWS A2.4-91, *Symbols for Welding, Brazing, and Nondestructive Examination*

ANSI/IEEE 200-1975 (R1989), *Reference Designations for Electrical and Electronics Parts and Equipment*

ANSI/IEEE 315-1975 (R1989), *Electrical and Electronics Diagrams (Including Reference Designation Class Designation Letters)*

ANSI/IEEE 623-1976 (R1989), *Grid and Mapping Used in Cable Television Systems*

ANSI/ISA S5.1-1984 (R1992), *Instrumentation Symbols and Identification*

ANSI/NFPA 170-1991, *Public Fire Safety Symbols*

LETTER SYMBOLS

Y10.1-1972 (R1988), *Glossary of Terms Concerning Letter Symbols*
Y10.3M-1984, *Mechanics and Time-Related Phenomena*
Y10.4-1982 (R1988), *Heat and Thermodynamics*
Y10.11-1984, *Acoustics*
Y10.12-1955 (R1988), *Chemical Engineering*
Y10.17-1961 (R1988), *Greek Letters Used as Letter Symbols for Engineering Math*
Y10.18 1967 (R1977), *Illuminating Engineering*
ANSI/IEEE 260-1978 (R1992), *SI Units and Certain Other Units of Measurement*

METRIC SYSTEM

SI-1, *Orientation and Guide for use of SI (Metric) Units*
SI-2, *SI Units in Strength of Materials*
SI-3, *SI Units in Dynamics*
SI-4, *SI Units in Thermodynamics*
SI-5, *SI Units in Fluid Mechanics*
SI-6, *SI Units in Kinematics*
SI-7, *SI Units in Heat Transfer*
SI-8, *SI Units in Vibration*
SI-9, *Metrification of Codes and Standards SI (Metric) Units*
SI-10, *Steam Charts, SI (Metric) and U.S. Customary Units*

At the time of publication all information in this appendix is correct. Some of the standards are, and may in the future be, under review. Information in this appendix is subject to change. Some standards may be out of print. Out of print codes and standards are available from *Global Engineering Documents* (800) 854-7179, *Document Engineering Co.* (800) 645-7732.

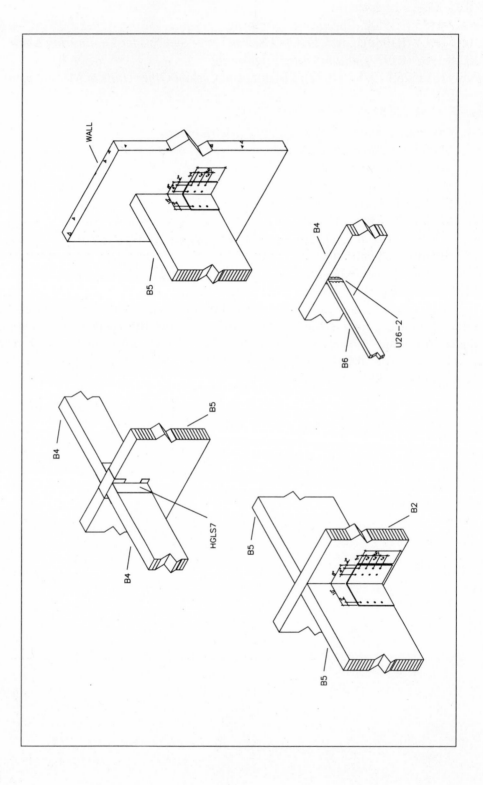

Joist hangers. (Mark Hartman)

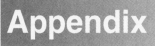

Appendix

Drafting Symbols and Standard Tables

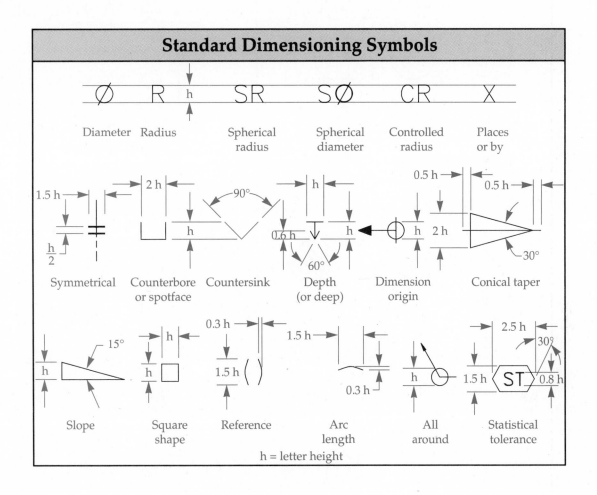

Standard Dimensioning Symbols

Ø	R	SR	SØ	CR	X
Diameter	Radius	Spherical radius	Spherical diameter	Controlled radius	Places or by

Symmetrical — Counterbore or spotface — Countersink — Depth (or deep) — Dimension origin — Conical taper

Slope — Square shape — Reference — Arc length — All around — Statistical tolerance

h = letter height

Geometric Dimensioning and Tolerancing Symbols

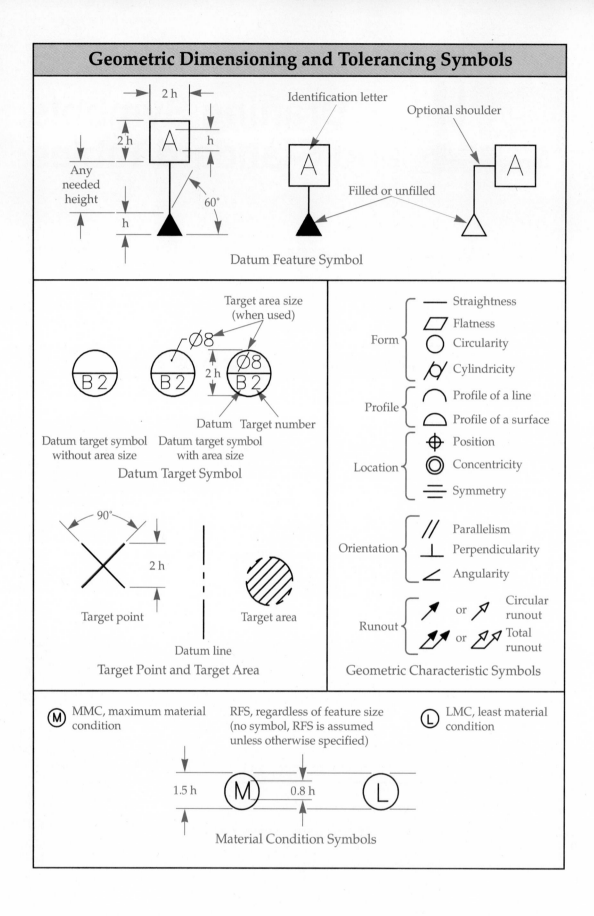

Datum Feature Symbol

Identification letter

Optional shoulder

Filled or unfilled

Datum target symbol without area size

Datum target symbol with area size

Datum Target Symbol

Datum   Target number

Target area size (when used)

Target point

Datum line

Target area

Target Point and Target Area

Geometric Characteristic Symbols

Form
— Straightness
⌭ Flatness
○ Circularity
⌭ Cylindricity

Profile
⌒ Profile of a line
⌓ Profile of a surface

Location
⊕ Position
◎ Concentricity
= Symmetry

Orientation
// Parallelism
⊥ Perpendicularity
∠ Angularity

Runout
↗ or ↗ Circular runout
↗↗ or ↗↗ Total runout

Ⓜ MMC, maximum material condition

RFS, regardless of feature size (no symbol, RFS is assumed unless otherwise specified)

Ⓛ LMC, least material condition

Material Condition Symbols

Additional GD&T information is found in *Geometric Dimensioning and Tolerancing* by David A. Madsen, and is available through Goodheart-Willcox.

Geometric Dimensioning and Tolerancing Symbols

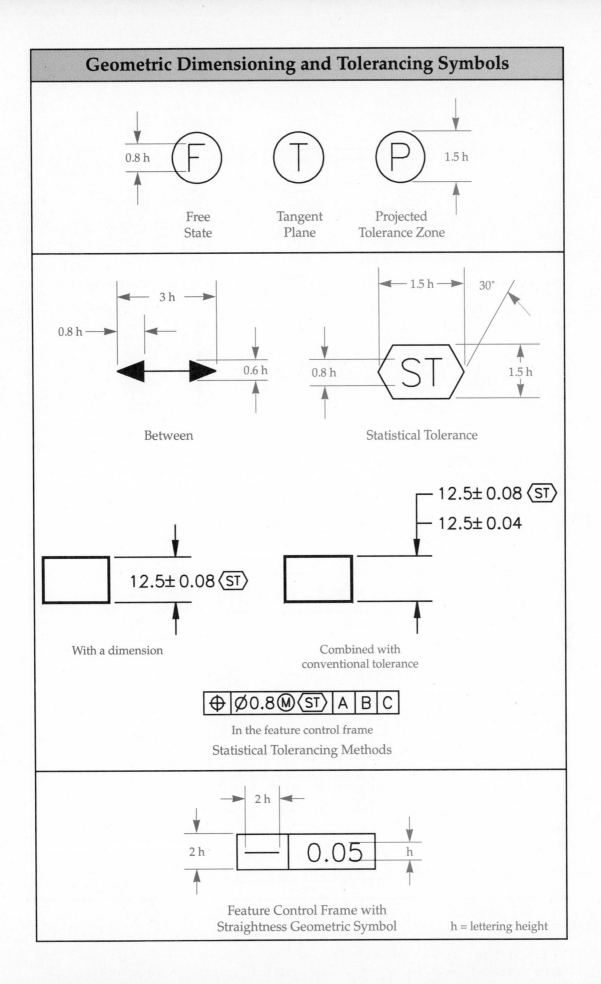

Free State

Tangent Plane

Projected Tolerance Zone

Between

Statistical Tolerance

With a dimension

Combined with conventional tolerance

In the feature control frame

Statistical Tolerancing Methods

Feature Control Frame with Straightness Geometric Symbol

h = lettering height

Geometric Dimensioning and Tolerancing Symbols

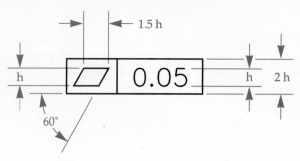

Feature Control Frame with the Flatness
Geometric Characteristic Symbol

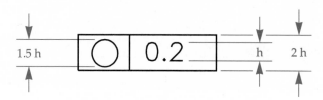

Feature Control Frame with Circularity
Geometric Characteristic Symbol

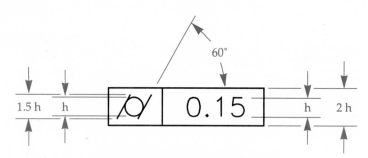

Feature Control Frame with Cylindricity
Geometric Characteristic Symbol

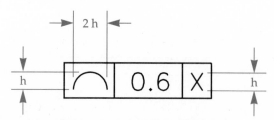

Feature Control Frame with Profile
of a Line Geometric Characteristic
Symbol and a Datum Reference

h = lettering height

Geometric Dimensioning and Tolerancing Symbols

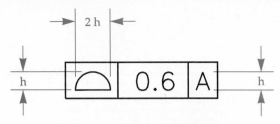

Feature Control Frame with Profile
of a Surface Geometric Characteristic
Symbol and a Datum Reference

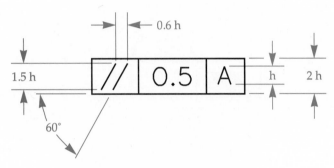

Feature Control Frame with
Parallelism Geometric Characteristic
Symbol and a Datum Reference

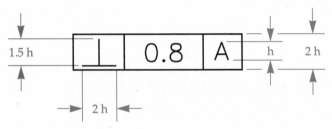

Feature Control Frame with
Perpendicularity Geometric Characteristic
Symbol and a Datum Reference

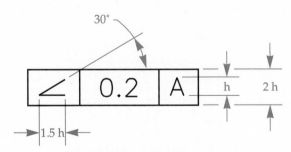

Feature Control Frame with
Angularity Geometric Characteristic
Symbol and a Datum Reference

h = lettering height

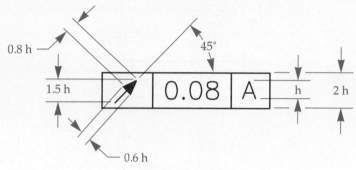

Circular Runout

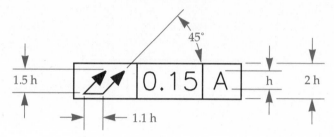

Total Runout

Runout symbols may be drawn open or filled

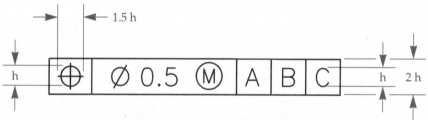

Positional Geometric Characteristic
Symbol and Tolerance in a Feature Control
Frame with Three Datum References

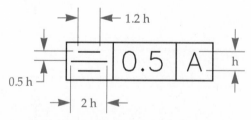

Feature Control Frame with Symmetry
Geometric Characteristic
Symbol and a Datum Reference

h = lettering height

Single Line Piping Symbols

Name	Screwed			Buttwelded		
	Left side	Front	Right side	Left side	Front	Right side
90° Elbow						
45° Elbow						
Tee						
45° Lateral						
Cross						
Cap						
Concentric Reducer						
Eccentric Reducer						
Union						
Coupling						

Additonal pipe drafting information is found in *Process Pipe Drafting* by Terence M. Shumaker, and is available through Goodheart-Willcox.

Common Symbols for Electrical Diagrams

Amplifier		Triode with directly heated cathode and envelope connection to base terminal		Fluorescent, 2-terminal lamp	
Antenna, general				Incandescent lamp	
Antenna, dipole		Pentode using elongated envelope		Microphone	
Antenna, dipole				Receiver, earphone	
Antenna, counterpoise		Twin triode using elongated envelope		Resistor, general	
Battery, long line positive				Resistor, adjustable	
Multicell battery		Voltage regulator, also, glow lamp		Resistor, variable	
Capacitor, general				Transformer, general	
Capacitor, variable		Phototube			
Capacitor, polarized				Transformer, magnetic core	
Circuit breaker		Inductor, winding, reactor, general			
Ground					
		Magnetic core inductor		Shielded transformer, magnetic core	
Chassis ground					
Connectors, jack and plug		Adjustable inductor			
Engaged connectors		Balast lamp		Auto-transformer, adjustable	

Common Architectural Symbols

Exterior door

Interior door

Pocket door

Bifold door

Bipass door

Window

Lighting outlet

Recessed lighting outlet

Wall lighting outlet

Fluorescent light fixture

Duplex convience outlet

Special outlet

Single pole switch

3-way switch

Toilet

Wall hung toilet

Urinal

Oval vanity sink

Rectangular vanity sink

Single kitchen

Double kitchen

220V outlet

Weather-proof outlet

Thermostat

Doorbell

TV outlet

Water heater

Shower

Shower w/seat

Tub

Washer/dryer

Range

Refrigerator

Fan

Conduit

Fraction, Decimal, and Metric Equivalents

INCHES FRACTIONS	INCHES DECIMALS	MILLIMETERS	INCHES FRACTIONS	INCHES DECIMALS	MILLIMETERS
	.00394	.1	15/32	.46875	11.9063
	.00787	.2		.47244	12.00
	.01181	.3	31/64	.484375	12.3031
1/64	.015625	.3969	1/2	.5000	12.70
	.01575	.4		.51181	13.00
	.01969	.5	33/64	.515625	13.0969
	.02362	.6	17/32	.53125	13.4938
	.02756	.7	35/64	.546875	13.8907
1/32	.03125	.7938		.55118	14.00
	.0315	.8	9/16	.5625	14.2875
	.03543	.9	37/64	.578125	14.6844
	.03937	1.00		.59055	15.00
3/64	.046875	1.1906	19/32	.59375	15.0813
1/16	.0625	1.5875	39/64	.609375	15.4782
5/64	.078125	1.9844	5/8	.625	15.875
	.07874	2.00		.62992	16.00
3/32	.09375	2.3813	41/64	.640625	16.2719
7/64	.109375	2.7781	21/32	.65625	16.6688
	.11811	3.00		.66929	17.00
1/8	.125	3.175	43/64	.671875	17.0657
9/64	.140625	3.5719	11/16	.6875	17.4625
5/32	.15625	3.9688	45/64	.703125	17.8594
	.15748	4.00		.70866	18.00
11/64	.171875	4.3656	23/32	.71875	18.2563
3/16	.1875	4.7625	47/64	.734375	18.6532
	.19685	5.00		.74803	19.00
13/64	.203125	5.1594	3/4	.7500	19.05
7/32	.21875	5.5563	49/64	.765625	19.4469
15/64	.234375	5.9531	25/32	.78125	19.8438
	.23622	6.00		.7874	20.00
1/4	.2500	6.35	51/64	.796875	20.2407
17/64	.265625	6.7469	13/16	.8125	20.6375
	.27559	7.00		.82677	21.00
9/32	.28125	7.1438	53/64	.828125	21.0344
19/64	.296875	7.5406	27/32	.84375	21.4313
5/16	.3125	7.9375	55/64	.859375	21.8282
	.31496	8.00		.86614	22.00
21/64	.328125	8.3344	7/8	.875	22.225
11/32	.34375	8.7313	57/64	.890625	22.6219
	.35433	9.00		.90551	23.00
23/64	.359375	9.1281	29/32	.90625	23.0188
3/8	.375	9.525	59/64	.921875	23.4157
25/64	.390625	9.9219	15/16	.9375	23.8125
	.3937	10.00		.94488	24.00
13/32	.40625	10.3188	61/64	.953125	24.2094
27/64	.421875	10.7156	31/32	.96875	24.6063
	.43307	11.00		.98425	25.00
7/16	.4375	11.1125	63/64	.984375	25.0032
29/64	.453125	11.5094	1	1.0000	25.4001

AutoCAD and its Applications—Basics

Chord Length—Segments of Circles

Length of arc (l=radians), height of segment (h), length of chord (c), and area of segment (A) for angles from 1 to 180 degrees and radius = 1. For other radii, multiply the values given for distance by the radius, and the values given for the area by r², the square of the radius. The values in the table can be used for U.S. customary or metric units.

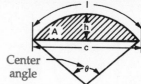

Center angle θ

Center Angle θ, Degrees	l	h	c	Area of Segment A	Center Angle θ, Degrees	l	h	c	Area of Segment A	Center Angle θ, Degrees	l	h	c	Area of Segment A
1	0.01745	0.00004	0.01745	0.00000	61	1.065	0.1384	1.015	0.09502	121	2.112	0.5076	1.741	0.6273
2	0.03491	0.00015	0.03490	0.00000	62	1.082	0.1428	1.030	0.09958	122	2.129	0.5152	1.749	0.6406
3	0.05236	0.00034	0.05235	0.00001	63	1.100	0.1474	1.045	0.10428	123	2.147	0.5228	1.758	0.6540
4	0.06981	0.00061	0.06980	0.00003	64	1.117	0.1520	1.060	0.10911	124	2.164	0.5305	1.766	0.6676
5	0.08727	0.00095	0.08724	0.00006	65	1.134	0.1566	1.075	0.11408	125	2.182	0.5383	1.774	0.6813
6	0.10472	0.00137	0.10467	0.00010	66	1.152	0.1613	1.089	0.11919	126	2.199	0.6560	1.782	0.6950
7	0.12217	0.00187	0.12210	0.00015	67	1.169	0.1661	1.104	0.12443	127	2.217	0.5538	1.790	0.7090
8	0.13963	0.00244	0.13951	0.00023	68	1.187	0.1710	1.118	0.12982	128	2.234	0.5616	1.798	0.7230
9	0.15708	0.00308	0.15692	0.00032	69	1.204	0.1759	1.133	0.13535	129	2.251	0.5695	1.805	0.7372
10	0.17453	0.00381	0.17431	0.00044	70	1.222	0.1808	1.147	0.14102	130	2.269	0.5774	1.813	0.7514
11	0.19199	0.00460	0.19169	0.00059	71	1.239	0.1859	1.161	0.14683	131	2.286	0.5853	1.820	0.7658
12	0.20944	0.00548	0.20906	0.00076	72	1.257	0.1910	1.176	0.15279	132	2.304	0.5933	1.827	0.7803
13	0.22689	0.00643	0.22641	0.00097	73	1.274	0.1961	1.190	0.15889	133	2.321	0.6013	1.834	0.7950
14	0.24435	0.00745	0.24374	0.00121	74	1.292	0.2014	1.204	0.16514	134	2.339	0.6093	1.841	0.8097
15	0.26180	0.00856	0.26105	0.00149	75	1.309	0.2066	1.218	0.17154	135	2.356	0.6173	1.848	0.8245
16	0.27925	0.00973	0.27835	0.00181	76	1.326	0.2120	1.231	0.17808	136	2.374	0.6254	1.854	0.8395
17	0.29671	0.01098	0.29562	0.00217	77	1.344	0.2174	1.245	0.18477	137	2.391	0.6335	1.861	0.8546
18	0.31416	0.01231	0.31287	0.00257	78	1.361	0.2229	1.259	0.19160	138	2.409	0.6416	1.867	0.8697
19	0.33161	0.01371	0.33010	0.00302	79	1.379	0.2284	1.272	0.19859	139	2.426	0.6498	1.873	0.8850
20	0.34907	0.01519	0.34730	0.00352	80	1.396	0.2340	1.286	0.20573	140	2.443	0.6580	1.879	0.9003
21	0.36652	0.01675	0.36447	0.00408	81	1.414	0.2396	1.299	0.21301	141	2.461	0.6662	1.885	0.9158
22	0.38397	0.01837	0.38162	0.00468	82	1.431	0.2453	1.312	0.22045	142	2.478	0.6744	1.891	0.9314
23	0.40143	0.02008	0.39874	0.00535	83	1.449	0.2510	1.325	0.22804	143	2.496	0.6827	1.897	0.9470
24	0.41888	0.02185	0.41582	0.00607	84	1.466	0.2569	1.338	0.23578	144	2.513	0.6910	1.902	0.9627
25	0.43633	0.02370	0.43288	0.00686	85	1.484	0.2627	1.351	0.24367	145	2.531	0.6993	1.907	0.9786
26	0.45379	0.02563	0.44990	0.00771	86	1.501	0.2686	1.364	0.25171	146	2.548	0.7076	1.913	0.9945
27	0.47124	0.02763	0.46689	0.00862	87	1.518	0.2746	1.377	0.25990	147	2.566	0.7160	1.918	1.0105
28	0.48869	0.02970	0.48384	0.00961	88	1.536	0.2807	1.389	0.26825	148	2.583	0.7244	1.923	1.0266
29	0.50615	0.03185	0.50076	0.01067	89	1.553	0.2867	1.402	0.27675	149	2.601	0.7328	1.927	1.0428
30	0.52360	0.03407	0.51764	0.01180	90	1.571	0.2929	1.414	0.28540	150	2.618	0.7412	1.932	1.0590
31	0.54105	0.03637	0.53448	0.01301	91	1.588	0.2991	1.427	0.2942	151	2.635	0.7496	1.936	1.0753
32	0.55851	0.03874	0.55127	0.01429	92	1.606	0.3053	1.439	0.3032	152	2.653	0.7581	1.941	1.0917
33	0.57596	0.04118	0.56803	0.01566	93	1.623	0.3116	1.451	0.3123	153	2.670	0.7666	1.945	1.1082
34	0.59341	0.04370	0.58474	0.01711	94	1.641	0.3180	1.463	0.3215	154	2.688	0.7750	1.949	1.1247
35	0.61087	0.04628	0.60141	0.01864	95	1.658	0.3244	1.475	0.3309	155	2.705	0.7836	1.953	1.1413
36	0.62832	0.04894	0.61803	0.02027	96	1.676	0.3309	1.486	0.3405	156	2.723	0.7921	1.956	1.1580
37	0.64577	0.05168	0.63461	0.02198	97	1.693	0.3374	1.498	0.3502	157	2.740	0.8006	1.960	1.1747
38	0.66323	0.05448	0.65114	0.02378	98	1.710	0.3439	1.509	0.3601	158	2.758	0.8092	1.963	1.1915
39	0.68068	0.05736	0.66761	0.02568	99	1.728	0.3506	1.521	0.3701	159	2.775	0.8178	1.967	1.2084
40	0.69813	0.06031	0.68404	0.02767	100	1.745	0.3572	1.532	0.3803	160	2.793	0.8264	1.970	1.2253
41	0.71558	0.06333	0.70041	0.02976	101	1.763	0.3639	1.543	0.3906	161	2.810	0.8350	1.973	1.2422
42	0.73304	0.06642	0.71674	0.03195	102	1.780	0.3707	1.554	0.4010	162	2.827	0.8436	1.975	1.2592
43	0.75049	0.06958	0.73300	0.03425	103	1.798	0.3775	1.565	0.4117	163	2.845	0.8522	1.978	1.2763
44	0.76794	0.07282	0.74921	0.03664	104	1.815	0.3843	1.576	0.4224	164	2.862	0.8608	1.981	1.2934
45	0.78540	0.07612	0.76537	0.03915	105	1.833	0.3912	1.587	0.4333	165	2.880	0.8695	1.983	1.3105
46	0.803	0.0795	0.781	0.04176	106	1.850	0.3982	1.597	0.4444	166	2.897	0.8781	1.985	1.3277
47	0.820	0.0829	0.797	0.04448	107	1.868	0.4052	1.608	0.4556	167	2.915	0.8868	1.987	1.3449
48	0.838	0.0865	0.813	0.04731	108	1.885	0.4122	1.618	0.4669	168	2.932	0.8955	1.989	1.3621
49	0.855	0.0900	0.829	0.05025	109	1.902	0.4193	1.628	0.4784	169	2.950	0.9042	1.991	1.3794
50	0.873	0.0937	0.845	0.05331	110	1.920	0.4264	1.638	0.4901	170	2.967	0.9128	1.992	1.3967
51	0.890	0.0974	0.861	0.05649	111	1.937	0.4336	1.648	0.5019	171	2.985	0.9215	1.994	1.4140
52	0.908	0.1012	0.877	0.05978	112	1.955	0.4408	1.658	0.5138	172	3.002	0.9302	1.995	1.4314
53	0.925	0.1051	0.892	0.06319	113	1.972	0.4481	1.668	0.5259	173	3.019	0.9390	1.996	1.4488
54	0.942	0.1090	0.908	0.06673	114	1.990	0.4554	1.677	0.5381	174	3.037	0.9477	1.997	1.4662
55	0.960	0.1130	0.923	0.07039	115	2.007	0.4627	1.687	0.5504	175	3.054	0.9564	1.998	1.4836
56	0.977	0.1171	0.939	0.07417	116	2.025	0.4701	1.696	0.5629	176	3.072	0.9651	1.999	1.5010
57	0.995	0.1212	0.954	0.07808	117	2.042	0.4775	1.705	0.5755	177	3.089	0.9738	1.999	1.5184
58	1.012	0.1254	0.970	0.08212	118	2.059	0.4850	1.714	0.5883	178	3.107	0.9825	2.000	1.5359
59	1.030	0.1296	0.985	0.08629	119	2.077	0.4925	1.723	0.6012	179	3.124	0.9913	2.000	1.5533
60	1.047	0.1340	1.000	0.09059	120	2.094	0.5000	1.732	0.6142	180	3.142	1.0000	2.000	1.5708

Area Equivalents

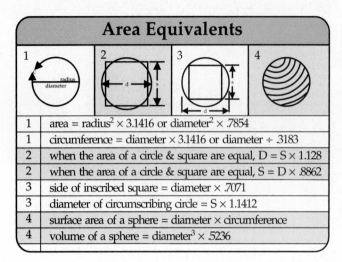

1	area = radius^2 × 3.1416 or diameter^2 × .7854
1	circumference = diameter × 3.1416 or diameter ÷ .3183
2	when the area of a circle & square are equal, D = S × 1.128
2	when the area of a circle & square are equal, S = D × .8862
3	side of inscribed square = diameter × .7071
3	diameter of circumscribing circle = S × 1.1412
4	surface area of a sphere = diameter × circumference
4	volume of a sphere = diameter^3 × .5236

Equivalents

Fahrenheit and Celsius
°F = (1.8 × °C) + 32
°C = (°F − 32) ÷ 1.8

Weight
1 gram = .03527 oz (av.)
1 oz = 28.35 grams
1 kilogram = 2.2046 pounds
1 pound = 0.4536 kilograms
1 metric ton = 2,204.6 pounds
1 ton (2000 lbs in U.S.) = 907.2 kg

Volume
1 U.S. quart = 0.946 liters
1 U.S. gallon = 3.785 liters
1 liter = 1.0567 U.S. quarts
1 liter = .264 U.S. gallons

Rutland Tool and Supply Co., Inc.

Length Conversions

multiply	by	to obtain
Inches	25.4	Millimeters
Feet	304.8	Millimeters
Inches	2.54	Centimeters
Feet	30.48	Centimeters
Millimeters	.03937008	Inches
Centimeters	.3937008	Inches
Meters	39.37008	Inches
Millimeters	.003280840	Feet
Centimeters	.03280840	Feet
Inches	.0254	Meters

Square Area Conversions

multiply	by	to obtain
Millimeters	.00001076391	Feet
Millimeters	.00155003	Inches
Centimeters	.1550003	Inches
Centimeters	.001076391	Feet
Inches	645.16	Millimeters
Inches	6.4516	Centimeters
Inches	.00064516	Meters
Feet	.09290304	Meters
Feet	929.0304	Centimeters
Feet	92,903.04	Millimeters

Rutland Tool and Supply Co., Inc.

Solutions to Triangles

$A + B + C = 180°$ $S = \dfrac{a + b + c}{2}$		Right B c a A b 90° C	Oblique B c a A b C
Have	**Want**	**Formulas for Right**	**Formulas for Oblique**
abc	A	$\tan A = a/b$	$1/2A = \sqrt{(s-b)(s-c)/bc}$
	B	$90° - A$ or $\cos B = a/c$	$\sin 1/2B = \sqrt{(s-a)(s-c)/a \times c}$
	C	$90°$	$\sin 1/2C = \sqrt{(s-a)(s-b)/a \times b}$
	Area	$a \times b/2$	$\sqrt{s \times (s-a)(s-b)(s-c)}$
aAC	B	$90° - A$	$180° - (A + C)$
	b	$a \cot A$	$a \sin B/\sin A$
	c	$a/\sin A$	$a \sin C/\sin A$
	Area	$(a^2 \cot A)/2$	$a^2 \sin B \sin C/2 \sin A$
acC	A	$\sin A = a/c$	$\sin A = a \sin C/c$
	B	$90° - A$ or $\cos B = a/c$	$180° - (A + C)$
	b	$\sqrt{c^2 - a^2}$	$c \sin B/\sin C$
	Area	$1/2a \sqrt{c^2 - a^2}$	$1/2 \, ac \sin B$
abC	A	$\tan A = a/b$	$\tan A = a \sin C/b - a \cos C$
	B	$90° - A$ or $\tan B = b/a$	$180° - (A + C)$
	c	$\sqrt{a^2 + b^2}$	$\sqrt{a^2 + b^2 - 2ab \cos C}$
	Area	$a \times b/2$	$1/2ab \sin C$

Rutland Tool and Supply Co., Inc.

Configuring the Digitizer

If you have a digitizer, the AutoCAD standard tablet menu is an alternative to keyboard entry or using screen commands. The tablet menu template measures 11″ × 12″. It contains most of the commands available in AutoCAD. Some commands are accompanied by small symbols, or icons, that indicate the function of the command. The menu is helpful because it provides a clear display of various AutoCAD commands.

If you are using your digitizer as the sole pointing device for all your Windows applications, you will require a driver called WINTAB. The WINTAB driver configures a digitizer to act as a mouse for Windows-based applications, but permits you to use the tablet screen pointing area and menus when running AutoCAD. You must install the WINTAB driver as your system pointing device in Windows before starting AutoCAD. These drivers are supplied by the digitizer tablet manufacturers, not by Autodesk. Most drivers can be downloaded from on-line services.

Like the screen menus, the tablet menu can be customized. Notice the empty spaces at the top of Figure J-1. This space is available for adding commands or symbols to aid picking and inserting functions. You can have several overlays for this area.

You do not have to use the template supplied with AutoCAD. Most people discover that many of the AutoCAD commands are not used for specific types of drawings, so they construct their own tablet menus. This is similar to creating screen menus, but there are different techniques involved when making tablet menus. Customizing tablet menus is discussed in *AutoCAD and its Applications–Advanced, Release 14.*

Using the AutoCAD Tablet Menu

The AutoCAD tablet drawing file is found in the Sample folder of the AutoCAD R14 file folder. To access this drawing, start AutoCAD and use the **OPEN** command to access the **Select File** dialog box. Open the AutoCAD R14 folder followed by opening the Sample folder. The Sample folder contains several sample AutoCAD drawings. One of the drawings is tablet14.dwg. Open this drawing to get the AutoCAD template shown in Figure J-1. You need to print or plot the template full size. The template can be printed on a durable material such as polyester film, or on paper and covered with clear plastic film for protection. The template can then be mounted to your digitizer tablet using small stick-on tabs that are available. These stick to the digitizer and are aligned with the punch-holes at the top of the template. You can also tape the template to the digitizer surface.

Figure J-1.
The AutoCAD tablet file is found in the Sample folder. (Autodesk, Inc.)

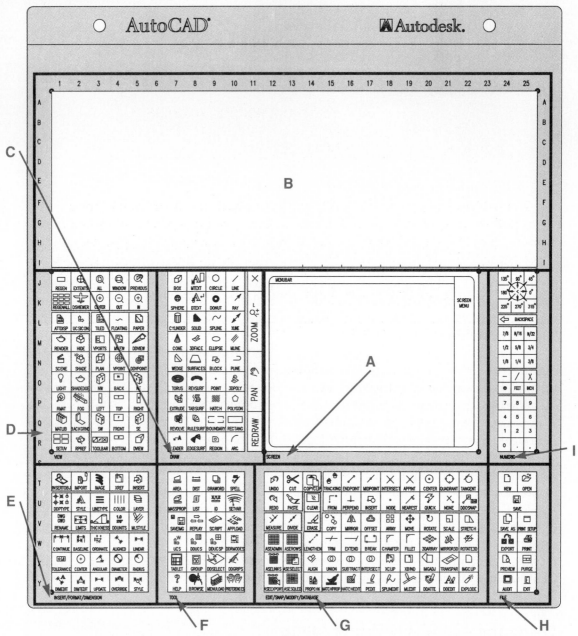

To use a tablet menu, the digitizer must first be configured for the specific menu you have. When you initially configure AutoCAD to recognize a digitizer, the entire surface of the tablet represents the screen pointing area. The **TABLET** command allows you to configure the digitizer to recognize the menu. This includes telling AutoCAD the exact layout of the menu areas and the size and position of the screen pointing area.

Tablet menu layout

The AutoCAD tablet menu presents commands in related groups. See Figure J-1. Notice the headings below each menu area.

Item	Group
A	SCREEN
B	User area
C	DRAW/ZOOM/PAN/REDRAW
D	VIEW
E	INSERT/FORMAT/DIMENSION
F	TOOL
G	EDIT/SNAP/MODIFY/DATABASE
H	FILE
I	NUMERIC

Configuring the tablet menu

The **TABLET** command allows you to tell AutoCAD the layout of the tablet menu. It prompts for three corners of each menu area and the number of columns and rows in each area. The screen pointing area is defined by picking two opposite corners. Three corners of each menu area are marked with small doughnuts. As you read the following example, look at Figure J-2. It illustrates how the standard AutoCAD tablet menu is configured and shows the doughnuts marking menu area corners.

Figure J-2. Small doughnuts mark the corners of the menu areas on the AutoCAD template. (Autodesk, Inc.)

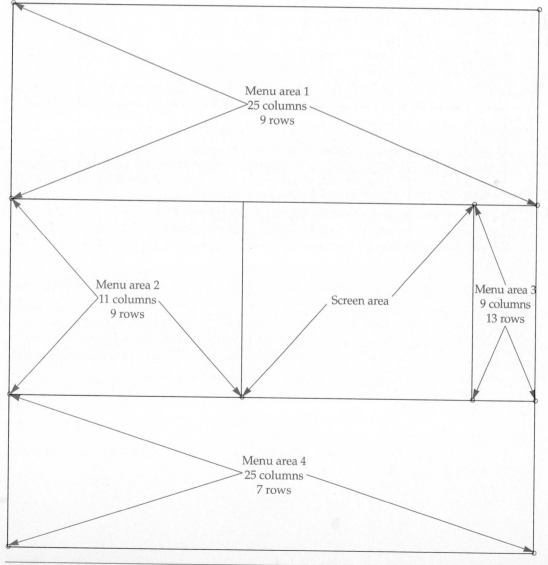

Menu area 1
25 columns
9 rows

Menu area 2
11 columns
9 rows

Screen area

Menu area 3
9 columns
13 rows

Menu area 4
25 columns
7 rows

The **Configure** option of the **TABLE T** command can be accessed directly by picking **Configure** in the **Tablet** cascading menu of the **Tools** pull-down menu, or using the **CFG** option after entering TA or TABLET at the Command: prompt as follows:

```
Command: TA or TABLET↵
Option (ON/OFF/CAL/CFG): CFG↵
Enter number of tablet menus desired (0-4) ⟨0⟩: 4↵
Do you want to realign tablet menu areas? ⟨N⟩ Y↵
Digitize upper left corner of menu area 1: (pick the doughnut at the upper-left corner)
Digitize lower left corner of menu area 1: (pick the point)
Digitize lower right corner of menu area 1: (pick the point)
Enter the number of columns for menu area 1(n - nnnn)⟨25⟩: ↵
Enter the number of rows for menu area 1(n - nnnn)⟨9⟩: ↵
```

You have now given AutoCAD the location of menu area 1 and specified the number of boxes that are available. The command continues with menu area 2:

```
Digitize upper left corner of menu area 2: (pick the point)
Digitize lower left corner of menu area 2: (pick the point)
Digitize lower right corner of menu area 2: (pick the point)
Enter the number of columns for menu area 2(n - nnnn)⟨11⟩: ↵
Enter the number of rows for menu area 2(n - nnnn)⟨9⟩: ↵
Digitize upper left corner of menu area 3: (pick the point)
Digitize lower left corner of menu area 3: (pick the point)
Digitize lower right corner of menu area 3: (pick the point)
Enter the number of columns for menu area 3(n - nnnn)⟨9⟩: ↵
Enter the number of rows for menu area 3(n - nnnn)⟨13⟩: ↵
Digitize upper left corner of menu area 4: (pick the point)
Digitize lower left corner of menu area 4: (pick the point)
Digitize lower right corner of menu area 4: (pick the point)
Enter the number of columns for menu area 4(n - nnnn)⟨25⟩: ↵
Enter the number of rows for menu area 4(n - nnnn)⟨7⟩: ↵
```

Next, you must locate opposite corners of the screen pointing area:

```
Do you want to specify the Floating Screen Pointing Area? ⟨N⟩: Y ↵
Do you want the Floating Screen Pointing Area to be the same size as the Fixed Screen
    Pointing Area? ⟨Y⟩: (enter Y or N; If you enter Y, digitize the lower-left and upper-
    right corners of the floating screen pointing area when prompted.)
The F12 key will toggle the Floating Screen Pointing Area ON and OFF.
Would you like to specify a button to toggle the Floating Screen
    Area? ⟨N⟩: (enter Y or N)
Command:
```

If you choose to use a digitizer puck button as the toggle, press the button of your choice. Do not press the pick button.

The tablet configuration is saved in the acad14.cfg file, which is in your AutoCAD R14 folder. The system reads this file when loading AutoCAD to determine what kind of equipment you are using. It also determines which menu is current. Use this same process when configuring the tablet for your custom menus.

Index

E

EDGEMODE system variable, 451
Edit Attribute Definition dialog box, 909
Edit Attributes dialog box, 917
Edit Multiline Text dialog box, editing dimensions with, 786
Edit Text dialog box, 339–340
Edit vertex option, 612, 614, 616
Editing,
    copying objects, 457–459
    creating multiple objects, 515–524
    drawing chamfers, 440–444
    drawing rounded corners, 444–448
    extending lines, 453–454
    length of object, 467–471
    lines and circles, 455–456
    mirroring object, 459–461
    moving object, 456–457
    moving and rotating object, 463–464
    removing section from object, 448–450
    rotating existing objects, 461–463
    selecting objects before editing, 471
    selecting objects for future editing, 472
    size of object, 464–465
    stretching object, 466
    trimming, 450–452
    See also Automatic editing
Editing dimensions, 733–750
    associative dimensioned objects, 738–742
    changing, 742–744
    editing text, 733–736
    erasing, 733
    extending, 740–741
    moving text, 739–740
    paper space dimensioning, 745
    stretching, 738–739
    trimming, 741–742
    using DIMOVERRIDE command, 737
    using UPDATE command, 737
Editing polylines,
    changing corner or point of tangency, 612
    changing appearance of linetypes, 618–619
    changing width, 611–612
    converting into individual line and arc segments, 619
    inserting new vertices, 613–614
    joining, 610–611
    making breaks in, 612–613
    moving vertices, 614
    opening and closing, 609–610
    revising as one unit, 609–619
    revising using PEDIT command, 609
    smoothing corners, 619–621
    using Spline option, 617
Editing splines, 624–630
    editing fit data, 625–627
    moving vertex, 628
    opening or closing, 627
    reshaping, 628–629
    reversing control point order, 629
Effective area, 419
Element Properties dialog box, 580–581
Elements, 576
ELEV command, 955–956, 967–968
ELLIPSE command, 201, 204, 206
    used as isometric circle, 941–944
Ellipses,
    drawing, 201–206. *See also* Drawing ellipses
    rotation angles, 203
Elliptical arcs, 204–205
Endpoint object snap, 224–225, 234
Engineering layouts, 970
Enter Attributes dialog box, 911–912, 923–925
EPS files, 562
ERASE command, 138–149, 496
    Box selection option, 147
    cleaning up the screen, 142
    CPolygon selection option, 144–145
    Crossing selection option, 141
    cycling through stacked objects, 148–149
    Fence selection option, 145
    Last selection option, 139
    making a single selection automatically, 139
    Multiple selection option, 147–148
    Windows selection option, 140
    WPolygon selection option, 143
[Esc] key, 53
EXPLODE command, 208, 590, 609, 619
    exploding dimensions, 849
Explorer, 542–549
    actions performed on selected files, 1014
    arranging folder and file icons, 1015–1016
    automatic startup, 1021–1026
    basic functions, 1013–1016
    copying disks, 1033–1034
    copying files, 545
    creating new folders, 548–549
    deleting files and folders, 547

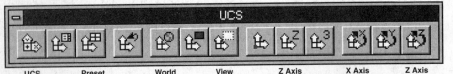

UCS

UCS · Preset UCS · World UCS · View UCS · Z Axis Vector UCS · X Axis Rotate UCS · Z Axis Rotate UCS
Named UCS · UCS Previous · Object UCS · Origin UCS · 3 Point UCS · Y Axis Rotate UCS

Insert

Insert Block · Image · OLE Object
External Reference · Import

Reference

External Reference · External Reference Clip · External Reference Clip Frame · Image Attach · Image Adjust · Image Transparency
External Reference Attach · External Reference Bind · Image · Image Clip · Image Quality · Image Frame

Zoom

Zoom Window · Zoom Scale · Zoom In · Zoom All
Zoom Dynamic · Zoom Center · Zoom Out · Zoom Extents

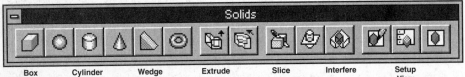

Solids

Box · Cylinder · Wedge · Extrude · Slice · Interfere · Setup View
Sphere · Cone · Torus · Revolve · Section · Setup Drawing · Setup Profile

Inquiry

Distance · Mass Properties · Locate Point
Area · List

Render

Hide · Render · Lights · Materials Library · Background · Landscape New · Landscape Library · Statistics
Shade · Scenes · Materials · Mapping · Fog · Landscape Edit · Render References

Surfaces

2D Solid · Box · Pyramid · Sphere · Dish · Edge · Revolved Surface · Ruled Surface
3D Face · Wedge · Cone · Dome · Torus · 3D Mesh · Tabulated Surface · Edge Surface

Bonus Standard Toolbar

Extended Change Properties · Move Copy Rotate · Extended Clip · Copy Nested Entities · Extend to Block Entities · Revision Cloud · Pack 'n Go
Multiple Entity Stretch · Extended Trim · Multiple Pedit · Trim to Block Entities · Wipeout · Quick Leader · List Xref/Block Entities

External Database

Administration · Links · Export Links
Rows · Select Objects · SQL Editor

Bonus Text Tools

Text Fit · Change Multiple Text Items · Arc Aligned Text · Explode Attributes to Text
Text Mask · Explode Text · Find and Replace Text · Global Attribute Edit

Bonus Layer Tools

Layer Manage · Change Current Layer · Freeze Object's Layer · Lock Object's Layer
Match Object's Layer · Isolate Object's Layer · Turn Object's Layer Off · Unlock Object's Layer

Internet Utilities

Attach URL · List URLs · Open from URL · Save to URL · Internet Help
Detach URL · Select URLs · Insert from URL · Configure Internet Host

Viewpoint

Named Views · Bottom View · Right View · Back View · SE Isometric View · NW Isometric View
Top View · Left View · Front View · SW Isometric View · NE Isometric View